WESTERN CIVILIZATION

A Social and Cultural History

SECOND EDITION

Volume 2: 1500–The Present

MARGARET L. KING

Brooklyn College and the Graduate Center
City University of New York

Prentice Hall Inc., Upper Saddle River, NJ. 07458

Published 2003 by Prentice Hall Inc.
A Division of Pearson Education
Upper Saddle River, New Jersey 07458

A CIP catalog record for this book is available from the
Library of Congress.
ISBN 0-13-045004-9

10 9 8 7 6 5 4 3 2 1

This book was designed and produced by
LAURENCE KING PUBLISHING LTD.,
London, www.laurenceking.co.uk

Senior Managing Editor: Richard Mason
Senior Editor: Samantha Gray
Commissioning Editors: Damian Thompson, Melanie Hill
Design: Ian Hunt Design
Cover Design: Design Deluxe
Picture Research: Peter Kent
Maps: Andrea Fairbrass and Ailsa Heritage
Printed in Hong Kong

Cover: Hans Holbein, *The Ambassadors* (National
Gallery, London)
A. E. Harris, *King Edward VII receiving maharajahs and
other dignitaries* (Roy Miles Gallery, London/Bridgeman
Art Library)

CONTENTS

Preface

Where is the West?   xiii

What, Then, is the West?   xiv

The West and the Rest of the World   xv

Changes to the *Second Edition*   xv

Walkthrough

Why is *Western Civilization, Second Edition,*
    Organized Thematically?   xvii

Features of the *Second Edition*   xviii

Supplements   xxii

CHAPTER 15

ABSOLUTE POWER
War and Politics in Early Modern Europe

(1500–1750)

Power and Gunpowder   418

Knights and Guns   418

Military Organization   419

War Games   422

Wars over Faith and Turf, 1500–1648   422

States in Competition, 1648–1763   425

An Age of Kings   426

Spain: Religious Zeal and Royal Absolutism   426

*Witnesses: The Experience of War in Works
    of Shakespeare and Voltaire*   427

France: The Apogee of Absolutism   429

England: The Sharing of Power   431

Windows On: Warriors and Peacemakers   432

Three New Empires: The Reshaping of
    Eastern Europe   434

Mirrors for Princes   438

The Idea of the Prince   438

Witnesses: A King's Right to Rule   440

Halls of Mirrors   440

Witnesses: A Queen's Right to Rule   441

Roman Law and Natural Right   441

*Witnesses: The Origins of Government in the
    Consent of the Citizens*   442

**Conclusion: Power, Resistance, and the
    Meaning of the West**   444

Review Questions   445

Suggested Resources   445

CHAPTER 16

EUROPE REACHES OUT
Global Voyages and Cultural Encounters

(1500–1750)

The Open Seas   448

Portugal Takes the Lead   448

Old World Ventures   452

Windows On: Mapping the World   453

Brave New World   455

Exploration and Conquest   455

Witnesses: Exploration and Conquest   458

Patterns of Settlement   461

Encountering Others   463

Witnesses: New World Peoples and Customs   464

The African Solution   467

Witnesses: Voices of Protest   470

The Wealth of Nations   471

Bringing Home the Bacon   471

Witnesses: The Profits of Trade   473

Trade Wars   474

**Conclusion: The Expansion of Europe
    and the Meaning of the West**   479

Review Questions   480

Suggested Resources   480

PART FIVE
THE WEST EXPANDS
Science, Enlightenment, and Revolution

(1500–1900)

CHAPTER 17
THE AGE OF REASON
Science, Schooling, and Thought in Early
Modern Europe

(1500–1780)

New Heaven, New Earth: The Scientific
Revolution   484
  The Advent of Infinity   484
Witnesses: Pioneers of a New Cosmology   486
Witnesses: Science and Religion in Conflict   488
  "Man the Machine": Exploration of the
    Human Body   489
  Hard Facts and Pure Reason: New Modes
    of Thinking   491
Witnesses: Pioneers of New Scientific
    Methodologies   493
  The End of Magic   495
The Lights Go On: The Enlightenment   496
  Common Sense   497
  Social Contracts   499
Witnesses: Visions of a Just Society   500
  Other Places, Other Customs   501
A Little Learning: Literacy and Education   502
  Pleasure Reading   502
  A Cat and a Catte: Women and Learning   504
Witnesses: Women, Men, and Learning   506
Windows On: Women and Science   507
  Halls of Reason: The Social Context   509
Conclusion: Descartes' Dilemma and
    the Meaning of the West   510
Review Questions   511
Suggested Resourcess   511

CHAPTER 18
TOWN, COURT, AND COUNTRY
Privilege and Poverty in Early
Modern Europe

(1500–1780)

Honorable Pursuits: The European Nobility
  of the Early Modern Age   514
  Lines and Houses   514
  Patterns of Nobility   518
  Courtiers and Kings   520
Witnesses: Courtier Graces, Bourgeois
    Self Control   521
New Ways with New Wealth:
    The Early Modern Bourgeoisie   524
  The Ranks of the Bourgeoisie   524
  At Home   525
Witnesses: Women Protest against Husbands
    and Predators   527
  Downtown   527
  Workers and Strangers   529
Witnesses: Being Poor: in Town and Country   530
Windows On: Women's Lives   531
Field and Village: The Boundaries of
    Peasant Life   535
  Bread, Beans, and Flocks   536
  Varieties of Labor   536
  Festival and Riot   539
Conclusion: The Privileged, The Poor,
    and the Meaning of the West   540
Review Questions   541
Suggested Resources   541

CHAPTER 19
INALIENABLE RIGHTS
Revolution and its Promises in Anglo-
and Latin America

(1500–1880)

Old and New in the New World   544
  Brazil and the Caribbean: Plantation Nations   544

Spanish America: Mine, *Hacienda*, and Village 546
Witnesses: Native Laborers in Spanish America 547
The North Atlantic Coast: The Beckoning
    Wilderness 549
Windows On: African Laborers in a Harsh
    New World 551
Witnesses: Native Removal in Anglo-America 554
Declarations of Independence 555
Atlantic North America:
    War for Independence 556
Revolution in Haiti and Mexico 558
Transition in Brazil and Paraguay 560
Spanish South America: Victory at Ayacucho 560
Witnesses: A Different Path for Spanish America 560
Fulfilling the Promise 561
The Reign of the *Caudillo* 561
By the People 565
Witnesses: Foundations of Freedom in
    Anglo-America 570
Witnesses: African Bondage in Anglo-America 571
Conclusion: Jefferson's Promise, Lincoln's
    Pledge and the Meaning of the West 574
Review Questions 575
Suggested Resources 575

Witnesses: Revolution Turns Radical 595
Reaction Sets In: The Directory 596
The Imperial Adventure 596
The Coming of Napoleon 596
Napoleon's France 597
Windows On: Revolution in Fashion 600
Witnesses: Napoleon, According to Himself
    and to an Enemy 603
Napoleon and the *Grande Armée* 603
The Tide Turns 606
Conclusion: Revolution, Empire, and
    the Meaning of the West 607
Review Questions 608
Suggested Resources 608

PART SIX
THE WEST BECOMES MODERN
Industrialization, Imperialism, Ideologies

(1750–1914)

CHAPTER 20
REVOLT AND REORGANIZATION IN EUROPE
From Absolute Monarchy to the Paris Commune

(1750–1871)

Preludes to Revolution 578
Resistance to Absolutism 578
Peasant Revolts and Free Trade 579
The War of Ideas 580
The Rights of Man 581
The Work of the National Assembly 581
Witnesses: The Collapse of the Old Regime 584
The Legislative Assembly and National
    Convention 585
The Birth of a Nation 586
Peasants and Sans-Culottes 586
Witnesses: The "True" Rights of Man—Burke
    vs. Paine 588
The Culture of Revolution 591
Windows On: The Radical Revolution 592

CHAPTER 21
MACHINES IN THE GARDEN
The Industrialization of the West

(1750–1914)

Before Industrialization 612
Medieval Foundations: The Urban Grid 612
Early Modern Changes 613
Witnesses: Buying and Selling Before the
    Industrial Age 614
Britain Industrializes 615
Cotton and Water 615
Windows On: In the Factory 618
Coal and Water 619
Iron, Coal, and Steam 620
Windows On: Power from Steam 621
Witnesses: The Coming of the Machine Age 622
Railroad and Steamship 622
Catching Up 626
The First Imitators 626
The Rest of the West and the Asian
    Vanguard 631

*Witnesses: Catching Up in Argentina,
  Germany, and Russia*   633
  Postponed Industrialization   635
**Conclusion: Despoiled Gardens and the
  Meaning of the West**   636
Review Questions   637
Suggested Resources   637

CHAPTER 22

LIVES OF THE OTHER HALF
Western Society in an Industrial Age
(1750–1914)

Workers and Workplace   640
  Mine, Mill, and Factory   640
Witnesses: The Factory Observed   641
  The Birth of Labor   642
Windows On: Men and Work   643
Witnesses: Workers' Lives   644
Windows On: Women and Work   648
The Industrial City   649
  Boom Towns   650
  Structure and Infrastructure   652
  On the Streets   654
*Witnesses: Friedrich Engels' Portrait of the
  Industrial City*   655
The Two Halves at Home   656
  In the Tenement   656
Witnesses: The Two Halves at Home   657
  In the Townhouse   659
**Conclusion: The One Half, The Other Half,
  and the Meaning of the West**   662
Review Questions   663
Suggested Resources   663

CHAPTER 23

THE CONCERT OF EUROPE
Mass Politics and the Triumph of the State
(1815–1914)

Power to the People: 1815–1848   666

After Napoleon: The Conservative Response   666
Liberalism and Nationalism in Central Europe   667
Revolution in Russia, the Iberian Peninsula,
  and Greece   668
Pressure for Change in Great Britain   669
France: Laboratory of Revolution   670
*Witnesses: To the Barricades: Paris, France,
  1848, 1871*   671
One People, One Nation: 1848–1871   673
  The Creation of Austria-Hungary   673
  The Unification of Italy   674
  The Unification of Germany   675
The State Trumphant: 1848–1914   676
  Britain: The Challenge of Mass Politics   676
  Russia: An Autocracy Attempts Reform   677
  France: From Second Empire to
    Third Republic   677
  Central Europe: The German and Austro-
    Hungarian Empires   678
*Witnesses: The Meaning of Country: German
  and Italian Nationalism*   679
*Witnesses: Statesmen Look Ahead: Austria,
  Germany, Britain*   682
  Mediterranean Europe: Italy, Spain,
    and Portugal   683
  Wars and Alliances   683
Windows On: Power to the People   684
**Conclusion: The Triumphal State and
  the Meaning of the West**   686
Review Questions   687
Suggested Resources   687

CHAPTER 24

THE WESTERN IMPERIUM
European Migration, Settlement, and
Domination around the Globe
(1750–1914)

**Lands of European Settlement: Colonial
  Ventures**   690
  The Anglo-American Pattern   690
  The Spanish-American Pattern   691
  Autralasia: Another Anglophone Success   693
  The Russian Empire   693
Old World Encounters: Imperialism in Asia   694
  India: A Sub-continent Subdued   694
  The Philippines and East Indies   696

Witnesses: Britain's Empire in India   697
   China, Korea, and Indochina: Forced Entry   698
Witnesses: The European Arrival in East Asia   700
   Japan: Point, Counterpoint   700
Old World Encounters: Imperialism in
   the Middle East and Africa   702
   The Middle East: The Last Islamic Empire   702
Witnesses: Europe in Africa and the Middle East   703
   Sub-Saharan Africa: Divided and Despoiled   705
Dominion Within   707
   The Irish: Despised and Persecuted   707
   The Jews: The Intimate Enemy   708
Witnesses: Dominion Within: the Jews and the Irish 709
   The Psychology of Domination   710
Windows On: Colonized Europeans:
   The Jews and the Irish   711
Witnesses: Europe's "Burden" or "Benefit"?   713
Migrants and Money   713
   The Global System: Money and Goods   713
   The Global System: Peoples and Culture   715
Conclusion: The Western *Imperium* and
   the Meaning of the West   716
Review Questions   717
Suggested Resources   717

Conservatism: Valuing Tradition   730
Nationalism: A Sacred Purpose   731
Socialism: Sharing the Wealth   731
Witnesses: Idealists and Ideologues (I)   732
   Marxism, Communism, Anarchism   733
Witnesses: Idealists and Ideologues (II)   734
   Feminism: Rights for Women   735
***Fin de Siècle* and the Advent of the Modern**   737
   The Death of God   737
   New Visions   738
Witnesses: The Fin de Siècle *and the Advent*
   of the Modern   739
Windows On: Fin De Siècle *and the Advent*
   of the Modern   740
Conclusion: The Advent of the Modern
   and the Meaning of the West   741
Review Questions   742
Suggested Resources   742

PART SEVEN
TOWARD A NEW WEST
Post-War, Post-Modern, Post-Industrial
(1914–2000)

CHAPTER 25
STORM, STRESS, AND DOUBT
European Culture from Classicism to
Modernism
(1780–1914)

CHAPTER 26
THE MIGHTY ARE FALLEN
The Trauma of World War I
(1914–1920)

From Romanticism to Realism   720
   Romanticism and Revolt   720
   Realism and Disenchantment   721
Windows On: The Cycle of Styles: Classicism,
   Romanticism, and Realism   722
Witnesses: Pioneers of Literary Style:
   Romanticism and Realism   723
The Sciences and the Schools   723
   The Past as It Really Was   724
   The World as It Came to Be   724
Witnesses: Pioneers of the Intellectual Disciplines:
   History, Social Science, and Science   725
   Sciences of Society   727
   Schooling the Masses   728
Ideals and Ideologies   729
   Liberalism: Freedom and Rights   729

Pathways to War   746
   Hot Spots   746
Witnesses: The Onset of War   747
   Men and Boys at War   748
In the Midst of Battle   748
   Stalemate in the West   748
Windows On: Drama in Russia   751
Witnesses: At the Front   753
   The Eastern Steamroller   754
   At Sea and Abroad   755
   At Home   757
   Russia Turns Back   759
Witnesses: Revolution in Russia   762
In Search of Peace   763
   Peace Plans   763

Witnesses: In Search of Peace   764
  Settlement at Paris   765
  Outcomes   767
**Conclusion: Global War and the
  Meaning of the West**   768
Review Questions   769
Suggested Resources   769

CHAPTER 27

THE TRIUMPH OF UNCERTAINTY
Cultural Innovation, Social Disruption, and
Economic Collapse

(1915–1945)

Uncertainty in the Arts and in Thought   772
  Montage: the Disrupted Narrative   772
  Indeterminacy   777
Witnesses: The World Becomes Uncertain   778
**Uncertain Boundaries: the New Women, the
  Shrinking Family, the Nurturant State**   780
  The New Woman   780
*Witnesses: Rethinking Women's Roles and
  Possibilities*   782
  The Shrinking Family and the
    Nurturant State   784
**Economic Uncertainty: From Prosperity to
  the Breadline**   786
  Happy Days   786
Windows On: Highs and Lows   789
Witnesses: Living Through the Great Depression   790
  On the Dole   791
**Conclusion: Uncertain Lives and the
  Meaning of the West**   794
Review Questions   795
Suggested Resources   795

CHAPTER 28

STATES IN CONFLICT
Communism, Fascism, Democracy,
and the Crisis of World War II

(1917–1945)

Bolsheviks and Communists   799
  Lenin: Rewriting Marx   799
  War Communism and the New Economic
    Policy   799
Witnesses: Bolsheviks and Communists   800
  Stalin: Gravedigger of the Revolution?   801
  Socialism in One Country   803
*Witnesses: Communist Totalitarianism Repression
  and Terror*   804
  Socialist Realism, Soviet Realities   804
The Faces of Fascism   807
  Fascism   807
  Mussolini and His Imitators   808
  Imperial Japan, Imperialist Ventures   809
*Witnesses: Fascism and Nazism: the Flight
  from Reason*   810
  Nazism: the German Form of Fascism   811
The Second World War: Fascism Defeated   814
  The Dictatorships   814
  The Democracies: Frailty and Confusion   817
  The Spanish Civil War: Rehearsal for
    World War   817
  First Hostilities   818
Witnesses: Fighting the Second World War   819
  From Appeasement to Victory   820
Final Solutions   824
Windows On: The Holocaust   825
Witnesses: Final Solutions   827
**Conclusion: The Defeat of Fascism and the
  Meaning of the West**   828
Review Questions   829
Suggested Resources   829

CHAPTER 29

THE END OF IMPERIALISM
Decolonization and Statebuilding
around the Globe

(1914–1990s)

**Fading Empires: Anti-Colonialism and
  Decolonization**   832
  The Sun Sets on the British Empire   832
*Witnesses: Asia: Independence for India and
  Vietnam*   834
  Reluctant Disengagement   836
**New World Orders: Statebuilding in Africa,
  the Middle East, and Asia**   837

Statebuilding in Africa   837
Witnesses: Africa: Post-Colonial Quandries   841
*Witnesses: African Debates: Algeria and
     South Africa*   842
Statebuilding in the Middle East   842
Witnesses: New Orders in the Middle East   845
Statebuilding in Asia   847
Witnesses: Asia: Permanent Revolution in China   849
**The Last Imperialist: The United States
     Abroad and At Home**   851
Good Neighbors   851
*Witnesses: The Americas: a United States
     Protectorship in Cuba and the Mexican
     Nationalization of the Oil Industry*   852
The Domino Game   855
The Color Line: Conflict at Home   860
*Witnesses: The Americas: Racial Equality and
     Racial Separatism in the United States*   861
Windows On: Civil Rights for African Americans   862
**Conclusion: The Shadows of Imperialism
     and the Meaning of the West**   864
Review Questions   865
Suggested Resources   865

CHAPTER 30

BACK FROM ARMAGEDDON

From the Bomb to the Internet

(1945–1990)

Apocalypse Now?   868
Postwar Polarization   868
Witnesses: The Prospects of Nuclear War   871
Cold War Confrontations   871
The Cold War on the Global Stage   873
Witnesses: The Origins of the Cold War   874
Armageddon Deferred: 1985–1991   876
*Witnesses: As the Cold War Ages: Two United
     States Presidents Discuss the Soviet Threat*   879
All You Need is Love   879
*Witnesses: The Breakdown of Communism
     and the End of the Cold War*   880

Rolling Stones   881
Witnesses: Culture and Politics in the 1960s   883
   Women of Worth   883
Witnesses: Women and the Post-War World   886
   Love Your Mother   888
Windows On: Women, Poverty, and War   890
*Witnesses: Love Your Mother:
     The Environmentalist Movement*   893
Witnesses: The Age of Human Rights   895
**Conclusion: Retreat from Armageddon and
     the Meaning of the West**   896
Review Questions   897
Suggested Resources   897

EPILOGUE:
THE FUTURE OF THE WEST

(SINCE 1990)

Coming Together   898
Witnesses: Through a Glass Darkly   900
   The Ties that Bind   901
   Last Battles   903
*Witnesses: Why Some are So Rich and
     Some are So Poor*   905
Witnesses: Let's Roll: the War on Terror   908
Witnesses: The Future of the West   910
The End of the West   911
**Conclusion: The Past, the Future, and
     the Meaning of the West**   912
Suggested Resources   912

Picture Credits   E–1
Literary Credits   E–2
Acknowledgments   E–2
Glossary   E–3
Index   E–8

WITNESSES

Witnesses: The Experience of War in Fiction and Fact (Henry V threatens the French city of Harfleur; An eyewitness describes the destruction of his city during the Thirty Year's War)   427

Witnesses: A King's Right to Rule (Jean Bodin on the king's right to impose laws; Jacques-Bénigne Bossuet on kings as God's ministers)   440

Witnesses: A Queen's Right to Rule (John Knox on a woman's incapacity for rule; Queen Elizabeth I on her sovereignty)   441

Witnesses: The Origins of Government in the Consent of the Citizens (Thomas Hobbes on citizens' consent to sovereign power; John Locke on surrendering freedom to form civil government)   442

Witnesses: Exploration and Conquest (João de Barros on the sack of Mombasa by the Portuguese; Vasco da Gama arrives in Calcutta; An eyewitness to Magellan's Pacific crossing)   458

Witnesses: New World Peoples and Customs (Columbus arrives in the New World; Montezuma's spies report on Cortés' men; Explorer Jean de Léry on how the Tupinambá treat war captives)   464

Witnesses: Voices of Protest (Spanish priest Bartolomé de las Casas on native Amerindians; Former slave Olaudah Equiano on slaves sold at auction; A British physician on slaves bound for Brazil)   470

Witnesses: The Profits of Trade (French Minister Jean-Baptiste Colbert instructs Louis XIV on the kingdom's finances; Economist Adam Smith argues for free trade)   473

Witnesses: Pioneers of a New Cosmology (Copernicus claims that the earth rotates; Newton explains the universal system)   486

Witnesses: Science and Religion in Conflict Galileo on scientific and theological inquiry; Newton explains God's role in the universe)   488

Witnesses: Pioneers of New Scientific Methodologies (Francis Bacon advocates the Inductive Method; William Harvey defends the Empirical Method; René Descartes and rationalism)   493

Witnesses: Visions of a Just Society (Voltaire calls for toleration; Locke on government; Condorcet on reason and human progress)   500

Witnesses: Women, Men, and Learning (François Poulain de la Barre on the two sexes; Mary Astell declares men are superior)   506

Witnesses: (Castiglione on how to live at court; Benjamin Franklin recommends self-discipline and hard work)   521

Witnesses: Women Protest against Husbands and Predators (Venetian woman lambasts the tyranny of men; Artemisia Gentileschi at trial of her rapist)   527

Witnesses: Being Poor: in Town and Country (A view from the top and the bottom)   530

Witnesses: Native Laborers in Spanish America (What natives owed two *Encomenderos*; Spanish missionary describes miners of Potosí)   547

Witnesses: Native Removal in Anglo-America (Lewis Cass discusses Indian removal; Andrew Jackson on the need for Indian removal)   554

Witnesses: A Different Path for Spanish America (Simón Bolívar's address at Angostura)   560

Witnesses: Foundations of Freedom in Anglo-America (Declaration of Independence; Rights for women; Gettysburg Address)   570

Witnesses: African Bondage in Anglo-America (Colonial slave code; Laura S. Haviland on former slave who bought daughter's freedom)   571

Witnesses: The Collapse of the Old Regime (Abbé Sieyès questions meaning of Third Estate; Decrees passed in response to "Great Fear"; Declaration of the Rights of Man and the Citizen; The National Assembly attempts to secularize the Church   584

Witnesses: The "True" Rights of Man—Burke vs. Paine Edmund Burke distinguishes between civil and natural rights while Thomas Paine sees civil right as an extension of natural rights   588

Witnesses: Revolution Turns Radical The National Assembly declares war on Austria; the Jacobins warn against the king; the National Convention promises the support of the French people against tyranny; Decree establishing the *Levée en masse*; Abbé Carrichon describes execution by guillotine of group of nobles)   595

Witnesses: Napoleon, According to Himself and to an Enemy (Napoleon defends his record; Madame de Staël describes the dictator)   603

Witnesses: Buying and Selling Before the Industrial Age (Daniel Defoe describes cloth market; British government bans import of Indian calicoes; Friedrich List on industry in the German states)   614

Witnesses: The Coming of the Machine Age (Edward Baines describes textile factory; M. A. Alderson on the steam engine)   622

Witnesses: Catching Up in Argentina, Germany, and Russia (Juan Bautista Alberdi celebrates the railroad; Friedrich List on England's industrial lead; Sergei Witte on Russia's need to industrialize)   633

Witnesses: The Factory Observed Andrew Ure on child labor; P. Gaskell describes factory workers; Flora Tristan on factory conditions)   641

Witnesses: Workers' Lives (Yorkshire Chartist recalls boyhood; Irish stevedores at Liverpool docks; Patience Kershaw describes coal mines; Luise Zietz recalls childhood; Female servants' duties)   644

Witnesses: Friedrich Engels' Portrait of the Industrial City (1844) (Manchester; London)   655

Witnesses: The Two Halves at Home (The urban poor; The wealthy)   657

Witnesses: To The Barricades: Paris, France, 1848, 1871 (Alexis de Tocqueville foretells the Revolution of 1848; Alphonse de Lamartine comments on how the Revolution began; A British journalist describes the suppression of the Paris Commune)   671

Witnesses: The Meaning of Country: German and Italian Nationalism (Johann Gottlieb Fichte examines love of country; Giuseppe Mazzini calls upon the workers of Italy to love their country)   679

Witnesses: Statesmen Look Ahead: Austria, Germany, Britain (Prince Clemens von Metternich urges the states of Europe to suppress liberalism and dissent in society; Otto von Bismarck urges his fellow Germans to be strong; William Gladstone asks the House of Commons to accept the reality of mass politics)   682

Witnesses: Britain's Empire in India (Lord Wellesley defends East India Company; Thomas B. Macaulay on education in India; Dalpatram Kavi's "The Attack of King Industry")   697

Witnesses: The European Arrival in East Asia (Modern historian on First Opium War; Ito Hirobumi on learning from the West)   700

Witnesses: Europe in Africa and the Middle East (Ernest Linant de Fellefonds in conversation with Kabaka Mutesa; Jamal al-Din al-Afghani speaks on science)   703

Witnesses: Dominion Within: The Jews and the Irish (Heinrich von Treitschke condemns the "Jews Among Us"; Engels on British rule of Ireland)   709

Witnesses: Europe's "Burden" or Benefit? (Rudyard Kipling on the "white man's burden"; Lord Lugard on Britain's expansion into Africa)   713

Witnesses: Pioneers of Literary Style: Romanticism and Realism (Walt Whitman's "When I Heard the Learned Astronomer"; Emile Zola on a miner's life)   723

Witnesses: Pioneers of the Intellectual Disciplines (Leopold von Ranke on historical sources; Thomas Malthus on population increase; Emile Durkheim on sociology; Darwin on natural selection)   725

Witnesses: Idealists and Ideologues (I) (John Stuart Mill defines human liberty; Edmund Burke warns of chaos; Johann Gottlieb Fichte and Giuseppe Mazzini describe nationhood)   732

Witnesses: Idealists and Ideologues (II) (Marx and Engels define history; Pierre-Joseph Proudhon on government; Emmeline Pankhurst explains why women are militant) 734

Witnesses: The Fin de Siècle and the Advent of the Modern (Dostoevsky's "Underground Man"; Nietzsche repudiates morality and religion; Freud on civilization's discontent; Apollinaire discusses art) 739

Witnesses: The Onset of War (Heinrich von Treitschke describes nationalist and militarist sentiments; Sir Edward Grey on war; Bertrand Russell on the bloodthirstiness of the populace) 747

Witnesses: At the Front (Wilfred Owen describes a gas attack; song sung by British troops; Jaroslav Hasek describes his commanding officer; a German soldier writes home; Jessie Pope celebrates war girls) 753

Witnesses: Revolution in Russia (Lenin on need for Vanguard Party; Nadezhda Krupskaya on return to Russia; Lenin's April Theses) 762

Witnesses: In Search of Peace (Woodrow Wilson's Fourteen Points; Guidelines from the Treaty of Versailles) 764

Witnesses: The World Becomes Uncertain (Paul Valéry on World War II; Albert Einstein's Theory of Relativity; Sigmund Freud on the effect of war; Werner Heisenberg discusses the effect of war; Vasily Kandinsky on art as expression) 778

Witnesses: Rethinking Women's Roles and Possibilities (Charlotte Perkins Gilman criticizes women; Alexandra Kollontai on Soviet communism; Emma Goldman celebrates free women) 782

Witnesses: Living Through the Great Depression (Calvin Coolidge speaks on the eve of the Crash; The condition of the unemployed multitudes; Malcolm X on the Depression's effects on poor blacks) 790

Witnesses: Bolsheviks and Communists (Decree on food procurement; Stalin urges industrialization; V. Zazubrin celebrates the industrialization of the Soviet Union) 800

Witnesses: Communist Totalitarianism (Kronstadt sailors denounce the communist dictatorship; M.N. Averbakh on liquidating the kulaks; Nadezhda Mandelstam recalls Stalinist terror; Nikola Bukharin testifies to the terror) 804

Witnesses: Fascism and Nazism (Mussolini defines Italian fascism; Hitler on Aryans and Jews; Lilo Linke observes Hitler) 810

Witnesses: Fighting the Second World War (Hitler muses on the war's future; Tokutomi Iichirō on declaration of war; Churchill rallies the nation against Nazism) 819

Witnesses: Final Solutions (Hermann Graebe testifies at Nuremberg; Rudolf Hoess at Nuremberg; Elie Wiesel reflects; President Truman on the atomic bomb; Wilfred Burchett reports from Hiroshima) 827

Witnesses: Asia: Independence for India and Vietnam (Gandhi on freedom for the starving; Vietnamese Declaration of Independence) 834

Witnesses: Africa: Post-Colonial Quandaries (Kwame Nkrumah promotes African unity; the All-African People's Conference) 841

Witnesses: African Debates: Algeria and South Africa (The Governor-General of Algeria says France will never relinquish control;
A spokesperson rejoices at Algeria's victory; Nelson Mandella speaks in his own defense at his trial; Archbishop Desmond Tutu asks for help) 842

Witnesses: New Orders in the Middle East (Establishment of State of Israel; Goals of the PLO; Ayatollah Ruhollah Khomeini on the victory won) 845

Witnesses: Asia: Permanent Revolution in China (Mao Zedong on communist revolution; The aims of the Cultural Revolution) 849

Witnesses: The Americas (The Platt Amendment; Lazlo Cardenas on the nationalization of the oil industry) 852

Witnesses: The Americas: Racial Equality and Racial Separatism in the United States (Brown v. Board of Education of Topeka; Martin Luther King writes from jail; The Black Panther Party's demands) 861

Witnesses: The Prospects of Nuclear War (William Faulkner's Nobel Prize speech; Songwriter Sting on the likelihood of war) 871

Witnesses: The Origins of the Cold War (Winston Churchill notes the signs of Cold War; The "Truman Doctrine"; Andrei Zhdanov on United States "aid") 874

Witnesses: As the Cold War Ages (Jimmy Carter, Commencement Address; Ronald Reagan sees no compromise with evil empire) 877

Witnesses: The Breakdown of Communism and the End of the Cold War (Nikita Khrushchev denounces Stalin; Mikhail Gorbachev and *perestroika*; Václav Havel speaks of the past; Robert Heilbroner on the future of Socialism; Joel Barr renounces communism) 880

Witnesses: Culture and Politics in the 1960s (Bob Dylan, "The Times They are a-Changin' ") 883

Witnesses: Women and the Post-War World (The Redstockings Manifesto; China's marriage law; Women in Revolutionary Iran) 886

Witnesses: Love Your Mother (John C. Whitaker on the environmental movement; Ross Gelbspan on global warming) 893

Witnesses: The Age of Human Rights (UN Universal Declaration of Human Rights; UN Convention on the Prevention and Punishment on Genocide; UN Convention on the Rights of the Child) 895

Witnesses: Through a Glass Darkly (Paul Kennedy on the need for technology; Václav Havel discusses the advent of global society; Amartya Sen examines plural identities) 900

Witnesses: Why Some are So Rich and Some are So Poor (Economic theorists predict disaster for the global market; discuss the globalization of poverty; express concern over the futures of rich and poor; and see a solution to poverty in economic growth) 905

Witnesses: Let's Roll: The War on Terror (Rudolph Giuliani on the World Trade Center attack; Salman Rushdie on Islam; Osama Bin Laden declares America to be a target for "blessed terrorism") 908

Witnesses: The Future of the West (Francis Fukuyama on the future hegemony of the West; Bernard Lewis the place of the West in world history; Samuel Huntington predicts a decline in the West; Václav Havel looks at Europe's role for the twenty-first century) 910

TIMELINES

Society, Politics, and Economy	Religion and Ideas	Europe and the Americas	Rulers, Nations, Warfare, and Revolution

Civilization, Art, and Science	Africa, the Middle East, Asia, and Oceania	Beyond the West

15	Absolute Power: 1500–1750	416
16	Europe Reaches Out: 1500–1750	446
17	The Age of Reason: 1500–1780	482
18	Town, Court, and Country: 1500–1780	512
19	Inalienable Rights: 1500–1880	542
20	Revoltion: 1789–1815	576
21	Machines in the Garden: 1750–1914	610
22	Lives of the Other Half: 1750–1914	638

23	The Concert of Europe: 1815–1914	664
24	The Western *Imperium*: 1750–1914	688
25	Storm, Stress, and Doubt: 1780–1914	718
26	The Mighty are Fallen: 1914–1920	744
27	The Triumph of Uncertainty: 1915–1945	770
28	States in Conflict: 1917–1945	796
29	The End of Imperialism: 1914–1990s	830
30	Back From Armageddon: 1945–1990	866

MAPS

Map 15.1 The European States in 1526 423
Map 15.2 The European States in 1795 429
Map 16.1 World Economies and Movements of Peoples
around 1500 449
Map 16.2 Columbus' World 457
Map 16.3 European Exploration, 1450–1600 459
Map 16.4 World Trade and European Colonization, 1600–1750 472
Map 16.5 European Commerce, Industry, and Urbanization,
1550–1750 477
Map 17.1 The Major Scientific Thinkers and *Philosophes* 492
Map 17.2 Subscriptions to Diderot and d'Alembert's *Encyclopedia* 497
Map 18.1 The Emancipation of the Peasantry up to 1812 537
Map 19.1 The European Presence in the Americas on the
Eve of Independence (1750) 552
Map 19.2 Latin America from Independence to 1910 562
Map 19.3 Manifest Destiny: the Expansion of the United States,
Amerindian Relocation, and Consolidation of Canada 567
Map 20.1 The Revolution, 1789–1799 594
Map 20.2 Napoleon's Empire and Major Battles, 1799–1815 604
Map 21.1 Great Britain Industrializes, 1750–1850 616
Map 21.2 The Industrialization of Continental Europe,
1815–1860 627
Map 21.3 Industrialized Europe by 1914 631
Map 22.1 Charles Booth's Poverty Map, 1889 651
Map 23.1 Europe in 1815 as Established by the Congress
of Vienna 667
Map 23.2 Liberal, Nationalist, and Socialist Uprisings in
Europe, 1815–1871 672
Map 23.3 Unification and Differentiation—the Diverse Fates of
Ethnic, Religious, and National Peoples around 1870 680

Map 24.1 European Expansion in 1870 and 1914 691
Map 24.2 Europeans in Asia 692
Map 24.3 Europeans in Africa and the Middle East 704
Map 24.4 African States and People Before 1880 705
Map 26.1 Europe—A Two-Front War 749
Map 26.2 A World at War 757
Map 26.3 Redrawing the Boundaries 767
Map 27.1 European Debts to the United States, 1914–1925—
War Loans and Loans for Relief and Reconstruction 786
Map 27.2 Maximum Unemployment Rates for Industrial
Workers, 1930–1938 791
Map 28.1 Democratic, Authoritarian, and Totalitarian
Government, 1919–1937 798
Map 28.2 Expansion and Aggression West and East, 1930–1939 815
Map 28.3 Axis Advance and Allied Victory—World War II,
1939–1945 822
Map 28.4 Final Solutions, 1941–1945 824
Map 29.1 Colonial Possessions in Africa and Asia, 1939 833
Map 29.2 Independence Gained in Africa and Asia Since 1939 836
Map 29.3 African Political Systems, 1996 840
Map 29.4 United States Intervention in Latin America
and Asia 856
Map 29.5 The Fall of South Vietnam, 1975 858
Map 30.1 The Two Superpowers in a Bipolar World, 1955 869
Map 30.2 Collapse of the Soviet Bloc, 1989–1991 878
Map 30.3 Women of the World, 1990s 888–89
Map 30.4 Rates of Population Growth, 1993 892
Map 31.1 Europe: the Continent, the Union, the Alliance 902
Map 31.2 The Wealth of Nations: Developed and Developing
Nations of the World 904

WINDOWS ON

Windows On: Warriors and Peacemakers 432
Windows On: Mapping the World 453
Windows On: Women and Science 507
Windows On: Women's Lives 531
Windows On: African Laborers in a Harsh New World 551
Windows On: The Radical Revolution 592
Windows On: Revolution in Fashion 600
Windows On: In the Factory 618
Windows On: Power from Steam 621
Windows On: Men and Work 643
Windows On: Women and Work 648

Windows On: Power to the People 684
Windows On: Colonized Europeans: The Jews and the Irish 711
*Windows On: The Cycle of Styles: Classicism, Romanticism,
and Realism* 722
*Windows On: Fin De Siècle and the Advent of
the Modern* 740
Windows On: Drama in Russia 751
Windows On: Highs and Lows 789
Windows On: The Holocaust 825
Windows On: Civil Rights for African Americans 862
Windows On: Women, Poverty, and War 890

PREFACE

On September 11, 2001—a day that the citizens of the United States of America will not easily forget—four planes, hijacked by four squads of suicidal terrorists, were piloted deliberately toward four monuments that symbolized the achievements and strivings of our society. Three hit their targets; one crashed before it could do so, probably because of the prompt and courageous intervention of some of the doomed passengers. Nearly 4,000 people died in the four incidents, including hundreds of citizens of foreign nations resident in this country.

As these horrific events were pondered, while grief subsided and understanding dawned, the concept of "Western civilization" was mentioned rather more than it usually is in our bold and boisterous national discourse. Somehow, it was felt by many, these attacks had to be attacks on the fundamental structures of Western society: not just objections to American foreign policy, or resentment of American success, but a more basic blow to the values that sustain the democratic societies of the Western world. It is possible that some good will proceed from the great evil of September 11, and that one of the consequences of that day's events may be a renewed interest in the development of the West. The second edition of this book therefore begins with some very basic questions: where, and what, is the West?

WHERE IS THE WEST?

When I teach the introductory history course at Brooklyn College of the City University of New York, I start each semester by asking my students "Where is the West?" I send an unfortunate victim to the map of the world mounted on the back wall of the room. A finger roams around the continents of the globe. The class suggests many possibilities: western Europe? The western hemisphere? The wild west? The search goes on all semester—a search of special complexity for the many students who, speaking tens of languages, professing all the world's major religions, and hailing from all its inhabited continents, have no association by birth with Western civilization. To begin, I tell my students about Greenwich, England, where the Prime Meridian begins.

Visitors gathered outside the gates of the old Royal Observatory in Greenwich, England, may read a sign announcing that they now stand "at the center of time and space." From that spot an imaginary line circles the earth from pole to pole, slicing the globe in half. The two halves are the Eastern and the Western hemispheres. The line is the Prime Meridian, the first and last of the infinite series of lines of longitude by which any location on the globe, East or West,

can be accurately denoted by its precise variation in hours, minutes, and seconds from Greenwich time.

The packs of schoolchildren who come to Greenwich are often photographed grinning as they stand astride the Prime Meridian—each with one foot in the East and one in the West. Yet both feet are in England, in Europe, and in the zone of Western Civilization. Part of England and most of Europe (and all of Australia and New Zealand) lie in the Eastern hemisphere. Yet they belong to the West. A good fraction of Africa lies in the Western hemisphere. Yet it does not belong to the West. The people of the nations of Latin America lie in the western hemisphere, accept an official language which is European, and adhere for the most part to the Roman Catholic Church—is their civilization "Western?" Or does a struggling economy, or a large population of peoples of mixed indigenous and African heritage, mark them as non-Western?

What is the West? It isn't the "west" of the old movies, where for a brief moment cowboys prowled the frontier, and the native peoples of North America resisted the incursions of Europeans arriving from the East. It isn't the "west" of the Cold War era (1945–1991; see Chapter 30) when eastern and western zones of Europe adhered to different ideologies, and the boundary between their mental and political battles was designated by an Iron Curtain in part mythical, in part real. It is not only the zone of western, Catholic Christianity (which includes Poland, a nation solidly in "eastern" Europe), but embraces also the nations whose majorities embrace eastern, Orthodox Christianity: Greece, Serbia, perhaps even Russia. The West is not defined by any number of terms which contain, in their designations, the word "west": the Western hemisphere, the North American West, or Western Europe. What is the West? It is not, in fact, a place.

Neither is the West a specific people, or race, or set of nations. Although all of the nations of Europe are Western, so too are other nations far away—the nations of the Americas, Australasia, and the Asian zones of Russia—that were settled by Europeans who bore with them, along with their tools and skills, the elements of their civilization. In these scattered zones of Western civilization, and in the European homeland now as well, as migrations of peoples have altered its original population, people of greatly different origins—Asian, African—have adopted aspects of Western civilization. Just as anybody may learn French, or become a Methodist, anyone who so chooses may adopt and transmit the civilization of the West. Although at times in the Western past, theorists argued that civilization was linked to what

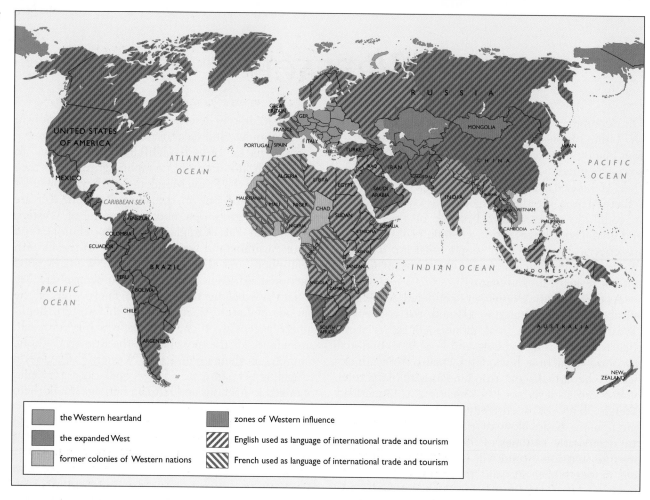

Where is the West: *Shown here is one way of thinking about the West geographically. Its heartland is Europe, where the cultural, social, and political traditions of the West developed their modern form after about 1000 C.E. "The expanded West" includes regions of European settlement, where Western civilization was transplanted from Europe after 1500 but where it has since developed in modified form because of contacts with other peoples. "Former colonies of Western nations" include those regions where Western civilization was imposed upon other nations, nations now largely liberated from colonial rule but still retaining some features of that civilization. Finally, areas designated as "zones of Western influence" have been largely free of any period of direct domination by Western nations, but have to a greater or lesser extent adopted selected Western political and economic institutions.*

was then, erroneously, called "race," the events of the last century have at long last obliterated those notions. Among the millions destroyed in the maelstrom of genocidal war were those considered to be by race outside the bounds of Western civilization; but their language and values were solidly Western, and their appeals for justice recapitulate the patterns of Western thought.

WHAT, THEN, IS THE WEST?

The West is a body of ideas, values, customs, and beliefs. These were forged over a period of centuries on the continent of Europe, which lay to the west of the then more advanced civilizations of the East. They triumphed during the centuries of European expansion: from approximately 1000 to 1900 of the Common Era, when Western values followed Western merchants, travelers, armies, and governors into every other corner of the inhabited globe. They are what the West means, and they are truly the meaning of the West.

Here are a few of the many concepts that have made the West and that constitute its core meaning:
• The principle of human dignity: that all human beings are equal in worth (if not in talents, beauty, or size), that they possess rights which cannot be taken away, and that to the greatest possible degree they are free.
• The ideal of justice: that no person should be unfairly privileged above another.
• The value of democracy: that the power to shape the future of a community belongs to its people as a whole and not to arbitrarily selected leaders.
• The method of rationalism, which assumes that all phenomena (even those pertaining to God, essence, or spirit) may be subject to the critical scrutiny of the human mind.
• The inclination to progress, to work toward goals to be achieved in the future.
• The habit of self-examination, which encourages human beings to examine themselves seriously and often to test whether they have fulfilled their promise and their responsibilities.

These, among others, are the habits and values that together characterize Western civilization, and which have caused it to develop in the directions it has—the very habits and values that have provoked the enemies to strike cruelly and violently against the innocent citizens of New York City and Washington DC on September 11, 2001.

THE WEST AND THE REST OF THE WORLD

We learn more about the Western world when we also examine the rest of the world. Some features of Western civilization are not unique to the West. They appear also in the cultural systems of other people around the globe, although not all of them appear in the same way in any other civilization. In many cases, particularly in the era of its origins, the West borrowed customs and ideas from the civilizations of Asia and Africa. More recently, a fully developed Western culture has lent, shared, or imposed its values on those civilizations and the newer ones of the Western hemisphere (see map, facing page).

This book will frequently pause in its narration of Western development to consider key aspects of non-Western civilizations. The ancient civilizations of the Mediterranean region, which confer upon the later West its first patterns of urbanization and political rule, its religious traditions and its alphabet, are considered. But so, too, are the ancient and medieval civilizations of China, India, Africa, and the Americas (Chapters 1, 2, 8, and 16). In the modern era, this book considers at length not only the process by which Western nations came to control much of the globe in the nineteenth century (Chapter 24), but also how colonized regions freed themselves from that domination in the twentieth (Chapter 29). To isolate the West from other regions which have helped shape it, and upon which it has impacted, makes no sense— especially in an age which is no longer dominated by the West but is truly **global**.

A global perspective transcends any claims for the superiority of one civilization to another. The civilization of the West is the focus of this book not because it is better (arguable) or because it is ours (it is not "ours" to many Americans by virtue of birth), but because it embodies principles of permanent value that will survive as long as there are those who learn them, reflect on them, and teach them to future generations.

It is hoped that this *Second Edition* of *Western Civilization: A Social and Cultural History* will help introduce students of the post 9/11/2001 world to the civilization that we all, whatever our origins or ethnicity, now share, and which can only be more treasured than it had been before. Please see the *Walkthrough* section of these preliminary pages for a detailed description of what is new in the second edition.

CHANGES TO THE SECOND EDITION

Drawing on the comments of the many reviewers of the original edition of *Western Civilization: A Social and Cultural History*, a number of changes and enhancements appear in this new edition.

The narrative has been changed at several points. Chapter 1 has been updated. In the modern era, the *Epilogue: The Future of The West* has been entirely rewritten. Chapter 20, which in the original edition had dealt with European politics from the Old Regime through the creation of the German and Italian states, has been split into two full-length chapters. The revised Chapter 20 deals with the French Revolution and Napoleon, while a new Chapter 23 carries the political narrative forward from the Congress of Vienna through the proclamation of the German empire and the Parisian Commune. Other chapters have been updated to reflect current scholarship or modified to improve the flow of the narrative.

Many elements have been updated or replaced. The *Witnesses* boxes, which contain, normally, two or more texts which "speak" to each other on an issue pertaining to the adjacent narrative, have all been equipped with brief introductions which aid the student in the critical reading of the selected passages. As well, 24 new *Witnesses* boxes or new *Witnesses* texts have been supplied, and some of the texts appearing in the original edition dropped.

In the same way, many of the illustrations in the original edition have been replaced, approximately 50 in color and 50 in black and white, and two new *Windows On* boxes have been created—most conspicuously a two-page spread on the impact of the French Revolution on both men's and women's costume. Moreover, each *Windows On* box now includes a *Windows On the Web* activity, which uses the Internet to continue the investigation presented in the text. In addition, new maps have been created for the Chinese world up to 800 C.E., German confessionalization in the sixteenth and seventeenth centuries, poverty in London, 1898–99, the fall of South Vietnam, 1975, and African political systems, 1996. There are also five new *How Many?* boxes, eight new *Must Reads*, and eight new *Who's Who* as well. Descriptions for these features can be found in the *Walkthrough* section that follows.

These changes to the narrative and features and updates throughout should make this *Second Edition of Western Civilization: A Social and Cultural History* more accessible to students than the original edition, and more appealing to faculty as well.

Margaret L. King
Brooklyn College and the Graduate Center
City University of New York
December, 2001

THE MEANING OF THE WEST, EXAMINED IN A LIVELY NEW EDITION OF

WESTERN CIVILIZATION

A Social and Cultural History

AVAILABLE IN THE FOLLOWING FORMATS:

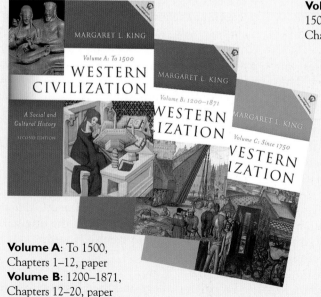

Combined Edition
Chapters 1–30, casebound

Volume 1
Prehistory to 1750
Chapters 1–16, paper
Volume 2
1500 to the Present,
Chapters 15–30, paper

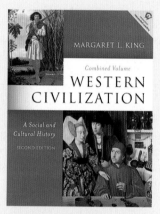

Volume A: To 1500,
Chapters 1–12, paper
Volume B: 1200–1871,
Chapters 12–20, paper
Volume C: Since 1750,
Chapters 20–30, paper

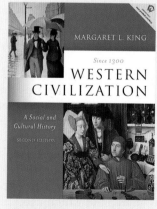

Since 1300
Chapters 11–30, casebound

WHY IS WESTERN CIVILIZATION, SECOND EDITION, ORGANIZED THEMATICALLY?

Because this book gives special attention to the history of culture and society, its organization is topical. Some chapters focus on politics, others on society, others on religion or ideas. Often two or three chapters in succession will deal with the same historical period, but from different topical vantage points. The chapters on the Middle Ages, for instance, examine the whole of that thousand-year period, stressing first politics and society (Chapter 9), then religion and ideas (Chapter 10), then commerce and urbanization (Chapter 11). A topical division has the virtue that students are introduced systematically to the variety of ways that historians study the past.

**Giovanni Boccaccio,
A Woman Copying a Manuscript,
fifteenth century**

The consequence of a focus on social and cultural themes is a deemphasis of the political narrative. That shift of priorities parallels the tendency of historical scholarship since 1960, which has elevated the richness of multiple themes, and highlighted the many voices of past reality. Accordingly, attention is paid to the experience of workers, the poor, and marginalized groups (modifying the traditional emphasis on rulers and elites), to the changing roles of women and children, to the structure and growth of cities, to war as an expression of social values, to religious experience and behavior (as well as doctrine and organization), to popular and high culture, to the settings of intellectual

**Hans Holbein, The Ambassadors,
1533**

discourse and the role of the powerful in shaping culture.

Although the development of states, the sequence of rulers, and the chain of wars and peace treaties are included, they are in briefer format than in most texts. No more than one of five chapters is devoted primarily to political discussion (Chapters 2, 15, 20, 23, 26, 29); only six others contain large sections dedicated to political narrative (Chapters 3, 5, 6, 9, 19, 28). Nearly two-thirds of the whole centers on social and cultural themes. Some chapters are particularly dedicated to language, religion, and ideas (Chapters 1, 4, 6, 7, 10, 13, 14, 17, 25, 27); others to social or economic problems, including world trade, migrations, urbanization, social structures, technology, development, and the environment (Chapters 3, 9, 11, 12, 16, 18, 21, 22, 30).

A topical organization means that students must read, and teachers must teach, different chapters in different ways. But in all cases, that reading and teaching is supported by maps, graphical, visual, and documentary materials that bring the material to life, and aid the student in gaining a rich and up-to-date vision of the past, and in developing an appreciation of Western civilization that is based not only on the recitation of its triumphs of war and state, but also on the impressive foundations of its social and cultural heritage.

**Etruscan sarcophagus
(coffin) from Veii,
c. 520 B.C.E.**

xviii *Walkthrough*

FEATURES OF THE SECOND EDITION

PART THREE

THE WEST TAKES FORM

Medieval Society, Politics, Economy, and Culture (500–1500)

Peasants and nobles created the society of the European Middle Ages. As Roman institutions crumbled and waves of invaders destroyed communities, medieval peasants devised new patterns of agricultural work and life, generally on the manors, or large estates, of noble landholders. The nobles, as an elite group of military men, warded off invaders and struggled among themselves for power.

Amid the bounds of mainly local authority, the first European kingdoms emerged, and kings employed violence and persuasion to assert their authority over nobles. The Crusades sent knightly armies east to the Levant (Palestine and Syria, on the eastern Mediterranean shores), while knights who stayed home at court developed the rituals of chivalry. In the late medieval centuries, which were gripped by famine and plague, peasant rebellions against landholders were frequent.

Providing cohesion to the disparate communities of Europe was the Catholic Church, centered in Rome under the pope, whose authority was at its height around 1300 after a process of reform, centralization, and resistance to the encroachments of secular rulers. A powerful Church summoned Christians to respect celibacy, the priestly administration of the sacraments, and the examples of saints and martyrs; and it disciplined those who strayed from orthodoxy. Providing access to libraries and schools, the Church trained most of Europe's intellectuals, who elaborated a rational system of theology and laid the foundations for modern philosophical, political, legal, and scientific thought.

As monarchical and ecclesiastical institutions crystallized, a new social group and setting emerged: merchants and towns. By 1300, towns stretching from the Mediterranean to the North Sea coasts housed artisans, merchants, bankers, and entrepreneurs. By 1500, their commercial ventures, extending to Africa, the Middle East, and Asia, made Europe rich and ready to expand.

9 Workers, Warriors, and Kings
Politics and Society in the Middle Ages, 800–1500

10 The Spiritual Sword
Religion and Culture in the Middle Ages, 500–1500

11 In the Name of Profit
Cities, Merchants, and Trade in the Middle Ages, 1000–1500

227

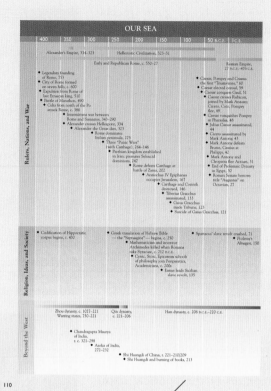

110

Part Opener

Western Civilization is divided into seven parts that group the chapters into a cohesive, thematic framework. Part-opening essays set the stage for discussions that follow.

Chapter Opener Timeline

Organized thematically, and arranged into color-coded sections, chapter-opening timelines show the chronology of major events and developments.

Map Opener

Map openers add a geographical and spatial dimension to each chapter's narrative. Inset maps put the the West in global perspective.

"I like the timelines and maps provided at the beginning of each chapter—these timelines will help."
WILLIAM BENTON WHISENHUNT,
COLLEGE OF DUPAGE

Contrasting colors, and a simple key, give clear information to ensure that the map is readily understood by students.

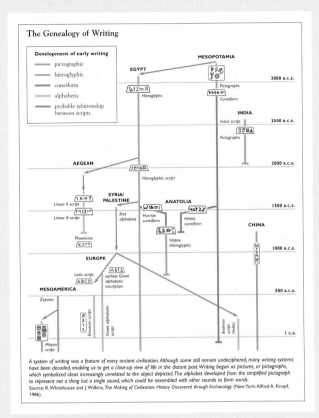

The Genealogy of Writing

Development of early writing
- pictographic
- hieroglyphic
- cuneiform
- alphabetic
- probable relationship between scripts

A system of writing was a feature of every ancient civilization. Although some still remain undeciphered, many writing systems have been decoded, enabling us to get a close-up view of life in the distant past. Writing began as pictures, or pictographs, which symbolized ideas increasingly unrelated to the object depicted. The alphabet developed from the simplified pictograph to represent not a thing but a single sound, which could be assembled with other sounds to form words.
Source: R. Whitehouse and J. Wilkins, The Making of Civilization: History Discovered through Archaeology (New York: Alfred A. Knopf, 1986).

Illustrated Information

Numerous tables, charts, and graphs display information visually. Complex processes and data are presented in an easy-to-read format that facilitates student learning.

Patterns of European Economic Development: 1850–1873

	1850	1869	1873
Britain			
Railroad	6,621	15,145	16,082
Coal	37,500	97,066	112,604
Steam power	1,290	4,040	
Pig iron	2,249	5,446	6,566
Raw cotton	266.8	425.8	565.1
Germany			
Railroad	3,639	10,834	14,842
Coal	5,100	26,774	36,392
Steam power	260	2,480	
Pig iron	212	1,413	2,241
Raw cotton	17.1	64.1	117.8
France			
Railroad	1,869	10,518	11,500
Coal	7,225	21,432	24,702
Steam power	370	1,850	
Pig iron	406	1,381	1,382
Raw cotton	59.3	93.7	55.4
Belgium			
Railroad	531	1,800	2,335
Coal	3,481	7,822	10,219
Steam power	70	350	
Pig iron	145	535	607
Raw cotton	10.0	16.3	18.0

By five measures of economic development—total railroad mileage (statute miles), coal production (1000 metric tons), steam power capacity (1000 horsepower), pig iron output (1000 metric tons), and raw cotton consumption (1000 metric tons)—Britain outpaced her three leading European rivals from 1850 to 1873. The gap narrowed, however, especially between Germany and Britain. Note Germany's sevenfold increase in coal production, compared to Britain's threefold increase, and Germany's sevenfold increase in cotton consumption, compared to Britain's, which slightly more than doubled.
Source: Based on D. Landes, The Unbound Prometheus (Cambridge: Cambridge University Press, 1969), p. 194.

Captions give a concise overview of visually presented information.

Map 10.1 Christianity and other World Religions, to 1500: Over many centuries, Christianity spread from Constantinople and Rome; from Celtic Ireland, Anglo-Saxon England, and the eastern Frankish kingdom; from Moscow and Novgorod. As Christianity expanded from its Mediterranean homeland to touch the remotest boundaries of Europe, it took its place as a major actor among the matured religious systems of the world.

Map 8.1 Migrants, Raiders, and Conquerors, 100–800 C.E.: Beginning in the first century C.E., nomadic peoples of the central Asian steppes began to expand both west and east, disrupting civilization in both the Mediterranean region and in China. China resisted determinedly, and had attained some stability by around 600. In the west, the movement of Asian peoples triggered the dispersion first of Germanic, and then of Slavic peoples, which was to cut western Europe off from the Mediterranean and the Eastern Roman Empire centered at Constantinople, and to result in the failure of Roman rule in the west. (Compare map 6.3, p. 179, showing the region when Rome, governed from its single capital, held unquestioned dominion over the region; and map 8.2, p. 235, showing the position of successor kingdoms to western Rome.)

Maps

In each chapter, a range of colorful maps (many featuring topography) help students to place events in their geographical context. Throughout the book, they chart the political, social, and economic changes that have taken place globally during the course of Western civilization.

"The colors of the maps and pictures should hold students' attention. With the emphasis of this book being social and cultural, this may be the type of book we are looking for."
CHARLES HOPE, TARRANT COUNTY JUNIOR COLLEGE

High Quality Art Reproductions

A stunning gallery of art focuses on the diverse experiences of people throughout Western history.

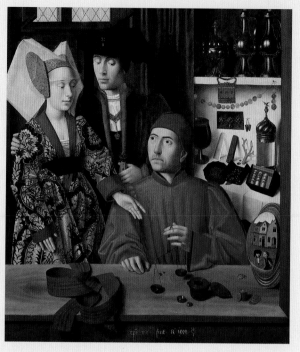

"I think the text is accessible, and the images are the best I have EVER seen in a textbook."

LINDA BREGSTEIN, MERCER COUNTY COMMUNITY COLLEGE

'Windows On' boxes

Windows On boxes illuminate subjects of high interest by gathering together a range of provocative visual sources.

"The text covers a vast amount of material and is extremely well written—college students will like the King text."

TIM CRAIN, UNIVERSITY OF WISCONSIN, MILWAUKEE

'Windows on the Web' activities extend the scope of the Windows On feature by combining documents, images, and Web-based material to explore concepts and problems in more depth. Each Windows on the Web activity can be found at **www.prenhall.com/king**

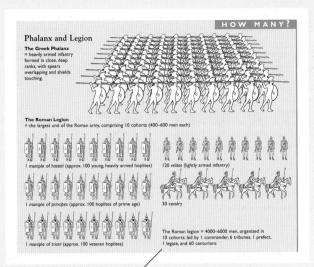

Phalanx and Legion

The Greek Phalanx
= heavily armed infantry formed in close, deep ranks, with spears overlapping and shields touching.

The Roman Legion
= the largest unit of the Roman army, comprising 10 cohorts (400–600 men each)

1 maniple of *hastati* (approx. 100 young, heavily armed hoplites)

1 maniple of *principes* (approx. 100 hoplites of prime age)

1 maniple of *triarii* (approx. 100 veteran hoplites)

120 *velites* (lightly armed infantry)

30 cavalry

The Roman legion = 4000–6000 men, organized in 10 cohorts; led by 1 commander, 6 tribunes, 1 prefect, 1 legate, and 60 centurions

'How Many' boxes

Unique to Western Civilization, How Many? boxes present useful data clearly and visually.

Women Protest against Husbands and Predators

In the sixteenth century, women's voices were finally heard—after centuries of near silence. Their works were composed mostly in the vernacular, which unlike Latin did not require an advanced education. The printing press made possible the publication of many copies, circulated widely, as in the case of Moderata Fonte's The Worth of Women represented in the first excerpt here. Women artists, too, became more conspicuous, as in the case of Artemisia Gentileschi, represented in the second excerpt. Both women protest against the actions of men: the first, broadly and theoretically, condemning them for "usurping" women's rights; the second, concretely and particularly, testifying in a trial against a man who raped her.

A Venetian woman lambasts the tyranny of men (1592): If men usurp our rights, should we not complain and declare that they have wronged us? Or if we are their inferiors in status, but not in worth, this is an abuse that has been introduced into the world and that men have then, over time, gradually translated into law and custom; and it has become so entrenched that they claim ... that the status they have gained through their bullying is theirs by right. ... And we would suffer it. ... if they did not insist on exerting such absolute control over us and in such an arrogant manner, treating us like slaves who cannot take a step without asking their permission or say a word without their jumping down our throats. ... As fathers, as brothers, as sons or husbands or lovers or whatever other relationship they have to us, they all abuse us, humiliate us, and do all they can to harm and annihilate us.
(Moderata Fonte (Modesta da Pozzo), *The Worth of Women, Wherein is Clearly Revealed their Nobility and their Superiority to Men*, 1592; ed. and trs. V. Cox, 1997)

Artemisia Gentileschi, painter, testifies at the trial of her rapist (1612): Agostino put his head on my breast ... and said "Let's walk together a while, because I hate sitting down." ... After we had walked around two or three times, each time going by the bedroom door, when we were in front of the bedroom door, he pushed me in and locked the door. He then threw me onto the edge of the bed, pushing me with a hand on my breast. ... Lifting my clothes, which he had a great deal of trouble doing, he placed a hand with a handkerchief at my throat and on my mouth to keep me from screaming. ... I felt a strong burning and it hurt very much, but because he held my mouth I couldn't cry out. However, I tried to scream as best I could.
I scratched his face and pulled his hair and ... I even removed a piece of flesh. ... And after he had done his business he got off me. When I saw myself free, I went to the table drawer and took a knife and moved toward Agostino saying: "I'd like to kill you with this knife because you have dishonored me."
(From M. D. Garrard, *Artemisia Gentileschi*, 1989)

'Witnesses' boxes

Bringing to life the events narrated in the text, authentic voices from the past provide personal accounts of social and political change. Brief headnotes introduce the documents and place them in comparative perspective.

"The Witnesses boxes are an excellent idea. I am pleased that primary sources are so numerous and varied."
MEAGHAN DUFF, WESTERN KENTUCKY UNIVERSITY

Books and Pamphlets from the French Revolution

Emmanuel Sieyès — *What Is the Third Estate?* (1789)

Edmund Burke — *Reflections on the Revolution in France* (1790)

Olympe de Gouges — *Declaration of the Rights of Woman and the Citizen* (1791)

Tom Paine — *Rights of Man* (1791)

Mary Wollstonecraft — *A Vindication of the Rights of Woman* (1792)

Key Books by Key Leaders

Vladimir Ilyich Lenin — *What Is To Be Done?* (1902)

Adolf Hitler — *Mein Kampf (My Struggle)* (1925)

Winston Churchill — *The Speeches of Winston Churchill* (1941–1945)

'Must Reads' boxes

Must Reads boxes list books of exceptional importance to the meaning of the West—books students may wish to read.

Fading Empires in Africa

Patrice Lumumba (1925–1961), first premier of the state of Zaire (formerly the Congo) upon Belgian withdrawal in 1960, but assassinated by rivals in 1961.

Joseph (Sese Seko) Mobutu (1930–1997), seized power in Zaire after Lumumba's death, and held it for 32 years, with US support.

Kwame Nkrumah (1909–1972), pan-Africanist prime minister of Ghana upon its independence in 1957, and president in 1960; ousted by a military coup in 1967.

Robert Mugabe (1924–), Marxist leader of Rhodesian revolutionary party which ousted prime minister Ian Smith; became head of nation re-named Zimbabwe.

Desmond Tutu (1931–), South African Anglican archbishop who aroused world outrage against the segregationist apartheid policy of the white Afrikaner government of South Africa; winner of the 1984 Nobel Prize.

Nelson Mandela (1918–), leader of African National Congress imprisoned in 1964 and released in 1960; in 1994, won election to the presidency of South Africa.

Muammar el-Qaddafi (1942–), seized power in Libya in 1969 after toppling the pro-Western monarchy, nationalizing foreign petroleum assets, and, during the Cold War, accepting Soviet aid and arms.

'Who's Who' boxes

Important figures are identified and listed in Who's Who boxes, and their principal contributions noted.

Conclusion
THE EARLIEST CIVILIZATIONS AND THE MEANING OF THE WEST

Much of what distinguishes human life today was first attained by the ancient people of the first civilizations. The ability to control nature, to manage food production, to build cities, to conduct trade, to develop technology, to understand science and mathematics, to create works of literature, to establish systems of law, and to ask thoughtful questions about the cosmos and our place in it—all of these were bequeathed to later generations by the first civilizations, and to the "West" specifically by the ancient civilizations of the Middle East. These civilizations offer lessons as well about the organization of the state and the fragility of power. The next chapter will consider this other dimension of life in antiquity.

'Conclusion' boxes

Conclusion boxes look at how the events discussed in each chapter influenced the course of Western civilization, and provide insights into their consequences.

Stone, Bronze, and Word, 2 million–500 B.C.E. 29

REVIEW QUESTIONS

1. Describe the evolution of the human species. Why were the advances in the New Stone Age so important? What role did women play in Neolithic society?

2. Where did the first civilizations arise? What functions did cities serve in these cultures? Why did iron implements largely replace bronze ones? Why were trade and cultural links significant?

3. Describe the social hierarchy of early civilizations. How did women's status influence these societies? How did the status of women differ in Egypt and Mesopotamia?

4. Why was the invention of writing in early civilization so important? Why did writing evolve from the first pictograms to the alphabet? What is the difference between writing and language?

5. How did the custom of sacrifice develop? Why were Akhenaten's religious innovations such a break with Egyptian religion?

6. By what process did the Israelites become monotheists? Why was the Israelite concept of a righteous God so radical in the ancient world? What role did ethics play in the development of early Confucianism and Buddhism?

SUGGESTED RESOURCES

Before History
Cavalli-Sforza, Luigi Luca, *Genes, Peoples, and Languages*, trans. Mark Seielstad (New York: Farrar, Straus & Giroux; North Point Press, 2000). Linking complex genetic and linguistic evidence, Cavalli-Sforza proposes to map the history of the migrations of all the world's peoples.

Fagan, Brian M., *The Journey from Eden: The Peopling of Our World* (London: Thames & Hudson, 1990). A critical overview of theories of human origin, arguing on the basis of recent historical, paleoanthropological, and genetic research that fully modern humans evolved in Africa and from there colonized the rest of the world.

Leakey, Richard and Roger Lewin, *Origins Reconsidered: In Search of What Makes Us Human* (New York: Doubleday, 1992). Reflections by a renowned paleoanthropologist on his own discoveries of early hominid life in East Africa. Leakey incorporates ideas from philosophy, anthropology, molecular biology, and linguistics to investigate not only how we evolved anatomically but how we acquired the qualities that make us human: consciousness, creativity, and culture.

McElvaine, Robert S., *Eve's Seed: Biology, the Sexes, and the Course of History* (New York: McGraw Hill, 2000). Fills in the history between the culmination of human evolution and the establishment of civilization, a period when women's role was dominant before envious men overturned power relations.

Civilization and the City
Diamond, Jared, *Guns, Germs and Steel: The Fates of Human Societies* (New York: W.W. Norton, 1997). A brilliant exploration of the geographical and material conditions that permitted Eurasian civilizations to advance and gain dominance.

Hodder, Ian, *The Domestication of Europe: Structure and Contingency in Neolithic Societies* (Cambridge, MA: Basil Blackwell, 1990). A bold if controversial attempt to reconstruct human societies in the Near East and Europe at the end of the Ice Age.

Kramer, Samuel Noah, *The Sumerians: The History, Culture and Character* (Chicago: University of Chicago Press, 1971). A classic history of Sumer, 4500–1750 B.C.E., with selected translations of Sumerian texts. Details Sumerian achievements in government, education and literature, philosophy, law, agriculture, and medicine.

Lerner, Gerda, *The Creation of Patriarchy I: Women and History* (New York/Oxford: Oxford University Press, 1986). A pioneering feminist study of the origin of women's subordination, linking it to the

rise of property-conscious agricultural societies in Mesopotamia, Israel, and Greece.

Nissen, Hans J., *The Early History of the Ancient Near East, 9000–2000 B.C.* (Chicago: University of Chicago Press, 1988). A balanced political and cultural history of Mesopotamia, based on archaeological sources and analysis of material culture.

The Indus Valley civilization:
http://www.historyofindia.com/indus.html
http://www.harappa.com/har/har0.html

Writing, Language, and Consciousness
Frankfort, H. and H. A., John A. Wilson, Thorkild Jacobsen, *Before Philosophy: The Intellectual Adventure of Ancient Man* (Baltimore: Penguin, 1949). A challenging description of ancient Egyptian and Mesopotamian mythopoetic interpretations of phenomena, in contrast to the philosophical outlook of later Hellenic culture.

Martin, Henri Jean (trans. Lydia G. Cochrane), *The History and Power of Writing* (Chicago: University of Chicago Press, 1995). A comprehensive study by a preeminent scholar of the book. Examines the technologies, forms, and structures of writing throughout history.

The Analects of Confucius:
http://classics.mit.edu/Confucius/analects.html

Evolving Religions
Bergmann, Martin S., *In the Shadow of Moloch: The Sacrifice of Children and its Impact on Western Religions* (New York: Columbia University Press, 1993). An eye-opening account of the ritual convention of child sacrifice and its shaping of ancient cultures.

Cross, Frank Moore, *Canaanite Myth and Hebrew Epic: Essays in the History of the Religion of Israel* (Cambridge, MA.: Harvard University Press, 1973; reprint 1997). Traces continuities between early Israelite religion and its underlying Canaanite culture. Explores re-emergence of Canaanite mythic material in the apocalypticism of early Christianity and the Dead Sea Scrolls.

Leeming, David A. & Jake Page, *Goddess: The Myths of the Female Divine* (Oxford: Oxford University Press, 1994). A biography of the "goddess," the compelling, commanding, threatening female divinity revered by human populations from the Ice Age to modern times, showing how ancient themes endure in modern religion and psychology.

Bible tools—text and history: http://bible.crosswalk.com

End of chapter matter

Review Questions stimulate critical thought and understanding. Suggested Resources direct students to further study by recommending books and websites.

SUPPLEMENTS FOR

WESTERN CIVILIZATION

Second Edition

PRINT SUPPLEMENTS

The Instructor's Manual with Test Item File combines teaching resources with testing material. The Instructor's manual includes chapter outlines, overviews, key concepts, discussion questions, and audiovisual resources. The Test Item File offers a menu of multiple choice, true-false, essay, and map questions for each chapter. A collection of blank maps can be photocopied and used for map testing or other class exercises.

The Study Guide (Volumes I and II) provides, for each chapter, a brief overview, a list of chapter objectives, study exercises, and multiple-choice, short-answer, and essay questions. In addition, each chapter includes a number of specific map questions and exercises.

The Documents Set (Volumes I and II) is a collection of additional primary and secondary source documents that underscore the themes outlined in the text. Organized by chapter, this set for each of the two volumes includes review questions for each document.

A Transparency Pack provides instructors with full-color transparency acetates of all maps, charts, and graphs in the text for use in the classroom.

Understanding and Answering Essay Questions suggests helpful analytical tools for understanding different types of essay questions, and provides precise guidelines for preparing well-crafted essay answers. This brief guide is available free to students when packaged with *Western Civilization: A Social and Cultural History.*

Reading Critically About History This brief guide prepares students with helpful strategies for reading a history textbook. Available free when packed with *Western Civilization, Second Edition.*

History on the Internet is a brief guide to the internet that provides students with clear strategies for navigating the Internet and World Wide Web. Exercises within and at the ends of the chapters allow students to practice searching for the myriad resources available to the student of history. Free to students when packaged with *Western Civilization: A Social and Cultural History.*

ELECTRONIC SUPPLEMENTS

The Companion Website™
www.prenhall.com/king
The Companion Website™ works in tandem with the text to help students use the World Wide Web to enrich their understanding of Western civilization. Built around the primary subtopics of each chapter, it includes study questions, web links, and document questions. Features new to the Second Edition include interactive map exercises, "Windows on the Web" activities and, for instructors, maps and graphics from the text available for downloading in Power Point presentations.

Instructor's Resources CD-ROM An ideal tool for classroom presentations, this CD-ROM contains all of the maps and charts from the text, PowerPoint lectures that match the sequence of topics in the text, and lecture outlines, chapter summaries, and test items.

Course Management Systems As the leader in course-management solutions for teachers and students of history, Prentice Hall provides a variety of online tools. Contact your local Prentice Hall representative for a demonstration or visit.
www.prenhall.com/demo

Prentice Hall Custom Test, a commercial-quality, computerized, test management program is available for Windows and Macintosh environments. This allows instructors to select items from the Test Item File in the Instructor's Manual and design their own exams.

Create Your Own Reader in Western Civilization with Penguin Custom Editions

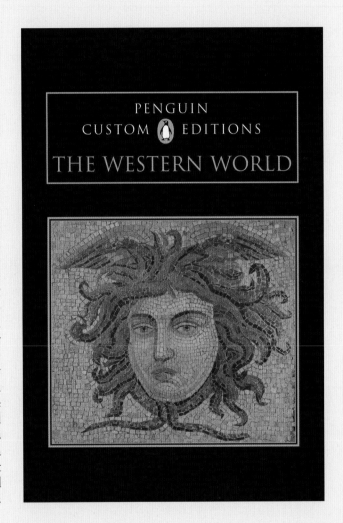

Developed by a team headed by leading historians, this superb new custom reader program from Penguin and Pearson Custom Publishing lets you choose the readings you want from an archive of 1,200 readings selected from the *Penguin Classics*™, the most comprehensive paperback library of Western literature, history, culture and philosophy available. For each excerpted reading, PCP's editors have prepared a brief headnote providing a quick biography of the writer and specifying the date of publication, the work from which the reading was taken, and the reading's historical context. Many important works are represented in readings of multiple lengths—brief (1–3 pages), medium (5–7 pages), and lengthy (10–15 pages). In addition to these selections, you have the option of adding your own writing, course notes, syllabi, and outside readings to your printed reader.

Go to Pearson Custom Publishing's online book building system—available through the **Penguin Custom Editions** web site at www.pearsoncustom.com/database/penguin.html—and you can quickly find the specific readings you need for your course using the powerful, multi-variable search engine provided. PCP has done the work for you and cleared all necessary permissions fees for you to use these materials in your **Penguin Custom Editions** reader. But that's not all. Once you create your custom reader online, you can order it shrinkwrapped with any Pearson Education text—including *Western Civilization, Second Edition*—and a selected list of Penguin Classics™ paperback books for a substantial discount. In just 4–6 weeks, we'll deliver a cleanly designed, beautifully printed paperbound reader you'll be proud to share with your students.

To request a free **Penguin Custom Editions** book building kit, or to obtain more information, contact your Prentice Hall sales representative or:

Project Editor, Penguin Custom Editions
Pearson Custom Publishing, 75 Arlington Street, Suite 300, Boston, MA 02116
Phone: 800-777-6872, Extension 2
Fax: 617-848-6366
Email: Dbase.pub@pearsoncustom.com
Web site: www.pearsoncustom.com/database/penguin.html

ABSOLUTE POWER

1500	1550	1600	1650	1700	1750	1800

Rulers, Nations, and War

French religious wars, 1562–94

Thirty Years' War, 1618–48

Anglo-Dutch Wars, 1652–74

Seven Years' War, 1756–63

Independence struggle in Netherlands, 1579–1648

War of Spanish Succession, 1701–14

Polish partitions, 1772, 1793, 1795

Elizabeth I in England, 1558–1603

English Civil War, 1642–51

Peter the Great in Russia. 1682–1725

Frederick the Great in Prussia, 1740–86

Philip II in Spain, 1556–98

Louis XIV in France, 1643–1715

Maria Theresa in Austria, 1740–80

◆ Fall of Granada, 1492

◆ Peace of Augsburg, 1555

◆ Treaty of Câteau-Cambrésis, 1559

◆ Defeat of Spanish Armada, 1588

◆ Henry IV assumes throne of France, 1589

◆ Peace of Westphalia, 1648

◆ Execution of King Charles I, 1649

◆ English Restoration, King Charles II, 1660

◆ Glorious Revolution, 1688

◆ Peace of Utrecht, 1713

◆ Treaty of Paris, 1763

◆ U.S. Constitution ratified, 1788

◆ French Revolution begins, 1789

Society and Economy

Plague endemic in Europe, 1347–1720

Atlantic slave trade, c. 1500–1888

◆ Expulsion of Jews from Spain, 1492

◆ Peasants' Revolt suppressed, 1525

◆ Spanish "New Laws" prohibit Amerindian slavery, 1542

◆ Approx. 10% of Europeans live in cities, 1600

◆ Bank of Amsterdam founded, 1609

◆ Stock Exchange completed, Amsterdam, 1611

◆ London's population tops 500,000, 1700

◆ Southern U.S. slave population tops 700,000, 1790

◆ London's population 1,000,000

Religion and Ideas

First century of printing, 1460–1560

The Enlightenment, 1685–1795

The Scientific Revolution, 1543–1687

◆ Erasmus' *Praise of Folly*, 1511

◆ Luther's *Ninety-Five Theses*, 1517

◆ Loyola's *Spiritual Exercises*, 1541

◆ St. Bartholomew's Day Massacre, 1572

◆ Jean Bodin's *Six Books of the Commonwealth*, 1576

◆ Edict of Nantes, 1598

◆ Thomas Hobbes' *Leviathan*, 1651

◆ Newton's *Mathematical Principles of Natural Philosophy*, 1687

◆ John Locke's *Letter on Toleration, Essay Concerning Human Understanding,* and *Second Treatise on Civil Government*, 1689–90

◆ Rousseau's *Social Contract*, 1762

Beyond the West

Mughal Empire, India, 1526–1857

Ming dynasty, 1368–1644

Qing dynasty, 1644–1912

◆ Columbus' first voyage, 1492

◆ Magellan sails the world, 1519–22

◆ Cortés conquers Mexico, 1521–2

◆ Chinese officials allow Portuguese trading, Macao, 1557

◆ Drake circumnavigates globe, 1577–80

◆ Jamestown founded, 1607

◆ Dutch East India Company, Batavia (Jakarta, Java), 1619

◆ Plymouth Bay Colony founded, 1620

◆ Dutch acquire Malacca from Portuguese, 1641

◆ East India Company founds port, Calcutta, India, 1690

◆ British control Dutch Cape colony, 1795

◆ Ireland incorporated into the U.K., 1800

CHAPTER

15

ABSOLUTE POWER

War and Politics in Early Modern Europe

1500–1750

KEY TOPICS

◆ **Power and Gunpowder:** The emerging nations of Europe gain new strength—and face mounting costs—as guns outpace swords, infantry displaces cavalry, and the demand grows for drillmasters and engineers.

◆ **War Games:** Wars fought increasingly for plain political advantage culminate in a struggle between France and Great Britain in the global struggle of the Seven Years' War.

◆ **An Age of Kings:** Kings aim to rule absolutely in Spain, France, England, Prussia, Austria, and Russia; in England, however, Parliament imposes limits on monarchy.

◆ **Mirrors for Princes:** Artists and intellectuals celebrate kings; some thinkers propose a social contract and the rights of citizens, which will in time undo the absolutist pretensions of kings.

T*he Perfect Prince* *Around the beginning of the sixteenth century, the Italian duke Cesare Borgia (1475–1507) was engaged in acquiring for himself a large chunk of central Italy. To bolster his authority in the city of Cesena, he decided to rid himself of the agent he had placed in charge of it. He waited for the right moment;* "*Then, one morning, Remirro's body was found cut in two pieces on the piazza …, with a block of wood and a bloody knife beside it.*" *The brutal message had its intended effect, keeping the citizens, at least for a while, "appeased and stupefied."*

This incident was narrated by Niccolò Machiavelli (1469–1527) in his handbook for the perfect prince (see Chapter 13). For Machiavelli, the concern of a prince is to gain and hold power—by any means necessary. He should crush enemies, rather than forgive them; inflict cruelties as necessary, swiftly and all at once. His subjects need not love him; better that they fear him, since "fear is strengthened by a dread of punishment which is always effective." Such a prince might possibly, Machiavelli thought, save Italy.

Machiavelli's prince never came. Hopelessly fragmented, Italy fell to nations beyond the Alps. Those nations embodied new dimensions of power, not seen since the days of the Roman Empire—enough to consume each other and to dominate much of the rest of the world. Their ascension owed much to their ambitious kings, who exemplified the principles that Machiavelli proposed.

The period from 1500 to 1750—often called the "early modern" era—saw a great concentration of power in Europe: the power of armies, of states, and, above all, of kings. Changes in military organization and funding, as well as terrible new weapons, made their progress possible and their ambitions urgent. (*How Many* on p. 428 shows the growth in army size and casualties.) Those ambitions erupted into a series of wars, fought at first in the name of religion and later for ***raison d'état***, "reason of state." The kings and princes who profited from these wars—who taxed their subjects, reined in their fractious nobles, and compelled ordinary men to fight—not only expanded their states but maximized their power. In several states, they reached for absolute power, which would allow them to execute law without the restraint of parliament or peerage. As monarchs gathered power, abetted by prime ministers, advisers, and **courtiers**, intellectuals developed theories of monarchy justifying the power of kings to the people who had none.

POWER AND GUNPOWDER

Machiavelli's hypothetical prince was armed with acute intelligence and supreme force of will. The states of Europe armed themselves with new weapons and new military methods. By 1500, armies that depended on the force of their **infantry** had supplanted armies of mounted knights. Lance and sword gave way to **arquebus** and **pike**, then to **musket** and **bayonet** (see p. 419); the cavalry charge, to rows and columns of uniformed soldiers; the simple medieval wall, punctuated by gates and towers, to elaborate systems of fortification, designed to foil the force of cannon fire. Military leaders—now required to be management experts as much as battle chiefs—forged armies that performed on the battlefield with the precision they learned on the drill field.

Knights and Guns

On late medieval battlefields, ordinary foot soldiers had already proved themselves a match for mounted knights. In Flanders, in 1302, a mob of urban workers smashed an army of French cavalry. Afterwards, the fragments of the noble warriors' expensive arms and armor littered the "Field of Golden Spurs," as the disaster was expressively named. In 1346, at Crécy, and 1415, at Agincourt, two battlefields of the Hundred Years' War, English peasants armed with longbows, made from the flexible wood of their native yew trees, mowed down heavily armed knights.

Within a century, the advent of guns clinched the triumph of infantry over cavalry. Basically, the gun is an iron tube in which gunpowder—a mixture of potassium nitrate, sulfur, and charcoal—is exploded to fire a missile. The Chinese and the Arabs had used gunpowder since the eighth century C.E., mainly for fireworks. The Mongols who attacked Sung Chinese fortifications early in the thirteenth century exploded gunpowder-packed bamboo stalks, the ancestor of the first guns. When Mongol armies swung westward to Poland and Hungary in 1240, Europeans first experienced the deadly might of gunfire. Soon European ironworkers—who honed their skills making swords and horseshoes, metal plowshares and great church bells—learned to manufacture guns.

Around 1400, the Ottoman Turks employed German and Hungarian metalworkers to construct the cannon they fired in their advance through the Middle East and the Balkans. Cannon fire figured in the Ottoman victory at Constantinople in 1453. Europeans soon surpassed the Turks, however, developing gun technology to an extraordinary degree. Guns would be the premier tool of European explorers, conquerors, and merchants as they penetrated other continents of the globe.

In the short run, guns prompted the creation of tougher suits of armor for mounted knights. In the long run, they spelled the death of knighthood. No cavalry force could withstand the direct assault of a battery of guns, although as late as the twentieth century some were still trying to. Ordinary foot

The Tools of War

The cannon: From the mid-fifteenth century, innovations in weapons changed the nature, costs, and social implications of warfare. The most dramatic changes affected the cannon, as shown here in Four Books of Knighthood, *1528.*

soldiers armed with better and better guns formed the heart of the modern army, replacing mounted warriors as these had once replaced the ancient legion and phalanx. In the sixteenth and seventeenth centuries, ranks of arquebusiers surrounded a core of pikemen (soldiers armed with long spears). In the eighteenth, lines or columns of musketeers—their more accurate weapons fitted with bayonets which made the pike obsolete—fired in unison, in precise rhythm on command, to halt an enemy charge.

At first, guns could not fire straight or very far. The main use of the new weaponry was in big guns, used to batter down gates and walls. Huge cannon, finely adorned by the talents of engravers and sculptors, were dragged by beasts or before the besieged town or castle. Firing ball after ball, they eventually breached the defenses. The greedy horde of soldiers then swarmed in to sack, rape, and burn. Among the first to use these tactics was the French king Charles VII (r. 1422–1461), who, in 1450, drove the English from their strongholds in France at the close of the Hundred Years' War.

Siege warfare had long figured in human conflict—as testified by the protective circuit of walls that ringed some of the most ancient communities. But now the siege became newly destructive. Innocent populations, trapped within their walls, hearing the cannon fire, awaited in fear the ending that must come as walls gave way to explosive force.

Responding to the challenge of cannon fire, military engineers designed a new type of fortification. The long, exposed **curtain walls** of medieval castles and towns were vulnerable to bombardment. The squat walls of the new-style fortifications, equipped with projecting **bastions** and thickened by earthworks, as shown in the illustration on p. 420, withstood cannon fire painlessly. The triangular bastions distanced the battle from the town within, and enabled crossbowmen, **musketeers**, and riflemen to rain missiles upon attackers from two sides at once. These fortifications required fat purses and master designers—among the first of whom were Leonardo da Vinci and Michelangelo. The craft of military engineering developed sophistication as the demand for fortifications increased, and was advanced by the experience of battle.

Although the development of land warfare was crucial, much of the fighting took place at sea. Europe's expanding dominion in the world, linked together by oceans and rivers, owed much to its naval power. Here, too, firepower proved its value, giving European navies an incontestable advantage over those of other civilizations precisely when the stakes of shipborne commerce peaked. Cannon mounted on shipboard or below deck could defend merchant convoys or fight all-out naval battles.

Guns and fortifications were expensive, as were the accoutrements of the new mode of warfare. Soldiers and sailors required not only weapons, but helmets and armor, ammunition and cannonballs, powder flasks and water canteens. Armies traveled with baggage wagons and construction gear, bringing in their wake servants, wives, mistresses, children, and spare horses. In the Greek *polis* or ancient Rome or medieval Europe, the soldier came to fight bearing his own equipment. Now the principality or nation supplied that equipment. The machinery of revenue collection strained to meet the cost of outfitting forces that numbered, by 1600, tens of thousands of men.

Military Organization

The use of guns and the greater reliance on infantry constitute major changes in methods of warfare.

The gun: The gun, which later developed to become a musket with bayonet, was also an important innovation (shown here in a 1508 drawing).

The castle: *The curtain walls of medieval castles, which were incapable of withstanding cannon fire, were replaced by massive fortifications like at Deal Castle in the sixteenth century, specially designed to face artillery attack from all angles.*

But these were only part of what some scholars have called the "military revolution" of the early modern period. Military organization also developed, as gifted leaders forged the modern, professional army.

Italy   Modern warfare first unfolded in Italy, where war was a paid profession. Unlike the armies of the north, which consisted of native noblemen and their peasant auxiliaries, those of the Italian cities consisted of hired warriors, paid with cash. Managing these hired, or mercenary, armies were generals called *condottieri* ("contractors"), one of whom is depicted in *Windows On* on p. 432. The *condottieri* were strategists, economists, and engineers, as well as soldiers. They were experts at recruiting troops, keeping them paid, pitching camp, and retreating in the face of danger. They fought to fulfill their contracted terms with their paymaster state. They aimed to spill as little blood, and to face as few battles, as possible. Thus Italian warfare was an efficient tool of statecraft, but it was not especially deadly.

It was on the shrewdest of such *condottieri* that Machiavelli modeled his prince (although he deplored the use of mercenary soldiers, who he thought would always fight less well than natives). Such men as Cesare Borgia (the son and agent of Pope Alexander VI) and Francesco Sforza (1401–1466, who in 1450 became Duke of Milan) battled their way to eminence and, in the case of the latter, even to sovereign power. Their skills of military organization lifted them far above the ranks of ordinary men and

close in line to the thrones of hereditary monarchs.

Switzerland   Among the mercenaries hired by the combative Italian states were soldiers from Switzerland. In that mountainous southwestern zone of the Holy Roman Empire, local regions called **cantons** had been engaged, since the late thirteenth century, in a struggle for independence. This struggle encouraged the development of native military skills. Swiss soldiers, like the hoplites of ancient Greece, fought on foot and side by side, mutually supporting each other. Armed with pikes and arrayed in tight squares from which their weapons bristled, they could withstand the cavalry charges led by the Empire's noblemen. The ordinary male citizen of a Swiss canton was nearly always of necessity a soldier. When the Swiss finally won their independence in 1499, these disciplined infantrymen sold their skills abroad.

Sweden   Far to the north, Sweden's King Gustavus II Adolphus (r. 1611–1632) led the way in creating a national standing army, rather than a knightly or mercenary one. Sweden was then a small and rather poor country whose role in European affairs before the seventeenth century was minimal. That role was changed with the outbreak of the Thirty Years' War. Gustavus Adolphus intervened in that conflict in 1630 to protect Protestant interests and to secure a footing on the south shore of the Baltic Sea. The supreme performance of his disciplined troops and mobile cannon won fame for Sweden, whose hymn-singing soldiers were forbidden by their pious king to pillage or rape—a unique prohibition in that era.

England   A generation later, the Englishman Oliver Cromwell (1599–1658), a leader of Parliamentary opposition to the king, organized the New Model Army, which defeated the Royalist forces in 1645. He personally led the military unit known as the Ironsides, men who as he said, "had the fear of God before them." Forming tight squares, their unflinching pikes projecting at set angles like a deadly, mechanical porcupine, his soldiers set a new standard for disciplined warfare.

France   Also contributing to the military revolution was France. In the mid-1400s King Charles VII reorganized the French army, building up a strong artillery and de-emphasizing the role of knights (who had once been so shamefully vanquished by England's bowmen). As knights became less important, the power of the nobility (which often challenged that of the monarch) could be curtailed. Charles ordered the castle towers of feudal strongholds cut down and extended his mandate into every pocket of regional power, seeking to create a national spirit and a national military organization.

Despite Charles's efforts, the French military remained a motley combination of individual units recruited by semi-independent generals. Then, in the later 1600s, King Louis XIV (r. 1643–1715) thoroughly reconstituted the army as an instrument of state policy. Its captains and generals became part of a hierarchy arrayed under the king's personal authority. Its soldiers wore standard uniforms, drilled and marched, and were provisioned by a central office. By the early 1700s, intensive recruiting had resulted in an increase from 100,000 to 400,000 men, making the French army the largest in Europe.

Prussia It was in Prussia, however, that the professionalization of the early modern army reached its zenith. Prussia was a new state, formed by the Great Elector Frederick William (1640–1688) from two non-adjacent territories—the imperial electorate of Brandenburg and the Polish duchy of Prussia. Geographically fragmented (it included several other small territories) Prussia required a powerful army for its defense. Its first ruler, the Great Elector Frederick William, made military values and needs the linchpin of his political strategy. Prudently providing for all other state expenses from the modest resources of his private purse, he dedicated all tax revenues to the maintenance of the army, while recruiting nearly the whole of the Prussian aristocracy—called the *Junkers*—to lead it. By these methods, he built the army up to 40,000 men, enormous for its time and for the size of the principality, which then numbered 1.5 million inhabitants. His successors in the next century raised that total to 200,000, one-half that of the army of France, with a population more than ten times that of Prussia.

By the eighteenth century, the miscellaneous cavalry contingents of the Middle Ages had been replaced by the modern army.

War and Diplomacy The eighteenth-century army centered on an infantry force armed with smooth-bore muskets, descendants of the earlier arquebus, which were transformed into spears by affixing a sharp dagger or bayonet. The infantry faced an enemy who had already been ravaged by artillery teams with mobile, increasingly accurate cannon. Salaried soldiers wore centrally-issued uniforms, slept in barracks, and drilled regularly the maneuvers that they would be called upon to perform in battle. Officers of noble origin learned the art of command at military academies such as those in Paris, Saint Petersburg, or Turin (modern Italy). Conducting a siege, according to King Frederick II, the Great, of Prussia (r. 1740–1786), was a craft "like that of carpenter or clock-maker." Battle itself—unlike the whirling charges of mounted warriors or the relentless pressure of a siege—was a formal, choreographed event in which two bodies of men faced each other across an open field and fired precisely on command.

*Titian, **Charles V on Horseback**, 1548: The Italian painter Titian (Tiziano Vecellio) painted this portrait of the Holy Roman emperor Charles V on horseback after the latter's victory in 1547 over Protestant armies at Mühlberg. The portrait evokes the energy and magnificence of the Roman emperors, to whom Charles, at this date the ruler in name of much of Europe, wished to think himself equal. (Prado, Madrid)*

Why did they fire? Because they were drilled to load, aim, and shoot in unison, and paid to do so—however meagerly and irregularly. Certainly, they did not fight for glory or territory, or for their faith; in the eighteenth century, religious differences did not spark wars. Nor did they fight from patriotism, a sentiment not yet invented. But if patriotism was not yet born, national and dynastic interests were very much alive. European wars were fought in the service of those interests, as rulers jostled for prestige, for land, and for power. To win those ends, they tolerated devastating losses of life and property, and incurred huge expenses borne by the citizenry.

Then, as now, talk was the main alternative to war. By the fourteenth century, especially in Flanders and Italy, the medieval herald, who conveyed messages between leaders, was beginning to develop into that of the modern **ambassador**. The ambassador also represented a state or ruler at the courts or assemblies of another. He brought information; conveyed messages of sympathy or congratulations; and presented terms for the settlement of disputes. Two are portrayed on *Windows On* on p. 432.

Even in the midst of hostilities, the ambassador enjoyed promises of personal security from all parties. By the sixteenth century, ambassadors were based in the main European centers and conducted negotiations between states. Those negotiations, constituting what is called **diplomacy**, prepared the peace treaties that followed upon war, or prevented war altogether. In 1619, an experienced Spanish diplomat advised that wars were no longer a test of strength, like a bullfight, to be decided by "mere battles"; "rather they depend on losing or gaining friends and allies, and it is to this end that good statesmen must turn all their attention and energy."

The citizens of *Utopia*, the ideal "nowhereland" envisioned by the sixteenth-century English writer Thomas More, did not go to war. If necessary, mercenaries were dispatched to do so. Utopian ambassadors arranged for a settlement of differences even at great financial cost. When diplomacy failed, Utopian policy called for the assassination of the enemy leader—an atrocity resorted to only to prevent the worse one of war. Europe was not yet so civilized.

WAR GAMES

Three centuries of war trace the shifts in the political configuration of Europe after 1500, as shown by Maps 15.1 and 15.2 and *How Many?* on p. 428. Cities and principalities lost to nations competing for dominance. Each sought security, territory, commercial advantages, and a share in the balance of power maintained by national leaders. Equipped with the latest military technology, rulers and statesmen employed war to reconfigure the map of Europe, playing a game that dealt its winners status, wealth, and power.

In the first phase of early modern warfare from 1500 to 1648, the enmity between two great players—France (successively under Valois and Bourbon rulers) and the House of Habsburg (Holy Roman Emperors, whose domains included Austria, Styria, Carinthia, Tyrol, the Netherlands, and Spain) stoked the fires of religious conflict. By the end of the Thirty Years' War, religious issues had waned, outpaced by political objectives. In the second phase, from 1648 to 1763, France again played a central role. Having emerged from the Thirty Years' War the most powerful nation in Europe, France ceded that title, in 1763, to the new dynamo on the world stage, Great Britain.

Wars over Faith and Turf, 1500–1648

From 1500 to 1648, religious controversies and territorial disputes between rival dynasties saw Europe in a nearly constant state of warfare. By 1500, Italy was overrun with Spanish, German, and French soldiers—"barbarians," they were called, but barbarians in such numbers as to overwhelm the once-proud Italian city-states. At the same time, the Protestant Reformation created the issues that precipitated warfare between Protestants and Catholics, especially in the Holy Roman Empire and in France. Religious differences also figured in a war for independence in the Netherlands and in a civil war in England, although these conflicts also had political dimensions. From 1618 to 1648, much of Europe became involved in the Thirty Years' War, fought largely on German soil. At its outset, religious issues were prominent. By its close, religious factors had been overshadowed by the contest between the dynasties of France and the German lands: the Bourbons and the Habsburgs.

The trends in international politics characteristic of the early modern era first emerged in Italy, where the experience of city-states prefigures that of the nations beyond the Alps. Intermittently at war, some of the principal Italian states, including Milan, Naples, Rome, Venice, and Florence, had arrived at an agreement by the Peace of Lodi in 1454. This truce aimed at maintaining a balance of power among contending nations. Within a generation, however, the five participants were at war again. Soon they looked for assistance to the nations on the far side of the Alps. Beginning in 1494, France, the Empire, and Spain sent their armies. Where the Italians had sought helpers, instead they stirred up conquerors.

The process of conquest rolled on for fifty years more on the slippery battlefronts of the Italian Wars (1494–1559). At the end, by the Treaty of Câteau-Cambrésis in 1559, the Spanish and allied imperial forces had bested the French and seized control of the peninsula. Of the major Italian states, only four remained independent: the two republics of Venice and Genoa, and the two principalities of Savoy and Tuscany (the region of which Florence was capital), now under the Grand Dukes of Tuscany, descendants of the Medici family of Renaissance days. Italy was mortally wounded, but the political system of balanced competitive states which it pioneered set the pattern for relations between European nations until World War I in the twentieth century.

As cities and nations contended on Italian soil, north of the Alps a series of conflicts arose as a consequence of the Protestant Reformation (see Chapter 14). Within the Empire, Protestant and Catholic princes and states maneuvered against and fought each other, as did Huguenot, Catholic, and *politique* nobles in France. In the German lands these wars lasted until 1555, when they ended with the Peace of Augsburg. War in France continued until the reign of Henry IV (1589–1610), drawing to a close with his conversion to Catholicism in 1593 and his issuing, in 1598, of the Edict of Nantes. These conflicts, ending in territorial settlements for Protestants and Catholics and some hope of reconciliation,

belong to the history of the Reformation. Although religion figured in other conflicts in the Netherlands, the Empire, and England, these were essentially struggles between competing nations and interests. The first was the Dutch war of independence against Spain, begun officially in 1579 (though fighting dated from 1568). The second was the Thirty Years' War (1618–1648), which began as a struggle between Protestant and Catholic rulers in the Empire, and ended as a European-wide conflict in which religious identification had lost political significance. The third was the English Civil War (1642–1651).

In the seventeen provinces of the Netherlands, in 1566, discontent with Spanish rule, especially among Protestants, gave way to full-scale protests and to riots. The Spanish responded by sending the Duke of Alba at the head of an army, to subdue these unruly subjects and administer the Inquisition. "Everyone must be made to live in constant fear of the roof breaking down over his head," ordained the Duke.

Map 15.1 The European States in 1526: *The map of Europe in the early 1500s was dominated by the House of Habsburg, with possessions in Spain, the Netherlands, southern Italy, and central Europe. Northern Italy and the German-speaking center of Europe were fragmented into hundreds of cities and principalities. To the east, the duchy of Muscovy was being transformed into Russia, bordering on the great expanses of Poland and Lithuania. The Ottoman Empire pressured Europe from the southeast.*

His Council of Troubles, set up to track down heretics, sentenced thousands of Protestants to death, and ordered the confiscation of many noble estates. In the face of this tyranny, Catholics and Protestants of all classes united in armed revolt.

In 1578, the more moderate Duke of Parma, sent by the Spanish to reestablish obedience, rallied the support of the largely Catholic southern provinces. These ten provinces returned to Spanish dominion calmly, and after 1713 to the Austrian Habsburgs. The seven largely Protestant northern provinces, led by Holland and Zeeland, formed the Union of Utrecht in 1579 and declared independence from Spain in 1581. Their leader was Prince William I, called "the Silent," of the House of Orange (1533–1584). Previously appointed *stadholder*, or lieutenant-governor in Holland, by the emperor Charles V, he had already begun, in the 1570s, to direct military and naval operations against Spanish rule.

The United Provinces, as they were called after 1579, were supported by England, which sent several thousand troops to assist in the struggle. It was partly to stop this support that Spain launched, in 1588, its fearsome Armada. Although the Armada boasted formidable guns, its ships were cumbersome. The sleeker, swifter English vessels, fitted with excellent guns, chased the Spanish fleet from the English Channel into the North Sea—and into oblivion. As England stood poised to enter into Continental power struggles, it perceived its success in this incident as providential.

Dutch and Spanish armies struggled until 1609, when the Twelve Years' Truce provided for a division between Catholic south and Protestant north. Dutch independence was officially recognized in 1648, and the new federal Dutch Republic took its place in the political arena. The Dutch had already greatly expanded their maritime ventures (see Chapter 16), which flourished as the English became involved in their Civil War. Emerging from that struggle, the English Parliament responded to Dutch competition by issuing the Navigation Act of 1651. This act (subsequently reissued several times) limited the shipment of goods to England to English-owned ships or the ships of the region of origin. The Navigation Acts challenged the Dutch carrying trade, the source of that Republic's wealth, and provoked war between these two Protestant powers—the First Anglo-Dutch War of 1652–54, followed by two others before 1674—who not long before had cooperated in resisting the Spanish.

The Thirty Years' War Sparked by rebellious Protestant nobles, the Thirty Years' War developed into a general European melee involving at least seventeen sovereign powers. The war was fought largely on German soil between, on the one hand, the Habsburg dynasty (both its Austrian and Spanish branches) and, on the other, the German Protestant princes and their allies, both Protestant (Denmark, Sweden, the United Provinces) and Catholic (France). The Habsburgs stood for a strong central European empire, backed by the Roman Catholic Church. Their opponents, both Protestant and Catholic, wished for political and religious reasons to preserve the autonomy of the states composing the Holy Roman Empire—now a nearly vaporous entity.

Coursing through several phases—Bohemian, Rhineland, Dutch, Swedish, and French—as different generals and interests came to the fore, the conflict was finally settled in 1648 by the Peace of Westphalia. That treaty provided for a balance of power between the main contenders (the Habsburg and French Bourbon powers) and associates. Granting virtual sovereignty to the component German states, it dictated the effective death of the Holy Roman Empire (although the Empire lingered in name until 1806) and created a power vacuum in central Europe, threatening danger to come. Finally, the treaty

War in Action

The Turkish army at Mohacs, 1526: *This miniature painting depicts the Battle of Mohacs, in Hungary, on the campaign road to Vienna in 1526. In it, Suleiman I, "the Magnificent," is shown directing his Turkish army from behind a row of cannon.* (Topkapi Museum, Istanbul)

recognized existing religious differences, thereby signaling the end of religious warfare in Europe.

What was indisputably accomplished by thirty years of battle was the devastation of Germany: its people, of whom perhaps 20 percent died; and its towns, its commerce, its blighted economy, its ruined fields, as the woodcut below and the passage reproduced in *Witnesses* on p. 427 testify. From the German perspective alone, this may have been the most catastrophic war in modern European history.

States in Competition, 1648–1763

The Thirty Years' War brought France to the front rank of European power. As she attempted to pursue that advantage, she collided with England, which had emerged from relative insignificance in the late Middle Ages to become a major presence in Europe. As the duel between them proceeded, other rivalries were pursued by the new nations of eastern Europe (the term denoting the lands of modern Poland, the Czech Republic, Slovakia, Hungary, the eastern German region, and Austria), Prussia and Austria, the most successful remnants of the Holy Roman Empire, and a reinvigorated Russia.

By the 1660s, France possessed the largest army in Europe and nurtured vast ambitions. It sought to limit Habsburg power on its borders, and to annex nearby lands, especially Alsace-Lorraine and the southern, or Spanish, Netherlands. The French strategy was checked in 1688 by a coalition of alarmed nations. It was contained again in the War of the Spanish Succession (1701–1714), when again most of the other major European powers united to combat it.

In Bauier men not left to bury the dead, but Rattes, and mice, devoured there carcasses.

Carcasses devoured by rats and mice: *There were many tragic consequences of war. Casualties from the Thirty Years' War, 1618–48, where bodies, left unburied, were devoured by rats and mice, are shown in this woodcut from* The Lamentations of Germany, 1638. *(British Library, London)*

This war was precipitated when the last Habsburg king of Spain, Charles II, died in 1700, having willed all of his possessions, to be kept intact, to the grandson of Louis XIV of France. Had the terms of the will been observed without protest, France would have dominated Europe (and much of the Western Hemisphere as well). An enormous alliance rose up against this possibility. The Peace of Utrecht of 1713 between England and France settled the conflict (although fighting continued between some parties for another year), and, together with the Peace of Rastatt (1714) drew new lines of authority in Europe. A French king of the Bourbon dynasty would rule in Spain and in Spanish America, but other Spanish dominions—principally the southern Netherlands and Spanish domains in Italy—were conveyed to Habsburg Austria. The rulers of the small states of Savoy and Prussia obtained territorial gains and the status of king, and the Dutch Republic received small concessions.

All contenders won something, but Great Britain (created by joining the crowns of England and Scotland in 1707) emerged the winner. She won the fortress of Gibraltar on the Spanish Mediterranean shore and parts of French Canada, which enabled her to pursue her maritime ambitions. Even more precious was the grant of the *asiento* ("contract") from Spain, giving Britain the right to carry African slaves to Spanish America (see Chapter 16). As a bonus, she also won a promise that France would not attempt to place a Catholic king on the British throne, which was now Protestant by law.

After some twenty-five years of relative peace, the European nations began fighting again in the 1740s, intent on gaining slips of territory and small advantages. An eight-year interlude between 1748 and 1756 was followed by the Seven Years' War (1756–1763), fought on three continents— not only in Europe but also in India and in North America, where it was known as the French and Indian War. Overarching all other issues was the continuing duel between Britain and France.

This time, the duel was fought largely overseas, as colonial possessions and foreign trade increasingly became the measure of national preeminence. By 1761, Britain had seized French possessions in India, and was poised for further ventures in the domination of that subcontinent. In 1759 a British force launched a surprise attack on the key French fortress at Quebec. After a ten-minute battle on the Plains of Abraham, outside the fortress, which the British won with disciplined musket volleys at close range, French prospects in North America were doomed. The Treaty of Paris of 1763 secured Britain's triumph over her main rival in India, in North America, and in Europe.

Eastern Europe   By 1700, three states dominated eastern Europe: Austria, Prussia, and Russia. The homeland of the Habsburg family, Austria had a strong monarchy and an expansive agenda. It absorbed Hungary, Bohemia, Transylvania, and parts of the northern Balkans, knitting its empire together through the figure of the king, who ruled as monarch in each kingdom. It held the southeast frontier of Europe against the Ottoman Turks, whose vigor had waned since the siege of Vienna in 1529, though it resurged in 1683 to threaten that outpost once again.

The kingdom of Prussia developed from the ancestral lands of the Hohenzollern family: Brandenburg, some tiny states in the Empire, and the duchy of Prussia itself. These lands were patiently acquired over generations and combined to form an independent state; it was granted the status of kingdom by the Peace of Utrecht of 1713. Farther east, Tsar Peter I (r. 1682–1725), called "the Great," who had toured the successful nations of western Europe, learned what he could, and imported trained experts to Russia, now built a new capital city on the Baltic Sea and reoriented his political goals. For the first time, Russia looked westward, ready to engage as a great power in European struggles for sovereignty.

In 1713, Prussia, along with most other European nations, had agreed to the Pragmatic Sanction. Issued by the Holy Roman Emperor Charles VI (r. 1711–1740), this provided that his daughter and heir, Maria Theresa (r. 1740–1780), would inherit all the Habsburg lands intact (although, as a woman, she was ineligible to become Holy Roman Emperor). In 1740, on the basis of no other principle than *raison d'état*, the young king of Prussia, Frederick II (r. 1740–1786) broke this agreement. Frederick needed Silesia—a prosperous province under Austrian domination. And so he took it. Other nations entered into the fray, nibbling at the Habsburg lands. By the 1748 Peace of Aix-la-Chapelle, which settled the War of the Austrian Succession, Silesia was his. A few years later, in the Seven Years' War, Austria allied itself with France and Russia, to block Prussia's further expansion. Bankrolled by Britain but left to fight on its own, Prussia stayed firm and retained its position.

In 1772, Prussia was still hungry for territory to round out the boundaries of its domain. Along with Austria and Russia, it annexed small bits of Poland, an ailing republic dominated by a fractious nobility under an elected king, fatally resistant to centralization. In 1793 and 1795, Poland's neighbors completed her dismemberment. In the final "partition," it disappeared from the map, not to be reconstituted until after World War I. Prussia, Austria, and Russia, fat with new territory, now held unrivaled domination of eastern Europe. As recently as 1500, they had been overshadowed by the Holy Roman Empire, now in tatters; by the Ottoman Empire, in retreat through the Balkans; and by Poland, devoured whole.

During the early modern era, the violence that had characterized medieval Europe in an era of invasion became the official tool of the state. As a result, the map of Europe was radically altered as winners took their prizes and losers shrank behind their borders. Soon after 1500, the Italian cities yielded their primacy, as Machiavelli had feared, to more powerful nations beyond the Alps. By 1600, the most potent states in Europe were monarchies poised on the Atlantic coast: Spain, France, and England. Emerging as major players soon thereafter were the kingdom of Sweden, the newly constituted Dutch Republic, and the German electorate of Brandenburg, subsequently the kingdom of Prussia. Meanwhile, the Holy Roman Empire withered, while the Habsburg dynasty, which had long held the imperial title, raised its hereditary domain of Austria to international importance. Portugal, the rising star of the early 1500s, languished, and Poland was obliterated. Led by a series of tsars, who considered themselves the successors of Roman Caesars, Russia moved into the European arena.

AN AGE OF KINGS

As the nations of Europe competed, they also developed forms of government that endured into the modern era. This process usually involved the refinement of monarchy, as the ability to make laws and exercise force was concentrated in the figure of the king—or, in a few cases, the queen. Such kings were "absolute" monarchs, because they tried to rule "absolutely" (believing in complete, unrestricted powers due to their divine right), unchecked by representatives of the people. By the end of the eighteenth century, that newly evolved monarchy would be challenged and, in some places, limited. In diverse ways, monarchy developed in the direction of **absolutism** in several European countries: in Spain, France, and England in the western zone; and in Prussia, Austria, and Russia in the eastern one (see *Who's Who* on pp. 437 and 439).

Spain: Religious Zeal and Royal Absolutism

The autonomous kingdoms that formed on the Iberian peninsula in the Middle Ages were united by a common dedication to the centuries-long crusade called the *Reconquista* (see Chapter 9). After the fall of the last Moorish fortress at Granada in 1492, the Inquisition fostered the crusading spirit by pursuing lapsed converts to Christianity, as well as heretics. The same crusading spirit inspired Spanish missionaries to the Americas, to convert the native population. Before it became a nation, Spain was a culture united by its dedication to Roman Catholic orthodoxy. On this basis, kings from the fifteenth and sixteenth centuries built a strong, centralized state.

Crucial developments in this unifying process were achieved in the reigns of Ferdinand II of Aragon

(r. 1479–1516) and Isabella of Castile (r. 1474–1504), whose marriage in 1479 linked their two kingdoms. (Portugal had already taken a separate path to nationhood before the events about to be described.) Although the component states of Castile and Aragon retained their separate judicial, political, and administrative laws and institutions, a strong commonality of purpose marked the reigns of their two respective sovereigns—displayed most decidedly and dramatically by their conquest of Granada.

In 1516, on Ferdinand's death, a now-united Spain passed to his grandson, Charles I. The grandson also of the Holy Roman Emperor Maximilian I and Mary of Burgundy, Charles inherited the Habsburg lands on Maximilian's death in 1519 and, as Charles V (r. 1519–1556), became Holy Roman Emperor. A portrait of him by Titian is illustrated on p. 421.

Ruler of several states, and required to manage the Italian Wars, the consequences of the Protestant Reformation, the rivalry of France, and the threat of Turkish invasion, Charles could not concentrate exclusively on Spain. When he abdicated in 1556, the Spanish inheritance (along with title to the Netherlands and parts of Italy) passed to his son Philip, and the Habsburg lands to his brother Ferdinand I.

Under Philip II (r. 1556–1598) the Spanish state rose to an apex of wealth and influence. Outside Madrid, Philip constructed the Escorial, a combined palace and monastery, vast and austere, which is depicted on p. 443. There he worshipped daily and ruled his far-flung possessions. Aided by diplomats and spies, he worked to extend Spanish rule and to reassert Catholic orthodoxy in Europe. Those goals were not implausibly grandiose, given that the great

The Experience of War in Fiction and Fact

Early modern Europe pioneered the war against civilians that some historians see as distinctively modern. Armies besieged walled cities, battered their walls and gates, gained entry, and loosed their soldiers to loot, murder, and rape at will. That fate is depicted vividly in the words of William Shakespeare's character Henry V, ironically the late medieval English king perceived as most heroic. It is also the fate of the city of Magdeburg, as described by its mayor, an eyewitness.

King Henry V threatens the French city of Harfleur with battery, capture, rape, and sack:

> How yet resolves the Governor of the town?
> This is the latest parle we will admit:
> Therefore to our best mercy give yourselves,
> Or, like to men proud of destruction,
> Defy us to our worst; for, as I am a soldier,
> A name that in my thoughts becomes me best,
> If I begin the batt'ry once again,
> I will not leave the half-achieved Harfleur
> Till in her ashes she lie buried.
> The gates of mercy shall be all shut up,
> And the fleshed soldier, rough and hard of heart,
> In liberty of bloody hand shall range
> With conscience wide as hell, mowing like grass
> Your fresh fair virgins and your flow'ring infants. ...
> ... Therefore, you men of Harfleur,
> Take pity of your town and of your people
> Whiles yet my soldiers are in my command,
> Whiles yet the cool and temperate wind of grace
> O'erblows the filthy and contagious clouds
> Of heady murder, spoil, and villainy.
> If not—why, in a moment look to see
> The blind and bloody soldier with foul hand
> Defile the locks of your shrill-shrieking daughters;
> Your fathers taken by the silver beards,

> And their most reverend heads dashed to the walls;
> Your naked infants spitted upon pikes,
> While the mad mothers with their howls confused
> Do break the clouds, as did the wives of Jewry
> At Herod's bloody-hunting slaughtermen.
> What say you? Will you yield, and this avoid?
> Or, guilty in defense, be thus destroyed?

(Shakespeare, *Henry V*, 1600, III. iii. 1–14, 27–43; ed. J. R. Brown, 1998)

Eyewitness Otto von Guericke, mayor of Magdeburg, describes the destruction of his city by an imperial army during the Thirty Years' War (May, 1631):
[The imperial troops and allies breached a gate and flooded into the city.] Thus it came about that the city and all its inhabitants fell into the hands of the enemy, whose violence and cruelty were due in part to their common hatred of the adherents of the Augsburg Confession, and in part to their being embittered by the chain shot which had been fired at them and by the derision and insults that the Magdeburgers had heaped upon them from the ramparts. Then was there naught but beating and burning, plundering, torture, and murder. ... Then, what with blows and threats of shooting, stabbing, and hanging, the poor people were so terrified that if they had had anything left they would have brought it forth if it had been buried in the earth or hidden away in a thousand castles. In this frenzied rage, the great and splendid city that had stood like a fair princess in the land was now, in its hour of direst need and unutterable distress and woe, given over to the flames, and thousands of innocent men, women, and children, in the midst of a horrible din of heart-rending shrieks and cries, were tortured and put to death in so cruel and shameful a manner that no words would suffice to describe, nor no tears to bewail it. . .

(*Readings in European History*, vol. 2, 1906; ed. J. H. Robinson) wealth then pouring into Spain from its American possessions (see Chapter 16) could fund a formidable military organization. Philip succeeded in acquiring Portugal in 1580. With his marriage in 1554 to the queen of England, Mary Tudor (r. 1553–1558), came the opportunity, never realized, to add that kingdom to his other possessions and to restore it to the roster of Catholic nations.

The great success of sixteenth-century Spain faded during the seventeenth, as its silver imports from the Americas failed to enrich the nation. After 1665, the deterioration was rapid. Charles II, who ascended the throne in that year as a child, was sickly, stupid, and impotent. It was his death in 1700 that precipitated the War of the Spanish Succession, resulting in the importation to Spain of a French Bourbon dynasty. Spanish fortunes revived in the 1700s as Bourbon monarchs and ministers created administrative systems on the French model, but Spain no longer played its earlier role of foremost European monarchy.

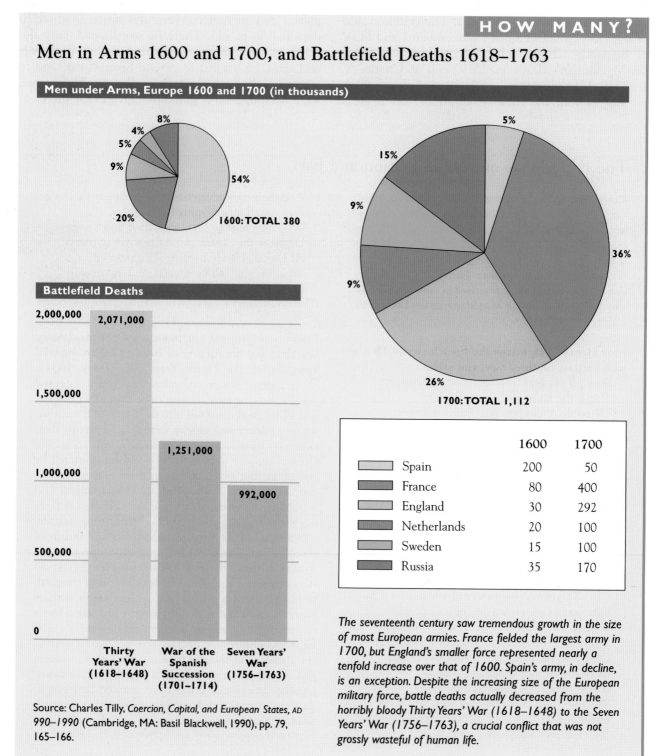

HOW MANY?

Men in Arms 1600 and 1700, and Battlefield Deaths 1618–1763

Men under Arms, Europe 1600 and 1700 (in thousands)

1600: TOTAL 380
54%, 20%, 9%, 5%, 4%, 8%

1700: TOTAL 1,112
36%, 26%, 9%, 9%, 15%, 5%

Battlefield Deaths

	Thirty Years' War (1618–1648)	War of the Spanish Succession (1701–1714)	Seven Years' War (1756–1763)
Deaths	2,071,000	1,251,000	992,000

	1600	1700
Spain	200	50
France	80	400
England	30	292
Netherlands	20	100
Sweden	15	100
Russia	35	170

Source: Charles Tilly, *Coercion, Capital, and European States, AD 990–1990* (Cambridge, MA: Basil Blackwell, 1990), pp. 79, 165–166.

The seventeenth century saw tremendous growth in the size of most European armies. France fielded the largest army in 1700, but England's smaller force represented nearly a tenfold increase over that of 1600. Spain's army, in decline, is an exception. Despite the increasing size of the European military force, battle deaths actually decreased from the horribly bloody Thirty Years' War (1618–1648) to the Seven Years' War (1756–1763), a crucial conflict that was not grossly wasteful of human life.

Map 15.2 The European States in 1795: *By 1795, France and England had fought their battles for supremacy, with France the loser in the global conflict that ended in 1763. Yet France remained a contender under its revolutionary leadership, and would soon strike out under Napoleon's leadership for hegemony in Europe. To the east the Ottoman Empire had weakened; Russia, Austria, and Prussia dominated the region, and by 1795 had partitioned and obliterated the once enormous Polish state.*

France: The Apogee of Absolutism

That role fell to France, which had lain in Spain's shadow in the sixteenth century, but towered above it in the next. Thanks to a larger and more productive population, the kings of France were able to build an impressive administrative machine, field an enormous army, and claim cultural leadership in Europe.

The French kings had already traveled far along the road toward sovereignty during the medieval centuries. They had gained recognition from the feudal nobility of their preeminence in the realm, and from the pope of their rights over the French clergy—the "Gallican liberties" won by the Pragmatic Sanction of Bourges in 1438 and the Concordat of Bologna in 1516. They had defended French territorial rights against other claimants, particularly the English, against whom they ultimately prevailed in the Hundred Years' War. The ascension to the throne of Henry IV (r. 1589–1610), the first of the

Bourbon line, finally brought an end to the chaotic era of religious warfare. It also marked the opening of an especially fruitful era in the building of the French monarchy.

If Henry IV had done nothing else he would be remarkable for his promulgation in 1598 of the Edict of Nantes guaranteeing generous freedoms to his former coreligionists, the Huguenots. But Henry did much more. He saw to France's recovery from the civil wars, collected forgotten taxes and paid forgotten salaries, repaired roads and bridges and the mechanisms of government, administered justice, and promoted commerce. In the twenty-one years of his reign, he never summoned the Estates-General (an assembly of representatives of France's three **estates**, clergy, nobility, and commoners, comparable to the English Parliament). He thereby signaled the capacity of the monarch to rule without consulting a representative assembly. An unusually effective ruler, he laid the foundations for absolute monarchy in France.

After the death of Henry IV, the true ruler of France was neither his son Louis XIII (r. 1610–1643) nor his widow, Marie de' Medici (1573–1642), regent for Louis, then only nine years old. It was the nobleman and cardinal Armand Jean du Plessis, the Duke de Richelieu (1585–1642). This prudent cleric, who became secretary of state in 1616 and Louis's chief minister in 1624, devoted himself to the secular interests of the French monarchy. In the last phase of the Thirty Years' War he intervened on the Protestant side against the Catholic Habsburgs.

Cardinal Richelieu promoted commerce in France and in its overseas possessions, encouraging poor nobles to enrich themselves in business ventures and wealthy merchants to gain titles of nobility by funneling cash to the royal treasury. He reined in aristocratic pretensions, prohibited private dueling, and destroyed fortified castles not in royal service. He also stripped the Huguenot community of its right to bear arms and live in fortified towns, although he reaffirmed the freedom of worship guaranteed by Henry IV.

Cardinal Richelieu's protégé, the Italian-born Jules Mazarin (1602–1661), followed his mentor's model. Made Cardinal in 1641, Mazarin effectively ruled France from 1643 to 1661 as the chief adviser to Anne of Austria, widow of Louis XIII and regent for Louis XIV. Like Cardinal Richelieu, Mazarin managed domestic and international affairs in the interests of the French monarchy, deftly succeeding in surviving a rebellion of restive nobles and peasants called the Fronde.

The Bourbon dynasty benefited from the service of yet a third royal servant: Jean-Baptiste Colbert (1619–1683). The son of a merchant, Colbert began his career by monitoring Mazarin's investments. In 1665, recommended by his mentor, Colbert was employed by Louis XIV (r. 1643–1715) as France's chief financial minister, a position he held until his death in 1683. Colbert reduced France's debt, systematized its accounting methods, and attempted (unsuccessfully) to equalize tax burdens. Aiming at economic self-sufficiency, he encouraged commerce and discouraged misuse of natural resources, built roads and canals, set standards of quality for manufactured goods and agricultural products, increased foreign tariffs and reduced internal ones—all features of the strategy of **mercantilism**.

The French kings were brilliantly served by their ministers Richelieu, Mazarin, and Colbert. It was the genius of the third Bourbon ruler, Louis XIV, himself to raise the monarchy to a new zenith of power. Already under Henry IV, the Estates-General had ceased to function. After 1614, when a fruitless meeting of the Estates-General was dismissed, it was not summoned again until 1789. Those 175 years mark the span of royal absolutism in France—its achievement due principally to Louis XIV.

The Sun King Louis was four years old when his father died. His mother, assisted by Mazarin, ruled in his stead. He was ten when the Peace of Westphalia was signed, preparing the ground for France's assumption of European leadership. In 1661, Mazarin died and Louis, aged twenty-two, undertook personal rule. He guided France until 1715, when he was succeeded by his great-grandson. At that point he had reigned for seventy-two years and outlived two generations, his sheer endurance unmatched by other monarchs. Heir to the achievements of Richelieu and Mazarin, Louis labored for the supremacy of France in Europe, and of the king within France.

Louis may have said, as it is reported, "I am the state." If so, it would have been an accurate statement of the role of the absolute monarch, in whom were centered all the capacities of the political realm. Louis's central role in the French state and culture was expressed visually as well as politically: in the architecture, gardens, and rituals of the royal complex he built at Versailles, twelve miles outside the ancient capital of Paris.

Beginning in the 1660s, Louis converted the small royal hunting lodge at Versailles into the most splendid palace in Europe (see p. 443). According to the statesman Montesquieu, there were "more statues in [the king's] palace gardens than there are citizens in a large town." Palace and gardens, 1400 fountains (fed by a river diverted from its natural course), a panoply of nobles, administrators, and servants (more than 10,000 in all) and nearly as many well-stabled horses—all served to furnish an image of royal grandiloquence. Ranks of courtiers and servants attended the king's daily acts, from waking up to eating dinner to strolling through the gardens or meeting with important officials. Their attendance in itself, their rank and privilege indicated by their dress and proximity to the king, was the business of the court, where all of life was a ceremony underscoring the importance of the king—*le Roi Soleil*, as he was called, "the Sun King." As the prestige of the king rose, the status of the aristocracy sank and the patterns of French culture—costume, behavior, and diet, as well as music, literature, drama, and dance—became the standard in the West.

As Louis gathered the tamed nobles of France at Versailles to dance and play, he centralized in his court the administration of justice and the determination of law, eroding the authority of regional courts and assemblies (the **parlements** and "estates"). To supervise affairs in the provinces, he dispatched bureaucrats called **intendants**, directly responsible to the crown. Royal appointees were often men from the middle classes who had purchased both their office and a title of nobility. These were members of the "nobility of the robe," to distinguish them from the ancient "nobility of the sword." In a further assertion of royal authority, Louis repealed the Edict of Nantes.

French Huguenots who wished to continue to worship as Protestants—among them many productive merchants and artisans—fled to the Dutch Republic, to England and to the Americas. An absolute monarch could not abide religious diversity.

In 1715, a child again ascended the throne of France—Louis XV (r. 1715–1774); again the country was governed by a regent. The aristocracy, which had been brought to heel by Louis XIV, now sought to recover their prestige and to curtail royal authority. The local *parlements* reasserted themselves, insisting on the right to register legislation and to assent to taxation. In this atmosphere of resurgent feudal claims, Louis XV and his grandson and successor, Louis XVI (r. 1774–1793), never enjoyed the absolute authority of their great ancestor. Louis XVI enlisted the aid of a series of capable and reform-minded finance ministers but never succeeded in winning the cooperation of the nobility. Indeed, he saw the principle of absolutism utterly defeated by the Revolution of 1789, which even cost him his life.

England: The Sharing of Power

The career of absolutism in England was different from the one it followed in Spain or France, for two principal reasons. First, England had a long tradition of the political rights of groups represented in its representative assembly, called Parliament. Second, England was, by the early 1600s, a Protestant nation; thus its kings could not bolster their authority, as did the Bourbon and Habsburg monarchs, by alignment with the Catholic Church. These realities tended against the accumulation of royal authority. Nevertheless, England achieved a strong, centralized monarchy; and, thereafter, a strong, centralized state, of which a limited monarch was titular head.

In 1485, the first king of the Tudor line, Henry VII (r. 1485–1509), acquired not only a throne, but the job of patching together a nation torn by the Wars of the Roses, fought between claimants from the York and Lancaster families. He succeeded in this task, organizing national finances, promoting trade and exploration, avoiding foreign entanglements, subduing rebellious nobles, and establishing the court of Star Chamber as a central judicial authority.

In 1509, his son Henry VIII (r. 1509–1547) succeeded him. Supported by shrewd ministers, Henry VIII pursued his father's centralizing strategies (but not his fiscal prudence). His concerns about the succession led him into a controversial series of marriages—six in all. Four of his unlucky wives were dismissed or beheaded; one died, and one survived him. The surviving progeny of these marriages were two daughters and, the youngest, a son—all of whom would accede to the throne, in 1547, 1553, and 1558 respectively: Edward (d. 1553), son of Henry's third wife, Jane Seymour; Mary (d. 1558), daughter of his first wife, Catherine of Aragon; and Elizabeth (d. 1603), daughter of his second wife, Anne Boleyn.

Great controversy surrounded the dissolution by annulment of Henry's first marriage. To effect it, Henry repudiated the pope and had himself declared the "supreme governor" of the Church in England, precipitating the Reformation in that country. His role as head of the Church enhanced Henry's authority. Later, religious controversy would flare up several times under his successors.

A child during most of his six-year reign (he died at fifteen), Edward VI was unable himself to act to shape the English monarchy. His advisers tended to the business of foreign affairs and the establishment of Protestant Christianity in England. On Edward's premature death, their labors on behalf of a Protestant Church were rendered futile. The young king's elder half sister Mary succeeded, having been passed over earlier in favor of the male heir. Granddaughter of Ferdinand and Isabella, raised by her mother an earnest Catholic, and married the year after her succession to the zealous Philip II of Spain, Mary sought to reestablish Catholicism in England. This attempt was thwarted by her death and the accession of Henry VIII's middle child, Elizabeth, whom Catholics considered illegitimate.

Elizabeth, portrayed on p. 434, overcame this liability and that of her sex in a forty-five year reign that is among the most remarkable in all of European history. A moderate Protestant, a classical scholar, and an extraordinarily intelligent leader, Elizabeth completed the task of forging an absolute monarchy begun by her Tudor forebears. Guided but not overshadowed by her very effective covey of ministers—notably Sir William Cecil (1520–1598), Sir Francis Walsingham (c. 1532–1590), and Robert Cecil (1563–1612)—she clarified the nature of English Protestantism, rallied popular support in foreign affairs, and guided financial and judicial institutions. Refusing to marry, she was able even as a woman to maintain authority in her own person and to command the respect of people and Parliament alike. Meanwhile, England's naval successes and deft diplomacy brought it recognition as a major nation.

In 1587, Elizabeth reluctantly authorized the execution—after eighteen years of imprisonment—of her cousin Mary Stuart (r. 1542–1567), the exiled queen of Scotland. (A Catholic with French ties, Mary was implicated in plots against Elizabeth just at the moment when Spain was planning to launch its Armada against England.) On her deathbed, in 1603, Elizabeth named as her successor the son of the woman she had executed, James VI, the reigning king of Scotland. As James I (r. 1603–1625), he assumed the thrones of England and Ireland as well, becoming the first of England's Stuart dynasty.

Twice a king, James was an advocate of absolutism in theory and reached for it in practice. As king in

Gentile Bellini, Muhammad II, c. 1480

Warriors and Peacemakers

Hans Holbein, The Ambassadors, 1533

Gentile Bellini's portrait (above left) from the life of Muhammad II, the Ottoman Turkish ruler who conquered Constantinople and destroyed the Byzantine Empire, depicts its subject as poised and statesmanlike, in retirement from battle.

The two splendidly attired ambassadors painted by Holbein (above right), experts in the avoidance of war, are surrounded by astronomical and musical instruments, appropriately remote from the field of battle.

In contrast, the bronze statue by Verrocchio of the Italian mercenary captain Bartolommeo Colleoni (left) epitomizes the early modern warrior possessed of power and determination.
(top left: National Gallery, London; top right: National Gallery, London)

Andrea del Verrocchio, Bartolommeo Colleoni, Venice, c. 1481–1496

To continue your investigation of this topic, please go to www.prenhall.com/king for the related **WINDOWS** on the **WEB** activity

Scotland, he established royal authority over warring Protestant lords, his mother's Catholic friends and kin, and leaders of the Calvinist (called Presbyterian in Scotland) church. An author and scholar, he wrote in defense of royal absolutism: *The True Law of Free Monarchy*. In England, he chose to challenge or evade the authority of Parliament, acquiring the funds to manage the state and his lavish court from unpopular customs taxes or grants of monopoly.

The Parliament James antagonized included a growing number of Puritan representatives who were critical of the practices of the established Anglican Church. He also antagonized Catholics, who sought an amelioration of the civil disabilities under which they suffered. And the flagrant immorality of his court aroused general disapproval. Serious tensions persisted when James died in 1625 and his son Charles I (r. 1625–1649) succeeded.

Civil War and Commonwealth Married to a French Catholic Bourbon Charles soon revealed a tendency toward absolutism and was suspected of favoring his wife's religion. Whether or not that was so, he certainly did his best to impose the Anglican faith upon all of his subjects. His ministers took repressive measures against nonconforming Protestants, and angered the Presbyterian Scots to the point of armed rebellion. Charles followed his father's lead in relations with Parliament, ignoring it when it did not vote him funds and, not long after the French king's dissolution of the Estates-General, dismissing it altogether in 1629. Eleven years later, desperate for more funds, he recalled Parliament. In 1642, Parliament demanded to be granted greater powers, including approval of the king's ministers. Charles now raised his military standard against Parliament.

At least some of the members of the Parliament that assembled in 1640—called the Long Parliament —continued to meet until 1653 (after 1649, consisting of a remnant of some 100 members, it was called the "Rump" Parliament). They presided over a war between royalists and parliamentarians, and between Anglicans and other Protestants, which permanently changed the course of government in England. In 1649, the victorious parliamentarians created a High Court of Justice, which tried Charles for treason and condemned him to death. His execution followed. At the very moment of the triumph of royal absolutism on the Continent, the English had demonstrated the superiority of assemblies to kings. Although Charles I's sons would later reach for absolute power, the possibility of establishing such power in England had been gravely wounded.

In 1653, the leader of the parliamentary army, Oliver Cromwell (1599–1658), engineered his own elevation to "Lord Protector" of the new Commonwealth of England under a written constitution called the Instrument of Government. Cromwell enforced Puritan policies that suppressed, among other activities, theatrical performances and Sunday games on the village green. He repressed political dissent, such as that offered by the sectarian Ranters and Quakers, and harshly persecuted the Irish, whose religion and culture he attempted to crush. He did, however, favor religious tolerance within a Protestant community. Generally hated, Cromwell was a curious amalgam of religious zeal and military skill, a dictator who had destroyed a monarch. At his death in 1658, Englishmen from all sectors turned from his path and looked forward to the Restoration of the monarchy, which was accomplished in 1660.

Restoration and "Glorious Revolution" The Stuart line returned in the person of Charles II (r. 1660–1685), son of the executed Charles I. Mindful of the need to conciliate parliamentary opponents, Charles agreed to all the demands made by those groups—including a general amnesty to nearly all of those who had opposed and killed his father. He further conciliated both elites and people by setting a new cultural tone. During the Restoration, as the years of his reign are called, Puritan repression ended and the quest for pleasure was back in fashion.

Nevertheless, in the course of his reign Charles repeated the patterns that had led to friction before. He tended to Roman Catholicism, to a pro-French foreign policy, to noncooperation with Parliament, and to absolutism. Worse, as Charles had no legitimate children, his successor was his brother James, an avowed Catholic. One parliamentary faction, called "Whig," called for the exclusion of James from that inheritance, while another, called "Tory," supported the king. James in fact succeeded on Charles' death in 1685, with little opposition.

But Tories and Whigs joined in opposition to James II when, in 1688, his wife gave birth to a son, assuring the continuance of a Roman Catholic monarchy. Parliamentary leaders offered the throne jointly to Mary II (r. 1689–1694), James's elder and Protestant daughter, and her husband William III, the Prince of Orange (r. 1689–1702), zealous opponent of French expansionism in the Netherlands. William arrived with his army, the king's commanders disbanded, and James took refuge in France. These events constitute the "Glorious Revolution," a bloodless rechanneling of authority in perfect contrast to the Civil War which had resulted in the execution of a king and the elevation of a dictator.

By accepting Parliament's Declaration of Right of 1689, William and Mary accepted, as a condition of their joint rule, limits on monarchical power articulated in the Bill of Rights (also 1689). The Bill of Rights reaffirmed constitutional principles that had developed over the previous few stormy decades, providing that the king would not be able to suspend a law of Parliament nor raise taxes nor maintain an army without parliamentary consent; nor could any subject be arrested without full due legal process. Furthermore, the throne would pass to the descendants in turn of Mary and her younger sister Anne; but no Roman Catholic could ever succeed to the English monarchy. The Act of Settlement of 1701 reaffirmed these principles and extended the provisions for the succession. The Toleration Act in the same year protected the rights of non-Anglican Protestants to worship, though it continued to exclude them from political office—as Catholics had been so excluded since the Test Act of 1673. The guarantees in these key documents were added to the traditional rights of Englishmen inherited from medieval custom.

By the complicated events of the 1600s, the government of England achieved a delicate but fruitful balance between the king and Parliament, and of both with the established Anglican Church. The king could not hold absolute power, but would yield to decisions of Parliament. Kings and public officials could be neither Catholics nor non-Anglican Protestant dissenters, although private worship was tolerated (not, however, in Ireland, where Catholicism was illegal and vital). Even Jews, who had been expelled from England in 1290, had been permitted by Cromwell to return without conversion.

Over the next century, the struggle between kings and Parliament gave way to a government dominated by political parties, prominent ministers, and the policies of the Bank of England. Great Britain in the eighteenth century, under the last Stuart monarch, Anne, and the first three kings of the House of Hanover, all Georges, was a different world from that ruled by Stuart kings before 1688.

Three New Empires: The Reshaping of Eastern Europe

The Thirty Years' War left central and eastern Europe in fragments. The Holy Roman Empire was a mere shell. Its more than 300 component cities and principalities, populated largely by German speakers, proceeded to develop independently. To the east of a line formed by the Elbe River and the mountains of Bohemia, largely Slavic and Hungarian peoples lived under Polish, Russian, or Ottoman overlordship. After 1648, three strong monarchies expanded to fill the vacuum of authority in central and eastern Europe—Austria, Prussia, and Russia. The main rulers are listed in *Who's Who* on p. 439.

Austria   The Habsburgs had long ruled the principality of Austria and had held the title of Holy Roman Emperor since 1438. By 1714, these Austrian rulers had gained sovereignty over Bohemia, Hungary,

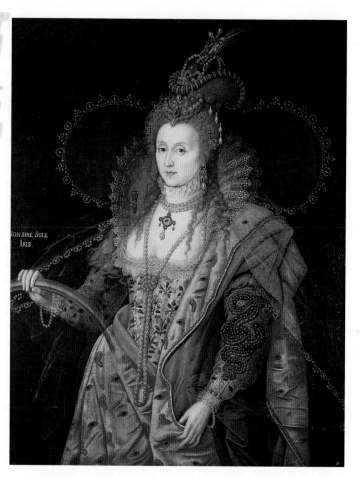

Kings and Queens

Anonymous, Elizabeth I: *The kings and queens of Europe were the subjects of celebratory art. This sixteenth-century "Rainbow Portrait" of Elizabeth I shows her possessing the authority of a ruler, youthful despite increasing age.* (Hatfield House, Hertfordshire; Courtesy, Marquess of Salisbury)

and parts of the Balkans (wrested from the Ottoman Turks by 1699), as well as, in the west, the southern Netherlands, parts of Italy, and some Mediterranean possessions (taken from Spain). They were emperors over many different peoples who spoke different languages, practiced different religions, and possessed very different historical traditions.

Although Habsburg rulers managed this disparate empire with a fair amount of skill, it continually threatened to disintegrate. Ethnic rivalries among Magyars, Germans, Czechs, Poles, Croatians, and Italians were inevitable. Religious tensions were also severe. Austria had been re-Catholicized during the Thirty Years' War, and now imposed strict Catholic uniformity in all of its possessions. Yet the Polish and Czech nobility had strong Protestant leanings, and Eastern Orthodox (and later Muslim) subjects in the Balkans resisted Catholic preeminence. Partly to win over the landowning classes, Habsburg rulers permitted the enserfment or reenserfment of the peasantry, now an oppressed group perpetually liable to restlessness and revolt.

With the Pragmatic Sanction of 1713, Charles VI attempted to guarantee the inheritance of his daughter and only heir, Maria Theresa (r. 1740–1780). Yet on her succession in 1740, she faced the aggressions of other European states which little respected a female ruler when there was so much land to be had. Nevertheless, Maria Theresa managed to hold the bulk of her lands and even acquired additional territory by the first partition of Poland in 1772.

By that date Maria Theresa was ruling jointly with her son Joseph II (r. 1765–1790). After her death in 1780, Joseph ruled alone. He continued his mother's policy of centralizing authority, attempting agrarian reforms, and making the capital, Vienna, a center for the arts and learning. But he attempted more fundamental reforms than his mother would ever have countenanced. These included, notably, the abolition of serfdom in 1781; the creation of a civil service based on the principle of merit; and the reform of the justice system, including the abolition of torture and capital punishment. These and other of Joseph's projects aroused substantial opposition and were suspended after his death in 1790.

Prussia By the time of Joseph's death, Prussia was overtaking Austria as the major power of the fading Holy Roman Empire. Piecing together the small states of Brandenburg, Prussia, and Pomerania, lands scattered across the southern coast of the Baltic Sea, the "Great Elector" Frederick William (r. 1640–1688) had assembled a small nation. He had also built up a mighty army to defend it. His successor was granted the title "King in Prussia" in 1701 and reigned as Frederick I (r. 1688–1713). Frederick's son Frederick William I (r. 1713–1740) continued in his grandfather's path, hoarding his wealth, promoting the landowning class, from which he drew his officers, and modernizing and expanding the army.

These achievements were the inheritance of his son, the capable Frederick II, the Great (r. 1740–1786). The edifice of Prussian power rested on the army. Civil servants, the middle class, the serfs, were all subordinate to its needs and to the will of the aristocracy, who led an enormous military force consisting of 200,000 soldiers out of a population of only 6 million. The prince who ruled this successful state was also a flute-player and author of note, who corresponded easily with the finest minds of the age and shared their skeptical spirit. An absolute monarch himself, Frederick thought little of the theory of the divine right of kings (see below).

Russia By the time of Frederick the Great, Russia had developed from the medieval duchy of Muscovy to become a modern state, governed by an absolute ruler. Having won independence from their Mongol overlords after 1480, the grand princes of Muscovy continued a policy of annexing adjacent territories.

Francisco de Goya, **Family of Charles IV:** *A more critical portrayal of a king and queen is seen in Goya's depiction of the Spanish royal family in 1800. The opulence of attire of Charles IV and his family does not disguise a weakness of intellect and will.* (Prado, Madrid)

Peter Paul Rubens, Marie de' Medici, Queen of France, Landing in Marseilles, 1622–25: *In 1622, Marie de' Medici, the widow of French king, Henri IV, called the Flemish artist Rubens to her court in Paris to paint a series of 21 canvases for her palace walls. Although her activities were only routine—like the one depicted in this painting—Rubens brilliantly employed mythological figures, sumptuous color and texture, and dramatic compositional strategies to elevate and glorify his patron. (Louvre)*

Under Ivan III, called "the Great" (r. 1462–1505), and Ivan IV, called "the Terrible" (r. 1533–1584), the new state of Russia became a powerful kingdom. The "Terrible" Ivan earned his designation by crushing the traditional landowner caste, the boyars, installing his own supporters as territorial lords, and supplying them with serfs. He further inspired fear when he established a corps of state spies, the *oprichniki*, the ancestor of the much-hated tsarist political police of the nineteenth century; and when, in 1581, he killed his own son in a fit of rage. Viewing himself as the heir to the Roman and Byzantine empires, Ivan had himself proclaimed "tsar" ("caesar") at his coronation in 1547. Anarchy followed his death in 1584, but in 1613, the establishment of the Romanov dynasty, destined to rule until 1917, restored stability.

Traditionally eastward-looking because of its history and because of its Orthodox Christianity, Russia turned westward under Peter I, "the Great" (r. 1682–1725). From 1689, when he ended the regency of his mother, Peter guided Russia to participation in the European cultural realm. He promoted the commercial and intellectual innovations of the West in order to develop the skills Russia needed to become a modern, sovereign state. The Church, too, was put

under his control. He suppressed the old landed nobility and created a new aristocratic elite, subservient to the tsar but granted extraordinary powers over their serfs, who, since 1675, were reduced to the condition of slaves; that is, they could be bought and sold separately from the land. He required the sons of the nobles to gain a Western education, and directed the printing presses to publish newspapers and books like those read in such cities as Paris and London. He created a Baltic fleet, completely rebuilt the army, and encouraged industry (while punishing financial failure). Totally ruthless, he had his own son and heir condemned to death when that young man balked at the Tsar's cultural revolution.

By the time of Peter the Great, Russia had swollen far beyond the limits of old Muscovy. It extended eastward to the region of the Volga River, dominating the Asian descendants of the once-victorious Mongols, called Tatars. Passing the Ural Mountains, Russia reached still father across the arc of northern Asia into Siberia and to the Pacific shore. Pushing northward into the region of the Baltic Sea, it faced Sweden, which it stripped of vital territory in the Great Northern War (1700–1721). Here Peter constructed a new capital, facing west across the Gulf of Finland, named after himself: Saint Petersburg.

Pushing southward to the Black Sea, gateway to the Mediterranean, Russia faced Tatar chiefs who paid tribute to Ottoman Turkish rulers. To the west, it bordered the regions of Belarus and Ukraine, then under Polish domination. Much of this territory it acquired by the three eighteenth-century partitions of Poland accomplished under the most capable of Peter's successors, Catherine II, called "the Great" (r. 1762–1796).

A German princess by birth, Catherine came to the throne by the assassination of her husband, the grandson of Peter the Great. Although at first a committed reformer, seriously educated in political thought, she nevertheless worked to enhance the nobility's power over their serfs, at the same time insisting upon their obedience to herself. In foreign affairs she succeeded in expanding Russia's presence in the Middle East, and she acquired land from both Poland and the Ottoman Empire, including a precious outlet on the Black Sea. Considered an "enlightened" monarch, like her contemporaries in Austria and Prussia, Catherine, too, retained absolute power.

By the late eighteenth century, Europe was unique in being largely organized into nation-states (sovereign states containing a population linked by language, ethnicity, or history), and most Europeans were the subjects of monarchs who ruled, or wished to rule, absolutely. Of the continent's major political units, only Venice, the Swiss cantons, and the Dutch republic were not monarchies. Britain, though a monarchy, was a limited one, its king hedged around with constitutional restrictions. Yet although this was an age of

---

WHO'S WHO

Europe's Rulers in an Era of Concentrating Power, I

Charles V (r. 1519–1556, d. 1558) Habsburg emperor who briefly ruled much of Europe from the Iberian peninsula to the Ottoman border, including Italian possessions and Mediterranean islands, and much of the New World in addition.

Philip II (r. 1556–1598) Habsburg king of Spain, who from his monastic fortress (the Escorial) reigned over a Spanish Empire reaching to the New World and Italy, and defended Spanish naval supremacy and Atlantic monopoly.

Elizabeth I, "the Great" (r. 1558–1603) Queen of England who presided over the Anglican religious settlement, victory over the Spanish Armada, and the New World exploration.

Gustavus Adolphus (r. 1611–1632) King of Sweden who led reorganized Swedish army in Thirty Years' War.

Louis XIV (r. 1643–1715) King of France and patron of the court of Versailles, who best illustrates the concept of "absolute monarch," reportedly claiming: "I am the State."

Oliver Cromwell (r. 1653–1658) Parliamentary leader in English Civil War; subsequently, as Lord Protector, uncrowned ruler of England.

kings, the forces that would someday dethrone them were already gathering strength.

MIRRORS FOR PRINCES

In the thirteenth century, the saintly French King Louis IX (r. 1226–1270) had administered justice in a grove of trees, reclining against a great oak in order to hear the petitions of his subjects. In the seventeenth, his successor the "Sun King" Louis XIV was surrounded by circles of advisers and bureaucrats, laws and institutions, rituals and splendor. The four centuries that lie between saw the development of the notion of monarchy and the apparatus of the court—and, concurrently, the arguments for resistance to unjust power, and the theories of natural law and inborn rights that would in time dismantle both.

The Idea of the Prince

Almost as soon as kings appeared in Europe, writers began telling them how to rule. The same university-trained clerics who wrote on philosophy and theology wrote works on the ideal king. These "mirrors for princes," as they were called, urged moral values on the ruler: he should be kind, just, generous. The prince or king was to look into such books and see a perfected image of himself, which he was to emulate.

The idealized model of kingship projected by these works was remote from kingship in the flesh. Medieval monarchy had rested largely on force—military, judicial, personal. A theoretical understanding of the role of the sovereign, the figure in whom all authority resided, had not yet crystallized. Still less had the idea of the state as an abstract entity served by the king for the benefit of the people. From the fourteenth through seventeenth centuries, these concepts developed, culminating in the theoretical model of absolute monarchy.

The struggle between popes and emperors, originating in the eleventh century, stimulated in the fourteenth works challenging the notion of papal supremacy. Political theorists such as John of Jandun, Marsilius of Padua, and William of Ockham, as well as the poet Dante Alighieri aimed to free politics from papal ambitions and proposed the model of a universal monarchy. They observed that rulers operated in a realm of necessity separate from the realm of spirit, and made the decisions most beneficial to the state. These theories helped dismantle the secular authority of the papacy, which had peaked in the previous two centuries, and paved the way for the development of discrete secular monarchies in the two that followed.

Machiavelli's lawless prince, with whom this chapter opened, enters into consideration here. Italy, the arena where the struggle between pope and emperor took place, had no national monarchy until the nineteenth century. It was a patchwork of autonomous city republics and principalities. This region of fragmented authority and endemic violence was the context for Machiavelli's prince, a figure representing an abrupt departure from medieval tradition. He was to act unburdened by piety, compassion, or ideals of any sort. He was calculating, opportunistic, and ambitious for power. His aim was only to secure his state; the purpose of the state merely to exist, to avert conquest by another prince.

Machiavelli's contemporary Erasmus developed his own conception of the ideal monarch, in his *Education of the Christian Prince*, as well as in other treatises and letters. Like the subject of the medieval mirrors for princes, that figure was to be just, well-advised, and all-provident. But he had particularly Erasmian features, in addition: he would have a classical education, he would avoid war at all costs, and he would support with special diligence the productive middling and poorer citizens of his state. Erasmus's prince resembles not at all his Machiavellian counterpart.

Although Erasmus and Machiavelli differed in their view of the ideal monarch, they agreed that the modern world required a modern type of monarch. For Machiavelli, that new monarch, the "prince," would need to be ruthlessly focused on the problem of maintaining his power. For Erasmus, he would need to assume increased cultural, social, and economic responsibilities, and his ability to perform these primary duties would be jeopardized by the enormous costs of warfare.

Both were right. The ideal of the monarch developed by later sixteenth- and seventeenth-century theorists had both Machiavellian and Erasmian dimensions. The monarch would be truly sovereign, concentrating in himself all authority and pursuing all

> ### HOW MANY?
>
> # European Wars, 1500–1763
>
> **The Italian Wars:** 1494–1559 (Italian states, Papacy, Habsburg armies, France)
>
> **Dutch wars of independence:** 1579–1648 (Provinces of Northern Netherlands, Spain)
>
> **Thirty Years' War:** 1618–1648 (States of Holy Roman Empire [Bohemia, Palatinate], France, Austrian Habsburg Empire, Sweden)
>
> **English Civil War:** 1642–1651 (England [Parliamentary and Royalist forces], Scotland)
>
> **War of the Spanish Succession:** 1701–1714 (Spain, France, England, Netherlands)
>
> **Seven Years' War:** 1756–1763 (Spain, France, England, Netherlands)

WHO'S WHO

Europe's Rulers in an Era of Concentrating Power, II

Peter I, "the Great" (r. 1682–1725) Tsar of Russia who labored on political, commercial, and cultural fronts to bring Russia into the world of western European nations.

Frederick II, "the Great" (r. 1740–1786) King of Prussia who continued to build his nation's military strength and who struck aggressively to annex further European territory.

Maria Theresa (r. 1740–1780) Habsburg Queen of the Austrian Empire, who struggled to secure and expand the multinational state left her by her father.

Catherine II, "the Great" (r. 1762–1796) German-born Tsar of Russia who extended her nation's boundaries, invited *philosophes* to St. Petersburg, and established a school for girls (see Chapter 17).

means necessary to further the interests of the state. At the same time, he would set standards in the cultural realm, promote the economic welfare of his subjects, secure peace and administer justice, and serve in his person as the symbol of national unity. He was an absolute monarch, who ruled by divine right.

The notion of the "divine right of kings" is implicit in the medieval worldview, with its hierarchies of perfection culminating in God. It was but a step more to declare that the king in his kingdom was comparable to God in the universe. Answering only to God, an absolute monarch might free himself of the laws passed by parliaments or urged by the Church or embodied in traditional customs. The king himself, deriving his powers from God, was the embodiment of law.

The French philosopher Jean Bodin (1530–1596) presented a classic statement of the theory of absolute monarchy in his *Six Books of the Commonwealth* of 1576 (see *Witnesses*, p. 440). Just as families fell under the authority of the father (a definition of patriarchy), so communities of families fell under the authority of the state and its prince. The sovereign power could maintain peace, make laws, ensure justice, promote well-being. He was not all-powerful, but was limited, like his subjects, by natural law. Those subjects, too, had rights, which the monarch was to respect. Bodin's theory implies an abstract state, a sovereign power embodied in the monarch but conceivable without him as an independent entity.

In his *Politics Drawn from the Very Words of Scripture* published posthumously in 1709 and quoted in *Witnesses* on p. 440, another Frenchman, Bishop Jacques-Bénigne Bossuet (1627–1704), allowed kings more authority than did Bodin. As God's representatives, kings naturally produced judgments that were reasonable and just, like the will of God. While the king conformed to the divine law that reigned over all, what he willed, in the secular state, was the law itself. Bossuet verbalized the assumptions of power made by his own prince, Louis XIV.

Across the English Channel, too, the monarch's claims for absolute power were voiced—as in the *True Law of Free Monarchy* written in 1598 by James VI of Scotland, the future James I of England. James argued for the elevation of the king's will over Parliament, law, and custom. It was precisely such a claim that caused English absolutism to fail in the next generation, when Parliament dispatched monarchy for eleven years and absolute monarchy forever.

Yet in 1651, amid the throes of that revolution, the *Leviathan* (a reference to the Biblical monster appearing in the Book of Job, chapter 41) of Thomas Hobbes (1588–1679) promoted a different kind of absolutism: that of the state itself (see *Witnesses*, p. 442). Viewing human nature in an infamously negative light, Hobbes argued that people allowed their freedom would descend to anarchy, corruption, and violence—a "state of war." They must be reined in by a "Leviathan," a stern and vigilant government (not necessarily a king), to which they voluntarily conferred their obedience in an implicit contract. Thenceforth, the state would order the lives of those made desperate because their existence was, in Hobbes' memorably succinct and sad expression, "solitary, poor, nasty, brutish, and short."

The "Monstrous Regiment of Women" As theoreticians elevated the status of the king, the question of female monarchy was reexamined. What if the heir to the throne were a woman? A woman, it was believed, was unfit to rule. She would be fickle, deceitful, incapable of leading an army, obsessed with male relationships. In France, women were legally barred from ascending the throne.

Yet the early modern era boasts many female rulers. Isabella of Castile presided jointly with her husband, Ferdinand, over the *Reconquista* and the Spanish expansion into the New World. The British Isles saw three women rulers in the sixteenth century alone: Mary I, Elizabeth I, and their cousin Mary, Queen of Scots. In seventeenth-century Sweden, Christina (r. 1632–1654; d. 1689) succeeded her father Gustavus Adolphus. In the eighteenth century, Russia had four reigning empresses: Catherine I, Anna, Elizabeth, and Catherine II. The empress Maria Theresa (r. 1740–1780) ruled the disparate German, Hungarian, and Balkan areas of the Habsburg empire. In France, where a woman could not reign, Catherine de' Medici, Marie de' Medici, and Anne of Austria all ruled France as regents for their sons, its future kings.

Facing the ascension of Elizabeth I to the throne (in the wake of Queen Mary I) and with his native Scotland under the rule of Mary Stuart, the Protestant reformer John Knox (c. 1514–1572) wrote, in 1558, his *First Blast of the Trumpet against the Monstrous Regiment of Women* (see *Witnesses*, p. 441). For Knox, women were defects in nature, and rule by women was a hideous contradiction in terms. Assembling the various misogynist views of ancient

philosophers, pagan poets, the Bible, and Church Fathers, he thundered that the English and Scottish nobility were worse than "brute beasts" for tolerating female sovereignty: "for that they do to women which no male amongst the common sort of beasts can be proved to do to their female, that is, they reverence them, and quake at their presence; they obey their commandments, and that against God."

In order to withstand such criticism, women who ruled often adopted the guise of androgyny. Queen Elizabeth I of England played with such male/female images—positive ones, of course—in representing herself to her subjects. She was a prince, and manly, she asserted, even though she was female, as recorded in *Witnesses* on p. 441. She was also (she claimed) a virgin, a condition essential to avoid the attacks of her opponents, for whom female nature always inclined to lust. In her last years, she defied the limits of female sexual identification. "My sex," she said, just before her death, "cannot diminish my prestige."

Catherine de' Medici skirted the boundaries of male and female identifications in the imagery she adopted to define her position. She chose as one symbol the figure of Artemisia, an androgynous ancient warrior-heroine, who combined a female persona with masculine powers. Thus clothed in androgynous imagery, these women rulers could, like their male counterparts, claim to be princes and absolute sovereigns.

Some later female rulers readily acknowledged and even exploited their gender. Maria Theresa, devoted to her wayward husband and to her thirteen children, was the embodiment of the motherly queen, while at the same time being an outstanding monarch. Catherine the Great indulged her own sexual appetites with the same freedom shown by male monarchs, taking numerous lovers—but never allowing them to distract her from affairs of state.

Halls of Mirrors

Just as political philosophers developed the theory of absolute monarchy, architects designed spaces in which those monarchs might display their power. On grand staircases and in splendid reception rooms, such as the huge Hall of Mirrors built for Louis XIV at Versailles (and imitated in other royal courts) the king shone in glory; and those gathered around him, like glass, reflected his brilliant image. In addition to the crowds of courtiers pressing forward to catch a glimpse of majesty, the monarch was attended by poets and playwrights, composers and painters, all competing for the honor (and financial rewards) of royal patronage.

During the Middle Ages, as before, events of importance to the community had been celebrated with processions—solemn ritual marches, featuring a display of special objects. In the early modern era, kings adapted the ritual device of the procession to

A Queen's Right to Rule

Although the sovereignty of the male monarch could be vigorously defended, the sovereignty of a woman monarch remained in question. In the first passage the Scottish reformer John Knox, whose own country and neighboring England were (to his fury) ruled by queens, denies that women can exercise authority as men do. In the second, Queen Elizabeth I presents herself to the English army, and declares her readiness and capacity to rule.

John Knox blasts his trumpet against rule by women (1558): The empire of a Woman is a thing repugnant to Nature. ... For who can deny but it is repugnant to nature, that the blind shall be appointed to lead and conduct such as do see? That the weak, the sick, and impotent persons shall nourish and keep the whole and strong? And finally, that the foolish, mad, and frenetic shall govern the discrete, and give counsel to such as be sober of mind? And such be all women, compared unto man in bearing of authority. For their sight in civil regiment [government] is but blindness; their strength, weakness; their counsel, foolishness; and judgment, frenzy, if it be rightly considered.

(John Knox, *The First Blast of the Trumpet against the Monstrous Regiment of Women*, 1558; ed. D. Laing, 1864, modernized)

Queen Elizabeth addresses the troops encamped at Tilbury (9 August 1588), asserting her sovereignty even in a military situation—the naval battle against the Spanish Armada had commenced–where her enemies might hope she would weaken: I know I have the body but of a weak and feeble woman; but I have the heart and stomach of a king, and of a king of England too, and think foul scorn that Parma or Spain or any prince of Europe should dare to invade the borders of my realm; to which, rather than any dishonor should grow by me, I myself will take up arms; I myself will be your general, judge, and rewarder of every one of your virtues in the field ... not doubting but by your obedience to my general, by your concord in the camp, and your valor in the field, we shall shortly have a famous victory over those enemies of my God, of my kingdoms, and of my people.

(Elizabeth I, "To the Troops at Tilbury, 1588"; ed. G. P. Rice, Jr., 1951)

their purposes. When a ruler was scheduled to enter a city, a team of artists, architects, and mechanics constructed props and scenery to make the arrival more imposing. Costume, music, and the careful choreography of the prince's retinue also enhanced the effect.

In the prince's private dwelling, too, sound, imagery, and movement were designed to reflect the sovereign's power. The paintings on the wall, the carving of the furniture, the patterns of the glass in the window, or the carpet on the floor—all could be designed to label the space inhabited by the prince. Throughout the Middle Ages, works of art and literature had been mainly religious, whether commissioned by the Church or by a private individual. In the early modern age, in the precincts of royal power, to communicate the authority and prestige of the prince was itself the business of the arts.

To convey their grandeur, kings built palaces increasingly distinct, in size and magnificence, from the homes of the subjects they ruled. Both the Escorial, near Madrid, and Versailles, near Paris, were not mere palaces, but immense complexes engineered to express the raw fact of royal power. The Austrian princes built palaces of commensurate grandeur and Peter the Great, of Russia, built a whole city, Saint Petersburg, in his image. Even the dukes and despots of Italy and the petty German princes of the Holy Roman Empire surrounded themselves with splendor.

The arrogance of royal power is nowhere expressed so eloquently as in these palaces, whose purpose was frankly not to live or to rule but to overawe. The claim to absolute power made by the kings of Europe and portrayed in stone, glass, and gilding would be challenged by other currents of early modern culture. In time these new ideas would variously reshape monarchy or abolish it, and would make of those palaces what most of them are today: museums, displaying the customs and values of a remote past.

Roman Law and Natural Right

As European monarchs accumulated power and as writers and artists celebrated it, traditions of law evolved that variously supported or undermined royal claims to authority. Concepts of natural right, based on both legal and philosophical traditions, also emerged to pose a challenge to political absolutism.

When Roman authority evaporated in the fifth century C.E., the peoples of Europe outside the old Empire—Celtic, Germanic, and Slavic—continued to follow the customs of their ancestors: tribal law. These customs satisfactorily regulated community life and disciplined criminal behavior so long as those communities remained simple. As tribes and villages became incorporated into nations, the increased complexity of life required the development of more complex systems of law. In many parts of western Europe, the sophisticated apparatus of Roman law, which had served the needs of the largest empire of the ancient Mediterranean world, was drawn upon to alter and even replace customary law.

While medieval philosophers fitted the concepts of Christian theology into the framework of Aristotelian metaphysics, medieval jurists studied the *Code* of Justinian. Centered at Bologna from the

The Origins of Government in the Consent of the Citizens

While some political theorists labored to bolster the theory of monarchy, others thought about why and how citizens formed themselves into a political community. Foremost among these are Thomas Hobbes and John Locke, whose very different understandings of "civil society" are still important in political thought. Here Hobbes explains why subjects should and must obey a sovereign authority (who might or might not be a monarch), while Locke explains why individuals freely sacrifice some of their rights and join forces to form a civil body.

Thomas Hobbes shows how all citizens consent to the sovereign power (1651): II.17. The only way to erect such a common power, as may be able to defend [men] from the invasion of foreigners, and the injuries of one another, and thereby to secure them in such sort, as that by their own industry, and by the fruits of the earth, they may nourish themselves and live contentedly, is, to confer all their power and strength upon one man, or upon one assembly of men, that may reduce all their wills, by plurality of voices, unto one will. ... This is more than consent, or concord; it is a real unity of them all, in one and the same person, made by covenant of every man, in such manner, as if every man should say to every man, "I authorize and give up my right of governing myself, to this man, or to this assembly of men, on this condition, that thou give up thy right to him, and authorize all his actions in like manner." This done, the multitude so united in one person is called a "commonwealth," in Latin *civitas*. This is the generation of that great LEVIATHAN, or rather, to speak more reverently, of that "mortal god," to which we owe under the "immortal God," our peace and defence. For by this authority, given him by every particular man in the commonwealth, he has the use of so much power and strength conferred on him, that by terror thereof, he is enabled to perform the wills of them all, to peace at home, and mutual aid against their enemies abroad. And in him consists the essence of the commonwealth . ...

And he that carries this person is called "sovereign," and is said to have "sovereign power"; and every one besides, his "subject."
(Thomas Hobbes, *Leviathan*, 1651, 2:17; ed. E. Weber, 1990)

John Locke explains why people will surrender their freedom to form civil government (1690): Men, being, as has been said, by nature all free, equal, and independent, no one can be put out of this estate and subjected to the political power of another without his own consent. The only way whereby anyone divests himself of his own natural liberty and puts on the bonds of civil society, is by agreeing with other men, to join and unite into a community for their comfortable, safe and peaceable living one among another, in a secure enjoyment of their properties, and a greater security against any that are not of it. ... When any number of men have so consented to make one community or government, they are thereby presently incorporated, and make one body politic, wherein the majority have a right to act and conclude the rest. ...

If man in the state of nature be so free as has been said ... why will he part with his freedom? Why will he give up this empire, and subject himself to the dominion and control of any other power? To which it is obvious to answer, that though in the state of nature he has such a right, yet the enjoyment of it is very uncertain. ... This makes him willing to quit this condition which, however free, is full of fears and continual dangers; and it is not without reason that he seeks out and is willing to join in society with others who ... unite for the mutual preservation of their lives, liberties and estates, which I call by the general name—property.

The great and chief end, therefore, of men uniting into commonwealths, and putting themselves under government, is the preservation of their property. ...
(John Locke, *The Second Treatise on Government*, 1690; ed. E. Weber, 1990)

twelfth century, a series of jurists wrote commentaries showing how Roman law could be applied to the patterns of Christian society and medieval communities. Soon Roman legal concepts were employed by the advisers to the kings of Europe. Roman law had been developed for a state in which power was centered in a ruler, the emperor. Its concepts were now useful to kings seeking tools by which to discipline their nobility, administer their states, and become "emperors" in their own lands. Indeed, the very concept of a "state" was made available in the language of Roman law. It was the precondition of the further development of the nations of Europe.

In England, newly revived concepts of Roman law encountered an independent tradition of common law, developed during the Middle Ages and rooted in Anglo-Saxon and Norman practice. English common law was based on the principle that previous judicial decisions, rather than codes or statutes, established right. The jury system and the system of criminal procedure based on "grand" and "petty" inquests are components of English common law. The kings of England promoted common law, which was the law administered in the kings' courts, and shaped its procedures to the benefit of royal authority. In time, they also incorporated elements of Roman law into

The Royal Palace

Pierre Patel the elder, View of Versailles: *In the sixteenth and seventeenth centuries, Europe's rulers built palaces to match their claims for glory. Greatest of these was Louis XIV's palace at Versailles, built between 1669 and 1686. This painting is an aerial view of the palace and its walks, fountains, and gardens.*

the tradition, especially those that tended to exalt the authority of the monarch. As elsewhere in Europe, the law of the Roman Church, or "canon law," which was modeled on Roman principles, also helped to shape common law.

If Roman law served to bolster the authority of the state and its ruler, it also conveyed another concept important in the development of modern politics: that of natural law. Roman jurists distinguished between the positive law by which Roman citizens were bound—the "law of nations" which regulated interactions between peoples—and natural law, which mirrored eternal principles of good and evil that were intrinsic in nature. Those concepts were transmitted in Christian Europe through the work of medieval jurists, and flourished anew in the early modern era. "The law of nature is a dictate of right reason," wrote the seventeenth-century Dutch theorist Hugo Grotius (1583–1645); an act is judged morally worthy if in accord with rational nature, or

View of the Escorial: *The Spanish king Philip II's gloomier palace, the Escorial, was built outside Madrid between 1563 and 1584 more for labor and penitence than for the leisured elegance of Versailles.*

base if it is not. Human law, God's law, nature's law were all different, he maintained, but they could exist in congruence.

If medieval and Reformation thinkers wished to bring human activity into accord with divine mandates, some political thinkers of the early modern era wished to limit the state by the principles of natural law. Whereas Roman law favored state-building, the theory of natural law encouraged the building of states according to principles of right and justice which were unattached to any specific nation or people or system of belief.

Another school of political theory developed to justify resistance to states perceived as unjust. Some religious communities fostered an ethic of skepticism toward those in power, and even sanctioned disobedience to governments that violated independent standards of justice. These attitudes often prospered in radical Protestant groups, and in many cases they were extinguished as the adherents of such groups were suppressed. But similar attitudes also characterized the reformed churches radiating from Calvin's Geneva, born of a man who had himself fled a persecuting regime. "Obedience to man must not become disobedience to God," wrote that sober reformer. Next to God, Calvin acknowledged, we are subject to kings—but only so long as their command is godly. "If they command anything against Him, let it go unesteemed."

The right to resist unjust governors, cautiously but clearly stated here, is the proto-democratic germ of Calvinist political theory. The theme was not so prominent in Geneva (where Protestants were in power) as in the further reaches of the Calvinist network, where the reformers were opposed to the majority: in England, Scotland (until the late 1600s), Huguenot France, and Hungary, Poland and Bohemia before their re-conversion to Catholicism in the Thirty Years' War. Later Calvinist theorists went so far as to propose the notion that sovereignty lies in the people, who have the authority to make laws, appoint magistrates, and create kings.

It was but a step further to propose that government was based on a contract between the ruler and the ruled. Sovereignty resided in the people, who, by a kind of contract, agreed to surrender their independence in order to gain the benefits of a well-regulated state. These views form part of the famous analysis of civil government forged in the late seventeenth century by the English liberal John Locke.

A university-trained philosopher who witnessed in his youth the struggles of the English Civil War, John Locke (1632–1704) worked as secretary to a nobleman of the Whig party, which engineered the 1688 Revolution. By that time, Locke himself was living in the Dutch Republic, a center for the circulation of the latest and most daring ideas. From there in 1689–1690 he published four fundamental works: the *Letter on Toleration*, the *Essay Concerning Human Understanding*, and *Two Treatises on Civil Government*. Each was a groundbreaking work of momentous significance. The second of the two *Treatises* is specifically relevant here.

According to Locke, human beings were born absolutely free to pursue their own welfare as best they might amid the natural abundance that God provided at the Creation. All were born with fundamental rights: to life, to liberty, and to the pursuit of property. Some chose to labor diligently and acquire private property. When the others, propertyless, sought to seize what they had not labored to accumulate, the property-owners joined together to create civil government—which was, in effect, the result of a contract. That contract was reminiscent of that called for by Hobbes, but unlike his, it was reversible.

The participants chose representatives to a legislature, which reported to a king. If the government failed to perform the functions for which it was created, it could be dismantled and refounded on the original principles. If the king abused his position and interfered with the proper function of a just government, he could be removed. Locke's treatise is a roadmap at once for the creation of a society based on capitalist notions of the accumulation of property and for the founding of a government rooted in the consent and will of the people. These views passed directly to the authors of the American Declaration of Independence and inform its core principles.

Conclusion

POWER, RESISTANCE, AND THE MEANING OF THE WEST

Although Machiavelli's prince never appeared and Italy was lost, elsewhere the European monarchs of the early modern era adopted the objective that Machiavelli defined: the pursuit of power. By the mid-eighteenth century, the states of Europe were the most powerful in the world, and the rulers who governed them were, in most cases, absolute. Yet the possibility of resistance to unjust monarchy had also become apparent—in the example of the English Revolution on the one hand, and, on the other, in the philosophical vision of the proponents of natural law and social contracts. The tendencies to the concentration of power and, at the same time, to its limitation would both continue to characterize the civilization of the West, as Westerners set out to explore and to dominate the rest of the globe.

REVIEW QUESTIONS

1. Name major developments that changed the nature of power in the "early modern" era. How did gunpowder change warfare? Why did the foot soldier achieve dominance on the battlefield?

2. Explain how the following changed warfare: Italy, mercenary soldiers; Sweden, Gustavus Adolphus; England, Oliver Cromwell; France, Louis XIV; Prussia, Frederick the "Great Elector."

3. Explain the importance of the following wars: wars of Reformation; Dutch revolt in Spain; wars of Louis XIV; colonial conflicts in the New World; War of Austrian Succession; Seven Years' War.

4. What was the importance of Philip II's reign? Why did Spain decline as a great power? Why did France emerge as the strongest power in Europe? What were the contributions of Louis XIV?

5. How did England's development differ from Spain, France, and Austria? What were the issues that divided the English Parliament and the king? What was most significant about the Restoration and the Glorious Revolution?

6. How did the Thirty Years' War affect the development of emerging states in central and eastern Europe? Why did Prussia emerge as a major power? Explain the importance of Ivan the Terrible; Peter the Great; Catherine the Great.

SUGGESTED RESOURCES

Power and Gunpowder

Black, Jeremy, ed., *European Warfare, 1453–1815* (New York: St. Martin's Press, 1999). Nine historians look at major conflicts in Europe—in their social, cultural, and political contexts—painting a comprehensive picture of warfare from the Ottoman conquest of Constantinople to the fall of Napoleon.

Brewer, John, *The Sinews of Power: War, Money, and the English State, 1688–1783* (New York: Knopf, 1989). A methodical analysis of the fiscal-military complex that powered the English state through a period of nearly continuous warfare.

McNeill, William H., *The Pursuit of Power: Technology, Armed Force, and Society since A.D. 1000* (Chicago: University of Chicago Press, 1982). Argues that the emergence of free enterprise in Europe allowed wealth, technology, and political power to reinforce each other.

Parker, Geoffrey, *The Military Revolution: Military Innovation and the Rise of the West, 1500–1800*, 2nd ed. (Cambridge: Cambridge University Press, 1996). A classic description of a "military revolution" that was a major factor in Europe's achievement of global power during the early modern era.

Phillips, Carla Rahn, *Six Galleons for the King of Spain: Imperial Defense in the Early Seventeenth Century* (Baltimore: Johns Hopkins University Press, 1991). A study of shipbuilding, the logistics of naval defense, and the problems of the effort to defend the Spanish Atlantic Empire.

War Games

Anderson, Fred, *Crucible of War: The Seven Years' War and the Fate of Empire in North America, 1754–1766* (New York: Knopf, 2000). Traces the events that led to the Seven Years' War and its expansion over three of the continents, which shaped the development of Britain into a world empire.

DuPlessis, Robert S., *Lille and the Dutch Revolt: Urban Stability in an Era of Revolution, 1500–1582* (Cambridge–New York: Cambridge University Press, 1991). Shows that Lille remained loyal to Philip II during the Dutch revolt due to the political response of its ruling class.

Parker, Geoffrey, *The Thirty Years' War* (London–Boston: Routledge, Kegan Paul, 1984). A masterful account of this most devastating conflict of the early modern era.

An Age of Kings

Bonney, Richard, *The European Dynastic States, 1494–1660* (Oxford: Oxford University Press, 1991). An excellent overview of the political development of Europe's nation states in the early modern era.

Burns, J. H., *Lordship, Kingship and Empire: The Idea of Monarchy 1400–1525* (Oxford: Clarendon Press of Oxford University Press, 1988). An examination of lordship in late medieval and early modern France, England, Spain, the papacy, and the Holy Roman Empire.

Elliott, J. H. & L. W. B. Brockliss, eds., *The Age of the Favourite* (New Haven: Yale University Press, 1999). The absolute kings did not rule absolutely but shared power, tacitly, with their "favorites," men who gained importance because of their privileged access to and command over the monarch, and depicted in a variety of European settings in these essays.

Major, J. Russell, *From Renaissance Monarchy to Absolute Monarchy: French Kings, Nobles, and Estates* (Baltimore: Johns Hopkins University Press, 1994). Considers kings, aristocrats, and assemblies in the struggle for power, with the monarchy edging ahead in the end.

Mirrors for Princes

Brown, Jonathan and J. H. Elliott, *A Palace for the King: The Buen Retiro and the Court of Philip IV* (New Haven: Yale University Press, 1980). Analyzes the 1630s construction of the Buen Retiro palace, showing how the palace was a contrived presentation of kingship, intended to awe spectators and subjects.

Burke, Peter, *The Fabrication of Louis XIV* (New Haven–London: Yale University Press, 1992). An imaginative analysis of the staging of the French kingship during the high point of absolutism.

Frye, Susan, *Elizabeth I: The Competition for Representation* (Oxford: Oxford University Press, 1993). How Elizabeth appropriated the image-making machinery around her to advance her own construction of herself as both woman and monarch.

Life and Times of Queen Elizabeth I: http://www.elizabethi.org

Louise XIV, biography (Versailles): http://www.chateauversailles.fr/en/210.asp

Constitutional goovernment, works of all periods, including Machiavelli, Grotius, Hobbes, Locke, Bodin, and Bossuet: http://www.constitution.org/liberlib.htm

EUROPE REACHES OUT

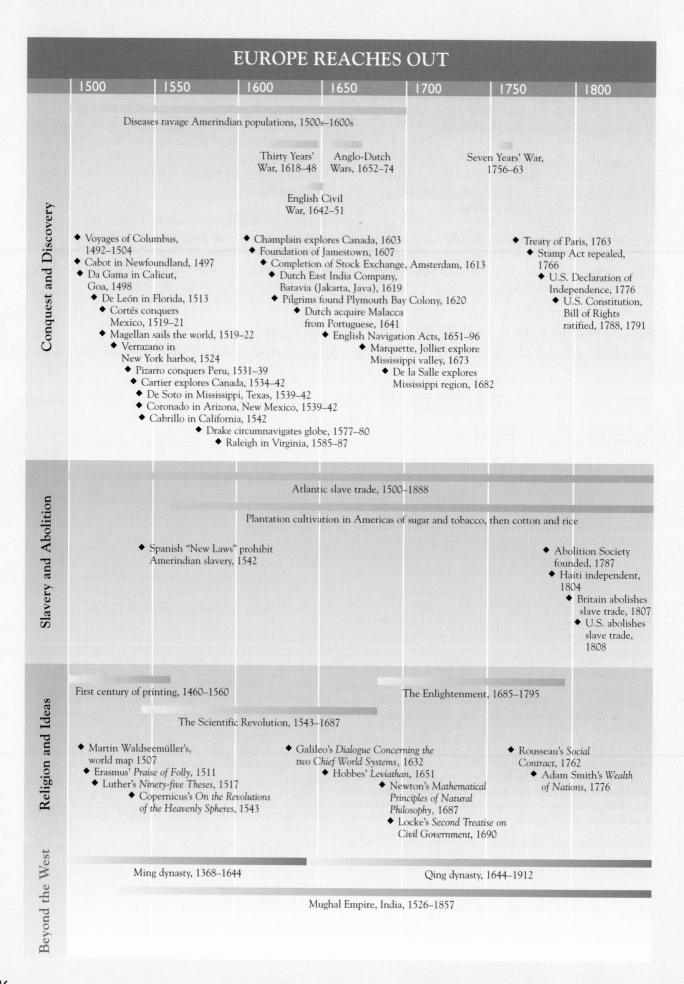

	1500	1550	1600	1650	1700	1750	1800

Diseases ravage Amerindian populations, 1500s–1600s

Thirty Years' War, 1618–48

Anglo-Dutch Wars, 1652–74

Seven Years' War, 1756–63

English Civil War, 1642–51

Conquest and Discovery

- Voyages of Columbus, 1492–1504
- Cabot in Newfoundland, 1497
- Da Gama in Calicut, Goa, 1498
- De León in Florida, 1513
- Cortés conquers Mexico, 1519–21
- Magellan sails the world, 1519–22
- Verrazano in New York harbor, 1524
- Pizarro conquers Peru, 1531–39
- Cartier explores Canada, 1534–42
- De Soto in Mississippi, Texas, 1539–42
- Coronado in Arizona, New Mexico, 1539–42
- Cabrillo in California, 1542
- Drake circumnavigates globe, 1577–80
- Raleigh in Virginia, 1585–87

- Champlain explores Canada, 1603
- Foundation of Jamestown, 1607
- Completion of Stock Exchange, Amsterdam, 1613
- Dutch East India Company, Batavia (Jakarta, Java), 1619
- Pilgrims found Plymouth Bay Colony, 1620
- Dutch acquire Malacca from Portuguese, 1641
- English Navigation Acts, 1651–96
- Marquette, Jolliet explore Mississippi valley, 1673
- De la Salle explores Mississippi region, 1682

- Treaty of Paris, 1763
- Stamp Act repealed, 1766
- U.S. Declaration of Independence, 1776
- U.S. Constitution, Bill of Rights ratified, 1788, 1791

Slavery and Abolition

Atlantic slave trade, 1500–1888

Plantation cultivation in Americas of sugar and tobacco, then cotton and rice

- Spanish "New Laws" prohibit Amerindian slavery, 1542

- Abolition Society founded, 1787
- Haiti independent, 1804
- Britain abolishes slave trade, 1807
- U.S. abolishes slave trade, 1808

Religion and Ideas

First century of printing, 1460–1560

The Enlightenment, 1685–1795

The Scientific Revolution, 1543–1687

- Martin Waldseemüller's, world map 1507
- Erasmus' *Praise of Folly*, 1511
- Luther's *Ninety-five Theses*, 1517
- Copernicus's *On the Revolutions of the Heavenly Spheres*, 1543

- Galileo's *Dialogue Concerning the two Chief World Systems*, 1632
- Hobbes' *Leviathan*, 1651
- Newton's *Mathematical Principles of Natural Philosophy*, 1687
- Locke's *Second Treatise on Civil Government*, 1690

- Rousseau's *Social Contract*, 1762
- Adam Smith's *Wealth of Nations*, 1776

Beyond the West

Ming dynasty, 1368–1644

Qing dynasty, 1644–1912

Mughal Empire, India, 1526–1857

CHAPTER
16

EUROPE REACHES OUT

Global Voyages and Cultural Encounters

1500–1750

KEY TOPICS

◆ **The Open Seas:** Led by skilled Portuguese navigators, European merchants establish footholds in Africa, India, the East Indies, and East Asia.

◆ **Brave New World:** With Christopher Columbus in the vanguard, Spanish and Portuguese conquerors settle much of South and North America; the English, Dutch, and French follow them, as native Amerindians are increasingly

displaced, and African slaves are imported to work the mines and the fields.

◆ **The Wealth of Nations:** New world commodities flood Europe, which exports its manufactures to the new colonies of the Western Hemisphere and the ancient markets of the east; "mercantilist" strategies are challenged by the proposition that free trade is an even better tool for building the wealth of nations.

Who is the Cannibal? *The Tupinambá, wrote the sixteenth-century French essayist Michel de Montaigne (1533–1592) of the* **Amerindian** *inhabitants of Brazil, roasted and then ate their war captives. As the victims awaited their fate, they suffered without flinching the winners' abuse and mockery. A well-bred European of the ruling noble class, Montaigne did not quite admire this behavior, but neither did he condemn it. Did not Europeans perpetrate worse cruelties? "I think there is more barbarity in eating a man alive than in eating him dead," wrote Montaigne referring to then current judicial punishments, "and in tearing by torture and the rack a body still full of feeling, in roasting a man bit by bit, and mangled by dogs and swine …, than in roasting and eating him after he is dead."*

Montaigne's attitude—at once curious, skeptical, and tolerant—could have crystallized only after Europeans began their great expansion into the other inhabited continents of the globe. During that 500-year venture, European peoples encountered the diverse peoples of Asia, Africa, Australia, and the Western Hemisphere. Non-Europeans and Europeans were transformed by the interactions that followed.

As Maps 16.1, 16.3, and 16.4 show, from the mid-fifteenth to the mid-seventeenth century, Europeans ranged over the globe, buying and selling, measuring and mapping, conquering and settling. First tiny Portugal ranged beyond the Mediterranean, and around the African coast to India and east Asia. Portugal's competitors quickly joined the race and extended the European presence in Asia. In the Western Hemisphere, European nations explored and settled the Americas, the setting for unanticipated encounters among Amerindian, African, and European peoples. Stimulated by European colonization, a global commercial system of unprecedented complexity developed, while conflicts flared up among competing nations which had committed their wealth and their people, and other peoples and their wealth too, in the quest for greater profits.

THE OPEN SEAS

In the late 1400s, European ships which had rarely ventured beyond the Mediterranean Sea launched out into the open ocean: the Indian, the Pacific, and the Atlantic, called the "Ocean Sea." These waters were the key to Europe's powerful leap forward in the early modern era. They were conquered by sturdy ships, refined navigational tools, cast-iron cannon, and better maps. The tiny Iberian state of Portugal took the lead, establishing footholds in Africa, India, China, Japan, and the famed "Spice Islands" or

Moluccas (in modern Indonesia). Immense profits flowed into the port of Lisbon and the Portuguese royal treasury. Dutch, French, and English merchants followed their lure. By 1700, these nations had footholds of their own on the African coasts and in south and east Asia and the Pacific islands.

Portugal Takes the Lead

Since the earliest days of civilization, world trade had centered on the Mediterranean. In the Middle Ages, Byzantine, Arab, and Italian merchants carried across the Mediterranean goods hauled overland and over water from the three continents that surrounded it. Driving this commerce was the demand for luxury products from India and China, the islands of southeast Asia, and the African interior. These were, above all, spices—pepper, cloves, nutmeg—craved as preservatives and flavorings; also silks and cottons, exotic woods, ivory, and gems. Much as Europeans craved these luxury commodities, European merchants craved even more the gold with which to buy them.

It was in order to find both gold and spices that, in the fifteenth century, the captains of Portuguese ships set out on unprecedentedly long journeys. The little kingdom of Portugal bordered the Atlantic Ocean on the western edge of the Iberian peninsula. Under Moorish domination until the twelfth century, it was isolated both from the main currents of European life and from Mediterranean commerce. But Portuguese merchants had knowledge of Arab science and navigational tools, and enjoyed royal patronage, assets enabling them to win the prize they sought: direct access to the trading depots of the Old World.

Navigation Aids Previously, the impediment to exploring the open ocean had been the difficulty of knowing where you were, where you were going, and where the winds might blow you. Late in the Middle Ages, several technical advances came together to solve the problem. The **astrolabe**, invented by the Greek scientist Hipparchus in the second century B.C.E. and later refined by Arab scientists, permitted the navigator to measure the apparent height of a star and thus determine his latitude. Meanwhile, astronomers worked out detailed tables of the positions of the stars. These tables allowed the technician with an astrolabe to determine a ship's position.

The **quadrant** and, later, the more advanced **sextant**, also measured the altitude of heavenly bodies and thus determined position. Mechanical clocks could check the bearing of the sun—although longitude could not be measured until precision chronometers in the eighteenth century. The **compass**, used by Chinese navigators from around 1100, was adopted by Europeans, who designated as its four cardinal points the fixed directions North, South, East, and West. The device pointed to a magnetic, and therefore variable, north, rather than a true north, which limited its usefulness.

As nautical tools improved, so too did maps. **Portolan** charts gave sailing distances in clear quantities and bearings in straight lines. Lacking parallels and **meridians**, or any indication of the curvature of the earth, they could be used for enclosed seas, but not on the open oceans. Better charts became available as geographical knowledge improved.

Early in the fifteenth century, a copy of the *Geography* by the Greek scientist Ptolemy (c. 90–168 C.E.), began to circulate in western Europe, spurring the creation of a new generation of world maps. These first ventures of modern **cartography** (the science of mapmaking) sadly preserved Ptolemy's errors. He underestimated the circumference of the earth by one-sixth and imagined a huge "unknown land" covering much of the Southern Hemisphere. Portuguese expeditions enabled cartographers to partially correct the maps and charts and called for the drawing of at least one meridian and lines of latitude. By the mid-sixteenth century, map projections regularly described the earth as a sphere, as shown in *Windows On*, p. 453. Thereafter maps were more accurate than Ptolemy's, as science and experience improved on the knowledge inherited from antiquity.

As shipbuilding also improved, so too did ships (see Chapter 11). The ships of medieval Europe were square-masted and depended on oars for maneuverability and speed. Arab ships called **dhows**, designed for the deep waters of the Indian Ocean, were rigged with triangular, or **lateen**, sails. From these two types of vessel, Spanish and Portuguese shipbuilders developed the small, fast **caravel**. The key to the caravel's

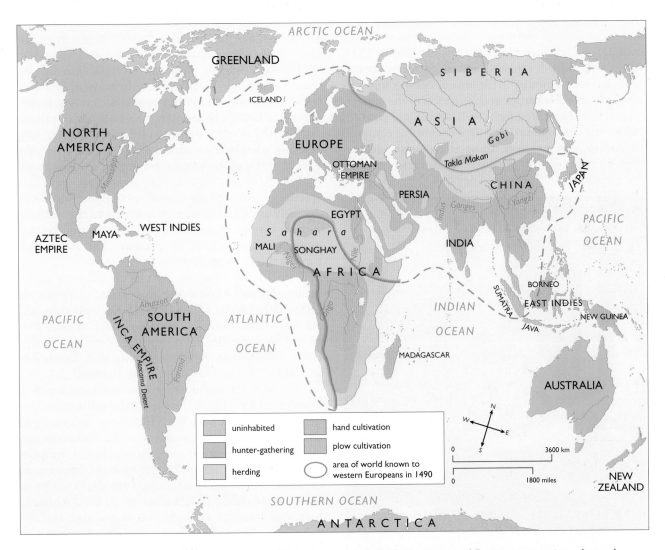

Map 16.1 World Economies and Movements of Peoples around 1500: *On the eve of European expansion, advanced economies based on cultivation with the plow were found in Europe, Asia Minor and the Near East, South and East Asia and some of the Pacific islands, and a small fraction of mostly Mediterranean Africa—the areas of the original Eurasian civilizations and those regions that developed from contact with them. Here the production of food surplus had also made possible the intensive development of urban centers. Food gatherers, hand cultivators, and pastoralists occupied the rest of the inhabited globe, the major part of its surface. Beginning in the late fifteenth century, peoples from the more advanced areas and especially Europeans began the settlement, expansion, and transformation of those unvisited areas.*

speed was its enlarged sail area, achieved by increasing the number of masts and rigging the middle mast with a square sail or sails, the fore and aft with lateen sails. The stern rudder, a recent innovation, allowed for quick, precise steering. Navigators learned to overcome the westerly winds of the Atlantic and to make use of wind patterns on the Indian Ocean. Because oarsmen were unnecessary, their places could be taken by sailors, cargo, or soldiers.

These superior sailing ships also developed fighting capacity. In the 1400s, they carried cannon on deck, as well as soldiers armed with crossbows and arquebuses. By the early 1500s, guns were permanently mounted between the decks so as to fire broadside through special gunports. Hulls were strengthened, and the whole structure braced by multiple decks, so that the ship could withstand enemy bombardment and cannon recoil. Wherever they went, the new men-of-war (as these warships were called) out-powered other ships and even coastal defences. "At the rumor of our coming," a Portuguese general wrote his king in 1513, "the native ships all vanished, and even the birds ceased to skim over the water." This armed, oceangoing craft made possible the European domination of the seas.

Safe, fast, and formidable, well-steered and powered entirely by sails, manned by a smaller crew but equipped to sustain long journeys, these ships constituted an improvement over the Mediterranean carriers used by the Genoese and Venetians. They brought explorers to the New World, and escorted convoys of heavy merchant vessels across the oceans. (The "New World," designating the lands of the Western Hemisphere, was isolated from the Old World civilizations of Afro-Eurasia until Columbus' arrival in 1492.) By 1600, European ships, once inferior, were the best in the world.

The African Route   The first nation to benefit from this improved technology was Portugal. Emerging from the wars of the *Reconquista*, Portugal entered upon its most glorious age around 1400, during the long reign of King John I (r. 1385–1433). John was not only a state-builder but the founder of Portugal's maritime success, even more brilliantly patronized by his brother Prince Henry the Navigator (1394–1460). In 1415, Henry participated in the Portuguese capture of Ceuta, a Moorish depot opposite Gibraltar. The next year he summoned cartographers and seamen to form an institute for navigation. Under Henry's patronage, dozens of vessels sailed straight from the shore into unknown waters, to Africa and beyond.

Plucking up the Atlantic archipelagoes of the Azores and Madeiras Islands on the way (while Spain took the Canaries), Portuguese sea captains turned south to plant garrisons along the west African shore. By the 1470s, they had founded permanent trading stations, where they loaded the gold, spices, ivory, and exotic woods of the interior on ships bound for home. Although their original objectives were gold and spices, they quickly developed an appetite for slaves. As early as 1433, Prince Henry approved the traffic in human cargoes. Soon the crown was taxing the revenues of this trade at 20 percent. The slave trade funded the Portuguese state.

Late in the fifteenth century, Portuguese exploration reached beyond the west coast of Africa. In 1488, Bartolomeu Dias (1430–1500) looped around Africa's southern tip (later named the Cape of Good Hope) and continued northeast along the further coast. Repelled by Arab merchants, and daunted by unfamiliar winds, Dias returned to Portugal.

Ten years later, and under Dias' tutelage, Vasco da Gama (c. 1460–1524) completed the mission his predecessor had launched. With four ships, he sailed past the Cape of Good Hope and into the Indian Ocean, previously the preserve of Arab merchants. In 1498, he anchored off Calicut, on the west (Malabar) coast of India, one of the main depots for the Asian spice trade, as described in *Witnesses* on p. 458. Although hostilities erupted between the Portuguese and the ruler of Calicut, Da Gama managed to return to Portugal with a quantity of pepper. That pepper signaled the accomplishment of a route to the east that started from the western coast of Europe.

Soon the Portuguese established a firm base at the city of Goa, farther north on the west coast of India. This would serve as the Asian capital of their commercial empire of "the Indies" (meaning at the time all of

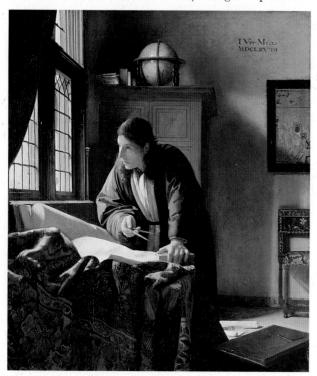

The Lure of Faraway Places

Jan Vermeer, The Geographer: *In this painting of 1669 by the Dutch artist Vermeer can be seen different articles of navigation: a compass, maps, and a globe.* (Städelsches Kunstinstitut, Frankfurt)

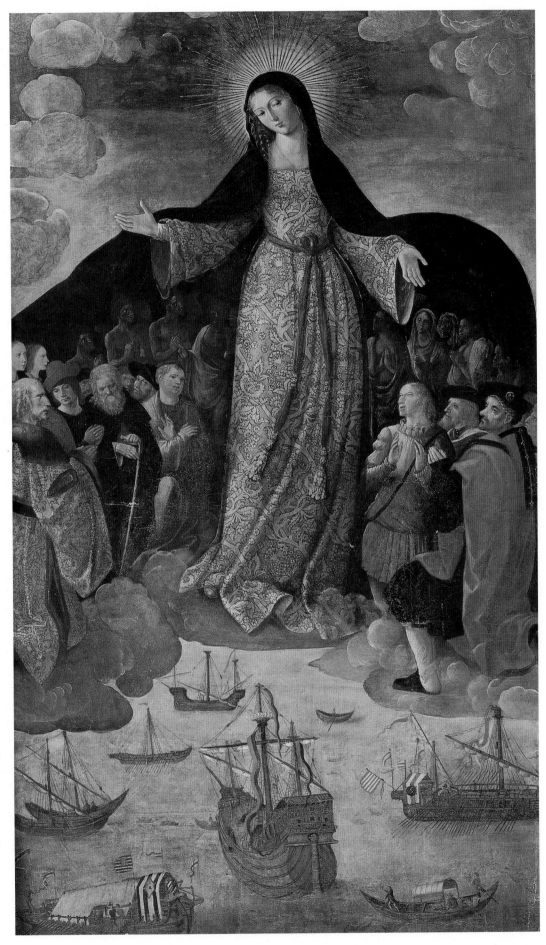

Alejo Fernandez, Our Lady of the Navigators: *This 1535 painting of the Virgin Mary as protectress of several known bold explorers (Columbus may be the figure at the left), and depicting some of the kinds of ships in which they would have sailed, was painted for the Casa de Contratación, or Trade House, in Seville, the center for New World shipping in Spain.*

Asia) which embraced merchant depots in the spice-rich Molucca islands, China, and Japan. Governor-general Afonso de Albuquerque (1453–1515) wrested the depot from Arab merchants and military forces who had long-established colonies there, committing terrible atrocities in the process. Portuguese merchants sent the precious commodities of the east directly back to Lisbon on an average of twelve ships per year. There they sold cheaply (the prices uninflated by the middle-men costs that Venice had had to pay), but at profits sufficient to make the tiny country rich. The kings of Portugal took 20 percent of the profit.

The Portuguese achievement was unprecedented. With a population of only 2 million, Portugal quickly acquired an empire vastly greater than itself. Its ships pierced the zone of Arab mercantile supremacy, crossed the Indian Ocean, and opened a European sea route to India, Indonesia, and China. The port at Lisbon now rivaled once-mighty Venice. After 1600, her mastery of the Mediterranean devalued by Portuguese competition, Venice was reduced to enjoying the small profits of Middle Eastern commerce. The future of merchant ventures lay on the open ocean.

Old World Ventures

In the early 1500s, the Dutch, English, and French followed the Portuguese into the commercial heart of the Old World, and had usurped their position by 1700. They did so by developing merchant empires, consisting of far-flung networks of garrisoned depots, often managed by **joint-stock** merchant companies which acted like nations in themselves.

Joint-stock companies were corporations more complex than the partnerships created by medieval Italian merchants. Now hundreds or thousands of individuals contributed funding for an ongoing commercial enterprise, and awaited, passively, a share of profits in return. The company itself had an identity independent of its participating partners, or shareholders. It sold its shares where merchants gathered—at the *bourse* (French for "purse"), or stock market, such as the one in Antwerp (Europe's first), founded in 1531, or the more important one in Amsterdam, completed in 1613. The company developed its own bureaucracy and hierarchy of officers and agents, and even its own security force, which looked much like a small army. A joint-stock company had the power not merely to buy and sell, but also to settle, manage, and defend a merchant **colony**.

The European agents of merchant companies pressed for trade privileges everywhere along the coasts of southern and eastern Asia. They succeeded especially well in establishing themselves in India, where most of the local rulers, possessing no naval capacity and at odds among themselves, were accustomed to commercial interaction with foreign merchants. Portuguese merchants maintained the base at

Goa until it was reclaimed by an independent India in 1961. By 1700, English and Dutch competitors had taken over Indian trade with Europe. Their various enterprises in India were organized by the English East India Company, established in 1600, and the Dutch East India Company, established in 1602 (see *How Many?*, p. 454).

India As the Portuguese, English, and Dutch planted their commercial colonies on the coasts of India, great changes occurred in the interior. Since the Gupta kings died out on the Indian subcontinent in the mid-sixth century C.E., India had split into a multitude of states and kingdoms, but it still sustained a lively commercial life. By 1192, Islamic invaders from the frontier Sind region had conquered much of northern India and established a sultanate at Delhi which gained sovereignty in the northern part of the subcontinent. Meanwhile, Arab Muslim traders established commercial depots along the coasts. The Delhi sultanate fell in 1398 to the Mongol-Turkic conqueror Tamerlane (c. 1336–1405), to be succeeded by small Muslim kingdoms. After 1526, Tamerlane's descendant Babur (1483–1530) swept in, defeated the different petty states of the north, and established the Mughal Empire. The Great Mughals, as the emperors were called, gained dominion over much of the region, creating a united empire, and presided over a blossoming of culture.

By the early 1700s, the Hindu kingdoms of the center and south reasserted themselves, however, and by mid-century, the Mughal Empire had weakened, leaving India in a disarray the British then exploited. By 1757, the English East India Company, with bases at Bombay, Madras, and Calcutta, and employing its own army and diplomats, had become the principal power in the subcontinent (see Chapter 23). Over the next century it would defeat one regional power after another until it came to rule all of India—about two-thirds directly, and one-third indirectly.

China In China, European merchants never controlled local rulers as they did in India. Prosperous China was uninterested in the goods and services proffered by Europeans. Under the Ming dynasty (which replaced the Mongol Yuan dynasty in 1368), the Chinese people were better fed, clothed, and educated, and perhaps better ruled than peoples anywhere else. Even a poor boy from one of the remote farming villages could aspire to pass the difficult examinations that permitted entrance to the ruling bureaucracy. Steeped in the ancient Confucian tradition, these mandarins advocated self-sufficiency and disdained commercial enterprises and projects of territorial expansion.

Such attitudes had not always prevailed in China. Between 1405 and 1433 (two generations before Columbus' voyages), the emperor's Muslim eunuch Zheng He had made a quite remarkable series of

Mapping the World

Grazioso Benincasa, Portolan chart of the east coast of Africa, 1468

Anonymous, Amerigo Vespucci, 1673

Perhaps the most important navigational device was the map. But advances in map creation had consequences beyond just practical considerations. Improved, realistic world maps based on data collected by acute explorers provided Europeans with an entirely new concept of the globe on which they lived. Shown here (above) is an example of a Portolan chart (showing the east coast of Africa), which guided navigators before the development of modern maps. The intersecting lines connect known locations, and the coastline is drawn freehand based on the careful observation of experienced sailors.

Amerigo Vespucci, Italian navigator, is shown (above right) complete with a compass, a map, and a globe.

Hondius' sophisticated map (below) shows the route followed during Sir Francis Drake's circumnavigation of the globe in 1580.

(top left: British Library, London)

Hondius, World map showing Drake's voyage (1580), seventeenth century

To continue your investigation of this topic, please go to www.prenhall.com/king for the related **WINDOWS** on the **WEB** activity

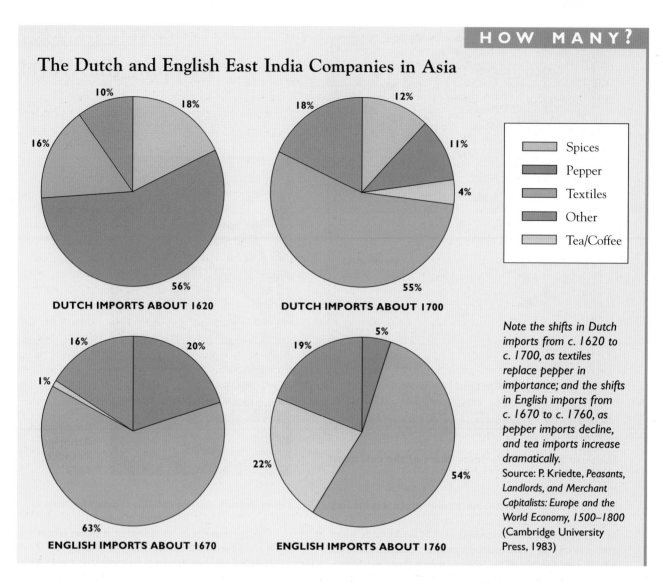

HOW MANY?

The Dutch and English East India Companies in Asia

DUTCH IMPORTS ABOUT 1620
- 18%
- 10%
- 16%
- 56%

DUTCH IMPORTS ABOUT 1700
- 12%
- 18%
- 11%
- 4%
- 55%

ENGLISH IMPORTS ABOUT 1670
- 20%
- 16%
- 1%
- 63%

ENGLISH IMPORTS ABOUT 1760
- 5%
- 19%
- 22%
- 54%

Legend:
- Spices
- Pepper
- Textiles
- Other
- Tea/Coffee

Note the shifts in Dutch imports from c. 1620 to c. 1700, as textiles replace pepper in importance; and the shifts in English imports from c. 1670 to c. 1760, as pepper imports decline, and tea imports increase dramatically.
Source: P. Kriedte, *Peasants, Landlords, and Merchant Capitalists: Europe and the World Economy, 1500–1800* (Cambridge University Press, 1983)

expeditions through the Indian Ocean to the east African coast. On the first occasion, Zheng had sailed with a fleet of sixty-two vessels, carrying 28,000 men. Advised by mandarin officials, Chinese rulers later halted these expeditions, and even banned the building of ships. Commerce had low priority for the ruling Chinese. But Europeans yearned to sell Chinese goods to the west—especially since the decline of the ancient caravan link between the Middle East and China, through which had flowed Chinese silks and luxury products. Chinese rulers stood firm, however. They might grant Europeans a trading base, such as that gained by the Portuguese at Macao in 1557, but they continued to insulate Chinese society from Europeans.

Japan   Japanese rulers felt much the same way. From the twelfth century, Japan had been dominated by a class of warrior landowners—the **samurai**, roughly similar to the knights of medieval Europe—who owed obedience to an overlord, or shogun. Shoguns and samurai overshadowed the emperor, isolated in his court but protected from challenges by his divine descent. This

Japanese elite opposed European influence. In 1636, the Japanese abandoned all seafaring activity and sealed themselves within their borders. In the 1630s, they expelled all Europeans except the Dutch, who were allowed to dock one ship each year and remain, segregated, on an island near Nagasaki. But the Dutch were to have no contact with Japanese, nor even learn that language; and the Japanese, similarly, were prohibited from learning Dutch, with the result that the two merchant communities were forced to converse in the language of the now-absent Portuguese. The Dutch merchant colony was the main link between Japan and the West until the nineteenth century.

The Dutch Initiative   The Malay Peninsula (part of modern Malaysia), the islands of the South Pacific (including modern Indonesia and the Philippines), and other Pacific islands, including New Zealand and the continent of Australia, all became known to European merchant fleets between 1500 and 1800. The prime commercial target was the Moluccas, or Spice Islands, producers of cloves and nutmeg. In this vast Pacific region, as in India, the Portuguese were the first venturers, establishing a base at Malacca (in modern Malaysia) by 1511. But farther east the Dutch outpaced the Portuguese to win the prize. They gained title to the Moluccas by 1613, and in 1619 established an administrative center at Batavia (now Jakarta, in modern Indonesia). Dutch merchants became the main exploiters of the spice trade, and they were the first Europeans to sight New Zealand and Australia. The Dutch explorer Willem Schouten discovered the southern tip of South America in 1616 and named it Cape Hoorn (or Horn) after his birth place. In 1652 the Dutch settled the African Cape of Good Hope, indicating their leadership in world trade by their presence at these two southernmost outcroppings.

In the seventeenth century, the immense Pacific looked like a Dutch sea. How could such a tiny nation command so far-flung and efficient an empire, if only a merchant empire? The answer lay in its familiarity with the sea—a constant threat to the low-lying Dutch terrain but also a stimulus to shipbuilding. By 1600, the Dutch had 10,000 ships, which sailed the Baltic and Northern seas, as well as the Atlantic and Pacific oceans. The *fluyt* or "flyboat," a Dutch innovation, was an efficient vessel designed for inexpensive, utilitarian hauling. The Dutch became the common carriers of Europe, transporting both utilitarian and luxury goods and linking ports all over the globe. Of these entrepreneurs, the English writer Daniel Defoe (1660–1731) wrote with some awe: "They buy to sell again, take in to send out, and the greatest part of their vast commerce consists in being supplied from all parts of the world that they may supply all the world again."

From the coasts of Africa, across the Indian Ocean and on into the Pacific, merchant vessels probed the ports of the Old World. The next frontier lay on the far side of the Atlantic.

BRAVE NEW WORLD

As the human species evolved and developed communities in the Old World, the New World of the Western Hemisphere remained uninhabited. It acquired its first human immigrants around the time of the last Ice Age (which ended about 10,000 years ago). These peoples developed their own varied cultures and civilization in isolation from Old World influences. After 1492, explorers, conquerors, and settlers came in turn to the Western Hemisphere, overwhelming the New World's tens of millions of Amerindian natives, importing more than 10 million African strangers, and planting the seeds of new cultures descended from those of Europe. The New World became part of Western civilization; but its Amerindian and African inhabitants, whose labor enriched merchant and professional elites on both sides of the Atlantic, remained, to varying degrees, alienated from it.

Exploration and Conquest

The first explorers to visit the Western Hemisphere entered a world inhabited by defenseless peoples, rich in resources, and ripe for exploitation. They learned the extent and nature of the land and claimed it for the European nations that had sent them. Conquest followed exploration, resulting in the destruction of two advanced New World civilizations.

During the last Ice Age (from about 30,000 to 10,000 years before the present), Asian hunters wandered over the land bridge that stretched some 50 miles (80 km.) from Siberia (modern Russia) to Alaska—a region Europeans later called "Beringia," after the straits named for the Danish explorer Vitus Bering (1681–1741), (see Chapter 8). Others may have come from Asia by sea. These Asian migrants were the true discoverers of the lands of the Western Hemisphere. Material remains of their culture testify to their residence at various sites of North and South America from between 20,000 and 10,000 years ago.

Over thousands of years, the Amerindians migrated across the land mass to its southernmost tip, developing into numerous tribes and nations, speaking hundreds of languages. Most had not progressed beyond a Neolithic condition before the arrival of Europeans. Some remained hunters and gatherers, while others, beginning about 7000 years ago, learned to farm. More than half of them lived in Mexico and the Andes regions, where they developed, respectively, the Aztec and Inca civilizations. Perhaps 4 to 6 million lived in what is now the continental United States, and as many more in the Caribbean. In all, perhaps as many as 75 million Amerindians inhabited the Western Hemisphere before Europeans "discovered" that world and proclaimed it "new."

As early as the late tenth century, Viking sailors were exploring the waters of the north Atlantic near the coast of modern Canada. In 982 Erik the Red founded a settlement on the island of Greenland (so named by him to make it more attractive to

MUST READS

Tracing the Spanish Conquest of the Americas

Bernal Diaz del Castillo *The Discovery and Conquest of Mexico* (c. 1527)

Bartolomé de las Casas *Brief Relation of the Destruction of the Indies* (1552)

Christopher Columbus *Diaries*

Hernán Cortés *Letters*

colonists). A few years later some Viking sailors are believed to have accidentally discovered the Atlantic coast of North America; they reported their discovery to their compatriots in Greenland. Erik's son Leif Eriksson repeated the journey in 1003, naming the site of his landing as that of Vinland (possibly in Newfoundland). Two subsequent expeditions failed to establish a lasting settlement, and the Viking adventure was forgotten except in Greenland sagas. Nearly 500 years later, as Vasco da Gama and Dias were skirting Africa, a European expedition again arrived on the fringes of the Western Hemisphere. This time the newcomers stayed, and were followed by many others.

Columbus and the Spanish In 1492 the Genoese sea captain Christopher Columbus (1451–1506), funded by the Spanish monarchs Ferdinand and Isabella, set out with three ships on a daring expedition on the open ocean. His goal was to sail to the rich markets of the Indies, claiming for Spain any islands or mainlands he discovered en route. Assuming that Japan and China lay only 3000 miles (4380 km.) to the west, Columbus planned to reach Asia by traversing the Atlantic. This "Admiral of the Ocean Sea" died in 1506 still thinking he had reached Asia, called the "Indies", (see Map 16.2).

In fact, Japan lay more than 13,000 miles (20,900 km.) to the west—over half the circumference of the globe. Just under 4000 miles (6440 km.) away were the continents of the Western Hemisphere. Columbus first landed on the island he named San Salvador in the Bahamas, then visited other Caribbean islands. On a second journey, he established a base on the island he named Hispaniola (now shared by Haiti and the Dominican Republic). In two subsequent voyages he reached what is now Venezuela (1498) and the shores of Central America (1502)—and realized that his expedition had encountered not just some islands, but at least one huge land mass.

Columbus wanted to find gold, as he wrote in his notebook soon after the discovery: "I do not wish to delay but to discover and go to many islands to find gold." In Hispaniola, he established a trading depot. This was the first of a circuit of fortified mercantile settlements which, within a generation, ringed the Caribbean Sea along the coasts of Mexico, Central America, northern South America, and Florida, and on various islands including Cuba.

Within weeks of his arrival in the New World, Columbus had formed an opinion of its aboriginal residents, whom he named *Indios*, or Indians, thinking he had reached the Indies, or Asia. He concluded that the native Amerindians "would make good and industrious servants" and were "fit to be ruled" (see *Witnesses*, p. 464, and illustration on p. 461). Columbus's men put the Taino natives to work hauling the goods to be sent back to Spain. Appointed viceroy of the island, Columbus sparked a native

revolt by his authoritarian rule. He was sent back to Spain in disgrace, but allowed to return again. In 1503, Queen Isabella granted his request for permission to enslave the Taino tribespeople. "Being as they are hardened in their bad habits of idolatry and cannibalism, I hereby give license and permission … to capture them … and to sell them and utilize their services. …" Thus used, the Tainos were extinct within a century.

Meanwhile, Portugal laid claim to Spain's new possessions, announcing that they were an extension of the Atlantic islands of the Azores. Spain appealed to the reigning pope, Alexander VI (r. 1492–1503), who was Spanish by birth. In 1493, Alexander issued a series of papal bulls confirming Spanish possession of the new lands, and drawing an imaginary boundary between Spanish and Portuguese zones: a north-south line about 300 miles west of the Portuguese Azores. By the 1494 Treaty of Tordesillas between Spain and Portugal, the north-south line was redrawn farther west. The effect of the Treaty was that Portugal retained title to what is now Brazil, and Spain to the remaining lands of North and South America claimed by her explorers.

Papal intervention into the realm of geopolitics had a sound foundation. According to medieval theology, all property came from God. Who better to determine its allocation than the pope—according to Roman Catholic thought, God's representative on earth? Later Protestant participants in the race for New World properties were naturally unpersuaded by this line of reasoning.

Spurred by Columbus's example, a stream of explorers now journeyed across the Atlantic. Most were Italians or Portuguese in the employ of other nations. Soon after Columbus's first voyage, the Italian explorer Amerigo Vespucci (1454–1512), scion of an important commercial family of Florence and portrayed in *Windows On* on p. 453, set out in the employ of Spain and (later) Portugal. Probing the coast of South America, he found and explored some of the vast expanse of the Amazon River. He was the first to conclude that the new lands were not part of Asia but part of a previously unknown continent. He called it the "New World." The New World, ironically, was later named after him. In 1507, the German cartographer Martin Waldseemüller published an updated world map in which the New World lands were designated, in honor of the pioneering Florentine, "America."

Over the next fifty years, Spanish explorers crossed Panama to the Pacific Ocean (Vasco Nuñez de Balboa, 1475–1517), and claimed the lands of Florida (Juan Ponce de León, c. 1460–1521), Mississippi and Texas (Hernando de Soto, c. 1496–1542), Arizona and New Mexico (Francisco Vásquez de Coronado, c. 1510–1554), and California (Juan Rodríguez Cabrillo, d. 1543). Their expeditions in search of gold and of a miraculous "fountain of youth" were largely

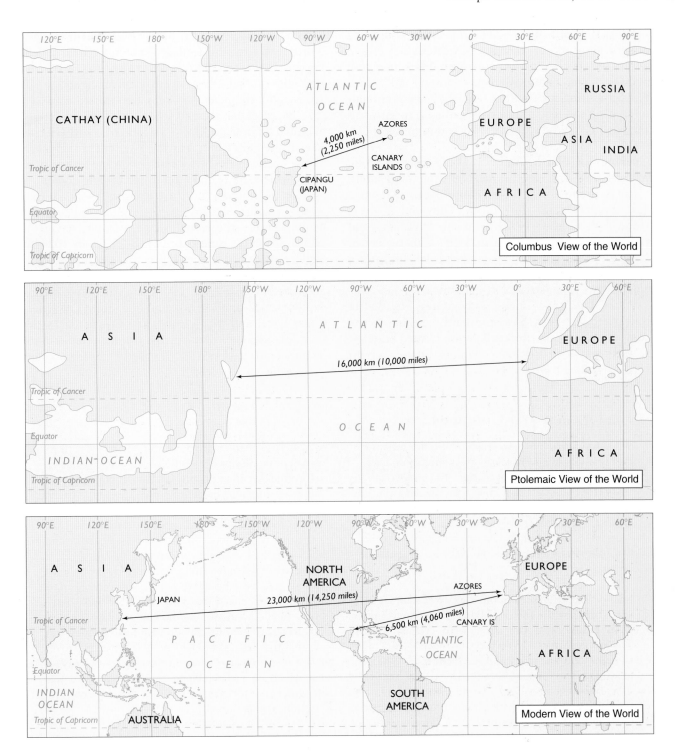

Map 16.2 Columbus' World: *Columbus fully intended to reach Japan after a westward journey across some 3000 miles of the Atlantic—"correcting" the prevailing Ptolemaic (ancient Greek) model that placed Asia at a distance nearly three times that. Both theories were wrong, as the unknown continents of North and South America and the unknown Pacific Ocean lay between the coast of Spain and the coast of Asia. (Scientific Americans, November 1992, p. 103)*

fruitless, but they acquired for their Spanish overlords the lands of western North America stretching as far north as Utah.

The venture of the Portuguese navigator Ferdinand Magellan (c. 1480–1521) was of another sort. In Spain's employ, Magellan set out in 1519 to reach Asia. He sailed from Atlantic to Pacific through

the strait near the tip of South America later named after him, the Strait of Magellan, and then across the Pacific, with a starving crew for sixty-eight days, described in *Witnesses* on p. 458, before reaching land (on the island of Guam). Touching on some islands which were later named the Philippines (after the future King Philip II of Spain), Magellan died in a battle with hostile natives. The expedition continued under the second in command. Of the five ships and 270 men who began the journey in 1519, one ship and a mere eighteen men returned in 1522. Accomplishing for the first time the feat of circumnavigating the globe, they had learned how vast was the Pacific, and how distant Asia was from Europe.

Opening up North America   The other Atlantic nations now entered the race for American lands, focusing their efforts on the coast of North America. The English sent the Italian Giovanni Caboto (John Cabot, 1450–1499) with one small ship and eighteen sailors to explore in 1497. Cabot reached Newfoundland (in modern Canada), establishing a foothold on the basis of which England would later claim rights to much of North America.

Years later, the English adventurer Sir Walter Raleigh (c. 1552–1618) journeyed three times to the coast of what is now the southeastern United States—a land he named Virginia, in honor of the "Virgin Queen," Elizabeth I. On Roanoke Island (in modern North Carolina) he formed a colony, which failed. Francis Drake (c. 1540–1596), famed for his persistent raids on Spanish Atlantic commerce, repeated in 1577–1580 the feat of circumnavigation achieved first by Magellan's crew. Henry Hudson (d. 1611) explored for England Canada's immense northern bay, later named after him. For the Netherlands, Hudson explored the New York river also named after him, along which the Dutch established trading depots.

Hoping to find a "northwest passage"—an alternative northern route through the American land mass to the Pacific—the French sent the Italian navigator Giovanni da Verrazano (c. 1485–1528) in 1524 to explore the North American coast. Venturing south from Newfoundland, he entered what is now New York harbor. For over 200 years, French captains explored the Canadian coast and the Saint Lawrence, Great Lake, and Mississippi waterways as far as the Gulf of Mexico. Among the most notable were Jacques Cartier (1491–1557), Samuel de Champlain

Exploration and Conquest

The expansion of European ventures into other regions of the world was accomplished with great brutality at times, yet also, at times, with great courage. The first passage reports the Portuguese plundering of an African town. The second presents the first, disappointing attempts by Vasco da Gama to open trade at Calicut, in India. The third describes the enormous hardships suffered during a portion of the journey by a participant in Magellan's expedition to circumnavigate the globe.

João de Barros describes the sack of Mombasa, eastern Africa, by the forces of Portuguese grand-captain Dom Francisco d'Almeida (15–16 August 1505): The Portuguese attack and burn the town; the fire raged all night long, and many houses collapsed. ... [The next morning.] The Grand-Captain ordered that the town should be sacked. ... Then everyone started to plunder the town and to search the houses, forcing open the doors with axes and iron bars. ... A large quantity of rich silk and gold embroidered clothes was seized. ... [The next day] they also carried away provisions, rice, honey, butter, maize, countless camels and a large number of cattle, and even two elephants. ... There were many prisoners, and white women among them and children, and also some merchants. ...
(From G. S. P. Freeman-Grenville, *The East African Coast*, 1962)

Vasco da Gama arrives in Calicut, India (20–29 May 1498), according to an eyewitness: The king was in a small court, reclining upon a couch covered with a cloth of green velvet ... and upon this again a sheet of cotton stuff, very white and fine, more so than any linen. ... On the right side of the king stood a basin of gold, so large that a man might just encircle it with his arms. ... The canopy above the couch was all gilt. ...

On Tuesday the captain [da Gama] got ready the following things to be sent to the king, viz., twelve pieces of *lambel* [a striped cloth], four scarlet hoods, six hats, four strings of coral ... a case of sugar, two casks of oil, and two of honey. ... [The king's officials came] and when they saw the present they laughed at it, saying that it was not a thing to offer to a king, that the poorest merchant from Mecca, or any other part of India, gave more, and that if he wanted to make a present it should be in gold, as the king would not accept such things. When the captain heard this he grew sad, and said that he had brought no gold, that, moreover, he was no merchant, but an ambassador; that he gave of that which he had. ... Upon this they declared that they would not forward his presents, nor consent to his forwarding them himself.
(*A Journal of the First Voyage of Vasco da Gama, 1497–1499;* trs., ed. E. J. Ravenstein, 1848)

Eyewitness Antonio Pigafetta describes Magellan's Pacific crossing (1521): We were three months and twenty days without getting any kind of fresh food. We ate biscuit, which was no longer biscuit, but powder of biscuits swarming with worms, for they had eaten the good. It stank strongly of the urine of rats. We drank yellow water that had been putrid for many days. Rats were sold for one-half ducado apiece, and even then we could not get them. ... Had not God and His blessed mother given us so good weather we would all have died of hunger in that exceeding vast sea. ...
(From L. Wright, *Gold, Glory, and the Gospel*, 1970)

Map 16.3 European Exploration, 1450–1600: *By 1600, Spanish and Portuguese explorers and traders established settlements in South America and the Caribbean, and commercial depots on the coasts of Africa, India, the Pacific islands, China, and Japan—at a time when English, Dutch, and French explorations of North America had just begun.*

(1567–1635), Louis Jolliet (1645–1700), along with the priest Jacques Marquette (1637–1675), and Robert de la Salle (1643–1687).

The Aztecs   Even before the English, French, and Dutch embarked on North American ventures, Spain had completed its conquest of much of the Americas. Most Amerindian communities succumbed quickly to European force. The Aztec and Inca empires, centered respectively in modern Mexico and Peru, promised serious resistance. In 1521 and 1533, two *conquistadores*, conquerors from a nation with a long history of conquest, destroyed these civilizations within a brief time and with only a handful of men.

Spain had only just completed the reconquest of the Iberian peninsula from the Moors when it set out to conquer the lands of the New World. Behind it was a centuries-old military tradition, fueled by a religious zeal tinged deeply with intolerance. Ahead was a project that also invited the use of arms and the missionary muscle of the Roman Catholic Church. The goal of the medieval *Reconquista* was the recovery of Iberian land from foreign domination. That of the American conquest was gold. The extraction of gold from the earth—and later silver, in much greater abundance—was the major economic activity of the Spanish in the New World.

The Amerindian people who constructed the civilization that Europeans called "Aztec" (they called themselves the Mexicas) had moved into central Mexico in the middle of the thirteenth century, establishing a harsh dominion over existing tribal groups. There they claimed inheritance of the culture of the Olmecs and Maya, creators of successive Mesoamerican civilizations (see Chapter 8). On an

460

New World Encounters

Columbus' first voyage: *This woodcut by Giuliano Dati, 1493, depicts the imminent arrival of Columbus' ship in the Bahamas, with idealized representations of natives on the shore.*

island in the middle of Lake Texcoco, the Aztecs built their capital of Tenochtitlán (incorporated in modern Mexico City), the preeminent metropolis of pre-Conquest culture.

Tenochititlán bristled with temples, sculptures, and shrines, with palaces and schools, workshops and markets, interspersed with floating gardens and equipped with roads and movable bridges to the mainland. It had a population of about 100,000; few cities in contemporary Europe were larger or more splendid. A Spanish chronicler described the reaction of the soldiers—some of whom had seen Constantinople and the cities of Italy—who reported that "so large a market place and so full of people, and so well regulated and arranged, they had never beheld before."

The Aztecs worshiped many gods, especially a sun god having male and female attributes, the dual deity represented by an eagle on a cactus. Guided by Mayan traditions recorded in sacred picture books (for they had no written language), Aztec priests supervised religious life according to calendar cycles of worship, sacrifice, and feasting. Rite and sacrifice shaped the civilization—including human sacrifice, a celebration of the spilling of blood, in which the victim's still-beating heart was ripped from their chest and offered up to the divinity, as illustrated on this page. The need to secure sacrificial victims to appease the sun god stimulated wars of conquest. From childhood, young warriors were trained to capture rather than slay enemies, so that prisoners might be brought back for ceremonial deaths—"the flowered death by the obsidian knife"—on temple stones.

This was the civilization that fell to the conquistador Hernán Cortés (1485–1547). Arriving in 1519

with about 600 men and 11 vessels, in defiance of an order of recall from the Spanish governor of Cuba, Cortés and his troops made their way to Tenochtitlán. Having been received cordially, they proceeded to take prisoner the Aztec emperor, the oddly compliant Montezuma II (the familiar form of the name; more properly Moctezuma, r. 1502–1520). Cortés had burned his own ships, thereby closing off any escape for his men. He sallied from Tenochtitlán to meet a force of his own compatriots who had come to put an end to his mission. Defeating the leaders, he persuaded the men to return with him and pursue the conquest of Mexico.

In Cortés's absence, warfare broke out in Tenochtitlán, triggered by a Spanish massacre of a group of natives during a religious festival. Cortés returned; Montezuma died (possibly as a result of stoning by his angered people, possibly at the hands of the Spanish); and Cortés withdrew again during a "Sad Night" in which half his men were killed. Regrouping, the Spanish forces returned in 1521 to besiege the city, having constructed a fleet

Human sacrifice: *The Aztec practice of human sacrifice by excising the heart of a living victim, pictured in this sixteenth-century* Florentine Codex, *was condemned as barbaric by the conquerors. (Biblioteca Medicea Laurenziana, Ms. Laur. Med. Palat. 218, c. 175v, Florence)*

of twelve small oar- and sail-powered boats to do so. A few months later, after firing cannon from the decks of their ships, they seized and razed Tenochtitlán. A few Spanish soldiers armed with arquebuses and cannon achieved this military conquest (assisted by epidemic, caused by microbes for which the Aztecs had no immunity) over thousands of Mexicans armed merely with arrows and swords carved from obsidian, a volcanic glass. (An account of the Spanish forces is given in *Witnesses* on p. 464.) A cultural conquest followed. In an attempt to extinguish Aztec religion, the conquerors burned the sacred books and erected Christian churches, often on the sites of native temples.

The Incas   The other great indigenous civilization was the Inca Empire at Cuzco (in modern Peru), in the Andes Mountains. The Inca domain, extending 2000 miles (3200 km.) along the Pacific coast of South America, included parts of modern Bolivia, Chile, Argentina, and Ecuador, as well as Peru. The empire had reached its greatest extent just prior to the arrival in 1531 of the Spaniard Francisco Pizarro (1475–1541), whose forces conquered and destroyed it.

The Inca emperor was an absolute monarch, whose legitimacy was marked by ceremonies of veneration for the mummies of his deceased ancestors. The emperor commanded the obedience of his subjects and was considered responsible for their welfare. The state owned virtually all property, which was sustained by the labor of the inhabitants. The agricultural wealth thus generated, and stored in an elaborate warehousing system, supported an elite of priests, government workers, and merchants, as well as the elderly, the ill, and widows. The priests managed the feasts, ceremonies, and sacrifices (including human ones) necessary to gain the favor of a roster of deities, among whom the sun god held sway.

The Incas used advanced engineering to terrace, drain, and irrigate the mountainous terrain and maximize productivity on plots as high as 9000 feet (2745 m.) above sea level. They were also expert builders, working from models rather than plans (as they had no system of writing) to create large cities. A network of roads and bridges extended more than 12,000 miles (19,000 km.), negotiating chasms, rivers, and solid rock. Metals buried in the earth, especially silver and gold, were reserved for the use of the emperor—until the arrival of Pizarro and his followers.

Pizarro arrived in Peru in 1531 with a mere 168 men, 67 horses, and 3 cannon, to assail an empire with a population of several millions and a military force of some 100,000. He captured, deceived, tortured, and executed the uncomprehending ruler Atahuallpa. Moving briskly to the capital at Cuzco, he began a conquest in which European guns and European steel swords overcame the force of wooden spears and clubs of the Incas. Pizarro's men accomplished the victory by unparalleled brutality, of which one participant has left this testimony: "I can bear witness that this is the most dreadful and cruel war in the world," in which both sides "give each other the cruelest deaths they can imagine." By 1539, the Spanish victors had quelled native resistance and established their colonial regime, subordinating almost as slaves a people who had administered one of the world's great empires. The Spanish soon opened the mines of Potosí (in modern Bolivia), an immense reservoir of silver, rich enough to supply the numerous Spanish **bullion** fleets for decades to come.

Patterns of Settlement

After the first phase of New World exploration and conquest, settlers built European communities in what seemed like an endlessly fertile expanse. The pattern of settlement varied from region to region. Two main colonial zones emerged: the southern zone, or "Latin" America (including those regions of South America, the Caribbean, and Mexico where Spanish, Portuguese, or French—all derived from Latin—are spoken); and the northern zone, including much of North America, predominantly English- and French-speaking. The southern zone was settled earlier, and its main characteristics established by 1600. The northern zone was settled in the period after 1600. The administrative blocs in both areas were called colonies, each related to its own European "mother" country, or metropolis.

Silver mines: *Once conquered, Amerindians were pressed into service as laborers. At the "Silver Mountain" mines in Potosí (modern Bolivia), as in this engraving, c. 1584, 40,000 poorly paid laborers were employed to mine the silver which was then shipped back to Spain and made into coinage. (Hispanic Society, New York)*

Latin America   By the mid-1500s, Spanish settlers had organized the main population centers of Peru and Mexico. Spanish administrators and landowners, drawn primarily from the lesser nobility of the metropolis, recreated so far as they could the culture of their homeland. Their native Spanish language soon developed into a **creole**—a colloquial language containing elements of local Amerindian and African dialects. Their cities, modeled on European cities, boasted cathedrals, palaces, theaters, printing houses, and universities (five by 1636, when the first university of Anglo-America, Harvard, was founded). The new American culture was a mixture of imported Spanish and native Amerindian customs.

The Amerindian inhabitants worked for the proprietors of the *encomiendas* (royal land grants to the conquistadors), or as domestic and agricultural laborers on *haciendas*, the large ranches or plantations owned by the Spanish-speaking elite. The natives who lived on the land granted in *encomienda* owed labor services to the proprietor—who in turn owed the laborers protection, security, religious training, and even education. Haciendas drew on the labor services both of permanent residents—often **peons**, or debt slaves—and of seasonal workers from nearby Indian villages. These arrangements seemed to promise advantage to both laborer and contractor or landowner. In practice, the laborers were abused while the proprietors got richer.

The kingdom of Castile directly ruled the Spanish colonies and closely supervised their governance. Two governors—called viceroys ("vice-kings"), respectively, of "New Spain" (modern Mexico) and Peru—administered the whole of Spanish territory (the number of viceroys increased after 1700). Each viceroy presided over a regional advisory council established in the principal cities, and sent out inspectors to report on local administrations. The position of viceroy conferred high status and attracted ambitious noblemen from Spain. There, a Council of the Indies, based in Madrid, scrutinized the records of each viceroy's service upon completion, and intervened to direct the course of colonial events.

In contrast, Portuguese settlement in the New World followed the pattern of Portuguese expansion in Africa and Asia. Garrisoned merchant colonies were planted at key locations on the coast of Brazil, as fueling stations for fleets bound for the Caribbean. Later, Portuguese governors and landowners took over the settled areas of the interior, intending to control the native population more than to establish European communities.

By the late 1500s, settlers had brought to Brazil the **plantation system** (with lands worked by slave labor under supervision) for sugar cultivation developed in the Portuguese Atlantic islands, especially the island of São Tomé, just off the African coast. English, French, and Spanish landowners later adopted this system in the Caribbean (where tobacco, generally farmed on a smaller scale and yielding lower profits, had previously been the main cash crop). The Dutch, although possessing small colonial bases in the West Indies and on the north Brazilian coast, were more interested in trade than in settlement. Their Dutch West India Company, established in 1621, organized a profitable trade in Brazil and the Caribbean. From the West Indies ports of Havana (Cuba) and San Juan (Puerto Rico), the Spanish bullion fleets took off twice each year, an irresistible lure for Dutch, English, and French raiders.

North American Colonies   After 1600, a northern zone of European settlement in the Americas established itself from Savannah (in modern Georgia) to Quebec (in modern Canada). Most of the settlers were English-speakers; some were French, German, or Dutch; there were even a few hundred Swedes. English settlement was at first organized by joint-stock companies. These obtained from the crown a charter enabling the creation of single agricultural communities, centered in Virginia and New England. Jamestown (in modern Virginia), settled by English emigrants, was founded on this pattern in 1607. The Virginia colony thrived, based as it was on the cultivation of tobacco as a cash crop.

In 1620, Plymouth (in modern Massachusetts) was the second English-speaking community to be established. The aim of the Plymouth **Separatists** (Puritans who had separated from the Church of England—later dubbed "Pilgrims") was not simply to gain farmland but also to secure the right to practice their own form of Protestant worship. Other Puritans settled the Massachusetts Bay Colony (1630), while other New England and mid-Atlantic settlements were also motivated by the quest for religious freedom.

By 1700, twelve colonies had been established (the thirteenth, Georgia, was founded in 1732), and about one-half million English-speakers dwelled in North America, equivalent to one-eighth to one-tenth of the population of England itself. Without initially planning to do so, the English had created a sizable empire abroad. Ruled theoretically by King and Parliament (although they had no representatives in Parliament), the colonies developed effective regional, representative governments.

The Dutch and French settlements more closely resembled the Portuguese pattern of coastal enclaves, and contained fewer colonists. These nationals established merchant colonies respectively in New Netherland (modern New York State) and New France (modern Canada, especially the province of Quebec). The Dutch merchants dealt in a variety of commodities, but the French (who competed with the Portuguese for fish in these northern waters) were particularly interested in the valuable furs that their hunters and traders obtained from the forested interior. French settlement was sparse. By the mid-1600s, there were only about 3000 Europeans in all of New France, many fewer than in the single English colony of Virginia. The French crown ruled its colony directly, sending military governors and financial supervisors responsible to officials in Paris.

In 1664 the Dutch lost their North American mainland possessions to their English challengers on the seas. The French would intermittently fight the British for theirs until an eventual British victory in 1763. By the time that the American War of Independence broke out in 1775 (see Chapter 19), the Atlantic region of North America was largely English both by language and tradition. Although the Spanish and the Portuguese had opened up the New World, the British eventually dominated in North America.

Religion played a major role in shaping the post-conquest civilizations of the New World. A main objective of many of the settlements, especially of the Spanish, was the conversion of Amerindian natives. In the English colonies of North America, as has been seen, a main motive for colonization was religious freedom—or freedom, in effect, from other Europeans. That impulse for liberation would express itself again, years later, when an ideology of political liberty took root in the same region. Meanwhile, the freedom sought by some colonists was steadily denied by all of them to the two "other" peoples with whom they interacted in the New World—the native Amerindians and the newcomer Africans.

Encountering Others

The "discovery" of the New World was more than the discovery by Europeans of lands previously unknown to them. It was a mutual discovery of different peoples, as European strangers, Amerindian natives, and, in time, African captives interacted. For the Amerindians, the encounter was deadly.

The Amerindians When Columbus and his sailors first landed on San Salvador, native Amerindian Tainos greeted them with an assortment of gifts. Impressed by the Europeans' unusual appearance, the Tainos concluded that they were gods. The European newcomers were equally startled by the appearance and customs of a people they had never seen before: largely naked, with painted bodies and long hair, smoking tobacco. The Tainos lived in stable communities, in well-constructed houses equipped with hammocks—an object the Europeans had never seen. Their enemies on nearby islands, the Caribs (after whom we name the Caribbean Sea), had a reputation for ferocity—specifically for cannibalism (although this is possibly undeserved). With such terrifying and amazing stories Columbus and later visitors impressed readers back in Europe.

The millions of natives inhabiting the Western Hemisphere before the European advent consisted of hundreds of nations and tribes and peoples too diverse to be considered as a single Amerindian culture. However, they did have some things in common. Their hundreds of languages ultimately descended from a common pool of Asian languages. None of these was a written language. Only the Mayan peoples acquired the ability to record spoken language in symbols. Although this skill vanished with their decline, the Maya transmitted to successor Mesoamerican peoples—who composed sacred texts using pictographs—a memory of writing and a respect for books.

Based on collectives of family, tribe, and clan, Amerindian societies could be highly stratified, with extended lineages generally traced in the male line. Some formed federations, while others developed representative assemblies. Respected priests, or shamans, were in charge of religious rites, medicine, and magic, all of which might overlap considerably. Some groups practiced human sacrifice, often of war captives. In many, women performed agricultural work.

Amerindians wielded as weapons spears, bows, and clubs of wood, stone, and, more rarely, copper or bronze; they had no iron and no sharp-edged swords, a key factor in their military defeat. They had no horses and no pack animals for hauling heavy loads long distances (the Andean llama could bear only a light burden) or for pulling plows—and perhaps for that reason never developed the wheeled vehicles

New World Peoples and Customs

Exploration? Expansion? Conquest? Encounter? How should the European quest for land, wealth, knowledge, and power around the globe be titled? "Encounter" is certainly a term that could be used to describe one facet of that process, as Europeans encountered peoples previously unknown to them, and as remote peoples looked at Europeans for the first time. In these passages, Christopher Columbus observes the natives of the island he called Hispaniola; the king of the Mexican Aztecs, Montezuma, hears his agents' report of the Europeans arrived in his land; and the French Huguenot explorer Jean de Léry describes the customs of the Tupinamba natives of Brazil.

From Columbus' Diary: The arrival in the New World (1492): In order that they would be friendly to us ... to some of them I gave red caps, and glass beads which they put on their chests, and many other things of small value, in which they took so much pleasure and became so much our friends that it was a marvel. ...

But it seemed to me that they were a people very poor in everything. All of them go around as naked as their mothers bore them. ... They are very well formed, with handsome bodies and good faces. Their hair [is] coarse—almost like the tail of a horse—and short. ... And some of them paint their faces, and some of them the whole body, and some of them only the eyes, and some of them only the nose. ... They should be good and intelligent servants ... and I believe that they would become Christians easily, for it seemed to me that they had no religion.

(Christopher Columbus, *The Diario of Christopher Columbus' First Voyage to America, 1492–1493*; ed. trs. O. Dunn, J. E. Kelley Jr., 1969)

Aztec King Motecuhzoma (Montezuma) hears his messengers' report of Cortés' men (who they think are gods), according to an Aztec account (1521): Motecuhzoma was also terrified to learn how the cannon roared, how its noise resounded, how it caused one to faint and grow deaf. The messengers told him: "A thing like a ball of stone comes out of its entrails; it comes out shooting sparks and raining fire. The smoke that comes out with it has a pestilent odor, like that of rotten mud. ... If the cannon is aimed against a mountain, the mountain splits and cracks

open. If it is aimed against a tree, it shatters the tree into splinters. ..."

The messengers also said: "Their trappings and arms are all made of iron. They dress in iron and wear iron casques [helmets] on their heads. Their swords are iron; their bows are iron; their shields are iron; their spears are iron. Their deer [horses] carry them on their backs wherever they wish to go. These deer, our lord, are as tall as the roof of a house. ... Their skin is white, as if it were made of lime. They have yellow hair, though some of them have black. ... Their dogs are enormous, with flat ears and long, dangling tongues. The color of their eyes is a burning yellow; their eyes flash fire and shoot off sparks. ... They bound here and there, panting, with their tongues hanging out. And they are spotted like an ocelot."

When Motecuhzoma heard this report, he was filled with terror. It was as if his heart had fainted, as if it had shriveled. It was as if he were conquered by despair.

(From M. L. Portilla, *The Broken Spears*, 1992)

Huguenot explorer Jean de Léry describes how the Tupinambá treat their war captives (1556): Now when the captive has hurled everything he could pick up near him on the ground—stones, even clods of earth—he who is to strike the blow ... approaches the prisoner with, for instance, "Are you not of the nation called Margaia, which is our enemy? And have you not yourself killed and eaten of our kinsmen and our friends?" The prisoner, more fearless than before, replies in his language ... "Yes, I am very strong, and have slain and eaten a great many." "... And for that reason," says he who is standing there ready to slaughter him, "since you are now in our power, you will presently be killed by men, and then roasted on the *boucan* and eaten by all the rest of us." "Very well," replies the prisoner ..., "my kinsmen will avenge me in turn." ... [He] who is there ready to perform this slaughter lifts his wooden club with both hands and brings down the rounded end of it with such force on the head of the poor prisoner that ... I have seen some who fell stonedead on the first blow. ...

(Jean de Léry, *History of a Voyage to the Land of Brazil, Otherwise called America*, 1556; trs., ed. J. Whatley, 1990)

such beasts might haul. They ate corn rather than wheat as a cereal staple. Where the climate permitted, they wore little or no clothing. They wore adornments crafted from stone and metal, shells, teeth, and feathers, and often painted their faces or bodies. Their skin was tawny.

The Amerindians worshiped many gods, among whom were gods of sun and sky like those the ancestors of the European newcomers had once worshiped. Their forests were alive with indwelling spirits—of

the trees, of the eagles, of the jaguars. The land, like the air, was free for the use of all, and sacred in its generative power. To these communities, the European languages and their artifacts—treaties, contracts, documents, treatises of theology—must have seemed inexpressibly strange. The tools and weapons and clothing and armor and horses of the newcomers were awesome. Their guns were "iron which has a spirit." Their white skin seemed to be luminous. At Roanoke Island (modern North Carolina) in 1584, an eyewitness reported, the natives "wondered marvelously … at the whiteness of our skins, ever coveting to touch our breasts, and to view the same." The religious rites, institutions, and personnel—the robed priests and friars with their crucifixes and sacred vessels—must have seemed odd and overwhelming.

The customs of Amerindian communities both shocked and surprised the European newcomers. They were impressed by the nakedness of the natives, and the brilliant hues of their adornments; their unfamiliar sexual customs, their generally meager technology and (in the European sense) their illiteracy; the ferocity and (from the European viewpoint) barbarous customs of a few—the cannibalism of the Caribs and the human sacrifices of the Aztecs and Incas. These permitted the invaders to label the inhabitants of the new land "primitive"; and because primitive, inherently suited to serve the new arrivals. Even if they

Huejotzingo Codex, 1531: *Constituting part of the testimony in a lawsuit brought by the Huejotzingo people in central Mexico to the Audiencia (high court) of New Spain, this detail shows a Christian image of the Virgin and child Jesus. Surrounding it are the objects representing the items brought in tribute by Amerindian workers to their masters. (Library of Congress)*

were not to serve, they were at least expected not to impede Europeans as they settled new lands that they considered to be empty wilderness.

Nevertheless, each group learned from the other. Europeans learned to eat corn and potatoes, to smoke or sniff tobacco, to equip their ships with hammocks (an improvement over the deck in terms of comfort and hygiene), and to employ some Amerindian methods of coping with the climate and cultivating crops. Amerindians learned to use horses and guns—to such an extent that some of them fundamentally changed their way of life. They craved European goods. One native hunter who delivered cherished beaver pelts to European fur traders observed contentedly that "the beaver does everything perfectly well"; and indeed, the beaver had netted him a fortune in "kettles, hatchets, swords, knives, bread."

Some Amerindians, often those who were kidnapped by settlers, learned to speak Spanish, Portuguese, English, or French, and served as translators and interpreters. The need to teach the natives the language of the conquerors encouraged the creation of language-teaching tools. The author of the first Castilian (Spanish) grammar, published in 1492, observed correctly that "language has always been the companion of empire."

So also was religion. Dominican, Franciscan, Augustinian, and, after 1540, Jesuit missionaries accompanied the Spanish expeditions. The Jesuits were especially active in Brazil. (Suspected of pursuing an agenda hostile to the monarchy, the Jesuits were expelled from several European nations in this period, and from the Portuguese colonies in 1759, the Spanish in 1767.) Missions constituted some of the first permanent European settlements in the Spanish American periphery, beyond the main regions of settlement in Mexico and the Andes. Missions were establishments modeled on European monastery communities; they offered medical assistance and skills training to Amerindian communities while urging conversion to Christianity. On a smaller scale, Protestant missionaries also attempted the conversion of native populations. Christian beliefs, institutions, and rituals were deeply alien to Amerindian belief systems. Conversions remained largely unsuccessful in the case of the Protestants, or incomplete in the case of the Roman Catholics, where native attitudes heavily colored alien doctrines. Each Amerindian group thought of itself as "the people," or "the true people," and were not disposed to adopt the spiritual habits of alien folk they considered inferior to themselves.

Over the same centuries, as Christian clergy attempted the conversion of the Amerindians, European farmers and landowners claimed their land. The original inhabitants were sometimes, initially, tolerated. More often, they were pushed away to more remote regions of the interior, or pressed into labor service. In the latter case, they worked as virtual serfs—dependent on a European owner and paid meager wages to work the land that had once been theirs. Others were labored under hideous conditions in the gold and silver mines that fed the Spanish Empire for nearly a century, as shown on p. 461.

Amerindian workers proved an unsatisfactory labor force—resistant to regimentation, prone to disease. The debased condition of the enslaved Amerindians prompted attempts at reform. The "Laws of Burgos" of 1512–1513 limited to 150 the number of forced laborers one person could maintain in Spanish America, but tacitly sanctioned the *encomienda* system. The "New Laws" of 1542 prohibited Amerindian slavery, even of war captives, and banned the *encomiendas*. The laws were not enforced.

During these years, the problem of Amerindian servitude aroused the attention of one of the West's most original and profound moralists: the priest Bartolomé de las Casas (1474–1566). As an owner of enslaved natives, de las Casas observed the harsh treatment of the Amerindians. In 1512 or 1513, he became a priest. In 1514, he gave up his slaves and committed himself to exposing the atrocities against American natives. His opposition was based on the view that natural laws and rights were common to all peoples, Christian and non-Christian. Moreover, the Amerindians were inherently a gentle, teachable, amenable people. He felt that if priests, and not armed conquerors, were sent to the New World, the Amerindians could be guided peacefully to live as Christians in a society based on European standards. Thus de las Casas did not propose to abandon plans to settle the New World and subordinate the Amerindians—but only to accomplish those projects without brutalizing them.

De las Casas described Spanish atrocities and his proposals for ideal Amerindian communities in works written over a long lifetime: in direct appeals to the Spanish monarchs, in a history of the new territories, in memoranda to the council that administered New World affairs, in a scathing *Brief Relation of the Destruction of the Indies* (see *Witnesses*, p. 470, and the illustration on p. 463). After the composition of this work, but before its publication in 1552, he held a public debate with the theologian Juan Ginés de Sepúlveda. Sepúlveda argued that slavery was natural, that the Amerindians were inherently suited to be slaves, and that the evils that accompanied the conquest were outweighed by the greater good achieved for civilization. In response, de las Casas swayed his audience by reporting vividly the tortures of innocent natives that he had witnessed.

In the end, he convinced King Philip II of Spain. In 1573, Philip approved new regulations decreeing that the occupation of the New World was not to be considered a "conquest," and that the natives were to be treated with love. "The Indians," read the ordinance, "[are] to be pacified and indoctrinated, but in no way are they to be harmed, for all we seek is their welfare and conversion." Such decrees ruled out the actual enslavement of the Amerindian population, but could not reverse (nor was that the intention) the destruction of its pre-conquest way of life.

The brutal conquest, the hideous conditions of labor, the disruption of Amerindian communities, the dispossession of the natives from their lands were terrible events. But these are responsible for only a small fraction of the Amerindian death toll that resulted from the European arrival in the New World. The rest were victims of "microbe shock."

Before the arrival of Columbus, the approximately 75 million Amerindian inhabitants of the Western Hemisphere constituted nearly one-fifth of the world population. A little more than 50 years later, only about 10 million remained. In Mexico, a pre-conquest native population of as many as 25 million inhabitants

had, by 1600, sunk to about 1 million. The number of Caribs sank almost to zero. Most of the natives of the Western Hemisphere vanished in the first century after the arrival of the Europeans. They died from disease: smallpox, diphtheria, influenza, measles, mumps, and other illnesses. The inhabitants of the Old World had been exposed to the microbes causing these diseases, and had developed some immunity against them. New World populations, isolated from Eurasia for many millennia, had none. (Perhaps the New World retaliated; some scholars believe that syphilis, which infected Europe about the time of Columbus, originated in the Americas.) More than guns, more than abuse and dislocation, the common illnesses of Europe battered and nearly consumed the flourishing societies of the Americas. The continent became, it appeared, what the first European visitors proclaimed it to be: a wilderness.

The African Solution

Amerindians became less available as a labor force because they were deemed not subject to enslavement, because they resisted the regimentation of the mines and plantations, and because they were ravaged by disease (imported from Europe) and declining in numbers. Europeans then turned to another labor source: that of African slaves. African slavery would have enormous consequences for the later development of American culture.

Two circumstances combined to trigger the exploitation of Africans in the New World by European landowners and entrepreneurs. The first was that the Portuguese had settled the west African coast at about the same time as the opening and exploitation of the Western Hemisphere. The second was that these same Portuguese had already experimented successfully, on their recently acquired Atlantic islands, with the plantation farming of sugar using African slave labor. Once the Portuguese inaugurated sugar planting in the Western Hemisphere, the importation there of the necessary slaves was inevitable. This happened in the 1530s, in Portuguese Brazil. Soon Dutch entrepreneurs had carried the system to the West Indies, where Spanish, French, and English landowners developed into a slakeless market for slaves.

Continuing a pattern begun in the first millennium C.E., the east African coastal cities, dominated by Arab traders, looked toward the mercantile zones of the Persian Gulf and Indian Ocean. Christian Ethiopia, facing the Red Sea, was also related to those trading centers. The states of North Africa were culturally Arab; their merchants traded south across the Sahara and on the Mediterranean, where they were trade rivals of Italian, Spanish, and Portuguese merchants. Egypt, in the northeast, previously part of the Arab network, and for nearly three centuries

---

HOW MANY?

Slave Imports to the Americas

5%

44%

43%

8%

APPROX. TOTAL NUMBER IMPORTED 9,299,000

North America excluding Mexico (400,000)

Caribbean (4,000,000)

Spanish South America including Central America and Mexico (769,000)

Brazil and Guiana (4,130,000)

Of nearly ten million Africans imported to the Americas and enslaved, the greatest numbers remained in Brazil (and nearby Guiana) and the Caribbean (totalling 87% of the whole), with lesser numbers dispersed over the great areas of Spanish America and North or Anglo-America (totalling 13% of the whole).
Source: H. Spodek, *The World's History* (Upper Saddle River, NJ: Prentice Hall, 1998), p. 448

(1250–1517) governed by the Mamluk sultans, became part of the Ottoman Empire in 1517.

In contrast to northern and eastern Africa, central and south Africa was characterized by village-based societies and small states. Though geographically more remote, these communities had been involved in local and even continental trade for centuries. West Africa was the zone of the great medieval kingdoms of Ghana, Mali, and Songhay, centers for commerce in gold and salt, and was still dominated by Songhay. Other, smaller states continued to form in west Africa. From these, and from the Kongo region to the south, flowed the stream of men and (in lesser numbers) women who were involuntarily removed to labor across the Atlantic Ocean.

Slaves were the major commodity that Portuguese merchants traded from their African depots. During the Middle Ages, most of the slaves exchanged in Mediterranean markets were Asian or Slavic—whence the word "slave" and its equivalents in European languages. The supply of these victims diminished in Europe after the conquest of Constantinople by the Ottoman Turks in 1453. Black African slaves took their place, and soon were exchanged in greater numbers than Eurasian captives had been earlier. Like the ancient Romans, Arab purchasers enslaved white and black workers indiscriminately.

North African Arab dealers supplied African slaves from the continent's interior to Mediterranean markets and to the courts and cities of Islamic Africa. After the Portuguese settlement on the west coast, mainly near modern Ghana, these dealers brought slaves also to the western coastal markets, where European traders waited to purchase them. European traders also recruited slaves directly from the nations and tribes of the interior, who willingly surrendered their war captives to the care of the new entrepreneurs.

In exchange, African suppliers received textiles and hardware, especially guns. The guns permitted more war, and war produced more slaves.

From the 1440s, Portuguese ships brought African slaves to Europe. After 1503, slaves were transported across the Atlantic. Their numbers rose into the nineteenth century, to constitute the largest instance ever of the mass-transplantation of captive peoples. This trade enriched the Atlantic nations of Europe.

Different estimates are given for the numbers of slaves transported across the Atlantic, but recent research indicates the magnitude of that transshipment. Some 9 to 12 million African slaves arrived in the Western Hemisphere (in addition to one to 2 million others who died during the voyage) between the first shipment in 1503 and the last in the 1880s, as shown in *How Many?* on p. 467. The numbers were low at first (a few thousand per year in the 1500s), but mounted rapidly in the 1600s (20,000 per year) to peak in the late 1700s (nearly 100,000 per year). Before 1800, more Africans than Europeans crossed the Atlantic, carried first by the Portuguese, and then the Dutch and the British. Realizing annual profits of close to 10 percent, after 1730 the British became the chief traffickers in slaves.

Of the 9 to 12 million transported, men outnumbered women by two to one. Most were put to work in the Caribbean and South America, where the lives of laborers were short—slaves being, as one Portuguese official commented, "a commodity that died with such ease." They were swiftly replaced. The impact on African society of the steady removal of mostly young men can well be surmised. Only about 400,000 slaves came to North America, where they were able to reproduce themselves, so that plantation owners did not depend so heavily on new importation.

A SLAVE-SHED.

Captives awaiting transportation, 1890: *From around 1500, human slaves were the most important commodity that European traders exported from Africa. Often African chieftains acted as intermediaries. Depicted here is a group of captives, including a young child, who are bound, leashed, shackled, and immobilized in locked devices, awaiting whatever fate that the slavemaster may assign.* (Century Magazine, 1890)

Commerce in Human Flesh

A slave ship: *In this drawing, 1789, of the slave ship* Brookes, *a slave cargo is arranged below decks for the horrific "Middle Journey" across the Atlantic. The slaves were squashed so tightly that they hardly had room to move. Contagious diseases spread quickly, leading to significant loss of life. (Wilberforce House Museum, Hull, England)*

The journey was punishing. Slavers brought the bands of new slaves to the ship, stripped them, and examined them—only the strong and healthy were valuable. For eight to twelve weeks, the slaves lived below deck, chained together and lying on shelves where they could neither sit up nor move about, as shown on this page. They were exercised on the deck, in which sessions females were vulnerable to rape. The food was scarce and shared from common buckets. Disease ran rampant. Vomit, mucus, excreta, and blood pooled in the slave quarters, breeding new waves of illness, described in *Witnesses* on p. 470. Despair drove many to suicide. The dead were thrown overboard. On the other side of the Atlantic, the survivors faced the degradation of the slave markets, depicted on this page and described in *Witnesses* on p. 470. Here, many were wrenched from family members and compatriots before being dispatched to a life of forced, unremunerated labor.

The system of African slavery developed to provide labor in places where Amerindians could not or would not work, and where Europeans were unavailable. Those circumstances differed in the northern and southern zones. In the south, especially in the Caribbean, African laborers were immediately impressed into labor on the sugar plantations—indeed, the numbers of slaves shipped rose directly in proportion to the increase of sugar farming. In the north, where sugar was not a key crop, slavery was slower to develop. In Brazil in later years, coffee plantations, displacing sugar as the main form of agriculture, eventually absorbed great numbers of slaves.

In the early years of North American settlement, European immigrants farmed the lands themselves. For additional labor services, they could employ convicted felons who had been transported to the colonies in lieu of punishment at home (a phenomenon also found in the West Indies). Or they could employ **indentured servants,** who worked without wages for a contractually

defined period of years in exchange for the price of passage to the colonies and clothing, room, and board while in service. From the employment of these workers—tantamount to temporary slaves—it was not a long distance to the use of imported African slaves.

The first African laborers in the English colonies were brought to Virginia by Dutch traders in 1619, twelve years after the colony's founding. They worked as indentured servants, however. So long as tobacco—the first cash crop—was farmed on a small scale, there was little reason to resort to slaves. As late as 1660, there were only 1700 black workers in Virginia, when slaves in West Indian Barbados numbered 20,000. As tobacco plantations grew, slavery was established in Virginia. In the Carolinas, the cultivation of rice—requiring intense labor under unpleasant and dangerous conditions—also encouraged the adoption of slavery. The introduction of cotton in the warmer colonies in the early 1700s gave a further impetus to the use of slave labor. By 1700, there were 20,000 African slaves in the Chesapeake

A slave auction: *A slave family is sold on the auction block in Virginia, 1861. The placard reads "Negroes for sale at Auction this day at 1 o'clock."*

Voices of Protest

The slave trade, rampant within Africa for centuries before the European arrival, entered a new and horrible "Atlantic" phase for nearly four centuries thereafter, during which it supported a colonial economic system that enriched the planters and merchants who became the governors of new American states. Yet there were those who opposed it, and whose opposition, in time, led to its extinction. Here the priest Bartolomé de las Casas protests against the exploitation of the Amerindians; his intervention prefigures later protests against the evils of colonialism. More than two centuries later, the former slave Olaudah Equiano deplores the evils of slavery; and a British physician reveals the awful conditions on the ship that was to transport human cargo out of Africa and into slavery.

The Spanish Priest Bartolomé de las Casas describes the native Amerindians and condemns Spanish atrocities (1552): And of all the infinite universe of humanity, these people are the most guileless, the most devoid of wickedness and duplicity, the most obedient and faithful to their native masters and to the Spanish Christians whom they serve. ... And because they are so weak and complaisant, they are less able to endure heavy labor and soon die of no matter what malady. ... They are very clean in their persons, with alert, intelligent minds, docile and open to doctrine, very apt to receive our holy Catholic faith, to be endowed with virtuous customs, and to behave in a godly fashion. ...

[Towards these gentle people, for the last forty years, the Spaniards have been] ... acting like ravening beasts, killing, terrorizing, afflicting, torturing, and destroying the native peoples, doing all this with the strangest and most varied new methods of cruelty, never seen or heard of before, and to such a degree that this Island of Hispaniola, once so populous (having a population that I estimated to be more than three millions), has now a population of barely two hundred persons. ...

(Bartolomé de las Casas, *The Devastation of the Indies: A Brief Account*, 1552; ed. H. Briffault, 1974)

Former slave Olaudah Equiano describes the sale of his fellow slaves at auction (1789): We ... were sold after their usual manner, which is this: On a signal given ..., the buyers rush at once into the yard where the slaves are confined, and make choice of that parcel they like best. ... In this manner, without scruple, are relations and friends separated, most of them never to see each other again. ... O, ye nominal Christians! Might not an African ask you—Learned you this from your God, who says unto you, Do unto all men as you would men should do unto you? Is it not enough that we are torn from our country and friends, to toil for your luxury and lust of gain? Must every tender feeling be likewise sacrificed to your avarice? ... Why are parents to lose their children, brothers their sisters, or husbands their wives? Surely, this is a new refinement in cruelty, which ... adds fresh horrors even to the wretchedness of slavery.

("The Life of Olaudah Equiano, or Gustavus Vassa, the African," 1789; ed. A. Bontemps, 1969)

A British physician inspects slaves on a ship bound for Brazil (1843): After the first paroxysm of horror and disgust had subsided, I remarked on the poop another wretched group, composed entirely of females. Some were mothers with infants who vainly endeavoring to suck a few drops of moisture from the lank, withered, and skinny breasts of their wretched mothers ... most of them destitute even of the decency of a rag. ...

While employed in examining the negroes individually ... I obtained a closer insight into their actual condition. Many I found afflicted with a confluent smallpox, still more with purulent ophthalmia, and the majority of what remained, with dysentery, ulcers, emaciation, and exhaustion. ... Not the least distressing sight on that pest-laden deck was the negroes whom the ophthalmia had struck blind, and who cowered in seeming apathy to all that was going around. This was indeed the ultimatum of wretchedness. ... Deprived of liberty, and torn from their native country, there was nothing more of human misery but to make them the victims of a physical darkness as deep as they had already been made a moral one.

(Thomas Nelson, "Remarks on the Slavery and Slave Trade of the Brazils," 1843; from eds. P. Riley et al., 1998)

Bay region of Virginia and Maryland; by 1775, some 331,000 African slaves in the North American British colonies, outstripping the number of those on the islands of Barbados and Jamaica together. These slaves, generally better treated than in the West Indies, enjoyed a higher birth rate and lower mortality rate and were able to reproduce themselves.

New World Women Women of all races and peoples, such as Amerindian natives and African slaves, were another kind of "other" in the New World: they did not number among the explorers, conquerors, settlers, and governors, but instead were subordinate to them. They had the main responsibility for domestic labor, and they were sexually exploited by the men of the ruling elite. Although all women shared this subordinate position, European women were by far the most privileged. The wives and daughters of upper-class men lived comfortable and protected lives. Even those who began their lives in the Americas as servants or laborers might improve their status by marrying rich planters or professional men—for women were in high demand in the largely male communities of European settlers, and found unusual opportunity for social mobility through employment or marriage.

Quite the opposite was true of Amerindian and African women. In their own cultures, they were already subordinated, and very often assigned responsibility (in addition to domestic service) for agricultural work held in low esteem. Additionally, they were vulnerable to the sexual demands of European males. Often they were coerced into such sexual relationships, ranging from rape to concubinage or marriage, from fleeting to long-term. From these sexual relationships was born a whole new population of persons of mixed ancestry. In Spanish America, where intermixture of races was common, persons with mixed Amerindian and European ancestries were called **mestizos**, meaning simply "mixed." Men and women with mixed African and European ancestries were called **mulattoes**, an insulting term derived from the Spanish word for "mule." In the West Indies, light-skinned mulattoes, often slaves, in some circumstances obtained higher status than their fully black peers and kin.

In addition to sexual services, African slave women labored hard as field hands or domestics, often, in the latter case, bearing full responsibility for the functioning of the slave-owner's household. They served as nurses for the infants and the elderly members of the slave-owner's family, and their young children were the companions of the slave-owner's heirs, until separated in adolescence.

In time, slavery received the detestation it deserved. The French theoretician Montesquieu concluded as early as 1721 that the institution of slavery was opposed to natural law (see Chapter 17). In Britain, Quakers proclaimed an ardent anti-slavery message. Later in the century, the former slave Olaudah Equiano (c. 1750–1797) raised his voice for the abolition of slavery. Using the name Gustavus Vassa given him by his English purchaser, he published his compelling autobiography in 1789. In it he described his capture in Nigeria at age eleven and the cruelties of his passage across the Atlantic, the slave market where he was sold, and the different masters for whom he labored. Eventually he bought his freedom, taught himself to read and write, settled in England, and publicized his story. In this case, one man was instrumental in changing public opinion.

The system of African slavery gradually ceased over a period of nearly a hundred years. The London-based Abolition Society, founded in 1787, and the French Declaration of the Rights of Man of 1789 spelled out the principle of the fundamental evil of slavery—which was also implicit, but without immediate fruit, in the "all men are created equal" clause of the Declaration of Independence (1776) of the new United States. In 1794, the French decreed the abolition of slavery at home and in its colonies; but the system was later reinstated in the colonies by Napoleon and lasted until 1848. In 1804, nevertheless, the Caribbean nation of Haiti, populated almost entirely by slaves, won independence from France. In 1807 and 1808 respectively, Britain and the United States banned the slave trade. The former abolished slavery throughout the British Empire in 1838; the latter abolished it only in 1865.

In 1813, the independent government of Buenos Aires (Argentina) decreed that all children born of slaves would be deemed free, thus launching the process of emancipation in Latin America. New World slavery ended only in 1886 and 1888, when the Spanish colony of Cuba and the nation of Brazil, respectively, decreed abolition. The scar left by the institution of slavery on the societies of the new nations of the Americas was indelible. Like the metropolitan nations of Europe, the nations of the Americas are heirs of the civilization of the West—in all aspects, good and bad. We are all the descendants of societies that profited from slavery; and that fact has had persistent and inescapable consequences.

In the same way, these nations are the children of societies that dispossessed the Amerindian inhabitants of the Western Hemisphere. That heritage, too, conditions the civilization that American nations, north and south, have inherited.

THE WEALTH OF NATIONS

Just as the encounter among European, African, and Amerindian peoples shaped the cultural systems that developed in the New World, so did the economic dynamics that developed during the first hundred years of European presence in this vast region. The commercial energies of Europeans, which in previous centuries had built mercantile cities and trading empires, now produced modern capitalism. The origins of today's global economy lie in the Atlantic age that Columbus, it might be said, "discovered."

Bringing Home the Bacon

Before about 1500, Europe's foreign trade was fundamentally unbalanced. Wealthy nobles, prelates, and patricians craved the spices and gems, exquisite porcelains and finished silks found in the East. Having little of value to offer in exchange, Europe paid mostly in **specie,** with gold or silver coin. That pattern shifted after the opening of the New World. The Americas provided not only new sources of silver and gold, but also beneficial new commodities and raw materials for Europe's many manufacturing enterprises. By the 1700s the products of these enterprises had found markets in Asia. Eastern luxuries still satisfied the appetites of the rich, but other imports fed the European economy in more productive ways. By 1750, instead of draining Europe of coin, trade with other regions of the globe had, in fact, contributed to Europe's wealth.

The conquistadors, it was said, set out from Spain for "God, gold, and glory." They found gold and silver in abundance, as indicated in *How Many?* on p. 476, although not as much of the former as they would have liked. From the mid-1500s, annual shipments of bullion loaded on twenty to sixty ships escorted in convoy by two to six men-of-war left American ports for Spain (mostly) and Portugal. One-fifth of the wealth went directly to the royal treasury. From Columbus's first voyage until 1800, the New World supplied 85 percent of the world's silver and 70 percent of its gold; Spanish coins (the **reales**, each one-eighth of a **peso**, or "piece of eight") circulated worldwide.

Profitable New Crops   Meanwhile, some people saw that a potentially greater treasure was present in a plant for which Europeans developed an enormous appetite—the sugar cane. In medieval Europe, honey was the principal sweetener, and sugar was rare. It was sold only in small pellets as a pharmaceutical, the ancestor of the modern candy bar. Sugar cane grew in Arab lands, including Sicily. From there, Portuguese entrepreneurs transplanted it to their newly settled Atlantic islands in the late fifteenth century, and to Brazil early in the sixteenth. From Brazil, sugar cultivation spread to the West Indies, where it grew on plantations owned by nationals of several different countries, with the labor of African slaves.

By itself, sugar constituted a whole economy, and its cultivation was a preeminent agricultural pursuit. It became doubly profitable when merchants learned to derive molasses and rum from it. In the eighteenth century, sugar and sugar products accounted for more imports to Britain (where their consumption reached huge proportions) than all the goods of the North American mainland, or all of those from Asia.

Of greater benefit to the European diet were some native American crops that proved to be cultivable in the Old World. None was more basic than the potato. Rich in vitamins, easily grown, capable of

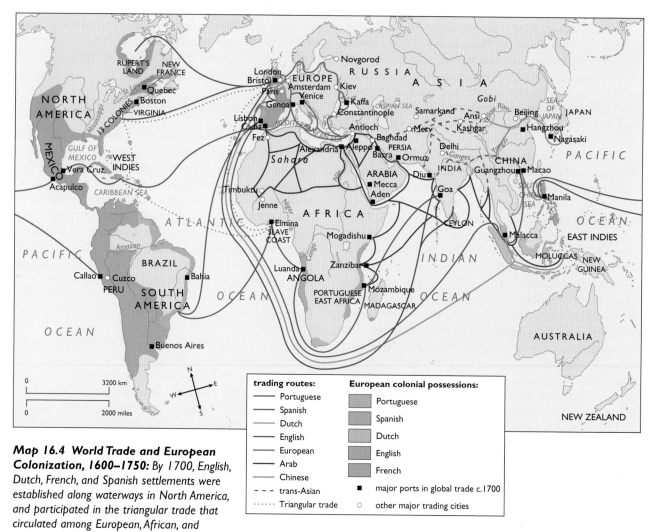

Map 16.4 World Trade and European Colonization, 1600–1750: *By 1700, English, Dutch, French, and Spanish settlements were established along waterways in North America, and participated in the triangular trade that circulated among European, African, and American ports. Meanwhile, French, Dutch, and English ships joined Portuguese and Spanish ones on the trade routes across the Indian and Pacific Oceans. Europeans had not yet fully explored the interiors of the Americas, Africa, and parts of Asia. They came to know of the existence of Australia and New Zealand only late in the eighteenth century.*

The Profits of Trade

It was trade that enriched Europe so that Europeans might venture beyond their borders to other parts of the globe; and then trade again that enriched Europe and supported her political and cultural modernization. In these two passages, the French finance minister Jean-Baptiste Colbert and the Scottish economist Adam Smith think about the benefits of the circulation of goods in trade. For Colbert, trade will increase the nation's wealth, and thus its tax revenues, which can in turn support the nation in the event of war. For Smith, the effect of trade is the generation of wealth, and more is generated as each individual separately attempts to acquire as much of it as he can—through which selfish activity, as though by an "invisible hand," he is led to increase the wealth of the nation.

French Minister Jean-Baptiste Colbert instructs King Louis XIV about finances (1670): The palpable reward ... will be that by attracting a great quantity of wealth into the kingdom by trade, not only will you soon re-establish that due proportion between the money circulating in trade and the taxes paid by the people, but both will be increased proportionately, so that revenue will rise and the people will be in a condition to assist more effectively in the event of war or other emergency.
(Jean-Baptiste Colbert, "Mémoire au Roi sur les Finances," 1670; from ed. A. Lossky, trs. G. Symcox, 1967)

Scots economist Adam Smith criticizes mercantilist theories and argues for Free Trade and the regulation of an "Invisible Hand" (1776): The annual revenue of every society is always precisely equal to the exchangeable value of the whole annual produce of its industry. ... As every individual, therefore, endeavours as much as he can both to employ his capital in the support of domestic industry, and so to direct that industry that its produce may be of the greatest value; every individual necessarily labours to render the annual revenue of the society as great as he can. He generally, indeed, neither intends to promote the public interest, nor knows how much he is promoting it. ... [H]e intends only his own gain, and he is in this ... led by an invisible hand to promote an end which was no part of his intention. Nor is it always the worse for the society that it was not part of it. By pursuing his own interest he frequently promotes that of the society more effectually than when he really intends to promote it.
(Adam Smith, *The Wealth of Nations*, 1776; ed. E. Cannan, 1987)

being prepared in innumerable ways, this root vegetable which was already a prime source of nutrition (unlike sugar) for the Amerindian soon became a staple of the European (and African) diet. Its consumption in some places increasingly came to rival that of bread, which in Eurasia had held pride of place since antiquity.

Corn, tomatoes, yams, beans, squash, and cacao beans (for chocolate) and cashews also traveled to Europe, and even the ungainly turkey found some consumers on the eastern side of the Atlantic. Other North American animals were valuable not as food, but for the products they yielded. The beaver's fur (for warmth and fashion), the whale's blubber (for heat and light) were readily available in the huge forests and waters of the new continent. From a Mexican insect came the valuable dyestuff cochineal, which produced a rich red hue.

Some crops and beasts made the journey the other way. European pigs, sheep, horses, cattle, and chickens; honey bees; apple, peach, and pear trees; and, of course, wheat came with European farmers and thrived on new soil. Europeans also transplanted from Asia white rice (the Amerindian cereals were corn and wild rice), coffee and bananas, indigo (another dye), and cotton.

One other American crop added much to European culture, though nothing of benefit to its health: tobacco leaves, grown in southeastern North America. Europeans learned from Amerindian users to dry, age, and pulverize it into a powder called **snuff**, to be inhaled, or shred it into a coarse mix to be smoked in pipes, cigars, or in cigarettes, invented as early as the sixteenth century but refined in the later 1700s. This new luxury product complemented the spices, silks, porcelains, and other luxuries already imported from Asia.

European planters in warmer regions of North America experimented with crops native to tropical regions of the Old World. Rice, the staple grain of much of Asia, thrived in the marshy lands of the Carolinas, whose economy it boosted from the 1690s. Slaves first undertook its cultivation, using their experience of growing rice in Africa. The cotton plant, the source of the principal textile of the Indian subcontinent, could grow throughout the North American southeast. Cotton cultivation was already established in the 1600s, but really took off after 1800 to become the "king" of American agriculture (see Chapter 19). Both of these were plantation crops, grown by methods that were first developed for sugar cultivation in the West Indies, and absorbed the labor of African slaves. Coffee grown in Brazil also used forced labor. New World products greatly invigorated the European economy and made the Atlantic a theater of world trade as great as, and soon greater than, those of the Old World. But the old trade routes still functioned. At the height of Dutch sea trade in the 1600s, one-third of this trade was committed to the Baltic Sea, where Dutch ships had supplanted those of the medieval Hanseatic League after the late 1400s. The Baltic route, which extended from London in the west to Novgorod in the east, carried tar and timber, flax and hemp, honey, wax, and, most important, grain from the plains of eastern Europe. That ready supply of grain permitted some western European laborers to leave the soil and tend to manufacturing tasks—a precondition of subsequent industrialization.

European-made products and those transshipped from Asia—textiles above all, plus tools, furniture, nails, and tea—won ready markets on the western side of the Atlantic. The American colonists required these high-cost goods for survival and comfort and paid for them with low-cost raw materials in bulk. In the Atlantic trading system, trade was again unbalanced, but now in Europe's favor.

Trade Wars

With the creation of the Atlantic trade system, Europe's role in the global economy changed dramatically. Now she became the pivot of world trade (the nations of east Asia remaining aloof from the West for three more centuries). Her manufactures diversified, her appetite grew, her need for markets expanded, her merchant fleets swelled, and her treasuries fattened. The quest for profit, which had once driven Italian entrepreneurs to scour the Mediterranean, now drove the capitalists of Spain and Portugal, Britain and France, the Netherlands and Germany to expand their business empires to the farthest possible limits. By 1750, Europe was the wealthiest region on the globe. On the wave of this expansion, prices increased, populations soared, cities grew; and the ancient rivalries between European states increasingly gave way to a new generation of commercial competition and trade wars.

In the race for wealth, the European nation states took the lead in a departure from the medieval trade pattern, in which Italian merchants won the first fortunes of the modern West. But as navigation and commerce increasingly shifted to the Atlantic, these states developed under the aegis of newly powerful monarchies, whose rulers and chief ministers understood wealth to be the wealth of the nation.

This outlook was the outlook of mercantilism. Mercantilist strategies involved both economic and political measures, which sought to increase the nation's wealth in various ways: by encouraging domestic industries (often by grants of monopoly right), by limiting foreign imports, by assuring a favorable balance of trade, by securing ample quantities of gold and silver bullion, and by outpacing rival nations, whose increased wealth meant a relative decrease of their own. In mercantilist logic, these objectives were to be won, if necessary, by force. "Trade cannot be maintained without war, nor war without trade," pronounced an official of the Dutch East India Company, stating a commonplace of mercantilist thought.

Thus mercantilism pitted nation against nation in the race for wealth. The Portuguese were at first in the forefront, then were displaced by the Spaniards, who had meanwhile acquired the gold and silver resources of the Americas. Spanish ships laden with gold and silver attracted pirates and privateers, the semi-official raiding ships of the northern Atlantic nations which were ready to steal from Spain, but not yet to compete with her. The Spanish bullion hoards

Engines of Commerce

The great crane at Bruges: *Machines in early modern Europe speeded up enterprise but were powered by the energy of human beings or beasts, as shown in the operation by human beings of a treadmill in this sixteenth-century manuscript illumination. (Bayerisches Staatsbibliothek, Munich)*

Jhiob Berckheyde, **A general scene at the Amsterdam Stock Exchange:** *At the Amsterdam stock exchange, completed in 1613, merchants might purchase shares in the commercial and industrial enterprises that fueled the prosperity of the age. (Private Collection)*

did not enrich the nation as planned (most of the money went to foreign bankers), and by the early seventeenth century Spain had fallen behind the Dutch.

For nearly a century, the Dutch were the masters of European trade, with England and France nipping at their heels. In those years, approximately three times as many Dutch ships as English ones set off for Asia. England's several Navigation Acts, passed between 1651 and 1696, aimed at undercutting Dutch competition. In the three Anglo-Dutch wars fought between 1652 and 1674, the English navy edged ahead of the Dutch. In the next century, with France as a primary rival, the British struggled to maintain economic supremacy, which it achieved at the close of the Seven Years' War in 1763.

From 1500 to 1800, foreign trade grew steadily, as more raw materials from the New World were used for European manufacture, and as more European products found markets in the west or in Asia. By 1700, almost half of England's merchant fleet was trading with America or India—the cargoes often guaranteed by Lloyd's, a new company which set the pattern for the modern insurance industry. In the following century, British exports to other parts of the world rose from a trickle to more than a third of the whole, while imports from those lands rose to over one-half of all imports. Meanwhile, France's foreign trade trailed Britain's and the Dutch share fell behind, while Spain and Portugal were no longer serious competitors.

The profits from this commerce went to merchant capitalists, but also to small investors, who sometimes greedily participated in unwise ventures: notoriously the "Louisiana bubble" (in France) and the "South Sea bubble" (in Britain). In these early-eighteenth-century episodes, private investors, sometimes pledging family estates and life savings, purchased stock in investment ventures that promised huge profits. Speculation proceeded unchecked, the stock values collapsed, and the investors were left with nothing from the exploded "bubble."

While western Europe's large nation-states seized the leadership of European trade, other areas were

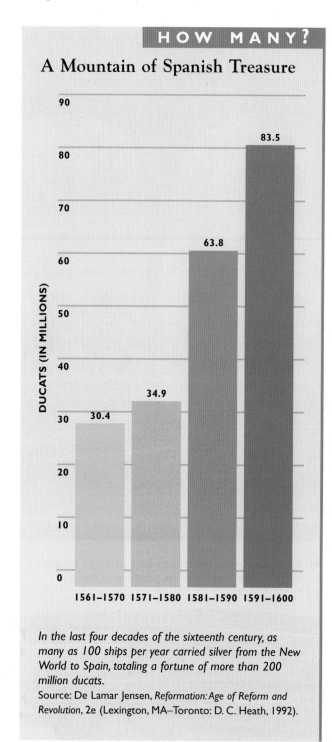

HOW MANY?

A Mountain of Spanish Treasure

DUCATS (IN MILLIONS)

83.5
63.8
34.9
30.4

1561–1570 1571–1580 1581–1590 1591–1600

In the last four decades of the sixteenth century, as many as 100 ships per year carried silver from the New World to Spain, totaling a fortune of more than 200 million ducats.
Source: De Lamar Jensen, *Reformation: Age of Reform and Revolution*, 2e (Lexington, MA–Toronto: D. C. Heath, 1992).

quiescent, and still mainly agrarian in character. Eastern Europe turned deliberately to more intensive agricultural production. Italy lost its commercial preeminence in trade, although some Italian cities continued to produce profitable luxury goods, such as Venetian glass and lace.

Proto-industrialization   Another way to enhance the wealth of the nation was to build up its manufacturing base. The old merchant and craft guilds that had generated economic growth during the Middle Ages had become restrictive, discouraging innovation

or the circulation of personnel. Mercantilist projects tended to enliven the manufacturing sector, stimulating certain crafts or inviting joint-stock companies to undertake new endeavors. For example, Colbert (1619–1683), finance minister to Louis XIV, encouraged a variety of manufacturing enterprises (including the famous Gobelins tapestry workshop). To promote commerce, Colbert also oversaw the construction of new roads and canals, harbors and shipyards, and built up the French navy. The failure of Spain to support its industries, especially as silver imports dwindled, helps to explain its economic decline.

The devices that promoted the wealth of nations also enriched individuals, who accumulated enough wealth to fund extensive investments. Still, the wealthy merchants of the early modern era must be distinguished from later industrial capitalists, whose great factories won them previously extraordinary profits. These earlier merchants took commodities made by others and shipped them to distant markets. Or they supervised manufacturing enterprises, especially textiles, which worked on the domestic or "putting-out" system. In this system, the merchant acquired raw materials, distributed them to country workers who labored in their own cottages, and collected the finished goods for sale. Employing men, women, and children, this system flourished into the eighteenth century. It constituted a "proto-industrial" phase of European manufacturing, featuring rural production and city-directed exchange.

Technological innovations also contributed to the growth of the European economy. By 1500, Europe already had put machines to work in productive ways. Waterwheels and windmills helped grind grain, brew ale, pump water, make paper, saw wood, and treat textiles. The circulation of goods was facilitated by the building of canal networks which in turn was made possible by the invention of locks. Changes in ship design and gun manufacture have already been noted. Over the next centuries, other new machines and industrial processes improved textile and glass manufacturing, coal mining, and iron production.

All this growth, however, had a disadvantage: rapid inflation. The injection of new quantities of bullion into the European economy, the deliberate devaluation of existing currencies, and the steady climb of the European population caused an explosion of values and prices. Prices rose for goods, while wages and rents lagged, with regional variations: in Spain, prices more than tripled in the century before 1600; in England, the prices of basic goods rose nearly sixfold during the same period. The pattern of steep price increases affected different groups differently—it allowed merchants to accumulate capital for investment in more manufacture and trade, while it mercilessly pinched peasants and urban workers.

The forward wave of commercial economy favored population increase, which in turn undergirded the economic boom. European population generally increased until about 1600, when it surpassed for the first time the pre-Black Death level of 73 million. During the seventeenth century, population growth slowed again, owing in part to the disastrous effect of the Thirty Years' War, which reduced the population of central Europe by 30–40 percent. The marriage age increased in many regions, showing that people were adopting a familiar strategy to reduce the birth rate. Spain and Italy fell behind the north Atlantic nations, and France's rate of growth fell behind England's. In the eighteenth century, the population began again to increase as mortality rates declined. After a last outbreak of bubonic plague in Marseilles in 1720, the plague left Europe (perhaps because of unfavorable shifts in the ecology of the black rat, the critical carrier of the deadly infectious flea). The cycle of famine receded too, and the proto-industrial cottage industries, which allowed young persons to make a profit from their labor without delaying marriage, drove the numbers upward.

Despite economic growth, the steady upward pressure on prices and the increasing population brought hardship, especially to the rural poor. Grain prices rose by factors of three, four, even six, while the average price of manufactured goods merely doubled. Bread was expensive or scarce, while landowners strove to extract more labor from their workers. The real wages of agricultural workers fell catastrophically, and the force of hunger, briefly subdued in the aftermath of the Black Death, returned. The numbers of the landless increased, and beggars proliferated.

The high price of grain resulted not only from general inflationary trends but also from a shortage of good soil due to over-plowing and little fertilization. In England and the Netherlands, farmers opened up new land for cultivation of more grain. They drained low-lying lands, fenced off fields to raise stock, and systematized crop rotation to increase the yield of already-plowed soil. These practices were only slowly diffused to the rest of Europe.

Urbanization   With economic growth came urbanization, as Map 16.5 below shows. Merchants concentrated in cities, where goods changed hands, where banks held funds, where artisans labored, and where consumers purchased. In the early modern centuries, towns became cities, cities expanded. For the first

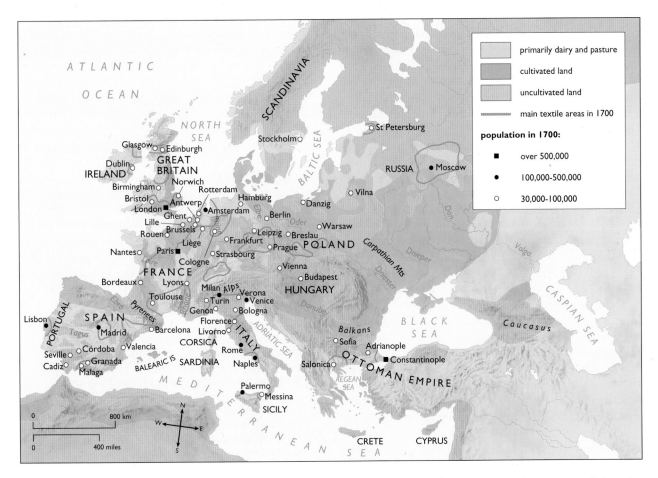

Map 16.5 European Commerce, Industry, and Urbanization, 1550–1750: *The medieval centers of commerce in Italy and Flanders expanded from the fifteenth through the eighteenth centuries, while new areas of textile production and zones of intensive mining enriched the European economic scene. Population increased overall, and especially in towns, many of which grew to be cities, two approaching the million mark in population, while others, like Amsterdam and Madrid, surpassed 100,000.*

time, many European cities grew to exceed the largest cities previously known in the Western world (London, Paris, Naples, and Milan). Not only did large cities grow larger, but a greater proportion of Europeans lived in cities and towns; even country workers often migrated to the city for part of their lives before returning to their villages, their mental outlook forever changed. No longer islands in a world of fields, the cities were open to the countryside and linked to each other in large regional networks of economic activity.

Before 1500, few people lived in concentrations greater than 10,000. Between 1500 and 1800, the number of western European cities larger than 10,000 more than doubled (from 154 to 364). At the same time, the number of people living in those cities more than tripled (from 3,441,000 to 12,218,000). From 1500 to 1750, the percentage of Europeans living in cities of more than 10,000 inhabitants increased from 6.1 to 9.9 percent. The growth was heaviest in areas of new urbanization—western and northern Europe—rather than in Italy, whose cities had been the power centers of medieval commerce. Farther east—in Russia, for example—urbanization was minimal, and only a few towns held populations as large as 30,000.

Some individual cities mushroomed. By 1600 the populations of Seville (Spain), Lisbon (Portugal), and Antwerp (modern Belgium), all involved in transatlantic trade, had jumped to 100,000—the size previously reached only by the largest Italian cities. By the same year, the populations of London and Paris approached 200,000; by the end of the eighteenth century, they reached 800,000 and 670,000 respectively. Lyons, France's second commercial city, had nearly 100,000 inhabitants. Smaller cities, with populations hovering around 20,000, were nevertheless important centers of regional trade. The major German cities (Augsburg, Nuremberg, Cologne), subject to the political fragmentation of the Empire, never exceeded this range in the early modern period.

Medieval cities, concentrated in Italy and Flanders, had flourished in the absence of strong national governments. In contrast, the largest early modern cities were the centers of powerful nations, often the capitals. They looked the part. Their streets were straightened, for displays of military and state power and for the carriages of the wealthy. Their secular buildings—palaces, banks, **stock exchanges** and theaters—began to rival cathedrals in grandeur, both secular and sacred buildings being designed in styles that raised classical forms to new levels of opulence.

Amsterdam The city of Amsterdam is a noteworthy example of early modern urbanization. In the Middle Ages, Amsterdam had been a town of little importance, but the political developments of the sixteenth century boosted it to eminence. Nearby Antwerp, a port city with access to the Atlantic, had preceded

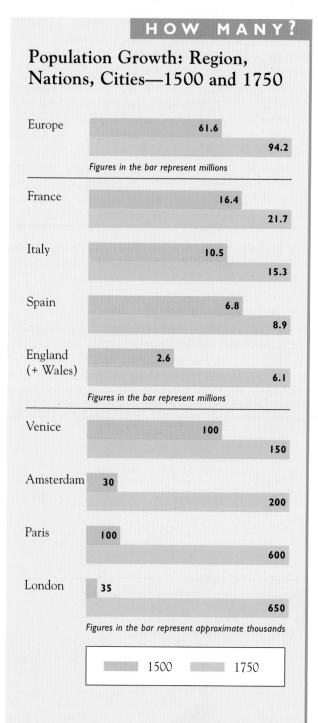

HOW MANY?

Population Growth: Region, Nations, Cities—1500 and 1750

Europe   61.6 / 94.2

Figures in the bar represent millions

France   16.4 / 21.7

Italy   10.5 / 15.3

Spain   6.8 / 8.9

England (+ Wales)   2.6 / 6.1

Figures in the bar represent millions

Venice   100 / 150

Amsterdam   30 / 200

Paris   100 / 600

London   35 / 650

Figures in the bar represent approximate thousands

1500   1750

The population of Europe increased more than 50% (from a base of about 60 million) from 1500–1750. But nations and cities increased at different rates. While the population of France increased only about 32%, the population of England increased 135%, to reach by 1750 more than twice its 1500 figure. Meanwhile Venice, the front-ranking city of 1500, fell to a poor fourth place by 1750, when London, having increased more than twentyfold, reached preeminence with a population of 650,000.

Source: J. de Vries, *European Urbanization, 1500–1800* (Cambridge, MA: Harvard University Press, 1984)

Amsterdam as the major port (and thus the commercial and banking center) of northern Europe. It reigned supreme in the sixteenth century, when it handled much of Portuguese trade as well as the commerce of the textile manufactures of the region. But Antwerp's career suddenly declined around 1650, when the newly independent United Provinces were allowed (by the Treaty of Münster, 1648) to close the Scheldt River, the city's route to the sea. Located not far to the north of Antwerp and in closer proximity to the sea, Amsterdam took its place.

In the seventeenth and eighteenth centuries, Amsterdam was the banking center of Europe, the fulcrum of world trade. Its population grew from 30,000 in 1567 to over 200,000 by the early 1780s. Its bank, founded in 1609 on the model of the Venetian Rialto banks, issued its own gold florin. By 1700, the bank provided safety for more than 2000 depositors and the lowest interest rates in Europe (4 percent or less) on investment loans. At its stock exchange (completed 1613), illustrated on p. 475, merchants participated in ventures around the globe, trading in as many as 491 commodities by 1674 (when London, its rising competitor, dealt in 305). A weekly bulletin listed options and gave updated prices.

Even after the 1713 Peace of Utrecht, when the Netherlands fell behind the British and French as a European power, Amsterdam remained the center of European financial life. During the eighteenth century, the city lived on the capital it had accumulated over the previous 200 years, which now helped fund, at profitable rates of interest, nearly every major commercial venture in Europe.

The growing mercantilist commercial system of the sixteenth, seventeenth, and eighteenth centuries enriched European nations, swelled their towns and cities, and lavishly rewarded the merchant investors. It seemed a great success. And yet it also had many defects. The intervention of government into the business of business, while often protective, also retarded the pace of commerce. Tariffs set to shelter domestic manufactures and monopolies created by royal edict interfered with the free flow of trade and the mechanisms which, as later experts argued, allowed the market to regulate itself.

Such problems of mercantilist organization encouraged the Scottish professor Adam Smith (1723–1790) to argue for an alternative organization of manufacture and commerce. In his *Inquiry into the Nature and Causes of the Wealth of Nations* (published in 1776, the same year as the Declaration of Independence), part of which is quoted in *Witnesses* on p. 473, he argued that the absence of intervention would enhance production within the nation, as individuals pursuing their own self-interest would both yield high profits and benefit the public. Free trade policies would allow the entrepreneurs competing for foreign trade to realize the greatest possible wealth, and thus enrich the nation. Directed only by merchant interest and buyer need, "as though by an invisible hand," free trade would more greatly increase the "wealth of nations" than a trade system controlled by jealous states and governors. The nation states that had just matured in the political life of Europe were now instructed to limit themselves to defense and security. They did not easily retreat.

Conclusion
THE EXPANSION OF EUROPE AND THE MEANING OF THE WEST

From 1500 to 1750, Europe expanded beyond its earlier borders physically, economically, and psychologically. The expansion had begun even earlier, with the commercial revolution achieved by Italian merchants and the foreign adventures of the Crusades. The cultural and religious movements of the Renaissance and the Reformation, although contained within the geographical boundaries of Europe, entailed an enormous broadening of Europeans' mental horizons. Now, however, the expansion was fundamental and taking place on all fronts: it sent people of many nations around the world on new ships driven by new technology; it stimulated Europeans to reconsider their view of themselves upon contact with human communities previously unknown; it changed what ordinary people ate and wore, their work and their homes; it impacted on the lives of nearly every European, from the Dutch ship hand to the Polish peasant.

The same expansion made Europe the master of the globe. Europeans were involved in the rout of Amerindian culture, in the mass enslavement of Africans, and in the enlistment of Indian and Indonesian (if not yet east Asian) producers into the economy of the West. At the beginning of the episode of European expansion, Montaigne wrote about the Amerindian Caribs who ate their war captives. But he had already detected that, much as his fellow Europeans feared and deplored the cannibal, the cannibal had much to dread in the advent to his world of European civilization.

REVIEW QUESTIONS

1. Why was Portugal a leader in African and Asian explorations? Who were the shoguns and samurai of Japan? What advantages contributed to the rise of Dutch power?

2. What were the strengths and weaknesses of Columbus' accomplishments? How were other avenues to North America discovered? Who were the Aztecs and Incas and why were Cortés and Pizarro able to defeat them?

3. Describe the culture of Amerindians before European colonization. What role did missions play in colonial development?

4. What led to the emergence of the African slave trade? What was the final destination of most African slaves and why? What role did women of African and Amerindian descent play in colonial development?

5. How did the New World contribute to Europe's wealth? Explain the European colonial trade routes. Why did Spain and the Netherlands decline as colonial powers?

6. What was proto-industrialization? What were the positive and negative economic and social effects of colonial trade for Europe? Why was the burgeoning city of Amsterdam a good example of early modern urbanization?

SUGGESTED RESOURCES

The Open Seas

Chaudhuri, K. N., *Asia before Europe: Economy and Civilisation of the Indian Ocean from the Rise of Islam to 1750* (New York: Cambridge University Press, 1990). A study of cultural practices and beliefs: food and drink, architecture, clothing, symbolism, land, nomadism, urbanism.

Fernández-Armesto, Felipe, *Before Columbus: Exploration and Colonization from the Mediterranean to the Atlantic, 1229–1492* (Philadelphia: University of Pennsylvania Press, 1991). A collection of essays on the pre-Columbian European expansion in northwest Africa and the Atlantic islands.

Smith, Roger C., *Vanguard of Empire: Ships of Exploration in the Age of Columbus* (Oxford: Oxford University Press, 1993). Explores the advances in ship technology that allowed the Spanish and Portuguese to venture out on the deep seas for exploration and exploitation.

Voyages of discovery and exploration, biographies and links: **http://www.win.tue.nl/cs/fm/engels/discovery**

Columbus navigation homepage: **http://www1.minn.net/~keithp**

Sir Walter Raleigh, biography, resources, and links: **http://www.britishexplorers.com**

Brave New World

Axtell, James, *Beyond 1492: Encounters in Colonial North America* (Oxford: Oxford University Press, 1992). Essays on themes relating to interactions between Amerindians and Europeans.

Blackburn, Robin, *The Making of New World Slavery: From the Baroque to the Modern, 1492–1800* (New York: Verso, 1998). A discussion of New World slavery in a comparative and historical perspective.

Clendinnen, Inga, *The Aztecs: An Interpretation.* (Cambridge: Cambridge University Press, 1991). A provocative study of Aztec rituals and human sacrifice in terms of an all-consuming religious world-view.

Crosby, Alfred W., *Ecological Imperialism: The Biological Expansion of Europe 900–1900* (Cambridge: Cambridge University Press, 1993). A survey of the biological impact of European contact on the Americas, Africa, Asia, Australia, and the Pacific islands.

Curtin, Philip D., *The Rise and Fall of the Plantation Complex: Essays in Atlantic History* (Cambridge: Cambridge University Press, 1990). A study of plantation agriculture from the medieval Mediterranean to the Atlantic islands and the American tropics.

Josephy, Alvin M., Jr., ed., *America in 1492: The World of the Indian Peoples before the Arrival of Columbus.* 2nd ed. (New York: Knopf, 1993). A collection of essays surveying the Indian peoples by region and by theme—language, religion, trade, technology, etc.

Pagden, Anthony, *Lords of All the World: Ideologies of Empire in Spain, Britain and France, c. 1500–c. 1800* (New Haven: Yale University Press, 1995). A brilliant and fascinating reconstruction of the different ideological traditions that authorized European conquerors to dominate other peoples.

Stannard, David E., *American Holocaust: The Conquest of the New World* (Oxford: Oxford University Press, 1993). Describes the European conquest and wholesale destruction of the Indian populations of the Americas as a deliberate act of genocide, whose origins lie within the Christian traditions of the West.

Thomas, Hugh, *The Slave Trade: The Story of the Atlantic Slave Trade, 1440–1870* (New York: Simon and Schuster, 1998). Splended overview written for a general audience, that evokes the whole tragedy of the Atlantic slave trade, taking into its purview the slave traders, purchasers, collaborators, and the slaves themselves.

Indigenous peoples of the Americas, all regions, articles, and resources: **http://www.hartford-hwp.com**

The Wealth of Nations

De Vries, Jan & Ad Van der Woude, *The First Modern Economy: Success, Failure, and Perseverance of the Dutch Economy, 1500-1815* (Cambridge: Cambridge University Press, 1997). Presents the Dutch as the first to create a truly modern economy, with an integrated profitable agricultural sector, foreign trade, and capital market.

Mintz, Sidney, W., *Sweetness and Power* (New York: Penguin, 1985). A study of sugar in the rise of plantations and the world economy.

Price, Jacob M., *Perry of London: A Family and a Firm on the Seaborne Frontier, 1615–1753* (Cambridge MA: Harvard University Press, 1992). Traces the history of one family, and firm, which imported American tobacco into Britain in the 17th and 18th centuries; reveals the connectedness of social, economic, and political power.

Tracy, James D., ed., *The Rise of Merchant Empires: Long-Distance Trade in the Early Modern World, 1350–1750* (Cambridge: Cambridge University Press, 1990). Thirteen essays by leading scholars on merchant networks, the transatlantic slave trade, trans-Saharan trade, and Central Asian trade.

PART FIVE
THE WEST EXPANDS

Science, Enlightenment, and Revolution (1500–1900)

17 The Age of Reason
Science, Schooling, and Thought in Early Modern Europe, 1500–1780

18 Town, Court, and Country
Privilege and Poverty in Early Modern Europe, 1500–1780

19 Inalienable Rights
Revolution and its Promises in Anglo- and Latin America, 1500–1880

20 Revolt and Reorganization in Europe
From Absolute Monarchy to the Paris Commune, 1750–1871

The social and cultural changes of the sixteenth through eighteenth centuries formed a prelude to the great political upheavals of the eighteenth and nineteenth centuries, together bringing the West to the threshold of modernity. The first scientists constructed a new model of the cosmos, discovered by observation and described with mathematics, while philosophers refined the logical and theoretical methods needed to explore both cosmic and human realms. In the intellectual movement known as the Enlightenment, critics questioned the bases of prevailing political and social systems, while an increasingly literate public joined in the conversation.

These new ideas challenged the system of social orders inherited from the Middle Ages—the Old Regime—prompting nobles to cling to the signs of their status and bourgeois hopefuls to try to "live nobly"; the peasantry, meanwhile, suffered the effects of economic change and political ambition. Across the ocean in the Americas North and South, the civilization of the West was reinvented in a new land and among new peoples, where opportunity beckoned to those who sought refuge from the cruelties of Europe. Along the Atlantic seaboard, the first Americans to cast off the rule of kings created a new nation, while in Europe the accumulated weaknesses of the French polity led to the French Revolution, which destroyed the Old Regime without establishing a society free of its defects.

The French Revolution bred sporadic later revolutions in France and elsewhere through 1871, when the Paris Commune was violently suppressed. The other major nations of Europe mobilized to suppress such revolutionary activity, while Britain, a unique case, gradually opened its political process to widening circles of ordinary citizens. Nationalist aspirations, meanwhile, another product of the French Revolution, culminated by 1871 in the unification of Italy and Germany, which for the first time took their place among the nation states of Europe.

THE AGE OF REASON

	1450	1500	1550	1600	1650	1700	1750	1800

Society and Politics

♦ "Glorious Revolution" in England, 1688

♦ Peter the Great of Russia creates "ciphering schools," 1714

♦ Frederick II of Prussia decrees obligatory elementary education, 1763

♦ American Declaration of Independence, 1776

♦ French Revolution begins, 1789

Scientific Developments

Scientific Revolution, 1543–1687

♦ Nicholas Copernicus' *On the Revolutions of the Celestial Spheres*, 1543

♦ Andreas Vesalius' *On the Structure of the Human Body*, 1543

♦ Tycho Brahe observes a comet, 1577

♦ Galileo makes first astronomical observations with telescope, 1609

♦ Johannes Kepler's *New Astronomy*, 1609

♦ Johannes Kepler's *Harmonies of the World*, 1619

♦ William Harvey's *Circulation of the Blood*, 1628

♦ Galileo's *Dialogue Concerning the Two Chief World Systems*, 1632

♦ English Royal Society founded in London, 1662

♦ Academy of Sciences founded in Paris, 1666

♦ Isaac Newton's *Mathematical Principles of Natural Philosophy (Principia)*, 1687

♦ Bernard de Fontenelle's *A Plurality of Worlds*, 1688

♦ Lady Mary Wortley Montagu champions smallpox innoculation in Britain, 1721

Art, Religion, and Ideas

First century of printing, c. 1460–1560

The Enlightenment, c. 1685–1789

♦ Peter Martyr's *Chronicles of the New World*, 1530

♦ Richard Hakluyt's *Principal Navigations, Voyages, Traffics and Discoveries of the English Nation*, 1589

♦ Francis Bacon's *The Advancement of Learning*, 1605

♦ Francis Bacon's *Novum Organum (New Method)*, 1620

♦ Galileo condemned by Roman Catholic Church, 1633

♦ René Descartes' *Discourse on Method*, 1637

♦ Poulain de la Barre's *On the Equality of the Two Sexes*, 1673

♦ Louis XIV of France revokes Edict of Nantes, 1685

♦ Aphra Behn's *Oroonoko*, 1688

♦ Locke's *Essay Concerning Human Understanding* and *Two Treatises of Government*, 1690

♦ Daniel Defoe's *Robinson Crusoe*, 1710

♦ Montesquieu's *Spirit of Laws*, 1748

♦ Denis Diderot and Jean d'Alembert's *Encyclopedia*, 1751–80

♦ British Museum established in London, 1753

♦ Jean-Jacques Rousseau's *The Social Contract*, 1762

♦ Voltaire's *Philosophical Dictionary*, 1764

♦ Immanuel Kant's "What is Enlightenment?", 1784

♦ Louvre Museum opens in Paris, 1793

♦ Condorcet's *Sketch for a Historical Account of the Progress of the Human Mind*, 1795

Beyond the West

Mughal Empire, India, 1526–1857

Ming Dynasty, China, 1368–1644

Qing Dynasty, China, 1644–1912

♦ Portuguese capture Malacca (Malaysia) and the Moluccas, 1511–13

♦ Ferdinand Magellan claims Philippines for Spanish crown, 1521

♦ Japanese expel Christian missionaries, 1614

♦ Dutch wrest Malacca from Portuguese, 1641

♦ Viceroyalty of New Granada created, 1717

♦ Viceroyalty of Rio de la Plata created, 1776

THE AGE OF REASON

Science, Schooling, and Thought in Early Modern Europe

1500–1780

KEY TOPICS

◆ **New Heaven, New Earth:** Scientists ranging from Copernicus to Newton transform Western models of the cosmos (now it would be infinite, governed by universal laws, and defined by mathematics); they explore the workings of the human body, search for clear, distinct truths, and discard magic and superstition.

◆ **The Lights Go On:** Demanding hard facts, and guided by clear reason, the *philosophes* question

the norms governing politics and society, and create the culture of the Enlightenment.

◆ **A Little Learning:** In an era of greater educational opportunities, as printing presses produce pamphlets, newspapers, and books, ideas are more rapidly disseminated than ever before and the rate of literacy rises.

Descartes' Dilemma *During a pause in the Thirty Years' War (1618–1648), the French nobleman René Descartes (1596–1650) turned his mind to a basic but important question: did he in fact exist? His senses of vision and touch told him that he was alive—but could he rely upon their evidence? In an anxious mental exercise, he stripped away from his consciousness everything he knew by means of his senses. Only one clear, distinct idea remained: his doubting, thinking mind. And if he was thinking, he concluded, he must exist. He announced his conclusion: "I think, therefore I am."*

Cogito ergo Sum

This statement in Descartes' *Discourse on Method* (1637), which is also quoted in *Witnesses* on p. 493, marks the beginning of modern **rationalism**, the principle that human reason is the source of knowledge. Where medieval rationalism had used logical arguments to prove the existence of God, Descartes would deduce God's existence from his own—the first step in a new way of thinking that would shift the attention of European thinkers from the divine to the physical world.

Descartes' thought epitomizes the intellectual culture of the early modern era. From 1500 to 1750, European thinkers remapped the universe and unveiled the workings of the human body. They created the scientific method, reformulated the rules of logic, and distinguished verifiable truth from magic and superstition. Applying the test of reason to social institutions and assumptions, they opened the door to fundamental change in the way Europeans lived. Making their ideas available to an ever-growing public, they even included in their number some women, who employed the tools of reason to advance the condition of their peers.

NEW HEAVEN, NEW EARTH: THE SCIENTIFIC REVOLUTION

During the early modern period, a series of thinkers including Descartes transformed the way Europeans viewed the universe and laid the foundations of modern scientific thought. In the Middle Ages, the universe had been seen as a closed system, controlled by God, centered on the earth and its human inhabitants. Now it became an infinite system that governed itself by immutable, natural laws.

While these scientists taught Europeans to see "a new heaven, and a new earth" (in the prophetic words of the Biblical writer of *Revelations*), others investigated the structure of the human body and the human mind—all became aspects of nature to be explored and known in their own right, not simply celebrated as evidence of God's creative powers. This expansion of the field of human inquiry, and the new

methods used to pursue it, constitute what some historians term the **Scientific Revolution**.

The Advent of Infinity

The creation of a new world system entailed a changed conceptualization of the place of the human and the divine in an immeasurable cosmos. The old model of the universe had prevailed for some 1400 years, since it was formulated by the ancient Greek mathematician, geographer, and philosopher Ptolemy (second century C.E.; see Chapter 5). It was geocentric—the earth stood at its center, circled by the planets and stars, including the sun. Complex patterns of the planetary paths were devised to make the geocentric model plausible. European philosophers of the Middle Ages added a Christian dimension to the **Ptolemaic** cosmos: they imagined the movements of

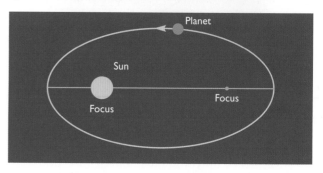

Anonymous, Portrait of Johann Kepler: *Johann Kepler (1571–1630), astronomer and imperial mathematician, lent new force to the Copernican hypothesis of a sun-centered system when he proved that the planets moved in regular and predictable ways that could be clearly explained mathematically—and thus opened a route that would lead to the work of Galileo and Newton. Also shown is a figure illustrating the first of his laws of motion in which orbits are not circles as previously believed. (Munster, Strassburg)*

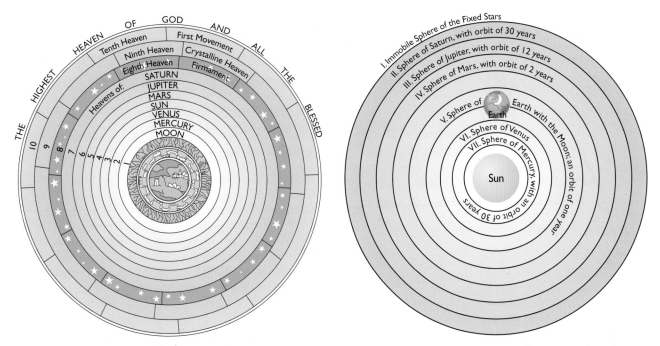

Mapping the heavens: *The Scientific Revolution saw the creation of a new cosmology (an understanding of the shape and structure of the universe). The medieval view had placed the stationary earth in the center of a finite universe composed of concentric crystalline spheres (above left). Each sphere rotated about the earth, carrying with it one or more of the heavenly bodies. God himself moved the outermost sphere, thereby causing all motion in the universe. This model was shattered by Nicholas Copernicus who in 1543 proposed that the sun was central and that the earth was the third planet from the center (above right). Copernicus retained other elements of the medieval view, however, in that his universe was still finite and composed of crystalline spheres.*

the planets and stars to describe a series of spheres within spheres, contained in a vast outer sphere on which were fixed the most remote stars. Outside the outermost sphere lay the realm of God and his angels, who guided the motion of the spheres. The diagram, top left, shows the medieval view of the universe in which the earth formed the stationary center.

Nicholas Copernicus   Nicholas Copernicus (1473–1543), a Polish cleric who had studied Greek, astronomy, and medicine in Cracow and Italian universities, was the first to challenge the Ptolemaic model. He rejected the accepted patterns of planetary motion. In his reading of Greek texts, he encountered the theory of a sun-centered system first proposed by Aristarchus of Samos in the third century B.C.E. (see Chapter 5). If the earth were understood to move around the sun, Copernicus argued, everything else fell into place: "if the motions of the other planets are connected with the orbiting of the earth … not only do their phenomena [movements] follow therefrom but also the order and size of all the planets and spheres, and heaven itself is so linked together that in no portion of it can anything be shifted without disrupting the remaining parts and the universe as a whole." Although he had formed his theory by around 1530, Copernicus did not publish his epochal work *On the Revolutions of the Celestial Spheres* until 1543, when he was on his deathbed and beyond the reach of critics (an extract is given in *Witnesses* on p. 486). The diagram on the right above illustrates Copernicus's ideas.

Against Copernicus' ideas were ranged centuries of tradition and the weight of orthodox Christian thought. The validation of his theory by later scientists over the following 150 years firmly established the new world order of the Scientific Revolution.

Brahe, Kepler, and Bruno   Born three years after Copernicus' death, the Danish nobleman Tycho Brahe (1546–1601) gathered meticulous astronomical records from a well-equipped observatory built to his own design. Situated in Brahe's castle on his private island—both gifts from his royal patron, Frederic II of Denmark, it contained a model of the globe 5 feet (1.5m) in diameter. While Brahe's astronomical observations, including sensational sightings of a supernova (a super-bright, exploding star) in 1572 and a new comet in 1577, led him to reject the Ptolemaic model, he never fully accepted the Copernican system. He maintained that the sun revolved around the earth, while the other planets revolved around the sun. Brahe nevertheless provided the data from which later scientists could pursue the implications of Copernicus' theory.

Some of the materials Brahe left unpublished on his death were edited by his assistant at the imperial court at Prague (where Brahe had settled in his last years), the German mathematician and mystic Johannes Kepler (1571–1630). Kepler employed Brahe's data of celestial motion to test the Copernican theory, concluding that nature operated in regular patterns that could be described mathematically. By 1619, Kepler

Pioneers of a New Cosmology

During the sixteenth and seventeenth centuries, European philosophers—the ancestors of modern scientists—fundamentally reconstructed the human understanding of the universe. Previously an expression of the divine will, the universe was now a giant machine that operated according to rational, indeed mathematical, principles. Nicolaus Copernicus was the first of a series of thinkers to generate this new cosmological understanding, which reached its culmination in Isaac Newton's work. Their principal claims are presented in brief in these passages.

Copernicus claims that the earth rotates (1543): [Copernicus criticizes earlier thinkers whose calculations did not explain planetary motion correctly and whose methods were inconsistent.] I pondered long upon this uncertainty of mathematical tradition in establishing the motion of the system of the spheres. ... I therefore took pains to read again the works of all the philosophers on whom I could lay hand to seek out whether any of them had ever supposed that the motions of the spheres were other than those demanded by the mathematical schools. ... [Copernicus soon finds that certain antique authors had suggested the earth itself moves.] Taking advantage of this I too began to think of the mobility of the Earth ... [and] ... by long and frequent observations I have at last discovered that, if the motions of the rest of the planets be brought into relation with the circulation of the Earth and be reckoned in proportion to the orbit of each planet, not only do their phenomena presently ensue, but the order and magnitudes of all stars and spheres, nay the heavens themselves, become so bound together that nothing in any part thereof could be moved from its place without producing confusion of all the other parts and the Universe as a whole. [Having established the motion of the earth, Copernicus carries on to describe other aspects of his cosmology including the order of the planets, with the sun at the center.]
(Copernicus, *On the Revolutions of the Celestial Spheres*, 1543; ed. M. Munitz, 1957)

Newton defines the whole burden of philosophy—to explain the universal system (1687): I offer this work as the mathematical principles of philosophy, for the whole burden of philosophy seems to consist in this: from the phenomena of motions to investigate the forces of nature, and then from these forces to demonstrate the other phenomena; and to this end the general propositions in the first and second Books are directed. In the third Book I give an example of this in the explication of the System of the World; for by the propositions mathematically demonstrated in the former Books, in the third I derive from the celestial phenomena the forces of gravity with which bodies tend to the sun and the several planets. Then from these forces, ... I deduce the motions of the planets, the comets, the moon, and the sea. I wish we could derive the rest of the phenomena of Nature by the same kind of reasoning from mechanical principles, for I am induced by many reasons to suspect that they may all depend upon certain forces by which the particles of bodies ... are either mutually impelled towards one another ... or are repelled and recede from one another. These forces being unknown, philosophers have hitherto attempted the search of Nature in vain; but I hope the principles here laid down will afford some light either to this or some truer method of philosophy.
(Isaac Newton, *Mathematical Principles of Natural Philosophy*, Vol. I, 1687; ed. Cajori, 1974)

An island of knowledge: *The astronomers of the sixteenth- and early-seventeenth centuries worked with relatively simple equipment. Tycho Brahe's observatory at Stjerneborg in Denmark was considered to be state-of-the-art in around 1600.*

had developed three principles or "laws" of planetary motion around the sun, still accepted today. The first demonstrated that the planets moved in ellipses, not circles around the sun. The second demonstrated that planets moved at varying speeds in their elliptical orbits, so that the area of the ellipse defined by their path and their radii drawn to the sun were equal in any period of time. The third revealed a mathematical harmony in cosmic relationships that was doubtless most gratifying to a mystic such as Kepler—namely that the square of the period of each planet's revolution is proportional to the cube of its mean distance from the sun. The planets danced like ballerinas according to a common script, written in numbers.

When Kepler was still a young man, the Italian philosopher and Dominican friar Giordano Bruno (?1548–1600) was burned at the stake, charged with pantheism (the concept that the universe and God are ultimately identical). Bruno's theories included the claim that the universe was infinite, and composed of innumerable irreducible elements. Bruno's theory of infinity was not based either on observations such as Brahe's or on the scholarly examination of ancient theories undertaken by Copernicus: he was an original thinker who believed that the perceptions of the human mind were conditioned by a person's spatial, chronological, and even psychological position. The universe might roll on for ever, and anything conceivable by the mind might be true, in some universe or other. Bruno's concept of an infinite universe contributed to the definitive revision of European ideas of the shape and extent of the cosmos, inaugurating the modern conception of the world.

MUST READS

Books that Made the Scientific Revolution

Nicholas Copernicus — *On the Revolutions of the Celestial Spheres* (1543)

Andreas Vesalius — *On the Structure of the Human Body* (1543)

Francis Bacon — *The Advancement of Learning* (1605)

William Harvey — *Circulation of the Blood* (1628)

Johannes Kepler — *New Astronomy* (1609)

Galileo Galilei — *The Starry Messenger* (1610)

Isaac Newton — *Mathematical Principles of Natural Philosophy* (1687)

Galileo Galilei The new spirit of inquiry emphasised the need to support theories about the material world with observation—the basis of modern scientific method. To make possible more accurate observation of the heavens, the mathematician, musician, and philosopher Galileo Galilei (1564–1642) employed techniques learned from a Dutch lens-grinder to construct the first astronomical telescope, which is illustrated on the right. From 1609, he used this to verify Copernican theory and record many

Galileo's telescope: *Galileo's remarkable telescope changed forever people's long-standing beliefs in an earth-centered system. Revealing for the first time new heavenly bodies for which existing cosmologies did not allow, and unanticipated fluxes and imperfections in those already known, it lent support to the Copernican hypothesis that the earth and other planets orbited around the sun. (Galileo Galilei, telescope, 1609; Museo delle Scienza, Florence)*

Science and Religion in Conflict

As the astronomer and physicist Galileo Galilei was to learn most powerfully in 1633—when his views were condemned by a tribunal of the Inquisition and he was forced, if insincerely, to abjure them—religion could act most powerfully against science. In the first of these passages, Galileo explains to the duchess of Tuscany that the truths of scripture, which are for human salvation, are distinct from the truths of natural phenomena, which derive from the evidence of our senses. In the second, Newton assures a clerical correspondent that his principles of motion argue for causation by a rational divine power.

Writing to Grand Duchess Christina, Galileo distinguishes scientific from theological inquiry (1615): I am inclined to think that Holy Scripture is intended to convince men of those truths which are necessary for their salvation, and which being far above man's understanding cannot be made credible by any learning, or by any other means than revelation. But that the same God who has endowed us with senses, reason, and understanding, does not permit us to use them, and desires to acquaint us in another way with such knowledge as we are in a position to acquire for ourselves by means of those faculties—that, it seems to me I am not bound to believe, especially concerning those sciences about which the Holy Scriptures contain only small fragments and varying explanations; and this is precisely the case with astronomy, of which there is so little that the planets are not [even] all enumerated. ... I think that in discussing natural phenomena we ought not to begin with texts from Scripture but with experiment and demonstration, for from the Divine Word Scripture and nature do alike proceed.
(From J. J. Fahie ed., *Galileo: His Life and Work*, 1903)

Writing to Reverend Bentley, Newton explains God's indispensable role in the Newtonian universe (December 10, 1692): When I wrote my treatise about our system [*Mathematical Principles of Natural Philosophy*, published in 1687], I had an eye upon such principles as might work with considering men for the belief of a Deity; and nothing can rejoice me more than to find it useful for that purpose. ... The motions which the planets now have ... could not spring from any natural cause alone, but were impressed by an intelligent Agent. ... Nor is there any natural cause which could give the planets those just degrees of velocity, in proportion to their distances from the sun and other central bodies, which were requisite to make them move in such concentric orbs about those bodies. ... To make this system, therefore, with all its motions, required a cause which understood and compared together the quantities of matter in the several bodies of the sun and planets and the gravitating powers resulting from thence. ... [A]nd to compare and adjust all these things together, in so great a variety of bodies, argues that cause to be, not blind and fortuitous, but very well skilled in mechanics and geometry.
(From M. Munitz ed., *Theories of the Universe*, 1957)

---

other observations. He saw the spots on the sun and the mountainous surface of the moon; he found that Jupiter had satellites and Saturn rings, and that the Milky Way was made up of innumerable stars.

Galileo announced his discoveries in his *Starry Messenger* (1610), winning public applause and offers of patronage. He also gained enemies as the forces of intellectual and religious orthodoxy turned against him, in particular church leaders who, still engaged in the mission of Catholic Reformation (see Chapter 14), maintained that the Copernican theory was contrary to faith. In 1632, a generation after his observations had finally consigned the Ptolemaic cosmos to the realms of fiction, Galileo published his *Dialogue Concerning the Two Chief World Systems*. Constructed as a dialogue between proponents of the Ptolemaic and Copernican cosmic models, it unequivocally supported the latter. Galileo chose to write in Italian, rather than in Latin, the language still used for scholarly publications throughout Europe, which meant that his work could reach a wider audience in his own country. In 1633, a church court examined Galileo and ordered him to repudiate his views. Threatened with torture, he acceded—an act that one modern philosopher termed "the crime of Galileo." (In 1992, more than six centuries later, the Church at last reversed Galileo's conviction.) Still, church condemnation did not halt the widespread circulation of Galileo's ideas. He had shattered existing frontiers to formulate the possibility of a universe that was wholly without center or boundary: an infinitude of bodies that was unthinkably remote.

Galileo was also a pioneer physicist. He used new equipment and experimentation to reveal flaws in prevailing beliefs about the nature and behavior of matter, which were largely derived from the writings of the Greek philosopher Aristotle (384–322 B.C.E.). Galileo described the law of falling bodies (that they fall at exactly the same rate of acceleration regardless of their weight) and discovered the law of pendular motion (that any pendulum takes the same amount of time to traverse its maximum and minimum arcs). He contested Aristotle's view that the natural condition of material bodies was to be at rest: according to Galileo (and modern physics since that time), matter was naturally in motion.

Isaac Newton It was the English scientist Isaac Newton (1642–1727) who went on to discover the principles that governed the limitless universe imagined by Bruno and investigated by Galileo, thus completing the early modern reconceptualization of the world system. In his *Mathematical Principles of Natural Philosophy* (1687; an extract from the introduction is given in *Witnesses* on p. 486), published in Latin, Newton defined the principle of universal gravitation. Gravity explained the movements of earthly and celestial bodies, providing the new world system with a unity and coherence that seemed to have been lost when Copernicus had removed the earth from the center of the cosmos a century and a half before. Newton further elaborated three laws of motion that have served as a framework for physical mechanics ever since. He also developed the branch of mathematics known as calculus and demonstrated using a glass prism that white light could be split into the sequence of colors that make up the spectrum.

Despite the breakthrough concepts they developed, early modern scientists worked squarely within the framework of the medieval intellectual tradition they transcended. They were considered "natural philosophers," whose range of inquiry embraced the whole material universe. This lack of more closely defined specialization helps explain the versatility of a Galileo or a Newton, who ranged easily from mathematics to physics to astronomy. Moreover, these early scientists used Latin, the universal language of learning in Europe, to communicate their findings across languages (Polish, Danish, German, Italian, English) and religious divides—Copernicus and Galileo were Roman Catholic; Brahe, Kepler, and Newton Protestant—while also permitting them to speak to the generalists among their educated public.

"Man the Machine": Exploration of the Human Body

Before about 1500 in Europe, the human body was unknown terrain. Ancient physicians had made extensive clinical observations and acquired some practical surgical experience, but they could not explain what they observed. In the sixteenth and seventeenth centuries, however, anatomists and physicians learned that the human being was an autonomous mechanism governed by natural laws. Exploration of the fabric of the body yielded a new model of the human being: in the words of one French writer, "man the machine." This breakthrough in medical thought was comparable to the breakthroughs in the realm of astronomy.

Ancient physicians had proposed the theory of **humors** to explain the functioning of the body. It was based on early Greek speculations, codified in the works of Galen (second century C.E.; see Chapter 6),

and repeated by Arab and Christian followers. It held that each healthy body possessed a balance of four bodily fluids: blood, black and yellow bile, and phlegm. These governed in turn four temperamental tendencies or humors—sanguine ("bloody," connoting optimism or good spirits); the black bilious (melancholic, depressed); the yellow bilious (choleric, hostile); the phlegmatic (slow and complaisant). Physicians examined their patients' bodily fluids and drained their blood, confident in their theory although dubious about the prospects of a cure. But they did not understand how or why the blood circulated, or even how a baby was conceived.

The course of medicine changed with direct exploration of the body. Renaissance artists seeking accuracy in the representation of the human form (notably Leonardo da Vinci) began to draw careful studies of its visible parts. Physicians, meanwhile, began to dissect cadavers. Progress was rapid, resulting in a new understanding of the body as a complex natural machine made up of interacting systems.

Among the first to practice the dissection of human cadavers was the Flemish anatomist Andreas Vesalius (1514–1564). He demonstrated his art at the university of Padua in Italy. In 1543, the same year as the publication of the Copernican theory, Vesalius published his *On the Structure of the Human Body*, which helped dismantle the Galenic system. The illustration from its title page on p. 490 shows him performing a dissection.

The ancient humoral theory, meanwhile, had already been challenged by the Swiss physician Theophrastus von Hohenheim, known by his Latin name Paracelsus (1493–1541). A systematic observer, inspired though he was by the false science of **alchemy**, Paracelsus experimented with a number of chemicals as therapies and developed some effective new treatments, such as opiates to kill pain. An experienced surgeon, Paracelsus also compiled in the German of ordinary readers the first practical surgical manual.

Vesalius' approach was pursued by the English physician William Harvey (1578– 1657), who proclaimed: "I profess to learn and teach anatomy not from books but from dissections, not from the tenets of philosophers but from the fabric of nature (see *Witnesses*, p. 493)". Having acquired his medical degree in Padua, he returned to London to practice and teach, serving eventually as court physician to James I and Charles I. His most important discovery was that the blood circulated through the body via arteries and veins, propelled by the heart functioning as a pump, as shown in the diagram on the left. The implications of Vesalius' observations, Paracelsus' experiments, and Harvey's hypothesis were not to be fully realized until the nineteenth century. In the mean time, however, some patients began to benefit from their proposals. On the battlefields of sixteenth- and seventeenth-century Europe, surgeons learned to close wounds without cautery (sealing with a hot iron), to improve amputation techniques on limbs that could not be restored to function, and to apply prosthetic devices. And in the domestic realm, doctors, shouldering midwives aside, began to deliver babies.

For the first time, anatomists began to understand how the female body functioned differently from the male. Ancient tradition on this issue was divided: according to the Aristotelians, the female body was that of a "defective male," and the male sperm was the sole cause of the creation of new life. The woman's uterus merely housed the growing fetus until the moment of birth. The Galenists took a more positive view of the female role in conception and gestation, hypothesizing that the fetus was formed by the conjunction of the male sperm and "female seed." This

theory accorded women's bodies greater respect than in the Aristotelian formulation, and was at least one step closer to what modern biology knows to be the case. In the seventeenth century, physicians began to develop the fields of gynecology and obstetrics (the study of the female body and of childbearing respectively). First among them was William Harvey, who made important observations of embryonic growth in animals, which resulted in a better understanding both of the female role in conception and gestation, and of general female dysfunctions and diseases.

At this point, the male medical establishment collided with the midwives. These were women who, over the generations, often from mother to daughter, transmitted what knowledge there was of the process of giving birth. Midwives guided women in their pregnancy and prepared them for labor; they knew when the fetus was well-positioned, and when its position needed to be adjusted by a skilled woman's hand (as shown in the woodcut above), and they knew when there was no hope, but that mother and child would perish. Midwives directed a team of female relatives and friends through the birth process. After the birth, they instructed the mother in the care of her child, and the personal care she needed to recover from the experience of giving birth.

Discovering the Human Body

Dissecting the body: *The sixteenth and seventeenth centuries saw a revolution in notions about human biology. An increasing reliance on experiment and empiricism began to replace subservience to the texts of the great anatomists of antiquity such as Aristotle and Galen. This illustration from the title page of Andreas Vesalius' On the Structure of the Human Body, 1543, shows Vesalius breaking with tradition by doing his own dissections.*

Over the early modern centuries, male physicians took over the power to manage birth. By the eighteenth century, the forceps had been developed to aid in the extraction of an infant in a difficult birth. Their use was limited to trained physicians, all male, who warned future mothers of the dangers they faced from "untrained" midwives.

Progress in medicine also made an impact in the treatment of disease. Although physicians did not yet know that microbes or viruses caused disease, they understood that disease had objective causes, and that it required strenuous treatment. In the early eighteenth century, during a stay in the Ottoman Empire, Lady Mary Wortley Montagu (1689–1762), wife of the English ambassador to Constantinople (modern Istanbul), observed the practice of smallpox inoculation, in effect the deliberate infection of the patient with a mild case of the disease. She had her own children vaccinated, and championed smallpox prevention in England on her return in 1721. Later in the century, Edward Jenner (1749–1823) refined the vaccine, and smallpox became the first disease to be conquered by medical science—both advances saving millions of lives.

Midwifery and childbirth: *Trained in the new culture of science, the male-dominated medical establishment frequently discredited earlier practices. In some cases, women were pushed out of fields they had traditionally dominated. Such is the case with midwifery, which had once been almost exclusively a female occupation, as shown here in this 1554 woodcut.*

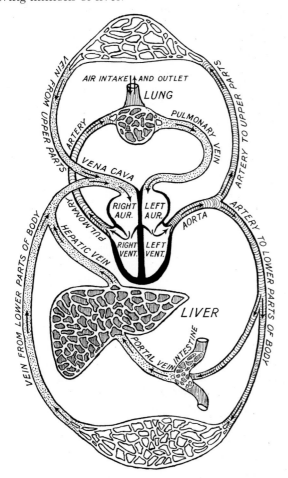

Circulation of the blood: *William Harvey's theories about the circulation of blood through veins and arteries, explained here in his diagram, were backed up by simple, yet highly effective empirical proofs.*

Hard Facts and Pure Reason: New Modes of Thinking

Advances in science in the early modern period owed much to the development of new modes of thinking. Trained in critical methods (and the Greek language) by Renaissance humanists (see Chapter 13), philosophers began to develop original systems of metaphysics. They created methods of reasoning that, unlike the propositions and syllogisms of medieval disputation, enabled scientific inquiry. They doubted everything, including the authority, once supreme, of Aristotle; and the assumptions, once self-evident, of Christianity. They studied nature more than reports of nature, and saw that its framework could be described in the language of mathematics. They accepted the evidence of indisputable facts, often gathered through experimentation. They trusted in, and could often demonstrate, the fundamental rationality of the world.

Aristotle continued to reign for 200 years after the humanist Lorenzo Valla (1405–1457) challenged his monopoly (see Chapter 13). While Aristotelianism stood for the old world order, it could also become a weapon against traditional ideas, as when the Italian

Map 17.1 The Major Scientific Thinkers and Philosophes: *Both the Scientific Revolution and Enlightenment were transnational movements, whose major exponents hailed from a variety of national, cultural, and religious backgrounds. Though it is true that the culture of science flourished best in Protestant countries, many of the most important thinkers came from, lived in, and wrote in Catholic countries.*

Pietro Pomponazzi (1462–1524) challenged the central Christian doctrine of the immortality of the soul: how could the soul be immortal, when it was so thoroughly enmeshed with the material body?

Such explorations of the possibilities of Aristotelianism during the sixteenth century paved the way for the development in the seventeenth century of philosophies spun out of pure reason. For the French nobleman René Descartes, the Dutch-Jewish lens-grinder Benedict Baruch de Spinoza (1632–1677), and the German nobleman and politician Gottfried Wilhelm von Leibniz (1646–1716), the universe, or nature itself, was perfectly rational. According to Descartes, everything in the universe

was either mind (a "thinking substance") or body (an "extended substance"), and the universe itself a vortex of matter directed by a thinking mind. Descartes' followers, who made up the Cartesian school, sustained this clean separation of matter from mind, substance from spirit.

For Spinoza, the universe was one single substance, alternately Nature or God himself, a perfect amalgam of matter and reason. In a significant break with Judeo-Christian thought, Spinoza saw God as enmeshed in nature, no longer a purely spiritual being capable of judging and directing the cosmos. His heterodoxy caused him to be expelled from the Jewish community of Amsterdam in 1656.

Leibniz, in contrast, won wide acclaim, and was courted by the princes of central Europe. He acknowledged the existence of a wholly immaterial God, the creator of the universe, and, like his own creation, infinite in space and time. But that universe was self-sufficient in its operations—consisting of a divinely ordained, perfectly ordered infinitude of immaterial particles, called "monads," each constituting a mirror of the whole, harmonious universe.

Other early modern thinkers, inspired by ancient texts, adopted the philosophical outlook of **skepticism**: an attitude of universal doubt. Whereas in the eleventh century the medieval philosopher Saint Anselm stated "I believe in order to understand," these men doubted in order to know. Descartes doubted the evidence of sense experience but proposed instead a logical method of **deducing**

further principles from essential first principles—this was the **deductive** method, based ironically on a faith in the capacity of pure reason.

French mathematician Blaise Pascal (1623–1662) doubted the capacity of reason to know anything: the only source of certainty for human beings, he argued, was a faith based not on tradition but on probability. For the Scots philosopher David Hume (1711–1776), even hard facts offered no truly dependable knowledge, let alone the vapors of mysticism. It may *appear* that the hammer strikes the nail, Hume argued, but the relationship can never be entirely proved, as the natural world is only a sequence of impressions.

Other early modern philosophers continued to believe in the reliability of sense perception, and in the evidence of hard facts. In late Renaissance Italy, the Dominican friar Bernardino Telesio (1509–1588)

WITNESSES

Pioneers of New Scientific Methodologies

How do we know what is true? Is it from the evidence of our senses, or reasoned demonstration—from an experiment, or from a logical proof? These were questions that occupied the philosophers of the new science in the seventeenth century. In these passages, two Englishmen, the philosopher Francis Bacon and physician William Harvey, argue for the empirical method, the derivation of knowledge from sense experience; and the French philosopher Descartes argues for the rational method, the deduction of true statements from prior truths.

From the senses to judgment—Francis Bacon advocates the Inductive Method (1620): There are and can be only two ways of searching into and discovering truth. The one flies from the senses and particulars to the most general axioms, and from these principles, the truth of which it takes for settled and immoveable, proceeds to judgment and to the discovery of middle axioms. And this way is now in fashion. The other derives axioms from the senses and particulars, rising by a gradual and unbroken assent, so that it arrives at the most general axioms last of all. This is the true way, but as yet untried.
(From H. G. Dick ed., *Selected Writings of Francis Bacon*, 1955)

Dissections not books—William Harvey defends the Empirical Method (1628): True philosophers, who are only eager for truth and knowledge, never regard themselves as already so thoroughly informed, but that they welcome further information from whomsoever and from whencesoever it may come; ... very many, on the contrary, maintain that all we know is still infinitely less than all that still remains unknown. ... Neither do they think it unworthy of them to change their opinion if truth and undoubted demonstration require them so to do. ... I profess both to learn and

to teach anatomy, not from books but from dissections; not from the positions of philosophers but from the fabric of nature. ... I avow myself the partisan of truth alone; and I can indeed say that I have used all my endeavors, bestowed all my pains on an attempt to produce something that should be agreeable to the good, profitable to the learned, and useful to letters.
(William Harvey, *Circulation of the Blood*, 1628; ed. C. D. Leake, 1931)

Truth firm and assured—the rationalism of René Descartes (1637): Inasmuch as I desired to devote myself wholly to the search for truth, I thought that I should ... reject as absolutely false anything of which I could have the least doubt, in order to see whether anything would be left after this procedure which could be called wholly certain. Thus, as our senses deceive us at times, I was ready to suppose that nothing was at all the way our senses represented them to be. As there are men who make mistakes in reasoning even on the simplest topics in geometry, I judged that I was as liable to error as any other, and rejected as false all the reasoning which I had previously accepted as valid demonstration. Finally, as the same percepts [i.e., perceptions] we have when awake may come to us when asleep without their being true, I decided to suppose that nothing that had ever entered my mind was more real than the illusions of my dreams. But I soon noticed that while I thus wished to think everything false, it was necessarily true that I who thought so was something. Since this truth, I think, therefore I am, was so firm and assured that all the most extravagant suppositions of the sceptics were unable to shake it, I judged that I could safely accept it as the first principle of the philosophy I was seeking.
(Descartes, *Philosophical Essays*, 1637; ed. J. Lafleur, 1964)

Cogito ergo Sum

argued for a systematic understanding of nature based on experience and observation in his giant work *On Nature According to Its Own Principles* (1565). Circulating widely at the end of the sixteenth century, it encouraged a preference for experienced-based, or **empirical** knowledge of the kind essential to the whole process of scientific inquiry.

Bacon, Galileo, and Locke   The English philosopher, essayist, and statesman Francis Bacon (1561–1626) took up Telesio's mission. He declared war on traditional Aristotelian philosophy, constructed from mere tissues of words, which could neither harness nature nor benefit humanity. Bacon aimed to reshape philosophy, planning to publish a *Great Instauration*, or "re-establishment," of knowledge. Parts of that project appeared in such works as *The Advancement of Learning* (1605) and the *New Method* (*Novum Organum*) (1620, a passage from which is quoted in *Witnesses* on p. 493). For Bacon, knowledge would have to be established on the observation of hard facts, without which the human being "neither knows anything nor can do anything."

First of all, the human mind must be freed of its prejudices and presuppositions, the glittering but false "idols" that people continued to worship. Bacon defined four classes of idols: the "idols of the tribe," those inherent in the human condition because of its essential nature and cultural heritage; the "idols of the cave," or the particular prejudices of individuals; the "idols of the marketplace," those shared commonplaces that arise from inaccurate understanding of words; and the "idols of the theater," the mistaken beliefs learned from unworthy others, including "the various dogmas of philosophers."

According to Bacon, the mind was to be cleared of these prejudices and presuppositions, so that it could apprehend hard facts with pure reason. Then, it would proceed by **inductive** reasoning: from observed data to more generalized statements "rising by a gradual and unbroken ascent, so that it arrives at the most general axioms last of all." The observer would systematically gather information about a phenomenon until a regular pattern emerged. From that pattern, he would form a theory, or **hypothesis**, about the phenomenon, which could be tested, verified, and expressed as a general statement. The accumulation of those general statements would amount to knowledge—or "science"—itself.

In Italy, Galileo developed the method of reasoning that would come to be called "the scientific method." Like Bacon, he held that the observation of clear facts led to universal statements. From data gathered about the movement of bodies in space, for example, theories might be devised to explain them. Impatient of waiting for sufficient data, however, and dissatisfied with their quality in the imperfect world around him, Galileo developed the method of

experiment: the staged and repeated "experiencing" of phenomena, controlled so that the factors of greatest interest are isolated and made visible. This method of inductive reasoning based on data gathered from the controlled observation of nature or from experiment remains the method of modern science.

It was Bacon the theorist rather than Galileo the experimenter who provided the inspiration for the English philosopher John Locke (1632–1704) in his advancement of the cause of inductive logic. His *Essay Concerning Human Understanding* is as important for philosophy, pedagogy, and psychology as his *Two Treatises on Civil Government* (both published 1690) (see Chapter 15) is for the development of political thought. In the former he argued against Descartes' contention that the mind contained true ideas of reality even at birth. Instead, Locke proposed that the mind at birth contained no ideas at all—it was a "blank slate," a *tabula rasa* as empty of thought as a teacher's empty blackboard. It is written on by experience. As the mind experiences things through the five senses, it forms ideas about the material world. The things come first; the mind fits thought to them, and after that, words. Everything in the mind arrives first through experience.

Consequently, evil thoughts and actions derived not from an innate evil in the soul, but from unfortunate experience in the world of things. Such moral deficiencies could be repaired, Locke implied, by a new round of more positive experience. The implications of Locke's theory of learning for social change were immense: immorality was not rooted in the soul, the blood, or the social order. It resulted simply from exposure to a poor environment. A correction of the environment would necessarily result in an improvement in mental condition.

While Bacon, Galileo, and Locke grappled with theories aimed at explaining the hard facts of material reality, others rushed to collect the facts themselves. Historians amassed documents chronicling their city's, country's, or religion's past. Others, following but surpassing Classical and Renaissance models, catalogued famous men or famous women. Surveys of topography, botany, geography, and mineralogy poured off the presses. How-to books described methods of zinc-smelting, fishing, or housekeeping; the biology of bees, birds, and silkworms; drainage and irrigation systems; the making of glass.

Other "moderns" (those who hunted for new truths in the present, in contrast to admirers of the "ancients," who studied them in the past) not only described things but also invented them. New pieces of equipment, specially devised for investigating the world with greater detail and accuracy, included the telescope, microscope, thermometer, and barometer. Measuring and calculating devices included the pendulum clock and adding machine (the last by Pascal), the mechanical pump, the flexible hose for fighting fires and lightning rod for preventing them (by the American philosopher and statesman Benjamin Franklin, see Chapter 20), new uses for windmills, and early versions of the typewriter, the sock knitter, and the sewing machine.

The new curiosity about, and desire to master, material reality is evidenced in the rush of discovery, invention, and data-collection that characterized the seventeenth and eighteenth centuries. That absorption in the concrete, the manipulable, the massive, and the movable contrasted both with the passive contemplation of the Middle Ages and the intellectual and aesthetic values of the Renaissance, with its passion for the past and its idealizing quest for truth, beauty, and perfection. The new age was more concerned with how things worked than whether they had reached the highest pitch of perfection—more interested in science, in sum, than in art.

The End of Magic

In a new world where facts were hard and reason prevailed, magical explanations of events were doomed. During the Renaissance, the possibilities of magic had expanded, boosted by learned humanists for whom ancient magical beliefs were as intriguing as ancient knowledge. Two centuries later, however, confidence in magical constructs withered among the learned, and took a last refuge in peasant huts and villages. Reason was the solvent that put an end to magic.

The most widely accepted form of secular magical thought was **astrology**, the study of the ways in which heavenly bodies supposedly affected human life. Until well into the seventeenth century, astrology remained a respectable branch of knowledge. Physicians, especially, were likely to boast secondary expertise as astrologers, and rulers routinely consulted astrologers about the best place to build a palace or the best time for a military expedition. The citizens of the republic of Venice included a horoscope of their city in public chronicles, knowing that it promised Venice a long and prosperous future, while an English astrologer accurately predicted the critical but unlikely 1645 Parliamentary victory in England's Civil War and the later, unprecedented execution of the king.

By the time Newton published his *Mathematical Principles* (1687), however, it was no longer possible for the educated elites to accept the principles of astrology. In a universe systematically ordered and governed by laws expressed in mathematical relationships, there was no room for mysterious communications between the heavens and the earth. Astrology retreated to the margins, to become a lure to the untutored and a pastime for the privileged.

Meanwhile, science made other inroads on the domain of the occult. Occult or "hidden" knowledge at the beginning of the early modern period included

---

HOW MANY?

Witchcraft Trials: Centres of Activity, Numbers Tried, and Percentages Executed as a Result

Place	Dates	Number of people tried (where outcome is known)	% executed
Dept of the Nord, France	1542–1679	187	48
Essex	1560–1672	291	24
Finland	1520–1699	710	16
Fribourg	1607–83	162	33
Geneva	1537–1662	318	21
Guernsey	1563–1634	78	46
Hungary	1520–1777	932	48
Luxembourg	1509–1687	547	69
Namur	1509–1646	270	54
Neuchâtel	1568–1677	341	63
Norway	1551–1760	730	38
Pays de Vaud	1537–1630	102	90
Scotland	1563–1727	402	54

Distribution of Witches Between the Sexes

MEN 24%

WOMEN 76%

Based on a sample of 8,738 people tried for witchcraft in Southwest Germany, the bishopric of Basel, Franche-Comté, Geneva, Namur, Luxembourg, Dept of the Nord, Castile, Aragon, Venice, Finland, Estonia, Russia, Hungary and New England (U.S.A) in the sixteenth–eighteenth centuries. The lowest percentage of women tried for witchcraft is in Russia, 1622–1700, where out of 136 people accused, only 32 percent were female. In Basel, 1571–1670, on the other hand, out of 190 people tried, 95 percent were female. In New England, 1620–1725, out of 242 people tried, 78 percent were female.

Source: *Brian P. Levack,* The Witch-Hunt in Early Modern Europe *(2nd edition, Longman, 1995)*

much of what later became modern physics, chemistry, and biology. Occultists were mainstream thinkers who strove to learn much about many things: among them were Paracelsus, Brahe, and Kepler. Newton, proponent of a grandly rational view of the cosmos, was an alchemist who believed in the possibility of transforming elements into each other and creating more valuable substances from baser ones. The varied range of experiments conducted by alchemists, which involved heating, mixing, dissolving, and generally observing the behavior of many different substances, contributed directly to the development of the modern science of chemistry.

As astrology became distinct from astronomy, and chemistry from alchemy, the field of magic was shrinking. "White" magic, in other words those practices, including astrology and alchemy, by which the course of nature could be understood and altered, was yielding to science. "Black" magic, namely practices intended to cause harm, was already in deep disrepute—the "witches" condemned of such practices were hounded into obedience or tried and executed (see Chapter 14 and *How Many?* on p. 495). By the mid-seventeenth century in much of Europe, however, the prosecution of witches had ceased. Rational thought could no longer entertain the possibility of nocturnal black sabbaths or aerial broomstick escapades.

As witches disappeared from towns and villages, so monsters disappeared from maps. **Cartography,** the science of mapmaking, which had been immensely stimulated by the discoveries and voyages of the fifteenth and sixteenth century (see Chapter 16), now became rationalized and, like astronomy, mathematicized. Legendary monsters vanished from their positions at the previously uncharted ocean peripheries of the maps of the world to be replaced with the parallels and meridians that quantified and codified space and dealt magic another blow.

Magic did not die entirely. Uneducated people continued to believe in what the learned called superstitions. Among the educated, the figure of the practitioner of magic—so much more than what modern people think of as a "magician"—had an afterlife in literature and drama as the passion-stirred individualist, ceaselessly but fatally curious and creative. That figure, epitomizing heroic modern humanity in its desire to stretch the boundaries of what can be known or achieved, was immortalized in the play *Doctor Faustus* by the English author Christopher Marlowe (1564–1593). Three centuries later, Faust returned in German drama and French opera.

By 1750, for intellectuals and their audience, magic had largely died and credence in traditional authority had faded. Replacing them were faith in pure reason and a commitment to hard empirical facts, in an infinite world perceived through the senses of the body, which was in essence a machine. The "disenchantment" of the world, in the words of the twentieth-century German sociologist Max Weber, had finally been accomplished.

THE LIGHTS GO ON: THE ENLIGHTENMENT

Science and philosophy cleared away the magical beliefs and stale orthodoxies of an intellectual tradition dating back to antiquity. In the clean air and bright light of a new mental age, intellectuals in late seventeenth- and eighteenth-century Europe turned from science and metaphysics to society. Now they inquired into how people lived and how they were governed. These thinkers are known by the French term *philosophes* (the most important books they wrote are listed in *Must Reads* below). They created the era known as the "**Enlightenment.**"

The Enlightenment was the predominant intellectual movement of the century extending from England's Glorious Revolution of 1688 (see Chapter 15) and the greatest works of Locke and Newton to the outbreak of the French Revolution in 1789 (see Chapter 20). Centered in France and England, it was also a powerful trend in Scotland, Italy, and the Netherlands, in some of the German courts and cities, and in the North American colonies. The *philosophes*

MUST READS

Books that Made the Enlightenment

Isaac Newton	*Mathematical Principles of Natural Philosophy* (1687)
John Locke	*Essay Concerning Human Understanding* (1690)
John Locke	*Two Treatises of Civil Government* (1690)
Voltaire	*Philosophical Letters* (1734)
Montesquieu	*The Spirit of Laws* (1748)
Jean-Jacques Rousseau	*The Social Contract* (1762)
Jean-Jacques Rousseau	*Émile: or On Education* (1762)
Denis Diderot and Jean d'Alembert	*Encyclopedia* (1751–81)
Condorcet	*Sketch for a Historical Picture of the Progress of the Human Mind* (1795)

Map 17.2
Subscriptions to Diderot and d'Alembert's Encyclopedia

Source: *Based on J. Merriman, A History of Europe, Vol. I: From the Renaissance to the Age of Napoleon (New York: W. W. Norton, 1996), p. 411.*

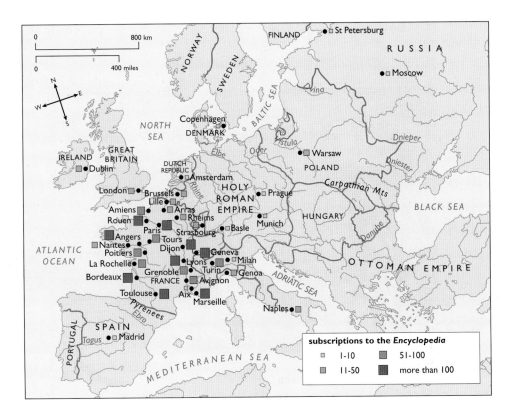

redefined the terms of Western thought and experience, discovered new foundations for political life, looked afresh at non-European places, customs, and beliefs, and drafted new blueprints for the future of humanity. At the core of the Enlightenment was the relentless deployment of reason to confront reality and to challenge traditional authority. In his 1784 essay "What is Enlightenment?," the philosopher Immanuel Kant (1724–1804) summarized the movement's mission as well as anyone can in the ringing imperative: "Dare to know!"

Common Sense

"I offer nothing but plain facts and *common sense*," wrote the English journalist and professional revolutionary Thomas Paine (1737–1809), explaining the purpose of his incendiary pamphlet (1776) of that name. Just as Descartes had sought "clear and distinct" ideas about universal reality, Enlightenment thinkers sought truths so plain and simple that they could be understood by everyone. Mere common sense would suffice.

"Common sense" was a deceptively innocent concept, as Paine well knew. It could be used as a weapon to slash through the obfuscations and pretensions of traditional culture, as by the French Huguenot refugee Pierre Bayle (1647–1706) in his *Historical and Critical Dictionary* (1695–1697). Bayle wielded common sense to demolish traditional concepts of society and thought as he redefined the very words that Europeans used. Reprinted frequently, translated, abridged, and extracted, Bayle's *Dictionary* was, as one

modern historian has called it, "a great engine of skepticism," and a "ponderous machine of war." With a copy propped on a shelf in every major library, it detached a generation of European intellectuals from traditional pieties and prejudices alike.

Some fifty years later, the French essayist, playwright, and literary critic Denis Diderot (1713–1784) masterminded the creation of a huge *Encyclopedia* (subtitled *A Classified Dictionary of the Sciences, Arts, and Trades*) that, like Bayle's *Dictionary*, redefined the outlook of the European public. The largest publishing venture of the age, it contained 60,000 brilliantly illustrated articles written by a team of authors. Publication of its thirty-five volumes took more than thirty years, beginning in 1751. The *Encyclopedia* aimed to encapsulate human knowledge. Its effect was to alter the way people thought. It provided information about such diverse subjects as farming and the soul, with entries on "history," "humanity," and the "slave trade." With a novel emphasis on science, crafts, and technology (coin stamping is illustrated on p. 498), the *Encyclopedia* told a spellbound public that dikes and waterwheels were as important as the symbols of heraldry or the calendar of saints. It sold widely, mostly in France, but also reached Madrid, Naples, and St. Petersburg at the fringes of Enlightenment Europe, as Map 17.2 above shows. In North America, Thomas Jefferson (1743–1826) and Benjamin Franklin (1706–1790) subscribed. The *Encyclopedia* won profits for the publisher and notoriety for the editors at the same time as it made the Enlightenment message the common property of the learned.

Work and Leisure

Diderot and d'Alembert's Encyclopedia: *Printed books and journals allowed a widespread diffusion of scientific ideas. The* Encyclopedia, *published in France beginning in 1751, gathered together in one easily accessible source virtually all the key ideas of the Scientific Revolution and Enlightenment. Practical subjects, such as coin stamping, illustrated here, were especially well represented.*

In his *Philosophical Letters*, Voltaire (1694–1778)—the most important *philosophe*—also sought to reinvent the universe of knowledge, urging his readers to cast off their inherited misconceptions. Its famous entry on "Religion," for example, blasted the injustices wrought in the name of God by Jews, Muslims, and especially Christians. Voltaire's savage criticism of traditional customs and beliefs is also the mainspring of his novellas *Candide, Zadig,* and *Micromégas.*

Voltaire's younger contemporary, the Swiss-born author Jean-Jacques Rousseau (1712–1778), saw in the human being an endless possibility for good that was stifled by the paraphernalia of schools, books, and teachers. In *Émile* (1762), a book now considered to be one of the foundations of modern pedagogy, Rousseau argued that the young child should learn from nature, not books, until the age of twelve. He should learn science by doing it, and history from his exploration of current issues: "It is not a question of knowing what is, but only what is useful." Tutored in this way, the child would gain a greater measure of self-confidence, as well as the good sense to learn whatever was necessary for success.

The war on tradition waged by Enlightenment thinkers necessarily involved a war on the Christian churches, whose whole history, they believed, was stained by indefensible notions and cruel practices. The whole Christian enterprise was snarlingly dubbed

by Voltaire, "*l'infâme*,"—an infamous, or detestable thing. To the apostles of common sense, the acceptance of rigid dogmas, and the act of faith itself, went directly against the imperatives of reason. The churches, in turn, had generally been either slow to accept or downright hostile to the discoveries of science, as in Galileo's case. Even the instigator of the Protestant Reformation (see Chapter 14), Martin Luther (1483–1546), cried out on first hearing of Copernicus' theory: "This fool wants to turn the whole of astronomy upside down!" Newton, however, found no contradiction between physics and faith, declaring that "the most beautiful system of the sun, planets and comets could only proceed from the … dominion of an intelligent and powerful Being … [who] endures forever and is everywhere present."

Even so, few Enlightenment thinkers were ready to do without religion altogether, and many adopted the stance of **deism**. Deists believed in "nature and nature's God," in the words of the American author of the Declaration of Independence, Thomas Jefferson, a "supreme being" and benevolent creator, who permitted the universe to operate according to natural law. They rejected wholesale the doctrines, rituals, and hierarchies of the churches—"truth has no sect," pronounced Voltaire. Others were agnostics or atheists who viewed Christianity as wholly irrelevant to the pursuit of truth; a religion full of miracles, grumbled Hume, which required a miracle for a rational man to believe in it. In such a climate of opinion, the cause of religious toleration, which was already championed by some well-known Reformation figures (see Chapter 14), acquired new support: John Locke's *Letter Concerning Toleration* (1689) urged openness to all religious expressions—except those of Roman Catholics and atheists, whom this early liberal Protestant thinker considered to be outside the margins of what could be tolerated!

One alternative to Christianity was provided in eighteenth-century Europe by Freemasonry. Blending beliefs supposedly from ancient Egyptian polytheism with the mysteries of medieval guild organization, it retained a belief in divine power and propounded an ethic of brotherly love. Opposed alike to the ceremonies of the old Church and the tyranny of traditional monarchy, it nevertheless involved the performance of complex and secret initiation rituals.

Learning from nature: *An aristocratic family puts into practice the new educational philosophies of Jean-Jacques Rousseau in this 1778 print by J. B. Simonet entitled "Here is the Law of Nature....". Rousseau criticized the earlier stress on strict discipline and book learning from an early age and stressed instead the importance of allowing young children the freedom to interact with nature, learn by experience, and develop their own innate and individual personalities.* (Metropolitan Museum of Art, New York)

Its members, who ranged from artisans and sailors to the great Voltaire, were undismayed, and Masonic lodges proliferated throughout Europe—numbering 800 in France alone on the eve of the 1789 Revolution. Freemasonry seemed to offer a secular religion to those who craved common sense.

Social Contracts

Common sense provided a corrective not only to traditional beliefs and prejudices, but also to over-abstract theory and bookish rationality. It persuaded men and women to think and act in new ways and to question the established framework of society and government. Enlightenment thinkers used it to undermine political authority in their development of the concept of a "social contract" (see Chapter 15).

In his *Second Treatise of Civil Government*, which is quoted in *Witnesses* on p. 500, John Locke saw government as a contract created by male property-owners, powered by their consent, and responsible to their interests. If government was an arrangement of this kind, its object was not to extract obedience from the subject but to avoid tyranny by the ruler. Locke's eighteenth-century followers included Montesquieu, Rousseau, and Thomas Jefferson.

In his *Spirit of Laws* (1748) the nobleman and professional *philosophe* Montesquieu (Charles-Louis de Secondat, 1689–1755) argued that laws determined the spirit of a nation, having evolved over time according to local conditions and historical accident. Public assemblies should act, in the preferred system he called "constitutionalism," to safeguard the freedom of citizens both from the arbitrariness of kings and the chaos of too free a democracy: "the government [must] be so constituted," he advised, "that one man need not be afraid of another." He also formulated the principle of the "separation of powers," in which each of the government's three functions—executive, legislative, and judicial—acts as a check and balance to the others. This distinction that Montesquieu saw as essential to good government and the preservation of liberty later became central to the world's first written national constitution, that of the United States (see Chapter 19).

Rousseau's *Social Contract* (1762) was concerned with the relation between the individual and the whole of society, whose intentions were expressed as a "general will." Each person willingly surrendered some of his natural liberty to the community of the whole in order to gain protection and security. He could do so with confidence, because the state was guided not by a monarch but by "a moral and collective body" of citizens. The individual, "in giving himself to all, gives himself to nobody." Nevertheless, the effect of Rousseau's reasoning was to elevate the "state" in relation to the individual. Freed from the usual constraints of royal or divine authority, it defined itself and decreed its own laws.

While Rousseau's theory of social contract allowed the state more power than did Locke, the English philosopher's more libertarian view was adopted by his eloquent follower across the Atlantic, the Virginian lawyer Thomas Jefferson. The core attitudes of the Enlightenment toward government are succinctly expressed in the American Declaration of Independence, which Jefferson authored (although his original language was modified by a cautious committee). In a few sentences, he recapitulated Locke's notions of government by consent and the

right to dissolve a government usurped by tyranny. To secure their natural rights of life, liberty, and happiness, he wrote, "governments are instituted among men, deriving their just powers from the consent of the governed." When the government no longer serves those ends, "it is the right of the people to alter or abolish it," and to start anew to design a government as "shall seem to them most likely to effect their safety and happiness."

The social contract theories of Enlightenment thinkers did not create, nor did they even recommend, democracy, in which all the governed participate in the machinery of government. It was still to be

WITNESSES

Visions of a Just Society

Enlightenment thinkers brought the daring and rigor of scientific exploration to the issue of human society: on what sound principles can we build a just society, they asked, and just what are the prospects for the human species? Here, Voltaire calls for universal toleration of other customs, beliefs, and opinions, to undo the legacy of hatred and conflict from the past; Locke envisions government as an agreement, or contract, between an accountable ruler and sovereign citizens; and Condorcet finds in the perfectibility of the human being the prospect of unlimited human progress.

Voltaire calls for toleration (1763): I no longer address myself to man, but to You, eternal God of all beings and of all worlds. ... You have not given us a heart to hate each other, nor hands to strangle one another. ... May You prevent our different clothes, insufficient languages, ridiculous customs, imperfect laws and foolish opinions from becoming causes for hatred and persecution. Let those who light candles in broad daylight in Your honor cherish those who content themselves with the light of the sun. ... And may the poor look upon the rich without envy, for You know that wealth and titles are unworthy reasons for vanity and pride. Have all men remember that they are brothers! ... If the plague of war is inevitable, let us not hate one another and torture each other in times of peace. And let us employ the short period of our existence in thanking You, wherever we may reside, be it in Siam or California, and in whatever language we command, for the life You have granted us.
(From V. W. Topazio ed., *Voltaire: A Critical Study of his Major Works*, 1967)

Locke sees government as a revocable social contract between ruler and ruled (1690): The reason men enter into society [create governments and laws] is for the preservation of their property; and the reason they choose and authorize a legislature is that laws may be made ... as guards and fences for the properties of all the members of the society, to limit the power ... of

every part and member of the society. ... Whenever the legislators endeavor to ... destroy the property of the people, or to reduce them to slavery under arbitrary power, they put themselves into a state of war with the people, who are thereupon absolved from any farther obedience, and are left to the common refuge, which

God has provided for all men, against force and violence. Whensoever therefore the legislature ... endeavors to grasp themselves, or put into the hands of any other, an absolute power over the lives, liberties, and property of the people; by that breach of trust they forfeit the power the people had put into their hands for quite contrary ends, and it devolves to the people, who have a right to resume their original liberty, and, by the establishment of a new legislature ... provide for their own safety and security, which is the end for which they are in society.
(John Locke, *Two Treatises of Government*, 1690; ed. C. B. Macpherson, 1980)

Condorcet envisions reason as the basis for unlimited human progress (1794): The aim of the work that I have undertaken ... will be to show by appeal to reason and fact that nature has set no term to the perfection of human faculties; that the perfectibility of man is truly indefinite; and that the progress of this perfectibility, from now onwards independent of any power that might wish to halt it, has no other limit than the duration of the globe upon which nature has cast us. This progress will doubtless vary in speed, but it will never be reversed. ... The time will ... come when the sun will shine only on free men who know no other master but their reason; when tyrants and slaves, priests and their stupid or hypocritical instruments will exist only in works of history and on the stage; and when we shall ... learn how to recognize and destroy, by force of reason, the first seeds of tyranny and superstition, should they ever dare to reappear amongst us.
(Condorcet, *Sketch for a Historical Picture of the Progress of the Human Mind*, 1795; ed. J. Barraclough, 1955, reissued 1979)

a long time before women, or men who did not own land or property, were to have any voice in the processes of government. Nevertheless, these theories formed a first step in the development of genuinely democratic political systems.

Other Places, Other Customs

As Enlightenment authors hammered out new frameworks for political life, they sometimes looked to the experience of other peoples in other places, who acted according to very different customs and beliefs. Travel literature is an ancient genre, in which a distinctly new phase began with the opening of the New World to European explorers (see Chapter 16). Inevitably, eye-witness reports of the pre-Columbian civilizations of the Americas, which had evolved quite separately from those in Europe and the East, prompted Europeans to reflect on the meaning for their own society of the other cultures of humankind. Such works as the Italian Peter Martyr's *Chronicles of the New World* (1530), the French Jean de Léry's *History of a Voyage to the Land of Brazil* (1578), and the English Richard Hakluyt's *The Principal Navigations, Voyages, Traffics and Discoveries of the English Nation* (1589) forced Europeans to revise their notion of the heroic, now played out in distant wildernesses.

In her 1688 novel *Oroonoko*, the English novelist and playwright Aphra Behn (1640–89) depicted the courageous martyrdom of a noble African king caught in the violent trap of South American slavery. A generation or so later Daniel Defoe celebrated the conquest of nature and "savage" alike by his hero Robinson Crusoe (1719), who survived abandonment in the wilderness because of his superior mental and practical skills. In his novella *Candide*, Voltaire empathized with the Amerindians of Peru, in his view victims of the extraordinary cruelty of European Jesuits. Montaigne, Diderot, and Rousseau respected, and even celebrated, the "savages" of the other hemisphere—in direct contrast to the English lexicographer Samuel Johnson (1696–1772), who grumbled that "savages" made up four-fifths of the inhabitants of the globe.

Asian and Islamic cultures also found European interpreters. China's Confucian traditions, which resembled those of the contemporary West in their lucid rationality, impressed Enlightenment *philosophes*, and Hindu and Buddhist mysticism won sympathetic students. The East, especially the Ottoman Empire—still a formidable political presence in eastern Europe although languishing—provided an exotic contrast to prosaic European customs. Voltaire situated his comic hero Zadig in ancient Babylon, and Montesquieu's satirical *Persian Letters*, supposedly written by Asian observers of contemporary France, drew on contrasting Eastern and Western perspectives in its disguised attack on French royal absolutism (see Chapter 15).

The geographical explorations of the early modern era opened up realms of previously inconceivable possibility—to one commentator, a "horizon that recedes without end." Not surprisingly, the encounter with other real worlds encouraged the creation of fictitious ones. An early example is the English author and statesman Thomas More's *Utopia* (see Chapter 14), which certainly drew on New World themes: the work's narrator is a survivor of a shipwreck in unknown seas, so that a seemingly real journey introduces a plausible but imaginary one. The Dominican friar Tommaso Campanella (1568–1639), a prisoner of the Inquisition for twenty-seven years and possibly insane, described a more extensive utopia in his *City of the Sun*. The people inhabiting a world based on the astronomy of Copernicus, Bruno, and Galileo are transformed into what they know, a condition that is defined as the only form of eternal life. Campanella's contemporary, the English philosopher Francis Bacon constructed a utopian "New Atlantis" described in a book of the same title, whose citizens utilized scientific principles as they worked to improve their daily lives. And in the Enlightenment period, the Anglo-Irish author Jonathan Swift's satire *Gulliver's Travels* (1726) criticized contemporaries and explored the indeterminacy of moral values while depicting imaginary foreign realms.

These authors shared an awareness of other worlds beyond the limits of Western civilization—known, imaginary, and possible—which allowed them to reexamine their own. In the wider arena of the unfolded globe, the old European boundaries of identity faded: "Once past the equator," wrote Denis Diderot, "a man is neither English, nor Dutch, nor French, nor Spanish, nor Portuguese"; he has become "nothing." In these shifting realities, European assumptions could be shown for what they were—intrinsically no better, sometimes more deceptive or more shallow, than those of other cultures.

Encounters with other realities stimulated European reflection on the future of humankind. One popularizer of science announced fantastically (as it then seemed) that someday human beings might walk on the moon, while the French *philosophe*, the Marquis de Condorcet (Marie-Jean-Antoine Caritat, 1743–1794) predicted phenomenal advancements for the human race. He foresaw the elimination of poverty, the extension of human life, the establishment of mass education, and the equality of the sexes in his *Sketch for a Historical Account of the Progress of the Human Mind* (1795), an extract from which is given in *Witnesses* on p. 500. It was written, ironically, while Condorcet was evading the grip of the revolutionary Terror (see Chapter 20), which perhaps prompted his suicide.

Optimism like Condorcet's, based on secular faith in reason, suffuses the products of the Enlightenment. Fundamentally, all things in heaven and on earth were perceived to be orderly, splendid, and benign. "Whatever is," as the English poet Alexander Pope (1688–1744) declared, "is right."

A LITTLE LEARNING: LITERACY AND EDUCATION

The order of the world might be essentially right, according to Pope, but understanding it was still a matter for the select few: "A little learning is a dangerous thing," he warned. Enlightenment, in his view, was for the well-educated only—it was not enough to be able to read; one needed to be widely read and intellectually well-equipped. This exclusive view did not reflect the enormous broadening of the audience for science, literature, and ideas that occurred in the early modern centuries. While the ruling classes retained their privileged access to education (for their male offspring, at least) schools in general took on a broader mission, printshops poured out books, more people read, and many wrote. Teachers and bureaucrats, women and amateurs possessing what Pope dismissed as a "little learning" now participated in the intellectual world, which extended beyond the study and university to include learned and artistic academies, fashionable salons, and public as well as private museums.

Pleasure Reading

The creation of a broader audience for the intellectual products of the early modern era can be ascribed to two institutions: the school and the printshop. Where medieval schools had trained priests and monks, and Renaissance schools the sons of wealthy merchants, despots, and noblemen, from the sixteenth through eighteenth centuries, more people in general had the chance to go to school and learn to read (the growth in literacy is shown in the table on the right). They became the reading public of the Enlightenment era, avid consumers of many types of literature and new ideas propounded in cheap, easily available printed books.

The seventeenth and eighteenth centuries saw many, varied educational initiatives as the ability to read became an increasingly essential skill. In both England and France, private endowments established hundreds of different schools for the children of certain cities, craft professions, or religious denominations. In 1698, King Louis XIV of France (r. 1643–1715) ordered the establishment of a school in each rural district. In 1714, Peter the Great of Russia (r. 1682–1725) ordered the creation of "ciphering schools" throughout the realm, to train future technicians in arithmetic and geometry. In 1763, Frederick the Great of Prussia (r. 1740–1786) decreed that elementary education was obligatory, and the Habsburg emperor Joseph II (r. 1765–1790) created

---

Literacy Rates: France and the German States

Literacy in Urban France	
1683	51%
1770	60%

Source: E. Le Roy Ladurie, The Ancien Regime: A History of France 1610–1774 (Cambridge, MA: Basil Blackwell, 1996), p. 309.

Literacy in Rural Normandy	Males	Females
Late 17th Century	37%	7%
Late 18th Century	73%	46%

Source: F. Furet and M. Ozouf, Reading and Writing Literacy in France from Calvin to Jules Ferry (New York: Cambridge University Press, 1982), p. 160.

Literacy in the German States	
c. 1500	3–4%
c. 1800	50% (Males 50–66%; Females 33–50%)

Source: J. Merriman, A History of Modern Europe: From the Renaissance to the Age of Napoleon (New York: W.W. Norton, 1996), pp. 38, 417.

The eighteenth century was a time when great numbers of Europeans learned to read and write for the first time. Though measures of literacy are notoriously inaccurate (partly because of problems defining specifically what level of ability constitutes literacy), the figures above provide a good guide to overall trends.

---

state schools in which students destined for bureaucratic positions were trained to read and write their native languages (including the Magyar, Croatian, Slovak, Romanian, and Ruthenian of the empire's ethnic minorities, in addition to German).

Some privately endowed schools were created specifically for girls, including two of the most famous schools of the era, at Port-Royal and Saint-Cyr, both in France. A century later, in Russia, Empress Catherine the Great (r. 1763–1796) founded the Smolny Institute, a school for 500 daughters of noblemen, modeled on Saint-Cyr. All of these girls' schools aimed to prepare their students for marriage and polite society, rather than for scholarship or public life, since the future leaders of society were overwhelmingly male. Wealthy boys were often tutored at home, while their sisters sometimes listened in.

At the advanced level, the European universities continued to train physicians, lawyers, clergymen, and philosophers. Their enrollments grew, however, as more laymen and students from the lesser nobility and the middle classes attended. A university education was a prerequisite for entry to the professions. Hence women, barred from universities into modern times, failed to enter professional careers. While the older universities in Italy and France experienced some stagnation, others flourished, especially in the Dutch Republic and in Scotland. New universities continued to be founded notably in the German lands, Spain, Spanish America, and British North America.

Elementary schools succeeded in raising rates of literacy in the vernacular languages in western Europe. Overall, more than fifty percent of city dwellers gained basic literacy, and not all peasants (as was once the case) were illiterate. While men attained higher literacy rates, women too experienced rising literacy. Women became an important component of the reading audience, and tended to support women authors, to read novels about women's experience, and to subscribe to periodical publications pertaining to women's lives.

While the sons of elite groups learned Latin and perhaps Greek, for most people literacy meant the ability to read the vernacular language of their state. In the early modern centuries, these vernacular languages were just becoming standardized, as on form or regional dialect took precedence over others. This process can often be linked to the emergence of a preeminent literary figure and the adoption of his works as national "classics." Dante (1265–1321) performed this service for Italian, and Luther, in his translation of the Bible, for German. The dramatist William Shakespeare (1564–1616) was a key figure in the creation of modern English, and the French language reached a similar peak in the mock-heroic works of François Rabelais (c. 1494–c. 1553). For Spanish, the novel *Don Quixote* by Miguel de Cervantes (1547–1616) is central. Some of the major scientific and philosophical works of the early modern period were likewise also written in vernacular languages, for example those by Galileo in Italian and Descartes in French.

By the seventeenth century, standardization of the grammar and spelling of European languages followed. Vernacular dictionaries became available in some languages, and boards of experts such as the French Academy, established in 1634, met to regularize and safeguard the newly formed modern languages. Latin remained into the nineteenth century (into the twentieth in parts of eastern Europe) a useful language for communicating philosophy, science, medicine, theology, law, and sometimes history. But from the seventeenth century most literature, political theory, and other ideas were expressed in the vernacular whose readership formed the widest possible circle.

The development of vernacular languages was aided by the printing press, while printing establishments benefited from larger audiences. The scope of printed material expanded as vernacular readers bought more books.

In the sixteenth century—the first full century of printing—religious and classical works dominated. The Bible, saints' lives, prayerbooks and other devotional works, were initially the works most favoured by presses and sought by readers. The war between the Protestant Reformation and Roman Catholicism from the early sixteenth century was waged in print. With regard to Classical works, the first aim was to produce clear, legible, and accurate versions of ancient Latin and Greek texts. By 1500, however, vernacular translations were being produced, making such authors as Cicero, Plutarch, and Tacitus available to a wider public.

The vernacular readership was interested in a diverse range of subjects. They bought almanacs and books on etiquette and history, animal husbandry, beermaking or viniculture, and collections of choral hymns. They read fairy tales and novels, kept abreast of things with newspapers (published daily in the big cities of the later eighteenth century) and laughed at satirical cartoons. They studied the explorers' narratives of their journeys to the New World, and sought advice about marriage, childrearing, and childbirth. These books opened a world of knowledge to audiences beyond the university and the monastery: with the Enlightenment, for the first time in Europe, the lights turned on in the homes of ordinary folk.

Major printing centers included Venice, Rome, Basel (Switzerland), Strasbourg, Antwerp, Amsterdam, London, and Paris. These cities were magnets for editors, translators, and authors from many countries, who joined intellectuals and artists in a process that stimulated new understandings.

Such a lively intellectual milieu led to the expression of unconventional ideas that often provoked official censorship, which in turn broached the issue of free speech. Many of the *philosophes'* books were censored but continued to be distributed via a covert trade in prohibited books. Bayle and Locke published their work in the safe haven of the Dutch Republic, where dissent was tolerated, but Voltaire and Diderot, in France, found some of their works condemned. Rousseau learned from a bookseller friend of the fate of his book on educational proposals: "I saw your *Emile . . .* publicly consigned to the flames in Madrid," he wrote, in front of a Dominican church one Sunday "in the presence of a whole crowd of gaping imbeciles." Demand for the book soared.

The English Puritan poet John Milton (1608–1674) addressed the problem of the regulation of ideas, hurling against a recent act of Parliament to censor "scandalous, seditious and libellous works" an elegant and impassioned defense of free speech

In Defense of The Worth of Women

Juan Luis Vives — *The Instruction of a Christian Woman* (1523)

Henry Cornelius Agrippa von Nettesheim — *On the Nobility and Preeminence of the Female Sex* (1529)

Moderata Fonte — *The Worth of Women* (1600)

Lucrezia Marinella — *The Nobility and Excellence of Women* (1601)

Marie de Gournay — *The Equality of Men and Women* (1622)

Anna Maria van Schurman — *Whether a Christian Woman should be Educated* (1650)

François Poulain de la Barre — *On the Equality of the Two Sexes* (1674)

and free thought. "For books are not absolutely dead things, but do contain a potency of life in them to be as active as the soul was whose progeny they are," Milton argued in his *Areopagitica*. "Who kills a man kills a reasonable creature, … but he who destroys a good book, kills reason itself." It is no accident that, in this environment of intellectual debate women thinkers began actively to assert the worth of the female sex and the unacknowledged capacity of the female mind.

A Cat and a Catte: Women and Learning

Marie de Gournay (1565–1645), close associate of the French essayist Michel de Montaigne, observed of the graceful creature adorning her room that there was no difference between *un chat* ("a cat") and *une chatte* ("a catte," or female cat): "the human animal is neither male nor female." That conclusion was reached—and even then, accepted by few—only after a struggle over the nature of female identity known as the *querelle des femmes* ("the debate on women").

The *querelle* had its origins in the deep misogyny of medieval literature, which presented women as vain, self-centered, deceitful, corrupting, and lecherous. Beginning with Christine de Pisan (1364–c. 1430) (see Chapter 12), a series of authors in most of the

Women and Learning

Louis Michel Dumesnil, Queen Christina of Sweden with Descartes: *Only a minority of major scientific and philosophical figures during the seventeenth and eighteenth centuries considered women to be intellectually equal to men. One such was René Descartes, who is seen here, seated at a table, engaged in tutoring Queen Christina of Sweden.* (Palace of Versailles, France)

Attributed to Jan van Belcamp, The Clifford "Great Picture": *The Englishwoman Lady Clifford, seen in the panel at left with her books in a painting from around 1646, was a contemporary of Queen Christina of Sweden and profited from a similar sort of tutoring. Contrast the portrait of Margaret Cavendish on p. 507, depicted in her library amid her fantasies but without books!* (Collection of Abbot Hall Art Gallery, England)

European languages—some male but mostly female—wrote in defense of women. Their defenses elicited a correspondingly large group of responses. Through the course of this *querelle* may be traced an increasingly sophisticated justification for the spiritual and intellectual equality of the female to the male.

The first stage of the debate included many catalogues of "women worthies"—powerful and important women in history and legend. More serious issues pertaining to women's spiritual and intellectual equality were developed by Italian humanists, especially among women humanists (see "Nogarola" in Chapter 13), whose arguments were elaborated in the sixteenth century by Erasmus (c. 1466–1536) and Vives (1492–1540), and especially by Henry Cornelius Agrippa von Nettesheim (1486–1535), a philosopher and physician who also dabbled in alchemy. Agrippa not merely defended women but proposed their supremacy. His work *On the Nobility and Preeminence of the Female Sex* was widely translated and imitated, influencing two notable seventeenth-century works: Marie de Gournay's *The Equality of Men and Women* (1622) and Lucrezia Marinella's (1571–1653) *The Nobility and Excellence of Women*. With Mary Wollstonecraft's *A Vindication of the Rights of Woman* (1792), this tradition reaches its culmination.

A closely related issue was women's capacity for education. Their defenders include the influential Dutch scholar Anna Maria van Schurman (1607–1678), whose Latin treatise *On the Capacity of the Female Mind for Learning* was widely read in translation, and her contemporary, the Englishwoman Margaret Cavendish, Duchess of Newcastle (c. 1623–1673), depicted in *Windows On* on p. 507 who grumpily complained about the limitations of her own training: "As for learning, that I am not versed in it, no body, I hope, will blame me for it, since it is sufficiently known, that our sex is not brought up to it, as being not suffered to be instructed in schools and universities." Around 1700, Cavendish's compatriot Mary Astell (1666–1731) urged the higher education of women in a kind of Protestant nunnery, set apart from male-dominated society, in her *Serious Proposal to the Ladies*. In France, meanwhile, François Poulain de la Barre (1647–1723) presented a comprehensive defense of female capacity for advanced education in his book *On the Equality of the Two Sexes*, quoted in *Witnesses* on p. 506 while Bernard de Fontenelle (1657–1757) designed his work on scientific popularization, *Conversations on the Plurality of Worlds*, as a dialogue between a philosopher and a woman. Finally, the Marquis de Condorcet advocated not only women's equal capacity for advanced education, but, additionally and unprecedentedly, their participation as citizens in public affairs. The illustrations above and on p. 504 show two women who benefitted from private tutoring; Queen Christina was taught by Descartes himself.

Women Writers   Even as the debate about women's nature and rationality reached a higher pitch, women had begun to write (see Chapters 10, 12, 13). Prior to the Renaissance, nearly all women's public writing

Women, Men, and Learning

The debate over women's capacity for knowledge began well before the Enlightenment. However, in an era that stressed reason as the essential human trait, it became all the more important for women to claim for themselves the capacity to reason. That claim is made effectively by two seventeenth-century thinkers, the male Poulain de la Barre, who argues the full equality of the sexes on the basis of their mental capacities, and Mary Astell, who advanced the argument that at least some women should pursue a serious education.

François Poulain de la Barre declares that the mind has no sex (1673): It is easy to see that sexual differences apply only to the body since ... it is only the body which is used for human reproduction; the mind is involved in reproduction only in giving its assent and, since it does this in the same way in everyone, one may conclude that it has no sex.

If one considers the mind in itself, one finds that it is equal and has the same nature in all human beings, and that it is capable of all kinds of thoughts. ... The difference between the sexes does not result from their minds. ...

This is even more obvious if we consider the head, which is the unique organ of the sciences and the place where the mind exercises all its functions. Our most accurate anatomical investigations do not uncover any difference between men and women in this part of the body. The brain of women is exactly like ours.

(François Poulain de la Barre, *On the Equality of the Two Sexes,* 1673; ed. D. M. Clarke, 1990)

Mary Astell explains why men seem to know more than women (c. 1700): There are strong and prevalent reasons which demonstrate the superiority and preeminence of the men. For in the first place, boys have much time and pains, care and cost bestowed on their education, girls have little or none. The former are early initiated in the sciences, are made acquainted with ancient and modern discoveries, they study books and men, have all imaginable encouragement. ... The latter are restrained, frowned upon, and beaten ...; laughter and ridicule, that never-failing scarecrow, is set up to drive them from the tree of knowledge. But if in spite of all difficulties nature prevails, and they can't be kept so ignorant as their masters would have them, they are stared upon as monsters, censured, envied, and every way discouraged.

(Mary Astell, *The First English Feminist: Reflections on Marriage and Other Writings;* ed. B. Hill, 1986)

was religious. Saints and nuns, writing themselves or through dictation to confessors or mentors, had contributed to the Western mystical tradition as well as to a female tradition of self-exploration. In the Renaissance, women humanists, while not departing from a Christian framework, used Classical models in their letters, orations, and dialogues, which often gave expression to strong feminist themes.

The next three centuries saw an explosion of female creativity, as the grip of a traditional intellectual culture, dominated by the university, Latin, and the priesthood, weakened. The humanist dethroning of medieval Scholasticism (see Chapter 13), the use of the vernacular, the proliferation of the printshop, the views of Locke and Descartes, which located the ability to think in a mind unformed by class, profession, or gender, and the new worlds opened by explorers or discovered by scientists, all combined to create a milieu in which women felt free to write and impelled to express themselves.

In Italy, the number of published women writers soared to around 250 for the period from 1500 to 1700. Of these, about a third continued to write on religious themes but others composed love poems (mostly courtesans), occasional letters, and moral treatises which were sought by publishers and purchased by the public in great quantity. In England and France, works by, for, and about women increased markedly in the seventeenth century.

What did women write about? Some wrote devotional works, but the proportion of these to the whole of women's production diminished sharply after 1600. Some wrote about the family, others wrote about themselves. Some joined in discussions of philosophy, science, language, and love; they wrote histories or biographies, or translated the works of famous men; they wrote poetry or **novels**, a genre which originated in the seventeenth century and was influenced by the need to address a female readership. One scholar counts 106 women authors of 568 novels writing in English before Jane Austen (1775–1817) became, as used to be thought, the "first" woman novelist.

Works about the family predominate. Women wrote diaries about their experience as mothers and wives, and guidebooks to life and manners for their children. The Jewish woman Glückel (1656–1724) of Hameln, a widow who had survived two husbands and raised twelve children, described in her memoirs the resourcefulness, diligence, and faith that allowed the family to survive in the world of seventeenth-century mid-European ghettos. Arcangela Tarabotti (1604–1652) wrote in protest of "paternal tyranny" in Catholic Italy, where fathers disposed of superfluous daughters in convents. Women wrote against the constraints of marriage, as did Mary Astell in her *Reflections on Marriage,* quoted in *Witnesses* on the left, and the Italian Moderata Fonte (1555–1592) in her dialogue on *Women's Worth.* The chief speaker

Anna Morandi Manzolini

Elisabetha and Johannes Hevelius, 1673

Margaret Cavendish, Duchess of Newcastle

Among Western nations, Italy offered perhaps the best environment for women scientists. Anna Morandi Manzolini (top), for example, made several original discoveries in anatomy and held a professorship at the University of Bologna from 1760 until her death in 1774. In many cases, women accepted and repeated arguments about their intellectual inferiority to men. Margaret Cavendish, Duchess of Newcastle (left), herself an active participant in the important scientific debates of her time, nonetheless stated that women's brains were "cold" and "soft" compared to men's. Women often worked alongside their more celebrated husbands as scientific assistants or, occasionally, as full partners. In a print from 1673 (above) Elisabetha and Johannes Hevelius take astronomical readings together using a sextant.

 To continue your investigation of this topic, please go to www.prenhall.com/king for the related **WINDOWS** on the **WEB** activity

Discourse in Salons and Academies

A. Lemonnier, The Salon of Madame Geoffrin: *Educated women played a key role in spreading Enlightenment culture through the many salons they ran. In this painting from 1812 an actor reads from Voltaire at the salon of Madame Geoffrin. Some of the most famous philosophes found a congenial atmosphere for debate and philosophy.* (Châteaux de Malmaison et Bois-Préau, France)

Members of the French Royal Academy of Sciences: *During the eighteenth century, learning became an important cultural accomplishment among the well-to-do. New ideas and philosophies were spread via various media. Of great importance were the growing number of scientific academies established from the seventeenth century on. In this 1666 tapestry by Henri Testelin, members of the French Royal Academy of Sciences gather for their inaugural meeting.* (Palace of Versailles, France)

in the latter work proclaims proudly: "I would rather die than subordinate myself to any man."

Women also participated in the discussion of pedagogy, defending the educability of women. They debated the theories of Descartes in France and Italy, and studied Platonism in England. In Italy, Lucrezia Marinella demonstrated an encyclopedic command of contemporary philosophical debates in the seventeenth century, and Laura Bassi pursued a professional scientific career in the eighteenth. The French noblewoman Emilie du Châtelet (1706–1749), Voltaire's patron and lover, worked daily on the latest problems raised by science and philosophy. In England, Lady Mary Wortley Montagu published a newspaper that discussed current philosophical and political issues.

In France, meanwhile, women acted as literary critics and promoted an elaborate, stylized manner of speaking and writing that earned them the name *les précieuses* (the precious ones). Brilliant women hosted **salons**, sessions in their homes attended by the leading men of letters of the day in which new ideas were debated and criticized. Although not themselves *philosophes* or authors, Madame Geoffrin (1699–1777), Madame du Deffand (1697–1780), and the latter's former protegée Julie de Lespinasses (1732–1776), were leaders of intellectual conversation in Paris at a time when to think was to converse, and when Paris led Europe in the generation of ideas. Madame Geoffrin's salon is shown on p. 508.

The English playwright and novelist Aphra Behn presents an outstanding case of the woman author who recognized the predicament she faced as an educated woman in a society dominated by men. During her adventurous youth she lived in the Dutch colony of Surinam in South America, served as a spy in the Netherlands, and married a Dutch businessman, whose death in 1666 when she was twenty-five freed her for a writer's career. Behn's distinctively feminist plays (successfully staged in London in the 1670s and 1680s) explored the realms of marriage and adultery, featuring plucky heroines who defied male power and greed. Her plays were among the first on the English stage to employ female actresses. Her thirteen novels may perhaps establish her, 150 years before Austen, as the first woman novelist in English. Among these is the extraordinary *Oroonoko*, set in the New World, with its uncompromising repudiation of slavery. In her own words, she faulted the prejudices that had for too long kept women from receiving a serious education:

> *Permitting not the female sex to tread,*
> *The mighty paths of learned heroes dead …*

Conscious of her talents and ambitious to win the fame due to her, she sought above all the freedom that male writers enjoyed: "If I must not because of my sex, have this freedom, I lay down my quill and you shall hear no more of me … I value fame as much as if I had been born a hero." Seeing no difference between a catte and a cat, Behn claimed her due place in the world of letters.

In the early modern centuries, women began to emerge from the subordinate position in which they had previously been placed by custom and belief. Women thinkers and writers, who first confronted on the level of language the assumptions that had kept them imprisoned, were the pioneers of that advance. Wider social change would follow later; at the end of the twentieth century, that process was not yet everywhere completed.

Halls of Reason: The Social Context

If the disputation was characteristic of the intellectual life of the Middle Ages, the collection was characteristic of the early modern period: collections of books, natural objects, and scientific instruments; and collections of people interested in intellectual pursuits.

In the early modern era, the passion for collecting (previously confined to kings) spread to members of the nobility, bourgeoisie, and learned elite. Objects that were precious or unusual because of their antiquity, craftsmanship, or materials; items brought from across the wide oceans now navigated by European ships; and exotic plants and animals found their way into famous collections. The apartments of the Habsburg emperor Rudolf II (1576–1612) were littered with clocks and machinery, books and statues,

---

Official Scientific Academies in Europe During the Eighteenth Century

	Official Scientific Societies in all Europe (excluding colonies)	Official Scientific Societies in France
1700	5	2
1789	65	29

Much more than universities, scientific academies were the vital institutions of scientific discourse during the Scientific Revolution and Enlightenment. The great increase in their number during the eighteenth century testifies to the growing interest in science among the governments, crowns, and other elites who funded them. The table above shows only official societies (ones formally recognized or funded by their respective governments).

Source: Based on J. E. McClellan III, *Science Reorganized: Scientific Societies in the Eighteenth Century* (New York: Columbia University Press, 1985), pp. 261–280.

while paintings lined the walls. Remnants of antiquity, contemporary art works, and scientific and musical instruments were heaped together as a kind of summation of all that was known and valued. More specialized collections developed in the hands of scholars, scientists, or wealthy amateurs. The sixteenth-century Italian Ulisse Aldrovandi (1522–1605) gathered specimens of rare and exotic creatures, which were visited by at least the 1579 persons who signed his guest book (at least ten percent were members of the nobility). By the eighteenth century the gentleman-collector's study and the dilettante prince's palace crammed with curios had given rise to the first modern museums: the Ashmolean in Oxford, the British Museum in London, the Brera in Milan, the Louvre in Paris.

The society of the learned gathered together in a range of associations. In Renaissance Italy, humanists met in the gardens of their patrons for polite conversations; later, during the sixteenth century, they moved into academies. These were associations in which both noble and commoner, and male and female participants mingled to discuss ideas, the arts, or the news of the day. In the informal and vivid setting of the academy, ideas and styles originated that could not have been heard in the hierarchical setting of the university or court.

In the seventeenth century, north of the Alps, academies took a different direction. More official and formal, they served as laboratories for the creation of new knowledge. The French Royal Academy of Sciences, established by King Louis XIV in 1666 (its members are depicted on p. 508), was expected both to explore technologies useful to the state and to reflect glory upon the monarch. Provincial academies encouraged both literary and scientific activities,

frequently sponsoring essay competitions or rewarding exceptional achievement. Private academies and literary societies on the Italian model also flourished, in France closely resembling private salons. The English Royal Society, founded like the French by royal initiative in 1662, left its members entirely free to pursue their own interests. By 1670 its membership numbered 200 and included, alongside amateur merchants and artisans, a number of the most prominent scientists, mathematicians, and philosophers in the nation.

Outside these gatherings of professional thinkers, people gathered informally in the hundreds of coffeehouses and clubs that sprang up in the cities of western Europe. The English insurance company Lloyds grew up in one London coffeehouse visited by businessmen engaged in international shipping; in another, courses on Newtonian mechanics and optics were available. Members of private clubs or Masonic lodges formed reading groups and developed lending libraries. The salons over which gifted women presided in the major European capitals brought together the wealthy, the learned, and the famous to discuss the latest literary or philosophical works.

Informal associations of the learned and talented, at first in Italy, subsequently in the Netherlands, France, and England, were the matrix of the new ideas and visions that fueled the Enlightenment. Superseding the monastery, the cathedral, and the court, more lively than the contemporary university, located in homes and shops that were magnets alike for those with a little or a great deal of learning, they were the halls of reason that characterize the age as much as the monarchs' halls of mirrors. Here the age of reason took form, guided by the transcendent discoveries of intellectual leaders and extended by the buzzing conversation of their readers, followers, and admirers.

Conclusion

DESCARTES' DILEMMA AND THE MEANING OF THE WEST

Because he thought, Descartes concluded, he must exist. And because he existed, he could know. It was confidence in the knowability of things that knit the intellectual world of the West into one system and that gave the Enlightenment its momentum. In the early modern centuries, the rationalism of Western culture that was already apparent in medieval thought was reaffirmed. But now reason reigned alone and triumphant, sharing no space with the Christian faith that had unified the West in the Middle Ages. Loosed from its moorings in faith, expanding around the globe, certain of the knowledge it garnered from the operations of reason, the civilization of the West approached the threshold of the modern age fired with confidence and titanic ambition.

REVIEW QUESTIONS

1. What did Descartes mean when he said, "I think, therefore I am"? How was the rationalism of the early modern era different from that of the Middle Ages? Why did the new rationalism clash with Christian beliefs?

2. What was the Scientific Revolution? How did the new discoveries in astronomy change the way Europeans thought about the cosmos? What was the significance of Newton's theory of gravity?

3. Why did the study of anatomy advance so rapidly in the sixteenth and seventeenth centuries? How did new knowledge about the human body affect the practice of medicine? Why did male physicians take over the power to manage births from midwives?

4. What is the scientific method? How was it different from Aristotelian philosophy? Why did belief in magic and the occult decline in the early modern era?

5. What was the Enlightenment? Why did the *philosophes* attack the Church? Why were the "social contract" theories a step toward democracy?

6. Why did the number of literate Europeans increase in the early modern era? Why did more women writers appear at this time? What was the debate on women?

SUGGESTED RESOURCES

New Heaven, New Earth

Biagioli, Mario, *Galileo, Courtier: The Practice of Science in the Culture of Absolutism* (Chicago: University of Chicago Press, 1993). Explains how Galileo rose to prominence by relying on practices of patronage traditional in courtly society.

Christianson, John Robert, *On Tycho's Island: Tycho Brahe and his Assistants, 1570–1601* (Cambridge: Cambridge University Press, 2000). Reveals Brahe as a master administrator of a scientific research organization and publicist of a scientific world view.

Dobbs, Betty Jo Teeter, *The Janus Faces of Genius: The Role of Alchemy in Newton's Thought* (Cambridge: Cambridge University Press, 1991). Far from being a rationalist who rejected religion, Newton is revealed in this major reconceptualization of his role as dedicated to bringing natural philosophical and religious truth together into one system.

Porter, Roy, and Mikulás Teich, eds., *The Scientific Revolution in National Context* (Cambridge: Cambridge University Press, 1992). Examines the interaction between science and scientists, and social, political, and cultural forces. Argues that the nature and fate of science in the 16th and 17th centuries varied significantly in different national contexts.

Schiebinger, Londa L., *The Mind Has No Sex? Women in the Origins of Modern Science* (Cambridge, MA: Harvard University Press, 1989). Argues that women, too, played a role in pioneering the new sciences of the 17th and 18th centuries.

Sobel, Dava, *Longitude: the True Story of a Lone Genius Who Solved the Greatest Scientific Problem of his Time* (Walker & Co., 1995). A vivid narration of how one British clockmaker created the sea-borne chronometer, which permitted sailors to determine with accuracy the longitude of their ship.

Johann Kepler, 1571–1630 (Rice University):
http://es.rice.edu/ES/humsoc/Galileo/People/kepler.html

The Lights Go On

Gay, Peter, *The Enlightenment: An Interpretation*, 2 Vols. (New York: Knopf, 1966–69). Probably the best synthesis of the Enlightenment.

Goodman, Dena, *The Republic of Letters: A Cultural History of the French Enlightenment* (Ithaca: Cornell University Press, 1994). Focusing largely on salons, argues that women provided sociability, discussion, and civility to the overall culture of the Enlightenment.

Outram, Dorinda, *The Enlightenment* (Cambridge: Cambridge University Press, 1995). An up-to-date synthesis, placing the remarkable intellectual motor of the Enlightenment in the context of changing social structures, gender roles, and global ventures.

Porter, Roy, *The Creation of the Modern World: The Untold Story of the British Enlightenment* (New York: W.W. Norton, 2000). Whereas Enlightenment surveys often dwell on French giants like Montesquieu, Diderot, Voltaire, and Rousseau, Porter gives the credit for the development of a modern world view to Britain.

A Little Learning

Chartier, Roger, *The Order of Books: Readers, Authors and Libraries in Europe between the 14th and 18th Centuries* (trans. Lydia G. Cochrane; Stanford: Stanford University Press, 1994). Relates how developments in the tracking, indexing, and ordering of books created a new world of knowledge between the late Middle Ages and the Enlightenment.

Eisenstein, Elizabeth L., *The Printing Press as an Agent of Change: Communications and Cultural Transformations in Early Modern Europe*, 2 Vols. (Cambridge: Cambridge University Press, 1979). Examines the revolutionary consequences of the change from script to print culture.

Goldsmith, Elizabeth, ed., *Going Public: Women and Publishing in Early Modern France* (Ithaca: Cornell University Press, 1995). Essay collection exploring how French women writers "went public" in the 17th and 18th centuries, seeking wider audiences for the memoirs, novels, and poems that had previously circulated in coterie circles.

Grafton, Anthony, *Cardano's Cosmos: the Worlds and Works of a Renaissance Astrologer* (Cambridge MA–London: Harvard University Press, 1999). Famed as a physician, mathematician, and scientist, Cardano was also known and courted throughout Europe as an astrologer, whose predictions were widely sought by the wealthy and powerful.

Lewalski, Barbara K., *Writing Women in Jacobean England* (Cambridge, MA: Harvard University Press, 1993). Focuses on educated, typically aristocratic, women and their relationship—either as patrons or writers—with print culture during the early 17th century.

Shakespeare's Globe Theater (University of Reading, UK):
http://www.rdg.ac.uk/globe/home.htm

Early Modern Women Online: bibliography and web resources (Folger):
http://chnm.gmu.edu/emw/bibliography.htm

Printing: history, resources, links:
http://www.digitalcentury.com/enyclo/update/print.html

TOWN, COURT, AND COUNTRY

	1450	1500	1550	1600	1650	1700	1750	1800

Society and Politics

- ◆ Jews expelled from Spain, 1492
- ◆ Columbus reaches the Americas, 1492
- ◆ Around 9% of Europeans live in cities, 1500
- ◆ Peasant Revolt in Germany, 1525
- ◆ Around 10% of Europeans live in cities, 1600
- ◆ Paris rules that beggars should be whipped, branded, and driven out of town, 1606
- ◆ Irish revolt, 1641
- ◆ The Fronde in France, 1648–53
- ◆ Climax of English Civil War, 1649
- ◆ "Glorious Revolution" in England, 1688
- ◆ Population of London tops 500,000, 1700
- ◆ Jews make up 4% of population of Amsterdam, 1700
- ◆ Some three-fourths of all Jews in world live in Poland, 1700
- ◆ Last major outbreak of Plague in Western Europe, 1720
- ◆ Peter the Great of Russia introduces Table of Ranks, 1722
- ◆ Around 11% of Europeans live in cities, 1750
- ◆ Emilian Pugachev leads peasant uprising in Russia, 1773–75
- ◆ Catherine the Great of Russia's "Charter of the Nobility," 1785
- ◆ Final partition of Poland, 1795
- ◆ Population of London exceeds 1 million, 1800

Art and Ideas

Scientific Revolution, 1543–1687

The Enlightenment, c. 1685–1789

- ◆ Peter Bruegel the Elder's *The Peasants' Wedding*, 1568
- ◆ Margaret Cavendish, Duchess of Newcastle's *Sociable Letters*, 1664
- ◆ Mary Astell's *Some Reflections on Marriage*, 1700
- ◆ Daniel Defoe's *Conjugal Lewdness, or Matrimonial Whoredom*, 1727
- ◆ John Gay's *The Beggar's Opera*, 1728
- ◆ Cesare Beccaria's *Essay on Crimes and Punishments*, 1764

Beyond the West

Mughal Empire, India, 1526–1857

Ming Dynasty, China, 1368–1644

Qing Dynasty, China, 1644–1912

- ◆ Portuguese capture Malacca (Malaysia) and the Moluccas, 1511–13
- ◆ Ferdinand Magellan claims Philippines for Spanish crown, 1521
- ◆ Japanese expel Christian missionaries, 1614
- ◆ Dutch wrest Malacca from Portuguese, 1641
- ◆ Viceroyalty of New Granada created, 1717
- ◆ Viceroyalty of Rio de la Plata created, 1776

TOWN, COURT, AND COUNTRY

Privilege and Poverty in Early Modern Europe

1500–1780

Europe in the 18th century

■ areas with a population of over 40 per square km

■ areas with a population of 20-40 per square km

● cities with populations of over 500,000

● cities with populations of 100,000-500,000

KEY TOPICS

◆ **Honorable Pursuits:** In the courts of early modern Europe, monarchs fashion exalted images of themselves, while nobles compete at court and consume art, music, and literature as indices of refinement and gentility.

◆ **New Ways with New Wealth:** Wealthier than ever before, bourgeois city-dwellers fill their townhouses with copious items of luxury; the urban poor, meanwhile, are dogged by hunger, disease, homelessness, and crime.

◆ **Field and Village:** In the countryside, some peasants gain new freedoms while others are newly enserfed, as agricultural improvements lead to increased grain yields, more diversified crops, and fatter, healthier livestock.

The Would-Be Gentleman The French playwright Molière (1622–1673) amused King Louis XIV (r. 1643–1715) with sprightly comedies lampooning hypocrites, pretentious ladies, hypochondriacs, and social-climbing members of the bourgeoisie—such as Monsieur Jourdain, the main character in The Would-Be Gentleman. In his desperate effort to turn himself into a nobleman, Jourdain hires a music master, a dancing master, and a philosopher—but fails hilariously. Molière's play, first performed in 1670, highlights the key social issue of the age: the exclusive hold on status and privilege retained by the nobility, and the subordination of all other social groups.

The would-be gentleman was laughable to his audience because he yearned to acquire a status to which he was not born. The early modern age (approximately the period from 1500 to 1750) was still one of social orders entered at birth, altered rarely, and only at great cost. The great representative assemblies of the emerging states of Europe (see Chapter 15) were constituted by delegates from the constituent orders of clergy (the first order or "Estate"), nobles (the second), and commoners (the third, understood to include everyone from the urban bourgeoisie to the peasant in the fields); the British Parliament reduced the three orders to two, creating a bicameral legislature of nobles or "Lords" and "Commoners." In terms of culture, too, each order had its customs. The aristocracy developed an elaborate code of behavior, that preserved their preeminence and set the standard for all subordinate classes. The artisans and merchants of growing towns and cities developed a new taste for luxury, education and the arts. The poor in town and country had neither the wealth nor leisure to cultivate a taste for luxury, but continued to engage in the rituals of village life, or to explore the new possibilities of gin lanes or the poorhouse.

The members of each order strove at least to maintain, or better, to surpass the social status they had inherited from their parents. As Molière's bourgeois gentleman strove to be like the nobility, nobles strove to be like kings, and kings raised themselves above humanity. Beneath the ranks of the bourgeoisie, artisans and shopkeepers also craved the marks of social prestige, lest they fall further down the ladder of social rank. There the quest for prestige dimmed. Workers, migrants, and servants fought to survive, along with deserted women and children and the destitute. The struggle of the poor for subsistence and the aspirations of the propertied for status in town, court, and country mark the social relations of the early modern era. They foreshadow the boundaries of social class that still prevail in the Western world today. The diagram on p. 515 show different patterns of social inequality.

HONORABLE PURSUITS: THE EUROPEAN NOBILITY OF THE EARLY MODERN AGE

Comprising between one and ten percent of the population in most parts of Europe, the nobility was the traditional landowning and military class. Noble prestige was defended by the idea of honor, which expressed pride in ancient heritage and moral code. Its status increased in the early modern era because of its monopoly of cultural refinement and its closeness to those who held real power: the kings.

Lines and Houses

Europe's most powerful noblemen came from ancient "**lines**" that held title to ancient "**houses**." The line was the series of family connections leading back through male ancestors to the earliest possessors of the land that gave the family its noble status. The "house" was the place or even the building with which the family was associated and from which it took its aristocratic title. For example, the Marquis de Lafayette (1757–1834), a participant in both the American and French revolutions (see Chapters 19, 20), was a member of the house of Lafayette; his family name, seldom used, was "du Motier."

The preeminence of the house in defining noble status stemmed from the nobility's original role in European society in the Middle Ages (see Chapter 9). Because land was originally the reward bestowed by a monarch for military service, it was the nobleman's identity as warrior that established his right as householder. It also provided the emblems of his high social status, the shield and the sword. The symbols decorating a nobleman's shield—his coat of arms—would once have served to identify fully-armed knights on the battlefield.

Shield and sword represented the value of **honor** that noblemen believed was uniquely theirs. To maintain noble status, it was not sufficient or even necessary to be wealthy; it was only necessary to preserve one's honor. In this cause, European aristocrats were willing to kill or be killed, often resorting to dueling as a ritualized form of private warfare. At the same time, the European nobleman could still win honor in the manner of his medieval forebears in the frequent real wars that engulfed Europe in the early modern era. The mounted knight became an army officer, in a transformation that helped the aristocracy to keep its hold into the twentieth century on senior military positions. Away from the battlefield, meanwhile, the nobleman was a hunter, intent on fine sport, good exercise, and dominion over the forest. When nobles entered their treed reserves, accompanied by their wives and servants, they were demonstrating their power over nature itself. Poor men might have the right to gather chestnuts or firewood

Social Inequalities

Percentage of Population Formed by the Nobility in Five Countries, c. 1750

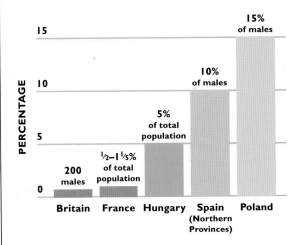

Source: *Based on J. Merriman,* A History of Modern Europe: From the Renaissance to the Age of Napoleon *(New York: W. W. Norton, 1996) p. 356.*

Distribution of Population and Wealth in Lyon, France, 1545

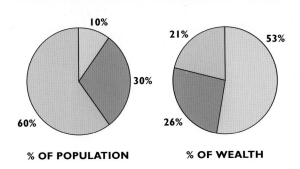

% OF POPULATION   **% OF WEALTH**

Note that 10% of the population controls 53% of the wealth, and 90% of the population the remaining 47%—less than half.

In the early modern period, social inequalities were a source of great tension. These graphs show four different patterns of social inequality. The percentage of the population formed by the nobility in five countries is seen in the first graph (top left). The other graphs show breakdowns of the population into groups designed by status or wealth: the city of Lyon in France in 1545 (above); England in 1688 (top right); Florence in 1457 (right); and France in 1698 (far right).

Source: *Based on C. M. Cipolla,* Before the Industrial Revolution: European Society and Economy, 1000-1700 *(New York: W. W. Norton, 1976), pp. 10, 11, 12, 13.*

Distribution of Income in England in 1688 According to the Calculations of Gregory King

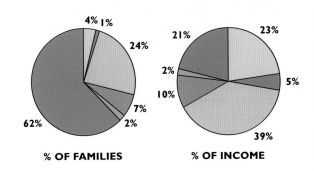

% OF FAMILIES   **% OF INCOME**

Socioeconomic Class

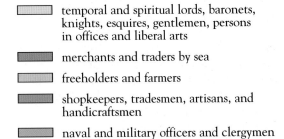

- temporal and spiritual lords, baronets, knights, esquires, gentlemen, persons in offices and liberal arts
- merchants and traders by sea
- freeholders and farmers
- shopkeepers, tradesmen, artisans, and handicraftsmen
- naval and military officers and clergymen
- common seamen, laboring people and outservants, cottagers and paupers, common soldiers

Classification of Florentine Families Based on 1457 Tax Rolls

Vauban's Classification of French Population in 1698

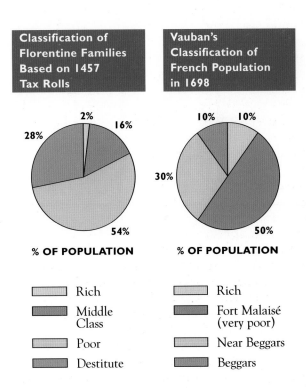

% OF POPULATION   **% OF POPULATION**

- Rich
- Middle Class
- Poor
- Destitute

- Rich
- Fort Malaisé (very poor)
- Near Beggars
- Beggars

there, or to let their pigs run through the brush, but they were barred from stalking the deer, boar, or hares that provided the well-fed nobility with an even richer diet of meat.

Men and women of other social groups were expected to show the nobility deference, by bowing or curtseying, making way for them in the street, or yielding to them the front pew in church. Such privileges of nobility were legally enforceable. The nobleman, in turn, was accustomed to wielding authority over those of lesser social status. The French writer Voltaire (see Chapter 17) had little recourse against a lofty nobleman who took revenge on him for insults in print by having him beaten and left in the street.

During the early modern era the intrusion into the old nobility of men possessed of wealth or professional skills changed the nature of the class. New nobles, called *noblesse de robe* ("of the robe") in France after the robes worn by judges, assimilated quickly to the old nobility "of the sword." They purchased land and

acquired coats of arms and army commissions. At the same time, they brought a new dynamism to a class whose political importance was fading.

Some commoners were ennobled because of service to the crown through their exceptional administrative talents. Trained lawyers often rose to become royal ministers and advisers. These new nobles swelled the bureaucracies of the nation states which increased in pace with royal budgets. Overall, the cost of government, the number of officials, and the size of the nobility, all tripled or quadrupled in the early modern centuries.

Townsmen who had grown numerous by commerce—an activity that was considered dishonorable for noblemen and in some places actually forbidden them—yearned to join the aristocracy. The cash-starved monarchs of Europe, with armies to supply and palaces to build, granted their wish through the sale of titles. This practice led to an increase in the nobility, which grew by one-half in seventeenth-century

Images of Power

Hall of Mirrors, Versailles: *In the Hall of Mirrors at Louis XIV's palace at Versailles, the king could see his sovereignty reflected as he proceeded from one formal appointment to the next. Versailles served to attract and distract nobles, who arrived from their country estates to vie with each other in elaborate rituals to win the king's favor.*

François Marot, Louis XIV Instituting the Order of Saint Louis: *In this 1710 painting, Louis XIV exercises his function as royal patron and rewards the efforts of his nobles at Versailles by conferring the Order of Saint Louis.* (Palace of Versailles, France)

Spain and doubled in France between 1715 and 1789. In the republic of Venice, nobility admitted 127 new families to their ranks between 1646 and 1718 for the enormous sum of 100,000 ducats apiece.

In England, a unique case, it was virtually impossible for a commoner to buy or insinuate his way into the restricted noble elite called the peerage. There were only about 200 peers in a nation of several million. But wealthy commoners regularly purchased country estates and so became members of the gentry. This non-noble landowning elite had access to power and privilege in England comparable to that of the nobilities of continental European countries.

By the eighteenth century, the presence among the nobility of many people who had been born commoners gave strong cause for reflection on what nobility was: was it determined by birth, wealth, virtue, or education? Such discussions led to a profound criticism of noble privilege in the Enlightenment (see Chapter 17), and ultimately to the revolutionary rejection of all that it stood for.

In the meantime, Europeans generally accepted the nobility as a hereditary ruling class. The aim of new nobles was to become assimilated as quickly as possible to the old elite: they acquired estates and coats of arms; they enjoyed exemption from some taxes in a number of countries; and they sought to marry their children to the children of the old nobles. As newcomers gained high status, however, some members of the traditional nobility were experiencing

difficulties. Where income from land declined, nobles could fall into poverty, possessing little but their sword and their coat of arms and the threadbare costume of a magistrate.

Some noblemen met the challenges of the early modern period by engaging in commerce, by vigorously managing their estates, or by marrying a wealthy commoner's daughter. Their willingness to accept a redefinition of what it was to be an aristocrat permitted them to survive into a new age in the position of dominance to which they were accustomed. Not all noblemen were free to adapt in this way, however. In France and Spain, a nobleman who engaged in trade was liable to "derogation"—to be struck from the rolls of nobility. In some localities, marriages between nobles and commoners were illegal. Those noblemen who survived best the transition from medieval to early modern society did so by playing an active part in the more sophisticated royal administration and growing bureaucracy required by modern states, and by adapting to the needs of the marketplace, both in their land management and in their cash investments.

Though the nobility was an ancient class, it was a dynamic one in the early modern centuries. New members entered the nobility, while poor nobles struggled to maintain their hereditary status. The wealthiest nobles, of the old sword families, continued to dominate the choicest positions and access to power and privilege.

The Italian Court

Just as Italy produced the classic manual (by Castiglione) instructing aristocrats of Europe how to behave at court, it also first elaborated the organization of the princely court. The courts of tiny Mantua, Ferrara, and Urbino (see Chapter 13) then served as models for the monarchical courts of France, England, Spain, and wealthier German states. Shown here is a structural representation of an Italian court.
Source: S. Bertelli et al, The Courts of the Italian Renaissance (New York–Oxford: Facts on File Publications, 1986).

Patterns of Nobility

The nature of the European nobility varied from region to region. Each community had its own particular set of relationships between nobleman and peasant, nobleman and king.

In Russia, an autocratic tsar distributed privileges to a nobility defined entirely by its service to the crown, and rewarded those servants with the right to dominate a nearly enslaved peasantry (**serfs**). Here the nobility originated not from the earlier landowning or military elite, known as the boyars, which had been suppressed, but from the decrees of the tsars. Ivan the Terrible (r. 1533–1584) and Peter the Great (r. 1682–1725) (see Chapter 15) transformed the Russian elite into a service nobility, a process culminating under Peter in the 1722 "Table of Ranks." The Table of Ranks set out the military and bureaucratic services in fourteen ascending categories. It was intended to replace promotion according to birth and ancestry by promotion according to a person's ability, and to open up the highest ranks of the nobility to those commoners who gave distinguished service as administrators or officers.

To compensate nobles for their lifelong commitment to government the tsars gave them total authority over their serfs, who became virtual slaves, bound not only to the land but also to their lords. Catherine the Great (r. 1762–1796), in her "Charter of the Nobility" of 1785, reaffirmed the privileges held by lords over serfs, and attempted to mold the Russian nobility into a cultural as well as political elite (constituting somewhere between two to three percent of the population).

In Prussia the ruler granted economic and judicial privileges to the nobles, called Junkers, in exchange for military service. Here, as in Russia, the near-total mobilization of the nation brought the interests of the nobility into line with national aims, at the expense of the peasant population.

Further east, in the aristocratic republic of Poland, a nobility comprising some ten to fifteen percent of the population tyrannized its peasantry while also having a say in the election of its king. Enriched by grain exports to the more urbanized areas of western Europe, the Polish nobility jealously guarded its medieval rights to assemble and vote on national issues. It possessed, in addition, the liberum veto ("free veto"), enabling any individual nobleman to thwart the intentions, for good or ill, of any monarch. This constitutional situation invited anarchy and contributed to the series of international maneuvers that culminated in the partition and final disappearance of the Polish nation in 1795.

Much of the rest of eastern Europe (excluding the Balkans, still largely under Ottoman rule) fell under the domination of the **Habsburg** dynasty. As in Poland, the Czech and Hungarian nobility constituted a large percentage of the population, and profited from commerce in grain. While they resented their subordination to German-speaking Habsburg emperors, they often filled posts in the royal administration. In the northern countries of Denmark and Sweden, as in Russia and Prussia, nobles received their privileges from the king in proportion to their service to the crown.

The principalities that made up the many German-speaking states of central Europe, as well as Sweden and Habsburg Austria, modeled themselves on the western absolute monarchies, and their nobility also resembled those in the west. In northern Italy, Switzerland, and the Netherlands, the nobility were not a preeminent political class, but shared authority in various ways with the wealthy urban bourgeoisie who controlled civic affairs, and frequently engaged in commerce themselves. As landowners, they were concerned with agricultural productivity, but did not necessarily supervise the work of tenant farmers. Nobles of once-great mercantile centers such as Venice, whose ancestors had scoured the Mediterranean for profit, lived in the countryside in leisured detachment.

In England, the nobility consisted of some 200 peers with long medieval traditions who played an important role in Parliament. Despite owning fifteen to forty percent of the land, they had little direct authority over a largely free peasantry. Both this nobility and the gentry often took great interest in the productivity of their landholdings, which were farmed largely by tenant farmers employing landless day laborers. An exception to the general European pattern, the English nobility had surrendered its tax privileges, but voted in Parliament to tax itself as required to supplement the monarch's own funds. With the gentry, it was deeply involved in government and unafraid of the power of the crown, limited decisively by the two revolutions of 1649 and 1688 (see Chapter 15).

In France and Spain, nobles stood at the apex of a steep social hierarchy, overseen by monarchs jealous of their autonomy. In Spain, the nobility (totaling some 500,000 adult males) ranged from powerful grandees to simple *hidalgos*. Seeking to maintaining the purity and distinctiveness of noble lines, the crown supported the *hidalgos* with modest state pensions, and until 1773 barred noble participation in trade or manual labor. That prohibition was a disability for the *hidalgos*, many of whom were impoverished and unable to keep themselves as befitted their status.

The French nobility also considered commercial activity incompatible with high status. Poor nobles suffered as land values fell, while the "grand" nobility managed well on its vast estates, advantageous marriages, financial investments, and royal patronage. Altogether, from 25,000 to 55,000 families claimed noble status, and owned a quarter to a third of all cultivated land. Of these, up to sixty percent were poor.

In the 1630s, Cardinal Richelieu (1585–1642) tried to strengthen the power of the crown in relation to these grand nobles. He restricted their role as generals of private armies, ordered their fortified castles and towers destroyed, and prohibited their duels of honor, labeling them crimes against the state. Aristocrats chafed at these restrictions, and seized the opportunity to recover their lost autonomy shortly after the deaths of the Cardinal and of his master Louis XIII (r. 1610–1643). The young king Louis XIV was still a minor, and France was ruled by the queen mother, the regent Anne of Austria (1601–1666) and her lover, the Italian-born Cardinal Jules Mazarin (1602–1661). In 1648 a protest against royal financial policies grew into a full-scale insurrection that engaged not only the nobility but also townspeople and peasants. The Fronde, named after the slingshot used by Parisian children to shoot pebbles at rich folk in carriages, was suppressed in 1653, resulting in the humiliation of the aristocracy and the triumph of the crown. Traumatized by his experience at age twelve of rebellious Frondeurs, Louis XIV later distracted his potentially troublesome grand nobles in the salons and gardens of his huge palace of Versailles outside Paris. Meanwhile, robe nobles wielded regional power in their judicial assemblies, or *parlements*, or transacted with efficiency the business of government.

Courtiers and Kings

Some members of the aristocratic elite were not only nobles but courtiers too. They attended Europe's kings, princes, and prelates in palatial settings that expressed the ruler's glory. These courts had a dual function: they served to subordinate the nobility to the greater power of the monarch, and—increasingly in the early modern period—they were places where elite arts and social graces were nurtured, setting a new standard for European culture. Those monarchs who still aimed to possess absolute power needed to win the cooperation of their nobles, to reward loyalty, and to discipline resistance. To this end, they drew their nobles to court, where the monarch stood at the center controlling the courtier nobility who, like planets, circled around their sun. This court system had its roots less in the rough, itinerant councils of medieval monarchs than in the lavish ritual systems of the local despots of the Italian Renaissance (see Chapter 13 and the diagram on p. 518). The jewelbox courts of Ferrara and Mantua, Milan and Urbino, spawned imitations on the grand scale in Madrid, Prague and Vienna, St. Petersburg, and London, but above all at Versailles.

The sparkle of aristocratic activity heightened the grandeur of the monarch. A throng of courtiers and servants busily engaged in little of importance formed a kind of collective human prop for the symbolic authority of the prince. Courts also attracted artists and intellectuals with the promise of royal patronage: their brilliant productions added further luster to princely authority. Architecture and the arts were designed to reflect the monarch's grandeur—literally in the case of Louis XIV's Hall of Mirrors at Versailles, illustrated on p. 516. Conspicuous expressions of wealth and high culture ranged from the gems sewn on courtiers' clothes or hung about the necks of their wives, to the silver forks that, for the first time in the history of the West, were used for the delicate science of proper dining; in an older and cruder age, the elite ate with their fingers, just like their peasant subjects. The early modern court system evolved through the need of monarchs to engage the cooperation of their nobles in their determination to retain absolute power. At the same time, bureaucrats, accountants, and secretaries began to carry on more of the business of government. Guided in that direction by the Italian city states and the papal curia, Europe's monarchs made great progress by 1750 in developing centralized and efficient methods of government, staffed by administrators, like the *intendants* instituted by Richelieu. Even so, monarchs still relied on nobles to recruit armies, keep order, and deal out justice.

A great weakness of the court system was that it was precisely those nobles who resided at court, closest to the monarch, who often turned out to be most likely to disobey him. This made court society rife with suspicion, aspiration, and deception, the perfect breeding ground for intrigue and rebellion. Both women and men joined in this intrigue and deception involved in playing for power. In this setting, women's general exclusion from warfare or government was irrelevant: they, like their menfolk, became easy experts in such methods as innuendo and gossip. The aim of intrigue was to gain power and privilege in a system of patronage in which monarchs bestowed rewards on loyal nobles. While lesser offices were filled by members of the lower nobility, gentry, or bourgeoisie, high positions were generally reserved for the high nobility. Salaries dispensed in this way took on the nature of bribes, and the whole system was, to modern eyes, corrupt. While official state payments often lined the pockets of those entrusted with distributing them, nobles who depended on royal handouts often waited for months or years for their promised rewards.

Court life also served as a school, in which the self-willed nobles of Europe learned the new arts of civility. Civility entailed far more than showing reverence to a monarch: it involved a code of manners and attitudes that would become the standard of proper behavior for the next few centuries. Nobles at court needed to know how to behave at table, in the bedroom, in the garden, and in the great halls; in what way and where to bow, speak, or attend to bodily functions; how to address people of different ranks; how to dress for each occasion. To advise the aspiring courtier there were etiquette manuals, supplemented by letters from parents and advice from patrons. The classic manual, a Europe-wide bestseller, was *The Book of the Courtier* by the Italian diplomat Baldassare Castiglione (1478–1529), a passage from which is given in *Witnesses* on p. 521. Translated into five languages, and circulating in 115 editions before 1600, it provided a model for the ideal courtier, who should combine the qualities of a sportsman and a warrior, a musician and a poet, a conversationalist and a counsel to the prince. He should possess all these virtues lightly, with a quality Castiglione called *sprezzatura,* translatable as lively nonchalance, an effortless display of the most refined and developed abilities.

The great chasm that divided the early modern courtier from the warrior knight of the Middle Ages can now be understood. The nobleman who wished to succeed in the new game played in the corridors of power must learn cultural skills unknown in the earlier era. The modern courtier went to school, watched his manners, and participated in music, dance, and theatrical events as both performer and spectator.

Noblewomen   Noblewomen too became expert courtiers. Except for female monarchs, women of the highest social class had been warriors only as surrogates for their husbands and held no public office. A woman's manners and artistry were her sole means of announcing high status, to which she claimed right through her father's line or the wealth of her husband. Woman's role as a civilizing force had roots in the

courtly games of the Middle Ages (see Chapter 9), in which a noblewoman might hold sway through the yearning love and admiration she inspired in young aristocrats and troubadours. Women's role as social arbiter persisted in the early modern era: in the model court described by Castiglione, women presided as moderators and judges of the conversation and behavior of men. "Society depends on women," Voltaire noted, however much men were the agents in realms outside the court. No wonder that the salon—a lady's sitting room—became in the Enlightenment the principal setting for the exchange of ideas (see Chapter 17).

Nevertheless, even noblewomen remained subject to their husbands, just as in the Middle Ages. Marriage choices were made by fathers, with an eye to family honor and prosperity. Women often were dispatched at young ages to older husbands. Bearing children in quick succession, who were quickly dispatched to wet nurses, they might find relief in early widowhood, or perhaps a discreet love affair—the

---

Courtier Graces, Bourgeois Self Control

During the seventeenth and eighteenth centuries, the nobility and the bourgeoisie—two elite social groups—developed codes of behavior suitable for their members. Nobles, or "courtiers," who ideally spent their life at court in the presence of the monarch, refined their previous warrior ideal to include the possession of verbal fluency and effortless grace. The bourgeois ideal was to save time, money, and energy, in order to focus on the transcendent duty of obtaining "wealth and distinction." The first ideal is represented here by the tremendously successful Book of the Courtier; *the second by American leader Benjamin Franklin's* Autobiography.

Castiglione tells the would-be gentlemen of Europe how to live at the courts of princes (1528): Now your request is that I should describe what, in my view, is the form of courtiership most appropriate for a gentleman living at the Courts of princes … in short, … what kind of man must be one who deserves the name of a perfect courtier. … I would have our courtier of noble birth and good family, since it matters far less to a common man if he fails to perform virtuously and well than to a nobleman. For if a gentleman strays from the path of his forebears, he dishonours his family name and not only fails to achieve anything but loses what has already been achieved. … The first and true profession of the courtier must be that of arms; and this above everything else I wish him to pursue vigorously. Let him also stand out from the rest as enterprising, bold and loyal to whomever he serves. … So I wish our courtier … demonstrate strength and lightness and suppleness and be good at all the physical exercises befitting a warrior. Here, I believe, his first duty is to

know how to handle expertly every kind of weapon, either on foot or mounted. … [One must always] steer away from affectation at all costs, as if it were a rough and dangerous reef, and … practice in all things a certain nonchalance which conceals all artistry and makes whatever one says or does seem uncontrived and effortless. I am sure that grace springs especially from this, since everyone knows how difficult it is to accomplish some unusual feat perfectly, and so facility in such things excites the greatest wonder; whereas, in contrast, to labour at what one is doing and, as we say, to make bones over it, shows an extreme lack of grace.
(Baldassare Castiglione, *The Book of the Courtier,* 1528; ed. G. Bull, 1967)

Benjamin Franklin recommends self-discipline and hard work (1771): Reading was the only amusement I allow'd myself. I spent no time in taverns, games or frolicks of any kind; and my industry in my business continu'd as indefatigable as it was necessary. … My circumstances, however, grew daily easier. My original habits of frugality continuing, and my father having, among his instructions to me when a boy, frequently repeated a proverb of Solomon, "Seest thou a man diligent in his calling, he shall stand before kings, he shall not stand before mean men," I from thence considered industry as a means of obtaining wealth and distinction, which encourag'd me, tho' I did not think that I should ever literally *stand before kings,* which, however, has since happened; for I have stood before *five,* and even had the honor of sitting down with one, the King of Denmark, to dinner.
(Benjamin Franklin, *The Autobiography of Benjamin Franklin;* ed. J. Bigelow, 1867)

Aristocratic Leisure

Giovanni Pannini, Gallery of Scenes from Ancient Rome: *During the seventeenth and eighteenth centuries, the European nobility enjoyed power, indulged in luxury, and consumed culture. Here, in a painting dated 1759, fashionably dressed aristocrats examine the accumulated artifacts and representations of Classical civilization, displayed floor to ceiling in the vast halls of an imaginary palace. (Louvre, Paris)*

latter a risky choice, since adultery on a wife's part was punishable in many places by death (although openly tolerated in high aristocratic circles). Or they might find amusement in court intrigue, salon conversations, or the world of fashion.

Fashion and Culture Fashion—the idea that we can choose what we wear and that this choice is meaningful—had arrived at the end of the Middle Ages, in courts and cities that had access to luxury fabrics, often obtained by foreign trade. First aristocratic, and then burgher dress became distinguished from that of peasants, the clergy, and lawyers and other professionals. The latter two groups continued to wear the long robe of the previous era, while peasants still dressed in homespun tunics and cloaks. The elites clothed themselves in silks, brocades, velvets, laces, luxury wools, and furs, adorned with jewels, ribbons, buttons, and clasps, as shown in *Windows On*, p. 600. Outlandish styles came and faded: shoes with long toes; detachable sleeves slashed to show the silk beneath; headdresses stacked high on wire frames

and wide skirts supported by wire basketwork; deep decolletés that revealed women's bosoms and stiff codpieces that accentuated, while covering, male genitals; stockings that ended below or over the knee, and breeches that closed over or above the stockings.

Amid this panoply, a few clear trends can be distinguished in upper-class fashion. First, at the beginning of the early modern era, men's clothing diverged from women's (they had both previously worn gowns, cassocks, robes, and cloaks). The main garment became the short doublet (a close-fitting jacket), while women's robes remained long. Then, toward the end of the seventeenth century, the doublet gave way to two garments, an inner sleeveless waistcoat and an outer coat, that are the forerunners of the modern vest and jacket. Finally, in the eighteenth century, women's dress for the first time became more elaborate and luxurious than men's.

In the realm of culture, the court replaced the church as the primary institution. It was initially through royal and noble patronage that modern European music, theater, dance, and the visual arts developed. During the early modern period, many of the great composers were still hired primarily to produce religious music, but the patronage of music was being assumed by the kings, princes, and prelates whose courts also supported the first orchestras of string, brass, and wind instruments. By the eighteenth century, most formal music was secular and performed in the courts. Elaborate festivals, ballets, and masques were organized for such occasions as weddings and victories, diplomatic visits and sacred events.

Art was also essential to the culture of the high nobility. Royal and aristocratic patrons competed with each other in amassing collections of works of art (an imaginary one is depicted on p. 522). These collections announced the good taste, learning, and wealth of the patron. Many works were created in styles that evoked the art of ancient Greece and Rome. A renewed interest in this art, gave birth to Renaissance Classicism. Classical features, such as balanced proportions and grand entrance porticos with columns, became the mark of high-prestige buildings, from country houses to churches and palaces.

In the seventeenth and eighteenth centuries the Baroque style prevailed, especially in Italy, Spain, Germany, and Austria. This was characterized by bold, dramatic rhythms, with strongly curving, often disrupted forms. A highly decorative variation of Baroque called Rococo won favor in France and eastern Europe in the early eighteenth century. Meanwhile, as the nobility and their favored architects and artists began to travel more widely, visiting ancient sites on the so-called Grand Tour, a more precise and scholarly form of Classicism, termed Neoclassicism, evolved. The Baroque style of architecture was especially suited for displaying the grandiose ambitions of the European royalty and nobility who commissioned the great building projects of the age. In Russia, Peter the Great constructed a whole new city, St. Petersburg, much of which was designed in the Baroque style by architects brought from western Europe. This gigantic enterprise was at once a display of the despotic power of an absolute monarch and an expression of civilized good taste on a grand scale.

Princes and nobles commissioned portraits of themselves and their families, which record the importance of the noble line and the luxury of the age. In England, Sir Anthony van Dyck (1599–1641) painted numerous portraits of Charles I (r. 1625–1649) and his family,

The Comédie Française, 1780: *Aristocratic culture found clear expression in theatrical performance, which in the early modern period became increasingly lavish, flamboyant, and formalized—as demonstrated in this contemporary drawing of the French national theater on the eve of the French Revolution. (Paris, Bibliothèque Nationale)*

while his contemporary in France, Pierre Mignard (1612–1695), immortalized the "Sun King" Louis XIV and his court. In Spain Diego Velázquez (1599–1660) painted forty portraits of King Philip IV. Family portraits carefully emphasize the role of the patriarch, and illustrate the fecundity and respectability of his wife.

Despite the changes forced on it during this period, the early modern nobility was a successful class. In many cases, it maintained its honor, its social and economic privileges, while ceding some political power to the monarch. At the same time, it had been transformed by the experience of the high noblemen and women who attended the kings of Europe at court. They created an ideal of behavior that set a new standard in European culture, at precisely that moment when European culture took precedence on a global stage. Into the twentieth century, to belong to the European elite was to possess as the accompaniments of power a superior education, refined manners, and cultivated taste.

NEW WAYS WITH NEW WEALTH: THE EARLY MODERN BOURGEOISIE

As the European nobility was transformed during the early modern era, so the bourgeoisie developed in size, complexity, wealth, and in the range of its aspirations. Europe's leading cities became cultural centers rivaling the kingly courts, as its once-modest private homes became showplaces of domestic virtues and lavish material consumption. Some members of the bourgeoisie, such as Molière's would-be gentleman, practiced the social and cultural skills that were now the earmarks of high status and sought to enter the ranks of the aristocracy. As they yearned to climb the social ladder, those beneath them sold their crafts in the shops and on the streets, labored in burgher homes as servants, or acquired their daily bread by theft or prostitution. Those who were idle and unpaid sought charity from the institutions that guarded well the wealth of riches commanded by urban patriciates.

The Ranks of the Bourgeoisie

The bourgeoisie derived from the merchants who lived as exceptions in a society that comprised clergy, nobles, and peasants—the three medieval social orders, or estates. They were called, in French, *bourgeois* (in English, German, and Italian: burgher, *Bürger*, *borghese*) because they lived in *bourgs* (borough, *Burg*, *borgo*), or towns. As towns multi-plied, the bourgeoisie also grew, early becoming an exceptionally prosperous and dynamic class in Italy and Flanders (see Chapter 11). By the seventeenth century, the bourgeoisie were the dominant social group in Europe's urban centers: in London and Amsterdam, for example, they rivaled the aristocracy in power and prestige.

The early modern bourgeoisie developed great social complexity. Constituting as much as ten percent of the population in England, France, and the Netherlands, although only a tiny percentage of the regions of eastern Europe, it included merchants, bankers, and entrepreneurs as well as patricians, professionals, guildsmen, and prosperous artisans. Among these were the dynamic leaders of Europe's economic expansion. Some were conservators of outmoded and restrictive mercantile traditions. And some, having amassed their wealth in commerce, invested it in land and lived like nobles. There was no longer a single but many bourgeois orders uncomfortably ranked among the commoners, mostly peasant, of the Third Estate.

The entrepreneurs and bankers, descendants of the great medieval merchant princes, were engaged in those activities that yielded the greatest profits: long-distance trade and the financial back-up that made it possible to fit out oceangoing ships and undertake other costly ventures. Resident mainly in the most populous cities of western Europe, these men invested in the joint stock companies that trade with Asia and the Americas, in the ships that carried African slaves across the Atlantic or wheat cargoes in the Baltic, and in the mines providing iron for guns and machinery. Bankers lent cash to monarchs and startup funds to other merchants. Energetic, creative, and risk-taking, these entrepreneurs opened up world markets and mapped out the commercial system that made Europe the foremost economic power in the world (see Chapter 16).

The patricians were the traditional elites of the European cities. These more conservative "city fathers" were outpaced in Amsterdam and London by dynamic entrepreneurs, but continued to flourish in smaller independent cities such as Strasbourg or Hamburg. Their merchant ancestors had accumulated the wealth that enabled later generations to live on rents and investments while maintaining control of town councils. Where the entrepreneurs drove forward the European economic engine, the patricians' outlook was often local and limited. Other members of the bourgeoisie whose prosperity was not primarily based on mercantile activity included bureaucrats and public officials, who were often trained lawyers.

In the frequent civic and religious processions that wound through streets and market squares, the patricians marched first, followed by guildsmen and artisans, costumed and accoutred according to their ranks. The guildsmen were artisans who were masters of their craft, as certified by the guild organization. Unlike entrepreneurs, whose mercantile activities had burst the bounds of guild-organized commerce, the guildsmen of the early modern period were a conservative force: they tended to resist change in production methods, trade patterns, and the social organization of industries. Below guildsmen in status

Going to market: *Trade and commerce (later industry) were the lifeblood and culture of Europe's urban bourgeoisie. In this anonymous contemporary painting buyers and sellers fill the cheese market in front of the Weighouse in the busy Dutch merchant city of Alkmaar. (Stedelijk Museum, Alkmaar)*

were journeymen ("day-laborers," from the French *journée*, a day) or craftspersons not admitted to guilds, or practicing crafts that had no guild structure. Very rarely, women workers, especially in such specialized textile crafts as gold embroidery or pursemaking, might belong to guilds in their own right, rather than as the widow or daughter of a master.

In Protestant regions, members of the clergy were considered as professionals with bourgeois or gentry status. In Catholic regions, they remained a class apart: privileged like most nobles, with freedom from taxation, they were accorded the highest social honors. In the nations of Catholic Europe, the clergy constituted the highest ranking social group, or "First Estate," technically followed by the nobility as second, although many high-ranking clergy were nobles.

The sons of the bourgeoisie—entrepreneurial, patrician, or artisan—often joined their fathers in commercial partnerships. But increasingly, following a pattern already seen in the towns of late medieval Italy, these young men proceeded from the elementary schooling that equipped them to be merchants to the secondary and advanced education that permitted them to be lawyers, clergymen, or physicians. From this professional order came not only most of Europe's administrators and bureaucrats, but nearly all its theorists and intellectuals. Other young men from wealthy bourgeois families sought to acquire the land that made it possible for a burgher to live like a nobleman, even without the official title of nobility. In the Dutch Republic, the distinction between wealthy landowner and nobleman was fine. In England, landownership of itself conferred social status, making it possible for a man rich from trade to become a member of the gentry: "Trade in England makes gentlemen and has peopled this nation with gentlemen," commented the novelist Daniel Defoe (1660–1731). The defection of successful bourgeois to the countryside, and worse, to the ranks of the nobility, tended to retard the development of the commercial classes and their most energetic members, the entrepreneurs.

At Home

Those wealthy bourgeois who did not emigrate to the countryside aimed, in town, to "live nobly"—which meant to have servants to do the menial work, and to spend lavishly on beautiful or useful things made by others' hands. In the intimacy of their well-furnished homes, however, townspeople seem to have experienced domestic lives more infused with sentiments of love and devotion than was typical of the aristocracy, or available to most of the laboring poor.

The interior spaces of burgher households began to shine with the kinds of luxuries—carved furniture, tiled or sculpted fireplaces, elegantly decorated chests, painted and glazed dishware, silver implements, and glass vessels—that had previously been the possessions of only wealthy nobles or the most successful of Italy's merchant princes. Less conspicuously lavish items were still expensive, including window glass, candles, and fine soap, and such foodstuffs as meat, fish, and cheeses in abundance, and imported wines, tea, and coffee. In a world where simply having enough to eat amounted to prosperity, bourgeois magnates reveled in material goods and consumables. In costume as in diet, they imitated aristocratic opulence, as far as their budgets and their mercantile prudence would allow.

Particularly in the Netherlands, where the bourgeoisie achieved a maximum of success in the seventeenth century, the contents of households and laden tables were enshrined in art. While painters elsewhere celebrated royalty and nobility, here such artists as Jan Vermeer (1632–1675) depicted the clean, ample, and tranquil space of the bourgeois household.

Already in the Middle Ages, the wealthier town-dwellers protected household wealth by adopting the system of giving daughters a "marriage portion," or dowry, and limiting inheritance either to the eldest son (primogeniture) or all males. Like noblemen (see Chapter 9), burgher patriarchs traced their descent in the male line, and carefully chose their children's marriage partners to enhance family status and prevent the drain of capital. Emotional ties between family members, including sentiments of affection for children, were often subordinated in these circumstances to the needs of household maintenance.

The prominent role of the father in this household system was further reinforced by the advent of the Reformation in some parts of Europe (see Chapter 14), and of absolutism in many (see Chapter 15). In Protestant families, the patriarch summoned the family to daily prayer and enforced discipline not just as the eldest male, but also as the minister of divine authority. The father was understood to be monarch in his family, as the ruler was in the state: to obey him was to learn to obey the king. "A family is . . . a little Commonwealth," wrote one English preacher, "a school wherein the first principles and grounds of government and subjection are learned."

In a family system dominated in this way by the husband and father, a wife's duty was to be subordinate—not a new obligation in the early modern era (see Chapter 12). Among the bourgeoisie, however, concerns for the preservation of family wealth

and advancement of social status made marriage a business of critical importance for many persons other than the bride. The complete surrender of personality required of a woman in marriage was often made without the woman herself having actively made a decision to marry, or to marry the man chosen for her by her parents, who were not bound to consider their daughter's inclinations. Sadly, wrote the English aristocrat Margaret Cavendish, Duchess of Newcastle (1623–1673) "daughters are but branches which by marriage are broken off from the root whence they sprang and grafted onto the stock of another family."

Once married, a woman was largely defined by the interests of the new household. Her dowry wealth was generally given over to her husband to manage (not until modern times were women completely free to manage their own, or their family's, finances), while her behavior and costume were assumed to reflect her husband's social position. Adultery was seen as a woman's crime: a man who had sexual relations with other women outside of marriage committed no wrong, except against the honor of the other woman's husband. A married woman who committed adultery injured her husband so grievously that, in Spain, he was entitled to execute her with impunity and, in France, with slight or no consequence.

Married women had only limited claim to their children, or to their own or their husband's property. Children belonged to their fathers. Only rarely did a married woman leave a household with her children, who were understood to continue her husband's lineage. Wealthy widows were discouraged from marrying again, especially if there were young children who might suffer if a woman's dowry was removed from the household; they were often encouraged to remain in the deceased husband's house, maintaining a chaste condition. Depending on local law, a woman might be entitled to any portion of his property.

Some women protested against the restrictions of marriage and women's status, as the passages quoted in *Witnesses* on p. 527 show. In *Some Reflections on Marriage* (1700), quoted in *Witnesses* on p. 506. Mary Astell (1666–1731) offered a powerful critique, centered on the need for women to develop their own personalities and faculties prior to becoming a wife. Women should not rely only on beauty and adornments—nor should men be satisfied with these, but should seek real companionship with an educated comrade. In all, a woman should consider before she married, since once wed, she was in her husband's power, "and if the matrimonial yoke be grievous, neither law nor custom affords her that redress which a man obtains." Lady Mary Chudleigh (1656–1710) put the matter succinctly in her poem "To The Ladies":

Wife and Servant are the same,
But only differ in the Name.

Women Protest against Husbands and Predators

In the sixteenth century, women's voices were finally heard—after centuries of near silence. Their works were composed mostly in the vernacular, which unlike Latin did not require an advanced education. The printing press made possible the publication of many copies, circulated widely, as in the case of Moderata Fonte's The Worth of Women represented in the first excerpt here. Women artists, too, became more conspicuous, as in the case of Artemisia Gentileschi, represented in the second excerpt. Both women protest against the actions of men: the first, broadly and theoretically, condemning them for "usurping" women's rights; the second, concretely and particularly, testifying in a trial against a man who raped her.

A Venetian woman lambasts the tyranny of men (1592): If men usurp our rights, should we not complain and declare that they have wronged us? Or if we are their inferiors in status, but not in worth, this is an abuse that has been introduced into the world and that men have then, over time, gradually translated into law and custom; and it has become so entrenched that they claim ... that the status they have gained through their bullying is theirs by right. ... And we would suffer it. ... if they did not insist on exerting such absolute control over us and in such an arrogant manner, treating us like slaves who cannot take a step without asking their permission or say a word without their jumping down our throats. ... As fathers, as brothers, as sons or husbands or lovers or whatever other relationship they have to us, they all abuse us, humiliate us, and do all they can to harm and annihilate us.

(Moderata Fonte (Modesta da Pozzo), *The Worth of Women, Wherein is Clearly Revealed their Nobility and their Superiority to Men*, 1592; ed. and trs. V. Cox, 1997)

Artemisia Gentileschi, painter, testifies at the trial of her rapist (1612): Agostino put his head on my breast ... and said: "Let's walk together a while, because I hate sitting down." ... After we had walked around two or three times, each time going by the bedroom door, when we were in front of the bedroom door, he pushed me in and locked the door. He then threw me onto the edge of the bed, pushing me with a hand on my breast. ... Lifting my clothes, which he had a great deal of trouble doing, he placed a hand with a handkerchief at my throat and on my mouth to keep me from screaming. ... I felt a strong burning and it hurt very much, but because he held my mouth I couldn't cry out. However, I tried to scream as best I could.

I scratched his face and pulled his hair and ... I even removed a piece of flesh. ... And after he had done his business he got off me. When I saw myself free, I went to the table drawer and took a knife and moved toward Agostino saying: "I'd like to kill you with this knife because you have dishonored me."

(From M. D. Garrard, *Artemisia Gentileschi*, 1989)

The wife's condition might have been more like a prostitute's than a servant's, suggested the writer Daniel Defoe. In *Conjugal Lewdness, or Matrimonial Whoredom* he argued that marriage often amounted to the legally protected sexual exploitation of women.

High rates of child-bearing and high infant mortality were both accepted facts of existence (see Chapter 12). The children of elite families often spent their first years with wet nurses. Sons returned to their mothers only briefly before they again left their parents' homes—perhaps around age fourteen, but possibly as early as eight—to serve an apprenticeship in their destined occupation, to enter a military academy or religious institution, or in other ways to embark on adult life. In another sense, they did not achieve adulthood until their later twenties, when they married themselves (often to a much younger wife, or an older widow), set up their own households, and perhaps succeeded to their fathers' positions.

Despite these bleak realities, the bourgeois families of the early modern era began to reconceptualize childhood. Evidence exists in diaries and letters of a deepened emotional involvement of parents in child-rearing, an increased concern for children's education and welfare. Around the mid-seventeenth century, the severe disciplining of children in school was questioned. Elite mothers increasingly breastfed their own babies; they also dressed them in special clothes (children had previously been dressed just like miniature adults), and supplied them with playthings. Mothers and fathers alike recorded their mourning for children who died, as so many did, by arranging elaborate funerals, commissioning monuments, or writing works describing their grief. In general, family life in the comfortable homes of bourgeois Europeans seems to have become more focused on personal identity and experience. Outside these homes, in the vibrant cities of early modern Europe, a new cultural world was also emerging.

Downtown

While some members of the bourgeoisie wished to buy land and noble status, those who remained based in the great European cities created a vital and refined cultural world that imitated, rivaled, and eventually replaced that of the court: the world of "downtown."

Medieval European cities had developed as autonomous commercial centers (see Chapter 11), in which merchant organizations determined the forms of town governments, which wrested political privileges from kings, bishops, and emperors. Each city developed distinctive social and cultural traditions, and different patterns of interaction with the immediate countryside, and with other independent cities.

By the sixteenth century, however, the medieval patterns were changing, in three ways (see also Chapter 16). First, the major urban concentrations shifted from the Mediterranean region to the Atlantic region, where new patterns of urbanization emerged, driven by explosive economic and population growth.

Second, the network of autonomous cities was replaced by networks of integrated regions, in which major cities were the economic focus of a large area that included many medium-sized and small towns. Often these regional supercities were also national capitals, as were London and Paris. As regional centers, these previously isolated centers of commercial endeavor now derived their wealth and resources from far beyond the urban core. They opened themselves up to the countryside beyond, whose goods they purchased and whose needs they supplied.

Third, the pace of urbanization accelerated overall. Not only did the populations of Europe's towns and cities increase, but the proportion of Europeans living in cities rose from under nine percent in 1500

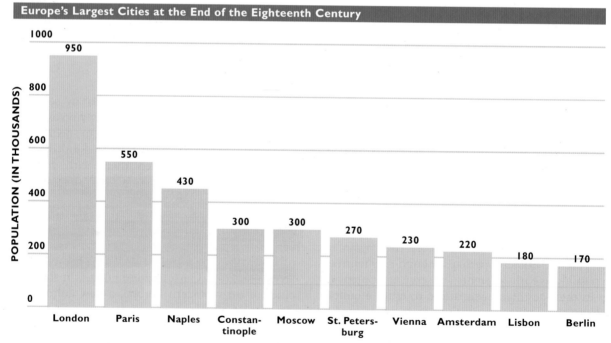

Population Takeoff in Europe

| | Approximate European Populations | | | | | |
	France	Prussia	Russia	Italy	Sweden	England
1600	10,500,000	N/A	10,000,000	12,000,000	1,000,000	4,066,000
1700	21,000,000	1,750,000	14,000,000	13,000,000	1,500,000	5,027,000
1800	29,000,000	9,000,000	30,000,000	19,000,000	2,500,000	8,728,000

Sources: *Based on* Atlas of World Population History *(New York: Facts on File, 1978) and B. R. Mitchell,* British Historical Statistics *(Cambridge: Cambridge University Press, 1988), pp. 7–9, 40–42, 52–54.*

Europe's Largest Cities at the End of the Eighteenth Century

POPULATION (IN THOUSANDS)

- London — 950
- Paris — 550
- Naples — 430
- Constantinople — 300
- Moscow — 300
- St. Petersburg — 270
- Vienna — 230
- Amsterdam — 220
- Lisbon — 180
- Berlin — 170

Source: *Based on J. Merriman,* A History of Modern Europe: From the Renaissance to the Age of Napoleon *(New York: W. W. Norton, 1996), p. 385.*

By 1500, Europe began to recover from the catastrophic population losses caused by the Black Death (see Chapter 12). After a slowdown in the rate of growth in the seventeenth century, steady gains were realized after 1700, and by 1800, Europe was densely populated. The first table shows the mounting population of selected European countries in 1600, 1700, and 1800, while the second shows the population attained by some of Europe's most important cities by around 1800.

to about twelve percent by 1750 overall (with a still higher proportion in the Mediterranean and north-western regions). The largest cities in the Middle Ages barely exceeded 100,000 inhabitants; by 1700, the largest broke the barrier of 500,000 and by 1800, approached 1 million, as the diagram on p. 528 shows. Smaller cities with fewer than 50,000 inhabitants continued to thrive. Constituting three-fourths of all European cities, they were hives of commercial activity and key to Europe's urbanism.

Increasing in size and in the range of their economic activity, the great European cities lost their walls: they were no longer the exceptional islands they had been in the sea of medieval society. No longer enclosed by gates and walls, the intensity of city life spilled out from busy port and market complexes into the surrounding region and beyond. Reflecting national and continental interests rather than merely local ones, urban planning and architecture adopted new forms. Broad avenues cut through the winding web of medieval streets to provide a stage for royal and religious processions and military parades, for personal communication and commercial traffic. Buildings sprouted up in the imposing Baroque and Neoclassical architectural styles borrowed from aristocratic mansions: official palaces, stock markets, and banks; the townhouses of the nobility and wealthy bourgeoisie. By 1750, the cities were displacing courts, palaces, cathedrals, and monasteries as centers of European civilization.

Against the backdrop of monumental buildings and planned streets, a new urban theater materialized. Medieval cities had been cultural centers, where ritual processions and special events occupied a good part of the annual calendar. Early modern cities engendered different forms of cultural activity. The elites travelled in carriages to visit government officials, business contacts, or personal friends. They promenaded in public gardens and along river embankments. They frequented coffeehouses and teashops, and went shopping on "high" streets lined with speciality shops, stocked with the manufactures of Europe and exotic produce from around the globe.

For the first time, the city also contained theaters in the modern sense. In the Middle Ages, plays based on Bible stories had been enacted in villages, monasteries, and courts, while the Italian Renaissance had seen the revival of Classical drama. In London from the late 1500s, and in Spain and France in the 1600s, dramatic performances moved into public theaters, where they were enjoyed by audiences mixed in gender and social origin, achieving glorious success. European playwrights of the early modern era included some of the greatest geniuses of the Western tradition: most notably William Shakespeare (1564–1616) in England; Lope de Vega (1562–1635) in Spain; Jean-Baptiste Racine (1639–1699), Pierre Corneille (1606–1684), and Molière in France.

Women also wrote for the stage, including the Italian Antonia Pulci (1452–1501) and the English Aphra Behn (1640–1689) (see Chapter 17).

The first operas had been staged for elite audiences in Renaissance Italy. By the 1700s, opera houses stood in most major European cities and played to crowds who came to applaud the brilliant virtuosity of the performers as much as to listen to the music. The Classical, tragic themes of the earliest operas were joined by comic themes, often boldly critical of contemporary society. One such was *The Beggar's Opera* by John Gay (1685–1732), which celebrated criminals and prostitutes in a subtle commentary on elite values, or *The Marriage of Figaro* by Wolfgang Amadeus Mozart (1756–1791), based on the play of the French adventurer Pierre-Augustin Caron de Beaumarchais (1732–1799), with its charms concealing a merciless critique of the aristocracy.

While theater developed in part from folk traditions, musical performance evolved from the royal and princely courts, which had provided patronage for composers and musicians. In bourgeois homes, meanwhile, families and friends joined in choral and solo singing, with amateur instrumental accompaniment.

This musical tradition erupted into the life of the city in the seventeenth century with the opening of public opera halls (such as Venice's Fenice), and in the eighteenth century with the creation of the concert hall. The virtuoso skills of composers, musicians, and singers could now be enjoyed by a bourgeois audience that did not reside at court.

The bourgeois outsiders of medieval society were the insiders of the early modern city. City-dwellers imitated the arts of the court to create the urban civilization of the modern Western world, centered not in halls of mirrors but amid the traffic of downtown. The bourgeoisie were not the only residents of the early modern cities, however: they shared their habitat with the poor, who, leaving the countryside, thronged there in search of work.

Workers and Strangers

The ranks of the bourgeois were the elites of the cities that they shared with a multiplicity of people, whose presence made urban life more turbulent and variable than life on the land. Migrants from towns and villages boosted the population levels of early modern cities, which could not be maintained by citizen births alone: migration accounts for much of the urban demographic growth in this period. Some migrants were educated professionals or skilled artisans, who found employment in the city councils, the schools and universities, or guild-regulated shops. But most were unskilled: they packed the streets and filled the rented rooms in cities that provided them with only limited opportunities and no remedies for the harsh realities of the marketplace.

Being Poor: in Town and Country

The condition of the poor remained dire in the early modern centuries, but had become more various than in the previous era. Some of that variety is indicated in the passages here. The first describes an attempt in the city of Venice to reduce the number of street beggars by removing those that had become sick to a hospital. In the second, the poor workers of Manchester, still angry and hungry in the aftermath of a harshly suppressed food riot, send a threatening letter to the local Justice of the Peace. In the third, a German poet gives expression to the plight of the peasant, as bleak as it had always been.

A view from the top—Sick beggars in Venice must enter the hospital of the *Incurabili* or be banished (1522): Many gentlemen and gentlewomen and others have been moved to take pity on numerous persons sick and sore of the French pox [i.e. syphilis] and other ills. Some of these persons in their bodily weakness languish in the streets and the doorways of churches and public places both at San Marco and at Rialto to beg for a living ... giving forth a terrible stench and infecting their neighbours and those with whom they live. ... Now, because the aforesaid charitable persons are making every possible effort to care for these sick people—who are plunged into the deepest destitution and misfortune—in a hospital of theirs at the Spirito Santo ... , we ... decree ... that, if from henceforth any men or women sore of the French pox or other ill are called upon by the agents of the aforesaid hospital to go and enter the place to be nursed and looked after, and yet refuse and will not go, ... they shall be ... banished from this our city.
(Decree of the *Provveditori alla Sanità*, February 22, 1522; eds. D. Chambers and B. Pullan, 1992)

The poor of Manchester write threateningly to Mr. James Bailey, J.P., following the violent repression of a food riot in July 1762: This is to asquaint you that We poor of Rosendale Rochdale Oldham Saddleworth Ashton have all mutaly and firmly agreed by Word and Covinent and Oath to Fight and Stand by Each Other as long as Life doth last for We may as well all be hanged as starved to Death and to see ower Children weep for Bread and none to give Them ... but take This for a shure Maxon, That if You dont put those good Laws in Execution against all Those Canables or Men Slayers That have the Curse of God and all honest Men both by Gods Laws and Mens Laws ... I know You all have Power to stop such vilonas Proceedings if You please and if You dont amaidatley put a Stopp and let hus feel it the next Saturday We will murder You all that We have down in Ower List and Wee will all bring a Faggot and burn down Your Houses and Wait Houses and make Your Wifes Widdows and Your Children Fatherless for ... Blood for Blood We Require. Take Care.
(From E. P. Thompson, "The Crime of Anonymity" in D. Hay, et al, *Albion's Fatal Tree*, 1975)

A German peasant describes his condition (1568):
I am a peasant.
My work is hard and bitter.
I must plow, seed, and harrow,
Then cut, reap, and beat.
I gather wood and make hay and grain.
Rents and taxes break my heart.
I live on plain bread and water,
As the Lord has commanded Adam.
(Jost Amman, "The Peasant"; ed. S. Ozment, 1980)

Unskilled men worked as common day-laborers who hauled goods, removed debris, swept chimneys, or groomed horses. Women worked as domestic servants, or as spinners, embroiderers, or seamstresses. Servants were a numerous (and increasingly female) class in all European cities of the early modern period, numbering in the tens of thousands in eighteenth-century London or Paris. Men and women alike were subject to economic cycles that brought high prices and unemployment: just as a migrant from the country could become a city worker, that worker might easily become one of the urban underclass of the desperately poor. After 1500, one of Europe's major problems was what to do with indigents.

Members of this impoverished underclass were variously called "beggars," "wanderers," "vagabonds," and "paupers." They were a significant presence, constituting about ten to thirty percent of urban population. In Roman Catholic cities especially, charitable institutions offered relief (such as the Venetian hospital cited in *Witnesses* above), though only to a very few, and almsgiving was still practiced. This vulnerable poor population was increasingly unwelcome, particularly in the Protestant cities of the north, which often expelled indigents. Even Catholic Paris ruled in 1606 that beggars should be whipped, branded, and driven out of town (and in 1749, imprisoned). In contrast to the medieval notion that poverty was an opportunity for compassion, poverty was redefined after 1500 as a criminal offense.

In England, poor laws dating from the reign of Elizabeth I (r. 1558–1603) distinguished the "deserving" from the "undeserving" poor. The former could be housed in workhouses (later poorhouses) supported by the local parish. The latter must be set to work, or expelled from the locality—as, frequently, were strangers and foreigners. Such regulations created two strata of poor folk: those immobilized in their

Artemisia Gentileschi, Judith Slaying Holofernes, c. 1620

Claudine-Françoise Bouzonnet, after a drawing by Jacques Sella, Family Evening, 1667

Attributed to the School of Murillo, Celestina and her Daughter

Women's lives in the early modern period revolved around their sexuality—primarily their roles as birthgivers within the family or as prostitutes. In the engraving of a peasant family (top right), shadings of light and dark separate the world of women from the world of men. A harsher reality is indicated by the image of two prostitutes, young and old (or perhaps a prostitute and an aged procuress) looking out from a barred window—a stark and tragic reminder of their total isolation from the respectable world (above). In a dramatic painting by the renowned woman artist Artemisia Gentileschi, a woman revenges herself on a tyrant (top left). The biblical heroine Judith slays Holofernes, who is an enemy not only of her nation but also of the women he victimizes. (above: State Hermitage Museum, St. Petersburg; top left: Uffizi, Florence)

To continue your investigation of this topic, please go to www.prenhall.com/king for the related **WINDOWS** on the **WEB** activity

parishes, and those adrift on the roads. In London, city officials extended poor relief to those considered "deserving" because of their lack of capacity (able-bodied men were unlikely to qualify) and high moral character. Applying such strictures soothed the tempers of the ordinary folk who paid designated taxes or "poor rents" that supported these enterprises, and who often grumbled that they had to support wastrels as an unwanted burden. The threat of social unrest stilled these complaints. It was better to pay the cost of poor relief than to suffer riot and upheaval.

In France, a workhouse system also supplemented the informal networks of private charity. The *hôpital* ("hospital") continued to house both the hopelessly poor and the hopelessly sick, two groups equally unsupported by home and family. Those able to work labored at menial tasks to pay the cost of their maintenance. Some of the able-bodied poor, willing to work but unable to find employment, were set to road-building and construction tasks organized by publicly funded "workshops." None of these institutions provided sufficient relief to fill the giant well of poverty.

Women and Children   Women who had lost the protection of fathers (through abandonment or death) and husbands (through desertion or death) figured disproportionately among the poor. They had less opportunity than men to find well-paid work, and they bore the additional responsibility of caring for children that no one else wanted. In workhouses and poorhouses, they performed the low-level textile work that had traditionally been done by women, while male artisans took on the more highly-skilled jobs of weaving and finishing. Some regions had convent-style asylums where poor women performed low-paid work, perhaps acquired job skills, and engaged in frequent devotions. Despite the variety of these places of refuge, many poor women at the bottom of what one modern historian has called the "hierarchy of hunger" found no support except among the community of those equally adrift, and lived on the profits of begging.

Poor mothers, whether married or single, were especially vulnerable to variations in the supply and cost of the food they needed both for themselves and for their children. In line with new economic thinking, towns and cities sometimes withdrew from subsidizing grain, as they had in the Middle Ages, with the result that prices soared to a natural high in times of scarcity. High prices, in turn, provoked riot, as the passage reproduced in *Witnesses* on p. 530 and the print on p. 534 show. In the eighteenth century, women were often in the forefront of those who rioted, their explosive speech and physical unrestraint contrasting with their accustomed condition of controlled subservience.

Poor women often took to prostitution to save themselves from homelessness and destitution. During the Middle Ages, prostitution was generally

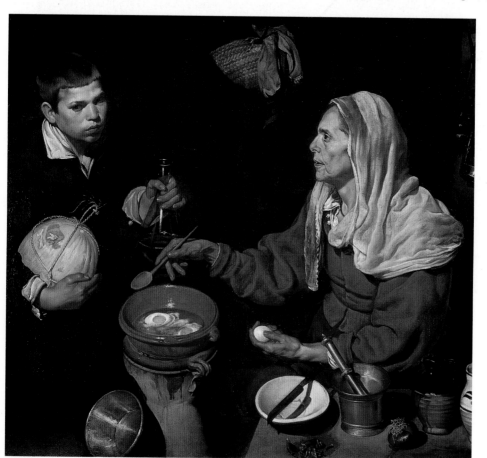

Ordinary Faces

Diego Velázquez,
Old Woman Frying Eggs:
This 1618 painting by the Spanish baroque artist Diego Velázquez features both the shimmering eggs in a pan, representing the perfect, desirable nutrition provided by women everywhere, but especially among the poor, and the deep, mysterious gaze of woman and boy, united in a central ritual act of food-preparation. Velázquez, who would paint princes and popes, here elevates the food and its cook to solemn and imposing rank. (National Galleries of Scotland)

legal, protected by civic authorities and kings alike as a way of forestalling more serious social problems. From the sixteenth century, that policy shifted: although prostitution was still tolerated and regulated in most urban areas, it was now perceived in both Roman Catholic and Protestant communities as a social evil that threatened the welfare of good citizens. A new category of institutions was created to house women who had been prostitutes, or who might turn to prostitution if not rescued from poverty and the streets. In late Renaissance Italy, asylums for the "badly married" allowed impoverished widows as well as former prostitutes to learn the skills that would enable them to leave the shelter for low-paying jobs.

Swift social intervention in the case of prostitution testifies that a social motive was at work beyond the desire to relieve poverty or punish crime. Measures taken to control prostitution attest to a readiness to discipline and monitor sexual behavior. That impulse is also evident in the intensified prosecution of sodomites (the term indiscriminately used for male homosexuals), infanticides, and alleged witches (the latter two groups mostly female). These trends mark an era also noted for the creation of modern science and Enlightenment rationalism.

Orphaned children formed another significant class of the poor. Orphanages had their roots in the early Christian era, but they were transformed in the eighteenth century by the number of abandoned infants they had to accommodate. Institutionalized in the first few months of life, most orphans were effectively presumed illegitimate, born as a result of rape or

William Hogarth, The Career of Gin: *William Hogarth's 1751 engraving is an indictment of the toxin of gin, to which the urban dwellers of eighteenth-century England became addicted, and the irresponsibility of the poor— drunken, suicidal, criminal, as seen in the many individual scenes that make up this unified image. At its center, representing the summit of irresponsibility, is the besotted woman, prominently seated on the stairs, her nursing breasts wantonly bared and legs scarred with syphilitic sores indicative of her manner of life, who allows her neglected infant to fall to his destruction over the railing.* (British Museum, London)

prostitution, or simply abandoned. With wet nursing still the only alternative to maternal breastfeeding, and with pediatric medicine still undeveloped, the orphanage system resulted in staggering death rates, in the range of fifty to ninety percent in European capitals. Those who survived the orphanage were placed still young as servants or apprentices.

Other children wandered the city, adrift and utterly alone. In many towns, most street beggars were children. Abandoned children swarmed down the roads that led to the cities, ideal recruits for the bands of beggars and thieves and disbanded mercenary soldiers whose gangs often "ruled" a whole neighborhood or district.

Crime and Disease The chronic poverty of so many encouraged crime, and elites suspected virtually all the poor of criminal intent. In cities, it is thought that crime was on a powerful upswing from as early as the seventeenth century. The increased incidence of crime stimulated the use of harsh punishments, such as physical mutilation, public humiliation, deportation overseas, and death. Judicially mutilated men and women could be seen everywhere, and capital punishment for minor property violations became common. Women were punished as harshly as, or more harshly than, men, unless they happened to be pregnant. The gallows alongside the gate reminded new arrivals of the judicial power of the city.

The gallows promised to bring order where society had descended to disorder. Critics horrified by this official use of violence, however, began to speak up against harsh punishment. The moral failing of the criminal, Sir Thomas More (1477–1535) pointed out in *Utopia*, was often a rational response to a harsh economic reality that made people choose between crime and starvation. The poor man stole, and was hanged, while wealthier offenders (often tried in different courts) might escape punishment altogether. A new generation of penologists, or experts on punishment, suggested that the end of justice was the reclamation of the criminal. In 1764, Italian jurist Cesare Beccaria published his influential *Essay on Crimes and Punishments* that heralded the end of torture and capital punishment. The English theoretician Jeremy Bentham later put Beccaria's views to work in his proposal for a model prison, the "Panopticon." Meaning "Total Surveillance," the Panopticon replaced the violence of the gallows with the relentless scrutiny of those committed to the rehabilitation and redemption, rather than the punishment, of criminals.

Early modern experts also sought remedies for disease. But the medicine of university-trained physicians, or surgeons with practical experience of wounds, or folk healers (mostly female) offered few remedies for illness (see also Chapter 17). Unaware of the real causes of infection, surgeons wielded a frightening array of unsanitary knives and scalpels to mend wounds or amputate limbs, or drained blood from patients already weakened by disease.

The main victory in the battle against illness was the end of bubonic plague in western Europe, a victory that owned everything to nature and nothing to health professionals. The plague, which had first arrived in 1347 and wrought unprecedented devastation on European populations (see Chapter 12), continued to return every few years to take new victims into the eighteenth century. When the plague exhausted itself in western Europe (although it remained endemic in eastern Europe into the nineteenth century, and in Africa and Asia into the twentieth). Its last outbreak was in 1720 in the French port of Marseilles. Thereafter, the disease faded out: by a

Urban Riots and Plague

The Fettmilch uprising in Frankfurt: *While drunkenness, crime, and disease oppressed the ordinary citizens, so too did the urban patriciate—an upper crust of the bourgeoisie that monopolized public magistracies. A ferocious urban riot in the city of Frankfurt in 1612–1616 was directed against the patriciate and, as often and tragically occurred, against the city's Jews.* (Historisches Museum, Frankfurt-am-Main)

Stürmung der Jüdengasse zu Franckfürt am Mayn.

Plague ward in a Hamburg hospital:
Pre- and early-industrial cities were notoriously harsh, unwelcoming environments. Poverty, squalor, overcrowding, and crime were ever-constant problems. Due to their concentrated populations, cities were also disproportionately at risk for experiencing major outbreaks of infectious disease. This 1746 depiction of a plague ward in a hospital in Hamburg offers few comforts. Note the crude conditions of amputation in the center. (Germanisches Nationalmuseum, Nürnberg)

benign historical accident, the black rat, which carried the flea that carried the killer bacillus, lost its ecological niche to a rival species. Meanwhile, prosperity (for some) and better nutrition also made it possible for the population to resist other diseases more successfully. Until just over a century ago, higher caloric consumption was the greatest cause of improved health for most Europeans.

Yet diseases still ravaged unprotected populations. The poorest Europeans, malnourished and badly housed, were the most vulnerable to such killers as typhus, typhoid, scarlet fever, and pneumonia, as well as the smallpox for which, at last, a preventive was found (see Chapter 17). Hospitals, which also housed the elderly and the destitute, were the refuge of the seriously ill whose own families could not assist them. A ward in a Hamburg hospital is illustrated above. At the margins of city life, the sick became strangers.

Other Outsiders The cities encompassed other outsiders: foreigners, dissenters, and Jews. Cosmopolitan centers such as Venice and Amsterdam had for years accommodated the needs of foreigners (Greeks and Turks, for example) by allowing them to build at their own expense a protected enclave, where they could pursue their own religion while trading with the local citizens. Dissenters were those adherents of minority (mostly Protestant) sects who were granted a grudging tolerance in England, and a more generous one in the Dutch Republic. Subject to various restrictions, they were at least protected by law, once Europe had weathered its outbreak of religious warfare.

The Jews formed another group of city dwellers whose presence of more than a thousand years among European Christians had won, at best, a reluctant tolerance. They had long since been expelled from some parts of western Europe, most recently (in 1492 and 1497) from Spain and Portugal (see Chapters 12, 14).

Still, large communities of Jews lived in the towns of the Holy Roman Empire, northern Italy, and the Netherlands. They flourished especially in Venice (where they were confined to the ghetto; see Chapter 12), and in Amsterdam, constituting in 1700 four percent of the population. In these regions, they enjoyed considerable freedom, although always subject to social restrictions. Further east, Jewish civic life thrived in the city of Prague in Bohemia. The strongest concentrations of Jewish population were to be found, however, in Poland, Lithuania, and the Balkans. By 1700, Poland alone probably sheltered more than three-fourths of the world's Jews, who constituted over four percent of the whole population.

Jewish communities from 1500 to 1750 benefited from the broadening of European culture stimulated by the Renaissance thirst for Classical learning and the Reformation rupture of Catholic uniformity. As those movements developed in scientific and enlightened directions, Jews continued to enjoy relative autonomy and security, while they were not yet liable, as later, to assimilation. Nevertheless, the horrors of the previous era, marked by anti-Semitic outbursts triggered especially by the Crusades and plague crises, did not wholly disappear. The Jews of Poland were harshly persecuted from 1648 into the 1650s, and blood-libel accusations by both Protestant and Catholic zealots pursued their communities in the Empire and Italy. As the modern age approached, the Jews were still strangers in Christian Europe.

FIELD AND VILLAGE: THE BOUNDARIES OF PEASANT LIFE

While city-dwellers enjoyed the riches of an urban environment now at the core of Western society, in the country, free peasants and bonded serfs, tenant farmers and sharecroppers, lost out both to the city and to enterprising landowners alike. For most of world history, most people were peasant farmers, and farming remained a struggle to wrest subsistence from the soil. Plowing, sowing, reaping, tool maintenance, and stock rearing were the framework of peasant life, as the passage quoted in *Witnesses* on p. 530 suggests. Changes in that great continuity in the early modern period allowed some Europeans to prosper as never before. Many others lost ground. Change and continuity characterized the rituals of village life, in which the sturdy cultural patterns of traditional Europe were both rehearsed and subverted.

Bread, Beans, and Flocks

The fields of grain—rye, barley, oats, wheat—that stretched across Europe's great plain provided the bread that led to improved health and increased population. Progress in medieval farming techniques lay behind the continent's demographic success: the use of the heavy plow, and the fallowing of one field in a two- or three-field system of rotation (see Chapter 9). After 1600 in the Netherlands and England, entrepreneurial landowners promoted farming techniques that further enhanced the fertility of the land, freeing some of it for the development of cash crops.

Urbanized from an early period, the Netherlands had scarcely enough land to grow the grain necessary for its ample population. In the seventeenth century, after the struggle of the largely Protestant northern provinces to free themselves from the rule of Catholic Spain had been resolved and the Dutch Republic created, Dutch landowners employed agricultural techniques that led to dramatically increased production of high-quality, high-priced agricultural goods. The merchant fleet that hauled grain from eastern Europe to home ports made these innovations possible. Freed from the need to produce wheat for bread, local farmers grew marketable vegetables and raised cows for dairy products. They rotated the sowing of crops in sequences planned so that nutrients lost in one planting would be restored to the soil in the next. In addition, ambitious land-drainage projects increased the amount of arable land that could be devoted to the new kinds of agricultural production. Fat cows and round, ripe cheeses, together with a variety of garden crops (among them the new species imported from the Americas), signified the improved diet and comfortable wealth of the Dutch. These innovations amounted to the first stage of what some historians have called the "Agricultural Revolution."

The English followed the Dutch in agricultural innovation, draining marshland, introducing crop rotation, and planning their agricultural ventures with an eye to the market. In so doing, landowners often displaced peasant cultivators, and installed tenant farmers directly responsible to them. Displaced peasants might become day-laborers or migrants to the cities.

The goal of landowner management was in some cases the increased cultivation of grain and vegetables. Often, though, it was to remove land from cultivation by erecting hedges or fences around common land previously used for grazing by an entire community or medieval-style open fields in the process known as enclosure. This made room for livestock—dairy cows, as in the Netherlands, and more importantly, sheep—which required only one man to oversee a whole herd or flock. English sheep had produced much of the wool woven into cloth in northern Europe throughout the Middle Ages. When an expanding market for wool led landlords to enclose the fields that had once supported numerous peasants, sheep grazed where once men had farmed.

Dutch and English landowners pioneered agricultural methods that would one day benefit farmers everywhere. In both countries, greater agricultural productivity freed land from grain production for the cultivation of high-profit cash crops, dairy products, and raw wool. While the changes had the potential to benefit all in the long run, they pressured some peasant farmers in the short run: many English farmers lost their land to the combined phenomenon of tenant farming and stock-raising. Many eastern European peasants suffered so that their masters might produce the quantities of grain that Dutch merchants paid well to acquire.

Elsewhere the pace of agricultural change was slow and uneven. In eastern Europe, landowners profited from the increased market for grain in the west. They increased their yields by extracting more labor from their serfs, rather than by improving their techniques. In Spain, increased acreage was devoted to sheep-farming organized by the guild of sheeptenders known as the Mesta. In Italy's rich Po river valley, maize (corn) and rice cultivation alongside traditional crops resulted in abundant harvests. Elsewhere, even in populous France, older farming methods remained in use up to the eighteenth century. Peasants living in manorial villages still plowed cooperatively, and grazed their animals on common land. Farmers eeking out a living on thin upland soil still used the wooden plow, and in the extensive forests of Russia and Sweden, slash and burn methods were used to carve out temporary farmlands.

Varieties of Labor

Alongside this great variety in the management of farmlands, a corresponding variety existed in the condition of farmers, as Map 18.1 on p. 537 shows. In the early modern centuries, differences in farmers' status became more pronounced, ranging from the prosperous English **yeoman** to the Russian serf. The most significant difference was between the mainly free peasantry of western Europe, and that of the oppressed serfs of eastern Europe. It is in this era that

Map 18.1 The Emancipation of the Peasantry up to 1812: *By the end of the eighteenth century, almost all of Europe's peasantry had won their freedom. The exceptions were Russia, Spain and Portugal, and the kingdom of Naples in southern Italy, where serfdom or other forms of unfree labor continued into the nineteenth century. Scandinavia (outside of Denmark) had never known serfdom. In Britain and the Netherlands (including Belgium) the peasants had emerged from serfdom after around 1200. The French Revolution (see Chapter 20) saw the destruction of the remnants of serfdom in France, and encouraged liberation in northern Italy, some of the Austrian lands, and Denmark.*

a marked disparity between the economic condition of those two European zones appeared.

In the west, the progress out of serfdom that had begun in the Middle Ages was largely completed. Most farmers were free men or women, legally bound neither to the landowner nor the land. Best off were peasant proprietors, who were freehold owners of a plot sufficient to feed their families and yield a marketable surplus. Even tenant farmers, who paid a landowner for the use of their land, could prosper if their farms were large and fertile. Then came the smallholders and sharecroppers. Smallholders might own just enough land to provide subsistence for their families in good years. In bad years, they borrowed in order to survive, or they starved. Sharecroppers, who owed landowners a share of up to fifty percent of all they produced, lived in a constant state of indebtedness. Even more vulnerable was the condition of day-laborers, who neither owned nor rented land but, continually in search of work, survived from day to day on the wages gained by their labor.

All peasants paid for the land they worked. Their plight is satirized in the cartoon on p. 538. Some paid "dues" to the landowner, obligations descending from medieval contracts, involving a certain amount of labor or a payment of cash, crops, or livestock. Others paid rent or a percentage share of the produce. Landowners could also collect fees from peasants for the use of the mill to grind grain or the winepress. To the king peasants owed taxes on the land, in addition to direct taxes on such commodities as salt, a hated levy that disproportionately burdened the poor. In Catholic regions, the church also took its tenth share or tithe. By the early modern era this was no longer used to support the local priest but rather drained to the big cities or to Rome itself to help fund the great prelates.

Peasant Lives

Cultivating and processing flax: *For most peasants, life in early modern Europe continued to revolve around a few fundamental certainties: the seasonal agricultural cycle, the village, hard labor, and the continual threat of crop shortages or outright famine. In this 1791 engraving, an entire family— except the youngest child who plays with the dog—is engaged in combing, cutting, and preparing the fibers of flax to weave into linen cloth. (Private Collection)*

In England, farmers were free of the tithe, yeomen could with hard work and good fortune hope to join the gentry, and even tenant farmers could prosper. But the English peasantry suffered greatly from the waves of enclosure, speeded by laws passed by Parliament, that gathered pace from the sixteenth to the eighteenth century. Those who lost their land might work in their homes in the "cottage industries" of textile manufacture (see Chapters 16, 21), or they might seek employment as migrant day-laborers.

The condition of the laborers of eastern Europe, consigned to a "second serfdom" in the early modern era, was worse. In Russia, for example, the tsar granted noble landowners the right to enserf their peasantry in exchange for loyalty and service. Russian nobles measured their wealth not by the extent of their acreage but by the number of "souls"—adult male serfs—who owed them labor.

Polish nobles acquired the same prerogatives without any concessions to the crown, driven by the lure of profits to be gained by exporting grain to western Europe through Baltic ports. Throughout eastern Europe, obligatory labor for the lord was increased to such an extent that peasants could scarcely cultivate their own land use. In Bohemia and Moravia, labor service called the *robot* (meaning "work") left the serfs only one day a week to cultivate their own land. Our modern conception of the mechanical robot descends from these laborers whose spirits were crushed by excessive exploitation. Landowners retained many rights over the peasants, and could demand gifts or prohibit a daughter's marriage. In many regions, nobles exercised judicial powers over serfs, their capacity to exact capital

Plight of the peasant: *The seeming stability of rural life masked important, and ultimately revolutionary, changes. This cartoon by Bulloz shows a struggling, elderly French peasant—a "commoner"—who is having to bear the full weight of the other two main continental social orders, or "estates," the privileged aristocracy and clergy.*

punishment signaled ominously by the presence of the gallows standing near the manor house.

Russian landholders attempted to stem the flight of overburdened workers by declaring their serfs bound to their land and village. Desperate serfs and other fugitives ran for the "borderlands," the region of Ukraine between old Muscovy, Poland, and the Crimea. Those who remained were virtually slaves, as the landowners might sell not only their land, with attached serfs, but the serfs, bodily, themselves.

Festival and Riot

Even in oppressed Russian villages, people danced, sang, and celebrated special occasions. The village community helped its members weather famine, cold, war, disease, and taxes. Its leaders met regularly to plan planting or harvest, and to address the demands of the landlord, or the misbehavior of the villagers. The villagers shared in joys and sorrows, and proclaimed in story and song the clever wiles by which peasants maneuvered and survived. Customs of village carnival and riot, disdained by the grandees of the court and city patricians, gave expression to the energy and talents of those who could neither read

nor rule. The village celebrations of peasants and serfs are the matrix of national traditions that have been inherited by modern states.

The life of the village was a whole world to the peasants. Together they celebrated the festivals of the Christian year, in rituals that were not wholly purged of pre-Christian, pagan practices. Together they feasted at harvest time, and at ceremonies marking births, deaths, baptisms, and weddings. At these events, they engaged in wrestling matches and tugs-of-war, brutal blood sports, and lighthearted entertainments. Self-trained experts played melodies distinctive to the region—"folk" music—on simple string, wind, and percussion instruments, accompanying village singers and dancers drawn from young and old, and men and women.

The young people of the village found wives and husbands in the same community where their parents had found theirs. Groups of adolescent girls paraded in front of the young men in rituals of courtship. Groups of adolescent boys courted them—but also joined in drunken and violent sprees, creating social and sexual disorder. Village healers or "good" witches could provide potions that aroused love, it was believed, in the opposite sex. Engaged lovers might

***Pieter Bruegel the Elder,* The Peasants' Wedding:** *Festive times provided welcome relief from work and were an important part of the peasantry's social and cultural life. Laden with symbolic meanings, at its simplest level this painting by Pieter Bruegel the Elder from around 1568 depicts such a scene. (Kunsthistorisches Museum, Vienna)*

decide not to wait to take their marriage vows before they consummated their understanding.

The village controlled its own members. Most premarital pregnancies resulted in hasty weddings under the guidance of village elders—although some were ended upon consultation of the midwife with herbal concoctions, often dangerous to the mother if not the fetus. In ritual enactments, adolescent gangs mocked those members of the community whose behavior was considered out of bounds—cuckolded husbands, scolding women, men who married women too young or who beat their wives. Also part of the festival celebration was the ritual of role reversal, where women dressed like men, beggars like nobles, in a safe but probing critique of social norms.

The festivities of village life were overshadowed by austerity. Peasants dressed in drab tunics and robes of black or gray, often bequests from dead relatives who had also worn them for a whole lifetime. They lived in huts of wood, clay, or rubble, consisting of one or two small rooms shared with animals who needed shelter and provided a source of heat. Unlike the wealthy bourgeoisie or nobles, their homes had no ornament, in fact scarcely any furniture at all: a bench, a table, perhaps a bed, a pot to cook the daily soup that was the main accompaniment of bread. About a pound of bread (of barley, rye, or wheat), if it could be had, was the standard poor person's diet, or porridge or potatoes if grain for bread was scarce, enriched by thin soups of vegetables and occasional eggs.

A famous depiction of a peasant wedding by the Flemish artist Pieter Bruegel (c. 1525–1569; see p. 539) shows solid peasants at table, amply supplied with round loaves and cheeses (but, correctly, no meat), boisterous in their celebration of the ample fruits of the earth. But the painting deceives. For the average European peasant's experience was of scarcity rather than abundance.

In the eighteenth century, scarcity was still a problem. In the Middle Ages, local governments often stockpiled grain in the event of crisis, but now it was sold on the open market, to the highest bidder, and its cost pressed ever upward. Periods of scarcity, together with the harshness of landowner exactions, inflamed many to rebel. Peasant unrest—often sparked by crowds gathered for festivals or processions—was ceaseless: the German peasants in 1525; dispossessed Irish Roman Catholics in 1641; the Russian followers of the false tsars Stephen Razin in 1670–1671 and Emilian Pugachev in 1773–1775, convulsed their nations. Amid the pages of a famous genealogy of Venetian noble families may be found periodically the telling comment on the disappearance of a patriarch, "murdered by the peasants."

During the English Civil War, members of two groups put forward radical solutions for social ills. The Levellers and the Diggers proposed the elimination of social distinctions and the assumption of real power by those below the elites. The Leveller leader Henry Denne denied that he wished to turn "the world upside down," yet his proposals for social reform were profoundly unsettling to those who ruled.

Resisting the demands of the landowner, the authority of the church, the tyranny of gender roles, or the rigidity of the whole social hierarchy, villagers had views of their own about their world that were far from those of the educated bourgeoisie or courtly aristocrats. Nevertheless, the ability of the peasant to present his point of view was nullified by the extraordinary refinement of verbal expression possessed by social superiors. His stories would be bound in volumes of folktales, his songs and dances worked into symphonies and operas, but he himself was voiceless.

In the seventeenth and eighteenth centuries, the elites declared war on the popular culture of the villagers. Catholic and Protestant clerics insisted on a "higher" standard of sexual morality than village custom allowed, and oversaw the regular religious instruction of peasant youth. Agents of absolute states called for obedience to the king, the court, and his officials from those who already supported those dignitaries with their tax contributions. Reformers and intellectuals attacked surviving "pagan" and magical beliefs, and brought the standards of urban and courtly refinement to bear on peasant custom. Priests and philosophers, pastors and journalists insisted that peasant culture be modernized, nationalized, and standardized—the peasant, too, should become a gentleman.

Conclusion

THE PRIVILEGED, THE POOR, AND THE MEANING OF THE WEST

In the early modern age, the system of ranked social orders inherited from the Middle Ages became more complex and more dynamic. The gap between the elites and the poor widened as status came to be determined by cultural refinement, in addition to wealth. Being poor became a problem, a reproach, a threat. To escape poverty, to approach nobility, were the aspirations of those in the middle—Europe's would-be gentlemen. An expanding group with seemingly limitless ambitions, these would-be gentlemen began their advance, which still continues today.

REVIEW QUESTIONS

1. Why did contemporary audiences find Molière's "would-be gentleman" ridiculous? To what extent was the nobility the ruling class in early modern Europe? How did newcomers seek to enter the ranks of the nobility?

2. Why did rulers establish elaborate courts? How did court life influence the high nobility? What roles could noblewomen play at court?

3. What groups made up the early modern bourgeoisie? Why were bourgeois women kept in subordination? How did the concept of childhood change in bourgeois households?

4. How did the medieval pattern of cities change in the sixteenth and seventeenth centuries? How did urban civilization come to rival court culture? Why was migration from the countryside crucial to the growth of cities?

5. How did European societies deal with indigents, poor women, and criminals? Why did so many poor women become prostitutes? To what extent did the position of the Jews in society improve in early modern Europe?

6. What was the "Agricultural Revolution"? Compare the status of peasants in western and eastern Europe. What role did the village community play in peasant life?

SUGGESTED RESOURCES

Honorable Pursuits

Arditi, Jorge, *A Genealogy of Manners: Transformations of Social Relations in France and England from the Fourteenth to the Eighteenth Century* (Chicago: University of Chicago Press, 1998). Examins etiquette manuals and courtesy books to show how the nobility of France and England created a code of behavior to assert social dominance.

Asch, Ronald and Adolf M. Birke, eds., *Princes, Patronage and the Nobility: The Court at the Beginning of the Early Modern Age* (London: German Historical Institute; Oxford: Oxford University Press, 1991). Focuses on the role of royal and princely courts as the contact point between rulers and local elites during the early modern era.

Bush, M. L., *The European Nobility* (2 Vols.); Vol. 1: *Noble Privilege* (New York: Holmes & Meier; Cambridge: Cambridge University Press, 1983); Vol. 2: *Rich Noble, Poor Noble* (Manchester: Manchester University Press, 1988). Detailed study of nobilities and their privileges in a variety of time periods and geographical locations.

Dewald, Jonathan, *The European Nobility, 1400–1800* (Cambridge: Cambridge University Press, 1996). An up-to-date, comprehensive overview of Europe's nobility from the late Middle Ages to the time of nobility, stressing the resourcefulness and flexibility of this elite class.

Almanach de la Cour—images and materials on nobility, royalty, and chivalry, from the Middle Ages through the 18th century: http://www.chivalricorders.org

New Ways with New Wealth

Amussen, Susan Dwyer, *An Ordered Society: Gender and Class in Early Modern England* (Oxford–New York: B. Blackwell, 1988). Explores popular notions of rank and gender, stressing the ruling classes' obsession with hierarchy and the role of the family as the basis thereof.

Beik, William, *Urban Protest in Seventeenth-Century France: the Culture of Retribution* (Cambridge: Cambridge University Press, 1997). Examines the struggle between angry crowd and town magistrates in more than 15 urban settings.

Franits, Wayne E., *Paragons of Virtue: Women and Domesticity in Seventeenth-Century Dutch Art* (Cambridge: Cambridge University Press, 1995). Uncovers the bourgeois ideals of domesticity and gender relations embedded in the art of the Dutch Golden Age.

Gottlieb, Beatrice, *The Family in the Western World: From the Black Death to the Industrial Age* (Oxford: Oxford University Press, 1993). A useful survey, including definitions of the family, kinship, marriage, sex, child-rearing, economics, and emotional life.

Safley, Thomas Max and Leonard N. Rosenband, eds., *The Workplace before the Factory: Artisans and Proletarians, 1500–1800* (Ithaca-London: Cornell University Press, 1993). Eleven essays examining the lives of early modern artisans in Europe (and New England), in such occupations as mining, textile manufacturing, shipbuilding, and printing.

Woolf, Stuart, *Domestic Strategies: Work and Family in France and Italy, 1600–1800* (Cambridge: Cambridge University Press, 1991). Explores how ordinary people dealt with markets and institutions in order to advance the interests of their households and families.

Wrightson, Keith, *Earthly Necessities: Economic Lives in Early Modern Britain* (New Haven: Yale University Press, 2000). How social systems adjusted to economic change between 1470 and 1750.

William Hogarth, painter and satirist of contemporary English life—images and biography:
http://sunsite.dk/cgfa/hogarth

Vermeer, Dutch painter of scenes of daily life—images, some accompanied by commentary:
http://www.kfki.hu/~arthp/html/v/vermeer/index.html

Field and Village

Hoffman, Philip T., *Growth in a Traditional Society: The French Countryside, 1450–1815* (Princeton: Princeton University Press, 1996). Shows how village economy responded flexibly to changes in policies and market structures—which suggests that revolution was not, as some have argued, the only path for peasant advancement.

Le Roy Ladurie, Emmanuel, *The French Peasantry, 1450–1600* (Berkeley: University of California Press, 1987). Explores the relationship between demographic changes and alterations in patterns of marriage, landholding, rent, and violence.

Manning, Roger B., *Hunters and Poachers: A Cultural and Social History of Unlawful Hunting in England, 1485–1640* (Oxford: Clarendon Press of Oxford University Press, 1993). Since hunting was the aristocracy's leisured form of war, and deer-hunting remained an aristocratic preserve into the 18th century, poaching was available to the poor and not-so-poor as a way at once to obtain meat and to resist authority.

INALIENABLE RIGHTS

| 1600 | 1650 | 1700 | 1750 | 1800 | 1850 | 1900 |

North America

French and Indian War, 1756–63

American Civil   Reconstruction
War, 1861–65   Era, 1865–77

War of Independence,
1775–83

◆ British colony of Jamestown
   founded, 1607
   ◆ First shipment of African slaves
      arrives in Jamestown, 1619
      ◆ British colony of
         Plymouth founded, 1620

◆ Coercive Acts, 1774
◆ First Continental
   Congress, 1774
◆ Second Contintental
   Congress, 1776
◆ Declaration of
   Independence, 1776
   ◆ *Federalist Papers*, 1787
      ◆ US Constitution ratified,
         1788–89
         ◆ Bill of Rights ratified, 1791
         ◆ Fugitive Slave Act, 1793
            ◆ "Louisiana Purchase," 1803
               ◆ War of 1812 against Britain
                  ◆ Missouri Compromise, 1820

◆ Monroe Doctrine, 1823
◆ Mexican War, 1846–48
   ◆ Seneca Falls Convention, 1848
◆ Compromise of 1850
   ◆ Dred Scott decision, 1857
      ◆ Lincoln elected President, 1860
         ◆ Thirteenth Amendment, 1865
            ◆ Fourteenth Amendment, 1868
            ◆ Fifteenth Amendment, 1870
               ◆ Dawes Act, 1887
               ◆ Wounded Knee
                  massacre, 1890

Latin America

Most Latin American states independent, 1804–28 Juan Manuel de Rosas rules in Argentina, 1829–52

Manuel Belzu rules in
Bolivia, 1848–55

Porfirio Díaz rules in
Mexico, 1876–1911

◆ Populaton of Potosí
   160,000, 1670

◆ Toussaint L'Ouverture
   controls Hispaniola,
   1801

◆ Population of Buenos Aires
   250,000, 1869
   ◆ Slavery abolished in
      Cuba, 1886
      ◆ Slavery abolished in
         Brazil, 1888

Europe

The Enlightenment, c. 1685–1789

◆ Revolutions in France, Belgium, Italy,
   Poland, 1830–31
   ◆ Irish potato famine, 1845–50
   ◆ Year of Revolutions, 1848
   ◆ Karl Marx and Friedrich Engels'
      Communist Manifesto, 1848
      ◆ Charles Darwin's *Origin of
         Species*, 1859
      ◆ John Stuart Mill's *On Liberty*,
         1859
      ◆ Serfdom abolished in Russia,
         1861

French Revolutionary
and Napoleonic Wars,
1792–1815

◆ French Revolution
   begins, 1789
   ◆ Mary Wollstonecraft's
      *A Vindication of the
      Rights of Woman*, 1792
      ◆ Congress of
         Vienna, 1814–15

Beyond the West

Ming Dynasty, China, 1368–1644

Qing Dynasty, China, 1644–1912

Mughal Empire, India, 1526–1857

British East India Company dominant in India, c. 1700–1857

Dutch East India Company in East Indies, 1619–1799

◆ First Opium War, 1839–42
   ◆ US Commodore Perry "opens"
      Japan, 1853
      ◆ Second Opium War, 1856–60
         ◆ Sepoy Mutiny, India, 1857
◆ Shaka leads   ◆ French gain control of
   Zulu nation,   Indochina, 1858
   Africa, 1817   ◆ Meiji Restoration, Japan, 1868

19

INALIENABLE RIGHTS

Revolution and its Promises in
Anglo- and Latin America

1500–1880

Map labels: Rockies, HUDSON'S BAY, Quebec, Philadelphia, Appalachians, Mexico City, GULF OF MEXICO, CARIBBEAN SEA, ATLANTIC OCEAN, PACIFIC OCEAN, Andes, Lima, Rio de Janeiro, Buenos Aires

Legend:
- extent of European settlement, 1750
- Amerindian peoples

KEY TOPICS

◆ **Old and New in the New World:** Settlers create a New World in the Americas north and south, blending elements of European, Amerindian, and African cultures; but it is a new world in which natives and slaves are compelled to labor for the benefit of a new colonial elite.

◆ **Declarations of Independence:** Inspired by the principles of the Enlightenment and guided by a written Constitution, the Americas give birth to

a new nation; the United States soon has many imitators around the western world.

◆ **Fulfilling the Promise:** Their independence achieved, the new nations of the Americas do not, in fact, extend to all their citizens the promises of freedom and equality that are inscribed in their constitutions; but by 1900 there is some progress toward that ideal.

Jefferson's Promise *Called upon to declare to the world why it was that North American colonists rebelled against their British masters, Thomas Jefferson (1743–1826) provided a concise statement of the political values of the Enlightenment (see Chapters 15, 17). Ironically a slaveowner himself, he asserted the "self-evident" truth that "all men are created equal," endowed with the "inalienable rights" of "life, liberty, and the pursuit of happiness." Government, said Jefferson, is created by men to protect these rights. When it fails to do so, "it is the right of the people to alter or abolish it," and to institute a new one.*

The points Jefferson stated so concisely were a concentration of the inherited political traditions of the West: behind them stand Aristotle and Cicero, Thomas Aquinas and Marsilius of Padua, Hobbes and Locke, Montesquieu and Voltaire (see Chapters 4, 10, 15, and 17)—above all, Locke.

The United States of America was the first nation in the world to be founded on these ancient, medieval, and Enlightenment principles. Soon the nations of Latin America would also declare their independence on the same principles. In neither region was the Jeffersonian promise of civic equality fulfilled at first. Yet an ocean away from the European homeland where those ideals were born, some progress was made toward the goal of securing for at least some citizens their inalienable rights.

This chapter explores the career of the nations of the Western Hemisphere during the four centuries after Columbus' first journey, examining the impact of the European legacy upon a world where Europeans, Amerindians, and Africans met, and considering the extent to which the Enlightenment principles Jefferson announced were realized in the Americas.

OLD AND NEW IN THE NEW WORLD

During the colonial period, from 1492 to about 1800 (see Chapter 16), the old and the new converged in different ways in British North America and in Latin America (including those parts of South America, the Caribbean, and Mexico where Spanish, Portuguese, or French, all derived from Latin, are spoken).

In the south, the imprint of European social, religious, and political institutions was heavy; in the north, it was light. In the south, large indigenous Amerindian populations molded colonial culture; in the north, the native presence was slighter. The economy of the southern region depended on plantations, ranches, or mines sustained by impressed Indian or slave labor; the economy of the northern region was more varied. The proportions of old and new in New World civilizations help explain their development.

Brazil and the Caribbean: Plantation Nations

During the colonial era, Brazil and the Caribbean islands developed plantation economies of a type unknown in Europe, but dominated by European elites. From the outset, Christopher Columbus (1451–1506) began building a New World economy different from the old. The climate was favorable, and the wilderness beckoned with fantasies of countless stores of gold. Columbus established a fortified city, and set six Dominican friars to convert and "civilize" the native Tainos. Within a generation, ships laden with New World treasures sailed regularly to Spain.

The Caribbean Tobacco was the first cash crop farmed in the Spanish-ruled Caribbean islands, followed by sugar, brought by Dutch merchants by way of Brazil. Having learned to grow sugar in Asia, the Portuguese developed the plantation system, sustained by slave labor, in their Atlantic islands of the Madeiras and São Tomé. Sugar cultivation was imported into Brazil, along with cargoes of slaves. From there, it reached the Caribbean islands.

The Amerindians of the Caribbean—the Tainos, Caribs, and Arawaks—could not supply the huge labor force required to grow, harvest, and mill sugar cane. By around 1600, some ninety percent of the Caribbean natives had died from overwork, heartbreak, and disease. African slaves replaced the natives. These provided a labor pool that the armed Europeans managed brutally. Since neither women's labor nor their fertility was deemed valuable, male slaves outnumbered females two to one, which meant that the slave population could not maintain itself through reproduction. New shipments of African captives were constantly required. The increase in the numbers of slaves imported into the New World is shown in *How Many?* on p. 565.

The existence of slavery informed every aspect of the new Caribbean culture. African song, dance, and storytelling figured more powerfully than the Christian rituals or European refinements of the elite. A mixture developed of Christian and African customs, particularly in western Hispaniola (modern Haiti), where it became known as **voodoo**.

Soon Dutch, French, and English competitors challenged Spanish dominion of the Caribbean and its coastal rim. With the foothold of Dutch Guiana (later Surinam) on the northern coast of South America, the Dutch continued to play a significant role in Caribbean shipping. The French acquired half of Hispaniola, as well as the islands of Martinique and Guadeloupe, and the north coastal colony of French Guiana. The British controlled the Bahamas and Jamaica, as well as some islands of the Lesser Antilles, the colony of British Honduras on the mainland of Central America (later Belize), and a British sector of

Guiana. The small European landowner class that dominated a much larger slave population relied on its mother countries for defense and supplies.

By 1750, the Caribbean had changed dramatically from the early days of the Spanish conquest. The large population of Africans outnumbered whites and **mulattoes** (persons of mixed African and European parentage) about ten to one. The Amerindian natives had virtually disappeared. The economy was dominated by the production of sugar and the Spanish monopoly had been broken.

Brazil   Spain was the principal metropolitan power in the Caribbean, but Portugal dominated Brazil. Early explorers recognized growing near the coast of the new continent a tree used for dyes that Portuguese merchants had previously exported from Asia. Brazil itself was named after this breselwood, or brazilwood. For a generation, the shipping of dyewoods occupied the Portuguese exploiters of the new territory. Later, the Portuguese brought sugar to Brazil, along with the plantation system of sugar farming. On the plantation, slaves tended the sugar plants, cut the canes, and milled the sugar for which Europeans developed an insatiable demand. The plantation farming of sugar, then coffee, became the backbone of the Brazilian economy. As many as 3 to 5 million African slaves were imported to labor on Brazilian plantations from the early 1500s, about one-third to one-half of all slaves imported to the western hemisphere. By 1800, blacks and mulattoes comprised more than half of Brazil's population. The practice of frequent manumission (release from slavery) resulted in a large group of free blacks and mulattoes, who gathered in the cities and intermingled with white elites. The indigenous Amerindians, on the other hand, isolated in the tropical forests of the interior, had little contact with Europeans concentrated on the eastern shore.

The Brazilian economy was more diverse than the Caribbean, which was wholly dependent on plantation crops. In addition to dyewoods, Brazil exported other products from the tropical forest (especially the drugs curare and coca), and mined gold and diamonds. A late-colonial gold rush encouraged the growth of Brazil's southern cities of São Paulo and Rio de Janeiro, which supplanted the original port city of Bahía in importance. Brazilian products amounted to as much as two-thirds of Portugal's exports; as was the case elsewhere, metropolitan prosperity depended heavily on colonial produce.

All three major Brazilian cities also supported small manufacture, whose artisans were often black or mulatto. Blacks and mulattoes also worked in the cities as servants, carters, peddlers, and prostitutes. As one Brazilian observer noted, "it was the black who developed Brazil."

The Portuguese regime in Brazil was similar to that in Spanish South America, although less restrictive. Advised by his overseas Council on New World concerns, the king appointed a viceroy to govern Brazil, who was surrounded by the ceremony and luxury befitting a European monarch. Law courts were headed by royal officials, and a tax commission oversaw the farming of revenues (i.e. the granting to individuals of the lucrative right to collect taxes).

Regional administrators were military officials called captains, who enjoyed considerable latitude. They launched a tradition of military leadership in civilian affairs, which saw Brazil push its boundaries westward by the 1700s to the Andes Mountains and south to the Plata River.

Captains were often native Portuguese who later returned to more prominent positions at home, but some were creoles (white Americans descended from European forebears on both sides). Creoles were a social group of critical importance in both

HOW MANY?

Death Comes to the New World—Amerindian Mortality in Mexico

1500   20-25

Figures represent millions

1600   1.5

1800   4

The numerous Old World diseases (principally smallpox) that the Spanish inadvertently brought to the Americas nearly annihilated various Amerindian populations, as shown here for Mexico. The Amerindian population recovered somewhat from 1600 to 1800, but remained well below its pre-conquest high.

Portuguese and Spanish America: from their ranks came the magistrates who headed the councils of local "municipalities," which dealt with land disputes, water supply, or security, in addition to various judicial procedures.

The Portuguese system of colonial rule had two main problems. The first was the inevitable tension between creoles and European-born *peninsulares* ("peninsulars," or people from the Iberian peninsula), who directed the colony's affairs. While creoles often believed that the peninsulars did not understand the American context, the peninsulars looked down on the creoles. The second problem was that of incompetence, caused by the neglect of duties or corruption. In the eighteenth century, the king's chief minister, the Marquis of Pombal (1699–1777) raised the standard of colonial administration, and reasserted the dominion of the motherland over the creole elite. Recognizing that Portugal's fortunes depended on Brazil's prosperity, he promoted industry and meticulously managed the royal treasury.

The Portuguese crown also closely monitored Brazil's economic life. It held monopolies of important commodities and collected tariffs on nearly all American imports. It permitted only Portuguese ships to carry Brazilian trade, and encouraged only those crops or manufactures that were considered to complement the Portuguese economy. Such restrictions were characteristic of **mercantilism** (see Chapter 16), and weighed heavily on colonial economies.

Nevertheless, some colonial landowners acquired immense wealth from estates as vast as whole provinces of the European homeland. Leading members of the creole elite resented their subordination to peninsular Portuguese and sought higher marks of status. The formation of militias for colonial defense provided an opportunity for such men, whose attainment of high military rank narrowed the social distance between them and peninsular governors.

Portugal also dominated Brazil's cultural and intellectual life, and saw to the firm establishment of Christianity. As elsewhere in Latin America, the conversion of the native Amerindians was a first priority. Unlike the placid Tainos that Columbus first encountered, Brazil's Amerindians resisted both Christianization and Europeanization into the eighteenth century, when decrees from Lisbon still called for natives to wear clothes like the Portuguese.

Brazilians of European descent remained within the cultural world of the motherland, journeying to Europe for study and intellectual discourse. By this route the ideas of the Scientific Revolution and the Enlightenment finally reached Brazil, which by the end of the colonial period still had not a single printing press or university, in contrast to the twenty-three universities in the Spanish zone. The Portuguese crown prohibited the establishment of printing, for fear of its revolutionary potential.

Spanish America: Mine, *Hacienda*, and Village

Spanish America stretched from California and Texas in North America to Cape Horn at the tip of South America. In this vast realm, as in the Caribbean and Brazil, explorers, conquerors, and settlers created a new economic and social system modeled on European patterns but shaped by local conditions.

Spanish settlements were concentrated in Mexico, called New Spain, and Peru (including also modern Bolivia, Ecuador, Colombia, and Chile), where the Aztec and Inca empires had flourished (see Chapter 16). In the pre-conquest era, the majority of Amerindians lived in this region, with sparser populations inhabiting Brazil, the Caribbean islands, and North America. During the first century of Spanish dominion, disease ravaged the native population, which in places sank to under ten percent of its former strength. While the native population recovered somewhat in the seventeenth century, their numbers remained low into the nineteenth century, well below their pre-conquest levels.

Mexico, for instance, had a population as high as 25 million at the time of the conquest. In the early 1800s, the population numbered no more than 8 million, counting European whites, mulattoes, **mestizos** (of European and Amerindian parentage) and Amerindians—the latter numbering about fifty percent of the whole. *How Many?* on p.545 shows this decline. In all of Spanish America at that date, the population numbered just under 17 million. Of this figure less than half was Indian, nearly one-third mestizo, one-fifth white, and a small minority African. Amerindians were the largest group in Mexico and Central America, while Indians and mestizos together constituted a majority elsewhere in Spanish America.

Changes in the ethnic composition of Mexico and Peru are shown in the graphs on p. 559. Low population and physical barriers discouraged the settlement of interior regions of South America. Instead Spanish settlers remained in the charted regions of the Mexican plateau and the Pacific coast (eventually extending along the Plata River, consisting of modern Argentina and Paraguay). Here they established an economy based on mining and agriculture, and oriented toward European markets.

The Economy   In the early years of the Spanish American settlement, the thirst for gold and silver prevailed. Hernán Cortés (1485–1547), the conqueror of the Aztecs, sent home shiploads of golden trinkets of native manufacture, while Francisco Pizarro (c. 1475–1541), the conqueror of the Inca empire, found the "silver mountain" at Potosí (modern Bolivia), one of the richest silver mines ever known. With a population of some 160,000 around 1670, Potosí became the largest city in the New World.

Native Laborers in Spanish America

Following quickly upon the Spanish and Portuguese exploration, then conquest, of large parts of the Americas were settlement and exploitation. The conquistadores and their successors acquired land and privileges, and put the native population to work in ways that pressed them into dependency. These passages report the conditions imposed on laborers subject to an encomienda, which resembled the European manorial system, and the reality of life in the mines, where laborers were essentially slaves.

What natives owed two *Encomenderos* who arrived with Hernando Cortés in 1517: [The Amerindians] are assessed each day two chickens and four loads of wood and two loads of maize, and fodder for the horses; and every eighty days twenty petticoats, and twenty shirts, and four loads of blankets of henequen [a plant fiber], and the labor on their plantings of peppers, beans, maize, and wheat, and the carrying of all this to the city, and the completion of the house, and they are not to be charged beyond this. ...

On April 21, 1553, by agreement, the services of the thirty-two Indians ... were commuted, so that instead ... they are to give from now on 192 common gold pesos per year in payments made every eighty days. ...
(Encomienda Records from Nestalpa, 1547–1553; ed. C. Gibson, 1968)

Miners of Potosí (Bolivia), described by a Spanish missionary (c. 1622): [Once] I went ... into the mine. ... The ore was very rich black flint, and the excavation so extensive that it held more than 3,000 Indians working away hard with picks and hammers, breaking up that flint ore; and when they have filled their little sacks, the poor fellows, loaded down with ore, climb up ... ladders or rigging, some like masts and others like cables, and so trying and distressing that a man empty-handed can hardly get up them. ... [To support the mine walls, the Indians] keep leaving supports or pillars of the ore itself. ... [Yet] There are men so heartless that for the sake of stealing a little rich ore, they go down out of hours and deprive the innocent Indians of this protection by hollowing into these pillars to steal the rich ore in them, and then a great section is apt to fall in and kill all the Indians, and sometimes the unscrupulous and grasping superintendents themselves....
(From Antonio Vazquez de Espinosa, *Compendium and Description of the West Indies*, 1942)

At first, native Amerindian laborers performed the dangerous work of mining, but as their numbers plummeted during the sixteenth century, African slaves were imported. Even so, the number of slaves brought to Spanish America was much lower than in the Caribbean and Brazil, and enforced Indian labor remained central to the mining enterprise.

Further gold and silver strikes were made, and the value of exports peaked in the period c. 1580–1630. Mining experts from Europe introduced the amalgamation process, which used mercury to separate silver from its alloy. At such ports as Havana in Cuba or San Juan in Puerto Rico, consignments of precious metals were loaded onto hefty Spanish ships that sailed in convoy twice a year, guarded by armed men-of-war from attack by Dutch and English privateers.

For nearly two centuries, gold and especially silver were Spanish America's major exports. They enriched neither the native population nor the people of Spain, but trickled through the royal treasury to profit merchants in Amsterdam or London. Later, other minerals, cacao beans and grain, and beef and hides were shipped to European markets. In the eighteenth century, trade increased from a few sailings per year around 1700 to 189 in 1760–1761. The Spanish government's "House of Trade" (*casa de contratación*), headed by the merchants of Seville or Cadiz, operated according to mercantilist principles and designated only a few ports of entry for European manufactures or for American exports.

Spanish America's second major economic activity was farming. Crops were sold locally, supplying villagers, city dwellers, and the large mining communities. European and creole elites sought to own farmland, a source of both wealth and prestige.

The first generation of settlers won ***encomiendas*** from the crown, which were similar to the medieval fief. These grants had been used as a tool of the Reconquest in Spain from the Moors in earlier centuries, and were now brought to the Americas. In exchange for military services, the recipient was granted land and the right to the labor of a certain number of native Indians. In a chronically depopulated region, land without the right to commandeer a workforce valued little. The effect of the encomienda contract was to enserf, if not enslave, the Amerindian workers, as suggested by the passage quoted in *Witnesses* above. It was controversial in Spain, where the king accepted the Church's arguments against the enslavement of native Americans.

In time, the encomienda gave way to the ***hacienda***, a type of large farm, embracing the owner's "great house," family and servants, the workshop and stables, the fields and villages of native Indian farmers, as illustrated on p. 548. While neither serfs nor

Life on a Hacienda

❶ Indian town
❷ Hamlet of Indian town
❸ Central site of hacienda
❹ Quarters of permanent workers
❺ Owner's residence
❻ Farmland of hacienda
❼ Town and market

The hacienda was more than a farm. It was a system for the exploitation of the labor of Indian villagers, some resident, some part-time, who were tied to the Spanish owner by contract and debt. A simplified scheme of a typical hacienda is shown here. Source: Based on J. Lockhart, S. B. Schwartz, Early Latin America: A History of Colonial Spanish America and Brazil (Cambridge: Cambridge University Press, 1983)

slaves, villagers worked on the owner's land, in addition to farming their own plots. Owners provided tools and seeds, or made loans, for all of which repayment was expected. Villagers thus became bound as debt slaves—the **peons**, who soon constituted the majority of native Indians in Spanish America.

The more fortunate peons worked on lands owned by the Roman Catholic Church, which became the largest single landholder in the Americas. The clergy often proved more flexible creditors and sympathetic managers than their secular counterparts. When, in the late eighteenth century, crown-appointed reformers sought to limit church power, everyone suffered.

The Church in Spanish America played a complex role. The Christian clergy were both oppressors, who sought to suppress native culture, and liberators, who guided the people to the best possible life in the framework of the European conquest. They worked for the conversion of the natives, enforcing conformity to European norms, but they were also dispensers of charity, and the directors of hospitals and schools. They learned the Amerindian languages, and translated oral histories and folktales into Spanish. In the South American universities, they included courses in Indian languages to train new generations of pastors to native populations.

Organized by the very different pursuits of farming for local markets and mining for export, the Spanish American economy at first seems to have defined a two-class society: that of farm and mine owners or managers, and workers. The real situation was more complicated due to the factor of race. Initially, the elite was white, of European descent, while the workers were mostly native Indian. Soon, those racial divisions blurred as a result of miscegenation, or racial intermixture. The shortage of European females encouraged concubinage, and even marriage was legally permitted across race lines as early as 1501. Spanish America was a truly trans-racial society, based on social and sexual contact between Caucasoid, Mongoloid, and Negroid peoples (often identified as the three principal races).

Racial mixing, however, did not yield social equalization. On the contrary, white elites maintained the distinction of their status from those of Amerindians, the majority group that possessed the lowest prestige, and of the intermediate group called **castas** (including Africans, mulattoes, and mestizos).

Government   Europeans from the homeland, meanwhile, claimed superiority to creoles. Creoles might participate in government at the local level of the "municipality," serve as officers in the militia, or even hold high rank in the Church hierarchy. But nearly all the high positions in the government of Spanish America were entirely reserved for peninsulars. These social tensions persisted despite the fact that creoles and peninsulars often intermarried.

The exclusion of creoles from senior government positions mattered, since Spanish America was heavily governed. Two huge viceroyalties were formed in the first generation after the conquest: the Viceroyalty of New Spain, of which Cortés was the first viceroy; and that of Peru. All the affairs of the colonial empire flowed through the viceregal offices. Each viceroyalty was subdivided into regional governments, or **audiencias,** with only the smaller subdivision of the municipality left to creole governors. Sometimes prone to corruption, the Spanish colonial administration was on the whole efficiently managed.

In the eighteenth century, Spain experienced a change of royal dynasty, when a European war installed Bourbon kings related to the monarchs of France in place of the Habsburg line (see Chapter 15). The Spanish Bourbons brought to colonial administration the tools of government developed under the able ministers of the French king Louis XIV (r. 1643–1715). The viceroyalties were subdivided, and the two new ones of New Granada (1717) and La Plata (1776) added. A higher standard of efficiency was instituted just at the time, ironically, when both absolute monarchy and the policy of mercantilism were under fire from Enlightenment critics (see Chapters 16, 18).

The creole elites of Spanish America resisted the Bourbon "reforms." Some were critical of the monarchy, many more were critical of mercantilism, and most resented the imposition of peninsular officials upon a society that, they believed, could be better led by themselves. Creole officers grew bold in native militias, while creole leaders centered in Buenos Aires directed large-scale smuggling operations designed to evade prohibitions on imports by sea. Creole elites helped build city centers whose baroque palaces, churches, and other public buildings mimicked European capitals in their elegance and cosmopolitan air. Blind to the possibility of resistance to their regime by native Indian villagers, they were preparing to resist the monarchy and its peninsular minions when the opportunity arose.

At the same time, creole elites supported a Spanish American culture that was deeply attached to Europe. Schools and universities followed European models, while American-born historians, philosophers, and mathematicians kept abreast of European currents in thought. Mexico City and Lima had printing presses already in the 1500s, and by 1800, nearly twenty presses published books for the small confraternity of learned creoles. Entering a convent at age fifteen in preference to marriage, in a career typical of many learned European women, Sor Juana Inés de la Cruz (1651–1695) wrote verse in a classical Castilian that is indistinguishable from the best produced in Europe.

In Spanish America, creole women continued to pursue the roles that were traditional in European society, where male patriarchs administered property and made decisions. Creole men, however, had few women of European descent available to them—a shortage contributing to the practice of concubinage and the resulting racial mixtures. In licit and illicit relationships, Indian and *casta* women were subject to white males by gender and by race. A European system of gender discrimination was thus unfortunately reinforced by the American phenomenon of racial discrimination.

In this arena as in many others, Spanish America was a blend of European social hierarchies and cultural outlooks with New World peoples and environments. The two realities met in the person of the creole, who would soon take charge.

The North Atlantic Coast: The Beckoning Wilderness

On the eastern coast of North America, as in Latin America, European newcomers created new societies in the seventeenth and eighteenth centuries that preserved features of the customs and outlook of their homelands. The lands of the future United States of America employed English models of judicial procedure and governance. Religious groups that in Europe had coexisted with difficulty developed side by side in a new environment. In the absence of a hereditary nobility or standing army, and given a nearly limitless expanse of undeveloped territory extending to the west, European settlers sensed possibilities that were unknown on the far side of the Atlantic. As they pursued their goals, they intruded upon Amerindian natives who were compelled to yield their land to the newcomers; and upon African captives who were compelled to do their labor.

The French, Dutch, and English who followed the Portuguese and Spanish to the New World found a land thinly settled by Amerindian natives—no Inca or Aztec empires here—lacking conspicuous sources of wealth or any sign of a sea link to the riches of Asia. The first resource that Europeans exploited in North America was a humble one: fish. In the seas of the north Atlantic off modern Newfoundland (claimed by the English) and Nova Scotia (claimed by the French), schools of cod beckoned to merchant shippers. Soon European woodsmen (mostly French) searched the forests for furs, and European farmers (mostly English and Dutch) scratched the new soil to see what it would yield.

Early Settlements The first enduring European settlements north of Spanish Florida were made after 1600. French expeditions reached from Canada to the Mississippi, establishing forts, trading depots, and missions. From Quebec, founded in 1608, French governors administered their American realm as an extension of the homeland. That realm numbered no more than 80,000 citizens in 1756, including fishermen, traders, and hunters clustered around fortified settlements. Valued as suppliers of furs and as wilderness guides, Amerindian natives were neither impressed into labor service, as in Spanish America, nor even displaced, as they were in the British colonies to the south.

In time, the British colonies of North America surpassed the French in population and importance. The first English colonies at Jamestown (1607) and Plymouth (1620) were agricultural ventures with modest aims. They were organized by the Virginia and Plymouth Companies, who provided funds and supplies to start the settlers off in a new land. The settlers too were modest people who sought land to farm and freedom from the economic and cultural restrictions of life in old Europe. These features of the first English settlements were to influence the whole later process of colonial formation.

Other colonies formed around the Chesapeake Bay and in Massachusetts, Rhode Island, Connecticut, and New Hampshire. South of these New England colonies, Dutch companies concentrating on the Hudson waterway founded the province of New Netherland in 1623, the capital of which, New Amsterdam, was seized by the British and renamed New York in 1664. Pennsylvania, New Jersey, and Delaware developed between New York and the Chesapeake region before 1700, absorbing Swedish and Dutch settlements. South of Virginia, the Carolinas were settled in part by migration from the British West Indies, features of whose economy the new colonies displayed. By 1700, all but Georgia (founded in 1732) of the eventual thirteen colonies had been established. They were sparsely populated communities, clinging to the ocean shore and the banks of rivers that emptied into the Atlantic. Several (Massachusetts and Georgia, for example) were assumed to extend from the Atlantic seaboard westward across the continent—from "sea to sea"— long before the nature of that expanse could be known.

Originally organized by joint stock companies or individual proprietors, the colonies built their own institutions of local government, which by 1700 displayed some common features. Most had a governor appointed by a far-away king. The colonists taxed themselves to pay the governor's salary. A legislature decided upon those tax levies and managed other local matters. Colonists meeting minimal property requirements voted for representatives (drawn from the wealthiest stratum of the population). These voters constituted only about forty percent of the adult male population; they excluded all slaves, Amerindians, and women, as well as the poor, the young, and recent immigrants. Experience in self-government over more than 150 years inclined many Anglo-Americans to resist new demands from Parliament in the decade before the eventual strike for independence.

No European-born nobility held sway in Anglo-American society. Immigrants were often fleeing poverty or repression. The nobility and the wealthier merchants stayed home. Even the governors did not form a cohesive elite, buttressed by ritual and luxury, as they did to the south. Instead, the colonial elite developed from within in a land where upward mobility was possible (see the diagram on p. 553). Colonial leaders were very different from the hereditary aristocracies who reigned in Europe.

No standing army policed the colonists. To defend against internal rebellion, foreign infringement, or Indian raids, the colonists raised their own militias. Regular army troops were not dispatched to the Americas until war broke out with the French in 1756 (see below). They provided a military education to the colonial militias, who would profit from their lessons a few years later.

At first, the colonial economy relied upon Britain's. Local artisans and merchants fulfilled local needs, although the colonies remained dependent on Britain (as the mother country wished) for manufactures. Mercantile restrictions encouraged the colonists were to produce goods useful to the metropolis, and to transport their goods on British ships. In the early years of colonial development, these restrictions were seen more as benefits than burdens.

The colonists lived in European-style villages, with central church, official buildings, and public spaces. As in Europe, all family members were expected to labor. Men were the main workers outside the house, assisted by the older boys. Women performed domestic chores, spun and wove cloth, tended the vegetable garden and small animals, and trained their daughters in these tasks. The products of their artistry, sold to supplement household income, included textiles, processed foods, soap, candles, and the like.

Families were larger, on the whole, than in the homeland. Once the hardships of the early years were past, families with six or eight surviving children were common. These patterns led to high rates of population growth: in 1700, the British colonies had a population of about 250,000 white Europeans; by 1800, about 5 million people of European descent resided in Britain's former colonies, almost one half of the total population of England. The custom of **primogeniture** that prevailed in Britain (see Chapter 18) was often bypassed, and family property was divided among all children, including girls. Women (especially widows) and children enjoyed a higher status than in British society.

The competition to inherit was eased in the colonies because of the open territory that lay beyond the last fenced plot in the village. Not even natural barriers restricted the opportunities for landownership: in eastern North America, there were no mountain ranges as high as the Andes, no rivers as vast as the Amazon, and no treacherous, disease-ridden jungles. The perceived promise of easy abundance just

African Laborers in a Harsh New World

Eastman Johnson, A Ride for Liberty—The Fugitive Slaves, c. 1862

Advertisement for sale of slaves, July 24, 1769

After early, unsuccessful attempts to impress Indians into labor service, Europeans in all parts of the Americas began to rely heavily on imported African slaves. A 1769 poster from Charleston advertises the sale of slaves originating in Sierra Leone (above left). The desperation of a slave family on the run in North America is captured in the dramatic image of A Ride for Liberty by the American painter Eastman Johnson (above right). Such attempts at escape rarely succeeded. In a more prosaic scene, slave women are shown working in the cotton fields, one accompanied by her child (right). (above right: Brooklyn Museum, New York)

Slaves picking cotton

To continue your investigation of this topic, please go to www.prenhall.com/king for the related **WINDOWS** on the **WEB** activity

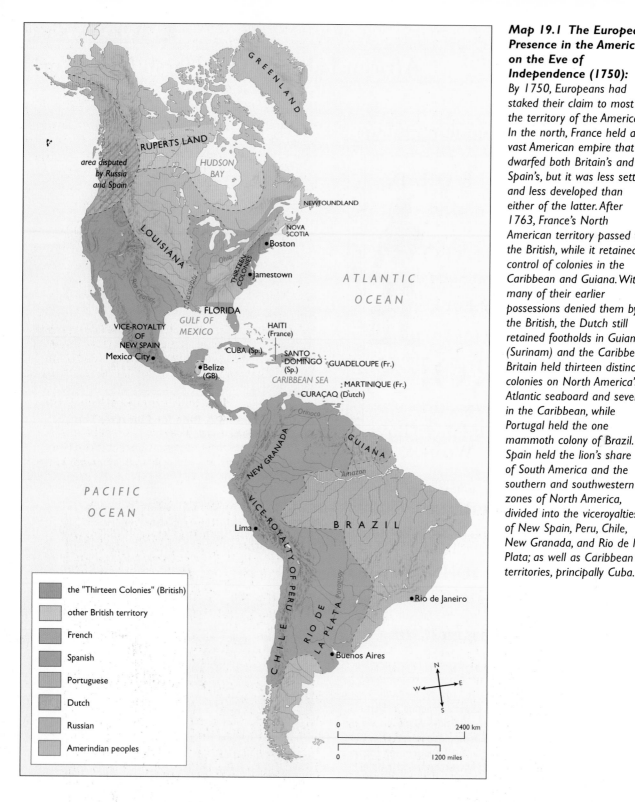

Map 19.1 The European Presence in the Americas on the Eve of Independence (1750): By 1750, Europeans had staked their claim to most of the territory of the Americas. In the north, France held a vast American empire that dwarfed both Britain's and Spain's, but it was less settled and less developed than either of the latter. After 1763, France's North American territory passed to the British, while it retained control of colonies in the Caribbean and Guiana. With many of their earlier possessions denied them by the British, the Dutch still retained footholds in Guiana (Surinam) and the Caribbean. Britain held thirteen distinct colonies on North America's Atlantic seaboard and several in the Caribbean, while Portugal held the one mammoth colony of Brazil. Spain held the lion's share of South America and the southern and southwestern zones of North America, divided into the viceroyalties of New Spain, Peru, Chile, New Granada, and Rio de la Plata; as well as Caribbean territories, principally Cuba.

beyond the next hill or stream shaped the American consciousness and persists to the present day.

Amerindians and Africans   That beckoning wilderness was not vacant, of course, but inhabited by some 1 million natives who possessed no concept of private property, considering the land to belong to their tribes and nations. In their first encounters with Amerindian natives, the colonists often established

friendly relations. In some cases, settlers negotiated a contract with Indian tribes for the use of their land. The Dutch famously purchased Manhattan island from the Indians of that name, and the Quaker William Penn (1644–1718) bought land as needed from his Indian "Friends." Such peaceful exchanges gave way to conflict. Occasionally, natives displaced from their lands responded by raiding colonial settlements. The colonists replied, fighting small-scale wars

The Social Pyramid in Colonial North America, 1775

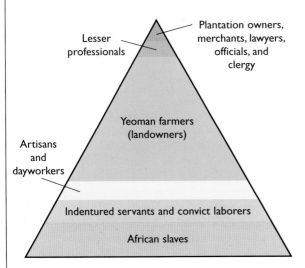

Britain's North American colonies did not avoid the social inequalities of the mother country, but exceeded them. "Merchant princes" and landed gentry sat at the very top of a pyramid that led all the way down to African slaves.
Source: *Based on T. A. Bailey,* The American Pageant: A History of the Republic, *Vol. I, 5th ed. (Lexington, MA: D. C. Heath and Co. 1975), p. 70.*

along the shores of the James or Connecticut rivers in Virginia and New England. Indian nations leagued together to protect their ancestral territories, sometimes allying with the French against British intruders, or with the British against the French.

Not all the interactions between Indian natives and European settlers involved violence, however. Religious and intellectual leaders called for the conversion and "civilization" of the Indians, and some were indeed converted to Christianity in the early decades of settlement. The Protestant missionary effort, however, was a lame thing in contrast to the extraordinarily successful conversion efforts of the Roman Catholic Church in Latin America.

New World Cultural Encounters

John White, **Indian Woman and Child:** *One of the earliest English observers of Amerindians and their culture, colonist John White painted this watercolor (far left) of an Amerindian mother and child—the latter holding a doll dressed in European style—in around 1585. (British Museum)*

Albert Eckhout, **Mulatto:** *Whereas in the north, European settlers and natives kept their distance, in Spanish America, Africans, Amerindians, and Europeans mixed freely, so that individuals of mixed racial background, such as this mulatto soldier painted in around 1641 (left) were increasingly common. (The National Museum of Denmark)*

Native Removal in Anglo-America

In Anglo-American North America, Amerindian tribes and nations presented a singular difficulty to a new nation intent on territorial and economic expansion. Tragically, finding that Amerindians did not readily assimilate European patterns of life, national leaders made the decision to push them westward, with hopeful but empty promises of a satisfactory new homeland. In this new homeland, uprooted Amerindians would suffer violence, poverty, and isolation.

Lewis Cass, Governor of Michigan Territory 1813–1831, discusses the case for Indian Removal (1830): The destiny of the Indians, who inhabit the cultivated portions of the territory of the United States, or ... their borders, has long been a subject of deep solicitude to the American government and people. ...

[V]arious plans for their preservation and improvement were ... pursued. Many of them were carefully taught at our seminaries of education, in the hope that principles of morality and habits of industry would be acquired. ... Missionary stations were established among various tribes. ... Unfortunately, they are monuments ... of unsuccessful and unproductive efforts. What tribe has been civilized by all this expenditure of treasure, and labor, and care? ...

The cause of this total failure cannot be attributed to the nature of the experiment, or to ... [those] who have directed it. ... [T]here seems to be some insurmountable obstacle in the habits or temperament of the Indians. ... [I]f [the Indians] ... are anxious to escape ... [from United States states' laws] ample provision has been made ... A region is open to them, where they and their descendants can be secured in the enjoyment of every privilege which they may be capable of estimating and enjoying. If they choose to remain where they now are, they will be ... subject, as our citizens are, to the operation of just and wholesome laws.

(Lewis Cass, *Removal of the Indians*, January 1830; eds. T. Purdue and M. D. Green, 1995)

Andrew Jackson, President 1828–1837, on the need for and progress of Indian removal (1835): The plan of removing the aboriginal people who yet remain within the settled portions of the United States to the country west of the Mississippi River approaches its consummation. ... All preceding experiments for the improvement of the Indians have failed. It seems now to be an established fact that they cannot live in contact with a civilized community and prosper.... .

The plan for their removal and reestablishment ... has been dictated by a spirit of enlarged liberality. [They are to be given ample lands, supplies of clothing and arms, and provisions sufficient for one year after their arrival.] In that time, from the nature of the country and of the products raised by them, they can subsist themselves by agricultural labor, if they choose to resort to that mode of life; if they do not they are upon the skirts of the great prairies, where countless herds of buffalo roam.... .

[Arrangements have been made to build schools, churches, dwellings for the chiefs, and to provide funds for poor relief, tools, steel, and iron.] And besides these beneficial arrangements, annuities are in all cases paid ... in all cases sufficiently great, if justly divided and prudently expended, to enable them, in addition to their own exertions, to live comfortably.

(From J. D. Richardson ed., *A Compilation of the Messages and Pages of the Presidents 1787–1897*, 1896–1899)

Trade flowed between Europeans and Indians. The former craved hides and furs, and the latter sought guns and other manufactures. European settlers also transmitted their diseases to the natives, who as in Latin America had no natural immunity to smallpox, diphtheria, and other illnesses. Disease caused an absolute decline in the native populations, so that the demographic balance between the two races shifted: the handful of settlers, who multiplied and prospered, became a majority among a shrinking community of natives. Weakened in numbers, diminished by their need for Western goods, undermined by quasi-legal land grabs and patronizing attempts at conversion, Indian communities were vulnerable as the colonies expanded across a continent they came to see as theirs.

While Indians were not forced to labor on settlers' farms, as in Latin America, African slaves were. The first shipment of slaves arrived in Jamestown on a Dutch ship in 1619, only twelve years after the colony was founded. Thereafter, slaves trickled into British North America, mostly to the southern colonies, where a sub-tropical climate promoted the cultivation of cash crops—first tobacco, then rice and indigo, and finally cotton—in a plantation system similar to that in the Caribbean islands. By 1700, the foundations of a plantation economy had been laid in Virginia and the Carolinas. In the northern colonies, too, a few African slaves labored as domestic servants, sailors, and artisans.

The slave economy supported a social organization in which African people were assigned the lowest rank. British elites in the West Indies had elaborated this racial perspective, which was adopted by North American planters. Racial prejudices did not prevent racial mixing, however, as slaveholders demanded the sexual cooperation of female slaves and permitted the raising of mixed-race offspring on their plantations.

Racial mixture followed a course different from that in Spanish America, however. In British America, there was little miscegenation of Europeans and Indians. The offspring of European men and slave women, moreover, were considered to be slaves and to be black, regardless of the fairness of their skin.

Slavery developed slowly in the British colonies because of the availability of "indentured servants." These were Europeans, male or female, who had contracted to come to the New World. In return for their passage, they sold their labor for a set number of years—generally four to seven. Unlike the Amerindian peon of Spanish America, or the African slave, the indentured servant might anticipate social opportunity equal to that of any other New World settler when the terms of indenture had been fulfilled.

A New Society   The opportunities offered by flourishing British colonies, and by a seemingly limitless wilderness beyond, attracted Europeans other than the English. There came the Scots, Welsh, and Irish from the British Isles, as well as Swedes and Dutch. Even in its first century, although strongly imprinted by its English heritage, the culture of North America was open and pluralistic.

In contrast to European countries, where memories of religious war, and of the demand for conformity, enforced by violence, were still vivid, in British America there was no **established religion**. Some colonies did align themselves with one branch of Christianity, collecting taxes for its support, and inviting dissenters to depart; but they never knew the Inquisition, the demands of an overweening clergy, or the presence of a monolithic Church as chief landowner or creditor. Religion remained a powerful force in British America, but not a unitary power.

Nevertheless, in Puritan New England especially, religion ruled sternly, demanding conformity to its understanding of God's will. Puritan austerity gradually waned and during the 1730s and 1740s a tide of religious expression called the Great Awakening swept the colonies. It demanded of worshippers not merely an outward conformity to religious norms but a deep commitment stemming from an experience of transformation, of being "born again" in faith. That religious current has persisted in American life.

Unburdened by an established church, a hereditary nobility, or the excessive control of royal government, the British colonists profited from their freedom. When, after 1763, in the aftermath of the French and Indian War, the British crown imposed a new round of economic demands and mercantile restrictions upon its North American colonists, the latter were unwilling to accept them. The French and Indian War had been the American phase of a worldwide struggle between the two powers of Britain and France, then preeminent in Europe. In its European phase known as the Seven Years' War (1756–1763),

Britain struggled to snatch primacy from France and its ally Spain. At the same time, Britain wrested from France the controlling position in the sub-continent of India. In North America, Britain won Canada in the north, and vast unexplored territories to the west which restive colonists were ready to investigate.

The war also brought the British face to face with their own American colonists, whose wealth, military capacity, and incipient claims for cultural and political autonomy became apparent. British citizens shouldered one of the highest tax rates in Europe, and Parliament looked to the colonists to pay a fairer share of the costs of the recent war. Parliament's pursuit of this objective, coupled with its enforcement of mercantilist restraints, was to lead to another war in North America—one the British would lose.

By this time, however, key features of Britain's political and cultural life had been re-rooted on American soil. There they produced new fruit. In British North America, as in Latin America, those who transplanted features of European life into the western hemisphere created exactly what the explorers thought they had stumbled upon: a New World.

DECLARATIONS OF INDEPENDENCE

Map 19.1 on p. 552 shows the European presence in the Americas in 1750. Within two generations of the Treaty of Paris (1763) that ended the French and

---

WHO'S WHO

Liberators of Latin America

François Dominique Toussaint L'Ouverture (c. 1748–1803), leader of the African slaves of Saint-Dominique who created Haiti, the first republic in the western hemisphere.

Miguel Hidalgo (1753–1811), Mexican priest who led an insurgent army of thousands of native Indians against the capital city in 1810, in the opening bid for Mexican independence.

Pedro I, Brazilian king (r. 1822–1831) who declared Brazilian independence in 1822 and accepted the title of "Constitutional Emperor."

Simón de Bolívar (1783–1830)

Antonio José de Sucré (1794–1830)

Bernardo O'Higgins (c. 1777–1842)

José de San Martín (1778–1850)

} four creole aristocrats who fought Spanish armies from 1810–1826, winning the independence of Venezuela, Colombia, Ecuador, Peru, Bolivia, Chile, and Argentina.

Indian War, most of the European New World colonies achieved independence. A North American rebellion against Britain unexpectedly succeeded, and led to the creation of a new nation. Fired by that example and by a favorable tide of events in Europe, the South American colonies rebelled a generation later. The monarchs of France, Spain, Portugal, and Great Britain were made to acknowledge that peoples who were once their subjects were now independent players in the concert of nations.

Atlantic North America: War for Independence

The United States of America was the first nation of the Western world successfully to graduate from colonial status to autonomy. The strength of its own, original institutions enabled the United States to win independence. So did the quality of its leaders, trained in European values and ideas which would soon find expression in a written constitution that was the legal foundation of the new nation.

The Roots of Revolution   The Treaty of Paris of 1763 granted Britain all the land between the Appalachians and the Mississippi River, as well as Quebec, the core of New France (in addition to Florida, ceded by Spain, France's ally). It also, as it turned out, laid the foundations for Britain's defeat in the American War for Independence that broke out twelve years later.

The Proclamation of 1763, as required by the Treaty of Paris, reserved the western territory to the Indian nations settled there, and denied it to angry colonists hopeful of expanding westward. In 1774, Britain further angered the mostly Protestant colonists by extending religious and civil liberties to the Roman Catholic French Canadians. Meanwhile, Parliament had imposed new taxes on the colonists, who believed themselves exempt from taxation, and Parliament powerless to tax them. Parliament for its part needed to repay the heavy costs of fighting the French and Indian War.

Parliament proceeded to levy a series of taxes, culminating in the Stamp Act of 1765, which required the purchase of a license or stamp to read a newspaper or send a letter or execute a legal document. After fierce and determined colonial resistance Parliament repealed the Stamp Act in 1766. At the same time, doggedly, it issued the Declaratory Act, a sullen piece of legislation that affirmed Britain's power to tax its colonies.

John Trumbull, **The Signing of the Declaration of Independence, July 4, 1776:** *This famous depiction (based on his own miniatures with portrait heads of Adams and Jefferson painted from life) of the moment of signing in Independence Hall in Philadelphia on the first July 4th was painted by John Trumbull, a veteran of the Revolutionary war, and mounted to much public acclaim in the United States Capitol in 1819. (Yale University Art Library)*

In 1767, Parliament imposed the Townshend Duties on imports. The new levies spurred a response from a network of cooperating colonial assemblies, led by Massachusetts. Active resistance in Massachusetts, punctuated by violence, led to military occupation. In 1770, British soldiers fired on unarmed protesters, killing five—the notorious "Boston Massacre."

By 1773, Parliament had removed all duties except a tax on tea, levied as a subsidy to the East India Company then suffering from foreign competition. American consumers protested by the ostentatious non-consumption of tea. The Boston Sons of Liberty, one of the groups of disciplined protesters the colonies had developed since the first resistance of 1765, responded colorfully to the arrival of a shipment in Boston Harbor. On December 16, 1773, dressed up like Indians, they slipped by night onto the anchored ships and threw the tea overboard. Parliament responded with the Coercive Acts of 1774, which ordered Boston Harbor closed until the tea was paid for and established martial law in the city.

The leaders of the colonial revolt against Parliament were members of the affluent merchant and planter classes, whose economic interests had been threatened by parliamentary actions since 1763. Yet it would be too simple to ascribe their opposition to Britain solely to economic self-interest. That would be to exclude the dimension of intellectual culture, at the very moment when, in Europe, its development was high in quality and particularly relevant to the American scene (see Chapter 17).

In America as in Europe, men gathered to discuss the latest ideas and world events in libraries, academies, and clubs. Schools and universities trained Americans on home soil, and literacy was high. American leaders were well-read, both in the Classics and in contemporary discussions of the purpose of government, individual rights, private property, and the social contract. Readers of John Locke (1632–1704) and the Enlightenment *philosophes*, they believed passionately in the quest for individual freedom, the need for toleration, the importance of representation and due process. They extended the Enlightenment analysis of the evils of despotism to the American context, where it no longer made any sense (they believed) for hereditary rulers to govern free men. Enlightenment theory combined with themes of resistance between 1763 and 1776, when the first modern nation declared its abdication from the world's first global empire.

It was not sufficient, however, for lofty minds to form theories; American leaders also had to unite and develop a sense of nationhood. A common purpose is evident in the Committees of Correspondence, established throughout the colonies to spread information about developments in Boston, and in 1774, twelve of the thirteen colonies (all but Georgia) sent fifty-six representatives to the First Continental Congress. Clearly, colonial leaders had begun to see their

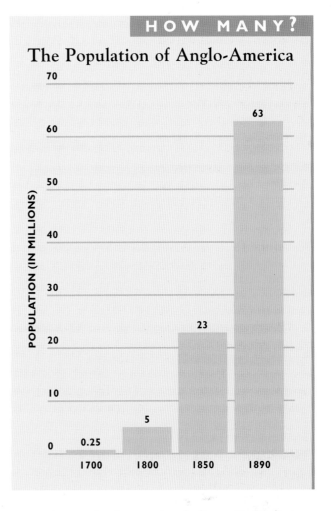

HOW MANY?

The Population of Anglo-America

(Bar chart. Vertical axis: POPULATION (IN MILLIONS), 0 to 70.)

- 1700: 0.25
- 1800: 5
- 1850: 23
- 1890: 63

enterprise as having national dimensions, distinct from its European roots. Then, in the spring of 1775, a swift series of events carried this movement forward.

Rebellion   Fearing a British offensive, Massachusetts militiamen had stockpiled ammunition at the town of Concord outside of Boston. The British dispatched troops to seize it. On April 19, as the redcoated soldiers marched through the village of Lexington, a shot rang out—the famous "shot heard round the world," prefiguring not only the American but subsequent revolutions around the globe. From Concord, where they faced American militiamen, the British returned to Boston harried by the local farmer-soldiers whose guerrilla tactics contrasted memorably with the strict order of the well-drilled redcoats. In Boston itself, martial law reigned.

The battles of Lexington and Concord forced the gentlemen in Congress to make some decisions during the winter of 1775–1776. Did they represent one nation or thirteen colonies? Did what happened in Massachusetts affect the other twelve colonies? If so, should they attempt to heal the break with Britain, or league together to oppose her? An impassioned printer, the recent immigrant Thomas Paine (1737–1809) sharply defined the issues in his pamphlet *Common Sense* (1776). An instant bestseller (some 100,000 copies were circulated), it called on the public to recognize what was already an accomplished fact: the American colonies were a new nation, dedicated to the pursuit of trade and liberation from the tyranny they had left behind in their common European past.

In the spring of 1776, the Second Continental Congress appointed a committee to draft a document declaring independence. The Virginian lawyer and slaveowner Thomas Jefferson largely composed the text of the Declaration of Independence that, with emendations, the members of Congress signed on July 4. This, the founding moment of the United States as a nation is depicted on p. 556. An extract from the text is given in *Witnesses* on p. 570.

Britain dealt brutally with rebels, and those who signed the Declaration of Independence placed their lives at risk. They were supported by some eighty percent of the colonists. The twenty percent who were **Loyalists** stayed in the wings of the British army, or fled to Canada.

The American Revolution, or War for Independence, was fought by badly trained and poorly supplied regular soldiers and militia contingents facing a highly efficient army. Nevertheless, after initial losses and hardships, and aided by a French alliance, the war ended with the surrender of the British general, the 1st Marquis Cornwallis (1738–1805), to George Washington (1732–1799) at Yorktown, Virginia, following a joint American and French blockade. Two years later in 1783 in Paris, diplomats negotiated a peace treaty that recognized the new nation, the United States of America, and granted it land from the Atlantic seaboard to the Mississippi River.

The New Nation   What kind of nation was the new United States to be? Would it be modeled on England, with a king and a parliament? Would the thirteen states be self-governing, or would they be subdivisions of one state, relating to each other through a central, or **federal** government? These issues were hammered out over the next generation.

Under the "Articles of Confederation" the thirteen former colonies each retained autonomy and cooperated in the war effort. In 1787, the Constitutional Convention convened at Philadelphia to consider a new framework for government. The former colonial leaders James Madison, John Jay, and Alexander Hamilton collaborated on the *Federalist Papers*, essays composed to convince the public of the need for a strong centralized, or federal government to guide foreign policy, oversee interstate commerce, adjudicate disputes between different states, and fund projects of interest to the whole nation. Despite a considerable amount of reluctance, the Constitution was adopted in 1788 after ratification by the necessary minimum of nine states.

The Constitution of the United States adopts principles from two political theorists of the Enlightenment: John Locke and Montesquieu (see Chapter 17). From Locke it takes the principle of rule by an assembly of representatives, whose interests must be respected by any executive power whose own potential for tyrannical rule is thereby curtailed. From Montesquieu it takes the principle of balancing the functions of government (executive, legislative, judicial), so that each checks and balances the others. These principles, committed to writing, have survived without serious challenge and have served as a model for emerging governments around the world.

In 1791, a Bill of Rights containing ten articles was ratified. These became the first ten amendments to the Constitution, guaranteeing freedom of speech, assembly, and the press; the right of citizens to bear arms and thus fight as a militia to defend the nation; the sanctity of the citizen's property and privacy; freedom in judicial matters from the requirement of self-incrimination, and from "cruel and unusual punishment," referring to the use of torture and abusive conditions of imprisonment in contemporary European judicial systems.

The American War of Independence, it has often been noted, was less a revolution than a nationalist revolt. Nothing was "turned over" except the leadership of the country: economy, society, and culture developed after 1783 along the same lines they had pursued prior to 1774. The leaders of the American Revolution nevertheless made two extraordinary conceptual leaps. For the first time in the history of the West, they had envisioned the possibility of a legitimate challenge to established political power by ordinary citizens. And they had created a written instrument of government, again the first in the history of the West, that guaranteed individual rights, guarded against arbitrary power, balanced the different functions of government, and provided a mechanism for its amendment. The government created by these programs was not yet a democracy; but it was a frame within which democracy could, and ultimately did, take form.

Revolution in Haiti and Mexico

The North American precedent of a war for independence soon found imitators in the Latin south. The first of the Latin American revolts occurred in the French Caribbean colony of Saint-Domingue (formerly part of the island of Hispaniola) renamed by the victorious rebels "Haiti." This, too, was a nationalist revolt, which replaced French colonial administrators with a local elite. It was even more a profound revolution, in which slaves rose up against masters, blacks against whites.

The revolution began in 1791, during the French revolution of which Caribbean slaves halfway around the world had heard. They rose up under the leadership of the educated son of African slaves, François Dominique Toussaint L'Ouverture (c. 1748–1803), a

Changes in the Ethnic Composition of Latin American Populations

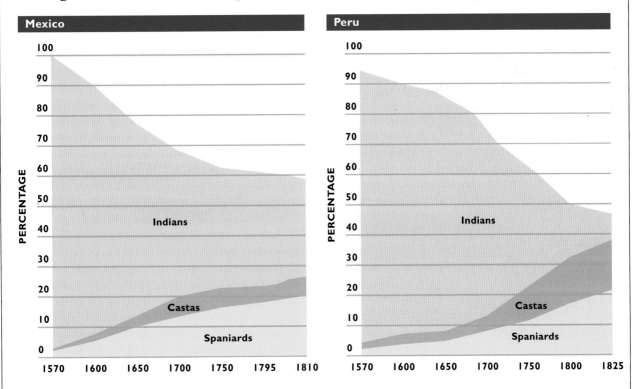

The heavy toll on Indian populations wrought by European diseases, the rise of immigration from the Old World to the New, and miscegenation among Spaniards, Amerindians, and African slaves profoundly altered the ethnic composition of Mexico and Peru during the colonial period. In both cases, the Amerindian component of the population fell markedly while the population of Spanish settlers rose. The population of castas (an intermediate group including Africans, mulattoes, and mestizos), a consequence of racial diversity and mixing, increased to form about fifteen percent of the Mexican, and thirty percent of the Peruvian population by their respective terminal dates.

Source: J. Lockhart, S. B. Schwartz, *Early Latin America: A History of Colonial Spanish America and Brazil* (Cambridge: Cambridge University Press, 1983), pp. 320, 342

slave himself. Leading a half-million slaves and some 25,000 mulattoes against 40,000 whites, by 1801 he had gained control of the whole of Hispaniola. The French, now ruled by Napoleon (1769–1821) (see Chapter 20), captured the insurgent slave. L'Ouverture died in 1803, a prisoner in France. His lieutenants persisted, and in 1804 they declared independence for the western half of the island, which they called Haiti. A state ruled by former slaves, Haiti became the second independent nation in the western hemisphere, the first in Latin America. Slaveowners everywhere trembled.

A struggle for independence in New Spain soon followed. This revolution remained unfinished, however, as more conservative forces seized power in the newly independent country, and creole and peninsular elites struggled for dominance in what later became Mexico. Their quarrel opened an opportunity for the priest Miguel Hidalgo (1753–1811), who in 1810 led an insurgent army of tens of thousands of native Indians against the capital city. He massacred the militia forces sent against him, abolished slavery, declared independence; then, believing his mission to be now fulfilled, he sent his followers home.

Captured and executed by the Spaniards in 1811, Hidalgo was the first leader of the Mexican revolution. The second was José María Morelos (1765–1815), also a priest. Following Hidalgo's lead, he raised an army, called for social equality and the redistribution of land; but in 1815 he, too, was captured and executed. In 1821, Mexico finally gained its independence from Spain. But independence was not accompanied by the social revolution envisioned by the priestly rebels Hidalgo and Morelos. A creole elite (who were joined by royalist peninsulars) established General Augustín de Iturbide (1783–1824) as emperor. Slavery continued, the Indians won no new land, and Mexico continued to swing from leader to leader for the next few decades.

Transition in Brazil and Paraguay

The violent revolution in Haiti and the unfinished one in Mexico contrast with peaceful transitions from colonial rule to independence in Brazil and Paraguay.

In 1807, as Napoleon blasted through the Iberian peninsula, the prince-regent of Portugal, John VI (r. 1799–1826), fled to take refuge in Brazil, where his presence united and animated the colony. When the king returned to Lisbon in 1821, he left his son and heir Pedro (r. 1822–1831) in Rio de Janeiro to preside over an American court now considered equal to the Portuguese. Creole officials were enthusiastic about the elevation of Brazil, but pressed for greater autonomy. Pedro yielded, declaring Brazil's independence in 1822 and accepting the title of "Constitutional Emperor." The constitution was ratified in 1824 and remained unchallenged until the monarchy fell in 1889. Local support for the constitutional monarchy increased in 1840, when Pedro's American-born son, Pedro II (1831–1889), ascended the throne. Brazil was now a wholly independent and wholly American nation.

Independence also came bloodlessly for Paraguay, accompanied by a profound social revolution. In 1811, while the king of Spain was a captive of Napoleon, a congress of Paraguayans declared their independence both from Spain and from the viceroyalty of La Plata. They chose a dictator: the lawyer and theologian José Gaspar Rodríguez de Francia (1766–1840), notoriously cruel but admired by historians for his competent administration of a poor and complex nation.

Aided by local creole elites, Francia nationalized the former crown and church lands, which he organized as a series of state ranches, rented for nominal fees to any Indians willing to labor there. Agricultural production increased, easing the poverty of the Indian population and enhancing the country's prosperity. With further improvements in education and manufacture to his credit, the unpleasant Francia emerges alongside the Portuguese monarchs, the former slave L'Ouverture, and the martyred priests Hidalgo and Morelos, as a hero of Latin American independence.

Spanish South America: Victory at Ayacucho

Spanish South America boasted heroes still more celebrated: Simón Bolívar (1783–1830) and his lieutenant Antonio José de Sucre (1795–1830) of Venezuela, Bernardo O'Higgins (c. 1777–1842) of Chile, and José de San Martín (1778–1850) of Argentina. From 1810 to 1826, these creole aristocrats fought Spanish armies and won independence for the regions of New Granada, Peru, and La Plata, from which were carved seven sovereign states

A Different Path for Spanish America

In his address at Angostura in 1819, the South American revolutionary leader, Simón Bolívar, calls for a republican constitution for the new state of Venezuela. This was to be centered on the principle of equality, in order to build a liberal society that would fully embrace the multiethnic peoples of the region.

I must say that it has never for a moment entered my mind to compare the position and character of two states as dissimilar as the English-American [i.e. the United States] and the Spanish-American. Would it not be most difficult to apply to Spain the English system of political, civil, and religious liberty? Hence, it would be even more difficult to adapt to Venezuela the law of North America. Does not [the French *philosophe* Montesquieu] state that laws should be suited to the people for whom they are made ... [and] that they should be in keeping with ... their inclinations, resources, number, commerce, habits, and customs? This is the code we must consult, not the code of Washington! ...

Our people are neither European nor North American; rather, they are a mixture of African and the Americans who originated in Europe. ... The greater portion of the native Indians has been annihilated; Spaniards have mixed with Americans and Africans, and Africans with Indians and Spaniards. While we have all been born of the same mother, our fathers, different in origin and in blood, are foreigners, and all differ visibly as to the color of their skin: a dissimilarity which places upon us an obligation of the greatest importance.

Under the Constitution, which interprets the laws of Nature, all citizens of Venezuela enjoy complete political equality. Although equality may not have been the political dogma of Athens, France, or North America, we must consecrate it here in order to correct the disparity that apparently exists. My opinion, Legislators, is that the fundamental basis of our political system hinges directly and exclusively upon the establishment and practice of equality in Venezuela. ... By this step alone, cruel discord has been completely eliminated. How much jealousy, rivalry, and hate have thus been averted!

(From H. A. Bierck and V. Lecuña eds., *Selected Writings of Bolívar*, 1951; trs. L. Bertrand)

of modern South America: Venezuela, Colombia, Ecuador, Peru, Bolivia, Chile, and Argentina. Bolívar's aspirations for the new state of Venezuela are quoted in *Witnesses* on p. 560.

Argentina swiftly won its independence, then joined the western armies that freed Chile, Peru, and Bolívar's "Great Colombia" (Bolivia, Colombia, Ecuador, and Venezuela). In 1807, British warships sailed into Buenos Aires. The creole militia resisted the attack and took charge of the nation. In 1817, its leader San Martín marched the Argentine army across the Andes to support the Chileans under O'Higgins. In 1820, he pressed on to Peru, the center of Spanish power in America. There, in 1822, he joined Bolívar. The final destruction of Spanish forces was wrought by Antonio de Sucre in 1824 at the battle of Ayacucho, which won independence for the new Latin states, and ensured the dominance of the creole elite.

The victory of these South American heroes was a victory for national autonomy, for Enlightenment values, and for free trade. It did not involve a social revolution, however, such as was dreamed of but abandoned in Mexico, and was secured for former slaves and Indian peons, respectively, in Haiti and Paraguay. The social and economic condition of the majority of the population was not affected by the achievement of independence.

As Map 19.2 on p. 562 shows, over the next generation, many of the modern nations of Spanish America emerged as free states, with the exceptions of Cuba, Panama, and Puerto Rico. The British, French, and Dutch retained their Caribbean and Guyanese possessions. As Europe, recovering from the Napoleonic wars (see Chapter 20), considered reviving its interests in the western hemisphere, the United States President issued a stern warning in 1823. The Monroe Doctrine stated that the Americas were not open "for future colonization by any European power," and that the United States would take any such attempt as "an unfriendly act." Protected by United States policy and, additionally, British interest in maintaining the Americas as a zone of free trade, the Latin American countries were free to pursue their own careers.

FULFILLING THE PROMISE

Both North and South America saw the triumph of liberal principles in the revolutions that occurred during the half-century following 1776. These enacted one of the ideals announced in the United States Declaration of Independence: the right of a people to abolish an abusive government, and institute a new one. They did not attempt to realize the other: the principle that all "men" are created equal. By 1880, the United States progressed some distance toward securing for all its citizens their "inalienable rights." In Latin America, that principle of liberalism was not yet even on the agenda.

The Reign of the *Caudillo*

From the 1820s through the 1880s, the nations of Latin America took form. Led by educated men descended from the creoles of the colonial era, economy, culture, and society were modernized. At the same time, traditional social patterns persisted, supported by two powerful conservative interests: the Church and the military. Consequently, most people found their condition no better, and perhaps worse, than it had been under colonial rule. To unify societies pulled between the ambitions of the elites and the needs of the masses, the autocratic strongman, or

Bolívar's Triumphal Entry into Caracas: *Born into an aristocratic Spanish family in Caracas, New Granada (today Venezuela) in 1783, Bolívar joined in the failed attempt to liberate his homeland in 1812, but succeeded in doing so in 1821. Here, Bolívar makes his triumphal entry.* (Private Collection)

caudillo, stepped in. Backed up by the military, the caudillos promoted the construction of new societies while suppressing any signs of disorder.

Trade with the Old World   In 1800–1880, the Latin American landowning elite developed its existing agricultural and mining enterprises. Commodities carried from the interior to port cities were transshipped abroad: coffee from Brazil and Central America; beef and hides from Argentina and Uruguay; tin from Bolivia and nitrates from Chile; from the great landed estates, or *latifundia*, all over Latin America a cornucopia of corn, cacao beans, nuts and bananas, medicinal plants and dyestuffs.

These goods traveled by railroad to waiting steamships, some fitted, after 1876, with refrigerated compartments for the shipment of beef. This new transportation technology had recently been developed in Europe (see Chapter 21), and rapidly found its way to assist the western hemisphere as it enlarged its role in the world marketplace. In 1815–1820, as few as two or three ships each year left Chile for England; in 1850, the figure was at least 300. During the same period, the value of exports shipped from Buenos Aires tripled. Boosted by coffee production, Brazil increased its foreign trade six- or sevenfold between 1883 and 1889. Overall, Latin American trade increased forty-three percent between 1870 and 1884, a period in which British trade increased just twenty-seven percent. While foreign trade boomed, local commerce between the regions of Latin America, where overland transport was difficult, lagged.

Map 19.2 Latin America from Independence to 1910: *From 1804 to 1838, most of Latin America gained independence from European empires. The Spanish, French, Dutch, and British all retained small islands and enclaves, especially in the Caribbean region, but most of these, too, became free by 1910. After achieving independence, the mainland territories fragmented into several states (with only Brazil avoiding fragmentation) to reach an eventual total of twenty autonomous republics for Latin America as a whole.*

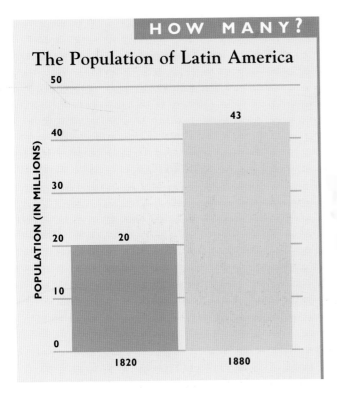

HOW MANY?

The Population of Latin America

Trade with Europe caused cities such as Buenos Aires, São Paulo, and Santiago to flourish. By 1869 the population of Buenos Aires rose to 250,000, then increased eightfold; by 1914, one of four Argentinians lived in that port city. In Chile, twenty-seven percent of the population was urban by 1875, forty-three percent by 1900. By 1850, Brazil's Atlantic coast was dotted with prosperous municipalities, with 500 more created between 1890 and 1914.

Some city-dwellers had migrated from the countryside, but many came from the impoverished zones of eastern and southern Europe in search of new opportunities. Those who succeeded joined native elites in striving to make their cities as much like European ones as possible. Adorned with grand boulevards and opera houses, railroad stations, senate buildings, and churches, these imitated the latest trends in European architecture and city planning, aspiring to be as grand as Paris.

Urban elites and landed proprietors purchased the manufactures of industrial Europe, especially Britain. In 1825, half of British exports to the western hemisphere were to Latin America, and half of these to Brazil alone. "Spanish America is free," one British official remarked considering the opportunities there for trade and investment, "and ... she is English." With competition from the fine products of Europe's new factories (see Chapter 21), the wares produced by local artisans sank in value. Latin American manufactures, poorer in quality and prestige, were destined primarily for local markets.

The Latin American economy came to depend on European capital, and financiers set up banks in the expanding cities. They funded the building of roads, ports, and eventually railroads for transporting goods from the interior to the harbors. They also funded the emerging Latin American states, which were often unable to service their debts and suffered bankruptcy. Despite wealth accumulated in some social sectors, government and society remained insecure—one consequence of an economy that produced, as was often lamented, "growth without development."

Divided Societies The beneficiaries of economic growth were the same elite who resisted colonial rule and led their peers to rebellion. They now ruled the fragile nations that had been formed in revolution. Sharing power with them were the leaders of the Church and the army.

As before, the Church's role was complex. On the one hand, it was a major landowner and, before the advent of complex banking, a source of finance capital. On the other, it was attuned to the native Indian population. Nevertheless, while the clergy sometimes supported the villagers against the interests of the great landowners, the Church's role was more often conservative, seeking to defend itself against the encroachment of liberal values.

The military, meanwhile, played a major role in Latin American society—and so it remains to this day. Elegantly uniformed officers represented the self-sufficiency of the new, otherwise illegitimate revolutionary societies of America. Nearly everywhere, they propped up the authority of the president, the king, or the caudillo. Their support was well rewarded. In the first generation of independence, expenditure on the military often took up more than fifty percent of the new nations' budgets. Mexico's military budget between 1821 and 1845 exceeded the total of all government revenues on fourteen occasions.

If colonial social patterns persisted in the Church and the military, the pre-Columbian past endured in the customs of the native masses. Wherever possible, they lived in their ancestral villages, and when displaced to haciendas, mines, or cities they retained their traditional culture, which had survived conquest and revolution alike.

Especially foreign to that culture was any notion of private property. Indians possessed their village lands in common. They cooperated in tasks, rather than compete and stand out beyond their comrades. Despite attempts to integrate the Indians into an economy based on private ownership, their assumption that land existed for communal use remained unshaken. Their village management of land, largely respected in the colonial era, was targeted by the post-revolutionary elites and rulers, whose land grabs enriched those who exported goods to foreign markets.

Nor did the economic prosperity of the post-revolutionary period advance the condition of the slave, before slavery itself was ended. Slaves were a minority in much of Spanish America, but in Brazil and the

Caribbean, they predominated. Slave rebellions were frequent well into the nineteenth century, and bands of runaway slaves were common in the remote interior.

Persons of mixed race belonged to the group called the *castas*, or "castes," who possessed a social status above that of Indian natives, and who sometimes benefited from economic growth. Those who pursued artisan or merchant careers came to occupy a middling rank. European immigrants—Spanish, Italian, Irish, German, among others—included many skilled laborers or professionals, and could prosper in Latin American society.

Latin American societies were thus divided between the interests, on the one hand, of the educated elites, assisted by a middling sector of professionals and merchants, buttressed by the Church and army; and, on the other, by those of the masses, Indian, black, and mixed (except in those nations—Chile, Argentina, and Uruguay—whose populations were mostly European). They somewhat resembled the societies of Europe in the eighteenth century but were, in fact, more perilously divided. In Europe the poor were not separated from their rulers by differences of race, culture, and history.

The Latin American economy was linked to the European in a pattern, not easily broken, in which one partner exported resources, the other manufactures. Though the Latin American market was thus subordinated to the European, the owners of the

Juan O'Gorman, **Porfirio Díaz, 1793:** *Political power in nineteenth-century Latin American states was generally monopolized by Creole elites and forceful caudillos—such as Mexico's Porfirio Díaz (r. 1876–1911) shown in this mural—who ruled primarily for the benefit of wealthy landowners, the church, and the military. (detail, Castillo de Chapultepec, Mexico City)*

mines, ranches, and *latifundia* reaped handsome profits and had no incentive to alter the arrangement. On the contrary: adopting the views of the French founder of **positivism**, Auguste Comte (1798–1857) (see Chapter 23), they held that an elite of highly trained experts justly led society to greater productivity, harmony, and happiness.

This program of "Order and Progress" would justify much of the social policy of the age, accepted by both "liberals" and "conservatives." Order meant the continuation of existing social patterns, and progress, the growth of profitable foreign trade in a free trade system. Liberals and conservatives were distinguished not by their economic strategies, but by their attitudes toward the Church. Liberals viewed the Church as an obstacle to progress, considered redistributing its property, and terminating its judicial and economic privileges. Conservatives saw the Church as a bulwark of the social order.

The dictatorial leaders who thrived in the first generation after independence would employ at will

Native and Elite Caudillos

Diego Rivera, A Sunday Afternoon in the Alameda Park: *Though Amerindians and* castas *were often marginalized within Latin American society, members of these "lower orders" did occasionally achieve political power. The Zapotec Indian lawyer Benito Juárez, for example, became President of Mexico in 1861 and is depicted at the center of this 1947 mural.*

both liberal and conservative stategies; the strongmen, or caudillos. These autocrats were usually drawn from the elite and nearly always promoted by the military. They well understood the effectiveness of the military in maintaining social order and protecting the interests of "civilization," as they saw it, over what they termed "barbarism." At the same time, caudillos of elite origin promoted the various economic interests of their class by allowing land takeovers and the manipulation of labor contracts.

Some caudillos, however, often of mixed race, were considered "popular." The popular caudillos pursued land policies that benefited native or mestizo workers. Popular caudillos garnered success as they awakened among the millions of their constituents an appetite for justice. The "throng of aristocrats," one told his followers, takes all wealth and privileges, "leaving you only with misery, disgrace, and work. ..."

Unlike these populist leaders, most of the caudillos stood for the maintenance of order. Typical is the Mexican caudillo Porfirio Díaz (1830–1915), a mestizo, who rose to the rank of general and battled his way to supremacy. He is depicted on p. 564. From 1876 to 1910, his autocratic, centralized government promoted economic growth while it protected the traditional interests of landowners, Church, and army—the usual recipe for success in Latin America.

While the old elites retained control, most nations had forged satisfactory constitutions and created representative assemblies which achieved at last the abolition of slavery. Beginning with "free birth" laws early in the century, which held free anyone born on native soil of slave parentage, abolition was attained nearly everywhere by 1880. The last two nations in the western hemisphere to accept abolition were Cuba (1886) and Brazil (1888).

Alone of the Latin American nations, Brazil was ruled by an emperor until the formation of a republic, one year after abolition. Cuba and Puerto Rico were the last of the old colonies to be ruled by Spain. While Haiti and the Dominican Republic were independent, most of the other Caribbean nations were under French, English, Dutch, or Danish rule. These regions did not experience the reign of the caudillo.

By the 1880s, most Latin American nations had developed governments based on limited representation. The majority of the people, Christianized and hispanized though they were, had little role in that government. Jefferson's vision of 1776, resting on the assumption that "all men are created equal," remained entirely alien to Latin America's leaders whose high prosperity demanded that some men—and all women—be left unequal.

By the People

The citizens of the United States of America were conscious of their nationhood. That consciousness emerged from the shared tragedy of war and the shared creation of a written Constitution with its statement of fundamental, inalienable rights. Over the next three generations, the nation would draw closer to the ideal implied in its founding documents: that all people were equal, and that the government was theirs. By the 1880s, the United States was nearly but was not yet a government "by the people."

HOW MANY?

Unwilling Strangers—Trends in the Trade of African Slaves

Figures represent slaves in thousands

Although the marketing of African slaves by European entrepreneurs began even before 1500, it peaked in the eighteenth century, reaching an apex on the eve of the American revolution.
Source: H. Spodek, *The World's History* (Upper Saddle River, NJ: Prentice Hall, 1998), p. 451.

The Expansion of a Nation   In the interim, the difficult question posed itself: who, and what, was an American? As the nation grew, it absorbed new immigrants and repulsed its own Amerindian natives. It freed its African slaves, and heard the protests of women subordinated to male leadership in the state, church, and family. As Map 19.3 on p. 567 shows, it expanded territorially from the Atlantic seaboard 3000 miles west to the Pacific shore past the barriers of the Appalachian Mountains, the Mississippi River, the Great Plains, the Rocky Mountains. With each new territory, the definition continued to broaden of who was an "American."

The first frontier lay between the Appalachians and the Mississippi, acquired by the United States in the 1783 settlement of the War for Independence. Pioneers poured into the region and formed the new states of Tennessee, Kentucky, and Ohio. In 1787, the Northwest Ordinance established guidelines for the admission to the Union of states, declared slave-free, to be carved out of the territory bounded by the Ohio and Mississippi Rivers and the Great Lakes.

The remaining additions to the territories of the continental United States occurred in three stages. The first was the Louisiana Territory, an expanse of over 800,000 square miles between the Mississippi and the Rocky Mountains. It was purchased for $15 million from the cash-poor French Emperor Napoleon (see Chapter 20) in 1803, and charted from 1804 to 1806 by the officer Meriwether Lewis and his colleague William Clark. In 1819, with the Spanish cession of Florida, the eastern half of the continent south of British Canada belonged to the new United States.

In 1846, the United States made its second large territorial acquisition. This was the Oregon territory, defined by an agreement with Britain establishing the United States–Canadian border at the 49th parallel of latitude. A third set of territories was acquired by war from neighboring Mexico between 1845 and 1853. This territory included much of the future states of Texas (which had previously won its independence), Arizona, New Mexico, Utah, Nevada, and California. A small adjunct to these, including parts of Arizona and New Mexico, was acquired in 1853 as the Gadsden Purchase. (Further additions to United States territory, none contiguous, include Alaska; the Hawaiian islands; Puerto Rico; and scattered Pacific islands; see Chapter 29).

Into the unknown west opened to settlement by purchase, treaty, and war, American settlers moved: pioneers on foot, families in carriages, caravans of covered wagons. The century-long experience of the frontier affected the notion that Americans had of themselves. They had cut loose from the European past and all its restrictive hierarchies and systems of privilege. They were a people engaged in the discovery of the world and themselves.

As the settlers' fortunes rose, those of the native Indian peoples sank. During the first years of colonization, European impact on the Indian way of life was limited. Natives and newcomers sometimes cooperated and sometimes clashed. Until the end of the eighteenth century, however, the natives largely retained their land and their traditional culture.

That situation changed during the first decades of independence. The victors of the War for Independence imposed treaties that forced the east coast Indians to cede their lands. With a combined population of about 150,000, these tribes were docile. They had long lived in proximity to the settlers; some were Christian converts, and some had acquired literacy. Some of their leaders were the mixed-blood offspring of Indian women and men of European background. Their marginality enabled them to guide their people in negotiations with the new Americans—negotiations they were destined to lose.

In the Northwest Territory opened in 1787, settlers encountered tribes unfamiliar with the habits of white Americans who were more easily deceived into surrendering their land. One American governor purchased much of the future state of Indiana from Miami and Delaware Indians for a mere $10,000. Although the Shawnee chief Tecumseh and his charismatic medicine-man brother resisted such land grabs, Chief Black Hawk (1767–1838) of the Sauk tribe surrendered his people's hunting grounds when, touching the fateful "goose quill," he unknowingly ratified a treaty with the United States government.

Systematic displacement of Indian populations began in the 1820s. Passages concerning the official policies are quoted in *Witnesses* on p. 554. Whole peoples were forcibly resettled in strange and less desirable lands, remote from ancestral graves and memories. This new policy affected Indian tribes from Florida, Alabama, and Georgia, and others on the border of Illinois and Iowa. Many were driven west and south to reserved "Indian territory" in modern Oklahoma, an arid region utterly unlike their

---

MUST READS

Calls for Revolution, Abolition, and Women's Rights

Thomas Paine	*Common Sense* (1775)
Frederick Douglass	*Narrative of the Life of Frederick Douglass, an American Slave, written by himself* (1845)
Harriet Beecher Stowe	*Uncle Tom's Cabin* (1852)
Elizabeth Cady Stanton	*Eighty Years and More: Reminiscences* (1898)

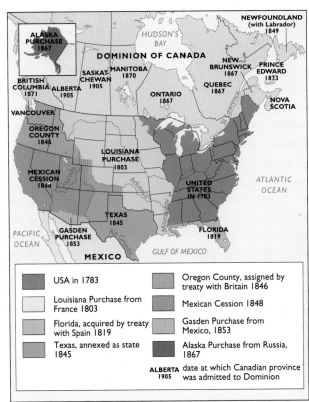

Map 19.3 (above and right) *Manifest Destiny: the Expansion of the United States, Amerindian Relocation, and Consolidation of Canada:*

After winning independence from Britain in 1783, and following its perceived "Manifest Destiny," the United States expanded westward at great speed. By expropriation, war, and purchase, it gained its present dimensions by 1898. Indigenous Amerindians paid a high price for the consolidation of the United States. Numerous battles, forced relocations, and the toll of Old World disease, reduced the pre-settlement population north of the Rio Grande from a peak of about 1 million—speaking 2000 languages—to just a few battered and isolated populations who were left languishing on reservations. The removal of Seminole, Creek, Cherokee, Chickasaw, and Choctaw Indians not only placed these groups in unfamiliar territory, but also made them immediate neighbors for the first time in their history. Meanwhile, Canada expanded and consolidated as a dominion of the British Empire, with similar pressure on indigenous peoples (right).

homelands. The illegal Cherokee forced migration along the Trail of Tears in the winter of 1838–1839, ordered by the Democratic President Andrew Jackson (1767–1845), is one of the saddest chapters in the history of the young United States.

After 1840, the conflict between American whites and native Indians shifted to the region between the Mississippi and the Pacific. While the southwest was home to **pueblo**-dwelling Indians with a long history of interaction with Mexican whites, on the Great Plains there roamed nomadic Indian peoples numbering about 360,000, whose limited contact with European peoples had enabled them to supply themselves with guns and horses. The Plains Indians used these to hunt bison herds, their main economic activity—the bison population of some 30 million could feed, clothe, and equip them indefinitely.

Mobile and aggressive, the Plains Indians resisted the advance of white settlers in a struggle which reached its final phase after 1865. As settlers streamed across the plains, they snapped up Indian land, confronted and killed Indians (who returned violence for violence), and slaughtered the bison. Railroad lines followed them, criss-crossing the Indians' realm in nine interlocking routes (see Chapter 21). Regular army cavalry and infantry, released from duty in the Civil War (see below), moved west to protect American migrants and their homes.

The last battles in this conflict occurred in the final decades of the nineteenth century. In 1881 the Sioux chief Sitting Bull (c. 1831–1890) surrendered his people and his lands to federal troops, by whose fire he was killed in 1890. The Apache leader Geronimo (c. 1829–1909) abandoned his long resistance in 1886. In 1890, at Wounded Knee, South Dakota, federal troops massacred 200 Indian worshipers who had gathered to dance the Ghost Dance, a newly invented ritual of desperation.

In Oregon, the salmon-hunting Nez Percé ("pierced nose," so named by French hunters for their distinctive form of adornment) refused to cooperate with federal officials. They fled to the north; weakened by starvation, just short of the Canadian border, their gifted leader Chief Joseph (c. 1840–1904) halted and surrendered, defeated by the suffering of his people. "I will fight no more forever," he announced in memorable words that seem to sum up the voice of the Indian peoples of North America.

By 1900, some four centuries after the Spanish conquest, the indigenous peoples of the Americas were no longer in possession of the lands that were the core of their identity. Nearly all the Indian nations under United States dominion had been relocated and dispirited, reduced permanently to a secondary status in the country that was once theirs.

Not all Americans approved of the government's "solution" for the Indian problem. Objections to the policy of Indian resettlement were voiced by Helen Hunt Jackson (1830–1885) in her explosive *A Century of Dishonor* published in 1881; and in 1883, the Women's National Indian Rights Association

Activists for Feminism and Abolition

Women's rights and abolitionism: *For women, and even more for former slaves, the full and equal inclusion into the American nation, as envisioned in the Declaration of Independence proved an elusive goal throughout the course*

of the nineteenth century. Shown as partners, Elizabeth Cady Stanton and Susan B. Anthony (left) supported both abolitionist and feminist causes, as did Frederick Douglass (right).
(left: Library of Congress; right: National Portrait Gallery, Washington, D.C.)

count as three-fifths of a person for purposes of representation and taxation. The effect was to guarantee to the southern states, where slavery was concentrated, more representatives in Congress than they would have obtained if slaves were not counted at all. Article I.9 guaranteed that the slave trade would not be impeded by law before 1808 (after which it was indeed ended), while Article IV.2 assured that the United States government would assist those whose slaves had escaped in the recovery of their property. For these provisions, abolitionists viewed the Constitution as flawed. They were further enraged by the passing of the Fugitive Slave Law of 1793, which reaffirmed the slaveowners' right to recover escaped slaves.

Ironically, circumstances conspired to boost the growth of American slavery exactly when political developments might suggest it was due to expire. In 1793, the northerner Eli Whitney invented the **cotton gin**, which mechanized the process of removing the small seed pods that grew amid the cotton fibers, making the large-scale production of cotton possible. That capability coincided, by chance, with the moment when British textile mills were converted into factories driven by steam power. The British factories were hungry for raw cotton, and the fertile fields of the American south were ready to provide it. Slavery and cotton thus worked together to dominate the economy, the social relations, and the culture of the south, especially the states from South Carolina to Mississippi, where Africans often outnumbered white Americans. The slave population of the south soared from about 700,000 in 1790 to 4 million in 1860. That surge fired the enthusiasm of Northern abolitionists. Other Northerners opposed slavery on economic grounds and opposed its extension into new territories. Some proposed resettling slaves in Africa.

Slavery drove a wedge between the interests of those states whose economy depended upon slave labor, and those where it did not—between the southern and northern states. Those sectional differences

formed to battle for victims of western expansionism. In 1887, the Dawes Severalty Act attempted to make private farmers of Indians whose tradition of land management was communal. It proposed to make gifts of land in parcels of 160 acres, and to grant full citizenship to participants. Seeking to impose European norms on Indian natives, it was a failure.

Slavery and Abolitionism The years of Indian displacement corresponded roughly to those of the rise and fall of African slavery in the United States. *Witnesses* on p. 571 and *Windows On* on p. 551 give insight into the lives of the slaves. Although at the foundation of the republic, most Americans accepted the institution of slavery, many deplored both the slave trade and the exploitation of unfree labor. Implicit in the statement that "all men are created equal" was the seed of **abolitionism**, the theory that slavery was morally wrong and should be abolished.

The Constitution, however, acknowledged and protected the institution of slavery at three critical points. Article I.2 contains the infamous "Three-Fifths Compromise," providing that a slave would

Foundations of Freedom in Anglo-America

The new United States based its constitution on a rich heritage of political philosophy. Yet a few fundamental documents from the era of its founding, and thereafter, encapsulate some of its essential principles. Represented here are the Declaration of Independence, with its promise of equality and its assertion that government must protect the rights of citizens; the Seneca Falls Declaration, deriving from the earlier one, which extends the thinking about equality and rights to women citizens of the republic; and the speech delivered by Abraham Lincoln to commemorate the Gettysburg battlefield of the Civil War. The latter recalls the initial promise of 1776 and restates the mission of the United States: government of, by, and for the people.

Separation from Britain: Thomas Jefferson's Declaration of Independence (1776): We hold these truths to be self-evident, that all men are created equal, that they are endowed by their Creator with certain unalienable Rights, that among these are Life, Liberty and the pursuit of Happiness. That to secure these rights, Governments are instituted among Men, deriving their just powers from the consent of the governed, That whenever any Form of Government becomes destructive of these ends, it is the Right of the People to alter or to abolish it, and to institute new Government, laying its foundation of such principles and organizing its powers in such form, as to them shall seem most likely to effect their Safety and Happiness.... .

The history of the present King of Great Britain is a history of repeated injuries and usurpations all having in direct object the establishment of an absolute tyranny over these States.... . [A list of "injuries and usurpations" follows.]

In every stage of these Oppressions We have Petitioned for Redress in the most humble terns: Our repeated Petitions have been answered only by repeated injury. A Prince, whose character is thus marked by every act which may define a Tyrant, is unfit to be the ruler of a free People.... .

We, therefore, the Representatives of the United States of America, in General Congress, Assembled, appealing to the Supreme Judge of the World for the rectitude of our intentions, do, in the Name, and by Authority of the good People of the Colonies, solemnly publish and declare, That these United Colonies are, and of Right ought to be Free and Independent States; that they are Absolved from all Allegiance to the British Crown, and that all political connection between them and the State of Great Britain, is and ought to be totally dissolved.... .
(The Declaration of Independence Made by the Original Thirteen States in Congress at Philadelphia, 1776)

Rights for women (1848): We hold these truths to be self-evident: that all men and women are created equal; that they are endowed by their Creator with certain inalienable rights; that among these are life, liberty, and the pursuit of happiness; that to secure these rights governments are instituted, deriving their just powers from the consent of the governed. Whenever any form of government becomes destructive of these ends, it is the right of those who suffer from it to refuse allegiance to it, and to insist upon the institution of a new government, laying its foundation on such principles, and organizing its power in such form, as to them shall seem most likely to effect their safety and happiness.... .

The history of mankind is a history of repeated injuries and usurpations on the part of man toward woman, having in direct object the establishment of an absolute tyranny over her. To prove this, let facts be submitted.... . [A list of "injuries and usurpations" follows.]

Now, in view of this entire disenfranchisement of one-half the people of the country ... in view of the unjust laws above mentioned, and because women do feel themselves aggrieved, oppressed, and fraudulently deprived of their most sacred right, we insist that they have immediate admission to all the rights and privileges which belong to them as citizens of the United States.
("Declaration of Sentiments and Resolutions, Seneca Falls, 1848". M. J. Gage, 1969, pp. 70–73)

The promise renewed: Abraham Lincoln's Gettysburg Address (1863): Four score and seven years ago our fathers brought forth on this continent, a new nation, conceived in Liberty, and dedicated to the proposition that all men are created equal.

Now we are engaged in a great civil war, testing whether that nation or any so conceived and so dedicated, can long endure. We are met on a battle-field of that war. We have come to dedicate a portion of that field, as a final resting place for those who gave their lives that that nation might live. It is altogether fitting and proper that we should do this.

But, in a larger sense, we can not dedicate—we can not consecrate—we can not hallow this ground. The brave men, living and dead, who struggled here, have consecrated it, far above our poor power to add or detract. The world will little note, nor long remember what we say here, but it can never forget what they did here. It is for us the living, rather, to be dedicated here to the unfinished work which they who fought here have thus far so nobly advanced. It is rather for us to be here dedicated to the great task remaining before us—that from these honored dead we take increased devotion to that cause for which they gave the last full measure of devotion—that we here highly resolve that these dead shall not have died in vain—that this nation, under God, shall have a new birth of freedom—and that government of the people, by the people, for the people, shall not perish from the earth.
(From R. P. Basler ed., *The Collected Works of Abraham Lincoln*, vol. 7, 1953)

ended in the **secession** of the southern states and the Civil War fought from 1861 to 1865. Even before that confrontation began, attempts had been made to deal with the issues of the abolition, preservation, and extension of slavery.

Twice, congressional leaders offered compromises in an attempt to silence the Sectionalist debates. In 1820–1821, the Missouri compromise provided that unorganized territory north of the 36°30′ parallel should remain free, while slavery could be extended to the south. Missouri would be admitted as a slave state, though north of that latitude, while Maine would be admitted as free.

The Compromise of 1850 reversed the principles of the Missouri Compromise. California was admitted as a free state, but the status of the Utah and New Mexico Territories were to be determined by the decision of the people. Among other provisions, slavery was allowed in Washington D.C., but the slave trade ended, and a stern fugitive-slave law was now imposed.

The 1850 Compromise did not settle the slavery issue for long. Four years later, a northern politician proposed the terms of the Kansas-Nebraska Act. It called upon the organization of Kansas and Nebraska as territories, with the slavery issue to be decided upon admission to statehood by the people there resident. Pro-slave and anti-slave activists rushed to Kansas, which became a battleground for the competing interests that soon turned to fraud and violence. "Bleeding Kansas" foreshadowed the horrors to come when, soon, the Civil War began.

The stiff fugitive slave rules of 1850 paved the way for the infamous Dred Scott case, upon which the Supreme Court ruled in 1857. Born a slave, Dred Scott had moved with his master to the Northwest Territory, where he lived for years on free soil. On that basis, he claimed his freedom upon his master's death. The Court ruled against him, and returned him to slavery.

The abolitionists were horrified by the ruling, which seemed to privilege slave-holders. Northerners in general now opposed the extension of slavery, though few favored its abolition where it already existed. That was the position held by Abraham Lincoln (1809–1865), an Illinois lawyer who in 1860 won the nomination for President of a new, northern political party; the Republican.

WITNESSES

African Bondage in Anglo-America

These two documents offer a glimpse of the two sides of slavery in the United States. The first, from the perspective of the slaveowner, calls for the recapture and punishment of runaway slaves. The second, from the perspective of those who had been enslaved, shows the determination to win freedom from slavery.

A colonial slave code (Virginia) aims to discourage runaway slaves: Whereas many times slaves run away and lie hid and lurking in swamps, woods, and other obscure places, killing hogs, and committing other injuries to the inhabitants ... if the slave does not immediately return, anyone whatsoever may kill or destroy such slaves by such ways and means as he ... shall think fit. ... If the slave is apprehended ... it shall ... be lawful for the county court, to order such punishment for the said slave, either by dismembering, or in any other way ... as they in their discretion shall think fit, for the reclaiming any such incorrigible slave, and terrifying others from the like practices. ...
(From H. Zinn ed., *A People's History of the United States*, 1980)

A former slave who had bought her own freedom in the antebellum South succeeds in buying her daughter's freedom, as recounted by abolitionist Laura S. Haviland (1889): We solicited over seventy dollars for a poor woman by the name of Jackson, from Marseilles, Kentucky, who had bought herself by washing and ironing of nights, after her mistress' work was done. During seven long years she did not allow herself to undress except to change. Her sleep was little naps over the ironing board. Seven years of night work brought the money that procured her freedom. She had a son and daughter nearly grown, and to purchase their freedom she was now bending her day and night energies. ... The master's indebtedness compelled him to sell one of them, and market was found for the girl of sixteen. Nine hundred dollars was offered, and the distressed mother had but four hundred dollars to pay. ...

In her distress she went from house to house, to plead for a buyer who would advance the five hundred dollars, and take a mortgage on her until she could make it. At length she found a Baptist deacon who purchased her daughter, and she paid him the four hundred dollars. He was to keep her until the mortgage was redeemed by her mother. ... After working very hard one year, she was able to pay but one hundred and fifty dollars toward the mortgage, when her health began to fail. The deacon told her ... he could not wait longer than another year, before he would have to sell her.

[Advised by sympathizers, the mother sought the aid of abolitionists in Cincinnati and Oberlin, including the author of the memoir.] A few weeks later the glad mother returned and redeemed the daughter. I saw them together ... happy in their freedom.
(Laura S. Haviland, *A Woman's Life: Work, Labors, and Experiences*, 1889; ed. G. S. Lerner, 1973)

Winslow Homer

The Bayonet Charge: *Winslow Homer's 1862 wood engraving of a bayonet charge captures the fury of a Civil War battlefield, yet still hints at the futility of an effort where brave men oppose hot guns with cold steel and face destruction.* (The Metropolitan Museum of Art, New York)

When Lincoln won the election, the slaveholding states of the lower south (South Carolina, Georgia, Florida, Texas, Mississippi, Louisiana, and Alabama) seceded from the Union, arguing the full sovereignty of each state within the nation. The secessionist states formed the Confederate States of America, loyal to all the principles of the United States polity except those related to slavery.

North Carolina, Virginia, Tennessee, and Arkansas soon joined the Confederacy. Four other slave states—Maryland, Delaware, Kentucky, and Missouri—which formed a border between the slaveholding regions and the north remained within the Union. In Western Virginia opponents of secession formed a new state, staunchly Unionist in allegiance.

Civil War and After   In 1861, South Carolina militia men fired on the federal garrison at Fort Sumter in Charleston harbor. Lincoln called a Special Session of Congress to ask for approval of the actions he had taken to counter the southern offensive. He argued against the theory of state sovereignty, calling

"States' Rights" a fiction—a "sophistry," or trick of logic. He called on Congress to reaffirm the supremacy of that nation which alone in human history, as he put it, had been called into existence to lighten its citizens' burdens. The Civil War began, the central and most tragic event in the nation's history (see Chapter 20).

It was not the purpose of the Civil War to put an end to American slavery. But that was its result. In 1863, the Emancipation Proclamation made all slaves in rebellious territories "forever free." That partial liberation affected neither northern states nor Confederate territory not under Union control. Yet it freed some half a million slaves by 1865 and struck a blow to the heart of the institution of slavery.

The war over, Congress set out both to reorganize and to punish the south. That mission they pursued until 1877 when "Reconstruction," as the process was called, ended. Former secessionists regained their civil rights. The crowds of reformers and opportunists who had streamed south dwindled, and the programs instituted to help freed men gain land and legal rights ceased.

In 1865, all slaves still in bondage were made free by the Thirteenth Amendment to the United States Constitution. In 1868, the Fourteenth Amendment guaranteed freed slaves the rights of citizens. In 1870, the Fifteenth assured them the right to vote.

Legislation could not adequately address the problems left by more than two centuries of slavery. Southern whites took steps to segregate blacks and deny them political rights. Black Codes, which reduced freed men to a condition of virtual serfdom, were banned, but their spirit prevailed and a host of customs and regulations barred African Americans from full civic participation. Black schools and black churches were targets for sporadic, illegal repression, and black leaders were victims of violence. Kept separate, illiterate, vulnerable, and poor, freed slaves did not yet benefit from the guarantee of rights found in the Declaration of Independence, the Bill of Rights, and the post-war amendments.

Yet the promise remained, as President Lincoln restated it in 1863 at the battlefield site of a recent Union victory in Gettysburg, Pennsylvania. In his brief speech honoring the thousands who died, quoted in *Witnesses* on p. 570, the president linked the moment to the moment of national founding: "Four score and seven years ago," which was to say in 1776, "our fathers brought forth upon this continent... ." He summoned his listeners to a second founding, there on the bloodied Pennsylvania fields, a sacred event. They were to "consecrate" themselves, pledging to fulfill the promise Jefferson once had made to create a government that nurtured the inalienable rights of all: one that was "of the people, by the people, for the people."

When Lincoln summoned Americans to fulfill that promise, slavery was not yet dead. The liberation of former slaves from the habits of discrimination that slavery had ingrained was still to come. Native Indians continued to languish in the bleak reservations built by federal officials. Other groups now sought inclusion in the circle of Americans. Poor white males, white immigrant males, and females of all origins claimed their place among those who called themselves "we, the people" of the United States.

In colonial America, as in England, property requirements limited the electorate. In seventeenth-century Massachusetts, just over half of all adult males

Winslow Homer, A New Field of Dead Men: *After the Civil War, soldiers who had been farmboys returned home to their farms; but they, and their fields, had changed—a metaphysical reality Winslow Homer captures splendidly in his huge 1865 painting of* The Veteran in a New Field. *The farmer back on the job is also the figure of Death wielding his scythe against innumerable, towering shafts of wheat, displayed in a brilliant yellow, who will each be cut down in their multitudes by the relentlessness of war.* (The Metropolitan Museum of Art, New York; Bequest of Adelaide Milton de Groot)

were eligible to vote; elsewhere the percentage approached twenty percent. After independence, the franchise gradually broadened. By the 1820s all white males had been granted **suffrage**, or the right to vote.

Immigrants, too, of whom some 5 million arrived between 1790 and 1860, sought inclusion in American civil life. Before the Civil War, they were mostly Irish or German, and often Catholics who found a hostile reception in a largely Protestant society. Later in the century, more waves of immigrants arrived from southern and eastern Europe as well as Asia and Latin America. Spurred by the discrimination they met, immigrants gained entry to politics in order to protect their communities as they struggled to succeed in a new world.

Women, like slaves, were denied full participation in American society; all, of whatever rank, were injured by the Jeffersonian statement that "all *men* are created equal." A feminist movement developed alongside abolitionism, leading to the 1848 meeting of women leaders and some male supporters at Seneca Falls, New York. Its outcome was the Declaration of Sentiments, quoted in *Witnesses* on p. 570, which called for an end to women's subordination to men. Prominent among the grievances were the limits on women's right to hold property or to have custody of their children; their prohibition from higher education or professional careers; their unequal status in the workplace and the unequal pay they received; and the sexual double standard that permitted males to ignore

moral norms while requiring women to obey them. The most urgent issue was the right to vote, which some hoped would be achieved for women when it was granted to freed black slaves. Among those supporting the Seneca Falls declaration were male abolitionist leaders, white and black.

After the Civil War, women leaders observed bitterly that while former male slaves now possessed the right to vote (if only in theory), no woman did. This injustice shaped the American women's movement, which now focused almost entirely on suffrage (finally obtained only in 1920). The circle of American citizenship had already expanded, and would continue to do so despite the opposition of those who stood to lose a monopoly on political power.

By the late 1800s, the question "Who is an American?" might be answered as follows: anyone born on American soil or, if born abroad, **naturalized**, or officially accepted as a citizen upon the satisfaction of minimal requirements. A second question still remained: "*What* is an American?" If not of English descent, would he or she speak English? If not of European descent—as the descendants of Africans, Asians, or Amerindians were not—would he or she identify with European culture, the civilization of the West? Though the question remains open, certain facts are clear: the political ideals, and the moral values behind them, that guided the American experiment, were the product of Western thought, the children of Western civilization.

Conclusion

JEFFERSON'S PROMISE, LINCOLN'S PLEDGE, AND THE MEANING OF THE WEST

From independence through the late nineteenth century, the United States proceeded in the direction of the inclusion of all its peoples in the task of government, and the recognition of their inalienable rights —goals that Jefferson promised, and Lincoln pledged. The nations of Latin America, where the task of inclusion was more difficult, did not.

In the north, the majority of the population was of European descent at the time the United States was founded. Amerindians numbered a sparse few hundred thousand, and Africans, slave and free, amounted to perhaps ten percent of the population. The cultural imprint of the European old world was therefore powerful.

In most of Spanish America, in contrast, the Amerindian population was a majority at the time that independence was won, while Africans dominated the Caribbean and Brazil. The elites of European descent who created the economic, political, and social foundations of their nations were a minority, who imposed their language and religion as a standard for all. Yet to this day the traditional cultures of native peoples are not wholly merged with that of the elites. Is Latin America an heir to Western civilization? It seems so. Not all of its people, however, belong to that civilization. Nor will they, or should they, unless they acquire through schooling the cultural values of the West—values responsible both for their domination in the colonial era and, subsequently, their liberation.

REVIEW QUESTIONS

1. What is Latin America? Why did colonial society in Latin America differ from that in North America? Why did the Plantation system dominate the economies of the Caribbean and Brazil?

2. Describe the economy of Spanish America. What role did the Church play in the Spanish colonies? Why did tension develop between the Creole elite and the Spanish government?

3. What were the origins of the British North American colonies? Describe their form of government. How did religion affect colonial society? Why did slavery develop in the southern colonies?

4. Why did the French and Indian War lead to conflict between Britain and its colonies? Why did the United States succeed in winning its independence? How did Enlightenment principles influence the United States Constitution?

5. Why did independence not lead to a social revolution in most of Latin America? What role did the caudillos play in the nineteenth century? Why did Latin American elites retain power after independence?

6. How did the expansion of the United States affect the Amerindians? Describe the rise and fall of African slavery in the United States. To what extent was the United States a "government of the people" at the end of the nineteenth century?

SUGGESTED RESOURCES

Old and New in the New World

Berlin, Ira, *Many Thousand Gone: the First Two Centuries of Slavery in North America* (Cambridge, MA: Belknap Press of Harvard University Press, 1998). Traces the evolution of African slave society in different regions of North America, integrating the history of these immigrants into the history of America's working peoples.

Calloway, Colin G., *New Worlds for All: Indians, Europeans, and the Remaking of Early America* (Baltimore: Johns Hopkins University Press, 1997). Describes the long cultural interaction between Europeans and Amerindians, including North and South America, and the Spanish, French, Russian, English, invaders.

Canny, Nicholas and Anthony Pagden, eds., *Colonial Identity in the Atlantic World, 1500–1800* (Princeton: Princeton University Press, 1987). Essays dealing with the colonial experience in Brazil, Spanish America, British America, Quebec, and Barbados.

Gutiérrez, Ramon A., *When Jesus Came, the Corn Mothers Went Away: Marriage, Sexuality and Power in New Mexico, 1500–1846* (Stanford: Stanford University Press, 1991). Explores the encounter between missionaries and natives, finding incomprehension on both sides.

Indigenous peoples of the Americas, all regions, articles, and resources: http://www.hartford-hwp.com/archives/41/index.html

Declarations of Independence

Draper, Theodore, *A Struggle for Power: The American Revolution* (New York: Time Books, 1996). Sees the Revolution as resulting from a struggle for power rather than from republican ideology or economic interest.

Harvey, Robert, *Liberators: Latin America's Struggle for Independence, 1810–1830* (London: John Murray, 2000). Vivid narrative of the process of liberation and state-formation in Latin America.

Kennedy, Roger G., *Burr, Hamilton, and Jefferson: A Study in Character* (Oxford: Oxford University Press, 2000). Thoughtful recent assessment of the unique personalities of three enormously important Americans in the era of founding.

Langley, Lester D., *The Americas in the Age of Revolution, 1750–1850* (New Haven, CT: Yale University Press, 1996). Offers a "comparative history of the revolutionary age," taking in both American continents.

Maier, Pauline, *American Scripture: Making the Declaration of Independence* (New York: Alfred A. Knopf, 1997). Views the creation of the epochal "Declaration of Independence" as a complex process involving many makers and ideas.

Wood, Gordon, *The Radicalism of the American Revolution* (New York: Knopf, 1992). Argues that insurgent egalitarianism and opportunism released by the revolutionary process resulted in radical transformation.

Biblioteca virtual de Simon Bolivar, depicted to his political philosophy: http://www.geocities.com/Athens/Acropolis/7609/eng

Fulfilling the Promise

Bushnell, David, and Neill Macaulay, *The Emergence of Latin America in the Nineteenth Century* (2nd ed.; Oxford: Oxford University Press, 1994). Up-to-date overview, balancing narrative history and interpretation. Covers most areas of Latin America and offers comparative national approaches to several major topics.

Gaspar, David Barry and Darlene Clark Hine, eds., *More than Chattel: Black Women and Slavery in the Americas* (Bloomington: Indiana University Press, 1996). Selection of essays exploring the intersection of race and gender within the slave systems of North America, Brazil, and the Caribbean.

Kolchin, Peter, *American Slavery: 1619–1877* (New York: Hill & Wang, 1993). A concise introduction explaining how slavery in the United States diverged from Caribbean and South American patterns.

Lynch, John, *Caudillos in Spanish America, 1800–1850* (Oxford: Clarendon Press of Oxford University Press, 1992). Traces the cultural, social, and political origins of the early caudillos.

Neely, Mark E., *The Last Best Hope of Earth: Abraham Lincoln and the Promise of America* (Cambridge, MA: Harvard University Press, 1994). Concise, updated biography focusing chiefly on Lincoln as political thinker and actor.

Thomas Jefferson: resources for his life and career, including electronic texts (University of Virginia): http://etext.virginia.edu/jefferson

Jefferson's house at Monticello: http://www.monticello.org

Abigail Adams Historical Society, resources in brief, with links: http://www.abigailadams.org/Abigail/abigail.html

Frederick Douglass, National Historic Site (US NPS), biography and images of his home: http://www.nps.gov/frdo/freddoug.html

Abraham Lincoln Online, texts and images, with links to further resources: http://showcase.netins.net/web/creative/lincoln.html

REVOLUTION

| 1750 | 1760 | 1770 | 1780 | 1790 | 1800 | 1810 | 1820 |

Revolution and Reorganization

American War of Independence, 1775–83

French Revolution, 1789–94

Napoleonic era, 1799–1815

- ◆ Tennis Court Oath, June 21, 1789
- ◆ Storming of Bastille, July 14, 1789
- ◆ Declaration of the Rights of Man and the Citizen, Aug 27, 1789
- ◆ March on Versailles, Oct 5–6, 1789
  - ◆ Civil Constitution of the Clergy, July 12, 1790
    - ◆ Declaration of Pillnitz, Aug 27, 1791
      - ◆ September Massacres, Sept 2–6, 1792
        - ◆ Louis XVI executed, Jan 21, 1793
        - ◆ Levée en masse, Aug 23, 1793
        - ◆ Festival of Reason, Nov 10, 1793
          - ◆ France ends slavery in colonies, 1794
          - ◆ Olympe de Gouges guillotined, 1794
          - ◆ "Thermidor": fall of Robespiere, July 28, 1794
            - ◆ Directory, 1795–99
              - ◆ Napoleon becomes First Consul, 1799
                - ◆ Concordat between Napoleon and Catholic Church, 1801
                  - ◆ Napoleon becomes Emperor, 1804
                  - ◆ Civil Code established in France, 1804
                    - ◆ Battles of Austerlitz and Trafalgar, 1805
                      - ◆ Napoleon invades Russia, 1812
                        - ◆ Congress of Vienna, 1814–1815
                          - ◆ Napoleon defeated at Waterloo, 1815

Society and Ideas

The Enlightenment, c.1685–1789

- ◆ Adam Smith's Wealth of Nations, 1776
  - ◆ Edmund Burke's Reflections on the Revolution in France, 1790
    - ◆ Mary Wollstonecraft's A Vindication of the Rights of Woman, 1792
      - ◆ Condorcet's Progress of the Human Mind, 1795

Beyond the West

Mughal Empire, India, 1526–1857

British East India Company in India, c. 1700–1857

Qing Dynasty, China, 1644–1912

Dutch East India Company in East Indies, 1619–1799

CHAPTER
20

REVOLUTION:
The End of the Old Regime
1789–1815

Empire of Napoleon, 1812

KEY TOPICS

◆ **Preludes to Revolution:** Nobles, peasants, and intellectuals resist the Old Regime.

◆ **The Rights of Man:** Liberal leaders declare the rights of men (but not women).

◆ **The Birth of a Nation:** Peasant protest and urban riot drive the French Revolution onward.

◆ **The Imperial Adventure:** Seizing power, Napoleon reconfigures Europe and returns France to autocracy.

***T**hermidor* On July 26, 1794—in the hot summer month the French revolutionaries had renamed "Thermidor"— Maximilien Robespierre (1758–1794) addressed the National Convention for the last time. For two years he had led that body of young radicals, unloosing a torrent of change and spilling a torrent of blood. But on this morning, a group of his former colleagues shouted him down. The next day, he was arrested and tried; the following morning, executed by the guillotine. The Terror he had launched with his decrees, and defended with his fiery orations, ended with his death.

Thermidor marked the end of the Revolution that destroyed absolute monarchy in France, along with the rest of the *ancien régime*, or "Old Regime", the social and political system previously established in that country. Yet it did not staunch the revolutionary impulse, which would erupt often in the next generations. In time, the French Revolution would transform all of Europe, inspiring bold hopes and triggering ruthless repression. It would lead to the creation of a new kind of nation, responsible not to a monarch but to its people—citizens now, not subjects. "The people" had made their presence felt and had announced their implacable demands.

Map 20.1 on p. 594 shows the progress of the Revolution. By 1789, the Old Regime was tottering. Nobles, burghers, peasants, and intellectuals had grown skeptical of kings, bureaucrats, the tax structure, and all the privileges and patronage that buttressed a failing system. Resistance broke out in 1789, and mounted rapidly, escalating in intensity over five years until the upheaval of Thermidor in 1794. Reaction then set in, but without wholly undoing the changes the Revolution had introduced. In 1799, the general

Napoleon Bonaparte seized leadership of France. Appropriating those features of the Revolution that suited him—while his armies exported throughout Europe the principles of "Liberty, Equality, Fraternity" that had energized revolt at home—he proceeded to impose strict control of the legal, political, and cultural life of the nation. Not a king, but a dictator, he transformed the revolutionary tradition and pointed it in the direction of the modern state.

PRELUDES TO REVOLUTION

The Enlightenment *philosophes* (see Chapter 17) had identified the faults of the French Old Regime and of similar despotic regimes elsewhere in Europe. Absolute monarchs, foolish laws, lazy aristocrats, intrusive clergy, and inquisitive censors all stifled human freedom and happiness. Their unjust dominion should be swept away. Attempts to do so were numerous in the years prior to the French Revolution. Nobles, gentry, peasants and intellectuals actively resisted those forces that stifled their freedom: absolutism, **seigneurialism**, mercantilism, and superstition.

Resistance to Absolutism

Even before Enlightenment thinkers framed their critique of absolute monarchy, the English had defied it. In 1649, the English Civil War culminated in the execution of Charles I by Parliamentarians (see Chapter 15). The principle that Parliament had authority even over the monarch was reaffirmed by the "Glorious Revolution" of 1689. During the following century, the influence of Britain's narrow aristocracy remained undiminished, and even representatives to the House of Commons were drawn from the wealthiest social strata. Still, the authority of the king was limited by Parliament.

Empty coffers: In this lampoon of the French financial crisis of the years before 1789, entitled "Le Défécit," Louis XVI and his chief finance minister contemplate the crown's empty coffers while a priest and an aristocrat exit with bags full of money. (British Museum, London)

578

In British North America the pretenses of monarchy received a more powerful rebuke in the War of Independence of 1776–1783 (see Chapter 19). Revolutionary leaders named as "tyrant" the same king whose powers, in Britain, were limited by its constitution, and their "Declaration of Independence" assailed him for violating their human rights.

Victory for the American colonists, in 1781, brought in its wake also victory for the republican ideas that had informed the debate about independence in 1776. The new nation rejected monarchy as its political form and created instead a government with balanced executive, judicial, and legislative powers defined by a written constitution. Thomas Paine, self-appointed scribe of both the American and French revolutions, proclaimed in his pro-independence tract *Common Sense* that in America, "the law is king".

Elsewhere, the challenge to monarchy was not nearly as strong as it was in the two English-speaking nations of Great Britain and the new United States. To be sure, the Italian republics (Venice, Genoa, Lucca) and the Swiss cantons managed without kings altogether, but only on the fringes of the main political currents of the age. The ailing Dutch Republic (created in the 1600s when the Northern Netherlands had gained independence from Habsburg Spain) was a republic still, though it was vulnerable to the aspirations of the princes of Orange, who sought to make their provincial title of *stadholder* hereditary. The once-mighty monarchs of Sweden and Poland were overshadowed by their nobles— those of Poland resisting not merely absolutism but any central order whatever. The refusal of its nobility to support a strong, centralized monarchy resulted in the annihilation of the Polish nation by its aggressive neighbors in the third partition of 1795 (see Chapter 15). The Hungarian nobles, fractious like the Polish and unconstrained by a monarch having no king of their own, resisted their Habsburg overlords. The Hungarians' struggle would erupt in the age of nationalism, during the next century.

A few "enlightened" monarchs adopted the *philosophes'* advice to promote the common welfare, fostering education, toleration, justice, and other human rights (see Chapter 17). In Prussia, Frederick II (r. 1740–1786) reformed the state bureaucracy and promoted industry and commerce. Yet he maintained a social system dominated by nobles, in which most people were voiceless. The Habsburg emperor Joseph II (r. 1765–1790) freed the Austrian serfs, among the most oppressed people of Europe. This farsighted action was undone by his brother and successor Leopold (r. 1790–1792), who, however, had some claim to the title of enlightened ruler, having introduced representative institutions when he ruled the Italian state of Tuscany (1765–1790).

In Russia, Catherine the Great (r. 1762–1796) supervised the reform of Russia's legal code, for which she personally composed an *Instruction* infused with Enlightenment principles. She promulgated the Statute of National Education, ordering the creation of state-funded schools. During her reign, more books were published in Russia than in all previous years combined. Yet much of what she started was left unfinished, and she was responsible for the extension of serfdom and deterioration of the condition of that already overburdened population.

"Enlightened" monarchs introduced reforms so long as they served the interests of the state and nurtured the institution of monarchy itself. They recognized that absolutism was unsustainable if it remained unleavened by any solicitude for its subjects. The monarch, as Catherine argued, "possesses all the means for the eradication of all harm and looks on the general good as its own."

In prerevolutionary France, aristocrats resisted the claims of absolute monarchy. In contrast to the era of Louis XIV (r. 1643–1715), when the most important noblemen of the realm were summoned to Versailles to dance attendance on the king, eighteenth-century aristocrats claimed greater independence. That independence was expressed through the *parlements*, or law courts, which often countered royal directives issued by centrally appointed administrators, or *intendants*. The Sun King's successors struggled to uphold royal authority over recalcitrant nobles.

In 1787, desperate for funds (in part because of the costly assistance lent to the American revolutionaries), the young king Louis XVI (r. 1774–1793) summoned an Assembly of Notables. He and his ministers hoped that these prominent men (including clergy, nobles, and bourgeois) would be willing to tax themselves in order to raise essential revenues. He was disappointed. The Assembly of Notables disbanded. Having nowhere else to turn, the king summoned the Estates-General, a legislative body of medieval origin which had not met since 1614, under his great-grandfather's grandfather, Henry IV. The principle function of this assembly was to vote tax levies. By forcing the kind to take this step, the "notables" had, in effect, signed his death warrant—and that of many of their own class. For the summoning of the Estates-General was the trigger of the Revolution that swiftly followed.

Peasants Revolts and Free Trade

While landowning elites resisted the pretensions of absolute monarchs, peasants often rose up in armed revolt against landowners. Peasant revolts were numerous, violent, and unsuccessful in European history—just as they were in antiquity or contemporary China. Peasant militias fell regularly to the superior force of professional armies. As if without memory of these earlier defeats (most had left no trace beyond what community elders recalled, when they became stressed by famine or landowner abuse, the peasants arose (see Chapter 18).

Why did peasants revolt? Because of landowners' demands and scarcity of food. The eighteenth century (an era, some scholars contend, of "feudal reaction" against absolutist centralization) saw a hardening of the landlords' position (see Chapter 18). This process occurred in western as well as eastern Europe, where the establishment of a "second serfdom" crushed the spirit of the workers. In a free-market economy, where agricultural surpluses could be sold for profit, landlords strove to increase the productivity of their lands. They moved to limit common lands and rights, such as the rights to graze livestock or glean forest products. And they squeezed what labor they could from the peasantry, insisting on the performance of "servile duties"—such as wall repair and road building— traditionally attached to their plots of soil.

The *philosophes* (and the economic specialists among them, known as "**physiocrats**") denounced these labor services, relics of a medieval economy. Ironically, however, the economic strategies of economic Enlightenment thinkers exacerbated the hardships of the poor. The "free trade" policies they advocated (*laissez faire*, or "let it be") might lift barriers to commerce and ease regulations. But they also interfered with traditional anti-famine practices of grain hoarding by local lords or municipalities. Now, in periods of famine, people could obtain grain only by paying a steep price; those who could not pay starved. The urban poor, being remote from any source of agricultural products and wholly dependent on inadequate mechanisms of distribution, were especially vulnerable. Hunger was often more severe in the eighteenth-century than it had been in earlier times. Those who suffered such experiences nurtured a potentially explosive hatred for those whom they blamed for their poverty: the local landowners.

Although the poor might suffer from the cycles of the free market, bourgeois businessmen and physiocrats opposed the traditional policy of mercantilism (see Chapter 16). They deplored the tariffs and fees that burdened trade with unnecessary costs, the granting of monopolies to favored companies, the obsession with bullion the costly competition between nations. In 1776, the Scots economist Adam Smith presented the anti-mercantilist and free-trade positions eloquently and at length in its influential *Inquiry into the Nature and Causes of the Wealth of Nations* (see Chapter 16). Mercantilism had been central to the foreign and domestic policies of absolute monarchs, and resistance to mercantilism as an important strike against the *ancien régime*.

The War of Ideas

As nobles and kings, landlords and peasants, mercantilist statesmen and entrepreneurs confronted each other, Enlightenment thinkers engaged in a war of ideas. Their enemies were superstition, ignorance, intolerance, and obfuscation, to which they opposed the probing force of reason.

Voltaire, the preeminent Enlightenment sage, had identified the Church as the sinister agent of superstition, and to his last moment he called for its destruction: "*Ecrasez l'infâme!*" (see Chapter 17). The objections to the privileged position accorded the Church in Roman Catholic countries were numerous. It promoted childish beliefs, critics argued, in saints and miracles. It persecuted heretics (the Inquisition was still busy in Spain and Portugal and their overseas colonies). It preached intolerance. It opposed the explorations of philosophy and social criticism. Above all, the clergy in general, and especially the elite order of Jesuits, were seen as defenders of absolute monarchy.

As two alternatives to established religion, Catholic or Protestant, intellectuals favored deism and Freemasonry. The first won favor because it was free of doctrine, positing only a "supreme being", the creator of the universe. The second gained adherents because it claimed authority in a pre-Christian and rationalist tradition, based on an ideal of brotherly love.

Both of these alternative "religious" movements formed part of a process of secularization that had been underway since the Italian Renaissance (see Chapter 13), when laymen in large numbers first joined the ranks of intellectuals. Thereafter, the growth of schooling, the spread of literacy, the advent of printing (which made cheap books, cartoons, and street ballads widely available) promoted a culture in which received dogmas were increasingly open to question (see Chapter 17). By the mid-eighteenth century, the cheap print media exposed even the poor to critiques of the powerful, and thus engaged them in the political debate.

By this time, a new form of subversive literature had emerged: pornography. Pornography not only busied the censors but also entered the realms of politics. What better way to sully the image of the mighty than by associating them with the prohibited fantasies of the pornographer? Among the targets was Marie Antoinette (1755–1793), the fastidious and hated consort of Louis XVI. According to the scandal-mongers, her lust was insatiable and her intimate "favorites" both male and female. Salacious accounts of her supposed debauchery inflamed popular resentment of the monarchy.

Thus, intellectuals, entrepreneurs, peasants, artisans, workers, and aristocrats all resisted, from their different motives, the established patterns of the old order. Although its vestiges would linger in places until World War I, it was already moribund by May 1789, in the more enlightened regions of western Europe. At that point, in France, there arrived at Versailles—the seat of the French court, situated at a distance of about 12 miles from Paris—the elected representatives to the Estates-General.

THE RIGHTS OF MAN

The arrival of these representatives opened the first phase of the Revolution: a liberal revolution which aimed to forge a government that would secure the "rights of man and the citizen." Those rights included the civil rights defined in the unwritten British constitution and the written American one. They also included more universal concepts of right derived from ancient philosophy via Thomas Hobbes (1588–1679), John Locke (1632–1704), and the *philosophes* (see Chapters 15, 17). These rights would be guaranteed in a newly framed constitution, to which the king would be subordinate.

A second phase of the Revolution began soon after the first and unfolded simultaneously: the radical revolution. Its effect was to transform French society. It would disenfranchise the "orders" or "estates" that had held sway for centuries and would reinvent the cultural values and religious beliefs of the people. These changes were to be achieved by the mobilization of masses of people, who, for the first time, gained access to the political process. The radical

nature of revolution provided no role whatsoever for a king, and he would not succeed in surviving it.

The Work of the National Assembly

In 1788, Louis XVI unknowingly launched the first phase of the French Revolution when he summoned the Estates-General to Versailles. The assembly consisted of representatives from the First, Second, and Third **Estates** (respectively, the clergy, nobility, and all commoners). During the winter of 1788–1789, the electorate gathered to ponder the history of that body, choose representatives, and construct an agenda by compiling *cahiers de doléances*, or "notebooks of grievances." All adult male taxpayers were eligible to participate. They met according to their "estate" in different local settings. The clergy and nobility met in large, elegant rooms, the peasants in parish churches, artisans and merchants in their guildhalls. *[Comparison to today?]*

Here they compiled some 40,000 *cahiers*, later digested into 615 general *cahiers*, of which most survive. The grievances included complaints about judicial incompetence, official misbehavior, the censorship of the press, religious intolerance, abuses by landlords, unjust taxation, and the condition of the roads. The *cahiers* amounted to a critique of the

Jacques-Louis David, Oath of the Tennis Court: *The Revolution proper began with the convocation of the Estates-General in May 1789 and the Third Estate's historic decision to constitute itself a National Assembly. Here in Jacques-Louis David's 1790 painting, members of the Third Estate, barred from the main meeting room, meet at a nearby tennis court and swear never to disband until a Constitution has been established. (Musée Carnavalet, Paris)*

Land Ownership by Social Category on the Eve of the French Revolution

	Clergy	Nobility	Bourgeoisie	Peasantry
Land in France owned by each group	6–10%	20–25%	30%	40–45%
Each group as a percentage of the total population	2%	1.5%	8.4%	82–87%

One of the long-term causes of revolution in France was the great inequality in wealth, measured in land ownership. This graph shows that two of the smallest groups in the population–clergy and nobility, or the First and Second Estates–together owned nearly one-third of all land in France.

existing political system, a critique that showed considerable agreement across class lines. A hefty seventy-four percent of the participants from the Third Estate demanded liberty of the press; and so did eighty-eight percent of the nobility. Free trade was advocated by forty-two percent of the Third and thirty-five percent of the nobility. The abolition of landlords' rights, in contrast, advocated by sixty-four percent of the Third, won the approval of only fourteen percent of the nobility, whose interests such a move would obviously injure.

One set of the complaints heard in that tense winter concerned the structure of the Estates-General itself. When it had last met, in 1614, it had consisted of the same number of representatives of each of the three estates, which voted as a body. As a result, the whole assembly produced only three votes, and (where there was not unanimity) always yielded a decision of two to one. Two estates could ally to determine the outcome, and often the First and Second Estates, the privileged orders, combined against the Third.

In 1788, these features of the composition and voting rules of the Estates-General aroused protest. A group composed largely of liberal aristocrats, called the "Society of Thirty", specially targeted for change these "forms of 1614"—and with good reason. Since 1614, the category of the Third Estate had become so complex that it could no longer be considered a single social order of "commoners." Comprising some ninety-eight percent of the French population, it included people from different regions, occupations, and levels of wealth, those who owned land and those who didn't; master craftsmen and unskilled laborers; those who wrote books and those who couldn't read; day workers and lawyers; entrepreneurs and servants. Nearly ten percent of the Third Estate consisted of members of the bourgeoisie, which was itself divided between merchants linked to the world of commerce, on the one hand, and the numerous public officials, *rentiers*, and professionals more closely tied to the traditional world of patronage relations, on the other.

How could so diverse a group be lumped together and given a single vote? Why should so large a group receive only one vote of three? The process of responding to the royal summons set in motion a series of provocative questions that would lead to the undoing of both the Estates-General and the monarchy.

As electors composed their *cahiers*, writers of tracts and pamphlets also explored the issues raised by the summoning of the Estates-General. One pamphlet, entitled *What is the Third Estate?*, stated the issues with particular clarity. Quoted in *Witnesses* on p. 584, it was the work of Emmanuel Joseph Sieyès (1748–1836), a young priest of bourgeois origin who began by championing the Revolution, then turned from its excesses, and finally supported its destroyer, Napoleon Bonaparte (see below). Sieyès concluded that the Third Estate had no need of the First and Second, but was in fact a complete nation in itself. Its members performed all the nation's productive work. On that account, they, and not idle clerics and aristocrats, were the nation. And they should be allotted votes accordingly.

Sieyès did not demand, as his argument suggested, the evisceration of the social elites. He modestly requested just two crucial changes—changes also requested by other pamphleteers and listed in many of the *cahiers*. The first was that the number of representatives of the Third Estate should equal the total number allotted to the other two. The second was that the votes be counted by head, rather than by order. The effect of these proposals would be that the Third Estate, by acquiring just one supporter from one of the other groups, would amount to a decisive majority.

Only the first of these proposals was approved. When the Estates-General arrived in Versailles, on May 5, 1789, the representatives of the Third Estate numbered about 600, double the number representing each of the other two. But when the elaborate preliminaries were over and the representatives of all three estates gathered, they were instructed by the king's ministers to vote by order and not by head.

What the people demanded

The method of voting was accordingly the first item of business taken up by the Estates-General. Debates consumed several weeks. The king and his advisers contemplated the possibility of an assembly in which the Third Estate possessed a majority. On June 17, the Third Estate announced itself to be the National Assembly, a body representative of the people of France. Cornered, the king struck back. On June 21, the delegates of the Third found their meeting hall barred. They reconvened in a tennis court.

There, the stakes of the debate were raised. The issue before the angry representatives was no longer the structure of the Estates-General, nor even the method of voting. Those matters had been resolved, to their displeasure, by the king's action—they were allowed neither to meet nor to vote under his aegis. The angry representatives, shown in David's painting on p. 581, consequently declared their intention to act: they swore an oath that they would not disband until they had written a constitution for France. That constitution would secure the rights of man, and the demotion of the king.

The Estates-General was no more. From 1789 to 1791 the representatives to the National Assembly would compose the legislation defining the new government. Most of them came from the educated bourgeoisie; they were young; nearly two-thirds were lawyers. They addressed several key matters. The first was the issue of landlords' rights: What was to be done about the remnants of customary authority that some landowners still had over some tenants, including those who were not serfs? The second was the Church: What was to be done about the excessive authority (as these representatives believed) of the clergy, and the excessively large share that the Church enjoyed of the territorial wealth of France? The third had to do with civil rights: What provision should be made to protect the political and personal rights of all citizens? The last had to do with the king: Where would he fit into the new constitution? Would he agree to accept the subordinate position that such a constitution would accord a monarch?

The events of summer 1789 drove the agenda of the National Assembly forward. Peasant rebellions broke out in several regions. Armed bands roamed the countryside, some of the rebels broke into the castles of their masters in search of documents specifying labor and monetary dues. These were burned—and often the houses too. Frightened aristocrats packed their belongings and fled to friendlier nations, remaining in exile for the course of the Revolution. The swift, violent rebellion was dubbed the "Great Fear." In response, the Assembly met in a tense all-night session on August 4, 1789. Its result was the dismantling of landlords' customary rights and the abolition of the system of noble privilege that had prevailed for a millennium. Some of the decrees are listed in *Witnesses* on p. 584.

Later that month, the National Assembly addressed the issue of civil rights. Combining elements of the English and American constitutions with some major principles of Enlightenment political theory, they promulgated, on August 26, the "Declaration of the Rights of Man and the Citizen", quoted in *Witnesses* on p. 584. The rights defined in this document constitute a digest of liberal political principles and establish the theoretical framework of a future constitution. Later versions of the "Declaration" were included in subsequent constitutions, and it forms part of France's constitution today.

Opening with the statement that "ignorance, neglect, or contempt of human rights, are the sole causes of public misfortunes and corruptions of Government," the "Declaration" proceeds to define those rights in full. It affirms that "men are born, and always continue, free, and equal in respect of their rights" and that the purpose of government is to preserve "the natural and imprescriptible rights of man." Human liberty is unrestricted, except by the need to allow for the liberty of others, and must not be limited by systems of law. Free speech and freedom of worship are also to be guaranteed, along with the civil protections (like those long embedded in Anglo-Saxon law) against improper arrest and prosecution. Citizens are accorded the right to consent to taxes levied upon them, and private property is acknowledged and protected. For all its brevity— fewer than 1000 words— the "Declaration" states the main principles of modern liberalism as developed by Enlightenment thinkers.

Article X of the "Declaration" provides for freedom of conscience and worship. To achieve that goal, revolutionary leaders needed to rein in the Roman Catholic Church, powerful because of its wealth and its hold on the consciences of the faithful. On November 2, 1789, the Assembly (now established in Paris) confiscated all church property—amounting to fifteen percent of the land in France, which had yielded an immense, tax-free income in tithes. The following month, it issues a new paper currency, backed by the huge value of former church lands, now considered *"biens nationaux"* ("national property"). Peasant entrepreneurs and bourgeois speculators eagerly purchased the land itself at auction. These provisions effectively destroyed the economic power of the Roman Catholic Church in France.

During the following year, the Assembly issued more restrictions on Church and clergy. On February 13, 1790, it suppressed the religious houses in Paris. On July 12, 1790, it promulgated the Civil Constitution of the Clergy, quoted in *Witnesses* on p. 584. That legislation dismantled the institution of the Church, just as the legislation of August 4, 1789, had dismantled the privileges of the nobility. All priests (of whom there were some 40,000) would receive salaries from the new secular state (rather

The Collapse of the Old Regime

The Old Regime collapsed because of anger, violence, the class of personalities, and unpredictable circumstances—but also because of words. Presented here are some of the words that were powerful enough to remake an entire nation. Abbé Sieyès questions the privileges of the nobility, while in three acts of legislation, from 1789 and 1790, the National Assembly dismantles all feudal relations, defines the civil rights of all citizens, and secularizes the Church by making the clergy responsible to the state. In 1791, the feminist writer Olympe de Gouges responds to the Declaration of the Rights of Man and the Citizen with her own Declaration of the Rights of Woman and the Citizen, calling for a broadening of the concept of citizenship in a direction not before anticipated.

Abbé Sieyès asks: "What is the Third Estate?" (1789): We have three questions to ask:

1st. What is the third estate? Everything.

2nd. What has it been heretofore in the political order? Nothing.

3rd. What does it demand? To become something therein. ...

What are the essentials of national existence and prosperity? *Private* enterprise and *public* functions. Private enterprise may be divided into four classes: [those engaged in agriculture; those engaged in industry and production; "dealers and merchants"; and the professional and service classes, ranging from scientists to domestic servants]. ... Such are the labors which sustain society. Who performs them? The third estate.

Public functions. ... may [also] be classified under four headings: the Sword, the Robe, the Church, and the Administration. ... [T]he third estate everywhere constitutes nineteen-twentieths of them, except that it is burdened with all that is really arduous, with all the tasks that the privileged order refuses to perform. ...

Who, then, would dare to say that the third estate has not within itself all that is necessary to constitute a complete nation?

(From J. H. Stewart ed., A *Documentary Survey of the French Revolution*, 1951)

Decrees passed the night of August 4, 1789, in response to the "Great Fear": 1. The National Assembly abolishes the feudal regime entirely, and decrees that both feudal and [other contractual] rights and dues ... are abolished without indemnity. ... 4. All seigneurial courts of justice are suppressed without any indemnity; nevertheless the officials of such courts shall continue in office until the National Assembly has provided for the establishment of a new judi-cial organization. 5. Tithes of every kind ... are abolished subject to the devising of means for providing in some other manner for the expenses of divine worship, ... and for all establishments, seminaries, schools, colleges, hospitals, communities and others, to the maintenance of which they are now assigned. ... 9. Pecuniary privileges, personal or real, in matters of taxation are abolished forever. Collection shall be made from all citizens and on all property, in the same manner and in the same form. ... 11. All citizens may be admitted, without distinction of birth, to all ecclesiastical, civil, and military employments and offices.

(From J. H. Stewart ed., A *Documentary Survey of the French Revolution*, 1951)

The foundations of liberal government are defined in the Declaration of the Rights of Man and the Citizen (1789): The Representatives of the French People, organized in National Assembly, considering that ignorance, forgetfulness, or contempt of the rights of man are the sole cause of public misfortunes and the corruption of governments, have resolved to set forth in a solemn declaration the natural, inalienable, and sacred rights of man, in order that such declaration, continually before all members of the social body, may be a perpetual reminder of their rights and duties. ... 1. Men are born and remain free and equal in rights; social distinctions may be based only upon general usefulness. 2. The aim of every political association is the preservation of the natural and inalienable rights of man; these rights are liberty, property, security, and resistance to oppression. 3. The source of all sovereignty resides essentially in the nation; no group, no individual may exercise authority not emanating expressly therefrom.

(From J. H. Stewart ed., A *Documentary Survey of the French Revolution*, 1951)

The "Civil Constitution of the Clergy" (1790) attempts to secularize the Church: The National Assembly, after having heard the report of the ecclesiastical committee, has decreed and do decree the following as constitutional articles: Title I, ARTICLE I. Each department shall form a single diocese, and each diocese shall have the same extent and the same limits as the department [thus bring the organization of the Church in line with the political organization of the nation. ... Title II, ARTICLE I. Beginning with the day of publication of the present decree, there shall be but one mode of choosing bishops and parish priests, namely that of election. II. All elections shall be by ballot and shall be decided by the absolute majority of the votes. ... [thus taking the selection of clergy out of the hands of the institutional Church.] Title III, ARTICLE I. The ministers of religion, performing as they do the first and most important functions of society and forced to live continuously in the place where they discharge the offices to which they have been called by the confidence of the people, shall be supported by the nation [thus secularizing the clergy, who become employees of the state]. II. Every bishop, priest, and officiating clergyman in a chapel of ease shall be furnished with a suitable dwelling. ... Salaries shall be assigned to each, as indicated below. ...

(From J. H. Robinson, ed., *Readings in European History*, 2 vols. [Boston: Ginn, 1906], 2: 423–427; taken from the website: http://history.hanover.edu/texts/civilcon.htm)

than from tithes levied on parishioners). Freedom of worship was extended to Protestants and Jews. By an addendum of November 27, 1790, priests were required to swear an oath of loyalty to the revolutionary government. Only about one-half complied. Many others, in hiding, continued to perform traditional religious functions for loyal parishioners and encouraged resistance to the Revolution.

On September 3, 1791, the Assembly approved in final form the constitution it had pledged in the tennis court to formulate. Reluctantly, the king acceded. Allowed to retain his title and permitted direct authority over foreign policy and the army, Louis XVI surrendered his claim to absolute power.

The Legislative Assembly and National Convention

At this point, the members of the Assembly surrendered some power of their own. Having completed their task, they intended to go home (thoughtfully awarding, before disbanding, a large gratuity to the owner of the tennis court where the critical oath had been sworn). A decree that none of their number would be eligible to serve in the next assembly (championed as a democratic measure by, among others, Robespierre) entailed the election of a new slate of delegates to a new institution. This new Legislative Assembly took up the reins of government in October. Its delegates were not only new, but also younger and less experienced that the representatives chosen in 1789.

The one-year term of the Legislative Assembly concluded in September 1792. At that point, a third assembly convened: the National Convention. Legislators who had served in the previous assemblies were eligible for election to this new body. Consequently, the National Convention included both experienced legislators from the original National Assembly and those with little or no legislative experience. It also included persons of different "parties," or sets of political beliefs and objectives. Since 1787, political clubs identified with different political viewpoints had sprung up all over Paris and in the provinces; by 1794 these would number some 4000. Among these clubs were the Girondins (named after the Gironde region in southwest France, from where the principles figures of this group hailed) and the Jacobins (named after the church of St. Jacques, or James, in which their party held its meetings, and led by Maximilien Robespierre). The average age of the delegates to the Convention was a youthful thirty-five, and most favored radical change.

The political clubs developed a range of rival strategies for the future of the Revolution. The more moderate Girondins had considerable influence from 1791 to 1792. But they were shouldered aside by the more extreme Jacobins, who emerged as leaders of the Convention and of the Revolution in the fall of 1792. Over the next three years, these revolutionaries put aside the issues of human and civil rights that had previously absorbed the National Assembly to attend to the unseating of the king and the transformation of society.

Meanwhile, events in Paris had captured the attention of observers from abroad. In that busy capital, the "rights of man and citizen" had now been inscribed in blood. The end had come, it seemed, of the reigns of kings, strongmen, warriors, and priests who had saddled the human race since the curtain lifted on the story of civilization. One man who responded to the lure of Paris was the Englishman Tom Paine (1737–1809) (see Chapter 17), a professional revolutionary and an incendiary author.

Author of *Common Sense* and *The Crisis*, pamphlets supporting the cause of American independence against Britain, Paine worked on a larger canvas in his monumental *Rights of Man*, quoted in *Witnesses* on p. 588. This two-part work, published during his stay in France in 1791 and 1792, interpreted the Revolution as a necessary struggle between liberty and tyranny. Elected as a representative to the National Convention, Paine then found that his views were insufficiently radical for its Jacobin leaders. He was imprisoned from December 1793 to November 1794, during the height of the Terror and the execution of Robespierre; he emerged to find the Revolution over. Like Sieyès, Paine managed to survive the Revolution he celebrated in his works.

Like Paine, the English writer Mary Wollstonecraft (1759–1797) lived in Paris during the Revolution and acclaimed the French quest for political freedom. Her *Vindication of the Rights of Man*, written in 1790—and, like Paine's *The Rights of Man*, written in response to an anti-revolutionary treatise by the British statesman Edmund Burke—defended the principle that a new society could be successfully based on abstract conceptions of natural rights. When the National Convention voted to exclude women from political life, however, Wollstonecraft responded with her *Vindication of the Rights of Woman* (1792), a revolutionary work of a different sort. The first major work of Western feminism, it argues that women should define goals and achieve careers equivalent to those open to men.

In his earlier work *Reflections on the Revolution in France* (1790; see *Witnesses*, p. 588), Edmund Burke (1729–1797) had challenged the basic assumption of revolutionary activity: that it is possible, having destroyed a traditional political system, to create a new one that is better. It was the wisdom of human communities successively evolving over time, Burke argued, that had produced kings, nobles, religious values, the rituals of civilized human association. They had defects. But could a single generation concoct new social institutions without also simultaneously planting the seeds of what would become new forms of injustice and cruelty?

Burke wrote during the first year of the Revolution. He seemed to predict the turmoil that would break out shortly after his *Reflections* spoke of the flawed premises of revolutionary zeal. Although Paine and Wollstonecraft wrote eloquently of political ideals, Burke's view of the French Revolution was more accurate. For the Revolution did rip apart old customs and institutions; it did assault the fundamental structure of radical society; and it did create new governmental agencies as ruthless, perhaps more ruthless, than those they replaced. Soon after its inception, the Revolution grew violent. It turned even more violent as its locus shifted from the legislative assembles into the streets and fields where the poor and excluded, energized by change, pushed the Revolution in unanticipated directions, creating for themselves not a just society, but one that was novel and full of possibility.

THE BIRTH OF A NATION

From 1789 through 1794, a second, parallel and complementary, phase of the Revolution unfolded. Whereas the first aimed only to defeat tyranny, the second sought the transformation of society—a *total* revolution. The first was accomplished by the power of legislation and used the written word as its weapon. The second was accomplished by action and movement and symbol, while words were recruited to justify actions taken or planned. The architects of the first were mostly middle-class male professionals. The architects of the second were the crowds of people, and their self-appointed agents, who heretofore had occupied no place in the political hierarchy. Their activity in the French Revolution marks the entry into history of a new political class: the "people"—consisting of artisans, peasants and dayworkers, city folk and country folk, the shabby servant and the respectable householder, and women as well as men—all those who traditionally had been excluded from power. In 1789, from the margins of the political realm, they watched deputies to the Estates-General reinvent themselves as the National Assembly. By 1794, they *were* the nation, at home and on the march.

Peasants and Sans-Culottes

The agents of this popular revolution consisted of two groups: the peasants, themselves a disparate class including both proprietors and landless laborers from the various regions of France and the laborers, artisans and shopkeepers of the cities, primarily Paris. These were the "**sans-culottes**"—so called because they wore long trousers of crude cloth rather than the elegant knee breeches (*culottes*) and silk stockings worn by the bourgeois or nobleman. Their wives, daughters, and mothers also joined in the drama of revolution, and at times were principals in the action. Within the first six months of the Revolution, peasants and *sans-culottes*, both armed and dangerous, had burst onto the political stage.

Revolution in the streets: *Parisian citizens stormed the Bastille on July 14, 1789 and provided themselves with gunpowder with which to defend the revolution. In this contemporary illustration by Cholat, ordinary people, male and female, engage in decisive action. Contrast the image on page 581, where male members of a well-dressed elite dedicate themselves to the project of defining a new political order. (Musée Carnavalet, Paris)*

The March on the Bastille In June 1789, disturbing rumors reached Paris from Versailles of the struggle between the king and the delegates of the Third Estate. Would the king send an army to subdue the Parisians as he had, apparently, used armed guards to intimidate the National Assembly? Fear permeated the city. On July 11, the king dismissed his finance minister, Jacques Necker, an act the people of Paris found ominous. Then, on July 14, a crowd of 80,000 rushed to the Bastille, an ancient royal fortress. Commanded by an old governor in charge of a small garrison, it interested the crowd because of its ammunition stores. They stormed in, released the prisoners (there were only seven), and killed soldiers and the governor himself—whose severed head they displayed on a pike. The attack is depicted on p. 586.

The assault on the Bastille is for the French today the symbol of their Revolution, and its anniversary is celebrated as a national holiday. Just as in the United States, a July 4 celebration (the day of the signing of the Declaration of Independence) commemorates the Revolution against Great Britain.

News of the fall of the Bastille reached the delegates in Versailles along with reports of peasant uprisings around the nation, and these events, as we have seen, stimulated them to pass new legislation abolishing the whole apparatus of the Old Regime and to issue the "Declaration of the Rights of Man."

The possibility of royal repression was not the only threat confronting the people of Paris: famine now prevailed. The grain crop had failed in 1785, 1787, and 1788; stores of food had vanished, while shipments of grain were few; and the price of daily bread soared to eighty-eight percent of a worker's daily wage. As so often in traditional society, it was women—whose responsibility it was to feed the children—who raged most bitterly at the food shortage. On October 5, 1789, around 10,000 Parisian women, armed with pikes, knives, clubs, and muskets, marched in a driving rain on the royal palace at Versailles. Accompanying them was a contingent of 12,000 soldiers of the Paris town militia, the National Guard, under the command of the liberal nobleman the Marquis de Lafayette (1757–1834), who had once fought with George Washington in support of the American Revolution. (He would survive the Terror to espouse, in 1830, the succession of Louis-Philippe, the last king of France.)

The women burst into the palace, where they killed some guards. They compelled the king, the queen, and their son to return with them to Paris, shouting as they walked alongside the royal carriage that they had gotten "the Baker, the Baker's wife, and the Baker's boy"—taunts voicing their hopes that the royal captive would somehow provide them with bread. With these words they accomplished not only the king's social demotion but his political demotion as well: he had been transferred from his zone of royal power at Versailles to the city of Paris, where the people held sway. The National Assembly followed soon afterward. Paris was now the center of the Revolution.

Defending the Revolution From October 1789 to September 1791, emotions in Paris simmered. Co-resident in the same city were the king, the National Assembly (and its successors), and the masses of the "people," the *sans-culottes*, both male and female, who milled in the streets and snatched up each morsel of news. The king aimed to preserve his authority and the remnants of the Old Regime. The Assembly attempted to design a new government through the mechanisms of proposal, debate, and vote. The people, now "citizens," demanded famine relief, a responsive government, and the destruction of their enemies. In revolutionary Paris, the people who had been ignored throughout the long story of civilization—the poor and the hungry—now entered history.

From 1791 to 1793, the presence of the king, the fervor of the crowd, and the anxieties of foreign monarchs reshaped the Revolution. On June 21, 1791, the king fled Paris with his family; caught and arrested at Varennes, near France's northeastern border, he returned five days later, a prisoner. All this time, aristocratic refugees urged other European rulers—who eyed nervously the events unfolding so near their borders—to intervene against the Revolution. On August 27, 1791, the monarchs of Prussia and Austria issued the Declaration of Pillnitz, announcing their intention to intervene in French affairs. Several months later, having joined into a coalition they provoked a French declaration of war (see *Witnesses*, p. 595). In August 1792, coalition forces crossed into France, and were met, and repulsed, by French armies (who, before the year was out, would be singing the angry battle anthem the "Marseillaise"). Here began France's military venture against the monarchies of Europe which was to last until 1815 and transform the shape of Europe.

As the coalition armies advanced, Paris responded. On August 10, 1792, Paris was declared a Commune, its citizens collectively dedicated to the defense of the revolutionary cause. Angry mobs stormed the royal Tuileries palace. In September, they invaded the prisons that held suspected enemies of the Revolution, whom they summarily tried and murdered with pikes, clubs, and knives. These September Massacres, shocking even to many revolutionary leaders, resulted in the slaughter of more than 1200 prisoners—one-half of those detained. On September 22, the day after its first meeting, the National Convention proclaimed France to be a republic. That day became the first day of the first month of the Year I of a new revolutionary calendar.

In December, the king faced trial. "The tree of liberty can only grow if watered by the blood of

The "True" Rights of Man—Burke vs. Paine

In 1790, having observed for himself events in France during the early stages of the Revolution, Edmund Burke published his Reflections on the Revolution in France, which questioned the legitimacy of the revolutionaries from a number of vantage points so thoroughly and subtly that his critique amounts to a foundation document of conservative thought. Two years later, Thomas Paine, who had already experienced the American Revolution firsthand and formulated important original arguments against mercantilism and hereditary monarchy responded to Burke in his Rights of Man. *Presented here are sections of their two works pertaining to the issue of the true rights of "man."*

Edmund Burke distinguishes between civil and natural rights, the latter necessarily surrendered in part upon entry into society (1790): Far am I from denying in theory, full as far as my heart from withholding in practice (if I were of power to give or to withhold), the real rights of men. ... Men have a right to live by that rule; they have a right to do justice, as between their fellows, whether their fellows are in public function or in ordinary occupation. They have a right to the fruits of their industry; and to the means of making their industry fruitful. They have a right to the acquisition of their parents; to the nourishment and improvement of their offspring; to instruction in life, and to consolation in death. Whatever each man can separately do, without trespassing upon others, he has a right to do for himself; and he has a right to a fair portion of all which society, with all its combinations of skill and force, can do in his favour. In this partnership all men have equal rights; but not to equal things. He that has but five shillings in the partnership, has a good a right to it, as he that has five hundred points has to his larger proportion. But he has not a right to an equal dividend in the product of the joint stock. and as to the share of power, authority, and direction which each individual ought to have in the management of the state, that I must deny to be amongst the direct original rights of man in civil society; for I have in my contemplation the civil social man, and no other. It is a thing to be settled by convention.

If civil society be the offspring of convention, that convention must be its law. That convention must limit and modify all the descriptions of constitution which are formed under it. Every sort of legislative, judicial, or executory power are its creatures. They can have no being in any other state of things; and how can any man claim under the conventions of civil society, rights which do not so much as suppose its existence? rights which are absolutely repugnant to it? ... Men cannot enjoy the rights of an uncivil and of a civil state together. That he may obtain justice, he gives up his right of determining what it is in points the most essential to him. That he may secure some liberty, he makes a surrender in trust of the whole of it.

Government is not made in virtue of natural rights, which may and do exist in total independence of it. Government is a contrivance of human wisdom to provide for human wants. Men have a right that these wants should be provided for by this wisdom. Among these wants is to be reckoned the want, out of civil society, of a sufficient restrain upon their passions. Society requires not only that the passions of individuals should be subjected, but that even in the mass and body, as well as in the individuals, the inclinations of men should frequently be thwarted, their will controlled, and their passions brought into subjection. This can only be done by a power out of themselves; and not, in the exercise of its function, subject to that will and to those passions which it is its office to bridle and subdue. In this sense the restraints on men, as well as their liberties, are to be reckoned among their rights. But as the liberties and the restrictions vary with times and circumstances, and admit of infinite modifications, they cannot be settled upon any abstract rule; and nothing is so foolish as to discuss them upon that principle.

Paine sees civil right as an extension of natural rights (1792): From this short review it will be easy to distinguish between that class of natural rights which man retains after entering into society and those which he throws into the common stock as a member of society.

The natural rights which he retains are all those in which the Power to execute is as perfect in the individual as the right itself. Among this class, as is before mentioned, are all the intellectual rights, or rights of the mind; consequently religion is one of those rights. The natural rights which are not retained, are all those in which, though the right is perfect in the individual, the power to execute them is defective. They answer not his purpose. A man, by natural right, has a right to judge in his own cause; and so far as the right of the mind is concerned, he never surrenders it. But what availeth it him to judge, if he has not power to redress? He therefore deposits this right in the common stock of society, and takes the arm of society, of which he is a part, in preference and in addition to his own. Society grants him nothing. Every man is a proprietor in society, and draws on the capital as a matter of right.

From these premises two or three certain conclusions will follow:

First, That every civil right grows out of a natural right; or, in other words, is a natural right exchanged.

Secondly, That civil power properly considered as such is made up of the aggregate of that class of the natural rights of man, which becomes defective in the individual in point of power, and answers not his purpose, but when collected to a focus becomes competent to the Purpose of every one.

Thirdly, That the power produced from the aggregate of natural rights, imperfect in power in the individual, cannot be applied to invade the natural rights which are retained in the individual, and in which the power to execute is as perfect as the right itself.

We have now, in a few words, traced man from a natural individual to a member of society, and shown, or endeavoured to show, the quality of the natural rights retained, and of those which are exchanged for civil rights.

[Note on sources: these are both taken from the Internet, which posts the documents from their original eighteenth-century editions.]

kings," asserted one deputy. By a majority of one, the Convention sentenced Louis XVI to death. On January 21, 1793, before 20,000 spectators, he was executed by a new invention, the guillotine designed to be relatively humane, as well as efficient and democratic, offering all its victims death by decapitation formerly reserved for aristocrats). The executioner displayed the royal head, for the "crowned fools" of Europe to see and reflect upon, as shown in *Windows On*, p. 592. The minutes of the Convention warned ponderously: "Peoples of Europe! Peoples of the World! Look carefully at the thrones and you will see that they are nothing but dust!" The European powers were completely undaunted: by early March, Britain, the Netherlands, Spain, and Sardinia had joined the First Coalition against France. Surrounded and isolated, the French mobilized furiously to defend their Revolution.

On April 6, 1793, the Committee of Public Safety was formed to do whatever was necessary to mobilize the nation. Its extraordinary actions had not only military, but also economic, psychological, and cultural dimensions. Led at first by the Jacobin Georges-Jacques Danton (1759–1794), it was soon taken over by Maximilien Robespierre, who, a year later, sent his rival to the guillotine. For a little over a year, Robespierre managed France and the Revolution, a single-minded dictator and ultimately the victim of his own stratagems.

On August 23, 1793, the Committee of Public Safety ordered a "mass levy" of troops—a target figure of 300,000 men. The decree is quoted in *Witnesses* on p. 595. Every adult male was eligible, with unmarried or childless men between eighteen and twenty-five to be called up first. The women were to be mobilized, too, "to make tents and clothes, and [to] serve in the hospitals." Even the old men had their assigned task: "to stimulate the courage of the warriors and preach the unity of the Republic and hatred of kings." The mass levy was a recipe for total war, calling for the dedication of each citizen of either gender and all ages to the success of the new **Republic**.

Robespierre's mass levy marks a new departure in warfare. Until now, the conduct of war had been primarily a nobleman's business. From the late fifteenth century, infantry and artillery forces had taken precedence over cavalry, and other changes in military organization occurred because of the crystallization of nations and constantly improving gun technology (see Chapter 15). But the men who led these forces, like those who commanded the cavalry, were almost invariably nobles—in Europe generally and in France, whose "nobility of the sword" were proud of their heroic past. These, however, were precisely the nobles who fled France in 1789. Some 60 percent of the officers in the royal army were now *émigrés*. With the ranks of noble officers drastically thinned, talented

leaders had to be recruited from among the people and promoted on the basis of merit. The mass recruitment of French villagers resulted in the sudden democratization of the army.

The million men—out of a population of 28 million—who marched for the Republic in the 1790s were defenders not only of their land but also of revolutionary ideals. These *enfants de la patrie* ("children of the fatherland"), in the words of the fearsome "Marseillaise," fought for France, the Revolution, and the Republic. In these armies of the 1790s was that that nationalism—an ideology centered on allegiance to the nation, its culture, and its people—that would spread throughout Europe and figure centrally in its political history thereafter (see Chapters 23, 25).

The French army mobilized not only against foreign enemies but also against counter-revolutionaries who threatened the Republic from within. In March 1793, a revolt erupted in the Vendée region, in northwestern France. It continued until December and was not totally pacified for years. Ascribed by members of the Convention to "the ignorance, fanaticism and subservience of the country people" or "the criminality and hypocrisy of the priests," it involved 60–100,000 artisans and peasants, encouraged by dissident clergy. Loyalist soldiers of artisan and peasant origin brutally suppressed the uprising. Citizens shot citizens in the Vendée, in massacres that prefigured those of modern times.

The Terror For Robespierre and his supporters, critics of the Revolution were as harmful to the Republic as armed counter-revolutionaries, and so must also be targeted for suppression. From June 1793 to July 1794, these presumed rebels, "guilty" only of political dissent, were hunted all over France. As many as 300,000 were imprisoned, and tens of thousands executed. (By contrast, not one person had suffered official execution for political crimes during the American Revolution; and all those who signed the Declaration of Independence died peacefully.) The victims included persons who were guilty only of having once been privileged—among them the chemist Antoine Laurent Lavoisier (1743–1794) and the *philosophe* Marie Jean Antoine-Nicholas Caritat, Marquis de Condorcet (1743–1794), author amid the violent torrent of a rosy *Sketch for a Historical Picture of the Progress of the Human Mind*. Condorcet died on his first night in prison, perhaps by suicide, cheating the guillotine.

Lavoisier and Condorcet were among a group of writers, intellectuals, and artists who, in 1789, constituted the 208 members, according to one scholar's count, of the French cultural elite. The Revolution hit them hard. Of those identified by this scholar, 19 were executed; 4 committed suicide; 25 were imprisoned; 17 were denounced, or "watched" by authorities; and 23 emigrated. Nearly half of France's cultural leaders suffered in the Revolution fought for, among other freedoms, that of expression.

This period of extreme repression is known as the Reign of Terror. Its main author, and last victim, was Maximilien Robespierre, whose activity foreshadows that of the totalitarian dictators of the twentieth century. Yet in his earlier career as a young provincial lawyer of poor family, Robespierre had been an idealist, a disciple of Rousseau. And in the National Assembly, where he pressed for the broadening of the electoral franchise, his principles stance won him the epithet "the Incorruptible." Assuming the leadership of the Jacobin club in 1791, he won election that same year as a delegate of the Paris Commune to the National Convention. In 1793, he supported the execution of the king and the purge of the Girondins. Elected to the Committee of Public Safety in July 1793, Robespierre became its spokesperson. In that role, he advocated the emergency measures undertaken to mobilize the nation and destroy political opponents, initiating the Reign of Terror—the perhaps inevitable consequence of his ominous creed that the Revolution was a "war waged by liberty against its enemies." The purges of the spring of 1794, consuming both his more moderate colleague Danton and the atheistic journalist Jacques René Hébert (1757–1794), worried even his supporters. A conspiracy of fearful members of the Convention had Robespierre arrested and tried on July 27, 1794 (9 Thermidor), in order to prevent more purges to come.

Jacques-Louis David, Death of Marat (1793): *The influential radical thinker Jean-Paul Marat, challenged by the more conservative Girondins, brought his Montagnard faction of the National Convention to its height early in 1793—just months before a young female opponent, Charlotte Corday, gained access to his rooms and stabbed him in his bath. David displays the 50-year-old martyr to the revolutionary cause with a stoic, Neoclassical starkness, all verticals (the arm holding the quill, the bathsheets, the rectangular block supporting the inkwell) and horizontals (the extended arm, the written sheet, the head that could no longer be supported by his body). (Musée Royaux des Beaux Arts de Belgique, Brussels)*

Along with more than a hundred of his supporters, he died the next day by the guillotine.

That the curtain fell thus swiftly on Robespierre's life was no doubt a blessing for the French people. Although Robespierre had capably managed the war effort and sustained the nation in a time of crisis, his call for the suppression of all dissent opened the path to even greater violence in an era already so stained by bloodshed that its epochal achievements could be called into question. In Robespierre's brilliant speeches, the fusion of democratic idealism and brutal repression is striking. His important speech of February 5, 1794, for example, identified democracy with virtue at the same time that it argued the need to defend virtue with "terror"—a theoretically just and ideal violence. The republic was in peril externally ("all the despots surround you") and internally ("all the friends of tyranny conspire"). It must "annihilate" both sets of enemies or "perish with its fall." The people must be guided by reason and the enemies of the people by terror." Both virtue and terror are essential in time of revolution: "virtue, without which terror is destructive; terror, without which virtue is impotent." In these startling phrases, linking the incongruous qualities of virtue and terror, Robespierre uses the manipulative language characteristic of the demagogue and dictator.

The Culture of Revolution

Amid the terror and political transformations of the early 1790s, revolutionary leaders also engineered a cultural revolution, which achieved the reshaping of religious and intellectual values, the democratization of society, and the remodeling of the family, which fell short, nevertheless, of obtaining for women full citizenship or sexual equality. It aimed to eradicate all the imprints of tradition on the human spirit, beginning with Christian belief and aristocratic privilege.

The attack on the property and privileges of the Roman Catholic Church had already begun in 1789. In the following year, the Civil Constitution of the Clergy secularized ecclesiastical institutions. In 1792, the Convention desanctified the church of Saint Geneviève, patron saint of Paris, and rededicated it to the celebration of "great men"; here Voltaire and Rousseau were honored. On October 5, 1793, in the midst of the Terror, Christianity was abolished. In November 1793, Hébert organized the Festival of Reason, which proclaimed the end of religion and the elevation of the human mind. Averse to atheism, Robespierre offered instead the deist "cult of the Supreme Being;" this was launched with the June 1794 Festival of the Supreme Being, shown in *Windows On* on p. 592, complete with its gaudy props designed by the quasi-official artist of the Revolution, Jacques-Louis David (1749–1825).

These efforts to deracinate Christianity from French soil and spirit did not succeed. Many people, especially in the villages, clung to their faith and their rituals. They protected the priests who had gone into hiding and they detested the Revolution. Later, Napoleon—who recognized that Christianity still lived and was useful to his purposes— permitted the Church a partial reestablishment.

The secularization and rationalization of values was pursued in the intellectual as in the religious sphere. The system of weights and measures was

FRENCH LIBERTY.　　BRITISH SLAVERY.

James Gilray, cartoon on the French Revolution: *The pioneering Scottish cartoonist James Gilray satirizes the achievements of the French Revolution in this 1792 image of two grotesque figures: a starving Frenchman on the left feeding his emaciated body on raw grasses, the traditional famine food of premodern crisis; and a bloated Englishman on the right—presumably the victim of an oppressive monarchy— scarfing down a tankard of ale and a side of beef. Who won the Revolution?*

The Radical Revolution

Anonymous, Execution of King Louis XVI, January 21, 1793

The Abolition of Slavery Proclaimed to the Convention on 16 Pluviôse, Year II, c. 1794

Festival of the Supreme Being

Villeneuve, Something to Ponder for the Crowned Fools of Europe, 1793

The Revolution entered a second, more radical stage after August 1792. The National Convention abolished the monarchy and proclaimed a Republic. On January 21, 1793, the deposed King Louis XVI went to the guillotine, as depicted in a contemporary painting (top). Supporters of the revolution vaunted the regicide, in a tone that echoed the message of the image shown here (right). The French inscription that accompanied the bloody, severed head of the king challenged the "crowned fools" of Europe to reflect on the fate of those who opposed the revolution. The radical phase of the Revolution brought huge, if only temporary, social and cultural changes. Among the most positive was the abolition of slavery throughout the French Empire, which was proclaimed to the Convention on February 4, 1794 (left center). With the demotion of Roman Catholicism, Robespierre attempted to create a new kind of religion, fully rational and free of superstition, as he saw it. The engraving here depicts the Festival of the Supreme Being held on June 8, 1794 (left).
(top and left center: Musée Carnavalet, Paris; right and left: Bibliothèque Nationale, Paris)

To continue your investigation of this topic, please go to www.prenhall.com/king for the related WINDOWS on the WEB activity

Mathematics + Standardization

reorganized on a decimal basis, requiring the creation of new units of measurement. The "meter," for instance, currently the basis of measurements in most Western nations, was defined in 1791 by the French Academy of Sciences as a precise fraction of the quadrant of the Earth's circumference running from the North Pole through Paris to the equator.

Calendar reorganized

The revolutionary spirit also called for the reorganization of the calendar, replacing names and dates derived from classical or Christian concepts with new ones. The names of months now reflect the natural year—"Germinal," or "budding," for mid-March to mid-April; "Thermidor," or "heat," for mid-July–mid-August; "Brumaire," or "foggy," for mid-October–mid-November. The years were renumbered to recognize revolutionary events. Year I was defined as beginning at the moment of the creation of the Republic (declared on September 22, 1792). This system of numeration, based on secular, political events, contrasted sharply with earlier calendrical schemes measured from a presumed date of the creation of the world (in the case of the Jewish calendar) or the irrelevant date, as it seemed to these deist revolutionaries, of the birth of Christ. In reordering the calendar, as in redefining measurements, the new government repudiated the experience of the past and began, brashly, anew.

Press

The same outlook may explain the great burgeoning of newspapers and pamphlets. Even ordinary people could read, or have read to them, these digests of the revolutionary events of the day. Among the revolutionary leaders, both Hébert and Jean-Paul Marat (1743–1793) (each a victim of the Revolution: the former guillotined, the latter assassinated, as depicted on p. 590) were journalists who used the press to forge a national consciousness.

New outlooks also shaped daily behavior, transforming the manners and customs established under the Old Regime. The deference formerly shown to persons of high social status was abolished. And where it was previously customary to address someone as "*monsieur*" or "*madame*"—or, in the case of a lord, "*monsigneur*"—now it was decreed that people address each other, without regard to status, as "*citoyen*" ("citizen") and "*citoyenne*." And each would address the other with the familiar form of "you," "*tu*," rather than the formal "*vous*." Men of the bourgeoisie adopted the long trousers of the *sans-culottes*. Wealthy women followed the fashion of simple dressing with plain (and sometimes translucent) fabrics.

The democratization of society extended to the matter of slavery. In 1791, the National Assembly had abolished slavery within the boundaries of France. In 1794, the National Convention extended abolition to the colonial possessions, whose economies depended upon the institution (see Chapter 19). In the French Caribbean colony of Saint-Domingue, located on an island shared with Spanish Santo Domingo, the abolition of slavery stimulated an independence

movement, under the capable leadership of a former slave, Toussaint L'Ouverture (c. 1748–1803). Although Toussaint would later become a victim of Napoleon's attempt to reconquer the colony, the new black nation of Haiti won and retained its independence.

Haitian Indep.

The family according to the revolutionaries, embodied a different kind of slavery—the result of patriarchal arrangements for the preservation of property. Fathers controlled the marriages of their children. Further, they directed inheritances away from daughters and toward elder sons, in order to preserve over generations the wealth of favored males. The Revolution introduced several laws that undermined this patriarchal structure. It legalized divorce, enabling women to be released from family ties (as some 6000 did in Paris alone between 1793 and 1795). It insisted on the sharing of inheritance among all heirs, female as well as male, in the event of an intestate death. It even, briefly, declared equal inheritance rights for illegitimate, as for legitimate, offspring. Wives and children, especially daughters, won unprecedented rights by these changes.

Women's rights

Despite the granting of these unprecedented rights, women did not gain the right to participate in civic life. Olympe de Gouges (1748–1793), the self-educated daughter of a butcher, an actress and playwright, detected the bias of revolutionary legislators from an early moment. In response to promulgation of the "Declaration of the Rights of Man" in August 1789, she published, in 1791, her "Declaration of the Rights of Woman." Her point was twofold. In the first place, women had heretofore suffered a double deprivation of rights: by the state, on the one hand, and by their husbands and fathers, on the other. In the second place, the male delegates to the National Assembly, had disturbingly, not thought to do anything about this.

These arguments, containing stern admonitions about the deprivation of women's rights within the family, De Gouges presents mainly in the preface to

MUST READS

Books and Pamphlets from the French Revolution

Emmanuel Sieyès	*What Is the Third Estate?* (1789)
Edmund Burke	*Reflections on the Revolution in France* (1790)
Olympe de Gouges	*Declaration of the Rights of Woman and the Citizen* (1791)
Tom Paine	*Rights of Man* (1791)
Mary Wollstonecraft	*A Vindication of the Rights of Woman* (1792)

her "Declaration." The main text, consisting of 17 articles, amusingly parodies of the "Declaration of the Rights of Man," revealing its misogynist assumptions. According to De Gouges, women, as much as men, are "born free," with the right to have their "imprescriptible rights" preserved by a government whose sole purpose for existing is to guarantee such rights. De Gouges pursues the implications of her own logic. In matters of criminal law, where women had traditionally been exempt from prosecution because of their presumed incapacity, she insists on their responsibility. Women, like men, might be "accused, arrested, and detained" for violations of law; indeed, women have the right "to mount the scaffold," to face the supreme penalty. De Gouges herself was guillotined in 1793. Before she died, she had composed the first feminist critique of the relation between the family and the state.

De Gouges had dedicated her "Declaration of the Rights of Woman and the Citizen" to the queen, Marie Antoinette, who she hoped would, as a woman, be sympathetic to women's interests. Marie Antoinette was herself a target of public criticism, fired in part by her taste for luxury and rumors of her sexual promiscuity but also, apparently, by her being a woman and a foreigner. In at least 126 pamphlets, she was charged with adultery, lesbianism, and more bizarre forms of sexual misbehavior. Like her husband, she was accused of being an enemy of the new state, and on October 16, 1793, she followed him to the scaffold. In the same year, de Gouges, too, was sent to the guillotine, a victim of the Reign of Terror which saw an activist for women's rights, however revolutionary, as an enemy of the Revolution.

The failure of male revolutionaries to undertake the civil liberation of women was not, in 1793,

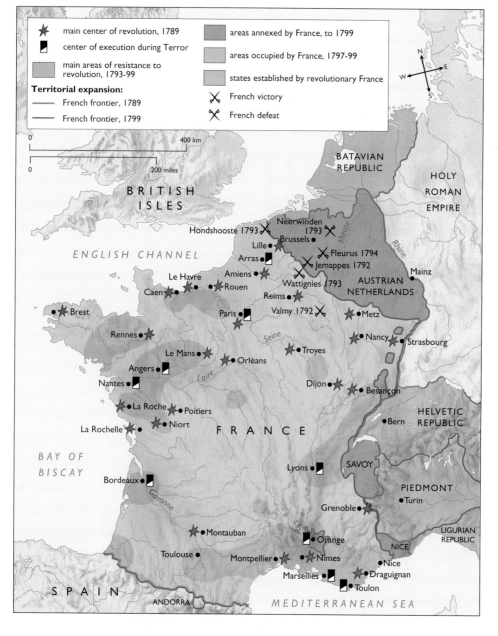

Map 20.1 The Revolution, 1789–1799: *The Revolution involved the whole of France, where entire regions were either loyal to the new government or in opposition. The Terror also affected the entire nation, although repression was centered in the capital. Even before Napoleon's advent, the revolutionary armies won victories against their European opponents. Shown here are main centers of revolutionary activity, executions during the Terror, and early battles.*

Revolution Turns Radical

The Revolution might have ended in September 1791, when the National Assembly achieved its goal of promulgating a constitution approved and signed by the king. Instead, the Revolution took a radical turn, some indications of which are seen in the documents here. In the spring of 1792, with Austria and Prussia poised to invade France, the French preempt them by declaring war against Austria and "the unjust aggression of a [foreign] King." The following August, the Jacobin faction pledges to struggle in "mortal combat" against the machinations of the king they now name "Louis the Last." In December, the National Convention offers fraternal aid to the nations of Europe in their struggle against tyranny. After the king was condemned and guillotined in January 1793, the Terror prevailed; one spectator describes the fate of a few of its victims.

The National Assembly declares war on Austria (April 20 1792). The National Assembly declares that the French nation, faithful to the principles consecrated by its Constitution *not to undertake any war with a view to making conquests, and never to employ its forces against the liberty of any people,* takes arms only to maintain its liberty and independence; That the war which it is forced to undergo is not a war of nation against nation, but the just defense of a free people against the unjust aggression of a [foreign] king: That Frenchmen will never mistake their brothers for their real enemies. ... That it adopts in advance all foreigners who, abjuring the cause of its enemies, range themselves under its banners and consecrate their efforts to the defense of its liberty. ...
(From J. H. Stewart, trans., *A Documentary Survey of the French Revolution* [N.Y.: the Macmillan Co., 1951], pp. 287–288)

The radical Jacobin faction reviews its gains, but alerts its members to the designs of the king (1792). Since the 10th of August [the] conspirators have expiated their crimes; public spirit has risen again [and] triumphs at length over the scoundrels leagued against its liberty and its welfare. Nevertheless, the people of Paris have felt the necessity of preserving an imposing attitude and of exercising a strict surveillance over the connecting links and agents of the conspiracy of the traitor, Louis the last! ... The head, the cause, and the pretext of the machinations still breathes! Despotism moves in the shadows; let us stand fast to engage it in mortal combat, whatever form it assumes.
(From J. H. Stewart, trans., *A Documentary Survey of the French Revolution* [N.Y.: The Macmillan Co., 1951]. p. 321)

In December 1792, the National Convention issues this Proclamation to the Nations, promising the support of the French people to all those proposing to rid themselves of tyrants: the French people to the people of ... brothers and friends: We have conquered our liberty and we shall maintain it. We offer to bring this inestimable blessing to you, for it has always been rightly ours, and only by a crime have our oppressors robbed us of it. We have driven out your tyrants. Show yourselves free men and we will protect you from their vengeance, their machinations, or their return. From this moment the French nation proclaims the sovereignty of the people, the suppression of all civil and military authorities which have hitherto governed you and of all which the taxes which you bear, under whatever form, the abolition [Page 450] of the tithe, of feudalism, of seigniorial rights and monopolies ' of every kind, of serfdom, whether real or personal , of hunting and fishing privileges, of the corvee, the salt tax, the tolls and local imposts, and, in general, of all the various kinds of taxes with which you have been loaded by your usurpers; it also proclaims the abolition among you of all noble and ecclesiastical corporations and of all prerogatives and privileges opposed to equality. You are, from this moment, brothers and friends; all are citizens, equal in rights, and all are alike called to govern, to serve, and to defend your country.
(From J. H. Robinson, ed., *Readings in European History*, 2 vols. [Boston: Ginn, 1906], 2: 449–450; taken from the website: http://history.hanover.edu/TEXTS/natcom.htm)

Decree establishing the *Levée en masse,* or mass levy of troops (August 23, 1793): Henceforth, until the enemies have been driven from the territory of the Republic, the French people are in permanent requisition for army service. The young men shall go to battle; the married men shall forge arms and transport provisions; the women shall make tents and clothes, and shall serve in the hospitals; the children shall turn old linen into lint; the old men shall repair to the public places, to stimulate the courage of the warriors and preach the unity of the Republic and hatred of kings. ... The levy shall be general. Unmarried citizens or childless widowers, from eighteen to twenty-five years, shall go first; they shall meet, without delay, at the chief town of their districts. ... The battalion organized in each district shall be united under a banner bearing the inscription: *The French people risen against tyrants.*
(From J. H. Stewart ed., *A Documentary Survey of the French Revolution,* 1951)

The Abbé Carrichon describes the execution by guillotine of a group of nobles (1793–1794): At last we reached the fatal spot. ... The moment was overwhelming. ... The sacrifice was due to begin. The noisy merriment of the spectators and their ghastly jibes add to the sufferings of the victims. ... The executioner and his assistants climb on to the scaffold and arrange everything. The former puts on over his other clothes a blood-red overall. He places himself on the left ... while his assistants stand on the other side. ... When everything is ready ... [the first victim] goes up the steps with the help of the executioners. The chief headsman takes him by the left arm, the big assistant by the right and the other man by the legs. In a moment they lay him flat on his face and his head is cut off and thrown with his body into a great tumbril, where the bodies swam in blood: and so it goes on. ... The Maréchale was the third to go up. They had to make an opening in the top of her dress to uncover her neck. Mme d'Ayen was the tenth.
(From G. Pernoud and S. Flaissie eds., *The French Revolution,* 1961)

surprising. At that time, women's voices had only, and only faintly, begun to be heard (see Chapter 17). They fought a misogynist tradition that denied that women were truly human, or capable of education or understanding at the level of men. The demand for political rights was wholly new in the early 1790s—as new as the meter and the Year I. It could have arisen only in the context of a male revolution against illegitimate authority. Although men did not welcome feminist claims during the French Revolution, the Revolution made the articulation of those claims possible for the first time in the history of the West, or anywhere on the globe.

The cultural revolution was as profound as the political one and ultimately as irreversible. And so it was that Robespierre—that precocious master of the corruption of language—fell from power not on July 27, 1794, but during Thermidor of the Year II. The Revolution would soon, once more, change course.

Reaction Sets In: the Directory

On Robespierre's downfall, his opponents took control of the National Convention. By August 1795, it had framed a new constitution, providing for the creation of a "Directory" as the nation's chief executive; this became effective the following November. The Directory, a five-man executive committee, presided over an assembly elected by limited suffrage. (The election of 1792 had been, in contrast, by universal manhood suffrage.) It proceeded to limit the freedoms gained by the Revolution to members of the high bourgeoisie, to shed many of its cultural innovations, to repress dissent, and to prosecute abroad the war, whose aim had shifted from self-defense to expansion.

Luxury and gaiety returned in the circles of those who had profited from the Revolution, or whose wealth had survived it. Hardship returned to the circles of the now-tamed *sans-culottes*, for the Revolution had not tamed the monsters of scarcity and inflation. The secret police monitored both royalist and popular conspiracies against the state. Repression and reaction reigned.

The liberal phase of the Revolution that began in 1789 had won for the French the same kinds of rights that Anglo-Americans had achieved in their War for Independence and recently ratified Constitution (see Chapter 19). The catalogue of those rights had emerged from Anglo-Saxon law, English precedent, and the different social and political theories that the Enlightenment thinkers had derived from earlier Western intellectual traditions.

The radical phase of the Revolution, also begun in 1789, had been characterized by peremptory decrees, by the abolition of long-established customs and the imposition of new ones, and above all by violence, directed against citizens and strangers alike. It was accomplished by the people *en masse*—the peasants of the countryside and the Parisian *sans-culottes*, then unloosed by bourgeois members of the legislative assemblies, whose modest programs for change escalated rapidly and unstoppably.

The achievements of both phases, the liberal and the radical, would be undone as the Directory yielded to Napoleon. Yet both would have an afterlife, in France and beyond, in years to come.

THE IMPERIAL ADVENTURE

The Directory governed for only four years. On one side, it faced resistance from royalists who wished to dismantle the Revolution and reinstate the Old Regime. On the other, it faced disenfranchised commoners, afflicted once again by the soaring price of bread, who still believed that the Revolution was theirs. It suffered, too, from its own inefficiency, incompetence, and corruption. Financial problems, dating back to the creation of a paper currency in 1789, went unresolved. Bourgeois investors suffered when, in 1797, more than half the national debt was canceled. The demands of the army aggravated the financial crisis; yet, the army was the key to the future.

The war begun in 1792 to defend France from encircling monarchies had become a ceaseless, roaming venture, which broadcast revolutionary ideas as it shifted political boundaries. The army won fine territorial prizes for France and glory for its generals. Preeminent among these was Napoleon Bonaparte (1769–1821), portrayed on p. 598, whose career began to develop amid the smoke of the dying Revolution. In just over 15 years, he would lead France to autocracy and transform Europe.

The Coming of Napoleon

Had Napoleon Bonaparte served in the pre-Revolutionary army, where only men of high rank succeeded, he would have remained a nobody. He was descended from a minor noble family of Corsica, a tiny and newly acquired Mediterranean island, whose native dialect was closer to Italian than to French. At the French military academy where he was sent to prepare for the best career open to boys of his background, he suffered the humiliation of being poor, short, and foreign. Even as a child, however, he displayed his talent for leadership—directing his classmates in snowball combat. In 1785, at the age of 16, he won a commission in the artillery, and in 1793, at age 24, seized the fortified harbor of Toulon for the Revolution in the face of a British naval assault. In October 1795, he won the gratitude of the Directory when he dispersed a crowd of royalist dissidents (killing about 100 of them) with, as he is said to have remarked, "a whiff of grapeshot." Rewarded with high command, he departed for wars abroad, where the effects of the Revolution in France were beginning to be felt.

By 1795, the First Coalition which had been formed against Revolutionary France had expanded to include Russia, Britain, the Netherlands, Spain, and Sardinia, as well as Austria. (Prussia had withdrawn, having just gorged itself in an independent political agreement with one-third of what remained of Poland—the balance assigned to Russia and Austria; see Chapter 15.) However, the coalition did not last long. One by one, France defeated or formed new alliances with most of its members, until only Austria and Britain remained. During the next four years, the French would oppose the Austrians in Italy and the British wherever they had interests—on the Mediterranean Sea and in North Africa, India, and the Caribbean. Napoleon took part in some phases of the war with both of these adversaries.

From spring 1796 to winter 1797, Napoleon stormed through northern Italy, then occupied by Austria. As he went, he transformed his troops into a dauntless force, capable of deadly speed and compact, focused attack. They defeated Austrian regular forces as well as Italian militias. By the Treaty of Campo Formio (October 17, 1797), Napoleon became master of northern Italy, which he reorganized as the Cisalpine Republic, a satellite of France. The peace settled, Napoleon returned to France in order to win support for his project to defeat the crucial enemy, as he saw it: Britain.

Napoleon's career in Italy already displayed the features that would characterize his later military ventures. He did not merely win battles; he also reshaped states and principalities, and did so with a purpose beyond territorial gain. He built more coherent, more centralized, more governable states than those he had defeated. Meanwhile, Napoleon's extraordinary charisma won him the devotion of his troops and impressed observers throughout Europe.

He was also, in his way, a revolutionary. Although he had cast his lot with the conservative Directory, there were elements of the revolutionary agenda that Napoleon actively promoted in the lands over which he held authority. For example, he fully embraced the Revolution's anti-clericalism. Throughout northern Italy, he suppressed religious orders and tore down moldering churches or converted them to secular uses. He imposed French law upon subject lands, abolishing serfdom, limiting aristocratic privilege, and insisting upon the inheritance rights of children of both sexes. His soldiers broadcast the Revolution's ideals of "liberty, equality, and fraternity." At the same time, their fierce patriotism awakened sentiments of national and ethnic loyalty among the peoples they encountered—sentiments that would inspire some of the great political movements of the coming century.

After returning briefly to France, Napoleon set out again in 1798, this time for Egypt. (Here, one of his adjutants found and arranged for the transport home of the Rosetta Stone, with its key to the late ancient demotic Egyptian language; see Chapter 1.) He saw Egypt—then controlled by the Ottoman Empire (see Chapter 15) and allied with Britain—as a stepping-stone to India and the heart of the British Empire. He defeated a Mamluk army at the Battle of the Pyramids; but soon afterward the British admiral Horatio Nelson (1758–1805) destroyed the French fleet at the Battle of the Nile, leaving Napoleon stranded in Egypt. The following year, Napoleon, along with companions, slipped past the British fleet and sped to France, where conspiracy was afoot.

There, he found a situation favorable to his ambitions: the government was foundering and France was in disarray. He joined forces with Emmanuel-Joseph Sieyès, author of the inflammatory 1789 tract "What is the Third Estate?" (see above). Now one of the Directors, Sieyès believed that a strong leader was needed to bring order to the state. He helped plan the events that occurred on 18 Brumaire (by the revolutionary calendar still in force), or November 9, 1799. With a small group of armed supporters, Napoleon marched into the assembly of the two ruling councils and announced that he would take charge. The deputies discussed the possibility of arresting him, but before they could vote on the matter, Napoleon's brother Lucien (1775–1840), president of the lower council, ordered the soldiers to expel those in opposition.

In this *coup d'état* (sudden seizing of power), Napoleon proclaimed a new government, of which he would be "First Consul" (with Sieyès and another supporter, for the moment, the second and third). For the next sixteen years, the story of France is the story of Napoleon.

Napoleon's France

The inexorable rise of Napoleon Bonaparte accelerated. In 1802, he made himself sole Consul for life; in 1804, emperor. Along the way, he paused briefly to consult the people of France, who had the privilege of approving each of these appointments by plebiscite. Having achieved a *rapprochement* with the Church, he invited Pope Pius VII (whom he would dispossess of the Papal States in 1809 and subsequently place under house arrest) to perform the coronation ceremony in Paris. But at the crucial moment, he grasped the crown and placed it on his own head; then he placed the consorts crown on that of his wife, Josephine de Beauharnais (1763–1814). There could be no doubt where the power lay. The moment is commemorated in David's painting, reproduced on p. 602.

As Napoleon's titles accumulated, republican institutions wasted away. After 1799, when he imposed the constitution of the Year VIII, the elected assembly was replaced by an appointed Senate and a Tribunal (eliminated by 1808), chosen by the

Napoleon at War

Antoine-Jean Gros, Napoleon Bonaparte on Arcole Bridge (1790): *Though he studied with David, Gros did not adopt the master's cool Neoclassicism. Here a romantic young Napoleon is hero and victor, a dauntless energy conveyed by the swirling forms of his sash, his hair, and his standard. (Hermitage Museum)*

Senators from a list of 6000 "notabilities." Those two bodies together disposed of legislation proposed by a Council of State, chosen by Napoleon. This whole government apparatus was approved by a plebiscite in which all adult males were permitted to vote. An overwhelming majority—99 percent— voted "Yes" to an authoritarian constitution. A little more than a decade since the promulgation of the first republican constitution, nearly all of its elements had been abolished with the approval of the electorate.

Pursuing the goals his royal Bourbon predecessors had mapped, Napoleon centralized and bureaucratized the government. In each *département*, or district, an appointed prefect executed his orders. Napoleon recruited his magistrates, like his army officers, from all social classes (including former members of the nobility) and rewarded loyal and efficient service well. To stabilize the currency and support commerce, he established, in 1800, the Bank of France. To ensure a steady flow of revenues, he regularized the system of taxation, including both direct taxes on property and indirect taxes on salt, tobacco, and liquor. To promote trade, he abolished most internal customs tolls and standardized weights and measures. To control the circulation of ideas, he censored the theater and the press, shutting down all but 13 of 73 newspapers, and unleashed a secret police force under the direction of a former agent of the Terror, Joseph Fouché. To underscore his eminence and that of his court, he created a new nobility from an assortment of former *émigré* aristocrats, loyal magistrates, and army officers—bestowing 3600 titles between 1808 and 1814. The former revolutionary Sieyès, who had engineered his rise to power, was made a count.

Napoleon also revised the legal system, creating the *Code Napoléon* (Napoleonic, or Civil, Code). This massive document, containing more than 2,000 articles, is still in force in France today, as well as in many other countries. It combined the comprehensive approach of Roman law with Enlightenment and, to some extent, revolutionary principles. To anxious bourgeois survivors of the Revolution, the Civil Code guaranteed the sanctity of private property. By contrast, it limited the rights of workers to form associations, or even to move about the country without official identification.

Within the family, the Code reaffirmed the father's traditional rights over household property and persons. A wife could not buy or sell property without her husband's approval, and her income was

***Gros*, Napoleon on the Battlefield of Eylau:** *A legislator, a critic, an educator, Napoleon was above all a war-maker—a successful one, too, until the last years of his career. In this 1808 painting he is seen with his loyal followers and soldiers on the field of the battle of Eylau in 1807.* (Louvre, Paris)

Revolution in Fashion

Pre-Revolution fashion worn by the upper-middle class, 1780

Pre-Revolution dress of the working class, c.1780

Fashion worn by the Incroyables, or Unbelievables, 1794

The momentous changes wrought by the French Revolution are written, among other ways, in how men and women dressed before and after the event. Shown here at top left are a representative couple of the upper-middle class just prior to the Revolution. She wears an elaborate flounced and frilled dress; he a vest, jacket, and culottes, or knee-length pants, which come to an end below the knee, atop silk stockings and elegant, heeled shoes. Modest though their dress is—aristocratic and courtly fashion was much more elaborate—it would become less showy after the Revolution ran its course. To their right is a working-class couple of the same era, dressed far more simply. Note especially the man's characteristic trousers, or sans-culottes, which extend, never gathered, below the knee to the ankles. The image upper right depicts soldiers and other participants in the Revolution in 1793–1794, the year of the Reign of Terror. Only the military drummer retains the culottes of the pre-Revolutionary era. At lower left, a wealthy couple strut the latest fashion at the climactic moment of the Revolution, 1794, just

Revolutionaries, 1793–94

before the fall of Robespierre and the institution of the Directory. These represent the Incroyables, or Unbelievables, the fast set of Revolutionary Paris at a tricky, transitional moment. At lower right, in a parlor scene from 1839, the effects of Revolution on fashion are displayed. The men, whether in military or sober civilian dress, now wear trousers like the proletarian sans-culottes that their ancestors would have disdained, while the woman, still beautifully attired, has moderated her frills and flounces. (top left: Private Collection; right: Costumes Historiques de la France; below left: Private Collection; Facing page, top: Private Collection; Facing page, below: Private Collection)

Post-Revolutionary fashion, 1839

To continue your investigation of this topic, please go to www.prenhall.com/king for the related **WINDOWS** on the **WEB** activity

considered to belong to him and his heirs. Divorce was possible but difficult, and, as in centuries past, adultery was considered a more serious violation for a woman than for a man. Napoleon thought little of women's rights, and saw their role as consisting chiefly in the bearing and rearing of children.

Thos children were, like their mothers, subordinated to their father's will, or that of their parents acting jointly. Parents could choose marriage partners for their children or reject their children's choices. Fathers could have their children jailed—one of the hated features of the Old Regime. The Code retained, however, the Revolution's bar against primogeniture (the practice by which the eldest son inherited the bulk of family property).

Just as he understood the importance of a coherent system of law, Napoleon also foresaw the need for a universal system of education. He did not institute such a system; nevertheless, under his guidance, France surpassed almost all other states in providing for the general education of the young. He ordered that each village should have a school for the elementary education of the young of both sexes. Secondary education was more limited; but the system of secondary schools, or *lycées* (open to boys—not to girls—who could afford the fees), was an

exceptional beginning to an educational system of high quality and, in time, universal access. Napoleon also organized a public university system.

Napoleon's settlement with the Roman Catholic Church was a complex matter. The Revolution had been anti-clerical from the start and, under Jacobin domination, wholly anti-religious. Its leaders had viewed priests and members of the religious orders as hypocritical, greedy, or superfluous, and the international church hierarchy as opposed to the interests of the French nation. One of the early acts of the National Assembly, moreover, had been to strip the Church of all its property. Yet many Frenchmen and women remained loyal Catholics, and even more wished to reestablish the Church to enforce moral standards, sanctify the key events of life—birth, marriage, and death—and to provide early schooling.

By the Concordat of 1801, the compromise negotiated with the Vatican, Napoleon reestablished the Roman Catholic Church in France under terms favorable to its ruler. The Church surrendered its claim to all property confiscated by the Revolution. Clergy must either swear allegiance to the state or resign. Priests could pursue their pastoral work unfettered, but were required to read official pronouncements

Jacques-Louis David, **Consecration of the Emperor Napoleon I and Coronation of the Empress Josephine in the Cathedral of Notre-Dame de Paris on December 2, 1804, 1806, and 1807:** *In an event of personal self-display that troubled Royalists and radicals alike, Napoleon brought the pope to Paris for his consecration and the coronation of his empress, Josephine de Beauhamais, in a moment that was to evoke memories of the papal crowning of Charlemagne in 800 C.E. At the last moment, Napoleon seized the crown and put it on himself; then crowned Josephine, as is depicted here. (Louvre)*

Napoleon, According to Himself and to an Enemy

Although the emperor Napoleon thought of himself as a champion of the Revolution, a restorer of the nation, a hero "who extended the limits of glory," others saw him as a despot, a danger, an anomaly. In these passages, the sketch of Napoleon by the feminist Madame de Staël stands in clear contrast to Napoleon's own self-portrait.

Napoleon anticipates most of the charges that history will make against him, and defends his record (c. 1815): I closed the gulf and cleared the chaos. I purified the Revolution, dignified Nations and established Kings. I excited every kind of emulation, rewarded every kind of merit, and extended the limits of glory! This is at least something! And on what point can I be assailed on which an historian could not defend me? Can it be for my intentions? But even here I can find absolution. Can it be for my despotism? It may be demonstrated that the Dictatorship was absolutely necessary. Will it be said that I restrained liberty? It can be proved that the licentiousness, anarchy, and the greatest irregularities, still haunted the threshold of freedom. Shall I be accused of having been too fond of war? It can be shown that I always received the first attack. Will it be said that I aimed at universal monarchy? It can be proved that this was merely the result of fortuitous circumstances, and that our enemies themselves led me step by step to this determination. Lastly, shall I be blamed for my ambition? This passion I must doubtless be allowed to have possessed, and that in no small degree; but at the same time, my ambition was of the highest and noblest kind that ever, perhaps, existed—that of establishing the empire of

reason, the full exercise and complete enjoyment of all the human faculties!

(From Marquis de Las Cases, *Memoirs of the Life, Exile, and Conversations of the Emperor Napoleon*, 1894; ed. J. K. Sowards, 1992)

Literary critic, novelist and *salonière* **Madame de Staël (1766–1817) gives her impressions of the dictator (1816):** I very quickly saw, in the various occasions I had to meet him during his stay in Paris, that his character could not be defined by the words we ordinarily use; he was neither good, nor fierce, nor gentle, nor cruel, like others we know. Such a being, having no equals, could neither feel nor arouse any sympathy: he was more than a human being or less than one. His appearance, his mind, and his speech were foreign in nature—an added advantage for subjugating the French.

Far from being reassured by seeing Bonaparte more often, I was made increasingly apprehensive. I had a vague feeling that no emotions of the heart could influence him. He considers a human being a fact or a thing, not a fellow man. He does not hate nor does he love. For him, there is nothing but himself; all others are ciphers.

Every time I heard him speak I was struck by his superiority: yet it had no resemblance to that of men educated and cultivated by study or by social intercourse, such as may be found in England or France. But his speech showed a feeling for the situation, like the hunter's for his prey.

(Madame de Staël, *On Politics, Literature and National Character*, 1818; ed. J. K. Sowards, 1992)

---

from the pulpit. At the same time, Napoleon guaranteed freedom of worship to all, including Protestants and Jews (who together numbered about five percent of the population). All clerical salaries, even those of Protestants, would be paid by the state. Loyal Catholics might return to their churches, but the Catholic behemoth that had saddled France, as the revolutionaries saw it, forever lost its privileges.

Did Napoleon restore the monarchy, buttressed by the nobility and Church? Not exactly. In the pattern of Robespierre, he was a new kind of ruler, more a prefiguration of a totalitarian dictator than a resurrection of ancient kingship. But his dictatorial intentions were expressed in his actions—in his undoing of the Revolution, his disenfranchisement of the people, his resurrection of court and nobility, his sweeping reconfiguration of government. Two views of him are given in *Witnesses* above.

Muscular, short and brilliant, Napoleon was a tireless worker, "never happier than in the silence of his own study," according to a modern historian,

"surrounded by papers and documents." After a day full of responsibilities, he retired at ten, to awake a few hours later to write letters (80,000 or so in the course of his career) and composing orders. On this impressive schedule, he accomplished the reorganization of France and the conquest of most of Europe.

Napoleon and the *Grande Armée*

Map 20.2 on p. 604 shows the expansion of Napoleon's empire. If Robespierre, in mobilizing the nation, was technically the founder of the modern French army, Napoleon was its true creator—the adored leader of the *Grande Armée* (Great Army) and one of the greatest military commanders in history (see Gros' painting of him on p. 598). Already a hero by virtue of his Italian campaign of 1796–1797, Napoleon seemed, in his campaigns of 1800–1815, to be invincible. The German poet Goethe marveled that "his life was the stride of a demigod from victory to victory." The composer Beethoven planned to

Map 20.2 Napoleon's Empire and Major Battles, 1799–1815: *Napoleon's empire consisted of a core of areas conquered and annexed to France, others conquered and ruled by members of his family, and a periphery of dependencies (where local governments survived but owed obedience to France).*

write a symphony in his honor—though he became disillusioned, and changed the dedication of the "Eroica" symphony to read, "Composed in Memory of a hero." All of Europe admired or dreaded him, and it took most of Europe to defeat him.

From 1793, France faced a series of coalitions (the First, formed in 1793; the Second, formed in 1798; the Third, 1805–1815) united at first against the Revolution and then against Napoleon. The First Coalition derived from the Prussian–Austrian alliance of 1792, and by 1795 it also included Britain, Russia, the Netherlands, Spain, and Sardinia. The Second included Britain, Austria, and Russia. The Third Coalition included the same combatants as the Second, with the addition of Prussia in 1806. Other coalitions formed in response to new defeats. Prussia and Austria supported Napoleon in 1812, but both

joined Russia and Britain and other allied forces against France in 1813, the last phase of this struggle, and in a seventh and final coalition in 1815, the allies at last liberated Europe from Napoleon.

To oppose these enemies required constant readiness and constant recruitment. From 1798, the institution of an annual draft meant that every young Frenchman faced the prospect of conscription (a situation that had not prevailed in France before the Revolution, nor would it after 1815 until the next century brought the experience of two world wars). Over the 23 years of revolutionary and Napoleonic warfare, some 2 to 3 million men served in the army, of whom about half a million died. Some resisted conscription, especially in rebellious regions of the south, where over fifty percent of those called failed to comply; and some draftees deserted, often swelling the ranks of criminal bands. For those who supported the war effort and showed courage or talent, the opportunity for promotion was open.

Napoleon's army employed tactics that marked a new stage in the evolution of warfare. For the sake of speed, it lived flagrantly off the land. Even those natives who welcomed the French initially as "liberators" had second thoughts when they saw the resulting devastation of their fields and homes. Thus unencumbered by the need for supply lines, the French could move swiftly (as much as 20 miles per day), a second feature of Napoleon's toolkit. They struck where they were not expected and wrung victory even from superior forces. Assisting them in the bold game of sudden attack were ample cannon mounted on mobile carts, handled by skilled gunnery crews. The French bombardment exhausted the enemy, who then succumbed to a powerful charge. Napoleon grouped combined forces of infantry, cavalry, and artillery into combat divisions and larger corps. Each corps acted as a disciplined entity, united by pride in shared experience and common symbols

and by gratitude for the rewards that the emperor distributed to those who served well.

Further, Napoleon exploited the possibilities of the infantry column. His opponents generally fought in line formation (even the British, whose excellent guns and peerless discipline allowed them withstand Napoleonic tactics), maneuvering into close formation for defense. Napoleon sent his soldiers forth in concentrated, marching columns, driven by drumbeat, terrible to behold and seemingly implacable. The powerful columns sliced through the lines of Austrian and Prussian opponents, scattering frightened soldiers, who now became the prey of the cavalry's sabers and their horses' hooves.

Napoleon's tactics were wasteful of men, as he knew. "A man such as I does not consider the deaths of a million men," he commented. Those in the front ranks were devastated by gunfire, but those in the rear moved up swiftly past their dead comrades to avenge them. It was France's large population—the largest of any European nation—that made Napoleon's tactics possible, while the emperor

Francisco Goya, The Executions of the Third of May, 1808: *Napoleon met his first serious setbacks in the Peninsular War in Spain, where French troops committed atrocities that aroused a significant amount of native resistance. Here in Francisco Goya's 1814 painting, a French firing squad executes guerrilla rebels, the chief victim's body extended in the form of the crucified Christ.* (Prado, Madrid)

succeeded in convincing the soldiers of this Grand Army that their sacrifice was warranted.

From 1800 to 1815, Napoleon's armies fought mainly in the German lands, Spain, and Russia. They won their greatest victory in the first area, where French armies absorbed the left bank of the Rhine, compensating Prussia, Austria, and some other German states for the loss of their domains. In 1798 Napoleon had imposed a constitution on Switzerland, now dubbed the Helvetic Republic, central Europe was briefly at peace.

At this juncture, some of Napoleon's troops attempted the reoccupation of Haiti and the reinstitution of slavery (see Chapter 19). The attempt failed—one of Napoleon's few early defeats. Although the architect of Haitian independence, Toussaint L'Ouverture, died in a French prison, Napoleon's soldiers died of disease; because of British intervention they could not be replaced. By the end of 1803, the island was lost. Meanwhile, Napoleon disposed of another colonial possession, the huge Louisiana Territory, which was sold in 1803 to the United States (see Chapter 19).

In 1805, returning to the German lands, Napoleon crushed Austrian and Russian forces at Ulm and Austerlitz. In 1806 he reorganized the hundreds of German principalities into the more rational Confederation of the Rhine, while overseeing the dissolution of the Holy Roman Empire, accomplished when its Habsburg emperor (Napoleon's future father-in-law) relinquished that title.

Alarmed by these new French victories, Prussia joined the Third Coalition; the next year it met, and lost to, Napoleon's army at Jena. In 1807, Napoleon defeated a Russian army at Friedland, forcing the tsar to agree to the Treaty of Tilsit, which made him France's reluctant ally. The three major continental powers had all been sidelined. Only Britain still stood undefeated against France.

The Tide Turns

It did so doggedly, benefiting from public support and the ingenuity of smugglers. In 1805, the naval commander Lord Nelson, who had previously chased Napoleon out of Egypt, destroyed the French fleet at Cape Trafalgar, near Gibraltar—and with it Napoleon's hopes of invading England. In 1806, Napoleon closed all continental ports to British ships, a strategy he called the Continental System. He aimed to cripple the British economy, already strained by military costs, by denying it European markets for its manufacturers and reexported colonial products. The painful effects for Britain included not only loss of income but an unsought war with the United States (the War of 1812). That young nation, a trading partner of France, bristled at British licensing demands and aggressive boarding and searching

of its ships. But smugglers managed to feed a trickle of British goods to the Continent, where demand was high, and Napoleon's Continental System failed.

Napoleon's will to conquer Britain led him south across the Pyrenees in 1808 to the Iberian Peninsula, where, beyond Spain, lay Britain's ally Portugal. A large French force marched toward the Portuguese capital, Lisbon, triggering the flight of the king to Brazil and the forced abdication of the Spanish king, Charles IV, and of his heir, Ferdinand VII, in favor of Napoleon's brother Joseph Bonaparte (1768–1844, r. 1808–1813). It also precipitated the combined opposition of Spain's powerful Church (resistant to Napoleon's plans for secularization), its nobility, and its peasantry, who, returning atrocity for atrocity, as shown in Goya's painting on p. 605, fought a modern guerilla war against the invaders. The British army, under Arthur Wellesley (1769–1852), later duke of Wellington, supported native resistance. It trapped more than 400,000 of Napoleon's Grand Army on the Iberian Peninsula and, in 1813, drove it out in tatters.

By this time, Napoleon's power had been fatally wounded elsewhere. His new alliance with the Habsburgs (divorcing Josephine, he had married the Habsburg princess Marie Louise) and his ambitions in the eastern Mediterranean, made Russia (which Austria viewed with distrust) his next target. In June 1812, with 450,000 men, he crossed the Polish border into Russia. Instead of the hoped-for rapid victory, however, he found himself pursuing the Russian army as it retreated, using scorched earth tactics, deep into the interior. After a costly and indecisive battle at Borodino, seventy miles to the west of Moscow, Napoleon captured the Russian capital in September. The city had been evacuated, and fire broke out the day the French entered. The Russian troops had escaped, with the tsar, to where the French could follow them no more. Napoleon was left stranded in hostile territory on the verge of the Russian winter. A 1500-mile retreat followed, fatal both to the emperor's men and to his ambitions. The abject Napoleon returned to Paris in December, ahead of the remnant of his army—130,000 soldiers. The others had died of cold and gunfire, disease and hunger in one of the worst episodes in the history of warfare.

The emperor's enemies were heartened by the Russian debacle. Wellington especially, fresh from his triumph in Spain, now concentrated all his military genius on securing the final defeat of Napoleon. The "Battle of the Nations" (Leipzig) in October 1813, was a resounding victory for the allies. Their armies pursued Napoleon back into France and, on March 31, 1814, entered Paris. From nearby Fontainebleau, Napoleon vainly tried to secure generous terms from the allies. In April, after a failed suicide attempt, he abdicated: first to his son then unconditionally. He was sent unharmed, an exile, to be the sovereign of the tiny island of Elba—tinier by far than Corsica, its neighbor in western Mediterranean waters. Then, after a few months he escaped.

Napoleon returned to France in March 1815, marching northward from the Mediterranean coast toward Paris. Troops and generals forgot their obligations to the restored Bourbon king, Louis XVIII, and joined his train, crying, as on the battlefield, "*Vive l'empereur!*" ("Long live the Emperor"). The allies were alarmed; though Wellington, at least, who did not underestimate his foe, was not surprised. Napoleon invited the next encounter, which took place at Waterloo, on the Belgian plains, where he had marched with 125,000 recruits. He was met by British forces, reinforced late in the day by Prussian allies who had been hastily summoned to the field. The French attack was fearsome, but the British would not fold. Victory went to the allies. "He has ruined us," a wounded French soldier lamented, "yet I love him still."

Napoleon was once again imprisoned, and once again exiled, unharmed. But instead of the quiet retirement in the United States or England that he had optimistically requested, he was exiled in the company of British guards to the remote island of St. Helena, in the south Atlantic. Located halfway between the west coast of Africa and the east coast of Brazil, it offered no chance of escape; had he escaped, there would have been no place to go. Napoleon sickened, lingered, and died six years later, still a British captive. The British feared even his corpse. They released it finally, in 1840, to the restored French monarch Louis Philippe (r. 1830–1840), who placed it reverently in the Hôpital des Invalides (formerly a military hospital), under the main dome. Thus did a descendant of Louis XVI, victim of the Revolution, honor the Corsican upstart who had appropriated the Revolution to further his own prodigious ambitions.

The victors of Waterloo, meanwhile, set about eradicating the joint legacies of the Revolution and Napoleon. Yet the impress of these phenomena on the consciousness of Europe could never be completely erased. Europe had seen monarchy bloodied and restored. It had beheld both liberation and conquest within an amazingly short timespan of just one generation. It had glimpsed the promise of universal rights and stirred with a new passion for national integrity. Which of these possibilities would bear fruit? "I live only for posterity," Napoleon said. His gift to posterity was a time bomb packed with a wealth of potentialities for both good and evil.

Conclusion
REVOLUTION, EMPIRE, AND THE MEANING OF THE WEST

The Revolution of 1789 ended with the fall of Robespierre, the installation of the Directory, and Napoleon's 1799 *coup d'état* and yet it did not end. From the Revolution in France burst the new flood tide of an awakened people eager for access to power. Over the next century, the people would often rush into the streets, raise their barricades, and fight for what they now saw as their rights. That expectation, the child of Revolution, is still alive in the West, and elsewhere, today.

Napoleon, too, contributed to the revolutionary legacy. By his legal, bureaucratic, and cultural initiatives, he acted to restore prerevolutionary social conditions, to maintain order, and to respect the privileges of rank. Yet the *grande armée* effected a massive dispersion of revolutionary ideals, promoted by the persuasive voices of those who believed that they had won liberation from the tyranny of the Old Regime. And Napoleon himself first disrupted, and then remade the political boundaries of Europe, discarding nations he deemed obsolete and creating new states from archaic ones. While he restored order and privilege at home, he unleashed forces for change abroad. It is Napoleon's Europe, refashioned by the destruction and renewal that he wrought, that became the foundation of the modern system of states which carried forward, in the century that followed, the traditions of the West.

Meanwhile, another agent of change had emerged, more disruptive and more violent than Robespierre's Revolution or Napoleon's wars: a machine, moved by non-human power, which, over that same century, would invade the fields and gardens of the nations of the Western world (see Chapter 21).

REVIEW QUESTIONS

1. How did aristocrats and intellectuals resist absolute monarchy? What role did Enlightenment thinkers play in undermining the Old Regime? Why did they attack the Church?

2. Why did Louis XVI decide to summon the Estates-General in 1789? Why did the French Revolution enter a new and more radical phase after 1789? Who were the *sans-culottes*?

3. What was the reign of terror? How did foreign opposition affect the course of the Revolution in France? How did the French Revolution transform the nature of warfare?

4. How did the Revolution change French society? To what extent did Napoleon improve the condition of women? Were the social changes introduced during the Revolution permanent?

5. How did Napoleon gain supreme power in France? To what extent did Napoleon undo the reforms of the Revolution? What were his most lasting achievements for France?

6. How successful was the Congress of Vienna in repressing the principles of the French Revolution? What victories did nationalism and liberalism win between 1815 and 1871? Why can we say that European politics were more liberal in 1871 than they had been in 1789?

SUGGESTED RESOURCES

Preludes to Revolution

Behrens, C. B. A., *Society, Government and the Enlightenment: the Experiences of Eighteenth-Century France and Prussia* (New York: Harper & Row, 1985). Useful comparison of these two states in the pre-Revolutionary period.

De Tocqueville, Alexis, *The Old Regime and the French Revolution*, trans. Stuart Gilbert (Garden City, NY: Doubleday, 1955). Timeless examination of the causes and consequences of the Revolution.

Hardman, John, *French Politics, 1774–1789: From the Accession of Louis XVI to the Fall of the Bastille* (London; New York: Longman, 1995). A detailed treatment of the French monarchy on the eve of the Revolution, stressing considerations of political power and place.

Higonnet, Patrice, *Sister Republics: The Origins of French and American Republicanism* (Cambridge, MA: Harvard University Press, 1988). Contrasts Americans' emphasis on individualism with the French stress on corporatism, finding therein an explanation of the different forms republicanism took in these two nations.

Roche, Daniel, *The Culture of Clothing: Dress and Fashion in the Ancient Regime*, trans. Jean Birrell (Cambridge: Cambridge University Press, 1994). Cultural history examining the production, distribution, and wearing of clothing for social, psychological, and other meanings.

The Rights of Man and the Birth of a Nation

Andress, David, *Massacre at the Champ de Mars: Popular Dissent and Political Culture in the French Revolution* (London: Boydell & Brewer, 2000). Traces the cultural systems and events in Paris that create the massacre of July 1791, as the Revolution enters its radical phase.

Censer, Jack Richard & Lynn Hunt. *Liberty, Equality, Fraternity: Exploring the French Revolution* (State Park, PA: Pennsylvania State University Press, 2001). New, up-to-date synthesis, with good coverage of the colonial dimensions of the revolt and historians' debates about it.

Chartier, Roger, *The Cultural Origins of the French Revolution*, trans. Lydia Cochrane (Durham, NC: Duke University Press, 1991). An important book, which asserts that the Revolution was caused neither by the Enlightenment nor by class tensions, but on the growing secularism, cynicism, and politicization of the French masses.

De Baecque, Antoine, *Seven Deaths under the French Revolution* (London: Routledge, 2001). Brilliant exploration of the cultural significance for contemporaries of the dead bodies of seven revolutionary victims, including King Louis XVI, Robespierre, and Marie Antoinette.

Hampson, Norman, *The Terror in the French Revolution* (New York: St. Martin's Press, 1998). Account of the bloodiest stage of the Revolution.

Hufton, Olwen H., *Women and the Limits of Citizenship in the French Revolution* (Toronto; Buffalo: University of Toronto Press, 1992). Essays on the disillusionment of women participants in the Revolution.

Lefebvre, Georges, *The Coming of the French Revolution, 1789* (Princeton: Princeton University Press, 1947). Its class-based interpretation of the Revolution is now out of favor, but this is still the basic reference point for later scholarship.

Schama, Simon, *Citizens: A Chronicle of the French Revolution* (New York: Knopf, 1989). The Revolution and its impact on a grand scale.

Notes and sources on Olympe des Gouges (Sunshine for Women): http://www.pinn.net/~sunshine/march99/gouges2.html

Robespierre, full text of his speech at the Festival of the Supreme Being (The History Place): http://www.historyplace.com/speeches/robespierre.htm

Napoleon Bonaparte Internet Guide: http://www.napoleonbonaparte.nl

The Imperial Adventure

Herold, J. Christopher, ed., *The Mind of Napoleon: a Selection from his Written and Spoken Words* (New York: Columbia University Press, 1955). Invaluable guide to the man's mind and character.

Markham, Felix, *Napoleon* (London: Weidenfeld & Nicolson, 1963). Classic, still compelling brief overview of Napoleon's career.

Schom, Alan, *Napoleon Bonaparte* (New York: HaperCollins, 1997). Updated, comprehensive biography.

Walter, Jakob, *Diary of a Napoleonic Foot Soldier*, ed. Mark Raeff (New York: Doubleday, 1991). Alternative perspective on the Napoleonic era and campaigns by a soldier participant.

Wolloch, Isser, *Napoleon and his Collaborators: the Making of a Dictatorship* (New York: W. W. Norton, 2001). Study of how Napoleon addressed the political, social, and economic needs of the nation.

Woolf, Stuart, J., *Napoleon's Integration of Europe* (London–New York: Routledge, 1991). Critical study of Napoleon's efforts to create a unified European system.

PART SIX
THE WEST BECOMES MODERN

Industrialization, Imperialism, Ideologies (1750–1914)

The arrival of the machine set Western civilization on the path to modernity that was largely completed by 1914. In Britain at first, then in Belgium and France, Germany and the United States, and finally in the rest of Europe and Japan, human beings made machines that produced commodities for use and export in quantities never before conceivable. Machines transformed Western society, where distinctions between rich and poor shifted and deepened. An increasingly bourgeois elite enjoyed a level of comfort previously known only to royalty and aristocracy, while a vast industrial working class experienced the unprecedented hardships of industrial work and urban life.

As European merchants, administrators, and generals ventured abroad to establish colonies and protectorates all over the globe, they recreated far from home the social rifts found in industrial cities. A European elite delighted in luxury as it managed the transmutation of native societies according to Western expectations, and enlisted laborers of many colors and customs to produce cheap goods. Success abroad encouraged Western ideologues to think that people of European descent had gained supremacy over the other peoples of the world because of their inherent racial, or genetic, superiority.

Critics of both social systems, the industrial and the colonial, denounced these injustices. Other thinkers fought to preserve liberal principles, to promote nationalist causes, to advocate rights for women or slaves, or toleration for Catholics, Protestants, or Jews. They spoke and wrote in a rich cultural milieu where, as Classical style gave way to Romantic and Realist movements, the modern repudiation of ancestral norms was already visible. By the end of the nineteenth century, with the death of God proclaimed by the German philosopher Friedrich Nietzsche, the self had lost its coherence, and the ability of the mind to apprehend a certain fixed reality was wholly cast in doubt.

21 Machines in the Garden
The Industrialization of the West, 1750-1914

22 Lives of the Other Half
Western Society in an Industrial Age, 1750-1914

23 The Concert of Europe
Mass Politics and the Triumph of State, 1815-1914

24 The Western *Imperium*
European Expansion Around the Globe, 1750-1914

25 Storm, Stress, and Doubt
European Culture from Neoclassicism to Modernism, 1780-1914

MACHINES IN THE GARDEN

	1700	1725	1750	1775	1800	1825	1850	1875	1900	1925

Britain

Britain industrializes, 1750–1850

◆ Thomas Newcomen's steam pump first used, 1712

◆ John Kay's flying shuttle, 1733

◆ James Hargreave's spinning jenny, 1764

◆ James Watt's steam engine, 1769

◆ Richard Arkwright's water frame, 1769

◆ Samuel Crompton's "mule," 1779

◆ Henry Cort's puddling process, 1783

◆ Edmund Cartwright's power loom, 1785

◆ Robert Owen opens factory in Manchester, 1789

◆ Richard Trevithick's locomotive, 1804

◆ Henry Bell's steamship *Comet* launched, 1812

◆ First railroad in England, 1821

◆ George Stephenson's "Rocket," 1829

◆ English railroad network almost complete, 1850

◆ The Great Exhibition at London's Crystal Palace, 1851

◆ Henry Bessemer's converter, 1856

◆ British steam engines' total output equals 40,000,000 men/6,000,000 horses, 1870

Western Europe and the US

American and French Revolutions, 1775–94

French Revolutionary and Napoleonic Wars, 1792–1815   Western and central Europe and North America industrialize, 1815–1900

◆ French introduce steam-driven cart, 1770

◆ French develop steam boat, 1783

◆ Eli Whitney's cotton gin, 1793

◆ Robert Fulton's steamship sails from New York to Albany in 32 hours, 1807

◆ William Cockerill's iron and steel factory system in Liège, Belgium, employs 2,000 workers, 1812

◆ First Atlantic crossing by sail-and-steam-powered ship, 1819

◆ German Customs Union, the *Zollverein*, established, 1834

◆ First transatlantic steamshipping line opened, 1838

◆ Transatlantic cable laid, 1866

◆ First transcontinental railroad in US, 1869

◆ French lose coal and iron fields in Alsace and Lorraine to Germany, 1871

◆ Alexander Graham Bell invents telephone, 1876

◆ Thomas Edison invents lightbulb, 1879

Eastern Europe and Russia

Russia industrializes, 1870–1918

◆ Steam engine used for cotton manufacture in Russia, 1805

◆ Henry Cort's puddling process introduced to Russia, 1836

◆ Railroad line opens from Dresden to Leipzig, 1839

◆ Moscow and St. Petersburg linked by railroad, 1851

◆ St. Petersburg has 900 factories, 1914

Beyond the West

British East India Company dominant in India, 1690–1857   Direct British Rule in India, 1858–1947

Japan industrializes, 1870–1918

◆ Shaka leads Zulu nation, Africa, 1817

◆ First Opium War, 1839–42

◆ Treaty of Nanjing, 1842

◆ US Commodore Perry "opens" Japan, 1853

◆ Sepoy Mutiny, India, 1857

◆ French control Indochina, 1858

◆ Meiji Restoration, Japan, 1868

◆ Suez canal opens, 1869

◆ First railroad opens in China, 1882

◆ "Scramble for Africa" begins, 1885

CHAPTER 21

MACHINES IN THE GARDEN

The Industrialization
of the West

1750–1914

areas of industrial concentration and development, 1914

KEY TOPICS

◆ **Before Industrialization:** The foundations of European industrialization are laid in the Middle Ages and early modern era: an urban grid, the putting-out system, agricultural innovation, military reorganization, and political centralization.

◆ **Britain Industrializes:** With the building blocks of cotton, water, coal, and iron, Britain leaps ahead, introducing steam-powered factories and

transportation systems amid a landscape of green fields and hills, and creating a modern industrial economy by 1850.

◆ **Catching Up:** France, Belgium, Germany, and the United States industrialize and modernize, suffering profound dislocations in the process. Their example is followed by the remaining European nations and Japan, and finally other nations of the world.

Satanic Mills The English author Charles Dickens (1812–1870) described in his novel *Hard Times* a town he dubbed "Coketown," transformed for the worse by the advent of the steam engine and the factory. "It was a town of machinery and tall chimneys," he wrote, "out of which interminable serpents of smoke trailed themselves for ever and ever, and never got uncoiled." It had a canal turned black, and a river turned purple from the pollutants that issued from the factory where a "steam-engine worked monotonously up and down like the head of an elephant in a state of melancholy madness." Into a peaceful natural world of clear sky and clean water, the machine had introduced poisons and dirt and demonic beasts—smoke serpents and mad elephants. Into the garden of pre-modern Europe the machine had burst with all its attendant maladies, staining the landscape of the pre-industrial paradise with, in the words of the visionary poet William Blake (1757–1827), "dark Satanic mills."

But the machine that despoiled the "garden," as wordsmiths nostalgically perceived it, of the pre-modern West was not simply destructive in its effects. Its arrival marked a new stage in the ability of the human species to create wealth and gain freedom from scarcity. Beginning in Britain in the late eighteenth century, the transformation of industrial production was accomplished on an astounding scale and with amazing speed, in barely a generation. This process of **industrialization**, often called the "Industrial Revolution," is the most significant change in the history of humankind since hunters and gatherers settled down to farm and live in villages at the end of the Neolithic era thousands of years earlier (see Chapter 1). For many historians and economists, it overshadows the French Revolution (see Chapter 20), or indeed any series of merely political events, in importance for the future of the human race.

This chapter explores the preconditions for industrialization in Britain and in Europe that existed well before 1780. It then describes the many innovations in technology and in the organization of work that together constituted the process of industrialization in Britain, well established by 1850. Finally, it traces the steps by which the industrial tide spread through Europe by around 1870, and thereafter to the rest of the globe where, far from Blake's England, there also sprang up "Satanic mills."

BEFORE INDUSTRIALIZATION

Long before Satanic forces, as Blake perceived them, planted machines in the garden of pre-industrial Europe, the foundations of an industrial economy and society had been laid. They were laid by men and women who could not have conceived of machine power, precision-made parts, or factory systems of production. Societies that had not pursued the European path of economic and social development were not, however, as well-equipped to develop new industrial methods. The features that made Europe the first region in the world to develop modern industry were these. First, from about the twelfth through the fifteenth centuries there developed an urban grid, home to extensive craft production, whose system of employment and distribution reached into the adjacent countryside (see Chapters 11, 12). Urban centers and their rural hinterland together provided a market for goods, stimulating production and exchange. Second, beginning in the sixteenth century, there occurred a rapid series of interconnected revolutionary developments in warfare, commerce, science, and agriculture (see Chapters 15, 16, 17, 18). Together, Europe's medieval social and economic framework, and the early modern advances in technology and knowledge, created the stage for industrialization.

Medieval Foundations: The Urban Grid

After the collapse of Roman power in western Europe during the fifth century C.E., Europe had few towns, and very few large ones. During the next several centuries, urban development ceased, as Europe fell prey to waves of invasion and suffered chronic economic recession. The exchange of goods never ceased, however, and as soon as circumstances permitted, it accelerated. Merchants who had previously journeyed with the goods they had for sale carried either on their own back or on that of a pack animal became sedentary. They settled in communities and the communities of merchants became the nuclei of European towns and cities.

In other civilizations—for example in China or Islam—a few enormous cities served as centers of political, religious, or intellectual life. Europe's cities, in contrast, were small, numerous, and commercial in character. They clustered in certain regions and exchanged goods among themselves, providing centers for both local and more extensive markets. Together, they formed a continuous urban grid that extended north to south from the lowland ports on the North Sea to the north Italian cities, both inland and coastal, of Tuscany, Lombardy, and Venetia. Numbering in the hundreds, most had only 2 to 3 thousand inhabitants; substantial towns had 20 to 30 thousand; and the biggest cities at their height reached about 100,000. At first, their residents were almost all artisans or merchants. In time, they also accommodated significant numbers of day workers, servants, migrants, vagrants, priests, and noblemen. But the merchants (who exchanged goods locally, regionally, and long-distance) and artisans (who produced and exchanged goods locally) were the key social groups in European cities, and impressed their character upon them.

By 1300, successful artisans and merchants formed craft guilds, associations of those engaged in the same kind of production or exchange. These self-governing associations established rules for the conduct of the craft or trade, defined procedures for training (apprenticeship) and entrance, and set standards for price and quality. The more important guilds and guildsmen were the city leaders, or "patriciate," who frequently negotiated **charters** with the noble or monarch who had sovereignty over the region. These charters made the towns independent of feudal networks, based on the exchange of land rights and services, and allowed townspeople to rule themselves.

Towns were centers of both trade and production. (A description of a cloth market is given in *Witnesses* on p. 614.) Merchants organized the import and export of raw materials, essential goods, and luxury commodities, the latter procured from distant locations in eastern Europe, Asia, and Africa. They developed commercial techniques that facilitated the keeping of accounts, the sale of goods, and the exchange of currencies. And they established networks of agents in remote European and non-European **entrepôts** or markets to manage long-distance trade. Those agents kept exquisite commercial records and wrote letters to their home offices describing foreign mercantile practices which their mastery of foreign languages permitted them to understand.

Artisans and merchants together participated in the production of Europe's main manufacture: textiles. Raw wool, especially from Spain and England, was processed in Flemish and Italian workshops, in grades ranging from the utilitarian to the highly refined. Linen and, in time, silk (from raw fiber processed in Italy and France) were also processed in similar ways. Metalwork was Europe's second most important manufacture. Swords and later guns joined bolts of cloth in the bellies of ships that traversed the Mediterranean to foreign markets.

The manufacture of both textile and metal products, though centered in towns, rested on an **infrastructure** that reached out to rural areas. Mining by its nature was a rural enterprise, that needed to be connected with purchasers and metalworkers in the towns. The raw materials for textile production, including not only the fiber itself, but also the materials for washing and dyeing, came from nearby as well as distant regions. Moreover, the country provided many of the textile workers, especially the myriad women who spun cloth on simple spindles or, after about 1300, the hand-operated spinning wheel.

In highly-urbanized Italy, the more advanced processes of textile production—weaving, fulling, dyeing, finishing—were performed in town, often in large workshops. In other less-urbanized areas (including parts of England, France, and central Europe), these processes might be performed in the cottages of workers in an arrangement called the "**putting-out system**" (see Chapter 16). Town and country were linked together, communicating through itinerant merchants or their agents, who distributed materials, collected finished products, and provided payment. These linkages multiplied and strengthened over time, and by the eighteenth century amounted to a "**protoindustrial**" system centered in towns and radiating out into adjacent rural areas.

The main features of Europe's urban grid were in place, and some were long-established, by 1500. They prepared the way for later industrialization, which harnessed merchant energies and commercial techniques while modernizing production methods.

Early Modern Changes

Soon after 1500, some revolutionary changes began to impact upon the social, economic, and intellectual realms, setting the stage for a later process of rapid industrialization. Historians sometimes refer to a "military," a "commercial," a "scientific," and an "agricultural" revolution. All occurred between 1500 and 1750, and all are preconditions for industrial development after 1780.

Changes in military technology and organization were developed especially by Italian generals and engineers just before 1500 (see Chapter 15). The cannon became more accurate and mobile, while improvements in hand-carried guns and muskets gave infantry an advantage over cavalry and precipitated changes in army organization. The plans of individual fortresses and strategies for national defense adjusted to new realities, guided by military theoreticians. Armies became larger and more expensive to equip and maintain, necessitating (as one among many factors) the centralization of nation states and the creation of new systems of taxation. By 1750, professional soldiers wore regimental uniforms, drilled in formation, fired in lines, and were subject to strict military discipline. Advanced gun technology and more intensive organization, discipline, and planning were related to the later process of industrialization.

Starting just before 1500, the Portuguese, Spanish, Dutch, English, and French—the Atlantic-facing nations of Europe—sent their ships around the globe in search of new commodities and new markets (see Chapter 16). The result was a remaking of the European economy, affecting prices, manufacturing methods, consumer habits, political administration, agricultural organization—just about every aspect of life. All of these were important for later industrialization, but none more important than the network of trade routes that now criss-crossed the globe like a web, and the ever-increasing value of foreign trade— effects sometimes called the "commercial" revolution.

Buying and Selling Before the Industrial Age

Since the earliest civilizations, and even before they formed, people have bought and sold commodities and crafted goods—artisans have sold their own wares; merchants have sold merchandise obtained from others; kings and states have sought to bolster the wealth of their nations, if only by excluding the goods of others to realize higher tax revenues. All these various activities were still ongoing in the eighteenth and nineteenth centuries when industrialization dramatically transformed first Europe's, then the world's, economies. In these passages, the English novelist Daniel Defoe describes a market scene in Yorkshire, England; the British government seeks to protect its domestic textile industries; and a German economist laments the tariffs that impede trade.

Daniel Defoe describes the Yorkshire cloth market (c. 1724): The Market itself is worth describing.... The street is a large, broad, fair and well-built Street, beginning ... at the Bridge, and ascending gently to the North. Early in the Morning, there are Tressels placed in two Rows in the Street, sometimes two Rows on a Side ...; then there are Boards laid cross those Tressels, so that the Boards lie like long Counters on either Side, from one end of the street to the other. The clothiers come early in the Morning with their Cloth; and as few clothiers bring more than one Piece, the Market being so frequent, they go into the Inns and Publick-Houses with it, and there set it down. At seven a Clock in the Morning ... the Market Bell rings; ... without hurry or noise, and not the least disorder, the whole Market is fill'd; all the Boards upon the Tressels are covered with Cloth ... and behind every Piece of Cloth, the Clothier standing to sell it. As soon as the Bell has done Ringing, the Merchants and Factors, and Buyers of all Sorts, come down.... [T]hey reach over to the Clothier and whisper, and in the fewest Words imaginable the Price is stated; one asks, the other bids; and 'tis agree, or not agree, in a Moment.... [I]n less than half an Hour you will perceive the Cloths begin to move off, the Clothier taking it up upon his Shoulder to carry it to the Merchant's House; and by half an Hour after eight a Clock the Market Bell rings again; immediately the Buyers disappear, the Cloth is all sold, or if here and there a Piece happens not to be bought, 'tis carried back into the Inn, and, in a quarter of an Hour, there is not a Piece of Cloth to be seen in the Market.
(From D. B. Horn and M. Ransome eds., *English Historical Documents, 1714–1783*, 1957)

The British government moves to protect domestic wool and silk manufactures by banning the use of printed calicoes, imported from India (1721): Whereas it is most evident, that the wearing and using of printed, painted, stained and dyed callicoes in apparel, household stuff, furniture, and otherwise, does manifestly tend to the great detriment of the woollen and silk manufactures of this kingdom, and to the excessive increase of the poor, and if not effectually prevented, may be the utter ruin and destruction of the said manufactures, and of many thousands of your Majesty's subjects and their families, whose livelihoods do intirely depend thereupon: for remedy thereof may it please your most excellent Majesty, That it may be enacted ... by and with the advice and consent of the lords spiritual and temporal, and commons, in the present parliament assembled, ... That from and after [25 December 1722], it shall not be lawful for any person or persons whatsoever to use or wear in Great Britain, in any garment or apparel whatsoever, any printed, stained or dyed callico, under the penalty of forfeiting to the informer the sum of five pounds of lawful money of Great Britain for every such offense.
(From D. B. Horn and M. Ransome eds., *English Historical Documents, 1714–1783*, 1957)

The economist Friedrich List describes impediments to trade and industry in the German states (1819): Thirty-eight customs boundaries cripple inland commerce, and produce much the same effect as ligatures which prevent the free circulation of the blood. The merchant trading between Hamburg and Austria, or Berlin and Switzerland must traverse ten states, must learn ten customs tariffs, must pay ten successive transit dues. Anyone who is so unfortunate as to live on the boundary line between three or four states spends his days among hostile tax-gatherers and custom house officials; he is a man without a country.... Only the remission of the internal customs, and the erection of a general tariff for the whole Federation [of German states], can restore national trade and industry and help the working classes.
(From W. O. Henderson, *The Rise of German Industrial Power, 1834–1914*, 1975)

Meanwhile, the revolution in science (see Chapter 17), began with astronomy, physics, and mathematics, later embracing biology, medicine, and chemistry. New paradigms for the structure and workings of the universe encouraged the kind of thinking about complex systems that later informed industrial organization. The use of the experimental method, developed by Galileo Galilei (1564–1642) and other early scientists to test their theories, further encouraged the understanding of material objects and processes, and required scientists, or the artisans they employed, to design new artifacts and make things work. Pumps, thermometers, telescopes, microscopes, and other pieces of special equipment invented to aid experimentation, observation, and measuring, littered the scientist's laboratory. More widely, the idea that specific requirements could be met by the invention of completely new artifacts was to underpin important aspects of the coming industrial era. Accumulating knowledge of the properties of chemicals and gases would similarly prove useful in industrial processes. Just as important as the tinkering inspired by science were the habits of thought that accompanied it: the attention to quantity and number; the zeal to find a simpler, more direct or elegant explanation; the desire to know even more, in the words of one historian (referring to the medieval magician, Dr. Faustus, who sold his soul to the devil in order to obtain unlimited knowledge), the "Faustian spirit of mastery."

Related to these earlier "revolutions" were profound changes in agricultural techniques developed from the seventeenth century in the Netherlands and, soon afterward, in Britain (see Chapter 18). Networks of ditches and dikes for drainage and flood control, and canals for irrigation, required advanced engineering skills and encouraged practical thinking about water supply, transportation, and communication. The elimination of the **fallow**, in some regions, opened new fields for experimental techniques of crop rotation, quickly resulting in enormously increased productivity and fertility. Increased yields meant improved nutrition, at the same time that specialized agricultural management of restricted fields radically changed the pattern of rural labor.

Enclosure of previously open, communal fields, especially in England in the seventeenth and eighteenth centuries, resulted in large-scale dislocations in the life of rural communities. Overall, the effects of the many initiatives in agriculture during this period were population growth, the practice of using hired labor, and the availability of large numbers of landless day laborers for agriculture and manufacturing. All were important for the process of industrialization, which required a mobile, flexible labor force, and a mass market for manufactured goods.

By 1750, the impact of revolutionary changes in these different but interconnected areas had been felt, especially in the northwestern region of Europe that had surged ahead of the Mediterranean region both in wealth and creativity. By this date in Britain, the process of industrialization was already under way.

BRITAIN INDUSTRIALIZES

Beginning soon after 1700, Britain experienced the first stages of industrialization, which accelerated rapidly after about 1780. Map 21.1 on p. 616 shows its development. By 1850, the process of industrialization had peaked. Britain was now the foremost manufacturing and trading nation in the world. The miracle of British industrialization was born from the interconnected histories of basic substances: coal, water, iron, and cotton.

Cotton and Water

Wool, not cotton, had been the lynchpin of medieval manufacture in Europe. The raw fiber came from sheep who grazed abundantly on Europe's relatively cool, well-watered fields. Complex workshop systems evolved to process the raw wool into a range of textiles for local as well as foreign consumption. Around 1700, wool was Britain's major export, amounting to some eighty or ninety percent of the total. Around the same time, however, British consumers, more numerous and more affluent as agricultural conditions improved, developed a taste for cotton cloth.

Bright, washable calicoes (fabrics from Calicut) were produced in India and imported by the British East India Company, which had by that time established virtual sovereignty in the Asian subcontinent. Cotton grew easily in India's hot climate. Indian women spun fine, strong yarn, which they wove into lightweight yet durable fabrics. Imports of these fabrics more than tripled in the last third of the seventeenth century—861,000 pieces for the period 1699–1701, compared to 240,000 pieces for 1663–1669. The passage quoted in *Witnesses* on p. 614 reveals a government attempt to restrict such imports.

British manufacturers, hoping to compete with the desirable new import, acquired raw cotton from American colonies, whose sub-tropical climate proved favorable to the recently transplanted Asian crop. British workers, however, or British techniques, could not produce a satisfactory cotton textile. They succeeded in interweaving cotton yarn with linen to make a product called fustian. But consumers wanted unblended cotton.

The Beginnings of Industrialization If there was no way to wean the public from a taste for cotton, could the means be developed to produce cotton cloth in Britain, entrepreneurs asked, so that they might reap the profit at home? The need for a solution to this problem stimulated a series of inventors to develop machinery that shattered traditional norms of textile manufacture once and for all. Those inventions were: the flying shuttle patented by John Kay (1704–1764) in 1733 and widely used from the 1750s; the spinning jenny, introduced in 1764 by James Hargreaves (d. 1778) and patented in 1770; the water frame, which automated the jenny, patented by Richard Arkwright (1732–1792) in 1769; the "mule," developed by Samuel Crompton (1753–1827) in 1779 (he couldn't afford to patent it), combining the jenny and the water frame to produce a fine, strong yarn; and the power loom, patented by Edmund Cartwright (1743–1823) in 1785.

Map 21.1 Great Britain Industrializes, 1750–1850: *From 1750 to 1850, Britain leaped ahead of the rest of Europe and the world in industrial production. Some of the causes for and consequences of that progress are illustrated here: natural resources (coal, iron, copper, lead, tin); natural and artificial waterways; large industrial and commercial centers with large concentrations of human populations; and a network of railroad links.*

Spinning and weaving are the two major processes of textile manufacture. (Other ancillary processes include washing, combing, fulling, dyeing, etc.) For centuries, weaving had been accomplished on a loom, which permitted the horizontal weft to be laced through the stretched vertical fibers of the warp. Kay's flying shuttle mechanized that process. The laborer had only to pull a cord to push the shuttle, and it wove the yarn horizontally through the warp threads. Not only did this innovation greatly speed the process of weaving (provoking some wrathful handloom weavers to destroy the inventor's model). It also put pressure on spinning.

Spinning was the real bottleneck in textile production. Traditionally, it was performed by women who worked with two rod-like tools, the distaff and spindle. The former held the mass of raw fiber, drawn out by fingers and spun to produce a twisted length of thread. The latter held the finished, weavable yarn yielded by the repeated, tedious process of separating and twisting fiber into thread and winding fine thread into durable yarn.

The innovation of the crank-operated spinning wheel speeded up the spinning process. The spinning-wheel, however, still produced only one thread of yarn at a time; it took between six and ten spinners to produce the yarn for one loom operator. Hargreaves' spinning jenny, illustrated in *Windows On* on p. 618, produced the first major breakthrough in spinning since the earliest days of textile work. It enabled a single laborer to produce several threads at once: six, twelve, twenty-four—the only limit was the force that could be exerted on the cranking mechanism. British laborers could now produce pure cotton yarn comparable to that spun by practiced Indian spinners, in virtually unlimited quantity.

As jennies became larger, however, spinning could no longer be done in the workers' cottages. The workers had mostly been women, who won welcome distraction from the tedium of the task by chatting with daughters, kinfolk, and friends engaged in the same work, and by supervising younger children also assigned useful labor. The invention of the jenny disrupted cottage-based spinning. Soon the new machines were being installed in specially constructed manufacturing shops, alongside several others. Workers, still women, walked from their cottages to the shop on a specified schedule. The children they brought with them performed ancillary tasks. A new kind of workplace was taking form.

Soon the jenny was linked by Arkwright's water frame (and later Crompton's mule) to an alternative source of power—the wheel. Water wheels, and more rarely windmills, were the sole forms of machinery known in the Middle Ages that were not driven by either human or animal muscle. Used mostly for grinding grain, their capacity to perform repetitive work had been known for centuries. With the creation of the jenny, and its placement in a workshop rather than a cottage, the opportunity offered by the time-tested wheel became apparent. The workshop was located next to a running stream, which turned a wheel that transmitted power to the moving parts of the jenny. The human laborer was no longer needed to turn the jenny's crank, but only to tend the machine, feed it raw fiber, and replace its bobbins (the machine version of the spindle) on which the strong, uniform yarn was wound, as suggested by the passage quoted in *Witnesses* on p. 622. Cotton and water came together, marking an important step toward industrialization.

With the availability of an infinitely expandable supply of cotton yarn, the burden of further development in textile production fell on weaving. The male laborers who had installed a loom in their cottages were now kept busy, and new entrants to the field

learned the skill. For a generation more (up to three generations in some regions) the handloom weavers commanded high rates. Their labor was essential if cloth production was to rise to the level of the availability of raw cotton and processed yarn.

Effects at Home and Abroad But how could weavers keep up with the enormous quantity of yarn spun by the tireless, ever-expandable jennies? Cartwright's power loom presented the solution. With water power driving the flying shuttle, little but supervisory attention was required from the laborer. As power-driven looms slowly took their place alongside jennies in the mills, weaving as well as spinning entered the industrial age. The handloom weavers lost their specialist niche in the manufacturing process, and faced demoralizing transformation into ordinary mill workers.

On two other continents, many more people suffered from the mechanization of cotton cloth production in English mills, which still nestled in the country alongside rushing streams. In India, the export trade in cotton cloth declined for a century and by 1830 was dead. For centuries, Indian spindles and looms had provided cottons throughout Asia and the Middle East. But with the advent of industrialization, these regions preferred to import cheap, durable cotton textiles from distant Britain. In India, workers lost employment in the textile sector, and the economy geared downward to export cash crops and resources. That shift amounted to the deindustrialization of India, which became a prelude to its political defeat (see Chapter 24).

In the British colonies of North America (more than the Caribbean, where sugar cultivation was the economic mainstay), increasing numbers of African slaves were imported to sow, tend, and harvest fields of cotton. The plant had only recently been introduced in the southern Atlantic colonies, where tobacco, indigo, and rice had preceded it as major cash crops. Cotton grew well in the Western Hemisphere, however. Its success encouraged the establishment of more and larger plantations, modeled on those created for the farming of Caribbean sugar and Virginian tobacco. British slave ships were never busier than in the century when cotton became established in the American south. By the late eighteenth century, Africans were a large minority of the residents of the continent, their enslavement encouraged by the yawning British market for raw fiber. And cotton production had not yet peaked.

The American phase of the story of cotton continued uninterrupted throughout the War for Independence (1775–1783). Not long after that conflict was resolved and the United States Constitution ratified, another invention, the creation of an American engineer, joined the new technologies that transformed cotton manufacture. In 1793, Eli

WHO'S WHO

Inventors of the Industrial Age: Textiles

John Kay (1704–1764) the flying shuttle

James Hargreaves (1720?–1778) the spinning jenny

Richard Arkwright (1732–1792) the water frame

Samuel Crompton (1753–1827) the "mule"

Edmund Cartwright (1743–1823) the power loom

Eli Whitney (1765–1825) the cotton gin

Interior of a cotton factory, Lancashire, England, 1835

The power of electricity: *By the 1870s, electricity was widely used for interior and street illumination and as a new source of power. Here a French factory is lit by electric "candles" in an 1883 illustration by Georges Dary.*

Factory production brought new efficiencies to tasks that had been accomplished by individual artisans or by family groups in traditional cottage industry. Nowhere was this change more visible than in the textile industries, where technology previously had permitted only one thread, or only a few, to be spun at a time. Now, as depicted above in a mid-nineteenth-century British factory, with the use of the mass-output "mule," multiple strands of thread were wound on multiple spindles simultaneously. So fundamental to textile production was the multiplication of spindles that factory capacity was measured in "spindlage"—not the number of machines, or workers, or even bolts of cloth, but of the spindles on which was wound mechanically produced thread. Iron and steel factories, now powered by steam engines, experienced similar efficiencies, as depicted in the illustration below of an iron and steel factory. By the late-nineteenth-century, factories that were lit by artificial electrical light, as seen in the image at right of a French factory in 1883, could continue production chores by night as well as day.

Iron and steel factory, nineteenth century

To continue your investigation of this topic, please go to www.prenhall.com/king for the related **WINDOWS** on the **WEB** activity

Whitney (1765–1825) was staying with a friend in Georgia, the manager of a cotton plantation. There he learned that one task above all slowed the process by which the cotton fibers were plucked from the plant, cleaned, and packaged for export. When first picked, the cotton fibers were tangled with seed. Valuable labor time was devoted to plucking and pulling out the seeds.

Familiar with industrial organization in New England mills, Whitney understood the value of this lost time and set out to find a way to reduce it. Within ten days, he had designed a model of the "cotton gin," a simple machine operated by human or horse power that spun the raw cotton, agitating and extracting the seeds. The cotton gin did efficiently what human workers did poorly. From 1793 to 1800, the amount of cotton exported jumped from 18 to 83 million pounds, more than a fourfold increase. In the end, however, the machine meant not less work for African slaves, but more. Speeding up the processing of fiber only encouraged the growing, picking, ginning, baling, and shipping of more cotton in the quest for greater profits. The gin inaugurated the reign of King Cotton in the American south, that did not falter until the Civil War (1861–1865) finally brought an end to slavery.

Meanwhile, the series of revolutionary technical innovations in cotton cloth manufacture already discussed made Britain the leading world producer of the textile. In due course, the new technology would be adapted for the manufacture of wool, linen, and silk textiles. But first, the cotton mill would undergo a final transformation. The water wheel made way for the steam engine, the end product of another story of successful technological innovation. That story is important and must be told before we return to see the mill reborn as the modern factory.

Coal and Water

The creation of the cotton mill resulted from the marriage of cotton textile production with the water-driven wheel. The steam engine resulted from a different combination of natural resources: coal and water. Coal heated water to produce steam. Steam was used to power the pumps needed to remove water from deep mines where coal (the principal fuel of the era, at least in Britain) lay hidden in the earth. The elegant circularity of these relations is important. It is precisely where these two substances lay in close proximity that the steam engine was developed to provide a solution.

Coal mining accelerated in Britain from the seventeenth to the eighteenth centuries. Charcoal, derived from wood, was the fuel previously used for a major task of traditional manufacture: the smelting of iron. But charcoal was in short supply. Most of Britain's forests had long since been felled to clear fields for

cultivation, and to provide fuel and construction materials. Timber for housing and shipbuilding was imported, from Russia and the American colonies. Unlike wood, however, coal was plentiful. In the 1600s, it began to be used for metallurgical and domestic heating purposes. With the increased use of iron in both machines and manufactures, demand for iron rose, and consequently also for coal. Mining boomed.

At first, coal was easily removed from near the surface. As those seams were exhausted, however, miners dug deeper into the earth, until mineshafts and tunnels reached well below the water table, and became liable to flooding. Flooding both weakened the tunnels and made it harder to remove the coal. Workers removed the water in buckets and carts. In places they adapted pumps of the kind used in the ships of the British Navy to keep the water that seeped in from sinking the vessels. Pumping by hand was constant, tiresome work. The need became apparent for a way to power pumps without wasting human effort.

At this juncture, the British inventor Thomas Savery (c. 1650–1715) adapted the design for a steam-powered engine already explored by the French Huguenot immigrant Denis Papin (1647–c. 1712). It utilized simple principles. When water turns to steam, its volume expands 1600 times. The force generated by that expansion can move a piston back and forth in a cylinder, and the piston can drive a pump—or, in later applications, virtually any machinery. The materials needed were also basic, both found nearby in the flooded mine: water and coal. These were the building blocks of the gigantic steam engine that Savery designed. He displayed it to fellow scientists at a meeting of the Royal Society, where Britain's leading experts gathered (see Chapter 17), and to King William III (r. 1689–1702) at one of his country residences, Hampton Court, and patented it in 1698.

Thomas Newcomen (1663–1729) invented an improved engine (first used 1712), illustrated in *Windows On*, p. 621. For the next half-century, the huge, awkward steam engines created by Savery and Newcomen loomed over the lips of coal mines, and pumped out water from the deep galleries below.

The early steam engines were inefficient, however. After the water was heated, and the resultant steam did its work, it needed to be cooled, and then heated again. Both time and fuel were wasted in the process. Having been commissioned to repair a Newcomen engine, the Scottish instrument-maker James Watt (1736–1819) began his search for a solution to these problems. Working over twenty years, he developed an efficient steam engine that burned only half as much fuel as its predecessors. Not only more effective in mining operations, it could also be adapted for other settings—as it would be for textile and iron production and, eventually, transportation.

Watt introduced several improvements to the original steam engines. First, he designed a separate condensing chamber where the water could be cooled and then recirculated. Second, he mounted an air pump to move steam into the chamber. Third, he insulated parts of the engine to prevent energy loss. Watt patented his improved engine in 1769, and in the 1770s, in partnership with the engineer and entrepreneur Matthew Boulton (1728–1809), developed a new engine capable of delivering rotary power. It is illustrated in *Windows On*, p. 621.

One of the problems Watt faced in developing an efficient engine was the need for precisely measured cylinders. Without them, the steam was not sufficiently contained in the cylinder, so that force was lost and fuel wasted. The solution he found for this problem is yet another illustration of how different technologies cross-fertilized each other in the development of modern industry. Watt employed the skill of gunmakers to craft his cylinders (what is a gun, after all, but a cylinder through which a missile is channeled and exploded?). A precision-made gun barrel insured both accuracy and safety. Its qualities also served well in the operation of the steam engine.

The efficient new steam engine was important in coal mining, where the results were evident: by 1830, Britain was responsible for four-fifths of the world's coal production. But now the steam engine could assist with other tasks—virtually any task that presented itself—greatly outpowering human or animal workers, as the passage quoted in *Witnesses* on p. 622 and the illustration on p. 624 show. Attention turned to the textile mills, recent innovations themselves, where water power, transmitted from rushing stream to turning wheel, drove the machines that spun yarn and wove cloth. By the 1780s, steam engines were utilized to drive these machines, marking the beginning of the history of the "factory" (derived from "manu-factory," a place where things were manufactured). In factories, machines made things; human "hands" (signified by the Latin "*manu*" of "manufacture") worked mainly to tend machines.

After 1785, when Edmund Cartwright patented his power loom, steam-powered textile factories multiplied. Factories no longer needed to be near streams. They could be established near to coal mines, and where bolts of finished cloth were easily transferred to canal barges or ships for export. Often they were near river or ocean ports or, in time, railroad depots. Profits were enormous. The industrialist Robert Owen (1771–1858) opened a factory in Manchester in 1789 for £100 in startup capital. Twenty years later, he paid £84,000 in cash to buy out his partners in the venture.

Outside of mining and textile manufacture, steam engines could be used to grind flour, brew beer, spin potting wheels, or prepare ceramic glazes, refine sugar, or power a printing press—and above all, to produce the parts of other machines. By 1800, 500 engines were at work in British factories, principally in the heavy industries (metals and textiles). By 1870, Britain's steam engines produced as much power as could have been generated by 6 million horses, or 40 million people—more than the nation's population.

While machines for textile manufacture greatly increased Britain's industrial output, and the steam engine raised that output still further, the availability of more and better iron drove it astronomically higher. That effect was achieved when the steam engine was applied to the manufacture of iron.

Iron, Coal, and Steam

From the earliest use of iron (see Chapter 1), the smelting process involved using high heat to melt the metal, release it from its ore, and remove impurities. In pre-modern Europe, first charcoal, and much later coke, distilled from coal, were used as fuels in this process. The availability of the steam engine permitted new innovations in iron manufacture.

Britain's own iron ores were of inferior quality, laced with impurities that injured the resultant metal's strength and malleability. Iron ore was imported from Sweden, Russia, and (after 1776) the United States. Meanwhile, some manufacturers experimented with coke, as opposed to charcoal, as a fuel for the production of raw or "pig" iron. In 1784, Henry Cort (1740–1800) patented his technique of "puddling," which allowed coke to be used throughout the process of iron manufacture. The process is shown in the diagram in *Windows On*, p. 621. The pig iron was heated with the coke to form a paste, which was stirred with iron rods, allowing impurities to be burned away. The molten iron was then passed between rollers, which pressed out any remaining impurities. A means had been found to use native ores in the manufacture of top-grade iron.

Innovations in iron manufacture meant a surge in production as shown in *How Many?* on p. 623. In 1750, Britain produced 28,000 tons of pig iron. By 1790, after puddling had been introduced, that figure more than tripled, to 87,000 tons; in 1818, it was 325,000 tons, in 1830, 700,000 tons, and in 1870, 4 million tons. Over 120 years, these staggering figures amount to a sum 142 times the original value—a rate of increase immeasurably beyond what could be achieved by human or animal power alone.

The steam engine permitted further advances in metallurgy. The engine could operate bellows to blast hot air into the molten iron—work previously done by hand. By 1856, Henry Bessemer (1813–1898) developed a method of using the steam engine to operate bellows and rollers in the process of iron refining, making the use of expensive, skilled "puddlers" unnecessary, and, by reintroducing carbon to the refined iron, to produce steel—harder and finer than iron. The steam engine, illustrated in *Windows On* on p. 621, operated in one continuous process to

Power from Steam

The ENGINE for Raifing Water (with a power made) by Fire.

Newcomen steam engine, 1717

Henry Cort's "puddling furnace," 1784

James Watt's design of a rotary engine, 1782

Bessemer converter, 1856

Like the breakthrough of multiple spindlage, the development of the steam engine burst the bounds of previous technology, increasing the power available for work not by a factor of two or ten or even hundreds, but by thousands and tens of thousands. Whereas power historically had been limited by the capacity of muscle, wind, or water, now it was virtually unlimited. The amazing machine that turned ordinary water into limitless power is seen in its early stage of development in Newcomen's 1717 model (top left; note the human figure on the left for scale), and in its later refinement in James Watt's elegant 1782 plan of a rotary engine, capable of turning a shaft for advanced industrial applications (bottom left).

Besides their use in textile manufacture and transportation, steam engines powered the new "iron age" (approximately 1760–1856), speeding up and improving iron and steel production. Henry Cort's "puddling furnace," patented in 1784, removed the impurities introduced into molten iron by the coke used for smelting it (top right). The transition from iron to steel was made possible in large part by the invention of the Bessemer converter in 1856 (bottom right).

To continue your investigation of this topic, please go to www.prenhall.com/king for the related **WINDOWS** on the **WEB** activity

Inventors of the Industrial Age: Power and Metallurgy

Thomas Savery (c. 1650–1715)

Thomas Newcomen (1663–1729) } the steam engine

James Watt (1736–1819)

Henry Cort (1740–1800) the "puddling" process (iron)

Henry Bessemer (1813–1898) the Bessemer converter (steel)

half-million tons worldwide in 1870 to almost thirty times that figure (14,600,000 tons) in 1895.

The iron and steel employed domestically or exported abroad had many uses. In Britain at first, and then elsewhere, these increasingly included the construction of new machines—steam engines to power factories, and the machines that produced goods in the factories. Once again, a circular process is observed: machines made it possible to produce the substance from which to make more machines. Interrelations such as this characterized the building of the industrial era, where each innovation was promptly applied to other purposes.

Railroad and Steamship

produce a high-grade metal capable of serving the needs of a machine age. Almost a luxury metal in the early years of industrialization, steel commanded a price more than ten times that of pig iron. But steel became cheap as production bounded from about a

Just as the power of the steam engine could be used to drive machines that stood in place, it could also be adapted to machines that moved. The possibilities of using steam to revolutionize transportation presented themselves from the beginning. In 1770, the French had attempted to develop a rudimentary steam-driven

The Coming of the Machine Age

The first observers of the machine-powered manufacturing process were often astonished by the speed, the capacity, and the productivity of the steam engine—a great beast with "iron fingers, teeth, and wheels," and "the noblest machine ever invented by man," as these two authors observe with understandable awe.

Edward Baines, a nineteenth-century student of industrialization, describes the great productivity of the machine-powered textile factory (1835): It is by iron fingers, teeth, and wheels, moving with exhaustless energy and devouring speed, that the cotton is opened, cleaned, spread, carded, drawn, roved, spun, wound, warped, dressed, and woven. ... All are moving at once—the operations chasing each other; and all derive their motion from the mighty engine, which, firmly seated in the lower part of the building, and constantly fed with water and fuel, toils through the day with the strength of perhaps a hundred horses. Men, in the meanwhile, have merely to check its slight and infrequent irregularities—each workman performing, or rather superintending, as much work as could have been done by *two or three hundred men* sixty years ago. ... When it is remembered that all these inventions have been made within the last seventy years it must be acknowledged that the cotton mill presents the most striking example of the dominion obtained by human science over the powers of nature, of which modern times can boast.
(Edward Baines, *History of the Cotton Manufacture in Great Britain*, 1835; ed. M. J. Daunton, 1995)

The steam engine as a living beast (1834): It is [in] the property which the steam-engine possesses of regulating itself, and providing for all its wants, that the great beauty of the invention consists. It has been said that nothing made by the hand of man approaches so near to animal life. Heat is the principle of its movements; there is in its tubes circulation, like that of the blood in the veins of animals, having valves which open and shut in proper periods; it feeds itself, evacuates such portions of its food as are useless, and draws from its own labours all that is necessary to its own subsistence. ... The motion of the fluids in the boiler represents the expanding and collapsing of the heart; the fluid that goes to it by one channel is drawn off by another, in part to be returned when condensed by the cold, similar to the operation of veins and arteries. Animals require long and frequent periods of relaxation from fatigue, and any great accumulation of their power is not obtained without great expense and inconvenience. The wind is uncertain; and water, the constancy of which is in few places equal to the wants of the machinist, can seldom be obtained on the spot, where other circumstances require machines to be erected. To relieve us from all these difficulties, the last century has given us the steam engine ... the noblest machine ever invented by man—the pride of the machinist, the admiration of the philosopher.
(M. A. Alderson, essay, 1834; ed. R. L. Hills, 1993)

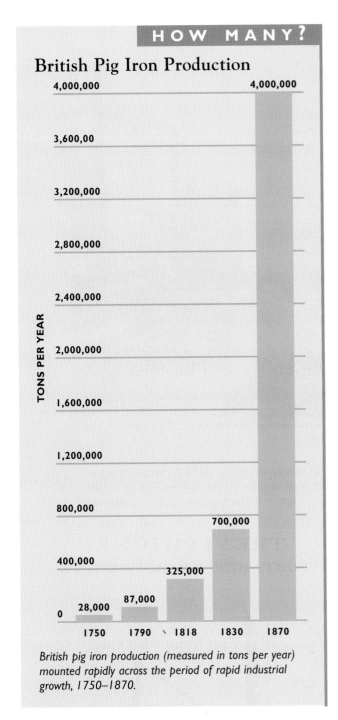

British Pig Iron Production

British pig iron production (measured in tons per year) mounted rapidly across the period of rapid industrial growth, 1750–1870.

ore from the rock face to the surface (when they did not carry baskets, or push crates). The rails, at first made of timber, were laid to permit the wheels of the carts to roll freely without becoming mired in mud. They were laid in the galleries of the mine or on the road from the mine to a depot by a river or canal, where the heavy mining products were loaded on barges for shipment to market. As early as 1556, a classic Renaissance treatise on metallurgy described the use of rails for just these purposes.

The carts, the rails, and the engine were first put together near the mines. They formed short railroad lines that ran from the mine to a coastal, river, or canal depot transporting coal. In 1804, the engineer Richard Trevithick (1771–1833) developed a locomotive, illustrated on p. 624, capable of carrying heavy loads on such truncated lines. The first expanded lines date from the 1820s, and in 1821, a rail line extended from Darlington, a mining center, to Stockton, a port; by 1825, this line was offering both freight and passenger services.

The next step in the development of the railroad came with the idea that the railroad could exist apart from the mine. It could link markets and ports, and could transport goods other than mining products. It might carry, for instance, bolts of cotton cloth, or loads of cabbages, to market centers. By 1829, George Stephenson (1781–1848) had developed the locomotive *Rocket* (which could clock a good 36 mph on a normal run—several times the speed of a horse pulling a cart). It operated on a line between the booming factory town of Manchester and the port of Liverpool, serving the Atlantic trade. By 1850, England was crisscrossed with a network of rail lines—an infrastructure that still exists in part 150 years later.

The railroad might be considered the most significant breakthrough in transportation since the days, millennia earlier, of the introduction of the wheel or the sail (see Chapter 1). Previously, in most parts of the world and certainly in Europe, the transportation of heavy materials over long distances was usually accomplished by water—whether on the sea or by river or canal. (Exceptions were the long pack animal trains that traversed the Silk Road in Asia, or the camel caravans across Middle Eastern deserts.) The railroad was faster, safer, and nearly limitless, reaching wherever rails could be laid. Railroad stations, the scenes of myriad comings and goings, as shown in Monet's painting on p. 625 became the new foci of industrial civilization. Timetables that clocked those goings and comings were objects of passionate scrutiny, offering the promise of arriving at a specified time at any given destination.

The steamship developed in tandem with the railroad, in due course replacing the sail, as rail replaced the wheeled cart. The American Robert Fulton (1765–1815) developed the prototype of the modern steamship from the unsuccessful design created by a

cart, followed by a steamboat in 1783. Useful steam-driven vehicles, however, were not developed until the early 1800s, when the necessary components—the steam engine, together with abundant supplies of iron and coal—were assembled.

A "railroad train" is a series of carts or carriages linked together (the train) whose wheels run on a pathway of parallel rails drawn by an engine (the locomotive). The steam engine itself, it has been seen, had origins intimately linked to the coal mine. Similarly, the railroad train was initially developed for mining work, assembling its parts from elements of the mining enterprise. The carts derived from those the miners used to transport coal or mineral-bearing

Steam Outdoes Men and Beasts

Sheffield, England, in 1879: *One of the industrial boom towns of the nineteenth century, Sheffield specialized in the production of steel and steel implements (such as cutlery and files). This scene displays the prominence of factories and belching smokestacks—and the continuity of traditional rural life in their midst, as is clearly evidenced by the presence of countryfolk and their cows.*

French inventor in 1783. In 1807, Fulton's 150-foot *Clermont*, powered by a Boulton and Watt engine, traveled upriver from New York City to Albany in thirty-two hours, averaging a little under five miles per hour. In Britain, Henry Bell (1767–1830) launched his steamship *Comet* in 1812. A steamship first crossed the Atlantic in 1819, powered partly by sail and partly by steam-driven paddlewheels, taking thirty days. The first transatlantic steamship line opened in 1838. By the 1850s, sturdy, reliable steamships fitted with screw propellers (which replaced the paddlewheel) were visiting all the major ports of the globe. The career of the sailing ship, which had opened the Atlantic and Pacific oceans to commerce, would soon close.

Industrialization took place in Britain first because of a number of favorable circumstances. Britain's colonial empire linked it with the cotton workshops

Advertisement for Trevithick's engine: *This advertisement for Richard Trevithick's primitive locomotive (developed in 1804, and called here a "portable steam engine") reads "Catch me who can!" and, even more defiantly, "Mechanical Power Subduing Animal Speed." This last concise phrase sums up the heroic achievement of industrialization.*

of India and the cotton fields of the Americas. Its own land yielded coal and iron in abundance, and its ample waterways and harbors made transportation and communication easy. Its sound banking system, ready capital, landlords friendly to profitable innovation, and entrepreneurs promoted investment in new ventures. Its government encouraged commerce but did not intervene too much to protect or restrict. Its large supply of unskilled laborers was available to work in the industries developed largely by a pool of talented artisans, who, unlike their continental colleagues, were unhampered by guild restrictions. Beyond these factors, a willingness to experiment seems to characterize the makers of what some historians call an industrial revolution in Britain.

By 1870, industrialization had transformed Britain. Machine power—"unconquer'd steam" (in the words of Erasmus Darwin, grandfather of naturalist Charles Darwin)—had demonstrated its superiority over animal strength, and machines were planted in the garden of the countryside. Over green fields loomed huge, brash factories (Blake's nightmare),

their smokestacks telling the tale of the storming, blasting steam engines within. Sleek, fast trains carried coal and iron, bolts of cloth, and the machines to make them to every corner of the country.

No other state could compete with Britain in output or market share, at home or abroad, as the passage quoted in *Witnesses* on p. 633 suggests. In 1851, the "Great Exhibition of the Works of Industry of all Nations" was held in London's Crystal Palace. In that building whose walls were fabrics of glass and steel, assembled on-site from factory-made components, more than 6 million visitors from around the globe admired 13,000 exhibits of British industrialization. After about a century of development, Britain remained unsurpassed in its industrial capacity. As the diagrams on p. 630 show, however, by 1870 four other nations had set out on the road to industrialization—Belgium, France, Germany, and the United States—two of which would overtake Britain in industrial capacity by 1900. Those other states had begun industrializing early, profiting from Britain's prior experience.

The Railroad and the Automobile

Claude Monet, Gare Saint-Lazare: *The 1877 work of French Impressionist painter Claude Monet captures the excitement of the railroad, which was the culminating symbol of triumphant industrialization. The huge and impressive Paris railroad station, with its multiple divergent tracks eliciting the wonder of distant lands, receives the mighty engine in its nimbus of gray smoke. (Musée d'Orsay, Paris)*

Karl Benz at the wheel: *The extraordinary century that opened with the development of the railroad closed with that of the internal combustion engine that powered the modern automobile, first available in the 1880s. Here is Karl Benz, creator of the Benz automobile, steering his new product in 1887.*

CATCHING UP

How does industrialization spread? Not like dye in water, or like an infection spread through droplets in the air. Each innovation in technology, in manufacture, in distribution had to be introduced on new ground by an individual engineer or merchant or investor. Energetic men (women did not figure noticeably in this process) from other nations visited, observed, and documented industrial processes in Britain. Or sometimes British experts, lured by the promise of bonuses or new opportunities, traveled abroad with a precious cargo of mental capital.

By a succession of such efforts—made covertly, as British law forbade the export of technology and the emigration of experts—other nations developed industrial foundations. As Map 21.2 on p. 627 shows, by 1870, much of western Europe and parts of North America were industrialized or had begun the process of industrialization. Between 1870 and 1914, other nations challenged and even surpassed the British lead, while other regions did not begin to industrialize until the twentieth century.

The First Imitators

The first imitators of industrial Britain were its neighbors in northwestern Europe—France, Belgium, and Germany—and its former North American colony, the United States. Beginning very soon after the Napoleonic settlement (see Chapter 20),

entrepreneurs in these regions began to expand the manufacture of textiles and metals, and to build railroad networks. By 1870, the industrial economies of these nations had developed to a point where they were competing directly with Britain. Germany and the United States proceeded to pass Britain's highwater mark by 1913. This later phase of industrialization, sometimes called the "Second Industrial Revolution," was characterized by the use of chemicals in manufacturing processes, electricity for power and light, and communication technologies.

France and Belgium   In the 1700s, France had been a vigorous producer of manufactures, but fell behind its rival Britain during the early industrial era of steam power. Until the late eighteenth century, France and Britain were not only the two main colonial powers, but the two leading manufacturing powers in Europe. Domestic or cottage industry flourished in France as well as Britain, producing textiles for local and foreign markets. France's iron production exceeded Britain's, while its cotton consumption was about the same.

Around 1760, Britain began to pull ahead in industrial capacity—even before the disruption caused after 1789 by the French Revolution. Signs of the quickening of Britain's economic progress are evident in the number of patents granted for new inventions, the volume of foreign trade, the rate of urbanization, and the production of textiles and iron. Though the French government actively intervened to promote the growth of manufactures, private entrepreneurship in Britain proved more effective, while economic blockades of revolutionary France reduced its ability to import raw materials. By 1800, Britain greatly exceeded France in all statistical measures of industrial activity.

Not only did Britain spurt forward at the end of the eighteenth century, but France dropped out of the race after 1789. Until Napoleon's defeat in 1815, France was preoccupied with a political and social transformation that left little opportunity, or wealth, for economic development. At the end of the revolutionary era, French manufacture had fallen below its level in 1789. In the meantime, Britain had enjoyed a near monopoly of foreign trade.

The period that followed, from the restoration of the monarchy through the inauguration of the Third Republic (1815–1871; see Chapter 20), was favorable to the development of an entrepreneurial bourgeoisie. Some of Napoleon's innovations proved helpful—the abolition of guilds, the removal of internal **tariffs**, and the standardization of commercial law. The mechanization of textile manufacture proceeded on the British model—French entrepreneurs often chose to hire skilled British workers, of whom there were as many as 15,000 working in France by 1830.

The French state actively intervened in economic matters. Through monarchical, republican, and imperial eras, official policy favored those who invested funds or launched companies, especially family firms. The government built the national railroad system (in place by the 1840s), then leased the component lines for terms of more than one hundred years to private companies. Napoleon III (r. 1850–1870) encouraged banking firms to invest in industrial ventures. Still, French industrialization was slowed by the commitment of so much of the economy to agriculture, and by the scarcity of coal and iron (exacerbated by the loss of Alsace and Lorraine to Germany in 1871, following the Franco-Prussian War). In 1870, France still lagged behind Britain, and would soon fall behind Germany and the United States.

The Belgian economy, which resembled that of France in 1789, followed its neighbor's lead and drew profitably on British expertise, in defiance of British law. A major coup was the enlistment of the Cockerill family of expert British manufacturers. William

Map 21.2 The Industrialization of Continental Europe, 1815–1860: As in Great Britain, industrial concentration in continental Europe occurred in the vicinity of mineral deposits and major ports. The continued flow of goods was encouraged by the elimination of tariffs and customs. The German customs union (the Zollverein, 1834), which incorporated most of the German states, was one of the most effective of these various free trade systems. Note the lower levels of industrial growth and railroad building occurring in southern and eastern Europe.

WHO'S WHO

Advocates of Industrialization

William Cockerill (1759–1832), British manufacturer who introduced the textile factory system to France and Belgium.

Friedrick List (1789–1846), German economist who advocated a free trade zone, or "Zollverein," by eliminating tariff walls among the various German states.

Alfred Krupp (1812–1887), called the "Cannon King," head of the German steel company that made possible the new nation's rapid development of machines, ships, and weapons.

Samuel Slater (1768–1835), New England entrepreneur who established the first water-powered textile mill in the United States.

Sergei Witte (1849–1915), Russian Minister of Finance who encouraged the industrialization of Russia and the construction of a continental railroad system that provided a link between St. Petersburg and Vladivostok.

Cockerill (1759–1832) (honored with French citizenship by Napoleon in 1810 for his introduction of textile manufacture to France) built a factory system for the combined production of metals and machines in Liège (modern Belgium, under French domination 1797–1815 and Dutch domination 1815–1830). In 1812, it employed 2000 workers; by the 1830s, it was the largest such plant in the world—reflecting a mission, as one observer thought, "to fill the whole world with machinery." The machines built in Cockerill's factory permitted the rapid development of mining, shipbuilding, and railroad systems. To set up their railroad system, the Belgians hired Britain's first expert, George Stephenson.

Germany   The German nation was only constituted in 1871, at about the time that German industrial activities surged ahead to new highs of production. The earlier stages of German industrialization had been undertaken primarily by Prussia. In the eighteenth century, Frederick the Great of Prussia (1712–1786), whose talents encompassed military management, literature, and music, had also been alert to his small state's economic interests. He outlined his goals neatly: first, to bring money in from abroad; second, to prevent its seeping out to foreign countries. He promoted silk, wool, and cotton manufactures, welcomed French Huguenot and Jewish immigrants whose diligence contributed to economic development wherever they settled, and seized Silesia from neighboring Austria in part to acquire its

mineral resources, especially coal. Still, outside of the industrial regions of Saxony and the newly acquired Rhineland (1815), Prussia was primarily an agricultural nation; its prosperous manufactures formed only a small part of its economy.

Napoleon's consolidation of the German states in the early nineteenth century was, ironically, a spur not only to German nationalism but also to economic progress. (His abolition of guilds and serfdom also promoted innovation and labor mobility.) In 1834, a further consolidation for economic purposes only—the *Zollverein*, or "Customs Union"—was voluntarily adopted by nearly all the German states. With the elimination of customs barriers among these still autonomous states, new enterprises, such as modern textile factories, could flourish, and new industries find markets and resources. Among these resources were coal, which from the 1840s began to be mined intensively in the Ruhr, Silesia, and Saar regions, and iron, smelted with coke from the 1850s. Coal production increased steadily in volume (more than doubling in the period 1851–1857 alone), until Germany, having incorporated the valuable provinces of Alsace and Lorraine, became Europe's greatest producer. Bismarck had said that Germany would be unified by "blood and iron" but, a modern economist has observed, it could be more truly said to owe its success to "coal and iron."

At the same time, even before the German nation formally came into being, a German rail system developed. By 1839, with the opening of a railway from Dresden to Leipzig, the German states were on their way to the development of a mature railroad system. Construction proceeded in the 1840s, and by 1860 total German rail mileage surpassed that of any other nation of continental Europe. As elsewhere, the creation of a railroad network stimulated industry and the labor market.

At first, German observers faithfully pursued the British model of industrial development. Like the French and the Belgians, they traveled to Britain and came home with new ideas. Alfred Krupp (1812–1887), called the "Cannon King," was the most famous member of a dynasty that controlled one of Germany's largest firms into the mid-twentieth century. Krupp visited Britain in 1838 to learn about metallurgical techniques. He later established the major German steel company that made possible the new nation's rapid development of machines, ships, and weapons later in the century. At the Crystal Palace in 1851, Krupp showed off his own 4300-pound steel block, impressing even the British with the quality and mass of the product, and a gun barrel of brilliant cast steel. By 1862, he had installed a Bessemer converter at the Krupp works in the Ruhr.

Krupp's enormous metalworks were typical of German industrialization after 1871. Germany's industries grew swiftly, rivaling British capacity by

1900. German businesses tended to be on a large scale for several reasons: first, Germany possessed the natural resources that fed heavy industry; second, the state actively subsidized and promoted new enterprises and investment; and third, funding was readily provided by modern credit banks, which especially encouraged exports to foreign markets. Patterns of investment encouraged the formation of **cartels**, in which one or two large firms dominated a whole industrial sector. Only two firms, for instance, controlled ninety percent of the electrical industry, which was pioneered in Germany. Germany's rapid industrial growth can be measured in its changing share of the world output of manufactured goods: from thirteen percent in 1870 to sixteen percent in 1900, while Britain's output gradually slid from thirty-two to eighteen percent.

The United States Like France, Belgium, and Germany, the fledgling United States learned to industrialize from Britain. Like Germany, its industrial economy surged in the last few decades of the nineteenth century during the "Second Industrial Revolution."

From early colonial days, the economy of the United States was tightly linked to Britain's. It had sent timber and tobacco to the motherland, and foodstuffs to her Caribbean colonies, enabling them to pursue the monoculture of sugar. By the middle of the eighteenth century, cotton cultivation in the southern Atlantic colonies grew steadily in volume, accelerating rapidly after the War for Independence. Cotton bound the United States economy to industrial Britain from 1783 until the 1860s, when the Civil War (1861–1865) disrupted the plantation system and put an end to slavery.

In the late eighteenth century, entrepreneurs returning from tours of inspection abroad established the first textile mills in the New England states. In 1793, Samuel Slater (1768–1835) established on the British model the first water-powered textile mill in the United States, in Rhode Island. Only fifteen more mills were built by 1808, but in 1809, eighty-seven additional mills were established. By 1814 in Waltham, Massachusetts, Francis Cabot Lowell (1775–1817) built a weaving factory designed on British models, its looms powered by steam engines. By 1831, the young industrial nation boasted 795 cotton factories, with a capacity of 1.2 million yarn spindles—nearly forty times the capacity of 1809. By the 1840s, sewing machines, invented by Isaac Singer (1811–1875), were busy in factories producing ready-made clothing.

British railroad construction won prompt attention from United States entrepreneurs. Beginning with the Baltimore and Ohio Railroad, local lines were already developed in the 1830s, and by the 1840s there were 3000 miles of interregional rail lines.

Private businessmen were the main developers of rail capacity, in contrast to France or Germany where the state dominated the establishment of railroad systems. The distances traversed by rail lines in the United States were huge, since railroads needed to carry manufactured products and migrating peoples from the Atlantic to the Pacific coast, 3000 miles away, and to return with grain and beef. The demand for boxcars and rails was consequently enormous, and stimulated steel and machine production.

Northern railroads supplied Union soldiers all along the battlefront and helped win the Civil War against the South, whose underdeveloped rail network served mostly to carry bales of cotton from farm areas to coastal ports. While the guns still roared, railroad companies began to stretch new lines across the belly of the nation. In 1869, with the war only four years over, rail lines extending from the Midwest and California met at Promontory Point, Utah, amid the peaks of the Rocky Mountains. The completion of the first transcontinental railroad anywhere on the globe was marked by the ceremonial driving of a golden spike, the hammer wielded by California entrepreneur John Leland Stanford (1824–1893). The Atlantic was now linked with the Pacific, from whose coast the West would find another vantagepoint on the East.

Railroad development encouraged other economic projects. It not only boosted machine and metal production, but facilitated the distribution of textiles and other manufactures, and foodstuffs. Another factor in industrial development was the existence of a large mobile labor force, augmented after the 1840s by immigration from Europe (especially refugees from the Irish famine) and, to a lesser extent, Asia. Government support in the form of federal land grants to entrepreneurs venturing westward was helpful, while government interference remained limited. By the 1870s, large corporations such as Andrew Carnegie's (1835–1919) steelworks employed hundreds or even thousands of workers, who shopped in company-run stores and were supervised by a private police force—maintained unapologetically by a man who would become one of the greatest United States philanthropists.

Although the economy of the United States remained heavily agricultural, its agricultural production was increasingly mechanized with the invention of tractors and harvesting machinery, and refrigeration systems for rail cars and steamships. The nation's seemingly limitless natural resources—both mineral and agricultural—and its ambitious, often ruthless entrepreneurs, had by 1914 made the United States the world's leading industrial nation.

The Second Phase By this late date—more than a century after the founding of the first textile mills, or the refinement of the steam engine—industrialization on both sides of the Atlantic had entered a second

Patterns of European Economic Development: 1850–1873

	1850	1869	1873
Britain			
Railroad	6,621	15,145	16,082
Coal	37,500	97,066	112,604
Steam power	1,290	4,040	
Pig iron	2,249	5,446	6,566
Raw cotton	266.8	425.8	565.1
Germany			
Railroad	3,639	10,834	14,842
Coal	5,100	26,774	36,392
Steam power	260	2,480	
Pig iron	212	1,413	2,241
Raw cotton	17.1	64.1	117.8
France			
Railroad	1,869	10,518	11,500
Coal	7,225	21,432	24,702
Steam power	370	1,850	
Pig iron	406	1,381	1,382
Raw cotton	59.3	93.7	55.4
Belgium			
Railroad	531	1,800	2,335
Coal	3,481	7,822	10,219
Steam power	70	350	
Pig iron	145	535	607
Raw cotton	10.0	16.3	18.0

By five measures of economic development—total railroad mileage (statute miles), coal production (1000 metric tons), steam power capacity (1000 horsepower), pig iron output (1000 metric tons), and raw cotton consumption (1000 metric tons)— Britain outpaced her three leading European rivals from 1850 to 1873. The gap narrowed, however, especially between Germany and Britain. Note Germany's sevenfold increase in coal production, compared to Britain's threefold increase, and Germany's sevenfold increase in cotton consumption, compared to Britain's, which slightly more than doubled.
Source: Based on *D. Landes*, The Unbound Prometheus (Cambridge: Cambridge University Press, 1969), p. 194.

phase. Joining the heavy industries (metals and textiles) of early industrialization, were newer industries concerned with producing chemicals or providing gas and electrical power. Chemical products (often derived from petroleum) were employed in textile manufacture, agriculture, mining, and construction in the form of dyes, fertilizers, or explosives. From the early 1800s, gas lamps illuminated streets, shops,

Map 21.3 Industrialized Europe by 1914: *By 1914, areas of industrial concentration in Europe had increased in number and the railroad system was greatly expanded (compare Map 21.2, p. 627).*

homes, and factories—"Gas has replaced the sun!" exclaimed one contemporary enthusiastically.

Electricity soon replaced gas as a source of power. In 1879, the American Thomas Edison (1847–1931) invented the incandescent light bulb, making electricity usable to light homes and public places. By the 1880s, electricity had taken over for the lighting of city streets, department stores, hotels, and public buildings. Gradually, ordinary homes were wired, and housewives felt privileged to have sewing machines, refrigerators, and vacuum cleaners that operated by electrical power. Electricity powered local transportation—the streetcars or "trolley" cars that first opened up suburban housing for workers, who were enabled to live in surroundings pleasanter than the immediate area of their industrial workplace. Bicycles, too, allowed workers to glide swiftly through city streets and in the countryside. By 1885, a workable internal combustion engine was available to power the first generation of automobiles. By 1909, a French observer announced: "It's finished, the tranquility of our streets, and the charm of promenading either on foot or in a carriage. ... Paris belongs to the machines."

Communications, meanwhile, had developed to meet the needs of entrepreneurs around the globe. First the telegraph (which could communicate even across the Atlantic ocean, thanks to a cable laid in 1866), then the telephone, patented by Alexander Graham Bell (1847–1922) in 1876, conquered the distances that modern economies traversed. From the

1890s, wireless communication was made possible by the work of Guglielmo Marconi (1874–1937), and by the early 1900s radio broadcasts could be received in ordinary households. During those same years, silent motion pictures began to be screened (by 1908, France had more than 1000 movie theaters), and couples could dance in their living rooms to music produced by the gramophone (see Chapter 26).

As Map 21.3 shows, by 1914, Western civilization had been transformed by industrialization, and could be called modern—for industry, which brought machines into the garden of traditional society, was in itself the creator of modernity.

The Rest of the West and the Asian Vanguard

By 1870, France, Belgium, Germany, and the United States had joined the select circle of industrialized nations. Over the next generation, other European nations entered—the Netherlands and Scandinavia, northern Italy, parts of Spain, Portugal, and Ireland, Poland and the region around Prague (the present-day Czech Republic), following in the footsteps of earlier neighbors. So too did Russia, as well as Canada, Australia, and Japan.

Tsar Peter the Great (r. 1682–1725) had put Russia on the path to industrialization. He traveled himself to western European nations, studying their military and shipbuilding technology especially. The

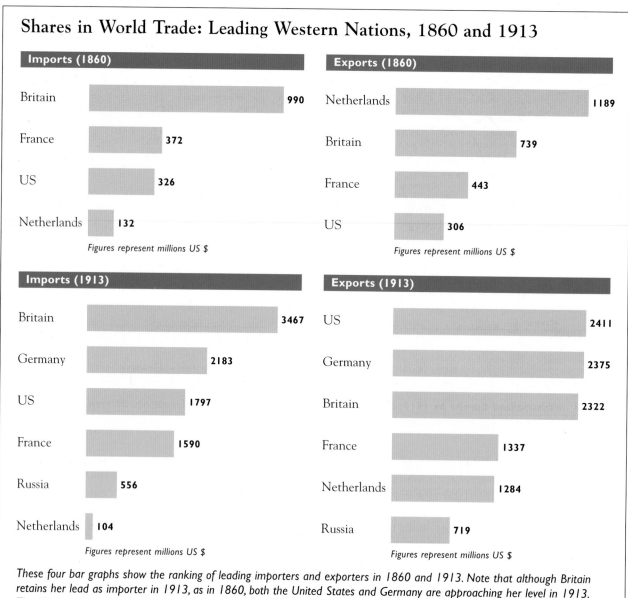

Shares in World Trade: Leading Western Nations, 1860 and 1913

Imports (1860)

Britain	990
France	372
US	326
Netherlands	132

Figures represent millions US $

Exports (1860)

Netherlands	1189
Britain	739
France	443
US	306

Figures represent millions US $

Imports (1913)

Britain	3467
Germany	2183
US	1797
France	1590
Russia	556
Netherlands	104

Figures represent millions US $

Exports (1913)

US	2411
Germany	2375
Britain	2322
France	1337
Netherlands	1284
Russia	719

Figures represent millions US $

These four bar graphs show the ranking of leading importers and exporters in 1860 and 1913. Note that although Britain retains her lead as importer in 1913, as in 1860, both the United States and Germany are approaching her level in 1913. The Netherlands is the leading exporter in 1860, but has fallen well behind the closely matched frontrunners Britain, Germany, and the United States—with the latter in the lead.

state supported the production of heavy manufactures, and eighty-six manufacturing enterprises were launched. By the end of the eighteenth century, Russia's iron production was second only to Britain's, and its urban populations had tripled.

These ventures had a limited impact, however, given the vastness of the nation and its entrenched system of agricultural production based on serf labor. In the nineteenth century, Russia industrialized but only slowly, on the model established by Britain in the previous century. In 1805, a steam engine was first used for cotton manufacture. In 1836, Cort's puddling process was introduced for the production of iron. Beginning in 1843, foreign consultants oversaw the importation and installation of updated machinery for textile manufacture, and planned the development of railroad and steamship systems. From 1820, a

steamboat regularly plied the river Volga. By 1851, a rail line ran from St. Petersburg to Moscow. The numbers of factories and free (non-serf) laborers multiplied, while serf workers labored in industrial workshops and serf entrepreneurs built and extended them.

But the economic base on which these impressive increases rested was inadequate. The nation was overwhelmingly agricultural (and continued demand for basic commodities—timber, grain, wax—encouraged it to remain so). Moreover, Russia had no tradition of artisan manufacture and only a tiny merchant class— about one-fourth of one percent of the population. The tsars' earnest support and the purchased services of Western experts had slight impact.

A transformation of the Russian economy along modern lines would only begin in the last years of the nineteenth century. By that time, a full generation after the abolition of serfdom, large numbers of laborers released from the land were available. These joined the skilled, mobile workers clustered in those cities large enough to support full-scale industrialization, funded by foreign capital. The exploitation of coal fields near the Black Sea, oil wells near the Caspian Sea, and iron lodes in the Ural Mountains, linked now by railroad to western Russian centers, made Russia competitive with the most advanced nations of the West. Urbanization gathered pace, the urban population rising from under 6 million around 1860 to more than 23 million in 1913. During this period, the population of Moscow increased from 500,000 to more than 1.5 million, and that of St. Petersburg from about 500,000 to

2 million. Despite a slow start, St. Petersburg, boasting 900 factories in 1914, was an industrial center among the largest in Europe.

In the Russian industrialization of the 1890s, Minister of Finance Sergei Witte (1849–1915), quoted in *Witnesses* below, labored to promote important enterprises and to lure foreign capital to fund them. Above all, he saw to the construction of an improved railroad system that linked Moscow and St. Petersburg to ocean ports and navigable rivers, and to manufacturing, agricultural, and mining centers. In 1899, under his direction, more than 3000 miles of the Trans-Siberian railway line had been completed. Arching across the whole continent of Asia, it opened Siberia to colonization. When he was dismissed in 1906,

Catching Up in Argentina, Germany, and Russia

By the middle and late nineteenth century, other nations of the Western world—including those across the Atlantic Ocean—were rushing in order to follow Britain's lead in industrialization. Here, policy advisers in Argentina, the German states, and the Russian empire greet with enthusiasm the challenge their nations faced to modernize and compete in a changed world.

Argentinian journalist and diplomat Juan Bautista Alberdi hails the railroad as a tool for unity and prosperity (1852): The railroad offers the means of righting the topsy-turvy order that Spain established in this continent. She placed the heads of our state where the feet should be. For her ends of isolation and monopoly this was a wise system; for our aims of commercial expansion and freedom it is disastrous. We must bring our capitals to the coast, or rather bring the coast into the interior of the continent. The railroad and the electric telegraph, the conquerors of space, work this wonder better than all the potentates on earth. The railroad changes, reforms, and solves the most difficult problems without decrees or mob violence. It will forge the unity of the Argentine Republic better than all our congresses. The congresses may declare it "one and indivisible," but without the railroad to connect its most remote regions it will always remain divided and divisible, despite all the legislative decrees.
(From B. Keen ed., *Latin American Civilization: History and Society, 1492 to the Present*, 4th ed., 1986)

Friedrich List on England's leadership in global industrialization (1841): Far from having been stopped in its progress by England, the world has received from her its strongest impulse. She has served as a model to all nations in her internal and external policy; in her great inventions and grand enterprises of every kind; in the advancement of the useful arts; in the construction of roads, railways and canals; in the discovery and cultivation of lands in a state of nature, particularly

in displaying and developing the natural wealth of tropical countries, and in the civilization of tribes, savage or subsiding into barbarism. Who can tell how far behind the world would have been if there had been no England?
(Friedrich List, *The National System of Political Development*, 1941; ed. T. H. von Laue, 1969)

Russian Finance Minister Sergei Witte argues that Russia must industrialize if it is to flourish (1900): The experience of all peoples clearly shows that only the economically independent countries are fully able to assert their political power. ... At present the political strength of the great powers which are called to fulfill great historical tasks in the world is created not only by the spiritual valor of their peoples but also by their economic organization. Even the military preparedness of a country is determined not only by the perfection of its military machine but by the degree of its industrial development. Russia ... needs ... a proper economic foundation for her national policy and her culture. ... International competition does not wait. If we do not take energetic and decisive measures so that in the course of the next decades our industry will be able to satisfy the need of Russia and of the Asiatic countries which are—or should be—under our influence, then the rapidly growing foreign industries will break through our tariff barriers and establish themselves in our fatherland and in the Asiatic countries mentioned above and drive their roots into the depths of our economy. This may gradually clear the way also for triumphant political penetration by foreign powers. ... It is possible that the slow growth of our industries will endanger the fulfillment of the great political tasks of the monarchy. Our economic backwardness may lead to political and cultural backwardness as well.
(Sergei Witte, "On the Condition of Our Industry," 1900; ed. T. H. von Laue, 1969)

Inventors of the Industrial Age: Transportation and Communication

George Stephenson (1781–1848) the locomotive

Robert Fulton (1765–1815) the steamboat

Thomas Edison (1847–1931) the incandescent lightbulb

Alexander Graham Bell (1847–1922) the telephone

Guglielmo Marconi (1874–1937) the radio

Russian industrialization, though still lagging behind the leaders of western Europe, was well under way.

The economies of colonial Latin America—Spanish and Portuguese, Caribbean and continental—were firmly linked, like the English and French ones of North America, to Europe (see Chapters 16, 19). The trade in tobacco, rice, and indigo, timber, fur, and fish in the latter case; silver, gold, and sugar in the former, formed chains across the Atlantic.

The silver and gold extracted from South American mines, mainly with native Amerindian labor, flowed through Spain and Portugal for three centuries, and provided Europe generally with the bullion necessary to trade with the nations of Asia. Sugar from Brazil and the Caribbean islands, raised and harvested mainly by imported African slaves, fed European appetites no longer content with a diet of bread and soup. In all these cases, the pattern is the same: the fruits of the earth, the produce of the mine, or the bounty of the fields were sent to Europe. In return came manufactured goods, especially metal products and textiles, such as the cotton fabric used to clothe plantation slaves, purchased in the Americas primarily by those of European descent. Thus supplied, they spurned the cruder handicrafts produced by native artisans. This trading pattern was distinctly unbalanced to the disadvantage of the dark-skinned laborers of Latin America.

Although the commodities traded changed with time, the same pattern prevailed for a century after the 1820s, the point at which most Latin American nations (all but Cuba and Puerto Rico, and the English and French Caribbean colonies) achieved their independence (see Chapter 19). The exports of silver and gold dwindled, to be replaced by other profitable products of the mines and large landed estates (**latifundias**): nitrates and tin, coffee, beef, and grain, medicinal plants and dyestuffs. The manufactured goods received in return were now machine-made textiles and metals, which competed with, and dispirited native artisans. Sugar exports from the Caribbean continued to flow, as Europeans continued to favor a variety of sweet treats and sweeteners for the exotic beverages, coffee and tea, that they had made their own.

In this context, Latin America failed to industrialize. Beginning in the 1850s, railroad lines were built to bring goods from the mines and the *latifundias* to the ports (see *Witnesses*, p. 633). Trade was directed toward Europe, and not toward the vast interior which remained largely untouched by the rail. Steam engines were employed in updated mines, thanks to foreign investment capital, mostly British. They also powered sugar refineries as early as 1815, requiring slaves to produce more and more raw cane to feed the vigorous new machines. But the failure to acquire the machinery for local manufacture was virtually total. As a consequence, Latin America as a whole lagged well behind the industrialized nations of the world into the twentieth century—despite its vigorous participation in foreign trade, and despite the wealth of a thin stratum of elite consumers, landowners, and entrepreneurs.

A quite different pattern holds for the far-flung British colonies of Australia, New Zealand, and Canada, later independent units of the Commonwealth, which was from 1931 the political association of former British colonies (see Chapter 27). These regions began to claim a stake in world trade (based at first on exports of abundant raw materials, such as foodstuffs, wool, and minerals) and industrial development by the late nineteenth century. As industrial powers, their fuller development, however, belongs to the twentieth century.

Apart from European nations, their colonies, and former colonies, Japan was the sole region to industrialize before the twentieth century. It did so because of the shocking challenge presented to its proud traditional culture by the advent, from the 1850s, of foreign economic intervention backed by the threat of force (see Chapter 24). Until that date, Japan, like China, considered itself economically self-sufficient. Although largely agricultural, it produced fine craft manufactures, and had some familiarity with Western gun technology (the gift of the Dutch merchants who, alone of Europeans, were allowed to deal with the Japanese through the port of Nagasaki).

Once "opened," however, by the arrival of the American Commodore Matthew Perry (1794–1858), the Japanese accomplished within a generation an astounding political and economic revolution. By the 1880s, Japan had established a textile-based industrial economy, which featured steam-driven factories, modern machinery, vigorous steel production, and an effective system of transportation by railroad and steamship. The Japanese economic miracle continued to flower into the next century, enabling it to defeat militarily a European rival—Russia—as early as 1905 (see Chapter 24).

Postponed Industrialization

By 1870, industrialization had reached maturity in several Western nations, and had begun in others, as it had in Japan. Elsewhere in Asia and Africa—in India, China, southeast Asia and Oceania; in the Middle East, North Africa, and Sub-Saharan Africa—industrialization had to wait until the twentieth century. During the 1800s, these regions exported cheaply-priced resources to the West, and in return purchased expensive manufactured goods, to their economic disadvantage (see Chapter 24).

Prior to the mechanization of British textile manufacture, as has been seen, India had been not only an active participant in Afro-Asian commerce, but also an active center as producer and exporter of cotton cloth. By the 1830s, it had become a consumer of British manufactures, including cotton textiles. In less than two generations, India had been transformed from a productive region to a non-productive one. The continued British presence (until 1947) meant that the Indian economy continued to serve British needs, as market and as provider of resources. The construction of a major railroad network from the 1850s, carrying both freight and passengers, increased mobility and stimulated commerce. But it did not encourage India to develop its own industries. Rather,

it facilitated the export of cash crops, including raw cotton, and the penetration of British manufacturers deep into the interior of the vast sub-continent.

Further east, China, like India, had played a central role in the Asian economy for many centuries. China produced prized manufactures, notably silk and porcelain, as well as tea, an expensive agricultural commodity. Her busy merchants carried these exports overland to India and western Asia, and shipped them throughout the South China Sea and western Pacific—to Korea and Japan, southeast Asia and Oceania. Despite China's strong economic position, however, it lagged behind with regard to the West at a critical juncture.

In China, the prevailing philosophy of Confucianism inhibited the development of industrialization. Confucianism denigrated merchants and profit-seeking, an attitude that was a disincentive to industrial development. Moreover, households with a surplus that could have been invested in commerce or manufacture generally preferred to invest in education for their sons, since the chief road to advancement was through the examination system to positions in government which conferred wealth and prestige. Any further surplus would have been invested in land, which became even more valuable as, especially with the demographic crisis of the

Liberia's first railway:
Industrialization has achieved global proportions in the twentieth century, as suggested by this photograph of Liberian workers building that nation's first railroad in 1950—one hundred years after Britain, the homeland of the steam engine, had completed its essential railroad grid.

eighteenth century forward, population pressures made it a scarce commodity. Precisely when innovation was needed, the reigning Manchu or Qing dynasty (1644–1912) finally began to weaken.

Meanwhile, Western nations sought greater access to Chinese ports, jealously closed to foreigners (see Chapter 24). In 1793 and 1816, the British sent representatives to China seeking more favorable treaty arrangements. Huge quantities of tea, which the British public craved, triggered these overtures. In this period, tea made up about half of British imports from China, which increased nearly eightfold between the 1780s and 1815. In exchange for tea, the British offered textiles, lead, and tin—and, covertly and illegally, opium processed from the poppy crop grown in India. Chinese officials were uninterested in the former, and furious about the latter.

In 1837, the imperial official Lin Tse-Hsu (1785–1850) addressed to the British Queen Victoria (r. 1837–1901) a stern letter about the opium trade. Whereas the Chinese exported many goods, all of benefit to humanity, he wrote, the British sent to China, along with benign products, an addictive poison. How could they sanction exposing Chinese people to a dangerous substance not permitted to their own citizens? To stop the traffic in drugs, the Chinese would severely punish any foreigner found participating in it—the penalty being decapitation. Not long after, the First Opium War (1839–1842) broke out, in which British warships shelled several Chinese ports that were completely defenseless against superior Western weaponry. By the 1842 Treaty of Nanjing, the British gained access to Guangzhou (Canton), Shanghai, and other ports.

Thereafter, several Western nations followed the British in "opening up" China to trade. As in India, the influx of Western manufactures had the unfortunate effect of retarding China's own industrial development. The first successful railroad, which was simply a short line for hauling coal to port, dated only from 1882. No factories for the machine production of textiles were established until the end of the century. The lofty Chinese empire sank rapidly to economic dependence upon contact with the West.

The experience of the Ottoman states of North Africa and western Asia followed a similar trajectory. These regions considered themselves superior to Europe in every regard—in religion, in statecraft, and in commerce. In the course of the nineteenth century, however, Western manufactures had their now familiar, and fatal, effects on native economies. Despite attempts, especially in Egypt, to establish factories under the guidance of Western advisers, these regions continued to fail to industrialize. They became exporters of agricultural and mineral commodities, locked into an unfavorable trade relationship with the European nations.

The nations of Sub-Saharan Africa were even less able than India, China, or the Ottoman Empire to withstand the economic dominance of Europe. With the cessation of the slave trade during the nineteenth century, their merchants were starved for cash. Despite a strong commercial tradition, and long experience in the manufacture of iron, Africans, too, became suppliers of raw materials to the industrialized West. That economic subordination, as will be seen, was merely a prelude to an even more complete subordination to those nations.

Conclusion
DESPOILED GARDENS AND THE MEANING OF THE WEST

By 1870, the productivity of the Western world far exceeded any measure imaginable in 1770. More things were made than ever before; exchanged faster; and sent further afield. The agent of this nearly inconceivable jump in material capacity was the machine operating by non-human, non-animal power—this was the first important innovation in the human ability to produce since the first human ancestor wielded the first tool.

Henceforth, humankind would share its earthly domain with the machine. For Enlightenment thinkers, the human being was much like a machine—a wholly rational being, a mechanism governed by mind. Julien Offray de la Mettrie (1709–1751), a case in point, argued in his aptly titled *Man the Machine* (1748) that the soul was nothing more than an extension of the body, itself a mechanical system. Now the machine approached the realm of the human. Like their human inventors, machines made things, and machines made machines. The machine commanded its human operator to tend it and feed it. If the human was a machine, could the machine be seen as possessing spirit, as it possessed heat and locomotion? Could the machine do good or evil?

The new machines caused Enlightenment optimism to cloud over, giving way to a darker, indeed Satanic, vision. The machines that invaded and despoiled the gardens of Western civilization promised abundance, but they devastated nature and deformed human lives. The following chapters will consider the impact of the machine on human society in the West and beyond, and on the ideas and images created by those who lived under its sway.

REVIEW QUESTIONS

1. What was the Industrial Revolution? Why was Europe the first region in the world to industrialize? Why did some thinkers call the new machines "dark Satanic mills"?

2. Why was Britain the first country to industrialize? How did the demand for cotton cloth spur industrialization in Britain? How did the steam engine transform mining and manufacturing?

3. Describe the improvements in iron and steel-making that occurred after 1750. Why were these improvements so important? How did railroads and steamships affect the growth of commerce?

4. What were the next states to industrialize, following the example of Britain? What role did the state play in industrialization in France and Germany? What was the Second Industrial Revolution?

5. Why did industrialization escalate in Russia in the late-nineteenth century? Why was Latin America so slow to industrialize? Why was Japan the only non-European nation to industrialize before the beginning of the twentieth century?

6. Why was the United States able to industrialize so rapidly toward the end of the nineteenth century? How did industrialization transform relations between the West and Asia and Africa? Why did China resist industrialization?

SUGGESTED RESOURCES

General studies

Landes, David S., *The Wealth and Poverty of Nations: Why Some Are So Rich and Some So Poor* (New York: Wal Mardon, 1998). Argues that what has made some nations rich and others poor is industrialization and the cultural patterns that tend either to promote or discourage it.

Mazlish, Bruce, *The Fourth Discontinuity: The Co-Evolution of Humans and Machines* (New Haven: Yale University Press, 1993). Imaginative exploration of the interactive development of humans and machines.

Stearns, Peter N., *The Industrial Revolution in World History* (Boulder, CO: Westview Press, 1993). Integrates and compares industrialization in Britain, Europe, the US, Russia, Japan, the Pacific Rim, Latin America, and elsewhere.

Before Industrialization

Ogilvie, Sheilagh C. & Markus Cerman, eds., *European Proto-Industrialization: An Introductory Handbook* (Cambridge: Cambridge University Press, 1996). Essays tracing the development of small-scale export industries between 1500 and 1800, constituting a stage of economic activity preliminary to the so-called "Industrial Revolution."

Overton, Mark, *Agricultural Revolution in England: The Transformation of the Agrarian Economy 1500–1850* (Cambridge: Cambridge University Press, 1996). General introduction to the changes in farming that helped create Britain's rising wealth and which ultimately facilitated industrialization.

Smail, John, *Merchants, Markets and Manufacture: The English Wool Textile Industry in the Eighteenth Century* (New York: St. Martin's, 1999). Notes the importance of product innovation and of export trade, describing not only what merchants and producers did, but how they thought about it.

Britain Industrializes

Hills, Richard, *Power from Steam: A History of the Stationary Steam Engine* (Cambridge: Cambridge University Press, 1993). A comprehensive history of the steam engine from Savery and Newcomen, to Watt, to the age of electricity.

Mokyr, Joel, ed., *The British Industrial Revolution: An Economic Perspective* (2nd ed.; Boulder: Westview Press, 1998). Five essays assessing recent views of the Industrial Revolution.

Timmins, Geoffrey, *The Last Shift: The Decline of Handloom Weaving in Nineteenth-Century Lancashire* (New York: St. Martins Press, 1993). Nineteenth-century handloom weavers are seen as the exemplar of skilled artisans replaced—and in many cases ruined—by technological advances in the textile industry.

Steam Engine Library, with links to contemporary texts about early industrialization: http://www.history.rochester.edu/steam

Age of Industry, links to biographies and texts relevant to the Industrial Revolution (Northwestern University): **http://history.evansville.net/industry.html**

Samuel Slater, Father of the American Industrial Revolution (geocities), text and images: **http://www.geocities.com/~woon_heritage/slater.htm**

Catching Up

Blackwell, W. L., *The Beginnings of Russian Industrialization, 1800–1860* (Princeton: Princeton University Press, 1968). Older but useful general introduction to the subject.

Gerschenkron, Alexander, *Economic Backwardness in Historical Perspective* (Cambridge, MA: Harvard University Press, 1962). Classic account comparing industrialization in several national contexts.

Henderson, W. O., *The Rise of German Industrial Power, 1834–1914* (California: University of California Press, 1975). Standard economic and political study of German industrialization. Includes discussion of the creation and significance of the *Zollverein*.

Johnson, Christopher H., *The Life and Death of Industrial Languedoc, 1700–1920* (Oxford: Oxford University Press, 1995). Studies a case of deindustrialization in a region of southern France which had begun to introduce new technology and build a modern wool industry, but began to decline in the later 19th century.

Milward, Alan S. and S. B. Saul, *The Development of the Economies of Continental Europe, 1850–1914* (Cambridge, MA: Harvard University Press, 1977). Detailed study of the economic history of European industrialization.

Morris-Suzuki, Tessa, *The Technological Transformation of Japan from the Seventeenth to the Twenty-First Century* (Cambridge: Cambridge University Press, 1994). Good, general economic history of Japan over several centuries. Synthesizes Japanese and Western scholarship.

LIVES OF THE OTHER HALF

	1750	1775	1800	1825	1850	1875	1900	1925

Society and Politics

American and French Revolutions, 1775–1794

French Revolutionary and Napoleonic Wars, 1792–1815

- ◆ Revolutions in France, Belgium, Italy, Poland, 1830–31
- ◆ First Reform Act in Britain, 1832
- ◆ Severe cholera epidemics in London and Paris, 1832
- ◆ Poor Law Amendment Act in Britain, 1834
  - ◆ Repeal of Corn Laws in Britain, 1846
  - ◆ Communist League founded in Britain, 1847
  - ◆ Revolutions in Europe, 1848
  - ◆ Public Health Act in Britain creates sewage system, 1848

- ◆ First underground (subway) system, London, 1863
  - ◆ School mandatory for children up to age of 10 in Britain, 1880
  - ◆ British population more than 67% urban, 1880
    - ◆ Nearly 75% of Parisian streets with sewers, 1887
  - ◆ School fees abolished in Britain, 1891
    - ◆ 75% of French population urban, 1900
    - ◆ Paris metro (subway) opens, 1900
    - ◆ New York subway opens, 1904

Labor and Economy

Britain industrializes, 1750–1850

Western and central Europe and North America industrialize, 1815–1900

Russia and Italy industrialize, 1870–1918

- ◆ Workers' combinations outlawed in France, 1791
  - ◆ Workers' combinations outlawed in Britain, 1799–1800
    - ◆ Luddites' industrial sabotage, Britain, 1811–12
      - ◆ "Peterloo Massacre," Manchester, England, 1819
        - ◆ British Combination Acts repealed, 1824
          - ◆ National Union of Cotton Spinners in Britain, 1829
            - ◆ British Factory Act, 1833
              - ◆ Robert Owen's Grand National Consolidated Trades Union, 1834
                - ◆ Chartist movement, 1838–48
                  - ◆ British Mines Act, 1842

- ◆ British Ten Hours Act, 1847
  - ◆ Karl Marx and Friedrich Engels' *Communist Manifesto*, 1848
  - ◆ National workshops set up in France, 1848
    - ◆ Amalgamated Society of Engineers formed in Britain, 1851
      - ◆ First International, 1864
      - ◆ Combinations legal in France, 1864
        - ◆ Second Reform Act in Britain, 1867
          - ◆ Paris Commune, 1870
            - ◆ Bismarck introduces social welfare for workers in Germany, 1883–89
            - ◆ Third Reform Act in Britain, 1884
              - ◆ Second International, 1889

Beyond the West

Qing Dynasty, China, 1644–1912

British East India Company dominent in India, 1690–1857

Direct British Rule in India, 1858–1947

Japan industrializes, 1870–1918

- ◆ Shaka leads Zulu nation, Africa, 1817
  - ◆ First Opium War, 1839–42
    - ◆ US Commodore Perry "opens" Japan, 1853
    - ◆ Mughal Empire in India ends, 1857
      - ◆ French gain control of Indochina, 1858
        - ◆ Meiji Restoration, Japan, 1868
        - ◆ Suez canal opens, 1869
          - ◆ "Scramble for Africa" begins, 1885

CHAPTER 22

LIVES OF THE OTHER HALF

Western Society in an Industrial Age

1750–1914

population density:

- under 50 per square mile
- 50-100 per square mile
- 100-200 per square mile
- over 200 per square mile
- ■ cities with a population of over 1 million

KEY TOPICS

◆ **Workers and Workplace:** Industrial workers laboring in the mill, mine, and factory under new and harsh conditions learn to unite as a social group and an economic force.

◆ **The Industrial City:** Burgeoning cities develop new structures and infrastructures as migrants arrive to work in factories and workshops, throng cafés and beerhalls, and spill out onto the streets.

◆ **The Two Halves at Home:** The divergent worlds of the townhouse and the tenement reflect the great rift between rich and poor in the industrial city; on the one hand, leisure, luxury, the duties of philanthropy, a culture of conformity, and the pursuit of "culture"; on the other hand, hunger, tedium, violence, dirt, disease, and hopelessness.

Domains of Rich and Poor In his 1890 book How The Other Half Lives, *the photojournalist Jacob Riis (1849–1914) revealed to middle-class New Yorkers the unhappy and desperate lives of the laboring poor and the hopelessly poor trapped in the seamier districts of their city. Only a few steps away from prosperity, he wrote, we encounter poverty. "We stand upon the domain of the tenement. … Suppose we look into one?" And so we shall.*

This chapter surveys the lives of rich and poor in nineteenth-century cities transformed by the advent of the machine. It peers into the places where workers labored and the places where they lived. Then it will cross town to visit other neighborhoods, not far away but a world apart, to consider the lives of the rich, whose wealth depended on the labor of those who owned nothing and commanded no one—those of the other half.

In industrial society, the poor were many and various. They were wageworkers who hauled loads and constructed homes, railroad stations, and public buildings; they were skilled **artisans** who tailored men's clothing or made precision tools; they were laundresses, prostitutes, thieves, and the jobless; and they were, most conspicuously, the new social group of **factory** workers, or **proletarians**. All lived together in the squalid streets of bursting cities, where they contended with filth, disease, and crime.

Across town (or sometimes just around the corner), lived the wealthy, not nearly so numerous, yet still various. Among the rich were the modern descendants of the old nobility, and the heirs of the old bourgeoisie—bankers, merchants, and professionals (including lawyers, physicians, engineers, accountants, and university professors). Preeminent among the bourgeoisie was a new group of factory owners, investors, and entrepreneurs: the capitalists, whose enterprises harnessed the power of machines to generate profits that were reinvested to create even more wealth. The rich lived in a world apart from the poor—a world filled with broad boulevards, grand homes, lavish consumption, and elaborate social ritual.

As the machine transformed the landscape of the Western world, it also transformed society, whose two halves in their separate domains, the rich and the poor, now faced each other in a new setting, across new and daunting barriers.

WORKERS AND WORKPLACE

As industrialization proceeded from the late eighteenth into the early nineteenth century (see Chapter 21), the nature of work changed. Machines established the framework of things, and workers obeyed the command of their clatter and roar. Machines transformed people just as they transformed the workplace, creating in the industrial proletariat a self-conscious working class—organized "labor."

Mine, Mill, and Factory

Workers in the mine pit, water-powered mill, and steam-driven factory experienced labor conditions harsher than those that rural workers knew in their villages, cottages, and fields. Workers of all ages and both sexes labored long days, in poor light and bad air, with little time to eat or rest. They were unprotected from dangerous equipment and subject to the peremptory commands and stern punishments of foremen or owners. Passages in *Witnesses* on p. 641 give an insight into the lives of factory workers.

The underground universe of the mine had always been a place of horror for those who probed the earth's recesses for tin and copper, gold and silver, iron and coal. In antiquity, slaves were employed to work the mines—an expendable workforce who could be subjected to heavy loads, noxious gases, and frequent cave-ins and explosions. The same risks attended mining in the early modern era, when heightened demand for iron and coal required deeper pits and more intensive production. These risks were often borne by the most fragile workers. Children, for example, were assigned to haul goods from the deepest mine tunnels because their slight bodies could adapt to the cramped underground spaces. Conditions in the mines only deteriorated as industrialization progressed and demand for their products increased.

Meanwhile, in the mills, rows of large machines wound newspun yarn on multiple spindles. Little was expected of their human operators, who were there to provide fresh raw fiber, realign yarn that had wandered or snapped, and keep up with the relentless pace of the machine. The machines themselves did the work, without artistry perhaps, but also without fatigue.

The relation between the worker and his work—more often her work in the early days of the mill—changed drastically. Previously a woman alone would spin all that was required for her family. Equipped with the simple distaff or spindle, she worked at home, amid childcare and household duties, assisted by unmarried female kin and neighbors. Her husband or some other local artisan would weave the thread into cloth in his cottage or workshop. In the proto-industrial "putting-out" system (see Chapter 16)—also called "domestic" or "cottage industry"—both spinning and weaving were performed on contract for production beyond household needs. The entrepreneur and his agents managed supplies, assigned fees, and collected profits, but left the village environment and the social world of the cottage unaltered.

With the advent of the mill, the cottage workers—men, women, and children—journeyed from the village to the river's edge. There they worked under the formal direction of an overseer and at the pace set by the machine. Just as, for centuries, many of the textile workers had been women, women were numerous among the employees of the mills. And just as their children had assisted with simpler tasks at home—washing, carrying, sorting—they, too, joined the labor force in the mill. The first generations of industrial workers consisted of all the members of the pre-industrial family, as yet unaltered by the requirements of modern industrial processes.

When the mills expanded to become factories—buildings containing many machines—the machine became a tyrant. Huge, belching, raucous steam engines, fed with mountains of coal by laborers' shovels, powered the machines which could be multiplied to the limit of the factory's power capacity. The workforce expanded to meet the demands of the machines. Battalions of workers streamed into the factories at a set hour, announced by the clocks and bells and whistles that governed precious industrial time.

Strict rules enforced by a system of fines and punishments disciplined this large and potentially restive labor force. Workers were required to report to work and depart at certain set hours. They were to avoid surly or aggressive behavior, keep their own workplace clean, and meet a work schedule. Corporal punishment, especially of children, kept the tired or the resistant properly at work, with summary dismissal as a final sanction. These oppressive regulations kept

WITNESSES

The Factory Observed

The first generations of factory labor were the harshest, as owners drove workers ruthlessly, and brought in women and young children to work under the most arduous conditions. Defenders of industry, like the author of the first excerpt given here, were not troubled by these conditions. The next two authors give the other, more accurate, view of the conditions of factory labor.

Andrew Ure, defender of industrialization, gives high marks to factory conditions for child laborers (1835): I have visited many factories ... entering the spinning rooms, unexpectedly, and often alone, at different times of the day, and I never saw a single instance of corporal chastisement inflicted on a child, nor indeed did I ever see children in ill-humour. They seemed to be always cheerful and alert, taking pleasure in the light play of their muscles,—enjoying the mobility natural to their age. ... It was delightful to observe the nimbleness with which they pieced the broken ends, as the mule-carriage began to recede from the fixed roller-beam. ... The work of these lively elves seemed to resemble a sport. ... As to exhaustion by the day's work, they evinced no trace of it on emerging from the mill in the evening; for they immediately began to skip about any neighboring playground, and to commence their little amusements with the same alacrity as boys issuing from a school.
(Andrew Ure, *The Philosophy of Manufactures*, 1835; eds. G. B. Kirsch et al, *ibid*, 1997)

P. Gaskell describes the appearance of English factory workers in 1833: Any man who has stood at twelve o'clock at the single narrow door-way, which serves as the place of exit for the hands employed in the great cotton-mills, must acknowledge, that an uglier set of men and women, of boys and girls, ... it would be impossible to congregate in a smaller compass. Their complexion is sallow and pallid—with a peculiar flatness of feature, caused by the want of a proper quantity of adipose substance to cushion out the cheeks. Their stature low—the average height of four hundred men, measured at different times, and different places, being five feet six inches. Their limbs slender, and playing badly and ungracefully. A very general bowing of the legs. Great numbers of girls and women walking lamely or awkwardly. ... Hair thin and straight—many of the men having but little beard, and that in patches of a few hairs. ... A spiritless and dejected air... .
(From P. Gaskell, *The Manufacturing Population of England*, London: Baldwin & Cradock, 1833
http://landow.stg.brown.edu/victorian/history/workers2.html)

Flora Tristan reports on conditions in English factories (1842): Most workers lack clothing, bed, furniture, fuel, wholesome food—even potatoes! They spend from twelve to fourteen hours each day shut up in low-ceilinged rooms where with every breath of foul air they absorb fibres of cotton, wool or flax, or particles of copper, lead or iron. They live suspended between an insufficiency of food and an excess of strong drink; they are all wizened, sickly and emaciated; their bodies are thin and frail, their limbs feeble, their complexions pale, their eyes dead. ... In English factories ... you will never hear snatches of song, conversation and laughter. The master does not like his workers to be distracted from their toil for one moment by any reminder they are living human beings; he insists on silence, and a deathly silence reigns. ... Between master and man there exist [no] ... bonds of familiarity, courtesy and concern ... bonds which soften the feelings of hatred and envy that the rich, with their disdain and harshness, their excessive demands and their love of luxury, always rouse in the hearts of the poor.
(*The London Journal of Flora Tristan*, 1842; ed. J. Hawkes, 1982)

workers in line although noise was deafening and light dim, meals swift and cheerless, and the machinery hazardous. Many workers lost fingers or limbs in the machinery, unshielded, unregulated by any law.

Even labor under these conditions, however, was preferable to the alternative—no work at all. Business cycles were volatile during the early expansion of factories. Workers often found themselves unemployed because of overproduction, when warehouses were full, or simply because of seasonal shifts in demand. As industrialization progressed, some craftsmen found their products, and their skills, became obsolete. Such was the fate of the English handloom weavers, who for a few brief decades had made out handsomely by processing into cloth the huge product of mechanized spinning jennies. Between 1805 and 1833 their wages fell by seventy-five percent.

Women and Children   Factories employed women and children well into the industrial era, an inheritance from the system of mill or cottage textile production. Owners found women to be useful employees on many counts. Women workers were strong enough to manage most machines, and offered little resistance to the demands of the workplace. They were cheap as well, earning as little as one-half a man's salary. During the early years of industrialization, they made up as much as one-third of the workforce. Yet in Britain, at least, women's factory labor was gradually curtailed. Legislation of the 1830s and 1840s limited their workday (and prohibited their employment in mines). After the mid-nineteenth century, British factory workers were overwhelmingly male. Women's labor did not end, however, but was transformed. In their homes, in the homes of others, and on the streets of the city, for lower pay and with lower status, they performed non-factory work.

The labor of children (technically those under age twenty, but in practice as young as eight or nine) was also essential in the early years of industrialization. One British historian has judged their exploitation "one of the most shameful events" of his nation's history, while a French scholar has termed it not only the exploitation but "martyrdom" of the young. Many children entered the factories alongside their parents, or at their bidding. Owners also procured child workers *en masse* by contracting with local orphanages and poorhouses. Children could be given simple jobs, such as sweeping or loading and switching bobbins of yarn. Their labor, like that of their mothers and older sisters, was cheap—a child earned about one-fourth the wage of an adult male. Like women, they were pliable and obedient to the commands of the foreman. If resistant, they could be physically punished, as children regularly were at home. Such abuse was only one aspect of their exploitation. The long hours of work, the lack of exercise, the absence of instruction and access to the open air, led to permanent physical and mental injury. The experiences of some children are narrated in *Witnesses* on p. 644.

Child labor was not officially or generally repudiated in the Western world until the twentieth century. It was, however, gradually restricted, at first in Britain and France. In 1833, the British Factory Act set a maximum of a nine-hour workday for children under thirteen. In 1847, further legislation reduced the workday of women and older children to ten and a half hours. In 1842, the Mines Act prohibited work for women and girls underground, as well as boys under ten. In France, where the state had never before intervened in employers' relations with their workers, a child labor law passed in 1841 banned factory work for children under eight, and limited the workday to eight and twelve hours respectively for children under and over age thirteen. Yet in Britain (as elsewhere), child labor remained an important component of the workforce as late as 1874, when fourteen percent of textile workers were children, and even 1900, when thousands of children under fourteen labored in mines and factories.

Children were not the only martyrs to industrialization. Workers throughout Europe suffered, especially in the early development of the iron and textiles production that made Europe the wealthiest region in the world. In the end, however, workers, too, benefited. They began to do so when they learned to join together to form organizations that could extract from a booming economy some fair share of the wealth that their labor helped generate.

The Birth of Labor

With industrialization, it became possible to produce and sell more goods. It was capitalism that made that potential actual. Capitalism is an economic system resting on the pre-industrial commercial achievements of European merchants, and theorized by Adam Smith in his embrace of market systems of supply and demand and his rejection of the state-managed economics of mercantilism (see Chapters 11, 16). In a capitalist system, entrepreneurs are free to invest their money, or capital, to acquire machines and factories (the astonishing capacity of which had only recently become a reality) and thereby to seek maximal profits with minimal government intervention. Proponents of capitalism argue that the great productivity achieved, and enormous profits gained, ultimately benefit every member of a society through an absolute increase in the amount of wealth, greater economic opportunity, increased availability of consumer products, and higher standards of living.

With industrialization, organized by capitalism, the history of the "working class" truly begins. Laborers began to think of themselves as a collective entity—as **labor** as opposed to "capital," the factory owners and entrepreneurs. They formed collective

Men and Work

Käthe Kollwitz, drawing from the series **A Weavers' Uprising,** *1897*

If the Industrial Revolution is the age of the voracious entrepreneur, it is also the age of the working man, the era when the "working class" took form—even though men, and women, had always worked throughout human history. The characteristic form of industrial labor was in the factory; yet factory labor was only one part of the story of work in an industrial age. Above, a group of determined weavers (whose artisan wages and conditions suffered from competition with factory machinery), their bodies expressive of the harsh conditions under which they lived, go out on strike in 1897, while at right, in 1895, three men with hand tools build the streets whose construction and repair was ceaseless in an era of exploding urbanization. Below right, workers at the Krupp plant in Essen, Germany, are seen tending to "Fritz," an enormous steam hammer originally invented in Britain. (top: Käthe-Kollwitz Museum, Berlin; center: Punch Magazine)

This illustration from Punch magazine shows road construction workers, 1895

Workers at the Krupp plant, Germany, 1903

 To continue your investigation of this topic, please go to www.prenhall.com/king for the related **WINDOWS** on the **WEB** activity

643

organizations to provide mutual support and to press for greater concessions from their employers. Eventually, **trade unions** gained the right to bargain collectively with their employers. Sometimes they used the device of the **strike**, withholding their labor in order to compel owners to accede to their demands. Trade unions worked toward two principal goals: to secure both better working conditions and higher living standards for their members. By 1900, industrial workers and their families lived significantly better than they did in 1800.

Early Labor Associations   The formation of modern trade unions was a complex process involving several intermediate steps. First, associations of skilled artisans formed to fill the vacuum left by the waning of the medieval guilds (see Chapter 11), which by the late eighteenth century were under pressure, especially in Britain and France, for their resistance to the mechanisms of the **free market**. A system driven by supply and demand, contrary to the ideals of the guild, might threaten product quality (which had been carefully specified) or allow profits to exceed

WITNESSES

Workers' Lives

These excerpts provide glimpses into the varied work lives, always difficult, of a range of laborers—an English boy who was both farm laborer and textile worker; Irish laborers hauling heavy sacks of goods in the dockyards; an English girl mineworker; a German girl who worked at carding and spinning; the servants in a French household, as described in a housekeeping manual.

A Yorkshire Chartist recalls his boyhood and youth experiences during the 1820s–1840s: Tom Brown's Schooldays would have had no charm for me, as I had never been to a day school in my life; when very young I had to begin working, and was pulled out of bed between 4 and 5 o'clock … in summer time to go … take part in milking a number of cows. … I went to a card shop [i.e., textile workshop] afterwards, and there had to set 1500 card teeth for a ½d. … I have been a woollen weaver, a comber, a navvy on the railway, and a [quarryman] … [and so] I claim to know some little of the state of the working classes.
(B. Wilson, *The Struggles of an Old Chartist*, 1887; ed. E. P. Thompson, 1964)

Irish stevedores unload sacks of oats at the Liverpool docks (1830s): These men … received the ful sacks as they were lowered by the crane off the hitch on their shoulders and carried them across the road. They pursued their heavy task during the working hours of a summer's day at a uniform, unremitting pace, a trot of at least five miles an hour, the distance from the vessel to the storehouse being full fifty yards. … At this work a good labourer earned, at 16d. per 100 sacks, ten shillings a day; so that consequently he made seven hundred and fifty trips … thus performing a distance of … forty-three miles.
(Sir G. Head, *A Home Tour of Great Britain*, 1835; ed. E. P. Thompson, 1964)

Seventeen-year-old Patience Kershaw describes her work in the coal mines to a parliamentary committee of inquiry (1842): My father has been dead about a year; my mother is living and has ten children … three lasses go to mill; all the lads are colliers [i.e., coal mine workers]. … I never went to day-school; I go to Sunday-school, but I cannot read or write; I go to pit at five

o'clock in the morning and come out at five in the evening; I get my breakfast of porridge and milk first; I take my dinner with me, a cake [a plain oatcake], and I eat as I go; I do not stop or rest any time for the purpose; I get nothing else until I get home, and then have potatoes and meat, not every day meat. I [work] in the clothes I have now got on, trousers and ragged jacket … sometimes they [the male workers] beat me, if I am not quick enough, with their hands; they strike upon my back; the boys take liberties with me … I am the only girl in the pit; there are about 20 boys and 15 men; all the men are naked; I would rather work in the mill than in coal-pit.
(Evidence given before Lord Ashley's Mines Commission, 1842; eds. G. B. Kirsch et al, 1997)

German socialist Luise Zietz (1865–1922) recalls her childhood in the 1870s: We had to pluck apart and oil the raw wool, to run it through the "wolf," which compressed it further, then it had to be put through the carding machine two times. A pair of dogs, who switched off, drove this machine by a large treadwheel, and when one of the large dogs died on us, we ourselves had to get down in the wheel. … Spinning was a terrible torture for us children. We crouched hour after hour on the low stool behind the spinning wheel at the horrible monotonous and exhausting work, just spinning, spinning, spinning.
(From B. S. Anderson and J. P. Zinsser, *A History of their Own: Women in Europe from Prehistory to the Present*, Vol. 2, 1988)

A French housekeeping manual describes the female servant's duties (1896): The maid of all work should get up at six, fix her hair, get herself ready, and not come down to the kitchen without being ready to go out to the market. From 6 to 9 o'clock, she has the time to do many things. She will light the furnace and the fires or get the stove going. She will prepare the breakfasts, do the dining room, brush the clothes and clean the shoes. When the masters arise, she will do their rooms, will put water in the water closets, carry up wood or coal, and carry down the excrement. For all these tasks, she will put on oversleeves and a white apron and take care to wash her hands. Then, … the dining room is restored to order, the tableware washed and put away, the cooking utensils cleaned.
(From B. S. Anderson and J. P. Zinsser, *ibid*)

what an older generation considered "just" (i.e. based on the cost of materials and labor rather than on the highest price obtainable in an open market). Guilds fought to retain their influence in many regions, but failed to do so in the wealthier nations. In Britain their power had faded by the late eighteenth century. In France, they fell victim to the Revolution, which tolerated no limitations on urban workers in the archaic name of quality.

Nevertheless, in the absence of any form of state welfare, workers still needed the protections the guilds had provided. The associations that emerged provided services to skilled artisans and their families, called "combinations," aroused alarm in the authorities. The British Combination Acts of 1799–1800 were intended to suppress them, while laws passed during the Revolution (1791) and under Napoleon outlawed them in France. Although these prohibitions were repealed in 1824 and 1864 respectively, workers' combinations continued to be suspect.

Skilled artisans often joined with their fellows to resist the mechanization of their trades. In Britain, France, and the German lands, such workers rioted. The English Luddites, textile-workers who rallied under the name of the (probably mythical) leader Ned Ludd, expressed their rage in 1811–1812 by smashing the machines that aimed to replace them. In 1831 and 1834 in the French city of Lyons, where thirty percent of the nation's exports were manufactured, journeymen weavers rose up against workshop owners (see *Windows On*, p. 643). During the same decade, the tailors of Paris, finding their incomes plunging as factory production undercut opportunities, took revenge on the machinery that threatened their economic status. In Prussian Silesia, linen-weavers rioted in 1844 against a factory-type system that threatened to turn high-skilled artisans into mere laborers.

Throughout the nineteenth century, the plight of the skilled artisan remained perilous. Tailors, shoemakers, and cabinetmakers figured among the leaders of revolutionary episodes and organizations—most conspicuously in Paris during the revolutions of 1830, 1848, and 1871 (see Chapter 20). It was precisely their kind of labor that was most threatened by competition from the factories that spewed out cheap goods at low prices.

Such outbreaks of violence fueled government determination to suppress workers' associations. At the same time, they prefigured the strikes of a more ordered labor movement that began to emerge around the mid-nineteenth century in Britain. There some groups of highly-skilled workers formed a new type of professional craft association, exemplified by the Amalgamated Society of Engineers, founded in 1851. A national organization supported by members' dues, it offered health benefits and unemployment protection, as well as a platform from which to negotiate for economic and political benefits. Such early trade unions sprang from the craft workshop tradition and not from the "Satanic mills" where unskilled workers still labored without any associations that could offer mutual consolation and assistance.

Skilled workers held high prestige and could command good wages (although these were still only a small fraction—one-third or one-fourth—of the income of a member of the bourgeoisie). Such privileges raised them well above the condition of the semi-skilled and unskilled workers whose numbers ballooned with the expansion of factory production, who earned only two-thirds or one-half as much. It is these new workers (called "proletarians" after the underclass of Roman citizens who were considered to serve the state only by reproducing and peopling the Republic) whose oppressed condition led to the formation of the modern labor movement.

The Proletariat   The condition of the proletarians, or proletariat, appeared permanent and inescapable. Not only did these workers labor long hours, in appalling conditions, for barely a subsistence wage, but they could aspire to little better. Moreover, they had no higher aspirations for their children, whom they generally introduced to the same form of employment. In the absence of any encouragement from employers or the state, and in the absence of a system of mass education, few workers expected their children to achieve greater wealth or status than they themselves possessed. It is unlikely that more than an exceptional few even pondered the possibility.

There were an exceptional few, however, who sought to improve their own understanding of the world to assist their advancement. They joined self-help movements, or attended voluntary lectures on science, business, and the arts, that offered a random but still advanced education. While working in his family's cotton mill in Manchester, the German industrialist and later **Communist** Friedrich Engels (1820–1895) was impressed by the popularity of such lectures, commenting in 1844, "I have sometimes come across workers, with their fustian jackets falling apart, who are better informed on geology, astronomy and other matters than many an educated member of the middle classes in Germany."

The workers who found their way to evening lectures on geology were greatly outnumbered by those who sought out taverns for relaxation or who returned to their beds to rest, after sixteen hours of labor. But even this more numerous group began, in the early years of industrialization, to seek each other out for solidarity, the necessary first step in the building of the labor movement. From the 1760s onward, they formed voluntary groups, variously called "friendly" or "mutual aid" or "cooperative" societies.

In the early nineteenth century, when such associations of workers were closely scrutinized by authorities, their objectives were limited. Funded by members' dues, they offered loans, unemployment and death benefits, and assistance to orphans. They established cooperative stores, where goods could be purchased at close to their wholesale cost, enabling working families to stretch their slight wages. By 1803, about 9600 friendly societies in Britain boasted over 700,000 members. By 1851, such organizations had founded 130 cooperative stores. The movement spread to the continent. By the mid-nineteenth century, cooperative banks sprang up in the German lands, with one in nearly every city by century's end. In France several thousand friendly societies enrolled about 800,000 workers by 1870, who constituted approximately thirteen percent of the workforce.

Utopia and Reform The originators of **socialism** (see Chapter 24), joined by some sympathetic entrepreneurs, encouraged worker cooperation. Early socialist thinkers envisioned a future society where workers lived in dignity, harvesting the wealth that workshops and factories produced with their labor and sharing equally in those profits. Families would live and work together and children would be educated. The patriarchal strictures that bound traditional families—requiring female chastity and obedience—could be abolished or at least modified. Relationships between men and women could be founded in love, not necessity. Women would enjoy the same sexual freedoms that men had always claimed. The state itself would be altered. Engineers and scientists might take the lead, qualified for the undertaking by competence rather than social origin. They would displace traditional leaders chosen from members of noble or bourgeois elites.

While most such **utopian** societies remained merely theoretical, some visionaries attempted to give them reality. In Britain, the successful self-made industrialist Robert Owen (1771–1858), an artisan's son, devoted much of his career to bettering the condition of the worker. Owen had prospered in cotton manufacture in the last decade of the eighteenth century, turning a £100 investment into a huge fortune (see Chapter 21). In 1800, struck by the miserable living and working conditions of his textile workers, he moved his operation from Manchester, England's greatest boom town, to New Lanark, near Glasgow, Scotland. There he established not merely a factory but an entire community, including housing, cooperative stores, a sewage system, schools for workers' children, and a humane workplace. The whole experiment, eagerly viewed by European industrial experts and visitors, embodied a new moral code based on cooperation, rather than competition.

In the 1820s, Owen journeyed to North America, to launch new cooperative ventures in an unfinished country where anything might be possible. He established an experimental community of New Harmony in the state of Indiana, where agricultural and

WHO'S WHO

Chroniclers and Builders of the Industrial Age

Jeremy Bentham (1748–1832) English political theorist, proponent of "Utilitarianism," and designer of the model prison, the "Panopticon."

Edwin Chadwick (1800–1890) disciple of Jeremy Bentham; promoted the building of systems for the delivery of water and the removal of sewage in his 1842 *Report on the Sanitary Condition of the Labouring Population of Great Britain.*

Robert Owen (1771–1858) self-made English entrepreneur, factory owner, experimentalist in utopian community building, and founder of the Grand National Consolidated Trades Union.

Louis Blanc (1811–1882) French socialist theorist and proponent of "national workshops" that would provide unemployed laborers with work and a decent wage.

Karl Marx (1818–1883) German-born intellectual; author, in collaboration with Friedrich Engels, of the *Communist Manifesto*; creator of modern socialist theory and progenitor of all modern communist systems.

Friedrich Engels (1820–1895) German industrialist and later communist; author of a classic study of life in British Manchester during a period of rapid industrialization.

Georges Haussmann (1809–1891) pioneer urban designer and adviser to French emperor Napoleon III; recreated Paris by razing its old structures to make way for a planned system of streets and monumental buildings.

Josephine Butler (1828–1906) British philanthropist and feminist; battled for the repeal of the Contagious Diseases Act of 1864 (mandating the medical supervision of prostitutes).

Jacob Riis (1849–1914) Danish-born crime reporter turned photojournalist; chronicler of how "the other half" lived in New York City during the industrial age.

industrial workers came together to form a self-sufficient society. It later disintegrated, but by then Owen had moved on to other things.

After his return from the United States, Owen organized a mass workers' movement in 1834: the Grand National Consolidated Trades Union. This was meant to be a single organization that would unite all workers in the country, who would therefore wield the irresistible negotiating weapon of a general strike. Owen's aim was not merely to improve

Socialist idealism

workers' pay and conditions, but also to influence the political process. His initiatives should be seen in the context of the politicization of labor (see below), that progressed as the century aged.

Owen's giant union soon collapsed, as had his perfect communities, and those of other designers of utopias. A new generation of social critics put utopianism aside and focused more concretely on solving immediate problems such as low wages and unemployment. In France, the socialist theorist Louis Blanc (1811–1882) proposed the creation of "national workshops." These would be funded by a benevolent state that guaranteed workers the right to work and a decent wage immune to the pressures of competition. The republican government formed in early 1848 committed huge sums to subsidize such workshops, intended to absorb workers unable to find employment elsewhere. They proved immensely popular, and their dissolution a few months later was one trigger of the workers' revolt and the suppression of the June Days (see Chapter 20).

In June, French workers' concerns turned from economic to political aims. Embittered by the closing of the national workshops, they exploded with antigovernment feeling, setting up street barricades in the time-honored fashion of French revolutionaries. This uprising was suppressed with excessive violence in which 4000 died. That outbreak was a major episode in the political history of workers' movements, but it was not the only one. Throughout industrialized Europe, urbanized, unskilled workers constituted a huge and potentially volatile part of the population. Wherever their demands became assertive, the possibility of political revolution loomed.

Well before the uprisings that took place in France, Germany, and elsewhere in 1848 (see Chapter 20), British workers had joined middle-class reformers to agitate for the Reform Act of 1832 (which broadened the franchise to middle-class men and made electoral reforms) and the Factory Act of 1833 and subsequent workplace legislation. They opposed the Corn Laws, which protected high-cost, local grain against cheaper imports, to the disadvantage of the poor—their opposition peaking in the notorious "Peterloo Massacre" (named for St. Peter's Field, Manchester, and the battle of Waterloo) of 1819 when mounted soldiers charged on a mass meeting. Workers also opposed the 1834 Poor Law Amendment Act, which withdrew support for unemployed able-bodied adults unless they were employed in state-run workhouses.

From 1838 to 1848, a movement to petition Parliament to pass a "People's Charter" harnessed workers' aspirations, which they determined to pursue "Peaceably if we may, forcibly if we must." Drafted by the London Working Men's Association, the Charter contained six points that were sure to alarm lawmakers. In addition to petitioning for electoral reform, these included a call for universal manhood suffrage. Presented to Parliament and rejected in 1839, again in 1842, and a final time in 1848, the Charter represented the heroic attempt of British workers to gain political objectives. Though it failed, those who participated in the Chartist movement had gained valuable practical experience of the political process.

Workers in the industrializing nations of continental Europe learned that same lesson later in the century, as the utopian socialism of its early decades gave way to an urgent, militant socialism in its latter half. Workers leaned to a variety of **"social democratic"** political parties, which proposed to win benefits for their supporters by gaining majorities in representative assemblies. Some joined the Communists, a group of socialists to whom a mission and a program were provided by the German intellectuals Friedrich Engels and Karl Marx (1818–1883) in their *Communist Manifesto* of 1848 (see Chapter 25). Both analytical and inspiring, the brief *Manifesto* is one of the key monuments of modern politics. It marks the moment when the possibility was first voiced of a complete reversal of the social order. Workers should throw off the chains that bind them by abolishing private property, eliminating the capitalist bourgeoisie, and taking control of both the factories and the state. These ideals animated the Communist League established in London in 1847, and subsequently the much larger International Workingmen's Association, or "First International," in 1864, and the "Second International" in 1889.

Even more threatening than the Communists to established elites were the French syndicalists and Russian anarchists. The former urged that workers gain their ends through coordinated, violent strikes against the state. The latter urged the annihilation of the state itself, which they saw as inherently alien to human welfare. In autocratic Russia, and in France where workers' revolts had twice been bloodily suppressed, syndicalism and anarchism won followers. But in Britain and other industrializing nations, trade unions were the primary institutions upon which workers relied in their quest for betterment.

Trade Unions Trade unions can be distinguished from both the "friendly societies" and utopian communities. They are workers' organizations whose main goal is to negotiate with employers for wage and workplace improvements. Trade unions continued to provide the kinds of benefits that mutual aid societies had offered, but they also attempted to deal with the managers and owners of large enterprises in negotiations known as **collective bargaining**. While capitalist entrepreneurs resisted the formation of trade unions, the trade union movement encouraged an orderly approach to workers' rights and pay, in contrast to outbreaks of riot and revolution that had

The Matchgirls' Union on strike, 1888

The Industrial Revolution created a variety of working environments for women. For much of the nineteenth century, women, often of a tender age, provided a major fraction of all industrial workers. They often worked long hours in poor conditions, like the women workers from the matchmaking factory who famously called a strike in 1888 (above). Not all women laborers worked in factories, however. Many were domestic servants, like the ones working in this kitchen (right). Others were pieceworkers, who, seated close to a small stove, sewed garments to be sold by the "piece" (below left).

Women of higher social standing tended not to work. Instead, they remained at home, where their main functions were to provide beauty, grace, and children. They could also go shopping in one of the new department stores, where they participated in a booming economy as consumers rather than laborers. The ribbons gallery of the great French department store, the Bon Marché was a vibrant, inviting space for those who had no need to work (below right).

(above: Hulton Getty; below left: Museum of the City of New York)

Maidservants in the kitchen, 1860s–1870s

Jacob Riis, **Sewing and Starving in an Elizabeth Street Attic,** *c. 1890*

Illustration of the Bon Marché from **Le Monde Illustré,** *c. 1875*

To continue your investigation of this topic, please go to www.prenhall.com/king for the related **WINDOWS** on the **WEB** activity

frightened entrepreneurs and only succeeded in stiffening their resolve to yield little to workers.

Where negotiation failed, trade unions wielded the weapon of the strike. In the early years of the labor movement, strikes were often violently suppressed, but by the late nineteenth century, they had matured to become a practical tool in the mission of organized labor to wrest from employers some of the wealth that their members' labors had generated.

The earliest trade unions formed in Britain soon after the repeal of the Combination Laws. Thus the National Union of Cotton Spinners was organized in 1829, the National Association for the Protection of Labor in 1830, and Owen's Grand National Consolidated Trades Union in 1834. But they soon collapsed, and from the later 1830s to 1848, the goals of Chartism took over from unionization. In the mid-century, skilled workers recruited from the artisan classes began to form crafts associations. After 1875, when the tactics of collective bargaining were finally recognized as legal, trade unions expanded in earnest. Their ranks were filled by unskilled and semi-skilled workers who were persuaded by such examples as the successful strikes of the London dockworkers in 1889, or the London match girls in 1888. By 1900, a century and a half after the beginnings of industrialization, membership in British trade unions had risen to over 2 million workers.

In Germany, too, union membership climbed from the 1860s to about 2 million around 1900, although the chancellor Otto von Bismarck (1815–1898) had tried to suppress the tactic of the strike. Here union members often supported the Social Democratic party, with a socialist, but not communist agenda, which militantly advocated workers' interests. In France, in the 1860s a nascent trade movement succumbed to the general repression following the 1871 Paris Commune (see Chapter 20). Driven underground, French unions or *syndicats* tended toward the violent solutions of syndicalism.

By the last two decades of the nineteenth century, workers had made considerable progress. Their standard of living had begun to rise. They now had more food and better food to eat than their fathers and grandfathers. Their wages were sufficient to purchase necessities and even to allow a small surplus for entertainment and brief vacations. If they suffered unemployment, or faced a strike, their trade union could assist with funds. They could not entirely put behind them the fear of want, nor had they yet attained the dignity that solid and regular pay afforded, but real gains had been made.

In the 1880s, the newly constituted state of Germany led the way to a new stage in the relations between workers and society. Bismarck instituted government insurance programs that would protect workers in the events of illness and disability, unemployment and old age. After 1900, Britain, France, the United States, and most other Western nations in turn instituted similar measures. Why was Bismarck, of all leaders the least indulgent to workers' petitions, the one to initiate a program of social insurance? He sought to lessen the momentum of social democracy by assuaging the workers with popular programs. Thus appeased, they might ignore calls for militant action against the state.

The modern working class suffered much in the formative stages of industrialization. Yet it achieved much before the end of the nineteenth century. Its members experimented with self-help groups and shopping cooperatives, utopian communes, riot and strike, with political initiatives and with collective bargaining. By 1900, although most still struggled to feed themselves and their families, the workers of the Western world had improved their standard of living beyond that achieved by any laborers of past ages.

THE INDUSTRIAL CITY

Cities had long been centrally important to the development of the European economy (see Chapters 11, 18). In the late eighteenth century, as population spurted as a result of improvements in agriculture, cities swelled prodigiously, as the table on p. 650 shows. Their populations approached and even (in the case of London) exceeded the 1 million mark that separates modern from pre-modern urban centers in the West. These already swollen cities, some of which became industrial centers after 1800, and others of which were major commercial centers, experienced an influx of workers that pushed population levels to several millions—exceeding those of any concentration of human beings previously known to have existed on the face of the globe. The table on p. 651 shows the changes in some major industrial nations.

As city populations exploded, urban structures and networks were transformed. The old, jumbled buildings and narrow, winding streets became overcrowded. As overcrowding fostered the spread of disease, the city developed systems of water supply and sewage removal. Streetcars moved people quickly across town, electric lighting made nighttime activities possible, and professional police and fire forces provided security. Neighborhoods developed distinctive personalities. Elegant boulevards designed by urban planners sliced through the districts where the wealthy resided. Narrow streets and alleyways, which the planners left untouched, snaked through the districts of the poor. These were an ideal setting for criminals and prostitutes—"streetwalkers"—who considered them their own. Whether they dwelled on mean streets or ample boulevards, city dwellers were prone to the **alienation** that haunted urban life, where the multiple goings and comings of many meant for some the atomization of humanity and the reduction of the human spirit.

Boom Towns

Already in the early modern era, streams of people flowed from the country to the city where jobs might be found. With the arrival of the factory, the din of the steam engines, the whirr of machinery, beckoned new throngs of migrants. The big cities which had reached nearly 1 million in 1800, reached several million by 1900, as shown in the table below.

The first nation to industrialize, Britain offers ample evidence of spectacular rates of urban growth. In 1750, Britain had only two cities with populations over 50,000. A century later, there were twenty-nine. The ten largest cities all at least doubled in the first half of the nineteenth century, with those centered in the new manufacturing regions near coalfields and seaports growing fastest. Leeds and Birmingham more than tripled; Manchester, Liverpool, and Glasgow more than quadrupled.

Manchester alone, nearly one-third of whose residents were engaged in the mechanized production of cotton cloth, doubled between 1801 and 1831 (from 70,000 to 142,000), then more than doubled again (to 409,000) over the next twenty years. Like "an industrious spider," as a contemporary remarked, from its center Manchester spun a web of roads and railways reaching out to swelling towns from where it received supplies and workers. Engels' description of Manchester is quoted in *Witnesses* on p. 655. Another commentator marveled: "From this foul drain the greatest stream of human industry flows out to fertilize the whole world. From this filthy sewer pure gold flows."

Though it did not increase at the pace of the northern manufacturing centers, the population of London increased from about 1 to 5 million by the end of the nineteenth century, when it was home to more than one-sixth of the nation's people. By 1850, more than fifty percent of Britain's population lived in cities; by 1880, more than two-thirds.

Rates of growth outside of Britain were slower but still substantial. Paris nearly doubled between 1800 and 1850, then doubled again over the next thirty years. By 1900, a majority of France's population lived in cities. Berlin (Germany) and St. Petersburg (Russia) doubled in the first half of the nineteenth century, and St. Petersburg then quadrupled, reaching a population of 2 million by 1914. From an 1800 population figure of 170,000, Berlin reached a total of 1.6 million by 1890. Vienna (Austria) increased about eighty percent, while Budapest (Hungary) more than tripled

---

Population of Europe's Largest Cities, 1750–1950

	1750		1850		1950	
Rank	**City**	**Population**	**City**	**Population**	**City**	**Population**
1	London	676,000	London	2,320,000	London	8,860,000
2	Paris	560,000	Paris	1,314,000	Paris	5,900,000
3	Naples	324,000	St. Petersburg	502,000	Moscow	5,100,000
4	Amsterdam	219,000	Berlin	446,000	Ruhr	4,900,000
5	Lisbon	213,000	Vienna	426,000	Berlin	3,707,000
6	Vienna	169,000	Liverpool	422,000	Leningrad	2,700,000
7	Moscow	161,000	Naples	416,000	Manchester	2,382,000
8	Venice	158,000	Manchester	412,000	Birmingham	2,196,000
9	Rome	157,000	Moscow	373,000	Vienna	1,755,000
10	St. Petersburg	138,000	Glasgow	346,000	Rome	1,665,000

European cities grew enormously during the era of incipient and maturing industrialization. Simultaneously, their rank order often shifted. Note in this table the mounting importance of Moscow and St. Petersburg (Leningrad in the third column) and the new British industrial centers of Manchester and Birmingham. As they escalated, traditional centers like Vienna and Rome, although growing respectably, fell to a lower place in the ranking of top ten cities. And three giants of early modern commerce—Lisbon, Venice, and Amsterdam—disappeared entirely from the top ten. London and Paris, whose populations exploded, maintained their top-rank positions.

Source: P. M. Hohenberg and L. H. Lees, The Making of Urban Europe, 1000–1950 (Cambridge, MA: Harvard University Press, 1985; 2nd ed., 1995), p. 227.

Map 22.1 Charles Booth's Poverty Map, 1889: *From 1886 to 1903, the philanthropist and businessman Charles Booth conducted a systematic and scientific survey of the condition of London's poor after three generations of rapid industrialization and urbanization. His famous poverty map of 1889 describes where the poor lived in Victorian London, geographically as they were culturally and economically isolated from the middle- and upper-classes who were at this moment the masters of the world.*

from 287,000 in 1867 to nearly 1 million in 1914. (Elsewhere in east-central Europe, where industrialization had scarcely started, large cities were few and increased only slowly.) The percentage of people living in cities, and the numbers of Europeans overall, both increased, resulting in a growth of urban populations by 1910 to six times their 1800 level.

These increases were achieved, for the most part, not through a growth in the birthrate but through migration to the cities. Only about one-half of those who lived in nineteenth-century London and Paris had been born there. Until the twentieth century, cities did not reproduce themselves. They required constant immigration from the countryside around, continuing on a larger scale a pattern that dated from the Middle Ages, when peasants sought employment and refuge in towns.

Urban migrants were of two sorts: those who came but left, and those who came and stayed. The former worked for a period in the city, then returned to country villages. When they did so, they brought with them the outlook of experienced urbanites, contributing to the increasing connectedness of country folk to city things. The second category of migrants came to

Levels of Urbanization in Leading European Nations (with the United States and Japan), 1800, 1850, 1910

	1800	1850	1910	
Belgium	20	34	57	As industrialization developed, more workers moved to cities. This bar graph shows the increasing percentage of urban-dwellers relative to the whole population in ten countries at three junctures in time. Note Britain's rapid and huge urbanization, by which it surpassed the citified Netherlands within the fifty-year span of its peak industrialization (1800–1850). Belgium, too, leapt forward to take second place in 1910, also ahead of the Netherlands. The level of urbanization in Britain, Belgium, and France approximately tripled in 1800–1910. In Germany, it increased more than fivefold, and in the United States, more than eightfold. In contrast, Italy, Spain, Russia, and Japan—even the Netherlands, despite its initial advantage—are slower to increase their levels of urbanization.
Britain	23	45	75	
France	12	19	38	
Germany	9	15	49	
Italy	18	23	40	
Netherlands	37	39	53	
Russia	6	7	14	
Spain	18	18	38	
US	5	14	42	
Japan	14	15	18	Source: P. Bairoch, Cities and Economic Development: From the Dawn of History to the Present, trs. C. Braider (Chicago: University of Chicago Press, 1988), p. 221

Figures represent approximate percentage of population living in cities

the cities and stayed, driving down (since most migrants were young) the average age of city dwellers. These migrants often joined the armies of the poor: those who labored in workshops and factories, who hauled and lifted and hammered, who cleaned and cooked in the well-kept houses of professionals, merchants, bureaucrats, and nobles.

For not all jobs in the city were factory jobs. Only in the handful of cities, such as Manchester, that were created during the process of industrialization, did industrial workers constitute a majority of workers. In most cities, there was a greater mix of occupations. In London in 1891, for instance, factory workers comprised about thirty-eight percent of all male, and thirty-three percent of all female workers. But servants also constituted a large group, comprising only seven percent of the more numerous male laboring population, but fifty-four percent of female workers. A group of kitchen servants is illustrated in *Windows On* on p. 648. After factory workers, servants (who were mostly female) were the largest occupational group in European cities. By 1900 in Britain, half of all working women worked as servants.

A notable development was the emergence of the category of **"white-collar"** workers, as they were later designated because they wore the clean clothes of the respectable middle classes rather than the heavy, durable blue of those who worked with their hands. They were bank tellers, secretaries in utility and insurance companies, draughtsmen and bookkeepers, tax-collectors and food inspectors, sales clerks in the new department stores and teachers in newly-mandated public schools. Their recruitment to government offices was rapid in the last decades of the century, when state bureaucracies in the advanced countries came close to doubling. Most white-collar workers were men, but women also prospered, especially as teachers, nurses, and sales and office clerks.

Although white-collar workers often aspired to enter the middle classes themselves—and sometimes succeeded—most workers were poor. For them, the **demographic** patterns of urban life were remorseless. The poor were less likely to survive childhood,

and more likely to die young than the wealthy in the cities of nineteenth-century Europe. Although birthrates among the poor were very high, their infants often died, with infant mortality running at up to fifty percent of all births. Toward the end of the nineteenth century, cities became more healthful and these demographic trends improved. Death rates fell, including infant deaths, and life expectancy increased. Meanwhile, although birthrates fell overall due to the increased practice of birth control, out-of-wedlock births rose—a marked characteristic of the modern era. These patterns meant that by around 1900, the city at last reproduced itself. No longer a killer of people, the city had also become the norm, rather than an exception in the social fabric of life in many European countries.

Structure and Infrastructure

Some of the headiest urban growth of the early years of industrialization involved new cities that suddenly developed—as did Manchester—from mere villages. More often, however, the greatly expanded urban areas of the nineteenth century involved a medieval or even ancient city, whose familiar buildings, streets, and walls were inadequate to house the influx of newcomers. The structures and infrastructures of these established cities became greatly strained as populations grew.

Where were people to live? They crowded into the existing building stock, squeezing in unrelated groups into **tenement** rooms. Or they occupied new, cheap housing hastily constructed on city outskirts. In some cities, wageworkers stayed in the city's poor districts in the dilapidated remnants of its older buildings. They doubled up, sharing rooms and facilities with strangers. This was the case in Paris, for example,

On and Under City Streets

Gustave Caillebotte, Rainy Day: *Slum clearance and the creation of wide boulevards offered easier traffic flow and broad urban vistas, though at the expense of the old neighborhoods. Baron Haussmann's program of urban renewal during the 1850s and 1860s transformed Paris from a crowded medieval town to a spacious modern city, shown here in a work from 1876–1877 by the Impressionist painter Caillebotte. (Musée Marmottan, Paris)*

Above and below ground in Paris: *The mid- and late-nineteenth century saw substantial improvements in urban life. The installation of municipal sewage systems greatly improved public health. This contemporary sketch of the Parisian system shows the complex of drains and sewers constructed below street level that gradually extended throughout the entire city, eventually bringing clean water and removing waste in poor as well as privileged neighborhoods.*

where the population increased by twenty-five percent in the period 1817–1827, while housing capacity increased by only ten percent. In other cities, such as Manchester, where there was no ancient building stock into which the poor might flow, entrepreneurs hastily constructed large, cheap, and anonymous buildings on the outskirts of the industrial core. Outside French and German industrial towns straggled rows of company-built, barracks-like houses or high-rise multi-residential buildings.

While poor residents crowded into old buildings, or spilled outward in shapeless, spreading suburbs, the wealthy bourgeoisie and aristocracy also found new housing. They either pushed outward, establishing new neighborhoods beyond the haunts of the poor, or established themselves in elegant enclaves within the city. Among the latter were the areas around the grand boulevards of western Paris, as shown on p. 652. These had been opened up by Baron Georges Haussmann (1809–1891), Napoleon III's adviser and pioneer urban designer, by tearing down the cramped, old housing of workers' districts. (Haussmann's project not only beautified the city, but also helped to control civil unrest by depriving would-be revolutionaries of their defenses and exposing them, when necessary, to gunfire.) Other

such areas were the *Ringstrasse* ("ring street," formed on the pattern of the old walls that had ringed the medieval city) of Vienna, and the streets bordering London's fine parks. These new developments were graced by elegant public buildings—modern museums and hospitals, post offices and monuments.

Until the late nineteenth century, the wealthier urbanites traversed the city by carriage, while workers walked. The absence of affordable transport for the poor meant that they had to live within walking distance of their workplace. This situation changed in the last decades of the century. New forms of transportation including trolley car systems powered by electricity, underground railroads, for example in London (1863), Paris (1900), and New York (1904), and bicycles made it possible for working families to move out to choicer and relatively cheaper suburban areas. By the mid-nineteenth century in major cities, gas lamps lighted the streets (replaced by electrical lamps by the end of the century), so that citizens of all classes could stroll abroad with confidence. By that era as well, running water and sewage lines had begun to challenge that great specter of urban life: infectious disease.

Cholera, spread through contaminated food and water supplies, was the great killer of city dwellers. It arrived in the early 1830s and returned periodically throughout the century. It struck London first in 1832, and then again in 1847, when 53,000 died throughout the nation, of whom 14,000 died in London alone. It visited Paris in 1832 and 1849, striking the poor more viciously than the wealthy. The death statistics revealed the outlines of a pitiless social classification, remarked one horrified observer, in itself "a savage denial of the doctrines of equality" that had supposedly been secured by the sacrifices of the Revolution. From 1892 to 1895, again, cholera took the lives of 300,000 Europeans, the great majority (270,000) Russians.

By that time, the work of Louis Pasteur (1822–1895) had uncovered the bacterial origins of disease (see Chapter 24), and the role of water as a vehicle for bacterial transmission was understood. Social reformers began to rank water supply systems as an issue of prime importance. In Britain, Edwin Chadwick (1800–1890), a disciple of the radical thinker Jeremy Bentham (1748–1832; see Chapter 24), urged the building of systems for the delivery of water and the removal of sewage in his 1842 *Report on the Sanitary Condition of the Labouring Population of Great Britain*. Here he argued that the consequences of disease were "greater or less ... according as there is more or less sufficient drainage of houses, streets, roads, and land, combined with more or less sufficient means of cleansing and removing solid refuse and impurities." According to the guidelines of the Public Health Act passed through Chadwick's advocacy in 1848, Britain built sewage lines, water delivery systems, and reservoirs. After the first cholera epidemic, the French slowly instituted a similar system. By mid-century, only one building in five in Paris received piped water, and sewage systems often served only privileged quarters of the city, leaving workers to use old collective toilets. By 1887, nearly three-quarters of Parisian streets had sewers.

Although cholera was the worst epidemic disease that Europeans faced in the nineteenth century, there were others. Smallpox still killed and destroyed, although vaccination, when used, was effective in controlling it. Venereal disease, whose spread was linked to the prostitution that thrived in cities, was a serious problem. Tuberculosis, which again ravaged the poor and malnourished far more cruelly than the wealthy, was judged responsible for about one-fifth of the deaths in England in 1839. The pollutants that increased mightily with industrialization also contributed to disease and death. These included the dyes and chemicals from shops and factories, as well as the black smoke produced by the coal burned to power the industrial machine.

On the Streets

Crime and Punishment   Meanwhile, other dangers roamed the streets. The concentration of wealth that was essential to city life was an invitation to crime, with the anonymity of urban life allowing predator and prey to coexist. Citizens succumbed to paralyzing fears of a hold-up in the solitary darkness, or a surreptitious and deadly assault. "For the past month," noted a French observer to his correspondent in December, 1843, "the sole topic of conversation has been the nightly assaults, hold-ups, daring robberies … [The assailants] attack rich and poor alike. … At one time the advantage of being poor was that at least you were safe; it is so no longer."

Urban police forces were established, and police records reported mounting instances of assaults on the innocent—if only because their record-keeping methods had become more sophisticated, so that every instance was noted. Newspapers daily reported the crimes of the night before, and devoted much of their space and lurid description to the executions of condemned perpetrators.

Criminals who were not executed were incarcerated or deported. Around 1830 in Paris, about 43,000 people (more than eighty percent male) were shut in prisons, or more than one in every thousand adults. Of these, the majority (seventy-one percent) were guilty of crimes against property. Imprisonment was increasingly the preferred form of punishment, following the influential theories of the Enlightenment theorist Cesare Beccaria (1738–1794). His influential *Essay on Crimes and Punishments* (1764) had heralded the end of torture and routine capital punishment, and his views were taken up by Jeremy Bentham in his proposals for a new form of prison, the "Panopticon" (see below). Deportation to the more remote and deadly colonies (in the Caribbean, North Africa, Australia) was also a commonly imposed penalty in France and Britain.

As the numbers of the imprisoned increased, prison reform initiatives sprang up. Christian activists (especially in Britain and the young United States) urged that the aim of incarceration be redefined as the redemption of the convicted, rather than their mere immobilization. The use of solitary confinement, the requirement of strict silence, the assignment of uniforms, and the imposition of compulsory labor came to characterize prison life. In Jeremy Bentham's Panopticon, constant scrutiny by officials would ensure the proper behavior of the inmates. The name, meaning "a place where all can be seen," suggested a psychological control over deviant behavior that, despite the author's humane intentions, heralded devices of modern totalitarian control.

Though crime was reported more regularly, policed more thoroughly, and punished more effectively, it was no more frequent in urban than it had been in rural settings. It became more terrifying, it seems, merely because the numbers of urban residents meant the multiplication of the fear aroused by malefactors.

The nocturnal voyager along the city's streets, in fact, was more likely to encounter a drunkard or a vagrant than a thief. The consumption of distilled alcohol (gin, vodka, whiskey) became widespread in the nineteenth century, competing with the more familiar beverages of beer and wine. Consumption of these latter favorites also soared—workers disbursed a large fraction of their wages on drink consumed before, during, and after work, while the wealthy considered dining incomplete without a trail of fine vintages. Alcoholism became a serious problem, even among women, previously excluded from the convivial settings of tavern and café where heavy drinking took place. The frustrations of industrial employment or the isolation of urban existence—which Engels remarked upon (see *Witnesses*, p. 655)—may have promoted excessive drinking in both sexes. Conversation accompanied social drinking. An abundance of both sometimes stimulated the formation of political attitudes, especially among workers—to such an extent that, in Paris, the café was deemed "the parliament of the people."

A vagrant or beggar was often only an unemployed drifter. Others belonged to gang-like groups, which sought mutual assistance and occasionally veered into criminal activity. Since the early sixteenth century, vagrancy had been eyed suspiciously by city officials, who often refused to distinguish between thieves and itinerant traders such as peddlers. Selling portable, cheap items, peddlers too had a marginal role in the world of shops, factories, and public spaces that made up the modern city.

Prostitution Walking the streets of the city were also the least fortunate of the prostitutes, whose trade reached a new importance in the nineteenth century. The large modern city had tens of thousands of prostitutes (London, for example, as many as 80,000). These ranged from wealthy, pampered **courtesans** who received their clients in well-furnished apartments, to the occupants of a brothel under the command of a madam or pimp. And they also included the stray, impoverished or part-time, often married, sexworker who picked up clients on the street. Some prostitutes were initiated by their own mothers, often poor and desperate, or prostitutes themselves. Some were forcibly recruited by abduction and rape, or turned to the profession when, as unmarried domestic servants discovered to be pregnant, they were cast out of their employers' homes on to the streets. Some adopted the career freely because it offered higher wages, easier work, and shorter hours than unskilled female wageworkers could otherwise command. Some remained prostitutes for only a brief interlude, before accumulating a dowry and marrying. Others were trapped in the dim underworld where prostitution, crime, and addiction converged.

Friedrich Engels' Portrait of the Industrial City (1844)

Engels' famous descriptions of urban life in an industrial age provided ammunition to those, like his associate Karl Marx, who saw unrestrained capitalism leading to the diminution of the human being, and the creation of a proletariat so hopeless that it would one day rise up and triumph over its exploiters.

Manchester: The view from the bridge—mercifully concealed from smaller mortals by a parapet as high as a man—is quite characteristic of the entire district. At the bottom the Irk flows, or rather stagnates. It is a narrow, coal-black stinking river full of filth and garbage ... out of whose depths bubbles of miasmatic gasses constantly rise and give forth a stench that is unbearable even on the bridge forty or fifty feet above the level of the water. ... Above Ducie Bridge there are tall tannery buildings, and further up are dye-works, bone mills and gasworks. The total entirety of the liquid wastes and solid offscourings of these works finds its way into the River Irk, which receives as well the contents of the adjacent sewers and privies. ... Below Ducie Bridge, on the left, one looks into piles of rubbish, the refuse, filth and decaying matter of the courts on the steep left bank of the river. Here one house is packed very closely upon another, and because of the steep pitch of the bank a part of every house is visible. All of them are blackened with smoke, crumbling, old, with broken window panes and window frames. The background is formed by old factory buildings, which resemble barracks.—On the right, low-lying bank stands a long row of houses and factories. The second house is a roofless ruin, filled with rubble, and the third stands in such a low situation that the ground floor is uninhabitable and is as a result without windows and doors. The background here is formed by the paupers' cemetery and the stations of the railways to Liverpool and Leeds. Behind these is the workhouse, Manchester's "Poor Law Bastille." It is built on a hill, like a citadel, and from behind its high walls and battlements looks down threateningly upon the working-class quarter that lies below.

London: [T]he inhabitants of London have had to sacrifice the best part of their humanity. ... The very bustle and tumult of the streets has something repugnant in it, something that human nature feels outraged by. Hundreds of thousands of people from all classes and ranks of society crowd by each other. Are they not all human beings with the same qualities and faculties: Do they not all have the same interest in being happy? Must they not in the end seek their happiness through the same means and methods? Yet they rush past each other as if they had nothing in common, nothing to do with one another. They are in (tacit) agreement on one thing only—that everyone keep to the right of the pavement so as not to interfere with the crowds that stream in the opposite direction. Meanwhile it occurs to no one that others are worth even a glance. The brutal indifference, the unfeeling isolation of each individual person in his private interest becomes the more repulsive and offensive, the more these individuals are packed into a tiny space. We know well enough that this isolation of the individual—this narrow-minded self-seeking—is everywhere the fundamental principle of modern society. But nowhere is it so shamelessly unconcealed ... as in the tumultuous concourse of the great city. The dissolution of mankind into monads, each of which has a separate purpose, is carried here to its furthest point. It is the world of atoms.

From this it follows that the social war—the war of all against all—has been openly declared. ... Men here regard each other only as useful objects. Each one exploits the other with the result that the stronger tramples the weaker underfoot, and that the few who are strong, the capitalists, seize everything for themselves, while for the many who are weak, the poor, there remains scarcely a bare existence.
(Friedrich Engels, *The Condition of the Working Class in England,* 1844; ed. S. Marcus, 1974)

All prostitutes depended on the demand created by men with money to purchase their services. These men came from all social classes, and, despite the rigid moral and social codes that governed, at least outwardly, the lives of the wealthier classes, their behavior was tolerated throughout most of Europe. Prostitution was considered (with the exception of some reformers) a necessary accommodation to the supposed realities of male sexual life.

If prostitution was tolerated, prostitutes themselves were kept under careful surveillance. As potential carriers of venereal disease, they posed a threat to public health. In many states (in France and Russia, for instance), brothels were frequently inspected by police, and prostitutes, who had to be licensed with the authorities, were examined for disease. (Their male associates, however, who were just as likely to be carriers, were spared the official scrutiny directed toward women sexworkers.)

In 1866–1869, the British parliament inaugurated the medical examination of prostitutes in garrison towns and seaports with the Contagious Diseases Acts, which provided for the isolation of those who proved to have the disease. The determined opposition of Josephine Butler (1828–1906), a clergyman's wife and an early campaigner for women's sexual freedom, led to the law's repeal in 1886. Still in Britain as elsewhere, the tendency was to isolate brothels to special "red light" districts where middle-class men would not willingly go.

The Problem of Poverty   The high incidence of prostitution, like that of crime and vagrancy, mirrored the existence of widespread poverty (there is a poverty map of London on p. 651). Urban poverty took on new dimensions in the bloated industrial cities, putting many individuals at risk of incarceration, violence, and abandonment, and inviting new sets of social attitudes and social policy. Before 1800, poverty was the concern of the churches or of small local agencies of government. By 1900, it was seen as a problem to be managed by the national state.

Britain pioneered in creating a national system of poor relief. The Poor Law Amendment Act of 1834 established a series of residential workhouses, to which the unemployed poor could be forcibly removed. These functioned much like prisons (see the photograph on p. 660). Strict discipline prevailed, work obligations were heavy, and food was plain and meager. Worse still, the workhouse system resulted in the break-up of families. Able-bodied men, who were expected to seek and find employment, were excluded. Women, children, and the old or infirm became the main beneficiaries—or victims—of the workhouse.

The British workhouse system found few imitators in other nations where, by the late nineteenth century, legislation in favor of workers served to moderate the effects of poverty. In Germany, as has been seen,

Bismarck instituted a system of benefits that cushioned employed workers and their families from unemployment, disability, ill health, and lack of income in old age. That model would be followed by many modern states. Trade unions, in addition, offered help in the case of unemployment, strike, or the death of a primary wage-earner. Private charities of a traditional sort continued to serve the poor, as did a new set of **philanthropic organizations**, which won the active support especially of some middle- and upper-class women.

Nevertheless, the poor continued to suffer particular disabilities. They were often uneducated or even illiterate. They had higher rates of illegitimacy and infanticide, suicide and mental illness than the rest of the population, less resistance to disease and lower life expectancy. They more often committed crimes, and were more often its victims. They ate less than the affluent, their nutrition deficit evident to the eye—the average laborer was several inches shorter than the average member of the middle class. In this pattern of starvation, that of poor women who were mothers of children—an "autostarvation" for the sake of their offspring—was a constant.

The poor were seen by the wealthy not merely as a class apart, but almost as a separate race, with a distinct culture and society. If the city was the site of the "dissolution of mankind into monads [very small units]," as Friedrich Engels observed—or the place where, uniquely, "the human heart is sick," according to the Romantic poet William Wordsworth (1770–1850)—surely those who were most deprived of selfhood and burdened with sick hearts were the dispossessed poor of the modern city.

THE TWO HALVES AT HOME

Crowding a new generation of industrial workers into the existing frame of urban life had tremendous consequences. The effects could be seen out on the street. The cityscape displayed sharp contrasts between the lives of the rich and those of the "other half." Such contrasts gain deeper reality, however, when the observer turns from the streets to the homes of workers and their employers. A chasm yawned between the tenement and the townhouse.

In the Tenement

However miserable the peasant's hovel (and some were mere piles of mud, or ditches covered with entangled branches), a peasant family normally had a place to live within an established village. The newly urbanized workers of the industrial age had nothing of the sort. As the photograph on p. 658 shows, they lived in one or two rooms shared with kin or strangers in the aging building stock of established cities, or in hastily-erected tenements in new towns or suburbs destined soon to deteriorate into **slums**.

In those rooms, heated if at all by a fireplace also used for cooking, they ate, slept, and gathered together. There were generally no separate rooms for food-preparation or dining, for bathing or toileting, for sleeping, or for intimate relationships of body or mind, as the passage in *Witnesses* below reveals. There was neither running water nor artificial light (well after these had become available to the affluent). For the performance of bodily functions, there were outhouses, or a pot inside, the contents of which were disposed of from windows by a centuries-old custom to add to the muck in the streets below.

The peasant household, moreover, possessed a stability the worker's household often lacked. In the countryside, male and female roles were distinguished.

While both men and women worked, sometimes side by side in the fields, they had different jobs. Men more often handled heavy tools, especially the plow, while women more often took care of barnyard chickens and other small animals, a cottage garden, housekeeping tasks, and above all the ceaseless labor of cooking and spinning. The worker's household instead was characterized by shifting, uncertain relations between the genders. In the early years of industrialization, men worked in factories alongside their wives and children. As women left the factories, they took up other work, still essential to family fortunes, while children often stayed in the factory. There they labored under dangerous conditions, subject to abusive employers, for the sake of a meager wage donated to support the family as a whole.

WITNESSES

The Two Halves at Home

Not only were the conditions of work very different for the poor and the wealthy in Europe's industrial age, but their living conditions sharply differed as well. These two passages present the filth and squalor of the worker's home, and the cultural emptiness and repressiveness of the bourgeois household.

The urban poor: description of domestic conditions among workers in Lille, France (1832): In their obscure cellars, in their rooms, which one would take for cellars, the air is never renewed, it is infected; the walls are plastered with garbage. ... If a bed exists, it is a few dirty, greasy planks; it is damp and putrescent straw; it is a coarse cloth whose color and fabric are hidden by a layer of grime; it is a blanket that resembles a sieve. ... The windows, always closed, are covered by paper and glass, but so black, so smoke-encrusted, that the light is unable to penetrate ... everywhere are piles of garbage, of ashes, of debris. ... One is exhausted, in these hovels, by a stale, nauseating, somewhat piquant odor, odor of filth, odor of garbage. ...

... I have seen individuals of both sexes and of very different ages lying together, most of them without nightshirts and repulsively dirty. Father, mother, the aged, children, adults, all pressed, stacked together. I stop. The reader will complete the picture, but I warn him that if he wishes it to be accurate, his imagination must not recoil before any of the disgusting mysteries performed on these impure beds in the midst of obscurity and drunkenness.
(From W. H. Sewell, *Work and Revolution in France: The Language of Labor from the Old Regime to 1848*, 1980)

The wealthy: Flora Tristan describes the life of the bourgeois Englishwoman (1842): It has long been the fashion to extol English liberties, but England is the seat of the most abominable despotism, where laws and prejudices submit women to the most revolting inequality! A woman may inherit only if she has no brothers;

she has no civil or political rights and the law subjects her to her husband in every respect. ...

This is what happens in wealthy families: the children are confined to the third floor with their nurse, maid or governess; the mother asks for them when she wishes to see them ... [and] she addresses them in a formal manner. As the poor little girl is starved of affection, her capacity for loving is never awakened ..., while for the father she hardly knows, she has a respect mingled with fear, and for her brother she keeps the consideration and deference she has been obliged to show him from her earliest childhood.

The system followed for the education of young girls seems to me fit to turn the most intelligent child into a blockhead. ... It is concerned solely to imprint on these young minds the *words* of all the European languages without the slightest thought for the *ideas*. ...

Young ladies have very few amusements: as family life is formal, arid, and intolerably boring, they plunge headlong into the world of the novel. Unfortunately, these romances revolve around lovers such as England has never known, and their influence gives birth to hopes that can never be fulfilled. ... [T]he fate of the married woman is very much sadder than that of the spinster; at least the unmarried woman enjoys a certain freedom, she can enter society and travel with her family or with friends, whereas once a woman is married, she cannot stir from the house *without the permission of her husband*. The English husband is like the *lord and master* of feudal times. ...

The English husband sleeps with his servant, casts her out when she is pregnant or after she has given birth. ... In England the wife is not the mistress of the household as she would be in France. In fact she is almost a stranger in her own home; the husband holds the money and the keys. ... [H]e has sole charge of everything.
(*The London Journal of Flora Tristan*, 1842; ed. J. Hawkes, 1982)

Getting by: *Many workers could not afford housing, not even in a slum. In one of journalist Jacob Riis's now classic photographs of working class existence in New York City, dated c. 1890, lodgers on Bayard Street rent a spot to spend the night for 5 cents. (Museum of the City of New York)*

Male heads of households depended for income on their children and wives. Frequently the householder was himself unemployed—for unemployment was a common, cyclical reality in the early industrial era—while his wife and children worked.

These different relations to work were reflected in personal relationships within workers' families. Women continued to bear complete responsibility for housework, the burden of which was added to paid labor outside the home. Since it was they who shopped for necessary supplies, they often controlled family finances. Managing the money that their husbands and children brought home, they sometimes rescued it from the hands of a spouse hoping to spend it at the local tavern.

Workers' wives could find employment as laundresses, daily servants, pieceworkers, and, later in the nineteenth century, laborers in the "**sweated industries.**" Piecework entailed sewing items of clothing, such as shirts, embroidering luxury items, or knitting stockings or caps, as shown in *Windows On* on p. 648. They might also market these products in the streets, as peddlers. The sweated industries employed a few laborers in workshops, or "sweatshops," outside the factory, generally dedicated to clothing manufacture. In all these cases, the wages they received were lower than those earned by male factory workers, or indeed by men doing work of equal difficulty. Overall, women may have earned about one-half the wages that men did for comparable work and hours.

Lower wages were not the only disability that women in working-class households experienced. They were often left to support whole families when the male head of household was unemployed or, as happened quite frequently, when he deserted his family altogether. They were often the victims of physical abuse from desperate and drunken husbands.

Single women workers were freer to move about to seek employment. In Britain, they often worked as domestic servants in the homes of bourgeois or aristocratic families (see below). As servants, they were frequently made pregnant by their masters or their masters' sons—a familiar cause for dismissal and social disgrace. Unmarried women in other job categories

Occupations of Women Workers in Milan (1881), London (1891), and France (1906)

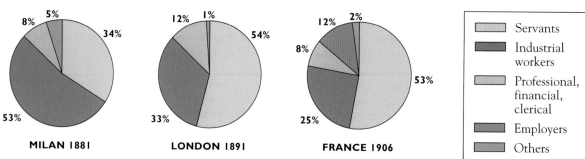

	MILAN 1881	LONDON 1891	FRANCE 1906
Servants	34%	54%	53%
Industrial workers	53%	33%	25%
Professional, financial, clerical	8%	12%	8%
Employers	5%	1%	12%
Others	—	—	2%

As in the early modern period, a great many of the women who worked found employment as servants. By the end of the nineteenth century, however, large numbers of women were working in factories, and in clerical and administrative positions in offices and stores—even as owners of shops and other enterprises.

Sources: Based on P. M. Hohenberg and L. H. Lees, The Making of Urban Europe, 1000–1950 (Cambridge, MA: Harvard University Press, 1985; 2nd ed., 1995), p. 210, and R. Price, A Social History of Nineteenth-Century France (New York: Holmes & Meier, 1987), p. 213

also often found themselves pregnant in the industrial city, where the restraints of village life had withered and died. Women who gave birth out of wedlock frequently abandoned their babies to the care of foundling homes or orphanages, now become numerous, and sometimes killed them. Many such women were forced into prostitution.

Whatever their circumstances, the laboring poor shared this characteristic with the incarcerated prisoner or the workhouse resident: they had nowhere to go. They had little expectation that conditions would improve for them, or that their children could aspire to higher positions than those they themselves occupied. Their wages purchased little beyond food and that food was mostly bread. Well over half a workers' wage was spent on food, and, after expenses of housing and clothing, barely ten percent was left—often dispensed on drink and entertainment. After their long workday, male and female workers alike sought recreation in tavern, café, or **music hall**, the social clubs of the poor. If they spent too much of their meager supply of cash on these amusements, pawnbrokers and loansharks were always available to lend them more, and bind them even more firmly to an unending condition of poverty.

By the late nineteenth century, and a little earlier in Britain (where workers' diets and prospects were somewhat better), standards of living for the working poor in northern and western Europe began at last to rise. In Britain, real wages increased by one-third between 1850 and 1875, and by nearly one-half again between 1870 and 1900. Advances in Germany were nearly as great. Improvements in agriculture resulted in lower food costs, at least in these privileged regions, falling to about half of the family budget. More money became available for housing, for clothes (cheap, well-cut ready-mades were now widely available), and for entertainment. Workers' diets became more varied, including grain and even meat, shipped in refrigerated compartments from the Americas and Australia. No longer a luxury, meat consumption among workers rose steadily.

Another step toward the eventual advancement of the working class was the advent of public schooling for its children (see also Chapter 25). By the eighteenth century, elementary schooling had become more widely available for the young children of ordinary folk in such areas as Prussia, Scotland, and parts of Anglo-America. The nineteenth century saw the expansion of mass secular education. From the 1880s, Britain and France instituted mandatory, free public schools for all children; most states of the United States had already done so by the end of the nineteenth century. With access to public education in at least these leading nations, all children—the tenement dweller just as much as the child of privilege—had the valuable opportunity to gain the skills by which they could strive for greater success.

In the Townhouse

Out in the countryside in pre-modern Europe, the grand manor house or castle of the local landowner dominated the huts or cottages of the peasants. The gulf between rich and poor was equally apparent in the city, which contained both the opulent townhouse or apartment of the bourgeois or nobleman and the worker's rented room. In the industrial era, as the dwellings of the poor became even bleaker in the multi-storied anonymity of the tenement, the homes of the well-off became softer, warmer and more comfortable than ever.

Domestic comfort had only recently become an important consideration for the upper classes as the industrial age opened. Since the fifteenth century, aristocratic homes had developed differentiated private and public spaces, both suitably adorned with fine furniture and tapestries. By the seventeenth and eighteenth centuries, aristocratic homes in country and city featured lush furnishings and expensive adornments—and the great luxury of windows. As industrialization proceeded in the nineteenth century, the ever-larger and ever-wealthier bourgeoisie imitated the pacesetting nobility and furnished their townhouses and apartments to suit their enhanced social and economic position.

The number of rooms multiplied, and more things filled those rooms. The homes of the wealthy now possessed parlors and studies, bedrooms and nurseries, and formal dining-rooms. Walls lined with brocaded cloth or richly designed papers were hung with prints and paintings, and adorned with fine wood or plaster moldings. Candelabras hung from the ceiling or were mounted on the wall. Scattered about were fine musical instruments—such as a piano in the parlor—showpiece clocks on pedestals or mantels, and collections of small precious things—crystal, silver, porcelain. Furniture included elegant tables and wardrobes and soft, deep chairs, resting on patterned carpets.

The dusting and cleaning of such large houses stuffed with so many possessions were the constant care of servants, who served in European cities in veritable armies. Most domestic servants were women who lived in closets and attics, consumed the same food as their employers' families, and could expect reasonable conditions of life and work despite their meager pay. Even in less wealthy bourgeois households, a single maid-of-all-work might clean the house, tend the fires, and wait at table, among a variety of other tasks. Servant labor made the zbourgeois style of life possible.

Ladies of Leisure   Like their female servants, elite women were also dedicated to the maintenance of the bourgeois or aristocratic household. Their lives are described in *Witnesses* on p. 657. They were expected to avoid work themselves—exemption from labor was essential to the status of "lady"—but to manage the labor of servants in housekeeping and food preparation tasks. The boundaries between the privileged and those considered to be "inferior" lay in these delicate, clearly understood social distinctions between the housewife who labored and the one who, having at least one female servant, did not.

Bourgeois and aristocratic women turned their skills and aptitudes instead to other household functions. They exercised their taste in the choice of furnishings and works of art, in the selection of schools and tutors for their children, and in the arts of hospitality—the entertainment of neighbors and business associates with afternoon tea, elaborate dinners (served in multiple courses by servants in formal attire), or for extended visits, all arranged by the genteel exchange of invitations in person or through written notes on luxury stationery. The elite household consumed much—food and drink, furniture and furnishings, the labor of servants—and women were charged with procuring these consumables. They hired servants, dealt with tradesmen, and visited the new department stores (the first of which appeared in Paris soon after 1850)—those palaces of consumerism which, observed the French writer Emile Zola (1840–1902; see Chapter 25), threatened to replace the churches in the hearts of many.

When not shopping or visiting, elite women stayed current by reading sentimental novels or ladies' magazines which had been published since the eighteenth century, filled with articles about fashion, entertaining, and childcare. They employed their leisure with activities that produced little of practical use but much of beauty: embroidery, knitting, and other forms of needlework. One advice book for young ladies explained: "The intention of your being taught needlework, knitting and such like is not on account of the intrinsic values of all you can do with your hands, which is trifling, but to enable you to fill up, in a tolerably agreeable way, some of the many solitary hours you must necessarily pass at home."

Women of the elites were responsible for the households in which they led lives of ease. At the same time, they had little connection with the public world beyond the household—the realm of work, wealth, and power. The distinction between a woman's life close to the household and a man's apart from it was not new to the industrial age, but it was to become even sharper as the "separate spheres" of home and work involved wholly different activities. Work had been wholly removed from the household, which was once itself a zone of productive activity, and it moved to the factory, the bank, the office building. The household now became the site for recuperation from work, a place reserved for the consumption of goods and services. Here women bore the responsibility of equipping their male kin for the distant, different place of work.

The widening gap between home and work among the elites, the spheres of female and male, was expressed in the new fashions of the industrial age. Some of these developments are illustrated in *Windows On*, pp. 600–601. A generation after the French Revolution, driven forward by the rage of the *sans-culottes* (see Chapter 20), bourgeois and aristocratic men abandoned knee-breeches for trousers, a fashion associated with practical, serious work, rather than the frivolities of the court. At the same time, they gave up powdered wigs and perfume, silks (except in the relic of the tie) and velvets, jewelry and high-heeled shoes. They dressed in black or grey, suggesting sober attention to duty, with the distinction between the wealthier and the less-wealthy evident not in the style of clothing but only in such details as the cut of the garment and the quality of the fabric. Elite women, however, continued to wear (after an interlude of simplicity during the Napoleonic era) the huge skirts, tight bodices, and brilliant colors of female aristocrats of the previous era. Their dress proclaimed their leisured status and

Workhouse and Café

Dinnertime in St. Pancras workhouse: *Significant numbers of poorer urbanites lacked even the most basic housing, and made their homes instead at workhouses or other institutional refuges. Here, women eat in the St. Pancras, London workhouse, in a scene from around 1900.*

their mission to bear children—their fertility announced to the world by the contrast between full skirt and corseted waist. Indeed, hoops and crinolines made women gigantic, larger than their menfolk but frailer, physically absurd in a way that suggested their continued rootedness to a natural world amid the frantic pandemonium of modern industrial life.

Although women's reproductive mission was thus displayed in their costume, privileged women in the wealthier nations were in fact beginning to bear fewer children—especially in France, where birthrates dropped drastically toward the end of the nineteenth century. Such declining birthrates witness the practice of birth control, especially the traditional but unreliable method of *coitus interruptus*, or male withdrawal. Condoms, though known, were crude, and mostly used with prostitutes, and the other possibilities (herbal remedies and home surgery) were unpleasant, dangerous, and often deadly.

Family Life A declining rate of infant mortality perhaps encouraged people to have fewer children. Economic factors were also important: increased costs associated with childrearing, especially private education, affected the middle classes, while, for working-class families, child labor laws and compulsory education meant that younger children could no longer contribute to family income. Whatever the case, fewer children in the family meant that non-working mothers could devote more time and care to their children's rearing. They worried over child health and education, seeking the opinion of experts and carefully selecting schools. For the first time in Western history, women of the elites breastfed their own infants, both to nourish them better, and to surround them with the maternal tenderness that so many infants through the ages had never known.

This trend toward the deepening attachment of middle-class women to their children (aristocratic women generally still consigned theirs to the care of servants) coincided with changes

in the medical treatment of childbirth. Male midwives, and then male doctors, took over the business of supervising birth for women of the upper classes (although they did so in women's homes rather than in hospitals, where poor women suffered the dangers of infection and neglect). The development of the forceps in the eighteenth century had helped infants and mothers to survive difficult births. A century later, two other developments assisted the mother. The first was the adoption of the principle of antisepsis (see Chapter 25), by assuring the cleanliness of surgical instruments and environment, which greatly reduced the rate of maternal mortality. The second was the introduction of anesthesia, initially by the use of chloroform—an innovation that Britain's Queen Victoria (r. 1837–1901) personally experienced and approved enthusiastically.

The intensifying involvement of better-off women with their young children was one aspect of a general intensification of family feeling. More often than in the past, men and women married partners of their choosing. Encouraged in part by the powerful cultural movement of Romanticism (see Chapter 25), whose message resounded in books, opera, and theater, they sought marriages founded on love. Meanwhile, marital love was valued by the public consensus as it had not been in earlier ages, when duty, obedience, or mutual affection was the expressed ideal. Advice books glorified family life, and manuals on conjugal love encouraged both men and women to seek sexual gratification within marriage for the sake of the harmonious community of mother, father, and children.

In the intense theater of family life, privileged women were the source not only of heightened sentiment, but also of a "higher" morality. It was the women who conveyed moral lessons, and saw to

Pierre-Auguste Renoir, Le Moulin de la Galette: *After dark, the city was full of opportunities. Working-class and middle-class urban-dwellers alike shopped, attended theaters and music halls, strolled in parks, and relaxed with friends in taverns and cafés. In Paris, cafés such as this one—painted by Impressionist artist Pierre-Auguste Renoir in 1876—were popular places to socialize. (Louvre, Paris)*

their children's moral as well as intellectual growth. Mothers supervised religious instruction, presiding over family prayers and seeking to instill the values of self-control and self-reliance that had become newly important in industrial society.

Women's association with the moral realm also reached beyond the household. Many engaged in charitable activities that took them across their own thresholds, and out beyond the boundaries of their neighborhood and caste to tend to the needs of those of the other half: orphans, unwed mothers, prostitutes, the sick, the poor. They gathered in clubs and organizations for charitable purposes, where as volunteer treasurers, secretaries, and presidents, they acquired the experience of management they were barred from in the professional world of work.

Despite their vigorous role in philanthropic activities (which also appealed to many men of the affluent classes), and their competence in running large and complex households, women were still expected to defer to men in matters concerning money. In most countries, a woman's dowry was still her husband's to use, if it was not absolutely his property. In some, women could own no property in their own name, and could negotiate loans only with the co-signature of a husband, father, or guardian. In France, where the Revolution had insisted on daughters' equal right to inherit, the Napoleonic Code (see Chapter 20) classed women as legal incompetents along with children, the insane, and criminals.

Nearly everywhere, a woman's adultery was still viewed by the law as a more serious offense than a man's—and in some countries, it was permissible for a husband who caught his wife in the adulterous act to kill her. Divorce, too (where it was obtainable at all), was more easily obtained by a man than a woman, who needed to prove amply and without question her husband's offenses. In the event of divorce or separation, it was fathers who generally held all custodial rights over children—and not their mothers, whose sentimental attachment to them was increasingly part of family life.

These barriers to women's independence would be resisted in the new feminist movement of the later 1800s (see Chapter 25). In the meantime, most propertied families functioned as though these problems did not exist, appearing to enjoy wholeheartedly the many opportunities their comfortable lives offered. Besides receiving visitors at home, and visiting others, men and women of the bourgeoisie and aristocracy eagerly attended concerts, the theater, and the opera, where they sat in halls among audiences who were much more orderly than in the past, and listened more attentively than had their ancestors—even entertainment was becoming a serious matter during the industrial age, requiring a disciplined and responsible attitude.

They also frequented teashops and cafés, strolled in well-groomed parks, borrowed books from libraries, attended lectures at literary or philosophical societies, and relaxed at their (mostly all-male) clubs. They traveled by the new railroad lines to the beach and to spas, where they bathed in and drank mineral-laden waters thought to be beneficial to their health. Equipped with guides to monuments, museums, and restaurants, they toured the cities of Europe, and, boarding steamships where they slept in luxurious staterooms and enjoyed elaborate dinners, they ventured to colonial centers abroad (see Chapter 24).

Far from home, the men and women of the privileged classes enjoyed comforts and refinements unthinkable in the tenements where the other half lived.

Conclusion
THE ONE HALF, THE OTHER HALF, AND THE MEANING OF THE WEST

During the nineteenth century, industrialization recreated the human and urban landscape of the wealthier Western nations. It created new social groups—that of the factory worker who bore the burden of the pain entailed by the reconstruction of the modern economy, and that of the capitalist, for whose profit the worker labored. At the same time, it created a new, previously inconceivable, kind of city—a huge and diverse place, embracing factories and libraries, department stores and brothels, all knit together by sewage and water pipes, gas lines, and electrical cable. Within that city the astoundingly rich coexisted with the desperately poor, and contrasts between wealth and poverty were vivid and shocking. The disparity between rich and poor, which had long been a concern of the Christian churches, would henceforth be taken up by the secular leaders of the Western world—a problem with moral, practical, and political dimensions, threatening both stability and conscience. At the dawn of the twenty-first century, the problem persists across the West still.

Even as rich and poor confronted each other in the different capitals of the Western world, the West was vigorously extending its influence in the world beyond the West, as the following chapter will show, confronting a different sort of poverty, and creating a new set of relationships between those who command and those who serve.

REVIEW QUESTIONS

1. What groups of people made up the poor in industrial society? How did the advent of machines change the nature of work? How did the factory system affect the social and economic roles of women and children?

2. What is capitalism? What effect did industrialization have on skilled workers? Who were the proletariat?

3. Why did workers join trade unions in the nineteenth century? What was the significance of the *Communist Manifesto*? How had workers' lives improved by 1900?

4. Why did European cities continue to grow so rapidly between 1800 and 1900? Who were the "white-collar" workers? How did industrialization act to transform the cities and why had they become more healthful by 1900?

5. Why were the lives of the urban poor so different from those of the rich and the middle class? How widespread was crime in nineteenth-century cities? In what ways did urban poverty affect the lives of working women?

6. What roles were elite women expected to play at home and in society? Why did the size of urban families decline in the late nineteenth century? How did smaller families affect attitudes toward children?

SUGGESTED RESOURCES

Workers and Workplace

Biernacki, Richard, *The Fabrication of Labor: Germany and Britain, 1640–1914* (Berkeley: University of California Press, 1995). Explores national differences in concepts of labor and wages.

Clark, Anna, *The Struggle for the Breeches: Gender and the Making of the British Working Class* (Berkeley-Los Angeles; University of California Press, 1995). Describes how male and female workers competed for jobs and household authority in the early industrial era, with the result that women lost the struggle for the breeches.

Horn, Pamela, *Children's Work and Welfare, 1780–1890* (Cambridge: Cambridge University Press, 1995). Useful introduction to an important and frequently under-examined area of industrial history.

Maynes, Mary Jo, *Taking the Hard Road: Life Course in French and German Workers' Autobiographies in the Era of Industrialization* (Durham: University of North Carolina Press, 1995). Sensitive study of autobiographies written by French and German workers, about one-third of them women, whose lives span the long 19th century, and whose memories help us to understand the impact of industrialization on the lives of real people.

Sewell, William, Jr., *Work and Revolution in France: The Language of Labor from the Old Regime to 1848* (Cambridge: Cambridge University Press, 1980). How French artisan-workers integrated collectivist demands with newer language of freedom and individualism.

The Plight of Women's Work in the Early Industrial Revolution in England and Wales (Women in World History Curriculum), brief history and texts: http://www.womeninworldhistory.com/lesson7.html

Child Labor (Victorian Web, Hartwick College): http://landow.stg.brown.edu/victorian/history/hist8.html

The Industrial City

Bairoch, Paul, *Cities and Economic Development: From the Dawn of History to the Present* (Chicago: University of Chicago Press, 1988). Examines urbanization and its significance in world history.

Jordan, David P., *Transforming Paris: The Life and Labors of Baron Haussmann* (Chicago: University of Chicago Press, 1995). A biography of the man responsible for the transformation of Paris from a medieval to a modern reality, in tune with the social and economic transformations of the century.

Landers, John, *Death and the Metropolis: Studies in the Demographic History of London, 1670–1830* (Cambridge: Cambridge University Press, 1993). Seeks the cause of London's high mortality rates, focusing on unhealthy environmental conditions and disease.

Reid, Donald, *Paris Sewers and Sewermen: Realities and Representations* (Cambridge, MA: Harvard University Press, 1991). The sewer is the emblem of 19th-century city transformation, as public health experts learn that the inflow of clean water and removal of sewage are essential for the control of disease. Reid explores the men who took on the heroic task of installing and maintaining the sewer system in Paris.

The Two Halves at Home

Corbin, Alain, *The Lure of the Sea: The Discovery of the Seaside in the Western World 1750–1840* (Berkeley: University of California Press, 1994). Traces the significance of the sea-shore as both a physical destination and a cultural artifact.

Fuchs, Rachel G., *Poor and Pregnant in Paris: Strategies for Survival in the Nineteenth Century* (New Brunswick, NJ: Rutgers University Press, 1992). How poverty and abandonment led to bleak outcomes.

Haine, W. Scott, *The World of the Paris Café: Sociability Among the French Working Class, 1789–1914* (Baltimore: The Johns Hopkins University Press, 1996). Identifies the café as the cultural center of French workers' lives in the 19th century.

Himmelfarb, Gertrude, *The Idea of Poverty: England in the Early Industrial Age* (New York: Knopf, 1984). Surveys of attitudes, ideas, and action regarding poverty and its relief.

Rappaport, Erika Diane, *Shopping for Pleasure: Women in the Making of London's West End* (Princeton: Princeton University Press, 2000). Describes how the habit of shopping developed by middle-class women transformed the life and the structure of London's West End.

Ross, Ellen, *Love and Toil: Motherhood in Outcast London, 1870–1918* (Oxford: Oxford University Press, 1993). Examines how mothers struggled to keep working families intact and nurture children.

Thompson, F. M. L., *The Rise of Respectable Society 1830–1900* (Cambridge, MA: Harvard University Press, 1988). Essays on Victorian society, including family, home, and leisure.

Jacob Riis, *How the Other Half Lives: Studies among the Tenements of New York* (New York: Charles Scribner's Sons, 1890), full-text hypertext edition: http://www.yale.edu/amstud/inforev/riis/title.html

THE CONCERT OF EUROPE

| 1810 | 1830 | 1850 | 1870 | 1890 | 1910 | 1930 |

Revolution and Reorganization

◆ Congress of Vienna, 1814–15
◆ Napoleon defeated at Waterloo, 1815
◆ Carlsbad Decrees, 1819
◆ Peterloo Massacre, 1819
◆ US Monroe Doctrine, 1823
◆ Decembrist Revolt in Russia, 1825
◆ Revolutions in France, Belgium, Italy, and Poland, 1830–31
◆ Greek independence, 1832
◆ First Reform Act in Britain, 1832
◆ Year of Revolutions, 1848
◆ Louis Napoleon restores Empire in France, 1851
◆ Victor-Emmanuel becomes king of Italy, 1861
◆ Austro-Prussian War, 1866
◆ Dual Monarchy of Austria-Hungary established, 1867
◆ Second Reform Act in Britain, 1867
◆ Unification of Italy, 1870
◆ Franco-Prussian War, 1870–71
◆ Paris Commune, 1870
◆ Unification of Germany, 1871
◆ Bismarck made Chancellor, 1871
◆ Congress of Berlin divides Ottoman empire, 1878
◆ Germany and Austria-Hungary form Dual Alliance, 1879
◆ Italy, Germany, and Austria-Hungary form Triple Alliance, 1882
◆ Third Reform Act in Britain, 1884
◆ Russia and France ally, 1894
◆ Britain and Japan ally, 1902
◆ Britain and France form Entente Cordiale, 1904
◆ Russo-Japanese War, 1904–5
◆ Balkan Wars, 1912–13

Society and Ideas

◆ Eugene Delacroix's Liberty Leading the People, 1830
◆ Factory Act in Britain, 1833
◆ German customs Union, the Zollverein, formed, 1834
◆ Poor Law Amendment Act in Britain, 1834
◆ Louis Blanc's The Organization of Work, 1839
◆ Potato Famine devastates Ireland, 1845–50
◆ Emancipation of serfs in Russia, 1861
◆ First International, 1864
◆ Slavery abolished in US, 1865
◆ British Parliament makes school mandatory for children up to 10, 1880
◆ Bismarck creates social welfare system for workers in Germany, 1883–89
◆ Combustion engine developed, 1885
◆ Second International, 1889

Beyond the West

Atlantic slave trade, 1500–1888

Qing Dynasty, China, 1644–1912

◆ Shaka leads Zulu nation, 1817
◆ First Opium War, 1839–42
◆ US Commodore Perry "opens" Japan, 1853
◆ Second Opium War, 1856–60
◆ Sepoy Mutiny, India, 1857
◆ French gain control of Indochina, 1858
◆ Meiji Restoration, Japan, 1868
◆ Suez canal opens, 1869
◆ Britain's Queen Victoria becomes Empress of India, 1877
◆ Berlin Conference sets off "Scramble for Africa," 1884
◆ Indian National Congress founded, 1885

THE CONCERT OF EUROPE:

Mass Politics and the Triumph of the State

1815–1914

newly unified or established states, with date

KEY TOPICS

◆ **Power to the People: 1815–1848:** With Napoleon gone, European leaders try to put a lid on the revolutionary impulse; but the people have been aroused, and all over Europe they take to the streets to demand their rights.

◆ **One People, One Nation: 1848–1871:** As much as they crave freedom, the peoples of Europe crave nationhood; Italy and Germany are created to meet that need, and Hungary are created to meet that need, and Hungary gains parity with

Austria under Habsburg rule; but minorities in that multiethnic empire are still dissatisfied as the century nears its end.

◆ **The State Triumphant: 1848–1914:** The states of Europe reassert their authority over their populations—in some cases with support from the electorate, in others by means of repression—as the state ultimately emerges triumphant after an era of revolution and turmoil.

The Paris Commune In 1870–1871, the workers of Paris resisted Prussian invaders and then their own countrymen, briefly creating the world's first socialist state amid the last spasms of the Franco-Prussian War. The Prussian siege brought starvation but did not quell the surge of political feeling within the city. Revolutionary clubs sprang up abundantly, while women's groups pressed for political and social rights, such as day care for working mothers. Workers' groups declared the "Paris Commune," a stateless society of free producers, engaged in what Vladimir Ilich Lenin (1876–1924) was later to call a "festival of the oppressed." In Versailles, in January 1871, the victors proclaimed the German Empire; in February, they settled an armistice with the French. In Paris, however, the war had not ended.

The attack on Paris that began in March 1871 was made not by Germans but by Frenchmen, the regular army of the new third Republic. In May they wrested Paris from its Communard defenders in the streets and marketplaces. neighborhood by neighborhood. It took a week—"Bloody Week," May 21–28—and the slaughter was immense. More than 20,000 Parisians were killed, both men and women, in the bloodiest episode in almost a century of sporadic revolution. As the photograph on p. 678 shows, their bodies were bundled into mass graves, dug in the lovely parks that the Emperor Napoleon had built for the recreation of the citizens.

The Paris Commune, crushed in March 1871, was the last of a series of revolts by the "people" against the "state" that mark the history of nineteenth-century Europe. Henceforth, the state would reign triumphant. But it could no longer do so without attending to the urgent needs of the people—which, if ignored, might erupt in violence. The age when kings and gentlemen could manage government by themselves was over, and the age of mass politics had begun.

The people raised their voices against their rulers, especially in the first half of the century, as they sought liberty from what they perceived as tyrannical regimes. Later in the century, it was often nationalist feelings that fired rebellions, and such uprisings were instrumental in creating the new unified states of Italy and Germany. By the last decades of the century, however, order prevailed, and the powerful states of Europe took up the task of governing and accommodating the masses of the people who had arrived at the political front and would not thereafter go home.

POWER TO THE PEOPLE: 1815–1848

In the waning days of Napoleon's empire, representatives of the nations who had defeated him came together in Vienna to create the "concert of Europe"—a harmonious balance among the most powerful nations, intended to secure a lasting peace. The plans devised at the Congress of Vienna (1814–1815) were, in fact, quite successful. They prevented war in Europe for more than half a century, and even managed to contain rebellious impulses for fifteen years. Thereafter, they could no longer mute the aspirations of bourgeois liberals, nationalists of all social classes, and workers. Most of the European monarchies that existed in 1815, or were reinstated thereafter, endured into the next century. But the people, seeking to be no longer subjects but citizens, demanded rights and recognition. Their aspirations exploded into action in 1830 and again, more forcefully, in 1848. These revolts were invariably suppressed. Yet they served to remind governments that peoples' demand for entry into the political arena could not be ignored or denied.

After Napoleon: The Conservative Response

To the representatives of the victor nations who met at the Congress of Vienna, Napoleon was the embodiment of all they disliked. The 1789 Revolution in France had tossed out monarchy, aristocracy, and Church. Under Napoleon, they were not restored, although the latter two received accommodations. In the eyes of the representatives, Napoleon was an illegitimate ruler whose intrusion among European leaders posed a profound threat, even after Napoleon himself had met his defeat.

The French Revolution itself presented an even greater threat. It had established a liberal agenda of human and civil rights, such as freedom of the press, freedom of assembly, freedom of religion, and the abrogation of class distinction, that challenged the authoritarian powers of European monarchs. Though the Revolution had foundered after the events of Thermidor, the French army had broadcast its message in all the lands it entered; and this message, it was feared, might inspire new revolutions abroad.

Moreover, the French Revolution had triggered a surge of patriotic sentiment, or **nationalism**, also exported by French soldiers alongside liberalism. To these two ideological threats, the diplomats of Vienna adopted an opposing ideological stance: that of **conservatism** (see Chapter 25).

The pioneering conservative Edmund Burke had cautioned against the destruction of institutions and beliefs built up over centuries, the work of multiple generations (see Chapter 20). He had foreseen what the consequences of revolution might be, but he died (in 1797) before they had materialized in the person of Napoleon. A harsher conservatism than Burke's emerged from the Vienna discussions, articulated by the principal Habsburg representative, Prince

Clemens von Metternich (1773–1859). Some of his ideas are noted in *Witnesses* on p. 682.

Metternich urged the following goals: to suppress revolutions everywhere; to restore legitimate rulers; to support the nobility and established churches; to limit dissent and even debate by controlling the press and establishing mechanisms of surveillance by secret police forces. Both liberal and nationalist movements threatened the stability of the allied nations; so they would have to be averted or destroyed. Just as Napoleon had suppressed the liberal aspirations of the Revolution, now monarchy, aristocracy, and Church would suppress the legacy of Napoleon.

By the time it ended, in June 1815, the Congress of Vienna had reestablished the monarchies disrupted by Napoleon and Revolution and the religious establishments that had supported them. Their distribution is shown on Map 23.1 below. As Map 23.2 on p. 672 shows, these governments set about suppressing liberalism and nationalism in the German and Italian states and in France; some anti-liberal measures were applied even in Britain, where the monarchy remained intact. European powers were, however, unable to stop revolutions in the colonies in South America and the Caribbean (see Chapter 19), and, ironically, supported a revolution in Greece against the Ottoman Empire. Within their own boundaries, they muzzled dissent by breaking up associations of workers and students, by censoring the press, and by unleashing secret police forces.

Liberalism and Nationalism in Central Europe

Austria was especially vulnerable to disruption by nationalist movements. Over the previous centuries, it had expanded from a mere duchy within the Holy Roman Empire to a principality; its Habsburg monarchs had held the imperial title virtually without interruption since the late 1400s. During the course of this expansion, Austria had absorbed a large part of central and southeastern Europe. Among its dominions were Bohemia, Moravia, and Hungary (including Transylvania); parts of Poland, Russia, and Italy; and the Ottoman Balkans, including parts of Croatia and Serbia. In addition to German-speaking Austrians, its

Map 23.1 Europe in 1815 as Established by the Congress of Vienna: *In 1815, the participants of the Congress of Vienna rearranged the map so as to put into reverse most of Napoleon's adjustments and in order to achieve the European balance of power that was a main object of their diplomacy.*

peoples included Italians, Czechs, Slovaks, Magyars, Poles, Romanians, Slovenes, and Croats. They spoke at least twenty different languages, and adhered to Roman Catholicism, Eastern Orthodoxy, Judaism, Islam, and varieties of Protestantism. Different political agendas guided the actions of these different ethnic groups.

The Austrian and Czech bourgeoisie shared the outlook of western European liberals. They hoped to limit Habsburg autocracy, to gain political rights and secure freedom of the press. Czech liberals were moved by nationalism, as were the powerful nobles of Hungary and Croatia. These aristocrats could be persuaded to cooperate with the Austrian government, which supported their domination over a subject peasantry, but they still demanded greater independence within the Habsburg regime. Other regions were more resistant to Habsburg rule; in Serbia and Moldavia, rebellions broke out in 1817 and 1821.

Northern Italians sought freedom from Habsburg rule. In 1831, insurrections broke out in Italy against Austrian and papal domination, calling for a unified Italian nation. Although those rebellions were suppressed, their cause was given increased muscle by the ardent patriot Giuseppe Mazzini (1805–1872), who became their leader. Some of his ideas are noted in *Witnesses* on pp. 679 and 732. He organized disparate groups of **carbonari** ("charcoal-burners") into the liberal–nationalist organization "Young Italy." It was not sufficient to have rights, Mazzini told his followers; one must belong to a nation: "Without Country you have neither name, token, voice, nor rights, no admission as brothers into the fellowship of the People." Organized as a secret society, admission to which involved oaths hedged with threats of retribution, Young Italy grew into a major movement which spurred progress toward national unification—a goal achieved in 1870.

Nationalist movements inspired by liberal principles flourished in the German cities and principalities, as indicated in *Witnesses* on pp. 679 and 732. Continuing the work begun by Napoleon, the Congress of Vienna created a Confederation of 39 German states (including Prussia and Austria), whose representatives attended a Federal Diet at Frankfurt. Instead of unifying Germany, however, this reorganization actually underscored the autonomy of the component states.

It was, rather, a combination of university students and their professors who spearheaded liberal and nationalist sentiment in Germany; and they faced tough opposition. The Carlsbad Decrees of 1819, which were conceived by Metternich and proposed jointly by the rulers of both Prussia and Austria to the complaisant Diet of the German Confederation, abolished the student proto-revolutionary clubs, and silenced the press: "No [daily or serial] publication …," came the decree to muzzle that voice, "shall go to press in any state of the union without the previous knowledge and approval of the state officials."

Censorship, however, could not choke off news of the 1830 revolt in France (see below), which sparked further rebellions in the Netherlands, Poland, and elsewhere. At Heidelberg and Frankfurt, university students gathered to call for a united Germany. The "Ten Articles," issued by the Diet of the German Confederation, scripted the suppression of liberal movements throughout the German states, but failed to silence a generation of young men who would become lawyers, magistrates, and professors of a new nation. Meanwhile, although political unification was postponed, the customs union (Zollverein) formed in 1843, which eliminated internal tariffs and promoted the economic unity of many of the German states, was of great significance for Germany's future.

Another creation of the Congress of Vienna was a united kingdom of the Netherlands, which included both the northern, largely Protestant provinces and the southern Catholic ones formerly under Habsburg rule. The new king, William I (r. 1815–1840), of the line of the princes of Orange, consolidated his position in the north. The southern provinces resisted amalgamation, and they revolted in 1830 (in the wake of the French revolt of that year). They eventually organized the separate nation of Belgium, headed by its own constitutional monarch supported by a representative assembly.

Revolution in Russia, the Iberian Peninsula, and Greece

The Russian empire, like the Austrian, had expanded territorially over the previous centuries. It now contained many Asian minorities, of which some groups were Muslims; and in 1815 it absorbed part of the kingdom of Poland which Napoleon had briefly reconstituted as the Grand Duchy of Warsaw. These subject territories were not, however, the main source of difficulty for Tsar Alexander I (r. 1801–1825). Rather, it was his nation's social rigidity. The great majority of the Russian people were virtually serfs, the personal property of the nobility.

Russia's minuscule bourgeoisie could do little to resist the autocratic regime, but a handful of dissident nobles attempted a coup in December 1825, on Alexander's death. Their attempt to place the former tsar's brother Constantine (believed to be more liberal) on the throne failed, and Alexander's son Nicholas became tsar. Nicholas I (r. 1825–1855) subdued the "Decembrist Revolt" (as it was called) and executed or exiled its leaders, inaugurating an era of even fiercer repression.

"Serfdom is a powder keg under the state," warned one of the tsar's noble advisers in 1839. From 1826 to 1849, serfs rose up in revolt on nearly 2000 occasions—not always with the success of the 54 peasants

The Growth of the Electorate in Nineteenth-Century Britain

Prior to 1832 Act — **Fewer than 500,000**

1832 — **813,000**

1867 — **1,994,000**

1884 — **All male householders**

By three giant leaps, those entitled to vote in Great Britain rose from less than 1 million to many millions as universal male suffrage was attained.

who in 1835 managed to kill 144 estate owners and 29 stewards before their rebellion, like the others, was suppressed. Meanwhile, dissident intellectuals, mostly aristocrats, fed on the thousands of foreign books smuggled into Russia and pondered nightly by impassioned student ideologies (see Chapter 25).

In Spain and Portugal, whose monarchs were restored by the Congress of Vienna, dissent still simmered; liberal revolutions, begun in both countries in 1820, were suppressed in 1823 and 1824, respectively. Across the Atlantic, several of the Spanish colonies revolted more on the pattern of the North American revolt of 1775 than the French one of 1789 (see Chapter 19). By 1825, the continental Spanish American colonies, as well as Brazil (formerly Portuguese), had been constituted as independent nations. European efforts to reverse these changes were halted by the policy declared in 1823 by U.S. President James Monroe and known as the Monroe Doctrine: the Americas, it announced, "are henceforth not to be considered as subjects for future colonization by any European powers"; and any intervention by European powers in the affairs of the Western Hemisphere would be seen as an "unfriendly act."

European powers might have intervened in Greece, but they did not. Here, insurrection broke out in 1821 against the Muslim Ottoman regime, which had ruled Greece since the fifteenth century (see Chapters 14, 15). In this case, the anti-revolutionary principles of the European states conflicted with their anti-Turkish and pro-Christian sentiments. Liberal writers, intellectuals, and young people all over

Europe, and especially in England, cheered on the Greek revolt, while their governments, though suspicious of all such movements, did nothing to protect the legitimate regime. By 1832, Greece had won its independence from the Ottoman Empire.

Pressure for Change in Great Britain

Britain, which had already undergone an industrial transformation (see Chapter 21), still shared the difficulties faced by the other principal nations during the post-Napoleonic period. Liberals demanded the broadening of the franchise and other civil rights, while workers sought to better their condition. As protest stirred, the Combination Acts of 1799 and 1800, which barred the formation of workers' organizations, were sternly enforced until their eventual repeal in 1824. "Corn Laws" (which protected landowners' profits) taxed grain imports, keeping the price of bread artificially high. The government suppressed mass protests against such restrictive tariffs and other inequalities. In 1819, in Manchester, soldiers fired on a crowd of 60,000 people gathered in St. Peter's Fields, demanding parliamentary reforms and repeal of the Corn Laws. Eleven people were killed in this "Peterloo Massacre" (named in imitation of Waterloo). Religious freedom was another contentious issue. Until 1829, Roman Catholics were barred from holding political office in Britain and Ireland. The Roman Catholic population of Ireland, subject to mostly Anglo-Irish Protestant landlords, suffered unremitting discrimination.

Over the next generation, however, Britain managed, without revolution, to open access to government and to nurse the wounds caused by economic change. The Reform Act of 1832 nearly doubled the franchise, as *How Many?* above shows. Now the wealthiest one-fifth of adult male citizens could vote for representatives in Parliament—an improvement, but still far short of universal suffrage.

The Poor Law of 1834 (see Chapter 22), which introduced new provisions for housing the destitute, signaled the government's readiness to address the social problem of poverty. In 1846, the repeal of the Corn Laws permitted the importation of cheaper grain; previously the Factory Act of 1833 and Mines Act of 1842 had done something to improve the conditions faced by the most exploited industrial workers.

More radical reforms were called for by the Chartist movement. This organization of working people acquired its name from a "People's Charter" drawn up in 1838 by the London Working Men's Association. The Charter demanded universal male suffrage, a secret ballot, and electoral reform, among other changes. Its supporters met and marched for ten years, engaging a generation of ordinary people in participatory democracy. Millions of citizens signed petitions, which were sent to Parliament in 1939 and

SOCIALISM

1842 but left unheeded. In 1848, stirred by news of continental revolutions, the Chartist movement culminated in a last great, but again futile, march.

Even more deeply estranged from British public life were the people of Ireland, saddled by absentee landlords and religious intolerance, unrepresented in Parliament, and unassisted by the government. In 1845, crisis struck (see Chapter 24).

Irish farmers had taken to growing potatoes (see Chapter 16), which grew easily and provided bountiful nourishment from a small area. In Ireland, where most peasants possessed only the tiniest of plots of soil from which to gain their whole sustenance, the potato took over, not merely as the chief but virtually as the sole crop. In 1845, the potato crop failed. A devastating famine, the "Great Hunger," seized Ireland, killing millions, leaving others malnourished, and driving hundreds of thousands more to emigrate (mostly to the United States). The long-standing hostility to British domination was to blaze still hotter among those who remembered the years of famine.

France: Laboratory of Revolution

In the years after Waterloo, France oscillated between revolution and reaction. In 1815 the Bourbon monarchy was again restored, in the person of Louis XVIII (r. 1814–1824), Louis XVI's younger brother, who had occupied the throne briefly the year before. (The young Louis XVII had died in prison in 1795.) He ruled subject to a constitution, appointing the upper chamber of a two-chamber assembly, while a tiny electorate of 100,000 adult males (in a nation of 30 million) chose the deputies to the lower chamber. The Napoleonic Code continued in force, and Napoleon's Concordat was retained, with modifications that effectively reestablished Roman Catholicism in France.

Upon Louis XVIII's death in 1824, his brother Charles X (1757–1836) succeeded him. Strongly supported by conservatives and royalists and determined to reinstate absolutism, Charles made new accommodations to the Roman Catholic Church, imposed stricter censorship, and generally protected the powerful. In July 1830, he issued the July Ordinances, which reduced the electorate even further to a thin stratum of wealthy men. The response was explosive: liberal bourgeois and angry workers spilled out into the streets of Paris. They threw together makeshift barricades of scrap wood and cast-off objects, and, in a pattern that would be repeated often in years to come, they faced, with their irregular weapons the king's regular troops.

Charles abdicated. In his place, Louis-Philippe (r. 1830–1848), member of a younger branch of the Bourbon dynasty, took the throne—without ceremony or pretense to absolutist principles. Unlike Charles X, he did not wear royal robes or a crown, but

the same kind of business suit as his banker might have worn. And in his hat he wore the tricolor cockade: a red, white, and blue ribbon rosette emblematic of the party of Revolution. This was a "Citizen King" who wished for no further revolution. He rules subject to a constitution, and the electorate—though still small—nearly doubled.

What happened in France in 1830 was precisely what Metternich and his colleagues had feared. But their day had passed; no longer could conservatives hope for a true counter-revolution and the return to a chessboard world of nobles, kings, and bishops. Indeed, even as liberals and nationalists clashed with conservative monarchs, they in turn faced opposition from below, as workers voiced their own claim to participation in political life. The arrival of the workers as a political force is viewed first in France.

France had not yet completed its career as a laboratory of social change. Between 1830 and 1848, French popular resistance to monarchial government displayed two main sets of interests. The first comprised the bourgeois businessmen and professionals who, even under the comparatively liberal regime of Louis-Philippe, were excluded from the suffrage. They sought the liberalization of the constitution and of economic policy.

The second set of interests was the growing class of urban workers, their ranks swollen by recent migrants from the countryside, who threatened disruption. They were encouraged by the theories of a new group of radical political thinkers, the socialists (see Chapters 22, 25). While embracing liberal notions of civil rights, socialists also maintained that states were responsible for improving the lives of their citizens through public policy and direct subsidies, requiring the redistribution of private property—a demand opposed by bourgeois liberals, who were disinclined to surrender a modicum of their accumulated wealth.

These two revolutionary streams—the bourgeois and the worker, the liberal and the radical— intersected in 1848. Late in February of that year, a mass demonstration turned into revolution when panicky soldiers fired on a crowd, killing 40 people. The crowd carried the martyred citizens through the streets, seized public buildings, and erected barricades to deter government troops. The events are described in *Witnesses* on page 671.

Louis-Philippe was forced to abdicate, and the Second French Republic was born. A provisional government proclaimed universal manhood suffrage and called for the election of a National Assembly to write a republican constitution. (It also abolished slavery in all French colonies—that institution having been reinstated by Napoleon.)

The February revolution was a bourgeois revolution. It would be followed by a revolt of workers and artisans, just as in 1789 the moderate revolution had given way to a radical one. From the onset, the

To The Barricades: Paris, France, 1848, 1871

In 1830 and 1848, the revolutionary impulse spread to the rest of Europe from France, as it had in the years after 1789—and indeed from Paris, where young bourgeois intellectuals and idealistic workers and artisans continued to take inspiration from the spirit of freedom and fraternity that the Revolution had embodied. In two of the passages presented here, Alexis de Tocqueville (1805–1859) and Alphonse de Lamartine (1790–1869), both writers of note, and both participants in republican government, comment on the 1848 revolt; de Tocqueville warns of its coming, and Lamartine describes its outbreak. In the third passage, a British journalist describes vividly what he saw during the suppression of the Commune in 1871, the last in the series of nineteenth-century revolts.

Alexis de Tocqueville, shortly before the Revolution of 1848, foretells its approach: I am told that there is no danger because there are no riots; I am told that, because there is no visible disorder on the surface of society, there is no revolution at hand. Gentlemen, permit me to say that I believe you are deceived. True, there is no actual disorder; but it has entered into men's minds. See what is passing in the breasts of the working classes, who, I grant, are at present quiet. ... Do you not see that there are gradually forming in their breasts opinions and ideas which are destined not only to upset this or that law, ministry, or even form of government, but society itself, until it totters upon the foundations on which it rests today? Do you not hear them repeating unceasingly that all that is above them is incapable and unworthy of governing them; that the present distribution of goods throughout the world is unjust; that property rests on a foundation which is not an equitable foundation? And do you not realize that when such opinions take root, when they spread in an almost universal manner, when they sink deeply into the masses, they are bound to bring with them sooner or later, I know not when nor how, a most formidable revolution?
(*The Recollections of Alexis de Tocqueville*, ed. A. T. de Mattos, 1896)

Alphonse de Lamartine, poet and politician, describes how the February revolution (1848) began: Towards ten o'clock in the evening, a small column of republicans of the young bourgeoisie passed through the rue Lepelletier. ... [soon] another column of workmen and men of the people presented itself, and halted there. ... A red flag floated amidst the smoke of torches over the foremost ranks of this multitude. Its numbers thickened as it continued to advance. A sinister curiosity became intent upon this cloud of men, which seemed to bear the mystery of the day.

In the front of the Hotel of Foreign Affairs, a battalion of the line, drawn up in battle array, with loaded arms, its commander at the head, barred the boulevard. The column suddenly halts before this hedge of bayonets. The floating of the flag and the gleaming of torches frighten the horse of the commander. Rearing and whirling on its hind legs, the horse throws itself back towards the battalion, which opens to surround its leader. A discharge of fire-arms resounds in the confusion of this movement. did it proceed, as has been said, from a concealed and perverse hand, fired upon the people by an agitator of the people, in order to revive by the sight of blood the cooling ardor of the struggle? Did it come from the hand of one of the insurgents upon the troop? In fine, what is more likely, did it come accidentally from the movement of some loaded weapon, or from the hand of some soldier who believed his commander was wounded when he saw the fright of his horse? No one knows. Crime or chance, that discharge of fire-arms rekindled a revolution.
(From Alphonse de Lamartine: *History of the Revolution of 1848* (Boston: Phillips, Sampson & Co., 1849.)

A British journalist describes the collapse of the Paris Commune (1871): The Versaillist troops collected about the foot of the Rue St. Honoré, were enjoying the fine game of Communist hunting. The Parisians of civil life are caitiffs [scoundrels] to the last drop of their thin, sour, white blood. [Only] yesterday they had cried "Long live the Commune!". ... To-day they rubbed their hands with livid currish joy to have it in their power to denounce a Communist and reveal his hiding place. Very eager at this work are the dear creatures of women. They know the rat holes into which the poor devils have got, and they guide to them with a fiendish glee. ... They have found him, the miserable [fellow]! Yes; they drag him out ... and a guard of six of them hem him round as they march into the Rue St. Honoré. A tall, pale, hatless man, with something not ignoble in his carriage. His lower lip is trembling, but his brow is firm, and the eye of him has got some pride and defiance in it. They yell—the crowd—"Shoot him; shoot him!"—the demon-women most clamorous, of course. ... He is down; he is up again; he is down again. ... But it is useless. They are firing into the flaccid carcase [*sic*] now. ... His brains spurt on my boot and splash in the gutter.
(From R. M. Golden and T. Kuehn eds., *Western Societies: Primary Sources in Social History*, Vol. 2, 1993)

The roots of Communism

economy descended into crisis, while prices and taxes soared. Workers pressed the government to provide work for unemployed laborers in national workshops—a program devised by the socialist Louis Blanc (1811–1882) which the provisional government initially had undertaken, but would later repudiate. In the midst of this disorder, Parisians and provincials enlisted in hundreds of political clubs of varying ideologies: liberal, radical, and even feminist in orientation (see *Windows On*, p. 684). Women now insisted not only on civil rights but on rights specific to women—the right to divorce their husbands, female suffrage, the equality of women before the law.

In April, eighty-four percent of the electorate (all adult males were now eligible to vote) chose the legislature; It was strongly conservative and monarchist; socialists and radical republicans gained only one in nine seats. When the radicals attempted to unseat the Assembly, the new government turned against them. On June 23, 1848, this new National Assembly announced the dismantling of the national workshops. The workers took to the streets. Once again the barricades went up in the poorer sections of Paris, defended by women as well as men, mostly workers and artisans, joined by a contingent of bourgeois sympathizers and intellectuals.

This three-day insurrection, known as the "June Days," was suppressed by the middle-class youth of the National Guard and by the lower-class youth of the Mobile Guard, a tactical force established by the Assembly to keep order—men as poor as those they faced across the barricades. The bourgeois Guardsmen shot hundreds of workers, and the Mobile Guard swept through the streets, killing about 1500 people, some of whom are shown in *Windows On*, p. 684. Some 12,000 insurgents were arrested, and about 8000 of these imprisoned; some 4000 were sent to penal colonies in Algeria and French Guiana, where they had but a scant chance of survival.

By November 1848, the political clubs had dissolved, censorship had been reinstated, women had withdrawn from view, and yet another constitution had been promulgated. Establishing France's Second Republic, it called for presidential elections the following month. On December 10, the victory went to Louis-Napoleon Bonaparte (1808–1837), nephew

Map 23.2 Liberal, Nationalist, and Socialist Uprisings in Europe, 1815–1871: *The French Revolution had many offshoots in the form of liberal, nationalist, and socialist uprisings between the Congress of Vienna settlement and 1871.*

of the defeated Napoleon. He would be reelected in 1851, with the approval of 90 percent of those voting; then, at the end of the year, he would dissolve the Second Republic he had twice been elected to lead. The following year, but another overwhelming vote, the empire was restored and Louis-Napoleon ascended the throne as Napoleon III (r. 1852–1870; the son of Napoleon I, had died in 1832). Having fought three revolutions and constructed two republics, the French, by the vote of a resounding majority, knelt once more to autocracy.

The rest of Europe studied Paris in 1848, as it had in 1789 and 1830. This revolt in France set off a series of insurrections in other European centers, reaching the Austrian empire, the German and Italian states, the Netherlands and Belgium, Russia, Spain, and Portugal—a total of more than fifty outbreaks (see Map 23.2, p. 672). In these places, bourgeois revolutionaries fought for written constitutions, freedom of the press, judicial equality, and a wider franchise. Nationalists in the Austrian empire and in German and Italian lands fought for autonomy. Students, professors, journalists, and workers took part in urban revolts which were violent and brutally suppressed.

Although not one of these 1848 revolts was successful, they left their mark upon Europe. While rejecting pleas for popular representation or autonomy, rulers nevertheless took note of the volcanic force that resided in the people, whose pleas could not go unheard forever. If 1789 spelled the beginning of a process that would put an end to the rule of kings, nobles, and bishops, 1848 offered further promise that that objective was in sight.

ONE PEOPLE, ONE NATION: 1848–1871

From 1815 to 1848, nationalism, as well as liberalism, was a spur to popular revolt. Nationalist impulses were especially strong in two settings: first, in the multinational Habsburg empire, where minority populations sought privileges or independence; later, in those regions united by language and culture but for centuries politically divided: Germany and Italy.

During the brief period from the 1848 revolutionary surge through the close of the Franco-Prussian War in 1871, nationalist aspirations were, to some extent, satisfied. The Habsburg empire was reorganized to give special status to the large Hungarian minority, and to recognize to a degree the separate cultures of Czech, Croat, and Slav minorities. The many component states of the Italian peninsula and of the German-speaking lands (except for Austria) achieved unification in the new nations of Italy and Germany. In both cases, though liberal nationalists had long championed the cause, unification was achieved from above by senior statesmen, who were themselves of noble birth. And in both cases, the

In Europe During the Revolutions, 1789–1871

Louis XVI (r. 1774–1793) King of France, and labeled "Louis the Last" by contemptuous revolutionaries; both unintelligent and unlucky, he was condemned on January 19, 1793 and guillotined two days later.

Maximilien Robespierre (1758–1794) inspired orator and determined Jacobin leader, who was head of the Committee of Public Safety, and engineer of the Reign of Terror that resulted in some 40,000 deaths in all.

Napoleon Bonaparte (1769–1821) conqueror of much of Europe during the period 1799–1815; trained under the monarchy and progressed rapidly to the rank of general in the French revolutionary army; seized power in 1799 and declared himself Emperor of France in 1804.

Clemens von Metternich (1773–1859) Austrian *—ultra-conservative* nobleman and diplomat, key figure at sessions of the Congress of Vienna of 1814–1815, and architect of the repressive strategy and counter-revolutionary principles of many European nations between 1815 and 1848.

Camillo di Cavour (1810–1861) nobleman, diplomat, and most notably the prime minister of Piedmont–Sardinia; achieved the unification of Italy under the leadership of his king Victor Emmanuel II.

Otto von Bismarck (1815–1896) Prussian nobleman, prime minister, and chancellor, who was responsible for the unification of Germany under Prussian rule.

new nations were monarchies. In other respects, the Italian and German cases are distinct.

The Creation of Austria-Hungary

Within the multinational Austrian state, the numerous minority populations sought independence or some form of cultural autonomy. Their distribution is shown on Map 23.3 on p. 680. The Habsburg government ignored these aspirations, although it did encourage economic development. Emperor Francis Joseph (r. 1848–1916) addressed dissent by firing his unpopular head of government (who directed the secret police) and experimenting ineffectively with new constitutions which gave greater representation to subject nationalities. Meanwhile, the emperor's reputation plummeted as Austria suffered repeated battlefield losses against Piedmont and Prussia.

Not until 1867 did the emperor accede to nationalist demands, agreeing, reluctantly, to legislation creating the Dual Monarchy of Austria-Hungary. The newly constituted state had two separate parliaments under a single Habsburg ruler. He remained king of Hungary, as well as emperor of Austria, but Hungary gained a separate political identity and the right of self-rule, while the Hungarian language became the official language of government. Hungarian resistance to Habsburg rule was thus neutralized. Other minority peoples, especially Czechs, Slavs, and Croats, were permitted to use their native languages in schools and in churches. They remained dissatisfied and the Slav minorities, especially in Hungary, remained restless.

The Unification of Italy

The Italian provinces, shown in the inset to Map 23.3 on p. 680, had a proud history. Long before they were reduced to third-rate status and subjected to Austrian, Spanish, and papal domination, the Italian city-states and principalities had been thriving political powers in their own right and cradles of the Italian

Renaissance (see Chapter 13). After Napoleon swept through the peninsula, Mazzini and Giuseppe Garibaldi (1807–1882) led a broad nationalist movement—known as the *Risorgimento*, or "Revival"—supported actively by bourgeois professionals. Joining these leaders after 1842 was the nobleman Camillo di Cavour (1810–1861), the new prime minister of Piedmont-Sardinia, a prosperous and constitutional monarchy. An intellectual with a taste for, and understanding of, economics, the graduate of a military academy, fired with republican sentiments, Count Cavour schemed, negotiated, and fought to achieve the unification of Italy.

Promising Napoleon III of France the provinces of Nice and Savoy, Cavour won the French emperor's support for his objective. A joint Piedmontese and French army pushed the Austrian army out of much of northern Italy in 1859, though Austria retained Venetia (the territory surrounding and including Venice). In 1860, several other states voluntarily ceded themselves to Piedmont. Meanwhile Garibaldi, a veteran Sardinian revolutionary, portrayed below, led an irregular volunteer force of 1000 "Red Shirts" in a daring invasion of Sicily. Joined by some of the men he had "liberated," Garibaldi then crossed to the mainland and swept up to Naples, bringing the whole of the south under Piedmontese dominion. The military victory was later confirmed by plebiscites. Before Garibaldi could reach Rome and challenge Cavour's monarchist state with a republican Italy, Cavour's troops rushed south to join Garibaldi in Naples.

Garibaldi's March: *Giuseppe Garibaldi's series of military victories, culminating in the capture of Naples, became one of the great legends of the nineteenth century. He is seen here leading volunteer soldiers in his "March" across the Italian mainland, which was seen by many as a vindication of the right of the individual to political self-determination. (Private Collection)*

The Parliament that Failed: *In the grand interior of the Church of Saint Paul in Frankfurt-am-Main (modern Germany), more than 800 delegates from tens of German states met to create a constitution for a future nation. Their well-laid plans to create a liberal modern state based on the rule of law under a constitutional monarch failed, however, when in 1849 the Prussian king Frederick William IV declined to become the figurehead monarch of a Germany governed by a parliament.*

In 1861, Victor Emmanuel II, king of Piedmont-Sardinia, was declared king of Italy. In 1866, as a result of Italy's support of Prussia in the Austro-Prussian War, the new nation acquired Venetia. In 1870, when French troops defending the papacy vacated Rome to face Prussian forces at home, Italian troops moved in and took the city. The following year, with the assent of Roman people, Rome was declared the capital of Italy. The pope, previously the ruler of the central 15 percent of the peninsula, retreated to the tiny precinct of the Vatican on the west side of the river Tiber. The political unification of Italy had been achieved. The great disparities in economic level and linguistic and cultural differences among Italy's varied regions were not yet overcome, and would remain an issue at the end of the following century.

The Unification of Germany

It was through the inspired and often ruthless methods of the Prussian nobleman Otto von Bismarck (1815–1896) that the unification of Germany was achieved. Bismarck completed a process begun by Napoleon and furthered by the Congress of Vienna, of rationalizing the many German cities and principalities into a coherent whole, as the inset to Map 23.3 on p. 680 shows. But the thirty-nine states of the German Confederation, established by the Congress, which included both Prussia and Austria, did not amount to a nation, as the events of the 1830s and 1840s demonstrated. In the spring of 1848, revolutions provided the impetus for a first attempt at unification. This forced promises of liberalization, which would be followed by the reassertion of central authority. In Frankfurt, in May 1848, more than 800 delegates from many of the German states met to design a constitution for a future nation, as depicted above. Over 80 percent of the delegates to this Frankfurt Parliament had attended universities, and two-thirds were judges, lawyers, professors, teachers, or bureaucrats—a cross-section of the liberal bourgeoisie, though tilted toward diligent and idealistic professionals, with few businessmen.

The liberalization of the Frankfurt delegates went only so far. Confining the franchise to propertied men, unfriendly to the needs of workers or peasants, and unwilling to admit to the union any state bringing with it territories having non-German populations, the Frankfurt Parliament had few supporters. In 1849, nevertheless, it promulgated a constitution for a united German state with a limited monarchy. When offered the crown of the new Germany, the Prussian king, Frederick William IV (r. 1840–1861), spurned it, and the bourgeois liberals who had made the offer, calling it a "crown from the gutter." The rejection of the new constitution by Prussia and (previously) by Austria, undermined the Frankfurt Parliament, and it dispersed.

In 1862, a struggle between the new king, William I (king of Prussia 1861–1888; German emperor 1871–1888) and the Prussian Parliament resulted in the appointment of Bismarck as prime minister. Aiming at any cost to defend the monarchy within Prussia, and Prussia's status in Germany and elsewhere in Europe, Bismarck pursued a strategy based on clear-sighted identification of the state's real interests, that would be dubbed *Realpolitik*. Accordingly, as a first step, he established the army's requirements as paramount within the state; he also suppressed liberalism in its various forms; liberal parties, supporters, and press. Next, he undertook war against Denmark (1864), Austria (1866), and France (1870–1871), in order to secure Prussian dominance within the German confederation and preeminence in a future united Germany.

The war against Denmark won the province of Schleswig-Holstein for Prussia. The Austro-Prussian War humiliated Austria militarily and resulted in the elimination of the German Confederation (which had included Austria) and the creation of the North German Confederation (which did not). The war against France saw Prussian forces defeat the French army, then besiege Paris—whose citizens responded by forming the revolutionary Commune (see above). The peace settlement of the Franco-Prussian War awarded Prussia the border provinces of Alsace and Lorraine, where many German speakers lived, and a cash indemnity. On January 18, 1871, in the palace of Versailles, the German Empire was officially proclaimed, with William I as emperor and Bismarck as chancellor (the event is depicted on p. 681). Bismarck's later speech to the German people, exhorting them to be strong, is quoted in *Witnesses* on p. 682.

[margin handwriting: German Empire]

THE STATE TRIUMPHANT: 1848–1914

Between 1848 and 1914, the political landscape of Europe fundamentally changed. Germany and Italy became nations; Austria-Hungary ceased to be the overweening power it once had been. France became a republic once again, and permanently, and Britain

approached democracy. After 1861, Russia no longer rested on the shoulders of its serfs, and even in laggard Spain and Portugal, forces were in action that would lead to the modernization of these states. In most of the European nations, by 1914, all adult men could vote; parliaments met to debate principles or make laws, and growing swarms of bureaucrats administered offices responsible for commerce, transportation, and education. Meanwhile, industrialization and modernization encouraged a swelling proletariat of displaced artisans and aspiring workers to press for a better life. The clamor of peoples—for nationhood, for food, for land, for security, for glory—could not be ignored by powerful states, even as they encroached in new ways into the lives of their citizens.

Britain: The Challenge of Mass Politics

The modernization of the state in Britain was fundamentally connected to the nation's liberalization and, especially, the broadening of its franchise. It was here that the liberal agenda won its greatest victory, as the expansion of the franchise in 1832 set Britain on the path it would follow for decades.

Despite the cautions of wealthy businessmen, aristocrats, and Queen Victoria (r. 1837–1901), a second Reform Act, in 1867, extended the franchise yet again, more than doubling the number of those entitled to vote in 1832. This new bill, which admitted all but the poorest laborers to the electorate, resulted in a more liberal Parliament, which reformed the army, legalized trade unions, and limited the privileges of the Church of England. In 1884, the franchise was extended once more to include virtually all adult males—an additional 2 million voters. The foundations for modern democracy were now solidly laid.

[margin handwriting: Suffrage]

Guiding Britain during this period were two capable prime ministers, William Gladstone (1809–1898) for the new Liberal party (which took the place of the former Whig party) and Benjamin Disraeli (1804–1881) for the Conservative (or Tory) party. Though responsible to very different constituencies, both supported the laissez-faire (free trade) policies which had prevailed in Britain since the repeal of the Corn Laws in 1846 (see above). Under Gladstone, whose speech to Parliament is quoted in *Witnesses* on p. 682, the Liberal party won broad support from the new voters admitted in 1867 and 1884. Under Disraeli, the Conservatives built nationalist and imperialist themes into their party platform in order to mobilize popular support outside of the landed elite and wealthiest business leaders. Other parties and interest groups pressed for a broader democracy—among them the suffragettes, who worked for women's political rights; reform-minded socialists (see Chapter 25); and, after 1901, the newly-formed Labour party. By the early twentieth century, British government was responsible to the masses of its people.

Russia: An Autocracy Attempts Reform

The autocratic Russian regime did not possess the flexibility of the British government. In 1848, the system was still based on a nobility whose loyalty was repaid with concessions over a serf population that included—since merchants and middle-class professional were few—nearly all of the Russian people.

By 1860, it was clear that serfdom must end. In a rapidly changing world, serfs had become inefficient: as workers, as soldiers, as citizens. Serf labor discouraged innovation—on the part of both landowners, who lived sufficiently on the labor of others, and serfs themselves, who clung to traditional methods of organization. Although freed serfs, as a large new class of taxpayers, might be a source of state revenue, escaped and rebellious serfs were a drain on the purse and a threat to order. If Russia were to rank alongside the great powers of the West, it was necessary to emancipate the serfs.

On March 3, 1861, Tsar Alexander II (r. 1855–1881) proclaimed the emancipation of the nation's 12 million serfs—roughly one half of all Russians then living. The state would recompense landowners for the loss of their land, which would be distributed among the former serfs by the village council of male householders. The former serfs would reimburse the state in forty-nine annual payments, with the village being collectively responsible for the debt. During that time, the serfs were rooted to their village. It would be almost two generations before large sections of the peasant population were truly free. In the meantime, former serfs were no longer counted among the "souls" with which landowners had reckoned their capital and could no longer be beaten or killed at a nobleman's nod.

Alexander also introduced further reforms. In 1864, he created village and regional *zemstvos*, or assemblies. In 1870, he created a similar structure of *dumas*, or councils, for cities. In both cases, the delegates were chosen by local officials and could not operate as representative institutions. Nevertheless, they were the first institutional structures of the kind in Russia and had potential for further political development. The tsar also instituted courts of justice (necessitated by the handover of judicial powers from landowners to the state) and reformed the army, which now relied on free peasant, rather than impressed serf, conscripts.

Freeing the serfs did not make Russia a liberal state. The tsarist Third Section (secret) police harried "political criminals" (anyone construed as an enemy of the regime) and tried to safeguard Russia from revolutionary ideas, which arrived between the covers of foreign books, smuggled in by the millions. In contrast to western Europe, where liberal intellectuals were often also teachers, journalists, or physicians, Russian society fostered the development of a permanent group of professional revolutionaries, largely from the nobility, many of whom became martyrs to the cause of social revolution. The benevolent tyrant himself, Alexander II, was also a martyr of sorts, assassinated in 1881 (after earlier attempts) by members of a radical political club.

From the 1880s until the outbreak of revolution in 1917 (see Chapter 26), a wide range of political activists and parties strove for preeminence— from democrats who wished to establish a parliamentary system to socialists representing the peasants' or workers' interests (see Chapter 25). Under Alexander's successor, Alexander III (r. 1881–1894), repression returned. The tsar launched a program of "Russification," supported by the Russian Orthodox Church, aimed at the 60 percent of the population that was not ethnically Russian (in Poland, Ukraine, and Belorussia; in the Baltic, the Caucasus, and Central Asia). Under Nicholas II (r. 1894–1917), Russia's expansionist policies led to the catastrophe of the Russo-Japanese War (1904–1905; see Chapter 24). Russia's defeat in that conflict, only 50 years after its defeat in the Crimea, pointed to the weakness of the regime and invited the revolutionary outbreak of 1905, to which the government offered only an inadequate response (see Chapter 26).

By the beginning of the twentieth century, attempts at reform in Russia had still failed to dismantle that nation's autocracy, increasingly untenable in an era of population aspirations.

France: From Second Empire to Third Republic

While Russia remained in thrall to its long-established policy of repression, France might have been expected—in the light of its recent history—to be a model of political and social progress. But the government in power from 1851 (when the Second Republic was dissolved) to 1870 discouraged the liberalization for which many clamored. To be sure, there had been significant gains. Napoleon III ruled an empire in which all adult males were eligible to vote (the only nation in Europe that could so boast); where strikes were legal (after 1864); and where the government encouraged commerce, urban renewal, and the construction of railroads. Yet it was a nation where the wealthy lived to excess; where the press was censored; where the Roman Catholic Church was privileged; where political patronage and favoritism reigned. Nowhere in Europe were the bourgeoisie more solid or content (in Britain, they still lived in the shadow of aristocracy). And nowhere in Europe were the strivings of workers—not factory workers, who were few (see Chapter 21), but rather artisans such as shoemakers and tailors—more fierce or explosive.

In September 1870, Prussian armies blazed through northeastern France; captured, deposed, and exiled the emperor Napoleon III; and marched on Paris. In Paris, the French proclaimed the Third Republic, established a provisional government, and laid plans to elect a National Assembly which would create a new constitution. The provisional government then withdrew to Tours, as the Prussians besieged Paris, abandoned to its poorest citizens—the Communards (see above). In January 1871, in the Hall of Mirrors at Versailles, where Louis XIV had flaunted the glory of France, the victors proclaimed the German Empire. In February, the Germans settled an armistice with the French government in exile. In March, the French government sent the regular army of the newly declared Third Republic to destroy the Paris Commune—which had, not long before, stood alone to block the Prussian advance.

The dead buried, the Third Republic resumed course. In the French National Assembly, as in the British Parliament, liberal and conservative interests wrested with each other. The political parties competed for support from the increasingly influential middle bourgeoisie of shopowners, teachers, and prosperous peasants. Moderate republican leaders tried to steer a center course between monarchists, supported by the Church, on the right, and militant socialists on the left. Liberals could rejoice that elections were based on universal manhood suffrage, that freedom of the press was guaranteed, that the Church was muzzled, and that a system of mass education had been instituted (see Chapter 25). Conservatives nursed nationalist sentiments and imperialist ambitions, stained by anti-Semitism (see Chapter 24).

Central Europe: The German and Austro-Hungarian Empires

The new German Empire was the old Prussian state writ large, even though individual states (there were twenty-five) were allowed considerable autonomy within their own boundaries. The parliament, or Reichstag, existed to approve what the emperor and his chief minister, the chancellor, proposed. It did not supply cabinet officers, nor did it propose legislation. Military and foreign policy were decided elsewhere, and positions in the army and civil service were staffed by members of the Prussian autocracy—the "Junker" elite. The preeminence of Prussian nobles in the administration of the German state was widely accepted by the high bourgeoisie, which in this period was engaged in the process of industrialization.

Corpses of the Communards: *French politics continued along a radical path after the Congress of Vienna. The short-lived Paris Commune, an autonomous state created by left-wing intellectuals and urban workers, ended with the massacre of the defenders. Note the corpse of the young woman lined up with those of her companions, a few among the thousands who were executed by government soldiers and then prepared for mass burial.* (Musée Carnavalet, Paris)

The Meaning of Country: German and Italian Nationalism

The French Revolution brought liberalism to all corners of Europe; and it brought nationalism as well. Just as the French gained a sense of themselves as a "people" when they became self-governing citizens, no longer subject to a king, they gained a sense of themselves as a nation, the patrie, or "fatherland." The foreign peoples whose lands they invaded—or "liberated"—learned from the French what it was to be a people, and longed for the true liberation of their nations, whether from the French invaders, or their own rulers. The passages here are by two nationalists whose compatriots struggled for and won independence by 1871: the German Johann Gottlieb Fichte (1762–1814) and the Italian Giuseppe Mazzini (1805–1872).

Johann Gottlieb Fichte examines the sentiment of love of country, which binds people on earth to an eternal principle (1807): Love that is truly love, and not a mere transitory lust, never clings to what is transient; only in the eternal does it awaken and become kindled, and there alone does it rest. Man is not able to love even himself unless he conceives himself as eternal; apart from that he cannot even respect, much less approve, of himself. Still less can be love anything outside himself without taking it up into the eternity of his faith and of his soul and binding it thereto. He who does not first regard himself as eternal has in him no love of any kind, and, moreover, cannot love a fatherland, a thing which for him does not exist. He who regards his invisible life as eternal, but not his visible life as similarly eternal, may perhaps have a heaven and therein a fatherland, but here below he has no fatherland, for this, too, is regarded only in the image of eternity—eternity visible and made sensuous, and for this reason also he is unable to love his fatherland. If none has been handed down to such a man, he is to be pitied. But he to whom a fatherland has been handed down, and in whose soul heaven and earth, visible and invisible meet and mingle, and thus, and only thus, create a true and enduring heaven—such a man fights to the last drop of his blood to hand on the precious possession unimpaired to his posterity.

Hence, the noble-minded man will be active and effective, and will sacrifice himself for his people. Life merely as such, the mere continuance of changing existence, has in any case never had any value for him, he has wished for it only as the source of what is permanent. But this permanence is promised to him only by the continuous and independent existence of his nation. In order to save his nation he must be ready even to die that it may live, and that he may live in it the only life for which he has ever wished.

(From Johann Gottlieb Fichte, *Addresses to the German nation* (New York: Funk & Wagnalls, 1898), trans. R. F. Jones & G. H. Turnbull (Chicago: University of Chicago Press, 1922).

Giuseppe Mazzini calls upon the workers of Italy to love their country, so as to serve all humanity (1844): O, my brothers, love your Country! Our country is our Home, a house God has given us, placing therein a numerous family that loves us, and whom we love. … Our Country is our common workshop, whence the products of our activity are sent forth for the benefit of the whole world; wherein the tools and implements of labour we can most usefully employ are gathered together; nor may we reject them without disobeying the plan of the Almighty, and diminishing our own strength.

In labouring for our own country on the right principle, we labour for Humanity. Our country is the fulcrum of the lever we have to wield for the common good. If we abandon the fulcrum, we run the risk of rendering ourselves useless not only to Humanity but to our country itself. Before men can associate with the nations of which Humanity is composed, they must have a national existence. There is no true association except among equals. It is only through our country that we can have a recognized collective existence. Humanity is a vast army advancing to the conquest of lands unknown, against enemies both powerful and astute. … Wheresoever you may be, in the centre of whatsoever people circumstances may have placed you, be ever ready to combat for the liberty of that people, should it be necessary, but combat in such wise that the blood you shed may reflect glory, not on yourself alone, but on your country. … Your country is the sign of the Mission God has given you to fulfill towards Humanity. The faculties and forces of all her sons should be associated in the accomplishment of that mission. The true country is a community of free men and equals, bound together in fraternal concord to labour towards a common aim. … Where the activity of a portion of the powers and faculties of the individual is either cancelled or dormant; where there is not a common Principle, recognized, accepted, and developed by all, there is no true Nation, no People; but only a multitude, a fortuitous agglomeration of men whom circumstances have called together and whom circumstances may again divide. …

(From Joseph Mazzini, *An Essay On the Duties of Man Addressed to Workingmen* (New York: http://history.hanover.edu/texts/mazzini/mazzini5.htm)

National and ethnic groups within Habsburg Empire

Slavonic:
- Czech
- Slovak
- Polish
- Slovene
- Croatians and Serbians
- Ruthenians (Ukrainians)

Teutonic:
- German

Romanic:
- Italian
- Romanian

Finno-Ugrian:
- Magyars (Hungarians)
- border of Habsburg empire

Unification of Germany, to 1871
- Prussia, 1815
- territory acquired by Prussia, 1815-66
- other German states absorbed into empire
- military campaigns, 1864-71
- boundary of North German Confederation, 1866
- boundary of German Empire, 1871

Unification of Italy, to 1870
- kingdom of Piedmont-Sardinia
- territory lost to France, 1860
- territory annexed 1859
- annexed 1860
- annexed 1866
- annexed 1870
- route of Garibaldi's forces
- Italian frontier, 1914

Map 23.3 Unification and Differentiation—the Diverse Fates of Ethnic, Religious, and National Peoples around 1870: *By 1871, both Italy and Germany achieved national unification, guided by the effective ministers of Piedmont–Sardinia and Prussia, respectively. During the same years, Europe's eastern empires (Austro-Hungarian, Russian, and Ottoman) contained numerous ethnic, religious, and national minorities whose aspirations remained a source of tension well into the next century.*

The Making of an Emperor, 1871: *Here, Prussian King William I and his Chancellor Otto von Bismarck celebrate the creation of the German empire, with the former as ruler, in January, 1871—even as Parisian workers and shopkeepers vowed to keep Paris free in the face of German invasion—in the Hall of Mirrors, a fitting setting from the age of absolutism, in the palace of Versailles built by an earlier absolute ruler, Louis XIV.*

Far more worrying to them than the pretensions of the nobles were the aspirations of the workers, which were voiced with increasing firmness after the German Social Democratic Party (or SDP) was founded in 1875. By 1912, this party would account for 35 percent of the popular vote.

Bismarck was extraordinarily effective in preventing further inroads of the SDP, instituting government-funded insurance programs which preempted the social democratic agenda (see Chapter 22). He also labored to limit the privileges enjoyed since antiquity by the Catholic Church in Germany—a church to which more than one-third of the population belonged. In his ***Kulturkampf***, or "culture war," he secularized marriage and the institution of the priesthood. In addition, he retained the ban on Catholic (and Jewish) participation in high government office and looked suspiciously at the center- and left-leaning Catholic political parties. In 1890, however, Bismarck's stern and vigorous management of the affairs of the Prussian state and the new German Empire came to an end. Unable to work with

the new emperor, William II (r. 1888–1917), a man of mediocre mind and lazy temperament, he resigned. Without his guidance, Germany became increasingly aggressive and nationalistic.

Whereas in Germany and other European countries, the struggles between liberals and conservatives, monarchists and republicans, Catholics and socialists were paramount, in Austria-Hungary the key issues remained ethnic: Where was there freedom, or even a sense of identity, for Slavs in a society dominated by Germans and Magyars, whose combined population amounted to less than one-fourth of the population. Croats and Czechs (the latter constituting the third-largest ethnic group in Austria-Hungary), especially, pressed for autonomy, their demands most strongly resisted by the Magyars, who launched a "Magyarization" campaign—resented all the more because the Magyar language, unrelated to the Slav or Germanic languages of other denizens of the Empire, was exceedingly difficult for non-natives to learn.

The task that fell to Emperor Francis Joseph was to hold the Empire together, in the face of these ethnic

Statesmen Look Ahead: Austria, Germany, Britain

Statesmen, diplomats, politicians won a new importance in the modernizing states of the nineteenth century. Here three such statesmen look to the future. Prince Clemens von Metternich (1773–1859), agent of the Habsburgs, urges the legitimate governments of Europe to band together to suppress the forces of liberalism and dissent. Otto von Bismarck (1815–1898), chancellor of the German Empire 1871–1890, urges the Germans, who were surrounded on all sides by "warlike neighbors," to be strong. William Ewart Gladstone (1809–1898), four times British prime minister and, from 1867, leader of the Liberal party, urges his listeners to accept the reality of mass politics and welcome the previously excluded working majority as participants in the nation-state.

Metternich calls on the states of Europe to save society from ruin (1820). Union between the monarchs is the basis of the policy which must now be followed to save society from total ruin. ...

The first principle to be followed by the monarchs, united as they are by the coincidence of their desires and opinions, should be that of maintaining the stability of political institutions against the disorganized excitement which has taken possession of men's minds. ...

Let [the Governments] in these troublous times be more than usually cautious in attempting real ameliorations, not imperatively claimed by the needs of the moment, to the end that good itself may not turn against them—which is the case whenever a Government measure seems to be inspired by fear. ...

Let them give minute attention to the financial state of their kingdoms, so that their people may enjoy, by the reduction of public burdens, the real, not imaginary, benefits of a state of peace.

Let them be just, but strong; beneficent, but strict.

Let them maintain religious principles in all their purity, and not allow the faith to be attacked and morality interpreted according to the social contract or the visions of foolish sectarians.

Let them suppress Secret Societies, that gangrene of society.

In short, let the great monarchs strengthen their union, and prove to the world that if it exists, it is beneficent, and ensures the political peace of Europe: that it is powerful only for the maintenance of tranquility at a time when so many attacks are directed against it; that the principles which they profess are paternal and protective, menacing only the disturbers of public tranquility. ...

(From Prince Klemens von Metternich, "Political Confession of Faith," 1820, in *Memoirs of Prince Metternich, 1815–1829*, ed. Prince Richard Metternich (New York: Scribner and Son 1881.)

Bismarck urges Germany, unified at last, to be strong (1888). When I say that it is our duty to endeavour to be ready at all times and for all emergencies, I imply that we must make greater exertions than other people for the same purpose, because of our geographical position. We are situated in the heart of Europe, and have at least three fronts open to an attack. France has only her eastern, and Russia only her western frontier where they may be attacked. We are also more exposed to the dangers of a coalition than any other nation. ... God has placed us where we are prevented, thanks to our neighbors, from growing lazy and dull. He has placed by our side the most warlike and restless of all nations, the French, and He has permitted warlike inclinations to grow strong in Russia, where formerly they existed to a lesser degree. Thus we are given the spur, so to speak, from both sides, and are compelled to exertions which we should perhaps not be making otherwise. The pikes in the European carp-pond are keeping us from being carps by making us feel their teeth on both sides. ... This will bring us to that state of being inseparable which all other nations possess, while we do not yet enjoy it. But we must respond to the intentions of Providence by making ourselves so strong that the pikes can do nothing but encourage us. ... Attack the German nation anywhere, and you will find it armed to a man, and every man with the firm belief in his heart: God will be with us.

(From Otto von Bismarck, "Speech to the Reichstag," 1888, in *The Age of Bismarck: Documents and Interpretations*, ed. T. S. Hamerow (New York: Harper & Row, 1973), pp. 290–293; from Rogers 2.218–20.

William Gladstone asks the House of Commons to look into the future (1866). Let us for a moment consider the enormous and silent changes which have been going forward among the labouring population. ... Let us try and raise our views above the fears, the suspicions, he jealousies, the reproaches, and the recriminations of this place and this occasion. Let us look onward to the time of our children and our children's children. ... Is there or is there not, I ask, a steady movement of the labouring classes, and is or is not that movement a movement onwards and upwards? ...

But a very few words more, and I have done. May I speak briefly to honourable gentlemen opposite (i.e. the Conservative party]. ... You cannot fight against the future. Time is on our side. The great social forces which move onwards in their might and majesty, and which the tumult of our debates does not for a moment impede or disturb— those great social forces are against you; they are marshaled on our side; and the banner which we now carry in this fight, though perhaps at some moment it may droop over our sinking heads, yet it soon again will float in the eye of heaven, and it will be borne by the firm hands of the united people of the three kingdoms, perhaps not to an easy, but to a certain and not too distant victory.

(From Gladstone, "Speech to the House of Commons, 12 April 1866." http://www.csn.ul.ie/~debates/gladstone.htm.)

demands, by the symbolic power of his Habsburg ancestry and with support from the long-established Catholic Church. The army, too, was a force for unity, its soldiers drawn from the twelve different constituent nationalities of the empire (although a disproportionate number of its officers were German-speaking). A new threat to imperial unity emerged after 1878, when Austria-Hungary absorbed Bosnia and Herzegovina, which included a population of Muslims (in a Catholic empire) and Serbs (sentimentally linked to their kin in independent Serbia, and supported by the Russian Pan-Slavic policies). These tensions would lead to the Balkan wars of 1912–1913 and to a series of terrorist incidents, and would create the immediate conditions for the outbreak of war in 1914 (see Chapter 26).

Mediterranean Europe: Italy, Spain, and Portugal

In southern Europe, the patterns of democratization and modernization best seen in Britain, and recognizable elsewhere, are obscured.

The unification of Italy, completed in 1871, was imposed by a northern literate bourgeoisie upon the massive poor, illiterate, and fervently Catholic population of the southern part of the peninsula, who sought neither the culture nor the politics of a liberal age. Here, the authority of the local priest, landowner, and small merchant was respectfully acknowledged, with order maintained by the highly organized criminal networks, the Camorra (in Naples) or the Mafia (in Sicily). The northern regime brought taxation and conscription. The pope, meanwhile, forbade Catholics even to vote for federal politicians, while political leaders unseated the Church from the schools, from its land, and even from its jurisdiction over marriage and divorce and other areas traditionally subject to **canon law**.

In the north, under the aegis of the monarchs Victor Emmanuel II (r. 1861–1878), Umberto I (r. 1878–1900), and Victor Emmanuel II (r. 1900–1946), ministers and deputies came and went, knitting together loose political coalitions which opposed both militant workers and the disestablishment of the Church, while sometimes trumpeting nationalist and imperialist themes. When the liberal prime minister Giovanni Giolitti (1842–1928), the most successful of these transient figures, drew too close to an agreement with the Church after 1912, the socialists won an enormous victory, forcing Giolitti out—just on the eve of impending war (see Chapter 26). By that juncture, the Italians had not succeeded in democratizing, modernizing, or even truly unifying their state.

Church and monarchy also remained powerful forces in the two nations of the Iberian Peninsula. Spain under Queen Isabella II (r. 1833–1868) (who

had been preferred to her brother Don Carlos, promoted by a reactionary faction) was a turbulent scene of coup and counter-coup, in which monarchists, moderates, republicans, and separatists contended. The period from Isabella's death until 1876 oscillated between monarchy and republic, until a constitutional monarchy was established under King Alfonso XII (r. 1868–1885). Isabella's son. By this time, constitutional monarchists had to contend with socialist and anarchist parties which had begun to make inroads among enclaves of workers, especially in Asturias and the Basque region; the first socialists were elected to the Spanish Parliament in 1909. Frequent strikes were met with severe repression, and political life remained unstable well into the new century, up to the brink of the Civil War of the 1930s (see Chapter 28). Portugal, too, struggled between liberal and reactionary monarchical regimes throughout the nineteenth century.

Wars and Alliances

If the last decades of the nineteenth century were a period of state consolidation, they also saw the increasing belligerency of some European nations who sought to expand their territory or their military capacity. That belligerency expressed itself in wars, which broke out in the Balkans, in response to Russian ambitions, and also, spurred by Prussian aggression, in central and western Europe. In seeking protection from their neighbors' expansionist tendencies, European states cast about for friends and supporters, creating a network of alliances and counter-alliances which would themselves ultimately become a cause of political instability.

The Congress of Vienna of 1814–1815 had envisioned a grand "Concert of Europe," a peaceful coexistence of nations whose mutual difficulties would be resolved through diplomacy and compromise. To a greater extent, that vision had been realized. Congresses held at Berlin in 1878 and 1884–1885 attempted to settle Balkan affairs and to mediate among the European states pressing to enter and exploit Africa. Another international gathering held at The Hague in 1899, discussed the restraint of armament levels, and became the world body known as the International Court of Justice. Yet unresolved conflicts between states resulted in sporadic European wars: the Crimean War (1853–1856), concerned with Russian advances in the Balkans; the Prussian invasion of Denmark of 1864; and the Austro-Prussian (1866) and Franco-Prussian wars (1870–1871).

In 1853, the post-Napoleonic calm was first ruptured when Russia invaded the Ottoman principalities of Moldavia and Walachia in the Balkans. Russia sought to support its Slavic brethren in these lands and also to push its way to Constantinople, where the

The French Revolution of 1789 was the mother of many revolutions, most clustering around the sparkpoints of 1830 and 1848. In the illustration above right by J. N. Lewicki, entitled "Great Saturday," Polish nationalists seeking independence from Russia establish a provisional government in 1831 following a major revolt. Russia soon crushed the revolt, and established full control. A newly-installed bourgeois government sent the national army to suppress the revolt of Paris workers and artisans in 1848, of whom a few martyrs are depicted below left, in a painting by Ernest Meissonier, fallen alongside the barricade built of cobbles spanning the narrow street of their humble quarter. A common theme in the Parisian revolts of 1789, 1848, and 1870–1871 was the assertion of women's rights and right to speak in the political clubs that sprung up spontaneously once the grip of authority relaxed. Such a woman's club is depicted below right, as a woman of great personal presence addresses an audience of enthusiastic listeners. (top: National Museum, Cracow; below left: Louvre, Paris; below right: Musée d'Art Moderne de la Ville de Paris)

J. N. Lewicki, Great Saturday, 1831

Ernest Meissonier, La Barricade, rue de la Mortellerie, Memory of the Civil War, June 1848

Women's Club, Paris, c. 1848

To continue your investigation of this topic, please go to www.prenhall.com/king for the related **WINDOWS** on the **WEB** activity

Turks held sway, and thus open the Mediterranean waters to the Russian navy. The British, who had friendly trade relations with the Ottomans and feared Russian encroachment in this region, soon came to the support of the Turks. Napoleon III of France, in turn, supported Britain, partly because he felt that a military victory abroad would be likely to play well at home. Camillo di Cavour, premier of Piedmont-Sardinia, lent his aid to France in exchange for French aid in the unification of Italy. And Austria-Hungary, always opposed to a strong Russian presence in the Balkans, also joined the allies.

Most of the fighting took place on the Crimean peninsula, then a Russian possession, on the Black Sea (hence the name "Crimean War" for this conflict). Poorly armed, Russia was unable to prevent the destruction of its naval base at Sevastopol; its defeat was total. Britain had demonstrated its leadership as much as Russia had its military weakness; the Ottoman Empire was saved; and, in 1858, the two principalities of Moldavia and Walachia, whose occupation by Russia had triggered the war, were united to form the independent state of Romania. The Russians returned home to digest the meaning of their failure, which would soon stimulate political reforms and an accelerated program of industrialization.

Ten years after the end of the Crimean War, Austria, too, would know defeat—at the hands of its rival Prussia. Whereas earlier in the century Austria had enjoyed ascendancy over Prussia in the German Confederation, now Prussia had become powerful; and in 1866, in a conflict lasting only seven weeks, it dismantled Austrian influence among the German states. That achieved, the way was prepared for the next step, which followed shortly, of German unification under Prussian auspices.

The political diminution of France, the plaything in the nineteenth century of two Napoleons, was accomplished by the Franco-Prussian War. It was fought over the same strip of territory west of the Rhine about which Charlemagne's grandsons had struggled in the ninth century, and it resulted in the annexation by Prussia of some of that corridor: the provinces of Alsace and Lorraine, including the prosperous cities of Strasbourg and Metz. The war also precipitated the collapse of the Second Empire, the departure of Emperor Napoleon III, and the inauguration of the French Third Republic.

On their own territory, the European states showed some restraint in confining themselves to these few wars. Abroad, they battled freely as they saw fit in pursuit of colonial interests (see Chapter 24). The swift, brisk wars of the nineteenth century, often won by simple superiority of firepower, were not greatly dangerous (except that they encouraged complacency about the frightening possibilities of full-scale war). Diplomats, meanwhile, labored to ward off potential conflicts by constructing complex (and

secret) defensive alliances. Toward the end of the nineteenth century, these began to proliferate.

An overview of the nineteenth century reveals two general patterns of alliance, one succeeding the other, with Russian Pan-Slavism serving as the hinge. Until the 1880s Austria and Prussia (later Germany) were allied with Russia, while France and Britain remained aloof. But from the 1880s, Russian Pan-Slav policies antagonized those central European empires. Russia eventually found support from France and Britain—the latter two nations, who had faced each other in the Hundred Years' War of the late Middle Ages and in the colonial struggles of the eighteenth century, finally uniting in an epochal joining of hands on the eve of world war.

The earlier of these two alliance systems began with the Holy Alliance (1815) of Austria, Prussia, and Russia, an immediate outgrowth of the counterrevolutionary agenda of the Congress of Vienna. Central to Metternich's strategy was the buttressing of monarchical power with the authority of the Church. In the Holy Alliance, the three emperors of central and eastern Europe sought to protect the interests of their churches and to gain enhanced reputation from their role as protectors of religion. The three-party alliance was revived at Bismarck's instigation in the Three Emperors' League of 1873 (renewed in 1881), even after Austria-Hungary had joined Britain and France in punishing Russia in the Crimea.

The later of the two alliance systems emerged in the aftermath of the Crimean War, with the development of Russian Pan-Slavism. Russia's earlier solidarity with the two central European emperors had been shaken in the Crimea and destroyed in 1878 by the Congress of Berlin (see Chapter 26). After 1890, which contained Russia's expansion on

HOW MANY?

Great Power Battle Deaths in European Wars, 1803–1918

Napoleonic Wars (1803–1815)	1,869,000
Crimean War (1853–1856)	217,000
Franco-Prussian War (1870–1871)	180,000
World War I (1914–1918)	7,734,300

Source: C. Tilly, *Coercion, Capital and European States, AD 990–1990* (Cambridge, MA: Basil Blackwell, 1990), pp. 165–166.

Triple Entente

the Balkan peninsula, Russia sought the support of the two other great powers, France and Britain. France was a natural ally of Russia, as long-standing cultural ties bound the two nations together, recently strengthened by a flow of French capital eastward to fund Russia's railroads and burgeoning industries. By 1894, Russia and France had forged a joint defensive alliance.

At first, Britain, sheltered by the power of her navy, refused to join any of these alliance systems. Her natural sympathies lay with Germany, and she had long been hostile to France. However, rapid German naval buildup in the 1890s, seemingly aimed specifically at dismantling British superiority, eroded those sympathies. By 1904, Britain's diplomats had tilted to France, with whom it signed the Entente Cordiale (a "cordial agreement"). The European nations were rapidly becoming entangled in a complicated web of mutual assurance and fear.

Britain did not as yet turn to Russia, with whom it competed for influence in Persia and Afghanistan. To complicate matters, Britain supported the world's newest great power, Japan, after 1902, in response to Russia's new presence at Port Arthur, and Japan would best Russia in the conflict of 1905–1906. Nevertheless, by 1907, Britain had decided that Russia was less of a threat than Germany, and the two nations settled their differences over the Middle East. The Entente Cordiale with France was now enlarged by the participation of Russia, and renamed the Triple Entente. Meanwhile, in response to Russia's apparent hostility, Germany and Austria-Hungary formed between themselves the rock-solid Dual Alliance of 1879; three years later, Italy joined them to make the Triple Alliance. In the last years before 1914, when war would break out again, Triple Entente and Triple Alliance faced each other, tense with mutual fears (see Chapter 26).

Conclusion

THE TRIUMPHAL STATE AND THE MEANING OF THE WEST

The period from Napoleon's defeat to the outbreak of world war, nearly one hundred years later, was punctuated by confrontation between the state and its people: official power versus the power of populations energized by liberalism, nationalism, socialism, and other vision of self-advancement (see Chapter 25). In 1830, in 1848, in 1871, the power of the state reasserted itself. As the European nations crossed into the twentieth century, their leaders were wary but contented. They did not doubt the strength, the competence, the rightness of their governments to do what they were doing. The same confidence would be observed on the continents of Asia and Africa and in the Americas, as these triumphal modernized western states ventured out to control most of the rest of the globe.

At the same time, the European state system was fragile. Officials often held on to power by repressing opposition. Increasingly, that opposition came not from angry mobs of protestors, who could easily be shot down by a detachment of well-disciplined troops. Instead, it came through the organized institution of a political party—moderate, liberal, left, conservative; centrist, socialist, democratic, republican constitutionalist, anarchist, syndicalist, agrarian socialist, Christian democratic, Catholic worker. These, too, could be suppressed. But they could also negotiate and compromise and build new alliances, win seats in the national parliament, and bring the voice of the people to the chamber where decisions were made that impacted on the lives of all.

The state emerged triumphant from the trials of the century from 1815 to 1914. But the state had a new partner. The millions of citizens freed by the forces of modernization and industrialization from bondage to the land, and by the words of post-Enlightenment theorists from bondage to authority (see Chapter 25) would not willingly return to their former condition of servitude.

REVIEW QUESTIONS

1. What were the main goals of the representatives to the Congress of Vienna? How effectively did the post-Congress-era leaders manage crises in Latin America, Greece, and Russia?

2. What were the origins of nationalism, and what were its main victories and frustrations during the period 1815–1871? What were the main differences between the processes of unification of Italy and of Germany? What were the experiences of the different ethnic minorities of the Habsburg empire?

3. How did the principles of liberalism enter into the politics of the period 1830–1848? To what extent were attempts to suppress liberalism successful? Was Europe more liberal in 1871 than in 1789?

4. To what extent did the powerful nation-states that prevailed during the period 1870–1914 rely on repression? To what extent did the derive their support from the mass of the population, and how did they win that support?

5. How did Russia's policies in eastern Europe and the Balkans impact upon the European nations? How successful was Russia in pursuing those policies?

SUGGESTED RESOURCES

Power to the People: 1815–1848

Church, Clive H., in *Europe 1830: Revolution and Political Change* (London–Boston: Allen & Unwin, 1983). Focuses on this often under-explored revolutionary year.

Droz, Jacques, *Europe Between Revolutions* (New York: Harper & Row, 1967). General account of the period 1815–1848.

Gould, Roger V. *Insurgent Identities: Class, Community, and Protest in Paris from 1848 to the Commune* (Chicago: University of Chicago Press, 1995). Comparing the Revolution of 1848 with the Commune, finds that social class identity was critical in the first, but small-group and neighborhood solidarity more important in the later conflict.

Sperber, Jonathan, *The European Revolutions, 1848–1851* (Cambridge: Cambridge University Press, 1994). Synthesis of recent scholarship.

Traugott, Mark, *Armies of the Poor: Determinants of Working-Class participation in the Parisian Insurrection of June 1848* (New York: Transaction Publishers, 2000). A sociologist analyzes the effects of organization upon the political beliefs and behavior of rebellious workers and Mobile Guard soldiers in the 1848 Revolution.

Encyclopedia of the 1848 Revolutions—brief essays on scores of figures and problems pertaining to the 1848 revolutions, by an international set of contributors, with bibliographies (1999, Ohio State University): http://www.cats.ohiou.edu/~Chastain/index.htm

One People, One Nation: 1848–1871

Blackbourn, David & Geoff Eley, *The Peculiarities of German History: Bourgeois Society and Politics in Nineteenth-Century German* (Oxford: Oxford University Press, 1984). Seeks to understand German developments in terms of the specific nature of German society within the European setting.

Deák, István, *The Lawful Revolution: Louis Kossuth and the Hungarians, 1848–1849* (New York: Columbia University Press, 1979). Classic study of Hungary's struggle against Habsburg rule in 1848, arguing that the revolutionary Kossuth acted within the bounds of constitutionality.

Salvatorelli, Luigi, *The Risorgimento: Thought and Actions*. Trans. Charles F. Delzell (New York: Harper & Row, 1970). Classic anti-fascist account of Italian unification and the creation of a liberal state, first published in Italian in 1943.

Smith, Dennis Mack. *Cavour* (New York: Knopf, 1985). Superior biography of a central figure in Italian unification.

Waller, Bruce, *Bismarck* (2nd ed.: Oxford–Cambridge MA: Blackwell, 1997). Studies Bismarck as maker of modern Germany, including militarism, Catholic strategy, and state construction.

The Monroe Doctrine (Avalon Project, Yale Law): http://www.yale.edu/lawweb/avalon/monroe.htm

The Anthony P. Campanella Collection of Giuseppe Garibaldi— images and materials, originally exhibited summer-fall 1997 (University of South Carolina): http://www.sc.edu/library/spcoll/hist/garib/garib.html

The State Triumphant: 1848–1914

Greenfield, Liah, *Nationalism: Five Roads to Modernity* (Cambridge, MA: Harvard University Press, 1992). The development of nationalism in four major European states and in the U.S., which argues that nationalism was an important factor promoting modernization, rather than a result thereof.

Hause, Steven, C., with Anne R. Kenney, *Women's Suffrage and Social Politics in the French Third Republic* (Princeton: Princeton University Press, 1984). Study of the political movement for women's suffrage in late nineteenth-century France.

Hobsbawm, E. J., *Nations and Nationalism since 1780: Programme, Myth, Reality* (new ed.; Cambridge: Cambridge University Press, 1993). Explores the origins of nationalisms, its efflorescence during the period 1870–1914, and its twentieth-century consequences.

Nord, Philip G., *The Republican Moment: The Struggle for Democracy in Nineteenth-Century France* (Cambridge, MA: Harvard University Press, 1995). Explores how, after the shock of revolutions and the experience of authoritarian government in the Second Empire, France achieved democracy due to the civic-minded solidarity of the people at large.

Okey, Robin, *The Habsburg Empire: from Enlightenment to Eclipse* (New York: St. Martin's Press, 2000). Utilizing sources reflecting its diverse ethnicities, traces how the Habsburg empire responded to the challenges of revolution and nationalism from the reign of Joseph II to the end of World War I.

Rich, Norman, *Why the Crimean War? A Cautionary Tale* (Hanover, NH: University of New England Press for Brown University, 1985). Synthesizes recent historical studies why the war happened and who won, and points to the greater conflict of World War I.

Simpson, William, *The Second Reich, 1871–1918* (Cambridge: Cambridge University Press, 1995). Overview of the whole era, attending to the competing views of contemporary historians.

THE WESTERN *IMPERIUM*

	1750	1775	1800	1825	1850	1875	1900	1925

Europe

Seven Years' War, 1756–63

French Revolutionary and Napoleonic Wars, 1792–1815

World War I, 1914–18

◆ Irish patriot Wolfe Tone rebels against Britain, 1798

◆ The Great Exhibition at London's Crystal Palace, 1851

◆ Roman Catholic Emancipation Act in Britain, 1829

◆ Serfdom abolished in Russia, 1861

◆ Potato famine devastates Ireland, 1845–50

◆ Alfred Dreyfus falsely accused of treason, 1894

◆ Theodore Herzl's *The Jewish State*, 1896

◆ Year of Revolutions in Europe, 1848

◆ J. A. Hobson's *Imperialism, a Study*, 1902

◆ 400 Jews killed in pogrom in Odessa, 1905

The Americas

Atlantic slave trade, 1500–1888

American Revolution, 1775–83

Most Latin American states independent, 1804–28

American Civil War, 1861–65

◆ Haiti first independent Latin American nation, 1804

◆ Canada becomes constitutional monarchy within British Empire, 1867

◆ Brazilian independence, 1822

◆ Transcontinental railroad completed in US, 1869

◆ Panama Canal opens, 1904

◆ Trans-Andean railroad completed, 1910

Africa and the Middle East

South African War, 1899–1902

◆ British take control of Dutch Cape Colony, 1795

◆ Berlin Conference sets off "Scramble for Africa," 1884

◆ Shaka leads Zulu nation, 1817

◆ Ethiopia defeats Italy at Battle of Adowa, 1896

◆ France annexes Algeria, 1830

◆ Suez canal opens, 1869

◆ "Young Turks" topple Ottoman sultan, 1908

◆ Britain occupies Egypt, 1882

◆ Italy occupies Libya, 1911

◆ Spain and France partition Morocco, 1912

Asia and Oceania

Qing Dynasty, China, 1644–1912

British East India Company in India, 1690–1857

Direct British rule in India, 1858–1947

Dutch East India Company in East Indies, 1619–1799

First Opium War, 1839–42

Second Opium War, 1856–60

Trans-Siberian railroad constructed, 1891–1904

◆ Britain acquires Australia, 1788

◆ Treaty of Nanjing, 1842

◆ Chinese lose Sino-Japanese War, 1895

◆ Dutch government absorbs Dutch East India Company, 1799

◆ American Commodore Perry "opens" Japan, 1853

◆ Japan victorious in Russo-Japanese War, 1905

◆ British gain "overlordship" of India as Mughal power declines,1803

◆ Sepoy Mutiny in India, 1857

◆ Japan annexes Korea, 1910

◆ French gain control of Indochina, 1862–1897

◆ Chinese Republic declared, 1911–12

◆ Meiji Restoration in Japan, 1868

◆ Indian National Congress founded, 1885

CHAPTER 24

THE WESTERN IMPERIUM

European Migration, Settlement, and Domination around the Globe

1750–1914

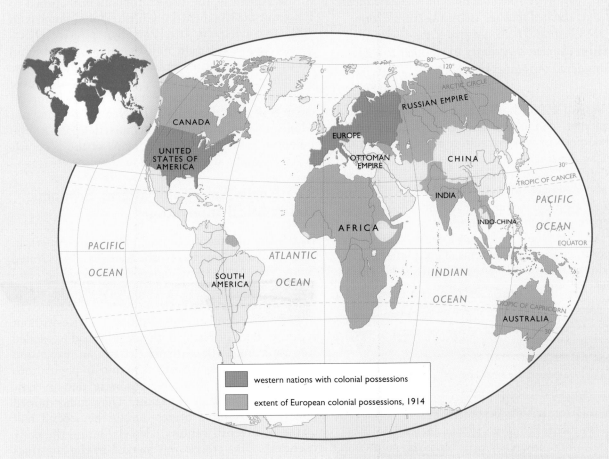

western nations with colonial possessions

extent of European colonial possessions, 1914

KEY TOPICS

◆ **Lands of European Settlement:** Europeans transplant the civilization of the West in the Americas, Australasia, and greater Russia.

◆ **Imperialism in Asia:** European merchant companies gain dominance in India, the Philippines, and East Indies, while China and Japan are forcibly opened to European trade.

◆ **Imperialism in the Middle East and Africa:** European nations establish protectorates in the

Middle East and participate in a "scramble for Africa" that results in partitioning that continent.

◆ **Dominion Within:** Within Europe itself, the Irish and the Jews are persecuted minorities.

◆ **Migrants and Money:** European ventures abroad result in an integrated world economic system, where money, goods, and peoples cross boundaries and transform cultures.

The Better Bookshelf In 1835, in a "Minute on Indian Education" prepared for the British Parliament, the English historian Thomas Babington Macaulay (1800–1859) declared that "a single shelf of a good European library was worth the whole native literature of India and Arabia." Thus he dismissed all of India's lofty literature, whose sacred texts rested on traditions at least as old as those of the Hebrew Bible. Although Macaulay promoted the cause of education in India, then part of the British Empire he betrayed an attitude characteristic of the Europeans who, by 1914, dominated much of the globe. Just as the Romans, who once ruled the ancient Mediterranean world, had dubbed that sea mare nostrum ("our sea"; see Chapter 5), the forgers of the Western **imperium** claimed superiority to all other peoples and considered the planet theirs.

From around 1500, the Western *imperium* expanded as explorers, conquerors and entrepreneurs established outposts of Western culture and customs in the Americas, Australasia, and elsewhere (see Chapter 16 and Map 24.1, p. 691). European commercial ventures also extended into Asia, the Middle East, and Africa. In all these regions, the system of coastal trading depots established by European merchants centuries earlier would be transformed during the nineteenth century into systems of economic or territorial domination, while Western thinkers developed theories of the racial superiority of peoples of European descent. Western imperialism brought about the globalization of the world's economy and culture: a system of interconnected regions across which goods, money, and people freely circulate.

The process of European expansion and domination of remote peoples is here called **imperialism**. The term **colonialism** is reserved for those cases where Europeans established settlements in undeveloped lands with no existing state system. In practice, these terms are often interchanged. European politicians might refer to their "colonial" policies, even in regions such as India, which was not a "colony"; and those who lived under European domination resisted "colonialism." More recently, the economic policies of the wealthier nations of the world are often referred to as "**neo-colonialism**."

Two contrasting views on imperialism are cited in *Witnesses* on p. 713. The Western *imperium* burdened the peoples and civilizations it engulfed. Yet the imperialist legacy is not entirely negative. The West spread abroad principles of human rights and parliamentary democracy, later embraced by non-Western nations as they forged their own liberation (see Chapter 29). And although the West imposed its own cultural norms on often unwilling peoples, these have

also led to improved health care, expanded educational systems, and agricultural and industrial modernization. The West has also learned much from the other cultures of the rest of the world, and became enriched by its global ventures.

LANDS OF EUROPEAN SETTLEMENT: COLONIAL VENTURES

In the lands settled by European migrants, the culture of the West developed new economic, social, and political patterns that would transform the world. Nowhere were these innovations more profound than in the Americas, the two continents first opened to European development by Christopher Columbus in 1492 (see Chapters 16, 19). Their positive effects do not excuse the pain inflicted over four centuries on the two populations enlisted to serve the interests of European settlers: those of displaced native Amerindians and imported Africans. Yet the European creators of what they called the New World were not wholly hostile in intent. The mixed legacy of the European settlement includes many of the acknowledged strengths and benefits of modern society.

The Anglo-American Pattern: Economic and Political Innovation

By the late nineteenth century, two Anglo-American societies had emerged in North America—the United States, from 1783 an independent republic, and Canada, from 1867 a constitutional monarchy within the British Empire. In both, a system of law rooted in English precedents promised citizens justice without regard to rank or birth. Both societies had expanded westward from the Atlantic coast, an expansion which came at huge cost to Amerindian populations (see Chapter 19). Both regions were rich in agricultural and mineral resources. They industrialized rapidly—the United States during the second half of the nineteenth century, Canada during the early twentieth. This process was marked by the construction of railroad lines extending across 3000 miles of mountain, plain, desert, and prairie. The more densely populated United States, especially its northern states, industrialized dramatically: by 1914 it had overtaken its European competitors to become the world's leading producer of steel.

From 1860 to 1865, those northern states fought a ferocious war with secessionist southern states whose economy depended on the plantation system of agricultural production, and thus on slave labor (see Chapter 19). In consequence, the southern states were returned to the Union and slavery was abolished, with pathbreaking legislation promising full citizenship rights, including the suffrage, to former slaves. Those promises were gainsaid by formal and informal systems

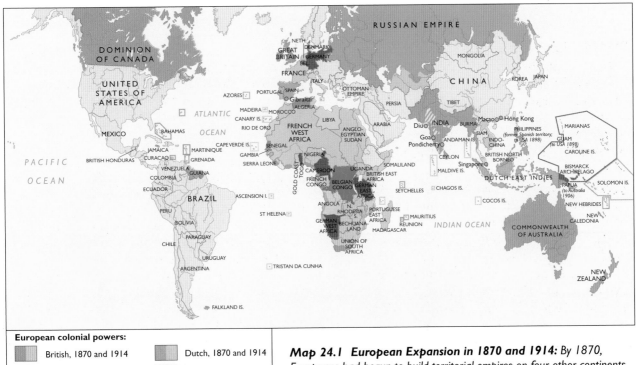

European colonial powers:

British, 1870 and 1914	Dutch, 1870 and 1914
French, 1870 and 1914	Belgian
Spanish, 1870 and 1914	German
Portuguese, 1870 and 1914	Danish
Russian, 1870 and 1914	Italian

Map 24.1 European Expansion in 1870 and 1914: *By 1870, Europeans had begun to build territorial empires on four other continents. By 1914 Europeans and European culture ruled outright, dominated, or heavily influenced the vast majority of the world's peoples.*

of segregation that barred those of African heritage from the enjoyment of their presumed civil rights. Women, too, in the United States as in Canada, did not enjoy political emancipation before the end of World War I (see Chapter 27). Yet by the early twentieth century Anglo-American societies had created vibrant economies and free polities, where opportunities abounded for many of those who sought them. Race, gender, and poverty kept some from reaching for those opportunities. Nevertheless these societies were more nearly free, and the principles upon which they rested embraced the principle of equality more firmly than any others in the world.

Both Anglo-American states respected and cultivated European traditions. During the colonial era, elementary and secondary education followed European patterns, while eleven universities, founded by the time of the American Revolution, authoritatively transmitted the heritage of European ideas to later generations. Cultural institutions such as academies and concert halls offered cultural opportunities available mostly to elites.

The English language created the cultural unification of North America, and was adopted even by immigrants from non-English speaking European regions. One significant exception was the Canadian province of Quebec, where French settlers taught their children the language and Roman Catholic religion of their forebears. Elsewhere, Anglo-Americans were generally Christians who came from a variety of Protestant denominations.

In language, religion, educational traditions, and political and social values, Anglo-America continued to remain firmly tied to established European patterns into the twentieth century.

The Spanish-American Pattern: Racial Mixture and Persistent Autocracy

In the Spanish-speaking regions of the Americas a new civilization also took form. By 1900, the colonies that Spain ruled for centuries had become independent nations. Cuba was the last to do so (while Puerto Rico was shifted from Spanish to United States rule) as a result of the Spanish–American war of 1898. At that point Spanish-American nations were only beginning to develop democratic institutions. Most were still ruled by despots and dominated by the military. A few had adopted constitutions that protected civil rights, limited church privileges, and abolished slavery.

The societies of these Spanish-American nations were also markedly different from those of Anglo-America. Centuries of cross-ethnic sexual relations meant that many Spanish-Americans had mixed Amerindian, African, and European ancestry. Persons of all skin colors were found among the ruling and commercial elites, as well as among the poor. In the country villages, however, peasant populations were heavily Amerindian.

The Spanish-American economies generally depended on the export of agricultural and mineral produce. They did not undergo the industrialization and consequent modernization that occurred in Europe and Anglo-America. This economic system

Map 24.2 Europeans in Asia: *European territorial expansion in Asia prior to 1914 includes gains made by the British, the French, the Russians, and the Dutch. The British dominated India in 1857 (at the time of the Sepoy Mutiny) and parts of southeast Asia in 1826–1915. To the east of Burma in Indochina, the areas of Vietnam, Laos, and Cambodia long under Chinese influence fell to the French after 1884. Thailand, however (indicated on the map under its old name, Siam), remained independent. The lands of the Dutch East India Company in the East Indies were ceded in 1799 to the Dutch government, which by 1910 controlled most of Indonesia. Though often overlooked as one of the major European colonial powers, Russia greatly expanded its authority in central and east Asia during the nineteenth century, building a contiguous empire with many parallels to the more far-flung holdings of other European powers.*

benefited the owners of mines and land, who relied on the exploitation of impressed Amerindian workers.

As in Anglo-America, the cultural institutions of Spanish America were modeled on European ones. Roman Catholic priests, monks, and missionaries, saw to the creation of cathedrals and parish organization, monasteries and convents, and the Inquisition. Churchmen persuaded native peoples to accept Christianity, and where possible provided elementary education in the Spanish tradition. Male members of the creole elites often finished their education in European cities and universities. European traditions also prevailed in the realm of the arts (where native Amerindian artistic styles influenced the visual arts) and ideas, and Spanish-American capitals resembled the great cities of Europe.

By 1900, Spanish America had not entirely shaken off its colonial past. The economic and political innovations that had transformed Anglo-America failed to take root in its southern neighbors. The intermixture of peoples invigorated the civilization, but did not result in its democratization.

Much of the rest of Latin America followed the Spanish-American pattern. Exploited mainly for their sugar crop during the colonial era, the French, English and Dutch-speaking societies of the Caribbean and Central America were heavily populated by African slave laborers until abolition was finally achieved in 1886. African religions, speech, and customs strongly influenced the cultures of these regions, although Christian practices and European languages remained dominant.

In Portuguese-speaking Brazil, the plantation economy likewise resulted in a huge presence of Africans, and many Brazilians had some African ancestry. In contrast, the Amerindians of the Amazon resisted both Europeanization and Christianization. Although Brazil's ample mineral and agricultural resources contributed to a vigorous economy, it remained an economy dependent on the export of cash crops and minerals, and had comparatively few industrial manufactures to export.

Australasia: Another Anglophone Success

More than 200 years after the Spanish and Portuguese first settled in the Americas, Britain launched a similar undertaking in the south Pacific. Australasia (including Australia, the world's smallest continent, and the nearby islands of New Zealand) had first been sighted by the Dutch and was charted by the British navigator Captain James Cook (1728–1779).

Australasia resembled North America in that the indigenous peoples had attained only a simple level of technical development. The **Aborigines** (meaning "those there from the beginning"), were expelled from the most desirable lands as British migrants and deported criminals settled after formal possession by Britain in 1788. New Zealand was home to nearly 150,000 Maoris, a native group of Polynesian origin. Here British settlers established a colonial society based on an agreement in 1840 with native peoples (the Treaty of Waitangi), subsequently violated, assuring equal rights. In both regions European settlers developed a prosperous economy based on the exploitation of natural resources and the development of sheep and dairy ranches.

Australia and New Zealand remained British colonies during the nineteenth century, developing as European enclaves of Anglophone culture. Their vigorous cultural institutions resulted in the attainment of high levels of literacy and health for their European populations, although the New Zealand Maori and Australian aboriginal peoples remained largely excluded from these benefits.

The Russian Empire: Russification Across Five Thousand Miles

By 1500, Russia had become the largest nation in the world. Throwing off Mongol suzerainty (see Chapters 8, 9, 15), Muscovite rulers pressed into Asia, reaching the Caspian Sea with the conquests of Kazan (1552) and Astrakhan (1556) and then beyond the Urals to Siberia. In the seventeenth century, fur traders and explorers crossed Siberia to the Pacific.

In the eighteenth century, Tsars Peter I ("the Great"; r. 1682–1725) and Catherine II ("the Great"; r. 1762–1796) eroded Ottoman claims in the southeast while simultaneously intruding westward into Poland and the Baltic. In the later nineteenth century, recovering from the humiliation of the Crimean War (1853–1856; see Chapter 20), Tsars Alexander II (r. 1855–1881) and Alexander III (r. 1881–1894) advanced in the Caucasus, central Asia, Siberia, and even North America. With these gains, Russia established sovereignty across northern Asia and south to a belt of natural mountain, desert, and river borders with Persia, Afghanistan, India (later Pakistan), and China.

By 1914, the Russian empire's vast dimensions were nearly double those of any of the other modern behemoths—the United States, China, India, or Brazil. An expression of its gigantic stature and industrial capacity was the Trans-Siberian railroad. Constructed between 1891 and 1904, it joined lines earlier constructed to arch from the capital of St. Petersburg to Vladivostok, founded in 1860 on the Pacific coast. Russia's further aims in Asia met traumatic defeat during a conflict with newly-vigorous Japan—the Russo-Japanese war of 1904–1905.

Russian expansion in Asia involved the exploitation of ample natural resources and the imposition of European traditions on sparsely-settled peoples of different origins. The European nucleus of Russia was already well-endowed with mineral resources and fine, flat fields. Subsequent additions in the Caucasus, the Urals, and Siberia brought great wealth in the form of natural gas and oil, coal and iron, gold, diamonds, and furs—even though much of the eastern region is too cold for crop cultivation.

Resident in these Asian lands were peoples of nearly a hundred nationalities, ethnicities, or language groups. Many groups resisted Russian domination in an ongoing pattern of tension and rebellion that continues into the twentieth century, creating problems for tsarist, communist, and post-communist rulers. The largely Muslim peoples of south central Asia, dwelling along the route of the ancient Silk Road (see Chapters 5, 6, 8), had old and distinct cultural traditions, and remain unassimilated.

In the Asian zone of the Russian empire, as in Australasia and the Americas, European colonists opened huge regions to economic development and exploitation. One result was the displacement, or subjugation, of native peoples. Another was the implantation of European cultures in a distant and distinct context. In all these regions, Old World traditions developed under the stimulus of changed conditions, leading to the creation of new forms of wealth, new social structures, and new political traditions.

OLD WORLD ENCOUNTERS: IMPERIALISM IN ASIA

Europeans did not rest with the establishment of colonies in the remote and sparsely populated regions of the Americas, Australasia, and northern Asia. They also pressed their commercial interests in the crowded Old World zones where established states and advanced civilizations did not welcome intruders from the West, but were compelled to admit them.

Europeans had sought for centuries the luxury goods of Asia (see Chapters 5, 6, 8, 11). Merchants had traveled overland by foot, horse, or camel, or by ship across the Indian Ocean and on to the South China sea, to acquire expensive silks, perfumes, and spices. The quest for spices drove Portuguese navigators to hazard the Atlantic currents, and sent Columbus westward to seek a direct route, as he thought, to Japan (see Chapter 16).

During the sixteenth century, Portuguese, French, Dutch, Spanish, and English merchant depots dotted the coasts of India, the East Indies (the Malay archipelago and Indonesia), and the Philippines, and even remote China and Japan. By the eighteenth century, cotton textiles, porcelains, and tea joined the list of important commodities that the West sought in the East. European entrepreneurs and the states that backed them, responding to increased commercial demand, insisted upon greater access to the economies of the Asian nations and in some cases seized dominion over them. In this process of imperialism, here as elsewhere, European nations exploited the resources of other regions for their own benefit, and imposed upon other peoples European political, economic, and cultural systems.

The Western encounter with Asia is pursued here by examining, first, those regions where systems of trading depots became the basis for the later establishment of direct imperialist rule (the Indian sub-continent, and the island regions of the East Indies and the Philippines). The account then turns to those regions that were relatively isolated (China, Korea, Indochina, and Japan), resistant to penetration, and "opened up" to European trade only by the threat, or the reality, of force. Map 24.2 on p. 692 traces the spheres of European influence in Asia.

India: A Sub-continent Subdued

In 1500, various kingdoms, both Muslim and Hindu, flourished in the huge Indian sub-continent. In the 1700s, it fell increasingly under the control of the British East India Company. After 1858, it was directly ruled by the British government.

Established by Muslim Turkic invaders from central Asia, the Mughal Empire was the first large, centralized state on the Indian sub-continent since the Gupta empire more than one thousand years

before (see Chapter 8). Its founder was the occasional poet and memoirist Babur (1483–1530), a remote descendant of the feared conqueror Tamurlane (1336?–1405) who had not so long before ravaged western Asia. Defeating native armies at Panipat in 1526, deep within the Ganges region, Babur united the squabbling Muslim princedoms of northern India into a state further consolidated by his successors.

Notable among these were Babur's grandson Akbar (r. 1556–1605), Akbar's grandson Shahjahan (r. 1627–1656), and Shahjahan's son Aurangzeb (r. 1658–1707). Akbar won the support of Hindu leaders from the Rajput region, thus forging a mixed Hindu–Muslim state efficiently managed by bureaucrats ranked in a hierarchy modeled on that of his army. Encouraging literature and the arts, he presided over a golden age which saw a synthesis, especially in miniature painting, of Persian and native forms.

Shahjahan shared Akbar's artistic tastes. He was renowned as the patron of the Taj Mahal which he had built as a mausoleum (completed in 1643) for his young wife (who had died prematurely in 1629). Symbolizing the paradise in which the royal couple would be reunited, the bejewelled monument is considered one of the world's finest buildings. Aurangzeb oversaw the expansion of the empire to its maximum by 1680, then faced the crises that pointed to its eventual decline. Rajput revolts in the northwest, and the sudden growth of the Marathas, a dynamic Hindu people of western India, undermined the Mughal system.

By that date, English officials of the East India Company had shouldered aside their Arab, Dutch, Portuguese, and French competitors (see Chapter 16). Soon after 1600, the merchants of the British East India Company arrived, establishing themselves at Bombay on the west coast, and on the east at Madras and Calcutta, where they founded an administrative center in 1690. Meanwhile, the French seized footholds at Pondicherry and Chandernagore (now Chandarnagar) in 1697. The military forces of the French and British merchant communities came into conflict after 1740, just as their national armies faced each other in the War of the Austrian Succession (1740–1748) and the Seven Years' War (1756–1763; see Chapter 15). In 1757, the British general Robert Clive (1725–1774) defeated a native force supported by the French at Plassey in Bengal. When the Seven Years' War was concluded by the Treaty of Paris of 1763, Britain gained Canada, territories in the Caribbean and Africa, and control of India. The British East India Company was now the chief European power on the Indian sub-continent, and would soon acquire mastery over native states as well.

This company of profit-seeking merchants dominated India from the 1700s, although increasingly regulated by the British government. Deploying an army of about 100,000 mostly native troops, the governors of the British East India Company absorbed

The importance of prestige: *European nations saw their empires—in Asia and elsewhere—as sources of both prestige and economic benefit. The benefit of prestige is well illustrated by A. E. Harris's illustration of the British King Edward VII as he receives a group of maharajahs and other dignitaries, who are clothed in their finest garments for the honor, in 1901. (Roy Miles Gallery, London)*

the native princedoms or reduced them to vassal status. As the Company's success mounted, and rumors of corruption surged, the British government intervened to supervise. As a result of the Regulating Act of 1773 and the East India Company Act of 1784, Parliament scrutinized the administration of Indian territories. By these steps, an imperial realm took form in the sub-continent (see *Witnesses*, p. 697).

India was a site of imperialism in action, as British officials exploited India economically, ruled it peremptorily, and often denigrated native culture—although many British officials and visitors admired India's civilization. The region's yield of spices, tea, and cotton textiles was cheaply purchased and sold profitably at home, without modernizing agricultural production in India itself (although British governors did promote the construction of irrigation and drainage systems). The trade in those commodities now left India poor as returns on agricultural commodities diminished, as the poet Dalpatram Kavi laments, in *Witnesses* on p. 697. Textile exports also dwindled as the Industrial Revolution (see Chapter 21) transformed British textile production and flooded world markets with cheap cotton cloth. Industrialization made India an importer of manufactured cottons, reversing for the first time in history its favorable balance of trade.

As India sank into the adverse economic relationship with a colonial power that characterized South America, its people became the target of European attitudes of racial superiority. Indian natives were barred from political decision-making, from military and administrative offices (although permitted to compete in examinations for lesser positions in the Civil Service, which grew to number about 1000 British and Indian members). They were excluded from the social circles of the resident British elite.

That elite also often dismissed India's impressive literary and religious heritage (see Chapter 1 and *Witnesses*, p. 697)—Hindu, Buddhist, Muslim—as alien and inferior. Missionaries converted few of these adherents of ancient faiths to Christianity. (Missionary efforts to improve health services and education did, however, bear fruit.) Certain customs that the British elite found repugnant—such as the caste system, that relegates millions to permanent social disability, or *suttee*, the supposedly voluntary burning of wives on a husband's funeral pyre—are still viewed as contrary to universal moral concepts. Others, such as the Hindu refusal to eat beef, or the Muslim refusal to eat pork, were rejected only because unfamiliar.

Economic exploitation, inflexible rule, and cultural incompatibilities stimulated the mutiny of native soldiers (called **sepoys**) in the Company's Indian army that erupted into war in 1857 and changed the nature of British sovereignty in India. Over the previous century, common soldiers had been recruited from among Hindu and Muslim natives, and trained to modern European standards. Some native soldiers rose in rebellion in May 1857, provoked perhaps by a perceived religious insult (their cartridges of ammunition, which they needed to break open with their teeth, were rumored to be coated with beef or pork fat, each kind offensive to either Hindu or Muslim troops) as well as deeper grievances.

Over the next fourteen months, sepoy rebels resisted British forces, while atrocities occurred on both sides. In the aftermath, the British Parliament instituted some reforms, including the guarantee of religious toleration, changes in land administration and military procedures, and the admission of Indian natives to some advisory councils and offices. In the India Act of 1858, having disposed of the British East India Company, the British Parliament declared it would henceforth administer India directly. In 1877, India was constituted as a monarchy subordinate to the British crown, and the British Queen Victoria (r. 1837–1901) was crowned empress. Some 1000 British administrators staffed the Indian Civil Service and lower offices, which ruled the sub-continent through the agency of hundreds of thousands of subordinate, native bureaucrats. Indian subjugation, as illustrated in the photograph above, was complete, and Indian nationalism was born.

From 1858 to 1917, though the British grip on India was firm, new cultural currents pointed toward eventual emancipation—a promise indeed envisioned by discussions between British and Indian leaders in 1917–1918. Extensive railroad construction facilitated interior trade and communication, and some native entrepreneurs were able to insert themselves in the foreign-dominated commercial system. These developments, together with the effects of the opening of the Suez Canal in 1869 (see below), resulted in a sevenfold increase in India's foreign trade.

For ordinary families, uncontrolled population increase outpaced gains in domestic product. The high-status natives who succeeded in entering the provincial civil service educated their children at schools recently instituted on the European model, or at British boarding schools and universities. This educated native elite was able to criticize British rule in its own terms. Its representatives in the Indian National Congress founded in 1885, the sub-continent's first national political movement, began to press for independence. Between 1907 and 1916, the Congress split into moderate and radical factions. Later on, Muslim–Hindu hostilities further split the Congress, fracturing the religious unity that Babur had tried to construct four centuries earlier. In the years following World War I (1914–1918), the Indian sub-continent nourished the intellectual and political leaders who would one day lead it to independence.

The Philippines and East Indies: Enduring Mercantile Empires

In the Philippines and the East Indies (including modern Malaysia and Indonesia), small European merchant settlements founded in the 1500s led, as in India, to enduring domination by European powers.

The huge tropical archipelago of the East Indies, extending more than 3000 miles west to east and lying on the sea route between India and China, was a magnet for merchant adventurers. It was originally populated around 1000 B.C.E. by migrants from the Asian mainland, and had seen the arrival of earlier traders in two waves: first, Indians around the seventh century C.E., who introduced Buddhism and Hinduism, and second, Arabs from the fourteenth century onward, who introduced Islam.

In contact with the advanced civilizations of the region, island natives developed states of their own. On Sumatra and Java, two native kingdoms emerged, respectively Buddhist (the Sri Vijaya) and Hindu (that of the Majapahits). These kingdoms flourished successfully from the seventh through the fifteenth centuries. Soon thereafter, Islam was established throughout the region, which splintered into separate political units.

The islands later named the Philippines (after King Philip II of Spain) form another tropical archipelago, extending about 1200 miles north to south. They were first populated about 30,000 years ago, and from about 1000 C.E. they had commercial relations with Chinese, Japanese, and Malaysian merchants (carriers of Buddhism), and with Arab merchants (who introduced Islam) from the fifteenth. Century.

The first European to arrive was the Portuguese navigator Ferdinand Magellan (c. 1480–1521; see Chapter 16) who claimed the islands for Spain in 1521. In 1571, merchants established a permanent station at Manila, after which the "Manila galleon" regularly journeyed between New Spain (modern Mexico) and the Philippines. Filipino companies exchanged native commodities for American silver in a commerce protected from foreign interlopers into the 1830s: spices, sugar, and coffee.

Spanish governors and armies, meanwhile, established a regime that endured until 1898. Ruled by a viceroy advised by an appointed royal council, or *audiencia*, it fought off pirates and competitors, and was disturbed by stirrings of rebellion only in its last years. Just as nationalist forces were poised to win independence from their Spanish overlord, Spain lost a decisive naval battle in Manila Bay (1898) to the United States. Within the year the United States had acquired sovereignty over the Philippines, to the dismay of many public figures opposed to such foreign ventures.

Their dismay deepened when Filipino leaders turned to guerrilla warfare, capitulating only in 1901. The United States spent more money, and sacrificed more lives in suppressing the revolt than it had in the Spanish–American War (1898)—a measure of Filipino determination. In 1914, the largely Christian Filipinos (converted by Spanish missionaries) were English-speaking dependents of the United States.

The East Indies were colonies first of the Portuguese and then of the Dutch. Portuguese interest in the region came when spices were the most valued commodity in the European trading system and the East Indies archipelago was the world's principal source of spices (especially the sub-group of nearly 14,000 islands known as the Moluccas, and formerly as the Spice Islands). In 1511 the Portuguese captured the city-state of Malacca, poised on the Malay straits that were the gateway to the Indies. By 1513, they had reached the Moluccas, and controlled the spice trade.

In the seventeenth century, Portuguese mastery yielded to the merchants, admirals, and governors of the Dutch East India Company. Over the next three centuries they acquired in the East Indies a total dominion comparable to that achieved by the British East India Company in India. Establishing their headquarters at Batavia (present-day Jakarta), founded in 1619 on the island of Java, they seized Malacca from the Portuguese in 1641, then the Moluccas, outposts on the island of Sumatra, and, by stages, the whole of the islands of Java and Bali. In 1910, all of modern Indonesia (except for the Portuguese enclave of East Timor) was in Dutch hands. After 1799, when the Dutch East India Company was dissolved, the Dutch government took direct control.

The Dutch now possessed the world monopoly of the Moluccan spice trade. In the eighteenth century the Dutch also promoted a range of other exports: coffee, for which Europeans soon developed an enduring passion, along with tea and tobacco. As in Spanish America, an economy based on the processing of agricultural commodities succeeded in short-circuiting any native attempts at modernization or diversification. Native resistance to Dutch policies exploded in rebellion in Java in 1825–1830 and on all three major islands—Java, Bali, and Sumatra—from the 1880s. At the beginning of the twentieth century,

---

Britain's Empire in India

The British takeover of the various peoples and nations of India was entirely to the advantage of the Indians—or so the British argued, as do the first two authors here, for whom British institutions and the English language were self-evidently superior to any others. A different view is expressed in the third passage, by an Indian poet, who calls on his countrymen to industrialize and grow wealthy so that they may reclaim their own nation from foreigners.

Lord Wellesley defends the East India Company (1813): There never was an organ of government, in the history of the world, so administered, as to demand more of estimation than that of the East India Company. There might ... be points of error to correct; but if their Lordships looked at the general state of our Empire in India— ... if they adverted to the state of real solid peace, in which countries were now placed, that had in previous times been so constantly exposed to war and devastation ... they would see that ... the administration ... of the East India Company had been productive of strength, tranquillity and happiness. The situation of the natives had been meliorated and improved—the rights of property, before unknown, had been introduced and confirmed. ... A judicial system had been established which, though not perfect, contained with it all the essentials of British justice.
(Lord Wellesley, Speech in the House of Lords, April 9, 1813; *English Historical Documents*, 1959, vol. XI)

Historian and statesman Thomas B. Macaulay urges that the British Parliament establish an English-language educational system in colonial India (1835): We have a fund to be employed as Government shall direct for the intellectual improvement of the people of [India]. The simple question is, what is the most useful way of employing it?

All parties seem to be agreed on one point, that the dialects commonly spoken among the natives of this part of India, contain neither literary nor scientific information, and are, moreover, so poor and rude that, until they are enriched from some other quarter, it will not be easy to translate any valuable work into them. It seems to be admitted on all sides, that the intellectual improvement of those classes of the people who have the means of pursuing higher studies, can at present be effected only by means of some language not vernacular amongst them. ... The whole question seems to me to be, which language is the best worth knowing. ...

I have no knowledge of either Sanscrit or Arabic.— But I have done what I could to form a correct estimate of their value. I have read translations of the most celebrated Arabic and Sanscrit works. I have conversed ... with men distinguished by their proficiency in the Eastern tongues. ... I have never found one among them who could deny that a single shelf of a good European library was worth the whole native literature of India and Arabia. ...

How, then, stands the case? We have to educate a people who cannot at present be educated by means of their mother-tongue. We must teach them some foreign language. The claims of our own language it is hardly necessary to recapitulate. It stands preeminent even among the languages of the west. ... Whoever knows that language has ready access to all the vast intellectual wealth, which all the wisest nations of the earth have created and hoarded in the course of ninety generations. It may safely be said, that the literature now extant in that language is of far greater value than all the literature which three hundred years ago was extant in all the languages of the world together. ... The English tongue is that which would be the most useful to our native subjects.
(Thomas B. Macaulay, "Minute of 2 February 1835 on Indian Education"; ed. G. M. Young, 1957)

The Bombay poet Dalpatram Kavi laments "The Attack of King Industry," which has transferred all wealth into the hands of foreigners (1861):
Fellow countrymen, let us remove all the miseries of
    our country,
Do work, for the new kingdom has come, its king is
industry.

Our wealth has gone into the hands of foreigners. The
    great blunder is yours
For you did not unite yourselves—fellow countrymen.

Consider the time, see for yourselves, all our people
    have become poor,
Many men of business have fallen—fellow countrymen.

        ...

Introduce industry from countries abroad and achieve
    mastery of the modern machinery.
Please attend to this plea for the Poet Dalpat—fellow
    countrymen.
(Dalpatram Kavi, "The Attack of King Industry"—"Hunnarkhan-ni Chadayi"; eds. C. Trivedi and H. Spodek, 1998)

the so-called Ethical Policy provided greater educational and administrative opportunities for talented natives. But in 1914, Dutch imperialism in the region remained repressive and entirely unyielding.

China, Korea, and Indochina: Forced Entry

In India and the East Indies, European merchant depots were the wedges that opened vast regions to direct domination by European nations. That pattern was not repeated on the mainland of east and southeast Asia. Although merchant footholds were established from the 1500s at Malacca, Macao, and Nagasaki (in present-day Malaysia, China, and Japan), these were scant. Before 1800, the advanced societies of the Asian mainland were little affected by European presence in the South China Sea.

After 1800, however, when Asian nations faced European states possessing military and technological superiority, the situation changed. They were unable to withstand the insistent demand for access to sources of wealth as yet untapped by European commerce.

In 1800, China was the oldest and most secure monarchy in the world (see Chapters 2, 8, 16). For centuries, it had imposed its law on neighboring states in Korea, Indochina, and Mongolia—over which states, at times, it exercised sovereignty. China collected tribute from these and even more distant regions. It exported prized commodities and manufactures: silk textiles, porcelain and lacquer goods, tea and other agricultural produce. Its merchants carried on a busy commerce within China and abroad, reaching India, the East Indian archipelago, and parts of Oceania, as well as central Asia and Mediterranean ports via the ancient Silk Road.

Along these routes, China also diffused its high literary and philosophical culture—Buddhist, Taoist, and Confucian. Trained in that Confucian tradition, China's scholars and poets were also its government officials (if they succeeded in passing licensing examinations). They administered the mammoth empire for the most part judiciously and efficiently. Science and technology also flourished in China, the world leader in those endeavors until the seventeenth century. China first gave the world paper, gunpowder, and block printing, among other inventions.

These patterns prevailed over a series of dynasties extending back to the Shang, Zhou, and Qin of the Bronze and Iron Ages; and to the Han, Tang, Song, and Yüan that ruled from the period of ancient Rome to the threshold of the European Renaissance (see Chapters 1, 2, 8, 16). They continued thereafter under the Ming (1368–1644) and Qing, or Manchu rulers (1644–1912). With the latter, who were exhausted, corrupt, and subjected to European overlords, the venerable procession of emperors and dynasties ended.

In 1368, after thirty years of popular resistance to Mongol Yüan rule, rebel leader Chu Yan-chang established the Ming dynasty. He and his Ming successors rebuilt the region, which had been devastated by the wars leading to Mongol victory in 1279. The imperial economic policy favored agriculture over commerce. That decision resulted in conservative government in the countryside, exercised by gentry landowners who belonged to the same social stratum as Confucian political officials.

Under Ming rule the economy flourished. Textiles, raw cotton, and grain, the main domestic commodities, traveled to and from the major trading centers in the Yangzi delta (especially Nanjing) and the newly founded (1421) capital at Beijing, which provisioned a large network of frontier garrisons in the north. Population soared from a depressed 60 million at the time of Ming takeover to more than 100 million in the late 1500s. At that time more people lived in China than in all of Europe.

Early successes permitted the Ming to challenge the Mongols, invade Vietnam (in Indochina), and reduce Korea to vassalage. From the late sixteenth century, they withdrew to a defensive posture, as Japanese pirates harried their coasts, boldly entered the Yangzi, and challenged China's preeminence in Korea. Ineffective emperors ceded authority to corrupt eunuchs, who had withstood government reform efforts. From 1627, a rash of rebellions left China vulnerable to incursion once again from the north. In 1644, the Ming fell to a new dynasty which was to be China's last: the Qing.

The Manchu, a non-Chinese people who originated in Manchuria, swept into the Chinese region from the 1620s, established themselves as the Qing dynasty at Beijing in 1644, and consolidated their sovereignty in the resistant south and west by 1680. During the following century, they expanded into Mongolia, central Asia, and Indochina, as the costs of expansion injured an already precarious economy.

By 1800, economic crisis loomed. Virtually all the arable land of China was under cultivation, and had reached the limit of what it could produce. Food supply was further strained by a population increase from about 100 million in 1650 to more than 300 million by 1800 and 420 million by 1850. The hungry peasants rebelled, as did subject states corralled unwillingly into the Manchu Empire.

Meanwhile, by the 1830s, the importation of opium by the British had begun to destabilize the Chinese economy. Since the 17th century, the British had paid in silver coin for Chinese tea, as tea-drinking became a regular custom at home. Seeking to balance their trade deficit, the British had exported Indian-grown opium to China—an import which not only led to the depletion of Chinese silver reserves, but threatened to corrupt Chinese workers in seaport regions. The free-trade policies of the British collided with the

Confucian principles of Chinese officials, for whom government must exert a moral influence that included commercial relations. When Chinese officials acting on the highest authority confiscated and destroyed more than 19,000 chests of opium in 1839, the conflict between world views erupted into the First Opium War of 1839–1842. Its result was a mandate for the economic opening of China by European merchants and states.

Since 1557, Chinese officials had allowed the Portuguese to maintain a trading station at Macao on the southern coast. British and French merchants later obtained a foothold at nearby Guangzhou (Canton), and the Dutch, briefly, on the island of Taiwan. From these depots, they exported the Chinese tea and luxuries craved by Western elites. Unsatisfied, they sought greater access to Chinese markets. The British, particularly, hoped to gain buyers for cotton textiles from Britain's new mills (see Chapter 21); or opium, in quantities of close to 2000 tons annually, imported from British-held India.

The imperial government rebuffed British pleas for greater access. Opium carried on British ships, in violation of Chinese law, succeeded in corrupting port officials and causing the addiction of millions of natives. Chinese bureaucrats investigated and condemned the trade, and protested to Queen Victoria, advising her of the penalty decreed for European peddlers of opium: decapitation. In 1839, responding to Chinese confiscation of opium stores, British warships trained their cannon on several coastal cities. Overwhelmed by Western superiority in weaponry, as related in *Witnesses* on p. 700, the Chinese capitulated.

The Treaty of Nanjing (Nanking) of 1842 put an end to the First Opium War and compelled China to open its gates to Western commerce and control. Protected by the new policy of "**extraterritoriality**" (which exempted Westerners from Chinese law), European trading stations operated at Macao, Guangzhou (Canton), Shanghai, and other ports. In addition the British gained control of Hong Kong, an island later (1898) leased to Britain for ninety-nine years.

In 1856, the Second Opium War erupted as the Chinese attempted to block European encroachments. A British and French force destroyed the imperial summer palace outside Beijing, and occupied the city. In 1860, China backed down, accepting a treaty that delivered some fifty ports to foreign control, permitted European diplomatic residents in Beijing, allowed Christian missionary activity, and, a final blow, legalized the importation of opium.

The humiliation of China continued for another generation. From 1848 to 1865, the Chinese government spent its energies suppressing the massive Taiping Rebellion, whose leader, a Christian-trained mystic and moralist, offered promise of national regeneration. Between 1862 and 1897, the French seized Vietnam and Laos in Indochina, previously dominated by China. An updated Japanese army claimed Taiwan and other smaller territories in the Sino-Japanese War of 1894–1895. Russia, meanwhile, crept into the northeast and briefly dominated Manchuria. By 1900, France, Britain, Germany, and Russia had imposed on the Qing government a system of **concessions**, or economic spheres of influence. These effectively partitioned China, weakened by famine and unrest. Progressive officials attempted to modernize and reform the Chinese government, in a program known as "self-strengthening." Their efforts came too late. Western subjugation of a once great, now decadent state was nearly complete.

The expropriations of European merchants, the arrogance of military leaders, the contempt of European officials for an ancient civilization, and the alien promptings of Christian missionaries, stimulated explosive and violent native resistance movements. The most famous of these was the rebellion of the Boxers (1898–1901), as the Europeans called them. Properly named the "Righteous and Harmonious

E. Duncan, painting of the steamer Nemesis: *Western warships wreaked havoc on traditional societies that had no weaponry to defend themselves. Here, the steam-powered* **Nemesis** *swiftly destroys Chinese junks at Guangzhou, China in 1843, as the British force the opening of China to Western trade. (National Maritime Museum, Canada)*

Fists," this was a secret society hostile to all Western political and cultural influence encouraged by the dowager empress Tz'u-Hsi (1835–1908) and her conservative courtiers. The Boxers deplored not only China's political takeover by the West, but the demoralization of the Chinese by foreigners whose technical and military power they recognized but whose intellectual and religious culture they despised.

Although the Boxer rebellion failed, native intellectuals had begun to conceive of national independence—both from the failing Qing dynasts and from European interlopers. A series of uprisings in 1911 dismantled the Qing dynasty. Sun Yat-sen (1866–1925) became president of the resulting republic in 1912, but was pushed aside the next year by the dictator Yüan Shih-k'ai (1859–1916). That new government was forced to surrender some territories to Japan during World War I. In 1914, the great empire that had loomed over east Asia for more than two millennia faced an uncertain future.

The native kingdoms of Southeast Asia, meanwhile, which had for centuries been prey to Chinese incursions, fell to British and French expansionism. By 1885, Britain controlled all of Burma (now called Myanmar). In addition, between 1786 and 1819, she had acquired three strategic city-states on the Malay Peninsula (and a protectorate over the region) that assured access to Chinese ports: Penang, Malacca (by Dutch cession), and Singapore, the latter established as a free port. One of the four European concession powers in China, France took direct control of modern Laos, Vietnam, and Cambodia in a war waged from 1862 to 1897. By 1914, with the exception of Siam (modern Thailand), Indochina was part of the European *imperium*.

Japan: Point, Counterpoint

Alone of the non-Western nations of the globe, Japan successfully resisted Western encroachment, responding to aggression with a disciplined program of self-development that rendered it, by 1914, one of the major world powers. Unlike China, which suffered repeated disruptions between the fifteenth and nineteenth centuries, Japan was politically unified and well-poised to meet the challenge of Western intervention when it came in 1853.

In 1603, after the suppression of more than a century of disorder, the *samurai* Tokugawa Ieyasu (1543–1616) seized the supreme position of *shogun* (the military leader of Japan, appointed by the imperial court which itself wielded no effective power). He initiated a period of stability that lasted two and a half centuries, reining in the competing samurai

The European Arrival in East Asia

Two very different encounters of Asian peoples with the West are recorded here. The first passage describes the Chinese failure to resist British warships during the First Opium War. The second reports the success of a Japanese delegation which studied on-site the parliaments of Europe, to prepare for the creation of a Japanese constitution.

The futility of traditional resistance: a modern historian describes Chinese efforts to repel British ships during the First Opium War (1842):

[Chinese volunteer] Pei Ch'ing-ch'iao's ... assignment was to superintend the making of five hundred rocket mortars. The model was an ancient specimen supplied by the aged Commander Tuan Yung'fu, and came from Yünnan. Pei was ashamed, he says, that ... the best they could produce was a contrivance that looked as though it emanated from the pages of the *Fire-dragon Book*, a seventeenth-century treatise on artillery. These mortars were supposed to be used in setting fire to the sails and rigging of foreign ships, but do not seem ever to have come into action.

Someone suggested that fire-crackers should be tied to the backs of a number of monkeys, who would then be flung on board the English ships. The flames would spread rapidly in every direction and might with luck reach the powder-magazine, in which case the whole ship would blow up. Nineteen monkeys were bought, and ... were brought in litters to the advanced base. After the failure of the Chinese attack they accompanied the retreating armies. ...
(From A. Waley ed., *The Opium War Through Chinese Eyes*, 1958)

Ito Hirobumi, chief architect of Japan's modernizing Meiji Constitution of 1889, recounts his efforts to understand and learn from the West (1909): It was in the month of March, 1882, that His Majesty [the Japanese emperor] ordered me to work out a draft of a constitution to be submitted to his approval. No time was to be lost, so I started on ... an extended journey ... to make as thorough a study as possible of the actual workings of different systems of constitutional government. ... I took young men with me, who all belonged to the elite of the rising generation, to assist and to cooperate with me in my studies. I sojourned about a year and a half in Europe, and having gathered all the necessary materials ... I returned home in September, 1883. Immediately after my return I set to work to draw up the Constitution.
(Ito Hirobumi, *Reminiscences on the Drafting of the New Constitution*, 1909; ed. W. T. de Bary, 1958)

Commodore Perry's "Black Ship": *The threat of imminent attack on Japan was posed by the warship that the American Commodore Perry piloted into Japanese waters in 1853. Such naval force served ultimately to bring both China and Japan into the Western-dominated global economy during the nineteenth century.* (The Mariner's Museum, Virginia)

clan-leaders, or *daimyos*, who had established themselves as independent territorial lords. Rewarding loyal samurai with offices and privileges and suppressing those who resisted, he compelled the Japanese nobility to recognize a strongly centralized government: the *bakufu*, located in Edo (modern Tokyo), a capital distinct from the imperial court of Kyoto.

Tokugawa and his successors established a legal code, a highway system, and a network of fortifications from which to suppress any future challenge to the now-powerful state. Prosperity returned, and the population climbed from about 20 million in 1600 to about 30 million in the eighteenth century.

The Tokugawa shogunate enforced a policy of isolation, shunning the Western adventurers who sought a foothold in Japan. Portuguese traders had arrived in 1542, followed quickly by Jesuit missionaries. The Tokugawa expelled the missionaries in 1614, and Christianity was soon extirpated in a series of persecutions in the 1630s. Even Buddhism was subordinated to Shinto religious institutions (see Chapters 1, 8), which elevated the shogun (the emperor for the moment in eclipse) as a ritual leader. And Confucianism, an import from China, supported the development of a samurai code of conduct appropriate to the new regime. The shogunate discouraged all contact with Western customs and even Western technology. The European guns that Tokugawa forces used to gain sovereignty, quickly imitated by Japanese military technicians, were banned soon after.

The shoguns did, however, allow the Dutch, established in Nagasaki since 1567, to remain in carefully supervised isolation. The Japanese were instructed to have nothing to do with their culture, their religion, or even their method of writing with letters that ran oddly sideways, in contrast to the

vertical columns of Asian characters. Yet the West demanded access, as it had in China. Between 1793 and 1853, several Western ships visited Japan's key ports seeking permission to trade. The last and most famous visitor, in 1853, was the United States Commodore Matthew Perry (1794–1858), whose warship is shown on the left. Perry threatened the Japanese with bombardment if they did not cooperate. Japan admitted the foreigners, submitting to the humiliating Harris Treaty of 1858.

Nevertheless, the Japanese managed to avoid Western domination. By 1868, the capitulation had triggered a fantastic series of events. A group of young, determined samurai expelled the shogun and restored the emperor as titular ruler, removed from obscurity in Kyoto to the capital at Tokyo, and to power (although the revolutionary samurai continued to hold real power). This was the sixteen-year-old Mutsuhito (1852–1912) who, as the descendant of the sun goddess (according to tradition and official doctrine until 1945), was seen as destined to fulfill the divine plan for Japan's governance. The revolutionary event is known as the "Meiji" (the term means "enlightened rule") restoration.

These innovators created a new imperial bureaucracy in which promotion was based on talent, abolished feudalism, and created a conscript army (1873). They sent experts to the major Western capitals to study law codes and parliamentary constitutions, (see the passage reproduced in *Witnesses* on p. 700) and technicians to study industrial production. They introduced cabinet government, bicameral legislature, and a formal constitution (1885–1889). They set up schools (enrolling ninety percent of all school-age children by 1900) and universities to train future generations to manage a renewed Japan.

By 1914, Japan was a modern nation, having swiftly experienced the processes of industrialization and urbanization that had taken centuries in Europe. Using one-third of the revenues gathered from a reformed tax system, the government promoted industry, transportation, and communications. Textile and steel production sped forward in the 1880s and 1890s, boosting Japan's trade balance—the nation was now an exporter of manufactures, an importer of raw materials. Population continued to climb, and by 1914, about one-third lived in cities.

Streamlined, industrialized, and fully competitive with the West, Japan now pursued its own imperialist goals in east Asia. Seizing the adjacent Kuril and Ryukyu Islands in 1875 and 1879, as a result of the Sino-Japanese War of 1894–1895 she further acquired Taiwan and part of Manchuria. In the Russo-Japanese war of 1904–1905, the unanticipated Japanese victory announced that nation's entry to the circle of great world powers. In 1910, Japan annexed Korea and, as a participant in World War I, claimed for itself further

Chinese territories in its notorious Twenty-One Demands issued in 1915 (see Chapter 26).

Japan was the exception among Asian states. Not only did the Japanese resist foreign domination, but they acquired the military and technical skills that gave Europeans their edge in the age of imperialism. By 1914, Japan was an imperialist power, too.

OLD WORLD ENCOUNTERS: IMPERIALISM IN THE MIDDLE EAST AND AFRICA

More easily than in Asia, European powers came to dominate the native peoples of the Middle East and Africa. Map 24.3 on p. 704 shows how these regions were divided. In the Middle East, a weakening Ottoman Empire gave the principal imperialist nations opportunities to exert economic and political influence. In Africa, the European nations intruded swiftly and decisively in 1880–1900.

The Middle East: The Last Islamic Empire

From ancient times, a series of vigorous empires ruled the Middle East (see Chapters 1, 8). The last of these—that of the Turkish Ottoman dynasty—reached its peak in the sixteenth century, weakened in the seventeenth and eighteenth, and succumbed in the nineteenth to the commercial and military power of western European nations it once scorned.

From the seventh century, followers of the prophet Muhammad carried the religion of Islam (from the Arabic term for "submission" to God) through the Middle East and North Africa, into Spain, the Balkans, India, and the East Indies. From the eleventh century C.E., the regimes of the Arabic rulers, or caliphs, yielded to new incursions of Asian steppe nomads—Turkish and Mongol polytheists who converted to Islam and ruled in its name.

In 1500, three Islamic dynasties ruled in the Middle East: the Safavids in Persia (modern Iran); the Mamluks in Egypt and Syria (including modern Palestine/Israel, Lebanon, and Jordan); the Ottomans in Asia Minor (Anatolia, now Turkey) and south-east Europe, nearly as far north as modern Hungary (see also Chapters 14, 15, 16). By 1600, the Mamluk lands fell to the Ottomans, who had also absorbed the coastal regions of North Africa and the Black Sea while containing the Safavids to the southeast.

Meanwhile, the Ottoman navy seized most of the strategic island bases that were situated in the Mediterranean from Venice, Genoa, and Spain, capturing Euboea (Negroponte) (1470); Lemnos (1479); Rhodes (1522); Cyprus (1573); and Crete (1669). Their rivals stopped Ottoman maritime expansion only in 1571, at the battle of Lepanto off the Peloponnesian coast of Greece. On land, Ottoman armies had advanced by 1529 through Hungary as far as Vienna, where they were only narrowly repulsed by a combined force of European armies.

By 1600, however, the Ottoman Empire had already spent its first vigor. Over the next two centuries, the Austrian Habsburgs and the Russian tsars pushed back the Ottoman borders in southeastern Europe. In 1683, combined European armies repelled a second Ottoman attempt to take Vienna, and the Treaties of Karlowitz (1699) and Passarowitz (1718) opened southeastern Europe to Habsburg advance at Ottoman expense. From 1768 to 1783, Russia under Catherine the Great seized the northern shore of the Black Sea, finally acquiring an outlet to warm-water seas. Meanwhile, the British navy patrolled the Mediterranean to protect its trade link to India from pirate raids issuing from Ottoman-held ports.

By 1800, the Ottoman empire was, it was said, the "sick man of Europe"—a phrase repeated gleefully by several European monarchs who hoped to profit from its disease. The following century saw its disintegration. In 1914, the Ottoman Empire retained only one-third of the territory it had ruled in 1800. Moreover, the seeds had been planted for later resistance to Western intervention by Asian and African people previously under Ottoman rule.

In Europe, the dismantlement of Ottoman power began with the successful revolution from 1821–1830, by which Greece won its independence. The Balkan states to the north—Serbia, Montenegro, Albania, Bulgaria, and Romania—had all broken away from Ottoman dominion by 1914. Bosnia–Herzegovina and Bessarabia were wrested away from Ottoman rule and incorporated, respectively, by Austria and Russia.

In Syria, Ottoman officials continued to rule ineffectually (with Lebanon under Christian governors after 1861) as British, French, and Russian interests took hold. The regions further east and south—Iraq and the Arabian Peninsula—came under British influence during the years prior to 1914, while Russian influence prevailed in Iran and in the Caucasian states of Georgia, Armenia, and Azerbaijan.

In North Africa, independent local rulers asserted themselves in Egypt (which dominated Sudan to its south), Libya, Tunisia, and Algeria; Morocco, an independent sultanate, never fell under Ottoman rule. All of these, including Morocco, became subjected to European states as their economies faltered due to the disruption caused by foreign intervention. France annexed Algeria (1830) and Tunisia (1881); Britain dominated Egypt (1882); Spain and France together partitioned Morocco (1912); and Italy occupied Libya (1911). By 1914, European powers had absorbed the whole of North Africa.

Shocked into an awareness of modern warfare and administration by Napoleon's presence in 1798–1801 (see Chapter 20), the Ottoman governors of Egypt detached the region from the parent state. The Macedonian governor, Muhammad 'Ali (1769–1849)

Europe in Africa and the Middle East

*M*uch *misunderstanding and resentment accompanied Europeans in their contacts with the people of Africa and the Middle East. In the first passage here, a French missionary speaks admiringly, but patronizingly, of a native African leader and his people. In the second, an Islamic reformer urges his coreligionists to recover their ancient greatness in the sciences, the springboard of commerce and wealth, so as to compete with the European nations that have taken over so much of the world.*

Ernest Linant de Fellefonds, a French Catholic missionary, recounts a conversation with Kabaka Mutesa (M'Tesa), the ruler of Buganda, East Africa (1875): In answer to all M'Tesa's questions concerning the earth, the sun, the moon, the stars and the sky and in order to make him understand the movement of the heavenly bodies, I had to make shapes on a board, the heavenly bodies being represented by little glass balls. The lecture took place today. ...

M'Tesa grasped everything perfectly. ... [and] was able to inspire ... in many of his people this quest for understanding, for self-instruction and for knowledge. ... They are an inquiring, observant, intelligent people with minds longing for the learning of white people whose superiority they recognize ...

(From D. A. Low, *Mind of Buganda: Documents of the Modern History of an African Kingdom*, 1971)

Jamal al-Din al-Afghani, an Islamic reformer, speaks on science (1882): The Europeans have now put their hands on every part of the world. The English have reached Afghanistan; the French have seized Tunisia. In reality this ... conquest has not come from the French or the English. Rather it is science that everywhere manifests its greatness and power. ...

If we study the riches of the world we learn that wealth is the result of commerce, industry, and agriculture. Agriculture is achieved only with agricultural science, botanical chemistry, and geometry. Industry is produced only with physics, chemistry, mechanics, geometry, and mathematics; and commerce is based on agriculture and industry.

Our *ulama* [Islamic leaders] ... have not understood that science is a noble thing that has no connection with any nation, and is not distinguished by anything but itself. ...

The father and mother of science is proof. ... The truth is where there is proof, and those who forbid science and knowledge in the belief that they are safeguarding the Islamic religion are really the enemies of that religion.

(Al-Afghani, *On the Importance of Science*, 1882; ed. M. R. Keddie, 1983, 2nd ed.)

---

reorganized the tax system, imported Western technology, encouraged factory construction, created public schools, modernized the army, and established his own dynasty—which failed to implement further the changes he had initiated. Under his successors, native entrepreneurs became financially dependent upon British and French bankers who poured into the European quarters of Alexandria. In 1882, the country went bankrupt. The British occupied this strategic region (extending into the Sudan) to protect its bankers' investments and its merchant navy's access to the Suez Canal.

Under the direction of the French entrepreneur Ferdinand de Lesseps (1805–1894), the Canal had been constructed to solve an ancient problem: how to connect the goods that came to Mediterranean ports from the interiors of Africa and Europe with the Indian Ocean trade routes that led to India, the East Indies, and east Asia? Portuguese explorers had a water route around the southern tip of Africa (see Chapter 16). But that journey was now shortened by the creation of a water link between the Mediterranean and the Red Sea—the Suez Canal—completed in 1869. A British-built rail link from Alexandria to Cairo and the Canal, completed in the 1850s, further facilitated the export of African goods to Asia.

The Middle Eastern regions of the failing Ottoman Empire had already lapsed into economic decline before 1800. Thereafter, they further suffered from the **economic imperialism** of European companies and states. Their traditional crafts and artisanal organizations weakened as these regions became suppliers of primary materials for European factories. Middle Eastern workers produced cotton, most importantly, but also sugar and tobacco for export, in exchange for high-priced European manufactures. The resulting balance of trade favored European interests, while it was ruinous to the natives, creating underdevelopment where there had once been prosperity.

European economic domination aroused native resistance under the influence of Islamic leaders called **ulamâ**, and judges, or **qâdi** (see Chapter 8). Islamic rebellions erupted, especially following the French and British interventions in northern Africa in 1881 and 1882. In Egypt, there was a call for a revival of Islamic traditions, and a new **jihad**, or religious struggle, against the infidel intruders. An Islamic resistance inspired by the **Mahdi**, the charismatic prophet Muhammad Ahmad (1849–1885), controlled the Sudan from 1881 to 1898, targeting both Egyptians, who had subjugated their nation, and the Europeans who now ruled Egypt.

While popular resistance movements flared, Muslim intellectuals faced a stony reality: adherence to Islam meant clinging to tradition, but independence from European domination could only be achieved by

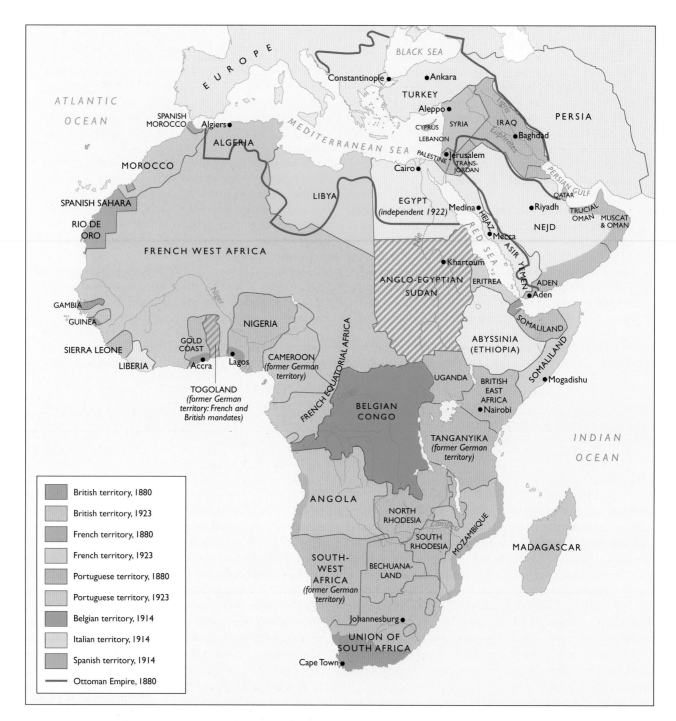

Map 24.3 Europeans in Africa and the Middle East: *As the Ottoman Empire's control of the Middle East and North Africa disintegrated after 1800, European powers rushed in to grab what they could. In the former region, they established protectorates, direct dominion, or zones of influence by the achievement of the post-World War I settlement of 1923. Africa in general, both northern and sub-Saharan, was partitioned by the European powers between 1880 and 1913. The national boundaries of modern African states reflect the interests and are largely the creation of Western imperialists. They bear little relationship to pre-existing African political borders or to African boundaries of ethnicity, language, or tribal community (see Map 24.4 opposite).*

modernization of ideas and institutions. The debate took place in schools and academies, and in the press, itself modeled on the traditions of Western journalism. The cultural elite was divided. Traditionalists looked backward to a purer era of Islam. Modernists, such as the teacher and journalist Jamal ad-Din al-Afghani (1838–1897), called for a new orientation of Islam in

scientific rationalism, recalling the great age in the ninth through twelfth centuries when Islamic scientists and philosophers were the world's most innovative thinkers (see Chapter 8 and *Witnesses*, p. 703).

Attempts to modernize through direct political action came in the early twentieth century. Protest following the 1890 concession to foreign merchants of

Map 24.4 African States and People Before 1880

other nations of the Middle East still lay under the sway of European entrepreneurs and governments.

Sub-Saharan Africa: Divided and Despoiled

By 1914, the economic exploitation of Africa south of the Sahara had resulted in its division. Every corner of the region, except the states of Ethiopia and Liberia had by this time fallen under European sovereignty, as Map 24.3 on p. 704 shows.

In 1500, the European presence in Africa was minimal (see Chapters 8, 16, 19). The Islamic states and settlements on the northern and eastern coasts were far more important for the internal development of the continent. From the north, Arab traders crossed the Sahara, visiting the rich cities of the Sudan to acquire gold, spices, the exotic products of the jungle, and slaves. These cities were not only commercial nodes stimulated by Arab trade, but also the religious and cultural capitals of Islamized native African states—including Songhay, the successor to Mali and Ghana—that had developed over previous centuries and now extended almost continuously across the grassland region to the south of the desert.

To the east, along the Red Sea and Indian Ocean coasts, stretched a string of Islamic centers that traded with the peoples of the interior. By 1500, Islamic Adal near the Horn of Africa was in stiff competition with Ethiopia just inland. Further south, intense commercial activity had stimulated the development of interior states, notably the rich, fortified center of Zimbabwe, whose exports were sent as far as China.

Other native states flourished in interior regions, created by the iron-using farmers and herders of sub-Saharan Africa, as yet untouched by Christianity or Islam (see Map 24.4 above). A cluster of small states developed between Lakes Tanganyika and Victoria. Further south, the Bantu states of Luba and Lunda supplied eastern coastal depots, but also the western native state of Kongo, just inland of the Atlantic coast south of the Congo river. North and west of Kongo, stretching west of the Niger delta along the "Gold" and "slave" coasts, native states developed after about 1500 (Benin, Oyo, Asante), stimulated by trade with Songhay and the Hausa states of the western and central Sudan, whose flourishing cities impressed European travelers.

In this western region, as well as around the Cape and, to a lesser extent, on the eastern coast near the mouth of the Zambezi River, European merchants established their trading centers. The process began with the Portuguese just before 1500. The Dutch, British, French, Spanish, Germans and even Danes followed in the seventeenth century. In 1652, the Dutch settled the Cape, and over the next centuries expanded toward the interior. Between 1795 and 1803, Britain occupied the Dutch settlement.

the tobacco production and export by the **shah** (ruler) of Iran culminated in the revolution of 1906, which established a representative assembly on Western models. The shahs subsequently suppressed the assembly and ruled autocratically until deposed decades later not by a liberal parliament but by an Islamic revolt that established a **theocracy** (see Chapter 29).

Modernization was desperately needed at the core of the Ottoman Empire, in what would in 1921 become the nation of Turkey. Here a succession of corrupt or ineffective sultans and advisers had permitted the empire to weaken. From 1839 to 1876, reformers introduced the policy of Tanzimat, or "reordering," which involved changes in areas of justice, taxation, education, and minority rights. But these did not stop the decline. In 1875, the Ottoman sultan declared that interest would no longer be paid on the public debt; the state was bankrupt. As in Egypt, that economic collapse opened the gates to European bankers. In 1881, a foreign commission undertook to supervise the imperial finances. In 1878, European powers at the Congress of Berlin saw to the further fragmentation of the Ottoman Empire, apportioning Bosnia-Herzegovina to Austria-Hungary, while Britain received Cyprus, and France, Tunisia.

These humiliations at last stimulated a movement of young native intellectuals, or "Young Turks." Their resistance culminated in a 1908 revolution that deposed and replaced the sultan, and eventually replaced his government by one that was more modern but not less brutal. Among the defeated nations in World War I (see Chapter 26), the last of the Islamic empires expired in 1918. Its remnant, Turkey, adopted a Western model of political order, and contended on equal ground with the nations of Europe, while the

European merchants sought the same commodities from African kings and chieftains as Arab merchants had long done. Following the European settlement of the Americas after 1500, however, one economic activity became preeminent: the trade in slaves (see Chapter 16). Kidnapped, captured, or purchased by native leaders, often from Arab intermediaries, and sold or resold to Europeans, some 10 million black slaves, mostly male, were compelled to sail the Atlantic "middle passage" in wretched conditions prior to further resale and lifelong unpaid labor. Arab merchants also dealt in slaves, transporting them in growing numbers from the east coast to Mediterranean and Indian Ocean ports.

After 1807, Western prohibitions of the slave trade pressured the economies of African states. Slave-trading now shifted south and eastward, where slave-hunters joined elephant hunters in the search for human beings and ivory tusks. Asian and European consumers wanted ivory for luxury objects such as billiard balls and piano keys, and native communities grew wealthy from the trade. A good share of the profit was spent on guns to equip the armies of militaristic native states springing up on the eastern coast to exercise dominion over the interior.

No longer in the market for slaves, nineteenth-century European merchants sought tropical products such as peanuts, palm oil, and rubber which they exchanged for European industrial manufactures—textiles, metals, and guns. There were goods more valuable still to be found. Gold and diamond deposits made the fortunes of many European companies formed to mine them—the source of the great wealth and influence of the British imperialist and entrepreneur Cecil Rhodes (1853–1902)—along with iron, coal, and copper. Entrepreneurs enlisted armies of migrant laborers to work their mines for starvation wages and in horrific conditions.

As knowledge of Africa grew, the extent of the continent's mineral wealth became clear. From the 1790s through the 1870s, the promise of the interior stimulated a series of expeditions (mostly by British explorers, with African guides and servants) to investigate its topography and peoples. (Such expeditions were made possible, in part, by the European discovery of **quinine**, derived from cinchona bark native to the Andes of South America, to control the effects of malaria.) The contribution of late nineteenth-century explorers was to map the major river highways that led to the African interior: the upper Nile, the Zambezi, the Zaire. Their aims were in part scientific, and their expeditions culminated in reports to learned societies; they were also in part religious, in part commercial. The missionary David Livingstone (1813–1873) explored the lakes and rivers of central Africa for more than twenty years, striving to promote the two civilizing forces, as he saw it, of Christianity and commerce. The journalist Henry Morton Stanley

(1841–1904), employed variously by United States, British, and Belgian interests, explored the Congo during the 1870s and 1880s to assess the commercial value of its jungle abundance.

Pressing further into the interior, Europeans sparked religious conflict. Christian missionaries established themselves in the vicinity of European settlements, especially in west Africa. They opened schools and hospitals, providing needed services even as they battled African **animist** and magical beliefs. Soon, native converts began missions of their own, adapting Christianity to local customary belief, song, and dance. Although many Africans resented the imposition of Western religious and cultural values, others were ardent converts themselves and proponents of Christian expansion. The Christian presence also encouraged Islamic jihads, especially in the central and western Sudan, where recently-converted Muslims sought zealously to impose a strict orthodoxy on nominal believers and proselytes. Islamic influences intensified on the eastern coast as the trade in ivory and slaves increased.

In only a few places did European states exercise direct domination over African territory before 1880: the French in Algeria; the Spanish in Guinea; the Portuguese in Angola and Mozambique; and the British at the Cape. The displaced Dutch settlers, called **Boers** (from the Dutch word for farmer), plunged in stages deep into the interior—most famously in the "Great Trek" of 1835–1837—where they founded the Orange Free State and the state of Transvaal, first recognized, then absorbed by the British. In these regions, they came in contact with several African peoples who, in their turn, were driven to migrate to distant lands by the consolidation of the Zulu nation in 1817 under their brilliant chief Shaka (c. 1787–1828). Shaka's Zululand, centrally administered, like his disciplined army of 40,000 conscripts, eventually fell to the British after the founder was treacherously murdered by his half-brothers.

From 1880, the major European powers effected the complete partition of Africa. The Berlin Conference of 1884 established the principle that sovereignty in Africa would be determined by "effective occupation." In the ensuing "scramble for Africa," the main feature of the "second" or "New" imperialism, all these European powers raced to occupy effectively what territory they could.

The occupation of the African interior swept inward from the coasts. The British and the French moved south from the Mediterranean coast, establishing colonies in the Sudan (French West Africa and, in condominium, the British–Egyptian Sudan). From the east, the Italians, Portuguese, Germans, and British snatched up the lands they called Eritrea and Somaliland, German and British East Africa (Tanganyika and Kenya), and Mozambique. From the Cape, the British expanded north to the Rhodesias

German invasion of Tanzania

Europeans and Africans

Europeans had a popular notion of themselves as bearers of civilization, commerce, and culture. Here, a less optimistic portrait of European–African relations—a battle between German and native troops in Tanzania—is drawn by early twentieth-century African artist Maru Bomera (left).

Most Africans were brought under European domination and integrated into the imperial economies. Here, African workers in Dakar, Senegal carry heavy sacks of peanuts for export (bottom).
(left: Tanzania National Museum)

(named after Rhodes) and Bechuanaland. In the Anglo-Boer War (1899–1902), they recaptured the Orange Free State and Transvaal from the Boer or **Afrikaner** settlers (after the dialect they now spoke, which was composed of Dutch and African elements), who had once been permitted to settle there. Of these different units, it was the British who forged the Union of South Africa.

On the west, proceeding north from the Cape, the Germans, Portuguese, and French established German South West Africa, Angola, and French Equatorial Africa, while along the Congo river the Congo Free State fell to Belgium, and specifically to its king Leopold II (r. 1865–1909), who set a new and terrible standard for the brutal exploitation of native labor. Further north along the Atlantic coast, the British, Germans, Spanish, and French established, respectively, Nigeria and the Gold Coast; the Cameroons and Togoland; Rio de Oro and Spanish Morocco; French Morocco (as a protectorate, while Islamic sultans continued as nominal rulers) and Senegal. French, Italian, and British-dominated states, part of the Middle Eastern cultural zone, now stretched along the Mediterranean. In 1914, nothing of Africa was left to the Africans but Liberia, which had been founded by freed American slaves, and Christian Ethiopia, which repulsed Italian invasion at the Battle of Adowa in 1896.

The partition of Africa accomplished the final partition of the inhabited globe, reorganized as nation states according to European definitions made without regard to native custom or ethnicity. Domination stretched and altered the European consciousness; Europeans dominated everywhere, and they dominated even those, a little different from themselves, who dwelled within their own domains.

DOMINION WITHIN

By 1914, Europeans had spent four centuries establishing their dominion over other peoples of the world in Africa and the Americas, Asia and Oceania. Their imperialism was not restricted to these remote regions only. It also affected cultural, religious, or other types of minorities who existed within their own boundaries. Among those groups whose histories prepared them to be viewed as targets for oppression in Europe were the Irish and the Jews.

The Irish: Despised and Persecuted

In the early Middle Ages, after their conversion to Christianity under Saint Patrick (see Chapter 10), the Celtic peoples of Ireland created a splendid civilization that in many ways outshone those of the Anglo-Saxon, Frankish, and Lombard kingdoms. From these regions, a significant number of capable youths traveled to study in Irish monasteries, the most disciplined and productive in Europe, and home to an unrivaled school of manuscript illuminators. Ireland also sent its missionaries and teachers abroad. Outside of the monasteries, the chiefs of the Irish clans, though they fought each other, supported cultural development and patronized poets who served as historians and theologians as well, the scribes of national memory and conscience.

Struck hard by Viking raids in the eighth and ninth centuries (see Chapter 9), Ireland lost its cultural preeminence. In the twelfth century, the pope placed it under the protection of the king of England, Henry II (r. 1154–1189). English nobles acquired Irish lands and exploited the native peasantry. From

African workers

the twelfth through the sixteenth century, Ireland was England's colony. Engels' description of its subjugation is given in *Witnesses* on p. 709.

Ireland's subjugation took a harsher turn when, in the 1530s, King Henry VIII (r. 1509–1547) repudiated the pope and created a new Protestant Church of England, with himself as its head (see Chapter 14). As England's colony, Ireland, too, was supposed to accept the new religious settlement, which made the king supreme head of the Church of Ireland in 1537. As in England, monasteries were dissolved, nonconverting priests dismissed, and the people required to abandon ancient customs. But in Ireland, the people identified the new prayers and rites with their English oppressors. As often elsewhere, the attempt to convert a subjugated nation to the religion of its masters was unsuccessful. Religious difference added to the tension between the Irish and the English, whose domination was now not only political and military, but also cultural.

From 1537 until 1798, the discord was intense. English absentee landlords confiscated Irish lands and peonized the laborers. From the early seventeenth century, the English sent more willing colonists—loyal and Protestant—to settle in the remote north of the island, where their descendants live still. English monarchs and the English Parliament twice sent their armies across the Irish Sea to suppress rebellions and punish the population. The brutal occupation of Ireland in 1649–1650 by Oliver Cromwell (see Chapter 15), then head of the Parliamentary army, is unforgotten in that nation's history.

The worst period of anti-Catholic repression followed. British authorities shut down Roman Catholic schools, and hounded and slaughtered the priests, often hidden at great risk by peasants and nobles. In 1798, the Irish patriot Wolfe Tone (1763–1798), the Protestant founder of the Society of United Irishmen, received support from French revolutionary forces in launching a rebellion against their common enemy, the British. The rebellion was harshly suppressed, and Tone committed suicide in prison, evading the reprisals that once again ravaged Ireland.

The plan first outlined by the British prime minister William Pitt the Younger (1759–1806) for settling what was delicately called the "Irish problem" involved two key actions. By the first, taken in 1800, Ireland was incorporated into a new political entity, the United Kingdom of Great Britain and Ireland, and ruled directly by the British Parliament to which it would elect 100 members. Irish leaders condemned this coerced unification, and now pressed for "home rule" by their own national assembly.

The second, realized in the Roman Catholic Emancipation Act of 1829, was more conciliatory. For the first time, Roman Catholics were able to take a seat in Parliament. By 1800, Roman Catholics had already regained some economic and political

rights denied them since the reign of Henry VIII: the rights to worship freely, and to educate their children, to marry, and to conduct their personal lives according to that faith. Further, they were permitted to hold some public offices, upon the taking of a loyalty oath, and to enter the military forces and the universities. Subsequently, in 1869, the resented Protestant Church of Ireland—to which some one million Irish Protestants adhered—was disestablished.

Some progress had been made in settling the differences between the British and the Irish when, in 1845, the great potato famine began. The Irish peasantry had become dependent upon the potato as a primary, often their sole crop. Introduced from the Americas and established as a field crop by the eighteenth century, it edged out the cultivation of grains that required fallowing if they were not to exhaust the soil (see Chapter 16). Infestation by a fungus specific to the potato resulted in catastrophe. Famine struck, and persisted for four years. An estimated 1 million died, and 1 million emigrated, causing the population of Ireland to drop by some twenty-five percent between 1845 and 1850. Over the next decades, 2 million more persons emigrated, leaving a population of about 4 million in 1900, half the pre-famine figure. The devastation was comparable to that wrought by the Black Death of 1348–1349, the greatest demographic catastrophe in European history.

Britain's perceived failure to assist Ireland, coupled with its record of persecution and oppression, convinced many Irish leaders of the necessity of national independence, even as significant progress was being made toward greater autonomy for Ireland within the United Kingdom. Indeed, Parliament voted to permit home rule in 1914. The coincident outbreak of World War I (see Chapter 26), however, prevented its enactment, and Ireland was poised for revolution.

The British who ruled Ireland came to detest the Irish peasantry. Their Roman Catholicism was seen as dangerous, their poverty an affront—even though it was British land policies and taxation that exacerbated it. The Anglo-Irish writer Jonathan Swift (1667–1745) had assailed British attitudes in his satirical essay "A Modest Proposal," which outlined a solution to the crisis of poverty and overpopulation: the children of poor parents might be boiled and eaten. Around 1800, as Britain industrialized, Irish immigrants squeezed into urban slums and performed the most despised jobs. Drunkenness, laziness, and criminality were all seen as the attributes of the Irish, the people whom the British had themselves reduced to desperation (see the cartoon in *Windows On*, p. 711).

The Jews: The Intimate Enemy

By 1750, European Jews had already experienced many centuries of persecution (see Chapters 12, 14, 18). They suffered mob violence; discrimination, including special dress requirements and exclusion from certain professions; and expulsion, from England and France in the thirteenth and fourteenth centuries, from the German lands in the fourteenth and fifteenth, and finally from the Iberian kingdoms in 1492 and 1497. Pushed into eastern Europe, by the eighteenth century most lived under the rule of Russian, Polish, Prussian, or Austrian monarchs. Here, in village *shtetls* or city ghettos, they labored as tailors, soapmakers, tanners, furriers, and as financiers, raising fortunes for kings, and moneylenders, serving the poor who resented their wealth.

During these years, Jews maintained their religious traditions. The center of every Jewish community was the synagogue: a place for learning, judgment, prayer, and the exercise of charity, supporting a sizeable elite of learned males—students, cantors, scribes, and rabbis—who committed themselves to learn and transmit the traditions of the Jewish people. The primacy of learning, and the respect for tradition, enabled an isolated people to survive and to flourish.

Since the fall of the Temple (see Chapter 7), the tradition of learned and logical commentary in Judaism coexisted with a mystical, more emotional tradition of worship. During the thirteenth century,

the former tradition reached its apogee in the work of Maimonides (Moses ben Maimon; 1138–1204). Maimonides presented the foundations of Jewish thought in his scholarly works including the classic *Guide of the Perplexed*, composed in Arabic but circulated in Hebrew and Latin translations. Combining Jewish law and Greek philosophy into one rational system, his work paralleled that of contemporary Islamic and Christian philosophers, who were also building rational theological systems on the foundations of ancient thought (see Chapters 8, 10).

Meanwhile, an alternative, mystical tradition flourished, based on the study of **kabbalah**, a body of orally-transmitted "secret" knowledge—expressed in patterns of ten divine numbers and the twenty-two letters of the Hebrew alphabet—that would allow the worshiper to approach directly to God. Such studies culminated in the Zohar, a thirteenth-century southern French work that presented a mystical interpretation of Old Testament passages and themes.

A series of messianic movements erupted in the seventeenth and eighteenth centuries, the most famous being that of Shabbetai Zevi (1626–1676). In 1665 in Smyrna (Izmir, modern Turkey), Zevi proclaimed himself to be the long-awaited Messiah. The

Dominion Within: The Jews and the Irish

Even as Europeans invaded the far corners of the globe and exploited the goods and labor of foreign peoples, at home they acted similarly towards two peoples in their midst: the Jews and the Irish. In the first of these passages, a German theorist warns his readers about the threat to German culture that he felt was posed by the Jews—a situation exacerbated by Jewish immigration. In the second passage, Friedrich Engels reflects on the destruction and demoralization brought about by the centuries-long British occupation of Ireland.

The German historian Heinrich von Treitschke condemns the "Jews Among Us" (1889): The instinct of the masses has ... identified a severe danger, a threat to the new life of Germans and one to be taken quite seriously. ...

Our Eastern border delivers year in, year out, a swarm of young [Jewish] men ... who are content for now to sell trousers but whose children and grandchildren will run stock exchanges and newspapers. Immigration grows before our eyes, and the question of how we can melt this alien folk element together with our own keeps getting more serious. ...

The loud agitation of the moment emerges as a brutal, but natural, reaction of German folk feeling against a foreign element which has begun to take up too much space. ... Let us not deceive ourselves: the movement is deep and strong. ... Even in the high-

est-educated circles, among men who would denounce every thought of religious intolerance or national arrogance, the words resound with a single voice: "The Jews are our misfortune!"
(Heinrich von Treitschke, *Ein Wort über unser Judenthum*, 1889; ed. P. Riley, 1998)

Friedrich Engels characterizes the centuries of British rule of Ireland: Characteristic of this country are its ruins. ... The most ancient are all churches; after 1100, churches and castles; after 1800 the houses of peasants. ...

The country has been completely ruined by the English wars of conquest from 1100 to 1850 ... [so that the people themselves] feel that they are no longer at home in their own country. ... The Irishman knows he cannot compete with the Englishman, who comes with means in every respect superior; emigration will go on until the predominantly ... Celtic character of the population is all to hell. How often have the Irish started to try and achieve something, and every time they have been crushed, politically and industrially! By consistent oppression they have been artificially converted into an utterly demoralized nation and now fulfill the notorious function of supplying England, America, Australia, etc., with prostitutes, casual labourers, pimps, thieves, swindlers, beggars and other rabble.
(*Marx–Engels, Selected Correspondence, 1846–95*, 1934; ed. N. Mansergh, 1965)

mystic and scholar Nathan of Gaza (1644–1680) promoted his cult in diaspora communities of the Ottoman Empire and Europe, resulting in mass enthusiasm and miraculous events across those regions. In 1666, Zevi journeyed north from Palestine to Smyrna. Denounced and imprisoned, he appeared before the sultan's court and was offered the choice of death or apostasy. Zevi chose the latter, converted to Islam, and snared a good job as the sultan's gatekeeper.

In the next century, **Hasidism** developed in eastern European regions of dense Jewish settlement. This was a modern religious movement growing out of earlier medieval seekings of the "pious" (the *hasid*) for spiritual comfort. The Ukrainian spiritual leader Israel ben Eliezer (c. 1700–1760) devoted himself to serving the needs of ordinary people, who awarded him the name Ba'al Shem Tov, or "Master of the Good Name." He and his followers held that the pious man could be a poor man who reached God not through years of study, but through zealous piety. Their celebrations marked by joyous and even ecstatic song and dance, Hasidic communities flourished and spread throughout eastern Europe and, later, the United States.

Meanwhile, the rational strain of Jewish thought also produced new fruit. In seventeenth-century Amsterdam, home to many Sephardic Jews (descended from those expelled from Spain and Portugal), Baruch Spinoza (1632–1677) developed a pantheistic philosophy grounded in Jewish thought but transformed by contemporary gentile philosophy (see Chapter 17). In his *Ethics*, *Treatise on the Correction of the Mind*, and *Theological–Political Treatise*, Spinoza demonstrated the continuities between human and divine, the compatibility of religion with political stability and with free thought, and the historical understanding of scripture. Yet the work of this proponent of philosophical freedom was condemned during his life by the Amsterdam Jewish community.

Spinoza's focus on freedom was characteristic of the mental world of the seventeenth and eighteenth centuries, during which ideas circulated more freely than ever before. In that open atmosphere, many Jews flourished. Some became wealthy serving as financiers for nobles and kings, and had adopted aspects of the dress, the behavior, and the outlook of their employers. Others, like Spinoza, had involved themselves in the intellectual debates of the age. The Enlightenment raised the prospect that Jews, too, might enter mainstream European society, and even attain equal civil rights. In the mid-seventeenth century, Cromwell's regime in England and, in the 1790s, the revolutionary regime in France moved to exclude religion from the public realm, facilitating Jewish **assimilation**.

In the eighteenth century, small circles of privileged Jews within major western European capitals were able to enter the mainstream of culture, such as

Moses Mendelssohn (1729–1786), who wrote rational explanations of Judaism in modern languages for the non-Jewish audience. In the following century, Jews and converted Jews were among Europe's leading poets, musicians, and political and scientific theorists—Heinrich Heine (1797–1856), Felix Mendelssohn (1809–1847, Moses' grandson), Karl Marx (1818–1883), and Sigmund Freud (1856–1939; see Chapter 24) are famous examples. Among other eminent Jews who remained fully committed to Judaism as a religion and a community were members of the Rothschild family of international bankers.

Yet discrimination continued and indeed intensified under the conservative monarchs of eastern Europe, as the passage quoted in *Witnesses* on p. 709 indicates. Even the cosmopolitan West saw outbreaks of virulent anti-Semitism, as in the case of the French army captain Alfred Dreyfus (1859–1935) who in 1894 was falsely accused of selling sensitive documents to the Germans (see *Windows On*, p. 711). Although the case against him was flimsy (he was later proved innocent), high-ranking generals allowed Dreyfus to be publicly degraded and exiled to a penal colony on Devil's Island off the South American coast. An outcry from the French intelligentsia followed, the highlight of which was the rebuttal by novelist Emile Zola (see Chapter 25), headlined "*J'Accuse*" ("I Accuse You") and dramatically displayed in 1898 on the front page of the newspaper *L'Aurore* ("The Dawn"). Dreyfus was eventually released.

In the Russian Empire, an outbreak of **pogroms** shattered the precarious security of the Jewish communities in rural villages and big cities. From 1881 until 1917, with the tsar, bureaucracy, and police failing to intervene in time, anti-Semitic riots caused the murder of many Jews and the destruction of their communities, as in Odessa during four days in 1905, when 400 Jews were murdered. A steady exodus of Russian Jews streamed to western Europe and the Americas.

The pogroms convinced many Jewish intellectuals that there could be no safety for the Jews in Europe. "In countries where we have lived for centuries we are still cried down as strangers," wrote the Hungarian journalist Theodor Herzl (1860–1904). Herzl proposed a solution: the evacuation of European Jews to their ancient homeland of Palestine. His arguments, outlined in his 1896 book *The Jewish State*, constitute the original document of the program of **Zionism**, largely realized after awesome struggles in the following century (see Chapter 29).

The Psychology of Domination

If anti-Semitism is an extreme case of hostility directed against a people because of their cultural distinctiveness, it is far from the only one. During the late nineteenth century, Western intellectuals inscribed in their speeches, letters, treatises, and

Colonized Europeans: The Jews and the Irish

LE TRAITRE
Dégradation d'Alfred Dreyfus

"The Traitor—The Degradation of Alfred Dreyfus," cover of Le Petit Journal, January 13, 1895

Thomas Nast, "The Day We Celebrate," 1867

Like few other events in modern history, the Dreyfus affair focused the attention of educated Europeans on questions of anti-Semitism. In this illustration (above left), Dreyfus, wrongfully convicted of treason, looks on as the French Ecole Militaire strips him of his buttons and braids and breaks his sword.

Jews were more often victims of harsher persecution. Here, victims of a pogrom (anti-Jewish riot) are laid out in the Ukraine in a scene from around the end of World War I (bottom).

The Irish also suffered from discrimination and negative stereotyping. Thomas Nast's satirical cartoon (above) depicts the Irish as irresponsible, unintelligent drunkards and ruffians. (bottom: The Jewish Museum, New York).

Pogrom victims in the Ukraine, 1881–1917

To continue your investigation of this topic, please go to www.prenhall.com/king for the related **WINDOWS** on the **WEB** activity

dispatches to the press the inferiority of other peoples of the world—those of other "races." The use of the term "**race**" in these decades has no scientific basis, but emerged from discussions of the theory of evolution recently proposed by Charles Darwin (1809–1882; see Chapter 25) and was colored by assumptions of Western superiority reinforced by the experience of imperialist ventures. Racial theory relates differences between peoples to their ancestry, rather than to differences in their culture or history.

Among those contributing to late nineteenth century racial thinking were the French politician Jules Ferry (1832–1893), architect of that nation's system of public education and advocate of colonial expansion, and the British entrepreneur Cecil Rhodes. Rhodes exemplifies that outlook: "I contend that we are the finest race in the world and that the more of the world we inhabit the better it is for the human race." Social Darwinists (see Chapter 25) looked for progress to emerge from the competition between "superior" and "inferior" peoples. The statistician Karl Pearson (1857–1936), an advocate of **eugenics**, urged the systematic "improvement" of populations. It was his "scientific view" that a nation's people should be "substantially recruited from the better stocks," and kept efficient through competition in war with "inferiors," and in commerce with equals. "This is the natural history view of mankind," he wrote, "and I do not think you can in its main features subvert it."

Imbued with such attitudes of racial superiority, many Europeans considered it their duty to introduce Western values to the world: it was the "white man's burden," the title of a poem by the muse of British imperialism, the Indian-born Rudyard Kipling (1865–1936), which is quoted in *Witnesses* on p. 713. Liberty of the press, religious toleration, representative government, impartial justice, were the exports that European elites could bring to Asian and African states.

Christian missionaries believed that they brought sound truths to the peoples of the rest of the world, and many dedicated men and women lost their lives in seeking to accomplish that purpose. In Africa, they won many converts; and though their contempt for native customs aroused resentment, mission schools trained many of the new African nations' future leaders, and mission hospitals provided services not otherwise available. In Asia, loyalty to ancient religious traditions—Hindu, Buddhist, Confucian, Taoist, Islamic—and outright hostility to the missionary effort, resulted in few conversions. Missionaries did not (at least at first) understand, however, that their benevolence implied their assumption of the preeminence of their customs and values—the assumption that their supremacy was due to their inherent superiority.

Writers, politicians, and generals, and even priests, pastors, nurses, and nuns shared in the assumption that Asians and Africans and Amerindians and other indigenous peoples would benefit by acquiring Western culture. Nevertheless, there were those who criticized imperialism and its racist assumptions. The Polish-born English novelist Joseph Conrad (1857–1924) described the corruption of the spirit that came from dominion over others as in his account of Belgian occupation of the Congo in the *Heart of Darkness* (1902). English author George Orwell (1903–1950), Indian-born and employed in his youth as a colonial policeman in Burma, repudiated imperialism as a crime against others and a poisoner of the European consciousness. Hilaire Belloc (1870–1953), another English anti-imperialist, sardonically identified the source of the European power to enslave others: the machine gun.

> *Whatever happens we have got*
> *The Maxim-gun; and they have not.*

In the United States, opposition arose to United States involvement in crushing the independence movement that broke out in the Philippines after the Spanish–American War (1898). In the Platform of the American Anti-Imperialist League, leading intellectuals, businessmen, and politicians argued that such imperialist aggression violated the fundamental principles of the United States Constitution: in the land of George Washington and Abraham Lincoln, it should not be necessary "to reaffirm that all men, of whatever race or color, are entitled to life, liberty and the pursuit of happiness," they wrote, insisting that "the subjugation of any people is … open disloyalty to the distinctive principles of our Government."

The British economist J. A. Hobson (1858–1940), in his *Imperialism, a Study* published in 1902 and later used by the Russian Marxist theorist Vladimir Ilyich Ulyanov, called Lenin (see Chapters 25, 26, 28),

MUST READS

Imperialism, For ...

Joseph Chamberlain   *Foreign and Colonial Speeches* (1897)

Rudyard Kipling   *"The White Man's Burden"* (1899)

Karl Pearson   *National Life from the Standpoint of Science* (1905)

and Against...

Joseph Conrad   *Heart of Darkness* (1902)

Vladimir Ilich Lenin   *Imperialism, the Highest Stage of Capitalism* (1916)

John Atkinson Hobson   *Imperialism* (1902)

Europe's "Burden" or Benefit? Contrasting Views of the Purpose and Morality of Imperialism

When Europeans intervened in the lives of peoples in remote parts of the world, were they conferring a benefit or laying a burden upon the unwilling targets of Western expansion? The two authors here, both English, differ on the question. For the poet Rudyard Kipling, the British were rightly seen as the civilizers of the "new-caught, sullen peoples" they had conquered. For historian J.A. Hobson, the British were less nobly engaged in a quest for economic profit, seeking markets for their goods that would otherwise fail in competition with newly unfolding industrial nations.

The poet of imperialism, Rudyard Kipling, proclaims it the "white man's burden" to bring civilization to the natives of other continents, viewed as "sullen" inferiors: "half devil and half child" (1899):

Take up the White Man's burden—
Send forth the best ye breed—
Go bind your sons to exile
To serve your captives' need;
To wait in heavy harness,
On fluttered fold and wild—

Your new-caught, sullen peoples,
Half devil and half-child.
(Rudyard Kipling, *Verse*, 1899)

It was this sudden demand for foreign markets for manufactures and for investments which was avowedly responsible for the adoption of Imperialism as a political policy. ... They needed Imperialism because they desired to use the public resources of their country to find profitable employment for their capital which otherwise would be superfluous. ... As one nation after another enters the machine economy and adopts advanced industrial methods, it becomes more difficult for its manufacturers, merchants, and financiers to dispose profitably of their economic resources, and they are tempted more and more to use their Governments in order to secure for their particular use some distant undeveloped country by annexation and protection.
(John A. Hobson, *Imperialism*, London: Allen and Unwin, 1948)

identified the greed of capitalist investors as the source of a baneful European expansionism, whose effect was the impoverishment of peoples abroad as well as at home (see *Witnesses* above). Racial theories propounded by intellectuals and politicians were only a disguise, he suggested, for mere acquisitiveness: "biology and sociology weave thin convenient theories of a race struggle for the subjugation of the inferior peoples, in order that we ... may take their lands and live upon their labours."

The spectacle of money and goods, workers and refugees, flowing to and from Europe lends support to the notion that imperialist expansion was essentially economic in motivation.

MIGRANTS AND MONEY

Prodded by entrepreneurs, "opened" by foreign states, menaced by gunfire, warships, and armies, by 1914 the nations of the world had been joined into a single economic system. Steamships journeyed between continents, exchanging copper, rubber, and silk for machine parts and cotton textiles. Telegraph cables linked distant regions, railroads spanned whole continents and blasted through and under mountains, and two great canals in two hemispheres (see below) abolished barriers to trade.

From the industrial centers of Europe money flowed to fund development in China or Chile, Russia or the Sudan. And money flowed back to Europe and

the United States, a rich return on their investments, as the graph on p. 714 shows. In antiquity and the Middle Ages, trade abroad had been trade in luxuries. The quantities were limited, the value small, producers and consumers few. In the modern age, a global economy involves huge quantities and astonishing sums, and affects everyone.

People moved, too, across the globe, in search of work, safety, or freedom. Their movements, indicated by the graph on p. 715, changed the distribution of cultures and skin colors on all the inhabited continents, as populations rose. The world's wealth multiplied, but unevenly, enriching those living in industrialized regions more than those who did not, whose poverty, relatively speaking, deepened.

The Global System: Money and Goods

The trading system across Europe, Africa, and Asia that developed in antiquity expanded after 1500 to include the Americas and the great oceans. It expanded again after 1750 to embrace the whole globe.

By 1900, a pattern was established in which the regions outside of Europe mostly provided raw materials and foodstuffs to the now industrialized giants of the West. China supplied silk, porcelain, and especially tea; India tea, cotton, spices, and jute; southeast Asia spices and coffee, rubber and tin; and Australasia minerals, including gold and copper, and foodstuffs, especially meat and dairy products.

The Middle East grew raw cotton for European factories, and Asian Russia yielded furs and minerals. Africa supplied gold, diamonds, and other minerals, rubber, palm oil, and other tropical produce. In all of Afro-Asia, Japan alone exported manufactured goods in quantity. By 1918, forty percent of all its exports were manufactures, and only fifteen percent of imports. The value of its foreign trade increased about sixty-fold between 1878 and 1918.

Latin America, whose main products at the outset were silver and gold (see Chapter 19), soon also produced sugar, tobacco, and coffee (the Caribbean and Brazil), nitrates and meat (Chile and Argentina), and other minerals and foodstuffs. North America at first supplied the West Indies with grain and fish, and later both Canada and the United States exported foodstuffs round the world. By 1914, the United States was highly industrialized and a net producer of manufactured goods. Within Europe itself, the eastern regions shipped grain to west, which exported industrial manufactures and the skills to the rest of the continent.

This gigantic exchange of commodities and manufactures was accomplished especially by steamship and railroad, two new forms of transportation. In the British merchant marine, steam replaced sailing ships rapidly; elsewhere, steam triumphed only in the last generation before 1914. Large and powerful steamships carried more goods than sailing ships, conquering distances that had once been nearly insuperable.

Railroads were also critical in the world trade network, and their web expanded wherever money, ships, and merchandise traveled. In 1870, more than ninety percent of all the rail mileage in the world was in western Europe and North America, which region also saw the first great transcontinental links—the United States in 1869, Canada in 1885. The next generation saw the trans-Siberian railroad reach Vladivostok (1916) and the trans-Andean line in South America (1910). Later, railroad lines spread across Africa and the Middle East, India, and China. By 1911, one-quarter of world rail mileage lay outside of Europe and North America.

The telegraph and telephone also helped shrink the world. By 1914, telegraph cables connected the Americas, Europe, the Middle East, and Africa; before long, the network extended to east Asia. Two great canals cut across slivers of land in the Mediterranean and Central America to connect on different poles the eastern and western halves of the globe. The Suez Canal (see above), connecting the Mediterranean with the Red Sea, opened in 1869; the Panama Canal, connecting Atlantic and Pacific Oceans, in 1914. The latter was a United States project, which united the two coasts of North America and opened Asia to eastern American ports.

From 1800 to 1914, the total value of world trade more than quintupled and foreign trade as a proportion of all trade increased from three to thirty-three

Money on the Move, 1913–1914

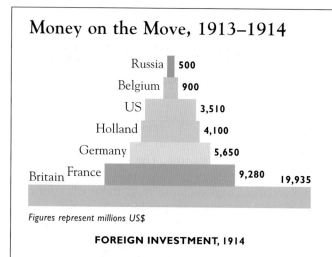

Russia 500
Belgium 900
US 3,510
Holland 4,100
Germany 5,650
Britain France 9,280   19,935

Figures represent millions US$

FOREIGN INVESTMENT, 1914

	imports	exports
Britain	3,467	2,322
Germany	2,483	2,375
US	1,797	2,411
France	1,590	1,337
Netherlands	1,189	1,284
Russia	556	719

Figures represent millions US$

IMPORTS AND EXPORTS, 1913

By the eve of World War I, the European nations were moving money and goods all over the globe. The graph on the left shows the relative amount of foreign investment disbursed by each of seven major nations. Note that British investments far exceed those of the nearest competitor, France, and that those of the United States lag behind four European colonial powers. The graph on the right shows the value of imports and exports for each of six nations on the eve of World War I. Note that the leading importers of goods are Britain and Germany, while the United States surpasses the other European traders. In exports, however, the United States is at the head of the class, exporting a greater value of goods than any European nation in absolute terms, and a much greater value relative to imports. Germany, too, has become a strong competitor to Britain. The increasing economic strength of Germany and the United States would be displayed in the political sphere over the next decades (see Chapters 26, 28).

Source: Times Atlas of World History, 4th ed. (London: Times Books, 1993), pp. 256–257.

percent. In this vast marketplace, the largest single player was Britain, which in 1860 was responsible for the value of one-quarter of all the world's trade. It was the pivot of international commerce, and the largest banking center. The total value of Britain's investments abroad was only slightly less than the total value of the wealth invested by France, Germany, Belgium, the Netherlands, and the United States together—no other countries approached these in the magnitude of their foreign investments. The British were especially active in South America, the French and British in the Middle East, the British again in India, China, and Australia. In addition, Europeans invested in North America, Russia, the Balkans, as well as the Ottoman Empire.

The Global System: Peoples and Culture

While money invigorated the economies of emerging nations, so too did the arrivals in new lands of hunted, hungry, and restless peoples from the old regions of the globe. After 1500, the distribution of the peoples of the world shifted: people of different nationalities, religions, and civilizations resettled far away from their homelands. Between 1800 and 1914, the most dramatic migrations were those of Europeans, especially to the Americas. Asian emigration within Asia and to the Americas was also significant.

About 40 million Europeans resettled in other continents during this period of global reshuffling. After 1845, driven by the Great Famine (see above), about 3 million Irish left, mostly for North American cities. After 1848, traumatized by the failure of political revolution in central Europe, about 5 million Germans resettled in the United States and South America (especially Argentina). Poverty drove 5 million Italians to the United States and South America (especially Argentina) in the later nineteenth century. Between 1881 and 1917, during a surge of pogroms in the Russian Empire, nearly 2 million Jews fled, again, to the Americas.

More than 12 million English, Welsh, and Scots emigrants—constituting the single largest national group—journeyed to the Americas or to even more remote Australia and New Zealand. Lured by cheap land, nearly 2 million Scandinavians came to North America. After 1900, another 2 million Italians settled mostly in the coastal cities of North and South America. More than 1 million French migrants established themselves in Morocco and Algiers in North Africa.

Chinese emigrants settled on the west coast of the United States and in the Caribbean, where they often worked as indentured laborers. Indian emigrants, similarly, became indentured workers in the Caribbean, while, in their settlements in South Africa, they formed a thin merchant stratum between white European bosses and African natives. Both Chinese and Indian entrepreneurs moved into the East Indies, the Chinese also to Indochina, where they formed merchant communities. Until the 1880s, the waning

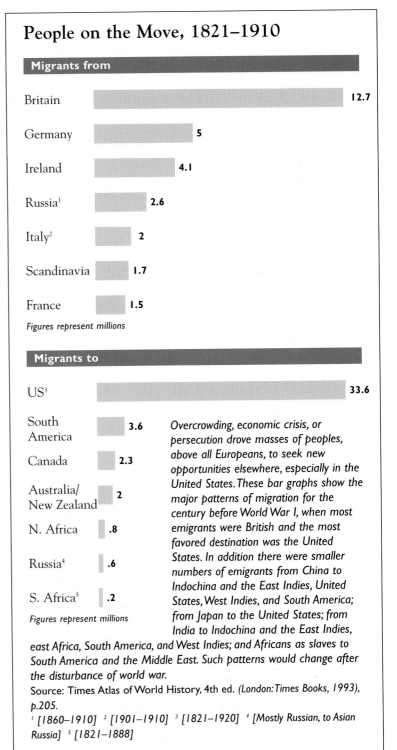

People on the Move, 1821–1910

Migrants from

Britain	12.7
Germany	5
Ireland	4.1
Russia[1]	2.6
Italy[2]	2
Scandinavia	1.7
France	1.5

Figures represent millions

Migrants to

US[3]	33.6
South America	3.6
Canada	2.3
Australia/New Zealand	2
N. Africa	.8
Russia[4]	.6
S. Africa[5]	.2

Figures represent millions

Overcrowding, economic crisis, or persecution drove masses of peoples, above all Europeans, to seek new opportunities elsewhere, especially in the United States. These bar graphs show the major patterns of migration for the century before World War I, when most emigrants were British and the most favored destination was the United States. In addition there were smaller numbers of emigrants from China to Indochina and the East Indies, United States, West Indies, and South America; from Japan to the United States; from India to Indochina and the East Indies, east Africa, South America, and West Indies; and Africans as slaves to South America and the Middle East. Such patterns would change after the disturbance of world war.

Source: Times Atlas of World History, 4th ed. (London: Times Books, 1993), p.205.
[1] [1860–1910] [2] [1901–1910] [3] [1821–1920] [4] [Mostly Russian, to Asian Russia] [5] [1821–1888]

slave trade still operated across the Atlantic to Cuba and Brazil and to Arabian ports.

Within Europe, English factories employed a large population of Irish workers, and Polish peasants found opportunity in the new Ruhr industrial zone of western Germany. About 7 million European Russians resettled in the great expanse of Siberia. In addition, Russian peasants moved seasonally, streaming to St. Petersburg and Moscow to find factory work during the winter months, returning to the countryside come spring to work on the land. In 1900, such peasant workers constituted nearly 1 million, or two-thirds, of St. Petersburg's population. Italian migrant workers journeyed in the same way to do seasonal work in southern France and Germany—and even distant Argentina.

Even as the poor, the frustrated, and the endangered folk of Europe piled on steamers bound for other continents, the population of Europe itself increased—faster than any other region of the world. While the population of the globe nearly doubled (increasing from 900 to 1600 million between 1800 and 1900), the European proportion of the whole increased from about one-fifth to more than one-quarter of this total (about 423 million), and the white proportion to about one-third.

By 1910, the sparsely-inhabited lands that Europeans had settled in the Americas, the southern Pacific, and Asian Russia contained 200 million people, most of European descent—nearly half as many as in the European homelands. From 1800 to 1900, the population of the United States nearly quintupled, while that of Mexico doubled, that of Brazil quadrupled, and that of Argentina had risen tenfold, from about one-half million to almost 5 million. European domination of the globe was mirrored in a surge in the quantity of Europeans.

That surge correlated to disproportionate wealth, as imperialism shifted the world's balance of wealth and poverty. One thousand years earlier, Europe had been poor; Islamic, Indian, and Chinese civilizations had been wealthy. In 1914, Europe and its offshoots were wealthy; and so, too, the Japanese. But now the peoples of Africa, the Middle East, and Asia labored to grow, mine, and process those products needed to supply Europe and its children. Wealth had shifted to Europe, and poverty to the non-Western peoples of the Old World, the Americas, and Australasia.

By 1914, nevertheless, nearly all the globe's inhabitants were part of one integrated economic system which held the potential of greater wealth for all. In Europe and in lands of European settlement, previously unsurpassed standards of living had been attained, and were enjoyed by a larger part of the population. Famine had been conquered in western Europe, North America, and Australasia. In time, as the newly-poor regions of the globe struggled free of European domination (see Chapter 28), they would not spurn the wealth of the West, but would struggle to attain such well-being for themselves. If that goal is one day achieved, it would be a fine, if unintended consequence of the Western *imperium*.

Conclusion
THE WESTERN *IMPERIUM* AND THE MEANING OF THE WEST

Between 1500 and 1914, Europe brought most of the world under its control. By 1914, Germany, France, and the Netherlands ruled millions of non-Europeans in Africa, Asia, and the Americas. The sprawling Russian Empire engulfed millions of Asian Muslims. The United States had acquired dominion over the Philippines and Puerto Rico. Britain flew its nation's flag over one-fifth of the surface of the globe, and ruled one-fourth of its inhabitants. Just as the ancient Romans proclaimed the Mediterranean "our sea" (see Chapter 5), Europeans might survey the planet Earth and declare it theirs.

The effect of Europe's expansion was not merely to control, but also to unify. Imperialist ventures integrated the world's peoples, nations, and civilizations. This was not the first attempt to unify the corners of the earth. The Persians, Hellenistic Greeks, Romans, Islamic caliphs, and Mongol khans had understood that challenge (though their empires lacked the racial dimension of later Western rule). The dominion these earlier conquerors won through violence did much to make disparate nations aware of each other, and promote the exchange of important technologies. The European nations also employed violence as they expanded, and brought about integration.

The European *imperium* was more successful than its precursors; it was also undeniably brutal. That brutality was encouraged by assumptions of cultural superiority. Western elites dismissed the customs and ignored the genius of the peoples they encountered—as did the genial historian Macaulay in his characterization of Indian culture with which this chapter opened. Their arrogance and their brutality were neither unprecedented nor unique. A glance back at Roman campaigns of conquest, or Mongol raids that left no creature alive, dispels that notion. Nevertheless, they committed deep injustices that would demand, in time, painful remedies (see Chapter 29). Few concerned themselves with that possibility during an era when Western civilization, as the next chapter will show, seemed unassailable.

REVIEW QUESTIONS

1. How is colonialism different from imperialism? What cultural and economic ties bound the Americas and Australasia to Europe before 1914? Describe the expansion of the Russian Empire which had occured by 1914.

2. How was Britain able to gain control of the Indian sub-continent? What currents in Indian life after 1858 were eventually to lead to independence? What were the bases of British rule in India?

3. Why were the advanced societies of the Asian mainland less able to withstand European states after 1800? Why did the Chinese Empire decline in the nineteenth century? Why was Japan able to resist Western imperialism and become a great power?

4. Describe the Ottoman Empire before 1914. Why were the Ottomans unable to resist European encroachment? How did economic imperialism affect the Near Eastern states in the nineteenth century?

5. What was the "scramble for Africa"? What role did religion play in British rule in Ireland? How strong was anti-Semitism in Europe before 1914?

6. What role did racism play in European imperialism? How did the West dominate the world economy before 1914? What benefits did Western rule bring to the rest of the world?

SUGGESTED RESOURCES

Lands of European Settlement and General Overviews

Clancy-Smith, Julia and Frances Gouda, eds., *Domesticating the Empire: Race, Gender, and Family Life in French and Dutch Colonialism* (Charlottesville: University Press of Virginia, 1998). How imperial ventures affected the domestic relations of colonized and colonizer.

Darby, P., *Three Faces of Imperialism: British and American Approaches to Asia and Africa, 1870–1970* (New Haven, CT: Yale University Press, 1987). How considerations of "power," "moral responsibility," and "economic interest" shaped foreign affairs.

MacDonald, Robert H., *The Language of Empire: Myths and Metaphors of Popular Imperialism, 1880–1918* (New York: St. Martin's Press, 1994). Explores the production and consumption of concepts of "Empire".

An On-Line History of the US: the Age of Imperialism (smplanet): http://www.smplanet.com/imperialism/toc.html

Imperialism, the Highest Stage of Capitalism, by Vladimir Ilyich Lenin (Lenin Works Archive): http://www.marxists.org/archive/lenin/works/1916

Old World Encounters: Asia

Arnold, David, *Colonizing the Body: State Medicine and Epidemic Disease in Nineteenth-Century India* (Berkeley: University of California Press, 1993). Explores how epidemic disease and ideas about its treatment shaped British conceptions of India and of their role as colonizers.

Beasley, W. G., *Japan Encounters the Barbarian: Japanese Travelers in America and Europe* (New Haven: Yale University Press, 1995). Describes the fact-finding mission in the 1860s and 1870s of Japanese observers in Europe and the United States, in the service of a modernized Japan.

Jayawardena, Kumari, *The White Woman's Other Burden: Western Women and South Asia during British Rule* (London: Routledge, 1995). Examines diaries and other writings of Western women in Asia, who pressed for the liberation of Indian women both from repressive native customs and from the oppression of a British imperial system. Johann

Old World Encounters: The Middle East and Africa

Edgerton, Robert B., *Fall of the Asante Empire: the Hundred-Year War for Africa's Gold Coast* (New York: Free Press, 1995). The struggle of a native African empire reorganized as the colony of the Gold Coast.

Goodwin, Jason, *Lords of the Horizons: A History of the Ottoman Empire* (New York: Henry Holt, 1999). An overview of the vast Ottoman Empire, which encompassed many ethnicities and religious groups, yet which thrived because of its tolerance and commitment to meritocracy, which allowed talented subjects to advance.

Hamilton, Carolyn, *Terrific Majesty: The Powers of Shaka Zulu and the Limits of Historical Invention* (Cambridge MA: Harvard University Press, 1998). Hamilton explores the figure of Shaka Zulu as a metaphor for leadership and national South African memory.

Pakenham, Thomas, *The Scramble for Africa: 1876–1912* (New York: Random House, 1991). Comprehensive study.

Joseph Conrad, *Heart of Darkness* (1899); (SUNY Buffalo): http://www.acsu.buffalo.edu/~csicseri

Dominion Within

Magnus, Shulamit S., *Jewish Emancipation in a German City: Cologne, 1798–1871* (Stanford: Stanford University, 1997). Examines the dynamics of Jewish emancipation and assimilation by focusing on Cologne, whose prosperous and innovative business community permitted the eventual recognition of Jews as citizens with full legal rights.

O Grada, Cormac, *Black '47 and Beyond: the Great Irish Famine in History, Economy, and Memory* (Princeton: Princeton University Press, 1999). Uses interdisciplinary social science concepts and comparative studies to write a rich and comprehensive account of the great disaster.

Steiman, Lionel B., *Paths to Genocide: Anti-Semitism in Western History* (New York: St. Martin's Press, 1998). Investigates the evolution of anti-Semitism in Europe and the West.

Beyond the Pale: The History of the Jews in Russia—with sections on the Dreyfus affair and late-19th-century anti-Semitism: http://www.friends-partners.org/partners/beyond-the-pale/index.html

National Archives of Ireland Research Guide, *The Great Famine, 1845–1850*: http://www.nationalarchives.ie/famine.html

Migrants and Money

Baines, Dudley, *Emigration From Europe, 1815–1930* (Basingstoke: Macmillan, 1991). Brief and accessible.

Cohen, Robin, ed., *The Cambridge Survey of World Migration* (Cambridge: Cambridge University Press, 1995). Encyclopedic, authoritative, and indispensable.

STORM, STRESS, AND DOUBT

| 1775 | 1800 | 1825 | 1850 | 1875 | 1900 | 1925 |

Politics, Society, and Economy

Congress of Vienna, 1814–15

World War I, 1914–18

- ◆ Revolution in France, 1830
- ◆ First Reform Act in Britain, 1832
- ◆ Factory Act limits child labor in Britain, 1833
- ◆ New Poor Law limits welfare benefits in Britain, 1834
- ◆ Year of Revolutions in Europe, 1848
- ◆ Serfdom abolished in Russia, 1861
- ◆ First International, 1864
- ◆ Slavery abolished in US, 1865
- ◆ Second Reform Act in Britain, 1867
- ◆ Education Act in Britain, 1870
- ◆ Unification of Italy, 1870
- ◆ Unification of Germany, 1871
- ◆ French establish compulsory schools, 1879–81
- ◆ Women's right to own property assured in Britain, 1882
- ◆ Third Reform Act in Britain, 1884
- ◆ Second International, 1889
- ◆ 94% of conscripts into French army literate, 1901
- ◆ Literacy rates in Russia around 43%, 1917

Arts and Ideas

- ◆ Thomas Malthus' *Essay on Population*, 1798
- ◆ Johann Wolfgang Goethe's *Faust*, 1808–32
- ◆ David Ricardo's *Principles of Political Economy and Taxation*, 1817
- ◆ Eugene Delacroix' *Liberty Leading the People*, 1830
- ◆ August Comte coins term "sociology," 1838
- ◆ Louis Blanc's *The Organization of Work*, 1839
- ◆ Charlotte Bronte's *Jane Eyre*, 1847
- ◆ Karl Marx and Friedrich Engels' *Communist Manifesto*, 1848
- ◆ Charles Dickens' *Hard Times*, 1854
- ◆ Gustave Flaubert's *Madame Bovary*, 1857
- ◆ Charles Darwin's *Origin of Species*, 1859
- ◆ Fyodor Dostoevsky's *Notes From Underground*, 1864
- ◆ Joseph Lister's first successful use of antisepsis on patient, 1865
- ◆ Gregor Mendel publishes work on genetics, 1866
- ◆ John Stuart Mill's *On the Subjection of Women*, 1869
- ◆ Ernst Renan's *Life of Jesus*, 1869
- ◆ Dmitri Mendeleev invents Periodic Table, 1871
- ◆ Émile Zola's *Germinal*, 1885
- ◆ Emile Durkheim's *Suicide*, 1897
- ◆ Marie Curie discovers radium, 1898
- ◆ Sigmund Freud's *The Interpretation of Dreams*, 1899
- ◆ Albert Einstein's special theory of relativity, 1905
- ◆ Eduard Bernstein's *Evolutionary Socialism*, 1909

Beyond the West

British East India Company dominant in India, 1690–1857

Direct British rule in India, 1858–1947

Qing Dynasty, China, 1644–1912

First Opium War, 1839–42

Second Opium War, 1856–60

- ◆ American Commodore Perry "opens" Japan, 1853
- ◆ Sepoy Mutiny in India, 1857
- ◆ Meiji Restoration in Japan, 1868
- ◆ Suez canal opens, 1869
- ◆ Indian National Congress founded, 1885
- ◆ South African War, 1899–1902
- ◆ Boxer Rebellion in China, 1900
- ◆ Panama Canal opens, 1904
- ◆ Japan wins Russo-Japanese War, 1905
- ◆ "Young Turks" topple Ottoman sultan, 1908
- ◆ Chinese Republic declared, 1911–12

CHAPTER 25

STORM, STRESS, AND DOUBT

European Culture from Classicism
to Modernism

1780–1914

countries with universal male suffrage:

- 1848-1900
- 1900-1914
- ■ major cultural centers

KEY TOPICS

◆ **From Romanticism to Realism:** The calm elegance of Classicism yields to the styles of Romanticism and Realism in the arts, literature, and thought—suitable complements to the revolutionary era and an age of disenchantment.

◆ **The Sciences and the Schools:** New disciplines in the sciences and social sciences take their place in the universities, as workers and peasants go to school for the first time.

◆ **Ideals and Ideologies:** New ideologies, expressing different interests, compete with liberalism in appealing to the masses of men and women who seek an active place in the political realm.

◆ ***Fin-de-Siècle* and the Advent of the Modern:** As some thinkers proclaim the death of God and an end to the centuries-long rule of good and evil, others lay the foundations of Modernism in literature, the arts, and thought.

Notes from Underground In 1864, the Underground Man—the narrator of Notes from the Underground by *Russian author* Fyodor Dostoevsky (1821–1881)—announced the failure of the Enlightenment principle of rationality. Reason, he conceded, "is an excellent thing, there is no disputing that, but reason is only reason and can only satisfy man's rational faculty." The human being will never abandon sensation and impulse for the presumed good that reason supplies. Our life may be worthless, concedes the Underground Man, "… yet it is life nevertheless and not simply extracting square roots." Given the choice between feeling and reason, human beings will always choose feeling in the end—even if feeling means suffering: "man will never renounce real suffering, that is, destruction and chaos."

FROM ROMANTICISM TO REALISM

This terrible message from underground is the voice of the "Modern," a complex and doubt-tinged world-view that evolved between 1789 and 1914. During that long century, the West accumulated great wealth and power. Industrialization stimulated global trade, while colonial and imperial ventures resulted in the European domination of much of the world (see Chapters 21, 23). These changes reshaped Western consciousness, and gave rise to new artistic and intellectual visions. In the arts, **Classicism** gave way to **Romanticism**, which elevated feeling over reason; and Romanticism to **Realism**, which inspected the contemporary world without sentiment or illusion.

Romanticism and Revolt

Enlightenment rationalism and Classical style, which mirrored its calm certainty, did not long survive the French Revolution (see Chapter 20). The post-revolutionary world invited artists and thinkers to put down their books and seek not to know but to feel.

Painted by the French artist Eugène Delacroix (1798–1863), *The 28th July: Liberty Leading the People*, which is reproduced in *Windows On* on p. 722, exemplifies the new spirit of Romanticism. In Delacroix's *Liberty*, all is in motion. A fierce female figure symbolizing Liberty represents the savage mother of a revolutionary generation. She signals the crowd of revolutionaries onward, over the bodies of dead and wounded comrades: a child wielding two revolvers, an artisan in frock coat. Such a painting celebrates change, passion, and action.

In a similar vein, the English Romantic artists J. M. W. Turner (1775–1851) and John Constable (1776–1837). spurned the idealised landscapes of Classical

style, and depicted nature in its primal, disorderly condition—in wild forests, burgeoning gardens, in storms, or at night. In Constable's landscapes of spreading green fields enveloping a few anonymous figures, nature, though benign, engulfs the human realm. Turner's spraying seas, as in *Shipwreck* illustrated on p. 722, or roaring railroads dissolve into mist, as all that is solid melts into the ambient natural world. Romantic artists also inclined to historical and exotic subjects, such as ruined castles or harems drawn from their fantasies about the Middle East.

Romantic musical style was also characterised by stormy variations of mood and tempo. The innovative later works of the German composer Ludwig van Beethoven (1770–1827), whose career bridged from Classical to Romantic, shock and stimulate. Writing often for the voice, the Austrian composer Franz Schubert (1797–1828) crafted contemporary poetry, with its celebration of love and loss, into art songs.

Opera especially benefited from the transition to Romantic style. Opera's sung drama is the ideal medium for grand themes such as love, death, sacrifice and betrayal, that Romantic style could portray with rich emotional power. The operas of the Italian composer Giuseppe Verdi (1813–1901), convey passion and grand idealism, whether the world of the Italian Renaissance is painted in *Rigoletto* (1851) or that of an up-to-date Parisian courtesan in *La Traviata* (1853).

Romanticism also infused literature, and especially poetry, the preeminent vehicle for the expression of emotion and the exploration of the self. The work of the English poet William Wordsworth (1770–1850) exemplifies the centrality of nature for Romantic poets. His friend Samuel Taylor Coleridge (1772–1834) depicted the poet as an inspired genius in his "Kubla Khan":

> *Beware! Beware!*
> *His flashing eyes, his floating hair!*
> *Weave a circle round him thrice,*
> *And close your eyes with holy dread:*
> *For he on honey-dew hath fed,*
> *And drunk the milk of Paradise.*

The centrality of heterosexual love, both marital and adulterous, as a literary theme prompted the participation of women in the culture of Romanticism. Women were often the subjects of Romantic works—betrayed wives, dying lovers, tormented courtesans. But they were also often creators in their own right. The wife of the English poet Percy Bysshe Shelley (1792–1822) was also a writer—Mary Shelley (1797–1851), the daughter of early feminist Mary Wollstonecraft (1759–1797; see Chapter 17). Likewise, the wife of the German poet Wilhelm von Schlegel (1767–1845), whose translation of Shakespeare stirred the Romantic imagination, was Caroline Michaelis (1763–1809), who left her first husband for the German idealist philosopher Joseph von Schelling (1775–1854). As in the Enlightenment, learned women sparkled in salons, but were now more likely to be themselves thinkers of stature—as was Rahel Varnhagen von Ense (1771–1833). Born Rahel Levin, a Jew, she converted to Christianity and, hosted an important Berlin salon during the decades from the 1790s to the 1820s.

Germaine de Staël (1766–1817), a salonière but much more, was the daughter of Jacques Necker (1732–1804), the Swiss finance minister of the former French king Louis XVI. As both hostess and author, she surveyed a turbulent period of French history, from Revolution to Empire and Restoration, interrogating the meaning of it all. She wrote novels featuring female heroines in tragic situations, but was even more important as a literary critic and political commentator. After traveling through Germany and observing at first-hand developments in literary, musical, and philosophical circles, she introduced the rest of Europe to some of the pioneers of Romanticism, the creators of the movement known as *Sturm und Drang* ("Storm and Stress").

Romanticism had first emerged in the German states. The German language, with its complex consonant combinations and surging rhythms lends itself to a poetry that represents emotion. Thus Johann Wolfgang von Goethe (1749–1832) expressed the uncontrollable strivings of the human spirit in his verse drama *Faust* (completed 1832), and the fatal power of love in his novel *The Sorrows of Young Werther* (1774). In *Faust*, the legendary late medieval sage and magician, who wished to know the hidden mysteries of the universe, suffers the consequences of his unbridled ambitions: death and damnation. The tormented young Werther, failing in love, commits suicide.

Historical settings evoked a powerful response among Romantic authors, who were fasinated by the medieval past. An interest in the past also related Romanticism to the nationalist movements of the nineteenth century, especially German, Italian, Polish, Czech, and Hungarian (see Chapter 20). History abounded with national heroes from an epic past, a shared heritage for people who otherwise knew only that they spoke the same language and worshiped in the same faith.

Romanticism also impacted upon philosophy, and found an advocate above all in G. W. Friedrich Hegel (1770–1831). History and feeling both played a central part in his work. Throughout history, the realm of the spirit evolved, which would one day reach its final culmination in the political state of Germany. It was not reason that made that nation great, according to Hegel, but its spirit, or will, or passion.

Realism and Disenchantment

If the powerful emotion in Romantic works rediscovered the passion in a world that the Enlightenment

had demystified, Realism accomplished for a second time the world's disenchantment.

Realist painters depicted ordinary human beings in everyday settings, eating, working, burying their dead. *The Man with the Hoe* by the French artist Jean-François Millet (1814–1875) for example, depicts a nameless worker identified by his labor: by his bent back, his rugged tool, and the invincible toughness of the soil (see *Windows On*, p. 722). He is a figure of the present moment, whose image bespeaks the condition of the peasant wholly identified with the work he must do.

A new medium, perfectly suited to Realism, was developed in the 1830s by L. J. M. Daguerre (1789–1851)—photography. The camera recorded a segment of reality, as seen by the eye, unmediated—so it was believed—by the adornments or fantasies of the artist. Photography shops sprang up in major cities, while expert photographers employed the camera as a witness to contemporary events, for example Jacob Riis (1849–1914; see Chapter 22) in his narrative and photographic account of the poor in New York, *How the Other Half Lives*.

Realist literature found its ideal vehicle in the novel, which created a convincing background of events against which the stories of struggling individuals unfolded. The French novelist Honoré de Balzac (1799–1850), for example, drew more than 2000 portraits of contemporary Parisians in the roughly ninety novels of the series *The Human Comedy*. His compatriot Gustave Flaubert (1821–1880) looked to the stultifying life of the provinces, where his fictional character, the adulterous Madame Bovary lived. His novel of that title (1857) tells the story of a woman who is compelled by soul-deadening tedium to disrupt moral boundaries and eventually to destroy herself. The novels of Emile Zola (1840–1902) examine

The Cycle of Styles: Classicism, Romanticism, and Realism

Eugène Delacroix, Liberty Leading the People, 1830

Jean-François Millet, **The Man with the Hoe**, *1860–1862*

Western art passed through three broad stages during the first several decades of the nineteenth century. The carefully controlled scenes created by Classicists such as the French Revolutionary-era artists Jacques-Louis David soon gave way to more emotional and romantic images. Eugène Delacroix's Liberty Leading the People (top)— which emphasizes the passion and action of the 1830 Revolution in France—epitomizes the new movement. Similarly, the English painter J. M. W. Turner challenges Enlightenment notions of the order of nature in his Shipwreck (bottom), stressing instead uncontrollable power and majesty.

By mid-century, however, Realist artists were turning from the heroic to the mundane and creating accurate depictions of the minutiae of ordinary life. Jean-François Millet's The Man with the Hoe (above right) illustrates this trend.

Photography, developed in the 1830s by L. J. M. Daguerre, provided a medium well suited for realism. It could capture life more or less in its actuality—as demonstrated here by the portrait of the American Lemuel Shaw (1851), when he was serving as chief justice of the Massachusetts supreme court (below right)—freeing artists later in the century to pursue more innovative approaches and styles referred to as Modernism.

(top: Louvre, Paris; bottom: British Museum, London; above right: The J. Paul Getty Museum, Los Angeles; below right: Metropolitan Museum of Art, New York)

J. M. W. Turner, **Shipwreck**, *1823*

Albert Sands Southworth and Josiah Johnson Hawes, Lemuel Shaw, *1851*

 To continue your investigation of this topic, please go to www.prenhall.com/king for the related **WINDOWS** on the **WEB** activity

Pioneers of Literary Style: Romanticism and Realism

Whereas Romanticism appealed to the beauties of nature and the wisdom innate in each individual, Realism looked at life as it actually was—often sordid; and people as they actually were—often debased by circumstances they could not help. The two passages here are by two exemplars of each approach: the American poet Walt Whitman and the French novelist Emile Zola.

A manifesto of Romanticism—Walt Whitman would rather look at the stars than listen to an expert (c. 1864):
When I heard the learn'd astronomer,
When the proofs, the figures, were ranged in columns
  before me,
When I was shown the charts and diagrams,
  to add, divide,
and measure them,
When I sitting heard the astronomer where he
  lectured
with much applause in the lecture-room,
How soon unaccountable I became tired and sick,

Till rising and gliding out I wander'd off by myself,
In the mystical moist night-air, and from time to time,
Look'd up in perfect silence at the stars.
(Walt Whitman, "When I Heard the Learned Astronomer," c. 1864)

A Miner's Life—an extract from a Realist novel (1885): That started them all off, and each threw in his word, while the fumes of the oil lamp mingled with the reek of fried onions. You worked like a beast of burden at a job that used in the olden days to be a punishment for convicts, more often than not you died in harness, and with all that you could not even have meat on the table at night. Of course you had food of a kind, you did eat, but so little that it was just enough to keep you suffering without dying outright, weighed down by debts and hounded as though you had stolen the bread you ate. ... The only pleasures in life were to get drunk or get your wife with a baby, and even then the beer made you too fat in the paunch, and when the child grew up he didn't care a bugger about you.
(Emile Zola, *Germinal*, 1885; trs. L. Tancock, 1954)

the lives of ordinary people—coal miners in his *Germinal* (1885), a passage from which is quoted in *Witnesses* above, a prostitute in *Nana* (1880)—as in a hostile environment. In England, Charles Dickens (1812–1870) depicted the squalor of the lives of the poor, the psychology of industrial capitalists, and the experiences of neglected or abandoned children.

Whereas Romanticism had resisted industrialization and retreated into nostalgia and the celebration of nature, Realism faced it ruthlessly. The ugliness of the physical environment, the deterioration of the laborer's body, the flattening of the spirit, and the endurance of the individual were grim subjects that called for unblinking investigation.

Did Realist writers have a political agenda? In their searing portrayals of poverty and exclusion, they present problems that begged for solutions. In the context of recurrent political revolution, and of the mounting force of socialism (see below), it would seem that literary Realism straddles the realms of art and politics. Some Realist authors indeed represented a new type of intellectual—an activist concerned with concrete and pressing issues. Zola's public championship of Alfred Dreyfus (see Chapter 24), a Jewish officer wrongfully convicted on charges of spying in 1894, marks the public birth of this phenomenon.

Novelists, among them women novelists, also considered the situation of women. The English novelist Jane Austen (1775–1817), focused on love and marriage as the central issues in women's lives and the social world. The sisters Charlotte (1816–1855),

Emily (1818–1848), and Anne Brontë (1820–1849), and George Eliot (the masculine pseudonym of Mary Ann Evans; 1819–1880) described the choices women made constrained by family demands and the desire for self-expression. In France, George Sand (a masculine pseudonym for Amandine A. L. D. Dudevant; 1804–1876) wore men's clothes and smoked cigars, while she pursued alliances with men of the intellectual elite and wrote novels, letters, and memoirs.

Music, too, took up some of the themes associated with Realism. Composers incorporated in their works melodic motifs from the song and dance of the peasants, or the "folk." Thus Polish and Hungarian motifs are showcased in the polonaises and mazurkas of Frédéric Chopin (1810–1849). Composers of Italian opera focused on contemporary settings and characters from the lower strata of society.

The Realists' immersion in the world linked them to socialism and **feminism** as it distanced them from both Classicism and the Romantics. Their role in literature was paralleled in the universities by the work of scientists, social scientists, and scholars.

THE SCIENCES AND THE SCHOOLS

Intellectuals promoted the development of new professional disciplines. Some of the principal ones are listed in *Who's Who* on p. 728. Meanwhile, the spread of public elementary education allowed talented young people access to professional careers.

The Past as It Really Was

The political and intellectual currents of nineteenth-century Europe are reflected in the writing of history, or **historiography**. In the Enlightenment, history was considered an art, and the author's opinions were allowed to color his view of the past. In the nineteenth century, historians saw themselves as the synthesizers of evidence, which, often in the form of original, official documents, bound them to the conclusions that emerged from their analysis. The product of this method, they believed, would be, in the famous words of the German historian Leopold von Ranke (1795–1886), a description of the past *wie es eigentlich gewesen ist*, "as it really happened." *Witnesses* on p. 725 quotes from his writings.

Pursuing this ideal, historians compiled extensive accounts of the development of major institutions, primarily the modern state. Von Ranke himself wrote histories of Germany, France, Italy, and England. Thomas Babington Macaulay (1800–1859) produced a history of England in five volumes; Jules Michelet (1798–1874) one of France in twenty-four volumes; and J.-C.-L. Simonde de Sismondi (1773– 1842) one of Italy in sixteen volumes.

Historians also looked beyond the sphere of the state. The nature of the historical Jesus, for instance, intrigued the French historian Ernest Renan (1823–1892), whose *Life of Jesus* (1863) shocked Christian Europe with its realist, anti-Christian stance. The English historian George Grote (1794–1871) chronicled ancient Greece, at a time when the non-Christian, Classical antecedents of Western civilization intrigued many intellectuals. The Swiss historian Jacob Burckhardt (1818–1897) described the Italian Renaissance as the birthplace of the modern spirit.

In these endeavors, historians took possession of the European past which they interpreted in terms that were meaningful for their own age. They established the writing of history as an academic discipline on a level with the traditional subjects of theology, medicine, or law in university faculties. Germany led the way in creating a multi-departmental university, in which the new historical discipline found a home. There it was joined by other humanistic pursuits such as Classics, the study of the civilizations of ancient Greece and Rome, modern languages and linguistics.

The World as It Came to Be

In establishing history as an evidence-based inquiry, historians were imitating scientists, who tested and proved their theories, or hypotheses, with evidence. Science made important advances during the nineteenth century, especially in the field of biology. Investigations in microbiology and genetics and the theory of evolution fundamentally changed the way human beings understood their place in the cosmos.

Microbiology and Genetics Louis Pasteur (1822–1895) was the culminating figure in a sequence of scientists who located the living organisms that caused many infectious diseases. With the aid of the microscope, Dutch, Italian, German, and French scientists opened a world invisible to the unaided eye, gazing at the tiniest independent animals, or protozoa; the different cells found in the brain, the blood, or the parts of plants; and bacteria.

Continuing these investigators' earlier work, Pasteur explained the processes of fermentation in yeast, and the souring of milk, both the result of bacterial activity. He developed the process to destroy bacterial contaminants in milk, called after him "**pasteurization**," and demonstrated that the apparent self-generation of **microorganisms** in non-organic media in fact derived from microorganisms introduced by contamination. Subsequently, he identified the bacteria responsible for forms of anthrax and cholera affecting farm stock, and the pathogens that ravaged silkworm populations essential for the textile industry. Finally, he isolated the bacterium responsible for rabies, a disease that terrorized rural populations exposed to infected animals. Pasteur's development of vaccines to prevent these diseases opened the road to the conquest of infectious disease. (Before Pasteur, only smallpox could be prevented through vaccination; see Chapter 17.)

The Austrian monk Gregor Johann Mendel (1822–1884) investigated the role of genes in biological reproduction through observations he made in his monastery garden. Like Pasteur, his work rested on that of early microscopists. Their analyses of animal and plant forms had contributed to the work of eighteenth-century **taxonomists**, who grouped and ranked the species of living things. The question of inheritance then presented itself: how did species transmit to their descendants their characteristic features?

Mendel's study of ordinary garden peas led him to the genetic theory of inheritance. The plants were long or short; their seeds were smooth or wrinkled. By carefully arranged cross-pollination of the plants in various permutations, he pointed to the existence of paired genes, of which some were dominant, which determined the characteristics of offspring. His genetic theory countered the prevailing theory, associated with the French scientist Jean-Baptiste Lamarck (1744–1829), that acquired characteristics could be inherited. Although his work was published in 1866, Mendel's obscurity meant that it was not circulated until after 1900.

Darwin's Theory of Evolution The work of the English naturalist Charles Darwin (1809–1882) depended, like Mendel's, on systematic observation. In the 1831 voyage of the British ship *Beagle*, in which he traveled as ship's naturalist, Darwin recorded his observations of species from many regions, notably

Pioneers of the Intellectual Disciplines: History, Social Science, and Science

New fields of knowledge took their places in European universities during the nineteenth century, filling out a curriculum that, since antiquity, had been based on philosophy, languages, and literature. Here, the German scholar Leopold von Ranke defines a new, more rigorous mission for the discipline of history; the English theorist Thomas Malthus lays down principles fundamental to economics and demography; the French theorist Emile Durkheim defines the new realm of the "social" sciences; and the English naturalist Charles Darwin opens a new era for the life sciences with the announcement of the theory of evolution by means of natural selection.

The German historicist Leopold von Ranke calls for the critical evaluation of historical sources (1824): One who for the first time confronts the multitudinous monuments of modern history must [feel like one] who confronted a great collection of antiquities in which genuine and spurious, beautiful and repulsive, important and insignificant, from many nations and periods, were heaped together without order. ... The material confronted would speak in a thousand voices. ... Some of the specimens ... attempt to derive from the past theorems for the future. Many want to defend or to attack. Not a few are zealous to develop the explanation of occurrences ... from the basis of subjective conditions and emotions. Then there are some which have only the purpose of passing along what has [actually] happened. ... The persons participating in the action speak. Original sources, alleged and actual, are present in abundance. Before all the question arises, "Which among many is a source of original knowledge? From which can we be truly instructed?"
(Leopold von Ranke, *Towards a Critique of Modern Historiography*, 1824; ed. A. W. Small, 1924)

Thomas Malthus gauges the implications of unrestrained population increase (1798): I have read some of the speculations on the perfectibility of man and of society with great pleasure. ... I ardently wish for such happy improvements. But I see great, and to my understanding, unconquerable difficulties in the way to them. [Malthus defines two premises affecting population growth and its outcome.]

First, That food is necessary to the existence of man. Secondly, That the passion between the sexes is necessary and will remain nearly in its present state. ...

Thus I say that the power of population is indefinitely greater than the power in the earth to produce subsistence for man. Population, when unchecked, increases in a geometrical ratio. Subsistence only increases in an arithmetical ratio. A slight acquaintance with numbers will show the immensity of the first power in comparison of the second. By the law of our nature which makes food necessary to the life of man, the effects of these two unequal powers must be kept equal. This implies a strong and constantly operating check on population from the difficulty of subsistence. This difficulty must fall somewhere and must necessarily be severely felt by a large proportion of mankind. ...
(Thomas Robert Malthus, *First Essay on Population*, 1798; Royal Economic Society, 1926)

Emile Durkheim insists that sociology is an independent science (c. 1901): A discipline may be called a "science" only if it has a definite field to explore. Science is concerned with things, realities. If it does not have a datum to describe and interpret, it exists in a vacuum. ... Before social science [or sociology] could begin to exist, it had first of all to be assigned a definite subject-matter. ... The subject-matter of social science is social things: that is, laws, customs, religions, etc. [which] are actual things, like all other things in nature; they have their own specific properties, and these call for sciences which can describe and explain them.
(Emile Durkheim, lecture, c. 1901; ed. A. Giddens, 1989)

Darwin outlines how species evolve by natural selection (1859): It has been seen ... that amongst organic beings in a state of nature there is some individual variability: ... But how is it that varieties, which I have called incipient species, become ultimately converted into good and distinct species... ? All these results ... follow from the struggle for life. Owing to this struggle, variations, however slight and from whatever cause proceeding, if they be in any degree profitable to the individuals of a species, in their infinitely complex relations to other organic beings and to their physical conditions of life, will tend to the preservation of such individuals, and will generally be inherited by the offspring. The offspring, also, will thus have a better chance of surviving, for, of the many individuals of any species which are periodically born, but a small number can survive. I have called this principle, by which each slight variation, if useful, is preserved, by the term Natural Selection.
(Charles Darwin, *The Origin of Species*, 1896; vol. 1)

the exotic species that had developed in isolation on the Galápagos islands (an archipelago 600 miles west of the coast of Ecuador). His observations led to questions: why and how did these creatures develop their distinctive characteristics? In response, he published in 1859 his *On the Origin of Species by Means of Natural Selection, or the Preservation of Favoured Races in the Struggle for Life.*

The theory of natural selection, summarized in *Witnesses* on p. 725, was an epochal breakthrough. It postulated that species of living things had constantly to struggle for existence. In the competition to eat and reproduce, individuals possessing certain biological characteristics were more successful than others. To the extent that those more desirable characteristics were inherited by subsequent generations, those descendants would win the struggle to survive, and accomplish the evolution of the species. Less desirable characteristics would result in the failure of individuals and of their offspring to compete successfully. Their biological future was bleak. No divine intervention, no special efforts of an individual to surpass his biological destiny, entered into the process. Nature itself made the decision.

Darwin's theory was the culmination of generations of biological and social thought. His understanding of the struggle for survival, for food and sexual reproduction, owed much to Malthus, while his understanding of the expanses of time over which species had evolved drew on the geological studies of Charles Lyell (1797–1875). His notion of a struggle for existence among competing animals had first been raised by his grandfather, Erasmus Darwin (1731–1802). Another influence was the work of Alfred Russel Wallace (1823–1913), who had studied the varied species of the Malay Peninsula, and was about to publish his account of biological evolution that threatened to preempt Darwin's.

The theory of natural selection explained, first, how existing species might have come into being without specific acts of divine creation. Second, it explained how variations in species characteristics might have developed other than by acquisition— that is, by the inherited behavior of individuals. Third, it embraced the animal, the vegetable, and even the human realms, claiming that the human being was firmly embedded in the natural order and subject to processes of change. This controversial point Darwin stated explicitly in his 1871 volume *The Descent of Man, and Selection in Relation to Sex*.

Darwinian theory, satirized in the cartoon on p. 727, posed challenges to religion, to humanism, and to liberalism. If nature selected some species for survival and others for extinction, what became of God? If human beings were simply accidents thrown up by the evolutionary process, where was the dignity of Man? If the fittest species alone survive, what did that imply for the status of persons whose race, nationality, class, or sex varied from the norm that Darwin himself represented—an upper-class Englishman?

Darwinian theory would soon be challenged on all of these points. Religious leaders protested immediately, while Social Darwinism (see below) applied the Darwinian model to the competition between classes, nations, and races, and feminists challenged Darwin's argument that women had reached a level of biological evolution lower than that attained by men.

Other Scientific Advances   The physical sciences also made advances, developing Newtonian principles in models of sub-molecular motion, of electricity, magnetism, and light. Chemists expanded the list of known elements ranked by atomic characteristics in the summary periodic table. The discovery of radium in 1898 by the Polish-born physicist Marie Curie (1867–1934) launched her and husband Pierre Curie (1859–1906) on the investigation of the phenomenon of radiation (the process by which energy is emitted from a body and absorbed by another). For this she received Nobel prizes in 1903 (with her husband) and 1911. On her husband's death in 1906, she assumed his university position, becoming the first woman to teach at the Sorbonne in Paris. The couple are portrayed on p. 727.

Of key importance for medicine was the development of antisepsis (killing or inhibiting bacteria). The British surgeon Joseph Lister (1827–1912), having studied with Pasteur, applied the principle of antisepsis to hospital environment. Now surgical patients would be treated in antiseptically clean hospital operating rooms, attended by teams of robed, masked physicians and assistants. From the 1840s, nitrous oxide, ether, or chloroform could achieve general anesthesia or mask the experience of pain. The physicians of the British Queen Victoria (r. 1837–1901) famously employed chloroform during her eighth childbirth in 1852: "the effect was soothing, quieting and delightful beyond measure," she reported.

WHO'S WHO

In the Sciences (1789–1914)

Charles Darwin (1809–1882) English naturalist; author of *Origin of Species*; created the theory of evolution by natural selection.

Gregor Mendel (1822–1884) Austrian monk and botanist; established the mathematical principles of the science of genetics.

Louis Pasteur (1822–1895) French biologist and pioneer of bacteriology; developed the concept and process of "pasteurization."

Joseph Lister (1827–1912) English surgeon and medical scientist; established the principles of antisepsis in hospitals.

Marie Curie (1867–1934) Nobel-prize-winning Polish-born French scientist; with her husband Pierre pioneered the study of radioactivity.

Albert Einstein (1879–1955) German physicist; creator of relativity theory and the notion that mass and energy are interconvertible.

Pioneers of Science

"Man is But a Worm": *In 1859, Charles Darwin published his* Origin of Species *establishing the theory of evolution, and in 1871, his* Descent of Man. *Darwinian theory, and especially its implications for the origins of humans, inspired frequent satire. One example is seen in this cover illustration from* Punch *magazine (December 6, 1881), where a circle of apes, having evolved initially from a worm, evolve in due course into a smartly dressed Englishman.*

Sciences of Society

Like history and the sciences, the social sciences found a place in nineteenth-century universities, with the emergence of political science, economics, sociology, psychology—fields of study that did not exist as such prior to the nineteenth century.

The science of economics had been pioneered by Adam Smith (1723–1790), author of *The Wealth of Nations* (see Chapter 16), who formulated the principles of supply and demand and the division of labor. Economics crystallized further because of the work of two Englishmen, the businessman David Ricardo (1772– 1823), son of Dutch-Jewish immigrants, and the clergyman Thomas Malthus (1766–1834).

What gave a commodity value, Ricardo asked—its intrinsic worth, or something else? If the former, why did prices often exceed the cost of materials? In answer to these questions he developed in his *Principles of Political Economy and Taxation* (1817), the "labor theory of value," later utilized by Karl Marx (see below). The value of an item derived not only from materials, and from the owner's proprietary (overhead) costs, but also from the cost of hiring the labor necessary to produce it.

Since it was in the interest of sellers to keep prices low in order to sell more, they exerted a downward pressure on labor costs. Workers' wages were kept as low as possible—and the lowest possible figure was always exactly the same: that sum that would allow the worker to subsist, and no more. Ricardo's explanation accorded well with experience. Workers' wages tended to devolve to subsistence level by what Ricardo called the "iron law of wages."

In his 1798 *Essay on Population*, (see *Witnesses*, p. 725), Malthus explored the mechanisms of population growth and the question of human happiness—why it had not been obtained by the great mass of people. He discovered that irrepressible appetites for food and sex constrained human beings mercilessly, as though by an iron law such as the one Ricardo described. Sexual activity resulted in more births, which led to more mouths to feed, and the eventual exhaustion of the food supply. When food supply could not keep pace with human population growth, that population became vulnerable to disease and starvation (two terrible forces that Malthus called "positive checks" on population), and soon shrank.

Marie Curie and Pierre Curie: *Nineteenth- and early twentieth-century women increasingly carved out places for themselves at the forefront of intellectual, scientific, and political life. The Polish-born French scientist Marie Curie, seen here in a scene from 1895 relaxing with her husband-collaborator Pierre, pioneered the study of radiation.*

Human communities that wished to eat needed to restrict their rate of fertility. Malthus advised them to do so through late marriage or abstinence, as historically they had done for centuries.

Both Ricardo and Malthus, though amateurs, contributed to social and political thought, which soon branched into autonomous professional disciplines. Auguste Comte (1798–1857), was the founder of sociology, the term he coined in 1838, the scientific study of human social behavior. Comte was a proponent of **positivism**, the creation of knowledge based on concrete evidence. Positivism looked carefully at hard facts and aimed at practical ends. The positivist study of human societies would lead, Comte argued, to sociology, which could then point the way to the creation of optimal human communities. Later, the French sociologist Emile Durkheim (1858–1917; see *Witnesses*, p. 725) was less certain that positivism led to well-functioning communities. Rather, cohesiveness derived from the set of moral and religious assumptions that a community collectively shared. When those shared assumptions broke down, misery set in. In *Suicide* (1897), Durkheim ascribed the phenomenon of suicide to the fragmentation of social values.

The English philosopher Herbert Spencer (1820–1903), less concerned with community, argued that superior individuals, derived from a superior inheritance—they were, in brief, racially superior. The most competent individuals—whom Spencer identified as those of the Anglo-Saxon race—would in time gain superiority over others. This theory of individual success based on competition and racial aptitude, seeming to mirror Darwin's theory of natural selection, acquired an air of scientific authority. Spencer's "Social Darwinism," however, has been repeatedly rejected by scientists, who note the confusion between Darwin's theory of the biological evolution of *species* and Spencer's notion of the willed competition between individuals *within* a species. Spencer's views, however, helped justify European imperial expansion over "races" presumed to be "inferior" (see Chapter 24).

The development of economics and sociology was important for political thinking, even as the liberalism that had displaced theories of monarchical rule was itself fragmented into conservatism and nationalism, socialism, communism, feminism, and anarchism (see below). Political thought, too, found a respectable university niche, and animated reformers and revolutionaries, whose work will be considered below. First, the system of schooling must be described by which youngsters were prepared to enter into the social mainstream.

Schooling the Masses

The principle of mass public elementary education is recent. Prior to the nineteenth century, nearly all elementary education was private. For the elites generally, such education aimed at Latin literacy. In some merchant circles, vernacular literacy was deemed sufficient, and mathematical skills were stressed. In Protestant communities, literacy was linked to Bible reading and basic religious instruction. Girls, along with literacy and perhaps some bookkeeping, needed to learn needlework skills. Privileged girls would also learn drawing, dancing, and music. Those at convent schools also received a thorough, and often tedious, religious training.

Most children, however, did not go to school. Children of working-class families might master a craft, do agricultural work, or labor as servants. Many did not learn to read, write, or perform arithmetic; many did not speak the official national language, but a non-standard dialect—as was the case with over ten percent of children in France as late as 1863.

The public schooling of the masses began in France and Britain in the late nineteenth century. It was schooling guided by a secular state that had begun to broaden its franchise, and looked to equip its citizens to participate in civil life. In France, anti-clerical republicanism called for a completely secular, public

---

WHO'S WHO

In Political, Philosophical, and Social Thought: the First Generation (1789–1914)

Edmund Burke (1729–1797) English statesman and philosopher of Conservatism.

Thomas Malthus (1766–1834) English clergyman, economist, and demographer; his *Essay on Population* (1798) foresaw the dangers of overpopulation.

Jeremy Bentham (1748–1832) English Utilitarian philosopher; argued that the only true standard for good was that which served the "greatest good for the greatest number."

G. W. Friedrich Hegel (1770–1831) German Idealist philosopher and important influence on Karl Marx.

F. M. Charles Fourier (1772–1837) Pioneer "Utopian" Socialist; proposed the creation of workers' communities based on a *phalange*, or communal association, of carefully selected personality types.

Auguste Comte (1798–1857) French Positivist thinker and founder of sociology.

Leopold von Ranke (1795–1886) German historian; promoted the use of official sources as the basis for writing history "as it really happened."

education. Its advocates wanted to terminate the clergy's long monopoly of the schools. From 1833 each commune (a local administrative unit) had been required to operate a primary school. Often the teachers were clergy who, though subject to secular standards, continued to teach religious doctrine. By 1847, nearly 4 million children attended these schools, and by 1875, literacy rates had climbed significantly.

From 1879 to 1881, the Minister of Education (later Premier) Jules Ferry (1832–1893) instituted a program of school reforms. These established free, secular, coeducational, and compulsory public schools in each village. Centrally-controlled teacher-training schools graduated idealistic school teachers of republican sympathies. By 1901, 83,700 primary schools of all types existed to instruct more than 5 million children (of a national population of 38.9 million) in basic subjects. By the same date an impressive ninety-four percent of army conscripts (a cross-section of the nation's male youth) were literate.

Secondary schools expanded as well, including girls as well as boys. Even so, few students, mostly from wealthy families, went on to secondary school (a fraction of a percent). Even fewer attended university (although attendance had tripled by 1900), the pathway to careers in law, medicine, and the civil service.

In Britain, Church-directed Sunday Schools were established from the late 1780s to provide poor children with basic skills. Hannah More (1745–1833), an early advocate, defined their aim "to train up the lower classes in habits of industry and piety." By 1833, nearly half of the school-age population was enrolled. The Sunday Schools could not by themselves produce educated workers (whose literacy rates in the early years of industrialization hovered depressingly around five percent for men, and two percent for women). Yet they laid the groundwork for a system of comprehensive, mass education.

Parliament mandated the operation of public schools by the Education Act of 1870. The Quaker member of Parliament William Foster (1818–1886), among others, had put the case: "On the speedy provision of elementary education depends our industrial prosperity, the safe working of our constitutional system, and our national power." In 1880, Parliament required school attendance for all children up to age ten; in 1899 it extended the requirement through age twelve; in 1891, it eliminated all fees. An educated citizenry and an educated workforce were now viewed as essential for an advanced nation.

Other European nations followed suit. In Italy prior to unification, the state of Piedmont in 1847 was the first to establish such a system. After unification, general progress was made, resulting in increasing the literacy rate from 1860 rates of about twenty-five percent for men and ten percent for women to an overall rate of seventy-five percent by 1914. That figure disguises the great division in Italy between the affluent,

largely literate northern provinces, and the impoverished, southern ones, where fewer than one-half of all children attended schools.

In Germany after 1870, an affluent, newly unified nation moved swiftly to train its youth. By 1900, less than one percent of the population failed to meet the standard of literacy. In Russia, where serfdom had been abolished only in 1861, the general literacy rate had risen to forty-three percent by 1917, with the countryside still lagging behind the cities, and women behind men. The government attempted to close higher education in Russia to all but the nobility, although some non-nobles did succeed in attending secondary school and university.

Although secondary and higher education remained exclusive, the elementary education now available to many meant a transformation in the intellectual world. Readers of all classes consumed novels, magazines, and newspapers—the latter evolving from monthlies to weeklies to dailies. As a result, the gap between the culture of the learned and the "popular" culture of workers and peasants, which had opened wide since the age of the Renaissance (see Chapters 13, 17), narrowed considerably. Reading and schooling encouraged national consciousness and culture that complemented the spirit of nationalism and the democratization of politics that characterized the age.

The establishment of public schooling in the wealthier nations of western Europe meant even the children of the poor might someday attend university, participate in the creation of new knowledge, and read, view, and listen to the cultural products of artists and intellectuals in what was then the dynamic center of the world's civilizations.

IDEALS AND IDEOLOGIES

Public education was one fruit of **liberalism**, the dominant **ideology** of the nineteenth century. (An ideology is a set of ideas linked to a program of social or political action.) Liberalism was, however, only one of several ideologies in this complex century whose political systems ranged from tsarist autocracy in Russia to republicanism, in France. Others included conservatism and nationalism, socialism and its offshoots (including communism), and feminism. The diagram on p. 730 shows their relationships.

Liberalism: Freedom and Rights

The ideas fundamental to liberalism derived from ancient, medieval, and Renaissance traditions. They were crystallized around 1690 by the English philosopher John Locke (see Chapters 15, 17), and further developed by Enlightenment thinkers. Liberalism assumes the rationality of the universe and the human capacity for rational thought. It values individual

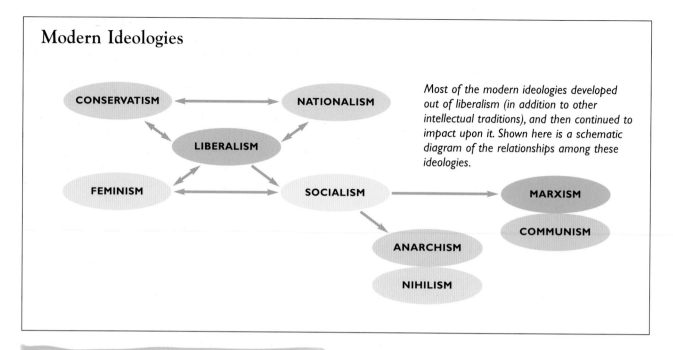

Modern Ideologies

Most of the modern ideologies developed out of liberalism (in addition to other intellectual traditions), and then continued to impact upon it. Shown here is a schematic diagram of the relationships among these ideologies.

freedom, including the possession of private property; the protection of civil rights, including the right to remove an abusive government; and government by a representative assembly with decisions made by majority vote. These principles inspired the American, French, and Latin American revolutions (see Chapter 19).

During the nineteenth century, liberalism reached its zenith. Supporters of constitutional monarchy called upon its principles, and free trade. Liberalism encouraged the toleration of minority religions—leading in Britain, for example, to the admission of Catholics, Jews, and Dissenters to political office. In multinational regions, it promoted the rights of ethnic minorities. It invited the expansion of the suffrage (the right to vote), first to male property owners, then to all male citizens, and eventually to women. Finally, liberal principles, buttressed by religious arguments, underlay abolitionist arguments for the elimination of slavery and serfdom (see Chapters 16, 19). Nineteenth-century liberalism did not, however, insist on the participation of all citizens in the political process—the fundamental principle of democracy, in which power resides in the people, who exercise it either directly or through elected representatives.

Several British thinkers developed liberal theory in the direction of social reform. The formulator of **utilitarianism**, Jeremy Bentham (1748–1832), extended liberal principles to argue that society as a whole, through government mechanisms, should work to secure "the greatest good for the greatest number." Such reasoning reduced liberalism's focus on the individual, and extended existing concepts of government's responsibility to the governed. The teaching of Bentham and his disciples led to the regulation of factory conditions, prison reform, the

installation of water supply and sewage systems, and the establishment of mass public education.

The philosopher John Stuart Mill (1806–1873), was the conscience of liberalism. While supporting the activist morality of utilitarianism, he returned to the issue of individual freedom. In his essay *On Liberty* (1859), published in the same year as Darwin's *Origin of Species* and quoted in *Witnesses* on p. 732, he elevated the liberty of the individual above communitarian needs. Free speech, for instance, must remain uninfringed, even if the speaker gives voice to ideas that are dangerous, offensive, or wrong.

Mill further advocated the rights of women, based on the same assumptions of individual freedom, in his *On the Subjection of Women* (1869). Mill's feminism had profited from a twenty-year collaboration with Harriet Taylor (1807–1858), who had previously written in favor of female suffrage, to whom he was married after her first husband's death in 1851.

Conservatism: Valuing Tradition

While liberal thinkers reaffirmed the freedom of the individual, conservatism argued reverence for traditional institutions, obedience to authority, and resistance to change. Conservatism as a theoretical position first emerged in Edmund Burke's (1729–1797) critique of the French Revolution, the *Reflections on the Revolution in France* (1790), which is quoted in *Witnesses* on p. 732. Burke argued that political institutions evolved slowly and expressed accumulated wisdom of many generations. They might be changed slowly and cautiously; but if destroyed rapidly, they would give way to new institutions that were no better than the old and perhaps far worse.

Those who gathered at the Congress of Vienna (1814–1815) to arrange the post-Napoleonic peace settlement of Europe, still shaken by the Revolution in France, were conservatives who wished to erase the effects of recent change (see Chapter 23). They were determined to restore monarchy in France, and to guarantee its supremacy elsewhere. They vowed to counter all revolutionary activity wherever it occurred—as it soon did in Latin America. They disliked constitutions, they detested the Enlightenment, and they distrusted university students with their dangerous talk of freedom and equality. They hated newspapers, many in the despised languages of ethnic minorities, that promoted disorder and disobedience.

How could traditional authority fight such enemies? Prince Clemens von Metternich (1773–1859), the key Austrian official at the Congress of Vienna (see Chapter 23), pointed the way, urging legislation that would impose censorship and halt revolutionary activity. Those aims were achieved for the German states in the Carlsbad Decrees of 1819. In Austria, Prussia, and Russia the secret police (an institution Napoleon had pioneered) hovered over revolutionaries and intellectuals.

Nationalism: A Sacred Purpose

Among those watched by the secret police were advocates of nationalism. Nationalism emerged in the 1790s from the fervor of French armies that fought to defend their new revolutionary order (see Chapter 20). More than patriotism; it was a mere passion that enthused the masses, a sense of sacred purpose and unity.

Nationalism could also be a powerful force among those who aspired to nationhood. The German peoples, conscious of a common language and a common past, had been splintered for centuries into hundreds of states, then reorganized by the Congress of Vienna into thirty-eight (see Chapter 20). Now, many of them yearned to be one. Intellectuals looked to German history for heroes and memories, in order to create a cultural unity that prefigured a hoped-for political unification. When that unification was achieved in 1871, it could draw on a sense of nationhood constructed by poets and philosophers.

Italy's aspirations for nationhood likewise emerged some time before its ultimate unification in 1870 (see Chapter 20). For centuries, the region housed a multiplicity of city-states and despotisms, some ruled by foreigners. These were eventually unified by capable political and military leaders, but also through the efforts of committed idealists and intellectuals who stirred nationalist feeling in the academies, the universities, and the daily press, while dodging the Austrian secret police.

Nationalist sentiment was especially strong among those peoples who, though possessing a cultural and historical identity, were subject to another nation. In the Americas, new nations emerged as a result of the nationalist strivings of the British, Spanish, and Portuguese colonists (see Chapter 19). Minority nationalities within the multinational empires of Europe also sought autonomy. These included the Poles within Prussia and Russia; the Belgians subject to the Netherlands (until 1830); the Norwegians subject to Sweden (until 1905); the Jews and Muslims of Central Asia within the Russian empire; the Hungarians, Croats, Serbs, Slovaks, Slovenes, and others within the Austrian Empire; and the Bulgarians, Romanians, Albanians, Serbs, and Greeks within the Ottoman Empire. National aspirations precipitated the Greek war for independence, several Balkan wars and other rebellions and terrorist episodes, including the one that precipitated World War I (see Chapter 26).

Nationalist feeling within Europe's dominant nations often coincided with theories of racial supremacy (see Chapter 24) and militarism. These were in turn both related to the imperialist ventures of the European states which reached their height in the generations before 1914. For example, English advocates of the preeminence of the "Anglo-Saxon race"—a version of nationalist thinking—often also advocated the use of military force in defending British interests. Similar statements could be heard in all the major European languages during an era when both nationalist and racial concepts peaked.

Nationalism also had a complex relationship to the kindred ideologies of conservatism and liberalism. In some settings (the Serbs under Ottoman or Austrian rule, for instance), nationalism was conservative, looking toward a lost past of cultural freedom, and finding strength in traditional religious affiliations. In others, as in Italy, nationalism was liberal, seeking to affirm human rights and throw off the yoke of abusive government. Nationalism's ability to sustain very different political agendas would also reveal itself in the twentieth century, when it was linked with Fascism (see Chapter 28), and even, as in the Nazi (National Socialist) program, with socialism.

Socialism, however, was essentially international, or transnational. It looked to a human community that preceded the state, and repudiated the system of private property that had led, according to liberal theory, to the creation of the state (see Chapter 15). For communism, which developed from socialism, national boundaries were also meaningless. The state itself would be obliterated when the workers of the world acquired the reins of power. Feminism, linked to liberalism as well as socialism, also saw the state primarily as an obstacle to the advancement of women, who even in the most advanced states had historically been denied political rights.

Socialism: Sharing the Wealth

Rooted in the French Revolution, and given urgency by industrialization, socialism flowered in the years following Napoleon's defeat. It employed liberal principles of equality and justice to critique the concentration of wealth, and envisioned society as a community of workers capable of exercising political power. It differed from liberalism in its repudiation of the principle that the ownership of private property was an essential human right, and looked to the community or state to provide for the welfare of all.

Socialist principles began to be formulated during the Revolution's second, more violent and creative phase. The notion that the state was immediately responsible to the people at large—not just those in the Convention, but those in the street—was preliminary to socialism. So were the ideas of such revolutionaries as François-Noël Babeuf (1760–1797) (who survived Robespierre to be guillotined by the Directory) who argued that the wealth of the rich should be redistributed to the poor.

A generation later, Henri de Saint-Simon (1760–1825) announced that it was a function of the state to assure a certain minimum of material welfare for its populace. So that it could do so efficiently, the state should be controlled by those endowed with the highest rational and administrative capacities—a consortium of industrialists and scientists. These views he presented in several works, beginning with the audacious *On the Reorganization of European Society* (1814). The positivist philosopher and pioneer sociologist August Comte supported Saint-Simon in this political program, until the latter developed, just prior to his death, a new mystical religion, centered on the relief of the misery of the poor. Compassion for the poor in the Saint-Simonian system linked the medieval religious and the modern socialist traditions.

Saint-Simon's compatriots and contemporaries F. M. Charles Fourier (1772–1837) and Etienne Cabet (1788–1856) further developed a visionary, or "utopian" socialism. Fourier proposed the creation of communities of workers—each group of workers a *phalange* (or phalanx, after the ancient Greek military unit), accommodated in a *phalanstère* (phalanstery)—

Idealists and Ideologues (I)

More than any previous century, the nineteenth century saw the airing of alternate and hostile views of society and politics. These passages represent three different currents: liberalism, in the words of John Stuart Mill; conservatism, in the words of Edmund Burke; and nationalism, both German and Italian, in the words of, respectively, Johann Gottlieb Fichte and Giuseppe Mazzini.

John Stuart Mill defines human liberty as limited only by the possibility of harm to others (1859): The sole end for which mankind are warranted, individually or collectively, in interfering with the liberty of action of any of their number is self protection. … The only purpose for which power can be rightfully exercised over any member of a civilized community, against his will, is to prevent harm to others. His own good, either physical or moral, is not a sufficient warrant. He cannot rightfully be compelled to do or forbear because it will be better for him to do so, because it will make him happier, because, in the opinion of others, to do so would be wise or even right. … The only part of the conduct of anyone for which he is amenable to society is that which concerns others. In the part which merely concerns himself, his independence is, of right, absolute.
(John Stuart Mill, *On Liberty*, 1859; Norton Critical Edition, 1975)

Edmund Burke warns of chaos to follow when the edifice of government is torn down (1790): The science of government … [is] a matter which requires … more experience than any person can gain in his whole life. … It is [thus] with infinite caution that any man ought to venture upon pulling down an edifice which has answered in any tolerable degree for ages the common purposes of society, or on building it up again, without having models and patterns of approved utility before his eyes. … When ancient opinions of life are taken away, the loss cannot possibly be estimated. From that moment we have no compass to govern us; nor can we know distinctly to what port we steer. …
(Edmund Burke, *Reflections on the Revolution in France*, 1790)

Two nationalists see nationhood as language, tradition, and culture: *Johann Gottlieb Fichte:* The first, original, and truly natural boundaries of states are beyond doubt their internal boundaries. Those who speak the same language are joined to each other by a multitude of invisible bonds by nature herself, long before any human art begins; they understand each other and have the power of continuing to make themselves understood more and more clearly; they belong together and are by nature one and an inseparable whole. … From this internal boundary, which is drawn by the spiritual nature of man himself, the marking of the external boundary by dwelling places results as a consequence. …
(Johann Gottlieb Fichte, "Thirteenth Address," 1806; ed. G. A. Kelly, 1968)

Giuseppe Mazzini: [The people of one nation] speak the same language, they bear about them the impress of consanguinity, they kneel beside the same tombs, they glory in the same tradition; … Nationality ought … to be … the assertion of the individuality of a human group called by its geographical position, its traditions, and its language, to fulfill a special function in the European work of civilization.
(Giuseppe Mazzini, "Europe: Its Condition and Prospects," 1852; ed. W. Clark, 1880)

who would live together, males and emancipated females, in harmony. They would engage in productive work, participate in artistic and musical projects, and enjoy fulfilling lives unfettered by conventional religious or moral restrictions.

Cabet also envisioned a harmonious workers' community. His *Voyage to Icaria* (1840) described an imaginary voyage to a workers' paradise organized by principles he called "communist" (the first use of the term). Cabet tried to put his ideas in action, setting off with hundreds of followers in 1848 to plant a communitarian settlement in Nauvoo, Illinois, on the site of one just abandoned by Mormon sectarians bound for Salt Lake City, Utah.

An opponent of the state (which he thought should be abolished) and of the capitalists who, he believed, were its principal beneficiaries, Pierre-Joseph Proudhon (1809–1865) envisioned workers' communities based on equity and justice. His 1840 book *What is Property?* posed that central question. Those who accumulate property, according to Proudhon, remove wealth from the common store and deprive the poor of basic necessities. He responded to his own question with an unequivocal reply: all property was theft. An extract from his writings on government is given in *Witnesses* on p. 734.

The attempts of Robert Owen (1771–1858) meanwhile to build real workers' communities in Britain and the United States (see Chapter 22) contributed to later socialist development. In France again, Louis Blanc (1811–1882) proposed in his 1840 book *The Organization of Work* a system of government-funded national workshops as a remedy for unemployment. These, too, were failures. At the same time, they were precedents for later workers' organizations. More, they announced the principle that government owed its citizens a right as substantial as the rights to free speech or worship: the right to work.

Marxism, Communism, Anarchism: Transfers of Power

After 1848, the utopian visions of the early socialists gave way to the pragmatic programs of workers' organizations, or trade unions, and social democratic political parties (see Chapter 22). Many of their leaders were influenced by the form of socialism that came to predominate in the latter half of the century, termed **Marxism** after its exponent Karl Marx (1818–1883).

Marxism combined economic analysis, social criticism, historical description, moral philosophy, and political theory into a weighty and complex intellectual system. It first appeared in a pamphlet written on the eve of the revolutions of 1848, the *Communist Manifesto*, on which Marx collaborated with fellow German intellectual Friedrich Engels (1820–1895). Together they had been founders of a political party that they called the "Communist League." Now,

dismissing as mere quackery the visionary socialism of Saint Simon or Owen, they outlined the fundamentals of a "scientific" socialism.

Surveying a society transformed by industrialization, they distinguished two major social groups, or classes: the bourgeoisie and the **proletariat**. For Marx and Engels, the term "**class**" denoted not merely a group of people, but a group that shared a certain relation to "the means of production," the tools for the creation of wealth. The "bourgeoisie" included those who manufactured on a vast scale in machine-powered factories, conducting business worldwide. It was the bourgeoisie who owned the "means of production"—the machines and factories of an industrial economy—and who used their financial resources (capital) in order to create even more wealth.

The workers whose labor was hired by bourgeois capitalists were themselves powerless and poor. These were the "proletariat," who participated in industrial society as mere "appendages" of the machines that made other people wealthy.

These two social classes were locked in an epochal battle; indeed it was history's final battle. All of history, Marx and Engels explained, was a history of "class struggle" (see *Witnesses*, p. 734). Earlier eras had seen the clash of landowners and slaves, of knights and serfs. In each age two primary classes emerged from the broader society to fight a duel, their struggle creating new social conditions that became the foundations of the next historical era. That process had continued to the present moment, when the class struggle was more intense than ever heretofore.

Its greater intensity derived from tangible, measurable conditions. Never before had so many people fallen into one of the two competing social classes. Never before had the wealthy been so powerful and their servants so deprived of power. History approached that moment when all but a few would be of one group—the proletariat—and only a few would oppose them—the bourgeoisie. At that moment, the many would seize power, and appropriate for themselves the means of production. Now wealth would belong to the workers, which is to say, to society as a whole. Socialism would have been achieved, and the resulting society, a workers' paradise, would be wholly classless, or communist.

Thus communism grew from socialism, systematized by Marx and Engels, who predicted as inevitable the destruction of private property and the victory of the industrial workers of the world. "Workers of the world, unite!," the *Manifesto* closes, "you have nothing to lose but your chains!"

Marx lived for thirty-five years after the publication of the *Manifesto*. During that time, he continued to write, (making regular use of the British Museum Reading Room in London, where he lived), and to organize, supported financially by Engels. Engels also contributed importantly to communist theory in his

The Conditions of the Working Class in England (1845) and *The Origin of the Family, Private Property, and the State* (1884). Marx's most important work was the three-volume *Capital*, an exhaustive analysis of the modern industrial economy. He also encouraged the formation of workers' unions and social democratic parties, and in 1864 organized the First International (the common name for the First Working Men's Association). After Marx's death in 1883, the Second International was formed in 1889.

In the late nineteenth century, Marxist theory developed most vigorously within the German workers' movement, where it branched in several directions. An "orthodox" school of thought, represented by Karl Kautsky (1854–1938) adhered to the original Marxian formulations. A "revisionist" school, represented by Eduard Bernstein (1850–1932), while respectful of the Marxist analysis, urged socialists to respond flexibly to emerging new conditions. These now offered the possibility of an evolution through a series of parliamentary reforms in the direction of communism, rather than the violent revolution that Marx prophesied. Christian Socialists—a seeming paradox, as Marx himself was militantly atheist—urged blending Christian values of compassion and mutual assistance with a Marxist analysis of society.

Socialist parties flourished according to the German pattern in Austria, Belgium, the Netherlands, and the Scandinavian countries. That pattern failed to crystallize in the United States, where Marxian socialism had little appeal in an environment of relative ease and freedom. The broad and flexible

---

Idealists and Ideologues (II)

Three further, this time "radical", outlooks on society and politics are represented here—"radical" because they challenged existing hierarchies and values. Karl Marx and Friedrich Engels define some basic principles of the communist agenda; Pierre-Joseph Proudhon, a proponent of anarchism, deplores all government control; and Emmeline Pankhurst explains why the goals of feminism may be won only with violence.

Karl Marx and Friedrich Engels define history as a series of class struggles (1848): The history of all hitherto existing society is the history of class struggles. Freeman and slave, patrician and plebeian, lord and serf, guild-master and journeyman, in a word, oppressor and oppressed, stood in constant opposition to one another, carried on an uninterrupted, now hidden, now open fight, a fight that each time ended, either in a revolutionary reconstitution of society at large, or in the common ruin of the contending classes. ... The modern bourgeois society that has sprouted from the ruins of feudal society has not done away with class antagonisms. ... Society as a whole is more and more splitting up into two great hostile camps, into two great classes directly facing each other—bourgeoisie and proletariat. ...
(Karl Marx and Friedrich Engels, *The Communist Manifesto*, 1848; ed. S. Moore, 1888)

Pierre-Joseph Proudhon—an anarchist—asks, "What is Government?" (1851): To be GOVERNED is to be kept under surveillance, inspected, spied upon, bossed, law-ridden, regulated, penned in, indoctrinated, preached at, registered, evaluated, appraised, censured, ordered about, by creatures who have neither the right, nor the knowledge, nor the virtue to do so. ... It is, under the pretense of public benefit and in the name of the general interest, to be ... extorted, squeezed, hoaxed, robbed; then at the slightest resistance, ... to be squelched, corrected, vilified, bullied, hounded, tormented, bludgeoned, disarmed, strangled, imprisoned, shot down, judged, condemned, deported, sacrificed, sold, betrayed . ... That's government, that's its justice, that's its morality! And to think that there are democrats among us who claim that there is some good in government—socialists who support this infamy in the name of Liberty, Equality, and Fraternity—proletarians who proclaim their candidacy for the Presidency of the Republic! Hypocrisy!
(From R. Hoffman ed., *Anarchism*, 1970)

Emmeline Pankhurst, the English feminist and suffragette explains why women are militant (1913): The extensions of the franchise to the men of my country [Britain] have been preceded by very great violence, by something like a revolution, by something like civil war. In 1832 ... it was after the practice of arson on so large a scale that half the city of Bristol was burned down in a single night ... that the Reform Bill of 1832 was allowed to pass into law. [This enfranchised middle-class males.] In 1867 ... rioting went on all over the country, and as the result ... the Reform Act of 1867 was put upon the statute books. [This enfranchised urban working-class males.] In 1884 ... rioting was threatened and feared, and so the agricultural laborers got the vote. Meanwhile, during the '80s, women, like men, were asking for the franchise. ... Meetings of the great corporations, great town councils, and city councils, passed resolutions asking that women should have the vote. More meetings were held, and larger, for Woman Suffrage than were held for votes for men, and yet the women did not get it. Men got the vote because they were and would be violent. The women did not get it because they were constitutional and law abiding. ...
(Emmeline Pankhurst, speech, October 21, 1913; ed. J. Marcus, 1955)

principles of the Socialist Labor Party formed by Eugene Debs (1855–1926) were more popular. In Britain, despite the presence of Marx, Marxist principles did not catch hold as on the continent. In their place, the Fabian Society (founded 1883/84) urged the gradual introduction of socialist values.

In France and Russia, socialist movements and their offshoots inclined toward violence. France's revolutionary past, and the recent bloody suppression of the Paris Commune of 1871 (see Chapter 23) led socialists in that nation to view the Fabian gradualism or Bernstein's revisionism as unimpressive. While Jean Jaurès (1859–1914), the pacifist assassinated on the eve of World War I, worked to build a vigorous socialism through parliamentary means, French **Syndicalists** (the term derived from the French word for trade union, or *syndicat*) planned instead for a violent revolution, to be engineered by workers' associations and precipitated by a general strike.

Anarchists, mostly Russian, advocated an immediate, violent assault on all government authority as the only means of acquiring social and political liberty. The theorist Mikhail Bakunin (1814–1876), having outlined the essential principles of **anarchism**, was expelled from the First International. But anarchism won followers in Spain and Italy, whose undeveloped economies provided fertile soil for extremism. **Nihilists**, specifically Russian, posited the non-meaning of everything, and promoted a violent and terroristic attack on all authority. Not surprisingly, terror ensued (see Chapter 26).

Feminism: Rights for Women

As liberals and socialists posed their different visions of the ideal life, women claimed for themselves a full role in contemporary society. Their movement, called feminism, drew on ideas developed from Renaissance humanism and the Enlightenment. Mary Wollstonecraft's *A Vindication of the Rights of Woman* (1792) had summoned women to construct lives for themselves outside of marriage and regardless of their sexual destiny. In the next century, modern ideologies introduced a new dimension to women's aspirations.

The seventeenth and eighteenth centuries had seen at least some real progress for women (see Chapters 17, 18). Elite women gained prestige from the occupation of childrearing, while many also extended their educative and nurturing activities into the wider society, engaging in philanthropic work. A few participated in intellectual circles as authors, critics, or patrons. Further down the social scale, some women found employment in theatrical and dance companies—marginal professions viewed by many as not differing much from prostitution, but offering talented women, nevertheless, greater independence and visibility.

The French Revolution saw female activism emerge in social groups outside of the elites. For such women, food crisis riots had been a characteristic form of political participation (see Chapter 20). Now they became revolutionaries: they shouted slogans, stormed prisons, cheered executions, marched on Versailles, and formed a network of revolutionary clubs. Meanwhile, revolutionary leaders passed legislation favorable to women, permitting divorce and facilitating inheritance of property by women. It appeared briefly as though substantial rights for women might be secured in the flux of revolution.

The Revolution itself, however, put an end to what it began. Never admitting women to the franchise (even as universal male suffrage was briefly instituted), in 1793 it ordered the women's political clubs closed down. In the same year, Olympe de Gouges, author of the provocative *Declaration of the Rights of Women* (1790) went to the guillotine (see Chapter 20). As the painter Elisabeth Vigée-Lebrun remarked in her memoirs, women had ruled before 1789, but "the Revolution dethroned them."

The Revolution's retreat from the matter of women's rights was seconded by the Directory and reaffirmed in Napoleon's Civil Code of 1804. The Civil Code returned women to the rule of the patriarch. Their property rights and personal freedoms were again sharply restricted, and they were restored to political nullity.

The Struggle for Women's Suffrage From that nullity, liberalism and socialism offered different possibilities of emancipation. Liberalism seemed to promise women the same freedom and rights that it promised men. In Britain and the United States, progress was made toward achieving that goal. John Stuart Mill advocated women's complete civil equality, to be marked by voting rights and the ability to hold political office. In 1867 he proposed a woman's suffrage amendment to the Reform Bill that expanded the male franchise. The amendment's failure prompted the formation the following year of the National Society for Women's Suffrage that would lead a growing movement for voting rights.

The suffrage movement came to a head with the protests of Emmeline Pankhurst (1858–1928), joined by her own daughters and other followers, whose demands for political rights turned militant in the early twentieth century. A speech of hers is quoted on p. 734. Imitating tactics employed by agitators for Irish independence, they smashed windows, cut telegraph wires, and vandalized post boxes. "The argument of the broken pane of glass," proclaimed Pankhurst, "is the most valuable argument in modern politics." Their acts of civil disobedience resulted in imprisonment and, when they protested with hunger strikes, painful and demeaning forced feeding.

Progress was also made in areas besides the franchise. By 1865, twenty-nine states of the United States granted married women the right to own and administer property. The British Parliament followed suit in 1882. Before 1900, women's colleges were established at the old English universities (Girton and Newnham at Cambridge; Somerville and Lady Margaret Hall at Oxford), and women gained admittance to the University of London, as they did to some colleges and universities in the United States. The British philanthropist Josephine Butler (1828–1906) defended women's rights by opposing the Contagious Diseases Acts (in force 1864–1886), which instituted the medical regulation of prostitutes. The *Englishwomen's Journal* and other publications kept readers informed of issues important to women.

The Struggle for Social Equality   Feminists also turned to socialism for a more radical analysis of the sources of women's social inequality. Why were women still kept subordinate to men, principally fathers and husbands? Why were their rights to own and dispose of property, especially if married, still limited? Why did their husbands, not they, have custodial rights to children? Why was divorce largely unavailable in the event of marital breakdown? Why was adultery still seen as a woman's crime? Why should women not enjoy the same sexual liberty that men had always claimed? Why were all women who lived outside the protected zone of the elite—servants and workers—considered the proper sexual prey of elite men?

Just as socialism, and especially Marxism, offered men of the laboring classes the dream of freedom from the domination by whose who monopolized the ownership of property, it offered women of all classes freedom from the domination of the very same men—as heads of propertied households, at once their employers and their male kin.

The early socialists already included the emancipation of women in their visionary plans to reform society. Though the household remained their fundamental unit, Fourier's phalansteries granted women complete economic and sexual freedom. Fourier himself saw the liberation of women as an index of human liberation, announcing that, as a general principle, "social progress and historic changes occur by virtue of the progress of women toward liberty." Saint-Simon and his followers posited women's right to inherit property and to full citizenship status. In 1832, the Saint-Simonian women's newspaper *La Tribune des Femmes* ("The Women's Tribune") argued for the combined struggle for emancipation of women and workers. After Marx's death, his benefactor and collaborator Engels delineated the historical progress of the subjugation of women in *The Origin of the Family, Private Property, and the State* (1884).

The confluence of socialism and feminism, seen especially in France, was most dramatically realized in the revolutions that periodically erupted there throughout the nineteenth century. In 1848, women's political clubs sprang up in Paris, much as they had after 1789. Their concerns were economic and political, but also addressed issues concerning the family and sexuality. In 1870, again, women's intense political activism embraced both the economic and political issues that concerned their male colleagues, and issues of particular interest for women. The suppression of the Commune marked a defeat not only for the working class, but for women as well.

Feminism drew on both liberal and socialist theory in its quest for the further liberation of human sexuality. Medieval restrictions on sexual expression were enforced by the Roman Catholic Church. Even harsher sanctions were introduced in the early modern era, which prosecuted the "crimes" of sodomy, infanticide, and witchcraft (linked to a variety of deviant sexual activities). The seventeenth and eighteenth centuries saw an upsurge of libertinism among the elites, accompanied by the circulation of pornography and obscene political art and writing. By the revolutionary era, the novels of the French nobleman, the Marquis de Sade (1740–1814), described practices, deemed deviant in the extreme, that caused pleasure through the infliction of pain.

During the nineteenth century, despite great reticence about sexual matters, evidence mounts of

---

WHO'S WHO

In Political, Philosophical, and Social Thought: the Second Generation (1789–1914)

Giuseppe Mazzini (1805–1872) Italian nationalist and founder of "Young Italy."

John Stuart Mill (1806–1873) English liberal philosopher; author of *On Liberty* (1859).

Mikhail Bakunin (1814–1876) Russian thinker and pioneer of the ideology of Anarchism.

Karl Marx (1818–1883) German philosopher; creator of Scientific Socialism and co-author (with Friedrich Engels) of the *Communist Manifesto*.

Herbert Spencer (1820–1903) English sociologist; best known for developing a theory of "Social Darwinism."

Friedrich Nietzsche (1844–1900) German anti-Christian philosopher who heralded the "Death of God."

Sigmund Freud (1856–1939) German psychologist and founder of psychoanalysis.

Emmeline Pankhurst (1858–1928) English radical feminist and suffragette; founder and leader of the Women's Social and Political Union.

the increased intensity of romantic courtship and love within marriage; so does that of resistance to restrictions on premarital and homosexual activity, and on women's sexuality within and outside of marriage. During the last decades before 1914, at least among the vanguard urban elite of western Europe, an era of greater sexual freedom began to dawn.

FIN DE SIÈCLE AND THE ADVENT OF THE MODERN

The *fin de siècle* ("end of the century") and the first years of the new century saw a riotous repudiation of traditional restraints on behavior, thought, and expression. The long weekend was cut short by the outbreak of war in 1914 (see Chapter 26). By then, Europe's cultural world had cut loose from its past; its religious and moral systems crumbled. Their place was taken by new understandings of the human mind, new models of the structure of the universe, and new ways of seeing the world, supplied by the scientists, philosophers, writers, and artists who created the Modern.

The Death of God

During the nineteenth century, the religious outlook that had hitherto characterized Western civilization came under general attack. The eighteenth century saw the growth of evangelical movements that appealed to the poor and lower middle-class—the **Methodists** in England, and the **Pietists** in the German lands, for example. Post-revolutionary conservatism and Romantic nostalgia had promoted Catholic revivals in France and England, an Anglican revival in England, and an invigorated orthodoxy among German Lutherans. But these revivals did not prevent the decline of the churches whose attendance dropped, especially among men, as Christianity, especially Roman Catholicism, became a woman's concern. Judaism, meanwhile, tended to secularization as some successful Jews assimilated with a mainstream culture. By 1914, though religion remained important for the rural poor and bourgeois homemakers, urban workers, self-confident elites, and cultivated opinionmakers had largely abandoned it.

Profound religious faith did not die out entirely among intellectuals, however. The Danish theologian and philosopher Sören Kierkegaard (1813–1855) powerfully argued for the centrality of religious experience. Tormented by the disintegration of spiritual confidence, seeing no certain or concrete demonstration of God's existence, he nevertheless advocated a radical choice for Christian theism. In England, the sermons and tracts of John Henry Newman (1801–1890) guided a revival of Anglicanism (the "Oxford Movement"). Following his conversion to Catholicism in 1845, Newman led many of his followers back to that faith.

The "death of God"—for thus the philosopher Friedrich Nietzsche (1844–1900) hailed the downfall of the religious outlook—followed from the twin onslaught of science and revolution. By its nature, the scientific outlook disputes the religious. In search of system and certainty, scientists pushed aside the mysterious nebula that necessarily enfolds religious experience. The unavoidable rivalry between science and religion began with the first phases of the Scientific Revolution (see Chapter 17), and troubled the careers of Copernicus, Galileo, and Bruno.

A new phase of that conflict began with Darwin's announcement of his theory of evolution. The theory of evolution ruled out neither the existence of God nor the human experience of worship. But it did refute the notion of a divine creation at one moment and for all time. God's creative activity, if that notion was not abandoned altogether, was confined to an earlier moment in cosmic history than the creation of the biological species. Those evolved continuously over vast reaches of time, without divine intervention, through entirely natural mechanisms. **Darwinism** outraged traditionalists all over the West, and outrages many still. It constituted a revolution in thought; as some would claim, the single most important one of the nineteenth century.

Darwin was not himself an enemy of religion; Marx was. For him, religious institutions were at best instruments of the bourgeoise in their oppression of the proletariat. At worst, they promoted obfuscations that kept the defenseless poor enthralled—religion was, as he succinctly put it, the "opiate of the masses." Aside from some mystical elements in utopian socialism, and the compassionate radicalism of the Christian socialist parties, nineteenth-century socialism and its descendants were unswervingly atheistic.

Contemporary philosophy also dispensed with God. During the Enlightenment, philosopher Immanuel Kant (1724–1804) had both elevated rational criteria of judgment, and shown their compatibility with a secular morality. During the Romantic era, Hegel marked the progress through history of supreme spiritual values. Neither Kant nor Hegel anchored their moral or spiritual views to Christianity. A generation later, Arthur Schopenhauer (1788–1860), influenced by both Romanticism and Indian mysticism, described a universe driven alternatively by "will" or "idea"—by an emotion-laden driving force or by rational thought, severing the two tendencies of Western thought that medieval philosophers had coaxed into a synthesis.

The irrational tendencies of Schopenhauer's philosophy reappeared in extreme form in Nietzsche's. With penetrating insight, Nietzsche lambasted all the shaky preconceptions and prejudices of his day—including, or so it seemed to him, the trite promises of religion. He unwrapped the hypocrisy of moralistic bourgeois shopkeepers, of self-satisfied politicians, of slogan-spouting demagogues, of silken-tongued professors, of Christianity (a "slave religion") and Judaism. Above all these ordinary folk, he elevated the "superman" (*Übermensch*)—an individual of supreme will and daring, who disdained to be bound by any strictures of morality or tradition. Modernism found its epitome in Nietzsche, whose trenchant prose disposed of dead ideals and transported Western civilization beyond the rigors of Good and Evil.

New Visions

The new worldview, termed **Modernist**, that emerges in Nietzsche's work was not merely destructive. A new world was emerging, as new visions of reality formed. Among the heralds of a dawning twentieth-century worldview, Sigmund Freud (1856–1939) and Albert Einstein (1879–1955) stand out.

Sigmund Freud A medical doctor specializing in neurology, Freud developed from his clinical work (notably with women suffering from mental illnesses that the nineteenth century diagnosed as "hysteria") the theory of the **unconscious**. This Modernist concept threw overboard the Western understanding of mind—that it was essentially rational. Instead, Freud described forces that operated below the level of consciousness—desires for pleasure, instincts of rage (the realm of the id, Latin for "it")—to modify behavior not quite successfully directed either by the rational, conscious self (the ego, or "I"), or the body of rules and conventions imprinted on the mind in early childhood (the superego, "above the ego").

From Freud's theories developed the modern fields of clinical psychology, psychiatry, and psychotherapy, with wide-ranging consequences for counseling, education, and social work. More, they yielded a more complex understanding of human personality as it functioned in life and in the arts. Modernism here gave birth to the modern human being.

Albert Einstein Einstein reshaped the Western understanding of the universe as Freud did that of the self, rupturing the Newtonian cosmos and describing one more complex, more dynamic, and more fraught with uncertainty. Two major contributions can be noted which profoundly affected general culture as well as the more specialized concerns of physicists.

The first of these is the theory of **relativity**, explained in *Witnesses* on p. 778. If the speed of light is constant, and natural laws prevail, then time and motion will be relative to the observer. For the scientist, Einstein's theory explains observed cosmic phenomena. For the lay person, what once appeared to be true had become relative, or mutable. What seems true here is not necessarily true there; what is true now is not necessarily true later; even the ideas of here, there, now, and then are fluid and undefinable.

The second contribution was the principle that the relation between mass and energy could be expressed in an equation; thus they were convertible, and one could be changed into the other. The equation is the famous $e = mc^2$, stating that a quantity of energy (e) can be obtained which is equal to the mass of a particle (m) times the square of the velocity of light (c). For scientists, this principle had many applications. For the world at large, it underlay the development of the most terrible weapon ever known, the atomic bomb, whose explosive force derives from the release of tremendous energy from a small quantity of matter. An idealist and pacifist, Einstein was horrified by the prospect of a bomb, understanding from the first the destructive potential of his equation (see Chapter 30).

Modernism and the Arts In a universe where things were relative and the human mind was not what it seemed, literature and the arts took new directions. Such writers as the Swedish dramatist August Strindberg (1849–1912), the American poet Ezra Pound (1885–1972), and the Irish novelist James Joyce (1882–1941), among others, hammered out forms of expression appropriate to a new age.

In the visual arts, Modernist tendencies appeared as early as the 1860s. From the Renaissance forward, the artist's skill was measured by his or her ability to represent clearly defined subjects—a building, a dramatic scene, or a beautiful woman (see Chapter 13). By the later nineteenth century, the primacy of the object yielded to a different imperative. The modern artist's goal became the depiction of the experience of a fleeting moment, to see with the artist's inner vision. The paraphernalia of daily life were matter to be manipulated by the artist's mind and hand.

The French Impressionists can be considered the first school of modern art, although this term is imprecise. Claude Monet (1840–1926) and Pierre Auguste Renoir (1841–1919), among others, painted domestic scenes, landscapes, and figures with a new intent. They studied the effects of light, which varies at different moments of the day, changing our perception of forms. In 1874, this group of young painters presented an exhibition of their paintings—disdaining the official annual Salon of the French Academy, which had previously refused their work. From the title of Monet's picture *Impression–Sunrise*, reproduced in *Windows On* on p. 740, they became known as Impressionists. Though attacked by art critics at first, by the 1880s the new style had triumphed; by 1886 it had been superseded.

Where the Impressionists tried to capture visual reality through the sparkling, momentary play of light, younger innovators focused on the turbulent inner world of emotions and the unconscious. The Dutch painter Vincent van Gogh (1853–1890) invested people, landscapes, and simple objects with

The *Fin de Siècle* and the Advent of the Modern

As *the nineteenth century turned and the twentieth dawned, modernism was born, as thought and art boldly cast off the bonds of traditional European culture, including both the prohibitions of Christianity and the confidence of the Enlightenment. Here, novelist Fyodor Dostoevsky defends irrationalism; philosopher Friedrich Nietzsche repudiates moralism; physician Sigmund Freud reveals the aggressive impulses driving human behavior; and poet Guillaume Apollinaire celebrates the new abandonment in the arts of the representation of nature so as to provide a higher order of truth and of pleasure.*

Fyodor Dostoevsky's "Underground Man" declares the primacy of the will, personality, and irrational urges (1864): Oh, tell me, who first declared ... that man only does nasty things because he does not know his own real interests; and that if he were enlightened, if his eyes were opened to his real normal interests, man would at once become good and noble. ... You see, gentlemen, reason, gentlemen, is an excellent thing, there is no disputing that, but reason is only reason and can only satisfy man's rational faculty, while will is a manifestation of all life, that is, of all human life including reason as well as all impulses. And although our life, in this manifestation of it, is often worthless, yet it is life nevertheless and not simply extracting square roots. ... But I repeat for the hundredth time, there is one case, one only, when man may purposely, consciously, desire what is injurious to himself, what is stupid. ... This very stupid thing ... this caprice of ours, may really be more advantageous for us, gentlemen, than anything else on earth ... because ... it preserves for us what is most precious and most important—that is, our personality, our individuality.
(Fyodor Dostoevsky, *Notes From the Underground*, 1864; ed. E. P. Dutton, 1988)

Friedrich Nietzsche repudiates morality and religion (1888):
What is good?—All that heightens the feeling of power, the will to power, power itself in man.
What is bad?—All that proceeds from weakness.
What is happiness?—The feeling that power *increases*—that a resistance is overcome.
Not contentment, but more power; *not* peace at all, but war; *not* virtue, but proficiency (virtue in the Renaissance style, *virtù*, virtue free of moralic acid).
The weak and ill-constituted shall perish: first principle of *our* philanthropy. And one shall help them to do so.
(Friedrich Nietzsche, *Twilight of the Idols/The Anti-Christ*, 1888; ed. R. J. Hollingdale, 1968)

The French poet Guillaume Apollinaire discusses the new trends in art (1913): [Modernist] painters, while they still look at nature, no longer imitate it, and carefully avoid any representation of natural scenes which they may have observed. ... Real resemblance no longer has any importance, since everything is sacrificed by the artist to truth, to the necessities of a higher nature whose existence he assumes, but does not lay bare. The subject has little importance any more. Generally speaking, modern art repudiates most of the techniques of pleasing devised by the great artists of the past. While the goal of painting is today, as always, the pleasure of the eye, the art-lover is henceforth asked to expect delights other than those which looking at natural objects can easily provide.
(Guillaume Apollinaire, *The Cubist Painters: Aesthetic Meditations*, 1913; ed. L. Abel, 1962)

the intensity of his personal world. His *Potato Eaters* (1885), portraying a family of miners, shows the impoverishment of the human spirit. His depictions of ordinary objects describe in worn leather and bent wood his own passionate and suffering nature. His *Starry Night* (1889), illustrated in *Windows On* on p. 740, portrays the modern cosmos, the explosive sky overwhelming the natural landscape, in which human beings must dwell.

In the twentieth century, artists turned from representationalism to paint **abstract** forms. The Russian Vasily Kandinsky (1866–1944) sought to express ideas and evoke emotions by the sheer power of line and color (see *Witnesses*, p. 778, and *Windows On*, p. 740). The Spanish master Pablo Picasso (1881–1973), who explored many stylistic approaches in the course of his long career, was a pioneer of

Cubism around 1907. This style fragmented forms into multiple facets, just as the eye in reality takes in objects from several angles. Like Kandinsky, he was painting a reality that dwelled in his mind alone—not what seemed, but what he knew to exist.

In music, also, where representation had never been a possibility, traditional norms fractured in the later nineteenth century. The operas of Richard Wagner (1818–1883) pushed to an extreme the Romantic understanding of music—that it was to express, and arouse, intense emotion. His overpowering musical compositions accompanied a vision of German history, the German soul, and German destiny informed by both Romanticism and nationalism. In this regard, Wagner is often seen as a forerunner of Nazism (see Chapter 28)—a possibility supported by his well-documented anti-Semitism.

Claude Monet, Impression–Sunrise, 1872

Fin de Siècle and the Advent of the Modern

Modernism arose as nineteenth-century notions of God, progress, order, and purpose collapsed before the twin onslaught of science (especially Darwinism) and Revolution. While Friedrich Nietzsche and Sigmund Freud helped dismantle the presuppositions of Western society—especially Christianity, traditional morality, and the presumption of human rationality—Impressionist, Post-Impressionist, Expressionist, and abstract styles inaugurated Modernism in the visual arts.

Impressionists such as Claude Monet—here represented by his Impression–Sunrise (top)—strove to describe their inner worlds rather than recreate the outer world represented by Western artists since the Renaissance. The Impressionists were soon overtaken by other artists and styles, each increasingly non-representational. In the Post-Impressionist Starry Night by Vincent Van Gogh (center), the heavens throb and pulse with light and energy, totally overwhelming the frail mortal realm that lies beneath.

During the twentieth century, artists including the Russian Vasily Kandinsky abandoned representation altogether in favor of purely abstract images (bottom).

(top: Musée Marmottan, Paris; center: Museum of Modern Art, New York; bottom: Städtische Galerie im Lenbachhaus, Munich)

Vincent van Gogh, Starry Night, 1889

Vasily Kandinsky, Study for Composition VII, 1913

 To continue your investigation of this topic, please go to www.prenhall.com/king for the related **WINDOWS** on the **WEB** activity

In the early twentieth century, Igor Stravinsky (1882–1971) and Arnold Schoenberg (1874–1951) took up a Modernist attack on traditional musical form that paralleled the rejection of representationalism in the visual arts. Stravinsky's ballet *The Rite of Spring*, performed in Paris in 1913, provoked the audience to outrage with its rhythmic and tonal violations of prevailing standards of composition, as well as its celebration of primal emotions and a pagan worldview. Audience members were horrified as dancers clad in bizarre costumes writhed obscenely, accompanied by music that to them was raucous and chaotic. It was the clarion call of the twentieth century.

Schoenberg's **atonal** music, the first examples of which were performed in 1909, aroused not so much horror as confusion. Listeners did not understand the composer's disavowal of the tonal structures that defied all previous Western music. The new, abstract structures of Schoenberg's compositions not only did not sound tuneful, but they did not seem to communicate any comprehensible human emotion or idea.

This creative ferment among artists and intellectuals scarcely affected the ordinary worker, or merchant, or leisured aristocrat—even as it transformed the mental universe their descendants would inhabit. To the extent that they could, they spent the last decades before World War I amusing themselves. The music halls and cabarets, theaters and beer halls provided light-hearted song and dance—heavily laden, nevertheless, with messages that overturned the moral values of an earlier era. Outside, and in the daylight, an equivalent disruption of norms was accomplished by the new world of speed. In automobiles and balloons, on motorcycles and bicycles, and especially in airplanes, people of all social classes and both genders soared beyond the confined worldview of their ancestors, who had been limited by the compass of nature to the speed of mammalian limbs.

In 1896, the Olympic Games were held again, for the first time since antiquity (see Chapter 4). But these were Modernist games. The ancient Greeks had

competed to win glory and to worship their gods. The races run by modern Europeans were complicated by nationalist resentments and by the convulsive efforts by competitors to go faster and get further. Such were the ingredients, too, of the cataclysm that put a stop to the joyous rebellion of the *fin de siècle* and the experiments of Modernism: the first war to engulf the whole of the globe.

WHO'S WHO

In the Arts: the Second Generation (1789–1914)

Frédéric Chopin (1810–1849) Polish-born French Romantic pianist and composer.

George Eliot (1819–1880) Pseudonym of Mary Ann Evans; English Realist novelist who developed techniques of psychological analysis used widely in subsequent literature.

Claude Monet (1840–1926) French painter; pioneer and advocate of Impressionism.

Emile Zola (1840–1902) French Realist novelist; his Rougon-Macquart series of twenty "naturalist" novels were presented as "social history."

James Joyce (1882–1941) Irish Modernist novelist; his major works, including *Ulysses* (1922) and *Finnegan's Wake* (1934), are bold experiments in language and method.

Pablo Picasso (1881–1973) Spanish Modernist painter; best known for his development of Cubism in the early twentieth century.

Igor Stravinsky (1882–1971) Russian Modernist composer; his "The Rites of Spring"—which violated accepted standards of tone and rhythm—outraged its audience when first performed in Paris in 1913.

Conclusion
THE ADVENT OF THE MODERN AND THE MEANING OF THE WEST

A giant creativity marks the era of Western culture bounded by the French Revolution and the outbreak of World War I. Artists, and intellectuals leapt from Classical, to Romantic, to realist, to abstract styles, and from the mission of depicting a reality that existed in fact to one that existed in the mind of the subject. Scientists discovered radiation and the cell, and introduced the theories of evolution, genetic inheritance, and relativity. Biology, chemistry, and physics, along with history, psychology, sociology, and economics, became academic disciplines housed in university departments. The children of peasants and workers went to school in their millions, as they would soon go to war. Liberals, conservatives, nationalists, socialists, communists, anarchists, and feminists devised their competing ideologies and contended for followers and for power. By 1914, Western culture was Modern and modern people cast aside the traditions that had both guided and constrained them. In 1914, as the following chapter relates, the elders whose values they rejected led the children of the Western world into the cataclysm of world war.

REVIEW QUESTIONS

1. Why did faith in reason decline after the French Revolution? How did Romanticism differ from Classicism in art, music, and literature? How did Romanticism promote the participation of women in cultural life?

2. Why was photography the perfect Realist medium? What was the goal of Realist novelists and historians? Why did historians try to emulate the practices of scientists?

3. What were the major advances in biology and the physical sciences in the nineteenth century? What challenges did Darwinist theory pose to religion and liberalism? How did the fields of economics and sociology develop in the nineteenth century?

4. How did public elementary education affect European society? Why did nineteenth-century liberalism lead to public reform?

5. Why was nationalism opposed to socialism and communism? What was the theory of Marxist socialism? What were the goals of parliamentary socialism before World War I?

6. What was the connection between feminism and socialism? How did scientists, artists, and intellectuals create the modern? Why were Freud and Einstein the "heralds" of the twentieth century?

SUGGESTED RESOURCES

The Cycle of Styles: Classicism, Romanticism, Realism

Honour, Hugh, *Romanticism* (New York: Harper & Row, 1979). Classic account of the historical, intellectual, and political background of European Romanticism.

Johnson, James H., *Listening in Paris: A Cultural History* (Berkeley: University of California Press, 1994). How and why people thronged to the concert hall in Paris during the years when Romanticism emerged, and how what they heard transformed contemporary culture.

Romantic Chronology, timeline of major works and styles interspersed with events, late-18th century to 1851: http://ucsb.edu.591/rchrono

The Sciences and the Schools

Bynum, W. F., *Science and the Practice of Modern Medicine in the Nineteenth Century* (Cambridge: Cambridge University Press, 1994). Examines the interaction of scientific theory and medical practice.

Desmond, Adrian J. and James Moore, *Darwin* (New York: Viking Penguin, 1991). Perhaps the best biography of this important figure.

Geison, Gerald L., *The Private Science of Louis Pasteur* (Princeton: Princeton University Press, 1995). Examines Pasteur's personal laboratory notebooks to reconstruct the scientist's motives and intentions in the world of powerful and learned men he inhabited.

Quinn, Susan, *Marie Curie: A Life* (New York: Simon & Schuster, 1995). Comprehensive account of this major scientist, placing her firmly in the context of women's history.

Vitezslav, Orel, *Gregor Mendel: The First Geneticist* (Oxford: Oxford University Press, 1996). Excellent biography, covering most aspects of Mendel's life and work.

Albert Einstein, Image and Impact (American Institute of Physics)—resources and links: http://www.aip.org/history/einstein

Ideals and Ideologies

Donner, Wendy, *The Liberal Self: John Stuart Mill's Moral and Political Philosophy* (Ithaca–London: Cornell University Press, 1991). Updated study of the philosopher's contributions to 19th-century liberalism.

Himmelfarb, Gertrude, *The De-Moralization of Society: From Victorian Virtues to Modern Values* (New York: Alfred A. Knopf, 1995). Stimulating comparison of Victorian and modern values.

Offen, Karen, *European Feminisms, 1700–1950: A Political History* (Stanford: Stanford University Press, 1998). A comparative account of the development of feminism in the West.

Stites, Richard, *The Women's Liberation Movement in Russia: Feminism, Nihilism and Bolshevism, 1860–1930* (Princeton, NJ: Princeton University Press, 1978). Traces the emergence in Russia of a feminism intimately tied from the first to radical political movements.

Wheen, Francis, *Karl Marx: A Life* (New York: W. W. Norton, 2000). The first major biography of Marx since the Cold War depicts him as a humane man whose aspirations summed up the issues of the century.

Guide to resources on Karl Marx, including electronic books (epistemelinks): http://www.epistemelinks.com/Main/Philosophers.asp?PhilCode=Marx

And from Bjorn's guide to philosophy: http://www.knuten.liu.se/~bjoch509/philosophers/mar.html

Fin de Siècle and the Advent of the Modern

Butler, Christopher, *Early Modernism: Literature, Music and Painting in Europe, 1900–1916* (Oxford: Oxford University Press, 1994). Synthetic examination of early modernism in painting, literature, and music.

Fritzsche, Peter, *Reading Berlin 1900* (Cambridge: Harvard University Press, 1996). Examines daily newspapers in the first years of the 20th century to understand the exciting urbanism of Berlin, a magnet for artists and writers, in an age of modernism.

Gilman, Sander L., *Freud, Race and Gender* (Princeton, NJ: Princeton University Press, 1993). Contends that *fin de siècle* medical science, and Freud's work, was permeated by notions of a racialized Jewish identity.

Mainardi, Patricia, *The End of the Salon: Art and the State in the Early Third Republic* (Cambridge: Cambridge University Press, 1993). Focusing on the institutions controlling the exhibition of new art, explains how modern style came to the fore in late 19th-century Paris.

Schorske, Carl E., *Fin de Siècle Vienna: Politics and Culture* (New York: Vintage, 1981; orig. Alfred A. Knopf, 1979). Classic collection of essays on the culture-transforming influence of the Viennese middle class, covering among others Freud, Klimt, and Herzl.

Wohl, Robert, *A Passion for Wings: Aviation and the Western Imagination, 1908–1918* (New Haven: Yale University Press, 1994). How flight captured the imagination of the adventurous minds of artists, intellectuals, and the leisured rich during one decade of the 20th century.

PART SEVEN
TOWARD A NEW WEST

Post-War, Post-Modern, Post-Industrial (1914–2000)

Three enormous conflicts overshadow the twentieth century and put the whole project of Western civilization in jeopardy: World War I, World War II, and the Cold War. World War I marked the point at which the West was no longer in the ascendant over the other regions of the world. A wounded civilization limped on to confront the various crises of economic collapse, social upheavals, and the advance of totalitarian states.

World War II purchased the defeat of fascism, which had threatened to reverse the Western tradition, at the cost of more than 40 million lives. The victory over fascism, won by an alliance of the democratic United States and Britain and the Communist Soviet Union, was a vindication of the civilization of the West.

The Cold War pitched two of the victors of the prior conflict against each other in an epochal duel between communism and capitalism. The two Superpowers faced each other in a bi-polar system that split the world, armed with weapons that could not be used—for they threatened the annihilation of human life itself. The face-off continued until, in 1989, communism began to self-destruct in Europe and the Soviet Union. Meanwhile, the regions of the earth that, in 1900, had been dominated by Europeans had won their autonomy, and claimed their stake in the world of nations. The transmission of knowledge edged out industrial manufacture in the world economy, as systems of communication and transportation came to unite the most remote regions of the earth.

In 1900, the West was secure in its political, military, and cultural superiority. In 2000, after the shock of three massive conflicts, the West inhabits a global world. It is a post-war, post-modern, and post-industrial West that enters the new millennium. Whether it maintains its identity and rediscovers its mission through a reflection on its traditions and achievements is in the hands of the present generation.

26 The Mighty are Fallen
The Trauma of World War I, 1914–1920

27 The Triumph of Uncertainty
Cultural Innovation, Social Disruption, and Economic Collapse, 1915–1945

28 States in Conflict
Communism, Fascism, Democracy, and the Crisis of World War II, 1917–1945

29 The End of Imperialism
Decolonization and Statebuilding around the Globe, 1914–1990s

30 Back From Armageddon
From the Bomb to the Internet, 1945–1990

THE MIGHTY ARE FALLEN

	1900	1905	1910	1915	1920

Politics and War

- Britain and Japan ally, 1902
- Lenin's What is To Be Done?, 1902
- Britain and France form Entente Cordiale, 1904
- Russo-Japanese War, 1904–1905
- Germany challenges France in Morocco,1905, 1911
- Revolution on Russia, 1905
- Britain launches first Dreadnought battleship, 1906
- Austria-Hungary annexes Bosnia Herzegovina, 1908
- Japan annexes Korea, 1910
- Balkan Wars, 1912–1913
- Archduke Franz Ferdinand of Austria-Hungary assassinated, June 1914
- Germany invades Belgium, Aug 1914
- Britain declares war on Germany; Battle of Tannenberg, Aug 1914
- Battles of the Marne and Masurian Lakes, Sept 1914
- Battle of Gallipoli, Apr 1915
- Germans sink Lusitania, May 1915
- Execution of nurse Cavell, Oct 1915
- Battle of Verdun, Feb 1916
- February Revolution in Russia, March 1917
- Lenin's "April Theses," Apr 1917
- Russian general Kornilov fails to overturn Provisional Government, Sept 1917
- October (Bolshevik) Revolution, Nov 1917
- Woodrow Wilson's "Fourteen Points," Jan 1918
- Treaty of Brest-Litovsk, March 1918
- Second Battle of the Marne, July 1918
- Armistice signed ending war, Nov 1918
- Treaty of Versailles, 1919

Society and Ideas

- 400 Jews killed in pogrom in Odessa, 1905
- St. Petersburg has 900 factories, 2 million population, 1914

Beyond the West

- Qing Dynasty, China, 1644–1912
- South African War, 1899–1902
- Boxer Rebellion in China, 1900
- Panama Canal opens, 1904
- Japan wins Russo-Japanese War, 1905
- "Young Turks" topple Ottoman sultan, 1908
- Republic declared in China, 1911–12

THE MIGHTY ARE FALLEN

The Trauma of World War I

1914–1920

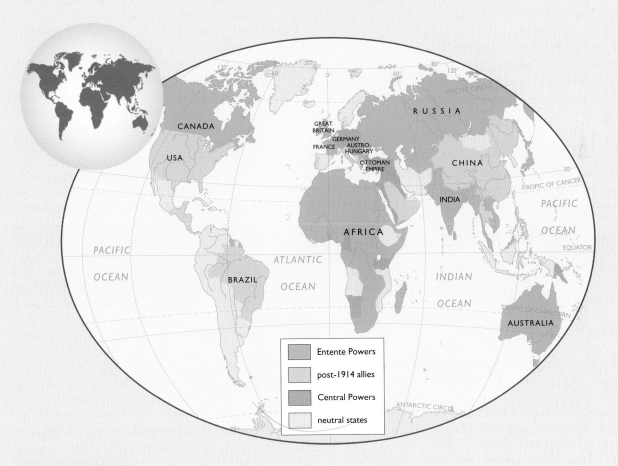

Entente Powers

post-1914 allies

Central Powers

neutral states

KEY TOPICS

◆ **Pathways to War:** The states of Europe avoid major conflicts between 1815 and 1914, until an assassin's bullet on the continent's southeastern rim sends a generation of young men off to war.

◆ **In the Midst of Battle:** On the western front, stalemate and carnage; on the eastern, slaughter; at sea, the stealthy assault of submarines; at home, factories, shops, and services manned by women; in Russia, revolution; repercussions around the world.

◆ **In Search of Peace:** Like the revolutionary Lenin, the visionary Wilson yearns for peace; but ironically his peace plans become the blueprint for more war to come.

The Generation of 1914 *In August 1914, European leaders sent a generation to war. In companies, brigades, and regiments, young men marched off to the cheers of parents, teachers, and kings, their minds set on honor and glory. Instead, they found slaughter, filth, vermin, starvation, and disease. More than 65 million fought. More than 21 million were wounded by bullets, bombs, and poison gas, or mentally ravaged by the horrors concocted by the most advanced civilization on the globe. More than 8 million died— "the unreturning army that was youth," wrote the English poet Siegfried Sassoon (1886–1967), one of the startling poets this war called forth. And, snarled the American poet Ezra Pound (1885–1972), for what purpose?*

> *For an old bitch gone in the teeth,*
> *For a botched civilization.*

When the smoke finally cleared, the mighty too had fallen—emperors, politicians, and generals were dead, and with them the complacency of an age irretrievably gone. The remnant of the generation of 1914 stumbled on into the rest of the twentieth century without a guide and stalked by despair.

This chapter traces the origins, course, and settlement of the war that tragically brought down the generation of 1914, and its elders, and radically altered the history of the West.

PATHWAYS TO WAR

Many paths led to global conflagration, the first major European conflict since the Napoleonic wars. During the "long century" between the post-Napoleonic settlement at Vienna in 1815 and the first hostilities of 1914, diplomats secured the cooperation of contending nations and resolved potential conflicts. Their efforts were largely successful; except for colonial ventures and brief outbreaks of limited war, Europe was at peace (see Chapters 24, 25). Even so, as the old century turned, threats to peace, at home and in faraway continents, asserted themselves. The furious signing of treaties of alliance, accelerating as the new century turned, testified to mounting political tensions. These radiated from several troublespots. All would figure in the conflict of world war, as Map 26.2 on p. 757 shows.

Hot Spots

In the decades before the outbreak of World War I, the map of the globe was dotted with "hot spots," or danger zones where long resentment and counterposed interests provided fertile ground for conflict.

French and German interests collided in the area west of the Rhine. French leaders and patriots saw the German seizure of the provinces of Alsace and Lorraine following the Franco–Prussian War as a tragic and unforgivable provocation.

Germany also faced a rival to the east. Here Russia, long dependent on western European technology and experts, was beginning to modernize and industrialize. A formidable military power, it had lost face, nevertheless, by its defeats in the Crimea and by the Japanese, and was troubled by revolution in 1905. Russia still looked strong, however, and with its Polish and Ukrainian territories loomed dangerously close to Germany's eastern border.

Russia also posed a threat to Austria-Hungary (a "dual monarchy" after 1867; see Chapter 20) and to the whole of Europe as a result of its policies in the Balkans. As Ottoman power in the region waned after 1699 (see Chapters 15, 20), the peoples of the Balkans sought to gain national autonomy, while Austria-Hungary sought to extend its sphere of influence southward into the peninsula. After the Berlin Congress of 1878, Austria-Hungary effectively ruled Herzegovina and Bosnia, which they annexed in 1908. Finding that their Ottoman masters had been replaced by Austrian ones, Serb nationalists vowed resistance.

The Slavic-speaking Balkan peoples who lived under Austro-Hungarian rule were ethnically related but culturally diverse. They included Roman Catholic Croats and Slovenes with allegiances to Rome and western Europe; Muslims converted under Ottoman rule; and Eastern Orthodox Serbs who had resisted Ottoman overlordship and had paid heavily for that resistance. The different interests of these diverse groups made for tension and instability.

Outside of the Austro-Hungarian zone, Orthodox Serbs, Bulgars, and Romanians (the latter speaking a Romance language), had won freedom from Ottoman overlordship and formed autonomous states in 1878. As a result of the two short Balkan Wars of 1912–1913, the Turks lost control of the region, except for a belt around Constantinople (modern Istanbul). In addition, the boundaries of the Balkan nations were redefined to the disadvantage of Bulgaria and the advantage of Serbia, while Albania and Montenegro gained national autonomy. Thereafter Serbia supported Slav resistance to Austrian rule in Bosnia and Herzegovina. So did that other, much larger Orthodox and Slavic nation—the Russian Empire, protector of Pan-Slavic nationalist aspirations. In the Balkans, nationalism was a disruptive force that drove the world to war.

As Russia supported Pan-Slav objectives in the Balkans, it sought to wrest from the decaying Ottoman sultans their strategic post at Constantinople. Constantinople was one of the world's major ports, strategically positioned at the entrance to the Black Sea from the Mediterranean. It had particular interest

The Onset of War

As war loomed, observers responded variously depending on their nationality, their beliefs, and their occupations. In these three examples, a German theorist welcomes war as ennobling; the British Foreign Secretary outlines apprehensively the risks that lay ahead; and the British philosopher Bertrand Russell, a pacifist, is horror struck by how much ordinary people actually welcomed the excitement and violence of war.

On the eve of war, nationalist and militarist sentiments abounded, as expressed in these words of the German theorist Heinrich von Treitschke (1915): When the State exclaims: My very existence is at stake! Then social self-seeking must disappear and all party hatred be silent. The individual must forget his own ego and feel himself a member of the whole, he must recognize how negligible is his life compared with the good of the whole. Therein lies the greatness of war that the little man completely vanishes before the great thought of the State.
(Heinrich von Treitschke, *Die Politik*, 1915; eds. M. Perry et al, 1995)

On the eve of Britain's declaration of war British Foreign Secretary Sir Edward Grey explains to the House of Commons why war must be fought and what war might bring (August 4, 1914): We have great and vital interests in the independence ... of Belgium. If Belgium is compelled to submit to allow her neutrality to be violated, of course the situation is clear. ... [I]f her [Belgium's] independence goes, the independence of Holland will follow. I ask the House from the point of view of British interests, to consider what may be at stake. If France is beaten ... [and] becomes subordinate to the will and power of one greater than herself ... and if Belgium fell under the same dominating influence, and then Holland, and then Denmark. ... We are going to suffer, I am afraid, terribly in this war whether we are in it or whether we stand aside. ...
(*Hansard's Parliamentary Debates*, 5th Series, vol. 65, 1809–1827)

In London as war is declared, Bertrand Russell, British philosopher and mathematician, is troubled by the bloodthirstiness of the populace (August 15, 1914): Although I did not foresee anything like the full disaster of the war, I foresaw a great deal more than most people did. The prospect filled me with horror, but what filled me with even more horror was the fact that the anticipation of carnage was delightful to something like ninety per cent of the population. ... I had supposed that most people liked money better than almost anything else, but I discovered that they like destruction even better.
(Bertrand Russell, Letter to London's *Nation*, August 15, 1914; eds. M. Perry et al, 1995)

for Russia, whose only warm-water ports lay in the Black Sea, and whose free access through the Dardanelles strait commanded by Constantinople's fortresses was essential for international trade. While Russia had designs on Constantinople, the other European powers, propping up the empty Ottoman suit, worked industriously to keep the city Turkish.

Weakening Ottoman influence prompted European maneuvers at the extremities of the Ottoman Empire as in southeast Europe. In North Africa, European nations now sought to acquire footholds through military or economic means (see Chapter 23). To the west, Spain and France held protectorates in Morocco. In 1905 and 1911, Germany challenged French authority in Morocco with shows of support for Moroccan autonomy. These moves precipitated two crises and drove France and Britain into alliance. In 1911, the Italians invaded Libya in the center of the north African littoral, while Egypt, where British and French financial interests had long competed, was occupied by British troops from 1882, becoming a protectorate in 1914. In the Middle East, Britain and Russia competed for influence in Persia, Iraq, and Afghanistan.

Far to the east, Japan had acquired the Chinese island of Formosa (Taiwan) in the Sino-Japanese war of 1894–1895. Ten years later, in the Russo-Japanese war, it obtained footholds on the Asian continent, in South Manchuria and Kwantung, as well as the southern half of the island of Sakhalin (Karafuto). In 1910, Japan annexed Korea; in 1914, declaring support for the Entente powers when war broke out in Europe, she swiftly seized German protectorates in China: Manchuria, Shandong, and Fujian, as well as several Pacific islands. The Chinese simply acquiesced to the territorial claims Japan announced in the Twenty-One Demands, lands Japan was allowed to retain by the 1919 treaties of Paris (see below). Chinese popular outrage at these losses triggered the student-led May Fourth Movement, a focal point in the later revolutionary politics of that nation (see Chapter 29).

In Europe, meanwhile, political tensions would soon erupt into war. On June 26, 1914, in the Bosnian capital of Sarajevo, a nineteen-year-old terrorist of the secret "Black Hand" society shot the Archduke Franz Ferdinand (1863–1914), fifty-year-old sportsman and heir to the Austrian and Hungarian thrones, and his wife. The assassination gave Austrian diplomats an opportunity to put pressure on Serbia. Encouraged by Germany, Austria issued an ultimatum; Serbia prevaricated, and Austria declared war, provoking Russian mobilization. These rapid exchanges in late July triggered the activation in early

August of the European system of alliances for mutual defense. The Serbian assassination and the Austrian ultimatum together cut the cord. For the next four years, the nations of Europe were at war.

Men and Boys at War

With the onset of war, old and young prepared to fight. The different points of view expressed are examined in *Witnesses* on p. 747. Elderly diplomats and generals, their experience shaped by memories of such conflicts as the Crimean War and colonial campaigns where Europeans easily outgunned native forces, planned to mobilize a generation of young men.

Even the battle plans of the generals were, on the whole, old. Although Europe's military elite had fought few battles during the nineteenth century, they had constructed many battle plans. German planning was especially intense, both because of the traditional militarism of the old Prussian **Junker** generals, and because of Germany's understandable fear of encirclement. Planted in Europe's center, with neither mountains nor seas as buffers, Germans knew that in any war they might have to face an enemy on two fronts, both west and east.

Addressing this difficulty, Alfred von Schlieffen (1833–1913), veteran of the Franco-Prussian war and former chief of the German General Staff, devised by 1905 the most important of Europe's battle plans. Upon his death, in 1913, never having had the opportunity to use it, he bestowed the "Schlieffen plan" upon Field Marshal Helmuth von Moltke (1848–1916), himself a man of advanced age. Von Moltke understood it to be his duty to follow the Schlieffen plan faithfully. The grand design that would determine the destinies of Europe's youth was a decade old.

Other nations had their battle plans, too. The French Plan XVII urged an offensive posture—"always the offensive!" French generals bellowed—by striking into Alsace and Lorraine and then, from that vantagepoint west of the Rhine, boldly on to Berlin. The British trusted in their new Dreadnought battleships—so named after the first hefty Dreadnought launched in 1906, imposingly armed with heavy-caliber guns—and their traditional naval strength. To support their ally, they would dispatch a small expeditionary force to France. The Austrians had plans, too, but deferred to leadership from Berlin. The Russian army had plans to modernize its weaponry and its communications, goals not yet achieved when war erupted. Its generals sent millions of young peasants off to the front, desperately undersupplied.

In another, subtler way, old men held the fortunes of young men on the eve of world war. In schools and homes, the old taught the young the unhealthy message that their duty to their nation surpassed all other duties, that honor surpassed all other values, and that greatness displayed itself above all on the battlefield.

The pseudo-scientific theories that circulated among late nineteenth-century intellectuals (see Chapters 24, 25) taught that some "races" were superior to others, and that the conflicts of nations, were part of an epochal natural struggle in which the "fittest" would survive. Cultural habits reinforced these beliefs and encouraged an escalating militarism. In the time-honored tradition, boys from elite families played sports as a preparation for war. As though the violent defeat of an adversary could be an elegant game, they strove to fence, hunt, and shoot as gentlemen should, impeccably dressed and in fashion.

When orders for mobilization went up on walls and were broadcast in the newspapers, a generation of young men lined up for battle, democrats, socialists, and former pacifists together. In Britain, they volunteered. Elsewhere, they were drafted. They went in high spirits, cheered on by their mothers, unaware of the horrors they were to face. The war would be over "before the leaves fall," said the pundits in August; before Christmas, at the very latest. The young men left home trusting the words of their elders, and the war plans that lay ready in the desk drawers of graying generals born in an older Europe. Wrote Rudyard Kipling (1865–1936):

> *If any question why we died,*
> *Tell them, because our fathers lied.*

The generation of 1914 marched as children to the front. Only half returned whole. When they did return, they too were old, grayed by the memory of slaughter.

IN THE MIDST OF BATTLE

Map 26.1 on p. 749 shows the fronts and major battles of the war. Fronts formed immediately where invaders met defenders, but both sides held their ground. Germany faced France and Britain at the western front, parallel lines of fortified trenches stretching from Switzerland to the English Channel. Germany faced Russia on the eastern front, among ravaged villages, swamps, and forests. On the seas, around the world, merchant ships laden with military hardware and foodstuffs bound for Allied ports ran a gauntlet of German **U-boats** (*Unterseeboote*, or submarines), while British battleships choked off the flow of such goods to German ports. At home, women were employed in munitions factories, making the numberless bullets and bombs needed at the fronts, and hoarded food to feed their children. In Russia, soldiers without food to eat or bullets to defend themselves left the military front for the one back home—the struggle for peace, bread, and land.

Stalemate in the West

The Schlieffen plan called for a rapid, disabling blow at France, making possible the concentration of forces

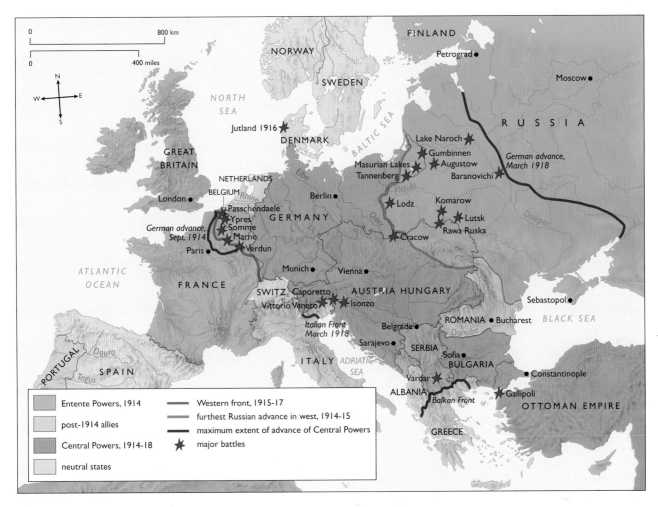

Map 26.1 Europe—A Two-Front War: *After the German army smashed through Belgium and pushed toward the French capital of Paris, war on the western front settled into a stalemate and was fought largely from trenches. Despite staggering loss of life on both sides, little movement was made in either direction. The eastern front was a different matter. While also a very deadly affair, war was fought here on the move, with trenches the exception rather than the rule. The Italians, however, were locked in futile combat with the Austrians during 1915 to 1917, fighting eleven battles at the river Isonzo with negligible result.*

on the east to deal with Russia, regarded as the major threat. Although France could be reached from Germany by crossing the Rhine and pounding through Alsace and Lorraine, that was not the route Schlieffen prescribed. Instead, he had proposed a giant encirclement of Paris from the north. German forces would cut through Belgium, violating that nation's neutrality, in a vast arc around Paris, edging so close to the coast that, as Schlieffen envisioned it, a soldier on the powerful right flank might "brush the Channel with his sleeve." Having taken Paris, they would swoop eastward to pounce on the French forces who, as it was rightly predicted, would have foolishly charged to Alsace-Lorraine, leaving the heart of their homeland undefended.

It was only a minor obstacle for the German general staff that Belgium was a neutral nation. When Belgium was constituted as a state in 1830, the combined nations of Europe had pledged themselves to protect its neutrality. As they grew aware of German designs, Belgian leaders attempted to convince their

incredulous allies of the impending crisis. By this time, the Germans were already on the move.

The First Moves The great fortifications at Liège, guarding the road to Brussels, were considered the best in Europe. The city was ringed by ramparts, and defended by a garrison; a circle of satellite fortresses surrounded it. It seemed, and should have been, impregnable. But the Belgian army had not yet moved up to defend it. And the Germans came with new long-range guns of an unprecedented destructive capacity. On August 16, 1914, the city surrendered, barely two weeks after the war began. The German invasion thrust on past the Belgian town of Namur, across the river Meuse and into the Ardennes forest.

The German advance through Belgium seemed to display a unique and novel brutality. The resisters who harassed the German advance provoked furious reprisals: the execution of hostages, including women and children, the burning of homes, the slaughter of livestock. At the university town of Louvain, angered

Execution of British nurse Edith Cavell: This French poster calls upon that nation's citizens to remember the martyrdom of British nurse Edith Cavell, executed in Brussels on October 12, 1915—"an abominable crime." Note the German officer holding a pistol over the dead woman's body—a scene that aroused horror in an era when women were held properly to be exempt from the first-hand sufferings of war.

by snipers, the German command ordered the citizens to be massacred and the city burned. The library was destroyed, a library that had guarded for centuries one of the finest collections in Europe.

The horrors of the German assault on Belgium were exaggerated further in the propaganda reports that circulated in Britain and France and beyond. Press reports, cartoons, and posters told of brutalized infants, and raped and murdered women, including the British nurse Edith Cavell (1865–1915), portrayed above, who was charged with assisting prisoners and refugees and executed in 1915. Propaganda aroused war fever among the allied nations of western Europe.

For by now, they had formally become military allies. For years, the French pressed the British to agree to a defensive treaty; for years, Britain evaded making that commitment. At last, the British recognized the threat to France, and thus to the Channel, and to themselves. How many men must they send the French as a sign of their support? Just one, responded the French, and we shall be sure that he gets killed—for one British soldier dead by a German bayonet would seal the alliance in the popular mind.

In the end, the British sent an expeditionary force across the Channel, while the French sent troops toward Alsace and Lorraine. The French did not yet comprehend the nature of the war they must fight. Their troops were brightly uniformed, with perky red hats; the Germans marched in a battlefront gray suited to modern warfare. The plan was to attack— "the offensive! Always the offensive!" shouted the French generals, who trusted in the *élan* (a quality of dash or verve) that they believed all Frenchmen to possess. In fact, by taking Alsace and Lorraine, they had diverted their main strength from the spot where the real enemy vanguard struck—in the Ardennes, where outnumbered French defenders fought German invaders blindly in the forest, with a disheartening number of casualties.

Meanwhile, the British were slow to arrive, slow to fight, and slower still than the French to understand the strength and determination of their opponents. At last, the British Expeditionary Force took its place alongside the French at Mons (Belgium), facing the right of the German offensive front. By August 24, this combined Allied force was in retreat, permitting the Germans to begin their arc toward Paris.

The German forces that set out on that arc were weaker than they should have been—weaker than old Schlieffen had wished, whose dying injunction was "only keep the right wing strong." Von Moltke had detached some troops to resist the French advance in Alsace-Lorraine, and he permitted one of his best generals to leave the western front and begin operations in the east. As a result, the German right wing did not, as intended, sweep west of Paris to encircle it, but slipped down to the east of the capital.

Informed of the German position, the general in charge of the Paris garrison acted promptly. Requisitioning whatever vehicles could be found— including famously the city's taxis—he sent soldiers from the garrison out to join with regular French forces and meet the Germans. Just thirty-five miles from Paris, on the river Marne, these French forces won on September 5–8 one of the most important Allied victories of the war. They stopped the German advance, denied them Paris, and forced them to retreat. Pushed back forty miles to the river Aisne, the Germans dug a trench, a fortification quickly available wherever there were soldiers with spades.

Digging In Before winter settled in 1914, the line of German trenches stretched from the Aisne north to the Channel, and south past the western face of Alsace to the Swiss border. Opposite those 466 miles of German fortifications stretched a parallel line of trenches dug with French and British spades. From 1914 until 1918, that line scarcely moved, though brave men on both sides hurled themselves repeatedly across the "no-man's land" that lay between the two lines of trenches. In 1915, French offensives in the north gained no ground. In February 1916, the Germans struck mightily at the border fortress of

The Russian Revolution

The 1905 uprising, a scene from **Battleship Potemkin,** *1925*

Above, a scene from Sergei Eisenstein's 1925 film Battleship Potemkin—conceived as part of a film cycle to tell the story of the revolution—commemorates a failed 1905 uprising. Here, the film's most famous scene is shown—the panic on the Odessa Steps as troops open fire on the crowd.

In Petrograd (now, as it was before, St. Petersburg) in 1917, the masses of the people had spilled out into the street. A woman's food riot in winter led to the tsar's abdication and the institution of a Provisional Government. In the spring, the Bolshevik revolutionary Vladimir Ilich Lenin arrived, won the allegiance of the surging crowds of soldiers and sailors and workers, and in November led the charge on the Tsar's Winter Palace—the decisive blow which delivered a radical faction control of a vast state. Once won, it had to be defended against armies in the field and enemies of the state within. Below, in Moscow's Red Square, Lenin addresses the troops responsible for defending the new Bolshevik regime against separatist and Tsarist rivals.

The assault on the Winter Palace, Petrograd 1917

Lenin addresses the troops in Red Square, 1917

To continue your investigation of this topic, please go to www.prenhall.com/king for the related **WINDOWS** on the **WEB** activity

Verdun, killing so many French soldiers that their proclaimed goal to "bleed France white" seemed fulfilled. Yet in this protracted battle that engaged 2 million men, the "victors" suffered casualties nearly as high (350,000) as the French "losers" (400,000).

In July 1916, the British countered with a huge offensive along an eighteen-mile front on the river Somme, memorialized by the song in *Witnesses* on p. 753. Here preliminary bombardment by the British guns ripped up the ground, slowing their own men's assault across a stretch of no-man's land while fully exposed to German machine guns. Those British soldiers who did reach the German line were trapped and shot down on the barbed wire. In the first day of battle alone, over fifty percent of the British force of 110,000 were casualties; nearly twenty percent died.

By the end of the Somme offensive, the tally sheet of casualties was again nearly even: 620,000 British and French to 650,000 Germans. The next year, the news was worse. In 1917, half the French army mutinied when, after another failed offensive, yet another was ordered. Launching a third offensive from the same Belgian town of Ypres that had seen terrible slaughter in 1914 and 1915, the British hurled themselves suicidally at the Germans at Passchendaele (Belgium)—and gained four miles. The German generals who resisted them began, for the first time, to despair of winning.

From 1914 to 1918, there was stalemate on the western front, where millions of corpses lay buried, some in the trenches they had defended. The trenches, as deep as men were tall, sheltered soldiers on an open field and fortified their position. Trench warfare was not new: it had been used by Napoleon's soldiers, and by both Northern and Southern forces in the American Civil War. But the trench was the hallmark of the western front, where men battled for a few more yards of ground beyond the enemy's entrenched position. If those few yards were taken, a new trench was dug, perhaps to be surrendered to the enemy when he counter-attacked.

In all, some 25,000 miles of trench scarred the elongated front, dug in parallel networked systems between a few yards and a mile apart. The most advanced German position, achieved early in the war, yielded to an Allied advance only when fresh American divisions arrived late in 1917. In the final campaigns of 1918, the now superior Entente forces pushed the Germans back to the Belgian border.

British, French, and German soldiers ate, slept, and passed time in the trenches—aware that, in safe positions to the rear, their generals dined well and plotted out the battle with sets of colored pins. Conditions were repellent: mud and excrement, rats and lice (no one escaped the lice, thus all the soldiers were "lousy"—the original meaning of that term),

Soldiers and horses in gas masks: *Among the horrifying innovations of World War I combat was the use of nerve gas by both sides to gain an advantage over the enemy in the stalemate of trench warfare. This scene of German soldiers, equipped with gas masks, riding their horses, also equipped with protective muzzles, presents an almost unbearably ironic contrast between traditional warfare conducted with horse-drawn carts and modern, total war, waged without mercy by machine-propelled cannisters of toxic agents.*

At the Front

The shocked reactions to battlefield horrors come to us from an enormous literature of poems, diaries, and letters written in the midst of war, of which a few are excerpted here. They speak vividly of the pain of seeing young men die, the lack of awareness and self-absorption of leaders, the absurdity of patriotic sentiments that once seemed noble, the immense courage of the ordinary soldier, and the inability of those far from the front to understand the immensity of the tragedy.

English soldier and poet Wilfred Owen describes a German gas attack (1915):
Gas! GAS! Quick, boys! – An ecstasy of fumbling,
Fitting the clumsy helmets just in time;
But someone still was yelling out and stumbling,
And flound'ring like a man in fire or lime ...
Dim, through the misty panes and thick green light,
As under a green sea, I saw him drowning.

In all my dreams, before my helpless sight,
He plunges at me, guttering, choking, drowning.

If in some smothering dreams you too could pace
Behind the wagon that we flung him in,
And watch the white eyes writhing in his face,
His hanging face, like a devil's sick of sin;
If you could hear, at every jolt, the blood
Come gargling from the froth-corrupted lungs,
Obscene as cancer, bitter as the cud
Of vile, incurable sores on innocent tongues,
My friend, you would not tell with such high zest,
To children ardent for some desperate glory
The old lie: *Dulce et decorum est*
Pro patria mori*.
[*"Pleasing and right it is to die for one's country."]
(Wilfred Owen, "Dulce et Decorum est ...," 1915; ed. S. Sassoon, 1920)

Song sung by the British troops who took their positions on July 1, 1916 for the battle of the Somme, in which thousands were slaughtered:
We beat them on the Marne,
We beat them on the Aisne,
   We gave them hell
   At Neuve Chapelle
And here we are again!
(From M. Gilbert, *The First World War: A Complete History*, 1994)

Czech draftee Jaroslav Hasek remembers his commanding officer, with no fondness (c. 1914):
Apparently by way of encouraging the rank and file ... [the commanding officer] asked where the young recruit came from, how old he was, and whether he had a watch. The young recruit ... said he hadn't got one, whereupon the aged general gave a fatuous smile ... and said, "That's fine, that's fine," whereupon he honored a young corporal, who was standing near, by asking him whether his wife was well.

"Beg to report, sir," bawled the corporal, "I'm not married."

Whereupon the general, with a patronizing smile, repeated, "That's fine, that's fine."

Then the general, lapsing still further [into] senile infantility, asked Captain Sagner to show him how his troops numbered off in twos from the right, and after a while, he heard them yelling, "One-two, one-two, one-two."

The aged general was very fond of this. At home he had two orderlies, and he used to line them up in front of him and make them number off: "One-two, one-two."

Austria had lots of generals like this.
(Jaroslav Hasek, *The Good Soldier Schweik*, c. 1914; ed. P. Selver, 1963)

A German soldier writes home from the trenches (1915): Our regiment has been transferred to this dangerous spot, Souchez. No end of blood has already flowed. ... A week ago the 142nd attacked and took four trenches from the French. It is to hold these trenches that we have been brought here. ... This letter has been interrupted no end of times. Shells began to pitch close to us—great English 12-inch ones. ... One ... struck the next house and buried four men, who were got out ... horribly mutilated. I saw them and it was ghastly!

Everybody must now be prepared for death in some form or other. ... [T]he newspapers have probably given you a different impression. They tell only of our gains and say nothing of the blood that has been shed, of the cries of agony that never cease. The newspaper doesn't give any description either of *how* the "heroes" are laid to rest. ... [U]p here ... one throws the bodies out of the trench and lets them lie there, or scatters dirt over the remains of those which have been torn to pieces by shells.
(Alfons Ankenbrand in A. F. Wedd, ed., *German Students' War Letters*, 1929)

Slaughter and horror are far from the mind of English poet Jessie Pope as she celebrates the women who will "keep their end up" until the khaki-uniformed soldiers come home (1916):
There's the girl who clips your ticket for the train,
   And the girl who speeds the lift from floor to floor,
There's the girl who does a milk-round in the rain,
   And the girl who calls for orders at your door.
     Strong, sensible, and fit,
     They're out to show their grit,
   And tackle jobs with energy and knack.
     No longer caged and penned up,
     They're going to keep their end up
   Till the khaki soldier boys come marching back.
(Jessie Pope, "War Girls," 1916; ed. C. W. Reilly, 1981)

tedium, and fear. Ordered to attack, they climbed out of the trenches and went "over the top" across "no-man's land," in the face of enemy fire, as a German soldier describes in *Witnesses* on p. 753. That mad charge of exposed men against an enemy's fortified position, repeated again and again over four years, explains the resulting slaughter.

If the trench defined the war's western front, it was not its only military characteristic. Machine guns firing 600 rounds a minute were concentrated in nests that could annihilate waves of charging infantry. Developed by American inventors Richard Gatling (1818–1903) and Hiram Maxim (1840–1916), these guns were employed in colonial wars to wreak devastation on native armies. They caused high losses in Europe as well. "Three men and a machine gun can stop a battalion of heroes," observed a French general of the battle at Verdun.

Barbed wire, used on American ranches, helped defend the lines of trenches. Enemy soldiers had to stop and cut wire before they could continue their charge. As they worked, howitzers lobbed shells at them from distant, unseen positions. Explosive grenades varied in shape, range, and deadliness. Poison gas, a recent invention first used by the Germans in 1915 but quickly imitated, disabled the enemy who could then be overcome, or evaded, by masked troops—or such was the intention; in fact the flow of gas could not be controlled and often disabled the users. The poet Wilfred Owen describes a gas attack in *Witnesses* on p. 753. The British developed tanks, heavily armored vehicles that crawled on caterpillar treads over trenches, wire, and ground churned up by bombardment. Both sides used airplanes for reconnaissance; the Germans were the first to set machine guns to shoot in rhythm with the rotation of the propeller. Zeppelin airships dropped bombs on enemy cities. As the instruments of death multiplied, the numbers of the dead mounted.

The Eastern Steamroller

The eastern front was another scene of carnage. Here Austrian and German infantry faced the immense army of the Russian Empire, one of the world's four most populous nations. The rest of Europe regarded Russia as an enormous military steamroller that could burst out of the east and unstoppably roll westward. In reality, the Russian soldiers, who were mostly peasants, set out to war with too little food, and too few boots and bullets. And the Russian officers, all nobles, were a mixed lot of the heroic, the undisciplined, and the treacherous. Within a few months of the start of warfare in the east, the steamroller had paused, and Russia was in peril. By 1917, its prospects had become desperate.

In the summer of 1914 in Petrograd (formerly St. Petersburg, renamed that year), Russian officers gallantly welcomed the war. Spurred by Pan-Slavic enthusiasm, and French persuasion, they marched promptly to battle. Too promptly; for the Russians were unprepared. Their supply lines were unready (and hampered in any case by their rail lines, constructed to a different gauge than those in western Europe) and their supplies were inadequate.

Yet the Russian army's first strike had been successful—they won the battle of Gumbinnen over a small German army on August 20—and their swift penetration of the German **salient** in eastern Prussia alarmed von Moltke. Contrary to Schlieffen's principles, the German commander detached from the western campaign one of his most competent younger generals (not yet fifty), Erich Ludendorff (1865–1937), prominent in the capture of Liège, and sent him along with Paul von Hindenburg (1847–1934), aged sixty-seven, an elderly hero plucked out of retirement, to block the forward thrust of the Russian steamroller.

The Russian generals made it easy for the Germans. Not only did they send hungry men and starved horses to the front lines, but they broadcast to each other uncoded messages detailing their positions that the German radio corps happily intercepted. The Germans delivered the uncoordinated Russian armies a crushing defeat at the Battle of Tannenberg (August 26–31). The war had barely begun, and Russia's failed Prussian offensive cost around 250,000 casualties—a fraction of the bloodletting still to come that would leave nearly 2 million of Russia's 12 million soldiers dead.

The following January (1915), Germany's Austrian allies attacked a Russian army in the Carpathian Mountains on the Hungarian border. A winter war at those elevated altitudes brought new miseries—both guns and fingers froze. In the spring, the Germans arrived to do the job their allies could not, driving the Russians 100 miles back from the front. Having secured east Prussia on the north of the eastern front, and taken the Carpathians on the south, the victorious Germans pushed through the center of Poland beyond Warsaw to Brest-Litovsk. By the end of 1915, a new front ran from the Baltic to the Black Sea, leaving much of Russia's richest territory under German command.

The butchery continued. On the Russian side, generals and commanders were disgraced and replaced, while trainloads of fresh conscripts arrived at the front to freeze, starve, and bleed. On the German side, Hindenburg and Ludendorff were relentless.

In 1916, the energetic Russian general Aleksey Alekseyevich Brusilov (1853–1926) launched a serious offensive on the south of the front into Austrian Galicia and German-occupied Poland. In 1917, as the Germans pushed back in an offensive that, by 1918, brought them deep into the interior, Russian soldiers mutinied. In Petrograd, revolution was afoot. In March 1917, the Petrograd workers' Soviet (or council) issued Army Order No. 1. Those in the ranks, it stated, need no longer obey their commanders, but should form committees and take power into their own hands. Soldiers streamed home from the front, disgusted with war and ready to throw their lot in with the revolution (see below).

The Russian military disaster was complicated by the nature of the army. The British and French armies (the German and Austrian less so) were effectively popular, or citizen armies, whereas the Russian army reflected a more traditional society. The officers were nobles and the soldiers peasants. They shared an allegiance to the tsar and a profound religious tradition. But history divided them. The peasants had always obeyed, whether on the land or at the front, and

the nobles commanded. The slaughter at the front, combined with starvation and disease, awakened in peasant conscripts the thought that perhaps they would obey no longer.

South of the Russian positions on the eastern front, Austro-Hungarian forces (with German assistance or, often, direction) battled in the Balkans and in Italy. Bulgaria and the Ottoman Empire had leagued with the Central Powers. Between these nations and the Austrian border lay Romania and Serbia, which joined the Entente, as did Greece, tempted by promises of key chunks of Ottoman territory at the war's end. By 1916, overcoming stiff resistance from Slav Serbs and Romanians, the Central Powers controlled the whole Balkan Peninsula north of Greece.

Further west lay Italy, which had secretly negotiated a favorable treaty with Britain and France which detached them from their prior allegiance to the Central Powers. Italian armies battled to regain the *terra irredenta* ("unredeemed land") arching north along the Adriatic toward Trieste which, their leaders held, was rightfully Italian. Eleven times they faced an Austro-German force at the Isonzo river from June 1915 to May 1917, where more than 500,000 Italians were wounded or killed while edging only a little closer to the Adriatic. Even that progress was reversed, when they were pushed back seventy-five miles from Caporetto to regroup only twenty miles from Venice; from there, in 1918, they plunged on to win, at last, a victory at Vittorio Veneto. With the eventual peace settlement, Italy recovered her *terra irredenta*, at the cost of hundreds of thousands of irredeemable lives.

At Sea and Abroad

Prior to World War I, the British navy was the most powerful in the world, and the British trusted it to shield their nation from European conflicts. But over the previous two decades, the Germans had begun to construct a naval force that rivaled Britain's, equipped with battleships that were modern and almost unsinkable. Alarmed, the British responded by developing the Dreadnought, launched in 1906, the fiercest battleship ever constructed, equipped with ten heavy guns of unprecedented 12-inch size.

Over the next years, German and British shipyards raced to build more ships on its pattern. At the same time, the Germans developed a fleet of more than 100 submarines (an American innovation) or U-boats. Capable of slipping secretly in and out of ports, their torpedoes threatened the enemy's mighty Dreadnoughts and the merchant carriers of its suppliers.

The big ships had few opportunities to meet each other in battle. They did so in only one significant open battle, at Jutland, off Denmark, in the North Sea on May 31, 1916. The British lost more ships and more men, but the Germans fled; the battle had no clear result. More serious than such encounters was the war of attrition in northern seas. In the North and Baltic seas, British ships blocked supplies—foodstuffs as well as military goods—from reaching German ports. British ships also brought European armies to fight the allies of the Central Powers in the Middle East, and to dismantle Germany's colonial empire, while distant Japan, an Allied power, seized German protectorates in the Chinese provinces of Shandong and Manchuria.

The blockade choked Germany and Austria-Hungary, whose citizens were near starvation by 1917. The Germans in return aimed to stop the flow of goods to British and Allied ports, targeting especially the richly-laden ships of the neutral United States (as that nation sought to retain its neutrality while continuing to reap profits from its Atlantic trade with European powers on both sides). In these attempts, the submarine was their best and only tool.

On May 7, 1915, a German U-boat sank the British liner *Lusitania* in the Irish Sea, as a result of which 1200 persons died (including 128 United States citizens). It was found to contain (although the United States denied it) American-produced ammunition bound for Allied use, encouraging Germany to view the United States as a potential enemy. In 1916, when more Americans were wounded in the

sinking of the French ship *Sussex*, President Woodrow Wilson (1856–1924) protested vigorously, eliciting a pledge from the Germans to renounce such tactics. In January 1917, nevertheless, Germany declared a policy of unrestricted submarine warfare against Allied shipping, and acted upon it. Until a convoy system was instituted in May of that year, one-fourth of all British ships that left port were sunk, as were one-fourth of all those seeking to make port.

Germany's U-boat tactics misfired. Now Britain was able to convince the United States that the Germans displayed a perfidy that could not be ignored with safety. Isolationist, pacifist, and even pro-German sentiments eventually yielded to such arguments. On April 6, 1917, the United States Congress declared war, sending the first United States forces (of an eventual total of about 4 million mobilized) to Europe the following summer.

Meanwhile, the war had expanded to other theaters. All the French and most British leaders thought it should be fought and won on the western front. Some British strategists, however, argued for pursuing hostile objectives further away from home. They would thus weaken their opponents on the European fronts, and at the same time secure some fine colonial territories abroad.

Their first objective was the Ottoman Empire, now under a military despotism headed by the Young Turks (see Chapter 24). The Ottoman navy attacked Russia's Black Sea ports in October 1914 and closed the Dardanelles straits in November, blocking Russia's access to the Mediterranean. A British strike at the Dardanelles would support their ally, and at the same time serve to protect British interests in the Mediterranean. In 1915, the British sent thirteen battleships and more than 400,000 men (mostly colonial troops from Australia and New Zealand) to take the straits. The infantry landed at Gallipoli, fought and lost horribly to Turkish defenders, and were forced to evacuate late in 1915 and early in 1916, after suffering casualties of fifty percent.

Assisted by the forces of rebellious Arabs from the Hejaz (the coastal region of the Arabian Peninsula), the British also fought Turkish armies in Palestine and Mesopotamia, eventually capturing Damascus and Baghdad. From the Mediterranean, the war spilled over to Africa and east Asia, where Germany's various colonies and protectorates fell to Britain (assisted by South African soldiers in Africa) or allied Japan (in China).

In still another way, the wider world contributed to the war centered in Europe. From all parts of the globe, the colonies supplied pack animals and automobiles, tools and blankets, guns and bullets. Colonial soldiers—from Senegal and South Africa, India, Australia, New Zealand, Canada, and Moroccoz fought alongside Europeans. More than 2 million were casualties.

WHO'S WHO

"Winners and Losers"

Archduke Franz Ferdinand (1863–1914), heir to the Austrian and Hungarian thrones, assassinated on June 26, 1914, by a Serbian terrorist.

Helmuth von Moltke (1848–1916), German Field Marshal, inherited the Schlieffen Plan which directed the German advance through Belgium to France in 1914.

Edith Cavell (1865–1915), British nurse, charged with assassinating prisoners and refugees and executed by a German officer in 1915.

Rosa Luxemburg (1870–1919), a founder of the Polish socialist party, later German socialist leader, imprisoned in Germany for opposition to the war, and killed in 1919 during Spartacist (communist) uprising against the new government that had been installed at the war's end.

Woodrow Wilson (1856–1924), US President who, though he had campaigned against his country's involvement in the war, sent US soldiers to fight in Europe and, in 1918, worked vainly to negotiate a peace in line with the ideals expressed in his "Fourteen Points."

Map 26.2 A World at War: *The truly global nature of World War I can be seen here. Note particulary the site of battles that took place in Germany's various African colonial holdings.*

At Home

As the European conflict spread around the globe, changes were occurring at home. The demand for military supplies sent women into the factories. Capital, too, was put to work, as bankers, speculators, and smugglers aided the army in prosecuting the war. These changes were meant to last for the duration. Their effects were far greater and longer.

War meant an accelerated demand for virtually everything that factories produced—textiles for uniforms, blankets, and bandages in addition to normal civilian use; metals, machines, and tools; weapons and ammunition (see *How Many?*, p. 758); packaged and canned food and, for the blockaded Central Powers, food substitutes. War production required the service of bankers, who floated loans for the new factories and the purchase of supplies, and reaped their interest on the huge sales of factory products. As huge quantities of goods needed to be distributed within each country and abroad, more investment was required to fund packaging and transportation. On an unprecedented scale, money circulated to sustain the war effort.

As the diagram on p. 758 shows, stepped-up war production meant the mass employment of millions of women, many of whom had never before been wage-earners. Women stood in assembly lines to make guns and shells, drove trucks, collected tickets, and read gas meters (see *Witnesses*, p. 753). Jobs that once were filled only by the poor, male or female, were now often held by middle-class women, whose social awareness expanded. Many later became involved in social movements to remedy the conditions of work and home life for the laboring class.

Exposure to the world of work triggered changes in women's behavior and outlook. For the first time in the history of the West, women's skirts rose above their ankles. The fashion for voluminous petticoats and crinolines of not so long ago disappeared, along with stifling corsets, to be replaced by flowing clothes that followed the lines of the body. Women publicly took up smoking and drinking, stayed out late unescorted, and walked briskly and alone through the streets of the city. It was a modern woman who emerged from the war years, independent in outlook, and often of necessity, with the death of so many young men, self-supporting.

While many women worked in factories, others supported the war effort by working as nurses. Once the province of the religious orders, nursing had recently become a modern, secular profession—a transformation largely due to the pioneering work of one determined upper-class British woman, Florence Nightingale (1820–1910), who had volunteered to serve in a hospital in Scutari (in Turkey) during the Crimean War. As in other pre-modern wars, disease was as much a killer as gunfire: thousands died from infected wounds, cholera, and dysentery. Nightingale introduced standards for sanitation, acquired funding for proper equipment and medications, and trained other women to attend properly to the needs of the ill and wounded. Her example would be followed in the American Civil War by Clara Barton (1821–1912); and during World War I by the courageous, mostly privileged women who staffed the field hospitals erected immediately adjacent to the killing fields and cared for the dying, wounded, and diseased men sent back from the front lines.

British Munitions Production 1915–1917

Bullets	1,820,000,000
Artillery shells	42,000,000
Grenades	19,000,000
Rifles	956,000
Machine guns	30,300
Heavy guns	4,600
Trench mortars	3,152

Among other features of life on the home front was the demoralization which followed upon the news of the mounting dead, when nearly every family lost a son, a father, a cousin, or a friend. The stresses of wartime encouraged behaviors that would have been condemned before 1914—heavy drinking and high rates of out-of-wedlock births. Food and other shortages meant rationing, price controls, and standing in line. Speculators profited from the shortages, and many became rich acquiring and selling such commodities as oil or rubber.

The mass mobilization required for world war had to be supported by the will of the whole nation—as the French revolutionary wars had been by drafted soldiers and commoner officers. Armies relied on conscripts (and in Britain, at the start, on volunteers), who could only be activated if their families stood behind the effort. Those families, safely at home, faced privations, too—especially in central Europe, where the peoples of the blockaded nations were starving by 1917. It was essential that the public of the combatant nations receive the right information—not always true information—circulated to the public in newspapers, through posters, and in broadcast speeches. Information, often sliding into propaganda, was a necessity on the home front. It was supplied by newswriters and war correspondents, whose new profession dated from the Crimean War.

Not all the news during the war years came from the battlefront. Much was going on at home. In Britain, the Liberal candidate David Lloyd George (1863–1945) became Prime Minister in a coalition government in 1916. Elsewhere, social democratic parties and labor organizations protested the war, at least at the outset—for many socialists believed, erroneously, that workers united to overthrow the capitalist order would never fire on each other. In Germany, the women pacifists and socialists Clara Zetkin (1857–1933) and Rosa Luxemburg (1870–1919) were imprisoned for their opposition to the war. Dutch socialists summoned an international peace conference. The French suffered a soldiers' mutiny, but German presence on their soil ultimately restored solidarity. Food shortages in Germany (caused by the British naval blockade) resulted in food riots in 1916, and the deaths of about 750,000 citizens by war's end. Domestic tensions, meanwhile, reached serious levels in Russia, which had already sacrificed millions of men to the butchery of the eastern front, when the soldiers made it known they would go on no longer.

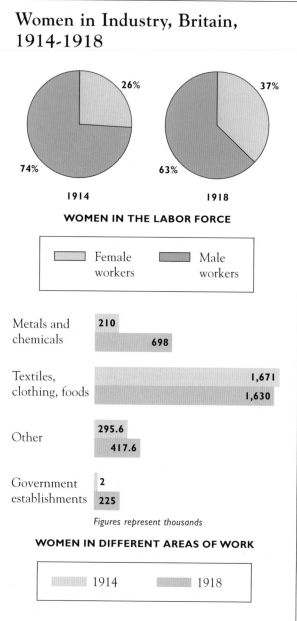

Women in Industry, Britain, 1914–1918

WOMEN IN THE LABOR FORCE

1914: 26% Female workers, 74% Male workers
1918: 37% Female workers, 63% Male workers

Female workers | Male workers

	1914	1918
Metals and chemicals	210	698
Textiles, clothing, foods	1,671	1,630
Other	295.6	417.6
Government establishments	2	225

Figures represent thousands

WOMEN IN DIFFERENT AREAS OF WORK

1914   1918

Labor shortages created by the mobilization of men for war brought huge numbers of women into a variety of employments during 1914–1918. Once hostilities ceased, however, the bulk of these new jobs disappeared again. Source: Women in Industry: Report of the War Cabinet Committee on Women in Industry (London: His Majesty's Stationery Office, 1919).

Russia Turns Back

In Russia, as further west, the factories roared furiously to produce armaments and supplies for the soldiers at the front. Russian industrialization had progressed rapidly in the generation before 1914 (see Chapter 21), and millions of workers—fully one-third of them women—crowded into the poorer districts of Moscow and Petrograd. However, as famine struck an already restive peasantry, production quotas drove the workers, and wounded or renegade soldiers returned from the front with tales of starvation and mayhem, the conditions for revolution crystallized. By the end of the single thunderous year of 1917, tsarist monarchy had yielded to a communist dictatorship.

The 1905 Revolution These things might have happened otherwise if the tsar had responded differently to the upheaval of 1905. But Tsar Nicholas II (r. 1894–1918) learned to rule from his predecessor, Alexander III (r. 1881–1894), who had pursued a dual policy of the repression of political enemies and the Russification of ethnic minorities—policies resulting in a succession of riots and pogroms (see Chapter 24) and the exile or execution of radical intellectuals.

Succeeding to the monarchy in 1894, Nicholas was determined to uphold the tsarist system of terror and repression. Backed up by the army, the secret police, obsequious ministers, the fanatically nationalist Black Hundreds, and an imperious, apparently hysterical wife—the German-born Alexandra (1872–1918), granddaughter of Britain's Queen Victoria—he met the demands for reform posed in 1905 uncomprehendingly and inflexibly.

In 1905, with Russian military failure in the war with Japan as somber backdrop, the demands of liberal nobles and bourgeois for a national parliament on the western European model coincided with the petitions of workers for political reform. In January, a group of the 100,000 factory workers then on strike in St. Petersburg presented to the tsar at his Winter Palace their petition for better working conditions and the right to unionize. The police ordered the workers to disperse; they refused. The police fired, killing about 100 people, including women and children. This "Bloody Sunday" massacre triggered strikes and rebellions throughout Russia.

Advised by his reform-minded chief minister, Sergei Witte (1849–1915), who urged concessions to the progressive agenda, Nicholas issued his October Manifesto. It called for the formation of a national representative assembly, or **Duma**, to be chosen by universal male suffrage. In addition, it permitted the formation of local and municipal councils, and allowed freedom of the press. Further unrest in December, however, and the return of the army from Asia, encouraged the tsar to take back many of his concessions. He ordered workers' leaders arrested and

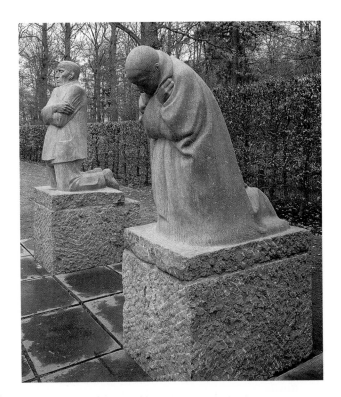

***Käthe Kollwitz*, Die Eltern (The Parents):** *As mothers, women mourned the millions of their sons, an unprecedented toll, who died terrifying deaths far from home. One such mother was the German artist Käthe Kollwitz, who tried to salve her grief after the conflict was over by producing a sculpture of the two stricken parents at their son's grave, forever weeping stone tears in his memory.*

minority uprisings suppressed, while unleashed forces of repression engaged in renewed anti-Semitic pogroms (see Chapter 24).

Nevertheless, the Duma met the following April (1906). Its largely liberal representatives (the more radical Social Democratic and Social Revolutionary delegates refused to participate) pressed for agrarian and political reform. To limit these reformist moves, the tsar created an upper assembly, of whom half the members were obedient appointees. When the Duma protested, it was dissolved. A second, more conservative Duma was elected. It, too, was dissolved. A third Duma elected in 1907 continued to press ineffectively for reform. Meanwhile, the reformist Witte had been dismissed and replaced by the more conservative chief minister Peter Stolypin (1862–1911).

In 1911, Stolypin himself was assassinated, having marked himself as too liberal by introducing reforms that allowed enterprising peasants (called *kulaks*) to establish their own farms. Nicholas retreated further into his circle of conservative supporters, who urged an ongoing campaign of repression and Russification and maintained a stubborn ignorance of the great storm that was brewing. Liberals and progressives chafed, while socialists of various shades of opinion discussed revolution.

Military Expenditures of the Great Powers, 1890 and 1914

	Year	Total Defense Expenditure ($ millions)	Cost per Capita Home Population
Japan	1890	24	0.6
	1914	96	1.75
Germany	1890	144	2.95
	1914	554	8.52
British Empire	1890	157	4.03
	1914	384	8.53
France	1890	186	4.87
	1914	287	7.33
Russia	1890	145	1.32
	1914	442	2.58
US	1890	67	1.06
	1914	314	3.20

The massive mobilization of people and resources in World War I meant a reorientation of economies and huge financial burdens on the citizenry. As this table shows, the increase in military costs per capita in wartime (1914 figure) ranged from about 150 percent (France) to about 300 percent (Japan and US) of their cost in peacetime (1890 figure).
Source: W. S. Morton, Japan: Its History and Culture, 3rd ed. (New York: McGraw Hill, 1994), p. 182.

Marxist parties, who advanced the revolutionary potential of industrial workers (the proletariat; see Chapters 23, 25). These included the pacifist Internationalists, and the Marxian Social Democrats, themselves split into **Bolshevik** (meaning "majority," as this faction once held a majority at the 1903 party congress) and **Menshevik** (meaning "minority") factions. Other revolutionary groups also proliferated, including those of the anarchists (see Chapter 25). The different parties produced their own newspapers to interpret political events for their readership. These were produced irregularly and distributed secretly, evading the censors.

Russian politics were further complicated by the fact that most of the revolutionary leaders were not in Russia. By 1900, the Okhrana, the tsarist secret police, had tracked most of them and seen them banished to Siberia. Once released, they often sought refuge in London, Brussels, or Zurich. From these cities, they published articles of political analysis for the party press or telegraphed instructions to

WHO'S WHO

Russia: Makers of Revolution

Nicholas II (r. 1894–1918), Tsar of Russia, head of a repressive regime, ardent supporter of the war, he was away at the front when revolution broke out in St. Petersburg; subsequently imprisoned and murdered by the revolutionary regime.

Grigorii Rasputin (1872–1916), charismatic, probably fraudulent mystic and healer, protected by Tsarina Alexandra through whom he manipulated policy decisions until he was finally murdered by aristocratic opponents.

Alexander Kerensky (1881–1970), moderate social democrat who led the Provisional Government of Russia upon the Tsar's abdication, and was himself ousted by Lenin in the October Revolution (November 6, 1917).

Vladimir Ilyich Ulyanov, known as "Lenin" (1870–1924), leader while in exile of the Bolshevik faction of Marxian social democrats, who returned to Russia (with German assistance) in 1917 and soon took up leadership of the young revolution.

Lev Davidovich Bronstein, known as "Trotsky" (1879–1940), returned to Russia in 1917 from exile in the US and joined forces with Lenin; organizer of the Red Army and negotiator of the Treaty of Brest-Litovsk; murdered in 1940 at the command of Lenin's successor Stalin (see Chapter 28).

Factions and Visionaries Between 1905 and 1917, Russian political parties were active and multifarious. They shared a determined opposition to tsarist autocracy (the latter supported by the high clergy and conservative nobles, along with officials whose loyalty had been purchased with privileges); otherwise they disagreed.

They were arrayed in three main groups. The first included the progressive nobles and bourgeois, professionals and liberal intellectuals, of whom the foremost were the Kadets (Constitutional Democrats), who aimed to establish a constitutional monarchy on European models. The second consisted of the several socialist parties intent on land reform (addressing the still unresolved condition of the eighty-five percent of Russia's population composed of former serfs), of which the best known were the Social Revolutionaries. The third group was that of the colleagues in St. Petersburg, and met with leaders of like-minded European parties at international congresses. Supported by party funds, parental largesse, or their own labor, they lived this existence of political exile for decades on end.

Such was the career pattern of Vladimir Ilyich Ulyanov (1870–1924), who adopted the revolutionary pseudonym "Lenin," the leader of the Bolshevik faction of Marxian social democrats. He is portrayed on p. 751. Radicalized by the execution in 1887 of his older brother, charged under Alexander III with participating in an assassination plot, Lenin committed himself to the career of professional revolutionary.

Arrested and exiled in 1895, Lenin departed in 1900 for Switzerland. A brilliant theorist as well as an active conspirator, Lenin produced analyses of capitalism and imperialism, and blueprints for revolution that adapted Marx to the circumstances of the Russian Empire. The essential points were outlined in his *What Is To Be Done?* (1902), quoted in *Witnesses* on p. 762. Revolution could be achieved in Russia, and a proletarian state created, but not by the workers alone. A disciplined **cadre**, or core group of committed and educated leaders, would lead the rank and file of workers, who would join with the peasantry (for Lenin, an unformed and unreliable group) to dethrone autocracy and create a revolutionary society.

Another exile who became a prominent leader of the Bolshevik revolt was Lev (Leon) Davidovich Bronstein (1879–1940), who adopted the pseudonym "Trotsky." In 1917, when news of mounting crisis arrived, he was living in the United States. Returning immediately to Petrograd, he joined with the Menshevik faction and became active as a leader of the Petrograd **Soviet**, an informal association of workers' councils. The Mensheviks hoped to work through such councils so as to be ready to act once bourgeois liberals had formed a constitutional government. As the events of 1917 unfolded, however, Trotsky joined with Lenin and the Bolsheviks.

Precipitating the Crisis The revolutionary year 1917 was preceded by the crisis of leadership of 1916, itself provoked by the experience of war. The tsar himself decided to go to the front to rally the troops, and left at the helm of the Russian Empire his obsequious ministers, his haughty wife, and her friend and counselor, the drunken, unstable but charismatic Grigorii Rasputin (1872–1916). Having won over the tsarina by convincing her that he alone could save her hemophiliac son, the heir to the throne, Rasputin exerted his influence in political affairs. Never has a state managed by such incompetents faced opponents of such intelligence and resolve.

In December 1916, a group of noble conspirators poisoned, shot, bludgeoned, and finally drowned Rasputin, who died at last beneath the ice of the Neva River. Now Russia was wholly without leadership. The pitiless winter descended, news from the front was bad, factory workers went on strike, and food shortages peaked. In March 1917, the women of Petrograd took to the streets—how often in the past women had rioted for bread! But rarely with such effect.

The women's protest turned into revolution—the "February" revolution by the old Russian calendar then in use. Workers joined the women, while mobs seized public buildings, and armed themselves with guns from the arsenal. Factory workers formed themselves into militias of self-appointed "Red Guards," and, prodded by Menshevik organizers, created the Petrograd Soviet of Workers' and Soldiers' Deputies. On March 12, Duma leaders created a Provisional Government to maintain order. Three days later, Tsar Nicholas abdicated, the last Romanov ruler of Russia, and the first emperor to lose his throne as a result of World War I.

Heading the Provisional Government was a committee of directors including both Kadets and socialists. Its aim was to restore order at home, manage food distribution, prosecute the war, introduce reforms, and arrange for the election of a constituent assembly that would, at long last, write a constitution. The moderate social democrat Alexander Kerensky (1881–1970), who emerged as its leader (and would die in exile in New York City fifty-three years later, one of the longest-lived of the generation of 1917), might have succeeded in meeting those goals had not the Petrograd Soviet formed other goals of its own.

In April 1917, Lenin returned from Switzerland. His triumphal arrival in Russia is described in *Witnesses* on p. 762. He had journeyed most of the overland distance in a sealed railroad car supplied by the German government, Russia's enemy, which recognized the profit to be gained from planting in Petrograd a Bolshevik agitator. The British politician Winston Churchill later described the transhipment of Lenin as a form of biological warfare—the transmission of a "plague bacillus" to destroy the enemy.

Safely arrived, Lenin joined the leaders of the Petrograd Soviet, which now had some 3000 members. By summer, his Bolsheviks controlled it. With their simple sociology (there were only two classes, the exploited proletariat and the exploiting bourgeoisie, and one must choose to serve one or the other) and their irresistible promises—"Land, Bread, Peace"—the Bolsheviks soon won influence in the workers' soviets of Moscow and other major cities. Taking the initiative, the Petrograd Soviet issued Army Order No. 1 (see above), an invitation to soldiers to disobey their officers with impunity. During the spring and summer of 1917, Russian soldiers "voted with their feet" (in Lenin's pungent phrase). They arrived in Petrograd from the front just in time to join the revolution.

Whereas Kerensky's Provisional Government wanted to win the war and secure a democratic constitution, the Bolsheviks wanted to end the war and

Revolution in Russia

Of the many ingredients of the Russian Revolution of 1917, the leadership of Vladimir Ilich Lenin, who became the first head of the new revolutionary state, was indispensable. In these passages, Lenin speaks—long before the Revolution broke out—of the need for a leadership group of professional revolutionaries; he is greeted by representatives of the volatile ranks of workers, soldiers, and sailors in Petrograd in April 1917; and, in the same month, he announces the strategy that the revolutionaries must follow in order to gain control.

Lenin defines the need for a Vanguard Party to lead the workers (1902): We have said that *there could not have been* Social-Democratic [revolutionary] consciousness among the workers. It would have to be brought to them from without. The history of all countries shows that the working class, exclusively of its own effort, is able to develop only trade-union consciousness. ...

I assert ... that no revolutionary movement can endure without a stable organization of leaders maintaining continuity ... that such an organization must consist chiefly of people professionally engaged in revolutionary activity. ... [who] will centralize all the secret aspects of the work—the drawing up of leaflets, the working out of approximate plans; and the appointing of bodies of leaders for each urban district, for each factory district, and for each educational institution. ...
(V. I. Lenin, *Collected Works*, vol. 5, 1973)

Nadezhda Krupskaya, Lenin's wife and secretary, describes their return to Russia (1917): The masses of Petrograd—workers, soldiers and sailors—came to welcome their leader. ... We were in the midst of a surging sea of people.

No one who has not lived through the revolution can have any idea of its solemn grandeur. Red banners,

a guard of honor of Kronstadt sailors, searchlights from the Peter and Paul fortress ..., armoured cars, files of working men and women guarding the road. ...

When Ilyich stepped out on to the platform, a captain came up to him, stood at attention and reported. Taken by surprise, Ilyich returned the salute. A guard of honor was lined up on the platform, and Ilyich was led past it. ... Then we were seated in motor-cars, while Ilyich was placed on an armoured car ... "Long live the socialist world revolution!" Ilyich shouted into the vast crowd swarming around us.

Ilyich already felt the beginning of that revolution in every fibre of his being.
(Nadezhda Konstantinovna Krupskaya, *Lenin*; ed. B. Isaacs, 1960)

Upon his return to Russia following the collapse of the Tsarist regime, Lenin proclaims his revolutionary strategy in the April Theses (1917):
2. The specific feature of the present situation in Russia is that the country is *passing* from the first stage of the revolution—which ... placed power in the hands of the bourgeoisie—to its *second* stage, which must place power in the hands of the proletariat and the poorest sections of the peasants. ...
This peculiar situation demands of us an ability to adapt ourselves to the special conditions of Party work among unprecedentedly large masses of proletarians who have just awakened to political life.
3. No support for the Provisional Government. ...
4. ... The masses must be made to see that the Soviets of Workers' Deputies are the *only possible* form of revolutionary government, ... therefore our task is ... to present a patient, systematic, and persistent explanation of the errors of [the Provisional Government's] ... tactics, an explanation especially adapted to the practical needs of the masses.
(Lenin's April Theses, proclaimed 1917)

---

seize power. The two sets of aims competed, much as the crowds of frock-coated officials in the Winter Palace jostled against the crowds of workers and soldiers in the street. In July, the moderate forces gained the upper hand; soon, though, the Bolsheviks rebounded and gained control. In September, the reactionary general Lavr Kornilov (1870–1918) attempted a coup, which Kerensky suppressed. Thereafter, enemies of the revolution were branded "Kornilovites," whether or not they had joined in the attempt at military putsch.

In October, as Kerensky's supporters awaited the formation of a constituent assembly, and as Lenin's supporters awaited the arrival of the delegates to the All-Russian Congress of Soviets, Lenin saw a moment of opportunity and grabbed it. As the delegates of the soviets arrived, but before they had the opportunity to oppose Lenin's move, supported by squads of workers, soldiers (from the Petrograd garrison), and sailors

(from the nearby naval base at Kronstadt) the Bolsheviks stormed the Winter Palace, described in *Windows On*, p. 751. Kerensky was expelled, and all power passed, as Lenin had wished, from the Provisional Government to the soviets. That event of November 6, 1917 marks the onset of the Bolshevik Revolution. By the old Russian calendar, the date was October 24; hence the event is known as the "October Revolution."

In Petrograd, the Bolsheviks seized the post office and telephone exchanges, government offices and ministries, the railroads, banks, and newspaper offices. In Moscow, they seized the Kremlin, the sacred center of the Russian state. Former Menshevik Leon Trotsky, head of the Military Revolutionary Committee that had coordinated the insurrection, organized the Red Army, and Felix Dzerzhinsky (1877–1926) the secret police, or Cheka.

The further course of the Bolshevik Revolution is a story to be told elsewhere (see Chapter 28). For the moment, its significance is that it resulted in Russia's withdrawal from the war. With the title People's Commissar for Foreign Affairs, Trotsky conducted the delicate negotiations with the Germans. An armistice was reached in December 1917. There remained the terms of the peace. When Trotsky rejected the German demands, they responded instantly by smashing into Ukraine, the Crimea, and Georgia to the east, and north to the Gulf of Finland, which lies barely 150 miles from Petrograd. Checked, desperate, on March 3, 1918 Trotsky signed at Brest-Litovsk in Belarus a peace treaty that left Russia mutilated. Russia sacrificed Poland, Moldova, Bessarabia, Ukraine, Georgia, the Baltic states, Finland—nearly one-fourth of the Russia the tsars had built, nearly one-third of its farmland, more than half of its industries, nearly all of its coal mines, cotton, and oil. The Bolsheviks who had wished to leave the war at any price paid a tremendous price; yet Lenin believed the losses unimportant, since they were bound to revert to Russia in the imminent world-wide communist revolution. Meanwhile, they were free to secure their revolution, and the Germans were free to return to the anguish of the western front.

Lenin the revolutionary was also a visionary. Seeing a new world ahead, he sacrificed all else—his own youth and livelihood, the lives of millions, the traditions of a nation—to make that vision real. Nearly halfway around the globe, a more prosperous nation with its own unique traditions had as its leader another visionary—the American president Woodrow Wilson (1856–1924)—for whom democracy and peace were imperatives that loomed as large as did revolution for Lenin. These two visionaries from the peripheries of the Western world foreshadowed its future more accurately than any of the leaders of the core nations of Europe, older now, after four years of war, exhausted, and transformed.

IN SEARCH OF PEACE

Woodrow Wilson was elected president in 1916 in part because he opposed American involvement in the war then raging in Europe—"He Kept Us Out of War" was his campaign slogan. The following year, he brought the United States into the war. As a fresh American army arrived in 1917 and, in 1918, swept German forces back through Belgium and across the Rhine, Wilson announced his blueprint for the future. Viewing this war as the "war to end all wars," he insisted that the settlement must provide for long-term goals: the establishment of democracy and the securing of a permanent peace.

In the event, the visionary Wilson did not succeed in realizing his plan. The peace settlement was achieved by deal-making and manipulations that left the work of building the future undone, and the defeated nations hungry for vengeance.

Peace Plans

On January 8, 1918, in an address to both houses of the United States Congress, President Wilson outlined his "Fourteen Points" (see *Witnesses*, p. 764). Underlying them were three fundamental principles. First, war must and could be avoided in the future if the nations in concert obeyed certain guidelines, above all the accomplishment of "open covenants of peace, openly arrived at." Second, national status should rest on ethnic self-determination—if a people considered themselves a unity, their living together "along historically established lines of allegiance and nationality" should be assured. Third (the substance of the crucial Fourteenth Point), an international body should be created, the League of Nations, to negotiate conflicts between nations before war erupted: "A general association of nations must be formed under specific covenants for the purpose of affording mutual guarantees of political independence and territorial integrity to great and small states alike."

Wilson's proposal also advocated free trade and freedom of the seas; a general disarmament "to the lowest point consistent with domestic safety"; the restoration of just boundaries and the protection of neutrality; an equitable settlement of colonial claims; and the relinquishing to Russia (then in the midst of civil war), in the spirit of self-determination, of its own destiny: "The treatment accorded Russia by her sister nations in the months to come will be the acid test of their good will, of their comprehension of her needs as distinguished from their own interests, and of their intelligent and unselfish sympathy."

Although Wilson's Fourteen Points may have been overly hopeful, he was the only world leader to grasp one essential desideratum: the avoidance of war in an age when war's destructive power could no longer be endured by humankind. To reach that end, he urged the embracing of democratic procedures under universal standards of justice.

The idealist Wilson was not alone in envisioning peace in 1918. On both sides of the conflict, people clamored for peace. In Britain, France, Italy, and Belgium they called for compensation and revenge.

MUST READS

Memories of War and Revolution

Erich Maria Remarque	*All Quiet on the Western Front* (1929)
Siegfried Sassoon	*The War Poems* (1983)
Wilfrid Owen	*Poems*
N.N. Sukhanov	*The Russian Revolution* (1917)

In Search of Peace

The idealistic president of the United States Woodrow Wilson saw an opportunity to make sense of the tragedy of World War I by establishing world politics on new principles of openness, freedom, self-determination, and negotiation. The treaties of Paris that were finally ratified—exemplified here by the Treaty of Versailles with Germany, designated the principal aggressor—instead aimed at containment and punishment, and thus pointed the way to an unstable peace and renewed war.

Woodrow Wilson's vision of the post-war order—the principles of justice and self-determination guide his "Fourteen Points" (1918): We [the US] entered this war because violations of right had occurred which touched us to the quick and made the life of our own people impossible unless they were corrected and the world secured once for all against their recurrence. What we demand in this war, therefore, ... is that the world be made fit and safe to live in; ... The program of the world's peace, therefore, is our program; and that program, the only possible program, as we see it, is this:

I. Open covenants of peace, openly arrived at, after which there shall be no private international understandings of any kind but diplomacy shall proceed always frankly and in the public view.

II. Absolute freedom of navigation upon the seas, outside territorial waters. ...

III. The removal ... of all economic barriers and the establishment of an equality of trade conditions among all the nations consenting to the peace. ...

IV. [International arms reductions]. ...

V. A free, open-minded, and absolutely impartial adjustment of all colonial claims, based upon a strict observance of the principle that ... the interests of the populations concerned must have equal weight with the equitable claims of the government whose title is to be determined.

VI. The evacuation of all Russian territory. ...

VII. Belgium ... must be evacuated and restored. ...

VIII. All French territory should be freed ... and the wrong done to France by Prussia in 1871 in the matter of Alsace-Lorraine ... should be righted. ...

IX. A readjustment of the frontiers of Italy should be effected along clearly recognizable lines of nationality.

X. The peoples of Austria-Hungary [including various Slavs] ... should be accorded the freest opportunity of autonomous development.

XI. Rumania, Serbia, and Montenegro should be evacuated; occupied territories restored; Serbia accorded free and secure access to the sea; and the relations of the several Balkan states ... determined ... along historically established lines of allegiance and nationality; ...

XII. The Turkish portions of the present Ottoman Empire should be assured a secure sovereignty, but the other nationalities which are now under Turkish rule should be assured ... an absolutely unmolested opportunity of autonomous development. ...

XIII. An independent Polish state should be erected. ...

XIV. A general association of nations must be formed under specific covenants for the purpose of affording mutual guarantees of political independence and territorial integrity to great and small states alike.
(*Congressional Record*, vol. 56, 1918, pt. 1)

From the Treaty of Versailles—guidelines for the containment and punishment of Germany as the instigator of war (1919):

Article 42. Germany is forbidden to maintain or construct any fortifications either on the left bank of the Rhine or on the right bank to the west of a [specified] line ...

Article 45. ... Germany cedes to France ... the coal mines situated in the Saar Basin. ...

Article 51. The territories [of Alsace and Lorraine] ... are restored to French sovereignty. ...

Article 80. Germany acknowledges and will respect strictly the independence of Austria. ...

Article 81. Germany ... recognizes the complete independence of the Czecho-Slovak State. ...

Article 84. German nationals habitually resident in ... the Czecho-Slovak State will obtain Czecho-Slovak nationality *ipso facto* and lose their German nationality. ...

Article 87. Germany ... recognizes the complete independence of Poland. ...

Article 116. Germany acknowledges ... the independence of all the territories which were part of the former Russian Empire on August 1, 1914.

Article 119. Germany renounces ... all her ... overseas possessions. ...

Article 159. The German military forces shall be demobilized and reduced. ...

Article 198. The armed forces of Germany must not include any military or naval air forces. ...

Article 231. The Allied and Associated Governments affirm and Germany accepts the responsibility of Germany and her allies for causing all the loss and damage to which the Allied and Associated Governments and their nationals have been subjected as a consequence of the war imposed upon them by the aggression of Germany and her allies.

Article 232. ... Germany undertakes that she will make compensation for all damage done to the civilian population of the Allied and Associated Powers and to their property ... as [elsewhere] defined. ...
(*Peace Treaty With Germany*, 66th Congress, 1st Session, Senate Document 49, 1919)

In Russia, sentiments for peace merged with the tide of revolution. Elsewhere in eastern Europe they were the platform of increasingly popular parties whose speakers called for peace without delay, without annexations of territory, without indemnities—a truce without winners or losers.

In Germany and Austria-Hungary, centrist socialists and republicans managed two revolutions during the last days of the war. These forced the expulsion of the Hohenzollern and Habsburg emperors, whose dynasties had reigned so long. The German revolution, sparked by naval mutinies and followed by general strikes, achieved the abdication of the emperor and the establishment of a democratic republic on November 9, 1918. The Austrians had already withdrawn from the war six days before. The flight of the last Habsburg, Charles (r. 1916–1918), who had succeeded Franz Joseph (r. 1848–1916) in 1918, meant the dismemberment of that multiethnic empire. Hungary and Austria declared themselves republics in October and November, free to pursue their separate paths.

These revolutions enabled new governments to sue for peace. But the transition from empire to republic in central Europe did not proceed without turmoil. As in Russia, a variety of political parties struggled to gain leadership. Whereas the Bolsheviks were victorious in Russia, moderate socialists held on to power in Germany and Austria. In Germany, centrist leaders weathered naval mutinies, a Bavarian socialist secessionist movement, and street rioting in Berlin. In that city, they faced the radical "Spartacist" faction of the Socialist Party (named after the slave who had led a revolt in ancient Rome; see Chapter 5). It was led by the brilliant theorists Karl Liebknecht (1871–1919) and Rosa Luxemburg, who guided the formation of workers' and soldiers' militias, modeled on those that had gained power in Petrograd in 1917. Fearful of a second Bolshevik revolution, the new German government unleashed the army to quell the uprising. Army agents were to murder Liebknecht and Luxemburg on January 15, 1919, just as the representatives of the victorious nations gathered at Versailles to decide on the terms of peace. The Spartacist socialists subsequently became the German Communist Party.

Meanwhile, the war reached closure on the military fronts. In a last, desperate offensive in March 1918, the Germans advanced westward with more than 1 million men, intending to finish what they had started in the fall of 1914. In June, some 300,000 still fresh United States troops responded with irresistible force, pushing the German armies back to Belgium, the Rhine, and beyond. In Germany, only the emperor and his generals still spoke of victory—and now the generals began to urge an armistice.

In October 1918, the German premier Prince Max von Baden (1867–1929) approached Wilson, expressing interest in the Fourteen Points and the promise of "peace without victory." But Wilson's patience had

HOW MANY?

What Germany Lost

100%	of her pre-war colonies
80%	of her pre-war fleet
48%	of all iron production
16%	of all coal production
13%	of her 1914 territory
12%	of her population

been tried by the loss of American lives. He left von Baden to deal with the British and the French, made pitiless by the experience of the slaughter on the western front. With these the Central Powers signed an armistice on November 11, 1918. Champagne flowed in London, Paris, and New York. The war was over, but peace would not easily follow. As the combatants had bloodied each other in battle, the victors now set out, with paper and pen, to bloody the losers at the conference called to set the terms of surrender.

Settlement at Paris

Attending the peace conference in Paris were the prime ministers of France, Britain, and Italy, and the president of the United States: respectively, Georges Clemenceau (1841–1929; known as "the tiger"), David Lloyd George, Vittorio Orlando (1860–1952), and Woodrow Wilson. In addition to these "Big Four," there were delegates from twenty-three other nations and four British dominions. No delegates represented the defeated powers; none were welcome from Russia, which had bled for the Allied cause but had exited the struggle early. The delegates wrangled, and the Big Four retired behind closed doors to work out the future of Europe. Clemenceau and Lloyd George looked for revenge and reparations; Orlando wanted land; and Wilson conceded much while fixing his sights on a future League of Nations.

The Peace of Paris resulted in a series of separate treaties with the defeated powers, each named after the Parisian suburb in which it was signed during 1919–1920. Of these the Treaty of Versailles, which settled affairs with Germany, overshadowed the others. In discussions held from January to June, these points emerged. First, Germany must be forced to admit its guilt as the aggressor and instigator of the terrible conflict. Second, it must repay the Allies the cost of war. Third, it must be demilitarized to the extent that it could cause no new conflict. Fourth, the defeated nations must surrender territory in Europe and possessions around the globe to the victor nations, who demanded a reward for their wartime sacrifice.

Germany, indeed, was humbled and stripped bare (see *Witnesses*, p. 764, and *How Many?*, p. 765). Article 231 of the Treaty of Versailles signed on June 28, 1919—the famous "war guilt" clause—stated that Germany accepted full responsibility for all losses and damages suffered by the Allies "as a consequence of the war imposed upon them by the aggression of Germany and her allies." Germany was ordered to pay a **reparation** of 132 billion gold marks (about $33 billion) over a period of years, a sum arrived at by rough calculation of the cost of war to the victor nations— a penalty of unimaginable dimension, little of which was ever paid. Their army was reduced to 100,000 volunteers, their airforce was eliminated, and their navy limited to six warships and no submarines. Even their merchant and fishing fleets were limited, and their shipyards assigned to supply the victor nations with new vessels at no cost. The Rhineland (the rich western sector) would be occupied by the French army until such date as the reparations were paid, and the coal-rich Saar region administered by an international committee until 1935, when a plebiscite would determine whether it became French or German. (The citizens of the Saar eventually chose German citizenship.) Kipling applauded the harsh settlement:

These were our Children who died for our Lands.
They were dear in our sight ...
The Price of our Loss shall be paid to our Hands ...
That is our Right.

Germany also accepted territorial concessions. The provinces of Alsace and Lorraine were returned to France; other German territory was ceded to Denmark, Belgium, and Poland, the latter reconstituted nation thus gaining "a corridor" to the Baltic Sea (except for the "free" city of Danzig, now Gdánsk) which divided East Prussia from the rest of the German homeland. German colonies in Africa and Asia were transferred to the Allied powers.

Austria, the remnant of the Austro-Hungarian Empire whose Balkan policies had triggered the war, gave up so much territory that its final dimensions were smaller than the crown lands the Habsburgs had ruled for centuries. From the lands it lost, whole new nations were constituted, their boundaries drawn (as much as possible) according to the Wilsonian principle of ethnic self-determination. Hungary became an independent republic. Czechoslovakia and Yugoslavia united, respectively, the Czechs and Slovaks and the southern Slavic Croatians, Slovenes, and Serbs. Romania doubled its territory. The south Tyrol (in the Alps) and parts of the Adriatic coast were conceded to Italy, which reclaimed thereby much of its *terra irredenta* but not enough to satisfy the Italian nationalists, who denounced this as a "mutilated peace."

A corridor of states was created of what was once western Russia—for, although the Brest-Litovsk treaty became invalid with the defeat of Germany,

Russia had still surrendered its destiny to the victorious powers. From its borderlands were formed the independent states of Poland, Lithuania, Latvia, Estonia, and Finland; while Bessarabia was ceded to Romania. Bulgaria gave up territory to Romania, Greece, and Yugoslavia.

The former Ottoman Empire, soon to be reconstituted as the modern nation of Turkey, was assigned to yield to Greece and Italy much of its European land, as well as key positions in Asia Minor and the island of Rhodes. These demands the Turks resisted, driving out the Greek forces that had rapidly moved into Asia Minor, and forcing the Europeans to accept a few Aegean islands in compensation. Leading the resistance was the young general Mustafa Kemal (1881–1938), who from 1923 until his death became Turkey's dictator (see Chapter 29).

The new state of Turkey was a truncated rump of the former Ottoman Empire. Although still a major power in the Middle East, on the European side of the straits (which were now open to all nations) it contained only the area around Constantinople (now Istanbul). Its North African and Middle Eastern territories were all lost. The belt from Morocco to Afghanistan became a patchwork of British, French, Spanish, and Italian colonies, protectorates, and "mandates." A mandate was the commission to administer a region (such as those of the former Ottoman Empire and former German colonies) under the auspices of the League of Nations, the institution Wilson had envisioned and which had a brief life between 1919 and 1939. It was the most hopeful, if flawed, outcome of the Paris conference.

The League of Nations was formed in 1919 to secure peace among nations so that the world, as Wilson had wished, would be made "safe fordemocracy." On its executive committee were British, French, Italian, and Japanese delegates. As at Versailles, delegates from the former Central Powers and communist Russia (now the Union of Soviet Socialist Republics, or USSR) were not represented. Neither was the United States. President Wilson had returned home from Paris to find his own nation in the grip of an isolationist mood. Republicans had a majority in the Senate (Wilson was a Democrat), while Irish, Italian, and German minority constituents all reported to their representatives their dissatisfactions with the peace settlement. In November 1919, the proposal that the United States join the League of Nations failed, and Wilson's spirits crumbled. Without American leadership, the League did not have the strength to fulfill its mission.

It certainly could not overcome the bitter feelings left by the peace treaties that the victor nations presented their former enemies: Versailles, with Germany, June 28, 1919; Saint-Germain, with Austria, September 10, 1919; Neuilly, with Bulgaria, November 27, 1919; Trianon, with Hungary, June 4,

Map 26.3 Redrawing the Boundaries: *Post-war Europe looked very different from its pre-war incarnation. Hoping to resolve the varied nationalist tensions blamed for provoking the conflict in the first place, negotiators broke up large multinational empires and created (or recreated) a swath of countries along supposed lines of "national self-determination." The settlement also destroyed, or weakened, numerous European empires. The Ottoman Empire, long considered the "Sick Man of Europe," was one of the chief casualties. Germany was compelled to yield her colonies to the protection of victor nations. They were greedy to assume their new "mandates" but too exhausted to manage them effectively (see also Map 23.4 on p. 704).*

1920; Sèvres, with Ottoman Turkey, August 10, 1920. No sooner issued, the treaties were challenged by the defeated nations. The next war was already in the making, as the French Marshal Ferdinand Foch (1851–1929) understood when he said of the Versailles agreement, "This isn't a peace, it's a twenty-year truce!" It lasted not quite twenty years.

Outcomes

In his 1865 Second Inaugural Address, President Abraham Lincoln reflected on the bitter experience of the American Civil War (see Chapter 19). It was longer and more cruel than anyone had anticipated. But its achievements were also monumental—the reestablishment of the American democracy, and the abolition of slavery. Had Lincoln spoken fifty-four years later of the record left by World War I, he would have noted a slaughter far greater, but an outcome less

hopeful. Its main effect was to increase, as the humanist Desiderius Erasmus (1469–1536) said of wars long before, the "empire of the dead."

Map 26.3 above shows the post-war boundaries. The chief outcome of World War I was the fall of the mighty—the rulers of four empires (German, Austro-Hungarian, Russian, and Ottoman); the values of European civilization that had reached its zenith in the century just ended; and an entire generation of young men. "How are the mighty fallen/ and the weapons of war perished!" (2 Samuel 1:25).

The first of these effects this chapter has already traced. The second will be described in Chapter 27. The third left a Europe populous with orphans, black-garbed widows, and mutilated men, who lived to visit the fresh-dug graves that crowded immense new cemeteries. Casualty rates in the armies of Germany, France, and Russia reached, respectively, sixty-three, seventy-one, and seventy-six percent; in Britain,

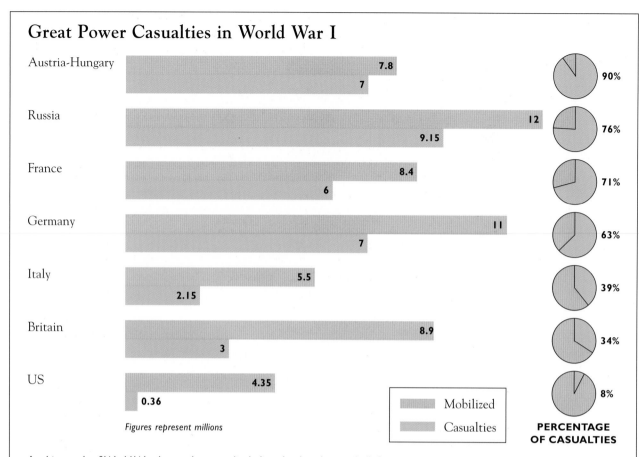

Great Power Casualties in World War I

Austria-Hungary — 7.8 / 7 — 90%

Russia — 12 / 9.15 — 76%

France — 8.4 / 6 — 71%

Germany — 11 / 7 — 63%

Italy — 5.5 / 2.15 — 39%

Britain — 8.9 / 3 — 34%

US — 4.35 / 0.36 — 8%

Figures represent millions

Mobilized
Casualties

PERCENTAGE OF CASUALTIES

As this graph of World War I casualty rates (including dead and wounded) for seven nations shows, Austria suffered catastrophic losses, followed by its opponents Russia (which had the largest commitment of soldiers), and France. The United States, a latecomer to the conflict, committed few soldiers and suffered only slight losses.
Source: J. L. Stokesbury, A Short History of World War I (New York: Quill, 1981), p. 310.

never invaded, and Italy, only peripherally engaged, the rates were thirty-four and thirty-nine percent. The United States, a late entrant, mobilized about 4 million men, and suffered only eight percent casualties. The Austro-Hungarian Empire suffered the highest rate of casualties, fighting simultaneously on two fronts, in cold, and amid mountains. Of the 7.8 million men mobilized, seven million—almost ninety percent—were killed or wounded.

Overall, some 8.5 million combatants died (not counting those dead of disease and other war-related causes)—thirteen percent of the 65 million mobilized. The French, German, Austrian, and Romanian dead were sixteen, sixteen, fifteen percent and a staggering forty-five percent of combatants respectively. The French dead, more than 1.3 million men of 8.4 million sent to war, were a number equivalent to one-half of all those who, in 1914, were between eighteen and thirty-two years of age—one-half a generation.

Thirty million more were to die in the aftermath of war—the victims of the worst ever influenza epidemic. Probably borne to Europe by United States soldiers in the spring of 1918, the disease raged among the undernourished survivors of war. The horrors of the battlefront nourished the still greater cataclysms that hostile Nature could wreak.

Conclusion
GLOBAL WAR AND THE MEANING OF THE WEST

World War I marked the point at which the West ceased to be in the ascendant over the other civilizations of the world. Its political influence had peaked and its cultural confidence was shattered—it seemed a "botched civilization," as Pound had written. Over the next three generations, though pressed by economic collapse (Chapter 27), the loss of empire (Chapter 29), the hell of totalitarianism (Chapter 28), and the joint terrors of genocide and the atomic bomb (Chapters 28, 30), the West would nevertheless endure.

REVIEW QUESTIONS

1. Why was there no general war in Europe in 1815–1914? How did the limited wars of the nineteenth century affect attitudes toward war? Why had two rival alliance systems been formed in Europe by 1914?

2. What role did rivalries outside Europe play in raising tensions among the Great Powers in the decades before World War I? What role did Pan-Slavism play in the road to war? Why did Austria declare war on Serbia in July 1914?

3. Why was there so much support for war in 1914? How did European leaders envisage the war? How did the war affect women in European society?

4. Why did the Schlieffen plan fail? Why could neither side win a quick victory on the Western Front? How did modern technology affect war? Why were the Germans more successful in the east than in the west?

5. Why did the United States enter the war? Why were the Bolsheviks able to get control of Russia? What territories did Russia lose?

6. How did the ideals expressed in Wilson's 14 Points compare to the terms of the Treaty of Versailles? Why was the Versailles Treaty not a lasting foundation for peace in Europe? What were the major political and territorial changes that the war brought about in Europe, the Near East, and Asia?

SUGGESTED RESOURCES

Pathways to War

Berghahn, V. R., *Germany and the Approach of War in 1914*, 2nd ed. (New York: St. Martin's Press, 1993). Written from a German point of view, a useful balance to more Anglocentric war studies.

Joll, James, *The Origins of the First World War*, 2nd ed. (London–New York: Longman, 1992). Argues that alliances and decisions made long before 1914 drove Europe almost irresistably to the brink, reducing freedom of action in the final, fateful days before hostilities began.

Langdon, John W., *July 1914: The Long Debate, 1918–1990* (New York: St. Martin's Press, 1991) Discusses six key questions concerning the outbreak of World War I, including the culpability of Germany, Serbian complicity in the assassination of Archduke Franz Ferdinand, and British diplomacy on the eve of war.

Stevenson, David, *Armaments and the Coming of War: Europe 1904–1914* (Oxford: Clarendon Press of Oxford University Press, 1996). Explores the military technologies of each of the major European powers during the late 19th and early 20th centuries.

In the Midst of Battle

Gilbert, Martin, *The First World War: A Complete History* (New York: H. Holt, 1994). Scholarly and detailed account of the war.

Grayzel, Susan R., *Women's Identities at War: Gender, Motherhood, and Politics in Britain and France during the First World War* (Chapel Hill: University of North Carolina Press, 1999). While men were combatants, women during wartime were mothers.

Keegan, John, *The First World War* (New York: Alfred A. Knopf, 1999). Masterful account of the failure of diplomacy that led to the War, and the horrors that followed thereupon, marking the end of an era and the beginning of the modern age.

Winter, Jay, *Sites of Memory, Sites of Mourning: The Great War in European Cultural History* (Cambridge: Cambridge University Press, 1995). The trauma of the war lingered long after the peace treaties were signed, marked by the cemeteries and monuments that sprang up as "sites of mourning" over the face of Europe.

Woollacott, Angela, *On Her Their Lives Depend: Munitions Workers in the Great War*, (Berkeley: University of California Press, 1994). Explores the lives, conditions, and consequences of women's work in munitions factories in Britain during the war.

The Russian Revolution

Clements, Barbara Evans, *Bolshevik Women* (Cambridge: Cambridge University Press, 1997). Studies of the women who made the Russian Revolution, from the pre-revolutionary generation of agitators to the death of the last female Bolshevik in the post-Stalinist era.

Fitzpatrick, Sheila, *The Russian Revolution*, 2nd ed. (Oxford: Oxford University Press, 1994). Assesses the revolutionary achievement from 1917 to the early 1930s, challenging notions of the Bolsheviks as merely totalitarian dictators.

Pipes, Richard, *The Russian Revolution* (New York: Knopf, 1990). Exhaustive and controversial account of the Revolution by one of its most outstanding and outspoken recent critics.

Read, Christopher, *From Tsar to Soviets: the Russian People and their Revolution, 1917–1921* (Oxford: Oxford University Press, 1996). A complex investigation of the revolution that recognizes both the propulsion given to events by a people detained too long by the tsarist authoracy, and a Bolshevik leadership intent on supreme power.

Service, Robert, *Lenin: A Biography* (Cambridge, MA: Harvard University Press, 2000). Brilliant and comprehensive post-Cold War biography that seeks to fathom Lenin's personality, formed in a vibrant home and fueled by immense ideas, while it does not excuse him from the decisions he made that led to oppression and devastation.

World War I: Trenches on the Web, a complete on-line resource for World War I (images, maps, sources, resources, bibliography, links): **http://www.worldwar1.com**

The Russian Revolution, on-line guide to sources, e-books, narrative, links: **http://www.barnsdle.demon.co.uk/russ/rusrev.hmtl**

Wilson on the Web, guide to resources, on Woodrow Wilson—speeches, bibliography, links (geocities): **http://www.geocities.com/Athens/2391**

In Search of Peace

Kolata, Gina, *Flu: The Story of the Great Influenza Pandemic of 1918 and the Search for the Virus that Caused It* (New York: Farrar, Straus and Giroux, 2000). As though the devastations of the 1914–1918 period were not sufficient, while thoughts turned to peace, the flu epidemic of 1918 took 40 million lives worldwide, spreading in the wake of war.

Schwabe, Klaus, *Woodrow Wilson, Revolutionary Germany, and Peacemaking, 1918–1919: Missionary Diplomacy and the Realities of Power* (Chapel Hill, NC: University of North Carolina Press, 1985). Woodrow Wilson's role in the post-war peace process.

THE TRIUMPH OF UNCERTAINTY

1900	1910	1920	1930	1940	1950

Politics and War

World War I and the Russian Revolution, 1914–21   World War II, 1939–45

◆ Mussolini's fascists march on Rome, 1922
◆ Adolf Hitler achieves power in Germany, 1933
◆ Italy invades Ethiopia, 1935
◆ Germany rearms, 1936

Society, Economy, and Ideas

◆ Max Planck's concepts of quantum mechanics, 1900
◆ Ellen Key's *The Century of the Child*, 1900
◆ First films play in "nickleodeons," 1900s
◆ American Federation of Labor (AFL) represents nearly one-third of US skilled workers, 1901
◆ Albert Einstein's special theory of relativity, 1905
◆ National Insurance Act in Britain, 1911
◆ Marcel Proust's *Remembrance of Things Past*, 1913–27
◆ D. W. Griffith's *The Birth of a Nation*, 1915
◆ Margaret Sanger establishes birth control clinic in New York, 1916
◆ Alexandra Kollontai forms *Zhenotdel* (Women's Department) in Soviet Russia, 1919
◆ New Economic Policy (NEP) in Soviet Union, 1921–28
◆ Luigi Pirandello's *Six Characters in Search of an Author*, 1921
◆ James Joyce's *Ulysses*, 1922
◆ T. S. Eliot's "The Waste Land," 1922
◆ Hyperinflation destroys German currency's value, 1923
◆ Dawes Plan reschedules German reparations payments, 1924
◆ Sergei Eisenstein's *The Battleship Potemkin*, 1925
◆ Virginia Woolf's *Mrs Dalloway*, 1925
◆ Franz Kafka's *The Trial*, 1925

◆ Quantum theory established, 1926
◆ John Maynard Keynes' *The End of Laissez–Faire*, 1926
◆ Werner Heisenberg formulates "uncertainty principle," 1927
◆ Bertolt Brecht's *Threepenny Opera*, 1928
◆ Sergei Eisenstein's *October*, 1928
◆ Joseph Stalin launches First Five Year Plan in Soviet Union, 1928
◆ US stockmarket crash and start of Depression, 1929
◆ Hawley-Smoot Tariff, 1930
◆ Austria's Creditanstalt bank fails, 1931
◆ 13 million Americans (30% of workforce) unemployed, 1932
◆ Franklin Delano Roosevelt establishes New Deal, 1933
◆ "Popular Front" alliances of Communists and Socialists, 1935
◆ Leni Riefenstahl's *Triumph of the Will*, 1935
◆ "Popular Front" left–liberal government under Léon Blum in France, 1936
◆ Jean Renoir's *La Grande Illusion*, 1937
◆ Sergei Eisenstein's *Alexander Nevsky*, 1938
◆ Jean-Paul Sartre's *Being and Nothingness*, 1943

Beyond the West

Korean War, 1950–53

◆ Amritsar Massacre, India, 1919
◆ British Commonwealth of Nations created, 1931
◆ Japan invades China, 1937
◆ Independence and partition of India, 1947
◆ UN partitions Palestine, Israel declares independence, 1947
◆ Communist victory in China, 1949

770

CHAPTER 27

THE TRIUMPH OF UNCERTAINTY

Cultural Innovation, Social Disruption, and Economic Collapse

1915–1945

US debtor nations, 1914-25

industrial unemployment, 1931-36:

countries reaching a maximum of 15-25%

countries reaching a maximum of 26-50%

KEY TOPICS

◆ **Uncertainty in the Arts and in Thought:** The wounded generation that survives World War I amuses itself with the illusions of cinema and the subversive sounds of jazz, while it ignores as much as possible reports that the cosmos is uncertain, indeterminate, and unknowable.

◆ **Uncertain Boundaries:** New Women go to work in short skirts and with short hair; neither thinking nor acting like their mothers; the family

shrinks, losing numbers and purpose, while the state takes on the nurturant functions that family and Church had provided.

◆ **Economic Uncertainty:** The post-war economic boom crashes, bringing bankruptcy and the dole, except where dictators rule; the shamed and doubt-ridden people of the West are vulnerable to their blandishments.

The Roll of Dice In 1930, the young physicist Werner Heisenberg (1901–1976) explained his "principle of indeterminacy" to a scientific gathering that included the giant of the scientific world Albert Einstein (1879–1955), creator of the theory of relativity (see Chapter 25). Since the behavior of subatomic particles could not be precisely known, Heisenberg reasoned, it should be described in terms of statistical probability. Einstein found the notion of a merely probable universe intolerable; a moral world, he insisted, depended on a rational universe. "God," he barked, "does not roll dice."

But Heisenberg's indeterminacy more accurately describes the realities in the Western world in the years after World War I (1914–1918) than does Einstein's vision of order. To most artists and intellectuals—for whom God had long since died (see Chapter 25)—the old certainties had vanished and the future was shadowy. Gender roles and social institutions were also in flux, as women sought personal freedom and citizenship, and as the traditional family lost many of its functions to social workers and state agencies. Western economies boomed and crashed, leaving millions without the savings that had promised security in old age, and millions more without work or without food. This catastrophe struck barely ten years after the close of a war that had left an unprecedented number mutilated and dead (see Chapter 26).

In this age of unknowns, the human condition was fragile. The mood of doubt and the tendency to irrationalism that had characterized the pre-war West mounted to a chronic condition of uncertainty. During the twenty years between the conclusion of the Paris peace treaties and the declarations that opened World War II, uncertainty triumphed in the arts and in thought, in social roles and institutions, and in economic life. Its shadow was not dispelled before the century ended.

UNCERTAINTY IN THE ARTS AND IN THOUGHT

The assault on rationalism that had begun with Romanticism around 1800 peaked in the early twentieth century. Pessimism prevailed about the nature of reality, the integrity of the self, as well as the limits of language. The visual arts abandoned linear narrative and realistic representation. Scientists and philosophers, despairing of certain knowledge, found a variety of ways to describe their uncertainty or even abandoned the search for absolute truths altogether. Literature looked inward, or focused on the perils of the human condition adrift in a world that was meaningless or menacing.

Montage: the Disrupted Narrative

Building on **avant-garde** developments in the last years of the nineteenth century, the pioneering artists of the twentieth no longer sought to represent objective reality. Whatever they painted, played, performed, or screened was not intended to imitate what existed in the world, but to present a creative reinvention of that reality. This Modernist project involved the abandonment of earlier artistic norms as new orthodoxies emerged in a rapidfire procession.

Moving Pictures Of the technical innovations, none was more novel than film. Its precursor the photograph had evolved from the 1830s to capture an image of objects in front of a camera—a great man, his family, a battlefield. Fifty years later, film was invented as a sequence of photographs, each viewed very rapidly in turn as the celluloid medium—the film—was drawn before the eye of the beholder. The effect was a moving picture created from the series of separate images. The art form popularly known as "the movies," "flicks," or "films" was more formally called **cinema**, short for "cinematograph" (from the Greek words for "motion" and for "drawing"), a picture engendered by motion.

The moving picture, however, existed nowhere on the film; It existed only in the mind of the viewer, whose brain supplied the continuity between separate still images. Whereas the photograph was the quintessential form of "Realist" art, claiming to reproduce perfectly the real object, film was essentially a modern medium, representing something that conceivably might exist but in fact did not.

In the 1900s and 1910s, fascinated viewers devoured early films in shopfront theaters called "nickelodeons" (because it cost a nickel, or five cents, to view) or peered into machines called "kinetoscopes" (from the Greek words for "motion" and "view"). An alternative to the live entertainment of the music hall or theater was provided by the soundless train rides, battles, robberies, or slapstick routines that formed the staple subjects of films. Studios sprang up as entrepreneurs sought to satisfy the public's appetite for the sixteen-minute-long films (the playing time of the celluloid strip that could be stored on one reel), of which hundreds, then thousands were produced each year. Mass entertainment had been born.

A motley cohort of artists turned film into the characteristic art form of the twentieth century. They were themselves actors, directors, or producers, with prior experience in provincial repertory, music hall, and circus. These were not intellectuals, but pragmatists willing to work fast and risk everything to exploit the moving image for expression and for profit.

Among the first great cinematographers were the American D. W. Griffith (1875–1948) and the

Russian Sergei Eisenstein (1898–1948), who boldly appropriated the technology of film to create a new kind of narrative form. Griffith was a Kentucky-born sentimentalist who longed for the patrician South of the United States before the Civil War—a culture based on slavery. His most famous film, *The Birth of a Nation* (1915), a still from which is illustrated below, was an American epic exploring the soul of the nation by retelling its history. It culminates with a scene repellent to modern audiences of the Ku Klux Klan (a secret society pledged to enforce the subordination of African Americans newly released from slavery) riding out on its nightmarish mission, and defeating the quintessential enemy—the African American soldiers of a United States Army force.

To arrive at his grandiose and unfortunate vision, Griffith introduced many innovations to the business of film-making. Films extended beyond their one-reel, sixteen-minute format to several reels, and two or three hours. And the photographic sequences were edited, so that the viewer saw an assemblage of images that did not necessarily occur in the same place or in sequence—a structural change that added a further element of unreality to the unreality that was already inherent in the medium. Griffith juxtaposed scenes that were to be understood as simultaneous in real time—robbers approaching, for instance, while the inhabitants of a house dread their arrival. Drama and suspense created by these juxtapositions enhanced the experience of viewing.

Eisenstein, making films under Communist rule from 1924 until his death in 1948, was a still more sophisticated manipulator of cinematic images. Eisenstein disrupted natural sequences, extracting images as his eye and his concept required to produce specific psychological effects in the viewer. This method of composition, based on disruption or discontinuity, is called **montage** (a French word referring to the ordering of images). The director rearranges reality to create a cinematic narrative that is abstract and idea-driven.

Using juxtapositions and interpolations in a pattern whose structure was rooted in the theory of **Marxian dialectic**, Eisenstein constructed sweeping, epic retellings of revolutionary events. His *Battleship Potemkin* (1925) retells an incident of the 1905 Revolution in Russia. Without sound or artificial lighting, or trained actors in major roles, by juxtaposing images of a sailors' rebellion, a popular demonstration, and the repressive violence of a military guard, he communicates the essentials of the revolutionary message: the innocence of the masses of the people, and the evil of those who hold power over them.

The work of Griffith, Eisenstein, and other early film-makers—German, French, Italian, and Swedish as well as American and Russian—paved the way for

the mature cinema of the 1920s and 1930s (by which time it had acquired synchronous sound). Many films aimed merely to entertain: grandiose historical epics, westerns, and gangster movies. Others presented social critiques, as did the comic films of Charlie Chaplin (1889–1977). The English-born son of two circus performers, Chaplin was grounded in the high comic tradition and used the persona of the clown in many of his films (which he directed, and in which he often acted) to reveal the absurdities of modern times.

Less comic but equally profound, Jean Renoir (1894–1979), the son of the Impressionist painter Pierre-Auguste Renoir, explored the meaning of World War I in his *La Grande Illusion* ("The Great Illusion") of 1937. Not a wartime adventure story, but an analysis of the disintegration of the traditional European world during World War I, Renoir's film juxtaposes a German and a French aristocrat, and these in turn with a worker and a Jew. Although the French gentleman is the German's prisoner, both are equally the social superiors of the other two—who nevertheless represent the vigorous world of the future, and who alone will survive the reality.

Whereas some films offered a critique of contemporary society, others were created in order to to celebrate the prevailing political regime. These were

D. W. Griffith, Birth of a Nation: *Pioneer film-maker D.W. Griffith portrays in 1915 the birth of a nation with novel techniques and old hatreds. Here in the wake of the Civil War, members of the Ku Klux Klan (a racist paramilitary group active in the American south after Reconstruction and into the first decades of the twentieth century) "build" the new United States, as Griffith sees it, through terror.*

René Magritte, **The Betrayal of Images,** *1928*

Uncertainty, Now and To Come

Like the performing arts, the visual arts reflected twentieth-century currents in thought and feeling. This painting by the Surrealist painter René Magritte (above) gives expression to the uncertainties of the age. A familiar object is labeled with a description that says it is not what it is: "Ceci n'est pas une pipe" ("This is not a pipe").

More confidently, Futurist artists looked ahead to new human triumphs over nature and history. In 1914, Antonio Sant'Elia imagined the city of the future—not very distant from our own cities today, but immensely different from those of Europe on the verge of World War I, where many buildings, streets, and squares were still defined by the architectural norms of previous centuries. (above: Los Angeles County Museum of Art; below: Paride Accetti Collection, Milan).

the propaganda films of the Communists and the German National Socialists, or Nazis, who recognized the capacity of the new medium to lend grandeur and conviction to their enterprise. In the Soviet Union, Lenin had recognized the importance of film (he called it the most important art form of the century), and his successor Joseph Stalin (1879–1953; see Chapters 26, 28) enlisted it to advance the interests of the new communist state. Film-making was placed under the supervision of an office of *agitprop*—the term abbreviating words meaning "agitation," denoting the arousal of revolutionary enthusiasm, and **propaganda**, meaning the diffusion of concepts favorable to the regime. Eisenstein, who had passionately hymned the Revolution in such films as *The Battleship Potemkin* and *October* (or *Ten Days that Shook the World*) (1928), was muzzled under Stalin by the artistic policy of **Socialist Realism**. Only as World War II approached (see Chapter 28) did his originality reappear in *Alexander Nevsky* (1938). Recalling a medieval confrontation between heroic defenders of Russian Muscovy and the faceless,

heartless ranks of Germanic invaders defeated in battle on a frozen lake, the film symbolized the imminent struggle with a modern enemy.

Similarly, the Nazi German leader Adolf Hitler (1889–1945) supported the creation of those films that advanced the Nazi agenda (see Chapter 28). He commissioned Leni Riefenstahl (1902–), Germany's first major woman director, to create the documentary film *Triumph of the Will* (1935), whose chilling message of German supremacy and romanticized aggression caused it to be banned in Britain, Canada, and the United States. Using unusual camera angles to maximize the awesome impression of Nazi leaders, and to announce the capacity for disciplined violence of massed Nazi troops, Riefenstahl advanced Hitler's project to install the third, final, and eternal Reich, or empire (the first was the medieval, Holy Roman Empire; the second lasted from 1871 to 1918).

Antonio Sant'Elia, **Electric Center**

Far from Russia and Germany during these inter-war years, the film industry installed itself in Hollywood, part of Los Angeles, California, a new city where the weather was almost always good. Promiscuity and gangsterism flourished in this root-less society of instant celebrities, awash (especially during the years of Prohibition, 1920–1933, when alcohol was officially banned) in a flood of alcohol, nicotine, and drugs. Hollywood became the capital of mass communications. It would communicate to vast audiences the reconstructions of reality assembled in a montage from photographic fragments—an unreal representation of a concrete reality.

Other Visual Arts Film may have been the most important medium of the visual arts in the twentieth century, as Lenin had said; but its career paralleled that of the others. In painting and sculpture, various schools of abstract art ("abstract" in that they consid-ered themselves free from the "concreteness" of the represented object) flourished in the major artistic centers, especially Paris: Cubism, Expressionism, Surrealism, and others (see Chapter 25). Novel and original, the artistic works produced shared a more or less marked tendency to distort, segment, displace, superimpose, or otherwise violate the recognizable objects of the real environment.

In architecture, despite its "concreteness," innova-tions also abounded. Architects rejected the tradi-tional vocabulary of building—the arches, columns, and domes, the grand entrances and deco-rated windows informed by Classical, Gothic, Renaissance, and Baroque forms. Instead, they designed the buildings needed by a modern age—factories, office blocks, railroad stations—that were expressive of their function, stripped of decoration, employing conspicuously the building materials of the modern age: concrete, glass, and steel (see *Electric Center* on p. 774).

The Jazz Age Unlike painting and sculp-ture, seen only in museums, architecture reached the eyes of multitudes. Like film, it was a medium of mass communication. In the same way, while some forms of music remained esoteric in the interwar years, a new form of music—**jazz**—became truly popular. Heard in bars and restaurants, on phonographs or radios, it gave its name to the era. The Jazz Age marked a new musi-cal genre, and a new kind of audience.

The new vocabulary of jazz distinguished it from the classical repertoire, naive folk song, and music hall ditties. North American in origin but quickly appreciated in Europe, jazz was a kind of musical mon-tage derived from the experience of African Americans, based on the sounds invented during

centuries of plantation slavery. A fusion of African harmony, melody, and rhythm with Western styles, these sounds were heard in work songs and lamenta-tions, in field shouts and Christian spirituals, and later woven into the new forms of jazz—**blues**, ragtime, Dixieland, swing, bop, and successive styles.

Jazz diverged sharply from the classical tradition both in sound and culture. In contrast to the sym-phony orchestra, jazz was played by bands (playing such instruments as trumpet, trombone, and tuba, saxophone and clarinet, bass, banjo, and guitar, drums, and piano). It was improvisational: the lead performer invented and varied both melody and rhythm at will backed up by a band that sponta-neously responded to the soloist's cues. Its rhythms were therefore freer than those heard in the concert hall, and its melodies featured non-standard repeti-tions, dissonances, improvisations, and the character-istic flattened thirds and sevenths of the chord that established the tonality of sadness supplied by the experience of slavery. The blues, generally vocal, highlighted that sadness in songs about poverty, aban-donment, and despair.

Jazz came from the other side of town—from the slums, ghettos, and working-class districts alongside the railroad tracks and the docks. Most of its perform-ers were black, although white bands and orchestras adopted the style and popularized it among audiences outside the South. At first, jazz was widely denounced by respectable people as music that celebrated sex

Louis Armstrong's jazz combo: *Just as film pieced together real images into a constructed new reality, modern dance and popular music utilized bits of classical art forms to construct patterns of movement and sound expressive of a modern age. Depicted here is Louis Armstrong (seated left), leader of the Hot Five combo that flourished in the 1920s, and the figure who brought the new sound of jazz from New Orleans in the American south to affluent urban audiences.*

WHO'S WHO

Writers and Artists in an Age of Uncertainty

Luigi Pirandello (1867–1936)   Italian novelist and playwright; his *Six Characters in Search of an Author* (1921) developed the technique of "theater within the theater."

D. W. Griffith (1875–1948)   American pioneer motion-picture director; his *The Birth of a Nation* (1915) has been hailed for its innovative technique and condemned for its racist message.

Eugene O'Neill (1888–1953)   Leading American dramatist; major works include *Long Day's Journey into Night* (produced posthumously in 1956) and *The Iceman Cometh* (1946).

Charlie Chaplin (1889–1977)   British-born American actor and film director; his "lovable tramp" character earned him critical and popular acclaim; major films include *Modern Times* (1935) and *The Great Dictator* (1940).

Jean Renoir (1894–1979)   French-born film director; son of the Impressionist painter Pierre-Auguste Renoir; his films—including *Madame Bovary* (1934) and *Grand Illusion* (1937)—are known for their dramatic realism.

Bertolt Brecht (1898–1956)   German playwright and poet; author of *Threepenny Opera* (1928); pioneered the use of theater as a vehicle for leftist political criticism.

Sergei Eisenstein (1898–1948)   Russian film director and Soviet propagandist; his *Battleship Potemkin* (1925), *October* (1928), and *Alexander Nevsky* (1938) combined major historical themes with ground-breaking cinematography.

and had wild jungle rhythms. Many of its performers, and many listeners, like the Hollywood stars and starlets, led a fast life that came to characterize the era: the 1920s are often called the "jazz age." Jazz was nevertheless a sophisticated musical form—popular in every sense—created by ordinary people, and from the experience of their unique past, and addressed directly to audiences of ordinary, untrained listeners; yet it was able to rival in expressive capacity and in audience appeal the classical forms of the high musical tradition.

At the same time that jazz challenged classical sound, the new compositions of classically-trained composers, now experimenting with atonality, were rapidly disenchanting concert audiences (see Chapter 25). As the new symphonies and operas became less comprehensible even to educated listeners, these demanded to hear the works of the older classical and Romantic repertory. Requiring a familiarity with a historical musical tradition, the concert hall became increasingly remote from contemporary experience—something to be enjoyed by well-to-do consumers of a specialized cultural product. Dance suffered a similar rupture: classical ballet was remote from the experience of most people, for whom dance meant the dances performed in music hall and cabaret, or by the audience of jazz bands, who became participants in the process of expressive improvisation. In the United States, modern dance freed itself from the rituals of ballet, formulated in royal courts, to incorporate some elements of folk dance movement, and convey emotion more expressively. In Europe, ballet continued to win popular attention in Russia, opera in Italy. Elsewhere, however, the repertoire of the Jazz Age dominated, as it did in the cabarets of Europe whose song and dance, jaded successors to the lighthearted fare of turn-of-the-century music halls, mocked society and its guardians.

The jazz idiom, and its message of a world where the disinherited and irreverent reigned was dramatized in the blazingly original plays of the German author Bertolt Brecht (1898–1956). Brecht's angry Marxism, seen in his savage critique of capitalists as exploiters of the poor, shocked his audience. So did his unblinking honesty which uncovered moral failings in the oppressed as well as the oppressor, and his break with the custom of theatrical illusion. Brechtian theater used some of the devices of cinematic montage. Narrative continuities were disrupted so as to arouse emotions—outrage, disgust, hostility—in the viewer. *Die Dreigroschenoper* (*The Threepenny Opera*, 1928), based on an eighteenth-century play about London's criminal underworld, *The Beggar's Opera* (1728), combines Brecht's drama with the jazz score of composer Kurt Weill (1900–1950) to yield a theatrical achievement—midway between the century's two world wars and on the eve of global economic crisis—that is the epitome of the Modern.

In challenging conventional morality, Brecht had allies in Britain and across the Atlantic. Irish-born playwright George Bernard Shaw (1856–1950) assaulted Victorian assumptions about class, religion, and sex in his plays, while American Eugene O'Neill (1888–1953) explored in his dramas the tragic hypocrisy of family relationships. Neither Shaw nor O'Neill, however, stabbed so viciously as Brecht at the comfortable assumptions of contemporary society.

Brecht's acid cynicism was more nearly matched by the humorous but black pessimism of the Italian author Luigi Pirandello (1867–1936). Pirandello's dramas are disturbing not because, like Brecht's, they violated moral and theatrical conventions, but because they invaded the boundary between reality and illusion and left viewers confused and doubt-ridden. Perhaps no play more accurately mirrors the uncertainty of the twentieth-century Western outlook than Pirandello's *Six Characters in Search of an Author* (1921), describing that world as a vacuum whose Creator has ceased to exist. Contemporary scientists and philosophers had similar doubts about a universe without author, purpose, or compassion.

Indeterminacy: the Limits of Knowledge and Action

In the nineteenth century, the biological sciences had flourished; the early twentieth century, in contrast, was the age of new discoveries in physics. These dismantled the Newtonian cosmos, which had affirmed the rationality, consistency, and predictability of all universal actions—a paradigm that had for two hundred years governed the thinking of experts and public alike. The cosmos that took its place was changing, bent, and uncertain.

The Anxieties of Science The principle of relativity announced by Albert Einstein in 1905 (see Chapter 25) shattered Newtonian certainties. In Newton's universe, definable laws acted uniformly on objects that behaved predictably and consistently. Into this ordered world, Einstein introduced the element of uncertainty. Time and space were relative to the observer. What was true in one set of conditions was not true in another. Instead of inspiring

faith in a Creator, the new condition of the universe that Einstein introduced aroused people's anxiety.

That anxiety increased with the investigation of the **atom** by the scientists Neils Bohr (1885–1962), Max Planck (1858–1947), and Werner Heisenberg. Previously, the atom had been understood as the smallest particle, irreducible and changeless, of any substance. That notion had originated with the ancient Greek philosopher Democritus (see Chapter 4), but it rapidly disintegrated after 1895, when the discovery of X-rays and the investigation of radiation by the Curies (see Chapter 25) inaugurated a new scientific venture: the investigation of subatomic particles.

Within the atom, scientists discovered an inconceivably small universe anchored by a nucleus about which other particles whirled (the electrons); and within the nucleus, further particles (protons and neutrons). Over the next generation, they attempted to align the model of the motion of subatomic particles with that of planetary bodies in the solar system. They learned that the particles' electrical nature—they were positive (the protons), negative (the electrons), or neutral (the neutrons)—caused them to repel or attract each other and hold the system in balance. They learned that the disruption of the nucleus resulted in the release of enormous stored energy—the fundamental principle behind the atomic bomb (see Chapter 28).

Planck proposed that the energy emitted by atomic particles did not flow smoothly but jumped in discontinuous spurts, or quanta (hence "**quantum theory**"). And yet the wave theory of light, or electricity, could not be entirely abandoned for a particle theory, if all phenomena were to be explained. Scientists concluded that both wave and particle theories, though seemingly contradictory, were correct, and that the two coexisted logically though absurdly—the theory of "complementarity."

Werner Heisenberg's 1927 formulation of the awesome "principle of indeterminacy" or "uncertainty," pointed out the limits of knowledge. Heisenberg demonstrated that it was impossible to know certainly both the position and the velocity of a subatomic particle. The more precise knowledge of one attribute became, the less precise knowledge of the other was rendered. Since certainty was impossible, the investigator should describe each by a range of statistical possibility. In a universe that was indeterminate, or uncertain, the scientist could never attain more than probable knowledge. It was this surrender to a permanent condition of uncertainty that Einstein—refused to accept. One day, he preferred to hope, the rationality of the universe, and thus its moral center, would be reaffirmed.

Philosophical and Religious Responses Philosophers studied the new science. In such an uncertain universe, some decided, philosophers should restrict

---

WHO'S WHO

Scientists and Philosophers in an Age of Uncertainty

Albert Einstein (1879–1955) German-born Jewish physicist; developed special and general theories of relativity, and the notion that mass and energy are interconvertible as expressed by the equation "e = mc²."

Werner Heisenberg (1901–1970) German physicist and philosopher; his Uncertainty Principle (1927) proposes that it is impossible accurately and simultaneously to measure the position and velocity of a particle.

Bertrand Russell (1872–1970) Nobel-Prize winning English philosopher and mathematician; ardent advocate of pacifism and nuclear disarmament.

Ludwig Wittgenstein (1889–1951) Austrian-born English philosopher, his *Tractatus Logico-Philosophicus* (1922) treated the nature and limits of language.

Jean-Paul Sartre (1905–1980) French novelist and existential philosopher; argued that the essential meaninglessness of existence presented humans with an opportunity for total freedom.

The World Becomes Uncertain

Modernism, which threw off traditional social and cultural norms, had already destabilized the European cultural world when war broke out in 1914, with traumatic effects. In these passages, the physician Freud and writer Valéry speak of the effect of war: it had caused "disillusionment" according to the former, and had "cruelly wounded" the mind according to the latter. The spirit of uncertainty that prevailed in the postwar era was also expressed in the science of the age, which departed from observable or inherited truths, and in the arts, which ceased to concentrate on depicting recognizable subject matter.

French writer and thinker Paul Valéry discusses the cultural and psychological effects of World War I (1922): We are a very unfortunate generation, whose lot has been to see the moment of our passage through life coincide with the arrival of great and terrifying events, the echo of which will resound through all our lives. ... You know how greatly the general economic situation has been disturbed, and the polity of states, and the very life of the individual; you are familiar with the universal discomfort, hesitation, apprehension. *But among all these injured things is the Mind. The Mind has indeed been cruelly wounded*; its complaint is heard in the hearts of intellectual man; it passes a mournful judgment on itself. It doubts itself profoundly.
(Paul Valéry, speech, 1922; ed. M. Cowley, 1954)

Albert Einstein's Theory of Relativity described by a peer (Lincoln Barnett) (1954): It [Einstein's Theory of Relativity] explains why all observers in all systems everywhere, regardless of their state of motion, will always find that light strikes their instruments and departs from their instruments at precisely the same velocity. For as their own velocity approaches that of light, their clocks slow down, their yardsticks contract, and all their measurements are reduced to the values obtained by a relatively stationary observer. ... From this it follows that nothing can move faster than light, no matter what forces are applied.
(Lincoln Barnett, *The Universe and Dr. Einstein*, 1954)

Sigmund Freud on civilization's discontent (1930): Men are not gentle creatures who want to be loved ... ; they are, on the contrary, creatures among whose instinctual endowments is to be reckoned a powerful share of aggressiveness. As a result, their neighbour is for them not only a potential helper or sexual object, but also someone who tempts them to satisfy their aggressiveness on him, to exploit his capacity for work without compensation, to use him sexually without his consent, to seize his possessions, to humiliate him, to cause him pain, to torture and to kill him. ... Civilization has to use its utmost efforts in order to set limits to man's aggressive instincts. ... Hence, therefore, the use of methods intended to incite people into ... relationships of love, hence the restriction upon sexual life, and hence too the ideal's commandment to love one's neighbour as oneself—a commandment which is really justified by the fact that nothing else runs so strongly counter to the original nature of man. ...
(Sigmund Freud, *Civilisation and its Discontents*, 1930; ed. J. Strachey, 1961)

Werner Heisenberg explains how war inspired his scientific thought (1952): When I left school in 1920 in order to attend the University of Munich, the position of our youth as citizens was very similar to what it is today. Our defeat in the first world war [*sic*] had produced a deep mistrust of all the ideals which had been used during the war and which had lost us that war. They seemed hollow now and we wanted to find out for ourselves what was of value in this world and what was not: we did not want to rely on our parents or our teachers. Apart from many other values we re-discovered science in this process.
(Werner Heisenberg, *Philosophical Problems of Nuclear Science*, 1952; ed. F. C. Hayes, 1966)

Painter Vasily Kandinsky learns that the artist's goal should be to express feeling and not represent objects, whose very existence science has called into doubt (1913): Previously I had only known realistic art ... and suddenly for the first time I saw a *painting*. That it was a haystack [by impressionist Claude Monet] the catalogue informed me. I could not recognize it. This nonrecognition was painful to me. I considered that the painter had no right to paint indistinctly. I dully felt that the object of the painting was missing. And I noticed with astonishment and confusion that the picture not only draws you but impresses itself indelibly on your memory. ... All this was unclear to me, and I could not draw the simple conclusions of this experience. But what was entirely clear to me— was the unsuspected power of the palette, which had up to now been hidden from me. ... And unconsciously the object was discredited as an indispensable element of a painting. ...
(Vasily Kandinsky, "Reminiscences," 1913; ed. R. Herbert, 1964)

themselves to discussing only what was indisputably true and knowable—only those logical deductions that were impenetrable to criticism, only those statements that were about things that were clearly "the case." Philosophy should cease to speculate about unseen or unknowable things, which should be left purely to spiritualists, novelists, and quacks.

These assumptions characterize the school of **logical positivism**, also called logical or scientific empiricism. Derived from the work on scientific logic of the British thinkers Bertrand Russell (1872–1970) and Alfred North Whitehead (1861–1947), and the investigations into the imprecision of language presented by George E. Moore (1873–1958), it was developed immediately following World War I by a group of mathematicians and philosophers known as the Vienna School. This circle published the writings of the Austrian Ludwig Wittgenstein (1889–1951), who had been Russell's student at Cambridge. Wittgenstein's *Tractatus Logico-Philosophicus* (1921) spelled out the philosopher's duty to clarify ideas, not to theorize about the unknown. Wittgenstein's understanding of the relations between language, the mind, and reality subsequently took root in Britain (where he taught from 1929 until his death) as well as the United States, where they are loosely described as the "analytic school."

Continental theorists who found Anglo-American logical positivism unsatisfying, offered different responses to the challenge of indeterminacy. **Existentialists** argued that, though the universe was admittedly unreliable and incoherent, and even the personal self was a great mystery, the actions taken by the conscious mind in themselves created a reality that, though dangerous, was genuine. Existentialism never formed a clearly demarcated school. Only the French thinker Jean-Paul Sartre (1905–1980) explicitly identified himself as an "existentialist." He expounded his view of the non-existence of God or meaning outside the unfettered, committed, acting self in novels and plays, as well as in his principal philosophical work *Being and Nothingness* (1943).

In the world presented by scientists and philosophers, either God did not exist or, if he existed, he did not control anarchic and obscure realities. Many turned from this psychological despair once again to religion and mysticism. Some embraced **spiritualism**, attempting to contact the spirits of the dead through professional mediums and special rituals. Others rediscovered the benefits of religious faith. Among Roman Catholics, interest in the miraculous swelled, and thousands sought healing and relief at shrines such as those at Lourdes (France) and Fátima (Portugal)—the latter founded as recently as 1917. In the United States, Protestant **fundamentalism** flourished in direct response to the destructive critique that Modernism made of religious principles and of the Bible.

Although most intellectuals remained aloof from orthodox religion, important exceptions included the French philosopher, paleontologist, and Jesuit priest Pierre Teilhard de Chardin (1881–1955). His views about cosmic evolution blended scientific theories of evolution with Christian humanist and cosmological views. Also French, the Jewish-born philosopher Simone Weil (1909–1943) turned to a mystical Roman Catholic Christianity in her quest for a greater closeness between humanity and God. In Germany a series of Protestant thinkers, much influenced by existentialism, such as Dietrich Bonhoeffer (1906–1945), adhered to fundamental Christian principles while restating biblical concepts in the light of the modern critique of religious faith. The Austrian Jewish theologian Martin Buber (1878–1965), influenced by both existentialism and Hasidic pietism (see Chapter 24), described in his influential *I and Thou* (1923) the intimate relationship attainable between God and worshiper.

By the twentieth century, the official pronouncements of Europe's largest church, the Roman Catholic, had become more open to modernization than when, in 1870, Pope Pius IX (r. 1846–1878) defined the doctrine of "papal infallibility." Pius' successor Leo XIII (r. 1878–1903) encouraged both a deep spirituality and social reform. His encyclical, or pronouncement, *Rerum novarum* ("Of New Things") in 1891 spoke against revolution and socialist utopianism, but in favor of equity in worker–employer relations, and the need for a just and adequate wage. Subsequent popes continued to speak for social justice within Europe, and for the easing of poverty and the need for peace throughout the world.

Nevertheless, the Church represented moral views now widely perceived as rigid and outdated. They seemed absurd to the progressive writers who flourished in the interwar years. Works of fiction such as *Ulysses* (1922) by the Irish novelist James Joyce (1882–1941) or the seven-volume *Remembrance of Things Past* (1913–1927) by the French writer Marcel Proust (1871–1922) ruptured at once the narrative continuities and moral certainties of nineteenth-century literature. The symbolic, sometimes surreal, stories and novels of the Czech Jew Franz Kafka (1883–1924) centered on threatened, anxiety-ridden individuals who reveal the terrifying truths behind bourgeois appearances. The hero of Kafka's *The Trial* (1925) experiences the annihilation of his identity when, faced with a tribunal governed by no discernible rules, he is accused of a crime he cannot remember committing.

While Kafka pointed to the menace implied in the modern world, the American-born expatriate poet T. S. Eliot (1888–1965) saw modernity as not so much menacing as empty, a meaningless vacuum, sliding toward destruction. His poem "The Hollow Men" (1925) sums up the feelings of a generation, shortly after World War I:

> *This is the way the world ends*
> *This is the way the world ends*
> *This is the way the world ends*
> *Not with a bang but a whimper.*

Here Eliot doubts not merely the prospect of human survival but more, its significance. In the great uncertainty of the age, the harshest uncertainty was this: whether human life had any value at all.

UNCERTAIN BOUNDARIES: THE NEW WOMEN, THE SHRINKING FAMILY, THE NURTURANT STATE

Just as intellectual pessimism and artistic sabotage assailed old truths and disrupted old forms, familiar notions of the role of women, the function of the family, and the mission of the state dissolved in the face of new social realities. Over the next generation, a "new woman" emerged. Economically independent, sexually liberated, she was in appearance and behavior everything her mother was not. The dismantling of the traditional family that had begun with industrialization (see Chapter 23) proceeded apace as the family's social, economic, and cultural functions dwindled. At the same time, the state assumed duties of nurturing and protection that had once been provided (if at all) by the family or religious institutions.

The New Woman

During World War I, women quite suddenly acquired unprecedented freedom along with exceptional responsibilities (see Chapter 26). Their fathers, sons, and brothers were at war, and the conflict generated an insatiable need for guns, bullets, uniforms, and bandages. To supply these, and to sustain the civilians in whose name the slaughter was undertaken, factories must produce overtime, buses run, schools and hospitals function, foodstuffs reach shops and pantries. With millions of men called away from their work to fight, millions of women poured into the workforce. Their successful performance of essential tasks brought them welcome prestige, wages, and aspirations for a new future.

At war's end, men returned to the factories and women, for the most part, to their homes. Governments and employers pushed women out of their wartime occupations. The jobs were needed for the returning men. Married women were deemed to be dependents of their husbands, whose labors earned a "family wage." Resuming the traditional roles forgotten for the duration of the emergency, they nurtured the children whose numbers would partly compensate for wartime fatalities.

Women in Politics   Women returned home often with ballot in hand. In appreciation of their wartime contributions, and in response to sustained pressure from the **suffragist** movement, many nations awarded women the right to vote (see the chart below).

From one point of view, the granting of female suffrage marked the culmination of women's long-expressed aspirations. From another, it was an insufficient response to the intractable problem of women's unequal condition, rooted in their enduring experience of subordination to patriarchal families and societies. The first view was that of most bourgeois feminists, whose outlook was shaped by the prevailing liberalism of the governing classes (see Chapter 25). Liberal theorists had argued for women's right to be "active" citizens, a status marked by the right to vote. Bourgeois women had embraced that goal. By 1900, bourgeois feminism had narrowed almost entirely to the suffragist agenda.

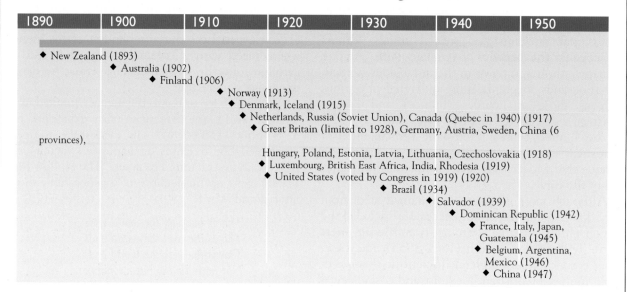

The Extension of the Franchise to Women through 1947

1890	1900	1910	1920	1930	1940	1950

◆ New Zealand (1893)
◆ Australia (1902)
◆ Finland (1906)
◆ Norway (1913)
◆ Denmark, Iceland (1915)
◆ Netherlands, Russia (Soviet Union), Canada (Quebec in 1940) (1917)
◆ Great Britain (limited to 1928), Germany, Austria, Sweden, China (6 provinces),
Hungary, Poland, Estonia, Latvia, Lithuania, Czechoslovakia (1918)
◆ Luxembourg, British East Africa, India, Rhodesia (1919)
◆ United States (voted by Congress in 1919) (1920)
◆ Brazil (1934)
◆ Salvador (1939)
◆ Dominican Republic (1942)
◆ France, Italy, Japan, Guatemala (1945)
◆ Belgium, Argentina, Mexico (1946)
◆ China (1947)

Many nations recognized the crucial role that women played in the economy of World War I by extending the franchise to women during the conflict or at least shortly thereafter. New Zealand, Australia, Finland, and Norway had already done so before the war. Others did so only at the end of World War II.

Many women of the laboring classes, in contrast, had aligned themselves with socialism and the social democratic parties that attracted large worker memberships during the late 1800s (see Chapters 22, 25). The socialist agenda for women was generally more ambitious than the liberal. It often included the right to divorce, to maternal custody of children, to property and contract, and to sexual freedom. In many social democratic parties, women met separately, created their own hierarchies, and had a significant role in the creation of policy. For socialist women, the granting of the right to vote in a political system they found inadequate offered little when compared to the elevation of the female condition.

German socialism was especially friendly to women's issues. Its early theoretician August Bebel (1840–1913) had written *Woman and Socialism* (1883), calling for women's civil, economic, and sexual rights, and dismissing as nonsense the notion that women were by nature limited to the tasks of childrearing and housekeeping. Later Karl Kautsky (1854–1938) predicted that by working alongside of men, women would gain equality with them: "[Woman] will be [man's] free companion, emancipated not only from the servitude of the house, but also from that of capitalism." On the eve of World War I, Clara Zetkin (1857–1933) criticized the suffragist movement as short-sighted, and called on women to fight for full economic and social freedom from both men and capitalism at once.

Russian socialism (which merged with the Bolshevik movement after 1917), was more militant than its counterparts (see Chapter 28). Women were prominent in the socialist parties active before World War I, as organizers, propagandists, agitators, and even assassins. Most notably, Alexandra Kollontai (1872–1952), an aristocratic Bolshevik advocate of free love, encouraged the factory women of St. Petersburg to embrace simultaneous feminist and socialist missions. An extract from her writings is given in *Witnesses* on p. 782. Some revolutionaries opposed Kollontai's approach, which they felt distracted everyone from the essential point, the class struggle. Kollontai survived the 1917 Revolution, however, to become a key figure in the new Communist government, whose leader Lenin (see Chapters 26, 28) detested women's subordination within the family and considered household drudgery to be "barbarously unproductive, petty, nerve-wracking, stultifying and crushing." As a leader of the Communist Party's Zhenotdel, or Women's Department (in existence 1919–1930), she was able to define feminist goals— female literacy and education, economic equality, freedom from housework and childcare, and sexual freedom—as part of that body's agenda.

The Bachelorette Few women, however, were socialist activists of the caliber of Zetkin or Kollontai.

The spur to more substantial change in women's lives came neither from socialism nor liberalism, but from the cultural explosions of the Jazz Age. Women's behavior—at least that of a vanguard of young, risk-taking women—reframed the issue of women's rights and women's place.

A New Woman emerged in the post-war years. She was a pleasure-seeking androgyne—a *"garçonne"* as the type was popularized in a daring 1922 French best-seller of that name, a "girl-boy" or "bachelorette." Her lean contours—a contrast to the bustled, corseted figure of her mother's generation—declared that her first function was not reproduction. She cut, or "bobbed," her hair, and applied lipstick, eyeshadow, rouge, and nail polish (previously regarded as the adornments of prostitutes). She wore slim skirts whose hemlines rose a shocking ten inches above her ankles, revealing more of the female body than had been seen (at least in fashionable dress) since antiquity. She was sexually liberated, and could use the devices and procedures made available by the medical profession to limit birth through **contraception** or **abortion**. Pressured by advertising and the advice of columnists in women's magazines, she might smoke cigarettes, drink cocktails, dance to the new sound of the jazz band, live alone or with a lover, have her own bank account, drive cars, and fly airplanes.

While the more expensive new recreations were restricted to rich young women, the attitudes of the New Woman were also adopted by working women. Such women might work in a shop, an office, or a profession. Certain professions enrolled large numbers of women, perhaps because of women's continued interest in gender-related matters. Teaching, nursing, and the new profession of social work were especially recognized as women's callings, where women could perform at the professional level the kinds of work seen as appropriate for women who, in the family framework, taught the young and cared for the sick and elderly. "She who cared only for her own flesh and blood," enthused the American economic theorist and feminist Charlotte Perkins Gilman (1860–1935), "is now active in all wide good works around the world."

The new field of social work emerged only after World War I in response to urban poverty in working-class and immigrant communities. Social workers aimed to assist individuals and families to improve their prospects by adapting to their communities and availing themselves of neighborhood resources. In the past, assistance of this sort had been provided by large family networks, or by religious institutions with long traditions of subventions to children, the poor, the elderly, the abandoned, the chronically ill, and socially-marginalized women—prostitutes, out-of-wedlock mothers, and widows. But family networks had often broken down among the urban poor and immigrant communities, and religious institutions

Rethinking Women's Roles and Possibilities

During the early twentieth century, feminist authors and activists conceived of deep reversals in the understanding of women's roles. Here, Charlotte Perkins Gilman posits the need for women's economic independence; Alexandra Kollontai announces the liberation of women from the anxieties of household management and childrearing; and Emma Goldman calls for women's freedom of choice in love, celebrating free love itself.

Charlotte Perkins Gilman criticizes women's economic dependence on men (1898): [M]en produce and distribute wealth; and women receive it at their hands. As men hunt, fish, keep cattle or raise corn, so do women eat game, fish, beef, or corn. … The economic status of the human race in any nation, at any time, is governed mainly by the activities of the male. … Although not producers of wealth, women [do, however] serve in the final processes of preparation and distribution. [Thus] their labor in the household has a genuine economic value. … The labor of women in the house, certainly, enables men to produce more wealth than they otherwise could; and in this way women are economic factors in society. But so are horses. The labor of horses enables men to produce more wealth than they otherwise could. The horse is an economic factor in society. But the horse is not economically independent, nor is the woman. …
(Charlotte Perkins Gilman, *Women and Economics*, 1898; ed. M. Schneir, 1972)

The end of women's work and the traditional family? Alexandra Kollontai describes life and work under Soviet communism (c. 1920): The individual household is dying. It is giving way … to collective housekeeping. Instead of the working woman cleaning her flat, the communist society can arrange for men and women whose job is to go round in the morning cleaning rooms. … Instead of the working woman having to struggle with the cooking … communist society will organise public restaurants and communal kitchens. … The working woman will not have to slave over the washtub any longer, or ruin her eyes darning her stockings and mending her linen. …

[T]he workers' state will [even] come to replace the family; society will gradually take upon itself all the tasks that before the [Bolshevik] revolution fell to the individual parents. … We already have homes for very small babies, creches, kindergartens, children's colonies and homes, hospitals and health resorts for sick children, restaurants, free lunches at school and free distribution of text books, warm clothing and shoes to school children. All this goes to show that the responsibility for the child is passing from the family to the collective. …
(From A. Holt ed., *Selected Writings of Alexandra Kollontai*, 1977)

Russian anarchist and United States immigrant Emma Goldman celebrates free love and free women (1910): Free love? As if love is anything but free! … Yes, love is free; it can dwell in no other atmosphere. In freedom it gives itself unreservedly, abundantly, completely. … Love needs no protection; it is its own protection. So long as love begets life no child is deserted, or hungry, or famished for the want of affection. I know this to be true. I know women who became mothers in freedom by the men they loved. Few children in wedlock enjoy the care, the protection, the devotion free motherhood is capable of bestowing. …
(Emma Goldman, "Marriage and Love," 1910; ed. M. Schneir, 1972)

had lost prestige and were insufficiently funded. Their place was taken by social workers.

Especially privileged and talented women sought careers as physicians, studying at those few European universities that from the 1890s opened their medical programs to women (or, in the United States, at the Women's Medical College of Philadelphia, established in 1851; the first medical program in the world available to female candidates). Women physicians inclined to those specializations which, like teaching and nursing, were extensions of activities traditional for females—pediatrics, gynecology, and obstetrics.

Although many working women of the post-war years pursued careers in teaching, nursing, medicine, and social work, most were office-workers, telephone operators, or shop-clerks. (Together with many male workers, they constituted the white-collar labor force, in contrast to blue-collar industrial workers.) Of these, many were young single women, who would cease work upon marriage and take up family responsibilities. But increasingly, they were married women who worked to supplement their family's income, or single women who chose not to marry (this group formed an increasingly large category).

Charlotte Perkins Gilman, editor of the journal *Forerunner* and author of *Women and Economics* (1898), quoted in *Witnesses* above, encouraged the trend for mature women to seek lifelong careers. Only financial independence, she argued, could give women genuine independence and dignity. Women who demonstrated their intellectual capacity and effectiveness in the workplace refuted the notions of nineteenth-century theorists (Darwin foremost among them; see Chapter 25) who held that women were biologically inferior to men. Men had reached a more advanced evolutionary stage, Darwin contended, than had women, children, or the pre-state peoples of the globe whom he termed "savages" (one instance of the linking of presuppositions about race or ethnicity with those about gender). Like proto-feminist thinkers from the Renaissance forward, Gilman rejoined that men and women shared a common, human nature. Women could as well as men, she argued, acquire the necessary expertise to work in the business and professional world.

Optional Motherhood In order to do so, women might need to shed the burdens of housework, and postpone (or abjure) motherhood, or limit the number of births. Modern medicine made birth-control options available to women as never before in history: the use of the diaphragm that permitted safe, effective birth control without any requirement of abstinence; and safe surgical abortion by trained experts in antiseptic conditions. These breakthroughs provided release from the cycle of childbirth and lactation that had previously determined the lives of most women. They are, some experts suggest, the preconditions of women's liberation.

Some methods of birth control had been known for centuries (*coitus interruptus*, or male withdrawal before ejaculation, is described in the Bible and was regularly used throughout the European Middle Ages). But modern birth-control procedures had a short history. Underground information circulated during the 1800s about condoms, douches, and diaphragms. In 1882, Aletta Jacobs (1854–1929) established the first modern birth control clinic in Amsterdam. Over the next generation, Dutch clinics trained socialist and sexual radical advocates from Britain and the United States. One of these, Margaret Sanger (1879–1966) founded a clinic in Brooklyn,

New York in 1916—so that every woman might "control her own body"—and was imprisoned for thirty days for doing so. At first socialist in outlook (she urged working women not to propagate children who would slave in capitalist factories and die in capitalist wars), she broadened her message after World War I to invite all women to the sexual freedom that existed with the availability of birth control.

The birth control movement also flourished in Britain and northern Europe (though not in the Roman Catholic countries to the south). In 1921, a clinic was established in London by Marie Stopes (1880–1958), author of two widely-read books that advocated planned births. These pioneering establishments operated in a hostile environment, where religious stricture and national law condemned or forbade the distribution of birth-control information and devices. Sweden was an exception: here, from the 1930s, the state both permitted and subsidized the use of birth control.

The availability of birth control marks a watershed in the history of women's quest for equality and autonomy. The ability to control their bodies had the potential to free women more profoundly than the acquisition of civil or political rights. So momentous a social change aroused objections from different quarters. Many religious leaders protested contraception on moral grounds. The Roman Catholic Church forbade it, holding that the creation of new life fell under God's authority, and not that of the woman who might bear the child. Many political leaders, mostly male, also opposed birth limitation. They adhered to a traditional model of the family in which women remained subordinate members, with special responsibility for childrearing and housework.

Abortion aroused even greater alarm than contraception. It was condemned by most religious groups (the Roman Catholic Church forbade it under any circumstances in 1869), and was

The Great Procession: *On the home front, liberation meant women's ability to control her reproduction. On the political front, it meant suffrage—the right to vote. In the Great Procession on June 18, 1910, members and supporters of the Women's Social and Political Union organized by British feminist Emmeline Pankhurst march for women's suffrage. Note that the women still wear the long skirts that had been the fashion for centuries but which would soon rise during World War I, a costume change marking a radical shift in the public role of women.*

generally illegal. Nevertheless, women desiring abortions could generally obtain them. Poor women often fell victim to untrained or unscrupulous practitioners, who cheated them, seriously injured, or even killed them. Wealthy, well-informed women, in contrast, could achieve perfectly safe abortions clandestinely in properly-equipped clinics or hospitals.

However restricted, the capacity women acquired to control their reproductive lives enfranchised them as powerfully as did the right to vote. This capacity has enabled modern women to act as full and equal citizens of their nations and their world.

The Shrinking Family and the Nurturant State

The liberation of women was one of several circumstances that has led to the diminished importance of the parent-headed household in modern Western societies. The twentieth-century family has been a shrinking family—shrinking in size, shrinking in functions, shrinking in prestige, and shrinking in its capacity to socialize its children. As the family unit became less influential, the state was summoned to nurture its citizens and provide physical and emotional support to unprotected individuals or families in crisis.

New Patterns of Family Life   The average western European family had been shrinking since the nineteenth century. The utilization on a large scale of some method of birth control meant lower fertility. As improvements in nutrition and medicine enhanced survival rates for infants and children, families deliberately limited the number of children born. Parents were therefore less burdened by dependents who required care and expense. Family limitation seemed to be in the interests of both children and parents.

Among the elites, smaller families meant that children became the objects of intense concern. Their health, schooling, and well-being preoccupied parents, who lavished wealth on vacations, tutors, and amusements. Those privileged youngsters, in turn, could expect to inherit a larger share of family wealth than had their predecessors. Among the poor, smaller families meant a greater chance at survival. Scarce resources insufficient to nurture five or six children might adequately feed two, and permit better-nourished parents to withstand disease and live longer. Poor women eagerly sought the services of birth-control professionals, when these became available, not so much for the selfish indulgence in unregulated sexuality (as critics charged), but so as to protect children already born from the competition of those not yet conceived.

In Soviet Russia, women were promised that they did not need to forego marriage or pleasure or children; the state would feed, nurture, and school their offspring. The early radicalism of the Bolshevik

outlook of the 1920s on sex quickly waned, however, partly because the resources to set up the new forms of housing were simply not available. The promise of elaborate social support for women was in any case lost after 1930 when, under Stalin (see Chapter 28), the Women's Department was abolished, marriage laws were stiffened, abortion outlawed, and women told both to work and to clean, shop, and care for their children, somehow, at home.

Although the Soviet state urged its young families to reproduce, most European societies experienced the opposite phenomenon. The decline in birthrates continued, as the chart below shows. By 1900 in France, they had fallen nearly fifty percent since 1810. From highs of about thirty-five births annually per thousand population in France and Britain in the early 1800s, birthrates slipped below twenty by the interwar period. As women tended to marry earlier and have fewer children, they found they were still in the prime of life when they no longer had major responsibilities for the welfare of their families. These trends freed women to take on other tasks.

Families were also shrinking in the range of functions they performed, and in the prestige that they enjoyed. In the twentieth century, the functions performed by a family were very different from those of the noble clans that had organized social relations in ancient Greece and Rome and during the European

Declining Birthrates in France and Britain, 1801–1951

During the nineteenth and into the mid-twentieth century, birthrates declined in the most affluent Western nations. The main reason for this was that as mortality declined and the demand for consumer and cultural goods increased, families adopted strategies for the preservation of household resources.
Source: B. Mitchell, European Historical Statistics, 1750–1970 (Columbia University Press, 1975).

Middle Ages. These families had waged war, apprehended and punished criminals, settled disputes, and appeased gods or saints. In the modern age, families (or their male heads) no longer took responsibility for war, justice, and religion, but had delegated these to national armies, to legal professionals, and to the clergy. There was little left for families to do. Their remaining functions were primarily social (they participated in community affairs) and cultural (they transmitted values and knowledge to their children).

The diminution of family functions meant that the performance of those that remained was the focus for heightened attention. Concerns with the feeding and rearing of children became obsessive. Manuals compiled by "experts" told mothers what to do, implicitly doubting whether mother would be able to measure up to the task. The ability of the family to perform its cultural mission was disrupted, moreover, by the emergence of the youth peer group as a culturally influential section of society. While families tried to instill traditional values, young people looked to each other for standards of behavior that would define them as a group apart. Popular music, reshaped now by jazz, especially marked the world of the youth peer group, which distanced the family further from the social formation of its children.

Changes in the way families functioned meant that many families lost control over their children, or might be unable to feed and nurture an obstinate or rebellious child. The economic failures of the 1930s exacerbated these tendencies. Fathers might not be able to provide sustenance for their young, who in turn left the family home to fend for themselves.

The readjustment of such families, if they were poor, became the business of social workers. They attempted to teach, counsel, comfort, and heal the wounds caused by poverty, delinquency, and dysfunction. In her mission to the poor immigrants of Chicago, as an instance, the American Jane Addams (1860–1935) established Hull House in 1889, the prototype of the "settlement house," a community center that served as the site for the distribution of middle-class largesse. Providing classes in English and gymnastics, and opportunities for socialization as well as social services, it was an enormous success, drawing more than 1000 participants each week. By the 1920s, privately and publicly funded social work endeavors of this sort had outpaced those of religious organizations in attending to the needs of poor and troubled families.

As Western families diminished in size and in functions, many looked back nostalgically to the imagined warmth of traditional families. But many celebrated the freedom that could be enjoyed as the power waned of the father and head of household to dominate his wife and children. Those who hailed this new freedom were unconcerned when national states began to assume some of the functions the family had relinquished.

New Roles for the State The growth of the nurturant, or "motherly" state—a state committed to the care of its citizens and not merely to their defense or moral discipline—was a phenomenon that marked the twentieth-century West. Earlier political theorists had proposed that the state might restrain the sinfulness of its members; or that it might act without regard to good and evil as a purely secular and autonomous entity; or that it must not intrude upon its citizens' private lives (see Chapter 15). In the nineteenth century, there developed the notion that the state was responsible for the welfare of every one of its citizens, and especially the weakest among them: the very young and very old, the disabled and the impoverished.

The modern state began to intervene in family life with the social welfare legislation of the late nineteenth century (see Chapter 22). In the 1880s in Germany, the chancellor Otto von Bismarck instituted programs that protected workers against loss of income due to disability, unemployment, or old age. Britain and France followed in the early 1900s. The experience of World War I stimulated further legislation in favor of the poor, of workers, and of families. So many millions had fought and suffered. The state, it was felt, must ease their financial pain and, however feebly, attempt to remedy their personal losses.

To this period may be traced the beginnings in the Western democracies of the modern **welfare state**. In addition to providing social insurance plans protecting workers against unemployment, disability, and old age, the state taxed its citizens—who were willing to bear the cost—to provide maternity leave, food subsidies, childcare centers and kindergartens, counseling, job training, and medical services, variously according to the customs and expectations of each society. The working-class population (lured away by such mechanisms from the bait of revolution) came to look to the state for support in the moments of crisis that had once been alleviated only by family or the Church.

Some theorists, while supporting state intervention in family life, resisted the trend toward a diminished maternal role in the socialization of children. The books of the Swedish writer Ellen Key (1849–1926) entitled *The Century of the Child* (1900) and *The Renaissance of Motherhood* (1914), both widely translated, elevated the role of the biological mother in childrearing at the same time that they called for the state to provide financial support for families and welfare guarantees for mothers without partners.

Proponents of **natalism**, especially in the fascist nations of Italy, Spain, and Germany, also stressed the mother's role and her need for state support. Their objectives were more complex than Key's. They sought to reaffirm the subordination of women within the family while encouraging the rapid birthing of new citizens (and new soldiers) for societies devastated by war fatalities. Birth control and abortion were accordingly banned. "The use of contraceptives means a violation of nature," announced German leader Adolf Hitler, "a degradation of womanhood, motherhood, and love."

In fascist societies, support of mothers was not part of a broader intervention in support of women, but was narrowly directed to bolstering the state's own aims. The Western nations under liberal or socialist governments also celebrated motherhood, awarding medals to mothers of multiple legitimate offspring and placing Mother's Day on the annual calendar. In these societies, support for mothers was balanced by support for other categories of the needy, including those who were outside of marital families.

For a variety of reasons, most Western nations took on nurturant functions in the decades after World War I. The reinvention of the state as the family of last resort was confirmed in the 1930s, at the nadir of worldwide economic catastrophe. How it did so will be observed in due course. First, it must be shown how that catastrophe came to be.

ECONOMIC UNCERTAINTY: FROM PROSPERITY TO THE BREADLINE

In the 1920s, the economies of Western nations and their allies, colonies, and trading partners around the globe struggled to recover from the dual trauma of world war and the Communist revolution (see Chapters 26, 28). Within a few years, prosperity, it

seemed, had returned. That prosperity was illusory. The nations of the West and the world followed the United States into a tenacious depression triggered by unrestrained speculation and a stock market crash. Efforts to tame the Great Depression failed until, ten years later, as another war began, military production defeated the monster of depression and put an end to the era of economic uncertainty.

Happy Days

After the war and the revolution, the shocked, grieving, and hungry peoples of the Western world longed to return to normalcy. The United States led them all as it rapidly recovered from a wartime economy and attained unprecedented prosperity. These were happy days for a young nation that had recently taken the lead in economic production and political affairs.

Boomtime in the United States   By the outbreak of World War I, the United States was world leader in industrial production and foreign trade. In the ten years following the Versailles settlement, United States production spurted forward. Its exports supplied half the manufactures produced in the world, as well as seventy percent of the oil and forty percent of the coal.

One of the secrets of that great productivity was the efficiency of American factories and their workforce. The assembly line, developed by entrepreneur Henry Ford (1863–1947) to speed up the manufacture of his automobiles, maximized the productivity of

Map 27.1 European Debts to the United States, 1914–1925—War Loans and Loans for Relief and Reconstruction: *Europe's economic landscape was transformed by four years of war. Victors in battle, the Allied nations found themselves hugely in debt to the United States for war loans and other assistance. Of these nations, only Finland ever paid its debt in full. The Soviets repudiated their war debt, refusing to acknowledge their tsarist obligations. Other nations had their debts canceled by the United States, or simply neglected to pay them. The vectors of capital transfer between Europe and North America are clear evidence of Europe's surrender of global economic leadership to the United States in the twentieth century.*

industrial labor. So too did the methods of industrial organization advocated by Frederick Winslow Taylor (1856–1915). Closely observing workers' behavior in his famous time–motion studies, he showed how reorganization of space, tools, and procedures could lead to greater productivity.

The workers who accepted these regimens were organized in trade unions, which crystallized into two main groups representing skilled and unskilled workers respectively. The former of these, the American Federation of Labor (AFL), at its origin in 1886 a gathering of twenty-five unions of skilled laborers, had grown by 1901 to represent nearly one-third of all skilled workers. The latter, the Congress of Industrial Organizations, emerged only in 1935 in opposition to the AFL's exclusionary policies.

Labor unions resisted employers who demanded too much work, for too little pay, under unsafe conditions. A series of strikes and riots, violently suppressed, marked the formative years of the American labor movement: the Great Railroad Strike of 1877; the Haymarket Square Riot (between labor unionists and police) of 1886; the 1892 steelworkers' strike against the mill in Homestead, Pennsylvania; the 1894 strike of railroad Pullman workers. A new series of strikes erupted in the 1930s. By that era, the unions had retreated from militant demonstration and even political activity, and elevated "bread-and-butter" issues—salaries and benefits. The trade unionists pressed for a minimum wage, and restricted child labor. The number of laboring children aged from ten to fifteen dropped by 1930 to a third of its 1910 high, before it was at last made illegal in 1938.

United States trade unions avoided socialism. Some workers were intrigued by international socialism and supported the presidential ambitions of Eugene V. Debs (1855–1926), but most did not support the Bolshevik takeover in Russia in 1917. American workers remained within established political frameworks, voting for Democratic and Republican presidents, as did their employers.

As in Europe, many wage-earners were not industrial workers. Agricultural workers, mostly non-unionized, were already suffering from an agricultural depression which had set in during the 1920s. White collar workers—salesmen and women, managers, clerks, and secretaries, as well as professionals such as accountants and engineers, teachers and professors, nurses, lawyers, and physicians, often better paid than industrial workers—were generally not unionized.

In the prosperous 1920s, American consumers purchased the goods produced by American factories—phonographs, telephones, vacuum cleaners, sewing machines, and, especially, automobiles. Spending for consumption, for leisure, for the home, they fueled a rapidly growing economy (see *Witnesses*, p. 790).

The companies producing these goods were traded on the stock market, or required investment loans.

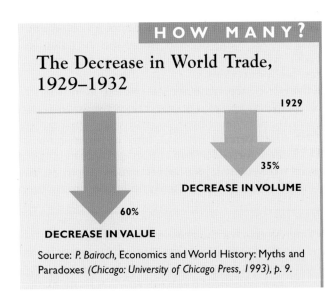

HOW MANY?

The Decrease in World Trade, 1929–1932

1929

35%
DECREASE IN VOLUME

60%
DECREASE IN VALUE

Source: P. Bairoch, *Economics and World History: Myths and Paradoxes (Chicago: University of Chicago Press, 1993), p. 9.*

These needs were handled by the brokers and bankers, many of them based in Wall Street, New York City, the home of the world's busiest exchanges.

The stock exchanges were closely linked with American banks, which purchased stocks, and made loans to domestic and foreign companies and governments. American bankers had by now displaced the British as the main players in an international money system. It was largely American money that had financed World War I, sending about $10 billion to some twenty nations. As those loans were repaid, others were issued. Gold flooded into the United States as a result of debt repayment, reaching unprecedented levels.

In 1900, the international currency system was anchored by the British pound sterling, itself tied to a gold standard—pounds were literally as good as gold. After World War I, the American dollar, also linked to gold, displaced the pound as the principal international currency. The gold standard supported the global trading system by ensuring convertibility among currencies. It was, however, inflexible. The supply of currency was limited to the value of gold the nation possessed. The government could not print more money to stimulate the economy. Without sufficient money to purchase goods and services, production could drop, and deflation follow.

As the world's greatest manufacturer and banker, the United States was central to the global trading system. So long as goods and money flowed smoothly out from the United States and back again, that commercial system was healthy. If the behavior of American investors or producers changed, the system was jeopardized. During the 1920s, trade barriers and the distractions of the stock market began to interfere with international commercial rhythms.

Many historians fault American foreign trade policy during the 1920s. It encouraged the export of manufactures and agricultural produce, and insisted that markets abroad should be kept open for all comers. But stiff tariffs limited imports of products that might compete with American merchandise. From its origins, the United States had inclined toward protectionism (while Britain in contrast adhered to free trade for the period from 1846 to World War I). Duties on the value of most imported manufactures amounted to thirty-five percent in 1816, forty percent by 1832, forty to fifty percent in 1875, and forty-four percent in 1913. These tariff walls were erected, proponents argued, to protect the "infant industries" of a newly industrializing nation and, later, to protect the wages of American workers from foreign competition. Employing the same logic, Congress enacted the Hawley-Smoot Tariff in 1930—raising the tariff rate on imports to the unprecedented high of about forty-eight percent. Foreign producers could not sell their goods in an American market which had made them artificially expensive; without those sales, they were unable to repay their debts to American bankers.

The investment mania that swept over Wall Street in the late 1920s further disrupted the free flow of global trade. Money that might otherwise have been sent abroad poured into American stocks and funds. From 1928 to 1929, the amount of capital sent abroad dropped sharply—loans to Germany, for instance, shrank from $277 to $29.5 million. Quick, dramatic returns appealed more to investors than the slow growth of distant enterprises. The richest people in the United States, the most powerful nation in the world, knew happy days were with them and did not consider that what went up fast might descend catastrophically.

Post-war Europe   As Americans rejoiced in their prosperity, Europe inched forward. Rebuilding commenced, and standards of living improved. By 1925, for the first time the production of food and raw materials surpassed their 1913 high.

Britain and France were strained by the need to assume the costs of new social programs. War debts burdened them. Productivity lagged. To protect manufactures, both nations imposed tariffs. In doing so, Britain broke with the free trade tradition in place since 1846. In the hope of bolstering British currency, in addition, the government returned in 1925 to the gold standard abandoned during the war (as did some forty nations in all); then repudiated it finally in 1931.

Both British and French governments also faced well-organized demands for higher wages and benefits from industrial workers. In Britain, the election of 1924 led to a Labour government (whose constituents were mostly union members) with Liberal support. Nevertheless, conservative interests continued to direct the economy. In 1931, a "National Government" (a coalition of Labour, Liberal, and Conservative ministers) took over, but failed to exercise effective leadership.

In France, socialist and communist parties competed, failing to capture a majority. Following the 1934 turnabout in policy announced by the Comintern (the Soviet organization monitoring extra-Soviet communist parties), communists, socialists, and other groups joined in a Popular Front against the menace of Fascism (see Chapter 28). In 1936, a left-liberal government was elected with a strong fifty-seven percent of the vote. One of the Popular Front governments linking left and central political parties, it was led by the Jewish socialist Léon Blum (1872–1950), who attempted to steer a course between the agendas of Left and Right. Although it liberalized the workplace, and established annual vacations and a forty-hour workweek, the Popular Front could not reverse an economic downturn, as productivity slipped and investment lagged.

Lackluster economic performance was the pattern in western Europe, as in France and Britain. Communist parties were springing up, branching off from social democratic parties, as communists and socialists competed for the loyalty of trade unionists.

In central Europe, the defeated nations of World War I faced disheartening economic problems. Germany, above all, was saddled with the burden of reparations—calculated so as to recompense the victor nations for the total expense of the war. These were not amounts that a demoralized and starving nation was willing to pay. To do so would have required a double sacrifice: a voluntary decrease in consumption of goods, and an increase in taxes. That two-pronged strategy was unacceptable. Instead, Germany defaulted through 1922. The next year French and Belgian forces occupied the coalfields of the buffer Ruhr region, intending to seize the value of the debt in the form of coal. Only the intervention of the United States and Britain in 1924 prevented a meltdown to violence (as the local population resisted) and chaos. By the terms of the Dawes Plan, a more acceptable payment plan was established. The United States would make loans to Germany according to a complex schedule, enabling Germany in turn to repay the French.

In the end, Germany never paid the reparations owed. Yet the reparations crisis had wreaked terrible damage upon the German economy. To raise funds to pay the Ruhr laborers while they resisted French occupation, the German government printed paper currency at will, shown in *Windows On*, p. 789. By November 15, 1923, the Deutschmark had fallen to twelve-billionths of its 1922 (July) value (from 493.2 to 4,200,000,000,000 marks per dollar). Viewed differently, it fell to a flabbergasting one-trillionth of its value of 4.2 marks per dollar in 1914 (July). This single fact bespeaks an economic trauma whose effects on the history of Germany and the world would be played out tragically over the next twenty-two years (see Chapter 28).

Highs and Lows

Issuing of the "Rentenmark," November 15, 1923

Wall Street, October 1929

A first surge of prosperity following World War I preceded a decade of economic turmoil. Above, German officials are ready to dispose of chests of bills which have lost much of their value in an era of devastating inflation. The hyperinflation that struck Germany in the early 1920s was a premonition of the depression and deflation that struck worldwide after the crash of the New York stock market in 1929. On the eve of that crash, the Wall Street brokers in the image shown here (right) happily read the news on slender lengths of ticker tape of their ever-mounting profits. Those highs would soon give way to cataclysmic lows, and the worst depression of the modern era. Depression followed the stock market crash, bringing unemployment to millions of workers around the globe. Ten years later, the Depression still lingered. Hunger and unemployment threatened to trigger outbreaks of social unrest. Below, a watercolor painting shows hunger marchers in 1932 being dispersed by London police.

Hunger marchers in London, 1932.

To continue your investigation of this topic, please go to www.prenhall.com/king for the related **WINDOWS** on the **WEB** activity

Living Through the Great Depression

Americans were unprepared for the Great Depression. Here, President Calvin Coolidge, only months before the Depression began, expresses confidence in American wealth. Over the next years, ordinary people without jobs or cash suffered hunger and humiliation, like the author of the second excerpt, and the young African American later known as Malcolm X, author of the third.

United States president Calvin Coolidge speaks to Congress on the state of the American economy on the eve of the Crash and Great Depression (1928): No Congress of the United States ever assembled, on surveying the state of the Union, has met with a more pleasing prospect than that which appears at the present time. ... The great wealth created by our enterprise and industry, and saved by our economy, has had the widest distribution among our own people, and has gone out in a steady stream to serve the charity and the business of the world. ... The country can regard the present with satisfaction and anticipate the future with optimism.
(President Calvin Coolidge, Message to Congress, December 4, 1928; ed. E. Hobsbawm, 1996)

The American economy—the general condition of the unemployed multitudes (1932): You are a carpenter. Your last cent is gone. They have cut off the gas. ... You can't get a job now for love or money. What do you do? ... [Y]ou go to the cop. He pulls out his directory and sends you to one of the listed charitable societies. ... You draw the Episcopal Family Relief Society. The Relief Society clears your name through the central agency to see that you are not receiving help elsewhere. ... Eventually it will allot you $2 to $8 a week, depending on the locality and the funds available. If its funds are exhausted it asks you to wait.
(From *Fortune* magazine, September 1932; ed. J. A. Garraty, 1986)

African American leader Malcolm X recalls the Depression's effects on poor blacks in Michigan (1934): By 1934, we really began to suffer. This was about the worst depression year, and no one we knew had enough to eat or live on. Some old family friends visited us now and then. At first they brought food. Though it was charity, my mother took it. ... In Lansing, there was a bakery where, for a nickel, a couple of us children would buy a tall flour sack of day-old bread and cookies, and then walk the two miles back out into the country to our house. ... But there were times when there wasn't even a nickel and we would be so hungry we were dizzy. My mother would boil a big pot of dandelion greens and we would eat that.
(From J. A. Garraty ed., *The Great Depression*, 1986)

With cheap—indeed worthless—marks, the government paid the Ruhr workers. But in 1923 devaluation caused hyperinflation that terrified the German people. The sturdy, prudent middle class found that their lifesavings had been made worthless by unbridled inflation. Those on fixed incomes became paupers, while workers had to be paid several times per day with bills of rapidly declining worth—and to carry their wages home in a suitcase or wheelbarrow.

Those scarred by hyperinflation would not forget the crisis. Yet Germany revived later in the decade, and the young entrepreneurs and managers who benefited most from that boom reveled in a new, though limited, prosperity.

To stimulate production in the Soviet Union, in 1921 the Communist leader Lenin, loosened briefly the economic controls imposed after 1917 (see Chapter 28). Under Lenin's New Economic Policy (NEP), retail trade and light industry were returned to private ownership and peasants were allowed to cultivate their own land. By 1929, with Lenin dead (in 1924) and Stalin in power, that policy was reversed. A series of Five-Year Plans set production goals for state-controlled industry that boosted the Soviet Union to the forefront of the developed nations.

The Scandinavian nations of Denmark, Finland, Norway, and Sweden found a "middle way" between the imposition of state controls in the Soviet Union and the free-market principles of the western European nations. Here the government promised benefits to every citizen from cradle to grave, paying for them with heavy taxation. Some major industries were nationalized, but many others were permitted to flourish in free-market competition. Economic experimentation yielded both industrial growth and improved living conditions. The Scandinavian system posed an alternative to the hectic buying and selling and uncertainty of outcomes that characterized the United States economy at this period.

In 1929, on the far side of the Atlantic, speculation in stocks, the spawning of holding companies, and the multiplication of unsecured loans marked an economy that might, at any point, go haywire. Speculation soared in the period from 1923 to 1929, years that saw the quadrupling of the volume of shares traded. Investors believed the market would never go down. They borrowed in order to buy, the only collateral being the value of the shares purchased. Such an unprecedented "bull market" led to catastrophe as stocks became desperately overvalued, and finance capital outstripped the capacity of consumers to buy. On October 24, 1929, "Black Thursday," disaster struck. That day, on which nearly 13 million shares were sold, and losses mounted to 3 billion dollars, marks the beginning of the Great Crash. Another plunge came five days later. Stock prices plummeted from an index of 216 to 145 by the end of November, and over the next three years pursued an unsteady descent to bottom out at 34—from $87 billion at their peak to $18 billion at their low. The financial giants of Wall Street trembled, shocked by their own losses and uncertain about what was to come. What came was a broadening of economic crisis into every corner of the United States, Europe, and the world.

On the Dole

The collapse in stock values in October 1929 set off a chain of events culminating in a profound, stubborn depression—the Great Depression. Banks had been involved in the speculative excess of 1928–1929. Pressed by their losses, they called in the monumental loans they had issued to fund the investment frenzy. Their debtors could not pay. Banks fell, pre-cipitating the failure of thousands of others, and cheating depositors of their savings. Those deposits were uninsured (insurance of small bank deposits was instituted only in 1933). Lifesavings were lost. Public confidence plummeted.

The banking crisis combined with larger economic trends to create monumental hardship. Production fell twenty percent from 1929 to 1930; by 1932, it stood at one-half its 1929 level. Wages fell, and work-ers were laid off. The passage in *Witnesses* on p. 790 describes their plight. The number of unemployed rose to more than 13 million by 1932—almost thirty percent of the workforce in the United States. Since workers were also consumers, spending slowed, espe-cially on big-ticket items whose high rate of sales was an index of prosperity—housing and automobiles. Even necessities were expensive, and consumers bought on credit, accumulating unmanageable debt.

The emergency deepened. Warehouses packed full with merchandise canceled their factory orders.

Map 27.2 Maximum Unemployment Rates for Industrial Workers, 1930–1938: *The Great Depression hit different regions at different times and with varying intensity. Shown here are the year and approximate rate of maximum unemployment during the period 1930–1938 for fourteen nations. The Soviet Union, in the midst of its Five Year Plans, remained wholly insulated from the unemployment that the Great Depression brought other nations. Japan, engaged in industrial expansion, suffered less than most. The maxima for Germany and the United States exceeded all others. The great disruption unemployment caused in these nations was expressed in divergent social and political responses: for Germany, the rise of Fascism (see Chapter 28), and for the United States, the launching of the New Deal.*

The Shame of Need, the Dignity of Work

New York during the Depression: *Unemployment forced millions of men and women into a poverty and degradation symbolized by, above all, the breadline. Scenes such as this one in New York were repeated in cities and towns around the world.*

The unemployed could not pay their rent. Homeless, they moved out into the streets, building shanties for their families of scrap lumber and debris. Shanty towns grew up outside the cities which a few years earlier had beckoned to newcomers with the promise of work and good fortune. Called "Hoovervilles" after Herbert Hoover, president from 1929–1933 when the Depression settled on the nation, they were visible monuments to the plight of the dispossessed.

The central symbol of the Depression, however, was not the shanty town. It was the breadline, or the "dole," the food handout that signaled the degradation suffered by the millions. Relief organizations opened soup kitchens and distributed food. Every day, lines of hungry adults and children reached outside and snaked around corners, as the hopeless and dishonored waited to eat from the giving hands of strangers. A breadline in New York is depicted above.

Effects in Europe   The stock market crash rocketed around the globe. American investment overseas dropped drastically from 1929 to 1933, then virtually ceased for the rest of the decade. While the flow of dollars abroad dried up, American bankers called in their loans from foreign borrowers (mostly European). The flow of gold and coin to the United States swelled, while European stores were depleted, and they still groaned under

the burden of war debt. At a conference in Lausanne, Switzerland, in 1932, an attempt was made to unloose the knot of debt obligations. France agreed to end reparations with a final transfer from Germany—which Germany never made. France defaulted, in turn, on its debt to the United States, which continued to insist, even as the demand paralyzed European economies, that all war debts be honored.

European banks failed if they could not respond to American calls for funds. In 1931, the Austrian giant Creditanstalt, drained by withdrawals of foreign funds, closed its doors. That move set off financial panic in Europe as depositors rushed to their banks to withdraw their endangered funds. In Britain, they withdrew gold, depleting the supply. Humiliated, Britain was forced finally to repudiate the gold standard that had anchored the pound. Now the pound inflated heavily, losing twenty-eight percent of its value in 1931.

Britain and her trading partners (including members of the newly-founded Commonwealth of Nations) fled gold, but the United States maintained the gold standard (aside from a brief interlude, and

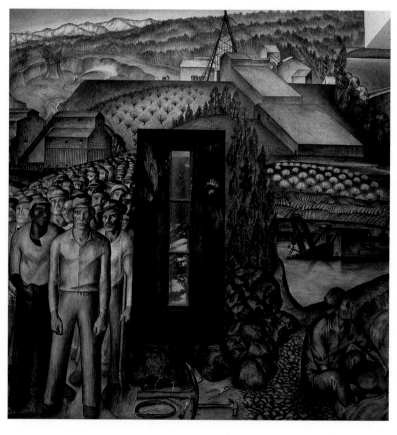

John Langley Howard, **California Industrial Scenes:** *The workers' faces painted in their honor by Paul Langley Howard in a mural series from around 1934 show great ethnic and racial variety but a single mood of determination, that is tinged by sadness.* (Coit Tower, San Francisco)

subsequent devaluation of the dollar), along with France, Belgium, the Netherlands, and Switzerland. These nations formed a separate trading bloc, distinct from the British. In addition to these two, a third bloc developed in central Europe, led by Germany. The barriers between these three isolated, exclusionary trading blocs were bolstered by high tariffs, installed to discourage foreign imports and protect domestic manufactures. The free and integrated trading network of the West in its boom years had vanished.

The remedies adopted for economic crisis only yielded more crisis. Currency inflation, economists reasoned, might help. With a cheaper currency, prices would decline and people could buy more goods. Protective tariffs would force them to purchase domestic manufactures, and sustain employment. These were illusions. Instead, trade declined, and production and employment levels fell, as Map 27.2 on p. 791 shows. At the depths of the Depression in the early 1930s, unemployment in the developed nations may have reached as high as 30 million—around one-fourth to one-fifth of the workforce, and in Germany as much as two-fifths (about 6 million workers)—with many others forced into part-time work.

The effects of stock market collapse, bank failure, production slowdown, and mass unemployment were felt around the globe. Many of the colonized nations of Asia, Africa, and Latin America were primary producers of agricultural commodities. Their fortunes had soared during World War I, when Europe needed their products. After the war, Europeans relied less on the importation of primary products from these markets. As the market became glutted with certain commodities, agricultural prices fell worldwide. The producers of wheat, sugar, rice, coffee, and other staples could not rapidly adjust to a changed marketplace. (India, an exception, took advantage of Britain's crisis to develop its own steel and textile industries.) The laborers deprived of the profits on their goods could not purchase the exports of the industrialized nations. Agricultural surplus and weakened sales exacerbated the international depression, as world trade sank by 1933 to nearly one-third of its 1929 level (see *How Many?* on p. 787).

The Soviet Union and Germany The Great Depression never came to the Soviet Union. It struck Germany hard, but was defeated. Between 1929 and 1938, these two nations ruled by totalitarian governments (see Chapter 28) had annual growth rates per capita of 4.3 percent and 4.2 percent respectively—the highest in the Western world, or indeed anywhere in the world except Japan (where the figure was 5 percent). By the 1930s, the Soviet Union had experienced a brief return to capitalism under Lenin's NEP (New Economic Plan) and was suffering the forcible creation of a fully industrialized and fully socialized economy under the terms of Stalin's First Five Year

Plan (see Chapter 28). Workers and peasants labored to meet Stalin's high quotas for agricultural and industrial production. While agricultural output remained weak, industry boomed, constantly fed by massive capital reinvestment allocated by the central government. Although the Soviet people suffered grievously from Stalin's policies, they were isolated from the depression that gripped western Europe.

Similarly, Germany benefited from the policies of the Nazi leader Adolf Hitler. Of the Western nations, Germany was hardest hit by depression. It had suffered a staggering unemployment rate and a catastrophic thirty-nine percent drop in production. That misery was Hitler's opportunity; he seized power in 1933 and brought the Depression to an end. His Four Year Plan launched in 1936 (financed by deficit spending on the **Keynesian** model also adopted in the United States by Roosevelt) aimed at economic self-sufficiency and a rapid increase in industrial production—especially military production. Commercial agreements made with Poland, Hungary, and Romania in central and eastern Europe assured Germany a supply of agricultural products and raw materials for industrial use. Meanwhile, German industrial scientists developed synthetic substitutes for exotic resources (cotton, wool, rubber) to bypass the need for foreign imports. The total control that Hitler exercised over economic life allowed him to mobilize people, commodities, and money to enhance industrial growth and assure military readiness.

Searching for Remedies Elsewhere the Depression persisted. People looked to their governments to take some action. Governments remained committed to deflation and steep tariffs. Workers defeated by hardship lined up for the dole.

In the United States, the election of Franklin Delano Roosevelt as president (1933–1945), brought fresh hope and the **New Deal**, which brought some relief and new aspirations. With an expression of compassion that had not been heard in American political life since perhaps Abraham Lincoln, Roosevelt defined the cause of the economic emergency, named the guilty parties, and announced the cure in his inaugural address as president. The cause was greed; the guilty parties were the rich speculators; and the cure was the largesse to be provided by the government for the "one-third of the nation" that was, as Roosevelt put it in his second inaugural address, "ill-housed, ill-clad, ill-nourished."

The first task was to organize cash relief. The Federal Emergency Relief Administration, created in 1933, handed out millions of dollars to states and agencies to help relieve hunger and homelessness. Two years later, the Social Security Act established for the first time in the United States the principle that those who could not work—children, the elderly, the disabled—should receive state benefits. It created a new social contract between government and people, superseding the system of private charity and self-help that had prevailed in the past.

In addition to these first steps toward establishing a modern welfare state—a state that assumes the obligation to sustain its citizens from cradle to grave—the New Deal set up programs to put the unemployed to work in public works projects and to sustain artists and writers by assigning them historical and cultural projects with a government salary. As a further measure to protect workers' interests, the New Deal created the National Labor Relations Act in 1935 that supervised unions and protected their right to engage in collective bargaining. To prevent future economic catastrophes, it passed legislation in 1933 and 1934 that insured bank deposits and supervised the stock exchanges.

All of these programs were expensive. Indeed, the New Deal sought to accomplish its goals by going into debt, with the government borrowing to support its programs. That tactic represented an abandonment of conventional views of government spending that dictated a balanced budget, especially during crisis periods. Instead, the New Deal embraced the novel economic theories of the British economist John Maynard Keynes (1883–1946), author of the 1926 work *The End of Laissez-Faire*. Keynes urged the state to engage in "counter-cyclical" activity: when times were hard, it should spend; when prosperity returned, it should raise taxes to enhance revenues and conserve wealth. The free market could not be relied upon to reequilibrate economic systems, which required the deliberate intervention of state spending stimuli and restraints. Keynes's theory seemed to offer a compromise position between capitalism, with its program of unrestrained profit-seeking, and socialism, with its tendency to deaden individual initiative. The New Deal set out to spend its way to recovery,

HOW MANY?

Rise and Fall of Annual Growth Rate in the United States, Japan, and the Soviet Union Before and After 1929

Legend:
- 1925–1929
- 1929–1938

Y-axis: ANNUAL GROWTH RATE IN PER CAPITA GNP

US: +2.3, −1.3
Japan: +1.1, +5.0
Soviet Union: +6.0, +4.3

The Great Depression played havoc with national rates of production and world trade (see Box on p. 820). Here the hard-hit United States suffers a steep decline in its annual growth rate, while the Soviet Union, turning from its NEP (New Economic Policy) developed under Lenin to the Five Year Plans developed under Stalin, suffers a more modest loss. Japan, arming itself for expansion in its Asian hinterland, experiences rapid growth.
Source: P. Bairoch, Economics and World History: Myths and Paradoxes *(Chicago: University of Chicago Press, 1993), p. 8.*

imbuing American liberalism with a new, pro-government ethos. As promised in Roosevelt's campaign song, "happy days" would come again, brought about by a newly activist state.

Conclusion
UNCERTAIN LIVES AND THE MEANING OF THE WEST

Roosevelt's Depression remedies may have alleviated some of the pain caused by economic collapse. But they did not reverse the economic trend. In 1938, unemployment was nearly as high as at the low point of Depression. World trade had stagnated, restricted by narrowly nationalistic economic policies. Only renewed military production was sufficient to stimulate the economy. By 1939, as European leaders rearmed their nations in preparation for another war, the factories hummed again, producing bullets, guns, and profits. The people of the Western world were able to go off the dole only because they were once again sent off to the front.

The economic volatility of the postwar years, and especially the Great Depression, had brought not only hardship but also anxiety to the people of the West and of the world. The era of the Modern had arrived—and then it crashed. Who, if anyone, was at fault? What, if anything, could be done? When would normalcy return? Amid the uncertainties born of economic crisis, many looked for strong leaders, who gave clear and positive answers, and promised that certainty would rise from despair. Those leaders came, promising the certainty that only totalitarian regimes can give a demoralized and disoriented populace; but with them came tragedy.

REVIEW QUESTIONS

1. How did the outlook of Western artists and intellectuals change after World War I? Why did Heisenberg's indeterminacy theory describe this outlook better than Einstein's theory of order? Why did the art of the 1920s and 1930s abandon the attempt to depict objective reality?

2. To what extent can cinema be called "the first form of mass entertainment"? How did the Soviet Union and Nazi Germany use the cinema to advance their political aims?

3. What made jazz and the works of dramatists like Bertolt Brecht "modern"? What was Existentialism?

4. How did World War I affect the position of women in Western societies? How did birth control help to liberate women? Why did bourgeois and working-class women have different political and social goals?

5. What services did the welfare state offer to its citizens after World War I? How did increased state intervention affect the attitude toward families and motherhood in the Fascist nations?

6. To what extent was Europe able to return to normalcy in the 1920s? Why did the stock market crash in 1929 cause the Great Depression? How did the European countries and the United States cope with the Depression?

SUGGESTED RESOURCES

Uncertainty in the Arts and in Thought

Bradbury, Malcolm and James MacFarlane, eds., *Modernism, 1890–1930*, 2nd ed. (New York: Penguin, 1991). Essays on Modernism in literature, art, poetry, drama, with its national variations.

Brian, Denis, *Einstein: A Life* (New York: J. Wiley, 1996). Comprehensive and up-to-date biography of this monumental figure.

Gamow, George, *Thirty Years That Shook Physics: The Story of Quantum Theory* (Garden City, NY: Doubleday Anchor, 1966). Accessible introduction to quantum physics.

Golan, Romy, *Modernity and Nostalgia: Art and Politics in France between the Wars* (New Haven: Yale University Press, 1995). Argues that French Modernism, from World War I to Vichy was permeated with nostalgic and traditionalist longings deriving from the trauma of the war.

Jelavich, Peter, *Berlin Cabaret* (Cambrdige, MA: Harvard University Press, 1993). Jelavich sees *cabaret* as a reshaping of older, popular forms of entertainment by artistic elites searching for new ways to express the nature of life in this key "modern" city.

Sklar, Robert, *Film: An International History of the Medium* (New York: Prentice Hall–H. N. Abrams, 1993). Surveys the development of cinema from its earliest days to the recent past, with an emphasis on the interaction of cinema, society, and technology.

Existentialism—links to essays and websites on existentialism: **http://www.knowdeep.org/existentialism**

Uncertain Boundaries: The New Women, the Shrinking Family, the Nurturant State

Chauncey, George, *Gay New York: Gender, Urban Culture and the Making of the Gay Male World, 1890–1940* (1994). Explores the creation of a gay culture in New York in the late-19th and early-20th century.

Gillis, John R., Louise Tilly, and David Levine, eds., *The European Experience of Declining Fertility: A Quiet Revolution, 1850–1970* (1992). Key collection of essays seeking to explain Europe's falling birth rates during the later nineteenth and twentieth century. Emphasizes cultural over socioeconomic factors, and local and national distinctions over pan-European trends.

Lee, W. Robert and Eve Rosenhaft, eds., *The State and Social Change in Germany, 1880–1980* (Oxford: Berg, 1990). Collection of essays exploring the roles of state and society in creating and developing the first modern welfare system.

Pedersen, Susan, *Family, Dependence, and the Origins of the Welfare State: 1914–1945* (Cambridge: Cambridge University Press, 1993). Comparative study of the movements pushing for family allowances in France and Britain during the first half of the 20th century.

Skocpol, Theda, *Protecting Soldiers and Mothers: The Political Origins of Social Policy in the United States* (Cambridge, MA: Belknap Press of Harvard University Press, 1992). Finds that the United States, although its "welfare state" was started later than European peers, nevertheless created many pioneering social support programs, especially maternalist ones, pressured by a multiplicity of vibrant interest groups.

Stites, Richard, *The Women's Liberation Movement in Russia: Feminism, Nihilism and Bolshevism, 1860–1930*, 2nd ed. (Princeton, NJ: Princeton University Press, 1991). Examines the historical development of the "woman question" in Russia during the 19th and early 20th centuries.

Women's Studies Database: History (University of Maryland): **http:// www.inform.umd.edu/EdRes/Topic/WomensStudies/Reading Room/History**

Economic Uncertainties

Brendon, Piers, *The Dark Valley: A Panorama of the 1930s* (New York: Knopf, 2000). Panoramic look at the lives of people and states in the United States, Europe, Russia, and Japan involved in the economic and political crises of the second interwar decade.

Eichengreen, Barry, *Golden Fetters: The Gold Standard and the Great Depression, 1919–1939* (Oxford: Oxford University Press, 1992). Focuses on policy decisions regarding the gold standard as key to the onset and nature of the Depression.

Kanigel, Robert, *The One Best Way: Frederick Winslow Taylor and the Enigma of Efficiency* (New York: Viking, 1997). Taylor pioneered time and motion studies and their application to work, helping create the 20th-century workplace.

Weber, Eugen, *The Hollow Years: France in the 1930s* (New York: W. W. Norton, 1994). Informative study of Depression-era France treating in detail the arts, culture, and ordinary life.

America from the Great Depression to World War II: 1935–1945, prints and photographs (American Memory, Library of Congress): **http://memory.loc.gov/ammem/fsowhome.html**

STATES IN CONFLICT

| 1910 | 1920 | 1930 | 1940 | 1950 |

World War I and the Russian Revolution, 1914–21

New Economic Policy in Soviet Union, 1921–28

Spanish Civil War, 1936–39

World War II, 1939–45

Fascism, Communism, and Prelude to War

- Treaty of Versailles humiliates Germany, 1919
  - New Economic Policy (NEP) launched, 1921
    - Mussolini's Black Shirts "March on Rome," 1922
      - Hitler's "Beer Hall Putsch" in Munich, 1923
        - Locarno Treaty, 1925
          - Stalin's First Five Year Plan, 1928
            - Lateran Treaty between Mussolini and papacy, 1929
              - Japanese invade Manchuria, 1931
- Hitler assumes German chancellorship, Jan 1933
  - "Night of the Long Knives," 1934
  - Brutal purges terrorize Soviet society, 1934–39
    - "Popular Front" alliances of Communists and Socialists, 1935
  - Nuremburg racial laws passed in Germany, 1935
    - Rome-Berlin Axis, 1936
      - "German Art" and "Degenerate Art" exhibitions, 1937
    - Guernica bombed, 1937
    - Japan invades China, 1937
      - *Kristallnacht* pogrom in Germany, 1938
      - Germany annexes Austria, 1938
    - Munich Conference, 1938
      - Germany annexes Czechoslovakia, 1939
      - "Pact of Steel", 1939
    - Nazi-Soviet Non-Aggression Pact, 1939
      - Trotsky murdered, 1940

World War II

- Germans invade Poland, Sept 1, 1939
  - Germans enter Paris, June 14, 1940
    - Germany invades Soviet Union, June 22, 1941
    - Japanese attack Pearl Harbor, Dec 7, 1941
      - Nazi "Final Solution" begins, 1942
        - Germans surrender at Stalingrad, Jan 31, 1943
  - Allies land in Sicily, July 10, 1943
    - D-Day, June 6, 1944
      - VE Day, May 8, 1945
      - Allies push Japanese from open Pacific, May 1945
    - Potsdam Conference, 1945
    - Hiroshima and Nagasaki bombed, Aug 6, 9, 1945
    - Japan surrenders, Aug 14, 1945
    - Nuremberg Trials begin, Nov 20, 1945

Society, Economy, and Ideas

- Ludwig Wittgenstein's *Tractatus Logico-Philosophicus*, 1921
  - James Joyce's *Ulysses*, 1922
    - Sergei Eisenstein's *The Battleship Potemkin*, 1925
    - Max Eastman's *Since Lenin Died*, 1925
    - Adolf Hitler's *Mein Kampf*, 1925
      - John Maynard Keynes' *The End of Laissez-Faire*, 1926
        - Great Depression begins, 1929
- Leni Riefenstahl's *Triumph of the Will*, 1935
- Sidney and Beatrice Webb's *Soviet Communism: A New Civilisation?*, 1935
  - Sergei Eisenstein's *Alexander Nevsky*, 1938
    - Anton Ciliga's *The Russian Enigma*, 1940
    - Arthur Koestler's *Darkness at Noon*, 1940
      - Jean-Paul Sartre's *Being and Nothingness*, 1943
        - George Orwell's *Animal Farm*, 1945
          - George Orwell's *1984*, 1949

Beyond the West

Korean War, 1950–53

- Amritsar Massacre, India, 1919
- Independence and partition of India, 1947
- UN partitions Palestine; declaration of state of Israel, 1947
  - Communist victory in China, 1949

28

STATES IN CONFLICT

Communism, Fascism, Democracy, and the Crisis of World War II

1917–1945

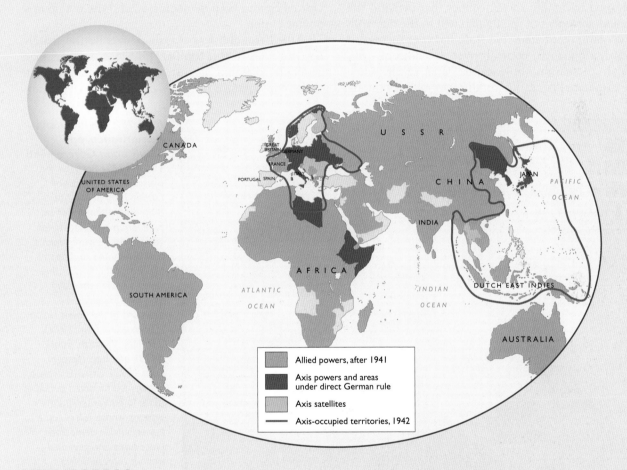

Allied powers, after 1941

Axis powers and areas under direct German rule

Axis satellites

Axis-occupied territories, 1942

KEY TOPICS

◆ **Bolsheviks and Communists:** In the Soviet Union, Lenin rewrites Marx, Stalin transforms the economy, and citizens have new access to jobs and opportunities—all at the price of autocratic rule, the censorship of the arts and thought, police surveillance, and terror.

◆ **The Faces of Fascism:** Many nations incline to fascism or quasi-fascist ideologies that combine nationalism and militarism with the cult of the

"leader" and, in German Nazism, with virulent and lethal anti-Semitism.

◆ **The Second World War:** As fascist leaders rearm and plan war, the democracies continue to seek peace, and wake up to find, by 1942, the Axis powers dominant in Europe and Asia; by 1945, victory is finally obtained in both theaters of war, but only after unprecedented slaughter and the terrible evil of "final solutions."

***T**he Omnipotent State* "*Everything within the state, nothing outside the state, nothing against the state!*" *With this summons, the Italian fascist leader Benito Mussolini (1883–1945) convinced the Italian people, in the uncertain years after World War I, to embrace the certainty that was offered by totalitarianism. The German Nazi leader Adolf Hitler (1889–1945) voiced a similar ideal: "Ein Reich, ein Volk, ein Führer!" ("one state, one people, one leader").*

These are the formulas of **totalitarianism**, a term often used to denote those regimes that demand the complete surrender of the human will to the demands of the omnipotent state. No state has ever succeeded in exercising such control over its citizens. But through persuasion, propaganda, and terror, some have attempted to do so. Totalitarian regimes (along with kindred despotisms or monarchies, often termed **authoritarian**) repudiate liberal principles of individual rights, freedom of conscience and expression, and access to political power.

As Map 28.1 shows, during the 1920s and 1930s, totalitarian governments came to power in many European nations: notably **fascism** in Italy and Germany (where it was known as Nazism); and communism in the Soviet Union (1917–1991, consisting of Russia and many of the lands of the former Russian Empire). In 1939, the aggressions of one of these states—Germany—provoked World War II. It ended in 1945 with the defeat of Nazi Germany, fascist Italy, and imperial Japan by the alliance of Britain and the United States, both democracies, and the communist Soviet Union.

Allied triumph was overshadowed by the matchless tragedies of the conflict. Of these one was mass **genocide**, directed against the Jews of Europe, the direct consequence of Nazi racial theory. The second

Map 28.1 Democratic, Authoritarian, and Totalitarian Government, 1919–1937: *Between the two great wars, most of Europe (and in Asia, Japan) drifted to authoritarian or totalitarian rule. Totalitarian governments—governments that attempted to direct all aspects of the lives of their citizens while repressing individual freedoms—prevailed in the Soviet Union (communism, from 1917), Germany (Nazism, from 1933), and Italy (fascism, from 1922). Other European nations fell for some period of years to authoritarianism—systems whose rulers came to power outside democratic procedures and governed without representative assemblies or through the manipulation of docile parliaments. Democracies survived, however, on the north and northwestern fringes of Europe and in Czechoslovakia—areas that had long parliamentary traditions, or had not suffered territorial loss as a result of World War I, or had advanced industrial bases.*

was the explosion in two Japanese cities, in August 1945, of atomic bombs, with their consequences of mass death, mutilation, and disease, and the threat of universal destruction.

This catastrophic war brought an end, however, to the interwar era of uncertainty (see Chapter 27). Certainty returned as the nature of Nazism became clear: it was an evil that could not be tolerated. Reluctantly at first but decisively at last, its opponents massed to defeat it.

BOLSHEVIKS AND COMMUNISTS

In Russia, the Bolsheviks who seized power in 1917 in the name of desperate masses (see Chapter 26) established a totalitarian state that employed modern tools of regulation, propaganda, and terror in order to compel the obedience of its peasants, workers, and intellectuals.

A generation of brilliant leaders accomplished the transformation of Russia from autocracy to the communist dictatorship called the Soviet Union (properly the USSR, the Union of Soviet Socialist Republics). Foremost among them were Vladimir Ilyich Lenin (1870–1924) and Joseph Vissarionovich Dzhugashvili (1879–1953), known as Stalin ("man of steel").

Lenin had reconstructed Marxian socialism (see Chapter 25) to suit Russian circumstances, as he perceived them. Stalin derived from Lenin a model for the forcible imposition of socialism. He also learned—from Lenin but also from Mussolini and Hitler—strategies for seizing and maintaining power. By 1939, when war once again engulfed Europe, Russian communism had reached maturity.

Lenin: Rewriting Marx

By 1917, Lenin had reconstructed the theories of Marxian socialism to suit Russian realities: a semi-industrialized country with a minuscule bourgeoisie, a nascent proletariat, and a vast peasantry. In 1917, his version of Marxism (Marxist-Leninism) became the political orthodoxy of the new communist state.

In his 1902 book *What Is To Be Done?* (see Chapter 26), Lenin announced the key points in his rewriting of Marx. An elite of trained intellectuals was necessary, he argued, to instruct and lead the proletariat. **Trade union** organizations were immature. Russian industrialization had been laggard. Many of the workers were not truly urbanized proletarians but peasants who labored for a season in the factory, then returned to the fields. They needed, Lenin believed, to be guided by a cadre of intellectuals, committed to the cause, who would serve as permanent, professional revolutionaries. Lenin's Marxism was thus modified not only by the condition of Russian workers, but also by the Russian tradition of a radical, elite intelligentsia (see Chapter 25).

MUST READS

Key Books by Key Leaders

Vladimir Ilyich Lenin	*What Is To Be Done?* (1902)
Adolf Hitler	*Mein Kampf (My Struggle)* (1925)
Winston Churchill	*The Speeches of Winston Churchill* (1941–1945)

When the revolution began in the spring of 1917 (see Chapter 26), Lenin expounded his principles in simple terms to mass audiences. At a ripe moment, the Bolsheviks acted, swiftly and almost unopposed, storming the Winter Palace and successfully ousting the provisional government. The Bolsheviks were only a faction of a faction, which in a nation of about 170 million had recruited perhaps 200,000 followers; now Bolshevism would shape the future of Russia. That nation was soon to learn that the dictatorship of the proletariat was, in the end, but another, and brutal, dictatorship.

War Communism and the New Economic Policy

It required three years of struggle to consolidate power, during which the Bolsheviks waged war against rival political factions, tsarist counterrevolutionaries, and foreign detachments. Even as Trotsky negotiated the Brest-Litovsk settlement (see Chapter 26), he built up the Red Army to safeguard the state Lenin had snatched in the October Revolution.

Establishing the Communist State   The Red Army faced a formidable task. In all directions, rival, or "White" organizations formed to oppose it. In the south, it faced troops of the general Lavr Georgyevich Kornilov (1870–1918; see Chapter 26) and his successors, joined at first by the Don Cossacks. In the Caucasus region, the Red Army needed to recover Georgia, Armenia, and Azerbaijan, which had declared their independence in 1918. In the east, they faced a conservative counter-government established at Omsk in Siberia, as well as an autonomous republic of social revolutionaries at Kuybyshev (now Samara). To the southwest, they aimed to recover Ukraine. In the north, Allied forces had occupied Murmansk and Archangel, ostensibly to protect Allied stores of war material. By 1920, the White opposition had been suppressed, rebellious nationalities brought to heel, and the foreigners dispersed. Russia was devastated. Between 10 and 30 million, mostly civilians, were dead.

Wartime atrocities, committed by both sides, were followed by the terror unleashed by the hated Cheka, a political police force organized in 1917 by the Bolshevik Felix Edmundovich Dzerzhinsky (1877–1926) to secure the new regime. The Cheka annihilated thousands of suspected enemies of the people, its persecutions mounting to 118 in the single month of February 1921. Modeled on its tsarist predecessor, the detested Okhrana, the Cheka surpassed that organization in the numbers of those executed, in the use of torture, and in the conditions of exile (now to forced labor camps) to which "politicals" (political prisoners) were subjected. The heritage of the Cheka endured in successor secret police organizations including: the GPU (State Political Administration), from 1922 (or OGPU, the word "united" added at the start, after 1923); the NKVD (People's Commissariat of Internal Affairs) from 1934; and the KGB (Committee of State Security) from 1953.

There remained the problem of disciplining not merely people, but thoughts. Censorship began promptly after the 1917 October Revolution with the closing of the "counterrevolutionary" press. By the summer of 1918, all independent dailies, weeklies, and monthlies had been suppressed. In 1920, suspect books were targeted. All but two copies each (these to be kept apart in "special reserve") of the works of ninety-four suspect authors—including Plato, Descartes, and Tolstoy—were removed from library shelves and destroyed. The instruction for this action proceeded directly from Nadezhda Krupskaya (1869–1939), member of the **commissariat** on education, and Lenin's wife and loyal companion during the years of exile.

Bolsheviks and Communists: Forging Communist Society

Two themes of early Soviet society emerged in the first years of the regime: the need to extract more wheat from the peasants to feed the industrial workers, and the need to create a modern industrial society as rapidly as possible. These imperatives are illustrated here in a 1918 speech on food procurement; in a 1931 speech of Stalin's to the managers of Soviet industry; and in a 1926 rhapsody by a loyal servant of the state about the imminent industrialization of Soviet society.

Among the other harsh measures that constituted "War Communism," a decree on food procurement orders the extraction of grain supplies from peasant proprietors (May 13, 1918): DECREE OF THE ALL-RUSSIAN CENTRAL EXECUTIVE COMMITTEE … While the consuming provinces are starving, great stocks of cereals, including the 1916 harvest and the 1917 harvest which has not yet been threshed, lie, as habitually, in the producing provinces. These stocks are in the hands of rural *kulaks* [better-off peasants] and wealthy people, in the hands of the rural bourgeoisie. … [T]his rural bourgeoisie remains deaf and unresponsive in the face of the moanings of starving workers and poor peasants; it refuses to dispatch cereals to the state station points … while at the same time it sells for its own benefit … at fabulous prices to speculators and bagmen. The obstinacy of the greedy *kulaks* and wealthy peasants must be brought to an end. … The reply to the violence of grain holders upon the rural poor must be violence upon the bourgeoisie.

Not a single *pud* [unit of weight] of grain must remain in the hands of the grain holders, except the quantity needed for sowing and subsistence of the household until the next harvest.
(From R. A. Wade, ed., *Documents of Soviet History, vol. 1: The Triumph of Bolshevism, 1917–1919,* 1995)

In a speech to the Managers of Socialist Industry, Stalin urges ceaseless efforts to industrialize for the sake of the fatherland (1931): To slacken the tempo would mean falling behind. And those who fall behind get beaten. But we do not want to be beaten. No, we refuse to be beaten! One feature of the history of old Russia was the continual beatings she suffered for falling behind, for her backwardness. She was beaten by the Mongol Khans. She was beaten by the Turkish beys. She was beaten by the Swedish feudal lords. She was beaten by the Polish and Lithuanian gentry. She was beaten by the British and French capitalists. She was beaten by the Japanese barons. All beat her— for military backwardness, for cultural backwardness, for political backwardness, for industrial backwardness, for agricultural backwardness. …

We are fifty or a hundred years behind the advanced countries. We must make good this distance in ten years. Either we do it, or they crush us.
(J. V. Stalin, speech to Managers of Socialist Industry, 1931)

Writer V. Zazubrin celebrates the coming industrialization of the Soviet Union as a necessary step in the creation of socialist society (1926): Let the fragile green breast of Siberia be dressed in the cement armor of cities, armed with the stone muzzles of factory chimneys, and girded with iron belts of railroads. Let the *taiga* [Russian forest] be burned and felled, let the steppes be trampled. Let this be, and so it will be inevitably. Only in cement and iron can the fraternal union of all peoples, the iron brotherhood of all mankind be forged.
(V. Zazubrin, speech to the 1st Congress of Siberian Writers, 1926; ed. B. Komarov, 1980)

Krupskaya also supported the campaign for the "liquidation of illiteracy" launched in 1919 for all citizens between eight and fifty. In 1917, the Russian masses were largely (fifty-seven percent) illiterate. On farms and in workplaces, adults labored to learn to read. Some progress had been made by 1926, when just over half—fifty-one percent—of Russians had attained literacy.

The need to communicate socialist theory to an uninstructed population gave impetus to film, theater, and art, which were charged to "agitate" audiences to revolutionary zeal. Krupskaya promoted the director Sergei Eisenstein (1898–1948), whose pioneering films presented historical and theoretical concepts through purely visual means (see Chapter 27). Theatrical performances celebrated heroic peasants and derided counterrevolutionaries. Posters presented bold images of ideal types—workers, peasants, soldiers—selflessly laboring for the creation of a new society.

Economic Measures To establish the socialist foundations of the new Soviet state, stern measures were also required in the economic sphere, as the passages in *Witnesses* on p. 800 show. Lenin had promised land to his peasant supporters and saw to the redistribution of landowners' property. Much farmland, however, was ravaged by the battles of the Civil War; while peasants, compelled to surrender their grain stores, had reduced their sown acreage. The consequence was a great famine in 1921, resulting in 5 million deaths. As people died in the streets where packs of starving, abandoned children roamed, the new government sought and received international aid to ameliorate the crisis.

Even as famine struck the countryside, Lenin requisitioned grain for the cities—workers would eat at the expense of the peasants. The workers, meanwhile, had been organized into self-governing soviets, which were responsible for meeting the production quotas set by a supreme council that regulated the industrial economy. They labored hard, at low wages and under unsafe conditions, compelled to forego consumer goods—housing, food, and clothing—to support maximum reinvestment in manufacturing enterprises.

People resisted the heavy economic burdens imposed by what was called "War Communism." Moscow and Petrograd shriveled, and industrial production plummeted. In 1921, Lenin adopted the more moderate approach announced in his NEP (New Economic Policy). It permitted small entrepreneurs to operate freely and peasants to acquire their own farms and livestock. This strategy encouraged a stratum of landowning peasants, called **kulaks**, and won popular support for communism at a crucial moment.

Commissars and Comintern The Communist government system also took form during these years. Immediately following the October Revolution (see Chapter 26), Bolshevik leadership had been affirmed by the National Congress of soviets then meeting in Petrograd (although only after the Mensheviks and Socialist Revolutionaries walked out). Lenin took the chairmanship of the newly constituted Council of People's Commissars, or "ministers". This new government council and the Politburo (short for political bureau) or policy committee of the Bolshevik party, soon relocated to Moscow.

In January 1918, the newly elected Constituent Assembly convened for the first time. But the Bolsheviks had not obtained a majority of its delegates, and so immediately disbanded the assembly—the last chance Russia had for a democratic, constitutional, and representative government. Instead, by the principle of "democratic centralism," the hierarchy of local and regional soviets sent recommendations upward, ultimately to the Communist central committee, which made a final decision—the "party line," binding upon all. Lenin hoped to stimulate new communist revolutions abroad, reminding his followers "that the interests of socialism, the interests of world socialism, are superior to national interests, to the interests of the state." In 1919, he launched the Third, or Communist, International, the "Comintern," which was to consist of foreign delegations under strict Soviet leadership. Its task was to subject all foreign communist parties to the discipline of Soviet communism and so to promote world revolution.

By 1920, the Comintern's "Twenty-One Conditions" for parties seeking affiliation outlined the essentials of "true" communism. The Comintern communicated to foreign communist parties the Soviet "line," or policy on international and domestic matters. From 1928, it instructed them not to compromise with liberal or socialist parties—a bold stand, since social democrats alone outnumbered foreign communist party members more than fifteen to one. In 1935, in a policy reversal, the Comintern directed otherwise. It now encouraged communists abroad to join with center and left parties in Popular Front coalitions aimed at combating fascism.

By that time, under Lenin's successor Stalin, the hope for spontaneous, world-wide communist revolution had been set aside. From 1928, Stalin had proposed a different goal for which to strive: "socialism in one country." Lenin had wished to establish world-wide socialism; instead, Stalin established a national communist state, under one-party rule, disciplined by the threat of violence, and governed by the *nomenklatura* (those who held positions, or "names"), the obedient servitors of the Politburo. Stalin then turned to transform the stubborn Russian economy according to socialist principles.

Stalin: Gravedigger of the Revolution?

To do so, he enlisted the labor and the lives of the peasants, the workers, and his own revolutionary comrades. He compelled the peasantry to work on collective farms, dispossessing the one rural class that had shown enterprise and leadership—the now vilified kulaks. He subjected industrial workers to harsh conditions dictated by rigid production quotas, while denying them consumer goods. He bullied and silenced his Bolshevik comrades, veterans of the 1917 takeover and the harsh Civil War, as well as millions of party functionaries, military officers, and citizens. Shocked by his despotism, Leon Trotsky called him the "gravedigger" of the Revolution. Perhaps; but at the same time, Stalin was, with Lenin, the builder of Soviet communism.

Stalin had always been different from the other leading Old Bolsheviks. A native of Georgia (in the Caucasus, and then part of the Russian empire) and the son of a shoemaker, Stalin became a Bolshevik in 1903. But he was not an intellectual, and did not join in the esoteric debates enjoyed before 1917 of fine points of Marxian theory.

Stalin was an effective manager who by the early 1920s had demonstrated his ability to execute instructions ruthlessly. This quality Lenin appreciated until, at the edge of death, he learned that it was accompanied by self-serving ambition. In declining health, having suffered from several strokes, and communicating only through written memoranda, Lenin dictated a "political testament" during his last weeks urging Stalin's removal from his post as general secretary of the party. But Stalin had already asserted himself. The testament was ignored, and then suppressed (it was not publicized until after Stalin's death in 1956). At his lowest moment, Trotsky was given the task of denying to Western skeptics that such a document existed. Thus he rescued a man he saw as an enemy—the "gravedigger of the Revolution."

In 1924, Lenin's embalmed body was laid to rest in a mausoleum in Red Square, Moscow's civic center, to be venerated as a deity in the public religion of communism. Now Stalin began in earnest to maneuver for power, "exposing" each of his colleagues in turn as extremists or deviationists. By 1930, he had expelled them all from the Politburo, and surrounded himself with lackeys. By 1940, every one of the six men with whom he shared power in 1924 had been killed. Trotsky, the last, was tracked by Stalin's agents to Mexico, and murdered by a Spanish NKVD agent with a mountaineer's ice pick.

As Stalin rose, debate ceased. All decisions proceeded from him, as once from the tsars. Even the information presented to him, in time, was filtered so as not to disagree with the dictator's presuppositions.

Stalin now proceeded to target new groups of supposed opponents, extremists, and "enemies of the people," who were paraded in "show trials" put on to instruct the Soviet people and the watching world. There were trials of engineers, of industrial managers, of party leaders and officials. Disoriented or impassive

after torture and threats, strangely compliant defendants confessed to crimes against the state before being sent to the labor camps or to death. In the course of trial, some of the accused went insane, committed suicide, or mysteriously died.

After the murder in 1934 of the Old Bolshevik Sergei Mironovich Kirov (1888–1934), who had spoken critically of Stalin's despotism in party meetings, the killing mounted to a frenzy. The murder was probably ordered by Stalin (who subsequently disposed of all the principals in the plot, including the assassin and his NKVD directors). But at the time, Stalin mourned Kirov's loss, and proceeded to "investigate" the murder.

Between 1934 and 1939 hundreds of inner-circle Communists were arrested, tried, and executed. Those killed included 98 of 139, or seventy percent, of Central Committee members; and 1,108, or fifty-six percent of the 1966 representatives to the 1934 XVIIth party congress held in 1934. Thousands, perhaps millions, of other public officials, artists, intellectuals, and ordinary people were also victims, (see *Witnesses* on p. 804). According to Roy Medvedev (1925–), a dissident survivor of the Soviet regime, the total arrested during 1934–1939 mounted to around 3 to 5 million, with hundreds of thousands shot. At the peak of the purge, over 200 executions were recorded per day in the Lubyanka, the NKVD central prison; "not streams, these were rivers of blood."

A purge of military officers in 1937–1938 complemented the purge of party officials. By 1939, Stalin had eliminated half of the Red Army officer corps—more than 40,000, of whom 400 were of the rank of colonel and above, including three of the five marshals, thirteen of the fifteen army commanders,

---

HOW MANY?

Stalin's Deathlist

Costs of collectivization, 1928–1933
People: about 10 million dead (the nation suffered a net loss in total population of 20 million from 1917–1934)

Livestock: 1 million head of cattle, pigs, sheep, and goats destroyed

Arrested, 1937–1938 5 million, of whom 1 million were executed

In jail, 1938 1 million

In gulags, 1935–1937: 6 million
                    1938: 7 million

Survival rate of purge-era prisoners: about 10%
Purged by 1939 of those active in 1934: Central Committee members: 98 of 139 (70%)
Representatives to the XVIIth Party Congress (1934): 1,108 of 1,966 (56%)

nine out of ten army generals, and six out of seven admirals. When the German army attacked the Soviet Union in 1941, two-thirds of its generals were novices.

Those arrested in the purges were imprisoned, tortured, sent to labor camps, or shot. Of these destinies, the labor camp or **gulag** is the special emblem of the Stalinist era (although its history begins under Lenin, with sixty-five in existence by 1922). Supervised by special government agencies, the labor-camp system went well beyond the penal regimes of the tsarist era. Prisoners worked at heavy tasks, for extraordinarily long work days under extreme conditions, especially of cold, as gulags were mostly in the Arctic. They were housed in barracks without heat or furnishings, denied adequate food (rations were deliberately withheld to present an incentive to productivity) and subjected to physical and psychological abuse. The labor of these prisoners dug canals, mined gold, and felled forests, contributing significantly if horribly to the nation's economic success.

Few survived. The camp served the combined purpose of work and extermination. Frequent shipments of fresh prisoners (criminals and politicals) restocked the labor gangs when their predecessors had died of hunger, exhaustion, or brutality. In just a few years, the special killing squads of the Nazi security force (the SS, or *Schutzsstaffel*)—these were the executioners, on the fronts or in the death camps, of Jews, Poles, and others—would show they had learned much from the Stalinist gulag.

Socialism in One Country

Among the political prisoners transported to the gulag were millions of kulaks. These small rural proprietors Stalin declared to be a peasant aristocracy that he would "liquidate as a class", as part of his program to attain "socialism in one country."

Small peasant proprietors were a relatively new social group. In the wake of the 1861 emancipation of the serfs, a handful of peasants had been able to establish themselves on small farms. With the Bolshevik confiscation of large estates in 1918, more were able to do so. The policies of War Communism bore heavily on this peasant elite, whose stores of grain were requisitioned for use by the Red Army and industrial workers. Under the NEP instituted in 1921, however, determined kulaks again increased their landholdings.

Even so, the peasant elite that existed in 1928 when Stalin launched his policy of **collectivization** was hardly a class of oppressors, as was charged. Kulaks (a term of abuse, signifying tight-fisted greed) typically owned seventy to eighty acres of land and two or three draught animals, and often hired their neighboring smaller peasants or day laborers to assist with farm tasks. Far from wealthy, kulaks more closely resembled a struggling middle class.

It was this social group that the collectivization campaign destroyed. Stalin's agents in the countryside demanded stated amounts of grain from each region. The grain was needed to feed the cities and industrial centers, where the proletariat labored to modernize a still-backward economy. The quotas were set so high that peasants were left with insufficient stores for themselves; at one point, the amount of grain requisitioned amounted to more than the total harvested.

The peasants resisted these demands. Sometimes they protested violently; sometimes they refused to grow the crops that they would not be allowed to enjoy. Inflamed, Stalin responded with a drive to remove the entire peasantry to collective farms, to be governed by soviets and supervised by official ideologues, or commissars. At the same time, he would boost grain yields (as he believed) by eliminating the kulaks who, he thought, clung to an outmoded, privatist model of rural production.

From 1928 to 1933, Communist officials confiscated kulak farms, seized grain stores, invaded cottages, and sent the occupants away homeless—if they did not shoot them or deport them to the gulag (see the photograph on p. 805 and *Witnesses* on p. 804). Millions starved to death, in their devastated villages or in the camps. Millions snatched their revenge in advance, burning their own farms and killing their livestock. In the winter of 1932–1933, this disruption of agriculture triggered famine. Peasants throughout Russia suffered through this induced scarcity which followed by only a few years the war-induced famine of 1921. The cost of collectivizing the countryside mounted to about 10 million deaths.

As Stalinist policies enforced socialism in the agricultural sphere, the industrial workforce also experienced the rigors imposed by a rapidly transforming economy. The workers, too, suffered shortages, and were harried by unrealistic production goals set by central economic planners. By their labors, nevertheless, Soviet Russia became a major world producer of steel, weapons, and machines. And a whole new elite of trained managers and engineers gained an autonomy their parents had never known.

The massive industrialization of the Soviet economy accomplished between 1928 and 1939 was guided by successive Five Year Plans. The first was approved in 1929, the second in 1933, the third in 1938, this last cut short by the outbreak of World War II. Each plan set production quotas to spur growth, especially in the heavy industries (metals, machines, and textiles). Although statistics were often falsified to give the illusion of success, the plans did lead to a dramatic expansion of Soviet infrastructure and industrial capacity.

The Five Year Plans accomplished nearly as much as they had ambitiously proposed. By 1938, the Soviet Union outdid Britain, and nearly equaled Germany, as a producer of pig-iron and steel. Agricultural production, too, eventually improved. But there had been deficits: rapid modernization required workers to endure low living standards, peasants to starve to feed the workers, and the most energetic stratum of the peasantry—the kulaks—to be sacrificed in order to achieve socialism in one country.

Socialist Realism, Soviet Realities

Social and cultural changes reshaped the lives of urbanized workers during the two interwar decades. Communism called for a transformation of the family and the repression of religion, the arts, and thought.

Communist Totalitarianism: Repression and Terror

Communism brought new opportunities to many Soviet citizens, especially by providing access to education and thereupon employment opportunities. Yet it was an undoubtedly, and horrifyingly, repressive regime. In these statements, the Kronstadt sailors who were eager participants in the 1917 Revolution denounce the communist dictatorship as it had emerged four years later; a novelist describes through fictional characters the brutal repression of the kulaks; a contemporary writer recalls the fear experienced by those who lived through the purges of the 1930s; and a Bolshevik hero, a victim of those purges, declares his innocence to posterity.

The Kronstadt sailors, participants in the 1917 October Revolution, denounce the communist dictatorship (March 1921): With the October Revolution the working class had hoped to achieve its emancipation. But there resulted an even greater enslavement of human personality. ... [But now there is resistance.] Here and there the land is lit up by the fires of rebellion in a struggle against oppression and violence. ... The Generals of Communism see clearly that it is the people who had risen, the people who have become convinced that the Communists have betrayed the ideas of Socialism. ... [L]ife under the Communist dictatorship is more terrible than death. ... [The Kronstadt rebellion was quickly crushed by Red troops.]
(Alexander Berkman, "The Kronstadt Rebellion," 1922)

An episode from the unpublished novel of M. N. Averbakh, member of a special brigade charged to liquidate the kulaks (1930): The door opened. The brigade burst into the house. The ... officer in charge of the operation was in front, brandishing a revolver.

"Hands up!"

Morgunov was barely able, in the gloom, to make out the frail figure of the class enemy. He was wearing white drawers and a dark undershirt, and was barefoot. ... The eyes, wide with terror, glanced from place to place. ... He kept blinking and crossing himself, shifting from one foot to the other, ... and suddenly he began to sob. ... His wife, not a young woman, jumped down from the high sleeping bench and began to wail at the top of her voice. The children began crying. A calf lying beside the stove, apparently not in very good health, began to bawl.

Morgunov looked around, aghast. He saw that the hut contained nothing but the one room and the big Russian stove. In the front corner ... were two simple wooden benches and a crude table made of planks. No chest of drawers, no beds, no chairs. ...

The class enemy!
(From R. Medvedev, *Let History Judge: The Origins and Consequences of Stalinism*, rev. ed., ed. G. Shriver, 1989)

Writer Nadezhda Mandelstam, whose husband, the poet Osip Mandelstam, died a prisoner in 1938, recalls the Stalinist terror: Anybody who breathes the air of terror is doomed, even if nominally he manages to save his life. Everybody is a victim—not only those who die, but also the killers, ideologists, accomplices and sycophants who close their eyes or wash their hands. ...

The principles and aims of mass terror have nothing in common with ordinary police work or with security. The only purpose of terror is intimidation. To plunge the whole country into a state of chronic fear, the number of victims must be raised to astronomical levels, and on every floor of every building there must always be several apartments from which the tenants have suddenly been taken away. The remaining inhabitants will be model citizens for the rest of their lives.
(Nadezhda Mandelstam, *Hope against Hope: A Memoir*, ed. M. Hayward, 1970)

Before his execution by Stalin's political police, Nikola Bukharin dictates to his wife a letter to a future generation of party leaders, to vindicate himself and testify to the terror (1938): I am leaving life. ... I feel my helplessness before a hellish machine, which ... has acquired gigantic power, fabricates organized slander, acts boldly and confidently. ...

Storm clouds have risen over the party. My one head, guilty of nothing, will drag down thousands of guiltless heads. ... I have been in the party since I was eighteen, and the purpose of my life has always been to fight for the interests of the working class, for the victory of socialism. ...

I appeal to all party members! In these days, perhaps the last of my life, I am confident that sooner or later the filter of history will inevitably sweep the filth from my head. I was never a traitor; without hesitation I would have given my life for Lenin's, I loved Kirov, started nothing against Stalin. ... Know, comrades, that on the banner, which you will be carrying in the victorious march to communism, is also my drop of blood.
(From R. Medvedev, *ibid*)

The war on the class enemy: "liquidate the kulaks": *Stalin's plan to build "socialism in one country" required the collectivization of agricultural production—which in turn required the elimination of small peasant proprietors (the kulaks). In this 1930 photograph, Russian villagers, who had been well-prompted by Soviet advisers, march with a banner asking to "liquidate the kulaks as a class."*

The Soviet Family   Dismantling the family meant the liberation of women from male authority (see Chapter 27). The first steps in this direction were taken as early as 1918, when a new Family Code declared women's equality, erased the distinction between legitimate and illegitimate births, removed marriage from religious to civil jurisdiction, and permitted divorce. Two years later, a further decree made abortion legal if performed by a physician. Married or unmarried, women were to participate fully in society—their labor was required to build the socialist economy. Women were also active in the Communist Party, and worked as teachers and bureaucrats to build the new society that Lenin envisioned.

Many of these measures were revoked under Stalin, however, whose Family Code of 1936 made abortion illegal and divorce difficult, restored the category of illegitimacy, criminalized homosexuality, and sought to rehabilitate the family.

The nurture and instruction of children was a responsibility the Soviet state took seriously. It undertook to rear and educate all of its young. Neighborhood and factory nurseries cared for infants from birth onward. Well-run elementary schools trained the offspring of parents of whom many were themselves illiterate. In an egalitarian setting, these schools prepared children for the technical requirements of a modern society, at the upper levels training engineers, research scientists, teachers, and officers. At the same time, schools and Komsomol (youth organization) units instilled communist values into their young charges—some of whom won favor, during the purges, for denouncing their parents.

The Manipulation of Culture   Those born in the early years of the Communist regime were raised to be uncritical supporters of the Soviet state. That state had replaced tsardom, aristocracy, and Church with a system that guaranteed social services to all and the opportunity for advancement to high position on the basis of merit.

As adults were retrained to participate in Soviet society, they were weaned from the Church that had for centuries been the mainstay of Russian culture. Official decrees desacralized churches, intimidated priests, and banned the performance of sacraments (restrictions briefly eased in 1941 when it was necessary to reaffirm traditional culture to support the "Great Patriotic War").

Communist censors understood very well the power of cultural expression in forming the minds of citizens. Writers, film-makers, and artists were gathered into unions that controlled the ideological content of books, plays, films, and paintings. Holding relatively high status in Soviet society, writers and artists largely followed the party line in matters of both taste and style.

So too did historians, linguists, psychologists, musicians, and even biologists, whose works were required to endorse the Soviet regime. Psychologists, for example, avoided Freudian psychoanalytic theories, as the notion of an unruly unconscious self countered Soviet understanding of the fully conscious and ideologically committed citizen. Biologists could not explore the field of genetics, as the notion of inherited characteristics countered the Soviet assumption of a wholly malleable human nature.

Stalin—father of his country: *This 1939 poster of Stalin as exultant master of an armed and ready Soviet Union expresses the nation's state on the eve of World War II—not a peaceful and democratic society but a militarist and despotic one. The words on the large unfurled banner exalt the leader: "Our army and our country are strengthened with the spirit of Stalin."*

By the 1930s, the bureaucratic control of the arts and ideas resulted in a serious loss of vitality. As the French author (formerly a communist sympathizer) André Gide (1869–1951) predicted, where there is no liberty, "art loses its meaning and its value … as … the assent of the greatest number … goes to the qualities the public is best able to recognize, that is to say conformity." In the visual arts, the officially sanctioned style of Socialist Realism prevailed, which celebrated the heroism of Soviet workers in a blandly academic manner. Film-making languished until, on the eve of World War II, Eisenstein produced his prophetic *Alexander Nevsky* (see Chapter 27).

The specter of the gulag kept many intellectuals in line. The novelist Maxim Gorky (1868–1936), an ardent participant in the debates of 1917, remained in favor as the leading intellectual of the new state that he never really endorsed. The poet Boris Pasternak (1890–1960), whose silence throughout the 1930s implied his hatred for the regime, was for the moment tolerated. The adventurous productions of the Old Bolshevik playwright Vsevolod Meyerhold (1874–1940?), however, invited repression in the

end; he was arrested, tortured, and probably executed. The poet Osip Mandelstam (1891–1938?), who had criticized Stalin, was exiled, and died *en route* to the gulag. The poet Anna Akhmatova (pseudonym of Anna Andreyevna Gorenko; 1889–1966)—whose two husbands were executed by Lenin and Stalin, whose son was exiled to the gulag, and who was herself twice denounced for the "bourgeois decadence" of her now widely-acclaimed work—succeeded in outliving the dictator.

Under Stalin, words were dangerous. For decades, some of the most important Soviet works of literature and thought were "published" only in manuscript and typescript, and circulated secretly (known as *samizdat*, "self-published"). Such was the case with the writings of Aleksandr Isayevich Solzhenitsyn (1918–), which at last escaped the censors to inform the peoples of the outside world about terror and the gulag in the world's first communist state.

Views from Abroad   Until the circulation abroad of Solzhenitsyn's *One Day in the Life of Ivan Denisovich* (1962) and *The Gulag Archipelago* (1973), exposing the Soviet labor camp system, ignorance about conditions in the Soviet Union was persistent. Idealistic sympathizers abroad, such as the British Fabian socialists Sidney and Beatrice Webb (see Chapter 25), enthusiastically praised the factories and labor camps in their *Soviet Communism: A New Civilisation?* (1935). The Dublin-born playwright George Bernard Shaw (1856–1950) approved of Stalin, who combined, he thought, the qualities of field marshal and pope. The novelist H. G. Wells (1866–1946) found him "candid, fair and honest," and the American industrialist Armand Hammer (1898–1990) commended his resourcefulness. These and other observers, including thousands of communist party workers around the world, ignored rumors and even hard evidence of the purges, the mass slaughter, and the bridling of free thought.

Some early followers did become disillusioned. The American writer Max Eastman (1883–1969), an enthusiastic supporter at first, soon renounced Bolshevism after visiting the Soviet Union in 1922. His *Since Lenin Died* (1925) unveiled the corrupt power plays of the 1920s. (It was to Eastman that an abject Trotsky denied the existence of Lenin's "testament" repudiating Stalin.) The English writer George Orwell (pseudonym of Eric Arthur Blair, 1903–1950), a socialist who had previously critiqued the hypocrisies of imperialism and absurdities of war, assailed communism for dehumanizing the individual in his epochal works *Animal Farm* (1945) and *Nineteen Eighty-Four* (1949).

The Yugoslav communist Anton Ciliga (1898–1992) clearly exposed the failures of Soviet society (where he lived from 1926 to 1936) in *The Russian Enigma* (1940). Arthur Koestler (1905–1983), a

MUST READS

Opponents of Totalitarianism

Arthur Koestler　*Darkness at Noon* (1940)

Anne Frank　*The Diary of Anne Frank* (1947)

George Orwell　*1984* (1949)

Alexander Solzhenitsyn　*The Gulag Archipelago* (1973)

Hungarian-born former Communist who was disillusioned by the 1930s purges, explored the phantom confessions of Stalin's victims in the classic *Darkness at Noon* (1940). Since the late 1980s, which brought the disintegration of the Soviet regime and the opening of the archives, scholars have been able to document the atrocities committed by a totalitarian state in the name of "the people."

Derived from the humane traditions of democratic socialism and liberalism, communism took a different turn in 1917, as Lenin and Stalin redefined its purposes. By the early 1920s, communism in the Soviet Union had crystallized as a totalitarian system sustained by terror and deception. The people it meant to serve benefited in many ways from its programs of economic modernization and mass education. But they suffered from the brutality of a state that elevated itself above the people it claimed to serve.

THE FACES OF FASCISM

In the decade after 1917, as Russian communism turned despotic, other European nations embraced different forms of fascism. Exalting a new type of charismatic leader—a *duce*, *Führer*, or *caudillo* (as these were named in Italian, German, and Spanish)—they chose nationalism, militarism, and corporatism over individual rights and freedom.

Why did so many Europeans abandon liberalism?—to the extent that, in 1938 when Hitler dismembered Czechoslovakia, it was the one remaining democracy, among all the nations of central or eastern Europe? The nations of Europe were unable to adjust to the outcomes of World War I. In some cases, their leaders were seen as having accepted too easily the grievous burdens of the Paris peace settlements. Or they could not manage the hammer blows in rapid succession, as in Germany, of inflation and economic depression. Or the people trusted too much the dynamic new leaders from the streets, who verged violence, youth, and unreason as antidotes to the ineptitudes of the politicians. For reasons such as these, support for fascist movements surged through Europe during the 1920s.

Fascism: an Ideology for the Twentieth Century

Fascism is a modern ideology, a child of the twentieth century. Unlike socialism or conservatism, rooted in a liberal past, it is the antithesis of liberalism, as the diagram on p. 816 illustrates. Fading toward monarchism or military despotism at one pole, toward anarchy at the other, but never toward democracy, the apparently inchoate phenomenon of fascism can be identified by some key features.

First, fascism is ultra-nationalistic—in contrast to the internationalism (or **cosmopolitanism**) of communism. It exhorts individuals to subordinate themselves to the whole "people." In the same anti-individualistic vein, fascism is **corporatist**, promoting identification with multi-class groups—industry-based councils or youth groups—which in turn support the nationalist agenda. Summoning individuals to identify themselves with nation rather than class, it is anti-socialist and anti-communist.

Second, fascism celebrates irrationalism, in contrast to communism's appeal to "scientific" theory. The elaborate symbols and images it devises appeal to myth rather than history, looking to memories of past greatness, and to premodern, even prehistoric episodes of heroic conquest. Fascism thrives on propaganda—the opposite of reasoned discourse—and specifically the propagation of pithy lies, slogans laden with hatred, resentment, or regret. Esteeming frenzy over reason, the will over the intellect, it prefers youth to age, and recruits its first followers among the discontented young.

Third, fascism promotes war and detests pacifism—in contrast, again, to Soviet communism, which came to power amid war's devastation promising "peace, land, bread." It exalts the qualities that accompany wartime heroism: courage, sacrifice, great efforts of will. "War alone brings all human energies to their highest state of tension," said Mussolini, "and stamps with the seal of nobility the nations which have to face it." Where war cannot be had, fascism admires bellicosity, if only in the form of terror.

Fourth, fascism advocates masculinism, and abhors any feminization of culture or politics. It upholds traditional gender roles in society—in contrast to communism which, in theory, denies gender inequality; or to liberalism, which must, in theory, recognize the rights of individuals irrespective of gender. Its vitalism and militarism are masculine ideals. It rejects pacifism and socialism as effeminate. Fascists are men. Women serve the fascist cause by tending to household needs and by bearing children, future mothers and soldiers.

Fifth, fascism is modernist—more so than communism, whose grand theoretical structures are rooted in nineteenth-century and even earlier streams of thought. The only one of the major Western ideologies to emerge in the twentieth century, fascism embraces novelty, especially new technologies and styles. Embracing **futurism**, it concocts visions of a mythicized future. It tends, consequently, to revolution, to the annihilation of existing structures and the fabrication of new ones: here, fascism does resemble communism, which also rejoices in the revolutionary meltdown of inherited institutions.

Finally, fascism is autocratic—at odds with communist theory, which promises power to a triumphant proletariat. It elevates an individual with charismatic qualities, who claims to represent the will of the people. To its *duce* or *Führer* it demonstrates allegiance in mass celebrations that turn the mere individual into a faceless servitor of his "leader" as of his state. It is by nature, therefore, anti-democratic (for democracy would give each person political power) and anti-liberal (for liberalism grants to each person inalienable rights).

Although fascism cannot coexist with communism ("the Left"), to which it is opposed in essence, it could and did make alliances with conservatism ("the Right"). Conservatism, which enlisted monarchists and militarists, honored the institutions and traditions that communism would dismantle. Accordingly fascists and conservatives could agree upon a nationalist, anti-communist, anti-pacifist program that excluded female activism and promoted a strong leader.

Europe's two principal fascist states arose in Italy and Germany. At the same time, Spain and Portugal, Hungary and Poland, Yugoslavia and Romania, and distant Japan among others had conservative governments with fascist components. By 1937, with the exception of the Soviet Union and the democracies of northwestern Europe (France, Britain, the Netherlands, Belgium, Switzerland, and the four Scandinavian nations), and Czechoslovakia, the sole democracy in central Europe, fascist or authoritarian governments ruled everywhere in Europe.

Mussolini and His Imitators

In Italy, the least of the Great Power victors of World War I, fascism first took form in the hands of Benito Mussolini, the least of the century's great dictators. A product of resentment, confusion, and force, Italian fascism was important as a role model for other authoritarian regimes.

Though a victor nation that gained territory as a result of the 1919 Paris treaties, Italy was disappointed with her reward for the terrible sacrifices made by her soldiers in the icy battlefields at the Isonzo River (see Chapter 26). Austria surrendered the Alto Adige (Italian Tyrol), the Triestino (Trieste and its environs), and Istria. But the newly-formed state of Yugoslavia incorporated a number of regions for which Italy felt it had bargained and bled.

Italians were also troubled by unrest in the streets and weakness in the parliament. Industrialized relatively late, the Italian economy had been greatly strained by wartime demands. Striking workers, often prodded into action by communist recruiters, poured into the streets. There they tangled with self-appointed black-shirted gangs of thugs and demobilized soldiers, the *fasci di combattimento* (combat "bundles," or squads) that sprang up in Italy after 1918. These *fascisti* ("fascists") detested communists and socialists, and suppressed their opponents by cudgeling, kidnapping, torture (castor oil, which they forced their victims to swallow in quantity, was a fascist trademark), and murder.

The Italian government—a constitutional monarchy dating only from the nation's unification in 1870—was dismayed by the disorder and looked for a leader who could contain it. King Victor Emmanuel III chose the easiest, most dangerous solution. He invited Benito Mussolini, leader of the black-shirted fascist gangs, and since 1921 a member of parliament for the new National Fascist party, to form a coalition government. Mussolini took a berth on the overnight train to Rome (this was his "March on Rome") to take up his appointment. By 1924, he personally dominated the government, having first dispatched by assassination his rival, the socialist leader Giacomo Matteotti (1885–1924), and quickly destroyed those who protested the act.

Mussolini in Genoa, 1938

The Duce: *Both Mussolini and Hitler were masters of self-presentation, staging spectacular processions and rallies that evoked high emotion and memories of past grandeur while they served to maximize the figure of the leader. Here, a triumphal Roman arch forms the theatrical backdrop to Mussolini's rousing public address in Genoa, underpinning the self-proclaimed magnificence of the duce.*

The man who acquired power so swiftly had been born poor. Like his proletarian father, a blacksmith, he was a committed socialist. From 1912, Mussolini edited the newspaper of the Italian socialist party *Avanti!* ("Forward"). He advocated worker activism and international pacifism until 1914, when, in an about-face, he joined those agitating for war. He fought, attaining (as did Hitler) the unexalted rank of corporal. After the war, he developed the political ideology of fascism (see *Witnesses* on p. 810), promoting it through violence and propaganda.

Once in power, Mussolini pursued a disparate agenda focused only in its ardent nationalism. He supported the large corporations by disabling trade unionism (while pretending to give workers a voice through corporation-based associations). In the Lateran Treaty of 1929, he forged an agreement with the papacy, which had lost the papal states in 1870. The pope was granted official recognition of his sovereignty over an autonomous Vatican state, and the Roman Catholic Church was permitted to resume its role in education while the state recognized the validity of Catholic marriage, which meant that there could be no divorce. In return for these concessions, the pope agreed to recognize the authority both of the Italian state and of Mussolini himself, who became the first leader of a unified Italy to be recognized by the Church.

In the arts, Mussolini promoted futurism, and cultural activities that magnified state interests. He centralized the bureaucracy and, famously, made the railroads run on time. He enforced the continued subordinate status of women, launching a natalist program, which encouraged women to reproduce prolifically in the interests of increasing national population (see Chapter 27). "Go back home," he told fascist party delegates in 1927, "and tell the women I need births, many births." As the photograph on p. 808 shows, he spoke to large, enthusiastic crowds gathered in vast cathedrals and arenas, monuments of past greatness, about Italy's ancient glory—Rome, he reminded them, had once ruled the Mediterranean world.

To recover that glory, Mussolini, too, must become a conqueror. He waited patiently to attain that status. In 1925, he took part with Britain, France, Belgium, and Germany in the agreement at Locarno (Switzerland) that guaranteed the maintenance of Germany's western (but not eastern) frontiers. In 1935, he joined once again with Britain and France in the agreement of Stresa (Italy), reaffirming the then allies' interest in preventing German aggrandizement. Later that year (on October 2, 1935), however, he struck at Ethiopia, which Italy had tried and failed to conquer in 1896 (see Chapter 24). The League of Nations punished Mussolini with weak economic sanctions; they did not, importantly, limit his access to oil, without which Mussolini could

not maintain his army. In 1939, Mussolini struck at Albania, across the Adriatic Sea.

Between Stresa in 1935 and the Albanian invasion in 1939, Italy edged gradually toward alliance with Germany. In the meantime, both Mussolini and Hitler had been sustaining a rebel Nationalist army in Spain as it battled the democratically elected Republican government (for the Spanish Civil War, see below). Mussolini sent divisions of "volunteers," fully equipped with aircraft and tanks, in support of the forces led by the Nationalist General Francisco Franco (1892–1975). In 1936, Mussolini and Hitler reached an agreement described as the Rome–Berlin Axis. In 1937, Italy joined Japan and Germany's Anti-Comintern Pact.

Other European nations followed the pattern of Mussolini's fascism, without necessarily adopting all of its ideological features. In the decade 1929–1939, they included Greece and the Balkan nations of Bulgaria and Yugoslavia; Hungary, Poland, and Austria; the Baltic states of Lithuania, Latvia, and Estonia; and Spain and Portugal. Here dictators with a nationalist agenda ruled in league with kings and military elites, sometimes, as in Italy, with the support of the Roman Catholic Church. Fascist movements surfaced even in democratic Britain (led by Sir Oswald Mosley, 1896–1980) and France.

Imperial Japan, Imperialist Ventures

Authoritarian government also took root in Japan, a country whose ancient imperial traditions and recent rapid modernization predisposed it toward despotism. Dominated by a military elite with expansionist plans and equipped with the latest technology, while Europe floundered, Japan was extending its power purposefully in east Asia.

In 1915 Japan imposed its Twenty-One Demands on China, claiming key footholds in Chinese territory and, in effect, made all China a Japanese dependency (see Chapter 25). Although Japan retained many of these claims in 1919, it was later forced to relinquish them. In 1921–1922, the Washington Conference, including Britain, France, Japan, and the United States, agreed to respect the independence and sovereignty of China. Japan agreed to restore the former German holding of Shandong to China, and to remove its troops from Siberia. It seemed that Japanese expansion had been contained.

The economic depression that gripped the Western world (see Chapter 27) also affected overpopulated Japan. Its poor peasants (its recent wealth was largely urban-based) could not afford to purchase Japanese products, and its industries relied on foreign markets. When the world demand for Japanese manufactures, especially silks, collapsed in the Depression, economic crisis in Japan followed. As in the West, crisis provided the cue for a militarist element to subvert the regular institutions of governance. A group of generals took over from the parliamentary regime that was reestablished after World War I. They now dealt directly with the emperor, believed to be the descendent of deities, who continued to inspire the sacrificial devotion of the Japanese people. They argued that Japan must expand on the mainland so that its people could eat. They were also concerned by the gathering strength of the Soviet Union to their north, and, to their west, by the concentration of power in the hands of the Chinese Nationalists under Chiang Kai-shek (Jiang Jieshi).

Upon the death in 1925 of revolutionary leader Sun Yat-sen (1866–1925; see Chapters 24, 29), Chiang took over the Nationalist, or Guomindang forces his predecessor had assembled. In 1926–1927,

with communist allies from whom he soon separated, Chiang drove north from Guangzhou on the South China Sea to the interior industrial center at Wuhan. His forces then wheeled eastward along the lower Yangzi River to prosperous Nanjing and the East China Sea port of Shanghai. By 1928, Chiang controlled a core of the eastern provinces from his capital at Nanjing. This regime he steadily expanded to the south and west, contending with local warlords, some his former allies. The rival communist factions withdrew into the countryside and began the recruitment of peasant supporters that would be the basis of their ultimate victory in 1949 (see Chapter 29).

Meanwhile, beginning in 1931, Japan began to tear at northeastern China, a region wedged between Soviet and Guomindang strongholds. Japanese forces

---

Fascism and Nazism: the Flight from Reason

Fascism was not one ideology, but a potpourri of notions; Nazism included some of these, and added some others. Together, the two were lethal. In these passages, the Italian fascist leader Mussolini defines some features of fascism— its repudiation of pacifism, Marxism, and democracy, and its idolization of the state; the German Nazi leader Hitler attacks the Jews and calls for the appropriation of eastern European territories; and a young girl who witnessed the rise of Hitler recalls the terrible impact that he made.

Benito Mussolini defines the principles of Italian fascism (1932): Fascism ... repudiates the doctrine of Pacifism. ... War alone brings up to its highest tension all human energy and puts the stamp of nobility upon the peoples who have the courage to meet it. ...

Such a conception of life makes Fascism the complete opposite of ... so-called scientific and Marxian Socialism, the materialist conception of history. ...

Fascism combats the whole complex system of democratic ideology, and repudiates it. ... Fascism denies that the majority, by the simple fact that it is a majority, can direct human society; ... and it affirms the immutable, beneficial, and fruitful inequality of mankind. ...

The foundation of Fascism is the conception of the State, ... Fascism conceives of the State as an absolute, in comparison with which all individuals or groups are relative. ... The Fascist state is itself conscious, and has itself a will and a personality. ...
(Benito Mussolini with Giovanni Gentile, "The Political and Social Doctrine of Fascism," *Enciclopedia Italiana*, 1932)

Adolf Hitler on Aryans, Jews, and *Lebensraum* (1925): What we see before us of human culture today ... is almost exclusively the creative product of the Aryan. ... If one were to divide mankind into three groups: culture-founders, culture-bearers, and culture-destroyers, then as representative of the first kind,

only the Aryan would come in question. It is from him that the foundation and the walls of all human creations originate. ...

The Jew forms the strongest contrast to the Aryan. ... The Jewish people, with all its apparent intellectual qualities, is nevertheless without any true culture, especially without a culture of its own. ... He is and remains the typical parasite, a sponger who, like a harmful bacillus, spreads out more and more if only a favorable medium invites him to do so. ...

[W]e National Socialists must cling un-flinchingly to our foreign-policy aims, that is to guarantee the German nation the soil and territory to which it is entitled on this earth. ... We take up at the halting place of six hundred years ago. We terminate the endless German drive to the south and west of Europe, and direct our gaze towards the lands in the east ... and proceed to the territorial policy of the future.
(Adolf Hitler, *Mein Kampf*, 1925; trs. R. Mannheim, 1943, 1971)

Lilo Linke observes Hitler as a girl in Germany (1935): For an hour and a half Hitler spoke, every few minutes interrupted by fanatic acclamations. ... He thrust his chin forward. His voice, hammering the phrases with an obsessed energy, became husky and shrill and began to squeak more and more frequently. His whole face was covered with sweat. ...

The audience was breathlessly under his spell. This man expressed their thoughts, their feelings, their hopes; a new prophet had arisen ... and had the power to lead them into the promised land if they were only prepared to follow him. ...

A single question as to reason or proof or possibility would have shattered the whole argument, but nobody asked it—the majority because they had begun to think with their blood, which condemns all logic. ...
(Lilo Linke, *Restless Days*, 1935, 1963)

invaded Manchuria in 1931, which they organized in 1932 as the puppet state of Manchukuo (under the last emperor of China, who had abdicated in 1912, a member of the last imperial dynasty, the Qing, or Manchu). Japan paid little attention to the mild rebuke issued by the League of Nations in 1933 and withdrew from that body. Manchukuo, rich in resources and laced with railroad lines, sustained the Japanese economy. The military resumed its advance, controlling much of northern China by 1935. In 1937, Japan would seize the major Chinese cities of Beijing, Tientsin, Shanghai, Hangchow, and Nanjing—subjecting the last, the capital, to pillage and massacre, resulting in between 200,000 and 300,000 Chinese civilian deaths. Taking Tsintao and Guangzhou the following year, and the province of Hainan in February 1939, Japan controlled China's eastern provinces and most important ports. Like Europe at this date, Asia faced the prospect of domination by a mighty power that aimed to take from its neighbors what land and wealth it desired.

For by this point, Adolf Hitler and his Nazi party had achieved dominion in Germany, and had set out to dominate Europe, and the world.

Nazism: the German Form of Fascism

In Germany, fascism developed the distinctive form of Nazism, a product of Germany's particular history and Hitler's unique personality. The events of World War I, and the Versailles treaty imposed at its conclusion, had left Germany abject and defeated. By the late 1930s, Hitler led a prosperous, armed, and nazified Germany that was fully prepared to take the next step toward war and mastery.

The Roots of Nazism Germany's military defeat in World War I had profound political consequences at home. Although the German generals had informed the government from the summer of 1918 that the war was unwinnable (see Chapter 26), the armistice of November 11 of that year was actually arranged by the centrist provisional government that had replaced that of Emperor William II (r. 1888–1918) only days earlier. Upon those Weimar politicians (named for the university town where the Constitutional Assembly of the new republic met) fell the duty of negotiating the Versailles peace treaty—a treaty that, its opponents felt, crippled and dishonored Germany. The generals who had failed to win the war presented themselves as having suffered a dastardly "stab in the back," when defeatist civilian leaders had signed the Armistice. The path was certainly now open to the rehabilitation of the military at the expense of parliamentary democracy.

The Versailles settlement stripped Germany of important territorial possessions. The industrial Saar district in the Ruhr region was placed (until a plebiscite in 1935) under international administration, the Rhineland was occupied and demilitarized, with Alsace and Lorraine, west of the Rhine, returned to France. The German army and navy were sharply cut back to the size of a police force barely capable of self-defense. Germany was effectively disarmed.

Moreover, the notorious "war guilt" clause in Article 231 of the Versailles treaty declared Germany responsible "for causing all the loss and damage" suffered by the Allies in a war "imposed upon them by the aggression of Germany and her allies." Crippled and starved by the conflict, Germany was to pay punitive "reparations." These provisions resulted in an ominous sense of national humiliation and deep resentment. Furthermore, the expense was unbearable. In an attempt to meet its costs, the government printed paper currency, leading to the ruinous hyperinflation of the 1920s (see Chapter 27).

In sum, the Versailles treaty amounted to a guarantee of renewed conflict. The Germans felt themselves dishonored, and plundered by the victor nations of World War I. Soon they would welcome a war of retaliation. But that war would be driven by other forces as well, including that of an explosive nationalism, fueled by popular racial theory.

Germany had only recently become a nation (see Chapter 23). It had developed an intense sense of nationhood from the experiences leading to unification in 1871: the Prussian resistance to Napoleon, the events of 1848, and Bismarck's construction of Prussian leadership (see Chapter 23). National pride was further bolstered by the cultural unity of the German-speaking domains.

The cohesion of German culture could be traced to the work of the reformer Martin Luther (1483–1546), who first distinguished national German interests from those of the cosmopolitan papacy. Since then, German-speakers had been among the leading figures of the scientific revolution and Enlightenment, and the Classical and Romantic movements in the arts (see Chapters 17, 25). In the nineteenth century, the German universities were the most advanced in Europe, training students in Classical and modern disciplines.

But German nationalism, as it emerged in the nineteenth century, also had deeper, troubling, dimensions. It was characterized by expansionist fantasies built on medieval precedents, and colored by racial theories. From the Middle Ages came the legacy of the *"Drang nach Osten,"* or "drive to the east," the movement of German-speaking peoples to open new territories in eastern Europe and to Christianize pagan Slavs. There lingered a sense of German entitlement to eastern lands, and of superiority over their peoples, who had indeed often been pressed into dependency in the Middle Ages.

German attitudes toward the Slavic peoples also had ideological origins. Imperialist ventures and

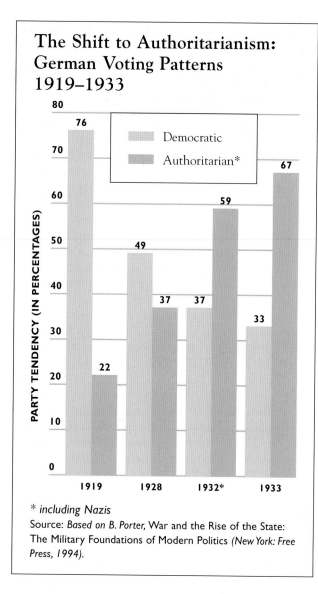

The Shift to Authoritarianism: German Voting Patterns 1919–1933

Democratic

Authoritarian*

PARTY TENDENCY (IN PERCENTAGES)

1919: Democratic 76, Authoritarian 22
1928: Democratic 49, Authoritarian 37
1932*: Democratic 37, Authoritarian 59
1933: Democratic 33, Authoritarian 67

* *including Nazis*

Source: Based on B. Porter, War and the Rise of the State: The Military Foundations of Modern Politics (New York: Free Press, 1994).

Darwinian theory encouraged the development of racial theories in the late nineteenth century (see Chapter 25). German academics constructed the notion of a superior Aryan race (related to ancient Indo-Aryan speakers of languages ancestral to those of modern Europe; see Chapters 1, 2). As Aryans, Germans were superior to Slavs, Jews, gypsies, and others, with a special place in the hierarchy of races.

The Rise of Hitler   These notions of German racial superiority, national destiny, the superiority of military to parliamentary rule, and the humiliations of the Versailles settlement, were the ingredients of the ideology of Nazism formulated by Adolf Hitler in his sprawling *Mein Kampf* ("My Struggle," 1925). To these Hitler added anti-Bolshevism and an economic justification for territorial expansion—the principle of Germany's need for (and hence entitlement to) *Lebensraum* ("living space").

Born in Austria–Hungary, the son of a government functionary and a doting mother, Adolf Hitler gave no evidence in his youth of the power he would wield.

With ambitions of becoming an artist, he gravitated to the political and cultural capital of Vienna. Living on the margins in those pre-war years, when philosophies stormed about, he picked up small jobs, slept in flophouses, and imbibed prevailing currents of thought (see Chapter 25): anti-Semitism, race theory, Nietzscheanism, socialism, and nationalism.

Hitler moved to Germany and joined the German army in Munich in 1914. He fought with distinction, achieving the rank of corporal and winning the Iron Cross. When an exhausted German government signed the armistice, Hitler, like his superiors, felt that he had been stabbed in the back.

With the war over, Hitler returned to Munich and became a political agent. In the confused, crisis-ridden 1920s, that meant recruiting like-minded comrades in beer halls and fostering squads of thugs who roamed the streets in search of enemies to maul. It also meant nursing the grievances the past had delivered: against Jews, against communists (among them, Jews), against rich speculators (among them, Jews), against the enemies of Germany, and politicians. As an informer in the pay of army intelligence, he infiltrated one of the fringe political parties—the NSDAP, or National-sozialistische deutsche Arbeiter-partei ("National-socialist German Workers' Party"), or Nazi for short—Hitler found a home.

Hitler was now a beer-hall orator, and commanded an armed gang of brown-shirted "stormtroopers," the later SA (*Sturmabteilungen*). In 1923, he led the Munich Nazis in a **putsch**, an attempted government takeover. Thrown in prison with a five-year sentence, he was released after a little more than six months. During that interlude, he wrote *Mein Kampf*. In contrast to the works of Lenin, characterized by their concision and logic, *Mein Kampf* impresses by the virulence of its ideas, the randomness of their expression, and the consistency of its maxims with the Nazi project Hitler later brought to culmination. A passage from it is reproduced in *Witnesses* on p. 810.

By the late 1920s, Nazis were as strong a presence as their chief political opponents, the communists, and began to win seats in the *Reichstag*, or parliament. When the Depression struck in 1929, Nazis and communists courted its victims. The communists recruited a following from among the industrial workers. The Nazis appealed to the lower and middle bourgeoisie, white-collar workers, small business proprietors, bureaucrats—those who were at once economically threatened, and fearful of Bolshevism.

By 1930, the Nazis gained a foothold in the Reichstag, winning 107 seats (of a total of 556) to the communists' 77; in July 1932, 196 seats. The graph above shows the shifts in voting patterns during these years. Meanwhile, the government floundered, as center-left leaders and ineffective chancellors came and went; the presidency remained in the hands of the elderly World War I veteran Paul von Hindenburg

(1847–1934; see Chapter 26), now nearly ninety. With conservative support, Hitler became chancellor on January 30, 1933, and formed a cabinet dominated by Nazis. It was to be the Weimar republic's last government. Twenty months later, after Hindenburg's death on August 2, 1934, the chancellorship and the presidency were merged. Hitler had reached the highest office in the German government by strictly legal means. He would now consolidate his power by force.

Hitler in Power On February 27, 1933, a fire broke out in the Reichstag building. Nazi arsonists were probably responsible, but blame was assigned to Hitler's communist opponents. The emergency gave Hitler the opportunity to suspend civil liberties and grab control. On March 23, 1933, the Enabling Act granted Hitler dictatorial powers. On August 19, 1934, a plebiscite approved the delegation of all executive power to Hitler as Führer, or "leader." Now Hitler moved to enact the nightmarish fantasies outlined so vividly—for any who had a mind to consult them—in *Mein Kampf*. "No human being has ever declared or recorded what he wanted more often than I," Hitler reminded an unseeing world.

Hitler's first goal was to climb out of the Depression (see Chapter 27). Two-fifths of German workers were without jobs, while production and foreign trade had dropped to disastrous lows. Hitler's solution for this crisis was threefold. First, he aimed at self-sufficiency, or **autarky**. With the institution of his Four Year Plan (October 19, 1936), the whole southeastern region of Europe was to trade almost exclusively with Germany. Second, Hitler encouraged barter exchange with other countries as an alternative to wealth-draining foreign trade, and had the chemical industries develop synthetic or "ersatz" equivalents of consumer staples and industrial supplies. Third, Hitler let loose the war machine. With factories producing guns, ammunition, and equipment, German workers found jobs, and a new appreciation for their Führer.

His economic program did not distract Hitler from the task of reshaping society. He encouraged groups of all sorts in a policy of *Gleichschaltung* (enforced conformity). Youth groups, choral groups, and sports clubs all offered opportunities for Nazi indoctrination and discouraged individualism. Christian organizations were a problem. Hitler did not like them; but many Germans did, and they were at least a force for social order. In 1933, Hitler made his peace with the Roman Catholics—and could not have been pleased to learn in 1937 that a papal encyclical denouncing Nazi racial policies had been read aloud in the churches. In 1933 he reorganized the mainstream Protestant churches into the nazified German Evangelical Church. More than sixty percent of German Protestants accepted the Nazi leader. Critics of Nazism formed a counter-church, the remnant of which resisted or fled.

Nazism promoted the sense of belonging to the *Volk*, or the people ("folk"), and history, legend, and song reinforced that sentiment. In art and in film, Hitler liked to see heroic images of the German people which defied the uncertainties of the twentieth-century world. In the painting reproduced on p. 814, he is shown as a knight in armor. In 1937, the Nazis mounted two art exhibitions: "German Art" paraded paintings of Aryan-type heroes, while "Degenerate Art" displayed the kind of images—Surrealist, Dadaist, Expressionist, Modernist, many by Jewish artists—that Hitler condemned.

In intellectual life, the Nazis required conformity, and burned books of which they disapproved. Some thinkers, such as the novelist Thomas Mann (1875–1955), refused to cooperate and lived in exile. Others, including the philosopher Martin Heidegger (1889–1976), gave the raised-arm Nazi salute on request and supported the regime.

Hitler directed women to resume their traditional roles. Central to Nazi ideology was the restriction of women to the realm of home and family—to *Kinder, Kirche, Küche* (children, church, kitchen). A Nazi "Women's Union," headed by the ideologue Gertrud Scholtz-Klink (1902–), supervised the political indoctrination of German women. In Nazi theory, the greatest service women performed for the state was bearing and rearing of Aryan children. The birthrate rose over forty percent between 1933 and 1939.

The Anti-Semitic Tide For none of Nazism's programs to promote fellowship and *völkisch* memory included Jews and other non-Aryans. Hitler's "racial laws" of 1935 were part of the process that became progressively uglier until it reached monstrous dimensions in the "Final Solution." This new era of persecution began with a call to boycott Jewish businesses. Jews were expelled from their positions in universities and the civil service. In time, they were denied citizenship; their properties were confiscated; they were forced to wear the yellow Star of David on their clothing. Slogans circulated: "The Jew is the cause and the beneficiary of our misery"; "The Jew is the plastic demon of the decline of mankind"; "The Jew is our greatest misfortune."

If it was still possible in 1933 for Jews to hope for a change of policy, over the next few years they should have abandoned all hope. Now stormtroopers beat up Jews on the street, destroyed Jewish places of business, and broke into Jewish houses to rob and rape. When Hitler seized Austria, Nazi agents burst into the Vienna residence of the founder of psychoanalysis, Sigmund Freud (see Chapter 25), a Jew. Mrs Freud, having watched the thugs tear apart her home, put some coins on the table and invited the brown-shirted gentlemen to take those as well. Freud himself was spirited out of the country to London. Less privileged Jews were left to face the full Nazi fury signaled by the

Hubert Lanzinger, Hitler as Knight: *Like Russian artists who adopted the style of "Soviet Realism" to give expression to communist ideology, German artists celebrated Nazi themes. In this painting by Hubert Lanzinger from around 1936, Hitler is portrayed as a knight in shining armor, bearing a swastika standard, in a determined pose that echoes the medieval image of the Teutonic Order of Knights who conquered and converted the Slavic peoples of eastern Europe.*

horror of Kristallnacht ("Crystal Night," the night of broken glass, November 9–10, 1938). SS Hitler Youth squads gutted 7,500 Jewish business and destroyed 177 synagogues. Ninety-one Jews were killed, hundreds more injured, and hardly anyone protested.

Nazism also targeted other groups for exclusion and extinction. The communist members of the Reichstag were arrested in 1933, and along with those swept up from the streets and factories, sent to detention camps and prisons. Gypsies, homosexuals, the disabled and permanently ill were all marked for persecution. Influenced by the theories of eugenics then in vogue, which discouraged the propagation of those seen as "unfit," Hitler's race theory dictated that the lives only of healthy Aryans were valuable—those likely to reproduce. The others served no purpose, and should be eliminated. Scientists and physicians cooperated; even non-Nazis made no effective protest against orders to neglect or kill these unfortunates. They instituted a full-scale "euthanasia" program, which some scholars have seen as a pilot program for the wholesale killing of Jews undertaken in 1942.

Hitler's economic and social projects were publicized by speeches, radio announcements, and press features that broadcast Nazi propaganda. With their simple rhetoric and bald misrepresentation of truth, these effectively shaped popular attitudes. The impact

of Hitler himself is observed in *Witnesses* on p. 819. The aim was not to educate the elite, but to win instant recognition from the ignorant. "The larger the mass of men to be reached," Hitler advised in *Mein Kampf*, "the lower its purely intellectual level will have to be set." In view of the "primitive simplicity" of the mind of the mass of the people, Hitler argued, the true leader must use a "big lie" to win their trust. Deception on a grand scale was necessary if the German people were to accept Hitler's views about Jews, communists, the Aryan Master Race, and *Lebensraum*.

Even those unconvinced by Nazi propaganda were impressed by the ruthless brutality with which Nazism could act. In a preemptive stroke on June 30, 1934, Hitler used his private army, the SS, to purge the brown-shirted SA that had raised him to power— about 2 million strong, the scum of the streets, career criminals, habitual killers. In the "Night of the Long Knives," about eighty SA leaders were killed. By this massacre, Hitler detached himself from his early supporters and aligned himself with the interests of the industrial and military elite. In 1938, a more discreet purge of army officers followed, many of them from the old aristocracy.

At this juncture, Hitler needed to rid himself of upper-level officers whose patrician upbringing might have intruded a tradition of civility and even moral principles. For he was embarked on a program that required the violation of Germany's agreements with most of the nations of Europe. The German form of fascism had reached its maturity. Now Nazism would lead the world into war.

THE SECOND WORLD WAR: FASCISM DEFEATED

Having seized power in Germany, Hitler rearmed and allied with the Axis powers of Italy and Japan. The principal European democracies stood by, their inaction and incomprehension facilitating the arms buildup and first hostilities.

Fascism advanced to a high tide in 1942. Over the next three years, it was beaten back to a total defeat by the Allied powers—at first Britain alone, then Britain with two latecomer participants from the peripheries of the West, the Soviet Union and the United States.

In 1945, an era of Western history came to a close with the explosion of two atomic bombs in Japan and the liberation of the Nazi concentration camps, which had annihilated the targeted victims of Hitler's Final Solution.

The Dictatorships: Rearmament and Realignment

From 1933, Hitler rearmed Germany and allied with Italy and Japan. By 1936, all three Axis powers had undertaken expansionist projects in Europe, Africa, and Asia, as Map 28.2 below shows.

In 1925, representatives from Britain, France, Belgium, Italy, and Germany met at Locarno in Switzerland to put a close to the issues that the Versailles peace had left unresolved. Those discussions brought voluntary recognition by Germany of its borders in the west (though not the east), left the matter of unpaid reparations in genteel silence,

and welcomed Germany back into the community of European nations. In 1927, Germany gained admission to the League of Nations. It joined the ongoing series of disarmament conferences that many hoped would assure the goal United States president Wilson had enunciated, that the Great War would prove to be the war to end all wars. Amid the glorious prosperity that characterized the late 1920s, such hopes flourished.

Map 28.2 Expansion and Aggression West and East, 1930–1939: *Between 1930 and 1939, the three nations that would become the Axis aggressors in World War II began programs of expansion in their separate spheres. Japan's expansion in east Asia and the Pacific had begun as early as 1895, advanced in 1905 as a result of the Russo-Japanese war, and culminated in the 1930s, with a push into Manchuria and northern and eastern China (and subsequently into Indochina, the Philippines, and other Pacific islands). Italy added to its existing African sphere of influence in Libya, Eritrea, and part of Somaliland by invading Ethiopia in 1935, and seized Albania in 1939, on the eve of war. Germany steadily followed up its first aggression of 1936—the remilitarization of the Rhineland—with annexations of Austria and the Sudetenland (Czechoslovakia) in 1938, and the rest of Czechoslovakia, the Baltic port of Memel, and Poland in 1939. The last aggression triggered the outbreak of war.*

International cooperation would not survive Hitler's advent to power. On July 15, 1933, Hitler joined with Britain, France, and Italy in signing the Four-Power Pact that affirmed adherence to the principles of the Locarno Treaty, the League covenant, and the Versailles treaty. But by the fall of that year, he began to repudiate all those principles and more. On October 14, 1933, Germany withdrew from disarmament discussions, and from the League of Nations itself. In 1934, the Soviet Union took Germany's place in the League of Nations.

Hitler rearmed. Army officers maximized the potential of the minimal forces allowed to Germany by the Versailles settlement, grooming an officer cadre and covertly sending pilots to train under Red Army instructors in the Soviet Union. On March 7, 1936, Hitler tested his military strength by reoccupying the Rhineland with a mere 22,000 troops (the Rhineland, German territory west of the Rhine, had been demilitarized by the terms of Versailles and evacuated by the French only in 1930). On March 16, he repudiated the disarmament clauses of the Versailles treaty. Hitler had sent a clear message to the European powers: he intended to take what he wished by force. They were surprisingly slow to grasp the reality of this message.

The remilitarization of the Rhineland challenged the authority of the Treaty of Versailles. In April, Hitler's former Locarno partners, Britain, France, and

Italy, met at Stresa in Italy to consider a possible response. France, meanwhile, signed a treaty of mutual assistance with the Soviet Union and explored treaties with Czechoslovakia, Yugoslavia, and Romania (the "Little Entente" from 1920). These diplomatic moves proved valueless. Hitler had negotiated an agreement (June 18, 1936) with the British, who sought to placate this alarming Führer, permitting Germany to build its navy up to thirty-five percent of British strength. The British government sought to use German strength as a bulwark against communism. The Soviet Union was seen as a greater threat than Germany, and there was considerable sympathy for Hitler at the highest levels of the administration. Thus was Hitler rewarded for invading the Rhineland and flouting international law.

In the fall of 1936, Hitler pursued alliances with Italy and Japan, who would become his partners in the coming war. On October 3, 1935, Mussolini had invaded Ethiopia. His democratic colleagues responded weakly; the League of Nations (before which the beleaguered emperor Haile Selassie, 1891–1975, had pleaded Ethiopia's cause), imposed toothless sanctions on Italy. Irritated, Mussolini secured the Ethiopian capital of Addis Ababa on May 5, 1936, and approached Hitler. The two agreed on an alliance, which Mussolini proclaimed on October 25, 1936 as the Rome–Berlin axis. A few weeks later (November 25), Germany and Japan joined in the

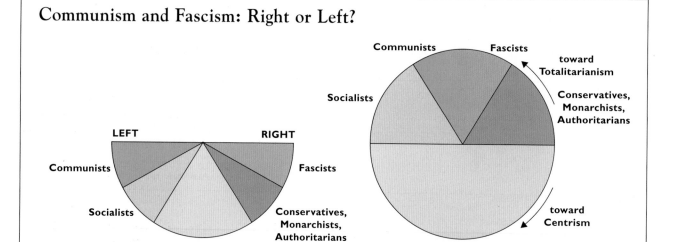

Communism and Fascism: Right or Left?

How are the phenomena of communism and fascism to be understood in relation to the more familiar spectrum of conservative and liberal political ideologies? A graphic representation can help, using the once again familiar categories of "left" for liberalism and socialism and their extremes, and "right" for conservatism and its extremes. For many scholars, communism, with its connection to democratic socialism, itself an outgrowth of liberalism, should lodge on the "left" of such a spectrum. Fascism, accordingly, with its links to conservative and authoritarian views, should lodge on the "right." These relationships are shown schematically in (a). Other scholars view communism and fascism as phenomena more closely related than that scheme implies, sharing such features as manipulation of mass sentiments through propaganda and indoctrination, futurism or modernism, anti-parliamentarianism, anti-liberalism, atheism, and inclination to violence. As totalitarian movements, then, they approach each other. This relationship is seen in (b).

Source: *Based on H.R. Kedward,* Fascism in Western Europe: 1900-1945 *(Glasgow: Blackie and Son Ltd., 1971), pp. 240–241.*

Anti-Comintern Pact that was ranged against the Soviet Union. Italy then joined a year later.

The Axis powers were now ready to expand. The Germans would recover what was justly theirs—its "unredeemed" lands that the last war had denied them, the lands of the Slavs, and racial and territorial dominance in Europe. The Italians would gain an overseas empire and the glory of the Roman Empire. Japan would seize dominion in eastern Asia so as to provide resources for its people and its factories, and achieve its supposed imperial destiny.

The Democracies: Frailty and Confusion

By the end of 1937, the Axis league had crystallized. Yet the Western democracies still misread the clear signal that catastrophe loomed. Were they misled? Were they inept? Were they so paralyzed by memories of the last war that they could not confront, when it was still possible to do so, those who would launch the next? These are difficult questions. Noting the following two factors may assist in finding answers.

First, the diplomacy of the principal democracies was aimed at maintaining the status quo achieved by the 1919 Paris treaties; the goal of their opponents, in contrast, was to subvert it. From 1919 through 1936, the League of Nations worked to achieve the "collective security" of Europe. In the 1920s, it sought to ease tensions in the Rhineland, and encouraged the settlement of the issues of reparations, war debt, and disarmament. In 1932, the League's Lytton Commission denounced the Japanese invasion of Manchuria as an "act of aggression." In 1935, when Italy invaded Ethiopia, the League imposed sanctions—but they were insufficient.

In each case, the League sought to diminish tensions, but nations set upon expansion reneged on international agreements. By 1936, the League had become ineffective. The nations that had depended upon it found themselves without a defender.

Second, political discussion in the free countries was marked by confusion and ideological fragmentation; in the Axis nations, in contrast, there was clarity of thought and unity of purpose. The major democracies cycled through coalition governments in the 1920s and 1930s; with the Popular Front coalitions of the 1930s, ideological variety reached a maximum, while the ineffectiveness of political leaders across the spectrum inspired little respect for any of the ideological alternatives represented.

Nor were those alternatives clearly distinguished. Apart from communists, there were on the left both democratic and anti-democratic socialists. Opposing them were conservatives and fascists. Fascism, however, in its appeals to group solidarity, and its repudiation of individualism, could tend toward socialism, in which it had its origins—Mussolini had really been a socialist; Nazism had originally embraced a working-class activism. Conservatives were so fearful of communism that they failed to see the more serious imminent threat of fascism. Liberal democrats, meanwhile, might be tempted by socialist, fascist, or communist alternatives, believing these to be the defenders of the working class, or the nation, or (as in the United States) of marginalized groups such as blacks and Jews.

Communism and fascism, finally, though viewed as opposites—both because of communist theory (which equated fascism with capitalism and imperialism) and fascist proximity to conservative aristocratic and clerical interests—had, ironically, strong resemblances. Both fascist states and the communist Soviet Union were ruled by dictators, repressed dissent, broadcast propaganda, and employed random terror to maintain control. Liberal democrats and democratic socialists occupied a weak center between wings that were not distinctly "right" or "left" on the political spectrum, but equally totalitarian.

In this stew of political alternatives, a well-meaning European could not easily make a rational choice. Neither could whole nations. They were rescued from perplexity by the advent of crisis: a preliminary crisis in Spain, followed by the graver one in central Europe.

The Spanish Civil War: Rehearsal for World War

From 1936 to 1939, civil war raged in Spain, on the periphery of continental politics. An elected center-left government faced a military revolt that eventually resulted in the creation of an authoritarian regime. While the European democracies stayed aloof, totalitarian powers both communist and fascist sent soldiers and supplies. Their intervention in the Spanish Civil War was a prologue to World War II.

The civil war was in origin a traditional conflict between liberalism on one side, and monarchy and entrenched elites on the other. Spain's era of greatness was long gone by 1898, when it lost the last of its major colonies (see Chapter 24). King Alfonso XIII (r. 1902–1931) ruled weakly thereafter as a constitutional monarch, bolstered by the Roman Catholic clergy and military leaders. Amid labor unrest and separatist revolts, Alfonso turned to the right and supported as prime minister José Antonio Primo de Rivera (1870–1930). In 1923, Primo de Rivera suspended the constitution, censored the press, and clamped down on the universities. When the Depression came in 1929, these tactics proved to be unsustainable.

In 1931, leftist Republican parties triumphed in municipal and national elections, forcing Alfonso to leave Spain. The new constituent assembly was dominated by socialists, communists, anarchists, and syndicalists. This body drafted a liberal constitution granting universal suffrage, basic freedoms, separation of Church and state, secular control of mass education, and the nationalization of church property. The disestablishment of the Roman Catholic Church was one platform on which nearly all agreed.

In 1933, new elections produced a rightist government which promptly undid earlier reforms. In 1936, the pendulum swung again; new elections yielded a left-center majority and a Popular Front government, alarming the wealthy, the clergy, and the military. On July 17, 1936, army officers in Spanish Morocco, North Africa, launched a revolt against the government. Ferried back to Spain in Italian ships, under the leadership of the general Francisco Franco, the Nationalists, as they were called, took control of the Spanish central region, which supported the rising. The Loyalists held the capital at Madrid, the Basque Country, and the developed eastern seaboard, including the region of Catalonia with its cosmopolitan capital at Barcelona.

By all rights, the legitimate, elected government should have won this struggle against a handful of insurgent generals. That it did not has to do with the behavior of the onlooker European nations. The ever-cautious democracies, fearful of war, would not intervene, even to provide the Spanish government with weapons and supplies. The dictatorships, however, intervened vigorously. Mussolini's Italy sent guns, tanks, planes, and men. Hitler unleashed his airforce, or Luftwaffe, including the elite Condor Legion, which practiced in Spain the tactics it would use in the larger conflict to come. Stalin's Soviet Union fed the Loyalists supplies and armaments, for which it required payment in full, and in gold. These were delivered along with the usual political commissars, urging allegiance to the party line.

Loyalist volunteers arrived in Spain as well—the International Brigades, about 40,000 volunteers from Europe and the United States, democrats, socialists, communists, and workers eager to fight for a new order. Thus strengthened, the Loyalists fought desperately against Franco and his supporters (including the Roman Catholic Church, of whom they murdered more than 1000 priests and nearly 300 nuns).

The efficient Franco—a soldier rather than a fascist, but in league with fascism none the less—made steady progress. His German allies pursued their experiments. Their blanket bombing on April 26, 1937 of the Basque town of Guernica was a tragedy not only for the Basques, but for the whole world, now introduced to a new tactic—the deliberate bombing of unwarned civilians. Its cruelty is conveyed in the coldly eloquent monochrome of Picasso's painting *Guernica.*

By the end of 1938, Franco's forces seized Catalonia; by spring 1939, Valencia and the capital of Madrid. The Loyalists and their international volunteers fled, or were captured, tortured, and murdered. Fascism was on the march.

Still the democracies did not act, and would not do so until they were forced to go to war once again, war total and world-wide.

First Hostilities

In 1938, Hitler moved on two fronts, the opening sallies of the next world war. He took over two neighboring regions: the state of Austria and the Sudetenland region of Czechoslovakia. In justification, he could cite the Wilsonian principle of self-determination (see Chapter 26): the ethnic Germans of Austria (the majority of Austrians) and Czechoslovakia (a majority in the Sudetenland) rightly wished to be part of Germany rather than exist as a minority, subject people. In March 1938, he accomplished the *Anschluss,* or annexation, of Austria—a kindred nation already under its own fascist dictator, with a strong native Nazi party and compliant populace to support Hitler's arrival.

Hitler's ingestion of Austria was scarcely noted by European onlookers. They were more disturbed when later the same year he annexed the Czech Sudetenland, which had a German majority and was dominated by a Nazi party. Poland joined in to pick up the district of Czechoslovakia with a strong presence of ethnic Poles.

Alarmed, the British prime minister Neville Chamberlain (1869–1940) met with Hitler three times in 1938, pursuing a policy of **appeasement.**

THE SCUM OF THE EARTH, I BELIEVE?

THE BLOODY ASSASSIN OF THE WORKERS, I PRESUME?

A meeting of dictators: *Stalin and his advisers may also have been deceived by Hitler when they agreed to a pact in the summer of 1939. The absurdity of this Nazi–Communist marriage was generally noted, as in this cartoon from London's Evening Standard on September 20, 1939. On a corpse-littered battlefield the two armed dictators greet each other: "The scum of the earth, I believe," says Hitler cordially; "The bloody assassin of the workers, I presume?" says Stalin.*

WITNESSES

Fighting the Second World War

As war burst, the intentions of the leaders of powerful states became painfully clear. Here, Hitler announces his ruthless intentions to dominate where he will; a Japanese nationalist argues for his nation's role as the unifier, and dominator, of all Asia; and a British statesman, the conservative, imperialist aristocrat Winston Churchill, rallies his countrymen to fight to the ultimate moment for victory over a "monstrous tyranny never surpassed in the dark and lamentable catalogue of human crime."

On the eve of war, Hitler muses on its future (1939): Since the autumn of 1938 ... I decided to go with Stalin. After all there are only three great statesmen in the world, Stalin, I and Mussolini. Mussolini is the weakest. ... So in a few weeks hence I shall stretch out my hand to Stalin at the common German–Russian frontier and with him undertake to re-distribute the world.

Our strength lies in our quickness and in our brutality; Genghis Khan has sent millions of women and children into death knowingly and with a light heart. History sees in him only the great founder of States. As to what the weak Western European civilisation asserts about me, that is of no account. I have given the command and I shall shoot everyone who utters one word of criticism. ... Who after all is today speaking about the destruction of the Armenians?
(Speech by Adolf Hitler, as recorded by a witness; from E. L. Woodward and R. Butler, eds., *Documents on British Foreign Policy, 1919–1939*, 1954)

Japanese nationalist writer Tokutomi Iichirō comments on the Japanese Imperial Declaration of War (1941): In Nippon [Japan] resides a destiny to become the Light of Greater East Asia and to become ultimately the Light of the World. However, in order to become [the former] ... we must have three qualifications. The first ... is strength. ... [W]e must expel Anglo-Saxon influence from East Asia with our strength. ...

The second qualification is benevolence. Nippon must develop the various resources of East Asia and distribute them fairly to all the races within the Greater East Asian Co-Prosperity Sphere. ...

The third qualification is virtue. ... It was the favorite policy of the Anglo-Saxons to make the various races of East Asia compete and fight each other and make them mutually small and powerless. We must, therefore, console them, bring peace and friendship among them, and make them all live in peace with a boundlessly embracing virtue.
(From R. Tsunoda et al, *Sources of the Japanese Tradition*, 1958)

In speeches to the British Parliament, Churchill rallies the nation that would soon oppose Nazism alone (1940): *May 13, 1940:* ... I have nothing to offer but blood and toil and tears and sweat. We have before all of us an ordeal of the most grievous kind. We have before us many, many long months of struggle and of suffering. If you ask what is our policy I will say it is to wage war ... war by air, land and sea, war with all our might and with all the strength that God can give us, and to wage war against a monstrous tyranny never surpassed in the dark and lamentable catalogue of human crime. That is our policy. If you ask us, "What is your aim"? I can answer in one word—victory ... victory however long and hard the road may be.
June 4, 1940 [after describing the evacuation of British forces from Dunkirk, on the far side of the Channel coast]:

We shall fight in France, we shall fight on the seas and oceans; we shall fight with growing confidence and growing strength in the air. We shall defend our island whatever the cost may be. We shall fight on the beaches, we shall fight on the landing grounds, in the fields, in the streets, and in the hills. We shall never surrender. ...
(Winston Churchill, speeches to British Parliament, 1940)

Britain and France were determined to avoid war at all costs. Their citizens had not yet recovered from the slaughter of the previous war (see Chapter 26). Moreover, they hoped that a pacified Germany would serve as a bulwark against communism. In the culminating journey to Munich, Chamberlain obtained (along with French and Italian representatives) a commitment, signed September 29, 1938, that in return for permission to occupy the Sudetenland, Germany would make no further territorial demands.

On that promise the appeasers rested their hopes. Returning to Britain, Chamberlain waved the piece of paper and exulted that it meant "peace in our time." In fact, it meant peace for eleven months. For the following spring, Hitler returned to Czechoslovakia. He

engrossed what remained of the western part (the provinces of Bohemia and Moravia) on March 16, 1939, and organized the eastern sector as the puppet state of Slovakia. Czechoslovakia was no more. In exchange for a brief and specious peace, the Western democracies had delivered Czechoslovakia—and soon the Slavs, the Jews, and virtually all of Europe—to the Nazis.

Hitler's actions caused even Chamberlain's confidence to crumble, and stirred his British and French colleagues to confront Germany's aggressions. Poland would likely be his next target; on March 31, Britain certified to Poland that, if Germany invaded, it would declare war. In the meantime, stifling their distrust of communism, Britain and France would seek an alliance with Stalin's Soviet Union. A diplomatic party set out in August 1939. But the Germans got there first. On August 23, 1939, Hitler's representatives signed with Stalin a Non-Aggression Pact, assuring mutual neutrality if either party was attacked; and some Polish and Baltic territories for the Soviets if war did ensue. Hitler's reasons are outlined in *Witnesses* on p. 819. The Germans, who detested the Soviets both as Slavs and as Bolsheviks, had bought freedom for their invasion of Poland. The Soviets detested the fascists no more than the democrats—to them, "imperialists"—whose war they did not wish to fight. The Comintern was alerted. Communist officials dictated the new party line to their followers: they had fought fascism in Spain, but now they must support, or at least cease their criticism of Nazism, and remain aloof from the "imperialist war." Consternation also struck Western diplomats, who had hoped to play Germany against the Soviets, or the Soviets against Germany—and now awoke to find that their playthings were arrayed against them. A contemporary cartoon is reproduced on p. 818.

Meanwhile, Hitler seized the Baltic port of Memel; Italy seized Albania on April 7, and on May 22 formed a ten-year military alliance with Germany—the "Pact of Steel." On September 1, 1939, Hitler let loose **Blitzkrieg** ("lightning war," war as stupendous as a bolt of lightning) on Poland. (On that same day he ordered, his racial theories always in the forefront of his mind, the execution of some 70,000 mentally ill patients in German hospitals.) On September 3, Britain and France declared war on Germany.

From Appeasement to Victory

Appeasement failed less than one year after Chamberlain announced he had won "peace in our time." The world was at war again in a conflict that was to involve Europe, east and southeast Asia, North Africa, and the Middle East—with combatants recruited also from the United States and the British dominions (see Map 28.3, p. 822). World War I had been fought with trenches, barbed wire, and nerve gas. World War II would be fought with airplanes, aircraft carriers, and amphibious landings; codebreakers, spies, and radar; resistance cells, suicide missions, and covert operations; tanks and bombs, conventional and atomic. Never had so much wealth been channeled to produce so many machines that killed.

In the European theater of the war, the German offensive pressed forward to 1942 when it received setbacks in the Soviet Union and Africa. Thereafter the tide turned in favor of the Allies, who concluded the war with encirclement of Germany.

The Nazi Invasion of Poland and Western Europe
By the end of September 1939, the German invasion of Poland was virtually complete. Now the invaders

subjected that country to a savage occupation, killing in all about 3 million Poles. As an inferior race, according to Nazi ideology, the Slavic Poles were to be reduced to a docile, illiterate serfdom. Poles were barred from schools, denied privileges and position, subjected to arbitrary violence, or deported. Their leaders and intellectuals were slaughtered, and the large Jewish population ghettoized. Eastern Europe learned quickly the nature of Nazi conquest as it swept beyond Poland and into the Balkans.

Nazi occupation seemed gentler, at first, when it came to the western nations of Norway and Denmark, the Netherlands, and Belgium, nations Hitler gathered up in the first six months of 1940. On June 14, 1940, the Germans entered Paris, having breached the supposedly impregnable fortifications of the "Maginot Line." The French swiftly capitulated, while the government, headed by Marshal Philippe Pétain, an aging hero of the previous war, entered into collaboration with the Nazi victors. He would run a puppet French state from the southern resort town of Vichy, while Germans held the north and west. From France, Hitler determined to take Britain.

The Air War: Germany vs. Britain   From June 1940, when its Expeditionary Force escaped the continent from the northern French port of Dunkirk in fishing boats and yachts, until June 1941, when the Soviet Union joined the conflict, the British faced the Nazi behemoth alone. It was, as Sir Winston Churchill, prime minister from May 10, 1940, both the poet and the chief strategist of the conflict, intoned, "their finest hour." Extracts from his speeches are given in *Witnesses* on p. 819. Britain had a small army, a still vital navy, and a trained, eager airforce—fortunately, for the Channel, which had sheltered the island from invasion, could now be bridged by air. In what came to be known as the Battle of Britain, Royal Air Force (RAF) pilots, aided by the sinvention of radar, narrowly staved off invasion by the numerically superior Luftwaffe. Never, said Churchill, had so few done so much for so many.

The Luftwaffe commenced the bombing of British military targets in July 1940; soon it bombed cities as well, including Birmingham, Manchester, Liverpool, and Southampton. Above all, London was a target—its children preventively evacuated since 1939, and its citizens taking nightly refuge in subway stations. The "blitz" of London peaked in September but continued through spring 1941. London's great cathedral of St. Paul's survived amid the surrounding wreckage. In the industrial Midlands region, the lovely cathedral of Coventry was destroyed. Later in the war, strategic bombing by the Allies was to destroy great swathes of the German cities of Hamburg, Cologne, and Dresden, whose churches were reduced to scarred debris, and whose "unavoidable" civilian casualties included the elderly and infirm, women and children.

Although the British fought mostly in the air, they had other, secret weapons. These included a squad of cryptologists (Polish exiles broke the German cipher early in the war) who intercepted tens of thousands of German messages per month, and the best intelligence operation in Europe, which kept the Germans ignorant or deceived about their opponents' actions.

At sea, meanwhile, the Germans initially had the advantage as their U-boats preyed on shipping along the western approaches to Britain. After 1941, they moved out to the mid-Atlantic (safe from British aerial patrol). After the United States entered the war late in 1942, they found new targets further west and in the Caribbean. Eventually, long-range planes equipped with radar were able to track the U-boats, and settle the "battle of the Atlantic."

The Germans in the East and in North Africa   By 1941, Hitler was planning a new venture for the spring: the invasion of his ally, the Soviet Union. On June 22, German armies launched a three-pronged assault on the Russian heartland. In the north, they targeted Leningrad; from the center, the capital, Moscow; to the south, the Crimean ports and lower river Don. The Germans dubbed this undertaking "Operation Barbarossa" in remembrance of the medieval German emperor Frederick I Barbarossa.

Until this moment, the Russians had observed their agreement with Germany. Two weeks after the Germans invaded Poland from the west, according to prior agreement, the Red Army did so from the east. One consequence of that invasion was the massacre in 1941, by Stalin's order, of 4443 Polish officers, in Katyn forest, near Smolensk. In 1944, Stalin shifted the blame for this massacre to the Nazis. Recent investigations assign it unequivocally to the Soviets—who were surely responsible also for 10,000 more Polish officers missing since the Soviet occupation. The incident is one relic of the brief period of Nazi–Soviet cooperation. In 1939–1940, Soviet forces allied with Germany also invaded the Baltic states, Finland, and Romania.

In June 1941, German forces smashed through the thin crust of Soviet defenses on the western frontier, taking Stalin thoroughly by surprise. The Red Army was not ready; it was in any case ill-trained. Stalin's Five Year Plans, however, had brought to a maximum the Soviet Union's capacity to produce armaments (it had nearly twice as many tanks at the front as the German attackers). And of people, it had an abundance. Communists around the globe celebrated Soviet strength—instructed now, after their abrupt about-face in 1939, to turn about once again.

In 1941 and 1942, the Germans advanced, tearing through Ukraine and the Crimea to the river Don, the Caucasus mountains, and almost to the Caspian Sea. But Soviet forces denied them Moscow, and the citizens and soldiers holding Leningrad—where a

siege of almost 900 terrible days cost over 1 million lives—saved that city as well (the left photograph on p. 823 shows Leningrad during the siege). In August 1942, German forces reached the industrial center of Stalingrad, on the river Volga, gateway to the Caucasus oilfields. They struggled for months with the city's defenders, commanded by General Georgi Konstantinovich Zhukov (1896–1974), in the streets, face to face, from house to house.

As winter arrived, the battle hardened. Soviet armies encircled the Germans, who froze and starved, and were soon to die as newly minted tanks emerged from the Stalingrad factories. On January 31, 1943, the remnant of 91,000 German soldiers surrendered to the Soviet army. German military morale never recovered from the humiliating defeat at Stalingrad.

The following summer, the Germans met the Soviets at Kursk. Here 9000 tanks came to grips, tough German Panzers ("panthers") against even heavier Soviet tanks, which won the battle. From Kursk, the Red Army surged westward, its sights on Berlin. The Soviets had borne the brunt of the German war and sacrificed an estimated 20 to 28 million soldiers and civilians, dwarfing casualty rates for Britain or the United States, or even Germany. For the Soviets, this had not been simply a struggle between communism and fascism, or communism and imperialism. It had been a war for Mother Russia, the Great Patriotic War.

The year 1943 was pivotal in other theaters too. In North Africa, German forces under General Erwin G. Rommel (1891–1944) had arrived early in 1941 to blast through to Egypt and the Middle East. But at El Alamein in Egypt in October 1942, British general Bernard Montgomery (1887–1976) bested Rommel, the mastermind of tank warfare, with his own tactics. (Montgomery had profited from reading the book Rommel wrote on the subject.) Soon thereafter, United States forces landed in northwest Africa under General Dwight D. Eisenhower (1890–1969) to complete the German rout by the winter of 1943.

The War in Asia   In east Asia also, 1942 was a turning point. In 1941, the Japanese had launched a campaign to control all the lands and islands of the western Pacific and southeast Asia (see *Witnesses*, p. 819). These were to form an outer zone of the Japanese Empire, complementary to the inner zone of home islands and Korean and Chinese possessions in a unified system called the Greater East Asia Co-Prosperity Sphere. Only the United States had a Pacific force capable of challenging them. To neutralize that potential enemy, the Japanese attacked, without warning, the United States naval base at Pearl Harbor in the Hawaiian islands, on December 7, 1941.

Until then, the United States had maintained an official neutrality, while supplying the Allies with armaments at first on a "cash and carry" basis, and after March 11, 1941 under the Lend-Lease program,

Map 28.3 Axis Advance and Allied Victory—World War II, 1939–1945: *The early years of the war saw the Axis powers expand in both the European and Asian zones almost to the point of total control. After 1943 turning points—the Russian victory at Stalingrad, the Allied invasion of Sicily and southern Italy—Axis-dominated Europe was put on the defensive. The June 1944 liberation of Rome and invasion of Normandy spelled the end of the Nazi empire, with final surrender in May 1945 following the Soviet sweep across eastern Europe and into Berlin. Meanwhile, the Allied war with Japan in the Pacific was effectively won by May 1945, although Japanese surrender followed only the epochal use of force—the release of two atom bombs—in August 1945.*

on the promise of future payment. But the Pearl Harbor attack prompted an immediate response. The next day, Congress declared war on Japan; soon after, Germany declared war on the United States. American factories soared into full production, and by spring 1942, troops were pouring into Britain, Africa, and Asia while a fleet strong enough to patrol two oceans gathered in the south Pacific. After Pearl Harbor the vigilant Churchill, the lone fighter, then wary ally of the Soviets, relaxed.

From September 1941 to early 1942, the Japanese roared through Asia, defeating native and colonial defenders, deporting survivors to concentration camps where many were tortured and starved. When the first United States ships arrived to join Allied defenders (British, Dutch, New Zealand, and Australian) in

spring 1942, Japan controlled mainland and islands to a vast perimeter. Its dominions included much of eastern China, parts of Indochina and the East Indies, and many islands, including the Philippines, seized immediately after Pearl Harbor and the evacuation of United States general Douglas MacArthur (1880–1964).

After some initial defeats, and victories at Midway and Guadalcanal, United States forces drove the Japanese out of the Pacific islands over the next two years. Japanese defenders (whose casualties exceeded those of the Allies ten to one) dug into foxholes, hid in caves, rushed in desperate, futile charges. As their code of honor dictated, encircled garrisons stood to the death, and both combatants and civilians often chose suicide over capture. The last defenders were suicide bombers, who blew themselves up with the enemy ships they attacked—the *kamikaze*, named after the seemingly miraculous wind that in 1281 had saved Japan from a Mongol invasion.

By May 1945, the Allies had swept the Japanese from the open Pacific. The Japanese airforce and navy were largely destroyed. Japan's home islands, gripped by hunger, suffered steady United States bombardment from island bases. The British launched land attacks from India, and the Chinese fought where they could. Yet, cornered, the Japanese resisted.

Victory in Europe   The drive to free Europe began in earnest in 1943. In July of that year, Allied troops recently victorious in the North Africa campaign crossed the Mediterranean to land in Sicily and, on September 3, to the Italian mainland. Germany's ally, and a belligerent since June 1940, Italy surrendered; the Italian people welcomed the Allied soldiers as liberators. The now hated Mussolini was dismissed by the (still reigning) king Victor Emmanuel III, then arrested and imprisoned. He was subsequently rescued by the Germans, but finally shot, with his Jewish mistress, on April 28, 1945, after a hasty court-martial by **partisans** (unofficial **resistance** forces).

The final liberation of Italy from tenacious German forces took many months. By June 5, 1944, the Allies had fought their way to Rome, but the Germans still held the north. Venice, the last major city to fall, was taken only nine days before the German surrender on VE Day ("Victory in Europe"). In the Tuscan hills and the Po Valley, resistance forces linked up with the Allies and aided the liberation.

Starvation, Siege, and Sack

Leningrad and Shanghai: *Among the many images of the brutality of war, this one from Leningrad (left) in 1942 (where starvation and terror endured during a siege of almost 900 days) and another from Shanghai (right) in 1937 (where Japanese forces bombed and sacked the city) are particularly poignant. In the first, parents pull a sled laden with the body of their dead child down Leningrad's Nevsky Prospect. In the second, an infant sits amid the wreckage of a railroad station.*

For there had been resistance groups in all the nations of occupied Europe. Active in many were communists receiving orders from Moscow; elsewhere nationalists who were instructed by governments-in-exile based in Britain; elsewhere Jews whose best choice was to fight Nazism wherever they could. The most effective were the Yugoslav partisans (divided between communist and monarchist units) who had fled to the mountains upon the German invasion of 1941, and there famously tied up twenty German divisions with their guerrilla tactics. Among the most daring perhaps were the German army officers whose attempt to assassinate Hitler on July 20, 1944, had it succeeded, might have saved the world millions of fatalities; but they were caught and savagely executed. The most ill-fated were the Poles of Warsaw, who perished on the brink of liberation in 1945, abandoned to Nazi fury by Stalin as he stalled outside the city. The French resistance groups pulled together at the end when on June 6, 1944, D-Day, Allied forces crossed the Channel to land on the Normandy coast, under the supreme command of United States general Eisenhower. In league with them were the forces of General Charles de Gaulle (1890–1970), who had escaped ahead of the Nazi takeover in 1940 and, from exile in Britain, organized the "Free French."

From Normandy, the Allied armies pushed eastward to meet the Soviets in Germany in April 1945. They moved swiftly, for the Soviets were storming westward, pushing the Germans out of Russia and Ukraine. By 1944, they had replaced the Germans as occupiers in Yugoslavia and Hungary, and, in 1945, Czechoslovakia and Poland. By April 30, 1945, the Soviets entered Berlin, and subdued it by May 2. On May 8, VE Day, with the surrender of German forces, the European war ended.

It was a dreadful liberation, accomplished with looting, terror, and the rape of tens of thousands, perhaps hundreds of thousands of women aged from ten to eighty in Germany alone. German prisoners could expect little mercy from Soviet avengers of their more than 20 million dead. But these cruelties could not equal what the Soviet troops found in the Nazi concentration camps they liberated—mass graves, machines of torture and death, a remnant of starved survivors—the evidence of unutterable evil, a secret and hideous **genocidal** war against the Jews.

FINAL SOLUTIONS

For the Jews, Hitler's chief advisers devised a "Final Solution," launched in spring 1942. The progress is shown on Map 28.4 below. From the start, Jews had been rounded up in the conquered nations. Some were shot, like the 100,000 at Babi Yar near Kiev in Ukraine, between 1941 and 1943 (see *Witnesses*, p. 827). A total of some 500,000 Jews would be killed in the Soviet Union before the German retreat. Some were ghettoized, like the 60,000 Jews of Warsaw, shown in *Windows On*, p. 825, who revolted in 1943 and were massacred, by April 20, to the last woman

and child. Others were transported to concentration camps—along with resisters, communists, gypsies, homosexuals, Russian and Polish prisoners, and others. There they were tormented, starved, and worked to death. Many died from the privations of the camps, the brutality of the guards, and the grotesque "scientific" experiments performed on these dehumanized subjects. The Final Solution was devised to ensure that they would all die. Its aim was to achieve the extermination of the Jews as a people—an aim it very nearly achieved.

The Germans established more than twenty concentration camps on German and Polish territory to warehouse their victims and extract what labor they could before they succumbed to starvation and disease. Of these, a few were designated as death camps—in German literally "places of annihilation"—whose purpose was the extermination of human beings: among them Auschwitz (which also served as a labor camp), Belsen (illustrated in *Windows On*, p. 825, Chelmno, Majdanek, Sobibor, and Treblinka. The Nazi extermination camps were unique. The Japanese,

Map 28.4 The Holocaust and the Bomb:
Hitler's Third Reich launched its "Final Solution" to the "Jewish question" in January 1942—the project to eliminate the Jews of Europe and their ancient culture, which continued until the Nazi defeat in 1945. One million Jews had already died, but now the killing became systematic: ghetto raids, massacres, deportations and death marches and, above all, the death camp, the machine designed especially for the destruction of human beings. The main map here shows the locations of the principal death camps, while the pie graphs document the extent of the destruction. The two atomic bombs that destroyed the Japanese cities of Hiroshima and Nagasaki on August 6 and 9, 1945, shown in the inset map, took fewer victims (see chart on p. 828), but aroused matchless terror. This previously inconceivable weapon had the potential to annihilate not merely thousands or millions but the entire human race.

The Holocaust

Jews before their deportation, Amsterdam, 1943

Vicious anti-Semitism, culminating in the Final Solution (the attempt to exterminate all European Jewry) earned Nazism its special recognition as uniquely evil. Here, respectably dressed and unsuspecting Dutch Jews carry their belongings with them as they are about to board the train that will take them to concentration camps and, for most of them, their deaths (top left). Their clothes bear the yellow star they were required to display by Nazi regulations. Nazi soldiers supervised the massacre of Jews (top right), and the rounding-up and deportation of Jews to the Warsaw ghetto (bottom right). This last photograph was presented in evidence at the Nuremberg trial of those accused of war crimes. The Allied forces that liberated the Nazi death camps, such as the Belsen camp (bottom left), found a few starved survivors amid heaps of corpses and bones. The remains of some 9 million people were located, about 6 million of them Jews.

Kovno pogrom, Lithuania, July 27, 1941

Belsen death camp, 1945

Jews removed to Warsaw ghetto, April 1943

To continue your investigation of this topic, please go to www.prenhall.com/king for the related **WINDOWS** on the **WEB** activity

too, built concentration camps, and mistreated their prisoners of war—more than one-quarter of the Allied soldiers held captive died. But they did not use the camps for genocidal ends as the Nazis did.

Nazi managers invented a method of mass extermination: the gas chamber. SS guards packed hundreds, even thousands of prisoners at a time into the sealed rooms. They then introduced a precise quantity of Zyklon-B gas (crystallized prussic acid, normally used as a pesticide). Death followed in just a few minutes—between three and fifteen, reported a camp commander to the Nuremberg Tribunal for war crimes. His testimony is quoted in *Witnesses* on p. 827. Squads of Jewish slave laborers then ripped out gold teeth, and searched the bodies for gold, jewelry, and gems; then burned or buried them. In a few hours, all trace of the slaughter was removed—bones, blood, ashes, all vanished. At Auschwitz, the most efficient of the death camps, this pitiless system killed as many as 9000 people per day, and a total of perhaps 2.5 million during its years of operation.

Why did no one intervene to stop the slaughter? Much of it happened in secret. But enough was known. By 1942, the Allied governments knew that Jews were being killed on a large scale, but authorized no rescue missions. On the other hand, the occupied Danes managed brilliantly to ship most of their Jewish population to safety in neutral Sweden; and many individuals, at dire risk to themselves, from moral or religious motives, saved individual Jews.

Hiroshima bombed: *The devastation caused by the atomic bombs dropped by the United States planes on the Japanese cities of Hiroshima and Nagasaki was unprecedented, causing the obliteration of whole cities. This photograph shows the remains of Hiroshima after its bombing on August 6, 1945.*

The Nazis kept careful records of their extermination program. The death camps killed about 9 million people, of whom nearly 6 million were Jews (of these, more than 1 million were children, the first to be sent to die). Over the last half-century, some of the survivors have told their stories, and Jewish organizations have reconstructed the unforgettable part of the past now called the **Holocaust** (a Greek word meaning a sacrifice offered for burning, or a "sacred offering") or Shoah (a Hebrew word meaning "destruction"). Now schoolchildren and museumgoers learn, so that the events may never be repeated, of the unique evil rationally planned and deliberately executed by a presumably civilized people.

The deed did not go wholly unpunished. After the war, from November 1945 through October 1946, an international tribunal convened at Nuremberg in Germany to investigate the war crimes of Nazi leaders. Twelve were sentenced to death, others to long sentences; three were acquitted. A separate tribunal began early in 1946 to consider the crimes of twenty-five Japanese civil and military leaders, all of whom were found guilty, and of these seven executed. Of other collaborators tried in their own nations' tribunals, the eighty-nine-year old French general Pétain and the Nazi-appointed Norwegian president Vidkun Quisling (1887–1945), whose name has come to mean "traitor," were sentenced to death. (Pétain's life was spared at de Gaulle's request.) Hitler himself escaped. He had committed suicide in his Berlin bunker, to evade Soviet capture, on the night of April 28–29, 1945—the day after Mussolini's execution, and two weeks after president Roosevelt's peaceful death.

The discovery of the slaughter of the Jews began with the Soviet liberations of 1944–1945. Not long after its terrors began to be known, another horror was in preparation: the atomic bomb.

The lifelong pacifist Albert Einstein (1879–1955), who had foreseen the horror of the bomb (see Chapters 25, 27), wrote President Roosevelt in 1939, explaining how the power of nuclear fission could be harnessed to create a weapon of unprecedented force. Late in 1941, the "Manhattan Project" began for the development of that lethal device. A team of British, Canadian, and United States scientists labored over the next years to achieve its implementation. (Soviet, German, and Japanese scientists were also at work on the same project, but were well behind.) Roosevelt, Churchill, and their military strategists approved of the enterprise. It would be the weapon of weapons, the war-winner without equal, a tool that must be made and, if necessary, used.

On July 16, 1945, a test explosion showed the bomb was ready. At the Potsdam conference outside Berlin (July 17–August 2), the Soviet Union, United States, and Britain issued an ultimatum: Japan must surrender unconditionally. When Japan declined to do this, President Harry S. Truman (who had

Final Solutions

The end of the war was worse even than its outbreak, since it brought about two horrors barely conceivable in a world that had undergone many unbearable horrors: those of the Holocaust—the wilful attempt to exterminate the entire Jewish population of Europe—and of the atomic bombs dropped on two Japanese cities populated by non-combatants. These were the tragic "Final Solutions" of a war born more than anything else of the evil intent of individual men who rose to power. The first three passages describe a Nazi massacre of Jews and the administration of a German-run concentration camp, and argue the need to remember forever the terrible time when "law itself became immoral." The next two relate to the dropping of the atomic bomb: the reaction of President Truman to the announcement of the event, and a reporter's account of the devastation of Hiroshima, 30 days after the bomb changed its citizens' lives forever.

German engineer Hermann Graebe testifies at Nuremberg about a Nazi massacre of Jews in the Ukraine (1942): The people who had got off the trucks ... had to undress upon the orders of an SS man, who carried a riding or dog whip. They had to put down their clothes in fixed places, sorted according to shoes, top clothing and underclothing. ...

Without screaming or weeping, these people undressed, ... kissed each other, said farewells. ... I watched a family of about eight persons. ... An old woman with snow-white hair was holding the one-year-old child in her arms and singing it and tickling it. ... The couple were looking on with tears in their eyes. The father was holding the hand of a boy about ten years old and speaking to him softly. ...

At that moment the SS man at the pit shouted something to his comrade. The latter counted off about twenty persons and instructed them to go behind the earth mound. ... I walked around the mound and found myself confronted by a tremendous grave. ... [T]he pit was already two-thirds full. I estimated that it already contained about 1,000 people. ... The people, completely naked, went down some steps ... to the place to which the SS man directed them. ... Then I heard a series of shots.
(USGPO, *Nazi Conspiracy and Aggression* 1946; document PS 2992)

Concentration camp commander Rudolf Hoess testifies at Nuremberg (April 5, 1946): I was ordered to establish extermination facilities at Auschwitz in June 1941. ... The Camp Commander at Treblinka told me that he had liquidated 80,000 in the course of one-half year. ... He used monoxide gas and I did not think that his methods were very efficient. So when I set up the extermination building at Auschwitz, I used Cyclon B, which was a crystallized prussic acid which we dropped into the death chamber from a small opening. It took from 3 to 15 minutes to kill the people in the death chamber. ... We knew when the people were dead because their screaming stopped. ... After the bodies were removed our special commandos

took off the rings and extracted the gold from the teeth of the corpses. ... Another improvement we made over Treblinka was that we built our gas chambers to accommodate 2,000 people at one time, whereas at Treblinka their 10 gas chambers only accommodated 200 people each.
(USGPO, *Nazi Conspiracy and Aggression*, 1947; document PS 3868)

Survivor, author, and Noble Peace laureate Elie Wiesel reflects on the past (1987): In those days and nights, humanity was distorted and twisted in this city, the capital of a nation proud of its distant history, but struggling with its recent memories.

Everything human and divine was perverted then. The law itself became immoral. ... It became legal and praiseworthy to ... destroy human beings—sons and daughters of an ancient people—whose very existence was considered a crime. ...

Still, not all Germans alive then were guilty. ... Only the guilty were guilty.

Children of killers are not killers but children. I have neither the desire nor the authority to judge today's generation for the unspeakable crimes committed by the generation of Hitler.

But we may—and we must—hold it responsible, not for the past, but for the way it remembers the past. ... Memory is the keyword. ... [S]alvation, like redemption, can be found only in memory.
(Elie Wiesel, *The Kingdom of Memory*, 1990)

President Truman recalls the dropping of the atomic bomb (1945): On August 6 ... came the historic news that shook the world. I was eating lunch ... when Captain Frank Graham, White House Map Room watch officer, handed me the following message:

TO THE PRESIDENT
FROM THE SECRETARY OF WAR
Big bomb dropped on Hiroshima August 5 at 7:15 PM Washington time. First reports indicate complete success. ...

I was greatly moved. I ... said to the group of sailors around me, "This is the greatest thing in history. It's time for us to get home."
(*Memoirs by Harry S. Truman, I: Year of Decisions*, 1955)

English journalist Wilfred Burchett reports from Hiroshima (September 5, 1945): In Hiroshima, thirty days after the first atom bomb destroyed the city and shook the world, people are still dying, mysteriously and horribly, people who were uninjured in the cataclysm—from an unknown something which I can only describe as the atomic plague. Hiroshima does not look like a bombed city. It looks as if a monster steamroller had passed over it and squashed it out of existence. I write these facts as dispassionately as I can in the hope that they will act as a warning to the world.
(From P. Knightley, *The First Casualty: From the Crimea to Vietnam: The War Correspondent as Hero, Propagandist and Myth Maker*, 1975)

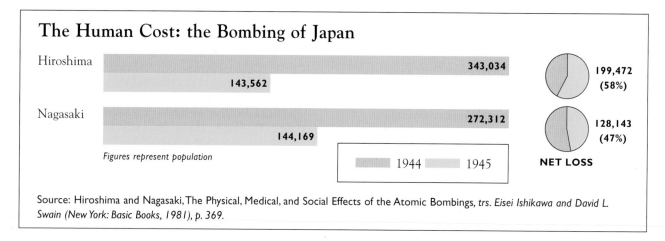

The Human Cost: the Bombing of Japan

Hiroshima — 343,034 / 143,562 — 199,472 (58%)

Nagasaki — 272,312 / 144,169 — 128,143 (47%)

Figures represent population

1944   1945

NET LOSS

Source: Hiroshima and Nagasaki, The Physical, Medical, and Social Effects of the Atomic Bombings, *trs. Eisei Ishikawa and David L. Swain (New York: Basic Books, 1981), p. 369.*

succeeded to the presidency on Roosevelt's death in April), ordered United States planes to drop on two Japanese cities the most powerful weapon ever made.

The bombs destroyed the cities in an instant, their destruction signaled by the mushroom-shaped cloud that immediately formed above the ruins. On August 6, the explosion of "Little Boy" (the bomb's name; the B-29 bomber was named Enola Gay, after the pilot's mother) immediately killed 78,000 of Hiroshima's 300,000 people—vaporized, burned, crushed. Many more were injured. The remainder lived to suffer mutilation and the horrible consequence of radiation (see *Witnesses*, p. 827). At Nagasaki, on August 9, "Fat Boy" killed more tens of thousands.

The deadly bombs brought a prompt result. Japanese leaders had already been discussing surrender before the bombing of Hiroshima. On August 10, the

Japanese government communicated to the Allied command Japan's surrender, which Allied Supreme Commander General MacArthur accepted on September 2 on board the battleship *Missouri*.

No war tribunals gathered to judge the scientists and politicians who unleashed the power of the atomic bomb on the human race. They believed the use of the weapon was justified. Indeed, their arguments are powerful. An Allied invasion of Japan would almost certainly have cost more Japanese (and American) lives. All arguments diminish next to the sheer magnitude of the destruction caused by that unimaginable weapon, and the threat of annihilation it posed and poses to all subsequent human generations (see Chapter 30).

Conclusion

THE DEFEAT OF FASCISM AND THE MEANING OF THE WEST

Nazism sprang from a combination of the worst of the Western traditions—irrationalism, extreme nationalism, racism. It failed because of the best of them—the traditions of liberty and justice that had evolved over centuries and had been inscribed in the constitutions of the Western democracies. The struggle of committed democrats against all forms of fascism, joined by Russian communist defenders of their ideals and their soil, spelled its destruction in 1945.

The cost of the war was enormous. Combatant and civilian deaths came to an estimated total of 46 million. The Soviet Union alone suffered 11 million military, and between 10 and 20 million civilian deaths, a tremendous toll from a population of about 190 million. Germany suffered over 4 million deaths, civilian and military; the Chinese perhaps 15 million; the Japanese nearly 2 million (and scarcely any wounded—the Japanese preferred death); the Jewish dead came to nearly 6 million, the Polish 3 million. Most lightly touched, the British, the French, the Italians, and the Americans together suffered a little over 1 million combat deaths; among the occupied French, an additional 350,000 civilians died.

The slaughter purchased the defeat of fascism. Yet it did not spell the end of totalitarianism in the West, where fascism in Spain and Portugal, and communism in the Soviet Union, endured until 1974–1975 and 1991 (see Chapter 30). In the postwar decades, new non-Western nations often inclined toward authoritarian or communist governments (see Chapter 29).

The future would also be burdened by memories: the destruction of cities and the willful deaths of non-combatants; the Holocaust; the atomic bomb. These horrors would haunt future generations. For many, the West had been discredited. Certainly the old world-system was dead. Another world was about to emerge, in which the meaning of the West and its vaunted traditions would be subject to question.

REVIEW QUESTIONS

1. How did Lenin adapt Marxist theory to fit conditions in Russia? Why were the Bolsheviks able to seize and retain power in Russia? What steps did Lenin take to impose communism within Russia?

2. How did Stalin gain control of the Communist Party? What did he hope to gain from the purges? How were the purges related to the collectivization of agriculture and the drive to industrialize Russia?

3. Why did so many Europeans find fascism attractive? How did it differ from communism? How did Mussolini seize and hold power in Italy? Which other European nations set up fascist regimes in the 1930s?

4. Why did the Weimar Republic fail? How did Hitler achieve supreme power in Germany by 1934? What role did racism play in his program for Germany and Europe? What did Hitler, Stalin, and Mussolini believe the role of women to be?

5. What were Hitler's goals in Europe? Why did Britain and France fail to stop Hitler in the 1930s? Why did Japan become an aggressor state after World War I? Why did Stalin reach an agreement with Hitler in 1939?

6. What were the decisive battles that led to the defeat of the Axis in World War II? Why was the war more brutal than previous wars? What was the Final Solution, and how did the Nazis put it into effect?

SUGGESTED RESOURCES

Bolsheviks and Communists *(see also Chapter 26)*

Brooks, Jeffrey, *Thank you, Comrade Stalin! Soviet Public Culture from Revolution to Cold War* (Princeton: Princeton University Press, 2000). Examines newspaper accounts of Soviet life to track the phenomenon of ceaseless elevation of the Communist state and its leaders.

Fitzpatrick, Sheila, *Everyday Stalinism: Ordinary Life in Extraordinary Times: Soviet Russia in the 1930s* (Oxford: Oxford University Press, 2000). Argues that attention should be paid, with regard to this decade of Stalinist terror, to the elevation of a new class of trained technical experts and bureaucrats, who were able to live productive lives regardless of the nature of the regime.

Getty, J. Arch & Oleg V. Naumov, *The Road to Terror: Stalin and the Self-Destruction of the Bolsheviks, 1932–1939* (New Haven: Yale University Press, 1999). Analysis of documents released from the Soviet archives which make clear the extent of the Stalinist purges.

Malia, Martin, *The Soviet Tragedy: A History of Russian Socialism, 1917–1991* (New York: Free Press, 1994). Argues that Stalinism was inevitable given Leninist principles.

Medvedev, Roy, *Let History Judge: The Origins and Consequences of Stalinism*, rev. ed., trs. George Shriver (New York: Columbia University Press, 1989). An impassioned account by a professional historian, dissenter, and survivor of the Soviet regime.

Service, Robert, *A History of Twentieth-Century Russia* (Cambridge, MA: Harvard University Press, 1998). Authoritative, balanced, and scholarly history of the Soviet Union.

Joseph stalin, Biographical Chronicle: http://www.stel.ru/stalin

The Faces of Fascism

Bullock, Alan, *Hitler and Stalin: Parallel Lives* (New York: Knopf, 1992). Juxtaposes Hitler and Stalin at parallel stages of their careers.

Carroll, Peter N., *The Odyssey of the Abraham Lincoln Brigade: Americans in the Spanish Civil War* (Stanford: Stanford University Press, 1994). Explores the motivations and impact of the participation of a meager battalion of about 3000 mostly young, mostly Jewish, mostly communist Americans who fought in Spain in 1937–1938 in the first phase of the struggle against fascism, supported only by Moscow.

De Grazia, Victoria, *How Fascism Ruled Women: Italy, 1922–1945* (Berkeley: University of California Press, 1992). Explores fascist Italy's efforts to enroll women in the political nation while demanding that they function essentially as producers of children.

Kaplan, Marion A., *Between Dignity and Despair: Jewish Life in Nazi Germany* (Oxford: Oxford University Press, 1998). Account of the attempts by Jews under German rule to maintain their traditions.

Kershaw, Ian, *Hitler 1889–1936: Hubris* (New York: W.W. Norton, 1998); *Hitler 1936–1945: Nemesis* (New York: W.W. Norton, 2000). Kershaw's comprehensive two-volume biography is likely to be the standard for years to come.

Mosse, George L., *The Fascist Revolution: Toward a General Theory of Fascism* (New York: Howard Fertig, 1999). Essays exploring the roots of fascism, focusing on the linked phenomena of nationalism, anti-Semitism, occultism, and the cult of the leader.

Payne, Stanley, *A History of Fascism, 1914–1945* (Madison: University of Wisconsin Press, 1995). Scholarly, a masterful disentanglement of Fascist theory and practice.

The Rise of Adolf Hitler, an online narrative in 24 chapters (History Place): http://www.bbc.co.uk/history
http://www.historyplace.com/worldwar2/riseofhitler

The Second World War: Fascism Defeated

Bartov, Omer, *Murder in Our Midst: The Holocaust, Industrial Killing, and Representation* (Oxford: Oxford University Press, 1996). The term "Industrial Killing" refers to murder that is organized by the state.

Duus, Peter, R. H. Myers, and M. R. Peattie, eds., *The Japanese Wartime Empire, 1931–1945* (Princeton, NJ: Princeton University Press, 1996). Essays on Japanese imperial practices in northeast and southeast Asia.

Goldhagen, Daniel Jonah, *Hitler's Willing Executioners: Ordinary Germans and the Holocaust* (New York: Knopf, 1996). Controversial book that focuses on the complicity of ordinary Germans in the Nazis' efforts to annihilate European Jewry.

Hicks, George, *The Comfort Women: Japan's Brutal Regime of Enforced Prostitution in the Second World War* (New York: W. W. Norton, 1995). Useful treatment of one of Japan's most notorious wartime activities.

Weitz, Margaret Collins, *Sisters in the Resistance: How Women fought to Free France, 1940–1945* (New York: J. Wiley, 1995). Examines the role of women and the limits and meaning of "resistance".

WWII oral history, women's experience of war:
http://www.stg.brown.edu/projects/WWII_Women/tocCS.html

THE END OF IMPERIALISM

1880	1900	1920	1940	1960	1980	2000

The Western World

World War I and the
Russian Revolution, 1914–21

World War II, 1939–45

◆ "Easter Rising," Ireland, 1916
- ◆ Great Depression
  begins, 1929
- ◆ Commonwealth of Nations
  created, 1931
  - ◆ Ireland ("Eire")
    independent, 1937
    - ◆ UN Universal Declaration
      of Human Rights, 1948

◆ Cuban Missile Crisis, 1961
- ◆ Civil Rights Act, 1964
  - ◆ NOW (National Organization for Women)
    created, 1966
    - ◆ Martin Luther King shot, 1968
      - ◆ Helsinki Accords, 1975
        - ◆ Soviet Union dissolved, 1991
          - ◆ European Union created,
            1994

Middle East and North Africa

◆ Balfour Declaration, 1917
- ◆ Ottoman Empire ends, 1919
  - ◆ Atatürk president of Turkey, 1922
    - ◆ Iraq independent from Britain,
      1932
      - ◆ Egyptian independence ends, 1937
        - ◆ UN partitions Palestine, 1947
          - ◆ Israel declares statehood, 1947

◆ Nasser nationalizes Suez Canal, 1956
- ◆ Algeria independent from France, 1962
  - ◆ Six-Day War, Israel, 1967
    - ◆ Oil crisis, 1973–74
      - ◆ Iranian Revolution, 1978
        - ◆ Palestinian "Intifada," 1987
          - ◆ Gulf War, 1991

Africa

South African War, 1899–1902

Many African nations gain independence, 1960–68

◆ National party takes control, 1948
- ◆ Bantu Education Act, 1953
  - ◆ Ghana independent, 1957
    - ◆ Sharpeville massacre, 1960

◆ Nelson Mandela freed, 1990
- ◆ Mandela elected
  president of South
  Africa, 1994

India, Pakistan, and Bangladesh

◆ Indian National Congress Party founded, 1885
- ◆ Amritsar Massacre,
  India, 1919
  - ◆ Gandhi's resistance campaign
    begins, 1919

◆ Independence and partition of India, 1947
- ◆ Gandhi assassinated, 1948
  - ◆ Indira Gandhi prime minister of India, 1966
    - ◆ Bangladesh established, 1971

East and Southeast Asia

Korean War, 1950–53   US military involvement in Vietnam, 1954–73

◆ Japanese annex Korea, 1910
- ◆ Chinese Revolution, 1911–12
  - ◆ Japan invades China,
    1937
    - ◆ Nagasaki and Hiroshima
      bombed, 1945
    - ◆ Vietnam declares independence,
      1945
      - ◆ French leave Indochina,
        1954

◆ China's "Great Leap Forward," 1958–60
- ◆ Cultural Revolution
  begins in China, 1966
  - ◆ Marcos regime overthrown,
    Philippines, 1986
    - ◆ Tiananmen Square protests
      suppressed, 1989
      - ◆ Hong Kong returns to
        Chinese control, 1997
        - ◆ Indonesia's Suharto
          ousted, 1998

Latin America

◆ Spanish–American War, 1898
- ◆ Mexican Revolution, 1911
  - ◆ FDR's "Good Neighbor"
    policy, 1933
    - ◆ Organization of American
      States formed, 1948
      - ◆ Castro seizes
        power in Cuba,
        1959

◆ Bay of Pigs fiasco, 1961
- ◆ Chile's Salvador Allende
  overthrown, 1973
  - ◆ Sandinistas take charge
    in Nicaragua, 1979
    - ◆ Democratic elections in
      Argentina, Brazil, Mexico,
      Nicaragua, and Paraguay,
      1980s

CHAPTER 29

THE END OF IMPERIALISM

Decolonization and Statebuilding around the Globe

1914–1990s

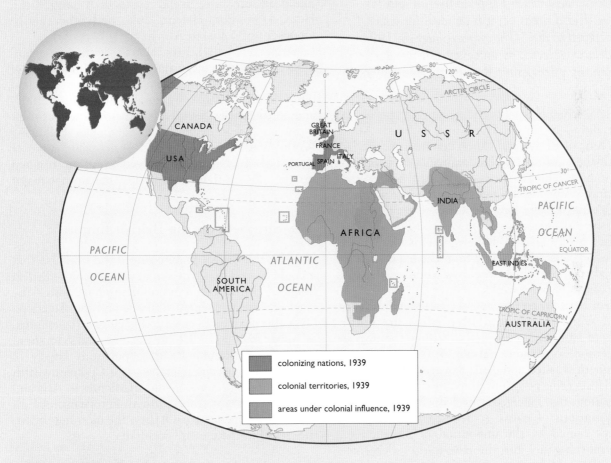

- colonizing nations, 1939
- colonial territories, 1939
- areas under colonial influence, 1939

KEY TOPICS

◆ **Fading Empires:** Anti-colonial resistance begins even before 1914, then flares up after World War I, and leads after World War II to a thirty-year process of decolonization; at the end, the European empires are no more.

◆ **New World Orders:** In Asia, Africa, and the Middle East, new states take form, shaped for better and for worse by their colonial experience, and representing a spectrum of political types—

democratic, monarchical, socialist, and communist, but most often autocratic.

◆ **The Last Imperialist:** A latecomer to imperialism, the United States acquires colonies in Asia and protectorates in Latin America, and intervenes as Cold War policeman in distant conflicts; at home the color line that divides the United States' own people is at last publicly acknowledged.

Sunset and Sunrise At his trial in 1964 for conspiracy against the government of South Africa, and on the eve of his imprisonment that would last twenty-six years, Nelson Mandela (1918–) spoke eloquently of his hopes for his people. All Africans should receive a living wage, have access to work and housing, be free to move about, and enjoy full civil rights, "because without them our disabilities will be permanent." Then he reaffirmed his commitment to democracy: "During my lifetime … I have fought against white domination, and I have fought against black domination. I have cherished the ideal of a democratic and free society … It is an ideal which I hope to live for and to achieve. But if needs be, it is an ideal for which I am prepared to die." Thirty years later, in 1994, Mandela was elected by universal suffrage the president of a democratic Republic of South Africa.

Mandela's triumph marks the passing of the age of imperialism—its sunset. The Union of South Africa was a relic of British and Dutch colonialism, the last area of the continent to be dominated by people of European descent. Now it would be African.

Mandela's words also mark the opening of a new age—a sunrise. The new Republic of South Africa would be a democracy with universal suffrage. With the fading of imperialism new nations were born, which had suffered tragically from the experience of colonial rule, but which would yet embrace the best ideals of the Western world.

From 1919, when the several treaties of Paris concluded World War I, until 1997, when the British colony of Hong Kong reverted to China, the imperialist ventures of Western nations in Asia, Africa, and the Americas faded and died. Sometimes the end of imperialism came peacefully, sometimes violently. The new nations that emerged struggled with its legacy— the distortions of native societies, economies, and cultures caused by the imposition of foreign rule. Some moved easily into the new world order; some have still not broken out of the impasse in which the colonial experience had left them. But the maps of the last decade of the twentieth century, in contrast to those of the first, display on every inhabited continent the free nations of a world that has outlived and surpassed imperialism.

FADING EMPIRES: ANTI-COLONIALISM AND DECOLONIZATION

By the outbreak of World War I, the principal European powers had devoured nearly all of the Old World (see Chapter 24). Exceptions were China, where the European presence was nevertheless strong,

Siam (now Thailand), Iran, Japan and its colonies in Asia; and Liberia and Ethiopia in Africa. Then the tide of empire-building turned. A first wave of colonial resistance to imperial claims swept through the Old World in response to World War I.

Even before 1914, European encroachment in Asia and Africa had not gone unchallenged. The British, Dutch, and French met fierce resistance, for example, to their dominion in the Sudan, Indonesia, and Indochina. So did the United States in its takeover of the Philippines. In India, as cultural elites pressed for independence, British rulers faced sporadic terrorist incidents. In North Africa and the Middle East, Islamic and nationalist movements threatened European suzerainty, as did revolts of Ashanti, Tutsi, Hutu, Hottentot, Herero, Zulu, and other native groups in sub-Saharan Africa.

Aroused colonial elites came to see the Europeans' political power as unwarranted, their exploitation of native economies unjust, and their imperialist and often racist outlooks intolerable. European armies and bureaucracies held the colonies in line, but their ascendancy was everywhere vulnerable. Following World War II, a second and unstoppable wave of resistance, a great quake of **decolonization**, resulted in the dismantlement of the remaining major European empires.

The Sun Sets on the British Empire

In 1919, the British Empire ringed the world, so that it could be said that "the sun never sets on the British Empire." British colonies and **dominions** dotted the maps of Africa, Asia, Australasia, and the Americas. Over the next half-century, this empire fragmented, as Maps 29.1 and 29.2 on pp. 833 and 836 show. Some former colonies with populations largely of British origin became members of a **Commonwealth** of equal and autonomous states. Colonies in Asia and Africa, in contrast (together with European Ireland), achieved independence. Of these the most important, the "jewel in the crown," was India.

Independence in India   In India, an elite of a few thousand military officers, civil servants, missionaries, and teachers (which included both British and Indian members, in roughly equal numbers) ruled a nation of 300 million people, subdivided by political, regional, caste, and religious affiliations (see Chapter 24). The persistent poverty of the population aroused the concern of foreign administrators, but had positive uses. The British were the beneficiaries of an unequal economic strategy, whereby India exported agricultural commodities and raw resources, and purchased British manufactures in exchange. Poverty had other causes as well, including early marriage and high fertility, which led to insupportably high rates of population increase. The more India grew, the more it ate.

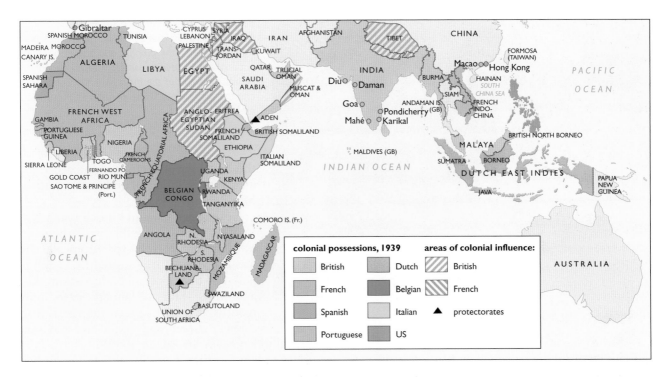

Map 29.1 Colonial Possessions in Africa and Asia, 1939: *In 1939, despite the shocks and realignments of World War I, much of Asia and Africa still lay under the domination of a European power. Native nationalist movements arose especially in colonized Asia and the Middle East, stimulated in some cases by the Japanese (who would soon occupy southeast Asia and the East Indies), the Chinese nationalist Guomindang, Soviet-dominated Comintern, or by Nazi Germany or Fascist Italy.*

From 1919 to 1947, India struggled toward independence. India's support of Britain in World War I—she supplied more than 1 million troops to serve with Allied forces—made Indian soldiers and political leaders more aware of their nation's place in the world system. After the war, British repression of popular political aspirations triggered outrage, as at Amritsar (April 13, 1919), when British troops fired on an assembly of unarmed civilians, killing 400 and injuring others. Nationalist leaders such as Subhas Bose (1897–1945) and Jawaharlal Nehru (1889–1964) called for independence, while Mohandas Gandhi (1869–1948) aroused popular support for nonviolent resistance to British domination. Nehru and Gandhi are seen in the photograph on p. 834.

Born a Hindu in India, trained as a barrister in London, Gandhi moved to South Africa in 1893 where he worked as an attorney. Shocked by the harsh discrimination suffered by Indians, he led a protest movement. From that experience he developed the strategy of nonviolent resistance against colonial rule, or *satyagraha*. It rested on an amalgamation of Hindu and Christian values and Western political philosophy. By suffering violence and causing none in return, his followers exposed their oppressors' injustice and their own righteousness.

Back in India in 1915, Gandhi instructed his followers in nonviolent resistance. Beginning in 1920, in response to British concessions he spurned as inadequate, Gandhi pursued his resistance campaign of protest marches and demonstrations. Although these

sometimes broke down into rioting, they had the effect intended: a worldwide awakening to the injustice of continued British colonialism in India.

Gandhi's opposition to foreign rule included a critique of colonialist economies. He urged Indians to boycott British manufactures, and to reestablish native industrial production, as the passage quoted in *Witnesses* on p. 834 shows. Modeling the sacrificial behavior he expected of others, he labored constantly at cotton-spinning. Gandhi also wanted to purify (but not end) the caste system that was so central a feature of Indian (specifically Hindu) society, and called for the abolition of the status of "untouchability."

Gandhi's leadership was crucial during the interwar years, his great moral authority signaled by the title given him of "Mahatma," or "great soul." But such leaders as Bose and Nehru, whose approach was both more secular and more militant, also found supporters. Growing opposition convinced the British that they would have to yield. In 1942 they promised to grant independence as soon as the war was over. Nationalist leaders repulsed the offer, demanding immediate independence and launching a "Quit India" movement. In 1942, the British imprisoned these opposition leaders, and suppressed the strikes and riots that erupted in protest. Bose fled India and raised an Indian National Army in Singapore with the assistance of Britain's enemy Japan.

After the war, Britain did quit India. While diplomats worked out the terms of independence with Indian leaders, the tension between Muslims and

Forgers of Independence for India:
Mahatma Gandhi (seated on the right, in traditional garb), the prophet and builder of Indian national independence, confers with Jawaharlal Nehru, president of the India National Congress and the first elected Prime Minister of that nation on July 6, 1946.

Hindus within India remained an issue. Massive conflicts causing more than 200,000 deaths resulted in the partition of India and the creation of a new state (Muslim Pakistan, with territory on the Punjab in the northwest and eastern Bengal in the northeast), the wrenching dislocation of some 10 million people, and

the slaughter of 1 million. India became an overwhelmingly Hindu state with a Muslim minority.

Although Gandhi himself had hoped to avoid religious conflict, strife between religious groups persisted. Ironically, he was a victim of it. Angered by Gandhi's policy of tolerance, a Hindu assassin shot and killed him in January 1948, only months after he had seen the last British soldiers depart and India and Pakistan declared independent in August 1947.

The Indian experience spelled the end of British dominion in Asia. Independence followed for Ceylon (now Sri Lanka) and Burma (now Myanmar) in 1948, and Malaya in 1957 (in 1963 merged with Singapore and other entities, it was reconstituted as Malaysia). In 1997, according to the terms set out in their

---

WITNESSES

Asia: Independence for India and Vietnam

The end of World War II brought about enormous shifts in global power relations. Independence for India, gained immediately after the close of World War II, was a cause for which Mohandas Gandhi had struggled throughout his career. In the first of these passages, he speaks of the need for a genuine freedom, which must begin with freedom from want, of which political independence, although essential, can only be one part. Vietnam, under French control, declared independence in 1945, in the document excerpted in the second passage here. However, a unified nation of Vietnam only came into existence following years of struggle against France and the United States.

Mohandas Gandhi weighs what freedom means for the starving (1926): A starving man thinks first of satisfying his hunger. ... He will sell his liberty and all for the sake of getting a morsel of food. ... Such is the position of millions of the people of India. For them, liberty, God, and such words are merely letters ... without the slightest meaning. ... They will extend a welcome to any person who comes to them with a morsel of food. And if we want to give these people a sense of freedom we shall have to provide them with work which they can easily do in their desolate homes and which would give them at least the barest living.

This can only be done by the spinning wheel. And when they have become self-reliant and are able to support themselves, we are in a position to talk to them about freedom. ...
(M. K. Gandhi, "Young India," in *The Collected Works of Mahatma Gandhi,* Vol. 30, 1968)

The Vietnamese Declaration of Independence repeats the American and French Founding Declarations, and asks for the same rights (1945): "All men are created equal. They are endowed by their Creator with certain inalienable rights; among these are life, liberty and the pursuit of happiness."
This immortal statement was made in the Declaration of Independence of the United States of America in 1776. ...
[After a recitation of French and other violations of Vietnamese autonomy.] For these reasons, we ... solemnly declare to the world that Vietnam has the right to be a free and independent country—and in fact is so already. The entire Vietnamese people are determined to mobilize all their physical and mental strength, to sacrifice their lives and property in order to safeguard their independence and liberty.
(Ho Chi Minh, "Declaration of Independence of the Democratic Republic of Vietnam," 1945)

ninety-nine-year lease, the British surrendered Hong Kong, their last Asian possession, to China.

The Middle East and Africa   In the Middle East and North Africa, Britain retained control during the interwar years. Her most significant possession was Egypt, where the Suez Canal was the lifeline of her international commerce. Spurred by a 1919 revolt, Britain granted Egypt independence by stages between 1922 and 1936, while maintaining a garrison zone around the Canal. At the same time, Egypt and Britain jointly administered Sudan; Sudan subsequently became independent in 1956.

Britain also gained control of Palestine and Iraq as **mandates** under the 1919 Paris settlement (and had considerable influence in independent Iran). Iraq gained independence in stages between 1921 and 1932, though Britain maintained military bases there. Iran (Islamic but not Arab) acquired in 1925 a new monarch, or *shah*, friendly to the British (and United States)—Reza Khan (1878–1944), a military officer who seized the ancient Persian throne, installing by force the Páhlevi dynasty that would rule until 1979. In Palestine, however, the British unhappily remained, as an influx of Jewish Zionist settlers from Europe competed with indigenous Palestinian Arabs.

In 1946, Britain gave independence to the state of Jordan, and attempted to suppress the bloody struggles of Palestinians and Jewish settlers. On November 29, 1947, the United Nations (successor organization to the League of Nations; see Chapter 30), recommended the partition of Palestine, with the assignment of one part to the Jews. On May 14, 1948, Britain withdrew, and Israel declared herself an independent Jewish state. The Jews began to hope that their historic longing for this land might at last be satisfied, and resolved to fight for Israel's survival. The move was a guarantee of future anguish, however, as some 600,000 Palestinians fled Israel and Arab neighbor states resisted what they perceived as Israel's alien presence (see below). Britain further withdrew from the region, when, in 1967, her Arab **protectorates** on the Persian Gulf and Arabian Sea became the independent states of South Yemen in 1967, and Bahrain, Oman, Qatar, and the United Arab Emirates in 1971.

After World War II, an exhausted Britain also released its colonies in sub-Saharan Africa. In west Africa, the Gold Coast (formed from the native Ashanti, or Asante, nation, plus neighboring Togo) gained independence as Ghana in 1957—the first African nation to do so outside of South Africa. Nigeria, Sierra Leone, and Gambia followed in 1960, 1961, and 1965. In east Africa, the British colonies of Uganda, Kenya, and Tanganyika won independence in 1961 to 1963; so did the protectorates of British Somaliland (1960) and Zanzibar (1963), while Tanganyika later merged with adjacent Zanzibar to form Tanzania in 1964.

In the southeast, Northern Rhodesia and Nyasaland became independent as Zambia and Malawi in 1964, Botswana (formerly Bechuanaland) in 1966, and the tiny Lesotho (formerly Basutoland) and Swaziland in 1966 and 1968. Southern Rhodesia broke from Britain in 1965, its European planter elite clinging to policies of racial division similar to those of South Africa. After bitter guerrilla struggle against an unyielding white regime, its black African majority finally won black enfranchisement and in 1980 the state was renamed Zimbabwe. South Africa, formerly under British rule, had been since 1910 a dominion within the British Empire. It would follow its own unique course (see below). But adjacent Namibia, illegally occupied by South Africa since 1914, became independent in 1990.

The Commonwealth and Ireland   The creation of the Commonwealth of Nations in 1931 permitted some former colonies, though independent, to continue to enjoy the benefits of privileged economic relations with Britian. Canada, Australia, and New Zealand, lands largely populated by those of European descent, were Commonwealth members and supported the motherland vigorously during World War II. Other former British colonies that have joined the Commonwealth include India and several African and Caribbean states.

Ireland alone remained an intractable problem for post-imperial Britain (see Chapter 24). The British government finally approved Home Rule for Ireland in 1914; but the bill was suspended when World War I broke out, and was never subsequently enacted. Ireland was uninterested in the war that now occupied Britain's attention—except for Protestant northern Ireland, or Ulster. The Irish nationalists, meanwhile, had formed political parties—the Home Rule party and, after 1902, Sinn Fein ("We Ourselves")—and events moved rapidly toward the secession of southern Ireland from Britain. The British suppressed a rebellion that broke out on Easter Monday, 1916, and executed its leaders. Repression garnered a mass following for Sinn Fein, whose candidates won seats in Parliament in 1918 but refused to take them up, declaring themselves an independent Irish parliament. Outlawed, they went underground, warring against the detested Black and Tans, the special troops Britain dispatched to tame the rebellion.

The war over, saner heads sought a peaceful settlement. In 1920, a bill partitioned Ireland into two self-governing areas within the United Kingdom, Northern Ireland and Southern Ireland. In 1921, the Irish Free State in the south was declared a dominion within the British Empire, and in 1937, the British relinquished sovereignty altogether. After nearly eight centuries of British rule, Ireland was free. But it was not united, and not at peace: the internal struggle between British and Irish, Catholic and Protestant, would continue sporadically, and violently, through to the end of the century (see Chapter 30).

Reluctant Disengagement: the End of European Empires

In contrast to the British, the Dutch and French were determined to win back their colonies at the end of World War II. Portugal, Belgium, and Spain retained their African dominions as well. A defeated nation, Italy lost hers, which temporarily were granted as mandates to other states before being freed. In time, all yielded to the current of decolonization.

By 1900, the Dutch Empire had largely shrunk to its lucrative core of East Indian possessions (see Chapter 24). Frequent nationalist uprisings persisted despite the Dutch government's concessions. In the 1930s the Japanese swept the East Indies into the "Greater East Asia Co-Prosperity Sphere" and drove out its Dutch rulers. After the war, nationalists under Sukarno (1901–1970) took power.

The Dutch soon returned and attempted to reestablish their dominion. In 1949 they agreed to a Dutch–Indonesian union, an alliance Sukarno cast off in 1954. In 1957, when the Dutch refused to surrender Netherlands New Guinea to the new Indonesia, he ordered a billion dollars in Dutch assets seized and severed diplomatic relations. In 1963, Indonesia forcibly acquired that last Dutch colonial enclave. (The Dutch, meanwhile, had granted Suriname (in South America) a parliament in 1954, and full independence in 1975.)

The French masters of Indochina had also been displaced by the Japanese during World War II. Before the end of the conflict, the French proposed granting their colonies self-governing status within the French Union. Cambodia and Laos agreed, but Vietnamese nationalists under the leadership of Ho Chi Minh did not. In 1945 Vietnam declared independence (see *Witnesses*, p. 834), and war broke out between French and nationalist forces. In 1954, badly beaten at the climactic battle of Dien Bien Phu, the French withdrew. The 1954 settlement signed at Geneva granted Vietnam independence. But it also left the country disunified, with the north in Ho Chih Minh's control, and the south scheduled to determine its own future in a 1956 election. That election never occurred.

In the Middle East, the war-weary French could not maintain authority in their mandates of Syria and Lebanon against spirited opposition from the league of Arab states. Persuaded by the British, the French yielded. Both nations attained independence in 1945.

In 1956, the French surrendered their North African protectorates of Tunisia and Morocco, held since 1881 and 1912 respectively, to native rulers. But Algeria, which the French had ruled since 1830, was considered to be an extension of France. Here many European French had settled (constituting ten percent of the population) and created a colonial civilization, much like the Spanish settlers of the Americas. But nationalist and Islamist groups demanded that they leave and revolts broke out in 1954 after the French defeat in Indochina. The subsequent conflict, marked by mutual atrocities,

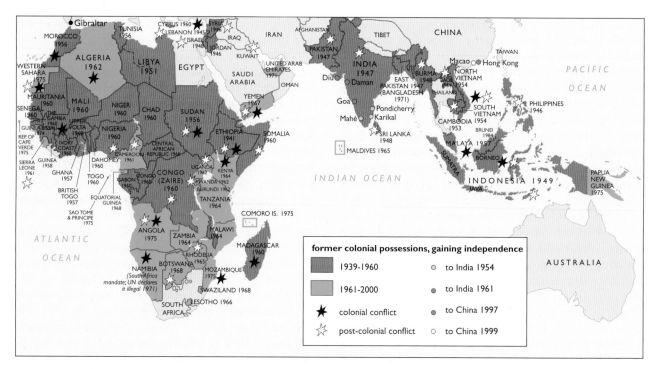

Map 29.2 Independence Gained in Africa and Asia 1939–1985: *The tired victors of World War II could not maintain their empires. The British and the French, the greatest imperialist powers, were the first to relinquish direct domination of Asian and African colonies. The last were Belgium, Spain, and Portugal. Decolonization was largely completed around the world by 1975.*

resulted in the deaths of some 250,000 Algerians (of a population of 9 million) and nearly tore France apart as opinion at home polarized. In 1958, a revolt of the French army brought World War II hero Charles de Gaulle (1890–1970) back from retirement. He was elected president, his supporters believed, in order to maintain "*Algérie française*," a French Algeria. Too good a strategist to battle in vain, de Gaulle returned Algeria to the Algerians in 1962.

The Algerian experience served as a model to avoid south of the Sahara. The French possessions of west and equatorial Africa (modern Guinea, Senegal, the Ivory Coast, Cameroon, Mali, Togo, Niger, Benin, Burkina Faso, Chad, Gabon, Mauritania, the Congo Republic, and the Central African Republic) gained their freedom with relative ease. Beginning in 1956, the French offered these colonies limited self-government within the French Union, an offer accepted by several. All had gained full independence by 1960 (but the east African colonies of the Comoros and Djibouti not until 1975 and 1977).

Portugal, the first of the European powers to win African and Asian footholds, was determined not to surrender colonies it had held so long and profitably. Nationalist movements in their colonies of Mozambique, Angola, and Guinea-Bissau, however, overwhelmed the military and economic capacity of Portuguese hard-liners. In 1974, military officers who recognized the impending failure of Portugal's colonial policy ousted the dictator Marcelo Caetano (1906–1980). With his fall came independence for Portugal's African colonies, as well as the island territories of Cape Verde and São Tomé and Principe. Portugal's neighbor Spain, having surrendered its section of Morocco, retained only a few African enclaves; nearly all were independent by 1968.

Belgium's African empire consisted of the great central Congo region and adjacent Rwanda and Burundi. Notorious exploiters of the people and resources of the Congo, the Belgians had failed to train a native managerial elite and the Congolese opposition was unprepared for political administration when the Belgians suddenly withdrew. The new nation achieved independence in 1960 as the state of Zaire (now the Democratic Republic of Congo), under Patrice Lumumba (1925–1961) as prime minister. Rival leaders representing ethnic minorities opposed Lumumba's nationalist strategy. They assassinated Lumumba and seized power. Rwanda and Burundi gained their independence in 1962.

In addition to their colonies in Asia, Africa, the Middle East, and the Americas, the European powers surrendered small islands in the Pacific, Atlantic, and Mediterranean. So passed the era of European imperialism. The new states that formed after independence repudiated that heritage. They found it was not easy to create better governments than those their masters had imposed upon them.

NEW WORLD ORDERS: STATEBUILDING IN AFRICA, THE MIDDLE EAST, AND ASIA

As the imperial powers exited, the stage was left to the premiers, presidents, and parliaments of the new nations of Asia and Africa. Newcomer states sought to form stable governments, stimulate economies, adopt new technologies, and provide for the health and education of their people, while still saddled with the legacies of imperial rule. Some met these goals readily; many others struggled or failed. In 1990, more nations lived under their own freely chosen leaders than ever before, and had begun the task of achieving security and prosperity for their peoples.

Statebuilding in Africa: from Village to Nation

Between 1945 and 1975, some forty independent states took form in Africa. (The African Resolution on Imperialism and Colonialism is cited in *Witnesses* on p. 841.) They experienced great disruption in their passage from subordinate colonies to modern democratic nations—even when the former colonial authority was supportive there was no easy transition.

The Legacy of Colonialism First, the national identities of the new states were inherently frail. Prior to the imperial scramble for Africa, the continent was governed by a variety of African kingdoms and pre-state, networked village communities. The European nations that partitioned Africa by 1914 created colonial territories whose boundaries were superimposed on traditional political divisions. When the European powers released their colonies, African nationalist leaders could not recover the political identities of pre-conquest times. But neither could they make the artificial new boundaries natural. Sometimes those borders divided ethnic or tribal groups, or encompassed two or more rival groups. Loyalty to the new nations was strained by ethnic tensions, linguistic divisions, and tribal memories. Pan-African congresses provided an important setting for the discussion of future projects, but did not lead to plans for political organizations larger than the colonial units.

Second, although colonialism had modernized the African economies, it had done so to benefit the metropolitan power rather than the colonized Africans. Once independence was won, the African nations found it difficult to reorient their economies in line with the broader needs of their peoples.

Colonized Africa had a cash crop economy. Peanuts, palm oil, coffee, cotton, and tobacco crops found foreign buyers. But the exclusive devotion of vast tracts of the best land to these profitable exports meant that less land was devoted to subsistence crops. The population was left vulnerable to food shortages, a situation exacerbated, as often in the 1970s and 1980s, by periodic drought. In addition, when the prices of export crops dipped, the whole economy staggered. From 1970 to 1990, food production declined, while the population grew unabatedly.

What was true of cash crops was also true of minerals. Their exploitation led to great wealth, but also to difficulties. Copper, gold, and diamonds were valuable exports, but these, too, were subject to commodity price fluctuation. Moreover, mineowners recruited large labor forces (generally all male) from the villages to work in the mines. With the men far from home, many women had to tend the fields alone. Not only did those women assume burdens of isolation and increased responsibility, but productivity often suffered, and the risk of famine increased.

New nationalist leaders found it difficult to shed the established model of the commodity economy—especially as it enriched an emerging urban elite of merchants, professionals, and bureaucrats. Turning to foreign capital to fund new enterprises led to

increased dependence on Western economies. Some leaders sought the solution of nationalizing some enterprises, or redistributing agricultural lands.

A third barrier to the establishment of modern democracy was cultural. Colonial administration had trained a small vanguard of Africans in European schools and universities. This elite was minuscule amid a vast sea of people untutored in political ideas. In the 1960s, at the peak of decolonization, scarcely three percent of the population had received a secondary education, and barely ten percent were literate. Religious allegiances—Muslim, Christian, polytheist, and **animist**—overlapped tribal and state boundaries, and did not serve to unify at the national level. Africa's divided, inexperienced, and ill-educated peoples were vulnerable to manipulation by propaganda and to control by dictators.

With these deficits, early efforts to establish democratic states understandably foundered. Nearly all the new African nations succumbed to authoritarian rulers who led one-party states that suppressed dissent. Their aims were not always malevolent: some pursued sound plans for economic development and human welfare. But even well-meaning dictators were tempted by wealth and power. Unchallenged by a democratic opposition, they became corrupt and inefficient. Often, these dictators were artificially sustained by Western nations or corporations which continued to seek advantage in the post-colonial era.

When corruption and inefficiency became intolerable, a military **coup** might oust a dictator and install the rule of generals—trained managers, but occasionally brutal ones, with little patience for claims of civil rights. Military governments might recivilianize the nation, once reform measures had been taken. But if the civilian governments failed again, military rule returned. During the 1950s and 1960s, military coups were frequent; during the 1970s and 1980s, they outpaced any other form of political change in Africa.

Several major African states experienced this rocky progression from hopeful independence to authoritarianism to military rule. Ghana, the former British Gold Coast colony, was governed by the pan-Africanist Kwame Nkrumah (1909–1972), a former teacher who studied in the United States and Britain. From 1948, he rallied urban elites and farmers to the cause of "Self-Government Now." Arrested, imprisoned, and released, he emerged in 1951 as key leader of the semi-autonomous state. Upon full independence in 1957, he became prime minister; in 1960, president (see *Witnesses*, p. 841). In that role, Nkrumah turned to authoritarianism and one-party rule. Having nearly bankrupted the nation with grandiose but often disastrous development projects, he was ousted by a military coup in 1966.

Patrice Lumumba, author, thinker, and nationalist leader, led an independent Zaire after the Belgian exodus in 1960. But leaders of tribal factions resisted

WHO'S WHO

Fading Empires in Africa

Patrice Lumumba (1925–1961), first premier of the state of Zaire (formerly the Congo) upon Belgian withdrawal in 1960, but assassinated by rivals in 1961.

Joseph (Sese Seko) Mobutu (1930–1997), seized power in Zaire after Lumumba's death, and held it for 32 years, with US support.

Kwame Nkrumah (1909–1972), pan-Africanist prime minister of Ghana upon its independence in 1957, and president in 1960; ousted by a military coup in 1967.

Robert Mugabe (1924–), Marxist leader of Rhodesian revolutionary party which ousted prime minister Ian Smith; became head of nation re-named Zimbabwe.

Desmond Tutu (1931–), South African Anglican archbishop who aroused world outrage against the segregationist apartheid policy of the white Afrikaner government of South Africa; winner of the 1984 Nobel Prize.

Nelson Mandela (1918–), leader of African National Congress imprisoned in 1964 and released in 1960; in 1994, won election to the presidency of South Africa.

Muammar el-Qaddafi (1942–), seized power in Libya in 1969 after toppling the pro-Western monarchy, nationalizing foreign petroleum assets, and, during the Cold War, accepting Soviet aid as well as Soviet arms.

Independence Day: *Independence came to most nations of Africa in the decades following World War II as colonial powers withdrew. As most African nations gained their independence, they began the process of state-building under their own leaders. South Africa, in contrast, had been under the control of white Europeans whose increasingly racist policies excluded African natives from power, education, and any type of high-paid employment. The opposition leader Nelson Mandela, imprisoned from 1964 and released after twenty-six years, is shown here speaking to the crowd in 1990. Mandela was elected President of the ANC (African National Congress) in 1991, at its first national conference. In 1994, he became president in South Africa's first post-apartheid elections.*

Lumumba's nationalist message, and one rich province seceded. In 1965, after Lumumba's assassination in 1961, a military coup put general Joseph (later Sese Seko) Mobutu (1930–1997) in power, in which position he remained propped up by the United States for thirty-two years.

These patterns reappeared in other settings. The brutal despot Idi Amin (1925–) held control of Uganda from 1971 until 1979; by then, he had caused the deaths of some 200,000 Ugandans, immigrants, and members of minority ethnicities. Nigeria, riven by tribal conflict, rocked between the corrupt authoritarianism of civilian and military governments.

In these states, authoritarian rule quickly descended into disorder and violence. In those nations where a large white settler caste had established itself in the pre-independence era, the potential for outbreaks of violence was even greater. In Kenya, African nationalists waged a guerrilla war for years before the settler elite finally yielded to native rule. In Southern Rhodesia, white settlers cut ties with Britain in 1965, before Britain could grant independence to the territory as a free African state in which blacks could vote. Rhodesian prime minister Ian Smith (1919–) fought guerrilla movements from 1973 until 1980, when Robert Mugabe (1924–), Marxist leader of one of the revolutionary parties, became head of the country that is now named Zimbabwe.

The Struggle against Apartheid   The largest group of white settlers lived in the Union of South Africa, from 1910 an independent state, and the one fully industrialized nation in Africa. Here, as of the 1970s, those of European descent numbered 4 million, "coloreds" 2 million (including Asians and those of mixed identity), and black Africans some 20 million—yet a white ruling caste controlled every aspect of the economy and the government. In 1948, white voters installed the National Party, dominated by the Afrikaner descendants of the original Dutch settlers. Against their policies stood the African National Congress, founded in 1912. From the 1960s, the ANC organized resistance to National Party principles, publishing its own Freedom Charter in 1955.

The National Party's goal was to forestall black independence. The 1950 Population Registration Act and Group Areas Act assured the permanent economic disability of black South Africans. The first established classification by race. The second assigned those of the African classifications to live in "Bantustans," or tribal "homelands," constituting a mere fourteen percent of the land. By the Bantu Education Act of 1953, they were barred from excellent mission schools and compelled to attend government-run schools that enforced racial hierarchies and taught only rudimentary subjects. As workers, they received lower wages than whites for similar work.

Other laws established the social norms of **apartheid** ("separateness"), mimicking the segregation laws of the southern states of the United States. Such laws barred blacks from white-designated public facilities, banned interracial marriage, and required blacks to carry an identity card. The efforts of African nationalist leaders to resist apartheid resulted in their arrest, but also in the worldwide condemnation of the government of South Africa. The killing of unarmed demonstrators at Sharpeville in 1960 (leaving 67 dead, 180 wounded) and Soweto in 1976 (where police fired on a crowd of 15,000, killing 575, including 134 children) aroused world opinion against South Africa. The Anglican archbishop Desmond Tutu (1931–), winner of the 1984 Nobel Peace Prize, carried the story of racial injustice around the globe. His speech to the United Nations is quoted in *Witnesses* on p. 842.

World opinion strengthened by economic sanctions forced President Pieter W. Botha (1916–) to resign in 1989. His successor Frederik Willem de Klerk (1936–) searched for a compromise between black aspirations and Afrikaner obduracy. De Klerk lifted the ban on the African National Congress in 1990 and released its leader Nelson Mandela after twenty-six years of imprisonment (see the photograph above, and also *Witnesses*, p. 842). The two leaders worked together for a multiracial and democratic society, calling for elections based on universal suffrage. Held in 1994, that election made Mandela president, De Klerk one of two deputy presidents. An African pledged to win justice for both Africans and Afrikaners led South Africa for the first time.

Varying Models of Independence   In other states, where independence was attained only after guerrilla struggle—as in the former Portuguese colonies of Guinea-Bissau, Angola, and Mozambique, or the former French colony of Algeria—socialism appealed to the embittered nationalist victors. In addition, by the 1970s, the animosities between the United States and the Soviet Union generated by the Cold War (see Chapter 29) intruded upon African politics, as each antagonist funded and supplied friendly guerrilla forces and client states.

In Angola in 1975–1976, Soviet arms and some 45,000 troops from Cuba, then a Soviet client state, aided one guerrilla group against another supported by the United States. The Soviet protégés won, and a Marxist government was formed. In Algeria, upon the final departure of the French in 1962, a socialist government took over foreign interests and nationalized industries. In Libya, army colonel Muammar el-Qaddafi (1942–) toppled a pro-Western monarchy

in 1969, nationalized foreign petroleum assets, removed United States and British military bases, and accepted Soviet aid and arms. In 1974, a self-proclaimed Marxist–Leninist regime took over in Ethiopia by overthrowing the last emperor Haile Selassie (r. 1930–1974). Ethiopia soon went to war with neighboring Somalia (pieced together in 1960 from former British and Italian Somalilands), also a Soviet client since 1974. For a while, the Soviet Union supplied both sides with arms and military experts. But on the whole, few African nations gravitated to the Soviet sphere of influence.

Among the conscientious African leaders who guided the continent into a modern age of political responsibility were the intellectuals Léopold Senghor (1906–) of Senegal, Patrice Lumumba of Zaire, and Jomo Kenyatta (c. 1893–1978) of Kenya. Senghor wrote several volumes of poetry; Lumumba wrote a study of his compatriots in *Congo: My Country* (1962); and Kenyatta wrote about the native traditions of his people in *Facing Mount Kenya* (1938) and *Suffering without Bitterness* (1968).

The socialist leaders Julius Nyerere (1922–) of Tanzania and Robert Mugabe (1924–) of Zimbabwe hoped to build African states on African principles, while serving citizens' welfare requirements according to Western political theory. Nyerere's controversial concept of *ujamaa* (familyhood), a politics based on village-centered popular rule, foundered in economic crisis, however. And Mugabe's achievements—building bridges to the economically important white minority of Zimbabwe, and seeking to create improved relations with South Africa—must be balanced against the

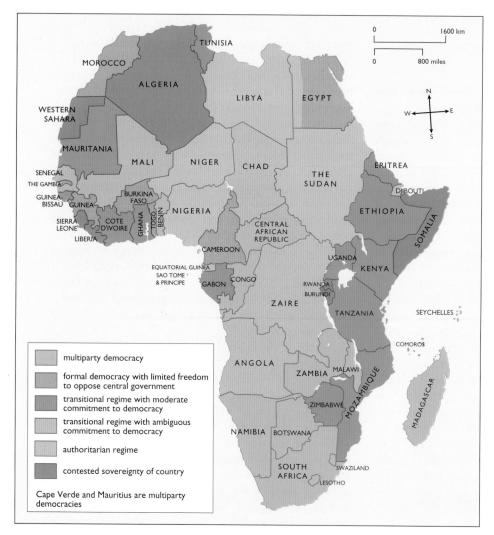

Map 29.3 African Political Systems, 1996: It is nearly 50 years since Africa came out from under the colonial yoke that had come to saddle it rapidly and completely in the decades before World War I. Yet Africa is not free. The political situation is heterogeneous and highly volatile, featuring a number of regimes which have not ascribed to the multiparty democratic model that appears today to be the preference of developing nations. This 1996 map shows a patchwork of authoritarian and democratic regimes, along with the many that are in transition (as Western observers hope) from the former to the latter.

defects of the increasingly repressive regime that he has inaugurated in Zimbabwe.

Under Nelson Mandela's leadership, notably, the African National Congress did not incline to Marxist socialism. Mandela staunchly adhered to democratic principles, displaying qualities for which, in 1993, he was recognized by the award of the Nobel Peace Prize. Mandela's 1994 election as president of South Africa with two-thirds of the popular vote was a triumph for democracy. But South Africa was not alone in the early 1990s. After decades of post-colonial experimentation and readjustment, and with the development of an indigenous educated and professional elite, many African states are moving in the direction of parliamentary procedures, multi-party elections, and economic privatization.

Africa: Post-Colonial Quandaries

As colonialist powers retreated, Africans considered the task that lay before them. Here the Ghanaian leader Nkrumah and the All-African People's Conference held at Accra in December 1958 call for a pan-African approach to end imperialism and promote economic development.

Kwame Nkrumah looks back to the past and ahead to the future, calling for an Africa that is politically unified and economically strong (1961): For centuries, Europeans dominated the African continent. The white man arrogated to himself the right to rule and to be obeyed by the non-white; his mission, he claimed, was to "civilise" Africa. Under this cloak, the Europeans robbed the continent of vast riches and inflicted unimaginable suffering on the African people.

All this makes a sad story, but now we must be prepared to bury the past with its unpleasant memories and look to the future. ... It is clear that we must find an African solution to our problems, and that this can only be found in African unity. Divided we are weak; united, Africa could become one of the greatest forces for good in the world.

Although most Africans are poor, our continent is potentially extremely rich. Our mineral resources, which are being exploited with foreign capital only to enrich foreign investors, range from gold and diamonds to uranium and petroleum. Our forests contain some of the finest woods to be grown anywhere. Our cash crops include cocoa, coffee, rubber, tobacco and cotton. As for power, ... Africa contains over 40 percent of the potential water power of the world. ... Yet so far, less than 1 percent has been developed. This is one of the reasons why we have in Africa the paradox of poverty in the midst of plenty, and scarcity in the midst of abundance.

Never before have a people had within their grasp so great an opportunity for developing a continent endowed with so much wealth. Individually, the independent states of Africa, some of them potentially rich, others poor, can do little for their people. Together, by mutual help, they can achieve much. But the economic development of the continent must be planned and pursued as a whole. A loose confederation designed only for economic co-operation would not provide the necessary unity of purpose. Only a strong political union can bring about full and effective development of our natural resources for the benefit of our people.

(Kwame Nkrumah, *I Speak of Freedom: A Statement of African Ideology,* London: William Heinemann Ltd., 1961)

At Accra, December 5–13, 1958, more than 300 delegates to the All-African People's Conference, representing more than 200 million Africans, agreed on the following "Resolution on Imperialism and Colonialism:"

1. That the All-African People's Conference vehemently condemns colonialism and imperialism in whatever shape or form these evils are perpetuated.

2. That the political and economic exploitation of Africans by imperialist Europeans should cease forthwith.

3. That the use of African manpower in the nefarious game of power politics by imperialists should be a thing of the past.

4. That independent African States should pursue in their international policy principles which will expedite and accelerate the independence and sovereignty of all dependent and colonial African territories.

5. That fundamental human rights be extended to all men and women in Africa and that the rights of indigenous Africans to the fullest use of their lands be respected and preserved.

6. That universal adult franchise be extended to all persons in Africa regardless of race or sex.

7. That independent African states ensure that fundamental human rights and universal adult franchise are fully extended to everyone within their states as an example to imperial nations who abuse and ignore the extension of those rights to Africans.

8. That a permanent secretariat of the All-African People's Conference be set up to organise the All-African Conference on a firm basis.

9. That a human rights committee of the Conference be formed to examine complaints of abuse of human rights in every part of Africa and to take appropriate steps to ensure the enjoyment of the rights by everyone.

10. That the All-African People's Conference in Accra declares its full support to all fighters for freedom in Africa, to all those who resort to peaceful means of non-violence and civil disobedience, as well as to all those who are compelled to retaliate against violence to attain national independence and freedom for the people. ...

(All-African People's Conference News Bulletin, Vol. I, No. 4, Accra: 1959

African Debates: Algeria and South Africa

Although a number of African nations were granted independence by colonial powers quickly after World War II, others underwent a longer and more painful experience. In Algeria, French settlers who had deep-rooted traditions as a colonial elite, refused to abandon the ideal of a "French Algeria," as a government official explains in the first of these excerpts. In the second, Frantz Fanon, a powerful anti-imperialist spokesperson, rejoices at Algeria's final victory. South Africa was already an independent nation when the War ended in 1945, but a nation whose native population was dominated by the descendants of older generations of European settlers from the Netherlands and Britain. The struggle of the African subjects of that colonial regime for civil rights in their own country lasted more than a generation, and was successful above all because of the sacrifice and determination of Nelson Mandela, eventually President of a renewed South African state, whose message was spread around the world by the native Anglican archbishop Desmond Tutu.

Jacques Soustelle, Governor-General of the French colony of Algeria, says France will never relinquish Algeria (1955): France is at home here, or rather, Algeria and all her inhabitants form an integral part of France, one and indivisible. All must know, here and elsewhere, that France will not leave Algeria any more than she will leave Provence and Brittany. Whatever happens, the destiny of Algeria is French.
(From K. Nkrumah, *I Speak of Freedom*, 1961)

Psychiatrist Frantz Fanon welcomes a new and autonomous Algeria (1959): On the Algerian soil a new society has come to birth. The men and women of Algeria today resemble neither those of 1930 nor those of 1954, nor yet those of 1957. The old Algeria is dead. All the innocent blood that has flowed on to the national soil [as a result of war with France] has produced a new humanity.
(Frantz Fanon, *A Dying Colonialism*, 1971)

Nelson Mandela speaks in his own defense at his trial at the Pretoria Supreme Court, Rivonia (1964): Africans want to be paid a living wage ... to live where they obtain work ... to be part of the general pop-

ulation, and not confined to living in their own ghettoes. ... Africans want to be allowed out after eleven o'clock at night and not to be confined to their rooms like little children. ... Africans want a just share in the whole of South Africa; they want security and a stake in society.

Above all, we want equal political rights, because without them our disabilities will be permanent. I know this sounds revolutionary to the whites in this country, because the majority of voters will be Africans. This makes the white man fear democracy. ...

During my lifetime I have dedicated myself to this struggle of the African people. I have fought against white domination and I have fought against black domination. I have cherished the ideal of democratic and free society in which all persons live together in harmony and with equal opportunities. It is an ideal which I hope to live for and to achieve. But if needs be, it is an ideal for which I am prepared to die.
(Nelson Mandela, *The Struggle is My Life*, 1990, 3rd ed.)

Archbishop Desmond Tutu implores the United Nations Security Council to help black South Africans gain their freedom (1984): White South Africans are not demons; they are ordinary human beings, scared human beings, many of them; who would not be, if they were outnumbered five to one? Through this lofty body, I wish to appeal to my white fellow South Africans to share in building a new society, for blacks are not intent on driving whites into the sea but on claiming only their rightful place in the sun in the land of their birth.

We deplore all forms of violence, the violence of an oppressive and unjust society and the violence of those seeking to overthrow that society, for we believe that violence is not the answer to the crisis of our land.

We dream of a new society that will be truly non-racial, truly democratic, in which people count because they are created in the image of God. ...

I say we will be free, and we ask you: Help us, that this freedom comes for all of us in South Africa, black and white, ... that it comes soon.
(Desmond Tutu, statement to the UN Security Council, October 23, 1984)

Statebuilding in the Middle East: Israel, Oil, and Islam

World War I accomplished the dismemberment of the last great Islamic empire in the Middle East—that of the Ottomans. Over the next decades, its component territories became independent states. After World War II, the inherent tension between Islamic traditions and modernization sharpened (see Chapter 24). The politics of oil, a sub-soil treasure concentrated

in the Arabian Peninsula, further destabilized the region. So too did the presence of Israel, created by European Zionists as a refuge for the Jewish people. These factors have made the Middle East a major trouble spot of the later twentieth century. Major Middle East leaders are listed in *Who's Who* on p. 843.

Turkey   The Ottoman Empire entered the twentieth century moribund. In 1914, it ruled only one-third of the lands it had held in 1800. Allied with the Central Powers in World War I, the Empire disintegrated at war's end. By the 1920 Treaty of Sèvres, it lost its North African, Middle Eastern, and European territories, along with some Aegean islands (confirmed as Italian possessions), leaving only Anatolia (in Asia Minor) as a homeland. Even in Anatolia, a valuable commercial strip near Smyrna was assigned to Greece, a reward for loyalty.

As Greek and Italian forces rushed to claim their prizes, Mustafa Kemal (1881–1938) led a swift counter-strike. An army commander during the recent war, Kemal was one of the Young Turks who had unseated the sultan in 1908. From 1919 to 1923, he recaptured Asia Minor and expelled the Greek occupiers. He won title not only to the whole of Anatolia, but also to a limited zone around Constantinople, now renamed Istanbul, on the European side of the Hellespont. The empire had been lost, but Turkey was born.

Made president in 1922 and henceforth known as Atatürk ("father of the Turks"), Kemal recast Turkey as a modern, secular state. He established compulsory public schools, for girls as well as boys, and by 1932 cut the illiteracy rate in half from its 1914 level. He established a civil law system (replacing traditional Muslim courts), discouraged Islamic customs, donned Western dress, made marriage a civil function, and transcribed the Turkish language in the West's Roman alphabet. He permitted elections (by universal suffrage) within a one-party system to a representative assembly whose decisions he consulted. By his death in 1938, Atatürk had transformed Turkey, which has since been further democratized by later constitutions (in 1961 and 1982).

Egypt   While Atatürk reshaped Turkey, the Arab regions of the former Ottoman Empire gained new contours. The most successful of these was Egypt, technically independent since 1936 but retaining a "preferential alliance" with Britain which ensured the latter continued control of the Suez and port of Alexandria and certain military privileges. In 1952, a military coup forced out the reigning king and, in 1956, obtained the independence of Sudan. In 1956, Egyptian president Gamal Abdel Nasser (1918–1970) seized and nationalized the Canal, the conduit through which passed two-thirds of the oil used by western Europe. Nasser's provocative strike nearly precipitated a military confrontation with Britain and her allies (who were restrained by the United States).

Nasser proceeded to nationalize banks and industries, dispossess the great landowners, redistribute lands to the peasants, and promote higher education. Funded by the Soviet Union, he built the Aswan High Dam (completed 1970). Aswan controlled the Nile floods that had for centuries irrigated the land and made Egypt the granary of the Mediterranean. A great project that he likened in scale to the pyramid

building of ancient pharaohs, it was intended to boost peasant productivity and generate electric power.

Nasser also galvanized the states of the Middle East, forging an international alliance for a pan-Arab, Islamic "socialism" that would be independent of both the West and communism. His successors have failed to resolve Egypt's economic problems, and f ace growing opposition from **Islamist** parties, which seek to unify Muslims and revitalize the religion and culture of Islam.

The Middle East   In the Middle East, Britain and France relinquished their post-World War I mandates and protectorates after World War II. Newly independent, these states confronted the tasks of creating a modern economy, transportation system, and institutions of health and education. Their accomplishment was complicated by the presence in the Middle East of the state of Israel, an abundance of oil, and increasing Islamic militancy.

A memo of November 2, 1917 by British minister Arthur Balfour (1848–1930) first approved the concept of a "national home for the Jewish people"— vague words that promised no support and gave no idea of how it would come into being. By 1917, Jewish immigrants had already founded a handful of settlements in Palestinian territory still under Ottoman rule (joining the approximately 68,000 Jews, mostly in Jerusalem, who had lived in Palestine for four centuries). From 1917 to 1948, tens of thousands of immigrants poured into Palestine, as Jewish settlers increased their share of the population from about one-tenth to a half.

The first settlers were committed Zionists (see Chapter 24) followed by refugees from Nazism. In time, these were joined by immigrants from other Middle Eastern states who had lived under Ottoman rule as a tolerated minority. With the financial assistance of Jews around the world, these pioneers installed irrigation systems and reclaimed once barren lands. When the new nation of Israel declared its independence in 1948 (see *Witnesses*, p. 845), it was more highly urbanized, better educated, better fed, and better armed than the surrounding Arab states.

Conflict was inevitable between the new state of Israel and its neighbors. Wars broke out in 1948, 1956, 1967, 1973, and 1982. In 1948, following the Israeli proclamation of independence on May 14, Arab forces from a league of neighboring states invaded the new nation. Highly motivated and better organized, the Israelis repulsed them. The territorial settlement based on the ceasefire lines gave them even more territory than had the United Nations' 1947 partition. Many Palestinian natives fled Israel; about half became refugees in neighboring Arab lands, while around 1 million still remain within Israel, as a significant minority in that nation whose population is currently about 5.5 million (see *How Many?* left).

Responding to border raids or threats of imminent invasion, Israel attacked Egypt in 1956, and its Arab neighbor states in 1967. At the close of the 1967 Six-Day War, Israel occupied lands south and west to the Suez Canal (the Sinai Peninsula) and east to the Jordan River (the region of the "West Bank," including the Old City of Jerusalem) as well as the Gaza Strip along the Mediterranean and the Golan Heights in Syria. Defying a United Nations injunction, Israel refused to leave until the Arab states agreed to negotiate; the Arabs refused to do so.

In 1973, after a six-year standoff, Egypt and Syria counterattacked. At the ceasefire they obtained a partial Israeli withdrawal from its 1967 high tide. In 1982, Israel invaded Lebanon to destroy the PLO headquarters. (The PLO, or Palestine Liberation Organization, was the official advocate of statehood for the uprooted Palestinians; some of its goals are listed in *Witnesses* on p. 845.) During these years, the United States provided Israel, and the Soviet Union its Arab opponents with arms, such activity serving to increase the volatility of the region's politics.

The problem remained that Israel occupied lands from which millions of now stateless Palestinians had been displaced. Over the next decades, some progress has been made toward resolving this intractable issue, which pits the moral right of the Jewish people to the homeland promised them against the moral right of Palestinian natives to the land which had long been theirs. In 1977, Egyptian president Anwar Sadat (1918–1981) bravely journeyed to Jerusalem to attempt to negotiate a settlement. That action culminated in the Camp David peace negotiations, hosted in 1978 by United States president Jimmy Carter (1924–). The resulting treaty between Egypt and Israel of March 26, 1979 obtained the complete Israeli

HOW MANY?

Palestinians Resident in the Middle East

Country	Resident Palestinians
Jordan	700,000
West Bank	675,000
Israel	350,000
Gaza	375,000
Lebanon	275,000
Syria	175,000
Egypt	25,000
Iraq	10,000
Persian Gulf countries	170,000
TOTAL	2,755,000

Estimated figures, March 1973

The destiny of 2.75 million stateless Palestinian Arabs, more than half of whom live as refugees in countries outside of Israel, is one of the greatest sources of tension in any region of the world.
Source: D. A. Schmidt, *Armageddon in the Middle East (New York: New York Times, 1974), p. 148.*

withdrawal from the Sinai. Egypt became the only Arab state to have made peace with Israel.

In 1981, Sadat was assassinated, the penalty for his peacemaking role. Fundamentalist groups, both Israeli and Arab, sprang up to resist the forces for peace. (Fundamentalists adhere strictly to the tenets of their religion and resist secular values and institutions; both Islamic and Jewish militancy may be linked to fundamentalist concerns.) In 1993, Israeli prime minister Yitzhak Rabin (1922–1995) and PLO chairman Yasir Arafat (1929–) signed a peace accord, following negotiations brokered by the United States and Norway. It allowed for Palestinian self-rule in the Gaza Strip and in the city of Jericho in the occupied West Bank, and called for a settlement by the end of a five-year transitional period. Further details within the same treaty framework were settled in 1995. These arrangements rankled nationalists on both sides. Recent years have seen a heightening of Arab resistance and Israeli nationalism. In 1987, young Palestinians in the Israeli-occupied territories of the West Bank and Gaza Strip launched the uprising called the *Intifada* ("shaking")—an informal campaign of stonethrowing, strikes, and demonstrations. In addition, Islamist groups (notably the Hamas and the Islamic Jihad) have launched random terrorist attacks, including suicide bombings, on Israeli civilians. These have inspired ferocious Israeli determination to resist. Assassinated in 1995, Rabin was replaced by Benjamin Netanyahu (1949–), of the conservative Likud Party, a figure reluctant to compromise with Palestinian groups. In 1999, the election of the moderate Ehud Barak (1942–) raised hopes for a new settlement.

WITNESSES

New Orders in the Middle East: Israel, the Palestine Liberation Organization, and Revolutionary Iran

In the troubled Middle East, one party's claim of justice often acts in contradiction to another's. That complexity is evident in the documents here. In the first, the nation of Israel—as the United Nations mandated—establishes itself as an independent state, claiming that it was "the natural right of the Jewish people to be masters of their own fate." In the second, a generation later, the Palestinian Liberation Organization, acting for the whole community of Palestinians (who had no state), declares the people's right of self-determination. In the third, the Iranian Ayatollah Khomeini, who had led his people in a successful revolution against rulers whose dynasty had been installed by Western governments, gives thanks for the nation's delivery from the power of the United States, that "global plunderer."

Declaration of the establishment of the State of Israel (1948): The land of Israel was the birthplace of the Jewish people. Here their spiritual, religious, and political identity was shaped. Here they first attained statehood, created cultural values of national and universal significance, and gave to the world the eternal Book of Books. ...

On the 29th of November, 1947, the United Nations General Assembly passed a resolution calling for the establishment of a Jewish state in the land of Israel. ... This recognition by the United Nations of the right of the Jewish people to establish their state is irrevocable. This right is the natural right of the Jewish people to be masters of their own fate, like all other nations, in their own sovereign state.

(From J. N. Moore, ed., *The Arab–Israeli Conflict: Readings and Documents*, 1977)

The goals of the Palestine Liberation Organization, founded to represent the interests of the Palestinians made stateless by the creation of Israel (1968):

#8: The Palestinian people is at the stage of national struggle for the liberation of its homeland. ...

#9: Armed struggle is the only way of liberating Palestine. ...

#26: The Palestine Liberation Organization ... is responsible for the struggle of the Palestinian Arab people to regain, liberate and return to their homeland and to exercise the right of self-determination in that homeland.

(From Zuhair Diab, ed., *International Documents on Palestine*, document no. 360, 1971)

Iranian revolutionary leader, the Ayatollah Ruhollah Khomeini, defines the nature of the victory won (1980): God Almighty has willed—and all thanks are due Him—that this noble nation be delivered from the oppression and crimes inflicted on it by a tyrannical government and from the domination of the oppressive powers, especially America, the global plunderer. ... It is our duty to stand firm against the superpowers, as we are indeed able to do, on condition that the intellectuals stop following and imitating either the West or the East, and adhere instead to the straight path of Islam and the nation. ... Beloved youths, it is in you that I place my hopes. With the Qur'an in one hand and a gun in the other, defend your dignity and honor so well that your adversaries will be unable even to think of conspiring against you. ... Know well that the world today belongs to the oppressed and sooner or later they will triumph. They will inherit the earth and build the government of God.

(Ayatollah Ruhollah Khomeini, "New Year's Message, 1980"; ed. M. Algar, 1981)

Oil and Fundamentalism   Meanwhile, Israel's Arab neighbors had grown wealthy. Oil had become the chief fuel of the twentieth century, and sixty percent of the world's oil lay under the sands of the Arabian peninsula (with other rich deposits in the United States and Canada, Mexico, Venezuela, Nigeria, Indonesia, Russia, and Kazakhstan). Since World War II, as the West and Japan became increasingly dependent on oil, the oil-producing Arab states reasserted control of their reserves. Suddenly wealthy, their economy has been sustained by the export of a single precious commodity.

In Africa and Latin America, commodity-based economies suffered with fluctuations in world markets. To control that volatility, in 1961 the Arab states united (with other oil-rich nations) as the Organization of Petroleum Exporting Countries (OPEC), with the aim of preventing outsiders from dictating the value of their principal resource by collectively setting oil prices. Between 1973 and 1975, they quadrupled the cost of a barrel of oil, triggering hardship in the oil-consuming West.

The wealth derived from oil profits has flowed to a variety of projects: construction, health, education, wages—and the personal enrichment of elites and rulers. By the late 1990s, though they eluded the worst dangers of a free marketplace, the Arab states had not succeeded in using the profits from oil to diversify their economies or to establish industrialization.

In nearby Iran, under the autocratic rule of the shahs, modernization and secularization proceeded rapidly at the expense of the exploited and zealously religious masses. By the 1970s, religious leaders denounced the Western moral values that pervaded urbanized and industrialized society. They identified the West as the enemy of traditional Islamic culture—which in Iran was **Shi'ite**, as opposed to the Sunni form of Islam practiced in most of the region—and particularly the United States, a supporter of the shah and a major source of foreign capital and ideas.

The tension between Islamism and modernization erupted in 1979 in a coup that took the West by surprise (see *Witnesses*, p. 845). The elderly ayatollah (the title of a senior Shi'ite expert in Islamic law) Ruhollah Khomeini (1902–1989) ousted the brutal and corrupt regime of shah Muhammad Reza Pahlevi (1941–1979). Khomeini proceeded to reverse the course of Iranian development, leading a revolution which in November 1979 seized the United States embassy and held sixty-nine officials and workers hostage, most of them for fifteen months. Further, he dissolved the hated SAVAK (the foreign-bankrolled secret police); confiscated United States properties and expelled United States military personnel; restructured schools and universities, and restored Islamic law. His agents policed morals, censored newspapers and broadcast media, and banned alcohol. Women once again wore the veil in a wholesale repudiation of the cultural values of the West—the

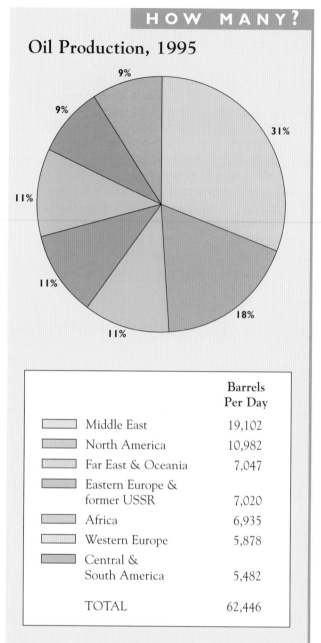

HOW MANY?

Oil Production, 1995

	Barrels Per Day
Middle East	19,102
North America	10,982
Far East & Oceania	7,047
Eastern Europe & former USSR	7,020
Africa	6,935
Western Europe	5,878
Central & South America	5,482
TOTAL	62,446

In 1995, world production of crude oil (still the most important source of fuel) reached 62,446 barrels per day. The chart above shows each region's share of global output, with the Middle East producing 19,102 barrels per day, or thirty-one percent of the total, compared to forty-one percent in 1929. In recent decades, Central and South America, western Europe, Africa, and the Far East and Oceania have significantly increased their share of world production.
Source: New York Times 1998 Almanac, p. 504.

homeland of the "Great Satan," the United States. After the death of Khomeini in 1989, deeply mourned by the Iranian people, his regime stayed the course, with recent elections and student resistance pointing toward a more moderate regime in the future.

Meanwhile, Islamic fundamentalism has proved to be a powerful force throughout North Africa and the

Middle East, and has been aimed not only at Western interests but also native, secular states. Islamist forces have supported terrorism in Egypt and Algeria, while in 1996, the Islamist Taliban faction fundamentalists swept into Afghanistan (previously a state within the Soviet sphere of influence) and transformed political culture and private life.

Not religion but nationalism and opportunism were the motives for the invasion by Iraqi leader Saddam Hussein (1938–) of adjoining Kuwait in 1990. His action provoked air attacks and ground invasion by the United States and allies (the Middle Eastern nations of Syria, Egypt, Saudi Arabia, and some smaller Gulf states as well as Western powers and Japan) in the second Gulf War. A swift victory for the Western forces in a fully televised conflict momentarily stymied Saddam's bid for territorial expansion and Arab leadership. The dictator contented himself with the brutal suppression of Shi'ite Muslim and Kurdish revolts at home.

By the end of the 1990s, the Middle East remains one of the world's most volatile regions. With the exception of Israel, its states are all dictatorships—military, princely, theocratic, oligarchic. Unifying forces include Islamic culture and pan-Arab nationalism—and the common hatred of Israel. But several factors destabilize the region: rivalries among even the Arab nations; the resurgence of Islamic fundamentalism; the abundance of oil, essential to power the industries of the West and Japan; the stockpile of sophisticated weapons supplied during the Cold War era by both superpowers and their allies; the presence of aggrieved minorities (Christian, Druze Muslims, Armenian, Kurd); and competing Israeli and Palestinian aspirations.

Statebuilding in Asia: Democracy, Communism, and Capitalism

The new post-colonial nations of Asia represent a variety of political forms. Some states (such as Pakistan and Indonesia) are reminiscent of those African nations that turned to autocracy when their colonial rulers left. But the major states of India and China offer contrasting models of democracy and communism, and the powerhouse micro-states of the Pacific Rim, resembling Japan more closely than India or China, are showcases of capitalism.

India and Pakistan   India has maintained its democratic institutions, with a brief interruption, from independence in 1947 until the present day. Its first head was the nationalist leader Jawaharlal Nehru (1889–1964), an associate of Gandhi's who ruled for seventeen years. Attempting to remain "nonaligned" (independent of either of the two Cold War superpowers), he imitated features of both kinds of states in his administration of India—and unfortunately slid,

like many of his fellow dictators, toward cronyism, distributing key posts to family members and friends. In 1966, after a two-year interim, Nehru's daughter Indira Gandhi (1917–1984) became prime minister. By 1975, her economic policies (the nationalization of banks and control of private enterprise) aroused opposition, and she was charged with corruption. She

> ## WHO'S WHO
>
> ### Fading Empires in Asia
>
> **Mohandas Gandhi (1889–1948)**, Indian Nationalist opponent of British rule and creator of the philosophy and strategy of "civil disobedience" as a form of non-violent resistance to unjust power.
>
> **Jawaharlal Nehru (1889–1964)**, Indian Nationalist leader, and first prime minister of independent India (1947–1964).
>
> **Indira Gandhi (1917–1984)**, Nehru's daughter, Indian prime minister (1966–1984), charged with corruption and abuse of power; assassinated in 1984; as was her son Rajiv (1944–1991), who succeeded her, in 1991.
>
> **Sukarno (1901–1970)**, Indonesian Nationalist leader who took power after World War II, cooperating with the Dutch administration until it was finally ousted in 1963.
>
> **Suharto (1921–)**, Indonesian who took power from Sukarno in a US-backed military coup in 1965; established an authoritarian regime, and joined the Southeast Asian Treaty Organization, or SEATO, a regional defense organization; he was finally expelled in 1998 because of his corruption and failed policies.
>
> **Mao Zedong (1893–1976)**, Chinese communist revolutionary leader who seized power in 1949, presiding over radical social, economic, and cultural policies (which resulted in the death of millions of people) until his death.
>
> **Deng Xiaoping (1904–1997)**, already elderly, replaced Mao in 1976, and continued his policies, which called for, in 1989, the violent repression of the student-led revolt in Tiananmen Square.
>
> **Ferdinand Marcos (1917–1989)**, autocratic and increasingly corrupt president of the Philippines from 1965–1986, when he fled following the election of Corazon Aquino (1933–), the widow of his former opponent.
>
> **Ho Chi Minh (1890–1969)**, Vietnamese Nationalist leader who opposed French domination after World War I, and the US-supported South Vietnamese government after 1954, whose supporters eventually attained Vietnamese unification and independence in 1975.

responded by suspending the constitution and ruling personally. In elections in 1977, Gandhi and her party were repudiated and democratic institutions restored. She was reelected in 1980, but was assassinated during 1984 riots between Sikhs and Hindus by Sikh members of her own security guard. Gandhi's son Rajiv (1944–1991) succeeded her as prime minister and retained the ministry until 1989. He too, however, was assassinated, in 1991.

India's democracy remained intact through the Nehru–Gandhi years. The security of India's political institutions, however, continues to be menaced by enduring social and cultural problems. These include religious and ethnic conflicts (Hindu–Muslim violence flared up again in 1992); resentment against powerful elites, who dominate government and cultural life; and a runaway rate of population growth that threatens prosperity even as productivity grows in both agricultural and industrial domains.

Neighboring Pakistan, mainly ruled by military dictators since 1958, has not enjoyed India's democratic experience. East Pakistan, now Bangladesh, broke away in 1971 to form an independent state—one of the world's poorest. It too has been subject to authoritarian government and one-party rule.

Indonesia The great archipelago of Indonesia also fell under authoritarian rule after winning liberation from the Dutch. Its president Sukarno, an architect of Indonesian independence, was still in power in the 1960s as that state slid into the orbit of communist China. In 1965, a United States-backed military coup under General Suharto (1921–) seized power (retaining Sukarno as figurehead until 1967), expelling communist officials and massacring their followers, along with about 750,000 ethnic Chinese. Suharto established an authoritarian regime, joining SEATO (the Southeast Asia Treaty Organization), a regional defense organization with close ties to the United States. He promoted economic modernization and attracted foreign investment, especially Japanese, while he suppressed dissent and restored Islamic law and customs. In 1998, mired in corruption and failed policies, Suharto was deposed by a mass movement led by university students demanding free elections and a democratic constitution.

China In China, the revolution of 1911–1912 brought freedom from emperors and the intrusion of Western powers (see Chapter 24). From 1912 to 1927, the armies of the Nationalist or Guomindang Party, eventually trained and bankrolled by the Soviets, gradually won control of much of eastern and southern China (see Chapter 28). Their commander Chiang Kai-shek (Jiang Jieshi, 1887–1975) fought against local warlords. Meanwhile, communist leaders (the Chinese Communist Party was founded in 1921) built up their power-base among the peasants in the countryside, whose loyalty and cooperation they won through practical means, with land redistributions.

In 1927, Chiang expelled or murdered the communists in the Guomindang, who fled to the interior regions of south China. In 1934, he attacked their stronghold at Jiangxi. Some 100,000 people, including thirty-five women, fled to the north in the heroic "Long March" (more than 6000 miles) of 368 days. Harried by Guomindang pursuers, barely one-tenth survived to establish a secure base at Yan'an in Shaanxi Province. Led by Mao Zedong (1893–1976), pictured on p. 849, their forces of some 1 million men cooperated cautiously with Chiang's armies of 3 million when the Japanese invaded in 1937.

The Japanese occupation of the industrial zones of eastern China deprived Chiang of his supporters among the commercial elites. Following the Japanese surrender in 1945, he resumed his struggle with the communists. In 1948, with United States air and naval assistance, Chiang rashly attacked strong enemy positions in the north. Communist troops smashed and rolled past him, armed by the Soviets. They swept southward and fanned out over the whole of China. Chiang and his followers escaped to the island of Taiwan, removed by the peace settlement from Japanese domination. Chiang declared himself head of the Chinese state in exile. In 1949, Mao became the leader of the new, Communist People's Republic of China. His speech is quoted in *Witnesses* on p. 849. With fewer than 3 million Communist supporters, he had conquered a nation of 600 million people. After a century of fragmentation (see Chapter 24), China was united under one leader.

From 1949 until his death in 1976, Mao Zedong consolidated the Communist regime and transformed Chinese economy, society, and culture. Fittingly for a nation where peasants constituted eighty percent of the population, Mao's revised Marxist–Leninist principles made agricultural production a priority. Peasant collectives seized great estates, without compensation to the owners—who were "tried" and often executed by peasant tribunals. Productivity mounted during the 1950s. To boost it further, Mao launched the Great Leap Forward in 1958, whose goal was the complete collectivization of agriculture. The countryside was organized into large communes whose leaders directed the peasants' life and work. The experiment was a complete failure, undermined by floods, drought, and peasant resistance.

Some 10 million peasants died in the resulting famine. After 1961, the peasants returned to their smaller village collectives and generated modest gains in productivity, which gave them a living standard higher than in recent memory. Production in excess of the government-set quota was theirs to sell in local markets. Enhanced agricultural production promoted industrialization. Heavy industries (metals and machinery) in urban centers were developed first,

对伟大导师毛主席心怀一个 "忠" 字
对伟大毛泽东思想狠抓一个 "用" 字

Chairman Mao and his Little Red Book: *Mao Zedong forged a unique form of communism in China based on peasant village organization and Marxist–Leninist principles. The poster shown here depicts youthful followers—with numberless others in the background—ardently studying the "Little Red Book" that contained the founder's philosophy. The poster gives an idealized vision of Mao's Communist regime.*

followed by more diversified factories in rural areas, offering employment alternatives for peasant workers. Organized as government-run enterprises, these industries invited foreign investment and trade.

Mao also undertook a profound reorientation of the traditions of ancient Chinese society and culture.

He had the prerevolutionary intellectual and political elites arrested, "reeducated," or silenced. The press was censored, and religious groups, including numerous Christian missions, disbanded. Government officials supervised each village and household, seeking to break down traditions of family loyalty and social deference in favor of revolutionary and collective behavior. The advanced skills needed in a modern society, along with Maoist principles, were taught in schools that all children, male and female, were required to attend. Individuals selected for higher training or leadership positions were identified by party officials and notified of their destinies. Party

WITNESSES

Asia: Permanent Revolution in China

The communist revolution in China happened not once but at least twice: first in the aftermath of World War II, when Mao Zedong consolidated his power and established a new kind of economy and government; and second, in 1966, when the same leader launched the Great Proletarian Cultural Revolution, which would ensure the permanency of the revolution by eliminating cultural tendencies that had strayed away from the proletarian base of communist society. Here, Mao explains the first of these revolutions, in 1949; and the Central Committee of the Communist Party accepts the second, in 1966.

Mao Zedong explains the goals of the communist revolution (1949): "You are dictatorial." … [T]hat is just what we are. … [We must] deprive the reactionaries of the right to speak and let the people alone have that right.

"Who are the people?" At the present stage in China, they are the working class, the peasantry, the urban petty bourgeoisie and the national bourgeoisie. These classes, led by the working class and the Communist party, unite to form their own state and elect their own government: they enforce their dictatorship over the running dogs of imperialism—the landlord class and bureaucrat-bourgeoisie. …

"Why must things be done this way?" … If things were not done this way, the revolution would fail, the people would suffer, the country would be conquered. (Mao Zedong, speech, "In Commemoration of the 28th Anniversary of the Communist Party of China," June 30, 1949)

The Central Committee of the Chinese Communist party on the aims of the Great Proletarian Cultural Revolution (1966): The Great Proletarian Cultural Revolution now unfolding is a great revolution that … constitutes a new stage in the development of the socialist revolution in our country. … The proletariat must … meet head-on every challenge of the bourgeoisie in the ideological field and use the new ideas, culture, customs and habits of the proletariat to change the mental outlook of the whole of society. At present, our objective is to struggle against and overthrow those persons in authority who are taking the capitalist road … and all other exploiting classes and to transform education, literature and art and all other parts of the superstructure not in correspondence with the socialist economic base, so as to facilitate the consolidation and development of the socialist system. (From J. Robinson, *The Cultural Revolution in China*, 1969)

Tiananmen Square, 1989: *More than twenty years after the Cultural Revolution, student-led demonstrations in Beijing's main Tiananmen Square protested against the repressive government that had succeeded Mao's regime. When on June 4, 1989, the government sent armed soldiers and tanks into the Square to end the protest, one lone and anonymous figure planted himself before the approaching column to prevent their advance. The famous photograph has captured a unique and moving moment of modern heroism.*

members themselves—a mere one percent of this officially egalitarian society—submitted to programs of indoctrination that denigrated prerevolutionary assumptions and values.

In 1966, detecting an ebb of revolutionary energy especially among party leaders, Mao launched the Great Proletarian Cultural Revolution (see *Witnesses*, p. 849). Its aim was to achieve "permanent revolution"—a state of constant criticism, by the yardstick of Maoist doctrine, of all in authority. In schools and factories, young people formed into revolutionary squads (the "Red Guards") to spread propaganda and denounce those lagging in communist exuberance—targeting senior officials and members of their own families. Thousands of intellectuals and party functionaries were deported to the countryside for "reeducation" as manual laborers. Others were persecuted, imprisoned, tortured, or murdered. Mao's wife Jiang Qing (1914–1991) participated in the hunt, naming "counterrevolutionary" intellectuals. As the purges of the Cultural Revolution subsided, the stunned survivors waited, and the world watched, to see who might succeed the titanic Mao at his death in 1976.

That event brought Mao's now elderly companions of revolutionary days to power, foremost among them Deng Xiaoping (1904–1997). Survivors and in some cases victims of the Cultural Revolution, their first act was to oust from power Mao's widow and her three colleagues (publicly reviled as the "Gang of Four"). Deng proceeded to liberalize economic policy, permitting material incentives, a return to family-centered farming and factory-based (rather than centralized) decision-making. He encouraged foreign investment and trade, and promoted the scientific and technical training arrested by the anti-intellectualism of the Cultural Revolution. Resulting gains in productivity positioned China in the 1990s to participate actively in the modern

system of global commerce. The price of this progress has been the continued curtailment of individual rights, backed up by censorship and repression of dissent. Especially controversial was the government's attempt to reverse rates of population growth by limiting family size to one child, with compulsory abortion for late pregnancies.

The children of the victims of the Cultural Revolution, who have no memory of the 1949 triumph, form a new generation. Many resist the regime of aging Communists who replaced Mao in 1976. In 1989, on the seventieth anniversary of the angry May Fourth Movement (see Chapter 26), university students led a massive demonstration in Tiananmen Square, the great central space of the capital of Beijing. The debates and demonstrations went on for weeks, and were televised worldwide, calling for an end to censorship and for free elections. Dissidents raised in the square a replica of the Statue of Liberty—a monument bestowed upon the United States by the French in 1886 to commemorate common republican traditions. Rechristened the "Goddess of Democracy," this icon made their provocative and dangerous message extremely clear.

China's leaders debated how they might respond, and decided, characteristically, on repression. The People's Liberation Army was dispatched to silence the dissidents. As the photograph above shows, tanks rolled into Tiananmen Square on June 4, 1989, crushing protestors who did not disperse, firing on unarmed demonstrators, killing about 1300, and arresting thousands more. Student leaders were rounded up and jailed without trial; some died from their injuries, some were executed. Witnesses to the repression told the story worldwide by telephone and fax machine; little was told through official channels. Since 1989, the government has released some of the jailed and tortured dissidents, but others are still held as political prisoners, even as China seeks admission to the club of modern nations who observe the rights of their citizens.

Japan and the Pacific Rim Defeated in war, Japan sprang quickly to the first rank in the global marketplace. With Japan occupied by Allied forces from 1945, under the command of United States general Douglas MacArthur (1880–1964), the revered emperor was permitted to remain, but as a figurehead, and only after he had publicly renounced the notion of his divinity. A new constitution emphasized that sovereignty lay with the people and parliament, founded an independent judiciary, and guaranteed civil rights for women as for men. Elementary and secondary education was made compulsory, labor unions made legal, landholding and corporate structures reshaped. The armed forces were disbanded (while the United States was permitted to maintain military bases on Japanese soil). In 1951, a peace treaty was signed and accepted by Japan and the Allies (except for the Soviet Union and China). National sovereignty was restored.

As a democratic, constitutional monarchy, Japan flourished. Its industries, banks, and commercial enterprises resumed their characteristic dynamism. Especially in the areas of electronics and automobile manufacture, Japan's products competed with the finest produced elsewhere, as enormous investment in research and development led to sophisticated technological products. By 1985, Japan was the world's second industrial power, after the United States. Wages were comparable to those in the affluent nations of the West. Until the slowdown that set in with the collapse of the Tokyo stock market in 1989, followed by a banking crisis in the late 1990s, Japan seemed to be on the way to claim first place.

Along with Japan, four other "Pacific Rim" states (so called because of their positioning on the east and southeast Asian coasts facing the Pacific) have emerged as economic powerhouses, albeit under authoritarian rule. Their activity, together with Japan's and China's, has nearly doubled East Asia's share of world production in the last generation, raising the region to parity with the West. From north to south, the first of these is South Korea. After recovering from the trauma of the Korean War in which one-tenth of its people died, it has flourished as a producer of electronic and automotive goods. The second is Taiwan, which has become a major commercial player under the Chinese Nationalist government established in 1949. The third is Hong Kong, British-owned from 1898 to 1997 and now reintegrated with China, an island-state that is a center of international finance capital. The fourth is Singapore, fully independent in 1965, another financial capital and exporter of labor-intensive manufactures. Especially in the latter two of these "Four Dragons" (or "Four Tigers") of the Pacific Rim, as they are called, forming a highly concentrated zone of economic endeavor, free enterprise reigns amid the ghosts of empires.

THE LAST IMPERIALIST

A latecomer to imperialism, the United States was among the last of the Western powers to renounce its dominion over other nations and peoples (see Chapter 19). After the war for independence from Britain (1776–1783), the new United States began a century of expansion across the North American continent, according to the self-defined privilege of **Manifest Destiny**. In that process of nation building, in the view of some observers, it acted as an imperialist power. It expropriated lands from native inhabitants, and annexed other territory from the independent nation of Mexico.

In the twentieth century, certainly, in Latin America, the Philippines, in Vietnam, and even its homeland, the United States has exercised dominion over unconsenting others, as Map 29.4 on p. 856 shows. In recent years, like its European peers, the United States has repudiated empire and its ambitions.

Good Neighbors: the United States in Latin America

The United States has played a contradictory role in Latin America (a region comprising Mexico and the nations of the Caribbean and South America whose people speak Spanish, Portuguese, or French, all derived from Latin). On the one hand, it has pretended to be a "good neighbor," the role urged by President Franklin Delano Roosevelt (1882–1945) in 1933. On the other hand, it has often intervened in the lives of the Latin American nations—to maintain order, to exclude other interests, to control the course of political events (even by invasion and occupation), to promote the economic interests of its entrepreneurs and investors, acting less like a "good neighbor" than the bully with a "big stick" envisioned by President Theodore Roosevelt (1858–1919).

Until 1898, the United States appeared to be a good, or at least an indifferent, neighbor toward the nations south of its borders. The Monroe Doctrine announced in 1823 declared the integrity of the Americas, warning that the United States would deem hostile any European attempt to recolonize the Western Hemisphere (see Chapters 19, 24). Except for the episode of the Mexican War, it remained detached over the next decades, engaged in its own expansion and traumatic Civil War (see Chapters 19, 24). After 1898, however, the United States frequently intervened in the political and economic life of the region.

The Spanish–American War of 1898 marked the shift in United States' strategy from indifference to intervention. Throughout the nineteenth century, the British had been the principal foreign presence in the region. British investors funded Latin America's mines and railroads, its manufactures flooded the

The Americas: a United States Protectorship in Cuba and the Mexican Nationalization of the Oil Industry

The United States' policy of interventionism—both official and commercial—with regard to Latin America is evident in these excerpts. In the first, the United States asserts its intent to remain involved, and in control, in a presumably independent Cuba. In the second, the Mexican president in 1938 offers as justification for his nation's takeover of foreign oil companies, including United States companies, their outrageous exploitation of the native population.

The Platt Amendment: United States conditions for the independence of Cuba (1902): I. ... [T]he government of Cuba shall never enter into any treaty or other compact with any foreign power or powers which will impair or tend to impair the independence of Cuba. ... III. ... [T]he Government of Cuba consents that the United States may exercise the right to intervene for the preservation of Cuban independence, [and for] the maintenance of a government adequate for the protection of life, property, and individual liberty. ... VII. ... [T]o enable the United States to maintain the independence of Cuba, and to protect the people thereof, as well as for its own defense, the government of Cuba will sell or lease to the United States lands necessary for coaling or naval stations at certain specified points to be agreed upon with the President of the United States.

(From C. I. Bevans, ed., *Treaties and Other International Agreements of the United States of America, 1776–1949*, vol. 8, 1971)

Lazlo Cardenas, president of Mexico 1934–1940, defends the nationalization of the oil industry (1938): It has been repeated *ad nauseam* that the oil industry has brought additional capital for the development and progress of the country. This assertion is an exaggeration. For many years, ... the oil companies have enjoyed great privileges for development and expansion ...; it is these factors of special privilege, together with the prodigious productivity of the oil deposits granted them by the Nation often against public will and law, that represent almost the total amount of this so-called capital.

Potential wealth of the Nation; miserably underpaid native labor; tax exemptions; economic privileges; governmental tolerance—these are the factors of the boom of the Mexican oil industry.

Let us now examine the social contributions of the companies. In how many of the villages bordering on the oil fields is there a hospital, or school or social center, or a sanitary water supply, or an athletic field ...?

Who is not aware of the irritating discrimination governing construction of the company camps? Comfort for the foreign personnel; misery, drabness, and insalubrity for the Mexicans. Refrigeration and protection against tropical insects for the former; indifference and neglect, medical service and supplies always grudgingly provided, for the latter; lower wages and harder, more exhausting labor for our people. ...

(From B. Keane, ed., *Readings in Latin American Civilization, 1942–Present*, 1967)

---

region's markets, and its navy protected British interests. After 1898, the United States replaced Britain as the region's main foreign investor, developer, exploiter, and master. It made the Caribbean its private lake, and the rest of the region its backyard.

After the 1898 war, Cuba and Puerto Rico, the last two Spanish colonies in the hemisphere, passed to the United States. Puerto Rico was ceded to the United States and, since 1953, has been a "commonwealth" under United States sovereignty. Cuba gained its independence as of 1898 under a constitution drafted according to United States guidelines. In 1901 the "Platt Amendment", part of which is quoted in *Witnesses* above, gave the United States the right to intervene in Cuban affairs in order to maintain order, and to keep a military force stationed at Cuba's Guantánamo Bay. The new state of Cuba was seen as a protectorate of the United States.

The terms of the Platt Amendment predicted future United States policy toward its Latin American neighbors. The point was reiterated in what is called the "Roosevelt Corollary to the Monroe Doctrine." In 1904 President Theodore Roosevelt defined

circumstances under which the United States might intervene in the internal affairs of a Latin American nation: evidence of "chronic wrongdoing," or an "impotence" that threatened civilized norms. Such wrongdoing and ineffectiveness, as defined by the United States, prompted that nation's takeover of Haiti and the Dominican Republic, making protectorates of those Caribbean states.

Panama also became a protectorate. In 1903, the United States encouraged Panama to break away from Colombia. When Panama became established as an independent nation, the United States secured from it on favorable terms (a rental of $250,000 per year, plus a $10 million one-time payment) the land needed to construct a canal across the fifty-mile waist of the isthmus. It obtained a perpetual lease to the ten-mile wide Canal Zone, over which it would exercise sovereign rights. The canal would be a major boon for United States and world shipping, which could span half the globe—from the Asian Pacific, to California, to Caribbean ports, to the European Atlantic ports—without the detour around South America's distant Cape Horn. It was the counterpart of the Suez Canal, built in Egypt by 1869 to link Mediterranean trade by way of the Red Sea with the Persian Gulf and Indian Ocean, avoiding the African Cape of Good Hope (see Chapter 24). Together, the two canals linked the oceans of the world.

When the Canal reached completion in 1914, the economic position of the United States in Latin America had strengthened. Between 1898 and 1914, United States investments in Latin America quintupled. Between 1914 and 1929, they tripled again, while British and other European interests receded. By 1929, almost forty percent of the region's imports came from the United States, which in turn absorbed almost thirty-three percent of its exports. United States businessmen funded copper factories in Chile, oil ventures in Mexico and Venezuela, tin mines in Bolivia, and two-thirds of Cuba's sugar production. Some companies—such as Boston's United Fruit, which built itself a "banana republic" in Central America—had huge territorial holdings.

Mexico   The stake that its investors had in Mexico prompted the United States to intervene when revolution broke out in 1910. The Mexican revolution was more than a revolt against the autocratic rule of Porfirio Díaz (1830–1915; see Chapter 19). It was also a broad protest of peasants and workers (mostly Indian and mestizo) against an oppressive social hierarchy topped by a landowner elite and foreign business interests.

Strongman Díaz had welcomed United States capital, and American citizens held Mexican land, mineral resources, and public utilities. Aiming to protect those interests and avoid disruption so close to its borders, the United States supported Mexican leaders it considered "moderate" and opposed those with revolutionary intentions—such as the peasant leader, Emiliano Zapata (1879–1913), and the colorful Francisco "Pancho" Villa (1877–1923), who headed a coalition of rebellious peasants, workers, and cowboys. In 1913, the United States President Woodrow Wilson (1856–1924) permitted arms shipments to the counterrevolutionaries. In 1914, with the unjustified arrest of United States sailors as a pretext, the United States navy occupied the port of Veracruz. In 1916, when Pancho Villa led a raid into New Mexico, Wilson dispatched General John J. Pershing (1860–1948) to capture him (which he failed to do).

These inglorious interventions altered nothing. Mexico formed a new government, whose 1917 constitution gravely threatened the interests of native and foreign elites. It seized estates and distributed land to the peasants; established collective organizations and a favorable labor code for workers; introduced limited suffrage (men could vote only for the official party's candidate, and women not until 1954); limited the role of the Roman Catholic Church; and confiscated without compensation all sub-soil rights,

including those of United States investors. Neither wholly revolutionary nor truly democratic, the new Mexican government achieved stability and promoted the general welfare, instituting public education, public health programs, and irrigation projects.

The Mexican revolution might have prompted a chain of revolutions in Latin America, as some feared. The Great Depression of the 1930s, which plunged the whole region into desperation (see Chapter 27), also threatened to do so. Dependent on the export of a few commodities, the Latin American economy suffered when demand sank. The elites found themselves without cash, while laborers and peasants grew restive as unemployment and hunger struck. Yet discontent did not lead to revolution. The region's strongmen, or *caudillos*, would not let it do so.

The Rule of the *Caudillos*   The enduring patterns of Latin American society—the intertwined elite of landowners, military officers, and churchmen—created the *caudillo* (see Chapter 19). The Latin American commodity economy called him into action. The wealth it generated was locked up for the consumption of the rich, and neither flowed to the poor nor stimulated more complex economic enterprises. This system yielded depressingly what some experts have termed "growth without development." It magnified social inequities and necessitated caudillo despots to keep order. From the 1930s through the 1970s, most nations of Latin America have experienced the rule of such bosses. Three may serve as examples: Argentina, Chile, and Brazil.

In Argentina, during the 1930s, dominated by landowning and military elites, the middle and working classes supported the rise to power of the army colonel Juan Perón (1895–1974), elected president in 1946. Backed by his dynamic and beautiful wife, Eva Duarte (1919–1952; "Evita," to her admirers), Perón redistributed wealth, promoted industrialization, and nationalized industries, measures that stimulated uncontrolled inflation and strained national finances. After 1949 the economy worsened, and Perón fled in the face of a military coup in 1955. For the next three decades, Argentina alternated between military and civilian strongmen (among them Perón and his second wife, who returned from 1973 to 1976). The vicious regime in power from 1976 to 1983 murdered more than 10,000 people, and imprisoned, tortured, and "disappeared" many more. The mothers of "missing" adult children, swept up in deadly raids by the military in charge, paraded regularly in the capital city of Buenos Aires to bear witness to their brutality. Since 1983, civilian, democratic governments have taken hold and spurred economic development.

In Brazil, a military coup elevated caudillo Getúlio Vargas (1883–1954), who ruled from 1930 to 1945, and again from 1951 to 1954. Vargas dismissed parliament and canceled elections, while he instituted censorship and a secret police force and encouraged rapid economic modernization. As leftist and liberal movements gained ground in the early 1960s, the military seized power in 1964 in a coup backed by the United States. Protests from the moderate middle class and the social revolutionary left were ruthlessly suppressed. Nevertheless, huge foreign investment spurred an economic miracle, in which industrial exports—rather than coffee and such commodities—generated real wealth for some Brazilians, without alleviating the poverty of others.

Brazil remained under military control from 1964 to 1985. Since then, democratically elected leaders have attempted to restore the free market, while confronting the problems of high inflation and debt. The exploitation of the Amazon River region, resulting in environmental degradation of global consequence, has raised concern, and prompted Brazil to host a United Nations conference on the environment in 1992. During its rocky postwar career, Brazil has industrialized and urbanized, its prosperity threatened still by the great poverty of the masses and rapid population growth.

In Chile, the working and middle classes forged coalition governments from the 1930s through the 1960s. In 1970, a moderate socialist government was elected with reformer Salvador Allende Gossens (1908–1973) as head. Allende's reforms included redistribution of land and the nationalization of banks and industries, especially copper-mining, in which United States entrepreneurs were heavily involved. But these measures triggered uncontrolled inflation and angered the middle classes.

In 1973, supported by the CIA (Central Intelligence Agency) of the United States, a military junta seized control, leaving Allende dead and his government finished. The new regime arrested 13,000 people immediately and, over the next seventeen years, killed some 2000. Under the repressive but modernizing regime of Augusto Pinochet (1915–), which lasted from 1973 until 1989, major industries were restored to the private sector, labor controlled, welfare services reduced, inflation lowered, exports increased, and the economy diversified. In 1989, free elections were reinstated.

The United States often supported the dictators and generals who protected the business interests of its nationals. Yet since the 1930s, it has moved away from the direct exploitation of the Latin American states. Franklin Delano Roosevelt announced the nation's benign intention to respect the rights of other nations in his "Good Neighbor" policy of 1933. In 1948, it helped form the Organization of American States to promote hemisphere solidarity against the threat of communist activity abroad. Postwar presidents Truman, Eisenhower, Kennedy, Johnson, and Nixon supported development in Latin America, as well as programs to bolster its military and police.

Response to Communism   In the 1950s and 1960s, the Cold War duel with the Soviet Union (see Chapter 30) added a new dimension to United States involvement in Latin America. Alert to the possibility of communist intervention in what it considered its own backyard, the United States assisted even corrupt and repressive anti-communist governments (see Chapter 30). **Counter-insurgency**—a crusade against leftist revolutionary activity—became a primary objective of United States foreign policy. The United States sent military advisers to lend assistance in Latin America, and trained and equipped native armies and police forces.

Occasionally United States forces intervened to direct the outcome of Latin American conflicts. In 1954, the United States sent troops to Guatemala to oust a left-leaning, reformist government. In 1979, it intervened in Nicaragua to prop up the conservative regime of Anastasio Somoza (1925–1980). The hostility aroused by this intervention boosted popular support for the Marxist regime of the Sandinistas who then took power. (The Sandinistas were named after the revolutionary hero Cesar Augusto Sandino, murdered in 1934.) Into the 1980s, through covert channels and without congressional approval, United States funds supported the Contra ("opponents") rebels against the Sandinista government. (In 1990, the Nicaraguan people themselves voted the Sandinistas out of power, electing a centrist government under Violeta Chamorro, b. 1929.) As recently as 1983, 1989, and 1993, United States troops intervened in the nations of Grenada, Panama, and Haiti.

Since 1960, the Latin American nation of greatest concern for United States policymakers has been Cuba, just ninety miles offshore of Florida. The United States managed the Cuban government during the early years of its nominal independence. In 1933, the strongman Fulgencio Batista (1901–1973) took over the government with United States support. For nearly thirty years, backed by the elites and the military, he ran a thoroughly corrupt administration deeply implicated with organized crime interests, which neglected and betrayed the island's already impoverished people.

In 1959, the revolutionary Fidel Castro (1927–), portrayed on p, 855, headed guerrilla forces that ousted Batista and his supporters; Cuba's wealthy and professional elites fled.   Castro installed a socialist regime that redistributed land, nationalized industries, and established health services and universal education for the people Batista had despised. The local Communist party embraced Castro's government, while the Soviet Union supplied Cuba with arms and loans, and purchased its sugar. Tiny Cuba became a major center of world communism.

The displacement of a tame dictatorship by a Communist state in its own Caribbean lake alarmed United States officials. Cautious diplomacy broke

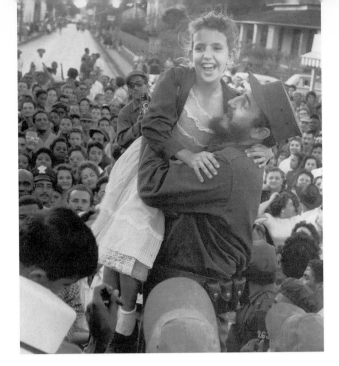

Castro's triumph: *In Cuba in 1959, the guerrilla forces of Fidel Castro drove out the corrupt government that had mortgaged the welfare of the people to American sugar companies. This photograph shows a triumphant Castro embracing one of his young supporters as he sweeps through Cuba to take power.*

down in 1961. The United States had backed an unsuccessful invasion by Cuban exiles at the Bay of Pigs. In response, the Soviets planted nuclear missiles on the island, which could easily reach the United States. In the tensest moment of his brief presidency, John F. Kennedy (1917–1963) "did not blink," as an adviser put it. His refusal to be intimidated forced the Soviets to back down. The United States agreed to plan no further invasions of Cuba.

The crisis past, relations between Cuba and the United States remained volatile, exacerbated by the activism of Cuban exiles who were now resident in the United States. By the 1990s, with the collapse of Soviet communism (see Chapter 30), together with the aging of the charismatic Castro, the tension of those relations finally eased.

Even in the early 1960s, at the zenith of the Cuban challenge, communism did not spread, as many had feared, to other Latin American nations. The containment of communism was due in part to United States-sponsored repression; but communism also failed because Latin American leaders made earnest efforts to reorient the economy so as to benefit the masses as well as the elites. They built new industries, adopted modern technologies, sought a broader spectrum of foreign investment, and diversified production. They accomplished the long-needed breakthrough, escaping the region's narrow dependence on a few export commodities. In addition, without taking the path of Cuban communism, they nationalized some economic functions, and instituted health and welfare programs.

By the 1980s, caudillism began to yield to democracy. A free electorate chose governments in

Argentina, Brazil, Mexico, Nicaragua, and Paraguay. Traces of older social hierarchies, concentrations of land ownership in elite circles, militarism, ethnic tensions, and abusive labor relationships persist in the region. But these appear to be yielding gradually to democratization and economic modernization. Whether Latin America's economic development can keep pace with its unrestrained population growth remains an open question.

The nationalist revolutions of the early 1800s promised an end to colonialism. That goal may at last have been accomplished at the close of the twentieth century. With the transfer of the Canal Zone to the nation of Panama in 1978 and the emancipation of a few Caribbean islands and mainland enclaves still in French, British, or Dutch hands, Latin America has crystallized as a region of largely independent, self-governing states. The United States, the last imperialist in the region, by its economic, political, and military interventions sometimes promoted, sometimes impeded, but in the end supports that achievement—as a good neighbor might.

The Domino Game: the United States in Asia

The United States might view the Caribbean as its lake, and the Americas as the paired continents of its hemisphere. But Asia was far away. Although the United States sought commercial access it had initially no large ambitions in that region. Yet the ideological struggles of the Cold War era defined Asia as a testing ground. The states of Asia were like dominoes, in the simile conceived in 1954 by United States president Dwight D. Eisenhower (1890–1969). If one fell to the alien destiny of communism, all would fall. To avert that outcome, the United States entered, and lost, the domino game.

The United States looked to Asia beginning in the 1850s, as it raced to share in the wealth that international commerce brought the old imperialists of Europe. Its goal, expressed in the "open door" policy enunciated in 1899, was commercial access to China, Japan, and other rich markets (see Chapter 24). Commercial activity, however, led to territorial acquisitions. To support its fleet in an age of steam power, the United States needed fueling stations and naval bases. It began to gather up Pacific islands. From 1851, the United States had a protectorate over Hawaii, acquiring the rights for a naval base at Pearl Harbor by 1887 and annexing the whole area in 1898. It also obtained rights to Midway (1867), Wake Island (1898), and American Samoa (1899). In 1898, it acquired the island of Guam and the archipelago of the Philippines.

The Philippines The Philippines, held by the United States from 1898 to 1946, was the United

Map 29.4 United States Intervention in Latin America and Asia: The imperialist ventures of the United States beyond the borders of North America began in 1898, with a series of interventions in Latin America. During the same period, as a result of their own internal development or, in some cases, provoked by the United States presence, the nations of Latin America seesawed between governments of the right and left, and many guerrilla movements took form in resistance to established powers. These complex political changes are indicated in simplified form above. In the Pacific, meanwhile, the United States acquired several possessions between 1867 and 1899, and intervened militarily in Korea (1950–1953) and Vietnam (1954–1975), as shown in the inset map.

States' first major non-continental territorial acquisition. The United States had claimed it with difficulty, overcoming ardent native resistance and opposition at home. During the 1930s, it negotiated with Filipino leaders a schedule for independence. In 1941, the Japanese invaded, causing the evacuation of the United States naval garrison and abandoning the inhabitants to a harsh occupation.

In 1946, the Philippines became independent according to schedule (although United States military bases remained until 1992). A landowning elite continued to exploit impoverished peasantry as parliamentary government gave way to increasingly despotic rule after 1965, with the election of Ferdinand Marcos (1917–1989). Marcos' regime became more and more corrupt and violent. Conservative elites supported his suppression of communist and Islamic opposition even as, in 1983, 1 million Filipinos defiantly marched in the funeral procession of his assassinated opponent Benigno Aquino. In 1986, Benigno's widow, Corazon Aquino (1933–), successfully challenged Marcos' reelection, which had been marred by irregularities. Marcos and his hated wife Imelda fled the country whose unsteady economic condition wad due in part to their depredations. Many social and economic problems remain unresolved, but the Philippines have attained democratic government under Aquino and her successors.

Korea   The postwar involvement of the United States in Korea and Vietnam developed in response to the perceived threat of communism, which had expanded into eastern Europe and Asia (see Chapter 30). Policymakers feared that communism threatened Africa and the Americas as well.

The partition of Korea at the thirty-eighth parallel of latitude at the end of World War II had positioned two hostile regimes face to face: the communist People's Republic of Korea in the north; and the Republic of Korea in the south. The Korean War broke out suddenly in 1950 when 100,000 northern troops invaded the south and seized the capital Seoul. The North Korean leader, trained and installed by the Soviets, had likely acted at Stalin's prompting. The United States, with a large occupation force based in Japan (see above), saw the invasion as an act of communist aggression that, if not contained, could spread throughout east Asia. It called upon other nations of the recently-constituted United Nations (see Chapter 30) to join in the defense of South Korea. Although a joint effort, the commander-in-chief was the American Douglas MacArthur, and most of the troops came from the United States.

The United Nations forces repulsed the North Korean advance and moved northward toward the Chinese border. About 200,000 Chinese troops swept in from adjacent Manchuria, repelled MacArthur's forces, and, early in 1951, took Seoul a second time.

MacArthur freed Seoul and proposed extending the war to China, his aggressive approach leading to his dismissal by President Truman. Peace talks began in the summer of 1951, concluding only in 1953. A new boundary was drawn between south and north, with a demilitarized zone at the crucial border.

Although the United States had not fought alone in Korea, the war was in many ways an American war, not least because United States forces suffered 34,000 fatalities. In addition, the United States had instigated the military response to what might have remained a civil war, setting a precedent for intervention in the internal affairs of other Asian nations. And the United States had declared its determination to battle communist advance in Asia.

Vietnam   The Korean war prefigured the Vietnam war, a conflict that occupied American attention for an entire generation. Part of the peninsula of Indochina, Vietnam had often suffered invasion—by the Chinese for centuries, and more recently by the French, who had seized almost all of Indochina by 1897 (see Chapters 8, 24). The French occupation triggered a nationalist movement, led by Ho Chi Minh (1890–1969) after World War I. In 1919, appealing to the principle of self-determination, Ho attempted and failed to persuade the drafters of the Paris treaties to free Vietnam as it had freed the subject nationalities of Europe (see Chapter 26). When they did not, he turned to communism, whose Comintern (see Chapter 28) offered friendly support to anti-colonial movements. In Moscow, Ho learned how to organize an insurgent struggle. In 1930, he formed the Indochinese Communist Party.

When the Japanese took over Indochina from the Vichy French during World War II, Ho formed the multi-party League for the Independence of Vietnam—the Viet Minh. In the meantime, nationalist fighters in Vietnam waged guerrilla war against the Japanese. Repatriated at war's end, Ho promulgated the Vietnamese Declaration of Independence, echoing principles drawn from the American Declaration and other classic sources of Western political thought. That document proclaimed the establishment of the Democratic Republic of Vietnam, with its capital at Hanoi.

Independence was not so easily won, however. Even as the Japanese evacuated, the British occupation forces yielded Vietnam to the French, who returned to reclaim their colonial rights. Vietnamese nationalists now fought the French in a prolonged struggle that ended only in 1954, with the obliteration of a French garrison at Dien Bien Phu, and the humiliation of that nation. Despite the sacrifice of tens of thousands of lives, the French had failed to quell the resistance of a people intent on independence, skilled in guerrilla tactics, and supported by the Chinese and the Soviets.

At first, the United States was also inclined to support Vietnamese independence. It reversed that policy and supported the French instead when the Korean War broke out in 1950. By 1954, the United States was paying seventy-eight percent of the costs of French operations in Vietnam. When the French pulled out, the United States went in.

The United States had no historic mission in Vietnam. What drove it to become involved in suppressing the Vietnamese struggle for independence? Why did a nation that had itself originated in a war for independence muster its resources to suppress another engaged in the same attempt?

The critical factor was the presence of communism. The Soviet Union's aims were patently expansionist. In 1949, moreover, a communist government had established itself in China, on Vietnam's border.

In 1950, a communist-inspired invasion of South Korea had dragged the United States into war. In 1954, president Eisenhower proposed his domino theory. Vietnam appeared to be the last bulwark against a communist Asia. The line, it was decided, must be drawn in Vietnam.

The 1954 Geneva Accords did not create an independent Vietnam, although Ho Chi Minh had badly beaten the French. It partitioned the nation at the seventeenth parallel of latitude, giving Ho the north, now communist. The last of the Accords, the Final Declaration, provided for elections throughout the country, north and south, in 1956. Without interference, the likely outcome in 1956 would have been a united Vietnam, under communist leadership. To forestall this event, the United States refused to sign the Final Declaration and assisted Ngo Dinh Diem (1901–1963) in his bid for power in the south.

Diem's actions triggered what came to be known as the Vietnam War. A French-educated Roman Catholic in a nation with a Buddhist majority, the corrupt autocrat Diem suppressed both political and religious opposition. He refused to hold the elections mandated by the Geneva settlement. That decision meant war. Ho Chi Minh's army mobilized. In 1960, thousands of pro-communist nationalists joined in the National Liberation Front to oppose Diem's autocratic government from within South Vietnam. They formed a guerrilla army supplied and guided from the north. These insurgents Diem contemptuously called the "Viet Cong" (Vietnamese communists). The combined activity of the North Vietnamese regular soldiers with the southern Viet Cong,

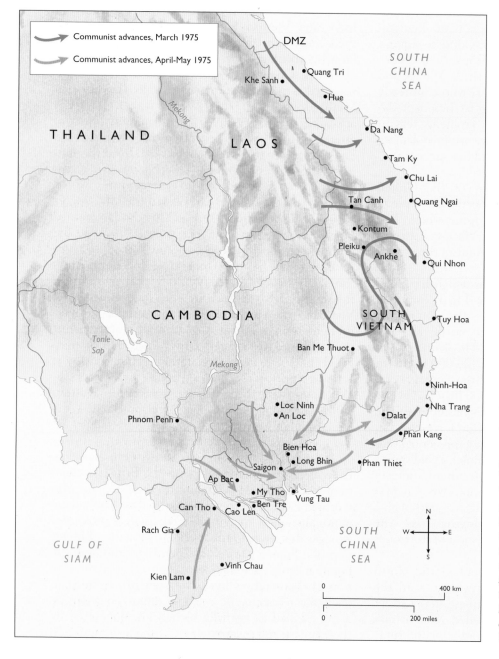

Map 29.5 The Fall of South Vietnam, 1975: *US forces left Vietnam in 1973, having achieved neither peace nor victory. In the spring of 1975, north Vietnamese troops and their southern allies swept rapidly from the north and from refuges in Laos and Cambodia to seize Saigon, capital of South Vietnam, whose anti-Communist regime had been sustained for so many years by a US dedicated to the cause of Cold War foreign policy.*

Give Peace a Chance: *American involvement in Vietnam dragged on fruitlessly, leading the superpower to employ tactics that discredited the aggressor without damaging the defender. In this famous photograph from June 8, 1972 (left) that aroused horror worldwide (though the attack was accidental), young children flee from an American napalm bombing.*

HOW MANY?

United States Military Personnel in Vietnam

Year	Personnel
1954	275
1960	685
1961	2,600
1963	16,500
1965	184,000
1966	385,000
1967	535,000
1969	542,000
1971	139,000
1972	25,000
1973	0

Source: W. R. Keylor, The Twentieth-Century World: An International History, 3rd ed. (Oxford: Oxford University Press, 1996), pp. 373, 375.

invisible within the southern population, frustrated all attempts to snatch the south from Ho's communist north.

Diem was a disappointment. Disgusted by his corruption, inefficiency, and intolerance—he ordered the destruction of Buddhist temples, among other atrocities—the United States withdrew support in 1963. That action encouraged a group of generals to assassinate Diem and seize power. A stream of generals ruled in turn in the south. The regime remained throughout an unsavory ally for the United States, difficult to defend to the public at home, and incapable of managing the war effort unassisted.

From 1954 to 1968, under presidents Eisenhower, Kennedy, and Johnson, the United States escalated its involvement in Vietnam, as *How Many?* left shows. In 1954, 275 Americans were advising the South Vietnamese army. By 1960, that figure had more than doubled to 685; by the end of 1961, it had risen to 2600; and by the time of President Kennedy's assassination in 1963, to 16,500. Meanwhile, the United States sent military aid rising to hundreds of millions of dollars annually. In 1965, the United States launched bombing raids in North Vietnam, and, for the first time, sent ground troops to the south—and the die was cast. By the end of 1965, there were 184,000 American soldiers in Vietnam; by 1966, 385,000; by early 1969, some 542,000. Now the United States was not merely an adviser to what it saw as the better side in a civil war. It was a combatant in an alien struggle on the other side of the globe.

As the numbers of ground forces mounted, Americans at home grew restive, then critical, then angry (see Chapter 30). A "credibility gap" grew wider as officials reported gains—measured in the daily "body count" of dead enemies, many of them civilian—while the Viet Cong and North Vietnamese regulars grew more numerous. Their Tet offensive of 1968, launched on a sacred Vietnamese holiday, showed that resistance was powerful and exposed the failure of United States officials to comprehend the depth of nationalist determination.

After 1968, the United States sought to find an exit from the Vietnam quagmire. President Johnson (1908–1973) signaled his awareness of the failure of his policies in Vietnam by withdrawing from the 1968 election. The new president Richard M. Nixon (1913–1994) promised to secure "peace with honor." By a policy of "Vietnamization," he gradually withdrew United States troops (only 25,000 remained at end 1972) and transferred military responsibilities to regular South Vietnamese forces. To cover the withdrawal, he intensified bombing in the north and in the contiguous states of Laos and Cambodia, thereby drawn into the maelstrom of the war. In 1973, Nixon accomplished the final withdrawal of United States troops—withdrawal, without honor or victory.

That withdrawal had the effect of abandoning the South Vietnamese to sure defeat. The 1973 settlement did not bring peace. By 1975, the North Vietnamese army had taken the southern capital of Saigon, and established dominion over a united Vietnam—an outcome for which Ho Chi Minh struggled for half a century before he died in 1969, just short of its fulfillment. Drawn into the conflict, Laos and Cambodia also fell to native communist movements, of which the Cambodian Khmer Rouge undertook an unprecedently vicious campaign against its own citizenry (see Chapter 30). Twenty years after the French withdrawal, a generation after the close of World War II, after nearly 58,000 American deaths and millions of Vietnamese deaths, after the rupture of confidence at home and the generation of implacable hostility abroad, Indochina (except for Thailand and Myanmar) was communist.

After Vietnam, the United States redefined its policy in Asia. Henceforth, it would seek commercial agreements, support friendly states, and promote a human rights agenda in the region. The domino game was over. The last imperialist limped home.

The Color Line: Conflict at Home

At home, the citizens and leaders of the United States faced the moral and social problems left by an earlier imperialist era. In pursuit of their Manifest Destiny, the European descendants of the first settlers, and the European immigrants who came in waves to join them, grabbed the land that stretched between the Atlantic and Pacific coasts. They seized it from peoples—Amerindian natives and Hispanic settlers of what had been Mexican territory—who became dispossessed of land and heritage alike. At the same time, the descendants of former slaves whose labor had sustained the economy of the old south remained still, as the twentieth century opened, unintegrated into society and barred from the means of progress.

A Visible Difference   Forgotten amid abundance, these groups shared one visible feature—their skin was ruddy, brown, or black. The exclusion of people of color from wealth and power in the world's wealthiest and most powerful nation became the foremost social issue of the century. Democratic principles and habits

of compassion for others alike had always faltered when they approached the color line.

By 1900, the Amerindian tribes of the United States had all been deprived of their lands and freedom (see Chapter 19). Some had been moved to territories set aside for the purpose; others resisted, and were forcibly driven into those **reservations**. They were wrested from the environment and the economy that had shaped their religion, language, and customs, and that were essential to their self-definition. In alien settings, they languished. Even when government programs offered opportunities for social and economic advancement, few individuals or tribes took advantage of them.

In the southwestern region of the United States, settlers wrested land from ranchers and planters of Mexican descent. Landless Mexican workers became subjects of the Anglophone United States. These were followed by waves of Mexican immigrants, for whom low-paid work in the United States offered a better opportunity than their homeland. Although some Mexicans assimilated into United States society, most remained a caste apart. Living in self-defined communities, or *barrios*, where they could practice their own religion and customs, they were isolated from most opportunities for education and progress. In systems of public education, their children tended to perform poorly, as poverty and cultural difference interfered with learning. The prejudice exhibited by bureaucrats, officials, and employers further disadvantaged Hispanic citizens and immigrants.

Most isolated of all the groups on the far side of the color line were those of African descent who carried as burdens not only their blackness but the terrible legacy of slavery (see Chapter 19). For two generations after the end of the Civil War, most continued to live in the south among the descendants of their former masters. The white population cooperated in the exclusion of blacks from the vote, from schooling, from housing, from economic opportunity. The Black Codes, laws passed by many states in the post-Civil War era, gave way to "Jim Crow" laws that limited the access of African Americans to housing, transportation, schooling, recreation, a lengthy list of possible avenues to advancement or happiness.

The condition of African Americans worsened as the twentieth century opened. The Supreme Court decision in the case of Plessy v. Ferguson (1896), quoted in *Witnesses* on p. 861, introducing the principle of "separate but equal," permitted the relegation of African Americans to separate institutions—schools, houses, public facilities—as long as those institutions were "equal" (which they were not). Blacks attended different schools, ate in different restaurants, drank from different water fountains, and sat in different sections of public buses.

Southern society prevented any deviation from these norms by a strategy of terror. The Ku Klux Klan, formed soon after the Civil War and reconstituted in 1915, was a loose network of secret societies that championed the white man's vision of the south. Disguised in fear-inspiring white robes and hoods, Klansmen terrorized blacks and their white supporters, leaving behind them as a sign of their implacable hostility a burning wooden cross. Klansmen often joined in lynchings, the illicit execution by hanging of those deemed guilty of crimes or hated without reason. In the 1880s, these had mounted to a high of over one hundred per year. They subsided, then returned, tripling in the key Depression year 1932–1933.

Despite terror, hatred, and discrimination, African Americans built their own neighborhoods and communities in the homeland they had never chosen. Christianized under slavery, they formed their own black churches (mostly Baptist and Methodist) headed by black pastors, who became the acknowledged leaders of African American communities. With the impediments to legal marriage and property ownership that slavery imposed now gone, they formed strong families and worked to secure land and housing, although they were more often forced into tenancy and sharecropping.

WITNESSES

The Americas: Racial Equality and Racial Separatism in the United States

Between the end of the Civil War in 1865 and the Civil Rights Act of 1964 lay an interim of just under a century in which Americans of African descent, most the offspring of former slaves, suffered great wrongs, including discrimination in housing, employment, and education. A major victory in the battle to turn that tide of discrimination was won in 1954, with the United States Supreme Court decision in the case of Brown v. Board of Education, excerpted in the first passage here. Martin Luther King, Jr., was the principal figure in the African-American struggle to gain the rights promised by the Amendments 14 to 16 of the United States Constitution. The second passage contains one of his statements giving the reasons for his resistance. During the 1960s, the struggle for civil rights for African-Americans became increasingly bitter and sometimes violent. The Black Panther Party, self-styled as revolutionary, announced its principles in its founding document, a party platform in 1966, of which some points are given in the third passage.

The US Supreme Court decision in the case Brown v. Board of Education of Topeka, overturning the "separate but equal" principle established by Plessy v. Ferguson (1896), orders school integration "with all deliberate speed" (1954): Today, education is perhaps the most important function of state and local governments. Compulsory school attendance laws and the great expenditures for education both demonstrate our recognition of the importance of education to our democratic society. ... In these days, it is doubtful that any child may reasonably be expected to succeed in life if he is denied the opportunity of an education. Such an opportunity ... is a right which must be made available to all on equal terms.

We come then to the question presented: Does segregation of children in the public schools solely on the basis of race, even though the physical facilities and other "tangible" factors may be equal, deprive the children of the minority group of equal educational opportunities? We believe that it does.

(Brown v. Board of Education of Topeka, 347 US 483–496, 1954)

Martin Luther King, Jr.: a letter from Birmingham Jail (1963): My Dear Fellow Clergymen:

... I think I should indicate why I am here in Birmingham. ... I am in Birmingham because injustice is here. ...

You deplore the demonstrations taking place in Birmingham. ... It is unfortunate that demonstrations are taking place ... but it is even more unfortunate that the city's white power structure left the Negro community with no alternative.

We [Black Americans] have been waiting for more than 340 years for our constitutional and God-given rights. The nations of Asia and Africa are moving with jetlike speed toward gaining political independence, but we still creep at horse-and-buggy pace toward gaining a cup of coffee at a lunch counter.

(Martin Luther King, letter from Birmingham Jail, April 16, 1963; eds. A. P. Blaustein and R. L. Zangrando, 1968)

In 1966, the extreme Black Panther Party announced in its Platform its demands for autonomy and for compensation from "white racist" Americans:

1. *We want freedom. We want power to determine the destiny of our Black Community.* We believe that black people will not be free until we are able to determine our destiny.
2. *We want full employment for our people.* We believe that the federal government is responsible and obligated to give every man employment or a guaranteed income. ...
3. *We want an end to the robbery by the white man of our Black Community.* We believe that this racist government has robbed us and now we are demanding the overdue debt [projected during Reconstruction, after the Civil War] of forty acres and two mules as restitution for slave labor and mass murder of black people. ...
4. *We want decent housing, fit for shelter of human beings.* ...
5. *We want education for our people that exposes the true nature of this decadent American society. We want education that teaches us our true history and our role in the present-day society.* ...

(from http://lists.village.virginia.edu/sixties/HTML_docs/Resources /Primary/Manifestos/Panther_platform.html)

As much as any colonized people abroad, Americans of African descent faced a long struggle for civil rights and guarantee of social and economic justice. Largely through the efforts of Martin Luther King, Jr.—shown here in August 1963 outside the White House (above)—a landmark Civil Rights Act was signed in 1964. Other battles remained. The fiercely committed Malcolm X is seen here summoning his followers to action (below right). He holds aloft a newspaper with the headline "Our Freedom Can't Wait!" The unfinished nature of the quest for equality is vividly illustrated in another photograph (below left), where striking

Memphis (Tennessee) sanitation workers, most African American, wearing placards saying "I am a man," parade in front of a row of National Guardsmen with rifles ready and bayonets affixed.

Memphis sanitation workers' strike, March 1968

Malcolm X, New York, 1963

To continue your investigation of this topic, please go to www.prenhall.com/king for the related **WINDOWS** on the **WEB** activity

Voices of Protest African American leaders had different visions of how best to promote their people. Scholars often note the classic opposition between two late nineteenth-century figures: Booker T. Washington (1856–1915), a freed slave; and William E. B. du Bois (1868–1963), the mixed descendent of Africans and Europeans, raised and educated in the north. Rising from the mine pits where he worked as a child immediately after emancipation, Washington became an educator, a reformer, and a public advocate on behalf of all African Americans and through his own efforts and intelligence. He urged upon his own community the values of hard work, especially in industrial tasks that would earn laborers respect and decent wages. He was cautiously non-revolutionary in his rhetoric, seeking to persuade white listeners of the diligence and benevolence of blacks rather than to frighten them with unsettling demands.

Du Bois took a different approach. A brilliant theorist and writer, he received a doctoral degree from Harvard (1895) and subsequently taught at Atlanta University in Georgia. Despite his mainstream credentials, Du Bois was no academic onlooker. He criticized Washington for kowtowing to white audiences and underestimating black competency. Calling on the "talented tenth" of black leaders to organize for political action, he formed the Niagara Movement in 1905, which in 1909, inspired the foundation of the National Association for the Advancement of Colored People (the NAACP), still a major force in the advocacy of equal rights for blacks. In 1961, concluding that American society would never truly welcome its black citizens, Du Bois joined the Communist Party, and moved to Ghana, in Africa, where he died in 1963. In such works as *The Souls of Black Folk* (1903) Du Bois argued for the radical emancipation of African Americans from deep-seated attitudes that he considered profoundly racist. In that work he diagnosed what he saw as the incapacity of white Americans to cross or erase the "color line," which he believed to be the defining issue of the twentieth century.

The color line grew bolder in the 1920s and 1930s when blacks emigrated in large numbers from the south to northern cities. As opportunities for unskilled workers shrank in the south (and most blacks were unskilled because segregation patterns barred them from high-quality schooling and training), they hoped to work in northern factories, on the railroads, and in the streets. Transplanted, they found that the north was also segregated. Denied access to the better schools and neighborhoods, they formed their own neighborhoods and church-centered communities. In isolated neighborhoods called ghettoes, African Americans led a life apart from other Americans—separate but not equal.

It was to these African Americans that Marcus Garvey (1887–1940) spoke most passionately. A Jamaica-born activist, Garvey lived in the United States from 1916 to 1927. Pointing to the long record of European mistreatment of non-Europeans, Garvey promoted rebellion and secession. He urged blacks "back to Africa," to build that continent from which their ancestors had been ripped centuries before. Convicted in 1925 of mail fraud in the management of his Black Star steamship line (founded to carry his followers back to Africa), Garvey was deported from the United States in 1927.

Among those who heard the voices of African American leaders calling for a new pride in the face of white dominance were the artists, performers, and writers of the Harlem Renaissance. The lights blazed nightly on New York City's Lenox Avenue and 135th Street where well-dressed blacks and radically chic whites visited clubs and theaters and conversed heatedly on the streets. Soon the voices were silenced by the Depression, which hurt black Americans even more than whites. Now movement leaders gathered into organizations such as the NAACP. The 1930s saw the political consciousness of the larger African American community broaden, as though in preparation for the vital struggles ahead.

The Harlem Renaissance was in full swing and the Great Depression had not yet stalled black progress when the greatest of African American leaders, Martin Luther King, Jr. (1929–1968), portrayed in *Windows On* on p. 862 was born. A minister and a minister's son, the recipient of a doctoral degree in theology, King was a worthy successor to Washington and du Bois. He combined Washington's understanding of the need to strive for advancement within a predominantly white society, with du Bois' deeper critique of that society's hostility to black success.

The Civil Rights Movement King began by protesting unjust barriers—the segregation of public transportation and public education. He became the prophet of the Civil Rights movement, which grew from resistance to bus segregation by a lone black woman, Rosa Parks (1913–), in 1955, to the high tide of 1964, when the Civil Rights Act was signed into law, barring discrimination by color in public facilities or in employment. More than any other single figure, he achieved widespread acknowledgment of the right—if not yet the reality—of black Americans to live, learn, and work as freely as their white counterparts. It may have been his great success that prompted an assassin to shoot King in 1968, when he was not yet forty and at the zenith of his career.

Du Bois' NAACP had prepared the way during the 1930s and 1940s for the drive against segregation that King led in the 1950s. Its team of lawyers brought cases that exposed segregationist practices. Chief counsel of the NAACP legal team from 1940 to 1961 was attorney Thurgood Marshall (1908–1993), appointed in 1967 the first African American justice of the Supreme Court. In 1954, the NAACP won a landmark judgment that effectively overturned Plessy v. Ferguson. In Brown v. Board of Education of Topeka, the Supreme Court ordered that "separate" schools were by nature unequal and discriminatory against black citizens. The next year, it ordered the twenty-one states that had segregated school systems to desegregate "with all deliberate speed." That mammoth victory opened the floodgates of reform.

In 1955, King led the boycott of the bus system of Montgomery, Alabama, that had been triggered by the arrest of Rosa Parks. In 1956, the Supreme Court vindicated that protest, declaring the segregation unconstitutional. The next year, with other leaders King worked to secure the enrollment of nine black students in the main white high school in Little Rock, Arkansas. A reluctant President Eisenhower sent federal troops to handle the crisis, which was resolved only in 1959.

These victories won, King and other civil rights leaders broadened their agenda. Through the SCLC (Southern Christian Leadership Conference), King urged a program of nonviolent resistance, based in part on the methods of Mohandas Gandhi. With the organizations CORE (Congress of Racial Equality) and SNCC (Student Nonviolent Coordinating Committee), activists confronted discrimination through nonviolent resistance. A dynamic coalition of young black southern activists, supported by northern white university students, won battles of conscience in lunch counters, waiting rooms, and polling booths across the south.

These resisters found violence turned against them, as segregationists with policemen and firemen fought against peaceful demonstrators. The rising tide of conflict compelled President John F. Kennedy to introduce a strong proposal for civil rights legislation. When King and 250,000 people came to Washington in August 1963, to proclaim their goal of racial justice, it was already in the works. By summer 1964, the Civil Rights bill was law—although Kennedy did not live to see its passage. The Voting Rights Act, passed the following year, added guarantees of access to the polls.

But these legislative victories seemed almost too late as the volume of protest rose. In the later 1960s, the militant Black Power movement rejected nonviolence and targeted the underlying racism that denied African Americans, even when accorded legal protections, their rights and their dignity (see *Witnesses*, p. 861). Riots broke out in urban centers from 1965 to 1967. The Black Muslim movement advocated black separatism. The courageous leader Malcolm X (1925–1965), a survivor of ghetto and prison cell, who is depicted in *Windows On* on p. 862. encouraged blacks to ceaseless struggle against white oppression, later accepting the possibility of racial integration. His former Black Muslim colleagues gunned him down in 1965. A lone gunman shot Martin Luther King in 1968.

In the end, the multiple movements for racial justice profoundly transformed the American consciousness. In 1964, activist Ella Baker (d. 1986) had proclaimed that seekers of freedom could not rest "until the killing of black mothers' sons becomes as important to the rest of the country as the killing of white mothers' sons." In time, it did. By the time of Malcolm X's death in 1965, by King's death in 1968, and certainly by Baker's death in 1986, most Americans had recognized the injustice of the tragic long night of exclusion, segregation, and prejudice. Government agencies officially repudiated those attitudes; in schools and houses of worship, they were assailed. A new liberal consensus had been established. Yet the full social and civil equality of African Americans was not yet a reality nor has it since been achieved. The color line still threads its way through the fabric of American life, the unlovely inheritance of slavery and the West's imperial ventures.

Conclusion

THE SHADOWS OF IMPERIALISM AND THE MEANING OF THE WEST

For 500 years, the most powerful Western nations imposed their will on the other regions of the globe. That age is over, but its shadows hover still. The exploitation of wealth that belonged to others, the coercive reshaping of societies and culture that had different roots and purposes, the demeaning of whole peoples—these actions performed by thousands of Westerners and approved by many millions have left deep wounds and great bitterness.

But though it imposed its will in ways now regretted, the reign of the West has not been without benefit for the other peoples of the world. Its industrial might, its political institutions, its cultural forms, even its religious values now have willing imitators around the globe, who can borrow from the West at will as they develop their own free and independent nations—just as dissident Chinese students, in Tiananmen Square in Beijing in 1989, erected a replica of the Statue of Liberty that stands in New York Harbor, and onlookers throughout the world beheld its message.

REVIEW QUESTIONS

1. Why did World War I weaken European rule? How did Ghandi act to advance the struggle for Indian independence? Why did Pakistan separate from India in 1947?

2. Which European powers fought to retain their African colonies? Why was Algeria so important to France? Why did so many African states suffer military coups?

3. What were the barriers facing nation-building in post-colonial Africa? Describe the system of apartheid in South Africa. How was apartheid brought to an end?

4. How did Atatürk create modern Turkey? Describe Arab–Israeli relations between 1948 and the 1990s. Why did the Arab states find it hard to accept Israel? Why does Islamism oppose Western influences?

5. How did Asian states seek to modernize their economies after World War II? Why has Japan become a democracy, but not China? Why did the United States become involved in the Vietnam War?

6. To what extent was the United States the last imperialist power? How has the United States intervened in Latin America since 1898? How does United States aggression abroad relate to racist attitudes at home? How did legal segregation end in the United States?

SUGGESTED RESOURCES

The Tide Turns: Anti-Colonialism and Decolonization

Hargreaves, J. D., *Decolonization in Africa* (London–New York: Longman, 1988). Excellent survey, attending to Portuguese, Belgian, and Italian, as well as British and French empires.

Judd, Denis, *Empire: The British Imperial Experience from 1765 to the Present* (New York: Basic Books, 1996). Emphasizes the tragedies, failures, and ultimately the decline of the British Empire.

Keay, John, *Empire's End: A History of the Far East from High Colonialism to Hong Kong* (New York: Scribner's, 1997). Covers the last 500 years, including the decline of foreign rule since the 1930s.

Read, Anthony & David Fisher, *The Proudest Day: India's Long Road to Independence* (New York: W. W. Norton, 1998). With a focus on liberation in 1947, the authors trace the British government's vacillation between benevolence and control in the preceding period, and the courage and determination of India's native leaders.

The United Nations and Decolonialization, current policies, declarations, and links (UN):
http://www.un.org/Depts/dpi/decolonization/main.htm

New World Orders: Statebuilding in Africa, the Middle East, and Asia

Carter, G. M and O'Meara, P. eds., *African Independence: The First Twenty-Five Years* (Bloomington: Indiana University Press, 1985). Essays examining inherited challenges and squandered opportunities on Africa's path to development.

Gerges, Fawaz A., *The Superpowers and the Middle East: Regional and International Politics, 1955–1967* (Boulder, CO: Westview Press, 1994). Surveys this key geo-political relationship during the High Cold War.

Irokawa, Daikichi, *The Age of Hirohito: The Making of Modern Japan* (New York: Free Press, 1995). Critical assessment of Japanese history during the 62 years' reign of the Emperor Hirohito, who died in 1989.

Jones, Eric, Lionel Frost, and Colin White, *Coming Full Circle: An Economic History of the Pacific Rim* (Boulder, CO: Westview Press, 1993). China was the world's economic center up to about 1400; according to the authors, it will resume this position in this century.

Meredith, Martin, *Nelson Mandela: A Biography* (New York: St. Martin's Press, 1998). Solid biography of this key figure of the late 20th century.

Spence, Jonathan, *Mao Zedong* (New York: Viking Penguin, 2000). Characterizes the revolutionary as committed to reform through upheaval, a theme borrowed from China's history and consistent with the subject's experience during the revolutionary struggle.

Wolpert, Stanley A., *Nehru: A Tryst with Destiny* (Oxford: Oxford University Press, 1996). Authoritative biography.

Mohandas Karamchand Gandhi, Man of Millennium, works, images, links (Institute of Advanced Studies, Nagpur, India):
http://www.mkgandhi.org

Nelson Mandela, biography and resources (African National Congress): http://www.anc.org.za/people/mandela.hmtl

The Last Imperialist: The United States Abroad and at Home

Cottam, M. L., *Images and Intervention: U.S. Policies in Latin America* (Pittsburgh: University of Pittsburgh Press, 1994). Explores connections between the image of Latin America held by the US and the latter's tendency to conduct foreign policy in Central and South America by means of military intervention and covert operations.

Garrow, D. J., *Bearing the Cross: Martin Luther King, Jr., and the Southern Christian Leadership Conference* (New York: W. Morrow, 1986). Explores King's role in the emergence of the Civil Rights movement.

Kaiser, David, *American Tragedy: Kennedy, Johnson, and the Origins of the Vietnam War* (Cambridge, MA: Belknap Press of Harvard University Press, 2000). First Vietnam history able to draw on a complete set of declassified documents. Kaiser argues that the roots of Vietnam policy date back to the Eisenhower era, and that Johnson, adopted the policy framework that Eisenhower had established, but Kennedy sidestepped.

Leogrande, William M., *Our Own Backyard: the United States in Central America, 1977–1992* (Chapel Hill: University of North Carolina Press, 1998). Comprehensive overview of United States policy in Latin America during the last phase of the Cold War.

Lischer, Richard, *The Preacher King: Martin Luther King, Jr. and the Word that Moved America* (Oxford: Oxford University Press, 1995). Examines the role played in King's thought by African-Baptist influences.

Young, Marilyn, *The Vietnam Wars, 1945–1990* (New York: Harper Trade, 1991). Unique account of the Vietnam conflict that gives equal consideration to the perspective of the Vietnamese themselves.

Martin Luther King, "I have a dream'" August 28, 1963:
http://odur.let.rug.nl/nusa

BACK FROM ARMAGEDDON

	1940	1950	1960	1970	1980	1990	2000

Korean War, 1950–53   Vietnam War, 1964–73

The Cold War and Global Politics

- ◆ Hiroshima and Nagasaki bombed, 1945
- ◆ United Nations founded, 1945
- ◆ Churchill's "Iron Curtain" speech, 1946
- ◆ Marshall Plan announced, 1947
- ◆ Truman Doctrine announced, 1947
- ◆ Berlin blockade and airlift, 1948
- ◆ UN Universal Declaration of Human Rights, 1948
- ◆ NATO formed, 1949
- ◆ China becomes Communist state. 1949
- ◆ Soviet Union explodes atomic bomb, 1949
- ◆ First hydrogen bomb, US, 1952
- ◆ Soviet Union has hydrogen bomb, 1953
- ◆ Ethel and Julius Rosenberg executed, 1953
- ◆ Warsaw Pact formed, 1955
- ◆ Sukarno hosts Bandung, Indonesia, conference, 1955
- ◆ Nikita Khrushchev denounces Stalin, 1956
- ◆ Hungarian uprising, 1956
- ◆ Suez Crisis, 1956
- ◆ Soviet Union launches *Sputnik I*, 1957
- ◆ United States sends *Explorer I* into orbit, 1958
- ◆ Berlin Wall erected, 1961
- ◆ Chinese–Soviet split, 1961
- ◆ Cuban Missile Crisis, 1961
- ◆ Nuclear test ban agreement, 1963
- ◆ Six-Day War, Israel, 1967
- ◆ Nuclear Non-Proliferation Treaty, 1968
- ◆ Prague Spring suppressed, Czechoslovakia, 1968
- ◆ *Apollo 11*, lunar landing, 1969
- ◆ Oil crisis, 1973–74
- ◆ Helsinki Accords, 1975
- ◆ Soviets invade Afghanistan, 1979
- ◆ Solidarity movement, Poland, 1980
- ◆ Marshall Tito dies, Yugoslavia, 1980

- ◆ Gorbachev launches *Perestroika* and *Glasnost*, 1985
- ◆ Chernobyl nuclear disaster, Ukraine, 1986
- ◆ Communism collapses in Eastern Europe, 1989
- ◆ Tiananmen Square protests suppressed, 1989
- ◆ UN Convention on the Rights of the Child, 1989
- ◆ START I treaty signed, 1991
- ◆ Yeltsin elected president of Russian Republic, 1991
- ◆ Anti-Gorbachev coup, Soviet Union, 1991
- ◆ Soviet Union dissolved, 1991
- ◆ Gulf War, 1991
- ◆ START II treaty signed, 1993
- ◆ Hutus massacre 500,000–800,000 Tutsis, Rwanda, 1994
- ◆ Bosnian Serbs massacre thousands in Srebenica, Bosnia-Herzegovina, 1995
- ◆ Dayton (Ohio) Peace Agreement, 1995
- ◆ Russian economic crisis threatens reform, 1998
- ◆ India and Pakistan carry out nuclear tests, 1998
- ◆ NATO bombs Serbia, 1999

Culture, Society, and Economy

- ◆ ENIAC computer developed, 1946
- ◆ Albert Camus's *The Plague*, 1947
- ◆ Simone de Beauvoir's *The Second Sex*, 1949
- ◆ European Economic Community (Common Market) formed, 1957
- ◆ Federico Fellini's *La dolce vita*, 1960
- ◆ NOW (National Organization for Women) formed, 1966
- ◆ Beatles' "All You Need is Love" broadcast worldwide, 1967
- ◆ Stanley Kubrick's *2001: A Space Odyssey*, 1968
- ◆ Woodstock Festival, 1969
- ◆ First Earth Day celebration in US, 1970
- ◆ Alexander Solzhenitsyn's *The Gulag Archipelago*, 1973

- ◆ UN General Assembly establishes World Commission on Environment and Development, 1983
- ◆ Spain and Portugal join the Common Market, 1986
- ◆ "Earth Summit" meets, Brazil, 1992
- ◆ European Union created, 1994
- ◆ Kyoto Protocol commits industrial nations to reductions in greenhouse gas emissions, 1997
- ◆ Debut of the euro, 1999

BACK FROM ARMAGEDDON

From the Bomb to the Internet

1945–1990

USA and Cold War allies

USSR and Cold War allies

KEY TOPICS

◆ **Apocalypse Now?:** With the fearful power of the atom unloosed, and with much of Europe under Soviet rule, people of the non-Communist West wonder whether the Apocalypse is about to arrive. Yet it is deferred when, in 1989, the Communist regime begins to unravel and the states of the former Soviet bloc turn to democracy and free markets.

◆ **All You Need is Love:** In the vanguard United States, the first generation born to face the prospect of nuclear annihilation ignores the Cold War, protests against the country's involvement in Vietnam, and invents a culture that is based on unhampered self-expression. The Sixties movement spurs sexual revolution and environmentalist activism, while religious and nationalist forces resurge and provoke small but deadly conflicts around the globe.

Reprieve from terror: 1989 On December 29, 1989, dissident playwright Václav Havel (1936–) became the first president of liberated Czechoslovakia as it set out on the path from dictatorship to democracy. "Your government, my people, has been returned to you," he proclaimed in his New Year's address a few days later.

Havel's ascendancy in a bloodless or "velvet" revolution marked the release of his nation from the Soviet-controlled communist regimes that had held sway since 1945. In 1989, Poland, Hungary, Bulgaria, East Germany (the German Democratic Republic), and Romania also threw off their former rulers, even as, in distant China, student democrats in Beijing's Tiananmen Square confronted the communist state (see Chapter 29). The events of 1989 preceded the dissolution in 1991 of the Soviet Union itself.

With its collapse, the terror eased that had gripped the nations of the West and of the world. From 1945 to 1989, two superpowers, the United States and the Soviet Union, both equipped with nuclear weapons, were locked in a condition of ideological stalemate and political confrontation known as the Cold War. For nearly fifty years, the prospect of Armageddon loomed—the great final battle of the nations of the world. That threat faded with the end of the Cold War, while internationalist movements to heal the Earth's ills flourished, rooted in the era of the 1960s when youthful activists proposed a worldwide agenda of human welfare and environmental concern.

APOCALPYSE NOW?

The last scene of World War II was the first scene of the age that followed. The atomic destruction of Hiroshima and Nagasaki in 1945 (see Chapter 28) struck a new kind of fear. "The life expectancy of the human species … [has] dwindled immeasurably," the *Washington Post* dismally announced. With the Soviet occupation of eastern Europe, the nations of the Western world divided into two hostile blocs—a communist East and a largely democratic West. For nearly fifty years, people wondered: would Apocalypse (a universal destruction prophesied in the Bible) come now? Or soon? Or could it be forestalled?

Postwar Polarization

From 1945 until 1953, the Soviet Union established its power in eastern Europe while the United States led an alliance of western European nations against further Soviet advance, pledging "massive retaliation" against any aggression.

Europe Divided By late 1945, the Soviet Union had already secured much of Europe. For two years after its

1943 victories at Stalingrad and Kursk (see Chapter 28), the Red Army swept German armies out of Russia and back to Berlin, where the enemy surrendered on May 8, 1945. The Soviet flag flew in Berlin and throughout the lands the Soviets now occupied.

Soviet territorial claims, rooted in older Russian ambitions, were sanctioned by wartime agreements between the Allies. The "Big Three"—United States president Franklin Delano Roosevelt (1882–1945), British prime minister Winston Churchill (1874–1965), and the Soviet leader Joseph Stalin (1879–1953)—convened twice during the war: at Teheran (Iran) in November and December 1943, and at Yalta in the Crimea in February 1945. (In addition, Churchill met with Stalin in October 1944 in Moscow.) A final meeting of the victors took place in Potsdam (Germany) in July 1945, where President Harry S. Truman (1887–1972) replaced Roosevelt, who had recently died; and Clement Attlee (1883–1967) replaced Churchill, defeated in British elections. These meetings yielded agreements that transferred to Soviet control a corridor of states from the Baltic to the Balkans—the European nations created in 1919 from the borderlands of fallen empires, promised by Hitler to Stalin in 1939.

This outcome was not what Roosevelt and Churchill had planned in the Atlantic Charter of August 1941. That charter stated that neither the United States nor Britain sought territorial aggrandizement, and called for the restoration of sovereign rights to nations that had been deprived of them, and the repudiation of the use of force to advance national interests—principles subsequently adopted by the twenty-six signatories of the January 1942 Declaration of the nascent United Nations. Those principles were ignored, however, as the Soviet Union, seeking to defend its borders and conscious of its extraordinary sacrifices in the battle against Nazism, took control of half of Europe. Now a communist megalith faced the nations to the west.

Between 1945 and 1949, Soviet-backed communist governments took over in East Germany, in Poland, Czechoslovakia, Hungary, Romania, Bulgaria, and Albania; Yugoslavia, alone, led by resistance hero Marshall Tito (Josip Broz, 1892–1980) broke with Moscow. In 1940, the Soviets had already annexed the Baltic states of Estonia, Lithuania, and Latvia; now they acquired parts of Finland, Romania, and Czechoslovakia. The citizens of these regions who had suffered Nazi brutality now lived under regimes answerable to the Soviet Union, a totalitarian state that imposed a command economy, agrarian collectives, press censorship, and one-party rule.

Western Europeans observed these developments with alarm. Having survived the Nazi threat, they now confronted a Soviet one. Their economies were in tatters, and their military capacity exhausted; Germany and Austria were wholly disarmed. They looked to the

Map 30.1 The Two Superpowers in a Bipolar World, 1955: *By 1955, Europe was divided between those states loyal to the Soviet Union (the members of the Warsaw Pact) and those aligned with the United States (members of NATO). Although many nations beyond Europe remained non-aligned, others also joined in alliances with one or another of the superpowers. The faceoff between the superpowers created, in effect, a "bipolar" world—oriented toward not one pole but two. Both contenders were armed sufficiently to destroy human life on earth.*

United States to guarantee their security. Would the United States renounce its former isolationism, and return to defend western Europe? In 1945, the answer was not yet clear. But the means were at hand with the terrible power of the atomic bomb.

European Recovery Meanwhile, the project of rebuilding Europe began. Nazi officials and collaborators were purged, and the destruction caused by bombs addressed. Cities were in ruins; some seventy to ninety percent of Germany's urban fabric had been destroyed, as had railroads and bridges, communications systems, and factories. Urban populations needed food and, for those driven to take shelter in warehouses or cellars, new housing. Millions of refugees awaited **repatriation**—Germans who had fled the advancing Red Army, forced laborers detained in Germany, former prisoners of war. Twelve million "displaced persons" were taken under the wing of Allied administrators.

German and Soviet prisoners of war unlucky enough to be released in the Red Army zone were shipped back to the Soviet Union; and then on to execution or the oblivion of the gulag.

In western Europe, parliamentary governments were restored and currencies stabilized—often at rates that caused the value of prewar bank accounts to plummet. British, French, and American armies settled down in western Germany and Austria. In the rest of Germany and eastern Europe, the Red Army dug in its heels.

Europe was vulnerable, analysts argued, its impoverished nations prone to communist takeover through open elections or covert design. Where the struggle against fascism had previously united the free world, now many saw communism as a primary global threat. American assistance would be needed for Europe's recuperation, not least as a counter-measure to communist influence. Proposed by Secretary of State

Weapons and Warriors

The Big Three: *The leaders of the major combatant nations—Churchill, Roosevelt, and Stalin (the so-called "Big Three")—met at Yalta in the Crimea in February 1945 to discuss Allied military strategy and the end of the war. At least as decisive—both in bringing the war in the Far East to a close and establishing post-War power relationships—was the atomic bomb.*

George C. Marshall (1880–1959) in 1947, the Marshall Plan (or "European Recovery Program") offered economic aid to any European nation—whatever its political commitments—upon the presentation of a reasonable proposal for its use. Prodded by their masters, the nations of the Soviet zone declined to participate; but the nations of western Europe responded enthusiastically, including the Germans whom Allied leaders had so recently labeled "beasts" and "barbarians."

Funneling United States wealth—$13.2 billion between 1948 and 1952—to the treasuries of noncommunist Europe, the Marshall Plan became in effect an economic corollary of the political strategy announced in the Truman Doctrine.

Early Cold War Activity   The Truman Doctrine, which energized foreign policy for more than two decades and culminated in the imbroglio of Vietnam (see Chapter 29), announced the strategy of "containment," outlined in 1947 by the State Department representative in Moscow, George F. Kennan (1904–).

Kennan viewed Soviet power as opportunistic and aggressive. The United States, he said, must offer an "unalterable counterforce" wherever the Soviets "show signs of encroaching upon the interests of a peaceful and stable world."

Crises in the eastern Mediterranean seemed to demand such a policy. In Turkey in 1946, the Soviet Union positioned itself to seize control of the Dardanelles, the straits connecting the Mediterranean and Black Seas for which the Russian tsars had long hungered. In response, President Truman deployed a naval force in the eastern Mediterranean. In Greece, meanwhile, communist opponents of the ruling monarchy were supplied by the new Balkan dictatorships. In 1947, the British Foreign Office informed the State Department that Britain could no longer afford to prop up its embattled ally. The United States assumed that task; communist opposition had failed by 1949.

These circumstances led Truman to define an aggressive international role for the United States. In March 1947, he announced that it "must be the policy of the United States to support free peoples who are resisting attempted subjugation by armed minorities or by outside pressures." This pledge to all nations confronted with the threat of communist takeover was the core of the "Truman Doctrine."

The mushroom-shaped cloud: *Hearing in 1939 that the Nazis had begun efforts to develop the world's first nuclear weapons, the United States strove successfully to beat them to the punch. By 1945 the United States had three bombs: one was tested at Alamagordo, New Mexico in July 1945, and the other two were dropped on Japanese cities in early August 1945. A later test of a similar device in the Nevada desert in 1946 is shown above.*

The Prospects of Nuclear War: Two Reflections

Fear of nuclear holocaust gripped a whole generation during the Cold War. In different ways, the words of author William Faulkner, at its outset, and songwriter Sting, near its end, express that fear.

Novelist William Faulkner speaks of the bomb during his Nobel Prize acceptance speech (1949): Our tragedy is a general and universal fear. ... There are no longer any problems of the spirit. There is only the question: when will I be blown up? ...

I decline to accept the end of man. It is easy enough to say that man is immortal simply because he will endure; that when the last ding-dong of doom has clanged and faded from the last worthless rock hanging tideless in the last red and dying evening, that even then there will still be one more sound: that of his puny inexhaustible voice, still talking. I refuse to accept this. I believe that man will not merely endure; he will prevail. He is immortal, not because he alone among creatures has an inexhaustible voice, but because he has a soul, a spirit capable of compassion and sacrifice and endurance.

(From Nobel Foundation, *Les Prix Nobel en 1950*, 1951)

Songwriter Sting considers the likelihood of war (1985):
How can I save my little boy
from Oppenheimer's deadly toy?
There is no monopoly on common sense
on either side of the political fence.
We share the same biology,
regardless of ideology.
Believe me when I say to you,
I hope the Russians love their children too.

[Sting's reference is to J. Robert Oppenheimer (1904–1967), one of the leading physicists on the atomic bomb project.]

("Russians," words and music by Sting, 1985)

Another early Cold War confrontation took place in the German capital of Berlin. In 1945, Britain, France, the United States, and the Soviet Union had occupied separate zones of Germany, as well as four separate sectors of Berlin—an awkward arrangement because the city was located 100 miles deep in the Soviet zone. By spring 1948, the division of Germany by four powers became a rupture between two: the consortium, on the one hand, of the British, French, and Americans in the west (who would organize the region as the Federal Republic of Germany the following year); and on the other, the Soviets in the east (who would respond by creating the German Democratic Republic).

In June 1948, wishing to isolate Berlin from the western zones of Germany (a policy to which the West Berlin municipal government refused to acquiesce), the Soviet Union shut down access to the city by road, rail, or waterway. For nearly a year the western powers organized an unprecedented airlift, supplying the besieged citizens with food and fuel. By May 1949, the Soviets dropped the blockade, having failed to detach Berlin from its ties to the West.

By the time of the Berlin crisis, the Western world had crystallized into two zones. The "free" and the "unfree" zones were separated by an "iron curtain" (in Churchill's phrase) constituted by the tanks and barbed wire that marked the borders between Soviet and non-Soviet states, and by the ideological gulf between them. As a response to the threat of aggression from the East, the United States, advised by Secretary of State Dean Acheson (1893–1971), guided the creation in 1949 of a multinational military alliance: the North Atlantic Treaty Organization (NATO).

The North Atlantic Treaty provided for mutual aid in case of attack against any of its members (originally twelve), with each nation later providing military units in proportion to its resources. It served not only a military purpose, but also provided a pattern for other cooperative projects. Just as the Marshall Plan had advanced the notion of economic cooperation, NATO nurtured the germs of political unity among the western European states. By 1951, several nations were cooperating in a European Coal and Steel Community, which led to the establishment of the European Economic Community [EEC], or Common Market, in 1957 (now the European Union).

In 1949, the achievement of NATO was to provide a "shield," and the nuclear-armed United States an atomic "sword" that could protect the continent from attack, delivering "massive retaliation"—"instantly, by means and at places of our own choosing," in the words of United States Secretary of State John Foster Dulles (1888–1959)—against any aggressor. This was not war, but it was like war, as both contenders (equally heirs to Western civilization) eyed each other warily.

Cold War Confrontations

In 1949, the year of NATO's creation, the Soviet Union demonstrated its nuclear capacity by exploding an atomic bomb. By 1952, the United States had developed the hydrogen bomb, 750 times more powerful than the one that destroyed Hiroshima. By 1953, the Soviets had one too. Now both superpowers were armed with weapons capable of annihilating the other—its cities, its people, its air and soil.

The citizens of the world took what comfort they could in the principle of "Mutual Assured Destruction," or MAD—an apt anagram, for the world certainly seemed to have become mad. With

Cold War Skies: Hope and Fear

The Berlin Airlift: *Angered by United States, British, and French plans to merge their zones of occupation in Germany, the Soviets attempted in 1948–1949 to blockade West Berlin— buried deep within the Soviet zone of occupation—and thus to cut it off from western Germany. The United States and Britain responded with the highly successful Berlin Airlift, making in all some 200,000 flights to drop off food and supplies to the besieged citizens, like those seen here.*

each superpower having the capability to annihilate the other, the reasoning went, neither would start a conflict; yet the possibility remained that one would. From 1948 into the 1960s, the tension between the two superpowers was at a zenith. It relaxed somewhat from the late 1960s into the 1970s, then mounted again during the 1980s.

In the early 1950s, both superpowers built up their arsenals. This "arms race" continued throughout the decades of the Cold War until the world had accumulated a total of some 50,000 nuclear weapons. Each contender had long-range bombers and radar detection systems to stop them. They had "inter-continental ballistic missiles" (ICBMs, developed in 1957) that could reach the enemy from a remote position of safety. They had intermediate-range ballistic missiles (IRBMs) that could be launched at an enemy from a nearby country. They had submarine-launched ballistic missiles (SLBMs), and anti-ballistic missiles that tried to find and stop incoming missiles (ABMs). Billions of dollars were dedicated each year to the goal of "Mutual Assured Destruction."

Each superpower mustered allies who might enhance its security. Already the chief figure in NATO, the United States promoted the organization of its non-European allies into a series of regional organizations. These included, in Asia, the Central Treaty Organization (CENTO) and Southeast Asia Treaty Organization (SEATO); and in the Americas, the Organization of American States (OAS). In 1955, the Soviets established the Warsaw

Treaty organization (or Warsaw Pact) with its east European allies, to defend the communist states from the West. In addition, it could rely on the support of the other major communist nations of the world— North Korea (from 1945), China (until 1960), Cuba (after 1960), and Vietnam (after 1976).

As the race for arms and allies spiraled upward, so too did technological competition in other strategically related areas—in space and in **cybernetics**. In October 1957, the Soviet Union sent up a first satellite, *Sputnik I*, to orbit the Earth. In January 1958, the United States responded to the challenge, sending *Explorer 1* into orbit. In April 1961, the Soviets again surpassed the Americans, launching a manned spacecraft. In July 1969, the United States upstaged the Soviets with the launching of Apollo 11, the first space mission to culminate in a lunar landing. From a lunar module detached from the spacecraft, astronaut Neil A. Armstrong (b. 1930) and his colleagues emerged and took "a giant step for mankind" on the moon's surface, watched on television by one-quarter of the people on earth. Thereafter, both superpowers maintained programs of space exploration, gathering information through satellites, probes, and space stations.

War stimulated the development of systems for the electronic storage and manipulation of data. The first computers were designed to help decipher intercepted messages during World War II. Such were Britain's pioneering Colossus, which could manipulate 5000 characters per second, or the massive ENIAC (Electronic Numerical Integrator and Computer) developed at the University of Pennsylvania in 1946.

Fallout: *If western Berliners looked to the skies for assistance, many Americans, fearing a Soviet nuclear missile attack, sought the doubtful security of home-made basement fallout shelters during the early Cold War years.*

Thereafter, the United States led the world in the development of computer technology in the new field of cybernetics. The ENIAC weighed fifty tons, had 18,000 vacuum tubes, and could store the equivalent of just twenty words in memory. In the late 1990s, computers based on the silicon chip (about ¼ inch across) could store in memory the equivalent of more than 50 million words. This powerful chip has given its name to "Silicon Valley" (a region of northern California), a site of intense technological innovation. In 1968, the film *2001: A Space Odyssey*, directed by Stanley Kubrick (1928–1999) marked the arrival of the cybernetic space age in popular consciousness. It starred the supercomputer "Hal."

The buildup of arms and strategic technology made nuclear war seem likely. People sought to protect themselves as best they could. In civil defense programs citizens, including schoolchildren, practiced taking shelter, at a signal, from falling bombs—an absurd response to a weapon that could incinerate hundreds of thousands in an instant and kill any survivors with invisible radioactive fallout. Some United States families constructed "fallout shelters" in their basements or back yards, equipped with food and water supplies for long-term hibernation. Mass circulation magazines also offered guidance on planning a well-stocked shelter.

The battle for which these Cold Warriors prepared was a contest not merely between nations, but between two ideas, almost two religions. To many, communism seemed an absolute evil; liberal democracy and capitalism, absolute goods. Thus the military and political bifurcation of the Western world was paralleled by an ideological bifurcation, especially in the United States where an extreme, and unique, anti-communism took hold. In Europe, in contrast, outside of Spain and Portugal (where a lingering fascism silenced communist opposition), communist parties and adherents were accepted and active within a parliamentary setting.

From 1948, a committee of the United States House of Representatives known as the House Un-American Activities Committee (HUAC) investigated people associated in any way with the Communist party. Its improper tactics—pressuring witnesses to implicate others, and presuming guilt by association with suspect persons or organizations— were challenged at the time and subsequently condemned. Among HUAC's targets was Alger Hiss (1904–1996), a highly placed former State Department official, convicted of perjury in 1950. He had perjured himself, it was charged, by denying his guilt in spying for the Soviets; a charge of espionage could not be pursued because the statute of limitations had expired. Although many defended Hiss's innocence, recent revelations from materials previously barred to public examination appear to confirm his guilt.

HUAC's activities prepared the way for the emergence of Wisconsin senator Joseph McCarthy (1908–1957), the leader of a furious crusade against presumed communists. McCarthy chaired Senate committee hearings from 1953 to 1954, in which hysterical and unsubstantiated accusations ruined many careers and lives. Eventually, both his Senate colleagues (who censured him) and the public at large denounced McCarthy's "witchhunt" (so called because of its resemblance to the witch persecutions of earlier centuries).

Although McCarthy was repudiated, anti-communist feeling was widespread. Many states made a "loyalty oath" a condition for the employment of government personnel and teachers. In this tense climate, a couple convicted of betraying atomic secrets to the Soviets were executed in 1953: Ethel Rosenberg (1915–1953) and her husband Julius (1918–1953), considered wholly innocent by numerous supporters. As in the case of Hiss, recently-released evidence appears to confirm the guilt of these Cold War martyrs, although their punishment was surely exceptional: they were the first civilians in United States history executed for espionage.

The Cold War on the Global Stage

The Cold War Outside Europe   The duel between the Soviet Union and the United States was fought in various settings around the world. In Latin America, the United States supported governments that took an anti-communist stance (see Chapter 29), including dictatorial regimes with unsavory reputations. It funded "counter-insurgency" programs to train military units in guerrilla tactics to be used against communist movements and states. Its CIA (Central Intelligence Agency) pursued the destabilization of pro-communist regimes, as in the coup that destroyed the elected government of Chilean socialist leader Salvador Allende Gossens (1908–1973) and in attempts to assassinate the Cuban communist leader Fidel Castro (b. 1927). In Cuba, an abortive invasion by an expatriate force (supported by the United States) and the Soviet installation on the island, in response, of missiles capable of carrying nuclear warheads triggered the most dangerous United States–Soviet confrontation of the era. The Cuban missile crisis of 1961 brought the two superpowers to the edge of nuclear war. A show of firmness by the United States persuaded the Soviets to dismantle their missile bases in exchange for an American promise not to invade Cuba again.

Although the emerging states of Africa were intent on their own internal problems (see Chapter 29), the Cold War contest between the United States and the Soviet Union inevitably intruded. From 1969, the Soviets supported strongman Colonel Muammar al-Qaddafi (b. 1942) in Libya. In 1974, it formed a pact with Somalia, providing weapons and military advice in exchange for naval and air footholds. In 1977, the Somalians cast off the Soviet alliance (and invited United States support) as it invaded neighboring Ethiopia, itself a Soviet client. The following year, Ethiopia defeated Somalia and compensated the Soviets with access to naval facilities. In 1975–1976, the Soviets sent weapons and some 19,000 Cuban troops to Angola to aid one group of insurgents against another supported by the United States. By the late 1970s, hundreds of Soviet advisers and more than 40,000 Cuban troops were deployed in a dozen African countries. The United States countered, enhancing its authority in Africa through programs providing economic advice and assistance. By the 1980s, the Soviets found it increasingly difficult to fund its African agenda. The Western bloc became the preeminent foreign influence on the continent.

In the Middle East, the United States backed Israel, while the Soviets embraced the cause of the dispossessed Palestinians, and supported the Arab states, especially Egypt (until its settlement with Israel in 1979), Syria, and Iraq (see Chapter 29). In east Asia a great communist state was formed in 1949, when Mao Zedong (1893–1976) led his triumphant forces into Beijing (see Chapter 29). Against this massive communist presence, the United States leagued with Japan, now a loyal ally after the period of postwar occupation. Another ally was the government of Taiwan (Formosa), established in 1949 by Chiang Kai-shek (Jiang Jieshi; 1887–1975) and the nationalist army that had taken refuge there from the communist forces that had overrun the mainland. Elsewhere in Asia, two major wars in Korea and Vietnam pitted revolutionary communist states against authoritarian, pro-Western ones backed by

The Origins of the Cold War

World War II had barely ended when, like its afterword, the Cold War began. Winston Churchill's "iron curtain" speech of 1946, from which comes the first excerpt here, marks its beginning. The "Truman Doctrine" announced by the United States president who had authorized the use of the atomic bomb, in the second excerpt, depicts a struggle between a "free" West and an enslaved Soviet zone. The Soviet official Andrei Zhdanov, in the third, views United States activities in Europe and elsewhere as aggressive and imperialistic.

Winston Churchill, wartime British prime minister, notes the signs of Cold War (1946): From Stettin in the Baltic to Trieste in the Adriatic, an iron curtain has descended across the Continent. Behind that line lie all the capitals of ancient states of central and eastern Europe. Warsaw, Berlin, Prague, Vienna, Budapest, Belgrade, Bucharest and Sofia, all these famous cities ... lie in the Soviet sphere and all are subject in one form or another ... to a very high and increasing measure of control from Moscow. The Communist parties ... have been raised to pre-eminence and power far beyond their numbers and are seeking everywhere to obtain totalitarian control. ... This is certainly not the liberated Europe we fought to build up. Nor is it one which contains the essentials of permanent peace.
(From *New York Times*, March 4, 1946)

United States president Truman outlines the "Truman Doctrine" (March 12, 1947): At the present moment in world history nearly every nation must choose between alternative ways of life. The choice is too often not a free one. One way of life is based upon the will of the majority, and is distinguished by free institutions, representative government, free elections,

guaranties of individual liberty, freedom of speech and religion, and freedom from political oppression. The second way of life is based upon the will of a minority forcibly imposed upon the majority. It relies upon terror and oppression, a controlled press and radio, fixed elections, and the suppression of personal freedoms.

I believe that it must be the policy of the United States to support free peoples who are resisting attempted subjugation by armed minorities or by outside pressures. ...
(US Congress, Congressional Record, 80th Congress, 1st session, 1947)

Soviet official Andrei Zhdanov interprets United States "aid" as imperialism (1947): With a view to consolidating America's monopoly position in the markets gained as a result of the disappearance of her two biggest competitors, Germany and Japan [due to their defeat in the war], and the weakening of her capitalist partners, Great Britain and France [a result of the toll of winning the war], the new course of the United States' policy envisages a broad program of military, economic and political measures, designed to establish United States political and economic domination in all countries marked out for American expansion, to reduce these countries to the status of satellites of the United States and to set up regimes within them which would eliminate all obstacles on the part of labor and democratic movement to the exploitation of these countries by American capital. The United States is now endeavoring to extend this new line of policy not only to its enemies in the war and to neutral countries, but in an increasing degree to its wartime allies [also].
(Andrei Zhdanov, address to conference, September 22–23, 1947; ed. Kirsch et al., 1997)

Stalin is Dead, Europe Lives

Repression and revolution: *Upon becoming the Czechoslovak Communist party secretary in January 1968 Alexander Dubček led his country's efforts to implement pro-democratic reforms and abolish censorship. Warsaw Pact tanks brutally repressed this "Prague Spring" later the same year. Here, Czech patriots vent their anger on a Russian tank (right). Anti-communist protest and reform—all across the Eastern Bloc—met virtually no such opposition in 1989, however. In the photograph below, the Berlin Wall is hacked down by ordinary German citizens.*

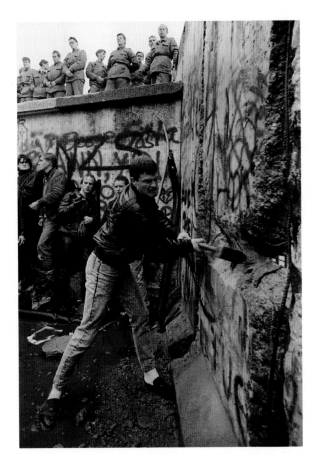

the United States (see Chapter 29). In Korea, a communist state retained power in the north. After United States disengagement, Vietnam was finally unified as a communist state.

India and Indonesia avoided identification with either Cold War position in a policy of "non-alignment," which aimed to advance the interests of the developing nations of what was now called the **Third World** by trading with both superpowers but declining participation in Cold War struggles. Indonesian leader Sukarno (1901–1970), an advocate of non-alignment, hosted an historic meeting of

Asian and African leaders at Bandung in 1955. In the Middle East, Egyptian leader Colonel Gamal Abdel Nasser (1918–1970) also led a bloc of non-aligned Arab nations.

De-Stalinization and Repression in the East While Soviet and United States interests collided abroad, at home the United States presidents from 1952 to 1973 pursued resolutely anti-Communist policies. They faced a shifting Soviet policy as the regime of Joseph Stalin yielded to that of Nikita Khrushchev (1894–1971), and, in due course, Leonid Brezhnev (1906–1982).

After Stalin died in 1953, Khrushchev battled his way to preeminence by 1955. On February 25, 1956, he surprised the Twentieth Congress of the Communist Party with a denunciation of "the crimes of Stalin." Even in Moscow some began to hope that the purges were over, that censorship of the press and the arts would lighten, and that the horror of the gulag would cease.

De-Stalinization in Moscow meant a brief moment of relaxation of Soviet control in eastern Europe, where leaders took the initiative in reaching for greater autonomy. In Poland in 1956, the election as first secretary of Władysław Gomułka (1905–1982), a "national" communist thought to be independent of Moscow, went forward despite a frown from Khrushchev. The same year, a popular revolt in Hungary under the liberalizing prime minister Imre Nagy (1896–1958) threatened the Soviet-backed regime. When Hungary announced its withdrawal from the Warsaw Pact, Soviet forces invaded and crushed the revolution. The victors installed leaders loyal to Moscow, executing Nagy and 2000 supporters. Some 200,000 Hungarians fled to the West.

The suppression of the Hungarian revolt silenced eastern Europe. Five years later, the Soviet Union again made clear its intention to limit dissent. Deep inside the German Democratic Republic, Berlin was the weakest point in the Iron Curtain. Refugees streamed from the eastern Soviet zone to west Berlin—more than 3 million people, including skilled workers and professionals. In August 1961, East Germany closed this gap by constructing the Berlin Wall, a structure of barbed wire and concrete dividing the city. The flow of refugees ceased, while all of Germany could observe in the microcosm of Berlin the great barrier that separated East and West.

In 1968, after Khrushchev had been pushed aside and the bureaucrat Brezhnev had emerged as Soviet leader, the Czech reformer Alexander Dubček (1921–1992) offered a new challenge to Soviet rule. His promise of "socialism with a human face" aroused widespread support, including that of student activists. A Soviet-led Warsaw Pact army of some 175,000 troops invaded (in its only coordinated effort), the largest mobilization of ground forces on the European continent since World War II. It swiftly suppressed the "Prague Spring" that had seemed so hopeful.

Once again, force muzzled protest in eastern Europe. Only after an interlude of more than ten years did there arise another movement of resistance to communist rule, this time in Poland. Here in 1980 the workers in the Lenin Shipyard in Gdánsk (German Danzig), led by electrician and anti-government activist Lech Walesa (b. 1943), formed an independent labor union. It served as the nucleus for a federation of unions, Solidarity, which constituted a democratizing political movement that won 10 million adherents and finally celebrated the collapse of the communist government in 1989.

Talking About Disarmament By the time of Walesa's resistance, relations between the United States and the Soviet Union had experienced a period of easing tension, or *détente*. The notion of "peaceful coexistence" between the superpowers had been aired as early as the 1950s. In 1954 and 1955, the Soviets had called in the United Nations General Assembly for limitations on conventional and nuclear weapons. In 1959, aware of the strain that the arms race put on the Soviet economy, Khrushchev advocated total disarmament within four years. To secure such disarmament, however, the United States insisted on on-site inspections; and these the Soviet Union refused to allow.

After the Cuban showdown of 1961, both superpowers sought to restrict the testing of nuclear weapons and to prevent their proliferation. In 1963, the United States, the Soviet Union, and Britain agreed not to conduct nuclear tests in the atmosphere or in the sea. In 1967, with France, they agreed not to permit the introduction of nuclear weapons into the Earth's orbit or on the moon. The same year, most Latin American states agreed to keep their region nuclear-free.

In 1968, the three signatories of the 1963 partial test ban and fifty-nine other states signed a Nuclear Non-Proliferation Treaty (NNT, extended indefinitely in 1995), by which the participants pledged not to supply non-nuclear powers with nuclear weapons or the technology required to produce them. By 1970, additional countries had signed (the non-nuclear powers further agreeing not to acquire such weapons). It was eventually signed by most of the countries in the world, including France and China (but excluding South Africa, India, Pakistan, and Israel). In addition, Iran, Iraq, Libya, and North Korea, who had signed the treaty, were thought to be in violation. Compliance with NNT was to be enforced by an international inspection team under the aegis of the UN International Atomic Energy Administration. This mechanism meant that the non-nuclear nations would be policed, while the nuclear superpowers remained free to develop more weapons—and they did.

Further agreements were necessary to limit all arms development, as well as to prevent the further proliferation of nuclear arms. In seven sessions between 1969 and 1972 held in Helsinki (Finland) and Vienna (Austria), United States and Soviet officials participated in SALT (Strategic Arms Limitation Talks). SALT I limited each superpower to fixed quantities of certain kinds of missiles (while others remained unregulated) over a five-year term to expire in 1977. President Jimmy Carter (1924–) signed a SALT II treaty with Brezhnev in 1979, while President Ronald Reagan (1911–) participated in Intermediate-Range Nuclear Forces (INF) talks beginning in 1981 and START (Strategic Arms Reduction Talks) from 1982.

Despite promising first steps, détente stalled from 1975 to 1985, as both superpowers stockpiled new missiles and bombs. Warsaw Pact armaments in Europe rose to several times more than those available to NATO, though they were generally less powerful, while the United States developed a neutron bomb, or Enhanced Radiation Weapon, that killed with radiation rather than explosive force. In 1979, Islamist rebels threatened the Soviet client state of Afghanistan, provoking a Soviet invasion. Resuming the policy of military containment, President Reagan stirred his listeners to the task of defeating once and for all the "evil empire," as he provocatively termed the Soviet Union in 1983. Still unreconciled, East faced West with distrust and fear.

Armageddon Deferred: 1985–1991

In 1985, four decades from its inception, the Cold War lingered on. Then the Soviet bloc disintegrated, surprisingly and suddenly, without bombs and without tanks. In 1991, it ceased to be. With its collapse, the fear of imminent nuclear catastrophe abated.

By 1985, it was clear that the Soviet economy did not work. Consumer goods, and especially housing, were in insufficient supply. The ample produce of distant farms was poorly distributed. The eastern

European satellites, the annexed Baltic states, and the Soviet republics of Central Asia all sought greater independence. Experts in the Soviet bureaucracy wanted a freer hand to implement reforms, and even the long-muzzled Russian Orthodox Church raised its voice. The United States was winning the arms race. Change was imminent.

In 1985, Mikhail Gorbachev (1931–), the first Soviet leader to possess university training, launched the twin campaigns of **glasnost** ("openness") and **perestroika** ("restructuring"). By inviting the open discussion of political and economic realities, and then the cautious restructuring of public policy, Gorbachev hoped to save the world's first communist society from disintegration. Instead, open discussion turned to bitter criticism. It appeared that modest repairs could not rescue Soviet society from its path toward self-destruction. The breakdown of the Soviet system was foreshadowed in the disaster that occurred in Chernobyl (Ukraine) in 1986. There a partial meltdown at a badly managed nuclear power plant killed many swiftly, and contaminated vast areas with radioactivity.

A loyal communist but resolute reformer, Gorbachev followed where *glasnost* and *perestroika* led until, by 1989, the communist *imperium* fragmented. The Soviet Union relinquished its military commitments abroad, leaving the communist states of Cuba, North Korea, and Vietnam to fend for themselves (while China had since 1980 been moving in the direction of capitalism). Soviet troops came home from Afghanistan, abandoning the struggle against Islamist rebels who, in 1992, seized power.

Under Gorbachev's leadership, the Soviet Union ceased to monitor eastern Europe, where in a single year revolutions in all six satellite nations rejected pro-Soviet communist governments. In Poland, a newly legalized Solidarity party negotiated reforms that led to free elections and the establishment of a free market economy. In Hungary, a government committee declared independence from Communist party control, rehabilitated the leaders of the 1956 revolution and threw open the border with Austria.

In Czechoslovakia, Václav Havel (1936–) was elected President, while the parliament chose as its speaker the architect of the 1968 Prague Spring, Alexander Dubček. In East Germany, reformers forced the Soviet loyalist leader to resign, flung open the borders, and permitted the jubilant citizens to batter down the Berlin Wall with crowbars, pickaxes, and bare hands—"Stalin is dead; Europe lives!" someone scrawled on the Wall just before its demolition. Massive protests sent the communist strongman

---

WITNESSES

As the Cold War Ages: Two United States Presidents Discuss the Soviet Threat

By the 1970s—after the United States had lived through the trauma and humiliation of the Vietnam War—who still believed in the Cold War? Two United States presidents offered different and opposing views. Jimmy Carter urged the nation to turn away from the "inordinate fear of Communism" and return to basic American principles. Just a few years later, Ronald Reagan insisted that the battle had been, and was still, worth fighting—against an opponent that was an "evil empire."

We are not afraid: Jimmy Carter, University of Notre Dame, Commencement Address (May 22, 1977): Being confident of our own future, we are now free of that inordinate fear of Communism which once led us to embrace any dictator who joined us in our fear. For too many years we have been willing to adopt the flawed principles and tactics of our adversaries, sometimes abandoning our values for theirs. We fought fire with fire, never thinking that fire is better fought with water. This approach failed, with Vietnam the best example of its intellectual and moral poverty. But through failure we have found our way back to our own principles and values, and we have regained our lost confidence.
(From *New York Times*, May 23, 1977)

No compromise with an evil empire: Ronald Reagan (March 14, 1983): [The Soviet leadership has …] openly and publicly declared that the only morality they recognize is that which will further their cause, which is world revolution. … I think the refusal of many influential people to accept this elementary fact of Soviet doctrine illustrates an historical reluctance to see totalitarian powers for what they are. … I urge you to beware the temptation of pride—the temptation blithely to declare yourselves above it all and label both sides equally at fault, to ignore the facts of history and the aggressive impulses of an evil empire. …

I believe that communism is another sad, bizarre chapter in human history whose last pages even now are being written. I believe this because the source of our strength in the quest for human freedom is not material but spiritual, and, because it knows no limitation, it must terrify and ultimately triumph over those who would enslave their fellow man.
(Ronald Reagan, *Weekly Compilation of Presidential Documents*, March 14, 1983)

Map 30.2 Collapse of the Soviet Bloc, 1989–1991: *Soviet leader Mikhail Gorbachev's policy of glasnost permitted the largely peaceable but rapid dissolution of the Soviet Union beginning in 1989. The nations of eastern Europe promptly declared their independence and undertook programs of economic and political liberalization. In the Caucasus region and Central Asia, nationalist tensions accompanied the disaggregation of the former empire. By 1991, the USSR disappeared as a state and Russia reappeared on the map for the first time since the Russian Revolution (1917–1921).*

of Romania, Nicolae Ceauşescu (1918–1989) into flight. But he was caught, convicted hastily of "genocide," and shot on Christmas day, the grisly image of his corpse displayed on television screens worldwide to an astonished public. In 1990, the two halves of the German nation reunited, and in 1991 the Baltic states declared their independence along with the former Soviet republics of Belarus, Moldova, Ukraine, Armenia, Georgia, Azerbaijan, Kazakhstan, Kyrgyzstan, and Uzbekistan.

Meanwhile, Gorbachev was negotiating an end to the arms race. Discussions begun with Reagan in Reykyavik (Iceland) in 1986 culminated in 1991 in a treaty signed by Reagan's successor, George Bush (1924–) and Gorbachev: the START I treaty, which achieved a twenty-five percent reduction in the nuclear forces of the Soviet Union and fifteen percent in those of the United States. In the meantime, both nations agreed to the CFE (Conventional Forces in Europe) treaty of 1990, which required a balance of conventional forces which was to be attained by the elimination of much of the Soviet arsenal of tanks, aircraft, and artillery.

In Moscow, the economy continued to decline. Gorbachev encouraged greater efficiency in state-run enterprises, and permitted some free-market reforms.

But he would not abandon the command economy, which would have caused massive unemployment and monetary stress while, pro-capitalist advisers argued, it opened the road to economic renewal. And he continued to court communist advisers who opposed the turn to a free-market system.

Thus Gorbachev was caught between old-line communists and democratizing reformers. Prominent among the latter was Boris Yeltsin (1931–) elected president of the Russian Republic in 1991. When in August that year a group of military and secret police chiefs imprisoned Gorbachev and attempted to restore the old regime, Yeltsin opposed them, bravely announcing his defiance from atop a tank outside Moscow's parliament building. Together Yeltsin and the reinstated but debilitated Gorbachev watched as the constituent republics of the USSR declared their independence. Together they accepted the dissolution of the Soviet Union, and the end of the seventy-four-year Marxist-Leninist-Stalinist experiment.

With the disintegration of the Soviet Union, anti-communist sentiment swept the region. In parks and city centers, citizens tore down statues of Lenin and Felix Dzerzhinsky, head of the Bolshevik secret police. Worshipers returned to Russian churches, and former communists saw to the baptism of their children. The borders were opened. Jews in large numbers fled the endemic anti-Semitism of their homeland and emigrated to Israel and the United States. Islamic fundamentalism stirred in the newly independent republics of central Asia, supported by Afghan insurgents across the border, and the governments of Iran and Pakistan. Ethnic loyalties surged after the long Soviet interim among the disparate peoples of the Caucasus.

On December 25, 1991, having no nation over which to preside, Gorbachev resigned, Nobel Peace Prize (1990) in hand, to tour the lecture circuit and write his memoirs. Yeltsin managed the remnants of the dissolved Soviet Union, twelve of its fifteen now-independent states joined in the voluntary federation of the Commonwealth of Independent States (CIS). Its technological and military assets, including its stores of nuclear weapons, were reallocated to the member states. The nuclear arsenal of the former Soviet Union had been located in four of the republics—Ukraine, Belarus, Kazakhstan, and Russia itself—all of which cooperated with the commissions established to oversee arms limitation. In 1993, Yeltsin and Bush signed the START II treaty, which obtained the reduction of strategic weapons by twenty-five percent on both sides. In 1994, the United States airlifted from Kazakhstan, with Russia's permission, enough strategic enriched uranium to make twenty-four atomic bombs, lest it fall into the hands of renegade nations or illicit dealers.

In Russia, free-market speculators and corrupt bureaucrats reaped profits from the nation's reorganization. Protests against Yeltsin mounted as the currency collapsed, state employees went unpaid, and living conditions deteriorated. In 1993, communist opponents barricaded themselves in the parliament building, while their supporters fought outside.

The military police quelled the revolt, firing on the parliament complex and killing more than 100 people. Yeltsin survived to face a nationalist opponent later that year, and a reelection race against a communist challenger in 1996. Amid domestic crises, while suppressing a revolt in the Caucasian region of Chechnya, Yeltsin endured, health failing, as the economy—beset by corruption, gangsterism, scarcity, and inflation, fueled by the uncontrolled printing of new rubles—went into freefall in 1998.

The dissolution of the Soviet Union meant the dissolution of the Warsaw Pact. In 1999, the Czech Republic (Czechoslovakia had divided in 1993 into the Czech Republic and Slovakia), Poland, and Hungary were admitted to NATO. Russia itself, the chief member of the "evil empire" NATO had been born to combat, received associate status.

In 1999, as a new century and a new millennium approached, the nations of the world had begun to hope that the deadly logic of "mutual assured destruction" would not end in a final struggle between East and West, communism and capitalism, the perceived good and evil. The world had escaped the test of Armageddon, and the Apocalypse, for the moment, had been postponed.

ALL YOU NEED IS LOVE

It was a different world, though, from the one envisioned at Yalta by the victors of World War II. The generation born in the shadow of the bomb—the product of a postwar demographic bubble, bulging in numbers, unique in self-absorption—transformed the world. This "baby boom" cohort, the first ever threatened from birth by global annihilation, reached adolescence during the 1960s when, especially in the United States, they erupted in protest against the Cold War and its makers. Summoned to fight during the unpopular Vietnam War, they retorted "Hell no! We won't go!"; then impudently commanded their elders to "Make love, not war!" "All you need is love," the

A Changing of the Guard: In many cases the collapse of Communism in Eastern Europe and the Soviet Union made outsiders insiders and vice-versa more or less overnight. Here, Czech dissident and renowned playwright Václav Havel— who under the Communists had spent time as a political prisoner— speaks as the newly elected president of Czechoslovakia in 1989.

The Breakdown of Communism and the End of the Cold War

The "evil empire," as President Reagan had deemed it, crumbled of its own weight, but took more than a generation to fall. The descent began with premier Nikita Khrushchev's denunciation of Stalin in 1956, excerpted in the first passage below. More than 30 years later, premier Mikhail Gorbachev announces the need for "restructuring," as seen in the second passage. In the third, on New Year's Day, 1990, the new Czech president Václav Havel speaks of communism in his country as a system defeated, and in the fourth a historian writing that same year predicts a bleak future for socialism. In the last passage, a man born in the United States, who had defected to the Soviets in 1950, admits in 1998 that he had made a mistake.

Soviet premier Nikita Khrushchev denounces Stalin three years after the dictator's death (1956): The negative characteristics of Stalin ... transformed themselves during the last years into a grave abuse of power by Stalin, which caused untold harm to our Party. ... Stalin acted ... by imposing his concepts and demanding absolute submission to his opinion. Whoever opposed ... was doomed to removal from the leading collective and to subsequent moral and physical annihilation. ...

Stalin originated the concept "enemy of the people." This term ... made possible the usage of the most cruel repression, violating all norms of revolutionary legality against any one who in any way disagreed with Stalin. ... In ... actuality, the only proof of guilt used . . . was the "confession" of the accused himself; and, as subsequent probing proved, "confessions" were acquired through physical pressures [ie, torture] against the accused.
(Nikita Khrushchev, US Congress, 85th Congress, 1st session, 1957)

Soviet premier Mikhail Gorbachev on the background and need for *perestroika* (restructuring) (1987): The Soviet Union is a young state without analogues in history or in the modern world. Over the past seven decades ... our country has traveled a path equal to centuries. ... Huge productive forces, a powerful intellectual potential, a highly advanced culture, a unique community of over one hundred nations and nationalities, and firm social protection for 280 million people on a territory forming one-sixth of the Earth—such are our great and indisputable achievements and Soviet people are justly proud of them. ...

At some stage—this became particularly clear in the latter half of the seventies—something happened that was at first sight inexplicable. The country began to lose momentum. ... Difficulties began to accumulate and

deteriorate, and unresolved problems to multiply. ... We first discovered a slowing economic growth. In the last fifteen years the national income growth rates had declined by more than half. ... As time went on, material resources became harder to get and more expensive. ...
(Mikhail Gorbachev, *Perestroika: New Thinking for Our Country and the World*, 1987)

Czech president Václav Havel speaks of the past and present at a New Year's address shortly after the overthrow of communism in his country (1990): For 40 years you have heard on this day from the mouths of my predecessors ... the same thing: how our country is flourishing, how many more millions of tons of steel we have produced, how we are all happy, how we believe in our Government and what beautiful prospects are opening ahead of us. I assume you have not named me to this office so that I, too, should lie to you. Our country is not flourishing. ... The state, which calls itself a state of workers, is humiliating and exploiting them instead. ... [In education] we rank 72nd in the world. We have spoiled our land, rivers and forests ... and we have, today, the worst environment in the whole of Europe. ... The worst of it is that we live [also] in a spoiled moral environment. We have become morally ill because we are used to saying one thing and thinking another. We have learned not to believe in anything, not to care about each other, to worry only about ourselves. ...
(From *New York Times*, "Havel's Vision—Excerpts from Speech by the Czech President", January 2, 1990)

The economic historian Robert Heilbroner on the future prospects for Socialism (1990): I am not very sanguine about the prospect that socialism will continue as an important form of economic organization now that Communism is finished. ... [T]he collapse of the planned economies has forced us to rethink the meaning of socialism. As a semireligious vision of a transformed humanity, it has been dealt devastating blows in the twentieth century. As a blueprint for a rationally planned society, it is in tatters.
(Robert Heilbroner, "After Communism" in *The New Yorker*, September 10, 1990)

Joel Barr, American-born Soviet spy and defector to the Soviet Union (1950), explains why he renounced communism (1998): I believe that now history will show that the Russian Revolution was a tremendous mistake. ... It was a step backward. The real revolution for mankind that will go down for many, many years was the American Revolution.
(From *The New York Times*, August 16, 1998)

popular rock music group called the Beatles proclaimed in 1967, in a live performance broadcast worldwide via satellite to some 400 million listeners.

During the next decades, the Sixties generation and its imitators sought to bind up the world's wounds. The needs of others for food, security, and dignity engaged a generation that had become traumatized by Cold War brinkmanship. The Earth itself languished, ravaged by the deadly machines that powered the mindless quest for wealth and power. It, too, cried for love, not war.

Rolling Stones

The Power of Protest The Sixties generation, like "rolling stones" (featured in a song by Bob Dylan, b. Robert Zimmerman, 1941) that had shed the moss of the past, set out to transform the politics, society, and culture of the West. They began by protesting against the bomb, joining pacifists of an older generation such as philosopher Bertrand Russell and physicist Albert Einstein (see Chapter 27), inspired by Erich Maria Remarque's *All Quiet on the Western Front* (1929) about the futilities of the first World War, or Joseph Heller's *Catch-22* (1961) about the absurdities of the second.

From protesting against the bomb, young activists joined with the civil rights movement, seeking to end discrimination against those of African descent (see Chapter 29). Student leaders who had experienced the thrill of mass mobilization and commitment to a cause were determined to defy the conformist culture of their parents with a new militancy.

In 1964, students at the Berkeley campus of the University of California protested against college officials who had interfered, as they saw it, with their right to form political organizations. This Berkeley Free Speech movement, in which the university itself came to symbolize all the repressive forces of society, prefigured the movements soon to emerge to protest against United States involvement in the Vietnam War (see Chapter 29).

That war, billed by the "establishment" as a campaign against communism, was identified by the young as one more chapter in the tedious tale of the strong bullying the weak. By 1967, when large numbers of young men were being drafted to serve in Vietnam, anti-war protests flared on college campuses that housed one-third of the cohort born between 1945 and 1949. At teach-ins, faculty mentors explained to a younger generation raised on television and rock 'n' roll where Indochina was, and why Vietnamese independence mattered. At rallies, hundreds or thousands gathered at a chosen moment to witness their opposition to the war. Sometimes protest turned violent, when participants taunted the security forces sent to keep order, or disrupted traffic, or broke windows.

To student observers, the spectacle of a superpower unleashing its vast arsenal against impoverished Vietnamese peasants in order to deny them the independence they ardently sought was both horrible and absurd. A "credibility gap" yawned wide as televised announcements of specious victories, and exaggerated reports of the number of the slaughtered made politicized students enduringly skeptical of government. "Hey, hey, LBJ, how many kids have you killed today?" they taunted the president in one ditty from the angry repertoire of student protest.

The anti-war frenzy climbed from 1968 to 1972. In 1968, following the debacle of the Tet Offensive, the dispirited President Lyndon B. Johnson (1908–1973) announced that he would not seek another term in office. Later that year, the despair of many Americans intensified with the assassination of two respected leaders: Martin Luther King, Jr. (see Chapter 28), champion of civil rights; and presidential candidate Robert F. Kennedy (1925–1968), younger brother of the charismatic President John F. Kennedy (1917–1963), the victim of another assassin in 1963. Violence seemed to be winning.

Meanwhile, the American model of youth protest had impressed Europe. In Paris in May 1968, students protested against government cuts in funding for social spending and universities. Provoked by police intimidation of the Parisian Left Bank community of intellectuals and artists, students set up barricades in the streets and harassed the forces sent to maintain order. Many citizens supported the students; industrial workers struck in sympathy. By early June, however, the deft maneuvering of president Charles de Gaulle (1890–1970) brought the revolt to a quick close. The Parisian example of student resistance to government inspired student revolts in Britain, Italy, and, with greater consequence, in Czechoslovakia.

In the United States in 1969, the new president Richard Nixon (1913–1994) implemented "Vietnamization" (see Chapter 29), a dual strategy of escalated bombing and troop reduction leading to an eventual withdrawal of all United States forces in 1973. In 1970, at Kent State University (in Kent, Ohio), National Guardsmen shot at rock-throwing students—their contemporaries—killing four. It seemed as though the nation had reached a nadir of depravity; it devoured its own children, whose one crime was to hate war. Public opposition to the war surged. The Nixon administration quieted the protest by ending the draft, making the United States military a volunteer force. Those who "would not go" did not have to.

The youth of "the movement"—an affluent and largely white minority—won their battle against their elders. Poor white, black, or brown young men from inner cities and rural towns had no choice but to go. They fought a vicious war without popular support and returned to a nation embarrassed by their presence. They did not figure in the perceptions of the youth who forged the counter-culture of the Sixties founded on the right of each individual to unlimited self-expression. Nor did the "silent majority" of citizens, young and old, who were untouched or dismayed by student radicalism.

A Changing Culture The American youth rebellion, led by a privileged few, had wide-reaching social and cultural impact. During the 1950s, the men and women who had endured the Depression and defeated Nazism pursued their careers, bought houses and cars, populated the suburbs, and settled down to enjoy unprecedented economic prosperity. In the 1960s, their children—or at least a rebellious vanguard—spurned those careers, those neighborhoods, that complacency. In their dress, their tastes, and their sexual mores, they cast aside norms that had so recently triumphed with a stunning wartime victory, and replaced them with provocative new ones.

Costume and style tell the story of cultural transformation. Spurning their fathers' gray-flannel suits and their mothers' crinolined dresses, they dressed in stark black, or in exotic peasant frocks, or, most often, in blue jeans, the dark denim uniform of the working class. Movement pacesetters might favor bizarre hats, or accessories with a military theme (camouflage, knapsacks, boots), or non-precious jewelry crafted by the indigenes of the Americas, Africa, or Asia. They spurned steak and potatoes for international menus (Mexican, Chinese, Indian, Vietnamese), or chose a vegetarian regimen. Where older adults sipped cocktails, the student rebels of the Sixties took up drugs.

The psychoactive drugs adopted by the young induced mental conditions that mocked conventional standards of decorum, rationality, and responsibility. They included marijuana preeminently (a substance that produced mild effects comparable to those produced by moderate alcohol consumption), but also "hard drugs" such as LSD (lysergic acid diethylamide), heroin, and cocaine.

Drug use for vanguard rebels had a range of purposes. Drugs might create states of heightened sensitivity. Drug use allowed the avoidance of social responsibility, inviting the initiate to "turn on and drop out." It helped the young create an alternative culture, a moral universe distinct from that of the adults who wielded power and authority.

The Sixties produced a musical style of its own of superb quality and genuinely revolutionary effect—"rock," or "hard rock," evolved from the "rock 'n' roll" of the previous decade. The drug culture shaped rock music in several ways. Listeners and performers alike often used drugs, while song lyrics often celebrated drug use. The lack of restraint induced by drug use may have spurred the innovations of rock artists. The relations between the drug culture and rock are important; yet rock is much more than the musical

accompaniment to the aimless leisure hours of the drug-consuming young generation.

Rock emerged from the American musical genres of the 1950s. "Pop," or popular music, featured easy melodies sung by polished performers—mainly white—for mainstream record companies. "Country and western" was a nostalgic regional style—also mainly white—that affirmed the customs of the old south and looked back to frontier days. "Rhythm and blues," or "blues," informed by jazz performance, communicated the depths of the African American experience (see Chapter 27). Spurned by most whites, it was the cultivated taste of an affluent few. Then in 1955, the southern white performer Elvis Presley (1935–1977) emerged to sing, gyrate, and sway a new kind of music, a compelling and shocking amalgam of black rhythms and sound.

By the 1960s, the generation formed by the experience of the Cold War had accepted Presley's musical challenge. Rock was not just a blend of musical motifs; it was social criticism. Adopting the simple, direct style of folk music traditions, such singers as Joan Baez (1941–) and Bob Dylan assailed the hypocrisy of mainstream culture. Meanwhile the British group the Beatles, which shot to stardom in 1962, developed Presley's style in a new mix of youth themes and counter-cultural challenges. Young people thronged to rock concerts and danced to the music of the Beatles and their disciples—as did the 450,000 who assembled in 1969, the apogee of rock, at the Woodstock Music Festival in New York State's gracious Catskill Mountains.

Rock's radical challenge to contemporary values was echoed in the cinema of the Sixties. In its visual reconstruction of reality, film had an inherently critical function (see Chapter 27), making it the ideal medium by which to convey the Sixties mood of rebellion. The anti-establishment heroes of *Bonnie and Clyde* (Arthur Penn, director; 1967), shockingly mutilated in the protracted montage of their death at the hands of police pursuers, and of *The Wild Bunch* (Sam Peckinpah, director; 1969), which opens and ends with brutal and senseless massacres, were emblems of the Sixties spirit.

European film had different concerns, elegantly communicated to select audiences while the larger public, fleeing such serious themes, sought primarily to be entertained. In France, Italy, and Sweden filmmakers meditated on the trauma of war and explored the deeper dimensions of the self. The films of Italian directors Federico Fellini (1920–1993) and Michelangelo Antonioni (1912–), notably *La dolce vita* ("The Good Life," 1960) and *L'avventura* ("The Adventure," 1959), evoke brilliantly the contradictions of postwar lives, while the Swedish director Ingmar Bergman (1918–) experimented with visual allegory to probe human emotion, as in *The Seventh Seal* (1956). The French directors of the *nouvelle vague* ("New Wave") that arrived in the 1950s celebrated human self-determination and freedom, as did *Les Quatre cents coups* ("The 400 Blows") by François Truffaut (1932–1984) and À *bout de souffle* ("Breathless") by Jean-Luc Godard (1930–), both released in 1959.

During the 1950s, the themes of human struggle against barbarism and death, a pensive reflection on the first half of a terrible century, found expression in a new generation of novelists, such as the French-Algerian Albert Camus (1913–1960), author of *The Plague* (1947). On the stage, the "theater of the absurd" is exemplified by the work of the Irish playwright Samuel Beckett (1906–1989), whose 1953 *Waiting for Godot* took up the theme of the dramatic exploration of meaning launched in the 1920s by Pirandello and Brecht (see Chapter 27). In the same way, the existentialism of Heidegger and Sartre (see Chapter 27), rooted in the 1930s and 1940s, found a new audience in the postwar era.

From the 1960s, the humanistic themes of the first flush of postwar culture shaded toward disillusionment. Many authors looked to Third World nations for models of political and cultural engagement, while others turned to revising or "deconstructing" established norms of thought and feeling. For instance, the French historian and philosopher Michel Foucault (1926–1984) exposed in his *Madness and Civilization* (1961) the repressive operation of common social practices.

On the other side of the Iron Curtain, where thought was governed by censors, cultural life was quite different (see Chapter 28). There novelists, poets, physicists, and historians covertly circulated in *samizdat* ("self-publication," by hand-delivered manuscript) their vision of a society distorted by communist repression. Boris Pasternak (1890–1960), an author who had experienced the 1917 revolution and its Stalinist aftermath, eluded the censors by publishing in Italy his *Doctor Zhivago* (1957), a novel breathing disillusionment with the whole Bolshevik experiment. *The Gulag Archipelago* by Alexander Solzhenitsyn (1918–), printed in Paris in 1973 after long *samizdat* currency, appalled the world with the story of Soviet forced-labor camps. The powerful voices of such dissidents as the physicist Andrei Sakharov (1921–1989) and historian Roy Medvedev (1925–) also circulated in secret.

Captivated by the popular culture that radiated from the United States, the commodified product of its protest movement, most Europeans were as indifferent to these trends in literature and thought as they were to art cinema. Rock music and movies, radio and television, the casual dress of anti-establishment youth, above all the uniform of blue jeans and T-shirts—these were the prizes consumers sought. Beyond the Iron Curtain, such treasures circulated in the underground, or "black" market.

To protest, drugs, music, film, and costume the youth movement added another ingredient: sexual revolution. In this most intimate sphere of human behavior, the young again defied the values of their elders. Courtship rituals, female chastity, monogamy, even fidelity in non-marital relationships—all these were questioned and rejected. Where the fear of unwanted pregnancy had once deterred women from the path of sexual radicalism, the new pharmacological discovery—the birth control "pill"—made it feasible. The custom of "swinging" gained popularity among some, which invited promiscuous and multiple sexual encounters, including adulterous, homosexual, and interracial relations.

The sexual radicalism of the Sixties accomplished a profound social revolution. In all previous civilizations, male elites had seen to the sexual regulation of their families. Now a vanguard group, harvesting the product of the socialist and feminist movements of the past two centuries, rejected all sexual regulation, with enduring effects on culture and society. "Your sons and your daughters are beyond your command ...," Dylan hissed at the elders, "for the times they are a-changin'."

Women of Worth

The sexual revolution born of the Sixties movement in the United States allowed women to reject conventional restraints. It also encouraged the forging of a new feminism that sought freedoms for women of all social classes and of all nations, races, and religions. Now all women everywhere were deemed to be, in the biblical phrase, "women of worth."

The Demand for Equality The new feminism of the 1960s was the culmination of earlier feminist ideals, restated vigorously in two important books.

WITNESSES

Culture and Politics in the 1960s

Bob Dylan, The Times They are a-Changin'
(1964):
Come mothers and fathers
Throughout the land
And don't criticize
What you can't understand
Your sons and your daughters
Are beyond your command
Your old road
Is rapidly agin'
Please get out of the new one
If you can't lend your hand
For the times they are a-changin'.
(Bob Dylan, *Lyrics, 1962–1985*, 1985)

Years of Protest

Flower power: *Fears of Communist expansion in Southeast Asia led the United States into a demoralizing and increasingly unpopular war in Vietnam, which aroused a whole generation to protest. In this photograph anti-war demonstrators in Washington, D.C. oppose guns with flowers.*

In 1949, the French writer Simone de Beauvoir's (1908–1986) brilliant manifesto, *The Second Sex*, made a post-war generation of women aware of the social denigration of women. In 1963, the American Betty Friedan's (1921–) *The Feminine Mystique* identified the cultural forces that denied women power and responsibility. The mirage of "femininity" controlled women's lives, Friedan argued. It confined their thoughts to their housecleaning and their hair-dos, and their days to shopping and self-doubt. In 1966, Friedan co-founded the National Organization of Women (NOW), the foremost institutional embodiment of the new feminism.

Women activists called for female autonomy in virtually every aspect of contemporary life. In the political sphere, women leaders pushed beyond the demand for suffrage, the key issue of earlier feminism (see Chapters 25, 27), to seek greater access to power. In many nations, women candidates were elected to political office, some reaching the highest political positions, as did Golda Meir (1898–1978) in Israel, Indira Gandhi (1917–1984) in India, and Margaret Thatcher (1925–) in Britain (1979–1990). Recently, women have gained the highest political positions in Iceland, Ireland, Norway, Portugal, and Poland in Europe; and in Argentina, Bangladesh, Dominica, Nicaragua, Pakistan, Sri Lanka, and Turkey else-where. In Europe, they have claimed twenty-five per-cent of the seats in the European Parliament; the percentage of women worldwide serving as national parliamentarians, in contrast, has changed little since 1975, remaining well under ten percent.

In the workplace as in politics, women's demands heightened. Although women made up an increas-ing proportion of the workforce in the postwar decades—they are now about one-half of all workers in the United States, about one-third in western Europe—they received lower wages than male work-ers. The demand for "equal pay for equal work" has brought about in some nations the narrowing, but not the elimination, of the "wage gap."

Expanded training opportunities gained women entrance to previously closed trades and professions. They now work in construction and truck-ing, as police and postal officials, in the armed forces, and as attorneys and judges, medical doctors and uni-versity professors. Professionalization of those careers that women tradi-tionally had entered, such as teach-ing and nursing, has enhanced their status and salaries. Increasingly, women have reached executive

Pro-choice: *The Sixties gave rise to the sexual revolution, encouraging a new wave of feminist activism in support of abortion rights. Here, a star-spangled "Wonder Woman" leads an angry pro-choice rally in New Zealand, 1977, demanding a woman's right to bear only "wanted" children.*

levels of modern corporations where (although an invisible "glass ceiling" retards their entry to the highest positions or levels of compensation) they enjoy great authority and high salaries.

Western women increasingly insist on the right to work unimpeded by verbal or physical intimidation from male co-workers seeking sexual relations or expressing hostility to females. Activists have engaged employers and government in the crusade against "sexual harassment."

Risks to women outside of the workplace have also concerned female activists, where women are victims of rape, including marital rape, and domestic violence—the latter the leading cause, after war, of harm and death to women worldwide. In many countries, feminists have brought these violations into public consciousness, and have had them legally defined as crimes. Liberalized divorce laws in most Western nations enable women to escape abusive marriages.

The Politics of Reproduction Women's rights must include, feminists insist, the liberty to make choices about their bodies. Thus the drive undertaken by early-century feminists (see Chapter 27) to make contraception available to all women has culminated in the "pro-choice" movement of the century's last decades, whose activists have sought to make contraception safe, cheap, and available.

These goals put feminists at odds with the guardians of traditional society, mostly male. That conflict became especially sharp over the issue of abortion. In many countries, clinical abortion was and has remained illegal; in others, the right of abortion has broad acceptance. The development since 1988 of an effective oral abortifacient (RU 486) promises a greater ease of access to abortion than heretofore. In the United States, a struggle between advocates for the right to abort (the "pro-choice" faction) and those opposed (the "pro-life" faction) has been a prominent feature of contemporary life.

Paradoxically, the demands of contemporary feminism for women's complete liberation contradicts the **maternalist** goals advocated by earlier feminist leaders (see Chapter 27). These contended that women's most powerful role was in the family. Recent emphasis on women's reproductive rights, however, points away from maternalism, insisting that women be free to have few or no children; and to make those choices independently of their fathers, or the men whose offspring they carry. Advocates of traditional family generally oppose both these assumptions, as well as abortion and other mechanisms—easy divorce, certain tax measures—they perceive as undermining the stability of the family.

The feminist position dictates that unmarried women should be as free as married women to choose to bear children, and would wholly eliminate the distinction between "legitimate" and "illegitimate" birth. The stigma associated with illegitimacy has largely faded in the developed nations, along with the economic sanctions and legal disabilities that "bastard" children so born once suffered. Furthermore, some feminist theorists argue that women who give birth outside of a marital family are entitled to government support for the raising of their children. Why, they ask, should some women be deprived of the right to raise future citizens merely because of their economic or social position, when modern democratic societies no longer bar access to educational or employment opportunities on those grounds?

The birthing of children, some feminists have argued, has been excessively medicalized. Whereas women in earlier societies (or outside of the West) often gave birth with the assistance of a female midwife, modernization has placed the process of birth in the hospital, frequently under the care of a male physician. Feminism has encouraged a revival of midwifery, and argued for a woman's right to safe and successful childbirth outside of the hospital environment. Where modern medicine may intervene too much with childbirth, however, it has not done enough for other aspects of women's health. Resources have been directed disproportionately to diseases suffered by men (prostate cancer), or to the male experience of diseases women also suffer (heart disease and stroke), and too little to diseases of women (breast cancer, osteoporosis).

Although feminists agree on most of these issues, they tend to disagree on two others: prostitution and pornography. Some feminists argue that prostitution degrades women. Others respond that women must be free to seek income from the use of their bodies, just as athletes or performers are. Similarly, some feminists see pornography as essentially antifemale, an extension of male acts of violence to representations of masculine power. Others see pornography as a form of expression that must be as free as all other forms of expression, and fear that imposing limits on pornography would open the way to reimposing restrictions on sexual expression so painfully and recently lifted.

Women Outside the West The feminist activists of the Western world have gained widespread support for women's freedoms. These are not equally recognized in other parts of the world. In communist and formerly communist states—the Soviet Union and its satellites, China, North Korea, Vietnam, and Cuba—women, in theory, possessed the same political and economic rights as men, and full freedom of reproductive choice. Yet women faced the dangers of sexual harassment, rape, and domestic abuse in communist societies as they did in the West. Despite official formulations, they have had a disproportionate responsibility for household tasks—housework, childrearing, care of the elderly. Although abortion has

Women and the Post-War World: Manifestos, Achievements, Promises

Although the agenda for women was clear from the early years of the twentieth century, and international in scope, many goals—the vote, citizen rights, and reproductive freedoms—did not begin to be realized, even in the advanced countries of the West, until after World War II. Here, a New York group of women declare their demands for fundamental freedom in the Redstockings Manifesto of 1969. Meanwhile, the communist Chinese government act to protect women's interests in marriage in 1949, and the Islamic republic of Iran reassert in 1979, within the framework of a traditional theocracy, that culture's high valuation of women as mothers.

The Redstockings Manifesto by a New York organization of feminists (1969): Women are an oppressed class. Our oppression is total, affecting every facet of our lives. We are exploited as sex objects, breeders, domestic servants, and cheap labor ... whose only purpose is to enhance men's lives. ... Our prescribed behavior is enforced by the threat of physical violence. Because we have lived so intimately with our oppressors, in isolation from each other, we have been kept from seeing our personal suffering as a political condition. ... In reality, every such relationship is a *class* relationship, and the conflicts between individual men and women are political conflicts that can only be solved collectively.
(Circulated in typescript, July 7, 1969)

A new order for Chinese women: China's marriage law, passed by the Communists (1949): Article 1. The arbitrary and compulsory feudal marriage system, which is based on the superiority of man over woman and which ignores the children's interests, shall be abolished. The new democratic marriage system, which is based on free choice of partners, on monogamy, on equal rights for both sexes, and on protection of the lawful interests of women and children, shall be put into effect. ...
Article 7. Husband and wife are companions living together and shall enjoy equal status in the home.
(*The Marriage Law of the People's Republic of China*, 1959)

Women and the family in Revolutionary Iran: from the Constitution of the Islamic Republic of Iran (1979): The family unit is the foundation of society and the main institution for the growth and advancement of mankind. ... It is the principal duty of the Islamic government to regard women as the unifying factor of the family unit and its position. They are a factor in bringing the family out of the service of propagating consumerism and exploitation and renewing the vital and valuable duty of motherhood in raising educated human beings. ... As a result motherhood is accepted as a most profound responsibility in the Muslim viewpoint and will, therefore, be accorded the highest value and generosity.
(T. Y. Ismael, *Iraq and Iran: Roots of Conflict*, 1982)

been freely available, gynecological and contraceptive services have, in fact, been restricted.

In China, women's reproductive freedom has recently been constrained by state policy decreeing that no couple should have more than one child. Abortion has been imposed even when not desired, in as late as the ninth month of pregnancy. Yet these restrictions should be seen in the light of the great progress towards women's equality that has been made under communism. In traditional China, patriarchal authority was absolute; women's bodies bore its impress, as the traditional practice of the binding of feet from infancy produced the effect of disproportionately tiny feet in adult women.

Women, ironically, have suffered from the collapse of communism in the Soviet Union and eastern Europe, even as civil liberties have been restored. Communist governments had (in theory) guaranteed access to childcare, maternity benefits, and abortion, and had instituted quotas assuring women's representation in national assemblies. With their fall, women resumed burdens they thought they had lost, and have borne disproportionately the hardships of

economic and cultural dislocation. In Poland, for example, the reinvigorated Roman Catholic Church has reaffirmed its uncompromising stand against birth control and abortion. In the central Asian republics of the former Soviet Union, where Islamic customs are being restored, many women are obliged to return to narrowly domestic roles.

Women of Islamic societies outside the communist realm also face special obstacles to their liberation. Islam is at once a faith and a way of life, and its law is both religious and civil (see Chapter 8). Its precepts with regard to women have not been secularized, as have been those of Western society. Women are understood to be under the protection of male kin at all times. In the more conservative Islamic societies, they are expected to be veiled in public, and may be barred from public life or even from such occupations as driving a car or going to university.

Non-Islamic Asian women also suffer disadvantages unknown in the West. In Japan, although some women obtain entry to elite universities and positions in a bustling corporate culture, traditional family norms keep many at home or, if in the workplace, in subordinate positions. In India, also, enduring social customs continue to disadvantage many women. Although the custom of *suttee*—where a widow went alive to the funeral pyre of her husband—has virtually disappeared, daughters are still valued less than their brothers in many Indian families. Often they are fed less, sold into prostitution (there are some 300,000 child prostitutes, mostly girls), or married to strangers for the advantage of other family members (and even murdered by their husbands if dowry demands are not met). The great poverty of peasant villagers exacerbates these problems. Women of the elite social strata, in contrast, are more likely to obtain secondary and university education, and to hold important public positions.

In Latin America, poverty also continues to disadvantage women, although maternal mortality rates are lower than in Africa, the Middle East, and southern Asia. A strong Catholic tradition has meant the limited availability of abortion, although contraception is widely used.

Perhaps the condition of women is nowhere more dismal than in Africa, where older social customs, including polygamy and slavery, burden many, and where exceptional poverty afflicts nearly all. Migrant labor patterns take men out of villages, and leave women behind to manage agricultural work and raise their children alone. Epidemic disease, including measles, tuberculosis, and AIDS (acquired immune deficiency syndrome; see below), has imposed upon women additional burdens of nursing and the trauma of child death. Most seriously, the rate of the heterosexual transmission of AIDS is higher in Africa than anywhere else in the world, resulting in the disproportionate infection of women. Of 3.8 million women worldwide who are infected with AIDS, 3.36 million, or eighty-eight percent, live in sub-Saharan Africa. Moreover, more women than men are carrying the HIV virus that promises the future development of the disease, implying that women will soon exceed men among the African victims of AIDS.

In a band of states cutting across Africa from Guinea in the west to Egypt, Ethiopia, and Somalia in the east, many women undergo at puberty the controversial surgical procedure of clitorectomy—also referred to as "female circumcision" or "genital mutilation". (In clitorectomy, the clitoris and all or part of the labia minora are excised; in the rarer practice of infibulation, part of the labia majora is excised as well, and most of the vaginal opening is stitched closed.) This operation is often performed by midwives without medical training and without anesthesia, in the absence of sterilized implements or a sanitary environment. It is estimated that 130 million women in the world today have undergone some form of genital cutting.

The consequence of clitorectomy performed by traditional methods is often infection and sometimes even death. In addition, the surgery results in the diminution of sensation in sexual contacts. That desensitization is at once the reason for clitorectomy, intended to promote the chastity of young brides; but also one reason for the opposition to it that has mounted in recent years. For feminists, clitorectomy is an assault on women's freedom and dignity. For members of those societies where the practice is common, it is a venerable tradition. The women concerned are themselves divided. Some have left their homelands in order to save themselves or their daughters from the experience. Others are proud to observe the customs of their people.

In a world still sharply divided into wealthier and poorer regions, women have different agendas. In the Western world (including Australia, New Zealand, and Japan), women are seeking equity in the workplace and in politics, reproductive rights, support in childcare and household responsibilities, and suitable medical attention. Elsewhere, women of the elites may share some of the concerns of their counterparts in the Western world. But most are poor, and suffer the greater likelihood that they will be undernourished, poorly educated, and exposed to epidemic disease; or sold into prostitution or slavery, or compelled to enter into unwanted or degrading marital relationships.

Perhaps the single greatest indicator of poor women's disadvantage in the developing world is their disappearance—for in several of these regions, women are missing in large numbers. Under normal circumstances, 95 girls are born for every 100 boys, and a similar sex ratio should be expected in the adult population. But there are ten percent fewer women than there should be in India, Burma, Pakistan in Asia; in Saudi Arabia, Kuwait, the United Arab Emirates, and Oman in the Middle East; and Libya in North Africa. In addition, several more nations have deficits of five percent, including China (where the deficit amounts to a monumental 20 million women), and several more with deficits up to that level. Almost all of the nations with such deficits are in the developing world (while many of the Western nations, in contrast, have a surplus of women). These aberrations result in a cumulative deficit of some 120 million women worldwide.

This disparity between the quantity of female and male life is an index of discrimination against women. More than men, women are denied nutrition, medical care, shelter, education, and other benefits. They are forced into servitude and prostitution, conditions often resulting in premature death. They are killed in childhood, or aborted prenatally, more often than male siblings. Whereas in affluent nations, abortion is a woman's choice, in poorer nations it is more often used to deny female life.

Abortion in general is more widely used in the emerging nations than in the wealthy nations of the world. Although twenty percent of pregnancies worldwide end in abortion, most abortions are performed outside of western Europe and North America. Ironically, the procedure is generally legal and medical facilities are advanced in those regions where abortions are less frequently performed. In regions with the highest rates of abortion, the procedure is more often illegal and improperly performed. Women in developing nations are 300 times more likely than their wealthier peers of the West and the North to experience complications (including death) as a consequence of abortion.

In the world's poorer regions, additionally, women are more likely to be pressed into prostitution and less likely to be educated. Especially in Asia, burdensome daughters are sold into sex slavery, and women without male protection seek income from prostitution. "Sex tourism," a custom where prosperous men from North America, western Europe, Saudi Arabia, and Australia seek recreational sex in certain cooperating markets in India, Indochina, Indonesia, and Brazil, has heightened the demand for child prostitutes.

Furthermore, women in Africa, the Middle East, and Asia show higher rates of illiteracy than men. Among the worst cases are Algeria and Zambia, where, respectively, eighty percent and seventy-four percent of adult women are illiterate, compared to thirty-eight and twenty-nine percent of adult men. These figures may be contrasted with those for most European nations and Japan, where fewer than one percent of women (but two percent in the United States) have failed to achieve literacy.

The disabilities suffered by those who are both female and poor have become the particular concerns of an international movement to uplift the condition of women around the globe. United Nations world conferences on women, attended by increasing numbers of women, met in Mexico in 1975, in Copenhagen in 1980, in Nairobi in 1985, and in Beijing in 1995. The last attracted an attendance of 30,000 women, and official delegates from 185 governments. Most nations of the world have signed the UN Convention on the Elimination of all Forms of Discrimination against Women. The recognition of the worth of women is now an international project.

Love Your Mother

Out on the American road in the 1980s, bumper stickers displayed a picture of the Earth, and beneath it the injunction: "Love your Mother." As family ties weakened and religious fervor waned, a devotion to the planet and the welfare of its peoples deepened among the activist young of the Western world.

Population, Disease, and Famine In an arithmetic to which the world was first alerted by Thomas Malthus (see Chapter 25), the welfare of human communities depends on the relation between two quantities: the size of the population and the resources that are

Map 30.3 (above and right) Women of the World, 1990s: *By the 1990s, the condition of women in the developed world (the West plus Japan) had improved greatly, while women in the rest of the world still suffered grave hardships. Some of the indices of women's welfare are indicated here: violence, literacy, and the female deficit. The female deficit is that number indicating "missing women": the shortfall in the number of women who should be alive given the number of men. Their absence can be explained by several factors, including differential levels of nutrition and selective feticide or infanticide.*

available in order to sustain life. Where population exceeds available resources, disaster results.

Statisticians note with alarm recent population trends. More than 5.8 billion people lived on the earth in 1996; more than twice the 1950 figure of 2.5 billion; more than three times the 1900 figure of 1.6 billion; more than thirty times the 170 million in the heyday of the Roman Empire. Not only has population soared since 1750, but the rate of increase is itself increasing. Some regions are growing at annual rates of two or three percent, portending the doubling of the population, respectively, in thirty-four or twenty-three years. Some experts fear a "population bomb," population magnitudes that will threaten the welfare of all.

Population pressures vary regionally. In the developed world, population has slowed since a peak rate of growth after 1750. Birth rates declined, witnessing the practices of contraception and family planning. At present, these nations are experiencing a growth rate under one percent. Some are actually decreasing in population, as new childbirths fail to match deaths.

In the developing world (most of Asia, Africa, and Latin America), population growth rates are much higher. These regions contain eighty percent of world population, and account for ninety percent of all births. Here modernization has permitted populations to increase far beyond traditional levels; but it has not progressed sufficiently to feed and nurture the resulting multitudes.

The most populous regions of the world experience deficits in the quality of life visible in lowered life expectancy, harsh conditions, and poor medical care. Whereas life expectancy is greater than seventy-five years in the world's wealthier nations, it sinks to less than sixty-five in India, Indonesia, Egypt, and Peru, among others; to less than fifty-five in most of Africa; to less than forty-five in a few desperate states, including Afghanistan and Uganda. High rates of child mortality correlate to decreased longevity. Among the nations with lowest life expectancy figures, as many as one in five of children under five years old die. That twenty percent rate of child

Zairian Tutsi refugees, 1996

Indian mother and daughter, 1993

Around the world, women's experience of poverty and war is sharpened because of their role as childbearers. At right, an Indian woman, desperate to conceive a male child, sits in 1993 with her unwanted two-year old daughter, whom she admits having "wanted to kill". She has, she says, already murdered a previous daughter. Genocidal war in Rwanda and Burundi between its Hutu and Tutsi peoples spilled over the border into Zaire and made refugees of thousands, including this Tutsi mother and child in the foreground of the photograph above. In Yugoslavia, a bewildering mix of ethnic, religious, and historical animosities engendered violent campaigns of "ethnic cleansing" and, in response, the NATO bombing of Serbia, perceived as the chief aggressor. In the photograph below an Albanian mother weeps for her son, killed in Kosovo in October 1998, by an explosive left by Serbian military police.

Albanian mother in mourning, 1998

To continue your investigation of this topic, please go to www.prenhall.com/king for the related **WINDOWS** on the **WEB** activity

mortality contrasts to a rate of one percent or less in the developed nations of the world. In 1993 in Great Britain and Germany, seven infants died per 1000 births; in Afghanistan, 163.

Harsh conditions—poverty, war, hopelessness—impel people to migrate to places of greater opportunity. Migrants from India and China, for example, have moved to the Middle East and South Africa; to Canada, the United States, and the Caribbean; to Great Britain, Australia, and other Asian nations. In 1960, the United States housed 200,000 Asian immigrants; by 1998, 10 million. Sometimes whole communities of a particular national or ethnic group will migrate, in what is called a **diaspora**, or "scattering." The immigrants' new skills, as well as native customs and languages, serve to enrich the host nations where they settle, even as they often become the targets of ethnic or racial discrimination.

Overpopulation not only strains resources, but also encourages disease. The unprecedented advance of medical science in the twentieth century made it possible to prevent most childhood diseases; to cure many known bacterial infections; to repair broken limbs; to control bleeding; and to relieve pain to an extraordinary degree. By World War II, medical researchers had learned to cure (with antibiotics) or prevent (by immunization, sanitation, and pest control) most fatal epidemic diseases: among them, malaria, smallpox (now eradicated), syphilis, tuberculosis, typhoid, and yellow fever. The vaccination of children lowered the death toll caused by diphtheria, pertussis (whooping cough), and, more recently, measles. The control of influenza, which took by different estimates, 15 or 40 or more million lives in a pandemic at the end of World War I (see Chapter 26), is improving, but is frustrated by the mutability of the viral agent. More recently, progress has been made in the treatment of cancer; with early detection, many malignancies no longer kill.

Medical success in confronting the diseases of the past has not yet been equaled in the case of the deadliest plague of recent times: AIDS, developed by those infected with HIV (or human immunodeficiency virus). The disease originated in Africa, perhaps as a mutation of a dormant, endemic disease of a species of chimpanzee, and spread suddenly to the Americas around 1980. Since then, it has reached Asia, Europe, Australia, and New Zealand. By 1996, more than 6 million people had died of AIDS worldwide, 1.5 million in that one year alone. More than 8 million have developed AIDS to date, and more than 29 million have been infected with HIV—figures predictive of millions more deaths in years to come.

An HIV-infected person may not develop the disease itself for several years. In the wealthier nations, drug combinations are used to delay the disease's progress or, in some cases, prevent death. That therapy is not available to most people in the developing world, where both HIV infection and the number of AIDS cases are soaring. About sixty-three percent of those with HIV or AIDS worldwide live in Africa, already stressed by overpopulation and low levels of technical development. In the tiny nations of Rwanda and Burundi, twenty percent of pregnant women (who transmit the disease to their offspring in twenty-five to thirty-five percent of cases) test positive for the disease.

Unlucky Africa suffers other epidemics at the same time—principally measles and tuberculosis, resurgent wherever poverty and insanitary conditions give it leave, and newly virulent due to the development of drug-resistant strains of the bacillus.

Physicians cannot solve malnutrition, the principal cause of human misery, which still afflicts more than one in ten people worldwide. The conquest of malnutrition in the Western world and Japan is virtually complete. Not only is food produced in sufficient quantity in these regions, but it is generally made available even to the poorest citizens through government programs or private charity. Individuals still suffer hunger amid affluence; but their cases are unusual and often involve collateral problems such as mental illness and extreme isolation.

The poorer regions of the world are by definition those that fail to nourish their inhabitants. In 1992, daily caloric intake averaged 1883 in Peru; 1707 in Haiti; 1505 in Somalia (in contrast to 3671 in the United States; 3504 in Italy; and a magnificent 3778 in Ireland, previously devastated by the Great Famine of 1845). Low productivity remains the principal cause of hunger. In these poorer regions, a natural disaster—drought, flood, extreme cold—brings famine. It is in the regions where the margin of survival is narrowest that distribution mechanisms are poorest. Central governments or international agencies may be unable to deliver needed food and fuel supplies.

HOW MANY?

World Population Figures, 10,000 B.C.E.–2025 C.E.

Year	Population
10,000 B.C.E.	4 million
1 C.E.	170 million
1900	1,625 million
1950	2,500 million
1996	5,800 million
2025 (projected)	8,250 million

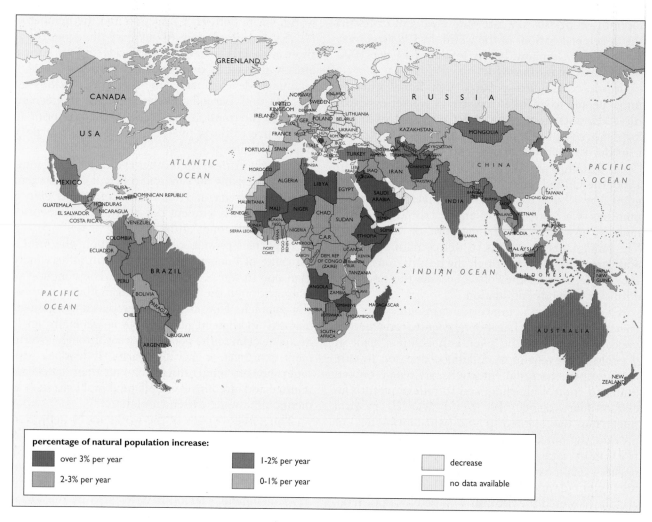

percentage of natural population increase:

over 3% per year   1-2% per year   decrease

2-3% per year   0-1% per year   no data available

Map 30.4 Rates of Population Growth, 1993: *Reaching a total of 5.5 billion in 1993, the world's population is unevenly distributed, as are rates of growth. In the lead for share of world population are China, with 21.4 percent, and India, with 16.3 percent. These nations are also growing at rapid rates of respectively one and two percent annually (with the effect that their populations will double in thirty-four and sixty-seven years respectively). They are not, however, among the most rapidly growing nations, with rates of growth at an annual three percent. Those nations are concentrated in Africa and the Middle East, and include Nigeria, Sudan, Iran, and Pakistan. In contrast, the nations of the Western world, and Japan, are either increasing at rates lower than one percent annually or actually decreasing.*
Source: M. Kidron and R. Segal, The State of the World Atlas, rev. 5th ed., (London: Penguin Reference, 1995) pp. 28–29.

Another kind of famine is caused not by natural disaster but by human decision-makers. Artificial famine seems all the more cruel because it is not merely preventable, but entirely willful. Warfare among private armies under fourteen different local strongmen led to mass hunger in Somalia, where over 300,000 starved in 1991–1992 as gunmen raided food shipments supplied by international agencies. In Sudan, the policies of strongman ruler Lt. Gen. Omar Ahmed al-Bashir who seized power in a 1989 coup have triggered a great famine, while his violations of human rights have led to the suspension of international aid efforts. These are small tragedies, however, next to those caused by collectivization of agriculture in the Soviet Union in the 1920s and in China in the 1950s, which each caused the deaths by starvation of some 10 million citizens (see Chapters 28, 29).

The Threat of Ecological Disaster Environmentalists are among the experts involved in the struggle against starvation, disease, and overpopulation. Environmentalism is a relatively new phenomenon, triggered by the brooding shadow of the atomic bomb. The possibility of the annihilation of humankind and the ruination of the planet moved a generation to arouse concern for the preservation of the earth which sustains us all.

In 1962, the publication *Silent Spring* by Rachel Carson (1907–1964) introduced a shocked audience to ecology, the beautiful (when undisturbed) interrelationships of plants, animals, and humans and to their natural environment. That wonderful equilibrium was jeopardized, Carson argued, by the use of toxic substances in materials used to promote agricultural productivity—chemicals that killed pests, fungi, and weeds. These agents entered and were retained by the soil, the water, and the air. They entered the tissues of plants and animals and, when ingested by humans, into our own bodies, where they caused disease. The protection of the environment became a pressing issue, especially for the young—whose perception was that their elders had irresponsibly plundered the natural world.

The environmentalist movement boomed as public education about endangered biological species and the benefits of recycling reshaped public consciousness. The first Earth Day celebration in 1970 (now celebrated annually in some 140 nations on April 22)

HOW MANY?

AIDS Cases per 100,000 Population

50 or more cases		
Africa:	**Congo**	85
	Malawi	
	Namibia	103
	Zimbabwe	
Americas:	**Bahamas**	104

25 to 49 cases		
Africa:	Burkina Faso	
	Burundi	
	Cote d'Ivoire	
	Rwanda	
Americas:	Barbados	
	Bermuda	

15 to 24 cases		
Africa:	Ghana	
	Tanzania	
	Togo	
	Uganda	
Americas:	US	

Figures are per 100,000 population (1992, or latest available data). Nations with the three highest rates are indicated by bold text, with the absolute number of cases given.
Source: M. Kidron and R. Segal, The State of the World Atlas, rev. 5th ed., (London: Penguin Reference, 1995), p. 54.

WITNESSES

Love Your Mother: The Environmentalist Movement

The shocks of war in the twentieth century, accompanied by genocide and weapons of mass destruction, encouraged a renewed appreciation of the goods of the earth. Here, a United States official reflects on the origins of the environmentalist movement in 1969 and, in 1997, a journalist announces that global warming, with its threat of catastrophic climate shifts, has arrived.

Under Secretary of the Interior John C. Whitaker on the emergence of the modern environmental movement (1969): As Americans traveled in their automobiles, ... they saw garish road signs, fields of junked automobiles, choked and dying streams, overgrazed and eroded hills and valleys, and roadsides lined with endless miles of beer cans, pop bottles, and the tin foil from candy wrappers and cigarette packages. They could no longer move a few hundred miles West: the frontiers were gone.
(From B. Kline, *First Along the River: A Brief History of the US Environmental Movement*, 1997)

Journalist Ross Gelbspan announces that global warming is here (1997): The recent weather record has been marked by more intense rainfalls and severe snowstorms; stronger hurricanes; unseasonal and prolonged droughts, resulting in crop failures and devastating forest fires from Texas to Mongolia; killer heat waves from India to Chicago; and record flooding from Yemen to Nepal. ... Environmentalists have been warning us about global warming for years. What is news is that global warming is no longer merely a future possibility. The heat is on. Now. Its early impacts, in the form of more extreme and unstable climate, are being felt even as I write.
(Ross Gelbspan, *The Heat is On: The High Stakes Battle over Earth's Threatened Climate*, 1997)

defined the areas of concern. Earth Day was followed by the United Nations Conference on the Human Environment, held in Stockholm (Sweden) in 1972, which resulted in the establishment of the United Nations Environment Program. In 1983, the General Assembly further established the World Commission on Environment and Development. In 1992, the United Nations Conference on Environment and Development (the "Earth Summit") met in Rio de Janeiro, attended by delegates from more than 178 countries. From the 1970s, "Green" parties joined the spectrum of political groups that contended for seats in European parliaments. The movement to protect the environment, in a brief generation, had leapt to the forefront of the international agenda.

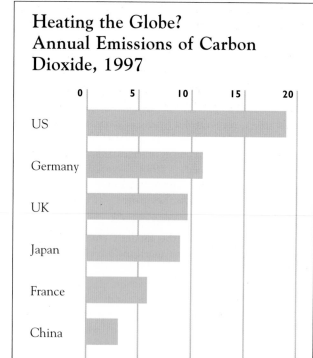

Heating the Globe?
Annual Emissions of Carbon Dioxide, 1997

Figures represent Tons per Head

The United States' current world lead in the production of carbon dioxide is projected to slim substantially in the near future as developing economies in highly populous states such as India and China begin to produce increased levels of this and other "greenhouse gases." The result will likely be much higher global emissions.
Source: Understanding Global Issues, ed. R. Buckley (Cheltenham, UK: Understanding Global Issues Limited, 1997), issue 11, p. 13.

Among the many issues environmentalists raised were those of pollution, the depletion of the stratospheric ozone layer, global warming, and the endangerment of living species and habitats. Pollution accompanies industrialization. But Europe and the West generally, pioneers of industrialization, had cleaned up its environment to some extent. The major polluters were now in the newly industrializing nations of eastern Europe, India, and China. Yet developed nations still polluted the air with chemical substances, spraying "acid rain" on humans, animals, and soil. They polluted the seas with waste from factories and naval vessels, imperiling whole categories of marine life. They built nuclear plants to generate power, which sometimes malfunctioned, releasing lethal radiation into the atmosphere.

Pollutants of a certain type, especially chlorofluorocarbons, have resulted in the thinning of the ozone layer, which is the protective gaseous zone of the earth's atmosphere that blocks the harmful effects of the sun's radiation. When released into the air, chlorofluorocarbons, used in aerosol sprays and in refrigeration and air-conditioning systems, cause the degradation of the ozone layer.

The emission of carbon dioxide and other gases, an accompaniment of industrial processes, is a cause, environmentalists argue, of the tendency toward "global warming". The air thickened by gaseous emissions traps the sun's heat close to the surface of the earth. Temperatures rise as a result; as they have been rising throughout the century.

Living things have suffered from the poisons that modern life broadcasts into air, soil, and water. Environmentalists created lists of "endangered species" and launched campaigns to save those injured by commercial ventures—whales poisoned by oil leaks from tankers, seals cruelly hunted, dolphins trapped in nets. As species are endangered, so natural habitats are jeopardized by the encroachments of modern society. Wetlands and rainforests around the world are shrinking—25 million acres of trees are lost each year—and with them the capacity for vegetable and marine life to replenish the earth and atmosphere.

Non-Governmental Organizations   Just as an array of international organizations promote environmentalist agendas, others support a variety of humanitarian causes. These "non-governmental organizations" (NGOs), many of them private or Church-related, some sponsored by the United Nations, have guided the movements for human health, welfare, and

Selected Nobel Peace Prize Winners Since World War II

1953   George C. Marshall, originator of Marshall Plan (US)

1964   Martin Luther King, Jr., civil rights leader (US)

1975   Andrei Sakharov (USSR), physicist, human rights campaigner

1978   Anwar el-Sadat, president of Egypt, and Menachem Begin, prime minister of Israel, for negotiation of peace accord

1983   Lech Walesa (Poland), Solidarity leader

1984   Desmond M. Tutu (South Africa), Bishop of Johannesburg, anti-apartheid leader

1990   Mikhail Gorbachev (USSR), initiator of Soviet reform and dissolution

1994   Yitzhak Rabin and Shimon Peres, prime minister and foreign minister of Israel, and Yasir Arafat, chairman of PLO, for negotiation of peace pact development. Constituting a new category of cooperative human effort—sometimes called "the third sector"—funded largely by grants from philanthropic foundations (notably the Ford or Rockefeller Foundations, both United States agencies) or private donations, they have become the primary agents of human welfare in a world that has turned from empire and values pluralism.

Senior among these NGOs is the International Red Cross, founded in 1864 (and since 1986 renamed the International Movement of the Red Cross and Red Crescent, to include Islamic national members), and honored with Nobel Peace Prizes in 1917, 1944, and 1963. The Red Cross serves the needs of the wounded and displaced in wartime, and brings food, clothing, medical care, and expert advisors to victims of natural disasters. Especially devoted to the medical needs of impoverished peoples or communities in crisis has been the French organization Médecins sans Frontières ("Doctors without Boundaries"), while

CARE tends to the needs of children worldwide. Amnesty International has pursued the cause of identifying prisoners of conscience (those imprisoned for no crime but criticism of government policies) and organizing international support for their release.

In addition, many agencies and programs of the United Nations are devoted to the control and prevention of disease (the World Health Organization, or WHO); the increase and distribution of food supplies (the Food and Agriculture Organization, or FAO); the welfare of children (the United Nations International Children's Emergency Fund, or UNICEF); the facilitation of world trade (the World Trade Organization, or WTO); and the promotion of knowledge (the United Nations Educational, Scientific, and Cultural Organization, or UNESCO). Informing the work of its agencies is the general mission of the United Nations: "to save succeeding generations from the scourge of war," as its Charter reads; and to "reaffirm faith in fundamental human

WITNESSES

The Age of Human Rights

Since the close of World War II, more and more of the world's nations have been moving toward consensus on some fundamental human rights and obligations. Some of that thinking is evident in the following sections from key documents of the United Nations: its 1948 Declaration on Human Rights; its 1948 Convention on Genocide; and its 1989 Conventions on the Rights of the Child.

UN Universal Declaration of Human Rights (1948):
Article 1. All human beings are born free and equal in dignity and rights. ...
Article 2. Everyone is entitled to all the rights and freedoms set forth in this Declaration, without distinction of any kind, such as race, colour, sex, language, religion, political or other opinion, national or social origin, property, birth or other status. ...
Article 3. Everyone has the right to life, liberty and security of person. ...
(From *United Nations Publication* No. 63.1.13, 1963)

UN Convention on the Prevention and Punishment of the Crime of Genocide (1948):
Article 1. The Contracting Parties confirm that genocide whether in time of peace or in time of war, is a crime under international law which they undertake to prevent and to punish.
Article 2. ... [G]enocide means any of the following acts committed with intent to destroy, in whole or in part, a national, ethnical, racial or religious group, such as: (a) Killing members of the group; (b) Causing serious bodily or mental harm to members of the group; (c) Deliberately inflicting on the group conditions of life calculated to bring about its physical destruction in

whole or in part; (d) Imposing measures intended to prevent births within the group; (e) Forcibly transferring children of the group to another group.
(From *Yearbook of the United Nations*, 1950)

UN Convention on the Rights of the Child (1989):
Principle 2. The child shall enjoy special protection, and shall be given opportunities and facilities, by law and by other means, to enable him to develop physically, mentally, morally, spiritually and socially in a healthy and normal manner and in conditions of freedom and dignity. ...
Principle 4. The child shall enjoy the benefits of social security. He shall be entitled to grow and develop in health; to this end, special care and protection shall be provided both to him and to his mother, including adequate pre-natal and post-natal care. The child shall have the right to adequate nutrition, housing, recreation and medical services. ...
Principal 6. The child ... needs love and understanding. He shall, wherever possible, grow up in the care and under the responsibility of his parents, and, in any case, in an atmosphere of affection and of moral and material security; a child of tender years shall not, save in exceptional circumstances, be separated from his mother. ...
Principle 7. The child is entitled to receive education, which shall be free and compulsory, at least in the elementary stages. ...
(From UN High Commissioner for Human Rights, 1997)

rights, in the dignity and worth of the human person, in the equal rights of men and women and of nations large and small."

Successor to the failed League of Nations, the United Nations was established in 1945, when representatives of fifty nations approved its charter. Consisting of a fifteen-member Security Council and a General Assembly, in which all member nations were to participate equally, the United Nations aimed to represent the concerted will of the nations of the globe in seeking peaceful resolution of conflicts and in promoting human welfare. By 1960, about fifty additional nations were admitted to membership, many of them newly independent states of Asia and Africa. By the late 1990s, the roster exceeded 180.

The United Nations has found multilateral solutions for several political confrontations in the postwar era, intervening in the Arab-Israeli crisis of 1947–1948, the Korean War in 1950, the Suez crisis in 1956, and the Congo crisis of 1960. Recently, it has coordinated international humanitarian and military "peace" forces, in the spirit of the 1992 "Agenda for Peace" outlined by Boutros Boutros-Ghali (1922–) of Egypt, UN Secretary-General 1992–1996. The World Court, the judicial organ of the United Nations, adjudicates disputes about territorial rights, sovereignty and nationality, immigration and asylum.

In December 1948, the United Nations adopted the Universal Declaration of Human Rights as a standard to which the nations of the world must be held. Among its principles were those contained in foundational documents of the liberal tradition such as the American Declaration of Independence and the French Declaration of the Rights of Man and the Citizen. To these were added guarantees of equality without distinctions of "race, color, sex, language, religion, political or other opinion, national or social origin, property, birth or other status"; assurances of the enduring right to national citizenship, and the right to flee or return to one's own nation; the legitimation of government by the will of the people, expressed in free and fair elections; the prohibition of both slavery and torture. The UN Declaration notably includes provisions about private matters, likely to be affected by local belief and custom, as well as by marriage (which must rest on the consent of both man and woman) and childrearing (children must receive education that would expand and multiply their life chances, and training in respect for human rights and freedom).

The UN Declaration of Human Rights was adopted unanimously (the Soviet bloc nations, along with South Africa and Saudi Arabia, abstaining). A less ambitious, but still pathbreaking agreement was reached at Helsinki (Finland) in 1975. The United States, Canada, and all the countries of Europe, except Albania (including the Soviet Union and its satellites)—signed the Helsinki Accords, pledging their acceptance of human rights standards in validation of the principles of the UN document of 1948. Meanwhile, in November 1989, the United Nations issued a Convention on the Rights of the Child, which was a corollary to its universal Declaration of Human Rights.

By the time the Cold War ended, consensus had been reached among the world's major powers on the preeminent values of peace and human dignity. But far from the centers of wealth and technological competition for wealth and power produced new paradigms of war—tragic battles, and it is generally wished, the last battles, in the long history of human conflict (see Epilogue).

Conclusion
RETREAT FROM ARMAGEDDON AND THE MEANING OF THE WEST

For more than fifty years after the bombing of Hiroshima signaled the end of World War II, the peoples of the Western world lived in fear. Their world was split between a communist "East" and a "free West," both armed with weapons of mass destruction and locked in mutual hatred. After 1989, with the disintegration of Soviet communism, deadlock eased.

Meanwhile, a younger generation, led by a prosperous and willful vanguard of American students, turned from the Cold War to promote personal liberation, sexual revolution, and global activism. They have learned that the world is divided not so much between the chimeras of "East" and "West," as between North and South, the zones of the developed and developing nations. Disturbingly, that region, which is most burdened by poverty, disease, and overpopulation, also suffers disproportionately from injustice, terror, and war.

Among the questions that emerge from the second half of the twentieth century are these: will a renewed West, freed from the prospect of Armageddon, reassert its commitment to the finest values of the Western tradition? And will it—or can it, or should it—lead the way in the building of a humane and prosperous global civilization?

REVIEW QUESTIONS

1. What was the Cold War? How did post-war Europe become divided into two rival power blocs? What was the Truman Doctrine?

2. What was the principle of "Mutually Assured Destruction"? How did anti-Communist influence United States domestic policy in the 1940s and 1950s? How did the United States–Soviet enmity play out in the Middle East, Asia, and Africa?

3. How did de-Stalinization affect Soviet rule in Eastern Europe? How successful was detente before 1985? Why did the Soviet Union undergo a collapse in 1985–1991?

4. What were the roots of youth protests during the 1960s and 1970s? What roles did the drug culture and rock music play in youth culture? To what extent did the activities of the Sixties generation change society in the West?

5. What was the sexual revolution? How did it influence the feminist movement? To what extent has women's place in Western society changed since the 1960s? Have similar changes occurred for women outside the West?

6. Why has the earth's population increased so rapidly? What are the effects of overpopulation? How successful has the UN been in resolving environmental and political problems?

SUGGESTED RESOURCES

Apocalypse Now?

Boyer, Paul, *By the Bomb's Early Light: American Thought and Culture at the Dawn of the Atomic Age* (Chapel Hill, NC: University of North Carolina Press, 1994). Compelling exploration of the cultural and psychological impact of the bomb on Americans.

Brands, H. W., *The Devil We Knew: Americans and the Cold War* (Oxford: Oxford University Press, 1993). Suggests communism might have collapsed even sooner in the absence of the Cold War.

Courtois, Stephane, et al., *The Black Book of Communism: Crimes, Terror, Repression* (Cambridge, MA: Harvard University Press, 1999). Controversial exploration of the death toll of communism in its manifestations around the world.

Daniels, Robert V., *Soviet Communism from Reform to Collapse* (Lexington, MA: D. C. Heath, 1995). Studies efforts to reform the USSR during the 1980s, asking why reform failed; and why the USSR collapsed so quickly.

Fursenko, Aleksandr, and Timothy Naftali, *One Hell of a Gamble: Khrushchev, Castro, and Kennedy, 1958–1964* (New York: W. W. Norton, 1997). Gripping account of relations among Cuba, the USSR, and the US from the Cuban missile crisis to Khrushchev's fall.

Haynes, John Early and Harvey Klehr, *Venona: Decoding Soviet Espionage in America* (New Haven: Yale University Press, 1999). Based on United States files only opened in 1995, reveals the vast extent of the post-war Soviet espionage network.

Volkogonov, Dmitri, *Autopsy for an Empire: The Seven Leaders who Built the Soviet Regime* (trans. Harold Shukman; New York: Free Press, 1998). The general who initiated the declassification of Soviet files narrates the Soviet story from the Bolshevik takeover to the regime's collapse in 1991.

Cold War International History Project, with document library, guides to institutes, links, resources (Woodrow Wilson International Center): http://cwihp.si.edu

All You Need is Love

Allyn, David, *Make Love, Not War: The Sexual Revolution: An Unfettered History* (London: Routledge, 2001). Consulting with advocates of sexual freedom, feminists, lawyers, prostitutes, and gays, Allyn retraces the history of the sexual revolution.

Buckley, Mary, ed., *Post-Soviet Women: From the Baltic to Central Asia* (Cambridge: Cambridge University Press, 1997). Essays on domestic conditions, the role of female politicians, women's economic status, national identity, and peace movements.

Ignatieff, Michael, *The Warrior's Honor: Ethnic War and the Modern Conscience* (New York: Metropolitan, 1998). Contrasts the mercenaries and warlords committed to the ethnic tribalism which informs so many modern wars with the well-meaning peace interventionists, diplomats, journalists, and medical teams who share an ideal of universal human rights.

Isserman, Maurice & Michael Kazin, *America Divided: the Civil War of the 1960s* (Oxford: Oxford University Press, 1999). Well-researched comprehensive study of the different issues that sparked the divisions of the Sixties and which still continue to inform a cultural divide within American life.

McNeill, J.R., *Something New Under the Sun: An Environmental History of the Twentieth-Century World*, (New York: W.W. Norton, 2000). Explores the progress of environmental degradation over the past century, and how it can be reversed without damaging the economy.

Nelson, Barbara J. and Najma Chowdhury, eds., *Women and Politics Worldwide* (New Haven, CT: Yale University Press, 1994). Vast essay collection, surveying women's varied experience in 44 countries around the world.

Rowbotham, Sheila, *A Century of Women: The History of Women in Britain and the United States* (London: Penguin, 1997). Assesses women's economic and political progress during the 20th century.

The Sixties Project Website, documents, resources, links (University of Virginia): **http://lists.village.virginia.edu/sixties/HTML_docs/Scholar.html**

Women in Philosophy: Feminism—resources on feminist women thinkers: **http://www.eraticimpact.com/~feminism**

United Nations homepage (English), with links to reports and resources on Peace and Security, Economic and Social Development, Human Rights, Humanitarian Affairs, and International Law: **http://www.un.org/english**

Two approaches to environmentalism: Greenpeace International homepage: **http://www.greenpeace.org**
The New Environmentalism (RPPI/NEPI): **http://www.newenvironmentalism.org**

EPILOGUE: THE FUTURE OF THE WEST

SINCE 1990

The Westward Journey When the Greek hero Ulysses (the Odysseus of Homer's *Odyssey*) returned home, after the Trojan war and twenty years of wandering, he did not, as imagined in a poem by the English poet Alfred, Lord Tennyson (1809–1892), stay home. Grizzled and old, yet "always roaming with a hungry heart," he set out to discover what lay beyond the western horizon of his Mediterranean world: "To strive, to seek, to find, and not to yield."

Ulysses' journey brings to mind the condition of Western civilization as it leaves behind the troubled twentieth century and opens the next millennium. The West is one of the world's youngest civilizations; but it is aging. Will it fade? Or will it continue the journey westwards, a "gray spirit yearning in desire," like Ulysses, venturing "to sail beyond the sunset":

> To follow knowledge like a sinking star
> Beyond the utmost bound of human thought?"

What is the future of the West? Will there still be a distinctively Western world, and a Western civilization, in this third millennium of the Common Era? Or will the West shrink to "a small and inconsequential peninsula at the extremity of the Eurasian land mass," as Samuel Huntington suggests? (see *Witnesses* p. 910). We cannot answer this question. But we can consider some of the main lines of the world's economic, political, and cultural development over the dozen years since the end of the Cold War in order to understand what may lie ahead for the civilization of the West. The prospect is unclear. On the one hand, the world of nations appear to be moving towards greater political integration and economic globalization. On the other, some peoples and cultures and civilizations are striking out against precisely these trends, retreating to ancient customs and reviving ancient hostilities against those whose message of modernization—and Westernization—is viewed as threatenings.

COMING TOGETHER

The breakup of the Soviet empire completed in the last days of 1991 (see Chapter 30) dramatically changed the world's political landscape. For nearly fifty years, two superpowers had faced each other with an intense antagonism; then one of those contestants slipped away. So momentous is the change that it can be said that the twentieth century ended in that year—in the same way that, in a sense, it began only in 1914 with the outbreak of World War I. This "short twentieth century" contrasts with the "long nineteenth century" (1789–1914), in which the nations of the West consolidated their power and prestige. Those nations then dragged the world into two calamitous world wars that resulted in mass slaughter and the prospect of universal destruction. Those conflicts in turn led to the Cold War and its bipolar geopolitical configuration that prevailed from the end of World War II until the moment when Gorbachev walked out of the Kremlin and the post-Soviet era began.

The end of the Cold War has facilitated the coming together of nations, beginning with the nations of Europe, the matrix of Western civilizaton. In 1945, Europe was divided between victors and vanquished, those whose cities had been bombed and populations ravaged from those who had survived with lesser injuries. A new barrier of suspicion emerged between the nations of eastern Europe, which became satellites of the mammoth Soviet Union, and the nations of western Europe which aligned themselves with the giant across the Ocean, the United States (see Chapter 30).

Yet from the exhausted, shattered European states that emerged from World War II in 1945, an increasingly united Europe formed. Those nations of western Europe which were free to do so proceeded to shape their futures through the parliamentary process. From the deep ideological rifts of the 1920s and 1930s, European politics have moved towards the center, with principal leaders chosen alternately from left-center and right-center parties. Thus Britain elected a

Labour government in 1945, then shifted back and forth between Labour and Conservative over the next fifty years. The 1997 election made centrist, Europe-conscious Labour candidate Anthony Blair (b. 1953) Prime Minister. Since 1949, West Germany has shifted between Christian Democrat and Social Democrat leaders, with the most recent election, in 1998, bringing Social Democrat Gerhard Schröder (b. 1944) and a socialist-Green (environmentalist) coalition to power.

Italy was largely under Christian Democrat control until 1983, when a socialist coalition took over, to be repudiated in 2001 by the election of the right-leaning ("Forza Italia", or "Forwards, Italy!") leader Silvio Burlusconi. In 1958, shifting from the leftwing government installed in 1945, France changed course with the election of Charles de Gaulle (1890–1970) and, in 1959, the institution of the Fifth Republic. Since De Gaulle's resignation in 1969, first conservative and then socialist and centrist leaders held the reins. In 1995, conservative Jacques Chirac became president, sharing power with socialist Lionel Jospin, elected in 1997.

In these and other European nations outside the Soviet sphere, transfers of power have been managed peacefully, while leaders of all parties presided over tax-heavy welfare states dedicated to protecting the citizens whose elders had begun, and suffered the consequences, of two world wars. In recent years, consensus seems to have formed in western Europe for a non-ideological "Third Way," neither "Left" nor "Right," a pragmatic politics that both cherishes the citizens while it promotes the conditions that generate greater wealth for the nation.

Over the same post-war period, two trans-national alliances formed which pointed towards the political and economic unification of the continent: the Common Market, formed in 1957, and NATO, formed in 1949 (see Chapter 30). The first allowed for the free flow of goods across the borders of member nations. The latter, led by the United States, sought to defend its members against possible aggression from the Soviet Union and its satellites (which in 1955 organized the Warsaw Pact of allied eastern European states under its leadership).

Since its founding, the Common Market has expanded to include more states and new forms of cooperation. It was replaced in 1967 by the European Community, and in 1993 became the European Union (EU). In 1999, the EU was a partnership of fifteen states. It is centered in Brussels (Belgium), with a written constitution and its own parliament (which meets in Brussels or Strasbourg, France). It aims to establish a common foreign policy for its members, and looks to their eventual political and economic integration. The collapse of communism in eastern Europe after 1989 has made the vision of a united Europe seem even more plausible.

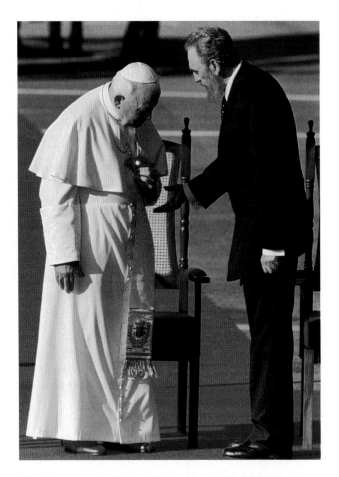

The Pope meets Castro: *The ending of the Cold War has brought into increasing contact societies and individuals long separated by mutual hostility and fear. Here, Pope John Paul II, the head of the Roman Catholic Church, meets Cuban leader Fidel Castro. Cuba is one of the last remaining communist states and is an officially atheist state.*

Eleven of the fifteen members of the European Union (all but the United Kingdom, Denmark, Greece and Sweden) joined in Economic and Monetary Union (EMU). Aiming to achieve the economic integration of the continent preparatory to its greater political integration, the EMU exercises strict discipline over member states in matters such as national indebtedness and monetary policy. On December 31, 1998, as one member proclaimed "the dawn of a new era in the integration of Europe," the EMU introduced its new currency, the "euro." In January 2002, the euro became Europe's single currency, and Europe was transformed into "Euroland," a vast new entity with 292 million inhabitants and a twenty-five percent share of the world's economic output (nearly equal to the United States' share of twenty-eight percent). At the outset of a new millennium, Europe was well on its way to continental unification at the levels of economic, political and cultural cooperation. It recalls the Europe of a millennium before, which, despite impoverishment and political fragmentation, was building the cultural unity of Christianitas, or Christendom, based on a

Through a Glass Darkly

Historians rarely dare to predict the future; but some do, and do so fearlessly. In these passages composed at the end of the twentieth century, historian Paul Kennedy in 1993 points to the need for technology to address the problem of population pressure; Czech president, author, and former dissident Václav Havel in 1999 envisions the creation of universal culture increasingly without political boundaries; and Nobel Prize-winning economist Amartya Sen in 2001 warns against the reduction of human nature to a single cultural identity.

Paul Kennedy on the Power of Technology versus the power of population (1993): The greatest test for human society as it confronts the twenty-first century is how to use "the power of technology" to meet the demands thrown up by "the power of population"; that is, how to find effective global solutions in order to free the poorer three-quarters of humankind from the growing Malthusian trap of malnutrition, starvation, resource depletion, unrest, enforced migration, and armed conflict ... The technology explosion is taking place overwhelmingly in economically advanced societies, many of which possess slow-growing or even declining populations. However, the demographic boom is occurring in countries with limited technological resources, very few scientists and skilled workers, inadequate investment in research and development, and few or no successful corporations; in many cases, their governing elites have no interest in technology, and cultural and ideological prejudices are ... tilted against change ... Simply because we do not know the future, it is impossible to say with certainty whether global trends will lead to terrible disasters or be diverted by astonishing advances in human adaption. What is clear is that as the Cold War fades away, we face not a "new world order" but a troubled and fractured planet, whose problems deserve the serious attention of politicians and publics alike. ...
(Paul Kennedy, *Preparing for the Twenty-First Century,* New York: Random House, 1993)

Václav Havel discusses the end of the nation-state and the coming of global society (1999): There is every indication that the glory of the nation-state as the culmination of every national community's history, and its highest earthly value—the only one, in fact, in the name of which it is permissible to kill, or for which people have been expected to die—has already passed its peak.

It would seem that the enlightened efforts of generations of democrats, the terrible experience of two world wars ... and the evolution of civilization have finally brought humanity to the recognition that human beings are more important than the state.

In this new world, people—regardless of borders—are connected in millions of different ways: through trade, finance, property, and information. Such relationships bring with them a wide variety of values and cultural models that have a universal validity. It is a world, moreover, in which a threat to some has an immediate impact on everyone ... in which all of us—whether we like it or not—must begin to bear responsibility for everything that occurs. In such a world, the idol of state sovereignty must inevitably dissolve. ...

If modern democratic states are usually defined by qualities such as their respect for human rights and liberties, the equality their citizens enjoy, and the existence of a civil society, then the condition toward which humanity will, and ... must, move will probably be characterized by a universal or global respect for human rights, by universal civic equality and the rule of law, and by a global civic society.
(Address to the Canadian Senate and House of Commons, April 29, 1999; pub. *New York Review of Books* (June 10, 1999); trans. from Czech by Paul Wilson)

Amartya Sen examines plural identities versus civilizational camps (2001): Dividing the world into discrete civilizations is not just crude. It propels us into the absurd belief that this partitioning is natural and necessary and must overwhelm all other ways of identifying people. That imperious view goes not only against the sentiment that "we human beings are all much the same," but also against the more plausible understanding that we are diversely different. ...

Each of us has many features in our self-conception. Our religion, important as it may be, cannot be an all-engulfing identity. Even a shared poverty can be a source of solidarity across the borders. The kind of division highlighted by, say, the so-called "antiglobalization" protesters—whose movement is, incidentally, one of the most globalized in the world—tries to unite the underdogs of the world economy and goes firmly against religious, national or "civilizational" lines of division.

The main hope of harmony lies not in any imagined uniformity, but in the plurality of our identities, which cut across each other and work against sharp divisions into impenetrable civilizational camps. Political leaders who think and act in terms of sectioning off humanity into various "worlds" stand to make the world more flammable—even when their intentions are very different. They also end up, in the case of civilizations defined by religion, lending authority to religious leaders seen as spokesmen for their "worlds." In the process, other voices are muffled and other concerns silenced. The robbing of our plural identities not only reduces us; it impoverishes the world.
("A World Not Neatly Divided," *The New York Times,* November 23, 2001)

common faith, language, and intellectual traditions (see Chapter 10).

As the major states of western Europe have drawn more closely together over the last decade, they are readmitting to their midst, and to the concept of "Europe," eastern European states that lay under the Soviet aegis before 1989. In 1990, at sacrificial cost, the western German Federal Republic reunited with the eastern German Democratic Republic, which has begun to catch up with the economic powerhouse that is its western half. During the 1990s, Poland, Hungary, and the Czech Republic launched new economic policies that were painful at first, but which have permitted those nations to become weaned from the command economies of the Soviet era and to compete and prosper in the European economic world. Russia itself, which lapsed into economic as well as constitutional confusion in 1992, its first post-Soviet year, and which reached a nadir of misery in 1998, at last in 2001 began to show signs of economic recovery. At the same time, under president Vladimir Putin—upon whom Boris Yeltsin suddenly conferred the mantle of power shortly before midnight on December 31, 1999, a position later ratified by election—Russia has sought to rejoin Europe and the West. Putin's rapprochement in 2001 with fledgling US President George W. Bush (elected 2000) moved Russia forcefully in that direction.

Bush, meanwhile, saddled from the outset with a controversial election that he scantily won, began his term with an approach towards Europe less open than his predecessor's, William Jefferson Clinton (president 1993–2000). The terrorist attack of September 11, 2001 (see below), however, recalled him to a position of solidarity with European allies, especially Britain. More locally, both Clinton and Bush worked to build hemispheric cooperation during the 1990s. The policies of the United States towards its Latin American neighbors had been colored by Cold War anxieties from the 1950s through the 1980s, resulting in the bolstering of authoritarian regimes and sporadic military interventions. At the same time, the United States extended considerable assistance to emerging economies, and was the source of important financial investment. By the 1990s, as the Cold War receded into memory, and leading Latin American states (such as Brazil and Argentina) developed powerful economies, it became more possible for these nations to cooperate with the wealthier nations to the north. These also benefitted from NAFTA (North American Free Trade Agreement), enacted in 1994, which facilitated trade between Canada, the United States, and Mexico. The possibility that some Latin American economies will "dollarize," or convert their currencies (already linked to the dollar) to United States dollars, suggests the consolidation of greater regional economic unity in the future, a goal called for at the Summit of the Americas held in Quebec in June 2000.

Both in Europe and the Americas, the quest for greater prosperity through barrier-free trade has helped bring nations together. That quest also drives the other nations of the world to embrace free market systems, and to bind them, if reluctantly at times, to the Western model of technological modernization, economic growth, and democratic values.

The Ties that Bind

The growing unity of the Western blocs, European and American, is part of a larger process towards the greater economic and cultural interconnectedness of the world—the process called globalization.

In economic terms, globalization means that the separate markets of the world—local, regional, and continental—are now linked into one. Not only do commodities purchased in the Western world, such as coffee, bananas, and oil, come from other continents, but clothing, carpets, and automobiles, among many other goods, are likely to have been manufactured in Asia, Africa, or South America where cheap labor markets lure Western investors. Business is international, carried on by itinerant entrepreneurs and speeded by modern technologies of transportation, communication, and computerization.

In the global economy, the processes of industrialization and urbanization that began in Europe before 1800 have become the model for regions remote from that source (see Chapter 21). But progress has been irregular and incomplete. The "developed" world, including the industrialized nations of the West, with Japan and the Asian "dragons" or "tigers" (see Chapter 29), is far wealthier than the "developing" world, including many Asian, African, and Latin American nations.

That inequality is a source of resentment and unrest among the present losers in the globalization process who suffer enormously during periods of economic transition or crisis caused by trade or currency imbalances—or by the corruption or inefficiency of local governments. The wealthier nations who control the major international organizations that promote free trade and manage international loans and currency transfers express sympathy; but persist regardless to effect those changes that will facilitate free trade, based on sound currencies, across national boundaries. In the end, free markets and global trade networks, they promise, will generate economic growth and benefit all.

It was this promise of greater wealth after transitional pain that US President Clinton extended to the Bulgarians in November 1999, when he assured them that "through freedom, you, too, shall overcome." A year later, he told the Vietnamese that "the key to the future" was "entrepreneurship, innovation, and competition," along with the free exchange of ideas. And British Prime Minister Tony Blair

Map 31.1 Europe: the Continent, the Union, the Alliance: *Europe is not only a continent and a set of nations. It also has a unity created by economic alliances, culminating in the European Union and the eleven nations adopting a unitary currency, and the political alliance of NATO (which also includes the non-European states of the United States and Canada).*

communicated a similar message in January 2000, addressing the annual meeting of the World Economic Forum in Davos, Switzerland: "far from impoverishing the world's poorer countries, trade liberalization is the only sure route to the kind of economic growth needed to bring their prosperity closer to that of the major developed economies."

The free trade consensus among the leaders of wealthy nations has recently fueled fierce protests from groups claiming to represent the world's poor and disenfranchised. Drawn from many nations and an enormous array of organizations from community groups to anarchist cells, these protestors have expressed themselves vigorously and sometimes violently at several economists' gatherings: most notably at the meeting of the WTO (World Trade Organization) in Seattle (Washington, USA) in December 1999, and of the G8 (a summit meeting of the leaders of eight of the world's major industrial nations) in Genoa (Italy) in July 2001. In these

settings, provocative and targeted acts of violence invited police repression, with consequent critiques by the press and the public. The Seattle meeting dissolved midway; the Genoa talks proceeded amid intense disturbance to their finish. This staged and bloodstained opposition to what protestors saw as an exploitative global capitalism did not deter the G8 leaders from their final statement—cushioned though it was with promises to assist heavily-indebted poor countries: "Sustained economic growth worldwide requires a renewed commitment to free trade."

The imperatives of free trade, open markets, fiscal discipline, stability of currency, have been in different ways and to different degrees embraced by those Asian, African, and Latin American nations that wish to participate in the international trade network and, ultimately, in the wealth that it may generate. Russia is returning from several years of trauma, as it adjusts to a market economy, still lacking the supports of rules of property and procedure. China, still

Communist, with a leadership committed to censorship and repression, is moving towards a free market economy and bracing itself for the tremendous transformations that are sure to come. After the Asian economic crisis of the mid-1990s, Japan is attempting to reform its over-protected economy. The major nations of eastern Europe have already made the transition to a modern market economy, while several Latin American nations have suffered through currency collapse and economic stress. Despite much tension and difficulty, significant increases in levels of wealth, as well as improvements in health and welfare, have been made worldwide.

The role of technology in economic globalization cannot be overstated. As manufacturing tasks have shifted to the "developing" zones of the world, the most highly developed have assumed the task of producing information and services rather than things. Rapid progress in cybernetics (see Chapter 30), with its origins in the military competition of World War II, has transformed the way business, government, and cultural institutions operate. The design and implementation of hardware and software systems require highly trained experts, while even the operation of these systems requires workers skilled beyond the level of the manual laborers who were once the core of the "working class." Those needs place huge demands on the educational systems of societies that aspire to excel in the enterprise of managing information: "in an economy dominated by information and knowledge," Blair points out, "education is king." Those nations whose people are not only poor but also, as often follows, illiterate, are doubly burdened.

Technologically updated transportation and communication networks have also facilitated globalization. A dense network of air routes links once-remote entrepots, while increasing efficiency and commercial competition have reduced prices for business and leisure travelers. In populous regions, high-speed trains are convenient and accessible. The Channel tunnel, or "Chunnel," opened in 1994, at last provides a non-stop connection between Paris and London, two main poles of European culture. Even as these networks for high-speed movement link the world's capitals, truck roads and rail links slowly multiply in the isolated interiors of the developing world.

Communications technologies are able to link even these parts of the world not yet well-served by transportation systems. By means of telephones, cellular phones, fax machines, the radio and above all, the Internet, vocal or digitalized information can be delivered almost instantaneously to governments, institutions, and individuals worldwide. In Africa, the radio has permitted long-distance communications where this was previously almost impossible. In China in 1989, fax machines distributed information about the Tiananmen Square demonstration and repression. In the late stages of the Yugoslav conflict, both Serbs and

Kosovars communicated with outsiders by e-mail, or "electronic mail." E-mail also connects entrepreneurs and intellectuals in New York, Moscow, or Milan, who conclude sales or arrange conferences with their counterparts in Germany, India, or Colombia.

Technology brought the promise of taming the great distances not only of the globe but also of the universe. Space programs began in the context of the Cold War arms buildup of the 1950s and 1960s, as the Soviet Union and the United States sought to demonstrate their capacity to extend their presence beyond the limits of the terrestrial world. Space exploration has since evolved into a cooperative effort to study the nature of the universe, and to gauge the ways that human or animal life can survive in the alien environments of space. The Russian Mir space station, launched in 1986, was finally dismantled in 1999 after a series of mishaps. Before its termination, the seven-storey, 35-ton International Space Station with linked Russian and American modules was launched into orbit late in 1998. It is designed to accommodate an international team that will pursue Mir's goals in seeking knowledge about space.

While the Internet annihilates distance and space missions conquer them, perhaps nothing unifies peoples of the world as their participation in a common culture—a mass culture of television shows and rock music, of youth fashion, sport, and film. Although these trends first appeared in the free, exuberant 1920s, they developed their present form during the Sixties (see Chapter 30), an era marked by political protest, sexual liberation, and countercultural transformations. In the 1990s, mass cultural style continued to be dominated by United States youth, whose pursuits of "sex, drugs, and rock and roll" now engage imitators on every continent—and evoke protest from traditionalists who see American popular or "pop" culture as a threat to traditional religious values and models of the family.

Even traditionalists, however, now inhabit a globalized world where the narrow boundaries of the past—of village, nation, denomination, language — are dissolving. The world is not yet one, and conflicts and hatreds disrupt it. But it is certainly a linked system, in which no one part stands alone, and every thought or deed has potentially worldwide impact.

Last Battles

The Polish-born Pope John Paul II, a trained philosopher and former anti-Communist, head of a church which numbers about one million billion adherents worldwide, periodically reminds his vast audience of the needs of the poor in a world bent on becoming rich. While proponents of theories of social justice sparred with proponents of globalization in the 1980s and 1990s, opponents of modernization, buttressed by the beliefs and infrastructures of traditional societies

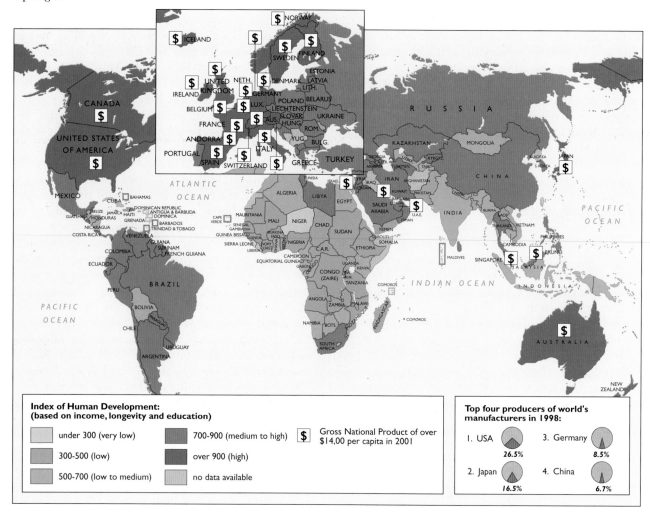

Map 31.2 The Wealth of Nations: Developed and Developing Nations of the World: *As the twenty-first century opens, the world appears to be divided between the wealthier nations, mostly Western, and poorer ones, mostly outside the West. With the exception of Japan, all the nations where the Gross National Product per capita in 1991 exceeded $10,000 were Western. Four nations—the United States, France, Germany, and Japan—produce over half of the value of the world's manufactured goods. The map shown here indicates relative levels of human welfare as indicated by the Human Development Index, a measure based on the three components of longevity, education, and income. Much of Asia and the Middle East, and all of Africa, rank below the highest levels.*

and goaded by dictators, warlords, and strongmen, armed themselves to resist any universal notion of a just and prosperous society that was modeled on those of the Western world. Tribal hatreds, ethnic rivalries, and religious jihads caused intense destruction, at first, in pockets of the world remote from the Western gaze, and then in the very heartland of the West. Far from the centers of wealth and technological advance, competition for power produced new paradigms of war—numerous small but tragic battles; many hope that they are the last in the long history of human conflict.

As the superpowers disarmed after the Cold War, other states of the world acquired massive military capacity. China and India stockpiled powerful weapons; so did Israel, Pakistan, Libya, North Korea, and Iraq. India refused to sign the Nuclear Non-Proliferation treaty until its requirements were universal and equitable. On 11 May 1998, she demonstrated her independence by exploding nuclear

devices about 70 miles from the Pakistani border. Also refusing to sign were India's neighbor Pakistan, South Africa, and Israel. Even without nuclear weapons, the militarized states of the developing world were dangerous. Some developed biological and chemical weapons (although international agreements prohibit their use), which are cheap, easily acquired, and difficult to monitor. Currently at least twelve nations are thought to have biological weapons; among them, Iraq, which has used its store of chemical weapons (banned by international agreements in 1925 and 1993) against neighboring Iran in the 1980s and its own citizens in the 1990s.

Conventional arms, however, are the main material of war sought by the upstart dictatorships of developing nations. These were acquired free from one or the other of the superpowers during the Cold War, or purchased on a growing open market. Armies as well as armaments are available for purchase, as mercenary bands, recruited from the veterans of military

Why Some are So Rich and Some are So Poor

*G*reater productivity in the Western world, driven by technological innovation and especially modern information systems, have markedly increased the gap between rich and poor within nations, as well as between rich and poor nations. Some economic theorists predict disaster ahead, such as William Greider, or blame the economic policies on wealthy nations, private corporations, and the international monetary agencies that speak for them, as does Michel Chossudovsky. Others, like David Landes and Nancy Birdsall, recognize that chronic divisions of wealth are erosive of our human community, but see the solution in greater economic innovation and growth—and not in the greater regulation or redistribution of wealth.

William Greider examines the global market and the coming storm (1997): Imagine a wondrous new machine, strong and supple, a machine that reaps as it destroys. It is huge and mobile ... but no one is at the wheel. ... It is sustained by its own forward motion, guided mainly by its own appetites. And it is accelerating. ...

The machine is ... modern capitalism driven by the imperatives of global industrial revolution. ... a free-running economic system that is reordering the world. ...

... The symptoms of upheaval can be found almost anywhere ... The convergence has no fixed center, no reliable boundaries or settled outcomes. ... The earth's diverse societies are being rearranged and united in complicated ways by global capitalism. The idea evokes benumbed resignation among many. The complexity of it overwhelms. The enormity makes people feel small and helpless.

(William Greider, *One World, Ready or Not: The Manic Logic of Global Capitalism*, New York: Simon & Schuster, 1997)

Michel Chossudovsky discusses the globalization of poverty (1998): The late-twentieth century will go down in world history as a period of global impoverishment marked by the collapse of productive systems in the developing world, the demise of national institutions and the disintegration of health and education programs. This "globalization of poverty" ... was initiated in the Third World coinciding with the onslaught of the debt crisis. Since the 1990s, it has extended its grip to all major regions of the world ... Famines at the local level have erupted ... health clinics and schools have been closed down; hundreds of millions of children have been denied the right to primary education. ... there has been a resurgence of infectious diseases including tuberculosis, malaria and cholera. ...

... The increasing levels of global poverty resulting from economic restructuring are casually denied by G7 governments and international institutions ... social realities are concealed, official statistics are manipulated, economic concepts are turned upside down. In turn, public opinion is bombarded in the media with glowing images of global growth and prosperity. ...

(Michel Chossudovsky, "Global Poverty in the Late 20th Century," *Journal of International Affairs*, Vol. 52, no. 1, Fall 1998)

David S. Landes expresses concern over the futures of rich and poor (1998): The old division of the world into two power blocs, East and West, has subsided. Now the big challenge and threat is the gap in wealth and health that separates rich and poor. These are often styled North and South ... but a more accurate signifier would be the West and the Rest ... Here is the greatest single problem and danger facing the world in the Third Millennium. ...

... Our task (the rich countries), in our own interest as well as theirs, is to help the poor become healthier and wealthier. If we do not, they will seek to take what they cannot make; and if they cannot earn by exporting commodities, they will export people. In short, wealth is an irresistible magnet; and poverty is a potentially raging contaminant: it cannot be segregated, and our peace and prosperity depend in the long run on the well-being of others.

(David S. Landes, *The Wealth and Poverty of Nations: why Some are so Rich and Some So Poor*, New York–London: W.W. Norton, 1998)

Nancy Birdsall on learning to live with inequality (1998): Belying Marx, the biggest story of the last 150 years has been the emergence in the West of a prosperous and stable middle class. But it took time. During a long transition from agriculture to industry, changes in production and in the structure of employment caused wrenching inequality. Much inequality today may be the natural outcome of what is an analogous transition from an industrial to an information age.

Still, there is no reason to despair. Some inequality is healthy and will speed the transition. The rapidly growing wages of the educated and skilled are making education and training much more attractive personal investments. As more people get greater access to education, their relative income advantage over the unskilled will decline. ... More fundamentally, people may care less about their current ranking in a static picture of global income distribution than about just and fair access to a better future, especially for their children. In an unequal world, good opportunities represent fair rules and matter at least as much as current status. Greater opportunities—which can be delivered today—are a better guarantee of a socially coherent global community than improved distribution tomorrow.

(Nancy Birdsall, "Life is Unfair: Inequality in the World," *Foreign Policy*, No. 111, Summer 1998) conflicts elsewhere in the world, take service under military strongmen who "buy war" in order to gain or keep power. Some states spend twice as much on the military as on health; others a mammoth ten times as much (Nigeria and Angola in Africa, for example, Iraq and Kuwait in the Middle East, and Pakistan and North and South Korea in Asia).

Thus armed, strongman follows strongman in a series of coups and comebacks, increasing the sum of violence. Between 1900 and 1990, 237 wars had been fought worldwide, compared to 205 in the previous century, or 68 in the eighteenth. Even relative to an increased population, the twentieth was the most violent century in human history. In the eighteenth century, wars caused about 5 deaths per 1000 people; in the nineteenth century, 6; in the twentieth, 46.

When the military gain power—and some 40 percent of the world's states today are controlled by military men—not only is there more violence, but there are violations of the standards of human rights established by the United Nations in 1948. Torture— revived by the Cheka under the Bolsheviks, the Nazis, and French colonial forces—is inflicted on prisoners around the world; citizens are raped, beaten, and slain; political opponents are murdered; the press, radio, television and the Internet are muzzled.

With the memory of the Nazi attempt to exterminate the Jews still vivid, the postwar world has also experienced recent episodes of genocide. Defined by the 1948 UN Convention on the Prevention and Punishment of the Crime of Genocide as "acts committed with intent to destroy, in whole or in part, a national, ethnical, racial, or religious group," modern genocide began early in the twentieth century with the Turkish persecution of their Armenian minority. More recently, genocidal warfare overwhelmed the neighboring African states of Rwanda and Burundi.

For centuries, the Tutsi tribespeople of Rwanda and Burundi had dominated a Hutu majority (about 80 percent of the population), in a pattern encouraged by Belgian administrators after 1918. Upon the achievement of independence in 1962, the Hutus were granted political rights. Yet persistent tensions erupted violently in 1965, 1969, 1972, and 1988, mounting to full civil war in 1994. As a Tutsi army drove Hutu forces to the frontier, fleeing Hutus massacred hundreds of thousands of Tutsi men, women, and children—at least 500,000, and perhaps as many as 800,000, out of a population of seven and a half million. Three million Hutus (including many of the killers) took refuge in Zaire and Tanzania, where, corralled in refugee camps, they suffered from starvation and disease. Many returned to Rwanda, where ethnic violence continues and resolution is not in sight.

In the Balkans, on Europe's southeastern frontier, enduring hatreds flared up in the 1990s between orthodox Christian Serbs, Roman Catholic Croatians, and Muslim Bosnians, all southern Slavs

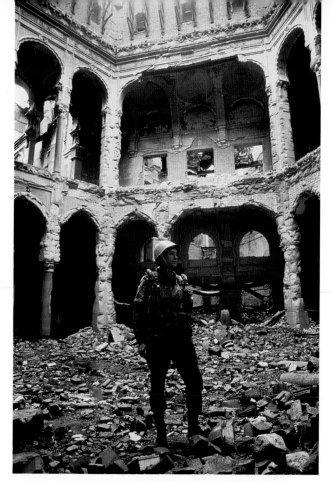

From civilization to barbarism: *Heavy and protracted fighting in the Bosnian capital Sarajevo (in the former Yugoslavia) reduced much of that city, a center of European culture, to rubble. Here, a UN peace-keeper surveys the city's wrecked library in February 1994.*

speaking the same tongue (although using different alphabets). For 35 years, the independent communist leader Marshall Tito (Josip Broz, 1891–1980) had kept these mutually hostile groups together in a union of "all Slavs," or "Yugoslavia." When Tito died in 1980, the union was shaken. It disintegrated with the collapse of communism in 1989.

Yugoslavia dissolved into six federated republics— Croatia, Slovenia, Bosnia-Herzogovina, Montenegro, Macedonia, and Serbia. The two "autonomous regions" of Vojvodina and Kosovo lay within Serbia, which maintained the army of the former Yugoslav state. Slovenia and Croatia withdrew from the federation in 1991, and many of the Serb minority joined the Serbian army to prevent their secession.

Meanwhile, Bosnia-Herzogovina also sought to secede from the Serbian-led federation. Its Orthodox Serb minority (about 33 percent of a population that was also 44 percent Muslim Slav and 17 percent Catholic Croatian) resisted the March 1992 plebiscite in which a majority voted for independence. Bosnian Serbs, including many Yugoslav army veterans, constituted themselves the "Serbian Republic of Bosnia-Herzegovina" and besieged the capital of Sarajevo. Over the next three years, backed by Serbia under Slobodan Milosevic (b. 1941) and the regular Yugoslav army, they starved and bombed the city. In a campaign of "ethnic cleansing"—the horrifying term born of this last European conflict—Serb forces persecuted, expelled, bullied, raped, and killed Bosnian Muslims. All contenders were guilty of atrocities, but the massacres by Serbs of thousands in Srebenica in 1995 especially outraged international observers.

The constituent nations of the European Union, NATO, and the United Nations (employing the US air force to enforce its decreed "no-fly zone") all attempted to halt the carnage in the Balkans. By the American-sponsored Dayton (Ohio) Peace Agreement of November 1995, the republic was divided into Serbian and Muslim–Croat entities, to be ruled by a single parliament, elected under the eye of United Nations peacekeeping troops. New Serb atrocities in 1999 against the Albanian Muslims of Kosovo provoked further warfare and refugee flight, as Milosevic pressed for ethnic Serb domination of an expanded Yugoslav state. The war finally ended only in October 2000, when a spontaneous coup in the capital at Belgrade resulted in the deposition of Milosevic and the election as president of Vojislav Kostunica, a professor of law, who has since led Serbia towards the rule of law.

Among the provisions of the Dayton accord was one that war criminals on both sides would be identified and prosecuted. Massacre, torture, and military rape, all considered illegal by international conventions (rape since 1996), were prominent features of the "ethnic cleansing" of Bosnia-Herzogovina, as they were of most recent wars. The determination to bring to justice those who violate the limits of permissible military violence is another aspect of the gathering world consensus on issues of human dignity and freedom. Several Serbian generals were arrested and put on trial in the Hague, the Netherlands, by the UN International Criminal Tribune. In 2001, they were joined by Milosevic—who had been indicted in 1999 for war crimes committed by Serbian forces in the 1998–1999 conflict in Kosovo—including rape (first defined as a war crime in international law in 1998), massacre, arson, and torture. Kostunica had said he would not send Milosevic abroad for trail, but his covert extradition was managed by Serbian Prime Minister Zoran Djindjic.

The prosecution of those who in positions of political or military leadership committed acts the world no longer deems acceptable or forgivable is a new feature of the international landscape, and promises to be frequent and diligent. Although the Cambodian Pol Pot (b. 1925/28) escaped prosecution (as leader of the Khmer Rouge faction he had been responsible for the death of nearly two million of the seven million Cambodian citizens between 1975 and 1979 by forced labor, starvation, disease, torture, or execution), having died peacefully of a heart attack in

1998, he was officially condemned for his actions. Similarly, the former Chilean president Augusto Pinochet (b. 1915), although excused from prosecution by a Chilean court, was held responsible by British and Spanish courts for violations of human rights committed following his 1973 rise to power. In other cases judicial retribution has been successful. In Tanzania in 2001, where the International Criminal Tribunal for Rwanda was in its fifth year of hearings in the summer of 2001, of 63 persons indicted as leading conspirators in the Hutu genocidal assault on Tutsi tribespeople in 1994, 49 were in custody, and 9 had been convicted. In such cases, the principle is firmly established that leaders, no matter how powerful, cannot escape responsibility for their actions.

Beyond the zone of the Western democratic states, and even beyond the structures of the nation-state, has emerged in recent years a new source of explosive violence: leaders and organizations who engage in terrorism. The prolonged standoff in the Middle East between Israel and the neighboring Arab states (see Chapter 29) has been a prime site for terror. For more than a decade, mostly young male Palestinians have resisted what they perceive as Israeli abuses and even the presence of the state of Israel with assaults on Israeli soldiers and suicide bombings in Israeli cities. While supporters of Israel are horrified by the trail of assassination and murder, supporters of the Palestinian cause recall the massacre of 29 Arabs at prayer in a mosque in Hebron in January 1997 by an Israeli zealot and, more recently, the retaliatory strikes by Israeli forces against Palestinian terrorist acts.

Outside of the Israeli theater, other incidents of terrorism have been a source of alarm. These include

Kostunica waving at crowds: *In October 2000, a coup in the capital of Belgrade resulted in the deposition of Serbian dictator Slobodan Milosevic (later extradited to the Hague, the Netherlands, to face trial for war crimes) and the election as president of Vajislav Kostunica, shown here greeting the crowd.*

Let's Roll: the War on Terror

On September 11, 2001, three of the four planes hijacked by terrorists of Osama Bin Laden's Al Quaeda organization hit their targets; one crashed, probably brought down by a few doomed passengers determined not to die without fighting, whose last words were heard by cell phone just before the plane exploded: "Let's roll!" Their action inaugurated the war soon launched officially by President George W. Bush against the terrorists and any nation that harbored them. Here are some voices from the early days of that struggle: of New York City mayor Rudolph Giuliani, whose heroic management of the catastrophic hit to the World Trade Center was admired across the US; of Muslim-born novelist Salman Rushdie, a victim and critic of militant Islamism; and of Bin Laden himself.

Rudolph Giuliani tells the United Nations that on the other side of democracy is tyranny (October 1, 2001): Our belief in religious freedom, political freedom, economic freedom—that's what makes an American. Our belief in democracy, the rule of law and respect for human life. That's how you become an American. ...

It's tragic and perverse that it's because of these very principles ... that we find ourselves under attack by terrorists. Our freedom threatens them because they know if our ideas of freedom gain a foothold among their people, it will destroy their power. ... The terrorists have no ideas or ideals with which to combat freedom and democracy. So their only defense is to strike out against innocent civilians, destroying human life in massive numbers and hoping to deter all of us from our pursuit ... of freedom. ...

But the long-term deterrent of spreading our ideals throughout the world is just not enough. ... The United Nations must hold accountable any country that supports or condones terrorism. ... It must ostracize any nation that supports terrorism. It must isolate any nation that remains neutral in the fight against terrorism. ... This is not a time for further study or vague directives.

The evidence of terrorism's brutality and inhumanity, of its contempt for life and the concept of peace is lying beneath the rubble of the World Trade Center less than two miles from where we meet today. Look at that destruction, that massive, senseless, cruel loss of human life and then I ask you to look in your hearts and recognize that there is no room for neutrality on the issue of terrorism. You're either with civilization or with terrorists. On one side is democracy, the rule of law and respect for human life. On the other is tyranny, arbitrary executions and mass murder.
(*The New York Times*, 10/2/01)

Salman Rushdie declares that, yes, this is about Islam: (November 2, 2001): "This isn't about Islam." The world's leaders have been repeating this mantra for weeks, partly in the virtuous hope of deterring reprisal attacks on innocent Muslims living in the West, partly because if the United States is to maintain its coalition against terror it can't afford to suggest that Islam and terrorism are in any way related.

The trouble with this necessary disclaimer is that it isn't true. If this isn't about Islam, why the worldwide Muslim demonstrations in support of Osama bin Laden and Al Qaeda? Why did those 10,000 men armed with swords and axes mass on the Pakistan–Afghanistan frontier, answering some mullah's call to jihad? Why are the war's first British casualties three Muslim men who died fighting on the Taliban side? ...

In recent weeks Muslim voices have everywhere been raised against the obscurantist hijacking of their religion. Yesterday's hotheads ... are improbably repackaging themselves as today's pussycats. ... If Islam is to be reconciled with modernity, these voices must be encouraged until they swell into a roar. ...

The restoration of religion to the sphere of the personal, its depoliticization, is the nettle that all Muslim societies must grasp in order to become modern. The only aspect of modernity interesting to the terrorists is technology ... a weapon that can be turned on its makers. If terrorism is to be defeated, the world of Islam must take on board the secularist-humanist principles on which the modern is based, and without which Muslim countries' freedom will remain a distant dream.
(*The New York Times*, 11/2/01)

Osama Bin Laden announces "Our Terrorism is Against America" (December 27, 2001): If their economy ends, they will busy themselves away from the enslavement of oppressed people ... It is important to concentrate on the destruction of the American economy.

Our terrorism is against America. Our terrorism is a blessed terrorism to prevent the unjust person from committing injustice and to stop American support for Israel, which kills our sons.

They (nineteen hijackers) used the enemy's planes and studied at enemy schools, without the need for training camps. But God helped them and taught this cruel lesson to those arrogant people who see freedom only for the white race and keep other nations humiliated and oppressed.
(Excerpts of Osama Bin Laden's videotaped comments aired on the Qatar-based Al-Jazeera television, December 27, 2001; *The New York Times*, 12/27/01)

American citizens and sites culminated, on September 11, 2001, in the greatest act of terrorism known to history. The earlier strikes included the bombing of an American plane over Lockerbie, Scotland in December 1988 (by terrorists protected by Libya); the failed attempt to bomb the World Trade Center in New York City in 1993, masterminded by an Islamist cleric; and the bombing of an US Air Force base at Khobar Towers in Dharan, Saudi Arabia in June 1996; of American embassies in Kenya and Tanzania in August 1998; of an American ship, the USS Cole, in Aden harbor, Yemen, in October 2000.

All of these last events are linked to militant Islamist movements in North Africa and the Middle East, apparently engaged in a crusade against modernizing secular states seen as corrupt and decadent, and especially against the United States. After 1993, and protected after 1995 by the radically conservative Taliban regime in Afghanistan, these groups have gelled under the leadership of the Saudi self-exile Osama Bin Laden in the Al Quaeda international terrorist organization. It was apparently Bin Laden who ordered and approved the September 11 strike— a suicide bombing by four planes targeting key US sites resulting in more than 3000 civilian deaths. In response to that incident, the US led a coalition of nations in a "War against Terrorism," marked by the highly focused and successful use of "smart" air power to obtain pinpoint objectives with minimum civilian or military casualties. That war effectively disabled Al Quaeda operations in Afghanistan as well as the Taliban regime which sheltered the

Terrorist Attack on World Trade Centre: *The horror and desolation of the scene in lower Manhattan, New York City, after the two great World Trade Center towers, emblems of American prosperity and daring, were struck by two different airplanes hijacked by squads of suicidal terrorists. Above, the upper floors of the towers are seen burning behind the landmark Brooklyn Bridge. Below, a lone observer in a wilderness of smoke and dust and the skeletal remains of the fallen towers.*

the attacks of Italy's Red Brigades, responsible for the 1978 murder of premier Aldo Moro, and repeated strikes by the Irish Republican Army, Basque separatists in Spain, and Kurdish rebels in Turkey. A sequence of terrorist attacks targeting mostly

The Future of the West

What role will the West play in the globalized world of the future? Here, Francis Fukayama argues that the Western liberal IDEA will continue to dominate in a new world; Bernard Lewis points out, in defense of the West, that it is the only civilization that has reflected upon and condemned its past errors; Samuel Huntington predicts a decline in the West, partly due to the failure of Western culture to value its own achievement; and Václav Havel pinpoints as the particular task of the West the dissemination of its "finest spiritual and intellectual traditions."

Francis Fukuyama looks at the future hegemony of Western Culture (1992): As mankind approaches the end of the millennium, the twin crises of authoritarianism and socialist central planning have left only one competitor standing in the ring as an ideology of potentially universal validity: liberal democracy, the doctrine of individual freedom and popular sovereignty. ...

What is emerging victorious ... is ... the liberal *idea*. That is to say, for a very large part of the world, there is now no ideology with pretensions to challenge liberal democracy, and no universal principle of legitimacy other than the sovereignty of the people. ...

(Francis Fukuyama, *The End of History and the Last Man*, Free Press, 1992)

Bernard Lewis asks if the place of the West in world history is a grossly undervalued achievement? (1994): In setting out to conquer, subjugate, and despoil other peoples, the Europeans were merely following the example set them by their neighbors and predecessors ... The interesting questions are not why they tried, but why they succeeded—and then why, having succeeded, they repented of their success as a sin. The success was unique in modern times; the repentance, in all of recorded history. ...

Imperialism, sexism, and *racism* are words of Western coinage—not because the West invented these evils, which are, alas, universal, but because the West recognized and named and condemned them as evils and struggled mightily to weaken their hold and to help their victims. If ... Western culture does indeed "go" [i.e. die out] imperialism, sexism, and racism will not go with it. More likely casualties will be the freedom to denounce them and the effort to end them.

(Bernard Lewis, "Eurocentrism Revisited, 1994" excerpted from *Commentary*, December 1994)

Samuel P. Huntington examines the decline of the West and the de-Westernization of the United States: (1996): Historically American national identity has been defined culturally by the heritage of Western civilization and politically by the principles of the American Creed on which Americans overwhelmingly agree: liberty, democracy, individualism, equality before the law, constitutionalism, private property. In the late twentieth century both components of American identity have come under concentrated and sustained onslaught from a small but influential number of intellectuals and publicists. In the name of multiculturalism they have attacked the identification of the United States with Western civilization, denied the existence of a common American culture, and promoted racial, ethnic, and other subnational cultural identities ...

The American multiculturalists ... reject their country's cultural heritage... [proposing] to create a country ... not belonging to any civilization and lacking a cultural core. History shows that no country so constituted can long endure as a coherent society. A multicivilizational United States will not be the United States; it will be the United Nations. ...

Rejection of the Creed and of Western civilization means the end of the United States of America as we have known it. It also means effectively the end of Western civilization. If the United States is de-Westernized, the West is reduced to Europe and a few lightly populated overseas European settler countries. Without the United States the West becomes a minuscule and declining part of the world's population on a small and inconsequential peninsula at the extremity of the Eurasian land mass.

(Samuel P. Huntington, *The Clash of Civilizations and the Remaking of World Order*, New York: Simon & Schuster, 1996)

Václav Havel discusses Europe's role for the twenty-first century (1996): Humanity is entering an era of multipolar and multicultural civilization. Europe is no longer the conductor of the global orchestra, but this does not mean it has nothing more to say to the world. A new task now presents itself, and with it a new meaning to Europe's very existence.

That task will no longer be to spread—violently or non-violently—its own religion, its own civilization, its own inventions, or its own power. Nor will it be to preach the rule of law, democracy, human rights, or justice to the rest of the world.

If Europe wishes, it can do something more modest yet more beneficial. It can become a model for how different peoples can work together in peace ... Moreover, Europe has one final possibility, if it so desires: it can reclaim its finest spiritual and intellectual traditions, ... and join ... in a search for the common moral minimum necessary to guide us all so that we may live side by side on one planet and confront jointly whatever threatens our lives together.

(*New York Review of Books*, 6/20/96, p. 41)

terrorists. Its unintended consequence has been the successful reassertion, as the world of nations opens a new century and a new millennium, of US primacy in military power.

Militarism, fanaticism, torture, genocide, and terror—these overshadowed the last decades of the twentieth century and the dawn of the twenty-first, even as the powerful nations of the developed world, the Cold War behind them, settled down to the business of building a prosperous global village based on technological innovation.

THE END OF THE WEST?

Where is the West in a global world? Has the West lost its importance, and its identity? Have its historical failings disqualified it for leadership, or require it to abandon its claims for greatness? Does the arrival of the post-Soviet, post-industrial, postmodern era mean the coming of the end of the West?

Western civilization has endured many vicissitudes, and will likely endure. In the twentieth century, two terrible wars threatened to destroy. But the West has recovered, and the principles of human rights, individual freedom, and parliamentary democracy have been vindicated. They are imitated worldwide. It is the primary goal of most of the nations of the developing world to establish civil societies on the model of those that exist in the Western world, resting on the core values of Western civilization.

Western civilization has evolved its core values over more than a thousand years. They include: (1) the principle of human dignity: that all human beings are equal in worth, that they possess rights which cannot be taken away, and that to the greatest possible degree they are free; (2) the ideal of justice: that no person should be unfairly privileged above another; (3) the value of democracy: that the power to shape the future of a community belongs to its people as a whole and not to arbitrarily selected leaders; (4) the method of rationalism, which assumes that all phenomena (even those pertaining to God, essence, or spirit) may be subject to the critical scrutiny of the human mind; (5) the inclination to progress, to work towards goals to be achieved in the future; (6) the habit of self-examination, which encourages human beings to examine themselves seriously and often to test whether they have fulfilled their promise and their responsibilities.

The last of these—the habit of self-examination— has yielded a rich harvest of criticisms of Western societies. Over the last centuries, the nations of the West arrogated to themselves power over the other regions of the world, drained them of wealth, and subjected their peoples to inferior status. They created and defended the Atlantic system of slavery, and more than a century after its abolition, have not yet wholly admitted the descendants of slaves into full

participation in the societies to which they were forcibly brought. In the name of Christianity, those nations have waged wars against other nations and peoples, compelled conformity through terror and torture, and excluded dissenters, if they did not actively persecute them, from participation in political and social life. In the service of its ideologies, most notoriously Nazism, Western civilization has spawned episodes of genocide. Characterized by patriarchal family structures, Western societies have injured the women and children whose destinies have been determined by the status concerns of authoritative males. Western expansionism has led to the unrestrained industrialization of regions of the world, resulting in environmental degradation and human misery.

All of these charges are, to some extent, true. It is also true, however, that other civilizations have been brutal and aggressive, characterized by patriarchalism, and buttressed by slavery. The Western world, however, is alone in repudiating those behaviors that, by its own moral standards, it has come to condemn. The West has rejected intolerance, terror, torture, and tyranny; it has admitted women and the descendants of slaves to full participation in civic life; it has recognized the need to protect the natural environment and to foster health and education of all its citizens. These stances, as much as the troubled legacy of past failings, are the harvest of the Western experience.

Astride the Prime Meridian: *These schoolchildren harbor no doubts about the meaning of the West. The West lies on one side of the line of longitude that runs through Greenwich, England, from pole to pole; on the other side is the East.*

Conclusion
THE PAST, THE FUTURE, AND THE MEANING OF THE WEST

As Britain battled its way to world empire during the eighteenth century, the astronomers in the Royal Observatory at Greenwich (southeast London) resolved the thorny problem of longitude with the aid of newly refined chronometers. Their system was anchored by the time current in Greenwich, at a point which, as an international conference held in 1884 established, would define the Prime Meridian. The Prime Meridian is that line of longitude that divides East and West, and serves as a universal standard of space and time. It runs from pole to pole through Greenwich, thus conceived to be the preeminent point on Earth. Its creation was an act both of scientific imagination and astounding arrogance. It is a reminder of the ease with which the West could once partition the globe. Then there was no ambiguity about the question: "where, and what, is the West?"

Nor should there be now. The West is not so clearly a place as it once was. It is not simply the western part of Europe, or the western hemisphere; parts of the West (Australasia, for instance) are not in the "west" in any geographical sense at all. The West is its civilization, its cultural heritage, and the moral and intellectual values that heritage has nurtured. A consideration of the map of the world shows that the West is everywhere—not only in the core area of Europe where its civilization was first developed, but in the regions of European settlement, and ultimately in every part of the inhabited world to which Western influence has extended.

And so the West, while it is no longer anywhere in particular on the globe, is everywhere. As a civilization, a cultural tradition, a set of moral and intellectual values, it exists wherever people take positive steps to study its past, value its wealth of attainments, and work for its future—people like the students who read this book. The future of the West lies with you, who may choose to take up the exciting mission Ulysses embraced when he resolved to sail westward, striving, seeking, finding, not yielding, but roaming ever with a hungry heart.

SUGGESTED RESOURCES

Evans, Gareth, *Cooperating for Peace: The Global Agenda for the 1990s and Beyond* (London: Allen and Unwin, 1994). Written by a foreign minister of Australia. Explores the abilities and role of the UN as an international peacekeeper. Argues too little emphasis has been accorded so far to pre-emptive diplomacy as a means of peaceful conflict resolution.

Fukuyama, Francis, *The End of History and the Last Man* (New York: Free Press, 1992). Controversial. Written immediately after the end of the Cold War. Argues that history is a teleological (i.e. goal-oriented) process that has effectively now come to an end with the triumph of free markets and liberal democracy across the world. Humankind's future—at least in terms of basic economic and political systems—will be much like the present, says Fukuyama.

Heilbroner, Robert, *Visions of the Future: The Distant Past, Yesterday, Today, Tomorrow* (New York: Oxford University Press, 1995). Capitalism has become supreme all across the globe, and is currently embarked on an unprecedented project of capital accumulation. Heilbroner, one of America's most important and readable economic historians, ponders the meaning and ramifications of these developments.

Huntington, Samuel P, *The Clash of Civilizations and the Remaking of World Order* (New York: Simon & Schuster, 1996). Views the coming century in relatively somber tones. Huntington foresees increasingly vigorous opposition among non-Western countries to the global hegemony of free-markets, democracy, and Western culture in general.

Kennedy, Paul, *Preparing for the Twenty-First Century* (New York: Random House, 1993). Stressing demographic pressures in the developing countries, foreshadows possible catastrophe if the wealthier nations do not take prior action.

Kindleberger, Charles, *World Economic Primacy: 1500–1990* (Oxford: Oxford University Press, 1998). Economic-historical study of economic primacy—what it is, which powers have wielded it and why, and so on. Covers great economic powers from Venice to the US, Britain to Japan. Kindleberger is generally pessimistic about America's future as a great economic power.

Landes, David S, *The Wealth and Poverty of Nations: Why Some Are So Rich and Some So Poor* (New York: Norton, 1998). Thought-provoking study of the global distribution of wealth. Landes argues that what has made some nations rich and left others poor is their success in industrializing their economies.

Sowell, Thomas, *Conquests and Cultures* (New York: Basic Books, 1998). Third of three volumes discussing the transfer of culture and its role in the creation of the modern world. Earlier volumes focus on race and migration; here Sowell concentrates on physical conquest as a means of effecting cultural transfer, and in particular on the reasons for the great success of European culture around the world.

White, Donald W., *The American Century: The Rise and Decline of the United States as a World Power* (New Haven: Yale University Press, 1997). Examines America's idea of itself as a nation with a world role. Focuses particularly on the 1940s as both the origin and apotheosis this "social myth."

World and political maps: http://www.atlapedia.com/

Elections around the world: www.electionworld.org

The World Factbook 2001: http://www.bartleby.com/151

PICTURE CREDITS

All numbers refer to page numbers (t=top; b=bottom; l=left; r=right; c=center)

CHAPTER 15
417 The Battle of Pavia (detail), 1525, Museo di Capodimonte/Scala; 419t AKG London; 419b Mary Evans Picture Library, London; 420 English Heritage Photo Library; 432b Cameraphoto Arte, Venice; 436 RMN-Jean/Lewandowski, Paris; 443t RMN-Gèrard Blot, Paris; 443b Institut Amatller DíArt Hispànic, Barcelona

CHAPTER 16
447 detail of 450; 450 Artothek, Peissenberg; 451 © Patrimonio Nacional, Madrid; 453tr, 468, 475 Mary Evans Picture Library, London; 453b, 469b Hulton Getty, London; 460t AKG London; 469t Bridgeman Art Library

CHAPTER 17
483 Rembrandt, sketch of a woman reading (detail), 1634, Library of Congress; 484t, 498 AKG London; 486 Science Museum/Science and Society Picture Library, London; 487 Scala, Florence; 491l from Charles Singer, *The Discovery of the Circulation of the Blood*, London, 1956, courtesy Mr. A.W. Singer; 491r, 507tl Wellcome Institute Library, London; 499 photo: © Metropolitan Museum of Art, New York. Harris Brisbane Dick Fund, 1930 (30.67.2); 504 RMN-Hervé Lewandowski; 507bl Mary Evans Picture Library, London; 507r from Hevelius, *Machinae Coelestis*; 508t RMN-Arnaudet; 508b RMN-Gérard Blot

CHAPTER 18
513 detail of 532; 516 © Paul M. R. Maeyaert, Mont de l'Encus (Orroir), Belgium; 517 RMN-Gérard Blot; 522 RMN-R.G. Ojeda; 523 AKG London; 525 Giraudon, Paris; 531tl © Studio Fotografico Quattrone, Florence; 531tr Bibliothèque Nationale, France; 531b The State Hermitage Museum, St. Petersburg, Russia/with the assistance of Petrushka Ltd, Moscow; 534 photo:Ursula Seitz-Gray; 538t The Art Archive, London; 538b Bulloz, Paris

CHAPTER 19
543 detail of 551tr; 551l courtesy American Antiquarian Society, Worcester, MA; 551tr Gift of Ms. Gwendolyn O.L. Conkling (40.59.A); 551br Hulton Getty, London; 553r photo: John Lee; 561 AKG London; 564l photo: Bob Schalkwijk; 564r Bridgeman Art Library, London; 572 Harris Brisbane Fund, 1929 (29.88.3[3])

CHAPTER 20
577 detail of 605; 581, 599, 602 RMN; 586 Photothèque des Musées de la Ville de Paris/Toumazet/P.H. Ladet; 590, 598 Bridgeman Art Library, London; 591 Mary Evans Picture Library, London; 592tl Photothèque des Musées de la Ville de Paris/Berthier; 592cl Photothèque des Musées de la Ville de Paris/Jean-Yve Trocaz; 600tl, 601b AKG London; 600bl+r Mary Evans Picture Library, London; 601t Hulton Getty, London

CHAPTER 21
611 detail of 621bl; 618t Mary Evans Picture Library, London; 618c Ann Ronan Picture Library/Image Select, London; 618b AKG London; 621tl Science Museum/Science and Society Picture Library, London; 621bl+br Hulton Getty, London; 621tr Courtesy Encyclopædia Britannica Inc./Permission by the Syndics of the Cambridge University Library; 624t The Illustrated London News Picture Library, London; 624b Mansell Collection/Time Inc./Katz Pictures, London; 625 Paul M.R. Maeyaert, Mont de l'Enclus (Orroir), Belgium; 626 Deutsches Museum, Munich; 635 United Nations/DPI, New York

CHAPTER 22
639 detail of 648tl; 643t AKG London; 643c Mary Evans Picture Library, London ; 643b © Fried. Krupp GmbH/Historisches Archiv Krupp, Essen, Germany; 648tl, 648tr, 658, 660 Hulton Getty, London; 648br Lauros-Giraudon, Paris; 652 Giraudon, Paris; 653 Bibliothèque Nationale, Paris; 661 RMN-Hervé Lewandowski

CHAPTER 23
665 detail of 684br; 674 AKG London; 675 Hulton Getty, London; 678 Photothèque des Musées de la Ville de Paris/Joffre; 681 Bismarck Museum; 684l RMN; 684br Bridgeman Art Library, London

CHAPTER 24
689 detail of 701; 695 Bridgeman Art Library, London; 707t © M&E Bernheim/Woodfin Camp & Associates, New York; 707b Hulton Getty, London; 711tl Bibliothèque Nationale, France; 711tr Harper's Weekly/Weidenfeld & Nicholson Archives; 711b Wiener Library, London

CHAPTER 25
719 detail of 740c ; 722tl RMN-Hervé Lewandowski; 727t © Punch Ltd; 727b The Curie and Joliot-Curie Association, Paris; 740t Giraudon, Paris

CHAPTER 26
745 detail of Otto Dix, *Wounded (Fall 1916 Bapaume)*/Private Collection; 750 Bibliothèque Nationale, France; 751t + c Novosti, London; 751b SCR Photo Library, London; 752 AKG London; 759 Paul M.R. Maeyaert, Mont de l'Enclus (Orroir), Belgium

CHAPTER 27
771 detail of 774b; 773 Culver Pictures, New York; 774t Bridgeman Art Library/© ADAGP, Paris and DACS, London 1999; 775 Tulane University, Hogan Jazz Archive; 783 Mary Evans Picture Library, London; 789tl AKG London; 789tr Corbis, London; 789b The Art Archive, London; 792t Topham Picturepoint; 792b photo: San Francisco Art Commission

CHAPTER 28
797 detail of 814; 805, 823l Novosti, London; 806 David King Collection, London; 814, 825tl AKG London; 818 David Low/Evening Standard/Solo Syndication, London/photo: University of Kent, UK; 823r Corbis, London; 825bl Camera Press, London; 825tr Yad Vashem Photo Archives, courtesy USHMM Photo Archives, Washington D.C.; 825br Topham Picturepoint; 826 Rex Features, London

CHAPTER 29
831 detail of 859; 834 Hulton Getty, London; 839 Rex Features, London; 849 David King Collection, London; 850 Stuart Franklin/Magnum, London; 855 Burt Glinn/Magnum, London; 859 Nick Ut/Associated Press, London; 862t Bob Henriques/Magnum, London; 862bl UPI/Corbis, London; 862r Associated Press, London

CHAPTER 30
867 detail of 870b; 870l Topham Picturepoint; 870r Archive Photos, New York; 872l Corbis-Bettmann, London; 872r Corbis-Bettmann/UPI, London; 875t+b Popperfoto, Northampton, UK; 879 Associated Press, London; 884t Paul Conklin/© Time Inc/Katz Pictures, London; 884b Ans Westra, Lower Hutt, NZ; 890tl Sayyid Azim/Associated Press, London; 890tr John Ward Anderson/The Washington Post, Washington, D.C.; 890b A.Chin/NYT Pictures, New York

EPILOGUE
898l+r, 909 Reuters/Popperfoto, Northampton, UK; 899 Popperfoto, Northampton, UK; 906 Epix/Sygma, London; 907 Rex Features, London; 911 Peter Kent, London

LITERARY CREDITS

Nancy Birdsall: from "Life is Unfair: Inequality in the World" by Nancy Birdsall from *Foreign Policy, Number 111* (Summer, 1998); **Blackwell Publishers**: "Decree of the Provveditori alla Sanità, February 22, 1522" from *Venice: A Documentary History, 1450–1630*, edited by David Chambers and Brian Pullan (Blackwell, 1992); **Georges Borchardt Inc**: from *The Kingdom of Memory* by Elie Wiesel (Elirion, 1990); **Michel Chossudovsky**: from "Global Poverty in the Late-20th Century" by Michel Chossudovsky from *Journal of International Affairs*, Volume 52, No. 1 (Fall, 1998); **The Gioi Publishers**: from "Declaration of Independence of the Democratic Republic of Vietnam" by Ho Chi Minh from *Selected Writings* by Ho Chi Minh (Hanoi: Foreign Languages Publishing House, 1977); **HarperCollins Publishers Inc**: from *A History of Their Own: Women in Europe from Prehistory to the Present, Volume 2* by Bonnie S. Anderson and Judith P. Zinsser (Harper & Row, 1988); **HMSO**: from *Documents on British Foreign Policy, 1919–1939*, edited by E. L. Woodward and Rohan Butler. 3rd Series (HMSO, 1954); **Houghton Mifflin Company**: from *Mein Kampf* by Adolf Hitler, translated by Ralph Manheim (Houghton Mifflin, 1943), © 1943, renewed 1971 by Houghton Mifflin Company; **Nikki Keddie**: "On the Importance of Science" by Al-Afghani from *Islamic Response to Imperialism: Political and Religious Writings of Sayyid Jam I al-Din n al-Afghani*, edited/translated by Nikki Keddie (University of California Press, 1983); **The New York Review of Books**: from Vaýclav Havel's *Address to the Canadian Senate and House of Commons* (April 29, 1999), translated by Paul Wilson, from The New York Review of Books (June 10, 1999), © 1999 NYREV Inc; **The Orion Publishing Group**: from "The Condition of the Working Class in England, 1844" by Friedrich Engels, in *Engels, Manchester and the Working Class* by S. Marcus (Weidenfeld & Nicolson, 1974); **Oxford University Press Inc**: from "Eurocentrism Revisited, 1994" by Bernard Lewis from *Cultures in Conflict: Christians, Muslims, and Jews in the Age of Discovery* by Bernard Lewis (Oxford University Press, 1995), © 1995 by Oxford University

Press Inc; **Penguin Putnam Inc**: from *Notes from Underground and the Grand Inquisitor* by Fyodor Dostoevsky, translated by Ralph E. Matlaw, translation © 1960, 1988 by E. P. Dutton; Penguin UK: from *The Book of the Courtier* by Baldassare Castiglione, translated by George Bull (Penguin Classics, 1967), © George Bull, 1967; **Prentice-Hall Inc**: from *A Documentary Survey of the French Revolution*, translated by J. H. Stewart (Macmillan, 1951), © 1951; "The Attack of King Industry" by Dalpatram Kavi, translated by Howard Spodek and Chimanbhai Privedi, in *The World's History* by Howard Spodek (Prentice-Hall, 1998), © 1998 Howard Spodek; **Random House Inc**: from *Restless Days* by Lilo Linke, © 1935 by Alfred A. Knopf Inc and renewed 1963 by Lilo Linke; from *Preparing for the Twenty-First Century* by Paul Kennedy (Random House, 1993), © 1993 by Paul Kennedy; **Salman Rushdie**: from article on Islam from *The New York Times* (November 2, 2001); Amartya Sen: from "A World Not Neatly Divided" by Amartya Sen from *The New York Times* (November 23, 2001); **Simon & Schuster Inc**: from *Hope Against Hope: A Memoir* by Nadezhda Mandelstam, translated by Max Hayward (Macmillan, 1970), © 1970 Atheneum Publishers, English translation © 1970 Atheneum Publishers; from *The Clash of Civilizations and the Remaking of World Order* by Samuel P. Huntington (Simon & Schuster, 1996), © 1996 by Samuel P. Huntingdon; A. P. Watt Ltd. on behalf of **The National Trust for Places of Historic Interest or National Beauty**: from "The White Man's Burden" by Rudyard Kipling from *Rudyard Kipling: Selected Poems*, edited by Peter Keating (Penguin Twentieth-Century Classics, 1993); **Yale University Press**: "The Peasant" by Jost Amman, translated by Steven Ozment, from *The Age of Reform, 1250–1550: An Intellectual and Religious History of Late Medieval and Reformation Europe* by Steven Ozment (Yale University Press, 1980).

Every effort has been made to trace or contact all copyright holders. The publishers would be pleased to rectify any omissions brought to their attention at the earliest opportunity.

ACKNOWLEDGMENTS

I am grateful to the staff at Laurence King Ltd. (Damian Thompson, Samantha Gray, Ian Hunt, Richard Mason, Nell Webb, Melanie White, Lee Greenfield, Judy Rasmussen, and especially Laurence King).

At Prentice Hall I would also like to thank Yolanda deRooy, President of the Humanities and Social Sciences Division, Charlyce Jones-Owen, Editorial Director for the Humanities and Social Sciences, and especially Charles Cavaliere, Senior Acquisitions Editor, who has been a fund of good ideas for revitalizing the second edition.

My colleagues in the History Department at Brooklyn College, especially Leonard Gordon, have contributed ideas and criticisms for which I am immensely grateful; as has former colleague Michael Mendle, now in the History Department at the University of Alabama (Tuscaloosa), former student and associate Michael Sappol, now at the National Library of Medicine (Bethesda, Maryland); and Brooklyn staffer Brian Bonhomme, now at the University of Arkansas.

My severest critics and most valiant sustainers have been my sons and my husband—David, Jeremy, and Robert Kessler.

Margaret L. King

The author and publisher would like to thank: **First Edition**: John F. Battick, University of Maine; Wood Bouldin, Villanova University; Blaine T. Browne, Broward Community College; Amy Burnett, University of Nebraska-Lincoln; Jack Cargill, Rutgers University; Anna Clark, University of North Carolina at Charlotte; Cyndia Susan Clegg, Pepperdine University; Jessica A. Coope, University of Nebraska Lincoln; Gerald Danzer, University of Illinois at Chicago; Steven

Fanning, University of Illinois at Chicago; Allan Fletcher, Boise State University; Neal Galpern, University of Pittsburgh; Richard Gerberding, University of Alabama; Gay Gullickson, University of Maryland; Jeff Horn, Stetson University; Patrick Kelly, Adelphi University; Mavis Mate, University of Oregon; John Mauer, Tri-County Technical College; Eleanor McCluskey, Broward Community College; Marion S. Miller, University of Illinois at Chicago; Joseph R. Mitchell, Howard Community College; Jim Murray, University of Cincinnati; Jasonne Grabher O'Brien, University of Kansas; William Percy, University of Massachusetts, Boston; John Powell, Penn State University at Erie; Thomas Preisser, Sinclair Community College; Carole A. Putko, San Diego State University; Timothy A. Ross, Arkansas State University; Roger Schlesinger, Washington State University; Hugo B. Schwyzer, Pasadena City College; James Smither, Grand Valley State University; Francis Stackenwalt, East Central University; Emily Sohmer Tai, Queensborough Community College; Robert W. Thurston, Miami University; Michael Weiss, Linn-Benton Community College; Norman J. Wilson, Methodist College; Michael Zirinsky, Boise State University. **Second Edition**: Linda Bregstein, Mercer Community College (vol 1); Tim Crain, University of Wisconsin-Milwaukee (comb); Meaghan N. Duff, Western Kentucky University (vol 1); Charles W. Hope, Tarrant County Junior College (comb); Herbert Luft, Pepperdine University (comb); Michael G. Paul, Boston College (vol 2); William Benton Whisenhunt, College of DuPage (comb); Steven Jay White, University of Kentucky Lexington Community College (comb); Raymond Kuyler, US Naval Ac.

GLOSSARY

absolution: In some branches of Christianity, the act of pronouncing forgiveness and the remission of sins, that is performed by a priest in the sacrament of penance.

absolutism: A political system or project that concentrates power in the hands of the monarch. Absolutism came to prominence in Europe during the sixteenth through the eighteenth centuries when monarchs sought to wrest power from the Church and the aristocracy, in order to create national states.

acropolis: The citadel of a Greek city, built at its highest point and containing the chief temples and public buildings.

agnate: A relative on the father's side, from a male line of descent. A cognate is a relative whose kinship is on the mother's side.

agora: A central feature of the *polis.* Originally a marketplace, the *agora* also served as the main social and political meeting place. With the acropolis, the *agora* housed the most important buildings of the city-state.

alumnus, alumna, alumni: In ancient Rome, abandoned infants who were picked up and "adopted" into families, usually as servants. In present-day usage, an alumnus or alumna is a person who has been graduated from a particular school or university.

ambassador: The highest-ranking diplomatic representative of one country to another, usually accorded the privilege of guaranteed personal security, even when the countries represented are at war.

ambulatory: A curved aisle running around the east end of a church, originally for processions.

Amerindians: Aboriginal peoples of the Western Hemisphere, American Indians. Preferred to "Indian" (used to refer to the peoples of the Indian subcontinent) and "Native American" (an anti-immigrant nineteenth-century American political party, called "the Know-Nothings").

animism: See **monotheism.**

anthropomorphism: The assigning of human characteristics to animals, natural phenomena or abstract ideas or, in the case of religion, to a deity or spirit.

anti-Semitism: The discrimination against, prejudice or hostility toward Jews.

anti-trinitarianism: See **unitarianism.**

apostle: An early follower of Jesus, including the original twelve disciples and the first missionaries.

apotheosis: See **deification.**

apprenticeship: Training in a craft or profession in which the master profits from the labor of the apprentice, and the apprentice receives training. See also **guild, master.**

apse: A domed or vaulted semicircular recess, especially at the east end of a church.

aristocracy: A government or social structure in which power and wealth is vested in a small minority, a hereditary nobility which claims to be best qualified to rule.

arquebus: A portable, long-barrelled gun, fired by a wheel-lock or match-lock, dating from the fifteenth century.

artisan: A skilled maker of things. Before mass manufacture, artisans produced earthenware, tools, jewelry, etc.

Aryan: Formerly a term that referred to the Indo-European language family, and an assumed racial category composed of people of Indo-European "blood." The notion of an Aryan race was created by nineteenth-century race theorists and adopted by Adolf Hitler. "Aryan" is now used to designate the Indo-Iranian language group, or, more narrowly, the Indo-Aryan (Indic) branch and the group of Indo-Aryan speakers who invaded the Indian subcontinent c. 1500 B.C.E.

astrolabe: The most important instrument used by astronomers and navigators from antiquity through the sixteenth century, used to measure the altitudes of celestial bodies. The altitude of the North Star yields the latitude, and the altitude of the sun and stars yields the time. In the eighteenth century, the astrolabe was superseded by the sextant.

atrium: The central rectangular, interior open-air hall of the Etruscan and Roman house, usually considered the most important room.

auto-da-fé: An "act of faith," a penal sentence by the Spanish Inquisition; also, the execution of that sentence by burning at the stake.

barbarian: In ancient Greece, a word applied to non-Greek-speaking peoples, assumed to be inferior and uncivilized. Similarly used in Chinese civilization. Later and more generally, a person or group believed to lack cultural refinement.

basilica: An oblong building that ends in a semicircular protrusion (an apse), used in ancient Rome as a court of justice and place of public assembly; early Christians adapted this plan for their churches.

bastion: A projecting work in a castle wall or other fortification which allows the defenders to fire along the face of the wall.

bayonet: A short sword attached to the muzzle of a rifle. First used by European armies in the seventeenth century as an infantry weapon for close combat, eliminating the need for a corps of pikemen.

Bible: The sacred writings of Judaism and Christianity, known to Christians as the Bible, consist of two parts. The first, called the Old Testament by Christians, stands alone for Jews as the Hebrew Bible. The second, called the New Testament, includes accounts of Jesus's life that are attributed to four of Jesus's disciples—Matthew, Mark, Luke, and John—known as Gospels (meaning "good news") or collectively as the Gospel.

Black Death: A fourteenth-century epidemic that killed one-fourth to one-third of the population of Europe (about 75 million people), caused by the bacterium *yersinia pestis* and spread by fleas harbored by the black rat.

bourgeoisie: See **burgher.**

bourse: See **stock exchange.**

brahman: A priest or member of the priestly caste in Hinduism.

Bronze Age: An age in which bronze, an alloy of copper and tin, was used to manufacture tools, weapons, and other objects. The term originated as part of the nineteenth-century three-age system (Stone Age, Bronze Age, and Iron Age), but bronze technology actually appeared at different times in different parts of the world. Around 3000 B.C.E. in Mesopotamia and Egypt, bronze alloys were developed to make stronger tools, shields, and weapons.

bull: A letter issued by the pope stating a religious doctrine. In very early times, papal bulls (from Latin *bulla,* "leaden seal") were sealed with the pope's signet ring. Today only the most solemn bulls carry a leaden seal.

bullion: Uncoined gold and silver, molded into bars or ingots.

burgher: In medieval Europe, a citizen of a town (*burg, borough, bourg, borgo*). Burghers were members of the class of enterprising merchants, bankers, and long-distance traders ("the bourgeoisie").

caliph: The supreme leader of the Islamic world after Muhammad's death in 632 C.E. Secular and religious authority were combined in the office of the caliph, who claimed to be appointed by God.

canon law: A single ecclesiastical rule or law, or the body of ecclesiastical law. By extension, a set of rules or fundamental texts pertinent in any art or discipline.

canton: In Switzerland, an independent unit of local government; the Swiss Confederation is divided into twenty-three cantons.

capitalism: An economic system organized around the profit motive and competition, in which the means of production are privately owned by businessmen and organizations which produce goods for a market guided by the forces of supply and demand.

caravel: A type of sailing ship, first developed in Portugal and widely used by fifteenth- and sixteenth-century explorers, equipped with square and lateen sails or entirely lateen rigged.

cartography: The art and science of mapmaking.

caste: A system of rigid hereditary social stratification, characterized by disparities of wealth and poverty, inherited occupations, and strict rules governing social contact.

castle: In the Middle Ages, the fortified residence of a European noble or monarch. At first only a wood or stone tower built on a mound encircled by walls or moat, castles later became more complex, with thick walls topped by a parapet.

catacombs: A complex of underground rooms and tunnels, especially in Rome, used as a cemetery, with niches for tombs and graves.

chancery: A record office; the court of a chancellor.

chivalry: The qualities expected of a knight; the code of values associated with the medieval nobility, developed in response to church strictures and elaborated at court.

Christendom: The part of the world in which Christianity predominates; the collective body of Christian believers.

citizen: In ancient Greece, a free male inhabitant of a *polis,* with landowning and voting rights. In modern times, this is a term applied to any legal member of the state.

civic humanism: An engaged form of humanism that responded to the moral concerns of those who lived in cities. See also **humanism.**

civility: The set of manners and attitudes that were developed in European princely and royal courts from the later Middle Ages and into the early modern period.

civilization: A condition of society characterized by high cultural achievement and complex social development. A society is a civilization if it has (1) class stratification; (2) political and religious hierarchies; (3) a complex division of labor; (4) an economic system that creates agricultural surpluses; and (5) the skills to create architecture, tools, and weaponry.

civil law: See *jus civile*

clan: A number of households that claim descent from a common ancestor.

classical: A term that refers to the ideals and styles of ancient Greek and Roman art, literature, and philosophy, and as reinterpreted by later generations. Classical ideals and styles have exemplified simplicity, harmony, restraint, proportion, and reason. Classicism also implies the finest period of artistic activity or the purest aesthetic. The era during which a society or art reaches its peak is often called classical, as in "Classical Greece" (fifth century B.C.E.).

clergy: A group ordained to perform religious functions. In Catholicism, the clergy is a hierarchical body headed by the pope.

cognate: See **agnate.**

cohort: A subdivision of the Roman legion, including infantry and cavalry.

coloni: In imperial Rome, the class of poor tenant farmers, often the descendants of manumitted slaves. The *coloni* were the forerunners of the serfs of medieval Europe.

colonialism: The control by a country over an area outside its borders. The ancient Phoenicians, Greeks, and Romans were colonizers. In the Middle Ages, Venice and Genoa had colonies on the banks of the Black Sea and in the Aegean. Modern European colonialism began with the discovery of America and of the sea route to the Far East.

comedy: A genre of humorous drama, typically with a happy or absurd ending, sometimes critical of social and political institutions, that was first developed in ancient Greece.

common: In medieval Europe, a centrally located area of land set aside for the free use of the community. Commons still exist in areas of England and the United States.

common law: A system of law developed after the Norman Conquest of England (1066), and still partly in use in most English-speaking countries. Unlike civil law (descended from the codified laws of the Roman Empire and from Napoleonic France), common law is not embodied in a text or code. Judges draw instead upon precedents that have been set by earlier court decisions.

commune: In the Middle Ages, a self-governing municipality with the right to regulate trade, collect taxes, and operate its own system of justice within the town walls. In northern Europe, communes were often granted charters by the royal government or local court. In Italy, communes were sworn associations of townspeople that arose in the eleventh century to overthrow local bishops or feudal magnates.

compass: A device that indicates direction on the earth's surface, and that is used as the principal instrument of navigation. A magnetic compass indicates movement relative to the earth's geomagnetic field.

condottiere: *See* **mercenary.**

confraternity: An association of laypeople linked by a common mission, which combined spiritual and charitable service.

conquistadors: Military adventurers who led the Spanish exploration and conquest of the New World during the sixteenth century.

consul: The two chief annual civil and military magistrates of Rome during the Republic.

contemplation: Quiet and solitary thought; the intellectual and religious ideal of medieval scholars who lived in monasteries and universities.

conversion: The act or experience associated with the decisive adoption of a particular religion and set of beliefs, often entailing the rejection of a previous religious identity.

cosmopolis: A culturally prestigious city whose population is composed of peoples from many parts of the world; an urban center where the most sophisticated customs, practices, and beliefs can be found.

coup d'état: The sudden, violent overthrow of a government by a small group.

courtier: A person in attendance at a court, and who seeks the ruler's favor.

creole: A fully-formed language that develops from a pidgin and becomes the primary language of a linguistic community. Most creoles have vocabularies derived from major European languages; some exist only or primarily in spoken form. The word also refers to combinations of European and non-European cultures, especially cooking and music, as well as to people of mixed racial heritage (*see also* **mestizo**).

culture: Learned behavior acquired by individuals as members of a particular group, in contrast to genetically endowed behavior. Each culture has different styles governing behavior and thought. "Culture" can include food preparation, politics, sculpture, architecture, painting, music, literature, philosophy, and a variety of other civilized pursuits.

cuneiform: A system of writing from Sumer and used for various Middle Eastern languages from c. 3000 B.C.E. until c. 100 C.E. It consisted of wedge-shaped characters that were inscribed on clay, stone, wax, or metal.

curtain wall: The plain wall of a castle or other fortified place, connecting two towers.

decurions: In cities of the Roman Empire, the elite hereditary class responsible for funding and administering municipal functions, and for collecting taxes.

deification: The process of attributing god-like attributes to a human being. In ancient Rome, a deceased emperor was often deified in a ritual known as apotheosis.

demesne: That part of a medieval landholding cultivated exclusively for the lord's use.

democracy: Term from the Greek words for "people" and "power." A form of government in which citizens monitor the state; as opposed to oligarchy or monarchy, where the state is controlled by a small minority or individual. In a direct democracy citizens vote in an assembly, as in ancient Athens. In an indirect democracy citizens elect representatives.

demotic: A simplified form of Egyptian hieroglyphic writing used for informal communication and by the masses; hieratic is a simplified form of writing used by the priesthood.

dhow: A type of sailing vessel with lateen sails, in common use from the Red Sea to the western coast of India.

dialectics: Logical argumentation, especially in the Western tradition according to the method of Aristotle and his followers. In modern times, the opposition or reconciliation of conflicting ideas or forces (as for Hegel and Marx).

dialogue: A literary genre favored by humanists, based on Classical models. Dialogue permitted an author to present two or more competing viewpoints and argue for each plausibly without committing himself.

diaspora: A Greek word meaning "dispersion," originally referring to the Jewish settlements of ancient Babylon and Egypt formed after the destruction of the Temple in 587 B.C.E. Later diasporas of Jews occurred, especially after Jewish revolts against Rome in the first and second centuries C.E. Today, "diaspora" is used of Jewry outside of the state of Israel and is also applied to other dispersions of peoples.

Diet: In the Holy Roman Empire, the assembly of the representatives of the estates.

diplomacy: Conducting negotiations in order to resolve differences, regulate commerce, make alliances, etc.

disputation: In medieval education, an exercise in logic that consists of arguments for and against a thesis, until a conclusion is reached. *See* **dialectics, sholasticism.**

distaff: A simple stick used in spinning. The distaff held raw fiber that was pulled and twisted into thread and wound on the spindle; later the spindle was the bobbin on the spinning machine that held spun thread.

dowry: The property a bride brings to her marriage. It correlates with the wealth or status of the bridegroom.

dualism: Any theory or system of philosophical or religious thought that recognizes two independent and mutually irreducible spiritual entities. The ancient Zoroastrian belief that the god of Good struggled against the god of Evil to determine human destiny was a form of dualism, influencing Judaism, Christianity, and Islam.

ducat: A gold coin with the portrait of the ruler (i.e. the duke, the doge) on it, first minted in 1284 by the city of Venice.

duchy: The territory of a duke or duchess.

dynasty: A succession of monarchs of the same line of descent; a group or family that maintains power for a long period of time.

elite: A small group of persons who control major institutions, exercise military and/or political power, possess superior wealth, or enjoy elevated status and prestige.

empiricism: The philosophy that knowledge derives from experience by the senses.

entrepreneur: A person who organizes and assumes the risks of a business.

epidemic: A contagious disease that periodically or episodically afflicts many people within a population, community, or region. Severe epidemics have killed large numbers of people, most notoriously the Black Death of fourteenth-century Europe.

estate: A social group, legally defined, invested with distinct powers, possessions, and property.

Eucharist: A central observance of the Christian churches, variously called the Lord's Supper, Holy Communion, and the Mass.

excommunication: The formal expulsion of a member from a religious group. In Roman Catholicism, the excommunicated are excluded from receiving the sacraments of the church.

façade: A French word meaning "face" or "front." In architecture, a façade is the side of a structure, normally the front, that is architecturally or visually most significant.

fallow: Cultivated land deliberately allowed to lie idle during a growing season in order to prevent soil exhaustion.

famine: A shortage of food sufficient to cause widespread privation and a rise in mortality. Famine may be caused by natural events; by war; or by certain agricultural practices that cause soil erosion.

feudal: *See* **fief.**

fief, feudal: Medieval relationships of lordship, landholding, and service are often called "feudal," and depended on the granting of a unit of land, the "fief," in usufruct.

florin: A coin first minted in 1252 by the city of Florence; later, any of several gold coins patterned after the Florentine florin.

fluyt: A "flyboat," in early modern Europe, a small, highly efficient vessel for inexpensive, utilitarian hauling, a Dutch innovation.

folk: The people as a whole; those who bear and transmit the cultural values of a people.

fresco: Italian for "fresh," a technique of durable wall painting used extensively for murals. In pure (*buon*) fresco paint is applied to a fresh wet layer of plaster; painting on a dry (*secco*) surface with adhesive binder is not permanent.

galley: A warship driven by oars in battle and with sails for cruising. It was the standard European battle vessel until the late sixteenth century, when the sail-powered, more heavily armed, galleon replaced it.

Gentile: A non-Jew, avoided by faithful Jews.

Geometric style: A style of Greek pottery produced in the ninth and eighth centuries B.C.E., marked by densely patterned lines, including zigzags and Greek key motifs.

ghetto: A segregated quarter where Jews were required to reside. In 1516, the first ghetto was established on the site of an iron foundry (the meaning of "ghetto") by the rulers of Venice. The term came to designate any urban area to which Jews were legally confined, or where Jews or any other socially marginalized group lived voluntarily.

Gospel: *See* **Bible.**

Gothic: An architectural style originating in twelfth-century France, which uses pointed arches and diagonal rib vaults.

grace: A central concept in Christian theology, referring to God's granting of salvation as a free and undeserved gift of love.

guild: An association of merchants or craftsmen. In medieval and early modern Europe, a guild normally comprised all self-employed members of an occupation in a town or district. Only guild members could practice that occupation.

gymnasium: In ancient Greece, a place where athletes exercised in the nude. Gymnasia served as meeting places for social events and intellectual exchange.

gynaeceum: The "women's quarters" of a Greek citizen's house; the workshop for women textile workers on an early medieval estate.

hegemony: The domination of one institution, sector, or state over others.

Hellas: The Greek name for Greece.

Hellenic: A term that designates the period of Greek culture and history from the Archaic Age (c. 700 to c. 500 B.C.E.) to the period of Alexander the Great (r. 336–323 B.C.E.).

Hellenistic: A term designating the period of Greek culture and history from the conquests of Alexander the Great until the eastern Mediterranean region fell under Roman domination (by 30 B.C.E.).

helot: In ancient Sparta, a serf who was forced to perform agricultural labor; originally, the Messenians, a group conquered by the Spartans and reduced to near slave status.

heresy: The rejection of the established doctrines of a group (e.g. a church) by a member or members of that group; from the Greek word meaning "to choose."

heterodoxy: Deviation from orthodoxy.

hierarchy: A series of persons, graded or ranked in order of authority.

hieratic: *See* **demotic.**

hieroglyph: Writing employing pictographic characters, developed in ancient Egypt.

hominid: The genus of human-like animals, comprising modern humans (*Homo sapiens*) and ancestral and related human and human-like species (*Homo sapiens neanderthalensis, Homo erectus, Homo habilis*). *See* **species.**

Homo erectus: *See* **hominid.**

Homo habilis: *See* **hominid.**

Homo sapiens: *See* **hominid** and **species.**

honor: A social value of growing importance in late medieval and early modern Europe, originally the reputation of a grand nobleman but also that of a patrician or bourgeois adult male; and dependent on the regulation of the sexuality of female kin.

hoplite: A heavily armored foot soldier of ancient Greece, who fought in close formation, each carrying a heavy bronze shield (a *hoplon*), a short iron sword, and a long spear.

hospice: A place of refuge for travelers and pilgrims. In the medieval context, very similar to the non-specialized hospital.

hospital: Generally church-related and increasingly funded by bequests, the hospital of the Middle Ages accommodated not only the sick but also abandoned children, "fallen" or deserted women, and the elderly. From the seventeenth century, it increasingly specialized in the treatment of the ill.

humanism: An intellectual movement that emerged in Italy in the late 1300s and spread throughout western and central Europe in the early modern period, centered around the revival of interest in ancient Greek and Roman literature, philosophy, and history.

icon: An image that represents a divine figure and is believed to possess some essential aspect of that divinity.

iconoclasm: A Christian religious movement opposed to the veneration of images (icons) of Christ and the saints. Controversy over the legitimacy of icons lasted for over a century (730–843 C.E.) in the Byzantine Empire. Iconoclasts (Greek for "image-breakers") often invaded churches, destroying the offending images, or icons.

illuminated manuscript: A handwritten book with pictures and ornamentation, "illuminating," or lighting up, the page.

immortality: Being exempt from death, also, human survival after physical death.

imperator: Originally, in ancient Rome, a person who commanded an army. Augustus Caesar was the *imperator* of all the armies and institutions of government, and thus of Rome and its territories.

imperium: The supreme command in war and in the execution of the law, granted at Rome to consuls and other magistrates; authority over a region or empire.

indentured servant: In the early years of North American settlement, a European immigrant who worked without wages for a contracted period in exchange for the price of passage to the colonies and clothing, board, and lodging while in service.

Indo-European: An extensive language family, originally derived from a common ancestor, Proto-Indo-European. The surviving languages include Hindi, Persian, Russian, Polish, Armenian, Albanian, Greek, Italian, French, Spanish, Portuguese, German, English, Dutch, and the Scandinavian languages.

indulgence: In medieval Catholicism, a document granting release from purgatorial punishment in recognition of extraordinary service.

infantry: Armed foot soldiers, as distinct from cavalry, air, or sea forces.

infidel: In Islam, a nonbeliever, someone who is outside the faith.

Inquisition: A church court to prosecute heretics. Inquisitory courts were harsh in their interrogation and punishment, obtaining confessions through torture.

intendant: In seventeenth- and eighteenth-century France, the absolute monarchy's key regional administrator, regarded by French monarchs as more reliable than hereditary officials.

investiture: The ceremonial conferring of high office and rank. The question as to which authority should have power to invest church officials was responsible for provoking the "Investiture Controversy" during the high Middle Ages between the papacy and secular rulers.

Iron Age: The period when iron replaced bronze as the material used for tools and weapons. Iron metallurgy began among the Hittites in eastern Anatolia, c. 1900–1400 B.C.E. and by 1000 B.C.E. had spread throughout the Middle East, Mediterranean region, and westward into Europe.

isonomia: The principle in ancient Athenian society that citizens are entitled to equality all before the law.

jihad: An Arabic word meaning "striving"; according to the Qu'ran, the religious duty of Muslims. Often translated as "holy war," it can be interpreted as a personal or collective spiritual battle against evil, or as a physical battle against unbelievers.

joint-stock company: A type of partnership similar to a corporation. A joint-stock company has transferable shares which are sold at a stock exchange. It is managed by a board of directors elected by the partners (shareholders) who, unlike modern corporations, are personally liable for the company's debts. The joint-stock company was instrumental in the expansion of mercantile capitalism and European colonialism.

jurisprudent: In ancient Rome, a citizen who was learned in law but who held no official position. Over time, jurisprudence came to mean a system or body of law, and jurisprudents became professionals in the imperial bureaucracy, whose documentation and analysis of past decisions constituted a system of law.

jus civile: In the Roman Empire, the "civil law," based primarily on codified statute, most famously the *Corpus Juris Civilis* of the sixth-century C.E. emperor Justinian, rather than court rulings and precedents. Today, used in the legal systems of certain western European countries and their offshoots in Latin America, Asia, and Africa. In contrast, the *jus gentium* ("law of nations") was based on unwritten customary practice and *jus naturale* ("law of nature") on an unwritten (and superior) divine or philosophical law.

justification: In Christianity, the process through which an individual, alienated from God by sin, is reconciled to God and becomes righteous through faith in Christ.

knight: In medieval Europe, a mounted warrior. Most were nobles of low rank who gave a military service to their lords in exchange for a land grant or maintenance. Higher-status nobles also acquired knighthood, by which they were admitted to military rank. A knight was named by a noble superior, and often went through an elaborate ceremony of knighthood.

koine: The form of Greek commonly spoken and written in the eastern Mediterranean in the Hellenistic and Roman periods, allowing people of many different cultures to communicate.

kore, pl. *korai:* A type of statue featuring a young, clothed female, developed in the Archaic Age (c. 700 B.C.E.).

kouros, pl. *kouroi:* A statue featuring a young, male nude, first introduced in the Archaic Age (c. 700 B.C.E.) and common in the Classical era.

lateen sail: A triangular sail on a long yard, used by dhows and other light sailing vessels.

latifundia: In Latin, literally "broad fields"; in Roman times a *latifundium* was a great landed estate, usually worked by slave labor.

layperson: A person who is not a member of the clergy; now commonly meaning a person who is not a member of a specific profession.

legitimacy: The claim of a right to power, which is based on hereditary succession, electoral rules, or natural law.

liturgy: The formal public rituals, prayers, and written texts of religious worship (from the Greek "people" and "work"), used of Christian services and the form of prayer in synagogues.

Lyceum: The philosophical school established by Aristotle; in the nineteenth century, the inspiration for secondary school education.

man of war: An armed, combatant naval vessel.

manor: In medieval Europe, a unit of social organization dominated by a lord, usually consisting of open fields, forest, and common grazing lands, a manor house and the lord's demesne, and one or more peasant villages. Peasants paid a portion of their produce and a number of days of labor each year to the lord. The lord was expected to provide military protection and to dispense justice.

manumission: The formal act of emancipating a slave, sometimes by written agreement or payment by the slave to his master.

martyr: A person who suffers the penalty of death (and/or painful torture) for adhering to a religion or cause.

Mass: The celebration of the Eucharist, the central religious service of the Roman Catholic Church and some other Christian churches.

master: An artisan who is self-employed or who employs journeymen, usually a member of a guild. A journeyman who could demonstrate truly superior skills might be admitted to the guild as a master. In the later Middle Ages, the guild membership was often limited strictly to the sons of masters.

materialism: A philosophical theory, first developed in ancient Greece, that physical matter is the only reality. In modern usage, also a cultural style in which the goal is the satisfaction of physical desire and comfort.

mendicant: Someone dependent on alms for sustenance. In the Middle Ages, the mendicant orders lived by begging or on charitable gifts. The first mendicant order grew out of the efforts of St. Francis of Assisi (c. 1182–1226).

mercantilism: An economic system developed in the early modern era to unify and increase the power and monetary wealth of a nation by regulating the entire national economy. From the sixteenth through the eighteenth century, western European governments practiced mercantilism to build up their military and industrial strength.

mercenary: A professional soldier who fights for pay in the army of a foreign country.

Messiah: The prophesied king and redeemer of the Jews, who would restore the Jews to Israel and bring divine justice to the earth; derived from the Hebrew term for "anointed one." Translated into Greek as "Christos," the term became applied to Jesus.

mestizo: A term of biological and cultural classification used in the Spanish-speaking world for persons of mixed Amerindian and white ancestry.

metaphysics: The branch of philosophy concerned with ultimate universal principles such as being and purpose.

metic: In ancient Greece, a merchant, usually a foreigner, who was a member of a class of resident non-citizens in the *polis*, with some, but not all, of the privileges of citizenship.

metropolis: A great city regarded as a center of business or politics. Applied to the ancient world, the term means the "mother" *polis* that established a colony. In that sense, it continues to be applied to nations that establish colonies.

Midrash: In Judaism, a method of interpreting biblical scriptures; later, compilations of stories and sermons commenting on, alluding to, or codifying biblical texts.

Milesian school: The first materialistic philosophers, Thales, Anaximander, and Anaximenes, who lived in the city of Miletus, in the sixth century B.C.E. They explained natural phenomena by reference to laws that governed growth and change, understood through observation and logic.

mintage, minting: The process by which metal money is coined by a government. A mint is the place where coins are manufactured from gold and silver bullion.

Mishnah: The oldest post-biblical codification of Jewish Oral Law, from the Hebrew "repetition" or "study." Together with the Gemara (later commentaries on the Mishnah), it forms the Talmud.

missionary: The missionary movement was the Christian effort to convert peoples. The first great missionary to the Gentiles, Paul, helped to spread Christianity until, by the end of the first century, it had reached most Mediterranean cities. The voyages of discovery in the fifteenth and sixteenth centuries and the expansion of European colonization began a surge of Roman Catholic missionary activity. Renewed missionary activity took place as part of nineteenth-century imperialism.

monarchy: Rule by a single individual, usually with life tenure and descended from a line of monarchs.

monasticism: The way of life of individuals who have chosen to pursue an ideal of perfection in a separate, dedicated religious setting. Monasticism is practiced in Buddhism, some forms of Christianity, and some other religions.

monotheism: Belief in a single God (as in Judaism, Christianity, and Islam). By contrast, polytheism is the belief that many gods exist; pantheism is the belief that God is suffused throughout, or is synonymous with, the universe; animism is the belief that spirits or divinities dwell inside objects and living things. Some religions are non-theistic (Confucianism, Buddhism), but permit belief in gods or spirits.

Moor: In medieval and early modern Europe, an inhabitant of Muslim North Africa, and, by extension, the Arab and Arabicized conquerors and inhabitants of Spain.

mosque: The Islamic place of public worship (from the Arabic *masjid*, "a place to prostrate one's self [in front of God]"), always oriented toward Mecca, the holy city of Islam. A mosque must have a place for ritual washing, a place from which a leader (*imam*) can start the prayer, and a minaret, a tower from which Muslims are called to prayer.

mulatto: In former colonies of Spain, Portugal, and France, and in the United States, a term for a person of mixed Negro and European parentage.

museum: An institution where objects of aesthetic, educational, or historical value are preserved and displayed.

musket: A large-caliber, smooth-bore firearm aimed and fired from the shoulder, which first appeared in Spain in the mid-1500s and was used to fire a lead ball.

Mycenae: An ancient Greek city which rose to military power around 1500 B.C.E. Mycenaean civilization, influenced by Minoan Crete and the ancient Middle East, flourished until approximately 1300 B.C.E.

mystery cults: In the ancient world, religious cults whose members believed that the performance of secret rituals would give them special knowledge and a mystical union with the divine. Initiates ritually reenacted the death and rebirth of the divinity at the center of the cult.

mysticism: Religious experience in which the believer has or claims direct contact with the sacred. In Christianity this can take the form of a vision of, or sense of union with, God.

myths: Stories that narrate in an imaginative and symbolic way the basic practices and beliefs upon which a culture rests. Mythology means either a certain body of myths (e.g. Greek or Scandinavian) or the study of myths.

nave: The central space in a church, usually extending from the west door to the chancel, and often flanked by aisles.

Neolithic Period: The prehistoric development that followed the Paleolithic Period and preceded the Bronze Age. In the Neolithic ("New Stone Age," c. 9000–3000 B.C.E.), chipped stone tool manufacture became increasingly sophisticated; agriculture and the domestication of animals were introduced; and pottery and polished stone tools were developed.

Neoplatonism: An interpretation of Plato's philosophy that developed in the third century C.E., which influenced Christian and Islamic philosophy and theology. It holds that knowledge is possible only through the understanding of archetypes, essences that structure the objects and beings that make up the world of human experience. According to Neoplatonism, the human soul has within it a vision of these ideal forms, which are dependent on and created by the One (i.e. is God).

nepotism: The practice of awarding jobs or privileges to a relative.

New Testament: *See* **Bible.**

nirvana: Release from bondage to physical desire and pain: a core belief of Buddhism, the ultimate state attained by the Buddha, and the goal of all Buddhists. In Hinduism, nirvana is achieved only through a complete cessation of the cycle of death and rebirth. In Buddhism a state of enlightenment can be achieved in this life, through spiritual or physical exercises.

notary: In medieval cities, a trained professional who drew up deeds, contracts, wills, and other documents essential for urban life.

oecumene: A Greek word referring to "the inhabited world"; in antiquity designating a distinct cultural community. The ecumenical councils in the early church were so called because they represented the whole church. Today, the term "ecumenical" is applied to the collective effort of all Christians to repair differences and manifest unity.

oikos: The household, the fundamental unit of private land and of domestic production in ancient Greece, consisting of a dominant man, his wife and children, and related and unrelated dependents, including slaves. The *oikos* was patrilineal and patriarchal.

Old Testament: *See* **Bible.**

oligarchy: A form of government in which a small minority holds ruling power in order to favor its own interests. Military dictatorships are often oligarchic, as are the political machines that sometimes run city governments in democracies.

Optimates: In late Republican Rome, die-hard defenders of patrician privilege (literally, the "best"). Opposing the Optimates were the Populares ("supporters of the people").

orthodoxy: The established (literally "correct") doctrine of a church or religious group.

ostracism: In ancient Athens, a method of banishment by popular vote, without trial. Each year the citizens would vote on whether anyone was so dangerous to the state that he should be ostracized, or exiled for ten years. Later, ostracism came to mean any form of political or social exclusion.

Paleolithic Period: Prehistoric cultural development that preceded the Neolithic Period. In the Paleolithic ("Old Stone Age"), which lasted from about 2.5 million to about 10,000 years ago, hominids and humans developed the manufacture of various chipped stone tools.

pantheism: *See* **monotheism.**

papacy: *See* **pope.**

papal bull: *See* **bull.**

papyrus: Writing paper made from the pith of a reed that grows wild in the Nile River, used from about 2400 B.C.E. by the people of Egypt, Palestine, Syria, and southern Europe. Connected together in strips and rolled up, it made scrolls, the books of antiquity.

parable: A brief moral tale (from the Greek *parabole*, "a setting beside"). In parables, a spiritual truth is articulated by telling a simple story. Well-known biblical examples include the Gospel stories of the Prodigal Son and of the Good Samaritan.

parlement: In medieval and early modern France, a regional supreme court of criminal and civil law. At first the *parlements* were staffed by royal appointees who supported medieval monarchs, but in the seventeenth and eighteenth centuries, they often actually obstructed the absolutist agenda of Bourbon kings. The revolutionary National Assembly of 1789 abolished the *parlements.*

pastor: In Protestantism, a leader or minister (Greek *pastor*, "shepherd") of a congregation who presides at the weekly Sunday celebration and whose role is to teach scripture, rather than to confer grace (the role of the priest in Catholicism). Pastors, unlike celibate priests, are allowed to marry.

patriarchy: Social organization marked by the supremacy of the father, the legal dependence of wives and children, and the reckoning of and inheritance from the male line.

patricians: The hereditary aristocratic class of ancient Rome, initially entitled to privileges denied to commoners (the plebeians). In medieval and early modern cities, a hereditary elite of bourgeois office-holders, *rentiers*, and high-status merchants, to be distinguished from ordinary guild merchants.

patrilineal: The tracing of ancestry and kinship through the male line. Female offspring are valued insofar as they help preserve the male line, mainly through marriage. Patrilineal families may also be patriarchal.

patrimony: The accumulation of familial wealth which can be inherited; originally the wealth that flows through the male line of descent.

patronage: The conferring of jobs, favors, and commissions by a powerful patron to a client, in order to promote the patron's interests.

pax romana: Literally, "the Roman peace." Under the empire consolidated by Augustus Caesar (27 B.C.E.), Rome's total domination of Europe, the Mediterranean, and the Middle East brought about 250 years of peace, albeit a peace secured by conquest and bloodshed.

pedagogue: In ancient Greece, originally a slave who accompanied children to school. Later, pedagogue came to mean a theorist of education or a teacher.

penance: A sacrament of the Roman Catholic, Eastern Orthodox, and some Protestant churches. The rite consists in the confession of sins to a priest, who then assigns the repentant sinner an act of penance in order to obtain forgiveness.

peon: A member of the landless agricultural laboring class of Spanish America; a person held in compulsory servitude to a master for the working out of a debt.

perspective: In art, the techniques used to represent three-dimensional spatial relationships on a two-dimensional surface; from the fifteenth century, one of the principal characteristics of western European art.

peso: In the early modern era, a widely circulated gold coin minted from gold mined in Spanish America (also known as a "piece of eight," because it was worth eight reales).

phalanx: In ancient Greece, a military formation in which heavily armed infantrymen lined up close together in deep ranks, which were defended by a wall of shields.

Pharisees: A major Jewish sect (flourished c. 100 B.C.E.–100 C.E.), noted for strict observance of rites and ceremonies and for their insistence on the validity of their own oral traditions concerning the written law. Pharisaism arose in opposition to the Sadducees; Pharisees argued that religious authority was not the sole prerogative of the priesthood. The Pharisees developed the idea of an afterlife and the resurrection of the body, and the concept of the Messiah. Pharisaism profoundly influenced the rabbinical Judaism of later centuries.

philosophy: The oldest form of systematic scholarly inquiry (Greek *philosophos*, "lover of wisdom"). Today "philosophy" has several related meanings: (1) the study of the principles underlying knowledge, being, and reality; (2) a particular system of philosophical doctrine; (3) the critical study of philosophical doctrines; (4) the study of the principles of a particular branch of knowledge; (5) a system of principles for providing guidance in everyday life.

phonogram: A character or symbol that represents a word, syllable, or language sound (phoneme) in writing.

pictograph: A simplified picture of an object that represents the object in writing.

pietas: In Roman culture, the highest virtue, a selfless regard for the father and ancestors, with a determination to preserve the lineage. Our term "piety" is derived from *pietas*, but now means religious devotion.

pike: A weapon consisting of a long wooden shaft with a pointed steel head, used by foot soldiers until superseded by the bayonet.

pilgrimage: The practice, common to many religions, of journeying to a holy place or shrine to obtain blessings from God or as an act of devotion or penance.

plantation system: Cultivating crops on extensive lands worked by slave labor, developed in the sixteenth century by the Portuguese settlers for sugar cultivation on São Tomé and elsewhere, and later adopted by other European colonizers.

plebeians: Most of the free citizens of ancient Rome, originally denied most rights accorded the privileged, hereditary patrician class.

plebs: The ordinary people of Rome; by the last century B.C.E., these were the increasingly dependent urban masses.

pluralism: In medieval and early modern Europe, the practice of holding several offices at the same time.

polis, pl. *poleis:* In ancient Greece, a city-state.

politiques: A faction that emerged in the sixteenth-century civil war between Protestants and Catholics in France, who rejected religious considerations in favor of the secular goal of order and national unity.

polyglot: A term describing geographical areas or states in which many languages are spoken.

polytheism: *See* **monotheism.**

pope: The pope (literally, "father"), or bishop of Rome, is claimed by Roman Catholics as the successor to the apostle Peter, who is traditionally assigned preeminence over other apostles. The papacy comprises the pope and the system of ecclesiastical government of the Roman Catholic Church.

Populares: *See* **Optimates.**

portolan: From the thirteenth century onward, charts that gave sailing distances in miles and bearings in straight lines. Lacking parallels and meridians, or any indication of the curvature of the earth, these charts could not be used on the open oceans.

predestination: A Christian doctrine according to which a person's ultimate salvation or damnation is determined by God alone prior to, and apart from, any worth or merit on the person's part.

prelate: A clergyman of high rank.

Presocratic philosophy: Greek philosophy (c. 660–440 B.C.E.) prior to Socrates. The Presocratic philosophers challenged religious explanations of reality and sought to explain rationally the natural world and physical processes.

primogeniture: The preference given to the eldest son and his descendants in inheritance. Practiced in many regions of medieval Europe to maintain estates whole and intact.

princeps: Literally, "first citizen," a title adopted by Augustus, the first Roman emperor. The system he created, based on the allegiance of the army and the people to the emperor (*imperator*) and on the collaboration between the emperor and the senatorial and equestrian classes, came to be known as the principate, meaning the rule of the first citizen.

proletarian: In ancient Rome, the poorest citizens; the only class of citizens who were not required to serve in the army. The word means literally "bearer of children": the proletarian's only service to the state was to provide new generations of citizens.

proscription: In ancient Rome, the posting of names of the opponents of a faction in the Forum. Those whose names were posted were murdered and their wealth confiscated.

quadrant: An instrument used by astronomers and navigators from medieval times to measure the altitude of the sun or a star and for surveying. At its simplest, the quadrant is a flat plate in the shape of a quarter circle marked with a degree scale along the curved side; two sights are attached to one of the radial sides and a plumb bob hangs from the apex.

Qur'an: The sacred scripture of Islam. Muslims acknowledge the Qur'an, or Koran (Arabic, "reading" or "recital"), as the actual words of God given to the Prophet Muhammad between c. 610 and his death in 632.

rabbi: The title given to recognized Jewish religious teachers, sages, and leaders. Originally a term of respect (Hebrew, "my master"), around the first century C.E. it became a formal title for men authorized to interpret and expound Jewish law.

race: A population group, subspecies, or variety within the species *Homo sapiens*, set apart from other groups on the basis of arbitrarily selected, commonly visible criteria. The criteria most often selected are: skin color; "blood"; hair type; the shape and form of the body, head, and facial features; and alleged moral and/or behavioral attributes.

raison d'état: French for "reason of state"; the justification given when the political interests of a nation-state override any moral principles governing the state's actions.

rationalism: The belief that the most fundamental knowledge is based on reason and that truth can be arrived at only by rational analysis of ideas, independent of empirical data, emotions, or prior authority.

real: In the early modern era, a small Spanish or Spanish-American silver coin, which was worth one-eighth of a peso.

regent: A person appointed to govern during the absence, childhood, or incapacity of a monarch.

relic: An object esteemed and venerated because of its association with a saint or martyr, often a body-part. Relics are often credited with curative or miraculous powers.

relief: A mode of sculpture in which forms project outward from a plane surface.

reliquary: A receptacle, usually richly decorated and made of precious materials, for the safekeeping or exhibition of a relic.

Renaissance: The period of European history from the early fourteenth to the mid-seventeenth century, derived from the French word for rebirth, originally referring to the revival of the values and artistic styles of Classical antiquity during that period, especially in Italy.

resurrection: The "rising again" to life of a dead person in the future or in heaven. The concept of resurrection from death is found in several religions, but is associated particularly with Christianity because of the central belief in the resurrection of Jesus.

rhetoric: The branch of written and oral discourse that concerns persuasion (Greek *rhetor*, "speaker in the assembly").

Romance languages: The family of languages that developed out of the provincial Latin spoken in various sections of the Roman Empire after its fall: Italian, French, Spanish, Portuguese, Romanian, and Romansch (spoken in some parts of Switzerland).

Romanesque: A style of art and architecture that flourished throughout western Europe from about 1050 to about 1200. The word originally meant "in the Roman manner"; Romanesque church architecture characteristically employs the Roman round arch and the major forms of antique Roman vaulting, and retains the basic plan of the early Christian basilica.

rosary: A circular string of beads used by Roman Catholics for counting recitations of such prayers as the Hail Mary (Ave Maria), the Our Father (Lord's Prayer), and the Glory Be to the Father (Gloria Patri).

sacrament: In Christianity, a sacred ritual used for conferring grace.

Sadducees: A powerful Jewish religious sect, identified with the priesthood and aristocracy, that flourished from about 200 B.C.E. until the fall of Jerusalem in 70 C.E. Unlike the Pharisees, the Sadducees did not believe in resurrection and the immortality of the soul, and opposed the use of Oral Law, holding only to the Pentateuch (the first five books of the Old Testament).

saint: A holy person (from the Latin *sanctus*, "holy") credited with the ability to work miracles of healing, or to pray effectively for others. In the New Testament "saint" refers to a baptized follower of Jesus Christ. Later the phrase "communion of saints" was used to refer to all members of the Church, living and dead. Still later, "saint" was defined as an individual who has died a heroic death for Christ (i.e. a martyr), or whose life has been marked by unusual signs of compassion. The Church came to regulate cults venerating such individuals by instituting a system of canonization in about 1000 C.E.

salvation: A religious concept that refers to the process through which a person is brought to ultimate, and eventually eternal, well-being. In Christianity, salvation (Latin *salus*, "health," "safety") refers to the process or state of being "saved" or "redeemed."

samurai: In medieval and early modern Japan, a class of warriors (from the Japanese *saburu*, "service"). The samurai were originally rural landowners who served as military retainers. Later they became military aristocrats and then military rulers.

Saracen: A term that Greek-speaking Byzantine chroniclers and other European peoples used for Muslim Arabs.

satrap: The governor of a province (satrapy) of the ancient Persian Empire.

schism: A formal division in a religious body. Two of the most important schisms in the history of Christianity were the division between the Eastern (Orthodox) and Western (Roman) Churches (traditionally dated 1054), and the period (1378–1417) during which the Western Church had two, and later three, competing lines of popes.

Scholasticism: A philosophical movement dominant in medieval European universities and writing from about the ninth century until the seventeenth century. Scholasticism combined Christian dogma, patristic philosophy (contained in the works of the Church Fathers), and Aristotelian philosophy.

sect: A dissenting religious body or political faction, often regarded as heretical or blasphemous by the larger body of believers.

secular: Of or relating to the worldly or temporal. Specifically in Catholicism, the term "secular" refers to a category of clergy that is not bound by monastic vows or rules.

Semitic: A branch of the Afroasiatic (or Hamito-Semitic) language group. Semites speak Semitic languages: Arabs, Aramaeans, Jews, and some Ethiopians, and in antiquity Babylonians, Assyrians, Phoenicians, Canaanites, and other groups. Speakers of a proto-Hamito-Semitic language may have migrated into Mesopotamia, the Middle East and the Arabian Peninsula from North Africa during the sixth millennium B.C.E.

Separatists: Seventeenth-century Puritans who separated from the Church of England and settled in North America in order to practice their form of worship.

serf: In medieval Europe, a peasant who was legally bound to the soil and obligated to give a portion of his produce to his lord. Up until about 1200, most peasants in western Europe were serfs.

sexagesimal: A numerical system based on the number 60, used by the Babylonians. Largely supplanted by the number 10 (decimal system), sexagesimal arithmetic presently survives in the use of 60 for the minute and hour cycle, the dozen, the foot (divided into 12 inches), and the 360° circle.

sextant: An optical instrument used in navigation since the mid-eighteenth century to measure the angles of celestial bodies above the horizon from the observer's position.

Shiite: One of the major branches of Islam, historically the dominant religious group in Persia (present-day Iran) and elsewhere a minority, in opposition to the dominant Sunnites. Following the death of Muhammad, disagreement arose as to who should succeed him as leader (imam) of the Muslim community. Shiites (from the Arabic *shiat Ali*, "the party of Ali") insisted that only descendants of Muhammad's son-in-law Ali could qualify.

Shintoism: The indigenous religious tradition of Japan, based on the worship of gods, nature spirits, and ancestors. After the eighth century C.E., Shintoism coexisted and blended with Buddhism and Confucianism.

shuttle: In weaving, a device or object used for passing the thread of the woof between the threads of the warp.

simony: In Christian canon law, the sale or purchase of a spiritual service or office.

slavery: A social practice in which a person is owned by and commanded to labor for the benefit of a master.

snuff: A preparation of dried, pulverized tobacco to be inhaled through the nostrils, chewed, or placed against the gums.

Sophists: A group of ancient Greek teachers of rhetoric, philosophy, and the art of living, fifth–fourth centuries B.C.E., known for their adroit and specious reasoning. "Sophistry" is now applied to any form of devious, but convincing, argument.

specie: Money in the form of coinage.

species: A biological classification designating a type of organism or population of animals potentially capable of interbreeding.

spindle: *See* distaff.

spinster: In medieval Europe, an unmarried woman who maintained herself by spinning thread. Later, the term came to designate an unmarried woman who is past the common age for marrying.

spiritualists: In sixteenth- and seventeenth-century Europe, inward-looking but radical Protestant sects, such as the Mennonites, Moravian Brethren, and English Society of Friends (Quakers). Spiritualist sects exalted the divine within the human and deliberately abstained from the demands of worldly existence.

stele, pl. stelae: An upright stone slab or column, decorated with inscriptions or figures, common in prehistoric and early historic cultures.

steppes: The Slavic term for the vast grasslands, flat, semi-arid, and subject to extremes of temperature, that stretch across central Eurasia.

stoa: A freestanding porchlike structure usually walled at the back with a front colonnade, designed to give pedestrians shelter and meeting places, often in the *agoras* of ancient Greek cities. The Stoic school of philosophy took its name from an Athenian stoa where its members first taught.

stock exchange, stock market: A place where brokers and dealers in stocks and bonds transact business together. Stock exchanges facilitated the financing of business and government activity by bringing together the buyers and sellers of the shares of joint-stock companies and, in later times, shares of corporations and bonds.

stratification: The division of society into separate groups, generally based on wealth, prestige, and/or ancestry.

suburb: A settlement immediately outside the walls of a city or fortification; in medieval Europe, sometimes the nucleus of a city.

sumptuary laws: Laws against luxury and extravagance (Latin *sumptus*, "expense"). Sumptuary laws prohibiting extravagance in dress or ceremony were designed to maintain moral standards and the distinctions between the social classes, and often particularly targeted women.

Sunnite: A follower of the Sunni branch of Islam to which most Muslims belong. Sunnites claim to strictly follow the *sunna* (practices) of the Prophet Muhammad, as defined and elaborated by the religious authorities (*'ulam*).

surrogate: A person who acts on behalf of another.

symposium: Originally, in ancient Greece, an all-male drinking party, where men composed drinking songs and engaged in lively conversation. The term is now usually applied to a meeting where speeches are given and discussions are held.

synagogue: A building where Jews gather for worship and religious instruction; the focus of Jewish communal life. In ancient Judaism, worship centered on the Temple in Jerusalem, where sacrificial rites were performed by a special caste of priests, with the masses excluded. In contrast, the synagogue is open to all Jews for prayer, ceremony, the reading of the Torah, religious instruction, and preaching. The synagogue provided the model for the Christian church and Islamic mosque.

syncretism: The fusion of cultural forms of different origin and character into a new formation.

Talmud: A compendium of law and lore that is regarded in Judaism as the sequel to the Hebrew Bible and the basis of Jewish religious life. There are two Talmuds: the Palestinian, composed in the third and fourth centuries C.E., and the Babylonian, completed about 500 C.E., with some later additions.

Tartars, Tatars: Descendants of the Mongols, who ruled part of eastern Europe and central Asia.

tax farmer: A free agent contracted by a ruler or state to collect taxes, from which he takes an agreed-upon commission or, more often, whatever percentage he can expropriate.

theocracy: Rule by a priesthood or religious elite, with rule of law based on religious doctrine or scripture.

tholos: The bee-hive shaped tombs built for of the Mycenaean kings.

tithe: A "tenth part" of agricultural or other produce, exacted to support the Church.

Torah: The entire body of Jewish teaching incorporated in the Hebrew Bible, the Talmud, and later rabbinical commentaries. Applied sometimes to the written Mosaic law that is contained in the first five books of the Bible.

tragedy: A genre of drama, developed in ancient Greece, in which a hero meets death brought on by a flaw of character and circumstances beyond personal control.

transept: The part of the church that crosses the nave; also, either wing of the transept.

transubstantiation: In Roman Catholic or Eastern Orthodox church dogma, the miraculous change by which bread and wine at their consecration during the ritual of Mass become the body and blood of Christ.

Trinity: The Christian understanding of God as a unity of three persons (triune): Father, Son, and Holy Spirit. The idea of the Trinity is an attempt to reconcile the diverse statements about God contained in the Bible.

triumvirate: A ruling group of three persons; originally, in the last years of the Republic, Julius Caesar, Crassus, and Pompey.

tyranny: Rule by an illegitimate leader, the tyrant, who seizes power and holds it by violence. In ancient Greece, tyranny was seen as the opposite of monarchy. Both forms of rule concentrate power in a single figure.

unitarianism: A form of Protestant Christianity asserting that God is one person, rather than three persons in one (the Trinity).

urban: Relating to the city. Urbanization is the process of becoming more urban through the concentration of population, the performance of economic tasks, and the development of the mental outlook of a city.

usufruct: The legal right of using and enjoying the fruits or profits of something belonging to another. In medieval Europe, land held in usufruct and granted by another noble, or a king or an agent of the church, was often called a fief.

usury: Money-lending for profit.

utopia: An ideal society in which social, political, and economic evils have been entirely eradicated, and in which the state functions to promote the happiness of all.

vassal: A person under the protection of a feudal lord, to whom he vows homage and fealty. The vassals of powerful rulers might also in turn have their own vassals.

vernacular: In medieval and early modern Europe, the native spoken language of a region or country; not Latin, which was the language used for the writing of high literary, scientific, legal, and religious works. In time the main modern national vernaculars such as French, German, and Italian displaced Latin in most intellectual tasks.

warp, woof: The warp is a series of yarns extended lengthwise in a loom and crossed by the woof (or weft), together constituting, when complete, a woven textile.

wergeld: Among the Germanic tribes that lived outside the borders of the Roman Empire, a vengeance or compensation payment, which varied according to a person's status.

wet nurse: A lactating woman who is hired to breastfeed the baby of her employers.

INDEX

Figures in **bold** refer to picture captions and maps.

Aborigines, Australian 693
abortion 781, 783–4, 785–6, **884**, 885, 886, 887–8
absolutism, 426, 433, 438, 439, 440; resistance to 578–9
abstract art 775; *see also* Kandinsky
absurd, theater of 883
academies 503, **508**, 509, 510, 593
Acheson, Dean 871
Addams, Jane 785
Advancement of Learning, The (Bacon) 487, 494
Afghanistan 847, 876, 879, 889, 891, 909
Africa: disease 887, 891, 893; European colonies **691**, **704**, 705, 706–7, **707**, **757**, 832, **833**, 835, 836, 837–8; explorers 706; independence 835, **836**, 838, 840; indigenous states **705**; missionaries 703, 706; Muslims 702, 703, 838; post-colonial political systems 838–41, **840**; radio 903; slaves 425, 450, 467–71, **468**, **469**; trade 450, 636, 837–8; women 887; *see* African slaves *and specific countries*
African-Americans 860–1, **862**, 863–4
African National Congress 839
African slaves: in Brazil 545; in the Caribbean 544, 545, 693; in North America/United States **551**, **553**, 554–5, 566, 569, 571, 572–3, 617, 706; in Spanish America 547, 634, 693
agriculture: Britain and Europe 535–8, 580, 615, 659, 793, new World 462; 892–3; Russia 536, 632, 802, 803,

805, 892; Spanish America 547–8; United States 629
Agrippa von Nettesheim, Henry Cornelius 505; *On the Nobility and Preeminence of the Female Sex* 504, 505
Ahmad, Muhammad 703
AIDS 887, 891, 893
Akbar 694
Akhmatova, Anna 806
Alabama 566, 572
Al-Afghani, Jamal al-Din 703, 704
Alaska 566, **567**
Alba, Duke of 423–4
Albania/Albanians 702, 731, 746, 809, **815**, 868, **890**
al-Bashir, Omar Ahmed 892
Alberdi, Juan Bautista 633
Albuquerque, Afonso de 452
alchemy 489, 496
Aldrovandi, Ulisse 510
Alexander I, Tsar 668
Alexander II, Tsar 677, 693
Alexander III, Tsar 677, 693, 759, 761
Alexander Nevsky (Eisenstein) 774, 806
Alexandra, Tsarina 759, 760, 761
Alfonso XII, of Spain 677
Alfonso XIII, of Spain 817
Algeria 702, 706, 715, 836–7, 840, 842, 847; women 888
'Ali, Muhammad 702–3
Alkmaar, Netherlands **525**
All-African People's Conference, Accra 841
All Quiet on the Western Front (Remarque) 763, 881
Allende Gossens, Salvador 854, 873
Almeida, Captain Dom Francisco 458
Al Qaeda 908, 909

805, 892; Spanish America 547–8;
United States 629

Alsace and Lorraine 627, 628, 676, 685, 746; and World War I 748, 749, 750, 766, 811
Alto Adige 808
Amalgamated Society of Engineers 645
Amazon River region 693, 854
ambassadors 422
Ambassadors, The (Holbein) **432**
American Civil War 568, 569, 571, 572, 629, 767
American Declaration of Independence 444, 500, **556**, 558, 561, 570, 579
American Federation of Labor 787
American War for Independence 514, 550, 556–7, 558, 579
Americas, the: the colonies 462, European settlement **543**, 544; *see* Amerindians; Canada; South America; United States
Amerindians **543**, 544; Caribbean 544, 545; and disease **545**, 546, 554; in Mexico and Spanish America 546, 547, **559**, 563, **564**, 693; in North America/United States 549, 550, **552**, 552–4, 553, 566–9, **567**, 574, 860
Amin, Idi 839
Amman, Jost: "The Peasant" 530
Amnesty International 895
Amsterdam 478,, 479, 503, 524, 535; Jews 492, 535, 710, **825**; population **528**, **650**; stock exchange 452, **475**, 479
anarchists 647, 728, 734, 735
Anglican Church **395**, 396–7, 398, 433, 434
Anglicanism 737
Anglo-Saons 442

Angola 706, 707, 837, 840, 874, 906
Animal Farm (Orwell) 806
Anne of Austria 520
Anselm, Saint 493
Anthony, Susan B. **568**
anthrax 724
anti-Semitism 535, 678, 681, 708–9, 710, **711**, 715, 813–14, 879; *see* Holocaust, the
Antonioni, Michelangelo 882
Antwerp 478–9, stock market 452
apartheid 839
Apollinaire, Guillaume 739
Aquinas, Thomas 544
Aquino, Corazon 857
Arabs 489, 756; and oil 842, 846; traders 705, 706; *see also* Palestine
Arafat, Yasir 843, 845, 894
Arawaks 544
architecture 523, 775
Areopagitica (Milton) 504
Argentina 546, 560, 561, 562, 563, 564, 633, 714, 715, 716, 853, 855, 901
Aristarchus of Samos 485
Aristotle/Aristotelianism 488, 490, 491–2, 544
Arizona 566
Arkansas 572
Arkwright, Richard: water frame 615, 617
Armenia 702, 799, 878
armies 418–19, 420–1, 425, **428**
arms trade 904, 906; *see* nuclear weapons
Armstrong, Louis **775**
Armstrong, Neil A. 872
art *see* painting
Artemisia, Queen 440

artisans 640, 644, 649
Aryans 812
Ashanti (Asante) 832, 835
Ashmolean Museum, Oxford 510
Astell, Mary: *Reflections on Marriage* 506, 526; *Serious Proposal to the Ladies* 505
astrology 495, 496
astronomy 484–5, 486, **486**, 487–8, 496, 501, **507**
Aswan Dam, Egypt 843
Atatürk *see* Kemal, Mustafa
atomic bombs 738, 799, 777, **870**
atonality, musical 741
Attlee, Clement 868
Augsburg, Peace of 423
Augustinians 466
Aurangzeb 694
Auschwitz death camp 824, 826, 827
Austen, Jane 506, 723
Australia 454, 634, 693, 713, 715, 716, 756, 835, 887
Austria 519, 579, 809, 813, 818, 868–9; *see also* Austria-Hungary; Habsburg dynasty; Vienna
Austria-Hungary 673–4, 681, 683, 685, 686, 705, 731, 746; World War I 747, 748, 755, 757, 763, 766, 768, **768**
Austro-Prussian War (1866) 676
autarky 813
automobiles **626**
Averbakh, M.N. 804
Axis powers **797**, 814, 816–17
Ayachucho, battle of 561
Azerbaijan 702, 799, 878
Aztecs 459–61, **460**

Ba'al Shem Tov 710
Babeuf, François-Noël 732
Babur 694
Bacon, Francis 493, 494; *The Advancement of Learning* 487, 494; *New Atlantis* 501; *The New Method* 494
Baden, Prince Max von 765
Baez, Joan 882
Bahamas 544
Baines, Edward 622
Baker, Ella 864
Bakunin, Mikhail 735, 736
Balfour, Arthur 844
Bali 696, 697
Balkans 685, 686, 702, 746, 906; wars (1912–13) 683, 731, 746
ballet 776
Baltic States (Estonia, Latvia, Lithuania) 763, 766, 809, 821, 868, 876; Jews 535, **825**
Balzac, Honoré de: *Human Comedy* 721
Bangladesh 848
Barak, Ehud 843, 845
Berents, Willem **459**
Barnett, Lincoln 778
Baroque style 523, 529, **532**
Barr, Joel 880
Barricade, La (Meissonier) **684**
Barros, Joo de 458
Barton, Clara 757
Basques 818, 909
Bassi, Laura 509
Bastille, storming the **586**, 587
Batista, Fulgencio 854
Battle of Britain 820
Battleship Potemkin (Eisenstein) **751**, 773
Bayle, Pierre: *Dictionary* 497, 503
Bayonet Charge, The (Homer) **572**
Beatles, the 881, 882
Beaumarchais, Pierre-Augustin de 529
Beauvoir, Simone de: *Second Sex* 884
Bebel, August: *Woman and Socialism* 781
Beccaria, Cesare: *Essay on Crimes and Punishments* 534, 654
Beckett, Samuel: *Waiting for Godot* 883
Beethoven, Ludwig van 603–4, 720, 721

Beggar's Opera, The (Gay) 529
beggars 530, 654
Behn, Aphra 509, 529; *Oroonoko* 501, 509
Beijing 698, 699, 811; Tiananmen Square demonstration 850, **850**, 903
Being and Nothingness (Sartre) 779
Belarus 878, 879
Belcamp, Jan van: *The Clifford "Great Picture"* 505
Belgium: colonies **691**, **704**, **707**, **833**, 836, 837; industrialization 627–8, **630**; painting **774**; trade **714**; urbanization **651**; World Wars 749–50, 752, 820
Bell, Alexander Graham 631
Bell, Henry: *Comet* 624
Bellini, Gentile: *Muhammad II* 432
Belloc, Hilaire 712
Belsen death camp 824, **825**
Bentham, Jeremy 646, 653, 728, 730; "Panopticon" 534, 654
Benz, Karl 626
Bergman, Ingmar 882
Berlin **528**, 650, 868, 871, 875–6; Airlift **872**; Wall **875**, 876, 877
Berlin, Congress of (1878) 705
Berlin Conference (1884) 706
Berlusconi, Silvio 899
Bernstein, Eduard 734
Bessemer, Henry: converter 620, **621**, 628
bicycles 631, 653
Bin Laden, Osama 908, 909
birth control 652, 661, 781, 783, 784, 785–6, 883, 889
Birth of a Nation, The (Griffith) 773, **773**, 776
birthrates *see* population
Bismarck, Prince Otto von 628, 649, 656, 673, 675, 676, 681, **681**, 682, 685, 785
Black Death 708
Black Hawk, Chief 566
Black Muslim movement 864
Black Panther Party 861
Black Power movement 864
Blair, Anthony (Tony) 899, 901–2, 903
Blake, William 612
Blanc, Louis 646, 647, 672; *The Organization of Work* 733
Blitzkrieg 820
blues 775, 882
Blum, Léon 788
Boers 706, 707
Bohemia 426, 444, 667, 819; *robot* 538
Bohr, Neils 777
Bolívar, Simón de 555, 560, **561**
Bolivia 546, 561, 562, 853; Potosí mines 546, 547
Bologna, Italy 441
Bolsheviks 760, 761–3, 765, 781, 784, 787, 799, 800, 801, 803
Bomera, Maru **707**
Bonaparte, Joseph 606
Bonaparte, Lucien 587
Bonaparte, Napoleon *see* Napoleon
Bonhoeffer, Dietrich 779
Bonnie and Clyde 882
Book of the Courtier, The (Castiglione) **518**, 520–1
books 502, 503, 580; *see* literature
Booth, Charles: poverty map **651**
Borgia, Cesare 418, 420
Bose, Subhas 833
Bosnia-Herzegovina 683, 705, 746, 747, 906–7
Bossuet, Bishop Jacques-Bénigne: *Politics Drawn from the Very Words of Scripture* 439, 440
Boston, Massachusetts: "Massacre" 557; "Tea Party" 557; United Fruit 853
Botha, Pieter W. 839
Boulton, Matthew 620, 624
Bourbon dynasty 422, 424, 428, 430, 433, 549, 607, 670
bourgeoisie, the 524–9, 677, 733
Boutros-Ghali, Boutros 896

Bouzonnet, Claudine-François: *Family Evening* **531**
Boxer Rebellion 699–700
boyars 518
Brahe, Tycho 485, 489, 496; observatory **486**
Brazil: 456, 462, 467, 469, 471, 472, 474, 545–6, 560, 669, 714, 716; slaves 563–4, 565, 693; trade 545, 546, 562, 563, 693; 20th c. 853–4, 855, 901
Brecht, Bertolt 776; *Threepenny Opera* 776
Brera Museum, Milan 510
Brest-Litovsk, Treaty of (1918) 763, 766
Brezhnev, Leonid 875, 876
Britain: absolutism 431; Act of Settlemeny 434; agriculture 477, 536, 538, 615; and American War for Independence 556–8, 579; Civil War 424, 433, 495, 540, 578; coal mining 611, 619, 620, 644; colonies 544–5, 550, **552**, 553, **553**, 555, 617, **691**, **692**, **704**, 705, 706–7, **833**, *see also* India; decolonization 832–5; common law 442–3; Deal Castle **420**; education 728, 729; emigration **715**; friendly societies 646; industrialization 611, 615–17, **616**, **618**, 619–20, 624–5, 626, **630**; interwar 816; jury system 442; Israel 844; literature *see* literature; navy 686, 714, 748, 755–6, 852; nobility (1750s) 514, **515**, 517, 518, 519; painting *see* painting; Parliament and politics 514, 519, 578, 581, 676, 788, 788, 898–9; philosophers *see* philosophers; population **515**, 784; poverty 530, 532; railroads 623, 903; religion 737; Restoration 433; Seven Years' War 555; suffrage **669**, 735; trade and economy 525, 626, 627, **632**, 636, 659, 698–9, **714**, 715, 788, 792–3, 851–2, *see also* cotton industry; urbanization 650, **651**; World War I 686, 747, 748, 750, 752, 754, 755–6, 757–8, 767, **768**; World War II 814, 818–19, 820–1, 823, 872; *see also* London
British Honduras (Belize) 544
Brontë, Anne, Charlotte and Emily 723
brothels 655, 656; *see* prostitution
Bruegel, Pieter, the Elder: *The Peasants' Wedding* **539**, 540
Bruges, crane **474**
Bruno, Giordano 487
Brusilov, General Aleksey A. 755
Bry, Théodore de: engraving **463**
Buber, Martin: *I and Thou* 779
bubonic plague 534–4, **535**
Budapest 650–1
Buddhism 501, 696, 698, 701
Buenos Aires 562, 563, 853
Bukharin, Nikola 804
Bulgaria 702, 731, 746, 755, 766, 809, 868, 901
Burchett, Wilfred 827
Burckhardt, Jacob 724
Burke, Edmund 728; *Reflections on the Revolution in France* 585–6, 588, 730, 732
Burma (Myanmar) 700, 834, 887
Burundi 837, **890**, 891, 906
Bush, George 878, 879
Bush, George W. 901
Butler, Josephine 646, 656, 736

Cabet, Etienne 732; *Voyage to Icaria* 733
Cabot, John 458, **459**
Caetano, Marcelo 837
Caillebotte, Gustave: *Rainy Day* **652**
California 566, 571, **792**, 873
Calvin, John 444
Cambodia **692**, 700, 836, 860, 907
Cambridge University 736

Camorra, the 683
Campanella, Tommaso: *City of the Sun* 501
Campo Formio, Treaty of (1797) 597
camps: labor (*gulags*) 803; Nazi death 803, 824, **825**, 826, 827
Camus, Albert 883
Canada 549–50, 566, **567**, 634, 690, 691, 714, 756, 835, 846, 901
cancer 885, 891
Candide (Voltaire) 498, 501
cannons 418–9, **419**; naval 419, 450
Capital (Marx) 734
capitalism 642, 647, 733, 902
capitalists 475
carbonari 668
Cardenas, Lazlo 852
CARE 895
Career of Gin, The (Hogarth) **533**
Caribbean, the 456, 461, 462, 467, 468–9, 471, 544–5, 561, 593, 617, 629, 634, 714, 855; Chinese and Indian immigrants 715; *see also* Haiti
Caribs 544
Carlsbad Decrees (1819) 668, 731
Carnegie, Andrew 629
Carolinas, the 550, 554, 572
Carrichon, Abbé 595
Carson, Rachel: *Silent Spring* 892
cartels 629
Carter, Jimmy 844, 876, 877
Cartesianism *see* Descartes, René
Cartier, Jacques 458, **459**
cartography 496
Cartwright, Edmund: power loom 615, 617, 620
Cass, Lewis 554
castas 548, **559**, 564
Castiglione, Baldassare: *The Book of the Courtier* **518**, 520–1
castles, medieval 419, **420**
Castro, Fidel 854, 855, **855**, 873, **899**
Catch-22 (Heller) 881
Catherine II (the Great) 437, 439, 440, 502, 519, 579, 693, 702
Catherine de' Medici 439, 440
Catholic Church 503; and birth control 783; in Britain and Ireland 669, 708, 737; in France 585, 584, 591, 602–3, 737; in Germany 681; in Italy 488, 580, 683, 809; in Poland 886; in Spain 817, 818; in Spanish America 548, 553, 563, 564; tithes 537–8
caudillos 561–2, **564**, 565, 853–4, 855
Cavell, Edith 750, **750**, 756
Cavendish, Margaret, Duchess of Newcastle 505, **507**, 526
Cavour, Camillo di 673, 674, 685
Ceausescu, Nicolae 878
Cecil, Robert 431
Cecil, Sir William 431
Celestina and her Daughter (school of Murillo) **531**
Celts 441
Central Intelligence Agency (CIA) 854, 873
Central Treaty Organization (CENTO) 872
Century of the Child, The (Key) 785
Century of Dishonor, A (H. Jackson) 568
Cervantes, Miguel de: *Don Quixote* 503
Chadwick, Edwin 646, 653
Chamberlain, Neville 818–19, 820
Chamorro, Violeta 854
Champlain, Samuel de 458–9
Chaplin, Charlie 773, 776
Charles I, of England 433, 489, 523, 578
Charles II, of England 433
Charles IV, of Spain 606
Charles V, Emperor **421**, 424, 427, 437
Charles VI, Emperor 426, 435
Charles VI, 426, 435
Charles VII, of France 420–1
Charles X, of France 670
Chartists 644, 647, 649, 669–70

Chechnyans 879
chemical industries 630
chemical weapons **752**, 753, 754, 904
Chernobyl disaster 877
Cherokee 567, **567**
Chiang Kai-shek 810, 848, 874
Chicago: Hull House 785
childbirth 490–1, **491**, 661, 726, 885
child-labor 640, 641, 642, 644, 645, 657–8, 661
children 525, 527, 533–4, 659, 784, 785, 888 see also child-labor; education
Chile 546, 560, 561, 562, 563, 564, 714, 853, 854, 873, 907
China 501, 635–6, 698–700, 713, 832, 847, 848–50, 857, 904; emigrants 715; famine 848, 892; and Japan 701–2, 747, 809–11, 848; trade and economy 698–9, 848–9, 902–3; women 849, 886, 887; see also Beijing
Chirac, Jacques 899
cholera 653, 654, 724
Chopin, Frédéric 723, 741
Chossudovsky, Michel 905
Christian Socialists 734, 737
Christianity 484–5, 498, 738; see also Catholic Church
Christina, Queen of Sweden 439, **504**, 505
Christine de Pisan 504
Chu Yan-chang 698
Chudleigh, Lady Mary: "To the Ladies" 526
Churchill, Sir Winston 761, 820, 822, 826, 868, **870**, 874; speeches 799, 819
CIA see Central Intelligence Agency
Cicero 503, 544
Ciliga, Anton: *The Russian Enigma* 806
cinema see films
circulation of the blood 489, **490**
cities see urban development
City of the Sun (Campanella) 501
Civil Rights movement 861, **862**, 863–4
Civilisation and its Discontents (Freud) 778
Clark, William 566
Classicism 523, 720, **722**; see also David, Jacques-Louis
Clemenceau, Georges 765
Clifford "Great Picture", The (Belcamp) **505**
Clinton, William Jefferson 901
clitorectomies 887
Clive, Robert 694
clothing 522, **600–1**, 659, 660–1
coalmining, British **616**, 619, 620, 644
Cockerill, William 627–8
Cold War 743, 840, 854, 855, **867**, 868, 871–7, 881, 898, 901
Cole, USS 909
Coleridge, Samuel Taylor: "Kubla Khan" 720
collections/collectors 509–10, 523
collective bargaining 647, 649, 794
collectivization 802, 848, 892
Colombia 546, 561
colonialism see specific countries
Columbus, Christopher 451, 455, 456, **457**, **459**, 460, 463, 464, 544, 546
Combination Acts 645, 649, 669
Comédie Française 523
"common sense" 497, 499
Common Sense (Paine) 557–8, 566, 579
Commonwealth of Nations 792, 832, 835
communication technologies 903
Communism/Communists 645, 647, 728, 733–4, 788, **816**, 817; in China 848–50; in Germany 765, 812; Soviet 743, 763, 799–807, 877, 878; and United States 854–5, 857, 858, 873
Communist Manifesto (Marx and Engels) 647, 733, 734
computer technology 872–3

Comte, Auguste 564, 728, 732
Concord, battle of 557
Condition of the Working Class in England, The (Engels) 654, 655, 733–4
Condorcet, Marquis de (Marie-Jean-Antoine Caritat) 501, 505, 589; *Sketch for a Historical Picture of the Progress of the Human Mind* 496, 500, 501
condottieri 420
Confucianism 501, 635, 698, 699, 701
Congo, Democratic Republic of 837
Conjugal Lewdness... (Defoe) 527
Conrad, Joseph: *Heart of Darkness* 712
Consecration of Napoleon and Coronation of Empress Josephine... (David) **602**
conservatism 666, 728, 730–1
Conservatives: British 676, 898; French 678
Constable, John 720
Constantinople see Istanbul
contraception see birth control
Conversations on the Plurality of Worlds (de Fontenelle) 505
Cook, Captain James 693
Coolidge, Calvin 790
"cooperative" societies 645–6
Copernicus, Nicholas 485, 487, 489, 498; *On the Revolutions of the Celestial Spheres* 485, **485**, 486
Corday, Charlotte **590**
Corn Laws 647, 669, 676
Corneille, Pierre 529
Cornwallis, Charles, 1st Marquis 558
corporatism 807
Cort, Henry: "puddling furnace" 620, **621**, 632
Cortés, Hernán 455, 460, 546, 547, 549
cosmology 484–5, **485**
cosmopolitanism 807
"cottage industries" 538, 613, 617, 640–1
cotton industry/plantations 473 **551**, 554, 569, 613, 615–17, **618**, 619, 622, 629, 699
counter-culture, Sixties 882
Courtier, The see Book of the Courtier
courts, European **518**, 520–1, 522
Creoles 545, 546, 548–9, 560, 561, **564**, 692
Crete 702
crime 534, 649, 654, 656, 683
Crimean War 677, 683, 685, 748, 757, 758
Crisis, The (Paine) 585
Croatia/Croats 667, 668, 674, 681, 731, 746, 766, 906
Crompton, Samuel: "mule" 615, 617, **618**
Cromwell, Oliver 420, 433, 437 708, 710
"Crystal Night" 814
Cuba 462, 547, 561, 565, 691, 840, 852, 853, 854–5, 873
Cubism 739
Curie, Marie and Pierre 726, **727**, 777
cybernetics 873, 903
Cyprus 702, 705
Czech Republic 879, 880, 901
Czechoslovakia/Czechs 668, 674, 681, 766, **798**, 807, 868, 877, **879**; literature 753, 779; "Prague Spring" **875**, 876; Sudetenland 818, 819; see Czech Republic

Daguerre, L.J.M. 721
d'Alembert, Jean see Diderot, Denis: *Encyclopedia*
dance 522–3, 776
Dante Alighieri 503
Danton, Georges-Jacques 589, 590
Darkness at Noon (Koestler) 807
Darwin, Charles 712, 724–6, **727**, 737, 782; *The Descent of Man* 726; *On the Origin of Species* 725
Dati, Giuliano: Columbus' first voyage **460**
Darwin, Erasmus 625, 726

David, Jacques-Louis 591, **722**; *Consecration of Napoleon and Coronation of Empress Josephine...* **602**; *Marat Assassinated* **590**; *Oath of the Tennis Court* **581**
Dawes, Philip: cartoon **569**
Dawes Plan 788
Dawes Severalty Act 569
Dayton Peace Agreement (1995) 907
Deal Castle, England **420**
Debs, Eugene 735, 787
"Decembrist Revolt" 668
Declaration of Independence 471
"Declaration of the Rights of Woman" (de Gouges) 593–4, 735
decolonization 832–5, 836, 837
deductive method of reasoning 493
Defoe, Daniel 455, 525, 614; *Conjugal Lewdness...* 527; *Robinson Crusoe* 501
deism 498, 580
de Klerk, Frederik Willem de 839–40
Delacroix, Eugène: *Liberty Leading the People* 720, **722**
Delaware 572; Indians 566
democracy 500–1
Democritus 777
demographic patterns see population
Deng Xiaoping 847, 850
Denmark **423**, 424, 519, 676, 683, **691**, 790, 820, 826
Denne, Henry 540
Depression, the see Great Depression
Descartes, René 484, 492, 493, 494, 497, 503, **504**, 505, 506, 510; *Discourse on Method* 484; *Philosophical Essays* 493
Descent of Man, The (Darwin) 726
Dialogue Concerning the Two Chief World Systems (Galileo) 488
Dias, Bartholomeu 450, 456, **459**
Diaz fel Castillo, Bernal 455
Díaz, Porfirio 564, 565, 853
Dickens, Charles 723; *Hard Times* 612
dictionaries 497, 503
Diderot, Denis 501, 503: *Encyclopedia* 497, **497**, **498**
Diem, Ngo Dinh 858–9
Dien Bien Phu, battle of 836, 857
Diggers 540
Discourse on Method (Decartes) 484
diseases 534–5, 653, 654, 885, 887, 891, 893
Disraeli, Benjamin 676
divorce 593, 662, 672, 885
Djindjic, Zoran 907
Djinljic, Zoran see Djindjic
Doctor Faustus (Marlowe) 496
Doctor Zhivago (Pasternak) 883
Dominican order 466
Dominican Republic 565, 852
Dominicans 487, 501, 503, 544
Don Quixote (Cervantes) 503
Dostoevsky, Fyodor: *Notes from the Underground* 720, 739
Douglass, Frederick **568**; autobiography 566
dowries 526
Drake, Sir Francis **453**, 458
Drang nach Osten 811
Dreadnought battleships 748, 755
Dreyfus, Alfred 710, **711**, 723
drugs, recreational 882
Dubcek, Alexander **875**, 876, 877
du Bois, William E.B. 863
du Châtelet, Emilie 509
du Deffand, Madame 509
"Dulce et Decorum est" (W. Owen) 753
Dulles, John Foster 871
Duma, the 759
Dumesnil, Louis Michel: *Queen Christina of Sweden with Descartes* **504**
Duncan, E.: *Nemesis* **699**
Durkheim, Emile 725, 728; *Suicide* 728
Dyck, Sir Anthony van 523
dyes 545, 654
Dylan, Bob 881, 882, 883; "The Times They are a-Changin'" 883
Dzerzhinsky, Felix 762, 800, 878

Earth Days 893
East India Company, British 615, 694, 695, 697
East India Company, Dutch **692**, 696
East Indies 696–8
Eastman, Max 806; *Since Lenin Died* 806
Eckhout, Albert: *Mulatto* 553
Economic and Monetary Union (EMU) 899
economics 580, 642, 727, 794; capitalism 642, 647, 733, 902; *laissez faire* 580, 676, 794; mercantilism 546, 547, 550, 578, 580; see also trade and economy
Ecuador 546, 561
Edison, Thomas 631
education/schools 502–3, 505, 557, 574, 579, 602, 659, 661, 678, 691, 701, 728–9, 805
Edward VII, of Britain **695**
Egypt 597, 636, 702–3, 835, 843, 844–5, 847, 874; Palestinians 844
Eighty Years and More... (Stanton) 566
Einstein, Albert 738, 772, 777, 826, 881; theories of relativity 738, 777, 778
Eisenhower, Dwight D. 821, 823, 854, 855, 858, 859, 864
Eisenstein, Sergei 773, 774, 801; *Alexander Nevsky* 774, 806; *Battleship Potemkin* **751**, 773; *October* 774
Electric Center (Sant'Elia) **774**
electricity **618**, 630, 631
Eliezer, Israel ben 710
Eliot, George 723, 741
Eliot, T.S. 779; "The Hollow Men" 779
Elizabeth I, of England 431, **434**, 437, 439, 440–1, 530
e-mails 903
Émile (Rousseau) 498, 503
empirical method 493, 494
EMU see European Monetary Union
encomiendas 462, 466 547
Encyclopedia (Diderot) 497, **497**, **498**
Engels, Friedrich 645, 646, 708, 709, 733; *Communist Manifesto* 647, 733, 734; *The Condition of the Working Class in England* 654, 655, 656, 733–4; *The Origin of the Family...* 734, 736
England see Britain; London
Enlightenment **483**, 496–502
environmentalism 892–4
Equality of Men and Women, The (de Gournay) 504, 505
Equiano, Olaudah 470, 471
Erasmus, Desiderius 505, 767
Erik the red 455
Eritrea 706, **815**
Escorial, Spain 427, 441, **443**
Essay Concerning Human Understanding (Locke) 494
Essay on Crimes and Punishments (Beccaria) 534, 654
Estonia see Baltic States
Ethiopia 705, 707, 809, **815**, 816, 817, 832, 840, 874
eugenics 712
European Union 871, 899, **902**
evolution, Darwin's theory of 724–6
Executions of the Third of May, 1808 (Goya) **605**
existentialism 779, 883
experimental method 494, 614

Fabian Society 735, 806
factories and factory workers **618**, **624**, 625, 640, 641–2, 654
Family Evening (Bouzonnet) **531**
family life 525–7, 657–8, 661–2, 781, 784–6
famine 670, 708, 848, 891, 892
Fanon, Frantz 842
farming see agriculture
fascism 731, 743, 785–6, 788, 798, 807–9, **816**, 817; see Nazism
fashion see clothing
Faulkner, William 871
Faust 496, 615

Faust (Goethe) 721
Federalist Papers (Hamilton, Jay, and Madison) 558
Fellini, Federico 882
Feminine Mystique, The (Friedan) 884
feminism: 15th-18th c. 505, **569**, 585, 593–4, 596; 19th c. **568**, 574, 662, 723, 728, 731, 735, 736; 20th c. 734, 780–3, 883–5, 886
Ferdinand II, of Aragon 426–7, 431, 456
Ferdinand VII, of Spain 606
Fernandez, Alejo: *Our Lady of the Navigators* **451**
Ferry, Jules 712, 729
festivities, village 539–40
Fichte, Johann Gottlieb 679, 732
films 631, **751**, 772–5, 882–3
fin de siècle 737, 741
"Final Solution" 824, **824**, **825**, 826, 827
Finland 763, 766, 790, 821, 868
Finnegans Wake (Joyce) 741
Flaubert, Gustave: *Madame Bovary* 721
Florence: population (1457) **515**
Florida 566, **567**, 572
flower power **884**
Foch, Marshal Ferdinand 767
Fonte, Moderata: *Women's Worth* 504, 506, 509, 527
Fontenelle, Bernard de: *Conversations on the Plurality of Worlds* 505
Ford, Henry 786
Foster, William 729
Foucault, Michel: *Madness and Civilization* 883
foundling homes 659
Fourier, F.M. Charles 728, 732–3, 736
France: absolutism 429–31; Academies 503, **508**, 510, 593; army 420–1, 425; agriculture 536; bourgeoisie 524, 670; Canadian and American settlement 549–50, **552**, 555–6; Catholic Church 583, 584, 591, 602–3; *Code Napoléon* 599, 602, 662, 670, 735; colonies 458–9, **459**, 544, **691**, **692**, **704**, 707, 833, *see also* Algeria; Declaration of the Rights of Man and the Citizen 583, 584; decolonization 836–7; Directory 596, 597; Dreyfus affair 710, **711**, 723; education 502, 602, 728–9; 1830/31 uprisings 645, 670, **684**; 1848 uprising 645, 647, 670, 671, 672–3, **684**; emigration 715, **715**; Estates General 579, 581–3; Freemasonry 499; friendly societies 646; the Fronde 520; Girondins 585, 590, **590**; and Indochina/Vietnam 700, 857, 858; industrialization 626–7, **630**; Jacobins 585, 590, 595; land ownership **582**; literature *see* literature; movies 631, 882–3; National Assembly **581**, 583, 584, 585, 586, 587, 595; National Convention 587, 589, 590, 591, **592**, 593, 595, 596; nobility **515**, 516, 517, 519–20, 579, 582, 589; painting *see* painting; peasantry **538**, 583, 586; philosophers 779, 883; population **515**, 784; postwar politics 899; *les précieuses* 509; salons **508**, 509; Second Republic 670, 672–3; Seven Years' War 555; syndicalism 735; theater 514, **523**, 529; Third Republic 677–8; Thirty Years' War 422, 424, 425; trade and economy 627, **632**, **714**, 788; trade unions 649; urbanization **651**; Versailles 430, 440, **443**; women 505, 593–4, 596, 599, 602, **658**, 672, 735; workhouse system 532; in World War I 748, 749, 750, 752, 767, 768, **768**; in World War II 819, 820; *see also* Franco-Prussian War; French Revolution; Napoleon; Paris; *philosophes*
Francia, José Gaspar Rodríguez de 560
Francis Joseph, Emperor 673, 681

Franco, General Francisco 809, 818
Franco-Prussian War 627, 666, 676, 677–8, 685
Frankfurt: Parliament **675**, 675–6; riot **534**
Franklin, Benjamin 495, 497, 521
Franz Ferdinand, Archbishop 747, 756
Frederic II, of Denmark 485
Frederick II (the Great), of Prussia 421, 426, 435, 439, 502, 579, 628
Frederick William I, of Prussia 435
Frederick William IV, of Prussia **675**, 676
free trade 580, 642, 644, 676, 901–2
Freemasonry 499, 580
French Revolution 514, 577, 578, 579, 581, 585–7, **586**, 589–91, **592**, 593–4, **594**, 595–6, 666, **684**, 731; and fashion **600**–1; and women 593–4, 735
Freud, Sigmund 710, 736, 738, **740**, 805, 813; *Civilisation and its Discontents* 778
Friedan, Betty: *Feminine Mystique* 884
"friendly" societies 645–6
Fronde, the 520
Fukuyama, Francis 910
Fulton, Robert: *Clermont* 623–4
futurism **774**, 808

Gadsden Purchase 566, **567**
Galen/Galenists 489, 490
Galileo Galilei 487, 488, 489, 494, 503, 614; *Dialogue Concerning the Two Chief World Systems* 488; *Starry Messenger* 488; telescope **487**, 487–8
Gallery of Scenes from Ancient Rome (Pannini) **522**
Gama, Vasco da 450, 456, 458, **459**
Gandhi, Indira 847–8, 884
Gandhi, Mohandas ("Mahatma") 833, 834, **834**, 847, 864
Gandhi, Rajiv 848
Gare Saint-Lazare (Monet) **625**
Garibaldi, Giuseppe 674, **674**
Garvey, Marcus 863
gas lamps 630–1, 653
Gaskell, P. 641
Gatling, Richard: gun 754
Gaulle, Charles de 823, 837, 881, 899
Gay, John: *The Beggar's Opera* 529
Gelbspan, Ross 893
genetics 724, 805
Genoa 579, **808**; G8 meeting 902
genocide 798, 824, 895, 906, 907; *see also* Holocaust, the
Gentileschi, Artemisia 527; *Judith Slaying Holofernes* **531**
Geoffrin, Madame: salon **508**, 509
Georgia 702, 763, 802, 878, 799
Georgia, USA 566, 566, 572
German Social Democratic Party 681
Germany: art **643**, **759**, 813; colonies **691**, 706, 707, **757**; communists 765, 812; cooperative banks 646; education 502, 729; emigration 715, **715**; immigration 716; industrialization 626, 628–9, **630**; interwar 765–6, 814–17, 815; literature 721, 763, 881; music and opera 603–4, 720, 721, 739; nationalism 679, 811–12, *see also* Nazis/Nazism; navy 686, 755–6; philosophers and thinkers 497, 710, 721, 728, 737, 813; postwar 868, 869–70; reunification (1990) 878, 901; scientists 777, 778; Thirty Years' War 422, 424, 427; trade and economy 614, **627**, 628, **632**, 659, 668, **714**, 788, **789**, 790, 793, 811, 813, 901; trade unions 649; unification 665, 666, 668, 675–6, 678, **680**, 731, 811; urbanization **651**; welfare 785; women 781, 813; World War I 686, 747, 748–50, 752, **752**, 753–6, 758, 763, 765, 767, **768**; World War II 814, 818–21, 823–4, 869; *see also* Berlin; Frankfurt; Hamburg; Prussia

Germinal (Zola) 723
Geronimo 568
Gettysburg Address (Lincoln) 570, 573
Ghana (Gold Coast) 468, 707, 835, 838
Gibraltar 425
Gide, André 806
Gilman, Charlotte Perkins 781, 782–3; *Women and Economics* 782
Gilray, James: cartoon **591**
Gin Lane (Hogarth) *see Career of Gin*
Giolitti, Giovanni 683
Girondins 585, 590, **590**
Giuliani, Rudolph 908
Gladstone, William 676, 682
glasnost 877
"global warming" 894
"Glorious Revolution" 433–4, 578
Glückel of Hameln 506
Godard, Jean-Luc 883
Goethe, Johann von 603, 721; *Faust* 721; *The Sorrows of Young Werther* 721
Gogh, Vincent van 738–9; *Potato Eaters* 739; *Starry Night* 739, **740**
Goldman, Emma 782
Good Soldier Schweik, The (Hasek) 753
Gorbachev, Mikhail 877, 878, 879, 880, 894, 898
Gorky, Maxim 806
Gouges, Olympe de: "Declaration of the Rights of Woman" 593–4, 735
Gournay, Marie de 504; *The Equality of Men and Women* 504, 505
Goya, Francisco de: *Family of Charles IV* 435; *The Executions of the Third of May, 1808* **605**
Graebe, Hermann 827
Grand National Consolidated Trades Union 646–7, 649
Grand Tour, the 523
Grande Illusion, La (J. Renoir) 773
gravity 488, 489
Great Depression 786, **789**, 790, **791**, 791–2, **792**, 861, 863
Great Exhibition, London 625, 628
Great Saturday (Lewicki) **684**
Greece 485, 489, 669, 731, 755, 766, 809; *see also* Aristotle
Greenland 455–6
Greenwich, England: Prime Meridian **911**, 912
Greider, William 905
Grenada 854
Grey, Sir Edward 747
Griffith, D.W. 772–3; *The Birth of a Nation* 773, **773**, 776
Gros, Antoine-Jean: *Napoleon Bonaparte on Arcole Bridge* **598**; *Napoleon on the Battlefield of Eylau* **599**
Grote, George 724
Guadeloupe 544
Guangzhou 699, **699**, 811
Guernica, bombing of 818
Guiana: British 544–5; Dutch 544, **552**
guilds/guildsmen 476, 524, 613, 644, 645
Guinea-Bissau 837, 840
Gulag Archipelago, The (Solzhenitsyn) 806, 883
gulags 803
Gulf War 843, 847
Gulliver's Travels (Swift) 501
guns 418–9, **419**
Guomindang 810, 848
Gustavus II Adolphus, of Sweden 420, 437

Habsburg dynasty/Empire 502, 509, 519, 549, 579, 606, 665, 666, **667**, 667–8, 673–4, **680**, 681, 683, 702, 765
haciendas 462, 547–8, **548**
Haile Selassie 816, 840
Haiti 456, 471, 558–9, 561, 565, 593, 606, 852, 854, 891; voodoo 544

Hakluyt, Richard: *The Principal Navigations...of the English Nation* 501
Hamas, the 845
Hamburg 524; plague ward **535**
Hamilton, Alexander *see* Madison, James
Hammer, Armand 806
Hard Times (Dickens) 612
Hargreaves, James: spinning jenny 615
Harlem Renaissance 863
Harris Treaty (1858) 701
Harvey, William 489, 490, 493; circulation of the blood 489, **491**
Hasek, Jaroslav: *The Good Soldier Schweik* 753
Hasidism 710
Haussmann, Baron Georges 646, **652**, 653
Havel, Václav 868, 877, **879**, 880, 900, 910
Haviland, Laura S.: *A Woman's Life* 571
Hawaii/Hawaiian Islands 566, 855
Hawes, Josiah Johnson: *Lemuel Shaw* **722**
Heart of Darkness (Conrad) 712
Hébert, Jacques René 590, 591, 593
Hegel, G.W. Friedrich 721, 728, 737
Heidegger, Martin 813
Heilbroner, Robert 880
Heine, Heinrich 710
Heisenberg, Werner 778; indeterminacy/uncertainty principle 772, 777
Heller, Joseph: *Catch-22* 881
Henry II, of England 707
Henry IV, of France 423, 429, 430
Henry V (Shakespeare) 427
Henry VII, of England 431
Henry VIII, of England 431, 708
Henry the Navigator, Prince 450
Herzl, Theodor 710; *Jewish State* 710
Hevelius, Elisabetha and Johannes **507**
Hidalgo, Miguel 555, 559
Hindenburg, Paul von 755, 812–13
Hinduism 501, 695, 696
Hipparchus of Nicaea 448
Hiroshima, bombing of **824**, **826**, 827, 828, 868
Hispaniola *see* Haiti
Hiss, Alger 873
Historical and Critical Dictionary (Bayle) 497
historians 494, 724, 725
Hitler, Adolf 793, 798, 809, 811, 812–13, 814, **814**, 816, **818**, 823; on contraception 786; *Mein Kampf* 799, 810, 812, 813, 814; prewar annexations 807, 818–20; and propaganda films 774; and Spain 818; speeches 810, 814, 819; suicide 826
HIV/AIDS 887, 891, 893
Ho Chi Minh 834, 836, 847, 857, 858, 860
Hobbes, Thomas 544, 581; *Leviathan* 439, 442, 444
Hobson, J.A.: *Imperialism...* 712, 713
Hoess, Rudolf 827
Hogarth, William: *Career of Gin* **533**
Holbein, Hans the Younger: *The Ambassadors* 432
"Hollow Men, The (T.S. Eliot) 779
Hollywood 775
Holocaust, the 824, **824**, **825**, 826, 827
Holy Alliance (1815) 685
Holy Roman Empire 422, **423**, 424
Homer, Winslow: *The Bayonet Charge* **572**; *A New Field of Dead Men* **573**
Hondius: world map **453**
Hong Kong 699, 832, 835, 851
Hoover, Herbert 792
"Hoovervilles" 792
House Un-American Activities Committee (HUAC) 873
housing: tenements 656–7, **658**; townhouses 659

Howard, John Langley: *California Industrial Scenes* **792**
HUAC *see* House Un-American Activities Committee
Huguenots 423, 429, 430, 431, 444, 464
Human Comedy, The (Balzac) 721
humanists 505, 510; women 505, 506
Hume, David 493, 499
humors, theory of 489
Hundred Years' War 418. 429
Hungary 444, 665, 667, 673, 674, 702, 766; nobility **515**, 519, 579, 668; 20th c. 809, 868, 875, 877, 879, 901; *see also* Austria-Hungary
Huntington, Samuel 898, 910
Hutu people 832, **890**, 906, 907
hypotheses 494
I and Thou (Buber) 779
Illinois 566
immunization *see* vaccination
imperialism 690; British 713, 716, 731; United States 833, 851
Imperialism, a Study (Hobson) 712, 713
Impression - Sunrise (Monet) 738, **740**
Impressionists 738
Inca civilization 455, 459, 461
indeterminacy (Heisenberg) 772, 777
India 847–8, 875; British in 690, **692**, 694–6, 697, 832; East India Company 452; European nases 450, 452, 458; independence 832–4; Mughal Empire 452, 694; nuclear power 904; poetry 695, 697; Rajput revolts 694; Seven Years' War 425; trade and economy 458, 615, 617, 635, 695, 712, 793; women 695, 887, **890**
Indian Mutiny (1857) 695
Indian National Congress 696
Indian Woman and Child (White) **553**
Indochina **692**, 698, 699, 700, 715, 836
Indonesia 454, 696, 697, 836, 846, 847, 848, 875
inductive method of reasoning 493, 494
industrialization 612, **631**, *see specific country*
Inés de la Cruz, Sor Juana 549
influenza 768, 891
Inquisition, the 426, 580
Instruction of a Christian Woman, The (Vives) 504
International Brigades 818
International Court of Justice 683
International Criminal Tribunal 907
International Red Cross 895
International Space Station 903
International Workingmen's Association (Internationals) 647, 734, 735, 801
Internet 903
Intifada 845
inventions 418–9; **419**; 476; **487**, 487–8, 494–5, 569, 615, 617, 619–20, **621**, 623–4, **626**, 629, 631, 714
Iowa 566
Iran 702, 705, 832, 835, 843, 845, 846; women 886
Iraq 702, 835, 844, 874, 904, 906
Ireland 669, 670, 707–8, **711**, 715, **715**, 716, 835–6, 891; writers 501, 708, 738, 741, 776, 779
Irish Republican Army 909
iron and steel industry: British **616**, **618**, 620, **621**, 622, **623**; Russian 632
Isabella II, of Spain 427, 431, 439, 456, 683
Islam/Muslims 693, 695, 696, 702, 703–4, 842, 843, 844, 845, 909; fundamentalism 846–7, 879; women 846, 886
Isonzo River, battles of the 755, 808
Israel 835, 842, 844–5, 847, 874, 879, 904, 907
Istanbul (Constantinople) 746–7, 766, 843

Italy 667; caloric intake 891; Catholic Church 488, 580, 683, 809; colonies **691**, **704**, 706, **833**; courts **518**, 520–1; decolonization 836; education 729; emigration 715, **715**, 716; expansionism 747, **815**, 816, 817; farming 536; nationalism 679; nobility 519; opera 529, 720; painting **522**, **531**, **774**; philosophy 493–4; postwar politics 899; Red Brigades 909; textile production 613; Triple Alliance 686; unification 665, 666, 668, 674–5, **680**, 683, 731; urbanization 612, **651**; women scientists **507**, 509; women writers 506, 509, 529; World War I 755, 767, **768**; World War II 814, 823; *see also* Genoa; Rome; Venice
Ito Hirobumi 700
Iturbide, General Augustín de 559
Ivan IV (the Terrible), Tsar 437, 519
ivory trade 706

Jackson, Andrew 554, 567
Jackson, Helen Hunt: *A Century of Dishonor* 568
Jacobins 585, 590, 595
Jacobs, Aletta 783
Jamaica 544
James I, of England (VI of Scotland) 431, 433; *True Law of Free Monarchy* 433, 439
James II, of England 433
Jamestown, Virginia 550, 554
Japan 448, **692**, 700–2, 832, 891; and China 701–2, 747, 809–11, 848; expansionism **815**, 817; Russo-Japanese War 634, 677, 686, 693, 702; trade and economy 454, 634, 698, 701, 714, 851, 903; and United States 634, 701, **701**, 851, 874; urbanization **651**; women 886, 887, 888; World War I 747; World War II 814, 819, 821–3, 824, 826, 828, 857
Jaurès, Jean 735
Java 696, 697
Jay, John *see* Madison, James
jazz **775**, 775–6, 781, 882
Jefferson, Thomas 497, 498, 499, 500, 544; Declaration of Independence **556**, 558, 570
Jenner, Edward 491
Jesuits 5466, 01, 580, 701, 779
Jewish State, The (Herzl) 710
Jews 506, 535, 709–10, 715; and Nazis 810, 812, 823, 824, **824**, **825**, 826; *see also* anti-Semitism; Israel
Jiang Qing 850
John of Jandun 438
John VI, prince-regent of Portugal 560
John Paul II, Pope **899**, 903
Johnson, Eastman: *A Ride for Liberty* **551**
Johnson, Lyndon B. 854, 859, 881
Johnson, Samuel 501
joint stock companies 452, 462, 524, 550
Jolliet, Louis 459
Jordan 702, 835; Palestinians 844
Joseph, Chief 568
Joseph II, Emperor 435, 502, 579
Josephine (de Beauharnais), Empress 597, **602**, 606
Jospin, Lionel 899
journeymen 525
Joyce, James 738, 741; *Ulysses* 779
Juárez, Benito **564**
Judaism 710, 737, 738
Judith Slaying Holofernes (Gentileschi) **531**
Junkers 519, 678, 748
jury system, English 442
Jutland, battle of 755–6

kabbalah 709
Kafka, Franz 779; *The Trial* 779
Kandinsky, Vasily 739, 778; *Study for Composition VII* **740**
Kansas 571

Kant, Immanuel 497, 737
Katyn forest massacre 821
Kautsky, Karl 734, 781
Kavi, Dalpatram: "The Attack of King Industry" 695, 697
Kay, John: flying shuttle 615, 616
Kazakhstan 846, 878, 879
Kemal, Mustafa 766, 843
Kennan, George F. 870
Kennedy, John F. 854, 855, 859, 864, 881
Kennedy, Paul 900
Kennedy, Robert F. 881
Kent State University killings 881
Kentucky 566, 572
Kenya 835, 839, 840, 909
Kenyatta, Jomo 840
Kepler, Johannes **484**, 485, 487, 489, 496; *New Astronomy* 487
Kerensky, Alexander 760, 761–2
Kershaw, Patience 644
Key, Ellen 785
Keynes, John Maynard: economic theories 793, 794
Khmer Rouge 860, 907
Khobar Towers airbase 909
Khomeini, Ayatollah Ruhollah 843, 845, 846
Khrushchev, Nikita 875, 876, 880
Kierkegaard, Sören 737
King, Martin Luther **862**, 863, 864, 881, 894; letter from Birmingham Jail 861
kings *see* monarchs
Kipling, Rudyard 748, 766; "The White Man's Burden" 712, 713
Kirov, Sergei Mironovich 802
Knox: *First Blast of the Trumpet against the Monstrous Regiment of Women* 440–41
Koestler, Arthur 806–7; *Darkness at Noon* 807
Kollantai, Alexandra 781, 782
Kollwitz, Käthe: *The Parents* **759**; *A Weavers' Uprising* **643**
Korea 698, 701, 747, 851, 857, 904, 906; Korean War 851, **856**, 857, 858, 874–5, 896
Kornilov, General Lavr 762, 799
Kosovo **890**, 906, 907
Kostunica, Vojislav 907, **907**
Kristallnacht 814
Kronstadt sailors 804
Krupp, Alfred 628; factory 628, **643**
Krupskaya, Nadezhda 800–1; *Lenin* 762
Ku Klux Klan 860–1
Kubrick, Stanley 873
kulaks (Russian 801, 803, 804, **805**
Kulturkampf 681
Kurds 847, 909
Kuwait 847, 887, 906

labor 642, 786–7; division of 727
labor associations 644–5; *see* trade unions
Labour Party, British 676, 788, 898, 899
Lafayette, Marquis de 514, 587
laissez faire policies 580, 676, 794
Lamarck, Jean-Baptiste 724
Lamartine, Alphonse de 671
Lancashire, England: cotton factory **618**
Landes, David S. 905
Laos **692**, 699, 700, 836, 860
Las Casas, Bartolomé de 455, **463**, 466, 470
latifundia 562, 564, 634
Latin, use of 489, 503
Latin America: and United States 851–3, 855, **856**, 901; *see also* Cuba; Mexico; South America
Latvia *see* Baltic States
Lausanne Conference (1932) 792
Lavoisier, Antoine 589
League of Nations 763, 765, 766, 809, 811, 815, 816, 817
Lebanon 702, 836; Palestinians 844
Lebensraum ("living space") 810, 812, 814
Leibniz, Gottfried W. von 492, 493

Leipzig, battle of 606
Lemnos 702
Lemonnier, A.: *The Salon of Mme Geoffrin* **508**
Lenin, Vladimir Ilyich 666, 712–13, **751**, 760, 761, 762, 763, 774, 799, 801, 802, 803, 806, 807; New Economic Policy 790, 793, 801, 803; *What Is To Be Done?* 761, 762, 799
Leningrad, siege of 821, **823**; *see* St. Petersburg
Leo XIII, Pope 779
Leonardo da Vinci 489
Leopold, Emperor 579
Leopold II, of Belgium 707
Lepanto, battle of 702
Léry, Jean de: *History of a Voyage to the Land of Brazil* 501
Lespinasses, Julie de 509
Lesseps, Ferdinand de 703
Letters Concerning Toleration (Locke) 499
Levellers 540
Leviathan (Hobbes) 439, 442, 444
Lewicki, J.N.: *Great Saturday* **684**
Lewis, Bernard 910
Lewis, Meriwether 566
Lexington, battle of 557
liberalism 670, **672**, 676, 678, 729–30
Liberal Party, British 676
Liberia 707, 832; first railway **635**
Liberty Leading the People (Delacroix) 720, **722**
Libya 702, 747, **815**, 840, 873, 904; women 887
Liebknecht, Karl 765
Liège, Belgium 749
life expectancies 889, 891
Life of Christ (Renan) 724
Lille, France: urban poor 657
Lin Tse-Hsu 636
Lincoln, Abraham 571–2, 767; Gettysburg Address 570, 573
Linke, Lilo: on Hitler 810
Lisbon: population (1750–1950) 448, 452, 478, **650**
List, Friedrich 614, 628, 633
Lister, Joseph 726
literature: American 566, 723, 738, 768, 779, 806–7; British and Irish 496, 501, 504, 505, 506, 509, 534, 612, 708, 712, 713, 720, 723, 738, 741, 746, 748, 753, 766, 779, 806; Czech 753, 779; French 498, 501, 504, 721, 723, 732, 779, *see also* Zola; German 721, 763, 881; Indian 695, 697; Italian 501; Russian 720, 739, 806, 883; Spanish 503, 529; World War I 753
Lithuania *see* Baltic States
Liverpool docks 644
Livingstone, David 706
Lloyd George, David 758, 765
Lloyd's Insurance Company 510
Locarno, Treaty of 815, 816
Locke, John 444, 494, 500, 503, 506, 544, 557, 558, 581, 729; *Essay Concerning Human Understanding* 494; *Letters Concerning Toleration* 499; *Treatises on Civil Government* 442, 444, 494, 499, 500
Lockerbie disaster 909
Lodi, Peace of 422
logical positivism 778–9
London 478, 503, 528, 655; Blitz 820; bourgoisie 524; British Museum 510; cholera 653; Great Exhibition 625, 628; parks 653; population **528**, **650**, 651; poverty 532, **651**; St. Pancras workhouse **660**; theater 529; underground 653; women's occupations **658**
London Working Men's Association 647, 669
Louis XIV, of France 421, 430–1, 437, 438, 440, 502, 510, 514, **516**, 519, 520, 524, 549, 579; *Louis XIV Instituting the Order of Saint Louis* (Marot) **517**

Louis XV, of France 431
Louis XVI, of France 431, 578, 579, 580, 581, 583, 585, 673, 721; execution 587, 589, **592**
Louis XVIII, of France 607, 670
Louis-Philippe, of France 587, 607, 670
Louisiana 566, **567**, 572, 606
Louvain, Belgium 749–50
L'Ouvrirte, François Dominique Toussaint 555, 558–9, 593, 606
Louvre Museum, Paris 510
Lowell, Francis Cabot 629
Lucca 579
Luddites 645
Ludendorff, General Erich 754–5
Lumumba, Patrice 837, 838–9, 840
Lusitania, sinking of the 756
Luther, Martin 498, 503, 811
Lutherans 737
Luxemberg, Rosa 756, 758, 765
Lyell, Charles 726
Lyons, France: population (1545) **515**; weavers' revolt 645

Macao 698, 699
MacArthur, General Douglas 822, 828, 851, 857
Macaulay, Thomas Babington 690, 697, 724
McCarthy, Senator Joseph 873
Macedonia 906
Machiavelli, Niccolò: *The Prince* 418, 438, 444
Madame Bovary (Flaubert) 721
Madeiras: plantations 544
Madison, James, Jay, John, and Hamilton, Alexander: *Federalist Papers* 558
Madness and Civilization (Foucault) 883
Mafia, the 683
Magellan, Ferdinand 457–8, **459**, 696
magic 495–6
Magrite, René: *"This is not a pipe"* **774**
Magyars 681
Mahdi, the 703
Maimonides 709
Malacca 696, 698
Malaysia 696, 698, 700, 834
Malcolm X 790, **862**, 864
Mali, kingdom of 468
malnutrition 891
Malthus, Thomas 888; *Essay on Population* 725, 727–8
Mamluks 597, 702
Man with the Hoe, The (Millet) 721, **722**
Manchester, England 530, 620, 623, 645, 646, 650, 652, 653, 655; Peterloo Massacre 647, 669
Manchu dynasty 698, 811
Manchuria 698, 811, 817
Mandela, Nelson 832, 838, 839, **839**, 841, 842
Mandelstam, Nadezhda 804
Mandelstam, Osip 804, 806
Manhattan Island 552
"Manhattan Project" 826
"Manifest Destiny" **567**
Mann, Thomas 813
Manzolini, Anna Morandi **507**
Mao Zedong 847, 848, **849**, 848–50, 874
Maoris 693
map-making 449, 496; Portolan charts 449, **453**
Marat, Jean-Paul 593; *Marat Assassinated* (David) **590**
Marconi, Guglielmo 631
Marcos, Ferdinand 847, 857
Marcos, Imelda 857
Maria Theresa, Empress 426, 435, 439, 440
Marie Antoinette 580, 594
Marie de' Medici **436**, 439
Marinella, Lucrezia 509; *The Nobility and Excellence of Women* 504, 505
Marlowe, Christopher: *Doctor Faustus* 496

Marot, François: *Louis XIV Instituting the Order of Saint Louis* **517**
Marquette, Jacques 459
marriage 521, 526, 661–2, 885
Marriage of Figaro, The (Mozart) 529
Marseilles, France 477
Marshall, George C. 894; Plan 869–70
Marshall, Thurgood 863–4
Marsilius of Padua 438, 544
Martinique 544
Martyr, Peter: *Chronicles of the New World* 501
Marx, Karl 646, 710, 727, 734, 737; *Capital* 734; *Communist Manifesto* 647, 733, 734
Marxism 733–5, 736, 761, 799
Mary, Virgin **451**
Mary I, of England 428, 431, 439
Mary Queen of Scots 431
Maryland 572
Massachusetts 462, 550, 557, 573–4
matchgirls' strike **648**, 649
Mathematical Principles of Natural Philosophy (Newton) 486, 489, 496
Matteotti, Giacomo 808
Maxim, Hiram: gun 754
Mazarin, Cardinal Jules 430, 520
Mazzini, Giuseppe 668, 674, 679, 732, 736
measles 887, 891
Médecins sans Frontières 895
Medici family, 423
medicine 489–91, 495, 534, 726, 885
Medvedev, Roy 802, 883; *Let History Judge* 804
Meiji Constitution (Japan) 700, 701
Meir, Golda 884
Meissonier, Ernest: *La Barricade* **684**
Memphis workers' strike **862**
Mendel, Gregor Johann 724
Mendelssohn, Felix 710
Mendelssohn, Moses 710
Mensheviks 760, 761
mercantilism 430, 474, 479, 546, 547, 550, 578, 580
messianic movements 709–10
mestizos 546, 548
metal production 613; see also mining
metaphysics 491
Methodists 737
Metternich, Prince Clemens von 666–7, 668, 673, 682, 685, 731
Metz 685
Mexico 546, 563, **564**, 565, 566, **567**, 716, 846, 852, 853, 855, 860, 901; War of Independence 559, 561
Meyerhold, Vsevolod 806
Miami Indians 566
Michaelis, Caroline 720–1
Michelangelo Buonarroti 419
Michelet, Jules 724
microbiology 724
Mignard, Pierre 524
migration 715–16, 891
Milan: women's occupations **658**
Mill, John Stuart 730, 735; *On Liberty* 730, 732; *On the Subjection of Women* 730
mill workers 640–1
Millet, Jean-François: *The Man with the Hoe* 721, **722**
Milosevic, Slobodan 906, 907
Milton, John 503–4; *Areopagitica* 504
mines/mining 640, 723; Africa 838; Britain (coal) **616**, 619, 620, 644; and child labor 640, 642, 644; gold 545, 547, 548, 634; silver 546, 547, 548, 634
Ming dynasty 452, 698
Ministry of an Egg (Velázquez) **532**
missionaries 426, 463, 466, 553, 599, 695, 701, 706, 707, 712
Mississippi 572
Missouri 571, 572
Mobutu, Joseph 838, 839
Modernism 719, **722**, 738; and the arts 738–9, **740**; and music 739, 741
Moldavia 668, 683, 685

Molière 514, 529; *The Would-Be Gentleman* 514
Moltke, Field Marshal Helmuth von 748, 750, 754, 756
Moluccas 448, 452, 454, 455, 696, 697
Mombasa, sack of 458
monarchs 520, 578–9
Monet, Claude 739; *Gare Saint-Lazare* **625**; *Impression—Sunrise* 738, **740** 778
Mongolia 698
Mongols 698, 702
Monroe Doctrine 561, 669, 851
montage 773
Montagu, Lady Mary Wortley 491, 509
Montaigne, Michel de 448, 501, 504
Montenegro 702, 746, 906
Montesquieu (Charles-Louis de Secondat) 430, 471, 499, 544, 558; *Persian Letters* 501; *Spirit of Laws* 499
Montezuma II 460, 464
Montgomery, General Bernard 821
moon landing (1969) 872
Moore, George E. 779
Moravia 667, 819; *robot* 538
More, Hannah 709
More, Sir Thomas: *Utopia* 422, 501, 534
Morelos, José María 559
Moro, Aldo 810
Morocco 702, 707, 715, 747, 756, 836
Moscow 632, 633, 716, **751**, 761, 801; population **528**, **650**
Mosley, Sir Oswald 809
Moulin de la Galette, Le (Renoir) **661**
movies see films
Mozambique 706, 837, 840
Mozart, W.A.: *The Marriage of Figaro* 529
Mugabe, Robert 838, 840–1
Mughal Empire 452, 694
Muhammad II (Gentile Bellini) **432**
Mulatto (Eckhout) **553**
mulattoes 545, 546, 548, **553**
Munich Appeasement 819
Munich Putsch 812
Murillo, school of: *Celestina and Her Daughter* **531**
museums 510, 662
music: classical 522–3, 603–4, 720, 721, 723, 741; jazz and blues **775**, 775–6, 781, 782; pop and rock 881, 882; see also opera
Muslims see Islam
Mussolini, Benito 798, 807, **808**, 808–9, 816, 817, 818, 819; death 823, 826; on fascism 810
Mutesa, Kabaka 703
Myanmar see Burma

NAACP see National Association for the Advancement of Colored People
NAFTA (North American Free Trade Agreement) 901
Nagasaki, Japan 698, 701; bombing of **824**, 828, 868
Nagy, Imre 875
Namibia 835
Nana (Zola) 723
Nanjing 810, 811; Treaty (1842) 699
Nant-y-glow Ironworks (Robertson) **643**
Nantes, edict of 423, 429, 430
Naples **674**; Camorra 683; population **528**, **650**
Napoleon Bonaparte 559, 560, 566, 578, 582, 593, 596–7, 607, 627, 628, 666, 668, 673; and Catholic Church 602–3; Empire 577, 600, **604**; *Grande Armée* 603–6; Russian débâcle 606; and secret police 731; Waterloo 607; and workers' combinations 645
Napoleon Bonaparte on Arcole Bridge (Gros) **598**
Napoleon on the Battlefield of Eylau (Gros) **599**

Napoleon III 627, 653, 672–3, 674, 677, 678, 685
Napoleonic Code 599, 602, 662, 670, 735
Nash, Paul: *We are Making a New World* **754**
Nasser, Gamal Abdel 843, 875
Nast, Thomas: *"The Day We Celebrate"* **711**
natalism 785–6
Nathan of Gaza 710
National Association for the Advancement of Colored People (NAACP) 863–4
National Organization of Women (NOW) 884
nationalism 589, 666, 668, 673, 676, 679, 728, 731
NATO (North Atlantic Treaty Organization) **869**, 871, 872, 876, 879, 899, **902**, 907
"natural philosophers" 489
Nauvoo, Illinois 733
navigation aids 448–9, **453**
Navigation Acts 424, 475
Nazi-Communist Pact (1939) **818**, 820
Nazis/Nazism 731, 739, 774, 793, 798, 799, 811–14, 828; death camps 803, 824, **825**, 826, 827
Nebraska 571
Necker, Jacques 721
Nehru, Jawaharlal 833, **834**, 847
Nelson, Admiral Horatio 597, 606
Nemesis (Duncan) **699**
Neoclassicism 523, 529; see David, Jacques-Louis
neo-colonialism 690
Netanyahu, Benjamin 843, 845
Netherlands 579, 668; agriculture 477, 536, 615; bourgeoisie 524, 526; colonies 544, 549, 550, 552, **552**, **691**, 692, 696–8, 705, **833**, 836; landowners 525; nobility 519; painting see painting; philosopher/scholars 492, 505, 710, 767; slave trade 554; trade and economy **525**, **632**, 696–8, 701, **714**; urbanization **651**; World War II 820; see also Amsterdam
Nevada 566
New Atlantis (Bacon) 501
New Deal 793–4
New England 462, 550, 553, 555, 619
New York State 462
New Field of Dead Men, A (Homer) **573**
*New Lanark, Scotland 646
New Method, The (Bacon) 494
New Mexico 566, 571, 853
New York 550, **797**; attack on World Trade Center 909, **909**; underground 653
New Zealand 634, 693, 715, 835; Maoris 693, 756; women **884**, 887
Newcomen, Thomas: steam engine 619, **621**
Newman, John Henry 737
Newton, Sir Isaac 489, 496, 498; *Mathematical Principles of Natural Philosophy* 486, 489, 495
Nez Percé 568
NGOs see Non-Governmental Organizations
Nicaragua 854, 855
Nicholas I, Tsar 668
Nicholas II, Tsar 677, 759, 760, 761
Nietzsche, Friedrich 609, 736, 737–8, **740**; *Twilight of the Idols* 739
Nigeria 707, 835, 839, 846, 906
Nightingale, Florence 757
nihilists 735
Nineteen Eight-Four (Orwell) 806
Nixon, Richard 854, 860, 881
Nkrumah, Kwame 838, 841
Nobel Peace Prize Winners 894, 895
nobility, European 514, **515**, 516–24, 538, 540, 579, 582, 589, 668
Nobility and Excellence of Women, The (Marinella) 504, 505

Non-Governmental Organizations (NGOs) 894–5
Normandy/Normans 442
North America: African slaves 551, 554–5; European colonies 549–50, 552, 555; religion 553, 555, 556; see also American War for Independence; Amerindians; Canada; United States
North Atlantic Treaty Organization see NATO
Northwest Territory 566, 571
Norway 731, 790, 820, 826
Notes from the Underground (Dostoevsky) 720, 739
novels 501, 503, 506, 509, 720, 721, 723, 741, 883; Russian 720, 739, 806
NOW see National Organization of Women
nuclear weapons 868, 871–2, 873, 876, 904
Nuremberg Tribunals 826
Nyerere, Julius 840

Oath of the Tennis Court (David) 581
occultists 495–6
October (Eisenstein) 774, 776
Odessa: massacre of Jews 710
Offray de la Mettrie, Julien: Man the Machine 636
O'Gorman, Juan: Porfirio Díaz 564
O'Higgins, Bernardo 555, 560, 561
Ohio 566
oil 842, 843, 844, 846, 847, 852
Oklahoma 566–7
Olmecs 459
Olympic Games (1896) 741
On the Capacity of the Female Mind for Learning (van Schurman) 505
On the Equality of the Two Sexes (Poulain de la Barre) 504, 505, 506
On Liberty (Mill) 730, 732
On Nature According to Its Own Principles (Telesio) 493–4
On the Nobility and Preeminence of the Female Sex (Agrippa von Nettesheim) 504, 505
On the Reorganization of European Society (Saint-Simon) 732
On the Revolutions of the Celestial Spheres (Copernicus) 485, 485, 486
On the Structure of the Human Body (Vesalius) 489, 490
On the Subjection of Women (Mill) 730
One Day in the Life of Ivan Denisovich (Solzhenitsyn) 806
O'Neill, Eugene 776
OPEC (Organisation of Petroleum Exporting Countries) 846
opera 529, 720, 739
opium trade/Opium Wars 636, 698–9
Orange, princes of 579
Orange Free State 706, 707
Organization of Work, The (Blanc) 733
Origin of the Family…, The (Engels) 734, 736
Origin of Species, On the (Darwin) 725
Orlando, Vittorio 765
Oroonoko (Behn) 501, 509
orphanages 533–4, 642, 659
Orwell, George 712, 806; Animal Farm 806; Nineteen Eight-Four 806
Ottoman Turks 418, 424, 426, 437, 467–8, 501, 519, 636, 667, 669, 683, 685, 693, 702–5, 704, 705, 731, 746–7, 755, 756, 766, 842–3
Owen, Robert 620, 646–7, 649, 733
Owen, Wilfred: "Dulce et Decorum est" 753
"Oxford Movement" 737
Oxford University 736

Pacific islands 566, 855
Padua, university of 489
Paine, Thomas 497, 585; Common Sense 557–8, 566, 579; The Crisis 585; Rights of Man 585, 586, 588

painting: abstract 775, 739, 740, 778; American 551, 556, 572, 573, 792; Belgian 774; British 523, 553, 643, 720, 721, 722, 754; Cubist 739; Dutch 539, 540, 738–9, 740; French 504, 508, 517, 524, 581, 590, 598, 599, 602, 625, 652, 661, 684, 720, 721, 722, 738, 740; futurist 774, 808; German 643; Impressionist 661, 738, 740; Italian 522, 531, 774; Mexican 564; Neoclassical 581, 590, 602; Post-Impressionist 738–9, 740; Realist 721, 722; Romantic 720, 722; Russian 739, 740, 778; Spanish 524, 531, 532, 605, 739, 818; Surrealist 774
Pakistan 847, 848, 904, 906; women 887
Palestine/Palestinians 702, 835, 844–5, 874, 907
Palestine Liberation Organization (PLO) 844, 845
Panama 561, 852, 854; Canal 714, 852–3
Pankhurst, Emmeline 734, 735, 783
Pannini, Giovanni: Gallery of Scenes from Ancient Rome 522
"Panopticon" (Bentham) 534, 654
Papin, Denis 619
Paracelsus (Theophrastus von Hohenheim) 489, 496
Paraguay 546, 560, 561, 855
Parents, The (Kollwitz) 759
Paris 478, 503, 528, 625, 631, 646, 651, 652, 652, 653, 749, 750, 820; cafés 661; cholera 653, 654; Commune 649, 666, 671, 672, 678, 678; department stores 648, 660; Louvre 510; Métro 653 population 528, 650; poverty 530; prisons 654; salons 508, 509; sewage system 653; student protests (1968) 881; women's political clubs 684, 736; workers' revolutions 645, see also French Revolution
Paris, Treaties of: 1763 555, 556, 694; 1783 558; 1919 747, 765, 835, 857
Parks, Rosa 863, 864
Pascal, Blaise 493, 494
Passchendaele offensive 752
Pasternak, Boris 806, 883; Doctor Zhivago 883
Pasteur, Louis 653, 724, 726
Patel, Pierre, the Elder: View of Versailles 443
Pearl Harbor 855; bombing of 821, 822
Pearson, Karl 712
"Peasant, The" (Amman) 530
peasantry, European 530, 535, 536–7, 537, 538, 538; festivities 539–40; rebellions 540, 579–80
Peasants' Wedding, The (Bruegel the Elder) 539, 540
Peckinpah, Sam: The Wild Bunch 882
peddlers 654
Pedro I, of Brazil 555, 560
Pedro II, of Brazil 560
peninsulares 546, 548
Penn, Arthur: Bonnie and Clyde 882
Penn, William 552
peons 548
Peres, Shimon 894
perestroika 877
Perón, Eva 853
Perón, Juan 853
Perry, Commodore Matthew 634, 701, 701
Pershing, General John J. 853
Persian Letters (Montesquieu) 501
Peru 455, 459, 461, 462, 546, 549, 560, 561, 891
pesticides 892–3
Pétain, Marshal Philippe 820, 826
Peter I, Tsar (the Great) 426, 437, 439, 441, 502, 519, 523, 631, 693
Peterloo Massacre 647, 669
Petrograd see St. Petersburg
philanthropy 656, 662

Philip II of Spain 427–8, 431, 437, 443, 466
Philip IV, of Spain 524
Philippines 454, 457, 696, 712, 832, 855, 857
philosophers/philosophy 737–8, 777–9; Austrian 779; British 487, 494, 544, 581, 728, 747, 777, 779, see also Locke, Mill; Dutch 492, 710; French 498, 779, see also Descartes, Montesquieu; German 497, 721, 728, 737, 813, see also Heisenberg, Marx, Nietzsche; medieval 484–5
philosophes 483, 496–7, 498, 501, 503, 578, 579, 580, 581
photography 721, 722; see Riis, Jacob
physicians 489–90, 495; women 782; see also childbirth
"physiocrats" 580
Picasso, Pablo 739; Guernica 818
Pietists 737
Pillnitz, Declaration of (1791) 587
Pinochet, Augusto 854, 907
Pirandello, Luigi 776; Six Actors in Search of an Author 776–7
Pitt, William, the Younger 708
Pius VII, Pope 597
Pius IX, Pope 779
Pius XI, Pope 809
Pizarro, Francisco 546
plague 534–5, 535, 708
Plains Indians 567–8
Planck, Max 777
plantations: coffee 469, 474; cotton 473; sugar 467, 469, 472; tobacco 462, 469, 473; Brazilian 545; Caribbean 544; North American 551, 554
Platt Amendment 852
Plessy v. Ferguson 860, 861, 864
PLO see Palestine Liberation Organization
Plutarch 503
Plymouth, Massachusetts 550
Pol Pot 907
Poland 426, 434, 437, 444, 667, 668, 684, 731, 766, 809, 868, 875, 879; emigration 716; Jews 535, 825; nobility 515, 519, 538, 579; Solidarity 876; women 886; World War II 820, 821, 823, 824
police forces 654; secret 667, 677, 731, 760
politics and political science 438–40, 441–4, 476–8, 557–8, 566, 579, 727, 728, 730, 898–9, 901
pollution 892–3, 894
Pombal, Marquis de 546
Pomponazzi, Pietro 491
Ponce de Léon, Juan 456, 459
Poor Laws 530, 532, 656, 669
pop culture 882, 903
Pope, Alexander 502
Pope, Jessie: "War Girls" 753
population 476–8 513, 528, 652, 639, 716, 725, 727–8, 784, 784, 888–9, 891, 892
pornography 580, 736, 885
Portolan charts 449, 453
Portugal 426, 606, 669, 683, 809; colonies 456, 462, 466, 468, 472, 472, 544, 545–6, 552, 691, 696, 704, 706, 833; decolonization 836, 387; explorers 449, 40, 457–8, 459, slave trade 467, 468; trade and trade wars 448, 450, 452, 454–5, 456, 467, 474, 701
positivism 564, 728; logical 778–9
Potato Eaters (van Gogh) 739
Potosí mines, Bolivia 461, 461, 546, 547
Poulain de la Barre, François: On the Equality of the Two Sexes 504, 505, 506
Pound, Ezra 738, 746, 768
poverty 530, 532, 533, 534, 535, 640, 645, 648, 651, 652–3, 654, 656–9, 903–4, 905; see also famine
Prague: Jews 535; "Prague Spring" 875, 876

Presbyterianism 433
Presley, Elvis 882
press censorship 583, 667, 668
Primo de Rivera, José Antonio 817
primogeniture 526, 550, 602
Principal Navigations…of the English Nation, The (Hakluyt) 501
Principles of Political Economy and Taxation (Ricardo) 727
printing 483, 503, 580; in South America 546, 549
prisons 654
processions, medieval 440–1
proletarians 640, 645–6, 733
propaganda 774
prostitution 531, 532–3, 649, 655–6, 661, 736, 885, 888
Protestantism 503, 779
Proudhon, Pierre-Joseph 733, 734; What is Property? 733
Proust, Marcel: Remembrance of Things Past 779
Prussia 425, 426, 435, 519, 628, 667, 668, 673, 678, 685, 731
psychiatry/psychology/psychotherapy 727, 738, 805
Ptolemy, Geography 449, 457; 484
Puerto Rico 547, 561, 565, 566, 691, 852
Pugachev, Emilian 540
Pulci, Antonia 52
Puritans 462
Putin, Vladimir 901
"putting-out" system 613, 640

Qaddafi, Muammar el- 433, 471, 838, 840, 873
Qing dynasty 698, 699, 700, 811
Quakers 552, 729
quantum theory 777
Quebec 549, 556
querelle des femmes 504–5
quinine 706
Quisling, Vidkun 826

Rabelais, François 503
rabies 724
Rabin, Yitzhak 843, 845, 894
racial theories/racism 710, 712–13, 731, 748; Nazi 798, 811–12, 813, 814, 820; see also anti-Semitism; genetics; Social Darwinism
Racine, Jean-Baptiste 529
radio 631, 903
railroads 616, 623, 625, 628, 629, 631, 632, 633, 634, 635, 662, 693, 714
Raleigh, Sir walter 458
Ranke, Leopold von 724, 725, 728
Rasputin, Grigorii 760, 761
rationalism 484, 493
Razin, Stephen 540
Reagan, Ronald 876, 877, 878
Realism 720, 721, 722, 723
Realpolitik 676
Red Brigades 909
Reflections on Marriage (Astell) 506, 526
Reflections on the Revolution in France (Burke) 585–6, 588, 730, 732
Reform Acts: 1832 647, 669; 1867 676
relativity, theories of 738, 777, 778
religion(s) 492, 498–9, 737, 779; Amerindian 460, 464, 465, 466; and science 484–5, 488, 492–3; see also Buddhism; Catholic Church; Hinduism; Islam; Judaism
Remarque, Erich Maria: All Quiet on the Western Front 763, 881
Remembrance of Things Past (Proust) 779
Renaissance Classicism 523
Renaissance of Motherhood, The (Key) 785
Renan, Ernest: Life of Christ 724
Renoir, Jean 776; La Grande Illusion 773 Moulin de la Galette 661
Renoir, Pierre-Auguste 738, 773; Le
Restoration, English 433
Reza Pahlevi, Muhammad 835, 843, 846

Rhodes, Cecil 706, 707, 712
"rhythm and blues" 882
Ricardo, David 727; *Principles of Political Economy and Taxation* 727
Rice cultivation, America 469, 473
Richelieu, Armand Jean du Plessis, Cardinal 430, 519, 520
Ride for Liberty, A (Johnson) **551**
Riefenstahl, Leni: *Triumph of the Will* 774
Rights of Man (Paine) 585, 586, 588
Riis, Jacob 646; *How the Other Half Lives* 640, **648**, **658**, 721
Rio de Janeiro 545, 560, 893
Risorgimento 674
Rite of Spring (Stravinsky) 741
Rivera, Diego: *A Sunday Afternoon in the Alameda Park* **564**
Robertson, George: *Nant-y-glow Ironworks* **643**
Robespierre, Maximilien 578, 585, 589, 590–1, 596, 603, 673
Robinson Crusoe (Defoe) 501
robot 538
Rococo style 523
Roman Catholicism *see* Catholic Church
Romania 702, 731, 746, 755, 766, 821, 868, 878
Romanticism 661, 720–1, **722**, 723, 737, 772
Rome 503, 675; population (1750–1950) **650**
Rommel, General Erwin G. 821
Roosevelt, Franklin D. 826, 829, 851, 854, 868, **870**; New Deal 793–4
Roosevelt, Theodore 851, 852
Rosenberg, Ethel and Julius 873
Rosetta Stone 597
Rousseau, Jean-Jacques 498, 499, **499**, 501, 590; *Émile* 498, 503; *Social Contract* 499–500
Royal Society 510, 619
Rubens, Peter Paul: *Marie de' Medici* 436
Rudolph II, Emperor 509
Rushdie, Salman 908
Russell, Bertrand 747, 777, 779, 881
Russia/Soviet Union **423**, 425, 426, 435, 437, 455, 667, 677, **691**, **692**, 693, **869**, 901; agriculture 536, 632, 802, **805**, 892; anarchists 647, 735; architecture 523; and Berlin 871; Crimean War 683, 685; and Cuba 854–5; dissolution of Soviet Union 877–9, 880; education 729, 805; emigration **715**; industrialization 631–4; Jews 710, **711**, 715; law reform 579; literature *see* literature; and Nazi Germany 816, 817, **818**, 819, 820; nobility 518–19; oil 846; and Ottoman Empire 746–7; painting 739, **740**, 778; and Palestine 844; population 716; railroad 632, 633, 693; Red Army 799, 802–3, 816, 821, 869; revolutions 668–9 (19th c.), **751**, 759, 773 (1905), **751**, 755, 761–3, 799, 800, 804 (1917); schools 502, 579; secret police 731, 760, 762, 800, 878; serfs 518, 538, 539, 632, 668; trade and economy 632–3, **714**, 790, 793, 801, 803, 876–7; urbanization **651**; women 784, 886; World War I 746, 747, 748, 754–5, 756, 758, 761, 763, 766, 767, **768**; World War II 814, 820, 821, **823**, 823–4; *see also* Bolsheviks; Cold War; Lenin; Stalin
Russian Enigma, The (Ciliga) 806
Russo-Japanese War (1905–6) 634, 677, 686, 693, 702
Rwanda 837, **890**, 891, 906

SA (*Sturmabteilungen*) 812, 814
Saavedra, Diego **459**
sacrifice, Aztec **460**, 465
Sadat, Anwar 843, 844, 845, 894
Saddam Hussein 843, 847
Sade, Marquis de 736

Safavids 702
St. Petersburg (Petrograd) 523, 632, 633, 716; population **528**, **650**; revolutions (1905) **751**, 759, (1917) **751**, 755, 761–3, 773, 799
Saint-Simon, Henri de 732, 736; *On the Reorganization of European Society* 732
Sakharov, Andrei 883, 894
salons **508**, 509, 510, 721
SALT 876
Samoa 855
samurai 454, 700, 701
San Martín, José de 555, 560, 561
San Salvador 456, 463
Sand, George 723
Sandinistas 854
Sanger, Margaret 783
"*sans-culottes*" 586, 593, **600**
San Salvador 456, 463
Sant'Elia, Antonio: *Electric Center* **774**
Santiago 563
São Paulo, Brazil 545, 563
São Tomé 544, 837
Sarajevo 747, 906–7
Sartre, Jean-Paul 777, 779; *Being and Nothingness* 779
Sassoon, Siegfried 746
Saudi Arabia 847, 887, 909
Sauk Indians 566
Savery, Thomas: steam engine 619
Schelling, Joseph von 720–1
Schleswig-Holstein 676
Schlieffen, Alfred von: Plan 748, 749
Schoenberg, Arnold 741
Scholasticism, medieval 506
schools *see* education
Schopenhauer, Arthur 737
Schröder, Gerhard 899
Schubert, Franz 720
Schurman, Anna Maria van: *On the Capacity of the Female Mind for Learning* 505; *Whether a Christian Woman should be Educated* 504
science and technology 484, 614, 724, 726, 777; female scientists **507**, 509, 726, **727**, 777; and religion 484–5, 488, 492–3; *see also* inventions
Scotland 425, 433, 440, 444
Scott, Dred 571
SEATO (Southeast Asia Treaty Organization) 848, 872
Second Sex, The (de Beauvoir) 884
seigneuralism 578
Sen, Amartya 900
Seneca Falls Declaration 574
Senegal 707, **707**, 756, 837, 840
Senghor, Léopold 840
Seoul, Korea 857
Sephardic Jews 710
Sepúlveda, Juan Ginés de 466
Serbia/Serbs 667, 668, 683, 702, 731, 746, 747–8, 755, 766, 906–7
serfs 535, **537**; Russian 518, 538, 539, 632, 677
Serious Proposal to the Ladies (Astell) 505
servants, female 644, **648**, 652, 658, 659, 660
Seven Years' War 425, 426, **428**, 475, 555, 694
Seville, Spain **451**, 478
sewage systems 649, **653**, 653–4
sewing machines 629
sex slavery 888
sexual matters 736–7, 883; *see also* birth control
Sforza, Francesco, Duke of Milan 420
Shahjahan 694
Shaka 706
Shakespeare, William: *Henry V* 427; 503, 529
Shanghai: Japanese bombing **823**
sharecroppers 537
Sharpeville massacre 839
Shaw, George Bernard 776, 806
Shaw, Lemuel **722**
sheep-farming 536
Sheffield, England **624**

Shelley, Mary 720
ships and shipbuilding 449–50, 455; slave ships 469, **469**, 470
Shipwreck (Turner) 720, **722**
shoguns 454
Siberia 455, 693, 716, 799; Trans-Siberian Railroad 633, 693
siege warfare 419, 426
Sieyès, Abbé Emmanuel Joseph 597; *What is the Third Estate?* 582, 584
Signing of the Declaration of Independence, The (Trumbull) **556**
Silent Spring (Carson) 892
Silesia 426
Silk Road 693, 698
silkworms 724
silver/silver mining 461, **461**, 466, 76
Simonde de Sismondi, J.-C.-L. 724
Simonet, J.B.: "Here is the Law of Nature..." **499**
Since Lenin Died (Eastman) 806
Singapore 851
Singer, Isaac: sewing machine 629
Sinn Fein 835
Sino-Japanese War (1894–5) 701, 747
Sitting Bull 568
Six Actors in Search of an Author (Pirandello) 776–7
skepticism 493
Sketch for a Historical Picture of the Progress of the Human Mind (Condorcet) 496, 500, 501
Slater, Samuel 628, 629
slavery: abolition 471, 565, 566, 571, 572–3, 593, 619, 670; African 425, 450, **467**, **468**, 468–70, **469**, 471, 544, 545, **551**, **553**, 554–5, 563–4, **565**, 569, 571, 617, 634, 693, 706, 911;
Slavs 441, 674, 681, 746, 811–12
Slovakia 879
Slovaks 731, 766
Slovenes 731, 746, 766
Slovenia 906
slums, city 656–7, **658**
smallholders 537
smallpox 491, 535, 654, 891
Smith, Adam: *The Wealth of Nations* 473, 479, 580, 642, 727
Smith, Ian 839
Social Contract (Rousseau) 499–500
Social Darwinism 712, 726, 728
social democratic parties 647, 649
social inequalities 514, **515**, 540, **553**; *see* poverty
socialism 646, 670, **672**, 723, 728, 731–3, 734–5; and feminism 736
Socialist Realism 774, 806
sociology 725, 727, 728
Solidarity 876
Solzhenitsyn, Aleksandr 806; *The Gulag Archipelago* 806, 883; *One Day in the Life of Ivan Denisovich* 806
Somalia 840, 874, 891, 892
Somaliland 835
Somme, battle of the 752, 753
Somoza, Anastasio 854
Songhay, kingdom of 468 705
Sorrows of Young Werther (Goethe) 721
Soustelle, Jacques 842
South Africa 832, 835, **839**, 839–40, 841, 842
South/Spanish America 546–9, **552**, 560–1, **562**,691–3; Amerindians 546, 547, 559, 563, 564; *caudillos* 561–2, **564**, 565, 853–4, 855; Church 548, 553, 563, 564, **564**, 693; industrialization 634; the military 563; population 563; slaves 563–4, 565; social divisions 563–5; trade and economy 562, 562–3, 564, 634, **714**; and United States 853–4, **856**; women 887
Southworth, Albert Sands: *Lemuel Shaw* **722**
Soviet Union *see* Russia/Soviet Union
Soweto massacre 839
space programs 872, 903

Spain 669, 683, 809; Catholic Church 817, 818; Civil War 809, 817–18; colonies **691**, 696, **704**, 706, 707, **833**; *conquistadores* 459–61, 472; and Dutch War of Independence 423–4; decolonization 836, 837; explorers 450, 456, **459**; under Ferdinand and Isabella 426–7; literature 503, 529; loss of Gibraltar 425; nobility **515**, 517, 519; painting *see* painting; under Philip II 427–8, 441; Reconquista 426, 459; sheep-farming 536; South American colonies 456, 461–2, **463**, 463, 472; and Thirty Years' War 425; trade and economy 474–5, 476; urbanization **651**; War of the Spanish Succession 425, 428
Spanish America *see* South America
Spartacist uprising 756, 765
spice trade 448, 450, 452
Spencer, Herbert 728
Spinoza, Benedict Baruch de 492, 710
Spirit of Laws (Montesquieu) 499
spiritualism 779
Sri Lanka 834
SS (*Schutzstaffel*) 803, 814
Staël, Mme Germaine de 603, 721
Stalin, Joseph 799, 801, **806**; atrocities 802–3, 806, 807, 821; cultural policies 774, 806–6; death 875; and Hitler **818**, 819, 820; and Korea 857; speech 800; trade and economic policies 793, 801–2, 803–4; and women 784, 805; at Yalta 868, **870**
Stalingrad, battle of 821
Stamp Acts (1765, 1766) 556
Stanford, John Leland 629
Stanley, Henry Morton 706
Stanton, Elizabeth Cady 568; *Eight Years and More: Reminiscences* 566
Starry Messenger (Galileo) 488
Starry Night (van Gogh) 739, **740**
START treaties 876, 878, 879
steam engines 619–20, **621**, 622; railroad 623, **624**
steamships 622, 623–4, 714
steel industry *see* iron and steel
Stephenson, George 628; *Rocket* 623
Sting: "Russians" 871
stock markets 452, **475**, 478, 479
Stolypin, Peter 759
Stopes, Marie 783
Stowe, Harriet Beecher: *Uncle Tom's Cabin* 566
Strasbourg 503, 524, 685
Stravinsky, Igor 741; *Rite of Spring* 741
streetcars 631, 653
strikes 644, **648**, 649; US 787
Strindberg, August 738
student activism 667, 668, 673, 881
Study for Composition VII (Kandinsky) **740**
Sturm und Drang 721
Sucré, Antonio José de 555, 560, 561
Sudan 703, 705, 706, 835, 892
Suez Canal 696, 703, 714, 835, 843
suffrage **669**, **719**; suffragist movement 734, 735–6, 780, **783**
sugar plantations 467, 469, 472, 544, 545, 634
Suharto 847, 848
Sukarno 836, 847, 848, 875
Sukhanov, N.N.: *Russian Revolution* 763
Sumatra 696, 697
Sun Yat-sen 700, 810
Sunday Afternoon in the Alameda Park, A (Rivera) **564**
Sunday Schools 729
superstition 578, 580
Surrealism **774**
Sweden 424, 426, **504**, 505, 731, 790; agriculture 536; birth control 783; nobility 519, 579
Swift, Jonathan: *Gulliver's Travels* 501; "A Modest Proposal" 708
Switzerland 579, 606; nobility 519
Syndicalists, French 647, 735
Syria 702, 836, 847, 874; Palestinians 844

tabula rasa 494
Tacitus 503
Tainos, the 456, 463, 544, 546
Taiping Rebellion 699
Taiwan 699, 701, 747, 848, 851, 874
Taliban 847, 909
Tamerlane 452
Tanzania 707, 835, 840, 906, 907, 909
Tanzimat 705
Tarabotti, Arcangela 506
taxonomists 724
Taylor, Frederick Winslow 787
Taylor, Harriet 730
technology 903; see computers; inventions; science
Tecumseh 566
Teilhard de Chardin, Pierre 779
telegraph, the 631, 714
telephones 631, 714
telescope, Galileo's 487, 487–8
Telesio, Bernardino: On Nature According to Its Own Principles 493–4
Tennessee 566, 572
Tenochtitlán, Mexico 460–1
terrorism 907, 908, 909
Testelin, Henri: tapestry 508
Texas 566, 567, 572
textile industry 536, 538, 538, 613, 614; see cotton industry
Thailand 692, 700, 832
Thatcher, Margaret 884
theater 522–3, 523, 529, 776–7, 806, 883
Thirty Years' War 420, 422, 423, 424–5, 425, 427, 430, 477
"This is not a pipe" (Magritte) 774
Three Emperors' League (1873) 685
Threepenny Opera, The (Brecht) 776
Titian: Charles V on Horseback 421
Tito, Marshal (Josip Broz) 868, 906
tobacco 462, 469, 473, 544, 554, 634, 705
Tocqueville, Alexis 671
Tokugawa Ieyasu 700–1
Tokutomi Iichiro 819
Tokyo 701
Tone, Wolfe 708
totalitarianism 743, 798, 798, 807, 828
towns see urban development
Tractatus Logico-Philosophicus (Wittgenstein) 777, 779
trade and economy 524, 613, 772, 786; free trade 580, 642, 644, 676, 901–2; and mercantilism 430, 474; world 713–15, 787, 901–3, 904; see also economics; European Union; and specific countries
trade unions: Britain and Europe 644, 645, 646, 647, 648, 649, 656, 676, 733; Russian 799; United States 787, 794
Transvaal 706, 707
travel literature 501
Treatises on Civil Government (Locke) 494, 499, 500
Treitschke, Heinrich von 709, 747
Trevithick, Richard: locomotive 623, 624
Trial, The (Kafka) 779
Triple Alliance 686
Triple Entente 686
Tristan, Flora: London Journal 641, 657
Triumph of the Will (Riefenstahl) 774
trolley cars 631, 653
Trotsky, Leon (Lev Davidovich Bronstein) 760, 761, 762, 763, 802, 806
Truffaut, François 883
Truman, Harry S. 826, 827, 828, 854, 857, 868
Truman Doctrine 870, 874
Trumbull, John: The Signing of the Declaration of Independence 556
tuberculosis 654, 887, 891
Tunisia 702, 705, 836
Turkey 705, 766, 842–3; see also Ottoman Empire
Turner, J.M.W. 720, 721; Shipwreck 720, 722

Tutsi people 832, 890, 906, 907
Tutu, Archbishop Desmond 838, 839, 842, 894
Twilight of the Idols (Nietzsche) 739
2001: A Space Odyssey 873
Tz'u-Hsi, dowager empress 700

Uganda 835, 839, 889
Ukraine 763, 799, 877, 878, 879; Jews 711, 827
Ulysses (Joyce) 741, 779
Ulysses (Odysseus) 898
Umberto I, of Italy 683
uncertainty principle (Heisenberg) 772, 777
Uncle Tom's Cabin (Stowe) 566
unconscious, theory of the 738
underground railroads 653
United Arab Emirates 835, 887
United Nations 835, 842, 844, 888, 893, 895–6, 907; Declaration of Human Rights 895, 896
United States 690–1; caloric intake 891; civil rights 860–1, 862, 863–4; Constitution 558, 565, 569, 573, 581; dance 776; education 557, 691; expansion 566, 567; films 773, 774, 775; and Gulf War 847; immigration 574, 715; imperialism 833, 851, see also Philippines; industrialization 617, 619, 626, 629; and Israel 844, 845; and Japan 634, 701, 701, 851, 874; and Latin America 851–5, 856; literature see literature; Monroe Doctrine 561, 669, 851; moon landing 872; New Deal 793–4; painting see painting; population 716; religion 779; 60s culture 881–2, 883; slavery and abolition 566, 569, 571, 572–3; socialism 734–5; trade and economy 632, 714, 714, 771, 786, 786–8, 790, 790–2; trade unions 787; urbanization 651; women's rights 568, 570, 574, 883–5, 886; World War I 756, 763, 764, 765, 768, 768; World War II 821–3, 826, 827, 828; see also American Civil War; Amerindians; Cold War; Korean War; New York; North America; Vietnam War
universities 503, 507, 557, 736; see also student activism
urban development 477, 477–8, 527–9, 612–13, 639, 649–53, 651
Ure, Andrew 641
Uruguay 562, 564
Utah 566, 571, 629
utilitarianism 730
Utopia (More) 422, 501, 534
utopia 646, 647; utopian socialism 732–3

vaccination 491, 535, 724, 891
Valéry, Paul 778
Valla, Lorenzo 491
Vargas, Getúlio 853–4
Varnhagen von Ense, Rahel 721
Vásquez de Coronado, Francisco 456
Vatican, the 675, 809
Vega Carpio, Lope Felix de 529
Velázquez, Diego 524; The Ministry of an Egg 532
Vendée, revolt in the 589
venereal disease 654, 656, 891
Venezuela 560, 561, 846, 853
Venice 495, 503, 530, 535, 579, 650, 823; nobility 517, 519, 540; Peace of Lodi 422; opera house 529; possessions (1526) 423
Verdi, Giuseppe 720
Verdun, battle of 752
Vermeer, Jan: The Geographer 450; 526
Verrocchio, Andrea del: Bartolommeo Colleoni 432
Versailles: Palace 430, 440, 443, 516, 520, 580, 582, 587, 676, 678, 681; Treaty (1919) 764, 765–6, 767, 811, 816
Vesalius, Andreas 489; On the Structure of the Human Body 489, 490

Vespucci, Amerigo 453, 456, 459
Victor Emmanuel II, of Italy 675, 683
Victor Emmanuel III, of Italy 683, 808, 823
Victoria, Queen 636, 661, 676, 695, 699, 726, 759
Vienna 702; population (1750–1950) 650; Ringstrasse 653; School 779
Vienna, Congress of 528, 666, 667, 667, 668, 669, 683, 730–1
Viet Cong 858–9
Viet Minh 857
Vietnam 692, 698, 699, 700, 834, 836, 857–8, 901
Vietnam War 856, 858–60, 859, 874–5, 879, 881, 884; casualties 860
Vigée-Lebrun, Elisabeth 735
Villa, Francisco "Pancho" 853
village festivities 539, 539–40
Vindication of the Rights of Man, A (Wollstonecraft) 585, 586
Vindication of the Rights of Woman, A (Wollstonecraft) 505, 585, 586, 735
Virginia, USA 458, 462, 463, 469, 469–70, 550, 553, 554, 571, 572
Vives, Juan Luis 505; The Instruction of a Christian Woman 504
Vojvodina 906
Voltaire (Jean-François Arouet) 498, 499, 500, 503, 509, 516, 544, 580; Candide 498, 501; Philosophical Letters 498; Zadig 498, 501
voodoo 544
Voyage to Icaria (Cabet) 733

Wagner, Richard 739
Waiting for Godot (Beckett) 883
Wake Island 855
Walachia 683, 685
Walesa, Lech 876, 894
Wall Street crash 789, 790–1
Wallace, Alfred Russel 726
Walsingham, Sir Francis 431
"War Girls" (J. Pope) 753
warfare 589, 903–4, 906–7, 911; see weaponry; World War I and II
Warsaw 823; Jewws 825
Warsaw Pact 869, 872, 875, 876, 879
warships 450
Washington, Booker T. 863
Washington, George 55
Washington, D.C. 571
Washington Conference (1921–2) 809
Waterloo, battle of 607
Watt, James: steam engines 619–20, 621, 624
We are Making a New World (Nash) 754
Wealth of Nations, Inquiry into…the (Smith) 473, 479, 580, 642, 727
weaponry 613, 620, 628, 712, 754; see nuclear weapons
weavers' revolts 643, 645
Weavers' Uprising, A (Kollwitz) 643
Webb, Beatrice and Sidney 806
Weber, Max 496
weights and measures 591, 593
Weil, Simone 779
Weill, Kurt 776
Weimar Republic 811, 813
welfare programmes 785, 793–4
Wellesley, Lord 697
Wellington, Arthur Wellesley, Duke of 606
Wells, H.G. 806
What is Property? (Proudhon) 733
What Is To Be Done? (Lenin) 761, 762
Whether a Christian Woman should be Educated (van Schurman) 504
Whigs 433
Whitaker, John C. 893
White, John: Indian Woman and Child 553
"white-collar" workers 652
Whitehead, Alfred North 779
Whitman, Walt: "When I Heard the Learned Astronomer" 723
Whitney, Eli: cotton gin 569, 617, 619
Wiesel, Elie 827
Wild Bunch, The 882

William I, Kaiser 676, 681
William I, of Orange 424, 668
William II, Kaiser 681, 811
William III, and Mary, of England 433–4
William of ockham 438
Wilson, Woodrow, US President 745, 756, 763, 765, 766, 853; "Fourteen Points" 763, 764
witchcraft 495, 496
Witte, Sergei 628, 633, 759
Wittgenstein, Ludwig 779; Tractatus Logico-Philosophicus 777, 779
Wollstonecraft, Mary 720; A Vindication of the Rights of Man 585, 586; A Vindication of the Rights of Woman 505, 585, 586, 735
Woman and Socialism (Bebel) 781
Woman's Life, A (Haviland) 571
women 531, 888; bourgeois and well-off 659–72; and democracy 501; disappearance of 887; enfranchisement 780; genital mutilation 887; humanist 505, 506; and learning 484, 502, 503, 504, 504–5; and Nazism 813; noble 521–2; physicians 782; and politics 684, 884; poor 532; salons 508, 509; scientists 507, 509; under Stalin 784, 805; workers 640, 641, 642, 648, 657–8, 658, 658–9, 781, see also servants; World War I and after 753, 757, 758, 780–3; writers 504–6, 509, 529, 720–1; see also childbirth; feminism; prostitution; women's rights
Women and Economics (Perkins) 782
Women's National Indian Rights Association 568–9
women's rights 888; France 593–4, 596, 599, 602, 672, 735; United States 568, 569, 570, 574, 691; see also feminism
Women's Worth (Fonte) 504, 506, 509, 527
Woodstock Music Festival 882
Wordsworth, William 656, 720, 721
workers 529–30, 537, 538, 640–2, 670, 733; see also trade unions; women
workhouses 656, 660
World War I 683, 700, 705, 743, 746, 747–50, 749, 754, 754–6, 757, 763, 765; casualties 767–8; home front 757–8; literature 746, 753, 763; munitions production 758; poison gas 752, 753, 754; and redrawing of boundaries 766, 767, 767; trench warfare 750, 752, 754; women 753, 757, 758, 780
World War II 743, 772, 798, 814, 818–24; casualties 828; see Holocaust
Would-Be Gentleman, The (Molière) 514
Wounded Knee, battle of 568

Yalta Conference 868, 870
Yeltsin, Boris 878, 879, 901
Yorkshire cloth market 614
"Young Turks" 705, 756, 843
Ypres offensive 752, 754
Yüan Shih-k'ai 700
Yugoslavia 766, 806, 809, 823, 868, 906

Zadig (Voltaire) 498, 501
Zaire 837, 838–9, 840, 890, 906
Zambia 835, 888
Zapata, Emiliano 853
Zazubrin, V. 800
Zeppelin airships 754
Zetkin, Clara 758, 781
Zevi, Shabbetai 709–10
Zhdanov, Andrei 874
Zheng He 452, 454
Zhukov, General Georgi K. 821
Zietz, Luise 644
Zimbabwe 705, 835, 839, 840–1
Zionism 710, 842, 844
Zohar, the 709
Zola, Emile 660, 710, 721, 723, 741; Germinal 723; Nana 723
Zulu nation 706, 832